T4-ADC-458

SOUTH UNIVERSITY
709 MALL BLVD.
SAVANNAH, GA 31406

Health Services Cyclopedic Dictionary

The Jones and Bartlett Series in Health Sciences

AIDS, Science and Society, Fan et al.

Anatomy and Physiology: An Easy Learner, Sloane

Aquatic Exercise, Sova

Aquatics: The Complete Reference Guide for Aquatic Fitness Professionals, Sova

Aquatics Activities Handbook, Sova

Basic Epidemiological Methods and Biostatistics, Page et al.

Basic Law for the Allied Health Professions, Second Edition, Cowdrey/Drew

The Biology of AIDS, Third Edition, Fan et al.

Bloodborne Pathogens, National Safety Council

A Challenge for Living: Dying, Death, and Bereavement, Corless et al.

Concepts of Athletic Training, Pfeiffer/Mangus

CPR Manual, National Safety Council

Drugs and Society, Fourth Edition, Hanson/Venturelli

Drug Use in America, Venturelli

Dying, Death, and Bereavement: Theoretical Perspectives and Other Ways of Knowing, Corless et al.

Easy ACLS: Advanced Cardiac Life Support Preparatory Manual, Weinberg/Paturas

Emergency Encounters: EMTs and Their Work, Mannon

Essential Medical Terminology, Second Edition, Stanfield/Hui

Ethics Consultation: A Practical Guide, La Puma/Schiedermayer

First Aid, National Safety Council

First Aid and CPR, Second Edition, National Safety Council

First Aid and CPR, Infants and Children, National Safety Council

First Aid Handbook, National Safety Council

First Responder, American Association of Orthopaedic Surgeons, National Safety Council

Fitness and Health: Life-Style Strategies, Thygerson

Fostering Emotional Well-Being in the Classroom, Page/Page

Grant Application Writer's Handbook, Reif-Lehrer

A Guide to Bystander Care at a Roadside Emergency, AAA Foundation for Traffic Safety

Health and Wellness, Fifth Edition, Edlin/Golanty/McCormack Brown

Health and Wellness Journal Workbook, Seaward

Health Education: Creating Strategies for School and Community Health, Gilbert/Sawyer

Healthy Children 2000, U.S. Department of Health and Human Services

Healthy People 2000, U.S. Department of Health and Human Services

Healthy People 2000—Summary Report, U.S. Department of Health and Human Services

Healthy People 2000—Midcourse Review With 1995 Revisions, U.S. Department of Health and Human Services

Human Aging and Chronic Disease, Kart et al.

Human Anatomy and Physiology Coloring Workbook and Study Guide, Anderson

An Introduction to Epidemiology, Timmreck

Introduction to Human Disease, Fourth Edition, Crowley

Introduction to the Health Professions, Second Edition, Stanfield/Hui

Managing Stress: Principles and Strategies for Health and Wellbeing, Seaward

Managing Your Health: Assessment and Action, Birch/Cleary

Mastering the New Medical Terminology: Through Self-Instructional Modules, Second Edition, Stanfield/Hui

Medical Terminology with Vikki Wetle, RN, MA, Video Series, Wetle

National Pool and Waterpark Lifeguard/CPR Training, Ellis & Associates

The Nation's Health, Fourth Edition, Lee/Estes

New Dimensions in Women's Health, Alexander/LaRosa

Omaha Orange: A Popular History of EMS in America, Post

Oxygen Administration, National Safety Council

Perspectives on Death and Dying, Fulton/Metress

Planning, Program Development, and Evaluation: A Handbook for Health Promotion, Aging, and Health Services, Timmreck

The Power of Positive Coaching, Nakumura

Primeros Auxilios y RCP, National Safety Council

Safety, Second Edition, Thygerson

Skill-Building Activities for Alcohol and Drug Education, Bates/Wigtil

Statistics: An Interactive Text for the Health and Life Sciences, Krishnamurty et al.

Stress Management, National Safety Council

Teaching Elementary Health Science, Fourth Edition, Newtens/Bender/Sorochan

Health Services Cyclopedic Dictionary

A Compendium of Health-Care and Public Health Terminology

Third Edition

Thomas C. Timmreck, Ph.D.
*Professor of Public Health and Health Care Administration
Department of Health Science and Human Ecology
California State University, San Bernardino*

Jones and Bartlett Publishers
Sudbury, Massachusetts

Boston   London   Singapore

Editorial, Sales, and Customer Service Offices

Jones and Bartlett Publishers
40 Tall Pine Drive
Sudbury, MA 01776

info@jbpub.com
http://www.jbpub.com

Jones and Bartlett Publishers International
Barb House, Barb Mews
London W6 7PA
UK

Copyright © 1997 by Jones and Bartlett Publishers, Inc.
Copyright © 1982, 1987 by Thomas C. Timmreck, Ph.D., and National Health
         Publishing

All rights reserved. No part of the material protected by this copyright notice may be reproduced or utilized in any form, electronic or mechanical including, photocopying, recording, or by any information storage and retrieval system without written permission from the copyright owner.

Library of Congress Cataloging-in-Publication Data

Timmreck, Thomas C.
  Health services cyclopedic dictionary / Thomas C. Timmreck. — 3rd ed.
    p.   cm.
  Previous ed. published with title: Dictionary of health services management.
    ISBN 0-86720-515-6 (hard cover)
    1. Health services administration—Dictionaries.   2. Medical care—
Dictionaries.   I. Title.
RA393.T56   1997
362.1'068—dc21   96-46403
                                                                   CIP

Vice President, Editor: Joseph E. Burns
Production Editor: Marilyn E. Rash
Manufacturing Manager: Dana L. Cerrito
Design/Typesetting: A-R Editions
Cover Design: Hannus Design Associates
Printing and Binding: Courier Companies

Printed in the United States of America
01 00 99 98 97   10 9 8 7 6 5 4 3 2 1

CONTENTS

Foreword vii

Preface ix

About the Author xi

Acknowledgments xii

Definitions

A	1
B	63
C	87
D	162
E	203
F	236
G	261
H	277
I	323
J	363
K	370
L	373
M	399
N	456
O	490
P	519
Q	607
R	615
S	672
T	767
U	795
V	808
W	819
X	830
Y	831
Z	833

Appendices   835

I	Epidemiology and Vital Statistics Rate Formulas	836
II	Abbreviations of Fellows of Colleges and Medical Diplomate Specialties	839
III	Medical Specialties and Their Abbreviations	841
IV	The Hospital Patient's Bill of Rights: American Hospital Association	842
V	Patients' Rights in Skilled Nursing Facilities	844
VI	Vital Signs of the Body	846
VII	Greek Alphabet	847
VIII	Numbers and Symbols Commonly Used in Charting Medical Records	848
IX	Abbreviations Used in Medical Records	849
X	Abbreviations Used in Charting in Medical Laboratories	853
XI	Abbreviations Used in Charting in Radiography	854
XII	Latin Abbreviations Commonly Used in Writing Prescriptions	855
XIII	Weight Equivalents	857
XIV	Volume Equivalents	858
XV	Code of Ethics for American Health Information Management Association	859
XVI	Privacy Act of 1974	860

FOREWORD

"Words, words, words . . . I hear words all day through. First from him, now from you," sang Liza Doolittle in Allen Jay Lerner's *My Fair Lady*. How empty they can be, or how full of meaning or misunderstanding. How pervasive they are in our personal and professional lives. How we struggle to find the right ones to denote our object or to connote our meaning and to communicate our intent. How deceptive or unintelligible our communications can be when our words have a particular meaning in our particular profession or discipline.

Dictionaries have served as the final arbiter in disputes over meaning, but many of the terms we use in specialized fields elude definition in standard, even unabridged, dictionaries. Many others carry specialized meanings that shift too swiftly in nuance with late-breaking research and changing auspices, legislative mandate, location, or discipline responsible for the specialized service. In English, we may turn alternatively to the *Oxford English Dictionary*, *Webster's, Gage's,* or *McQuarie's* depending on whether we practice in the United Kingdom, the United States, Canada, or Australia. Failing the search in these, we turn to the glossaries of textbooks in the specialized fields to find definitions. These glossaries typically yield only the particular meanings the particular authors intend when using the term in that particular book. Unabridged dictionaries cannot be revised fast enough to keep up with the pace of change and the emergence of neologisms in the health fields.

The health services have suffered the Babylonian fate of explosive growth, high stakes, multidisciplinary tongues, and aspirations to emulate the gods, all converging on a tower of jargon. The building blocks of the tower consist of oddly fitting etymological combinations: Classical Greek and Latin foundations overlaid with arcane Germanic scientific precision to cover the evidence-based side, the romance languages to cover the caring side. Loose bricks and mortar of bureaucratic acronyms, political finessing, congressional numbering, and economic obfuscation describe the organizational and pecuniary structures. Medical euphemisms cover the gory stuff, mixed with black humor to cope with the gore that cannot be covered. One-ups-professionship inflates the language of disciplines describing their roles and functions as they compete for health service territory and a piece of the inflated pie. Psychobabel on the motivational and behavioral side, business and commerce talk on the managed-care side, epidemiological epigrams and sociological sobriquets on the public health side, New-Age, quasi-religious terms on the spiritual and alternative healing sides, and postmodern discourse on the alternatives-to-the-alternative side provide the shaky pillars of this tower of Babel.

These characterizations are not to disparage the real contributions each of these language sources seeks to make to health services. They simply portray each in the light in which the others tend to see them, or more to the point, hear them and read them. Each accuses the other of imposing jargon on the field. Each justifiably defends its jargon as necessary to communicate with efficiency the complexity of its specialized part of the whole. Each addresses the same reality, but has a different slice of that reality to describe and comprehend. Then come the anti-specialists, the holistic specialists, the ecologists, the humanists, the systems analysts seeking to articulate a language of whole persons or whole health systems without segmenting them into specialized parts or reducing them to molecular levels of analysis. They add another layer of languages trying to synthesize rather than atomize, integrate rather than dissect. Their contributions to the language extend the boundaries and the richness of the health services lexicon, but they are no less given to jargon and specialized language despite their anti-specialization specialty.

Professor Timmreck has scaled this cyclopedic tower with courage, energy, and intelligence that has defied the breadth of knowledge to be comprehended and encapsulated. He has ventured where others have dared not go. Just defining their own terms in an article has eluded some authors. Constructing a glossary for a textbook has been too daunting for many authors. Some notables have attempted a dictionary for a particular discipline, but precious few bold pioneers have ascended the wall of the multidisciplinary tower. Take cover, because the product you hold in your hands will surely draw a withering crossfire of dissent from the various disciplines and subdisciplines. Some will argue for more encompassing definitions of their key terms (academic imperialism), or more specific definitions (disciplinary exclusivity), or more arcane definitions (professional mystification).

This book, *Health Services Cyclopedic Dictionary, Third Edition,* challenges us all to define more explicitly the specialized terms we use, or accept Professor Timmreck's definitions. Either way, with this publication, he and Joseph Burns at Jones and Bartlett will have made an incalculable contribution to greater clarity and understanding of communication in the health services.

Lawrence W. Green
Professor and Director
Institute of Health Promotion Research
University of British Columbia

PREFACE

This *Health Services Cyclopedic Dictionary, Third Edition*—a compendium of health-care and public health terminology—is the first major dictionary published for the fields of health care, health services, health-care administration, and public health. Now in its third edition, this reference represents a major effort to bring together all useful terms in their unique usage in the health services and public health fields. Prior to the first edition, published originally in 1982 as the *Dictionary of Health Services Management*, with over 6,000 terms, the author spent four years gathering terms and shaping the focus of the dictionary. The revised edition was published in 1987 as the *Dictionary of Health Services Management, Second Edition*, and was edited, updated, and expanded by 2,000 terms for a total of over 8,000. The third edition has been expanded to include all current terminology, including the National Health Security Program, universal coverage, managed competition, managed care, medical insurance, and health-care delivery. Also included is comprehensive coverage of epidemiology, public health, health promotion, and environmental health.

The *Health Services Cyclopedic Dictionary, Third Edition*, is not a medical dictionary. A number of fine medical dictionaries are available, so this one purposely avoids medical terminology or words readily available in medical dictionaries. When Noah Webster, LLD, an attorney by profession, first wrote his unabridged dictionary in the early 1800s, he used legal terminology as its foundation. Like Webster's work, the dictionary was originally developed using health law terminology as its foundation and started out as a student health law dictionary. The dictionary was expanded and made diverse enough to cover all facets of health services and to serve as a supplemental textbook for degree programs in health services, health-care administration, nursing, health education and health promotion, gerontology, and the allied health professions. This dictionary has also been recognized as a valuable tool for health-care professionals working in managed care, hospitals, acute- and long-term-care settings, medical group management, public and private health agencies, public health, and environmental health services and related areas.

The term *cyclopedic* has been included in the title to better represent how the terms are presented. *Cyclopedia*, according to several dictionaries, is a book that contains brief information on all branches of one subject and is alphabetically arranged. Longer explanations, rather than short one-line definitions, were used where appropriate, thus meeting the spirit of being cyclopedic in its presentation. Therefore, pronunciation guides, such as those found in traditional unabridged dictionaries, were not considered necessary.

The sources for terms are too numerous to mention or to identify readily. Terms were discovered in a multitude of sources, such as government documents, textbooks, professional journals, government publications, the expertise of health practitioners working in different health services settings, professional conferences, student input, and the media. In addition, the author drew on his own broad experience in health services, health administration, public health, environmental health, behavioral health, and health education and health promotion.

The following are some of the areas addressed by this *Health Services Cyclopedic Dictionary*:

Accreditation of health facilities
Aging services
AIDS and infection control
Allied health
Clinic management
Community health services
Emergency care
Environmental health
Epidemiology
General insurance
General safety
Gerontology
Health-care administration
Health-care delivery
Health-care finance
Health education
Health information management and computers
Health law
Health planning and evaluation
Health professions
Health promotion
Hospital administration
Human resources management
Long-term care and nursing home administration
Managed care and HMOs
Management of health services
Medical and health insurance
Medical group management
Medical specialties
Mental health services
Nursing services
Occupational health and safety
Omnibus Budget Reconciliation Act
Parliamentary procedure
Professional health associations
Program development, implementation, and evaluation
Psychiatric care
Public health
Rehabilitation
Rural health
Technology in medicine
Universal coverage and national health security programs

ABOUT THE AUTHOR

Thomas C. Timmreck, Ph.D., has been actively involved in the field of health care, public health, health science, and gerontology since his career began in 1971. His work has brought him to hospitals, nursing homes, public health departments, environmental health services, and both public and private social and health agencies. Dr. Timmreck has been a licensed nursing home administrator in two states and has taught health-care administration at Texas Tech University, Idaho State University, and Northern Arizona University and is currently a Professor of Public Health and Health Care Administration in the Department of Health Science and Human Ecology at California State University, San Bernardino. Dr. Timmreck has also taught management and organizational behavior in the M.H.A. and M.B.A. programs at the University of Colorado at Denver and the M.B.A. programs of the University of Redlands, the University of Denver, and Western International University in Phoenix. He has over fifty professional publications in a variety of subject areas—healthcare management, long-term-care administration, gerontology, health education, and behavioral health—and is the author of four books. Dr. Timmreck received his doctoral degree in health science from the University of Utah and a graduate certificate in gerontology from the Rocky Mountain Gerontology Center at the University of Utah. In addition, he holds two masters degrees—one in counseling psychology and human relations and behavior from Northern Arizona University and one in community health and health education from Oregon State University with a bachelors degree in Health Science from Brigham Young University.

ACKNOWLEDGMENTS

A reference book such as this could not have been brought to completion without the assistance of many of my scholarly and diligent students, both undergraduate and graduate, who over the years provided input and sources of terms. Gratitude is expressed to Ellen for her diligence in editing the entire manuscript.

No attempt has been made to compile a bibliography or listing of references because of the enormity of sources, which include a multitude of government publications, books, current periodicals (both scholarly and popular), newspapers, conferences, lectures, institutionally developed glossaries, television, films, and consultation with colleagues and professionals in the various areas covered by this reference book.

A

AA *See Alcoholics Anonymous, anesthesiologist's assistant.*

AAA *See Area Agency on Aging, American Academy of Addictionology.*

AAAHC *See Accreditation Association for Ambulatory Health Care.*

AABC *See American Association of Biofeedback Clinicians.*

AACN *See American Colleges of Nursing.*

AAFP American Academy of Family Physicians.

AAHA *See American Association of Homes for the Aging; American Academy of Hospital Attorneys.*

AAHC American Association of Healthcare Consultants.

AAHCF *See American Association of Health Care Facilities.*

AAHE *See American Association for Health Education; Association for the Advancement of Health Education.*

AAHPRD *See American Alliance of Health, Physical Education, Recreation and Dance.*

AAMC Association of American Medical Colleges.

AAMD American Academy of Medical Directors.

AAMSI American Association for Medical Systems and Informatics.

AAN *See American Academy of Nursing.*

AANP American Academy of Nurse Practitioners.

AAPA American Academy of Physician Assistants.

AAPCC *See adjusted average per capita cost; average adjusted per capita cost.*

AAP *See American Academy of Pediatrics; Association of American Physicians.*

AARP *See American Association of Retired Persons.*

abandon 1. To leave or give up entirely, completely, and finally. 2. To relinquish one's rights.

abandonee 1. The one who is abandoned. 2. The abandoned party. 3. The party to whom a right is abandoned or relinquished by another.

abandonment 1. To surrender one's rights, property, or obligations permanently with no intent of reclaiming them. 2. An emergency situation wherein a person leaves an injured or ill person without having another person to take over and provide care. 3. In health law, this occurs if a physician terminates a physician–patient relationship but fails to give the patient sufficient time, notice, or opportunity to obtain care by another physician and fails to properly inform the patient. A patient in an acute-care setting can be legally abandoned if a health-care provider ceases caring for a patient before he or she has found a new health-care provider. 4. The intentional desertion of a child with no thought of returning or searching for the child.

abandonor The one who does the abandoning.

ab ante (Lat.) 1. Prior. 2. Before. 3. To happen or occur in advance.

abatable nuisance A nuisance that is easily stopped or can be permanently prohibited without causing irreparable economic loss.

abate 1. To decrease. 2. To put an end to. 3. To diminish. 4. To destroy or end. 5. To lessen or reduce. 6. To stop.

abduction Criminally or illegally taking away another person. This could be of concern in health care if the one abducted is under the care of another.

aberration 1. Deviation from normal. 2. Mental illness.

abet 1. To encourage. 2. To aid or incite. 3. To order, help, or assist a person to commit an illicit act.

abettor (abetter) One who abets.

abeyance 1. Temporary inactivity. 2. Supervision of personal property. When there is no one to whom property can be given, it is in abeyance until a proper owner appears.

abilities In the management of personnel in a health-care facility, the worker's potential for doing specific work behaviors or acts.

ABIM American Board of Internal Medicine.

ab inconvenienti (Lat.) 1. From inconvenience. 2. An argument founded on the hardship of a case and the inconvenience or disastrous consequences as a result of a different course of reasoning.

ab initio (Lat.) 1. From its initiation or inception. 2. Since the very beginning.

ABMM American Board of Medical Management.

ABNA *See achievable benefit not achieved.*

abnormal 1. Deviating from the usual, expected, average or norm of behavior expected by society. 2. Out of the ordinary. 3. Having extreme characteristics or extreme behaviors. *See anomaly.*

abortion 1. The act of bringing forth or destroying a human fetus before it is capable of maintaining life. 2. Termination of a pregnancy before the fetus has attained viability (i.e., becomes capable of independent extrauterine life). Viability is usually defined in terms of the duration of pregnancy, weight of the fetus, and/or, occasionally, the length of the fetus. Viability is usually attained at 28 weeks of gestation, with a fetal weight of approximately 1000 g. This is based on the observation that infants below this weight have little chance of survival, whereas the mortality of infants above 1000 g declines rapidly. Different types of abortions are distinguished: early—less than 12 completed weeks of gestation; late—more than 12 weeks; induced—caused by deliberate action undertaken with the intention of terminating pregnancy; spontaneous—all abortions other than those induced. 3. The Centers for Disease Control counts legal abortions only. For surveillance purposes, legal abortion is a procedure performed by a licensed physician or someone acting under the supervision of a licensed physician. *See also stillbirth.*

abortion services A formalized, ethical program of pregnancy termination that exists in a health-care facility. These services may be inpatient (when a patient is admitted for at least an overnight stay) or outpatient (services provided on an ambulatory basis), and both must comply with local and state laws.

abortus When the fetus is expelled from the uterus or after an abortion, with no regard to its status, viable or nonviable, dead or alive.

above cited A phrase for "cited or stated earlier in this record."

abrogate 1. To repeal, annul, abolish, or destroy. 2. To cancel, as with a law.

ABS *See American Board of Surgery.*

abscissa side The horizontal side of a graph where values are presented.

abscond To hide or leave a jurisdiction to avoid legal process.

absence, day or leave of An authorized leave of absence, usually for 24 hours or a weekend, granted to a patient who is restricted to an inpatient facility.

absentees Employees of a health service organization who are scheduled to work but fail to show and are not present.

absenteeism In health administration and human resources management, this is the failure of employees to report to work as scheduled, whether or not such failure to report is excused. Vacations, holidays, and prearranged leaves or absences are not counted in absenteeism. Also referred to as "job absence."

absenteeism rates In health administration and human resources management, absenteeism rates are a good indicator of existing or potential personnel and management problems. Health services administrators can use an absenteeism rate to assess absenteeism occurrences. The absenteeism rate formulas follow:

$$\text{Absenteeism rate} = \frac{\text{Total number of absent days for 1 month}}{\text{Total number of employees}} \times 100$$

U.S. Department of Labor Formula:

$$\text{Absenteeism rate} = \frac{\text{Number of worker days lost through job absence during period}}{\text{Average number of employees} \times \text{Number of workdays}} \times 100$$

absolute address The binary number assigned as the location of memory on a disk, diskette, tape, or other information storage medium in microcomputers.

absolute assignment In insurance, this is a means of transferring the ownership of an insurance policy to another individual or organization permanently and authorizing the ownership and use of the policy.

absolute right A right given to a person that allows uncontrolled dominion over the subject, person, or item at all times and for all purposes.

absorption In health-care laser technology, this is the assimilation of laser light by tissue with the transformation of radiant energy to heat energy by the interaction of the light with matter.

absorption coefficient In health-care laser technology, this is the measure of a laser's wavelength capability to be absorbed in water.

absque (Lat.) Without.

abstention doctrine A doctrine that allows a federal court to refuse to decide a case, even if it has the power, including a medical malpractice case. This is a policy of the federal courts that grants another court discretion to decline to exercise its jurisdiction to hear a case.

abstinence Refraining from use of alcohol, drugs, food, sex, etc.

abstract 1. A summary or short overview of a subject with the substance of the document or paper presented. 2. In pharmacology, a drug in two parts, where one part of the abstract is compounded with milk sugar. Abstracts, unlike extracts, are double strength.

abstracter A person trained in medical record administration who pulls predetermined, selected, or specific information from medical records. *See medical record administration.*

abstract of record 1. A short, complete history of a legal case as found in a record. 2. An abbreviated overview of all the proceedings of a legal case complete enough to show that questions presented for review by an appellate court have been properly reserved.

abstracting 1. The process of writing or creating a summary. 2. Isolating or separating out a particular aspect of an object. 3. Extracting data or information from a medical record.

abstraction 1. The ability to do generalized thinking, form ideas, or sort out information. 2. In law, this is the fraudulent taking of money or items of worth.

abulia 1. Lack of ability to make decisions. 2. A lack of will.

abuse 1. To use improperly (i.e., abuse of drugs). 2. To mistreat or harm, as in child abuse or sexual abuse. 3. Improper or excessive use of program benefits, resources, or services by either providers or consumers. Abuse can occur, intentionally or unintentionally, when services are used that are excessive or unnecessary, that are not the appropriate treatment for the patient's condition, when cheaper treatment would be as effective, or when billing or charging does not conform to requirements. It should be distinguished from fraud, in which deliberate deceit is used by providers or consumers to obtain payment for services that were not actually delivered or received or to claim program eligibility. Abuse is not necessarily intentional or illegal. *See child abuse; sexual abuse; spousal abuse.*

abuse of discretion Unethical, unreasonable, or unsound decisions made by an administrator or other person in a position of authority through use or abuse of that authority; misuse of positional authority.

abuse of process In health-care law, this is the misuse of the legal system for improper purposes (can be a tort). Malicious prosecution or illegal involuntary commitment proceedings for psychiatric hospital admission are misuses of the legal system.

Academy of Management A national organization established in 1936 for college and university professors and executives in business. An assemblage of management specialists who create and foster growth in the field of administration and management. In addition to offering three levels of membership, it offers the honorary designation of "Fellow." The organization publishes two of the leading professional publications in management. One section of specialization in the academy is in health-care Administration.

acarophobia The fear of small objects such as spiders and needles.

acatelepsia Lack of ability to comprehend and reason.

accelerated clause In health-care finance, a special clause inserted in an installment note, mortgage, or deed of trust that allows the moneylender the right to demand full payment of the note in the event of certain circumstances (e.g., the failure to meet a payment by a certain date, change of ownership of the health-care facility, or any event that might endanger the security of a loan).

accelerated depreciation In health-care taxation management, this is a method of depreciation that is greater than a straight-line depreciation, as a greater amount of depreciation occurs early in the life of a piece of equipment or property. The writing off of the cost of an asset at a rate faster than using the straight-line depreciation method, which can use either a sum-of-years digits depreciation schedule or a double-declining balance method.

acceleration 1. To move faster. 2. To shorten the time for performance on a contract. 3. To cause something to come sooner, happen quicker, or become complete in a shorter time.

acceptability 1. In evaluating health-care services, this is a measure of consumer satisfaction with the services received, the manner in which the services are delivered, the ease with which services are obtained, and the level of consumer confidence in the providers of the services. 2. An individual's (or group's) overall assessment of available medical care. The individual determines acceptability by appraising such things as satisfaction, cost quality, results, convenience of care, availability, and provider attitudes. *See also accessibility; availability.*

acceptable provider panel In managed care, this is a group of health-care providers selected to provide care under a managed care contract based on availability, accessibility, specialty coverage, quality improvement, and care delivery.

acceptable risk In public health, occupational health, environmental health, or clinical treatment, the benefits of an action or a product must outweigh the hazards; the ability of medical and public health scientists to determine hazards associated with medical procedures or occupational or other health-related exposures.

"accept a committee report" In formal healthcare organizations' meetings using parliamentary procedure, this is the statement "I move to accept a committee's report" and is a formal motion made by the assembly that supports the action of the committee. A report can also be adopted by an eligible member stating, "I move that the committee adopt the report."

acceptance 1. In contract law, this stipulates an agreement that is bound by the precise terms of an offer, thereby creating a binding contract. 2. Willingness to pay a negotiable instrument.

access In health-care delivery, the potential to use or gain entry into the health-care system; ability to obtain medical care. The availability of health services to those who need them. Availability of health-care services, physicians, and transportation, as well as geographic location and proximity to health services, time delays in seeing health-care providers, cost of care, hours of operation, manner or source of payment, and satisfaction with the health-care services, are all determinants of access. *See acceptability; accessibility; availability; quality; quality of care.*

ACCESS Shortened form of abbreviation AHCCCS. *See Arizona Health Care Cost Containment System (AHCCCS).*

access time In data processing, the interval of time from when data are pulled from computer memory storage to when the data become available for use or processing.

accessibility 1. The degree to which a health service inhibits or facilitates the ability of an individual to gain entry and to receive services. Thus, accessibility includes geographic, distance, cultural, prejudicial, architectural, transportation, social, temporal, and financial barriers or considerations. 2. An individual's (or group's) ability to obtain medical care. Accessibility, with its many barriers and components, is very difficult to define and measure operationally. Many health-care programs or organizations have as their goal to improve access to care for specific groups or to provide equity of access for an entire population. Access is also a function of the availability of health services and their acceptability. In practice, access, availability, and acceptability collectively describe health system measures and characteristics. *See access; acceptability; availability.*

accessibility of services and facilities The ease with which residents can gain access to the existing health facilities and avail themselves of the services being provided. Barriers that impede access to health services and facilities may include factors such as architecture, geography, economics, cost, language, etc. *See access; accessibility.*

accessible radiation In laser technology as used in health care, this is laser radiation to which it is possible for the human eye or skin to be exposed in normal usage.

accession number In medical records, this is the number assigned to each medical record order as it is submitted.

accessory 1. Anything that is joined to, incident to, or part of another thing. 2. Contribution to; aiding. 3. One who helps another person commit an illicit illegal act.

accident 1. An unexpected, unplanned event that may involve injury. 2. An event or occurrence that was unforeseen and unintended. 3. Something done unintentionally. 4. A mishap that lacked intent. 5. An end occurrence in a sequence of events producing injury, death, or property damage that was not intended.

accidental bodily harm In insurance, this is injury to the body of an insured person as a result of an accident.

accidental death and dismemberment A form of insurance that provides coverage and benefits for either death or the loss of a limb and certain forms of disability.

accidental death benefit *See double indemnity.*

accidental injury A definite impairment of function or traumatic injury to a body structure resulting from an unexpected outside force or object, occurring without foresight or expectation at an identifiable time and place. Not to be confused with "medical emergency."

accident and health insurance A contract wherein the insurer, in consideration of premiums paid, agrees to pay the insured medical and hospital benefits, in the case of disease or accidental injury, or death benefits, in the event of accidental death.

accident and sickness policies A set of rules that

usually provides a minimum health-care stipend for a short time period (a few weeks to a half year) to help employees defray the loss of income while they are recovering from illness and injury.

accident incident rate *See incident; occupational health and safety; average lost workdays.*

accident investigation Concentrates on the gathering of all data and information about the factors that lead to accidents. An occupational safety and health program used to uncover factors that contribute to accident causes and conducted to prevent future accidents from occurring and to document facts, provide data on costs, and promote safety. Factors looked at in an accident investigation include 1) determining direct causes, 2) uncovering contributing causes, 3) preventing similar occurrences/accidents, 4) documenting facts, 5) providing information on the economic impact/costs of the accident(s), and 6) planning and promoting safety.

accident, operational *See operational accident.*

accident, other *See other accident.*

accident perils In health insurance underwriting, this is a classification used to evaluate the type and degree of peril represented by a particular occupation. Accident perils can include occupational exposure to risks such as fire, falling, dangerous equipment or machines, handling of heavy objects, etc.

accident type A description of the types or forms of occurrences that might lead to injury, death, or property damage.

accident while at work A classification of accidents where the injured is 18 years of age or older and was on the job at work or was doing official work activities at the time of an accident.

acclamation In parliamentary procedure and formal meetings, this is the voice vote expressed by stating "Aye" (or "Yes") or "No."

ACCME *See Accreditation Council for Continuing Medical Education.*

accommodation In mental health care, the progress or change in a person's cognitive processes to a sufficiently mature level, enabling the solving of problems that could not be solved previously.

accomplice One who intentionally participates in the commission or attempted commission of an illicit act.

account In finance, this is a segment of the ledger in which gains and losses are accumulated for separate assets, liabilities, equities, revenues, and expenses. The title of an account is called a "chart of accounts."

accountability 1. Being held responsible; accepting responsibility of one's actions to another. 2. In health administration, this is the fulfillment of administrative expectations through effectiveness and efficiency, how well employees are answerable for the use of their authority, and the handling of responsibility for achieving goals. 3. Responsible for and answering for the expenditure of money and the commitment of resources on the basis of gains or results achieved. 4. Having stewardship over money and other resources, with evaluation of acceptable use judged in relation to the reaching of specified goals. 5. With concern for the patient, this is an obligation to carry out responsibilities and to answer for administrative or patient care decisions and activities.

accountability hierarchy A formalized reporting, information flow, and responsibility structure to meet administrative expectations, performance, and productivity within a formal health-care organization.

accountable 1. Responsible, liable, explainable. 2. To provide or furnish justification, reason, or detailed explanation of financial activities or responsibilities. 3. To furnish substantial reasons or convincing explanations. 4. An obligation to periodically disclose, in adequate detail and consistent form, to all those interested parties directly and indirectly responsible for the purposes, principles, procedure, relationships, results, incomes, and expenditures involved in any activity, enterprise, or assignment so that they can be evaluated by the interested parties. The concept is important in health regulatory programs and agencies, which should be accountable to the public andto those affected by the actions of the agency.

accountable health partnerships (AHPs) An organization that integrates health-care providers and facilitates and assumes risk for groups of patients.

accountable health plan (AHP) Under managed care and managed competition, this is one financial arrangement and structure for managed care where the health plan is accountable to a governmental regulatory agency. Some universal coverage and managed competition proposals suggest that this be the mechanism to shift from a treatment and crisis intervention health services delivery approach to a health promotion and disease prevention driven system. These health plans would finance and deliver a full range of nationally defined benefit packages, be accountable to the public for satisfaction, comply with underwriting standards and community ratings, guarantee access, comply with renew provisions, and adhere to uniform forms and data reporting (Jackson Hole Group).

accounting Formal procedures used in compiling, recording, classifying, and analyzing money transactions using financial data and figures and including the interpreting of the results of all money transactions of an organization or business; a system of collecting, analyzing, and summarizing financial figures to obtain clear financial pictures needed to track money, make business decisions, and satisfy financial reporting requirements.

accounting department In a health-care organization, this is the administrative unit that maintains the accounting records and is responsible for bookkeeping and financial record management activities to ensure that the organization is being managed in a profitable manner. The accounting department is responsible for maintaining the company's general accounting records, preparing financial statements, and controlling receipts and disbursements and related financial records activities and money transactions while ensuring that all tax laws and related legal matters are within compliance.

accounting period In health-care finance, this is the time period that financial statements cover, usually monthly or quarterly.

accounting system All the records, ledgers, and procedures used in recording, retrieving, and reporting financial information, position, and operations. *See accrual basis of accounting; cash basis accounting.*

accounts payable 1. The money that is owed to others and is yet to be paid. 2. Liabilities on open account owed by the facility to other persons or companies for goods furnished and services provided.

accounts receivable 1. The money owed to an individual, organization, institution, or facility for services rendered, goods received, or use of the facility or services. 2. An open account of amounts of money owed to a business or health-care organization by outside persons or businesses for goods furnished and services provided by that organization. 3. In a health-care provider setting, the full amount of patient care charges that are owed to the health-care organization. *See average day of accounts receivable.*

accounts receivable turnover The net amount of money or billings for a period of time divided by the average balance of net accounts receivable. The formula is used to determine the effectiveness of collection policies.

accredit The act of officially recognizing or approving a health-care professional training program or an institution.

accreditation 1. The process by which an agency or organization evaluates and recognizes a program of study or an institution as meeting certain predetermined standards. The recognition is called "accreditation." Similar assessment of individuals is called "certification." Standards are usually defined in terms of physical plant, governing body, administration, medical and other staff, and scope and organization of services. Accreditation is usually given by a private organization created for the purpose of assuring the public of quality such as the Joint Commission on Accreditation of Healthcare Organizations (JCAHO). Accreditation standards are not always available for public review. In some situations, governments recognize accreditation in lieu of, accept it as the basis of, or require it as a condition of licensing such as in hospital or nursing home licensure. Public or private payment programs often require accreditation as a condition of payment for covered services. Accreditation may be either permanent once obtained or for a specified period of time. Unlike a license, accreditation is not a condition of lawful practice but is intended as an indication of high-quality practice, although where payment is effectively conditioned on accreditation, it may have the same effect. 2. A system for recognizing institutions and professional training programs for performance, integrity, and quality, entitling that organization to the confidence of the educational community and the public. 3. A determination that a health-care organization has complied substantially with applicable standards of care, quality, performance, productivity, and effectiveness (JCAHO for acute-care facilities). 4. The second highest level of accreditation awarded to a health-care facility. The second highest accreditation decision based on demonstrated high levels of quality and performance (JCAHO for acute-care facilities).

accreditation appeal The process through which an organization that has been denied accreditation can exercise its right to a hearing by an appeals hearing panel. The hearing is followed by a review of the panel's report, and a recommendation is made by the board of commissioners of JCAHO to affirm or reverse the accreditation denial (JCAHO for acute-care facilities).

Accreditation Association for Ambulatory Health Care (AAAHC) A nonprofit organization established to improve the quality of care rendered by ambulatory care organizations. The AAAHC develops uniform standards for ambulatory health-care organizations and provides consultants and educational services. It also conducts voluntary peer on-site reviews and inspections of ambulatory health-care facilities.

accreditation committee A committee of the Board of Commissioners of JCAHO that is responsible for overseeing the accreditation decision process (JCAHO for acute-care facilities).

Accreditation Council for Continuing Medical Education A national nonprofit organization that provides accreditation for continuing medical programs to assist physicians in meeting continuing medical education requirements.

Accreditation Council for Facilities for the Mentally Retarded A specialized accrediting organization that accredits institutions in the United States that provide housing and health care for the mentally retarded.

Accreditation Council for Graduate Medical Education A national nonprofit organization that provides accreditation for physician residencies and specialization clinical training programs.

Accreditation Council for Unified Medical Group Management Association A specialized accrediting organization that accredits medical groups in the United States. It is a division of Medical Group Management Association, with headquarters in Seal Beach, California.

accreditation cycle A designated time span used to determine how often accreditation is to expire and reaccreditation is to occur; under JCAHO this is usually a 3-year period. At the end of a time period, accreditation expires unless a new full survey is performed and passed (JCAHO for acute-care facilities).

accreditation decision On completion of the accreditation process, this is the conclusion reached by the accrediting body regarding the accreditation status of a health-care facility as a result of the survey. The decision to accredit or not accredit is based on the results of the on-site survey, recommendations of the surveyors, compliance with standards, correction of deficiencies, and evidence of recent improvements. The decision by the accrediting body is one of four types: 1) accreditation with commendation, 2) accreditation, 3) conditional accreditation, or 4) not accredit.

accreditation decision grid 1. A grid developed by JCAHO for use in the accreditation process for health-care organizations. The grid provides a summary of survey scores and a quick graphic presentation of the survey's findings. The grid uses a numerical summary of aggregated scores that reflect levels of compliance and represent standards of the survey. Each score on the grid reflects an assigned level of compliance in key performance areas such as infection control, safety management, etc. (JCAHO for acute-care facilities). 2. An aggregate of points acquired in the JCAHO survey process used to reflect overall performance and quality of a health-care facility as reflected in the accreditation decision grid. Each quality or performance area is weighted according to its importance, indicated by a roman numeral (I = most important). The performance areascore is multiplied by the weight to develop the percentage of a perfect score of 100% attained by the health-care organization.

accreditation duration The time period (usually 3 years) in which an accreditation is in force, as long as the health-care facility is in substantial compliance with accreditation standards. Satisfactory resolution of any limitation or problem is required to maintain an accreditation for the time period (JCAHO for acute-care facilities).

accreditation history An account of past accreditation decisions for the health-care facility. Accreditation history may be publicly disclosed by the JCAHO on request (JCAHO for acute-care facilities).

accreditation (JCAHO) A review and statement by the Joint Commission on the Accreditation of Healthcare Organizations (JCAHO) indicating that a health-care organization, such as a hospital, nursing home, or home health agency, has complied with quality standards set forth by JCAHO. *See accreditation*.

Accreditation Manual for Hospitals Two-volume publication of the Joint Commission on the

Accreditation of Healthcare Organizations (JCAHO). This manual provides the policies, procedures, rules, and accreditation standards that health-care organizations must follow to meet accreditation by JCAHO. Surveyors and health-care facility staff use the manual as a guide for the official accreditation survey. Standards used in accreditation and their justification are presented throughout the manual. Both volumes are designed for use in the self-assessment; volume 1 is the basis for the survey report forms used by surveyors during the on-site survey.

Accreditation Review Council for Educational Programs in Surgical Technology (ARC-ST) A national nonprofit organization that evaluates and reviews educational training programs in surgical technology. Training program curricula and accreditation standards are approved by the American Medical Association's Committee on Allied Health Education and Accreditation.

accreditation survey 1. The assessment of a health-care facility or health-care training program by a survey team. The team visits the site of the organization/facility to conduct a review and evaluation for compliance with accreditation standards and eligibility for accreditation. 2. An evaluation of a health-care organization done to assess the facilities level of quality and compliance with standards and to determine a facilities accreditation status. Accreditation surveys include evaluation of documentation of compliance provided by health-care facility personnel, verbal information disclosed with regard to the implementation of standards, examples of implementation of the standards, evidence of compliance, and on-site observations by surveyors. Education and consultation about standards and their compliance is also a part of the survey process (JCAHO for acute-care facilities).

accreditation survey, focused A specialized and specific survey conducted during the accreditation cycle used to assess the degree to which a health-care facility has improved its level of compliance on the basis of specific recommendations or deficiencies. The subject matter of this special survey is confined to those areas identified as being deficient (JCAHO for acute-care facilities).

accreditation survey report The document developed from the results of an on-site assessment of a health-care facility that sets forth the deficiencies, shortfalls, and instructions on how to come into compliance with accreditation standards and quality. The report sets forth the accreditation decision. Type I recommendations are stated about the implementation to be monitored by JCAHO through focused surveys or requests for written progress reports. A supplement to the report, which includes type II recommendations designed to assist the health-care organization in improving its performance, may also be provided (JCAHO for acute-care facilities).

accreditation survey team A group of health-care professionals who work together to perform an accreditation survey. The basic hospital survey team consists of a physician, a nurse, and administrator surveyors. A laboratory specialist and other surveyor specialist may be added to the survey team to evaluate certain areas and services of a health-care facility (JCAHO for acute-care facilities).

accreditation surveyor A physician, a nurse, an administrator, a specialist, or another health-care professional who evaluates quality and standards compliance and provides education and consultation regarding standards compliance in accreditation surveys (JCAHO for acute-care facilities).

accreditation, tailored survey A specialized survey where quality and survey standards from more than one set of standards (standards manual) are used to assess quality and accreditation standards compliance. The survey process might include the use of specialist surveyors needed to meet selected standards for specific areas (JCAHO for acute-care facilities).

accreditation with commendation The highest level of accreditation awarded to a health-care facility. The highest accreditation decision based on demonstrated exemplary performance.

accredited 1. To be officially authorized or vouched for. 2. The verification of having high quality and standards of service.

accredited facility Any health-care organization or institution that has met the standards of accreditation of an accreditation organization, usually, in the United States, by the Joint Commission on the Accreditation of Healthcare Organizations (JCAHO).

Accredited Records Technician (ART) An individual who has completed an accredited educational program in medical records systems and procedures and who has passed a national accreditation examination. One who has been certified may use the ART title after his or her name as proof of qualifications. ARTs are responsible for supervising the daily functions of medical records departments (assembling, analyzing, abstracting, and maintaining records). Records are reviewed for completeness and accuracy by the ART, who also indexes and classifies all diagnoses and operations performed during the course of a patient's hospitalization. This information is then retrieved and prepared for hospital statistics; reimbursement of Medicare, insurance, and HMO charges; reports of disease for public health authorities; special studies for the medical staff; and in response to authorized inquiries for insurance or legal purposes. *See also medical record administrator; registered records administrator.*

Accrediting Commission on Education for Health Services Administration (ACEHSA) The official accrediting body of university- and college-based graduate programs in health services administration education in the United States. The function of the ACEHSA is to foster excellence, encourage improvement, provide counsel, and endeavor to protect the educational programs of health services administration educational programs. ACEHSA is affiliated with the Association of University Programs in Health Administration (AUPHA). *See Association of University Programs in Health Administration.*

accrete As used in Medicare and managed care, this is the process of adding new members to a health plan with a Medicare contract.

accrual 1. In health-care financial management, the amount of money set aside to cover expenses. A best estimate of what expenses will be is based on data from accounting and financial reports. 2. A method of accounting that outlines expenses and income over a period of time, whether or not cash has changed hands during that period. 3. The process of gaining something. 4. In managed care, this is the amount of money set aside to cover medical costs; the managed-care plan's best estimate of what medical expenses will be on the basis of the authorization system, lag studies, and past provider activity and financial history. *See accrue, cash basis of accounting.*

accrual basis of accounting An accounting method used in health-care financial management that identifies money within the period in which goods or services are provided or consumed for a fee. Money is credited to the time period in which it is earned, regardless of when payments are received, and expenses are charged in the time period in which they occur, regardless of when cash is disbursed to pay the expenses. *See cash basis of accounting.*

accruals In health-care financial management, these are continued recurring short-term liabilities such as wages, accrued taxes, and accrued interest.

accrue 1. To gain, accumulate, or happen. 2. To come into fact or to come into existence. A "cause of action" can come into existence as a law when filed as a legal claim. The length of time allowed for a legal action to accrue is often determined by statutes of limitation. *See accrual.*

accrued expenses In health-care financial management, the funds a hospital or health-care facility has used or consumed through its normal operation but have not been billed by or paid to the supplier or vendor.

accrued liabilities In health-care financial management, the amount of money owed from past transactions, such as unpaid compensation, vacations or pensions, and unpaid accrued interest on loans.

accumulated depreciation 1. In health-care financial management, the account that shows the total depreciation recorded for an asset or a capital item since it was acquired. 2. The amount allowed for depreciation that contains the cumulative amount of depreciation of various fixed assets (equipment and property). Also referred to as "allowance for depreciation" or "reserve for depreciation." In health-care organizations, the depreciation allowance is generally calculated by the straight-line method. *See straight-line depreciation.*

accumulation As stipulated in some insurance policies, this is an increase in the amount of benefits provided as a reward to the insured for continuous renewal.

accuracy 1. In health-care strategic planning activities, this is how well a forecast of future activities comes to that of actuality when it occurs and can only be determined as it occurs. 2. In public health or medical science, the degree to which a measurement instrument or questionnaire is able to obtain the true value of the factor being measured.

accusation 1. A charge formally made in court stating that a person is guilty of committing a crime. 2. Any charge brought against a person or corporation. 3. An indictment or information.

accusatory instruments The official documents that charge a person with a crime.

accused 1. The defendant in a criminal case. 2. One against whom an accusation is made.

ACEP American College of Emergency Physicians.

ACGME *See Accreditation Council for Graduate Medical Education.*

ACHA American College of Hospital Administrators. *See American College of Healthcare Executives.*

ACHE *See American College of Healthcare Executives.*

achievable benefit not achieved (ABNA) A health-care quality management concept that specifies a target activity for quality management and reflects the relative quantity of improvement needed to be accomplished by systematic effort and available resources.

acid test ratio In health-care finance, this is the sum total of cash, saleable securities, and current receivables divided by current liabilities. Also referred to as the quick asset, or liquidity, ratio; used in determining liquidity of a business or corporation. The ratio is calculated by placing in the numerator total cash plus marketable securities, which is divided by the denominator, which is the current liabilities. The acid-test ratio formula follows:

<u>Cash and marketable securities</u>
Current liabilities

ACNHA *See American College of Nursing Home Administrators.*

ACNM American College of Nurse Midwives.

ACOG American College of Obstetricians and Gynecologists.

ACP American College of Physicians.

ACPE American College of Physician Executives.

acquaintance network In public health and epidemiological investigations, this is the group of people who have interpersonal contact and social interaction with other members of the group through which communicable diseases can be transmitted or have other health implications. Families, school classes, friendship groups, and extended families are a few examples.

acquiescence 1. A silent agreement. 2. The act of one remaining silent who knows about an act, behavior, or occurrence as it may be for his or her own betterment.

acquired immunodeficiency syndrome (AIDS) A complex of highly lethal infections and rare malignancies that first appeared in the United States in specific homosexual populations. The agent is the HTLV-3 retrovirus. The body's natural immune system is destroyed by this pathogen. The main means of transmission is by the exchange of body fluids, most specifically semen and blood. The disease has also been transmitted by injections related to intravenous drug use or blood transfusions.

acquisition In health-care finance, this is when one health-care organization purchases controlling interest in another health-care organization or hospital. If publicly owned, it usually is done by purchasing a controlling percentage of the company's stock.

acquisition charge In health-care finance, this is a financial charge assessed against the holder of a loan for paying it off early.

acquisition cost 1. In health-care finance, this is the actual cost of selling, underwriting, and issuing a new insurance policy, including clerical costs, commissions, advertising, and medical inspection fees. 2. The cost paid by a pharmacist or hospital to a manufacturer or wholesaler for a supply of drugs.

acquisition expenses In medical or other insurance, this is the cost of processing an application for the insurance and issuing the medical care policy.

acquit 1. To set free. 2. To be judicially discharged from an accusation.

acquittal 1. A formal legal judgment of a person's innocence. 2. To be released from a commitment or obligation.

ACR *See adjusted community rate.*

ACS *See American College of Surgeons; American Cancer Society.*

act 1. In health law, this is any behavior, occurrence, or action taken that may have legal consequences. 2. A law formally passed by a legislative body.

act in pais A judicial act that is not a matter of record and is performed out of court.

actio (Lat.) 1. An action. 2. A right. 3. Any legal proceedings that are taken to enforce a right. 4. A lawsuit.

actio damni injuria (Lat.) An action for damages.

actio ex delicto (Lat.) An action arising from a tort.

action 1. A judicial remedy. 2. To enforce a right. 3. To punish an offender. 4. A lawsuit. 5. The filing of a claim or answering to a charge. 6. As used in health promotion or health education, the behavior of individuals, families, groups, or community decision makers as well as administrators, government, and industrial policymakers and health professionals who might influence individual or community health status.

active labor In managed care and medical care, this is a mother who is in the imminent process of delivering of a baby, and there is inadequate time to effect a safe transfer to another health-care facility under a managed-care plan prior to delivery because a transfer may pose a threat to the health and safety of the patient/mother and/or the unborn child.

active listening Used in counseling, psychotherapy, and health-care management, this requires the listener to clear all preoccupation from his or her mind, stop talking, remove distractions, show patience, and be with another individual in every word they speak and to do so with empathetic understanding.

actively-at-work In managed care, this is a requirement found in some medical care and health plan policies that stipulates that, if the employee is not at work and actively engaged in employment on the day the health plan policy goes into effect, medical care coverage will not be provided until the employee shows up for work.

active medical staff The physicians, osteopaths, podiatrists, dentists, and psychologists who are responsible for medical and health-care practices within a hospital and perform patient care and staff, organizational, and administrative functions.

active medium In laser therapy, this is a substance that creates the laser light when pumped.

active physicians In assessing health-care delivery, these are professionally active physicians who are currently practicing medicine regardless of the number of hours worked per week. Public health statistics often distinguish between federally employed physicians and civilian physicians.

activities of daily living (ADL) A measure of disability, function, and dependency based on individual skills and ability related to basic self-care activities, including eating, bathing, dressing, transferring from bed to chair, bowel and bladder control, and ambulation ability.

activities therapists Persons who provide an ongoing program of activities designed to meet residents' interests and physical, mental, or psychosocial needs. This includes qualified therapeutic recreation specialists, activities professionals, qualified occupational therapists, or qualified occupational therapist assistants/aides spending 50% or more of their time as activities therapists. *See recreational therapist; recreational therapy.*

activity director One who directs recreational and social activities in long-term-care settings. *See recreational therapist; recreational therapy.*

activity expectation (procedure expectation) In health-care quality management, this is the expectation that any set of tasks of clinical care, such as injections or physical exams, be completed in the most effective and efficient manner and done with excellence each time.

activity leader Any individual qualified by training and experience to develop and implement activities programs in health-care facilities. *See recreational therapist; recreational therapy.*

activity services According to JCAHO, for psychiatric, alcoholism, and drug abuse facilities accreditation purposes, these are any structured activities designed to develop an individual's creative, physical, and social skills through participation in art, dance, drama, and recreational or social activities.

act of commission 1. In health law, this is an intentional act that is harmful or injurious. 2. Intentionally doing a criminal act.

act of omission 1. In health law, this is a failure to take necessary precautions to ensure that another person is not harmed. 2. Being negligent. 3. The lack of action when action is required to benefit another person.

actual cash value In health-care finance, this is the replacement cost of equipment or property less depreciation allowances. *See accelerated depreciation; depreciation.*

actual charge The amount a physician or other practitioner actually bills a patient for a particular medical service or procedure. The actual charge may differ from the customary, prevailing, and/or reasonable charges under Medicare and other insurance programs. *See fractionation.*

actual damage *See damages, actual.*

actuary 1. In insurance, a person trained in statistics, accounting, and mathematics who determines policy rates, reserves, and dividends by deciding what assumptions should be made with respect to each of the risk factors involved (such as the frequency of occurrence of the peril, death, illness, or injury; the average benefit that will be payable; the rate of investment earnings, if any; expenses; and persistency rates) and who endeavors to secure the most valid statistics on which to base his or her assumptions. Actuaries also calculate the premium rates of the insurance products and their companies' legal reserve liabilities. 2. An individual trained in statistics and quantitative methods who uses mathematical approaches to apply the theory of probability to the financial sides of managed care and insurance and provides advice and direction involving questions of probability, predictions, and projections.

actuarial In managed care and insurance, these are the statistical calculations and data used to determine rates and premiums based on projections of utilization and costs for a target population.

actuarial analysis In managed care, this is a prediction, using specialized actuarial analysis methods, of future events for the clientele population based on life expectancy, medical services utilization, hospitalization patterns, overutilization patterns, or other risks to the health plan's financial structure.

actuarial assumptions In managed care, these are the theoretical beliefs on which calculations are made about the cost and revenues of the health plan. Assumptions are made about utilization rates, age and sex mix, costs of care and services, levels and types of care utilized most or least, etc.

actuarial department An administrative unit within a managed-care plan or health insurance company that ensures that the plan's operations are conducted on a sound statistical and mathematical basis. This administrative unit utilizes data and information from throughout the organization and industry to design and revise services and the overall plan. Premium and dividend rates, as well as reserve liabilities, nonforfeiture, surrender, and loan values, are also determined. Research is conducted on mortality, morbidity, and vital statistics rates, and guidelines are established for determining and selecting risks and determining profitability of each service.

actus (Lat.) An act.

acuity 1. A measure of the level or seriousness of an illness or injury a patient experiences. Acuity is used to determine level of care used, resources utilized in providing care, and nurse staffing needs.

acupressure 1. A noninvasive approach to acupuncture where nerves are stimulated by pressure instead of the insertion of needles. 2. The compression of blood vessels by means of needles in surrounding tissues.

acupressure forceps Specially designed forceps with spring-loaded handles used for compressing blood vessels.

acupressure needles Special elastic needles used in acupressure for assisting in the compression of blood vessels.

acupuncture A Chinese treatment technique of puncturing specific nerve points on the body with needles to relieve pain or disease symptoms. This medical treatment is founded on a philosophy of body functioning based on the principles of Yin and Yang, both being distinct but inseparable poles of the life energy called TSJI. Together, both maintain a dynamic balance, neither of them being more valuable or better than the other. Treatment is based on the notion that an imbalance of Yin and Yang exists and may be restored by adding or distracting energy from diseased organs. This is accomplished through a combination of dietary advice, exercise, massage, and stimulating or blocking nerves at key points of stimulation. Special points on the human body have been identified as responding to either acupressure or acupuncture. Treatment is accomplished by producing regional anesthesia by passing long thin stainless steel needles into the skin and tissue at specific points. The needles are twirled or stimulated with a light electrical current. The anesthesia produced is often sufficient to permit surgery. Patients are allowed to retain consciousness during the surgery. This treatment method has been known in China and the Far East for centuries, but it was afforded little medical attention in Western civilizations until the 1970s.

ACURP American College of Utilization Review Physicians.

acute 1. Sharp or severe. 2. Short-term, short-stay. 3. Any severe condition or disease having a sudden onset and short course (as opposed to chronic).

acute administrative days Under Medicare and the prospective payment system and Medicaid, this is those days of care that have been approved for a higher level of care than usually needed by the patient in an acute-care inpatient facility; a patient's care that exceeds the level of care available in a skilled nursing care facility based on the judgment of a Medicaid consultant. The level, amount, and frequency of services necessary for the care of the patient that exceed the community standard for levels of nursing care found in a nursing home.

acute brain syndrome A reversible form of organic brain disease that results from acute diseases, pulmonary dysfunction, cardiac insufficiency (stroke), long-term high temperature, malnutrition, alcoholism, trauma, or other factors. Diagnosis of this syndrome is difficult. Symptomatology includes fluctuations in mood and mental capacity, confusion, easy distractibility, and possible hyperactivity. Early diagnosis and treatment are essential for recovery.

acute care 1. Short-term health care. 2. Services in a hospital setting intended to maintain patients for medical and surgical episodic care over a relatively short period of time. 3. Immediate medical care used to treat and cure any disease, injury, or condition near its onset with a short and limited time under physician or hospital services. 4. Short-term inpatient care provided in a general or specialty hospital.

acute-care days for heavy-care patients *See acute administrative days; heavy-care patients.*

acute-care hospital A short-term-care hospital with an average length of stay of less than 30 days. *See also average length of stay; hospital, acute-care; hospital, general.*

acute condition 1. Any spell of illness that lasts less than 3 months that involves either medical attention, care, or restricted activity, not one of the diseases considered chronic regardless of the time of onset. 2. Any illness or injury not associated with either at least one doctor visit or a least 1 day of restricted activity during the reference period is considered to be a minor condition. *See acute disease; chronic condition.*

acute disease A disease that is characterized by a single episode; is rarely permanent; produces no disability; requires little or no rehabilitation; and has a short duration, sharp symptoms, and a quick onset for the spell of illness, usually caused by a pathogen (some sources suggest that it lasts less than 3 months), from which the patient often returns to a normal or previous state and level of activity with medical treatment in a short time period. Patients can die from acute diseases; however, medical care often quickly cures most diseases in modern times. Although acute diseases are frequently distinguished from chronic diseases, there is no standard definition or distinction. It is worth noting that an acute episode of a chronic disease (an episode of diabetic coma in a patient with diabetes) is often treated as an acute disease. *See acute condition; chronic disease.*

ad (Lat.) At; by; for; to.

ADA *See American Dietetic Association.*

ADAMHA *See Alcohol, Drug Abuse, and Mental Health Administration.*

adaptation 1. Coping behavior. 2. The ability to handle the demands of the environment.

adapted physical education *See corrective therapist.*

adaptive mechanism *See mental mechanisms.*

ADC *See average daily census.*

ad curiam (Lat.) To court.

ad curiam vocare (Lat.) To summon to court.

ad damnum (Lat.) To the damage. In health law, this refers to money loss or damages claimed by the plaintiffs.

AD&D *See accidental death and dismemberment.*

addict A person who has a habit of use or abuse of a substance; who cannot resist the experience of the habit, especially with addictive drugs or alcohol; and who cannot exercise self-control over the use or abuse of these substances for psychological or physiological reasons.

addicting drug Any substance that produces both withdrawal symptoms and tolerance; is compelling in its attractiveness for use or abuse, either psychological or physiological or both; and causes an uncontrollable, overwhelming desire or need for the substance.

addiction Habitual use of a drug or alcohol where deprivation causes physical and/or psychological withdrawal symptoms that are distressing and produces a driving impulse to take the drug again. A state of an individual (or a laboratory animal) who succumbs to the uncontrollable, overwhelming desire or craving for a substance such as alcohol or drugs, and who is physically and/or psychologically dependent on its effects. *See addict; drug abuse; drug addiction; drug dependence.*

addictive Any substance or circumstance that produces a physical or psychological dependence.

additional drug benefit list In managed care, this is a preset list of a limited number of prescription drugs commonly prescribed by physicians for patients with chronic diseases and in need of long-term medication use. The list is put together by the health plan and is subject to periodic review and modification. Also referred to as the "drug maintenance list."

additives Any of a wide range of chemical substances added to foods or other products in low percentages to stabilize certain end products.

additur (Lat.) 1. It is increased. 2. An increase in the amount of damages awarded by the court, which usually is over the amount awarded by jury. 3. On a motion for a new trial, a plaintiff is denied the new trial on the condition that the defendant pay damages larger than those already awarded in a judgment, where a court believes the award to be too low.

address In data processing, this refers to a name or number that designates a location in the computer memory or on the disk, diskette, or tape where information is stored. *See absolute address.*

ademption 1. A revocation of a legacy. 2. A gift left in a will but given before death. 3. To credit a decedent's estate for gifts to an heir or a devisee already given before death.

adequate and well-controlled studies Investigations that must be conducted by a new drug sponsor to demonstrate that a new drug is effective. As amended in 1962, the federal Food, Drug, and Cosmetic Act requires that drug sponsors provide substantial evidence of effectiveness. Thus, this term takes on a special meaning: "evidence consisting of adequate and well-controlled investigations, including clinical investigations, by experts qualified by scientific training and experience to evaluate the effectiveness of the drug involved, on the basis of which it could fairly and responsibly be concluded by such experts that the drug will have the effect it purports or is represented to have under the conditions of use prescribed, recommended, or suggested in the labeling thereof" (Section 505[d]). Food and Drug Administration (FDA) regulations further delineate the types of studies that must be conducted to satisfy this requirement and permit waivers in certain cases. The study protocol must minimize bias and ensure comparability between test and control groups. Generally, four types of control are recognized: comparing treated and untreated patients, comparing results of new drug use with a placebo, comparing results of new drug use with results from a regimen of therapy known to be effective, and comparing results of new drug use with a historically derived experience. The statutes and regulations do not explicitly require that safety of a new drug be established by adequate and well-controlled studies, nor do they set forth explicit criteria for safety testing.

adequate staffing Under OBRA guidelines, long-term-care facilities require that an RN or LPN be on duty or available during certain periods of the day. A waiver can be granted in certain areas where nursing shortages exist. To provide quality care, increased nursing personnel are needed to monitor residents, and adequate staffing is needed to deal with the implementation of new guidelines on reduced restraints, both physical and chemical.

ADFS Alternative delivery and financing system.

adhere As used in health services hearings or formal board meetings using parliamentary procedure, when a motion is pending before the floor and other motions are added to it; thus, the added motions are said to adhere to the original motion. When the main motion is postponed or referred to committee, the added motions are subject to whatever the main motion is subject to because they adhere to the main motion.

adhesion A legally related insurance principle that states that any ambiguities or unclear wording in an insurance agreement will be construed against the insurer.

adhesion contract A contract presented in printed standard from, submitted on a take-it-or-leave-it basis. Adhesion contracts are common in situations where one party's bargaining position is substantially weaker than the other's. A court may refuse to enforce a contract of adhesion.

ad hoc (Lat.) For one special purpose; for example, an ad hoc committee meets only one or two times for a special purpose and disbands once its goals have been accomplished.

ad hominem (Lat.) To the person. A personal attack on another person rather than arguing against his or her position.

ad idem (Lat.) Proving the same point.

ad infinitum (Lat.) Without limit; infinity.

adjective law The rules governing legal procedure and practice. This is distinguished from substantive law, which determines rights and duties.

adjourn 1. In parliamentary procedure, to officially terminate a meeting. 2. To let out or dismiss. 3. To postpone.

adjourned meeting In formal health-care meetings or hearings, a special meeting that is a continuation of a regular meeting and is legally a part of that meeting.

adjourn sine die (French) 1. Without day. 2. In parliamentary procedure, an adjournment that officially ends a convention or conference.

adjudicate 1. To judge. 2. To evaluate or assess. 3. To finally decide.

adjudication In managed care or medical insurance, this is the process of reviewing claims to determine the services eligible for reimbursement; the process of making a decision on a claim.

adjunct Additional; added on or united with.

adjunct diagnostic or therapeutic unit A special ancillary unit of a hospital equipped and staffed to assist physicians in diagnosis, treatment, or therapeutic procedures; this is not an operating room, a labor and delivery room, or a medical care unit.

adjunct disability In the Veterans Administration health-care program, a non–service-connected disability associated with or considered as aggravating a service-connected disability.

adjunct staff Nonphysician members of a medical staff of a hospital or health-care facility who provide medical services such as nurse practitioners, physician assistants, nurse anesthetists, etc.

adjunction A permanent addition or attachment (e.g., a wing added to a hospital).

adjunctive radiotherapy physics services Treatments necessary to conduct radiation therapy for optimal patient care, performed in consultation with a qualified radiological physicist (e.g., patient dosimetry, design, and construction of beam-shaping devices).

adjuration 1. Swearing under a solemn oath. 2. Swearing under the penalty of a curse or commitment to a deity.

adjusted average daily census As used in hospitals and inpatient facilities, this is the average number of patients who received care each day during the reporting period, usually 1 year in length. Inpatients as well as outpatients are considered. The census figure is derived by dividing the number of inpatient day equivalents (adjusted inpatient days) by the number of days in the reporting period.

adjusted average per capita cost (AAPCC) Under managed care, this is one method of reimbursement used by the Health Care Financing Administration (HCFA) and an estimate of the cost to care for Medicare recipients under a fee-for-services basis. It is an actuarial measure of the cost that would have been incurred by Medicare on behalf of enrollees of an HMO if they had received their covered services from providers other than those under the HMO contract in the same geographical area served by the HMO. The AAPCC consists of 122 different rate cells, 120 of them factored by age, Medicaid eligibility, sex, institutional status, and whether a person has both Part A and Part B of Medicare. The other two cells are for end-stage renal disease.

adjusted community rate (ACR) In managed-care plans Medicare risk contracts, this is a calculation of which charges/premiums the HMO plan would charge for providing medical care services based on only the Medicare-covered benefits of a managed-care account, adjusted to allow for a greater utilization by Medicare recipients. A normal profit for the managed-care program is included, and the adjusted community rate may be equal to or lower than the Average Payment Rate (APR) but cannot exceed this rate.

adjusted death rate Basic to epidemiology and vital statistics, adjusted rates allow for the summarizing of rates. Adjustment of a rate, such as death rate, allows for the effects of differences in composition of variables between or among a group or population that often needs to be controlled by a mathematical procedure and thus is in need of adjustment. If two or more groups need to be compared and if the groups differ in risk, or if a third variable is present that confuses the issue, an adjustment of the data is needed. Death rates are usually adjusted most by age. *See age-adjusted death rates; case severity.*

adjusted expenses per admission The average expenses a hospital incurs in providing services and patient care for the total stay of one patient on an inpatient basis. Adjusted expenses are found by subtracting outpatient expenses from total expenses. The number that results represents inpatient expenses and is divided by total admissions, providing the average expense per inpatient hospital stay. *See adjusted expenses per inpatient day.*

adjusted expenses per inpatient day These are expenses incurred for inpatient care only. The amount is derived by dividing the total expenses by inpatient day equivalents, giving the adjusted inpatient days. A formula that helps clarify this follows:

$$\frac{\text{Total expenses}}{\text{Inpatient days} + \text{Outpatient visits} \times \frac{\text{Outpatient income}}{\text{Outpatient visit}}}$$

(which is equivalent to)

$$\frac{\text{Total expenses}}{\text{Inpatient day}} \times \frac{\text{Inpatient revenue}}{\text{Total patient revenue}}$$

Expenses per adjusted patient day does not mean the average expense of two services. By dividing the total expenses by the total composite figure representing inpatient days plus outpatient visits converted into equivalent inpatient days (top formula), this shows the removal of the expenses incurred for outpatient care and then is divided (bottom formula) by the remaining inpatient days.

adjusted inpatient days *See inpatient day equivalents.*

adjusted inpatient day equivalents *See inpatient day equivalents.*

adjusted rate of return The rate of return of money on a long-term project as determined by adjusting the cash flow of the project for the time value of money. Also called the "discounted rate of return."

adjusted rates A summary rate that presents one statistic or rate for a total population but is adjusted statistically to remove differences in population composition.

adjuster 1. A person employed by an insurance company who assesses, adjusts, or determines the dollar amount of a claim or debt. 2. A health insurance adjuster determines and settles medical care claims.

adjusting entry Any new entry made at the end of an accounting period to show a record of an accounting action that was not recorded during the regular accounting period or process.

adjustment 1. In psychology, the way a person relates to society and oneself. 2. In insurance, this is settling the amount an insured person is entitled to receive under his or her policy after experiencing a peril. 3. In public health and epidemiology, when rates have the effects of differences removed by mathematical procedures.

adjuvant A drug, that, when combined with a second drug, changes the action of the first drug in a predictable manner, such as antabuse, and its reaction with alcohol.

ADL *See activities of daily living.*

ad litem (Lat.) For the suit; to meet the needs of a lawsuit; for purposes of litigation.

administer 1. To take charge of and manage. 2. To take charge of a business or an organization. 3. To conduct, supervise, coordinate, or manage an organization, program, service, or project.

administration 1. Those management, supervision, and coordination activities of a health-care organization or facility that aim to accomplish the goals and objectives of the organization. The activities and functions of a chief executive officer and the administrative staff, including conducting the classic functions of a manager such as planning, organizing, directing, and controlling. 2. To take charge of the management or running of a public service, a health-care organization or institution, or a governmental agency. 3. The coordinating, staffing, supervising, planning, and controlling of an undertaking toward the achievement of its purpose. 4. The staff responsible for facility management such as an administrator, assistant administrator, department heads, and program or unit managers. In hospitals, this includes nursing administration, allied health, and, in some cases, supervisors. Administration and management are so similar that they are considered synonymous. However, some distinctions have been made—administration is applied to public and governmental activities, whereas management is applicable in the private sector or by describing one as concerned with the execution of policy and the other the formulation and implementation of the policy and the running of an enterprise. *See management; management by objectives; planning; goal; objective.*

administrative 1. According to JCAHO for psychiatric, alcoholism, and drug abuse facilities accreditation purposes, this is related to the fiscal and general management of a facility rather than to the direct provision of services to patients. 2. Refers to the activities, authority, responsibility, policy, and action of management.

administrative adjustment An accounting method used to show services provided but not billed to patients because costs of billing and collection would exceed the actual patient charge. It also reflects partial adjustment of charges in special situations.

administrative agency A branch of the government created to carry out laws and policies; for example, the public health department is a local health administrative agency and the Health Systems Agency is a regional or state governmental administrative agency.

administrative board A body of individuals designated by an agency or health-care organization to hold hearings and/or determine policy. *See also governing body.*

administrative costs 1. In managed-care and health-care financial management, the expenses and costs experienced by an insurance carrier for the administrative services and costs of doing business such as processing insurance claims, billing, enrollment services, forms processing, and other overhead expenses. Administrative costs are usually figured in as a percent of the premiums. 2. In administration and health-care financial management, the expenses, supplies, personnel, and related costs incurred in the process of carrying on the operations of a health-care facility or health service; those administrative activities that use up revenue and that are essential to doing business but do not directly generate revenue.

administrative decision A decision rendered by a commission established by legislation such as OSHA, SSA, or FDA. Decisions handed down concerning regulations from administrative agencies.

administrative diagnosis In health promotion planning activities, this is an analysis of the organizational structure and function, climate, policies, and resources that either hinder or accommodate the development of a health promotion program within an organization.

administrative discretion Decisions made by administrative officials not covered by a policy, regulation, law, or rule and that depend on professional judgment. On judicial review of an administrative decision, there is an area of such professional judgment that the court will not disturb in the absence of abuse of discretion.

administrative law 1. Laws made for the management of an administrative agency. 2. Regulations created by administrative agencies. 3. Branch of law dealing with government administrative agencies, regulations, power, and those responsible for determining regulatory activities. 4. In managed care and insurance, the law used to interpret and apply regulations established by state and federal governments to control and regulate the activities of managed-care and insurance companies.

administrative law judge An official charged with the responsibility of making decisions in governmental administrative and regulatory matters, including health regulations related to public health, environmental health, and health-care delivery.

Administrative Procedures Act (APA) Enacted in 1946 and revised several times, it has incorporated the Freedom of Information Act, Privacy Act, Government in the Sunshine Act, and Regulatory Flexibility Act. Each state has enacted a similar law to regulate the conduct of administrative agencies within each state. The APA provides rules to govern rule making, government regulations, and regulatory agencies in the United States. Agencies are required to publish activities, rules, regulations, and final opinions in the *Federal Register* to inform the public of its activities. This act sets forth the legal procedures for making, implementing, reviewing, approving, revising, changing, and removing regulations of governmental agencies. *See rule-making procedures.*

administrative remedy The provision of an internal solution to a problem related to certain regulations and the agency's jurisdiction prior to considering formal litigation. Generally, administrative remedies must be exhausted before seeking relief from the judicial system.

administrative residency A formal graduate-level internship for students in graduate programs in health-care administration. More lengthy and intense than undergraduate field experience, the graduate student is assigned to the chief executive officer (CEO) and management team of a health-care organization, such as a hospital, for mentoring and educational guidance. The graduate health administration student usually rotates through all departments in the institution and then is assigned to the CEO or other top administrator for direction, mentoring, and conducting significant projects. The administrative resident completes assignments common to top-level managers while producing reports and completing projects that are of value to the organization. Residency ranges from 450 to 2000 hours, and most graduate students receive some form of monetary compensation because of the time commitment and managerial contributions made to the organization. *See administrative resident; internship; externship; residency.*

administrative resident A graduate student enrolled in a health services or health-care administration program of a university who is assigned to a hospital, medical group, nursing home, health maintenance organization, public health department, or other health organization to complete the administrative residency requirement for a graduate degree in health-care administration. *See administrative residency; internship; externship; residency.*

administrative services Managerial activities related to the fiscal and general management of medical care facilities as well as management of the patient care environment. These do not include direct provisions of services to patients. 2. Activities used to ensure adequate management of medical care resources and a quality patient care environment such as supervision of health care resources, housekeeping, facility maintenance, business office management, etc.

administrative services contract (ASC) A contract between a managed-care organization and a self-funded care plan where the managed-care plan performs administrative services only and does not assume risk. An employer group handles administrative services for a fee per member, per month. Services often include utilization review management, claims processing, and payment but can include accounting services, actuarial analysis, utilization review, clerical activities, etc.

administrative services only (ASO) In managed care, this is when another company handles the administrative aspects of employer-based self-funded health-care plans. It performs administrative services only and does not assume risk, is not an insurance company, and requires the employer to be at risk for the cost of health-care services of employers.

administrative style Attributes, influences, approaches, and organizational values that management personnel ingrain in and invoke on an organization or institution.

administrator 1. A professional health-care executive who, under the direction of the board of governors or trustees, carries out the mission, goals, objectives, and specific functions and activities of the health-care facility, organization, or institution. 2. The chief executive officer or top-level position of a hospital, health maintenance organization, nursing home, group practice, government agency, or other health-care organization or institution; he or she is responsible for managing its internal day-to-day activities and functions and is in charge of policy development, activity coordination, procedural development, and planning. This person interacts with and evaluates the external environment of the facility and controls and coordinates the internal environment of the institution. He or she makes knowledge and information available to the governing body and to the internal administrative staff to attain the goals of the organization. 3. In long-term-care settings, this means a person licensed as a nursing home administrator by a state board of examiners of nursing home administrators or a person who has a state civil service classification or a state career executive appointment to perform managerial functions in a state facility.

administrator, clinic The chief executive officer responsible for the management of a medical group's administrative activities. The administrator is trained in management and business and reports to the board of directors, which usually consists of the physicians who own the medical group practice.

administrator, qualified In JCAHO long-term-care facility accreditation, this is an individual who is currently licensed by the state in which he or she is practicing, if applicable, and is qualified by training and experience for the proper discharge of delegated responsibilities. *See also administrator, skilled nursing facility; health administration; health services administrator; long-term-care administrator.*

administrator, skilled nursing facility A person who is licensed or who meets educational and training requirements in administration and management as approved by the appropriate state agency and may be required to have some supervised practical administrative experience in a skilled nursing facility or related setting. If a hospital has an attached nursing facility, the administrator of the hospital may also be required to be a licensed nursing home administrator or must meet federal or Medicaid requirements. *See also qualified administrator; long-term-care administrator.*

admissibility (of evidence) 1. The worthiness of evidence. 2. In health law and malpractice litigation, the evidence that meets the legal rules of evidence and is allowed to be considered by a jury.

admissible evidence In health law, these are

facts and proof that may be properly received by a court for consideration in a case.

admission 1. In health law, this is a voluntary statement admitting that a fact or set of events is true or happened and becomes a part of the record. 2. The formal acceptance by a hospital or other inpatient health-care facility of a patient who is to be provided with room, board, and continuous nursing service in an area of the hospital or facility where patients generally stay, usually overnight. Formal registration by a health-care provider of patients to receive medical care, nursing care, therapy, or treatment. 3. In psychiatric care, an individual who is classified as an admission to a psychiatric facility by being a new admission, a readmission, a return from leave, or a transfer from another service of the same organization or another organization.

admission by adoption In health law, this is a statement made in the presence of the defendant that is of such a character and is made under such circumstances as to require a denial if untrue.

admission certification A form of medical care review in which an assessment is made of the medical necessity of a patient's admission to a hospital or other inpatient institution. Admission certification seeks to ensure that patients requiring hospital level of care, and only such patients, are admitted to the hospital without unnecessary delay and with proper planning of the hospital stay. Lengths of stay appropriate for the patient's admitting diagnosis are usually assigned and certified, and payment by any program requiring certification for the assigned stay is ensured. Certification can be done before (preadmission) or shortly after (concurrent) admission.

admission, clinic outpatient See *admission, outpatient*.

admission/discharge/transfer (ADT) A method used by the admitting department for collecting, storing, and distributing patient data to the involved hospital departments. Such relevant information is maintained on all phases of hospital admissions, including inpatient, outpatient, emergency room patients, and ambulatory surgical patients.

admission, elective Any admission to a health-care facility for treatment of an injury, illness, or condition that can be delayed or is not life threatening.

admission, emergency The formal acceptance of a patient into the hospital's emergency room or freestanding emergency center for the purpose of emergency care and treatment when the patient's condition is of such a serious and immediate nature as to warrant immediate treatment.

admission, emergency department The formal acceptance to the emergency department of a hospital of patients in need of immediate definitive medical care who are treated on an outpatient basis and are not admitted as an inpatient in the hospital.

admission, inpatient The formal acceptance of a patient into the hospital for at least a 24-hour period to receive diagnostic services and medical treatment. Such a patient is assigned a hospital room in an area providing ongoing nursing services.

admission, newborn The formal acceptance of a newborn as an official patient in a hospital.

admission notice Communication from a hospital, skilled nursing facility, or other institution to a managed-care organization or medical insurance company to inform it of the admission and to determine a patient's eligibility for treatment and benefits.

admission of evidence See *admissibility of evidence*.

admission, outpatient 1. The formal acceptance of a patient into a hospital ambulatory care clinic, freestanding surgical center, or other outpatient clinic for the purpose of receiving diagnostic services or treatment in a specialized medical or surgical unit. No inpatient room is assigned, and the patient is not admitted to the hospital and does not remain overnight in the facility. 2. The formal acceptance of a patient by a hospital for medical care and treatment on an ambulatory basis only. The patient is not admitted to inpatient care in the facility and does not receive nursing care in one of the hospital inpatient medical units.

admission pattern monitoring The constant watching and following of the types of patients, kinds of conditions, and number of patients admitted to a health-care facility. The administration of a health-care facility uses the data and information gained from patterns of admissions to determine staffing levels, types of services, and type of personnel needed to care for the case mix of patients shown by the admission pattern.

admission, pediatric The formal admission by a physician of a child (post-newborn age to 21 years) as an inpatient in a hospital or other treatment facility.

admission, preadmission process for The formal acceptance of a patient by the hospital on an outpatient basis to conduct preliminary medical tests prior to that individual's admission as an inpatient. *See preadmission process.*

admission rate A mathematical expression of the number of admissions by an institution in a specific geographic area during a certain time period. Often expressed as the number of admissions per 1000 individuals of the total population of a particular geographic area.

admission, referred outpatient The formal acceptance of a patient by a hospital as an outpatient to receive certain specified services following referral by a physician or other medical facility.

admissions The number of patients accepted and admitted into a hospital for inpatient services during certain periods of time or reporting periods. Births are not considered admissions and are excluded in the reporting.

admissions office This department or administrative unit, also referred to as admitting, admitting department, or admitting office, that arranges and schedules paperwork for patients ready for admission and maintains a waiting list and a list of empty beds. The admissions office may assign rooms and beds and collect initial data and nonmedical information about the patient and his or her family for the patient's medical record before being taken to a room. Other areas of the hospital that are affected by the admission are identified and notified when the patient is admitted.

admissions/1000 *See admissions rate.*

admissions per thousand In managed care, this is the number of hospital admissions per 1000 health plan members. *See admissions rate.*

admissions rate In managed care, this is the number of hospital admissions per 1000 health plan members. The admissions rate is the number of admissions divided by member months. The admissions rate formula follows:

$$\frac{\text{Number of admissions to a hospital for a specific time period}}{\text{Member months}} \times 1000$$

admissions review The review of patient condition, status, treatment, and related issues to determine the medical necessity of that admission. The review is conducted shortly after the patient is admitted to the hospital. *See admission certification.*

admission, transfer 1. The formal acceptance of a patient by a hospital or other health-care facility from another health-care facility because the patient is being transferred for advanced or specialized treatment. 2. To move a patient from one department or unit within a hospital to another unit within the same health-care facility (e.g., to move a patient from the oncology unit to a medical–surgical nursing unit within the same hospital).

admission, urgent The admission of a patient with a serious illness for treatment in a health-care facility but who is not in need of immediate definitive care, as in an emergency admission, but whose condition is more urgent than of an elective admission.

admits 1. In health-care facilities administration, this is a shortened version of "admissions," indicating the types, number, status, frequency, and rates of patients admitted to a health-care facility. 2. In managed care as a measure of utilization, the number of admissions to a hospital or other inpatient facility.

admitted assets Revenue, property, and equipment of a managed-care organization, HMO, or insurance company recognized by a state regulatory body or other examining body in determining the company's financial condition.

admitting department The administrative unit of a health-care facility that ensures that paperwork is filled out properly, payment mechanisms are in place for each patient, and all legal and accreditation standards of patient rights and patient treatment are met. Some admitting departments are responsible for admissions, transfer, and discharge of all patients within the health-care facility.

admitting officer The hospital official responsible for arranging admissions and discharges of hospital inpatients and managing the administrative activities of the admitting department.

admitting pattern The percentage of patients admitted to a hospital, clinic, or other health-care facility compared to the number of patients admitted; the type, level of acuity, specialty used, occurrence of visits, etc., of all patients seen.

admitting physician The physician responsible for admission of a patient to a hospital or other inpatient health-care facility. This physician remains responsible for the care of the patient once admitted *(see private patient)*. In an indigent-care facility such as a city, county, or state teaching hospital, the house medical staff usually becomes responsible for admissions. Some government-controlled facilities have all admission decisions made by the admitting physician, typically a rotating responsibility.

admitting privileges Authority granted to physicians of a hospital's medical staff to admit patients. Physicians on the medical staff may admit and perform only those treatments and procedures within the scope of clinical privileges granted each individual physician by the facility's medical staff and governing board (JCAHO acute-care facilities). *See staff privileges.*

admonitory tort 1. An intentional tort. 2. A case in which a wrongdoer receives a mild punishment, where the injured party may feel that punishment is more important than his or her own compensation.

ADMS Alcohol, Drug Abuse, and Mental Health Services (Block Grants).

adolescent medicine A relatively new medical specialty focusing its practice on general medicine for the adolescent patient (11–21 years).

adopt 1. To put a law into effect. 2. To accept and to put a policy or program into use. 3. To establish the legal relationship of parent and child between parties not naturally related. 4. In parliamentary procedure, to accept, approve, or give effect to a motion or rule.

adopt a report The official and formal acceptance of a report under parliamentary procedure in official meetings. The adoption of a report commits the organization to all that is included in the report and is a show of approval of the committee's work. *See "accept a committee report."*

ad respondendum (Lat.) For the purpose of answering.

ad personam (Lat.) To or toward the person.

ad rem (Lat.) 1. To the thing; to the purpose; to the point. 2. To the point at hand; to the present or current issue.

ADS *See alternate delivery system.*

ADT *See admission discharge transfer.*

adult 1. Of legal age, a person over the age of majority as set by state law. 2. Refers to older patients or the special care or services offered to older persons such as adult day-care centers.

adult day care A whole range of community-based programs and special services and care provided in a facility for mostly elderly persons who, for physical or psychological reasons, cannot care for themselves during the day on a regular basis. These services are on an ambulatory basis but are not considered outpatient care. The services include planned, supervised activities and meals in group settings, for either all or part of a day, aimed at promoting social, physical, and emotional well-being through personal attention and group activities. This enables the disabled adult to live at home on weekends and evenings and allows the family to work during regular business hours. Two models have been developed to help understand the different types of services available. The "medical model" is an outpatient center provided for adults and the elderly in need of limited yet regular physical rehabilitation or other health services. Often meals and social activities are provided. The "multipurpose model" is a walk-in center that provides social interaction and certain social and medical services in a fixed location for a limited number of hours. Most states require licensure of these services by the Department of Social Services. In some states, developmentally disabled persons may receive funding for adult day-care services.

adult day-care center A community-based facility that provides supervised services, activities, and meals to disabled adults during the day, usually during normal working hours.

adult day health care Community-based services that provide medical, rehabilitative, and social services to elderly persons and other adults with disabilities or functional impairments, either physical or mental, for restoring and maintaining optimal capacity for self-care. An individual care plan is prepared for each client/patient and targets adults who are at the institutional level of care or at risk of institutional placement. Physical therapy, speech therapy, occupational therapy, social work services, psychiatric services, limited nursing care, and other medical-related services are provided. Patients can receive Medicaid benefits, and developmentally disabled persons in some states may receive funding for adult day health-care services and are usually licensed by the state's Department of Social Services.

adult day health-care center A community-based facility that provides supervised medical and rehabilitation services, social services and social activities, and meals to disabled adults during the day, usually during normal working hours. Some centers have special Alzheimer's programs.

adult day health services A special medical and health-care service provided during the day to patients who are ambulatory, who can be easily transported, and who do not require continuous care.

adult foster care A specialized social service that enables older adults to live with families or individuals who are willing to share their homes. This type of arrangement offers homelike accommodations and allows these adults to avoid entering a long-term-care facility.

adult protective services A special service that provides legal and financial counseling for those people who are unable to manage their own affairs or protect themselves. Such protective services are designed to prevent or remedy neglect and abuse of older adults or other vulnerable persons.

adulteration 1. The combination of a quality product with an item of lesser quality producing something inferior to the original genuine product. 2. Mixing inferior products or harmful materials in with quality ones to increase volume, increase profits, and lower costs. In health care, the adulteration of drugs is a legal concern.

adultery Sexual intercourse between a married person and another person who is not the legal husband or wife.

adult homes See *boarding homes; board-and-care homes.*

adult social day care Community-based adult day care that provides nonmedical services to meet the needs of functionally impaired or disabled adults. Services are provided according to care plans in structured comprehensive programs that provide a variety of social, psychological, and supportive services in a protective environment on a daily basis during normal business hours. Such services allow family members to work yet care for the adults outside of working hours. Developmentally disabled persons in some states may receive funding for adult social day-care services.

advance and arrears In managed care and in medical insurance, this is an accounting system used for industrial insurance. The corporate office charges an agent with the amount of all premiums due on the policies of the agent services. When the agent remits the collected money, the agent receives credit for the amount of the collected premiums.

advance appropriation An appropriation provided by the U.S. Congress 1 or more years in advance of the fiscal year in which the budget authority becomes available for obligation. Advance appropriations allow state and local governments sufficient time to develop plans with assurance of future federal funding. An advance appropriation is sometimes mistakenly referred to as "forward funding," which involves an agency in obligating funds in the current year for outlay to programs that are to operate in subsequent fiscal years.

advanced directive As part of the Patient Self-Determination Act (under OBRA 1990), the advanced directive is a formal document written in advance of an incapacitating illness or injury in which people can provide for decision making about medical treatment if they become unable to make their own decisions. Two types of advanced directives are used: those that appoint a legal agent to make decisions and those that state choices about treatment if the person is incapacitated. Advanced directives minimize legal risk and reduce the chance of conflict within the health-care setting. See *Patient Self-Determination Act; durable power of attorney for health care.*

advanced emergency medical procedures The medical care and treatment activities that paramedics are allowed to perform in the field. Emergency medical technicians (EMTs) fall short of advanced skills and the required formal training in advanced medical procedure areas and, thus, are not legally eligible to do them.

advanced emergency medical technician See *emergency medical technician; emergency medical technician, intermediate.*

advanced life support (ALS) In emergency medical care services, this is the use of specialized advanced treatment approaches such as the administration of certain injectable medications, intravenous administration of medications, defibrillation, and other advanced medical procedures.

adversary 1. One's opposition, foe, antagonist, or enemy. 2. In health law, this is the opposing party in a suit, writ, or action; the opponent in litigation.

adversary proceeding A trial court or a hearing where the contesting parties present opposing views.

adversary system The system in U.S. law where the judge serves as a decision maker between opposing parties.

adverse event An occurrence in a health-care setting when something happens to a patient to injure or harm the patient, resulting in a malpractice or liability lawsuit. Adverse events can be incidents or more serious occurrences such as patient injury, required unplanned surgery, any nosocomial infection that has developed, an iatrogenic occurrence, inpatient admission being required because of something going wrong in an outpatient surgery or treatment, a readmission caused by incomplete care that led to complications, inappropriate procedures that fell outside of the hospital's guidelines, blood transfusion problems, adverse drug reaction, cardiac arrest, respiratory arrest, fall or accident to a patient, or wrongful death situations. Also referred to as "adverse patient occurrences." *See incidence.*

adverse interest The needs or wishes of an individual that are in conflict with another individual.

adverse patient occurrence. *See adverse event.*

adverse selection 1. In managed care and insurance, this is the disproportionate insurance of risks (patients who use up a lot of health-care resources and who have above-average treatments and high utilization patterns) for people who are poorer or more prone to cause loss for the health plan or make claims than the average risk. It may result from the tendency for poorer risks or less desirable clients (sick people) to seek or continue insurance to a greater extent than do better risks (healthy people) or from a tendency for the insured to take advantage of favorable options in insurance contracts; favorable, as compared to adverse, selection (when intentional) is called "skimming." 2. When an insurance carrier accepts members who are a poorer risk than the average risk group. 3. A process of drawing a disproportionately high-risk membership as compared to a representative cross-section of the target population. 4. In managed care, this is also when the health plan population usually has a significantly higher utilization than was budgeted, resulting in premiums and fees failing to cover the cost of providing health care, often due to a segment of the plan population having a poorer health status than usual or being of increased age. *See also skimming; skimping.*

adverse witness A witness who shows opposition through prejudice and who, thus, is open to leading questions and cross-examination by the side that requested the witness appear.

advertising, health-care In strategic health planning and health-care marketing, this is the process of communicating to the customers or potential customers of the health-care organization the services offered and the advantages of using the organization's services. Some marketing and advertising approaches common to general business or manufacturing industries often do not work in health care. Promotional advertising can be used to promote a service or offering, and institutional advertising can be used to create an image of the organization in the community. Advertising approaches and methods can be used to change the organization's image and/or increase business activities through the use of all appropriate media sources and channels to assist in accomplishing the marketing plan's clearly defined objectives and well-developed marketing strategies. *See health-care marketing; customer, health-care.*

advisory board (group) 1. A committee of individuals that serves as an advice-giving body yet is unlike a board of governors or board of directors, as the advisory board has no authority or power over the organization that established it. 2. Under Professional Review Organization (PRO) programs, an organization required under Section 1162(e) of Public Law 92-603 to advise and assist a statewide Professional Review Council, or a PRO in a state without a statewide council, in carrying out PRO program objectives. An advisory group is an ongoing, formal mechanism whereby health-care practitioners other than physicians and representatives of hospitals and other health-care facilities participate in a PRO program. *See also Professional Review Organization.*

advocacy Actions taken by individuals and/or groups on behalf of others who have unmet needs. Working for political, regulatory, or organizational change on behalf of a particular interest group. A personal action on behalf of an individual on a personal level in assisting an older person with receiving some benefit to which that individual is entitled. An action may also be taken by a group or organization to secure its own unmet needs (e.g., a mass communication effort to persuade legislators to support or oppose a certain bill or law).

advocate 1. A person who pleads for another person or an organization. 2. A person who defends or pleads a "cause" of another.

A-EMT Advanced Emergency Medical Technician. *See EMT-A.*

aero- Prefix meaning "air."

aerobe Microorganisms that require oxygen for growth.

Aerobics and Fitness Association of America (AFAA) A national nonprofit professional organization for fitness practitioners. Fitness management of life is the philosophy of this group, headquartered in Sherman Oaks, California.

aerosols An environmental health and air pollution control concern, these are liquid droplets or microscopic particles (particulates) sprayed as a mist into the air that are fine enough to remain afloat and to disperse and remain suspended in the air for a long period of time.

aerospace medicine A medical specialty that specializes in the health and physiological effects of flying and space travel on the human body.

AFDC *See Aid to Families with Dependent Children.*

AFL-CIO *See American Federation of Labor and Congress of Industrial Organizations.*

AFCR American Federation for Clinical Research.

affect Emotions, as opposed to one's cognitive or intellectual domain. These are the inner feelings and the external reaction to feelings.

affect, blunted A disturbance in which emotions are dulled (can be observed in schizophrenia).

affected person In health planning and healthcare delivery, this is any person residing within the geographic area served or to be served by a change in health-care delivery capacity, Certificate of Need, or cost increases. This could involve individuals that have access to care changed by any health service agency, organization, hospital, or institution serving a contiguous health service area. Capacity can be affected if a competitive service is provided and could affect health-care providers and individual access in both a positive and a negative fashion within the target service area or in a neighboring health service area.

affective Based on, pertaining to, or arising from feelings, emotions, or certain mental states.

affective disorders Emotional problems marked by personality changes, alterations in mood, lack of self-esteem, and psychological confusion. Reactive depression and mania are frequently observed affective disorders.

affective interaction Interpersonal transactions that are emotionally charged.

affidavit Any voluntarily sworn or written statement or declaration of fact.

affiliate In health administration and organizational structures, this is when a service, program, or other facility is directly or indirectly financially or organizationally controlled by, answerable to, or associated with another similar facility or a parent organization and provides services to or receives services from it.

affiliated Includes any medical or allied health personnel who are associated with a health-care facility or program. Affiliation is based on a formal agreement between two organizations, often for shared resources, service, or educational training programs. *See affiliation.*

affiliated hospital or outpatient facility A healthcare facility that has a legal or a formal agreement and/or association with another health program, usually a medical school or school of health professions. Some definitions limit it to hospitals with close or extensive associations with a medical school or a school of allied health. Generally, this refers to a hospital or outpatient facility that is not owned by, but is formally associated with, a medical school or a school of allied health, nursing, health-care administration, osteopathy, or dentistry and that meets certain eligibility conditions and/or legal contractual and liability agreements.

affiliation An agreement (usually formal) between two or more otherwise independent programs or individuals that defines their interrelation. Affiliation agreements may specify procedures for referring or transferring patients from one facility to another, joint faculty and/or medical staff appointments, teaching relationships, sharing of records or services, or provision of consultation between programs. *See also affiliated hospital; outpatient facility.*

affinity Related to by marriage; a husband is related to his wife's sister by affinity.

affirmative action A legal requirement that government-related organizations take positive steps to avoid discrimination in hiring and promotion. Federal affirmative action laws prohibit discrimination on the basis of age, race, sex, religion, marital status, handicap, or Vietnam-era or disabled veterans status.

affirmative action programs This is an employer's administrative plan and policies implemented to ensure that equal employment opportunities occur within the organization; they set forth an organized plan to ensure that no one is discriminated against in employment or promotion because of age, sex, race, religion, marital status, etc., and is often administered by human resource departments or may be a separate administrative unit.

affirmative defense In health-care law, this is a defendant's legal answer that is more than a denial of facts to a complaint. It provides new facts and arguments that could cause the defendant to win even if the complaint is true.

affirmative relief In health law, the relief or compensation granted a defendant apart from any claim made against him or her by the plaintiff.

a force (Lat.) Of necessity.

aforesaid Said previously or already mentioned.

a fortiori (Lat.) A good possibility; having a strong reason to believe; for a greater reason.

AFP *See Aerobics and Fitness Association of America.*

aftercare 1. After hospitalization, continuous care on discharge from an acute-care hospital. It also refers to home health care provided after discharge from a hospital or nursing home when a patient still requires some skilled nursing or other care. 2. In psychiatric counseling, physical therapy, and occupational therapy, a continuing program of rehabilitation to help the patient make the transition to a new environment and the community's work setting. 3. According to JCAHO for psychiatric, alcoholism, and drug abuse facilities accreditation purposes, services provided to a patient after discharge that support and increase the gains made during treatment. *See home health care.*

against medical advice (AMA) The discharge status of a patient who leaves a hospital when it is medically inadvisable to do so. When a patient walks out or otherwise leaves a hospital without being formally discharged by the attending physician and does so against the advice of the physician or the hospital nursing and medical staff. If possible, the hospital staff requests that the patient sign a form that releases the health-care facility and physician from responsibility or liability.

age The years of life one has lived as reported as of one's last birthday. 1. For use in public health, vital statistics, and epidemiology, age in years is calculated by subtracting the date of birth from the reference date, which is the date of the examination, interview, or other contract with the individual. Age is recorded in single years and may be grouped in a variety of distributions depending on the purpose and use, as in the construction of an epidemiological table or chart. In determining epidemiological changes of morbidity and mortality within populations, age is the variable with the greatest influence on epidemiological outcomes and determinations. 2. Age is used to determine legal status, age of majority, minor status, and program eligibility for Medicare.

age-adjusted mortality (death) rate An adjusted death rate takes into account differences in a population caused by age, as age varies in different geographical areas. Mortality rates adjusted for age account for the high proportion of elderly living in a community having high numbers of deaths among the elderly. Adjustment takes into account the high proportion of elderly in a certain geographical area that may be no higher than national averages in terms of death rates. *See age adjustment; case severity; age-specific death rate.*

age-adjusted rate A total rate for a population, adjusted to ignore age distributions by multiplying each of its age-specific rates by the proportion of a standard population (state or national) in that age-group adding up the products.

age adjustment This uses the direct method and is the application of the age-specific rates in a population of interest to a standardized age distribution to eliminate the differences in observed rates that result from age differences in population composition. Adjustment is done when comparing two or more populations at one point in time or one population at two or more points in time. In most government epidemiological reports, death rates are age adjusted. It is standard public health practice to adjust age using the following age-groups: under 17, 17–44, 45–54, 65–74, and 75 and over.

age dependency ratio A demographic measure used to assess changing age composition in a population. It is based on an aggregation of those who are too young or too old to provide for their own financial or social well-being. The age dependency ratio is used to determine how many dependents every 100 working members of a group must support. Using simple statistics to reflect age distributions, this ratio can be calculated for various populations. Thus, it is possible to compare those who are age dependent across diverse societies.

age discrimination in employment Discrimination based on age related to employment is unlawful, with such law derived from both statutes and case law. The Age Discrimination in Employment Act of 1967 was passed to prohibit age-based employment discrimination for individuals between ages 40 and 70.

Age Discrimination in Employment Act of 1967 A federal law that prohibits discrimination in employment based on age, against those who are 40 and older.

Age Discrimination in Employment Act of 1975 (P.L. 94-135, 91 Stat. 269 [1975]) This act prohibits unreasonable discrimination on the basis of age in all programs receiving federal assistance; the act is not limited to persons between 40 and 65 years of age.

age distribution A statistical measure that describes the proportional age mix in a population.

age grading The classification of human behavior as appropriate or inappropriate for various age-groups in society such as young versus adolescent versus older adults.

ageism 1. The image of and attitudes toward an aged individual (either negative or positive). The extent to which the public in general perceives, stereotypes, and is prejudiced toward persons in their later years of life. 2. A process of systematic stereotyping of and discrimination against people because they are old, with younger generations seeing older people as different and subtly ceasing to identify older adults as human beings.

age limits Stipulated minimum and maximum ages below and above which a health insurance company will not accept new applications and may not renew old policies.

aged One who is advanced in age. Some authorities or programs classify anyone over 65 years of age as aged.

agency A relationship whereby one person represents or acts on behalf of another, under and by the other person's authority. *See master; servant; law of agency.*

agency bank In managed-care plans and insurance, this is a mutual saving type bank that does not sell its own insurance policies or plans to the public but sells policies as an agent for an issuance company. This bank accepts applications, collects premiums, and provides services for its own plans or policy owners.

agency, notice of availability In environmental health, the official public notification of an environmental impact statement usually published in the *Federal Register.*

age norms Guidelines used to determine age-appropriate behavior. Age norms provide a guide to acceptable behavior but do not supply detailed stipulations or exceptions for each and every possible case.

age of majority Legal age, ranging between 18 and 21 years, depending on the state. The age at which a person attains legal adult rights and obligations and can enter into contracts, drink alcohol, have adult status, and marry without consent of parents and is held legally accountable by law.

agent 1. In epidemiology, this is any factor such as a pathogen, microorganism, toxin, radiation, or chemical that invades or is present in the body in excess and, thus, causes a disease to occur; an organism or object which transmits a disease from the environment to the host. 2. In industrial health and safety, the principal object such as a tool or a piece of machinery or equipment involved in an accident and that contributed to the infliction of an injury or the cause of property damage. 3. In health law, any person who represents or acts on behalf of another with that person's implied or expressed permission and authority (e.g., a nurse who provides health care under the legal direction of a physician). 4. One who legally acts on behalf of the principal by carrying out the requests or orders of the principal. 5. In insurance, an insurance company representative licensed by the state who solicits, negotiates, or effects contracts of insurance and services the policyholder for the insurer. *See master; servant; law of agency.*

agent's statement In managed-care plans or insurance, this is a statement where the plan's agent reports anything known or suspected about the potential client that is not included in the formal application filled out by the client.

age/sex factor In managed care and insurance, this is a measure used by insurance carrier's underwriters to determine the level of risk of loss due to age and sex in medical care utilization and health care resource usage and the medical costs of one population relative to another based on age and sex factors. A group with an age/sex factor of 1.00 is average. An age/sex factor above 1.00 indicates a higher-than-average demographic risk of expected medical care claims. An age/sex factor below 1.00 indicates a lower-than-average demographic risk of expected medical claims.

age/sex rate (ASR) In managed care and insurance, this is a measure used by insurance carrier's underwriters to establish utilization by age and sex for a given employer group or enrollment group in which there is a separate rate for each grouping of age and sex categories. A single rate table serves a defined group of enrollees (group or product). Age and sex rates for a certain enrollment group are used to calculate premiums for group billing purposes. This type of premium structure is often preferred over single and family rating in small groups because it automatically adjusts for demographic changes for the enrollment group. Also referred to as "table rates."

age-specific birth rate The number of live births to a selected age-group per 1000, 10,000, or 100,000 population in that same age-group.

age-specific death rate The number of deaths reported in a selected age-group per 1000, 10,000, or 100,000 population in that same age-group.

age-specific fertility rate A rate that is used to determine the number of live births to females in a specific age range or age-group for a certain time period, usually 1 year and per 1000 females in that age range or age-group.

age-specific rate The rate of occurrence of an event, such as birth, marriage, death, or illness, for a specified age-group in a population; the incidence or number of events during a specified period for an age-group divided by the total number of people in that age-group.

age-specific rates In public health and epidemiology, these are the rates used in mortality and morbidity assessment for a specific age-group analysis; the numerator and denominator of the rate apply to the same age-group per 1000, 10,000, or 100,000 multiplier for the appropriate-sized population. The age-specific rate formula follows:

$$\frac{\text{Number of deaths in population, ages 40–65, in the geographical area per year}}{\text{Average population, ages 40–65, in the geographical area per year}} \times 100{,}000$$

age-standardized rate See *standardization*.

aggravation Actions that increase the seriousness of a crime, injury, or medical condition.

aggregate claims In managed care and medical insurance, these are equal to the claim frequency rate per insured multiplied by the average amount of claims and then multiplied by the number of insured lives. Aggregate claims expected under the terms of an HMO plan or a medical insurance contract are the primary element in calculating premium rates.

aggregate indemnity The maximum dollar amount payable for any disability, or period of disability, covered under an insurance policy; also called "policy limits."

aggregate mortality tables Death rates and mortality tables as used in life insurance that are based on the experience of all the lives of the insured, including mortality rates both during and after a given time period. Mortality rates of an aggregate mortality table fall between those of the selected and the ideal mortality tables.

aggregate standards compliance data See *aggregate survey data, hospital*.

aggregate survey data, hospital In the process of accreditation, information on key hospital performance areas and standards are collected from hospitals and compiled in a database to produce accumulated information on accreditation standards compliance of hospitals for a specific time period (JCAHO for acute-care facilities).

aggression 1. Forceful verbal or physical behavior. 2. The reaction of rage, anger, and hostility. 3. Any forceful physical, verbal, or nonverbal symbolic act.

aggressive collection In health care finance and business office management, this describes the use of a variety of methods to collect a debt, such as attachment, garnishment, etc.

aggressive drive In psychiatry, this describes destructive impulses aimed at others or at oneself; it may be known as the death instinct.

aggrieved party In health law, this is the legal party that has been injured or harmed or has had personal or property rights violated by another party.

aging The process of experiencing the passing of time and the growing old of body tissues wherein the function and capacities of the organism continue to decline. Several theories of aging have been suggested, ranging from the idea that a person ages from the time of conception to the belief that one grows to a certain point, usually in the late twenties, after which a decline in the body begins and continues until death.

aging accounts receivable In health finance, this is a method of reviewing and classifying accounts receivable in which one keeps track of the time elapsed since the receivable came due or the time that has passed since the last payment was made. This process is used for the purpose of evaluating credit and long-overdue bill collection policies. This process may also be used to estimate the amount of difficulty in collecting accounts receivable as of a given date. *See aging schedule.*

aging of the population The increasing proportion in the general population of older persons relative to younger persons. A measure of the distribution of older persons in the total population. Large numbers of cohorts of persons who move as a group into the later periods of life in the population. *See population pyramid.*

aging schedule In health finance, this relates to aging accounts receivable and is a report that shows how long accounts receivables have been outstanding. The report presents the percentage of receivables not past due and the percentage past due by 1 month, 2 months, 6 months, 1 year, etc. *See aging accounts receivable.*

agitation Anxiety associated with severe restlessness.

AGPA *See American Group Practice Association.*

agraphia Being unable to write.

agreement 1. Having unity in an opinion. 2. In contract law, the "meeting of the minds," where two or more parties have equal sentiment to enter into a contract. *See mutual assent.*

agreement number *See identification number.*

agromania An unhealthy interest in living alone or in seclusion.

AHA *See American Hospital Association.*

AHCA *See American Health Care Association.*

AHCCCS *See Arizona Health Care Cost Containment System.*

AHCPR Agency for Health Care Policy and Research (Public Health Service).

AHEC *See Area Health Education Center.*

AHIP *See Assisted Health Insurance Plan.*

AHP *See allied health personnel; accountable health plan; accountable health partnership; Association of Humanistic Psychology.*

AHPA *See American Health Planning Association.*

AHR *See Association for Health Records.*

AHSR *See Association for Health Services Research.*

AID *See automatic interaction detector.*

AIDA Automated Interactive Design of Applications.

aid and abet To know and intentionally help or encourage another to commit a crime.

aid codes In medical records administration and insurance coding, this is a 2-digit number code that links Medicaid participants to the Medicaid program (in California's MediCal). These are the third and fourth digits in a MediCal 14-digit identification number.

aide A worker in hospitals and nursing homes who helps with supportive nursing-related and personal care chores such as changing patients' clothes, changing diapers of incontinent elderly patients, showering patients, changing beds, etc. These workers are often female and require no specific education or credentials. Also referred to as a "nursing assistant." Individuals who do the same chores but with special training and experience and who pass special tests are called "certified nurse assistants" (CNAs). *See nursing assistant; orderly; certified nurse assistant.*

aider A procedure where a verdict has been reached and the facts on which the verdict is based are presumed to have been proven true.

AIDS Acquired immunodeficiency syndrome is an illness characterized by a positive test for human immunodeficiency virus (HIV) infection or the absence of specified causes of underlying immunodeficiency. AIDS includes the presumptive diagnosis of AIDS-associated diseases and conditions and to expand the spectrum of HIV-associated diseases reportable as AIDS. This list includes HIV encephalopathy, HIV wasting syndrome, etc.

AIDS/ARC unit A special care unit designated and equipped specifically for diagnosis, treatment, continuing care plan, specialized drug therapy, and counseling and support services for patients and their families.

AIDS support organizations *See The Aids Support Organizations.*

AIDS transplant pool In managed care, this is a pool of money set aside and shared between physicians/medical groups and a health plan/HMO to specifically cover all costs or services directly incurred by treating AIDS patients or transplant patients.

Aid to Families with Dependent Children (AFDC) A federal program created to provide medical aid and cash to families with dependent children. Any child under age 21 is eligible if the family is found eligible on the basis of children being deprived of parental support or care and their eligible relatives.

Aid to the Blind A federally created program that provides financial assistance to states for the provision of medical aid to the blind.

Aid to the Permanently and Totally Disabled (APTD) A federal program providing medical care to those permanently and totally disabled who are medically indigent.

AIMMS *See Automated Integrated Medical Management System.*

AIP *See Annual Implementation Plan.*

air pollution The contamination of the atmosphere with particulate materials, aerosols, dusts, smoke, fumes, or mists due to the discharge of noxious and sometimes toxic chemicals or substances into the air in sufficient quantity and of such a nature and duration as to be a hazard to one's health and to be injurious to humans, animal or plant life, and property. *See Ringlemann chart.*

air quality control region A geographical region where two or more communities share a common air pollution problem. Designated by the Secretary of Health and Human Services, these regions are required to set and enforce air quality standards.

airborne transmission When infectious agents such as bacteria or viruses are communicated among individuals or groups of people by water droplets, particles, or dust blown into and/or suspended in the air and then inhaled by other persons.

alarm reaction The initial and basic reaction of the human body to a stressor. *See stress.*

alcohol abuse Misuse or excessive use of alcoholic beverages or the unrestrained consumption or addiction to this drug, which may impair health or interfere with an individual's effectiveness on the job, in the family, at home, in the community, or in safe operation of vehicles. For some individuals, a single drink may constitute alcohol abuse.

alcohol and chemical dependency inpatient services Specialized programs that provide medical and rehabilitative therapy and treatment for patients who have a serious alcohol or other chemical dependency. Such patients require a 24-hour treatment program within a treatment facility or hospital with professional staff, specialized treatment facilities, treatment care plans, nursing services, psychiatric care, and the usual lodging and food services of a regular inpatient unit.

alcohol and chemical (drug abuse) dependency outpatient services Ambulatory hospital or specialized treatment facility services for persons who have a primary diagnosis of alcoholism or other chemical dependency that provide medical and rehabilitative therapy and treatment for alcoholism or other chemical dependency similar to those provided on an inpatient basis but without the patient being admitted to the facility.

alcohol and drug abuse specialist Personnel who have received specialized training and who work with patients and their families on problems of alcohol and drug abuse or dependence. Among their major functions are encouraging patient self-analysis and personality development, counseling, and providing emotional support and behavioral guidance, especially for institutionalized patients. They usually function as members of health teams that include physicians, psychologists, and social workers.

alcohol and drug abuse specialty A specialized educational program that trains individuals to counsel, guide, and assist persons addicted to alcohol or drugs to overcome alcohol and chemical dependency as well as help them overcome personal, family, and social problems that are manifested in alcoholism and drug addiction.

Alcohol, Drug Abuse, and Mental Health Administration (ADAMHA) A division of the U.S. Public Health Service that incorporates three other government health agencies: Drug Abuse and Mental Health, National Institutes on Alcohol Abuse and Alcoholism, and National Institutes of Health.

alcoholic An individual who habitually and uncontrollably consumes alcoholic beverages to excess and who suffers from alcoholism.

Alcoholic and Narcotic Addict Rehabilitation Amendment A public law passed in 1968 that provides additional provisions to the Community Mental Health Centers Act. This amendment provides funds for the construction of community mental health facilities as well as employment of medical personnel to provide treatment to addicts. Financing for special training programs was also provided.

alcoholic psychosis Mental illness from alcoholism, including organic brain damage. *See also delirium tremens; hallucinosis; Korsakof's psychosis.*

Alcoholics Anonymous (AA) A rehabilitation organization for alcoholics formed in 1935 that provides twelve steps to recovery from alcoholism based on the premise that alcoholics are powerless when it comes to alcohol use and they must turn their recovery over to God or a higher power. A fellowship in which recovering alcoholics help one another maintain sobriety and that recognizes that the desire to stop drinking must come from within; it is considered one of the most effective rehabilitation programs.

alcoholism 1. A progressive and chronic illness characterized by preoccupation with and loss of power to resist the drinking of alcohol. Once drinking is started, it leads to intoxication, and once drinking is halted, relapses are common. Marked physical disability, impaired emotional and social adjustment, occupational and work problems, and often job loss are typically associated with continued consumption and excessive use of alcohol. 2. Physical and psychological dependence on or addiction to alcohol. The definition of alcoholism in both theory and practice is highly variable, sometimes requiring only excessive drinking or interference with the drinker's functioning rather than both and sometimes requiring, in addition to the above, physical signs of drug dependence or being recognized as present without either. There are many variable systems for separating different types of alcoholism and grading its severity. Some medical professionals and behavioral scientists refer to alcoholism as a disease. Because no pathogen or similar agent is involved in the illness, many medical professionals and behavioral scientists view alcoholism as a behavioral, emotional, and psychological problem and not a true disease. *See also drug abuse.*

alcoholism and other drug-dependence services Health-care services that provide alcohol recovery and treatment for alcohol and drug dependency. In JCAHO accreditation, standards are applied to evaluate a health-care facility's performance in providing treatment and care for substance abuse.

alcoholism rehabilitation center A specialized treatment facility or treatment unit within a hospital staffed with trained professionals who offer treatment and rehabilitative services for the alcoholic. Treatment may be on either an inpatient or an outpatient basis.

alcoholism treatment services All specialized treatment and diagnostic services provided specifically for alcohol-related problems.

aleatory contract An agreement or contract that is contingent on an uncertain future event.

alexia The inability to grasp the meaning of written words and sentences.

algebraic method In managed care, this is a cost-finding technique involving the simultaneous distribution of general service cost center costs to both general service and financial cost centers.

-algia Suffix meaning "pain."

algorithm, clinical Health care providers, usually physicians or physician assistants or nurse practitioners, through the use of decision trees and all pertinent clinical data, follow an explicit set of steps in the care of a patient to ensure proper treatment. Also referred to as "clinical protocol."

alienable 1. That which can be sold. 2. That which can be transferred. 3. Subject to removal.

alienate 1. To estrange. 2. To transfer, convey, or dispose of property to another.

alienation 1. Feelings of detachment from society or from oneself. 2. Avoidance of emotional experience; to estrange oneself.

alienation clause A part of an insurance policy that voids or ends the policy if the insured item is sold or otherwise transferred.

alienist A psychiatrist or psychologist who provides expert opinion about mental illness or sanity.

alignment The positioning of bone structures or body parts that facilitates effective body function.

allay To subdue or reduce in intensity; to make quiet or calm or to reduce fear.

allegation 1. Something alleged, asserted, stated, or charged. 2. A statement in the pleading that provides the facts that one side expects to prove. 3. The first plea by the plaintiff in a case.

allege To declare without proof; to assert, charge, or make an allegation.

allergist A physician whose specialty is the diagnosis and treatment of allergies.

allergy immunology technician An individual trained to prepare and administer the materials prescribed by a physician, usually specializing in allergy immunology, to desensitize individuals to various environmental and food allergens.

all fours Two cases are on "all fours" if they are alike in a legal manner and are so factually similar that the rationale of one case with equal logic is equal to another.

alliance A formal organizational structure that works on behalf of its separate and individual members in the provision of services and goods and the promotion of activities and ventures in a way that is mutually beneficial to all participating members of the organization.

alliances In universal coverage and managed competition, this is a medical care insurance buying pool, purchasing pool, or purchasing cooperative. Uninsured or difficult-to-insure groups who lack purchasing power, such as small business and private individuals under an alliance, can band together to make a larger group and thus are able to get more competitive rates than if they tried to purchase medical insurance on their own. Under various American Health Security Act proposals, one or more regional health alliances would be established in each state to provide medical care for the region.

allied health The composite of instructional programs and semiprofessionals that assist physicians, osteopaths, dentists, and other qualified health care professionals in providing diagnostic, therapeutic, preventive, restorative, and rehabilitative services to patients under the direction of the qualified professional in health care facilities, the community, or the home.

allied health educator An individual who teaches in an allied health specialty in which he or she was trained to prepare students in the same discipline. The term is not specific to one occupation but refers to various allied health disciplines.

allied health manpower Educated or technically trained health care personnel who work with, support, and assist physicians and dentists in the provision of health services. Most allied health personnel do not engage in independent practice, or they work under a prescription written by a physician.

allied health personnel Those health-care workers who are specially trained and licensed to assist and support the work of the physician, dentist, podiatrist, osteopath, or psychologist. Often used synonymously with "paramedical personnel" and "paraprofessionals," the term is also used to describe those health paraprofessionals who assist environmental health engineers and public health personnel. Generally, the term refers to all health-care workers who perform tasks that must otherwise be performed by a physician. The term sometimes refers to health workers, health control officers, or others who engage in preventive medicine activities who do not usually engage in independent practice. Though considered a professional, in a legal sense nurses are allied health personnel, as the nurse is an agent of the physician or hospital and has to work under the orders of the physician, as he or she is the principal and can be held liable for the acts of the nurse or the allied health personnel if a working relationship exists and something goes wrong.

Allied Health Professions Personnel Training Act (1966) A federal law passed to establish programs for construction of facilities for training allied health-care providers such as nurses, medical technologists, and dental hygienists. Student loans, grants, and scholarships were also provided; however, loans for physicians and dentists who practice in rural areas were cancelled.

alien corporation A legal term that describes a type of corporation that is a legal organization incorporated under the laws of a country other than the United States.

all-line insurer An insurance company that has the authority to underwrite all types of insurance as well as the right to issue contracts on a variety of insurance, including life insurance.

allocated benefit provision A provision in a medical insurance policy or health plan under which payment for certain benefits (miscellaneous hospital and medical services such as X rays, dressings, and drugs) will be made at a rate for each benefit specified (scheduled) in the provision. Usually there is also a maximum that will be paid for all such expenses. An allocated benefit is one that is subject to such a provision. In an unallocated benefit provision, no specification is given regarding how much will be paid for each type of service, although the provision sets a maximum payable for all the listed services.

allocation 1. The setting up of an allotment or shares. 2. To set apart money or resources for a specific purpose; the distribution of resources to specific categories of expenditure or to a specific organizational subunit. 3. The total amount of money or resources that the administration of an organization, office of management, and budget or fiscal officer actually provides for the operation of a department or program. 4. The sum of money a foundation, government agency, or the U.S. Office of Management and Budget actually allots the grant or the project being funded.

allocation basis In health-care finance, this is a systematic budgeting and accounting method of assigning indirect costs to two or more cost areas. This method is useful in determining full costs that are then used for preparation of billing rates.

allocation of overhead In health finance and the financial statements or cost analysis, it is required to assign overhead expenses to patient care areas on the basis of statistical factors or accumulated data on items such as square feet, man-hours of labor, etc.

allocution A formality of the court whereby a defendant is asked whether he or she has anything to say on his or her own behalf to stop sentencing.

allograph 1. A legal paper or document written or signed by one person for another party who is not a party to the agreement. 2. A signature by proxy.

allograft When tissues or organs are transplanted from the same species but from one organism or person to another.

allopathic physician Usually used in contrast to "osteopathic" and "homeopathic," a physician practicing a philosophy of medicine that views the role of the physician as an active interventionist. This type of physician attempts to counteract the effect of a disease by using treatments, surgical or medical, that produce effects opposite to those of the disease. A homeopathic physician, on the other hand, generally uses a drug therapy that reinforces the body's natural self-healing process. Almost all physicians in the United States would be considered allopathic. *See homeopathy; osteopathy; osteopathic physician.*

allopathy The most common form of medical practice in the United States. This system deals with diagnosis and treatment through intervention and embraces a preventive approach to disease.

alloplasty 1. Adapting to stress by trying to change the environment. 2. Plastic surgery that uses inert material to repair or alter body tissue.

allowable charge A generic term referring to the maximum fee that a third party will use in reimbursing a provider for a given service. An allowable charge may not be the same as a reasonable or customary or prevailing charge. *See customary, prevailing, and reasonable charges.*

allowable costs Those items or elements of an institution's costs that are reimbursable under a payment formula. A reimbursement method where hospitals are reimbursed on the basis of certain costs but not for all costs. For example, allowable costs may exclude uncovered services, luxury accommodations, defensive medicine activities, costs that are not reasonable, and expenditures that are unnecessary in the efficient delivery of health services to persons covered under the program in question (e.g., in a seniors health plan it would not be allowable to reimburse costs involved in providing services to newborns).

allowable depreciation The actual depreciation of property and equipment as defined by the Internal Revenue Service.

allowance In health-care finance, this is any deduction from revenue, being the difference between gross revenue charges from services rendered at established rates and the actual amount received from patients, managed-care plans, or other third-party payers for services rendered. Allowances are not to be confused with bad debt or uncollectable losses. Three general allowances are recognized: 1) charity allowances, which are for indigent care; 2) courtesy allowances for services to clergy, physicians, employees, and their dependents; and 3) contractual allowances/discounts, which are selected allowed services covered by managed care, third-party payers, Medicare, or Medicaid.

all-payer DRG system All third-party payers of medical care in the states of Maine and New York use the diagnosis-related-groups and prospective payment system approach.

all-payer plan In managed care, this is a health plan in which all patients are under the same payment structure.

all-risk contract A special type of liability or property insurance contract that covers all risks of loss except those specifically excluded.

ALOS Average length of stay. *See average length of stay; case severity; length of stay.*

ALPHA Center A private nonprofit health policy center that stimulates and facilitates important changes in health-care financing and organization. Its mission is to provide policy and technical assistance to those making health policy decisions and managing health-care programs in federal, state, and local governments and in foundations and private organizations by offering technical assistance, policy studies, data analysis, intensive educational programs, strategic planning and consensus development, and intergovernment liaison. Headquartered in Washington, D.C.

alphanumeric In data processing, this refers to the subset of ASCII characters that uses the 26 letters of the alphabet combined with the 10 basic numbers.

ALS *See advanced life support.*

alteration Any construction work on health care facilities other than maintenance in an existing building that does not increase the floor or roof area or the volume of enclosed space.

alter ego (Lat.) 1. Other self. 2. When individual shareholders act through a corporation for personal rather than corporate purposes, they can be held personally liable for the consequences of the acts, as the corporation was their alter ego.

alternate delivery system (ADS) New methods of delivering health care (such as managed-care programs, i.e., PPOs, IPAs, HMOs, etc.) that emphasize preventive care, cost containment, new methods of payment, or other innovations.

alternating role A mental illness pattern characterized by the periodic switching from one type of behavior to another.

alternation ranking method In performance appraisals, the supervisor lists employees by certain characteristics and identifies the worker that best represents the expected characteristics. The supervisor identifies the employee who has the listed typical characteristics. The second best choice is selected, then the third choice, until all workers are selected and ranked.

alternative birthing center A labor and delivery service that can be an independent facility or adjoining a hospital. This specialized medical care facility strives to provide a homelike atmosphere with cheerful and comfortable surroundings. Nurse midwives, under the supervision of an obstetrician, are sometimes used to deliver the baby. If unexpected complications arise, the mother or child can be treated in adjacent high-risk units.

alternative delivery system 1. Various methods or arrangements of providing health-care benefits to groups of people that depart from the traditional indemnity methods; managed care is one example. 2. Medical care services provided in facilities other than acute-care hospitals, including intermediary nursing facilities, hospice programs, and home health care.

alternative facility licensure The process by which a state creates a new category of licensed health care facility or new licensure rules for existing categories of facilities for the purpose of maintaining the viability and accessibility of certain facilities or services.

alternative health system (AHS) *See alternate delivery system.*

alternative pleading 1. Declaring facts that exist separately but cannot exist at the same time in the same pleading. 2. A pleading in common law where separate facts are difficult to determine and it is unclear which set of facts a person is intended to rely on as the basis for recovery. "When a plaintiff pleads his case in the alternative, one version of which is good and the other not, his petition will, on demurrer, be treated as pleading no more than the latter, since it will be construed most strongly against him." (93 S.E. 2d. 3, 5)

alternative relief In health law, in a pleading, a plaintiff asks for relief in ways that might be contradictory (e.g., asking for either the return of a borrowed oxygen tank or the payment of its value).

alternative rural hospital project This rural hospital model project allows the hospital to drop the requirement of maintaining a 24-hour level of surgical staffing. A California model with eleven rural hospitals participating.

alternatives to long-term institutional care The whole range of health, nutritional, housing, home health, and social services designed to keep persons, particularly the aged, disabled, and retarded, out of institutions such as nursing homes and other facilities. The goal is to provide a range of services necessary to allow the person to continue to function independently in their own home environment. Some alternatives to institutional care include daycare centers, foster homes or homemaker services, home health agencies, and meals on wheels.

Alzheimer's assessment and diagnostic services (center) A specialized program or center used in the diagnosis and evaluation of people suspected of having Alzheimer's disease. Assessment can include medical, social, and behavioral conditions and the development of a treatment plan, including financial options and all medical concerns.

Alzheimer's disease One of the most frequent causes of irreversible dementia that occurs in adults, sometimes referred to as "presenility" because it can occur at uncommonly early ages. The disease is characterized by memory loss and intellectual impairment such as drowsiness, confusion, disorientation, delirium, forgetfulness, and decreased alertness. Symptoms, especially forgetfulness, progress to a final state of total disability. The causes of this disease are unclear and multifaceted, and multiple causes and changes in the structural surfaces of the brain have been noted. Patients who have this disease usually require care in a long-term-care institution, as the care needed is often more than the average family can handle or provide.

Alzheimer's disease day-care center This is a community-based ambulatory day-care center that offers respite for families who care for Alzheimer's victims. In addition to social day-care services, some centers offer training for families and professional caregivers. Sometimes referred to as "Alzheimer's day-care resource center."

Am. Jur. *See American Jurisprudence.*

AMA *See against medical advice; American Medical Association; American Management Association.*

ambit 1. Limits or scope of something. 2. A boundary line, limit, or border.

ambulance A vehicle especially designed to carry and transport sick, injured, or wounded persons at high speed to a health-care facility for advanced treatment. Advanced emergency care and resuscitation measures can be performed in the vehicle, as it is equipped with two-way radios, oxygen systems, suction devices, litters, blood pressure devices, stethoscopes, and other medical and safety equipment. The vehicle must have emergency vehicle markings and flashing lights. Most ambulances are now van-type vehicles. Helicopters and airplanes are also commonly used as ambulances.

ambulance chaser 1. A lawyer who follows ambulances to automobile accidents to get the legal business stemming from some negligent act. 2. Slang for any attorney who solicits legal business.

ambulance emergency medical technician Responds to medical emergency calls, provides first aid and emergency medicine, and transports the injured to medical facilities. Qualified to administer only basic life-support services, such as advanced first aid, artificial resuscitation, and cardiopulmonary resuscitation (CPR).

ambulant Able to walk or move about.

ambulation Walking or getting about in an upright position, unassisted by any walking device.

ambulatory 1. Movable; not fixed; changeable; revocable. 2. A patient who is not bedridden and is capable of walking. 3. In law, something that can be changed or altered; not fixed.

ambulatory automatism A form of automatism wherein a person unconsciously wanders about performing involuntary acts.

ambulatory care All types of health services that are provided on an outpatient basis in contrast to services provided in the home or for inpatients in health-care institutions. Although many inpatients may be ambulatory, the term "ambulatory care" usually implies that the patient has come to a location other than home and walked in to receive health-care services and has departed the same day. Health services provided without admitting the patient to the hospital. Services provided outside of an acute-care or long-term-care facility, usually performed in a doctor's office, clinic, medical center, surgery center, or hospital outpatient facility. *See ambulatory setting; hospital-sponsored ambulatory care department.*

ambulatory care center An outpatient facility with professional staff who provide a variety of medical and health-care services to those who do not require hospital admission as inpatients. This type of facility may be part of a hospital or may be freestanding.

ambulatory care system A set of health-care facilities, services, and providers that provides health care services organized to offer care to patients on a walk-in outpatient basis. Patients travel to the services and health-care providers, which include physician offices, outpatient departments of hospitals, public health clinics, health maintenance organizations, freestanding surgery centers, and other related services.

ambulatory health-care services *See ambulatory care.*

ambulatory patient grouping *See ambulatory patient groups.*

Ambulatory Patient Grouping software In medical information management for ambulatory care treatment clinics or settings, a specialized software used to group ambulatory diseases and treatments on the basis of the prospective payment system set forth by the Health Care Financing Administration (HCFA). *See ambultory patient groups.*

ambulatory patient group (APG) In health care finance under Medicare, this is a new prospective payment system developed by the Health Care Financing Administration (HCFA) for ambulatory and outpatient care settings implemented to reduce costs of medical care in these settings. Initially implemented for outpatient surgery, radiology, and diagnostic services, this system classifies outpatient services into 297 APG categories similar to those under the DRG/PPS arrangement. The initial software for this system was developed by 3M Company. *See diagnosis-related groups.*

ambulatory services building A freestanding building on a hospital campus or other similar site that has an array of services as well as physician offices. Services provided include typical office services for the physician as well as diagnostic, imaging, and treatment facilities, including ambulatory surgery suites. Such an arrangement enhances physicians' services and the role, function, and income of the hospital.

ambulatory service settings 1. Residential care wherein patients receive health-care services and are able to ambulate. These inpatients remain in a short-term health-care setting on a 24-hour basis and are allowed to walk about yet usually require medical assistance. 2. Outpatient services that are available to patients on a walk-in appointment basis.

ambulatory setting Any outpatient or walk-in health care service strategically located where organized health-care services are provided for patients who travel to the service or provider facility to receive health-care services. Such a health-care service has no provision for patients to be admitted on an inpatient basis or to stay overnight. *See ambulatory care; hospital-sponsored ambulatory care department.*

ambulatory surgery Surgical treatment provided to the patient on an outpatient, walk-in, same-day basis in an appropriately equipped and staffed health facility that may be freestanding or a part of a hospital outpatient department; a large range of especially selected and managed operative treatment procedures and anesthesia techniques are used that allow the patient to recover and recuperate at home immediately following the operation.

ambulatory surgery center An outpatient same-day care health facility specializing in the simpler types of surgical treatment on an outpatient basis by a licensed physician. A physician's office or the outpatient department of a hospital are not considered ambulatory surgery centers. An ambulatory surgery center is a separate freestanding, self-contained facility with all essential surgical equipment and personnel needed for quality surgery to be performed.

ambulatory utilization review In quality control management and health-care delivery evaluation, the assessment of frequency of visits; readmissions; and types of care, treatments, procedures, and therapy encounters rendered in outpatient walk-in treatment facilities. Patients who are admitted to inpatient hospital care after ambulatory care for the same diagnosis or problem are sometimes included in the review.

ambulatory visit group (AVG) A set of diagnostic groups and treatments that are common to outpatient care; they are similar to DRGs (diagnosis related groups) but are used in ambulatory care settings and are based on a prospective payment or capitation payment system structure.

ambulatory with assistance In nursing homes or long-term-care settings, this refers to a patient who can walk or move about with the aid of a walker, brace, cane, crutch, wheelchair, or another person.

AMCRA American Managed Care Review Association.

amelioration In occupational safety and public safety, these are those things done immediately following an accident to limit its consequences and to reduce the sensitivity of those consequences.

amenable Liable; responsible to answer.

amend 1. To change or revise; to improve; to correct; to review. 2. In parliamentary procedure, to add to or to change a motion, a previous motion, or information in a document by adding, deleting, or substituting words or provisions.

amendment 1. A change. 2. A revision. 3. The changing of a bill through legislation or changing a law that already has been passed.

American Academy of Medical Administrators (AAMA) A professional association for professional administrators of medical and health-care organizations that embraces a broad range of health services and those administrators who manage them, including physician administrators. AAMA was founded in Boston, Massachusetts, with the aim of uniting all specialties of medical administration. The academy is a professional organization dedicated to developing innovative concepts as well as promoting and advancing knowledge, professional standing, and personal endeavors through education and research in health administration.

American Academy of Medical Directors (AAMD) A national organization of physicians who serve in management or administrative positions in health-care organizations. Formerly the American College of Physician Executives.

American Academy of Pediatrics A national nonprofit private professional organization whose purpose is to advance knowledge in the medical care and preventive care of children and to provide continuing education, materials, and conferences for training of health-care providers who specialize in the care and treatment of children and to serve as a spokesman for children, for the care of children, and for pediatricians.

American Academy of Physician Assistants A national nonprofit private professional organization whose purpose is to advance knowledge and provide continuing education for its members who are certified as physician assistants. Headquartered in Alexandria, Virginia.

American Academy of Nursing (AAN) A national organization whose purpose is to advance knowledge in nursing and in nursing as a profession. On meeting adequate education, achievement, and professional qualifications advancement, members can achieve the status of "Fellow" and use the credentials FAAN.

American Agency System A national insurance marketing system where the local retailer or agent is an independent business yet represents several major insurance companies as a local agent.

American Alliance of Health, Physical Education, Recreation and Dance (AAHPERD) A national professional organization structured to support, encourage, and provide assistance to several various member groups, which include the American Association for Leisure and Recreation; the American School and Community Safety Association; the Association for the Advancement of Health Education; the Association of Research, Administration, Professional Councils and Societies; the National Association for Girls and Women in Sport; the National Association for Sport and Physical Education; and the National Dance Association.

AAHPERD seeks to initiate, develop, and conduct programs in health, leisure, and movement-related activities that in turn improve the quality of life.

American Association for Counseling and Development (AACD) An educational, scientific, and professional organization founded in 1952 whose members are dedicated to the enhancement of the dignity, potential, and uniqueness of each individual and to the service of society while serving the counseling, guidance, and human development professions.

American Association for Health Education The professional organization for health educators involved in school health education, community/public health education, health promotion, and academic-related health education programs. AAHE is one of the AAHPRD programs. *See also AAHPRD; SOPHE.*

American Association for World Health A private nonprofit professional society that is interested in global health challenges and promotes the increase of the health status of all individuals throughout the world. Headquartered in Washington, D.C., with former President Jimmy Carter the honorary president.

American Association of Biofeedback Clinicians (AABC) A professional society, organized in 1969, for clinical practitioners utilizing biofeedback techniques. The AABC awards four levels of certificates designed to judge competence at both theoretical and applied levels: 1) diplomat, 2) certified professional, 3) certified associate, and 4) certified technician.

American Association of Colleges of Nursing (AACN) An organization that promotes quality of education, research, and the development of leaders in colleges, universities, and institutions offering baccalaureate and graduate degrees in nursing.

American Association of Health Care Facilities (AAHCF) Organized in 1949 by a group of concerned leaders in the nursing home field to discuss the mutual goals and objectives of nursing homes. The membership of AAHCF consists of both proprietary and nonproprietary nursing home institutions.

American Association of Homes for the Aging (AAHA) A national organization of nursing homes and long-term-care facilities that operates on a nonprofit basis. Each state has its own state-level affiliate.

American Association of Medical Systems and Informatics (AAMSI) A national organization that advances and promotes the development, implementation, and application of information management systems and computers in health-care services and research.

American Association of Retired Persons (AARP) A national organization for people over age 50 that provides service, education, and lobbying on behalf of the elderly, including health-care issues and Medicare.

American Board of Internal Medicine (ABIM) A national organization responsible for examining physician candidates interested in certification in the specialty of internal medicine.

American Board of Medical Management (ABMM) A national organization responsible for examining physician candidates interested in certification in the specialty of medical management.

American Board of Surgery (ABS) A national organization responsible for examining physician candidates interested in certification in the specialty of general surgery.

American Cancer Society A national community-based voluntary health organization whose goal is to remove cancer as a cause of death and suffering in society through research, public affairs, fund-raising, community health education, and training.

American Chiropractic Association (ACA) A national nonprofit professional membership organization with a membership of more than 20,000 representing the majority of licensed practitioners in the United States. Headquartered in Arlington, Virginia.

American College of Healthcare Executives (ACHE) A professional, international society for health services administrators created in 1933 for the purpose of elevating the standards of hospital administration by establishing a standard of competence and promoting standards of education and training for hospital administrators. The college also aids in the education of hospital trustees and the public about the practice and training of hospital administrators and confers fellowships in hospital administration on those persons, known as fellows, who have made noteworthy accomplishments in the field of hospital administration. Until 1985, the organization was called the American College of Hospital Administrators (ACHA).

American College of Medical Group Administrators (ACMGA) A professional society for managers and administrators of medical clinics and medical group practices that have been organized into an administrative unit. The college confers fellowships on those medical group administrators who have met requirements of the college.

American College of Nurse Midwives (ACNM) A national professional organization that promotes professional development of nurse midwives and provides for their credentialing.

American College of Nursing Home Administrators (ACNHA) Organized in 1962 as an individual-membership professional society for long-term-care administrators, ACNHA assesses memberships through an advancement program, using experience, formal education, continuing education, professional activity, and civic/community activity as criteria for becoming a nominee, member, or fellow. Its major goals and purposes are to advance the quality of patient care in long-term-care institutions to the highest level possible, to promote the well-being of the public and maintain the dignity of nursing home administration, and to establish standards of performance for nursing home administrators.

American College of Preventive Medicine (ACPM) A nonprofit national professional society for physicians committed to disease prevention and health promotion. The college seeks to advance science and practice in preventive medicine by providing educational opportunities, advocating public policies consistent with scientific principles of preventive medicine, supporting the investigation and analysis of issues relevant to the field, participating in national forums to address public health concerns, and communicating developments in preventive medicine through a peer-reviewed journal, *The American Journal of Preventive Medicine,* and other publications. Headquartered in Washington, D.C.

American College of Surgeons (ACS) A national professional organization for physicians with a specialization in surgery.

American College of Utilization Review Physicians (ACURP) A national professional organization that promotes training and education in utilization review topics and management for physicians and others working in those areas.

American Dental Association (ADA) The major professional organization for licensed practicing dentists. Its board of trustees and house of delegates establish standards and policies and accredit professional dental school internships and residency programs. The association publishes professional journals, provides information services, and is involved in public health education, audiovisual service, research, statistics, etc.

American Dietetic Association (ADA) A professional organization responsible for establishing educational and supervised clinical experience requirements and standards of practice in the profession of dietetics.

American Digest System A collection of all of the summaries of law cases ever reported in America. *Century Digest* includes all cases up to 1896. For every 10-year period thereafter there is the *Decennial Digest* and the *General Digest*. Case summaries are presented by subject using the Key Number System.

American Druggist Blue Book (ADBB) The prices for each approved and manufactured drug are set and listed in ADBB, which is published on a periodical basis. This book is used by managed-care organizations and health maintenance organizations to provide monthly updates of drug prices on the basis of average wholesale prices set by the ADBB. *See drug price review (DPR).*

American Federation for Clinical Research (AFCR) A national organization limited to clinical investigators under age 41 who have completed significant and meritorious research in medicine and related fields.

American Federation of Labor and Congress of Industrial Organizations (AFL-CIO) A federation of national unions, this organization exists to provide a unified focal point for labor activities, to assist national unions, and to influence government policies that affect union members and working people.

American Group Practice Association (AGPA) Founded in 1949, AGPA represents private health-care group practice practitioners in the United States. The association is directed by a board of trustees selected from delegates representing AGPA institutional members. Membership size varies with physician staffs, ranging from three to many hundreds, with organization structures including partnerships, corporations, foundations, and associations. Most groups are single or multispecialty. Affiliated with AGPA is the American Academy of Medical Directors, which encourages educational and publications activities for physicians who serve as medical directors and/or have both management and health-care provider responsibilities. (The name was changed to the American Medical Group Association in 1996)

American Health Care Association (AHCA) The nation's largest federation of licensed nursing homes and allied long-term health-care facilities, AHCA was founded in 1949 to promote high professional standards in long-term health-care delivery and quality care for patients and residents in safe surroundings at fair payment for services rendered. All AHCA members must be licensed by their state governments, as must the administrators who manage them. AHCA represents its members on issues before Congress, the federal regulatory and executive authorities, and the press and public at large. AHCA and its affiliated state associations work closely with individual members to achieve their objectives at all levels of government and public opinion. The American Health Care Association, formerly the American Nursing Home Association, consists of skilled, intermediate, and residential care facilities as well as adult day-care, mental health, and child care services. Membership includes both proprietary (taxpaying) and nonproprietary (tax-exempt) facilities.

American Healthcare System (The) The official name of the "Clinton Plan" for health-care reform and the approaches to delivery of the new components to ensure medical care benefits to all citizens in the United States. Six components were included: 1) security—know that all citizens have health coverage even if they switch or lose their jobs or have a preexisting condition; 2) choice—have a choice of health-care plans and providers; 3) quality—quality of care is to increase by having a "report card" on health plans and health-care providers; 4) control costs—affordable health care will be provided, and escalating costs will be controlled, especially for businesses; 5) simplicity—eliminate fraud and abuse, reduce paperwork for physicians and patients, and reduce total bureaucracy; and 6) comprehensive—all citizens guaranteed a comprehensive benefit package.

American Health Planning Association (AHPA) A society of health planning professionals founded in 1971 with the desired goal of promoting changes that will make health care services more effective and more responsive to local needs.

American Heart Association One of the largest nonprofit voluntary health agencies in the

United States whose mission is fund-raising, health education, and research support aimed at reducing injury, illnesses, disorders, and deaths related to diseases and conditions of the circulatory system and heart. Major communities or regions have local chapters that are directly affiliated with the national organization.

American Hospital Association (AHA) The largest national professional hospital organization, representing most hospitals in the United States. This national association promotes hospital administration education, quality of care, publications and management training, healthcare delivery efficiency, and legislative activities that favor and assist hospitals nationally.

American Jurisprudence A legal encyclopedia, cited as *Am. Jur.* or *Am. Jur.* 2d (second series).

American Law Reports Reprints of significant American cases usually followed by an annotation of similar cases dealing with the same legal principle, cited as ALR, ALR 2d, ALR 3d, or ALR 4th, depending on the edition.

American Lloyds An unusual insurance agency, authorized to operate by some states, where owners assume much of their own risk as individuals, thus limiting the liability of the insurance company.

American Lung Association A national nonprofit private voluntary health organization that has the aim of preventing all lung diseases and disorders. Local chapters carry out the mission of the national organization, which participates in health education, health promotion, fund-raising, research, and support related to lung disease and respiratory disorders.

American Medical Association (AMA) The major physician association, founded in 1847, the AMA is a federation of subunits known as "constituent medical societies," which are composed of local, county, and city medical societies. The AMA is an educational and scientific nonprofit organization concerned with advancing medical knowledge and promoting high-quality, responsive medical care by evaluating medical education and examining health-care delivery systems.

AMGA *See American Medical Group Association.*

American Medical Group Association A medical group management professional society which represents large group medical practices/clinics and physician owned and physician managed independent practice associations. About 350 large groups and 40,000 physicians are represented. Education, advocacy services, outcomes research assistance and lobbying are some of the main goals of the organization. Headquarters are maintained in Alexandria, VA and Seal Beach, CA. Formed from a merger, this is the former American Group Practice Association and the Unified Medical Group Association.

American Medical Records Association The national professional organization for personnel involved with medical information records and systems.

American Medical Society on Alcoholism and Other Drug Dependencies (AMSAODD) A national organization for physicians and others interested in alcoholism and drug dependency and offering credentialing in these areas for physicians.

American National Standards Institute (ANSI) The key national organization responsible for coordinating the creation of voluntary business standards in the United States. Hospitals, nursing homes, long-term-care buildings and facilities, and public buildings are required by federal regulations to comply with the standards of the ANSI. These standards were developed to ensure accessibility and use by physically handicapped people. ANSI standards include detailed specifications for wheelchair accommodations on doorways, bathrooms, elevators, and ramps. Visual and auditory safety specifications are presented for the blind and deaf in the ANSI standards. *See National Uniform Billing Committee (NUBC).*

American Nurses' Association (ANA) The official national organization of registered nurses founded in 1896 to improve the standards of nursing and to promote the general welfare of professional nurses.

American Nursing Home Association *See American Health Care Association; American Association of Homes for the Aging.*

American Optometric Association (AOA) The professional organization for optometrists and doctors of optometry. This national official organization represents the interests and the educational and professional concerns of practicing optometrists.

American Organization of Nurse Executives (AONE) A national professional organization of directors of nursing/vice presidents or assistant administrators of patient clinical services, or of other nurse executives, providing a forum for education and professional advancement for nurse executive positions.

American Osteopathic Association (AOA) A national voluntary organization for physicians of osteopathy. This organization provides accreditation services for osteopathic hospitals and facilities similar to those of the JCAHO.

American Osteopathic Healthcare Association (AOHA) A national voluntary organization for acute-care health-care facilities and other related health-care facilities and services that are limited to and that specialize in patients treated by osteopathic physicians. AOHA represents 109 osteopathic hospitals in 24 states. Formerly the American Osteopathic Hospital Association (AOHA) (changed in 1993).

American Osteopathic Hospital Association (AOHA) A national voluntary organization for acute-care health-care facilities that are limited to and specialize in patients of physicians of osteopathy. The AOHA changed its name in 1993 to the American Osteopathic Healthcare Association (AOHA).

American Pharmaceutical Association (APhA) The professional organization for pharmacists. This national official organization represents the interests and the educational and professional concerns of practicing pharmacists.

American Psychiatric Association (APA) The official society for physicians who have completed medical school training and a residency in psychiatry. Its purpose is to advance the science, study, and treatment of mental, emotional, behavioral, and any related medical problems.

American Psychological Association (APA) Founded in 1892 and incorporated in 1925, this is the major psychological organization in the United States. The purpose of the APA is to advance psychology as a science, as a profession, and as a means of promoting human welfare. It attempts to accomplish these objectives by holding annual meetings, publishing psychological journals, and working to improve standards for psychological training and service.

American Public Health Association (APHA) Founded in 1872, this nongovernmental professional society represents all disciplines and specialties in public health. Together with the membership of its affiliated associations and regional branches, APHA is the largest public health association in the world, with a combined membership of over 55,000.

American School Health Association (ASHA) A national professional organization concerned solely with the health of the school-age child. It promotes comprehensive school health programs for school health services, health education, and a healthful school environment. Founded in 1927, it establishes guidelines for standards of excellence and competency for the school health team, including health educators, school nurses, physicians, dentists, dental hygienists, and other health-care professionals. It also serves as a professional liaison for the various disciplines in the field of school health. It provides cooperation with local, state, and national organizations on behalf of all school health personnel.

American Society for Bariatric Surgery (ASBS) A national professional association for physicians and surgeons specializing in the treatment of obesity, including surgery.

American Society of Clinical Investigation (ASCI) An exclusive national professional association of medical researchers who are allowed to join only on invitation and who conduct investigations with subjects under age 45.

American Society of Consultant Pharmacists The professional organization for pharmacists who serve as consultants to health-care providers. This national official organization represents the interests and the educational and professional concerns of consultant pharmacists, especially those serving nursing homes, home health agencies, and other long-term-care settings.

American Society of Law and Medicine A society devoted to education and training in the legal aspects of health care and medicine on an interdisciplinary basis, thus embracing both legal and health-care professionals who are concerned with the interrelationships between law and health care. Areas of interest of this society include but are not limited to medical malpractice, hospital law, patients' rights, health-care legislation, regulation, forensic medicine, bioethics, and related topics.

American Society for Quality Control (ASQC) An international nonprofit organization recognized for its expertise on quality improvement activities. The organization certifies quality professionals, helps set quality standards, and serves professionals who serve and are responsible for quality management in their organization. Members come from both manufacturing and services sectors, and many are from healthcare organizations. ASQC publishes the journal *Quality Progress* and is headquartered in Milwaukee, Wisconsin.

American Speech and Hearing Association The national professional organization for educators and practitioners in the fields of speech pathology and audiology. The organization is devoted to education, training, and professional development of its members and the profession.

American's with Disability Act of 1990 A federal law (P.L. 101-336) passed to establish a clear and comprehensive prohibition of discrimination on the basis of disability. The specific purposes of this act are to provide a clear and comprehensive national mandate for the elimination of discrimination against individuals with disabilities; to provide clear, strong, consistent, enforceable standards addressing discrimination against individuals with disabilities; to ensure that the federal government plays a central role in enforcing the standards established in this act on behalf of individuals with disabilities; and to invoke the sweep of congressional authority, including the power to enforce the fourteenth amendment and to regulate commerce to address the major areas of discrimination faced day to day by people with disabilities. Five major areas are covered by this law: employment, public services, public transportation, public accommodations and services operated by private entities, and telecommunications. It also includes some miscellaneous provisions. This law provides amendments to the Rehabilitation Act of 1973 to strengthen and clarify the law.

amicus curiae (Lat.) 1. Friend of the court. 2. One who is allowed to appear in court even though he or she has no standing as a party.

amnesty 1. Deliberately overlooking an offense. 2. Removal by the government of penalties or guilt of a crime. 3. Granting of a pardon.

amortization 1. Settling a debt. 2. The periodic payment of a debt that covers accrued interest and part of the principal. 3. The act or process of extinguishing a debt, usually by equal payments at regular intervals over a specific period of time.

amortize 1. To end, extinguish, or deaden. 2. To transfer or sell.

amortized loan In health care finance, this is a loan that the borrower gradually pays off by making periodic payments on the principal and interest throughout the term of the loan.

amphetamine A drug that is a central nervous system stimulant.

amplification To enhance or increase in strength or response. In laser treatment technology, the formation of a laser beam in the optical cavity, or resonator, of a laser. As the laser beam is reflected back and forth between mirrors defining the cavity, it is amplified through stimulated emission on each passage through the active medium.

ampule A small, sealed glass flask or container used to preserve a sterile medication or drug solution.

AMRA *See American Medical Records Association.*

ANA *See American Nurses' Association.*

anaerobe Any microorganism that can live and grow without the presence of oxygen.

anal incontinence The inability to voluntarily control bowel (fecal and gaseous) discharges. Also referred to as "loss of bowel control."

analgesia When one feels little or no pain.

analgesic A drug that relieves pain.

analog computer 1. A computer that measures variables by physical analogies in continuous form used primarily in scientific research and in hospitals. 2. A computer operating on analog data by performing physical processes on these data. This is contrasted with a digital computer.

analog forecasting In health planning and health services development, this is the prediction and estimation of future utilization based on similar experience in another time or place, treating some other experience as an analogy of future events.

analysis 1. The process of separating things into classes or parts for assessment and evaluation. 2. To examine information or circumstances to determine their parts or elements. 3. In computerized medical records or billing, used as an examination to distinguish the component parts of a record separately and in relation to the whole. 4. In psychology or psychiatry, this refers to psychoanalysis. *See qualitative analysis; quantitative analysis; vector analysis.*

analytical studies The use of scientific methods of research investigation and hypothesis testing to develop cause-effect associations in disease and medical conditions. In public health and epidemiology, several types of studies are used, including cohort studies, prevalence studies, and retrospective studies. Variables such as age, sex, race, education, occupation, economic status, environmental factors, and location of occurrence are analyzed.

anamnesis The patient's self-reported medical history, used in psychiatry to evaluate the patient's ability to recall.

anatomic pathology *See pathology, anatomic.*

anatomical pathology A specialized branch of medicine concerned with the body's structure and location of its various parts, tissues, and organs. The diseased states of the various parts, tissues, and organs is the major area of focus of practice. Samples from tissues and organs may be removed so that the physician can study and interpret the findings using microscopic study and analysis. This physician may also perform autopsies. *See autopsy; pathologist.*

anatomy The study of structures; the study of the structure, shape, and formations of the human body, including the location and form of organs and tissue.

anatomist An instructor who teaches medical, dental, allied health, and biology students about the human body's structure and function. As a researcher he or she may be involved in any aspect of biomedical research from problems at the molecular level to those concerned with the entire body. A graduate degree (possibly from a medical school) such as a masters or doctor of medicine degree is required.

ancillary A supportive role that helps a main function, effort, or proceeding (e.g., ancillary services of a hospital are support services that help in the daily functioning of the health care facility). Such support services include central supply, department of materials management, housekeeping, etc. Supplemental medical services that are supportive of the physician's medical care activities, such as lab, X ray, physical therapy, pharmacy, etc. *See also ancillary services.*

ancillary benefits Health or medical insurance that pays for tests, treatments, therapies, and procedures and other extra services provided or given to the patient.

ancillary charges 1. Those extra charges made to the patient for any unusual or special service, or diagnostic tests or treatments such as a CT scan, MRI scan, lithotripsy, lab test, X rays, etc. 2. In managed care, those fees billed to the health plan for medical care service beyond the usual treatment; additional services or services rendered beyond the primary treatment, such as anesthesia, laboratory tests, and specialized imaging procedures. Fees charged to the enrollee beyond any co-payment for prescriptions that are not on the health plan's maximum allowable costs (MAC) list.

ancillary expenses *See miscellaneous expenses.*

ancillary personnel Individuals who assist the medical and nursing staff of a hospital or clinic in the performance of routine duties by carrying out treatments or procedures for patients under the direct supervision of a physician, nurse, or other health care professional, often including operating room technicians, emergency room technicians, physical therapy technicians, occupational therapy technicians, orthopedic technicians, psych-techs, nursing assistants, aides, orderlies, attendants, medical assistants, etc.

ancillary services Hospital or other inpatient services apart from room and board and professional services. Services could include X ray, drug, laboratory, rehabilitation, or other services requested by the physician. *See also ancillary; miscellaneous expenses.*

ancillary technology Medical technology and equipment used to support basic clinical and medical services, such as diagnostic radiology, heart catheterization, radiation therapy, lithotripsy, etc.

andro- Prefix meaning "male."

andrologist A branch of medicine specializing in the treatment of males.

anesthesia 1. Absence of sensation, usually caused by a drug or a gas. 2. Loss of sensation or feeling; an induced loss of the sense of pain.

anesthesiologist A licensed physician who has specialized in, and whose practice of medicine is in, the science of anesthesiology. The physician who administers anesthetics for surgery and diagnostic procedures, possesses a medical degree with a specialization in the area, and is licensed to practice anesthesiology by the State Board of Medical Examiners.

anesthesiologist, qualified According to JCAHO for health-care facilities accreditation purposes, a doctor of medicine certified to practice anesthesiology and fully licensed to practice medicine.

anesthesiologist's assistant Performs diagnostic and therapeutic tasks under the supervision and direction of the anesthesiologist. Such activities may include care and proper usage of anesthesia equipment, monitoring of patients during anesthesia, and postanesthesia care.

anesthesiology 1. A clinical service provided in

hospitals that utilizes this specialty of medicine to administer local and general anesthetics, usually in surgery. The department often includes anesthesiologists and nurse anesthetists. 2. The medical study of and application of gases and agents that cause unconsciousness or insensitivity to pain.

anesthetic Any chemical substance or agent that numbs or suppresses feelings or sensations of pain.

anesthetist As used in JCAHO accreditation, a generic term used to identify anesthesiologists, physician anesthetists, or qualified nurse or dentist anesthetists.

angiogram A diagnostic method used to visualize the veins and arteries by introducing a radioactive dye into the bloodstream.

angioplasty A surgical or treatment procedure used to reconstruct or restructure blood vessels by surgical means or by nonsurgical techniques, such as balloon dilation or laser treatments.

animal technician Assists the veterinarian, biological or biomedical researcher, or other scientist in the care and management of animals. This technician is knowledgeable in basic principles of normal and abnormal life processes and in routine laboratory and animal health care procedures.

animal technology An allied health instructional program that prepares persons to become technologists or assistants to veterinarians, biological researchers, medical research scientists, and other scientists who care for animals or who use animals in research. Instruction includes basic animal anatomy and physiology, nutrition, and health and care procedures. Also referred to as "animal science."

animal unit month In ecology and environmental health, this is the amount of forage needed to sustain one cow and her calf, one horse, or five sheep or goats for 1 month. Used by the Bureau of Land Management of the federal government to determine grazing usage and charge ranchers' grazing fees.

anniversary *See anniversary date.*

anniversary date 1. In managed care, this is the date of the beginning of an subscriber group's or employer group's benefit year. 2. In personnel management, the date of employment.

annual claim costs In managed-care and medical insurance programs, the yearly costs that are equal to the expected numbers of claims for 1 year multiplied by the average amount payable for each claim. Annual claim costs are calculated each year for age, sex, occupational class, and geographical region or other pertinent variables of concern to claims.

annual debt service coverage ratio Used by financial institutions and bond-rating agencies to assess a hospital's ability to meet its long-term debt service obligations. The ratio of debt service to net patient revenue is compared. This ratio is associated with the organization's debt service burden on revenue. To financial institutions this is considered an important rating analysis in determining loans, lines of credit, and financial solvency. A rule of thumb is that, if the ratio exceeds 10%, the organization has an unfavorable financial condition due to either an excessive debt service load or insufficient patient income/revenues. The annual debt service coverage ratio formula follows:

$$\frac{\text{Debt service (principal and interest)}}{\text{Net patient revenue}} = \text{Annual debt service coverage percentage}$$

annual family income 1. The sum of the proportions of income contributed by each family member within a given yearly time period. 2. The total amount of income for a family from all sources for each person in the family, 14 years of age and over, in 1 year. Annual family income is prorated for each of the families in proportion to the amount of time each person spent in each family, as a person can change families within a study year. Annual income can be determined by dividing family income by the proportion of the year that the family existed and can classify persons by the annual family income of that family in which they spent the longest period of time during the study year.

Annual Hospital Report In health-care finance, this system of accounting that utilizes a specialized format to present the financial statement. This special system is imposed on the hospital or health-care facility by the finance agency providing loans and other financial assistance to the health-care facility. In this system, costs are grouped and reported according to function and are tied to reimbursement.

Annual Implementation Plan (AIP) 1. A part of the former National Health Planning and Resources Development Act of 1974 (P.L. 93-641), which required the former health system agencies to prepare or update annually a regional health plan specifying and describing how to implement and give priority to short-term objectives that were to achieve long-range goals of the agency detailed in the health system plan. Section 1513 of the act describes the place of AIPs in the larger context of an agency's function. 2. A document that presents the decisions reached by a health systems agency with regard to its short-range objectives and priorities and the tactical actions and resource changes that should occur within a coming year to bring about the long-term achievements set forth in the health systems plan. AIPs have value in strategic planning for hospitals, health maintenance organizations, and health systems if they are used as planning tools for annual plans, which are used to achieve the organization's strategic plans.

annual percentage rate The actual rate of interest paid, expressed as a percentage rate of a loan on a yearly basis (required by law to be disclosed).

annual premium The payment required to keep a medical insurance or managed-care policy in force for the benefit year. For a family this can include all charges for all policies that cover all eligible family members.

annual report An accounting report produced at the end of each fiscal year that includes a financial statement, income statement, and balance sheet and other important financial data that the organization deems necessary or important. Hospitals, managed-care organizations, and nonprofit or government-funded healthcare organizations often produce such yearly reports for review. Nonprofit community-supported organizations often make the annual report available for public review.

annual statement In managed care, this is a comprehensive report that includes detailed financial statements as well as accounting and statistical data that insurance company regulatory agencies use to evaluate the solvency of medical care insurance or managed-care insurance companies and their compliance with insurance laws.

annual survey The yearly inspection of a health care facility to ascertain compliance with state licensing regulations and/or Federal Conditions and Standards of Participation, which may be required by certain government programs or agencies.

annuity A fixed annual payment.

annul To void; to end, to nullify *ab initio*.

anomaly 1. A marked deviation from normal; an abnormality. 2. When a structure or organ is malformed or has an irregular formation (e.g., congenital anomalies are missing fingers or toes or heart defects).

anomie 1. Without a sense of association with society; experiencing lack of social cohesion. 2. A person with no fixed values or moral standards.

anorexia Lack or loss of appetite. Unlike hunger, which is considered a physiological phenomenon, appetite is considered psychological in origin. Anorexia can be stimulated by mental or thought processes, by environmental experience such as unattractive smells or food, or by drugs.

anorexia nervosa A serious, life-endangering emotional disorder manifested by a self-imposed lack of appetite and characterized by fasting, dieting, and excessive physical exercise.

answer 1. To reply to. 2. A counterstatement of facts in a pleading. 3. A response to a complaint. 4. A formal reply in a lawsuit.

antabuse A drug used in the treatment of alcoholics that causes a distressing physiological reaction (nausea and vomiting) if mixed with alcohol. Taken orally on a regular basis, disulfiram (as it is known pharmaceutically) discourages the use of alcohol.

ante- (Lat.) Prefix meaning "before."

ante (Lat.) Before.

antepartum care Includes usual prenatal services: initial and subsequent history, physical examination, recording of weight, blood pressure, fetal heart tones, routine chemical urinalysis, maternity counseling, etc.

anterior frame A frame on which the patient lies when in a prone position.

antero- or **anterio-** Prefix meaning "front."

anthropometric assessment Measurement and evaluation of height, weight, limb circumference, elbow breadth, skin-fold tests, total body fat assessment and other body measurements related to growth, development, and nutritional status. *See anthropometry; anthroposophical medicine.*

anthropometry A health-care approach that uses measurement of size, weight, and proportions of the human body.

anthroposophical medicine Considered an adjunct or addition to regular medicine, this form of healing distinguishes between body, mind, and soul and attempts to influence the three simultaneously in treating illness. Illness is interpreted in an attempt to reestablish harmony between the self and the cosmic surroundings, as illness is thought to result from a disturbance of the balance between vitalizing and disruptive forces. Therapy combines body/mind/soul treatments and remedies with expressive therapy, massages, and natural therapies, all based on the notion that mental forces are superior to physical forces. *See anthropometry.*

anti- Prefix meaning "against."

anti (Lat.) Against.

antianxiety drug A drug used to reduce the symptoms of pathological anxiety without influencing cognitive or perceptual functioning. It is both a minor tranquilizer and an anxiolytic drug.

antibiotic Any drug containing a quantity of any chemical substance produced by a microorganism that has the capacity, in dilute solution, to inhibit the growth of or to destroy bacteria and other microorganisms (or a chemically synthesized equivalent of such a substance). Antibiotics are used in the treatment of infectious diseases.

antibiotic certification An FDA program in which each batch of antibiotic drug for human use in anticancellation laws is certified by the FDA as possessing the necessary characteristics of identity, strength, quality, and purity to adequately ensure safety and effectiveness in use. Before an antibiotic is eligible for certification, the FDA must approve the drug as safe and effective under procedures that are substantially equivalent to those for approving new drugs. Similar procedures exist for batch certification of insulin. Both antibiotic and insulin certification services are supported by user fees.

anticancellation laws Insurance laws that restrict insurance companies from canceling their policies except under special circumstances or for specific reasons.

anticipatory breach In contract law, a breach prior to a duty to perform that indicates an intention not to perform.

anticipatory grief The foreknowledge that a death will occur and that permits one to adjust to and accept the inevitable without acute shock and emotional trauma after the actual death. It is believed that such knowledge lessens the emotional upset and stress of loss.

anticipatory socialization The preparation for obligations and rights of a new role, prior to actually assuming it, thereby making adjustment much easier.

anticoercion laws Laws that prohibit money-lending institutions from requiring that the person receiving the loan purchase insurance from the institution as a condition of receipt of the loan.

antidepressant drug A drug used to treat pathological depression.

antidiscrimination laws 1. In insurance, this can be a state law that prohibits insurers from giving preferential terms or rates not warranted by the rating of the risks involved. 2. In general use, this term refers to equal and fair treatment or selection for jobs, school, positions, etc.

antimanic drug A drug, such as lithium, that is used to reduce or alleviate the symptoms of mania.

antipsychotic drug Any drug used to treat psychosis, particularly schizophrenia. It could be a major tranquilizer.

antipyretic 1. A substance that reduces pain or fever. 2. A substance that is effective in treating burns.

antiquo (Lat.) 1. Since olden times. 2. Old rules or ideas.

antiselection In managed care and medical insurance, this is the tendency of individuals with a greater-than-average chance of loss to apply for or continue insurance to a greater extent than do other people. Also referred to as "selection against the insurer" or "adverse selection." *See adverse selection.*

antiseptic 1. Any agent that inhibits the growth of microorganisms. 2. A germicide. 3. Any substance that kills pathogens or living tissue.

antisocial personality Inability to get along with members of society; having repeated conflict with individuals and groups.

antisubstitution laws State laws that require the pharmacist to "dispense as written." The effect is to prohibit a pharmacist from substituting a different brand-name drug for the one prescribed or from substituting a generic equivalent drug in place of a drug prescribed by brand name, even if the drug that would be substituted is considered to be therapeutically equivalent to the drug prescribed and is perhaps less expensive. Drug reimbursement programs, such as the Maximum Allowable Cost Program, that will limit reimbursement to the lowest cost at which a drug is generally available will be more effective if they override antisubstitution laws.

antitrust acts Statutes that protect commerce from unlawful business trusts and monopolies.

antitrust laws Those laws that prohibit institutional mergers and acquisitions, exclusive contracts, joint ventures, and other business activities that may reduce competition or at least have a tendency to form a monopoly and detrimentally affect consumer choices, competition, and free enterprise. The Clayton Act (15 U.S.C. 12-2) is one example.

anxiety A mental state that is characterized by panic and anxious overconcern.

any willing provider Under universal health-care coverage proposals, this is a vague concept that suggests that any health-care practitioner —possibly including chiropractors and physician extenders or health-care facilities such as hospitals, regardless of affiliation—should be accepted as a health-care provider, as opposed to health-care providers being required to belong to some sort of medical care delivery alliance or management service organization to be allowed to participate. The legislation would prohibit or limit the ability of payers to exclude physicians and other licensed health-care providers from joining any network. This diminishes competition among networks and makes formation of specialty care networks difficult.

AOA Administration on Aging; American Optometric Association.

AODA Alcohol and other drug abuse.

AONE *See American Organization of Nurse Executives.*

AORN Association of Operating Room Nurses.

APA *See American Psychiatric Association; American Psychological Association; Administrative Procedures Act.*

Apache II A title given to a computer software program used in the assessment of the severity of illness of patients in an intensive care unit. Twelve physiological factors are used as the basis for the evaluation. The factors include age, certain blood tests, and vital signs. The measures can be applied to any patient at any time, as the severity is dependent not on the disease but on the condition and the physiological functioning of the body. The computer software programs were developed at George Washington University.

apathy Lack of feeling, interest, or emotional involvement.

aperture Any opening through which a substance can flow or pass. In laser treatment technology, this is an opening through which laser beams or laser radiation can pass.

aperture card A punch card with film attached to it used in medical records administration.

APGs *See ambulatory patient groups.*

Apgar scores Measurements taken soon after birth that are used to determine physical normality and are based on color, respiratory effort, heart rate, reflex action, and muscle tone. These scores are used routinely to detect the effects of drugs taken by pregnant mothers.

APHA *See American Public Health Association.*

aphasia 1. Disorder due to organic brain damage or dysfunction that manifests itself as the loss of the ability to write or speak coherently and to understand written or spoken language.

aphasia related to stroke The major problem related to aphasia for the stroke patient is the inability to understand language or to use language. There are three commonly used classes of aphasia: 1) expressive aphasia is observed in a patient when the inability to speak and write is predominant; 2) receptive aphasia is observed in a patient when the inability to understand speech and writing is predominant; and 3) mixed aphasia is most frequently found among aphasic patients, as it is unusual to see a clearly defined aphasia.

a posteriori (Lat.) 1. From the end result back to the cause. 2. An argument founded on fact or experimentation that demonstrates a cause.

apothecaries' measures A system of liquid measure used in pharmacy and the preparation of pharmaceuticals. Mostly replaced by the metric system. *See Appendix XIII, XIV.*

apothecaries' weights A system of dry measures and weights used in pharmacy and the preparation of pharmaceuticals. Mostly replaced by the metric system. 480 grains = 1 ounce. *See Appendix XIII, XIV.*

apothecary Related to the preparation and storage of drugs and medicines. One who prepares and sells drugs and medicines; a druggist or pharmacist. *See Appendix XIII, XIV.*

apparent defect A defect in a product that is not hidden and is readily discoverable on inspection, as distinguished from a latent defect.

appeal 1. Application to a higher court to challenge a decision of a lower court that is claimed to be in error. 2. In parliamentary procedure, an action of the presiding officer to send back a decision to the assembly, where a vote will make the final decision.

Appeal from the Decision of the Chair An incidental motion made in conducting formal health care organization meetings using formal parliamentary procedures. Any member of the board disagreeing with the chairperson's decision may put the matter to a vote of the board.

appeals In managed care, a formal request by a health plan member for a review of a denied claim or service. Customer service representatives usually have to exhaust all possibilities prior to utilizing an appeal.

appearance 1. To formally show up in court as a party to a lawsuit. 2. Being present in court.

appellant One who makes an appeal to a higher court.

appellate Pertaining to appeals.

appellate court Higher courts that hear appeals from lower courts and decide matters of law. Trial courts, in contrast, decide the facts of disputes.

appellate jurisdiction The authority given to a higher court to hear cases from lower trial courts with the power to make decisions about these cases without a retrial.

appellee The party appealed against by the appellant in an appeal to a higher court.

apperception The significance and meaning of one's own beliefs, experiences, knowledge, attitudes, thoughts, and emotions. *See also perception.*

appliance Any device used to assist the functioning of a part of the body. *See assistive device; durable medical equipment.*

applicant According to JCAHO for psychiatric, alcoholism, and drug abuse facilities accreditation purposes, an individual who has applied for admission to a program but who has not completed the intake process.

application In health insurance, this is a signed statement of facts requested by the insurance company on the basis of which the insurance company decides whether to issue a policy. This then becomes part of the health insurance contract if the policy is issued.

application form In human resource management in health-care organizations, a form designed for each health-care organization by its human resources department requesting specific information from applicants for various positions to identify appropriate job applicants and match qualifications with positions.

application program A computer program used to perform a specific function necessary for a special requirement of the department. This is usually not a regular part of the basic operating system.

applied research A study of practical problems that provides solutions that can lead to improved performance.

apply In parliamentary procedure, this is when one motion influences or is attached to another motion or alters or disposes of the first motion.

appoint 1. To fix by decree. 2. To constitute or establish. 3. To designate. 4. To give a person a job, duty, or responsibility. 5. To confer power on someone to carry out a responsibility.

appointment scheduling The management task of allotting time for patient/physician meetings.

apportion 1. To allot or portion out. 2. To divide something according to a predetermined plan. 3. To divide into fair shares.

appose 1. To put questions to. 2. To examine the Clerk of Records about one's records.

APR Annual percentage rate; average payment rate.

appraisal Estimating the quality or value of an item or other property by a fair and impartial appraiser.

apprehension 1. Taking into custody. 2. Fear of an upcoming event.

appropriate 1. To assign a particular use. 2. To claim an exclusive right 3. To acquire or take possession of something. 4. Suitable for a particular person, condition, occasion, or place; proper; fitting. A term commonly used in making policy, usually without specific indication of which aspects are to be judged appropriate or how and by what standard those aspects are to be judged. A good example occurs in P.L. 93-641, Section 1523(a)(6), which required state health planning and development agencies to periodically review institutional health services and make public findings "respecting the appropriateness of such services." No indication was given in legislative history of what the agencies were to find either appropriate or inappropriate (the costs or charges, necessity, quality, staffing, administration, or location of the services) or what methods and criteria were to be used.

appropriateness Proper level, amounts, and type of care provided to the right patient within an acceptable time period using proper quality care and not the misuse of or lack of care.

appropriateness of care For PRO programs purposes, this is used to describe proper settings for delivery of medical care (e.g., acute-care hospital when needed or long-term-care facility only).

appropriation 1. In the federal budget, this is an act of Congress that permits federal agencies to incur obligations and to make payments out of the Treasury for specified purposes. An appropriation usually follows enactment of authorizing legislation. An appropriation is the most common form of budget authority, but in some cases the authorizing legislation provides the budget authority. Appropriations are categorized by the period of availability (1 year, multiple years, no years), the timing of congressional action (current, permanent), and how the amount of the appropriation is determined (definite, indefinite). 2. A legislature's setting aside of money for a specific purpose. 3. The taking of property by the government.

approved According to JCAHO for psychiatric, alcoholism, and drug abuse facilities accreditation purposes, this means acceptable to the authority having jurisdiction.

approved charge The amount of money that Medicare, Medicaid, an HMO contract, or other managed-care contract has determined is appropriate payment to a physician for certain services, often based on historical charges for the organization or physician. *See usual, customary, and reasonable.*

approved cost In managed care, these are charges for services rendered and covered by the health-care provider. Approved costs may be controlled by the health plan through a contract between the health plan and an approved health-care provider subject to plan review, based on the terms of group subscriber agreements.

approved drugs and biologicals According to Medicare, such drugs and biologicals that are 1) approved for inclusion in the U.S. Pharmacopoeia, National Formulary, or U.S. Homeopathic Pharmacopoeia; 2) included (or approved for inclusion) in AMA Drug Evaluations or Accepted Dental Therapeutics, except for any drugs and biologicals unfavorably evaluated therein; or 3) not included (nor approved for inclusion) in the compendia listed in the above paragraphs of this definition. However, they may be considered approved if such drugs 1) were furnished to the patient during his or her prior hospitalization, 2) were approved for use during a prior hospitalization by the hospital's pharmacy and drug therapeutics committee (or equivalent), and 3) are required for the continuing treatment of the patient in the facility. (In the case of Medicaid, drugs approved by the state Title XIX agency are included.)

approved health-care facility (service, program) In managed care, any licensed health-care facility, service or program that has met licensure or certification under state laws as being approved to provide medical care, which in turn is approved by a health plan to provide health care to health plan members as set forth in a policy or contract.

appurtenance 1. That which is a part of something else. 2. An extra right. 3. Something annexed, attached to, or belonging to a major thing and that also passes with ownership.

appurtenant Belonging to or added on to.

a priori (Lat.) 1. From the first; from the preceding. 2. A form of reasoning that tries to discover what facts came first and in what order they follow.

APTD *See Aid to the Permanently and Totally Disabled.*

aptitude test A test used to predict an individual's ability to learn a specific job or be successful in a skill or training.

aqueo- Prefix meaning "water."

arbiter One authorized to judge or decide a controversy; an adjudicator.

arbitrament The decision of an arbitrator.

arbitrary 1. Not controlled by a principle; capricious. 2. Any action taken or made without any supervision or set of principles or policies used in decision making. 3. Left to the judgment of the court, not statutes.

arbitration A method of settling controversies or disputes by enlisting the services of an unofficial third party to hear and consider arguments to determine an equitable settlement. It has become common to have controversies of various natures reviewed for judgment by third parties with their decision being final and binding. Arbitration also serves as a screening mechanism that substitutes for the litigation process. Arbitration has been confused with mediation. The basic differences between these two are that the decision of arbitration is a binding decision that is often referred to as "award," whereas in mediation a compromise is sought in which a third party assists in reaching decisions. The concept of arbitration in recent years has been used in hearing malpractice suits prior to going to court.

arbitration clause A clause in a contract compelling the parties of the contract to settle differences and controversies that may arise from the contract.

arbitration, expedited *See expedited arbitration.*

arbitrator An unbiased third party through which a controversy is decided; an arbiter.

arbrovirus In epidemiology, this is a group of animal viruses that are capable of disease transmission between vertebrate host organisms via blood-feeding arthropod vectors such as fleas, ticks, flies, and mosquitoes. *See vector; vector-borne.*

ARC AIDS-related complex *See acquired immunodeficiency syndrome.*

Area Agency on Aging (AAA) A county-level agency found in most large county governments or district administration that is responsible for all home and social support programs for the elderly. Some of the programs include home-delivered meals, congregate dining sites, senior citizen centers, transportation programs, friendly visitor programs, and an information-referral office. Created in the early 1970s by the passage of the Older American's Act, which created the federal Administration on Aging. Originally called "Areawide Model Projects," the name Area Agency on Aging, or Triple As (for AAA), was used. Some counties call them the "Office on Aging."

Area Health Education Center (AHEC) An organization or system of health, educational, and service institutions whose policy and programs are frequently under the direction of a medical school or university health science center and whose focus is to improve the distribution, supply, quality, utilization, and efficiency of health personnel in relation to specific medically underserved areas. The primary objectives are to educate and train the health personnel needed for that underserved community and to decentralize health manpower education, thereby increasing manpower supplies and providing a link between the health and educational institutions in scarcity areas. In practice, each AHEC has as its nucleus one or more public or nonprofit hospitals, some distance away from the medical school or university health science center, whose educational efforts are under the effective guidance of such medical center. The development of AHECs was assisted by the former federal Department of Health, Education and Welfare.

area of responsibility A major aspect of the role that encompasses an aggregate of related functions.

area wage adjustment Under the Medicare Prospective Payment System (PPS), a payment formula used to account for and adjust the differences in wages in different hospitals and regions in the United States.

areawide agreement A single labor agreement made by one union that also makes the same agreement with many hospitals in the same geographical area.

Areawide Comprehensive Health Planning Agency (Areawide A agency, or 314[b] agency) A former substate (usually multicounty) agency assisted under the old section 314(b) of the PHS Act, created by the Comprehensive Health Planning and Public Health Service Amendments of 1966 (P.L. 89-749) and charged with the preparation of regional or local plans for the coordination and development of existing and new health services, facilities, and manpower. The agencies were authorized to review and comment on proposals from hospitals and other institutions for development of programs and expansion of facilities but had no significant powers of enforcement; up to three quarters of the operating costs of the 314(b) agencies could have been supported by federal project grants. The balance of the costs was obtained from voluntary contributions from any source, including the health-care providers affected by the agencies' plans. Under the provisions of the health planning law (P.L. 93-64 1), 314(b) agencies were replaced by health systems agencies that had expanded duties and powers. *See also health systems agencies.*

Areawide Model Projects *See Area Agency on Aging.*

arguendo (Lat.) Accepting something as true for the sake of argument.

argument 1. Debate and discussion using facts, reasoning, and legal documents to persuade a shift of opinion. 2. In-court presentation of facts and opinions to sway a decision.

argumentative 1. Stating reasons and facts with intent to prove something. 2. Stating conclusions and reasons.

ARIMA *See autoregressive integrated moving averages.*

arithmetic-logic unit In managed care and insurance, this is a computer or section of a computer that performs calculations and makes simple yes/no decisions through comparing data to determine if a given medical or other condition is true or false.

Arizona Health Care Cost Containment System (AHCCCS) A program developed in 1981 in Arizona, the only state that did not adopt Medicaid, to meet state health-care needs of the poor.

The program was implemented in October 1982. Some original differences between AHCCCS and Medicaid are the following: 1) eligibility for services for indigents is determined by income and resources rather than by participation in other public assistance programs; 2) the existence of an established stabilized risk pool; 3) the program offers eligible participants several plans to choose from in some areas; 4) choice of doctors within the health plan (the doctor serves as the control unit and is called the "gatekeeper"); 5) services to high-risk populations (those 65 years and older) continue to be provided by the counties; 6) most care is still provided on a cost-containment rather than a fee-for-service basis; 7) co-payment by all participants is required; 8) serves persons other than indigents in a cost-effective fashion with federal financial participation sought for these persons; and 9) noninclusion of family planning, home health care, transportation other than ambulance for emergency-only nurse midwives, and long-term care and nursing home care, all the costs for which are handled by the counties. Nursing home care (skilled nursing care) was the greatest limitation, and change in this area is expected. The private enterprise system was to be utilized in the management of the system, but this approach has met with difficulty.

Arizona v. Maricopa County Medical Society A landmark decision affecting HMOs and IPAs related to price fixing in the prepaid insurance settings, especially the fees paid to those physicians serving the prepaid programs. The court found that prepaid programs were not involved in price fixing.

arm board A special tablelike device, attached to an operating table, to aid in giving injections.

arraign 1. To bring a defendant before a court to hear charges, usually to enter a plea of guilty or not guilty. 2. To accuse or charge with faults.

arrears (or arrearages) 1. Something kept in reserves. 2. Debts that are owed or unpaid.

arrest 1. To seize or take by power or force. 2. To apprehend a person in a legal sense. 3. To take a person into legal custody to answer for criminal charges. This may involve the use of force if necessary. 4. To end or stop a disease, condition, or disorder or to stop it from getting worse.

arrest of judgment 1. The staying of a decision. 2. The temporary stopping of the court's judgment because of wrong proceedings.

arrogation 1. To claim something unwarrantedly. 2. To claim or take something in a manner that is overbearing or without having the right to.

ART *See accredited records technician; see also medical record technician.*

arthritis treatment center A specialized treatment center that is staffed and equipped for the treatment of joint disease and disorders related to arthritis.

art therapist 1. One trained to apply the principles and techniques of art to the rehabilitation of patients. These individuals work with mentally ill or mentally retarded patients and with those who may be temporarily or permanently disabled. 2. A person with a masters degree in art therapy, art education, or psychology with study in art, including an approved clinical internship in art therapy from an accredited college or university, and who is registered or eligible for registration as such with the American Art Therapy Association.

arteriogram A diagnostic method used to enable visualization of the arteries by introducing radioactive dye into the bloodstream.

arteriosclerosis A pathological condition in which the walls of the arteries become thick and hardened.

article 1. A part of a document. 2. A clause in a contract. 3. A distinct part of a document that has two or more parts.

articles 1. The separate parts of an instrument, document, policy, etc.

articles of incorporation A legal document used to create a corporation.

ASBS *See American Society for Bariatric Surgery.*

ASC Ambulatory surgery center.

ASC contract (administrative services contract) In managed care, this is a contract between an insurance company and a self-funded managed-care plan where the insurance company performs administrative services only and does not assume any risk. Services usually include claims processing but may include other services such as actuarial analysis, utilization review, etc.

Aschheim-Zondek test (AZT) A test for pregnancy detection where a urine specimen from a human female is injected into a female mouse.

ASCII American Standard Code for Information Interchange; a standardized computer code using a set of characters consisting of 8 digits coded for upper- and lowercase letters, numbers, punctuation, and special control characters.

asepsis The absence of disease-producing pathogens and microorganisms.

ASHA American Speech and Hearing Association. *See also American School Health Association.*

ASHFLCD Association of State Health Facility Licensing and Certification Directors.

asked price In health finance, this is the price at which bonds are presented for potential purchase.

aspects of care, important Patient care activities or processes that occur frequently or that affect large numbers of patients. Patient care or treatment activities that place patients at serious risk if not provided correctly, causing problems for patients and staff. For accreditation and quality assessment, certain aspects of patient care delivery cause more concern than others and are deemed "important" (JCAHO for acute-care facilities).

ASPH Association of Schools of Public Health.

asportation 1. Illicit removal of goods from where they are left. 2. Carrying away items illegally.

ASQC *See American Society for Quality Control.*

ASR *See age/sex rates.*

assault 1. An illegal threat of physical harm or an attempt to do harm. 2. Show of force or an action that could be taken to cause a person to feel in danger of physical attack or physical harm.

AS-SCORE A multiattribute clinical index of illness severity. In DRGs, this is a severity-of-illness system based on five characteristics of inpatients: 1) age; 2) organ or body system affected by the disease, illness, or injury; 3) stage of the disease; 4) complications; and 5) patient's response to procedures, treatments, and/or therapies. The system assigns the patient to one of four classes (I, II, III, IV) on the basis of the extent and seriousness of the disease or disorder. It is used as a health-care management tool to reduce length of stay and excessive charges for patients placed in one of the DRGs. This method can be used to check or measure DRGs to see if patients are homogeneous in a DRG category or if severity of illness is not being accounted for.

assembler A special and fundamental computer language that translates symbols as code into machine language by replacing the operation code with a binary code.

assembly In formal health-care meetings and hearings using parliamentary procedure, this refers to a group that gathers to carry on business in a formal meeting and that can include small executive meetings and large conference meetings involving the entire organization or society.

assent 1. To admit as true consent. 2. To approve an agreement. 3 Compliance.

assertiveness 1. Asking for and expecting a communication to be heard and respected while not allowing one's personal rights to be violated. 2. The ability to express oneself without dominating or humiliating or degrading others or abusing their rights. Assertiveness is contrasted with aggressiveness and is taught to improve the ability to achieve a person's rights, enhance communication, and allow compromises where neither party sacrifices basic integrity. *See also nonassertion.*

assertiveness training An educational process aimed at helping people lacking in assertiveness skills. Training programs have been developed for women, managers, administrators, supervisors, and other professionals to help them become more successful in management roles or in other roles usually reserved for men.

assess 1. To fix a sum against, such as a tax or fine. 2. To set an amount. 3. To place a value on something, usually for tax purposes.

assessed health status Self-reported self-assessment is used to determine one's health status on a continuum. This approach is used in the National Health Interview Survey and is based on the respondent's opinion, not on the clinical evidence.

assessed valuation Determining the value of real estate, usually less than market value, for tax purposes.

assessment 1. Estimation of the relative effectiveness, efficiency, quality, quantity, value, and importance of health services, programs, or projects; 2. In insurance, a charge on carriers to raise funds for a specific purpose, such as meeting the administrative costs of a government-required program (usually state government) or a special organization authorized by government and provided for in law or regulation. Applied to all carriers handling a specific line of coverage subject to regulation by the government in question and based on a formula. 3. According to JCAHO for psychiatric, alcoholism, and drug abuse facilities' accreditation purposes, the means by which a program evaluates an individual's strengths, weaknesses, problems, and needs.

assessment centers In health promotion, these are standardized employee appraisal systems that rely on multiple appraisal stations and raters who perform a range of evaluations, screening, and health appraisals. Any centralized location, clinic, or other service that provides comprehensive health appraisals to large groups of persons.

assessment criteria The focus of assessment standards and evaluation measures. The levels or variables used in assessment standards, such as that diastolic blood pressure should be under 90 mmHg or that overall cholesterol should be under 200.

assessment, program *See program evaluation; assessment centers.*

assessment standards Levels of outcome or performance; decision threshold levels, or benchmarks, for interpreting measures for certain tests, treatments, or performances, determined for a variety of health-related activities in medical care, medical testing, environmental health, psychological testing, etc.

assessment technology Machines, instruments, devices, computers, or procedures used to measure and evaluate medical or health activities or outcomes.

assets 1. Money, property, or any other item of value; items of value owned by a health-care organization.

assets, capital Any item of property with a life of more than 1 year.

assets, current Any item of property with a life of less than 1 year.

assets, fixed Any items of property that are of long-term value that are not bought or sold in the normal course of business and that add to the value of an organization (e.g., buildings, land, large pieces of equipment, etc.).

asset share In managed care and medical insurance, this is the amount of assets that insurance policies or an HMO contract will accumulate.

asset share calculation A projection based on computation of data that simulates the manner in which the assets of HMO contracts or insurance policies should financially grow, based on assumptions about interest rates, levels of morbidity in the clientele, mortality, expenses, use of resources, numbers of patient visits, etc.

assets, intangible Items of value but having no physical substance to them, such as copyrights, patents, reputation, and goodwill.

assets, noncurrent Property with a life of less than 1 year.

assets, tangible Items of property that have physical structure and substance, such as equipment, vehicles, buildings, and land.

assets-to-equity ratio In health-care finance, this ratio is used in equity financing. *See equity financing ratio.*

asset turnover The ratio of net sales to average assets representing the activity portion of the return on investment.

assign 1. To designate or appoint for a particular purpose or duty. 2. To transfer a contractual right to another. 3. An asset or belonging.

assigned risk A special type of insurance, such as malpractice insurance, underwritten by insurance companies only because it is required by law. A risk that underwriters do not care to insure (such as a person with hypertension seeking health insurance) but that, because of state law or other reasons, must be insured. Insuring assigned risks is usually handled through a group of insurers (such as all companies licensed to issue health insurance in the state), and individual assigned risks are assigned to the companies in turn or in proportion to their share of the state's total health insurance business. Assignment of risks is common in casualty insurance and less common in health insurance.

assignee The one to whom rights at law or whose property rights have been transferred for the benefit of others or oneself. An assignee may be designated by a court, specially appointed, or named in a deed.

assignment 1. An agreement in which a patient assigns to another party, usually a provider, the right to receive payment from a third party for the service the patient has received. This is preferred to a patient's paying directly for the service and then receiving reimbursement from public or private insurance programs. In Medicare, the process of assigning a patient's right to payment to the physician or supplier. If a physician accepts assignment from the patient, he or she must agree to accept the program payment as payment in full (except for specific co-insurance, co-payment, and deductible amounts required of the patient). Assignment thus protects the patient against liability for charges that the Medicare program will not recognize as reasonable. 2. A claim or right to another person or a second party. 3. The transfer of one's right to collect an amount payable under an insurance contract. *See also assignment of benefits.*

assignment of benefits An agreement where the patient assigns any or all benefits to be paid to the health-care provider by his or her health or medical insurance. If a provider accepts assignment, it accepts the amount paid by the third-party payer for that particular service. In most cases, the provider has the choice of accepting or rejecting assignment of benefits.

assignment of error A declaration made by an appellate court against a trial court that sets forth the errors complained of to determine from the record the effect of the alleged errors.

assignor One who assigns or transfers claims, property, or rights under law.

assimilation The process whereby a person is able to encounter and react to new situations by using existing defense or adjustment mechanisms.

assistant administrators An administrator holding a masters degree in health-care administration or the equivalent who works under the direction and supervision of the chief executive/administrator of a health-care facility. This member of a health-care facility's top management team assists in the areas of finance, organization, planning, personnel, clinical, voluntary services, etc.

Assisted Health Insurance Plan (AHIP) One of three parts of a proposed approach to national health insurance, the Comprehensive Health Insurance Plan. AHIP is designed to provide health insurance coverage for people of low income and high medical risk. It would be available to anyone electing coverage, at a premium no greater than 150% of the average group premium for private health insurance in the state. Premiums and cost sharing would be indexed to income. AHIP would replace Medicaid and would be state administered under contract with fiscal intermediaries. The plan would be financed by premiums and subsidized by state and federal revenues under a matching formula.

assistive device Any implement, prosthesis, or adaptive tool that assists a person in compensating for certain disabilities, impairments, or physical limitations, such as glasses for vision, a hook/hand for an amputee, a walker to assist ambulation, etc.

assistive technology Devices and other solutions that assist people with deficits in physical, mental, or emotional function.

assistive technology devices Implements, units, devices, and equipment that enhance the ability of an individual with a disability to engage in major life activities, actions, and tasks. Hundreds of devices are available, including mobility aids such as wheelchairs and walkers, orthotics, and prostheses, which are the more visible types. Other devices include microcomputers, powered mobility devices, myoelectrically powered prostheses, augmentative communication devices, optical pointers, headsticks, and alphabet boards. The most technically sophisticated devices are myoelectrically powered prostheses, infrared hearing systems, interactive computers, and text-to-speech software. *See Technology-Related Assistance for Individuals with Disabilities Act of 1988.*

associate degree program An educational degree–granting program providing 2 years of education at community colleges, junior colleges, and some colleges and universities. Usually, the student's classroom and laboratory instruction are principally provided at the college and clinical teaching at the affiliated hospital. Programs included in an associate degree program are those for nursing and other allied health areas. *See also diploma school; baccalaureate degree program; affiliated hospital.*

associate medical staff Physicians, dentists, podiatrists, psychologists, and other professional-level health-care providers who are new to the hospital staff and are under review for acceptance as regular medical staff.

associate membership Under union membership, this is when a person is allowed to be a member of the union but is not employed under a union contract. This person is allowed to affiliate with a union by paying fees and dues for union benefits.

association 1. In psychology, this is the relationship between ideas and feelings. 2. In research or epidemiology, the general name for a relationship between two variables identifying cause-effect relationships. Two related variables, such as age and the incidence of diabetes, are said to be "associated." Different types of association are recognized: artifactual, causal, and chance. The statistical relationship between two or more events. 3. A society or group of persons with common interests who create an organization for a common purpose to transact business and activities pursuant to the members' mutual advantage.

association, direct Cause-effect occurrence that does not occur via a third variable.

association, indirect causal In epidemiology, cause-effect occurrences in two different subjects from a third common cause. In epidemiology, a cause-effect occurrence in a third subject from a second subject who was infected from an original third subject.

Association for Health Records (AHR) A multidisciplinary society whose purpose is to exchange information between professionals in the field of medical records and health information.

Association for Health Services Research (AHSR) The only national organization representing the health services research community and dedicated to promoting and improving health services, health-care administration, and health-care delivery through empirical and research methods. AHSR represents its members in the development and implementation of national legislative and administrative policies concerning health services research. The organization also fosters cooperation among researchers, public and private funding agencies, health professionals, and the public.

Association for the Advancement of Health Education (AAHE) The former name of the American Association for Health Education. *See American Association for Health Education.*

association group A group composed of members of a trade or business association that purchases insurance under one master health insurance agreement.

Association of American Physicians (AAP) An exclusive national professional organization of physician scholars to which physicians who have made professional, academic, and scholarly contributions to the field of medicine must be extended an invitation to join.

Association of Humanistic Psychology (AHP) An organization that fosters the development of the human sciences in ways that recognize one's distinctive human qualities and works toward fulfilling one's innate capacities as an individual and member of society. Established to link people with a humanistic approach to interpersonal interaction and behavior, the organization encourages others to treat all in a humanistic way and to demonstrate that being humanistic to others can be realized in the life and work of all people.

Association of Schools in Public Health (ASPH) The only national organization representing the deans, faculty, and students of the official schools of public health. Established in 1953 to facilitate communication among the leadership of the Schools of Public Health, the association exists to provide a focus and platform for the enhancement of academic public health programs, to influence national policy, to serve as an information center for government and private groups whose concerns overlap with higher education for public health, and to assist in meeting national goals in public health and disease prevention. Headquartered in Washington, D.C.

Association of Superintendents of Insurance The Canadian equivalent of the National Association of Insurance Commissioners in the United States. Develops insurance legislation and encourages provincial legislatures to adopt the proposed ideas.

Association of Teachers of Preventive Medicine (ATPM) A national organization for medical educators, practitioners, and students committed to advancing the teaching of all aspects of preventive medicine. ATPM was founded in 1942 with three objectives: 1) advancing medical education; 2) developing instruction, scientific skills, and knowledge in preventive medicine; and 3) exchanging experience and ideas among its members. The aim of ATPM is to ensure the primacy and excellence of individual and community health promotion and disease prevention in the education of physicians and other health professionals and to extend the message of preventive medicine to new audiences of policymakers, health professionals, and the public. Headquartered in Washington, D.C.

Association of University Programs in Health Administration (AUPHA) An international cooperative effort to improve health services delivery through education for administration. The university programs are a primary resource for improving administrative technology, which is fundamental to high-quality and effective delivery of medical care. It is also fundamental to the appropriate allocation of scarce and expensive community health resources. Through graduate and undergraduate programs, community service, research, and continuing education, the member universities are advancing administrative technology and preparing qualified administrative leadership for health services. The association was organized as a corporation in 1948 to assist the participating universities in achieving their individual and collective objectives. Its work is supported by a unique partnership of industry, health organizations, individuals, foundations, government, and universities.

assuming insurance company *See reinsurance.*

assumption of risk Willingly exposing oneself or one's property to certain dangers with the knowledge that damages cannot be collected if any destruction occurs.

assurance Synonymous with "insurance."

asthenic personality One who lacks enthusiasm, lacks a capacity for enjoyment, has a low tolerance for stress, and tires easily.

Astler-Coller system A method used in classifying or describing the extent of tumors (called "staging").

astringent An agent or substance that causes contraction and that is usually applied topically.

asyndesis A language disorder common in schizophrenia where a person combines unconnected ideas and images.

ataxia The lack of either physical or mental coordination. In neurology, this refers to loss of muscular coordination. In psychiatry, the lack of coordination between feelings and thoughts (common in schizophrenia).

athletic trainer An allied health-care professional who treats athletic injuries and provides rehabilitation as prescribed by the team physician. Trainers give first aid, tape injuries, supervise diets, and assist in purchasing and fitting athletic equipment. A 4-year bachelors degree in athletic training is the minimum education. Graduate training is recommended, and some physical therapists become athletic trainers. College graduates without an athletic training degree can qualify by completing additional undergraduate and graduate courses and a minimum of 900 hours of supervised clinical experience. Formally trained physical therapists can also become athletic trainers.

ATOD Alcohol, tobacco, and other drugs.

atomic energy Energy released in nuclear fission or fusion; more correctly called "nuclear energy."

atomic power The production of thermal power in a nuclear reactor.

at risk 1. The state of being subject to some uncertain event occurring that connotes loss or difficulty. In the financial sense, this refers to an individual, organization (like an HMO), or insurance company assuming the chance of loss through running the risk of having to provide or pay for more services than paid for through premiums or per capita payments. If payments are adjusted after the fact so that no loss can occur, then there is no risk. Losses incurred in one year may be made up by increases in premiums or per capita payments in the next year, so the "risk" is somewhat tempered. A firm that is at risk for losses also stands to gain from profits if costs are less than premiums collected. For a consumer, being financially at risk usually means being without insurance or at risk for substantial out-of-pocket expenses. 2. The special vulnerability of certain populations to certain diseases or conditions. 3. In HMOs for the elderly under Medicare, this puts HMOs in the position of being paid fixed amounts on the basis of the average Medicare costs for all beneficiaries in the HMO's service area and requires that all health care for beneficiaries enrolled must be provided or authorized by the HMOs, except in emergencies. 4. In managed care, any medical care service, treatment, or therapy for which the health-care provider agrees to accept financial responsibility to provide or arrange for the provision of medical care in exchange for the capitation payment, which constitutes payment in full except for any stop-loss provision.

attachment The taking of goods, persons, property, or estates into custody for the purpose of satisfying a judgment. A hospital may attach a patient's bank account or property to make sure that a person pays a debt that occurred from a lawsuit.

attack rate A cumulative incidence rate used for a specific group with a unique set of possible exposures and limited time periods. This rate is commonly used in food poisoning or chemical exposures. Three types of attack rates are used:

a crude attack rate, a general attack rate, and a food-specific attack rate. The numerator of the attack rate has the numbers of persons ill and the denominator the number of persons attending the event or the number exposed or at risk, and all use the same time period per 100 or 1000. Attack rate formulas:

$$\text{Crude attack rate} = \frac{\text{Number of persons ill with the disease}}{\text{Number of persons attending the event}} \times 100$$

$$\text{Attack rate} = \frac{\text{Number of persons ill within the time period}}{\text{Number of persons at risk within the time period}} \times 100$$

$$\text{Food-specific attack rate} = \frac{\text{Number of persons who ate a specific food and became ill}}{\text{Total number of persons who ate a specific food}} \times 100$$

attending physician The physician who is the admitting physician or in charge of a certain patient's care and treatment; those physicians having hospital privileges for patient care and who are legally responsible for the care of their patients in a health-care facility. An attending physician is legally responsible for his or her private patients admitted to any health-care setting, including long-term care, home health care, outpatient treatment centers, or inpatient care settings. When treating public patients in teaching or government hospitals, a physician on the medical staff of the hospital may be assigned to a patient and then becomes the attending physician for that patient. *See physician, attending.*

attending physician's statement In managed care, this is a report to the HMO or insurance company from a physician who was responsible for treatment of a certain insured patient with a specific medical problem.

attenuation In laser technology, this is the decrease in the radiant flux as it passes through an absorbing or scattering medium.

attest 1. To swear, certify, or witness. 2. To put a person under oath. 3. To declare. 4. To bear witness to.

attestation 1. A testimony; an official declaration that supports fact or evidence. 2. Witnessing the execution of a written document. 3. Signing as a witness.

attest function The act of a noninvolved certified public accountant (CPA) auditing and reviewing the fairness of financial statements of an organization or a health-care facility and then explaining these findings to those having a direct concern.

attitude A constant belief, predisposition, or set of behaviors directed toward a person, situation, circumstance, or object.

attitude surveys An organized and scientific approach to ascertaining what employees think about the health-care organization in which they work. Surveys can be done through questionnaires, interviews, focus groups, telephone surveys, and other data-gathering methods. Results are given to administration and shared with the employees. Plans and actions are made to identify and resolve areas of concern and improve the work circumstances.

attorney's lien The right of an attorney to hold money or property already in his or her hands to pay for attorney's fees.

attractive nuisance Potentially dangerous property maintained so that children might be attracted to it (e.g., unfenced swimming pools or construction sites). The property owner can be held liable if the children get hurt, even if the children are at fault.

attributable fraction In public health, a concept that is occasionally used to refer to that part of a group or population that is exposed. It is a measure of the proportion of those diseased and associated with disease exposure within a group. Disease occurrence in a segment of a population is based on selected exposures to the disease-causing agent.

attributable risk In public health and epidemiology, the rate of disease in exposed persons that can be directly attributed to the exposure of the disease. Attributable risk is determined by subtracting the incidence rate or mortality rate of the disease of nonexposed persons from that of exposed persons.

attrition The loss of employees who leave a health-care organization or hospital; the turnover of health-care personnel.

attrition rate In managed care, this is the dropout rate or amount of disenrollment from a managed-care program expressed as a percentage of total membership; disenrollment as a percentage of total health plan membership. The amount of enrollment needed to maintain membership levels is determined by the level of dropout in membership from the health plan.

at-will employment In human resource management, this is the usual employment arrangement found in the free world where an employee works at the pleasure of the employee, and thus employment can be terminated at any time by either party without notice or specific reason.

atypical child A child with problematic personality development, often a brain-damaged or autistic child.

audi alteram partem (Lat.) To hear the other side. No man should be condemned without a chance to defend himself.

audiological assessment 1. The evaluation of an individual's hearing to determine if any hearing deficits exist. 2. According to JCAHO for health facilities accreditation purposes, certain audiological tests are given that delineate the site of auditory dysfunction, including such tests as pure-tone air- and bone-conduction thresholds, speech reception thresholds, speech discrimination measurements, and impedance measurements.

audiologist 1. A health-care provider who specializes in diagnostic evaluation of hearing and conducts research related to hearing disorders. Using electroacoustic instrumentation, an audiologist determines the range, nature, and degree of hearing function; coordinates audiometric results with other diagnostic data; and plans, directs, conducts, or participates in aural rehabilitation programs. These programs include such activities as hearing aid selection and orientation, auditory training, speech reading, speech conservation, counseling, and guidance. The audiologist may also provide consultant services to educational, medical, and other professional groups or teach audiology-related courses in educational institutions. 2. A person licensed by a board of medical quality assurance or who has a masters degree in audiology or who is authorized to practice under the supervision of a licensed audiologist. *See audiologist, qualified.*

audiologist, qualified According to JCAHO for health facilities accreditation purposes, this is an individual who is certified by the American Speech-Language-Hearing Association as clinically competent in the area of audiology or an individual who has documented equivalent education, training, and/or experience.

audiology The profession and associated training programs that provide the principles and techniques of the practice of restoring or partially restoring impaired hearing; the study of hearing and hearing impairment and methods of improving or restoring hearing impairment or loss.

audiology and speech pathology An allied health profession and education program that teaches the therapeutic techniques and theoretical foundations of the treatment of hearing and speech disorders.

audiology services A program of hearing testing, diagnosis, and treatment for patients with dysfunctional or impaired hearing.

audiometric screening According to JCAHO for health facilities accreditation purposes, this is a process that may include such tests as pure-tone air-conduction thresholds, pure-tone air-conduction suprathreshold screenings, impedance measurements, or observations of reactions to auditory stimuli.

audiometrician An individual trained to administer diagnostic and evaluative hearing tests to patients as prescribed by the audiologist or physician.

audio response unit A device that provides verbal replies to questions directed to a computer through a dial telephone input unit; an assistive device. *See assistive devices; assistive technology.*

audit 1. An examination of business or other records that may determine financial status.

audited financial statement In health-care finance, this is a balance sheet, a financial statement, and other financial documents that have been certified for accuracy by an outside accounting firm.

audit, financial According to JCAHO for health facilities accreditation purposes, this is an independent review by a public accountant certifying that a facility's financial reports reflect its financial status.

auditing The process of examining and assessing the records of a managed-care program, hospital, nursing home, clinic, or other health-care organization to determine if the records and accountability processes are accurate and effective.

auditing committee A committee of a board of directors that is responsible for supervising the organization's accounting functions and operations, overseeing external and internal audits, reviewing the organization's financial statements, requesting formal audits, hiring auditors, etc.

audit measurement The process of comparing the actual practice of medicine to preestablished criteria.

audit, medical The retrospective review of medical records by medical personnel to evaluate the quality and quantity of medical care in relation to acceptable predetermined standards.

audit of large dollar claims In managed care, these are the claims that exceed the identified thresholds and thus are reviewed in detail and compared against the medical records.

audit, patient care The retrospective review of selected medical records by various members of the professional staff to evaluate and assess the quality and quantity of medical care provided in relation to acceptable predetermined health-care standards.

audit, quality management An assessment of the level of effectiveness, efficiency, success, and overall quality of the management of a health-care organization. *See management audit; quality.*

audit report 1. In human resource management, this is a description of personnel activities covering both commendation for effective practices and recommendations for improvement. 2. In health-care finance, the final result of auditors, including a determination of the financial status of the organization, identified problems, and recommendation for improvement of the financial and accounting processes.

audit team In human resource management, these are individuals who are responsible for the evaluation of the performance of the human resource functions and personnel department of a health care organization.

audit, trial report In information management, this is the checking of a computer program for accuracy and its ability to run. Also, a portion of a data security check for the effectiveness and efficiency of programs generated by the computer.

auditor 1. An official authorized to examine financial accounts for accuracy.

AUPHA *See Association of University Programs in Health Administration.*

authenticate To prove the source or authorship of a legal or medical record by a stamp, initials, or a written signature.

authentication As used in JCAHO accreditation, proof of authorship. This may be by written signature, identifiable initials, or computer key. The use of rubber stamp signatures is acceptable only under the following condition: The individual whose signature the rubber stamp represents is the only one who has possession of the stamp and is the only one who uses it. The individual must place in the administrative offices of the hospital a signed statement to the effect that he or she is the only one who has the stamp and is the only one who will use it.

AUR Ambulatory utilization review.

authoritarianism The belief, held by persons in position of power or control, that there should be power differences in responsibility and status among people in organizations and that the proper placement and use of these differences is important to the success of the manager and the organization.

authority 1. The power or right to command or administer. 2. The power to act. 3. An official declaration. 4. A precedent or decision of a court. 5. In management and administration, the right of a worker to make decisions, direct and supervise others, spend money, hire and discharge workers, take action, and complete work assignments; having the right to command a worker to do a task and the subordinate having the duty to obey the request without the manager abusing the right to command. Authority has to be co-equal with responsibility for a manager to be successful. *See positional authority; responsibility.*

authority having jurisdiction According to JCAHO for health facilities accreditation purposes, this is the organization, office, or individual responsible for approving a piece of equipment, an installation, or a procedure.

authorization 1. To give authority; the power to act and make decisions. 2. In the legislative process, this is when the monies are allocated and authority determined and legally approved.

authorization cards In labor relations and union activities, these are forms that prospective union members sign as an indication that the worker has agreed to have an election to determine whether a labor organization will represent the workers in their dealing with management.

authorize 1. To make legal. 2. To give authority or official power. 3. To give the authority to act. 4. To officially permit.

authorized representative An individual approved under law, by a court order or a written statement signed by the patient (unless the patient has been legally deemed incompetent), to act on behalf of the patient. To be a legal authorized representative, a guardianship, conservatorship, or durable-power-of-attorney must be legally drawn up and approved.

authorizing legislation Legislation enacted by Congress that sets up or continues the legal operation of a federal program or agency indefinitely or for a specific period of time, often for 3 years. Such legislation is a prerequisite for subsequent appropriations or other kinds of budget authority to be contained in appropriation acts. It may limit the amount of budget authority to be provided subsequently or may authorize the appropriation of "such sums as may be necessary." In a few instances, budget authority may be provided in the legislative authorization. *See backdoor authority.*

auto- Prefix meaning "self."

autocorrelation In managed care, health-care delivery, and marketing, this is a forecasting technique based on the correlation between utilization in one period and the utilization in one prior period.

autodidactic Any person who is an inner-directed self-starter or self-teacher. This person questions reality and searches for underlying meanings and new ways of organizing information about the world. Believed by some professionals to be a personality characteristic of many creative persons.

autograft The surgical transplant of an organ or tissue from one part of a person's body to another part of the same person's body.

autogroup (AUTOGRP—Automatic Grouping System) The computerization of medical records by an interactive statistical analysis system that partitions data into groups using patients' medical records. The records are used to determine the reasons for day and cost outlier cases and to determine DRG classification. Homogeneous factors and related diseases are grouped into areas with commonalities, thus reducing the types and numbers of categories by placing them into one of the DRGs. Because the motivation behind DRGs is to reduce the cost and consumption of goods and services, length of stay has become a major basis for the analysis.

AUTOGRP *See autogroup.*

autologous To oneself; related to affecting oneself.

autologous blood transfusions In blood bank and blood transfusions, this is when a person uses his or her own blood that was stored previously for use by oneself later on, which may include storing the blood by freezing.

Automated Integrated Medical Management System In health-care utilization review and utilization management, a computer software program used to support utilization management activity.

automatic binding limit In managed care and insurance, this is a limit on the amount of reinsurance a reinsurer will provide to a company through an automatic reinsurance treaty. *See automatic reinsurance treaty.*

automatic interaction detector (AID) Under strategic health-care marketing and planning, DRGs are used in this statistical technique by health-care marketing personnel to place patients into groups according to demographic characteristics with the aim of identifying persons who have a greater demand for health-care services. In this way, appropriate strategic marketing can be developed to capture the health-care organization's market share. This method attempts to involve physician input by making the process medically meaningful. Clearly, this is vital because physicians play a strategic role in ordering and using health-care resources for patients.

automatic premium loan In managed care and medical insurance, this is an option that allows the insurer to pay overdue premiums on a policy by taking out a loan against the cash value of the insurance policy, which then avoids forfeiture of the policy.

automatic reinsurance treaty In managed care and insurance, an insurance company agrees to automatically provide reinsurance for all amounts of the policy in excess of the ceding company's retention limit up to a set amount, which is called the "automatic binding limit." *See automatic binding limit.*

automation 1. In medical records or the hospital business office, this is a process by which work is done with a minimum of human effort and that is largely self-regulating. 2. The investigation, design, development, and application of health-care or record-processing methods that renders processes automatic, self-moving, or self-controlling.

automatism Behavior that lacks direction and is not controlled by conscious thought and is more a reaction than a planned action.

autonomic Self-controlling; capable of independent function.

autonomous work groups In health-care administration, these are groups of individuals or teams of employees who lack a formal supervisor or manager at the head of the group and an appointed leader. The group chooses among themselves a leader and makes most decisions among themselves instead of having an organization-appointed manager making the decisions.

autonomy 1. Self; independence; self-governing; the right of an individual to govern himself or herself; separateness. 2. In health-care administration, having control over one's job, tasks, or professional activity.

autopsy Examination of the body after death to determine the cause of death; a postmortem. Consent for an autopsy is required from the dead person's survivors unless an exception is made by law.

autopsy data The information gained from the nonrandom autopsies of bodies in hospitals used to study the course, trends, and history of diseases.

autopsy, epidemiological Used to explore the disease states of bodies that would normally be autopsied for the cause of death. The new findings and discovered disease states are used in epidemiology to look for trends of disease states with populations or groups.

autopsy, hospital The postmortem examination of the body of an inpatient by a pathologist or other medical staff member to determine the cause of death or to investigate pathology that resulted in death.

autopsy rate The percentage of bodies examined as compared to the number of deaths in a given population for a given period of time and presented as a ratio per 100, 1000, or 10,000 population. The autopsy rate is sometimes considered a measure of the quality of a hospital.

autopsy rate, adjusted The number of postmortem examinations performed over a specified period in relation to the total number of inpatient and outpatient deaths minus those bodies not available for autopsy.

autopsy rate, gross The total number of postmortem examinations performed on persons who were inpatients in a hospital over a given period of time as compared to the total number of inpatient deaths and presented as a ratio of autopsies performed per 100 or 1000 deaths.

autopsy rate, net The total number of postmortem examinations performed on persons who were inpatients in a hospital over a specified period of time compared to the total number of inpatient deaths minus those bodies not available for postmortem examination.

autoptic evidence Information, facts, and insights as to the cause of death gained from the examination of a dead body.

autoregression In health services administration strategic planning, this is a specific type of correlation between health services utilization that occurs in different time periods expressed as a statistical regression.

autoregressive integrated moving averages In health services administration strategic planning, this is a computer-driven forecasting technique that combines moving averages with autoregression in analyzing past data as a method for predicting future utilization patterns.

auxilian Refers to one who participates in a hospital's auxiliary. This person may be a volunteer within the hospital or may work outside the hospital promoting the cause of the hospital and health care in the community.

auxiliary Supplementary; giving aid or support.

auxiliary computer storage A special information and data storage component that is external to the computer and has a greater capacity for storage. Information stored here takes more time to retrieve and is usually in the form of a hard disk, floppy disk, or tape.

auxiliary, hospital A group of volunteers formally organized from within the community to assist in promoting the cause and purpose of the hospital.

auxiliary services Those services within a health care institution other than hotel-related services (room and board), including professional services such as X ray, pharmacy and drug services, lab, etc.

availability 1. When a person can obtain health care at the time and place that it is needed. A measure of the type, volume, distribution, and location of the supply of health resources and services relative to the needs or demands of a given individual or community. Availability is a function of the distribution of appropriate personnel, resources, and services and the willingness of the provider to serve the particular patient in need. The appropriate supply and variety of health services and the capacity of the resources to provide care. 2. The extent to which health-care services are present in a specified geographic area. The mere presence or absence of a given service is the simplest measure of its availability. A better measure of availability is whether a particular service is present in the appropriate quantity and by its capacity for service. The extent to which health-care resources (manpower, facilities, equipment) are present in an area is often used as a substitute measure of service availability. *See also accessibility; acceptability.*

availability of service and facilities Those procedures a health-care consumer must follow to utilize existing health services. Refers to the existence of facilities and/or services on the basis of need regardless of the time at which the need occurs. *See also accessibility; availability.*

available bed days The average number of beds available in a health-care facility that can be used for patient care. This is determined by taking the number of beds available times the number of days in a given time period (e.g., a 100-bed hospital would have 36,500 available bed days per year).

aver 1. To affirm; confirm. 2. To prove. 3. To declare. 4. To justify. 5. To formally allege.

average annual rate of change (percent change) In public health and health services, the average annual growth rates are determined by the following formula:

$$[(P_n/P_o)^{1/n} - 1] \times 100$$

where
P_n = later time period
P_o = earlier time period
N = number of years in the interval

This geometric rate of change assumes that a variable increases or decreases at the same rate during each year between the two time periods.

average adjusted per capita cost In managed care, this is used by the Health Care Financing Administration (an administrative branch of Medicare), as a rate to calculate payments and is based on the average cost of providing health care to the Medicare beneficiaries in certain regions or geographical areas.

average cost Fixed costs plus variable total costs divided by the number of units of product produced or number of units of service rendered.

average cost per claim In managed care and medical insurance, this is the usual, regular, or average amount of administrative expenses or the amount of expenses generated and fees for medical care rendered for the unit of measure within each cost area or category of medical care delivery, such as admissions administration, health-care provider services, outpatient care, drugs, etc. The formula for average cost per claim follows:

$$\frac{\text{Total amount of all claims}}{\text{Number of claims}}$$

average daily census (ADC) The average number of persons in a hospital as inpatients who are served each day in a given period of time. Specifically, this is the total number of patients occupying a bed and receiving care as inpatients on any average day (excluding newborn infants). The average is determined by counting the number of patients in the hospital at a certain time every day, usually at midnight ("midnight census"). To calculate the ADC, the total number of patient days of care provided (not counting newborns) in the time period is divided by the total number of days in that time period. The formula and an example follow:

$$\frac{\text{Total number of days of patient care provided in a certain time period}}{\text{Total number of days in the time period}} = \text{ADC}$$

or

$$\frac{18{,}450 \text{ (patient days of care for one year)}}{365 \text{ (number of days in the time period)}} = 50.5$$

average days away from work, occupational health and safety As used in occupational health and safety and as set forth by the Occupational Safety and Health Administration (OSHA), this is the total days away from work (numerator) divided by total cases involving days away from work (denominator). *See average lost workdays.*

average days in accounts receivable In health-care finance, this is the average number of days it takes a health-care organization to collect the full amount of a bill for patient care charges.

average deviation The average or mean of all differences between each observation in a series of numbers and the median of the series of the numbers.

average function improvement *See function improvement.*

average length of stay (ALOS) 1. Using days as a measure of time, this is the average number of days a person stays as an inpatient in a health-care facility over a given time period. The number of days that services are rendered and care is provided to patients in a specified time period. The ALOS is determined by dividing the number of patient days that care was given by either the number of admissions or the number of discharges and deaths. The ALOS is most often determined by dividing the total number of patient days of services and care rendered to patients discharged during a period of time by the number of patients discharged during that period. The formula and an example follow:

$$\frac{\text{Total number of discharged patient days for care for that period}}{\text{Total number of patients discharged for that period}} = \text{ALOS}$$

or

$$\frac{17,500}{300} \frac{\text{(number of discharged patient days of care for the period)}}{\text{(total discharged for the period)}} = 58.3$$

2. In the National Hospital Discharge Survey, the ALOS is the total number of patient days accumulated at the time of discharge, counting the date of admission but not the date of discharge by patients discharged during a reporting period, divided by the number of patients discharged. 3. In the National Nursing Home Survey, length of stay for residents is the time from their admission until the reporting time, and the length of stay for discharges is the time between the date of admission and the date of discharge.

average lost workdays, occupational health and safety As used in occupational health and safety and as set forth by the Occupational Safety and Health Administration (OSHA), this is the total workdays (numerator) divided by total lost workday cases (denominator). *See average days away from work; incident rate; occupational health and safety.*

average nursing hours per patient day A nursing staffing approach that is rarely used. Average length of stay and occupancy rates affect the average nursing hours per patient day. Nursing services have much concern when inpatient facilities are at 100% occupancy because of the workload imposed on the nursing staff. Hospital administration discourages average nursing hours per patient day as a constant for staffing, as it affects quality and costs negatively as occupancy rates fluctuate greatly. Maximum staffing is desirable for the nursing personnel but not always cost-effective for overall hospital operations. *See staffing, nursing.*

average payment rate (APR) In managed care, this is the amount of money that the Health Care Financing Administration could pay a managed-care program under a Medicare risk contract. The amount paid is determined from the average adjusted per capita cost for the geographical area, adjusted for the characteristics that the enrollee population would be expected to have. The payment to the managed-care plan can be lower but cannot be higher than the average payment rate.

average per diem state rate The amount of patient care charges spent by a state for each Medicaid long-term-care resident for the average of each day of care.

average power In laser technology, this is the watts of total energy generated and passed during the treatment exposure divided by the duration of the exposure in seconds.

average wholesale price In materials management in health-care organizations, this is the average price for goods, including pharmaceuticals; used in purchasing contracts.

average workday lost *See average lost workdays; incident rate, occupational health and safety.*

averment 1. An offer to prove what is alleged. 2. A statement of facts to justify or prove.

aversion therapy A form of behavior therapy based on respondent conditioning. Stimuli related to undesirable behavior are paired with a painful or unpleasant occurrence, resulting in the elimination of the negative, undesirable behavior (e.g., the look, smell, and taste of cigarettes is paired with nausea induced by excessive use to diminish or eliminate the patient's desire to smoke).

aversive therapy *See aversion therapy.*

award 1. A document containing the decision of arbitration. 2. To formally give to or to grant. 3. The decision of an arbitrator in a dispute is an award. 4. To determine or to judge; to grant.

AWOL (absent without leave) As used in psychiatric care settings, this is when a psychiatric patient is on leave and has not returned on time or has left without permission.

axiom Self-evident truth or an established principle.

AZT *See Aschheim-Zondek test.*

B

Baby Doe (case) The landmark health law case of an infant born with Down syndrome and many serious medical conditions that prevented the child from eating normally and were possibly treatable with surgery. The parents refused consent for the surgery, and hospital administration turned to the courts and lawsuits (Indiana ex rel. *Infant Doe v. Monroe Cir. Ct.*, No. 482S140, Ind. Sup. Ct., April 16, 1982) to override the parents' decision, but the baby died first. As a result, legislatures have passed laws to protect newborns from similar situations. *See Baby Doe laws.*

Baby Doe laws As a result of the Baby Doe case, in 1985 attempts were made to pass laws to prevent the withholding of medical treatment from seriously ill newborn infants who have life-threatening conditions, but these attempts failed. Some legal efforts have been made to use the federal Child Abuse Amendments of 1984 by accusing such parents of child neglect.

baccalaureate degree program A 4-year educational program that trains nurses, health services administrators, radiological technologists, dental hygienists, public and community health workers, and related allied health professionals. Classroom and laboratory learning experiences are conducted at colleges or universities, and clinical training is conducted at affiliated hospitals and other health-care facilities and agencies. Because of the different levels of training available within the various programs, baccalaureate training in the health-care field has become a major concern. There is a perceived need for 4-year training programs rather than associate degree and diploma training, especially for nurses, dental hygienists, and radiological technologists.

backdoor authority Legislative authority that obligates funds from the federal budget outside the normal appropriation process. The most common forms of backdoor authority are borrowing authority (authority to spend debt receipts) and contract authority. In other cases (e.g., interest on the public debt), a permanent appropriation can become available without any current action by Congress. Entitlement authority is sometimes included as a form of backdoor authority, as the enactment of the basic benefit legislation may effectively mandate the subsequent enactment of the appropriations to pay the statutory benefits. Section 401 of the Congressional Budget and Impoundment Control Act of 1974 specifies certain limits on the use of backdoor authority. Examples of programs that have backdoor authority are the Environmental Protection Agency's construction grant program and the Social Security trust funds.

back pay In health-care personnel management, this is all parts of the worker's pay and benefits, including wages, salaries, and fringe benefits, that the worker was deprived of for some reason that should have been included in the normal pay and benefits provided and must be made up. A person who is dismissed and then reinstated must be paid all pay and benefits missed. On winning a lawsuit for wrongful termination, pay and benefits that were missed because of this action are required to be paid.

backup file In health-care information management, this is an additional copy of a computer file to be used in the event that the original file is lost or destroyed.

backup hospital A hospital that provides inpatient care and special services that could not be obtained in an HMO or a neighborhood health center. The backup hospital is the health-care facility affiliated with an HMO or neighborhood health center to provide those services not otherwise available for adequate patient care or treatment. The term also applies to managed care and HMOs, as some HMOs do not always have the ability to provide all needed hospitalization and have to rely on contracted backup inpatient care.

backup patients Elderly or handicapped patients who are in need of long-term-care placement but who are not preferred payment patients because of the type of payment they carry (Medicaid in some cases) or because of the severity of the case and level of care needed. These patients are kept in the hospital until placement is found. The prospective payment system under Medicare forces early discharge of these patients without placements being immediately available.

bacteria (plural) One-celled microorganisms. Of epidemiological and public health concern are those microorganisms of the pathogenic strains of this one class of microorganism that are capable of producing disease in humans and animals.

bactericide A bacteria-destroying substance.

bacterio- Prefix meaning "bacteria."

bacteriologist A microbiologist, physician, or medical technologist specializing in the study of bacteria for clinical, research, infection control, or public health purposes.

bacteriology The study of one-celled microorganisms.

bad debt Uncollectible money owed to a business or organization; the amount of income lost by a provider caused by the failure of patients to pay amounts owed. Accounts receivable that are written off in financial statements and under tax laws, as uncollectible, as the accounts remain unpaid for certain time periods. The impact of the loss of revenue from bad debts for proprietary institutions may be partially offset by the fact that income tax is not payable on income not received. Some bad debts are also written off as charitable care. Bad debt may also be recovered by increasing charges to paying patients by a proportional amount. Some cost-based reimbursement programs reimburse certain bad debts. *See reasonable cost.*

bad faith 1. Untrustworthy. 2. Dishonesty that may or may not involve fraud. The opposite of "good faith," implying a design to mislead another or to do fraud. 3. Neglect or refusal to complete a contract or fulfill a duty; not done by an honest mistake but by an unrighteous motive.

bait and switch Advertising a product or service at a low price to lure customers into the store (baiting) and then trying to persuade them to buy a totally different item (switching). This may be against the law if the item advertised is not available.

balance billing In health-care finance, this is when physicians or health-care services charge some patients one fee and others a different, higher fee for the same treatment or care, allowing an average charge to prevail, which is done to keep the medical practice profitable. This practice is also used to offset the lower payments taken in from managed-care contracts, capitation programs, Medicare, Medicaid, charity care, and bad debts.

balance sheet In health-care finance, a summary of the financial status of a company, hospital, or health-care facility at a given time. It usually provides an accounting of all assets and liabilities of the institution or organization.

Balkan frame A frame attached lengthwise over a bed to attach splints or traction to provide a means of raising or transferring bedridden patients or of assisting their mobility.

balloon payment or note In health-care finance, this is a financial note, usually a large sum of money, that is expected to be paid as the final payment on a loan because periodic payments were not sufficient to cover the full value of the loan.

ballot In official or formal health-care meetings or hearings using parliamentary procedure, this is the casting of a vote on paper or by means of a special mechanical or electronic device in order to ensure secrecy in voting.

bandage A special material used to wrap or bind a dressing to an injury or a body part.

banker's lien An interest in property or money owned by a banker as security to extinguish a debt. If proper legal steps are taken, a hospital or nursing home can use such a lien to secure a debt owed to the facility.

bankrupt 1. To be declared legally insolvent. Under the Federal Bankruptcy Act, a person may have all debts discharged once all property and money is turned over to a trustee to pay creditors proportionately. 2. A method by which an organization in financial trouble can be restructured by the courts and have property turned into cash to pay creditors.

bar 1. A system of law and courts. 2. An organized group of lawyers. 3. The practice of law in a particular court system.

Bar Act A law passed by a state mandating what type of law a lawyer may practice and how the practice is to be done to ensure ethical and legal standards.

barbiturate A highly addictive drug derived from barbituric acid that depresses the central nervous system. These depressants are most commonly used as hypnotics and sedatives. Phenobarbital and Seconal are commonly known barbiturates.

bar chart As used in public health reports, epidemiology, health plans, feasibility studies, hospital reports, and related documents, this is a group of rectangular graphs in the form of a bar or bars depicting the relationship of two or more variables or elements in graphic or pictorial form. All bars should be of standard width, and standard distances should be found between all bars in the graph.

bar code In information management systems, this is a pattern of bars that can be read by laser scanner computer systems. Uses range from inventory control to patient identification and medical records to laboratory controls.

bar diagram A graph similar to a histogram or bar chart in which the widths of the bars have no significance.

Bard-Parker forceps A special type of forceps commonly used to handle or transfer sterile supplies.

bargain 1. A contract or mutual agreement. 2. An agreement to buy, sell, or exchange.

bargaining agent 1. One who makes a bargain, contract, or mutual agreement. 2. A labor union that has the sole right to represent all the employees of a health-care facility or institution.

bargaining book Under labor union activities, this is a special journal that is a compilation of approaches, tactics, concerns, and issues of contract negotiation and that serves as the plan of action for the negotiation teams of both labor and management. In modern approaches, this book and its related information have been computerized.

bargaining committee In labor relations, this is the group of individuals representing the union and the stewards who negotiate with management's representatives to discuss and negotiate benefits, wages, working conditions, and other worker concerns that are to be a part of the labor agreement.

bargaining unit Employees in a health-care facility who constitute an in-house representative labor group for the purpose of being represented by a union.

bariatric medicine The branch of medicine that treats obesity by using anorectic drugs.

barium A metallic element commonly introduced into the body in solution as a contrast medium for X ray of the gastrointestinal tract.

barium sulfate White powder used as a contrast medium in radiology, given either orally or by enema, for radiographic diagnostic procedures.

barratry The practice of exciting, encouraging, or stirring up lawsuits; a lawyer's attempt to create lawsuits for his or her own financial gain.

barrier technique A medical practice used to control, destroy, or limit the spread of pathogenic disease or infection.

barrio (Spanish) The district, ward, or neighborhood in which most of the Mexican Americans of a city live.

BARS *See behaviorally anchored rating scales.*

basal metabolic rate The rate at which energy is expended by the body to maintain its functions at rest.

base 1. As used in epidemiology and vital statistics, this refers to the fundamental comparison number used to compare rates, which is *per*, as in *per* 1000. The *per* provides the base; the percentage that results from the formula calculation has a base of 1000. For example, an infant death rate of 8.3 per 1000 makes for easier cross-comparisons of populations, whereas percentages do not provide clear comparisons. 2. The beginning or a fundamental point of comparison such as a base year. 3. In chemistry, this refers to the range of acid to alkalinity, with base being the alkaline state.

base capitation In managed care and medical insurance, this is a set amount of money used to cover the costs of health care per member covered by a health plan less mental health and substance abuse services, pharmacy, and administrative charges.

base case *See reference projection.*

baseline data Basic information and facts about a patient.

base pay A starting, basic, or beginning rate of pay; the fundamental pay excluding bonuses, overtime, etc.

base unit The beginning, or starting point, of measure of a health-care unit-of-service. The cost of a unit of service is assigned a number of 1.0, and the relative values of all other related services are compared by multiples of the cost.

base year 1. A 12-month period starting from the month and day of establishment, initiation, or attachment. 2. The first, or start-up, year for a program.

BASIC Beginner's All-Purpose Symbolic Instruction. A computer language that combines English words and decimal numbers to create a simple standardized language useful for beginning computer programmers yet that is capable of handling business, health-care administration, and biomedical and health-care applications.

basic emergency medical services Rural hospitals that become limited-service rural hospitals and that are designated as rural primary care hospitals (RPCHs) are required to provide and/or arrange for the delivery of basic emergency medical care with 24-hour access to the broader emergency medical care system (EMS).

basic health insurance Health insurance does not insure against risks of health but against risks related to the cost of medical care treatment. The basic medical insurance plan provides first-dollar coverage for inpatient and hospital treatment and procedures. Basic coverage does not include major medical insurance and has lower maximum benefits.

basic health services 1. The minimum supply of health services that should be generally and uniformly available in a community to ensure adequate health status in and protection of populations from disease. Given that all possible services cannot be supplied to the entire population, little information exists as to what set of services constitutes appropriate minimum services and how to ensure their availability. However, federal laws concerned with HMOs and IPAs have established that basic health services in managed-care arenas should include 1) physician services, including referrals and consultations; 2) inpatient and outpatient services; 3) medically necessary emergency health-care services; 4) short-term (not to exceed twenty visits) mental health care (including evaluation and crisis intervention); 5) medical treatment and referral for the abuse of or addiction to alcohol and drugs; 6) diagnostic laboratory and diagnostic and therapeutic radiologic services; and 7) home health services and preventive health services, including immunizations, well-child care, periodic health evaluations for adults, family planning services, infertility services, and child eye and ear exams. The Oregon health care rationing plan for treatment of indigent persons under Medicaid has a list of over 700 different conditions and illnesses that will be treated and that are listed in order of priority, with the disease dictating treatment, not services or facilities. The assumption is that basic health services to treat each disease or condition on the list will be minimally available. 2. In managed care, these are the benefits that all managed-care health plans and HMOs must offer as set forth in the federal HMO regulations (Subpart A. 110.102). *See Oregon health care rationing plan; accessibility; acceptability; availability.*

basic life support Emergency care and first aid approaches used to restore life through artificial respiration, CPR, airway maintenance, bleeding control, immobilization of fractures, treatment for shock, and other injury treatment prior to acquiring advanced definitive medical care.

basic mortality tables Statistical tables of data on death. *See mortality rate; mortality statistical tables.*

basic nursing care Those nursing skills practiced and activities carried out solely by qualified nurses as found in primary and intermediate medical care settings. *See primary care; intermediate care.*

basis point In health care finance, one basis point is equal to one one-hundredth of one percent, numerically presented as .01%.

basket clauses In managed care, this is when the health plan or insurance company is called to invest a percentage of assets with no limitations imposed by regulatory restrictions.

baso- Prefix meaning "base."

bassinets Baby bed–type units (including incubators and isolettes) maintained for use in a hospital nursery for newborn babies. In public health research of hospitals, these are the number of newborn infant beds set up and staffed for use at the end of the reporting period. Bassinets are not included in the hospital bed count total and do not include isolettes or neonatal intensive care units, which are included under hospital bed counts.

batch processing In computerized medical records and business office data processing practice, this is the processing of data that has been accumulated into related groups and entered into the computer as a unit. Admission and discharge information compiled on a monthly basis could be a batch run. Related more to the older mainframe computers that ran cards organized in groups for entering information into the computer, a number of similar data items grouped and processed for a single computer run using the same computer program to be completed without operator intervention.

battered child syndrome Physical harm, injury, or damage to a child as a result of repeated beatings and abuse, usually inflicted by a parent or guardian.

battery 1. A legal principle describing any intentional, illegal, unwanted, or unprovoked beating, touching, or harmful physical contact to a person by an object or another person without that person's consent. 2. The act of beating or hitting another person with the intent of causing physical harm.

baud In computerized medical records and business office functions, this is an electronic computer signal speed rate used to run computer equipment or to allow different types of equipment to interface. If the signal is consistent and represents 1 bit of information, baud is equal to "bits per second"; if not, the equipment will not work.

BCA *See Blue Cross Association.*

BCHS Bureau of Community Health Services.

beam In laser treatment technology, this is a collection of laser rays that flow in a parallel form and may be divergent or convergent in their pattern.

bearer Any person holding, in possession of, or presenting a note or a negotiable instrument, such as a check.

BEC Behavioral emergency committee.

bed(s) 1. The basis of measurement of capacity in a hospital or inpatient health-care facility. Licenses may be granted for a certain number of beds or certain classes of beds. Each inpatient admission requires a bed, as a hospital admission usually also means an overnight stay and that the person is ill enough to require a bed. Hospitals have no accommodations for patients unless assigned a bed. 2. Any bed that is set up and staffed for use for inpatients is counted as a bed in a facility. In the National Master Facility Inventory, the count is of beds at the end of the reporting period; for the American Hospital Association, it is of the average number of beds during the entire period. The World Health Organization defines a hospital bed as one that is regularly maintained and staffed for the accommodation and full-time care of a succession of inpatients and that is situated in a part of the hospital where continuous medical care for inpatients is provided (National Center for Health Statistics). 3. Average number of beds, cribs, and pediatric bassinets regularly maintained (set up and staffed for use) for inpatients during the reporting period; also referred to as "statistical beds." Derived by adding the total number of beds available each day during the hospital's reporting period and dividing this figure by the total number of days in the reporting period (National Center for Health Statistics).

bed(s), acute medical/surgical A unit in a hospital that provides regular inpatient care for patients recovering from treatment or surgery by following physician's orders and treatment plans.

bed(s), acute pediatric A unit in a hospital that provides regular inpatient care for youth and child patients (usually under 21 years of age) recovering from treatment or surgery by following physician's orders and treatment plans.

bed(s), adult inpatient A bed maintained within a health-care facility for adult inpatients who are receiving medical care and nursing services on a continuing and regular basis. Each inpatient admission requires a bed, as a hospital admission usually also means an overnight stay and that the person is ill enough to require a bed. Hospitals have no accommodations for patients unless assigned a bed.

bed-bound When a patient has one or more chronic diseases that are severe enough to cause one to be restricted to or confined to bed because one is unable to walk or stand and move about independently. *See bed-chair patient (resident).*

bed capacity The actual space and rooms available for a certain number of patient beds that meets licensing and accreditation space standards; total number of beds by medical specialty or service category based on the use of formulas to calculate needed square footage. Bed count may not be related to the space available or the number of beds actually approved for occupancy; however, from a licensure and regulatory perspective, bed count cannot exceed bed capacity. *See bed need projection (net); bed need projection (gross).*

bed categories The various classifications through which hospitals report the type of unit, treatment, or care rendered or assigned, such as medical/surgical or intensive care, to various inpatient beds.

bed-chair patient (resident) Refers to a patient in a nursing home or long-term-care facility who is not bedridden but who cannot ambulate without the assistance of another person and thus is usually limited to being in a bed or a wheelchair.

bed complement All bassinets and inpatient and outpatient beds that are available, operational, and staffed for use by the health-care facility.

bed count The actual number of beds available for use by patients or residents of a health-care facility. Bed count may be broken down into specific categories such as adult inpatient, pediatric inpatient, bassinet (newborn), or outpatient. In nursing homes, bed count is often determined by source of payment.

bed, day A bed maintained in a health-care facility for use by persons who are inpatients only during the day because they are in need of only partial inpatient care such as rehabilitation.

bed days per 1000 (bed days/1000) In managed care, the number of inpatient days per 1000 health plan members. The bed days per 1000 formula follows:

$$\frac{\text{Total number of days}}{\text{Member months}} \times \frac{1000 \text{ members}}{\text{Number of months}}$$

bed day utilization Assessing and monitoring the use of inpatient beds; the total number of days that patients are inpatients and occupy a bed within a health-care facility.

bed disability day A day in which a person stays in bed for more than half of the daylight hours (or normal waking hours) because of a specific illness or injury. All hospital days are bed-disability days, which may also be work-loss or school-loss days. All inpatients in a hospital are considered to be days of bed disability even if they are not actually in the bed at the hospital. *See disability day; restricted activity day.*

bedfast *See bed-chair patient (resident); bed-bound.*

bed hold For acute hospitalization, this allows a bed to be maintained and held for a patient in a long-term-care setting and allows payment to be made to skilled nursing facilities, swing bed facilities, intermediate care facilities, developmentally disabled care facilities, or other approved long-term-care facilities for 7 days (in some states). For the patient to be sent to a hospital, he or she must have a physician's order, and the facility must hold the bed vacant for the hold period, unless notified in writing by the attending physician that the patient needs more days of inpatient care. The day of departure can usually be counted as 1 day. When a patient dies, the day of hold is terminated, and payment ceases.

bed, hospital A bed maintained in an acute-care facility to include medical and nursing services as well as hotel accommodations, including food, room, security, temperature control, housekeeping, and other related services used to restore the patient's health and to provide health care for patients. *See bed(s); hospital beds.*

bed, incubator Often counted with bassinets, this is a pediatric hospital bed with special features that allow for the control of temperature, environment, humidity, and oxygen and that serves as an isolation mechanism to protect the infant.

bed, inpatient 1. A bed regularly maintained in an acute-care facility for use by persons who are admitted to the facility as inpatients. Each inpatient admission requires a bed because a hospital admission usually also means an overnight stay and that the person is ill enough to require a bed. Hospitals have no accommodations for patients unless assigned a bed. 2. A bed regularly maintained in a long-term-care facility or nursing home for patients who enter the facility for a long-term stay.

bed, isolation One or two beds (usually in a separate room) maintained in a health-care facility that are used to separate persons with communicable diseases from contact with other patients and most health-care facility personnel. This is done to restrict the possibility of the spread of disease, as those persons who are placed in this type of bed (room) usually have acquired a communicable, infectious, or exotic disease that is a major medical concern and threat to the staff of the health-care facility.

bed, long-term-care A regularly maintained bed in a nursing home, mental health hospital, rehabilitation center, convalescent center, or other long-term-care facility that provides living accommodations, including lodging, food, laundry, bathing, housekeeping and other daily living needs, and nursing and medical care as needed.

bed need formula A mathematical equation used in regional health planning to predict the total number of hospital beds needed in a community or region. The number of specialized care beds needed by hospitals for a specific population for a certain time period can also be determined.

bed need projection (gross) A hospital use rate formula used to predict the number of patient days of hospital care per 1000. The gross bed need projection formula follows:

Hospital population served = Patient days per year ÷ 365 average daily census.

(Apply the desired occupancy rate to this number to yield a gross bed need)

Use rate of various services within the hospital (e.g., medical/surgical, obstetrics, pediatrics) × Population ÷ 365 = Average daily census ÷ Percentage of expected occupancy rate (i.e., 80%) = GROSS BED NEEDS

bed need projection (net) A formula used to predict the need for health-care beds in the future. Net bed need is from projected minimal use of various services. The net bed need projection formula follows:

Gross bed needs − Reduced current utilization − Reduced use as a result of long-term care − Reduced because of competition with other facilities, new construction, or other competition = NET BED NEED

bed, newborn A bed maintained only for babies born in the hospital; also called a "bassinet." *See bassinet*.

bed, night The keeping and maintaining of a bed in an acute-care facility (or long-term-care facility) for use only at night by persons who have unusual health-care or rehabilitation needs yet who can function outside the health-care facility in the daytime.

bed, occupied An administrative designation of the status of a bed. It is considered occupied whether or not it is physically being used because a patient has been admitted to a facility as an inpatient and has been assigned to the bed. For example, if a patient is sent to the hospital from a nursing home for surgery and will later return to the nursing home, the nursing home bed can be considered occupied for a certain length of time even though the patient is actually staying in the hospital.

bed, outpatient A bed maintained in a hospital or surgical center or other outpatient facility for use by patients who have a limited in-house duration of stay (less than 24 hours). The bed is usually for recovery from outpatient surgery or a short spell of illness, such as an ill college student who is put in a bed in a student health center while being kept under observation or waiting to be transferred to a hospital. In rural areas, some hospitals have converted to outpatient facilities and maintain several outpatient beds for short-term recovery from outpatient treatment or from short spells of illnesses or for stabilizing a patient who will be transferred to a hospital or who will go home.

bedpan A specially designed container used to allow bedridden patients to eliminate bodily wastes while remaining in bed.

bed, pediatric A bed maintained in a children's medical and nursing unit or in other specialized units that is specifically designated for use by children, other than newborns, who are to receive ongoing hospital services.

bed, resident A bed maintained in a residential care facility for use by persons who need some assistance yet do not require ongoing medical or nursing care. This type of bed is found in personal care or custodial care units of nursing homes or in freestanding personal care or custodial care facilities.

bedridden Being restricted or confined to bed; when a patient cannot ambulate or leave his or her bed to eliminate bodily wastes, move about, eat, or carry on usual daily activities.

bed size A measure of capacity for inpatient care for health-care institutions. Hospitals, nursing homes, and other inpatient health-care facilities are measured by the numbers of beds within the institution, thus determining their size.

beds, licensed The number of beds approved to be maintained in a health-care facility by licensing, certifying, or accrediting agencies.

beds, nonconforming *See nonconforming beds*.

beds, regularly maintained The actual number of beds that are kept, set up, used, staffed, and maintained on a day-to-day basis for ongoing and regular admissions of patients; the number is based on census and admission rates.

bed, specialty A bed maintained in a specialized medical and nursing care unit for a specific type of patient care, such as cardiac care, intensive care, or labor and delivery.

beds, statistical The average number of beds regularly maintained during a reporting period, including inpatient beds, adult beds, cribs, and bassinets. This figure is derived by adding the total number of beds available each day during the reporting period and then dividing this number by the total number of days in the reporting period.

bed, swing A hospital bed used for either acute or long-term care, depending on demand or need.

bed, temporary An extra bed maintained in a hospital when the regularly maintained beds are all occupied. The extra beds are used only until the census decreases.

bed-to-population ratio The number of health care beds needed for specific health-care services for every 1000 persons in a population or community (e.g., the number of nursing home beds needed per 1000 persons over age 70 or the number of pediatric beds needed per 1000 persons under age 21). *See bed need projection (net); bed need projection (gross)*.

bed turnover rate The number of patients occupying and vacating the same bed in a healthcare facility during a certain time period. Turnover rates can be averaged for admissions and discharges for the entire hospital, for a medical or nursing unit, or for specialized units, such as the intensive care unit.

behavior Any act or psychomotor response that is observable and has measurable outcomes that are specific in their frequency, duration, and purpose, whether emotional, based on beliefs or values, or conscious or unconscious in origin.

behavioral diagnosis Determining the specific health behaviors that are likely to affect a person's health status or need; delineating those health-related behaviors that can influence or affect health outcomes; the evaluation of the behaviorally related causes of a problem that an intervention can be used for or can be adjusted to by adaptation or behavior change.

behavioral emergency committee One of the many patient management and risk management committees often found in hospital organizations that deals with incidents that could involve unpredictable, assaultive, or violent behavior in patients. *See incident.*

behavioral epidemic An outbreak of conditions or disorders that are behavioral or emotional in origin. Examples are suicide pacts, from which large numbers of suicides occur; deaths or conditions from certain types of designer drugs, such as designer heroin, or glue sniffing; and binge drinking in fraternities. Modes of transmission are fads, social pressures, group reinforcement, television, and the media glorifying the issue. Many behavioral epidemic problems are substance abuse related.

behavioral evaluation 1. The assessment of behaviors or behavioral outcomes as compared to a standard, a norm, or an objective. 2. The clinical assessment of a client's human relations, social, interpersonal, work-related, or health actions; how they are effective; and how they may be dysfunctional or may interfere with normal or acceptable behaviors.

behavioral health A field of health care that uses patient education, health counseling, health promotion, health education, and behavioral therapy and procedures to alleviate problems of health or illness, disease, conditions, and disorders by changing self-defeating, self-destructive behaviors or behaviors detrimental to individual health status (e.g., smoking). Prevention, health education, health counseling, behavior change, and health activation are the major foci.

behavioral intention 1. Any act of an individual that produces a result that is indicative or representative of a held belief or a certain mental purpose behind the act. 2. A belief or psychological position taken by a person in which he or she can expect to do a specific action in the future.

behaviorally anchored rating scales (BARS) In personnel performance appraisal systems, a performance appraisal rating system that focuses on behaviors and acts rather than on personality traits. Behaviors are reviewed and then noted on a form by way of a line scale to indicate effective or ineffective performance. This method is superior to graphic rating scales, which use categorization on a continuum indicating, for example, "below average," "average," or "above average" rates for each work trait.

behavioral medicine 1. The use of behavioral procedures applied to problems of illness, disorders, disabilities, or behaviors, with attention focused on behavior change, prevention, diagnosis, treatment, and rehabilitation and with a goal of optimum health. 2. The interdisciplinary field concerned with the development and integration of behavioral and biomedical science, knowledge, and techniques relevant to the understanding of physical health and illness and the application of this knowledge and these techniques to prevention, diagnosis, treatment, and rehabilitation (Yale Conference on Behavioral Medicine). *See health psychology; behavioral health.*

behavioral modeling This depends on the example, emulation, or initiation of the desired behavior by a leader. Appropriate or expected responses or actions are acquired by repetition of behaviors or by examples being demonstrated or presented repeatedly.

behavioral objective A statement or plan that is created to achieve a desired outcome and that clearly outlines the specific steps to achieve the action; a desired measurable outcome statement indicating who is to do what of how much, by what activities, and by what time. Outcome activities are expected to result from the behavioral objective statement.

behavioral psychotherapy A type of therapy that uses observable behavior rather than focusing on thoughts and feelings. It aims at systematic improvement and the elimination of maladaptive behaviors. Various conditioning and learning theories are combined with a directive approach, including techniques adapted from other systems of psychotherapy.

behavior control Exercising influence over others by changing the environmental contingencies to achieve a goal or behavior change.

behavior modification The application of operant conditioning principles to behavioral problems with the intent of changing or managing behavior or health problems. Management of behavior is achieved by the control of reinforcers or consequences that change behavior. This behavior change modality has been utilized in changing both physical and mental disorders (e.g., smoking and obesity).

behavior therapy A therapy designed to modify the client's behavior. Behavior therapy is derived from learning theories and focuses on modifying observable and quantifiable behavior by means of manipulating the environmental and behavioral variables thought to be functionally related to the behavior that is to be changed. Some of the approaches are operant conditioning, behavioral reinforcement systems, shaping, token economy, and systematic desensitization.

belief A confidence, opinion, judgment, or expectation about the truth or knowledge of a case that is not based completely on fact; a perception or set of concepts or statements that are emotionally and intelligently embraced and accepted as being true by an individual or group.

bench 1. The place where judges sit. 2. A court of law. 3. Judges, collectively. 4. The seat of justice.

benchmarking In health-care management and quality management activities, this is a process of measuring services, work outcomes, and work practices against an organization's strongest competitors. The goal of benchmarking is to be the best in the field and to surpass all other competitive organizations. It is a tool used to identify, implement, and achieve standards of excellence that relies on continual updating and the constant integration of information on competitors, activities, roles, practices, and outcomes. Benchmarking is used to improve quality, effectiveness, and overall efficiency. This management process involves knowing one's competitors; applying proven knowledge within the health-care organization to adapt best practices; assessing internal and external environments; selecting functional and effective processes to implement the system; and developing business objectives, goals, and strategies and implementing action plans that will make the health-care organization the best in the field. This management approach may be a part of a "total quality management" program.

bench warrant An order issued directly by a judge or court to the police for the arrest of a person charged with contempt of court or a crime.

Bender-Gestalt test A psychological test used to measure the ability to reproduce a set of geometric designs. It is useful for detecting perceptual and visuomotor coordination difficulties, which might indicate brain damage.

bene- Prefix meaning "well" or "good."

benefice A benefit; a kindness; a favor; the doing of good acts.

beneficial occupancy In health-care finance and construction activities, this is the acceptable point in time when a health-care organization, as a tenant, can occupy a building and use it to conduct business even though the building is not completed.

beneficiary 1. A person designated in an insurance policy to receive a specified cash payment on the policyholder's accidental or natural death, injury, or illness. 2. In managed care or medical insurance, these are the enrollees or members, the ones eligible to receive benefits from the managed-care plan, or the one who is eligible to receive, or is receiving, benefits from a medical insurance policy or health maintenance organization. Usually includes both the people who have contracted for benefits and their eligible dependents. An individual accepted by an insurance company as eligible to receive insurance benefits. *See also subscriber; insured.*

benefit(s) 1. In insurance, a sum of money provided in an insurance policy payable for certain types of loss, or for covered services, under the terms of the policy. The benefits may be paid to the insured or on his or her behalf to others. 2. In managed-care prepayment programs (e.g., HMOs), benefits are the services the program will provide for a member whenever and to the extent needed, including limitations and exclusions. 3. The amount payable by the carrier toward the cost of various covered medical or dental services. 4. The medical or dental service or procedure covered by an insurance policy or program. 5. In health education and health promotion, this is the increase seen in quality of life or health status outcomes that can be directly attributed to health promotion or behavioral health interventions. 6. Under Social Security, this is the average pension elderly recipients are paid, which is 41% of their income at retirement. Those in the lowest-earning categories receive about 59%, whereas the highest-paid workers get 27% of their preretirement pay.

benefit achievable The optimum level of outcome or benefit that can be acquired within the level or amount of existing resources. *See efficacy.*

benefit-cost analysis Evaluating the relationship between the benefits and costs of a particular project or activity. *See also cost-benefit analysis.*

benefit/cost ratio In health-care financial management, a means to measure capital expenditure proposals. The ratio is obtained by dividing the present value of cash inflows by the net investment. If the ratio is greater than 1, the project or program is acceptable; if it is less than 1, it should be rejected. *See cost-benefit analysis.*

benefit design In managed care, this is used to reduce care of services and to include exclusions. Cost controls are implemented in health plans to affect patient utilization by limiting choices. Exclusions are aimed at excluding services that are hard to quantify, control, account for, or ascertain effectiveness for in use (such as mental health-care services).

benefit level In managed care and medical insurance, this is the degree, extent, or limit of medical care and health-care services a person is entitled to and eligible to receive under a health plan policy or the employer group's contract with a health plan or medical insurance company.

benefit maximum In managed care, this is the limit on what a health plan will cover or on what coverage will be paid for, which could be expressed as the allowable number of days of care or a given dollar amount.

benefit of health care The value that consumers receive from an encounter with a health-care provider or service and that can be measured in terms of value-scaled outcomes that occur in the form of health, economic, or personal gains.

benefit package 1. In managed care or medical insurance, these are the specific services provided in the health plan or insurance program to those persons enrolled; a list of covered services. The list of specific services, procedures, therapies, and other benefits that a health plan member is to receive and that a health plan organization is obligated to provide under the subscriber group's contract or the health plan policy. Medical and health-care services that a health plan, insurance company, or government health program offers to a group or to individuals as part of the health plan contract or the terms of the medical insurance policy. 2. In human resources management and/or employment contracts, the set of benefits that offset and assist the employees' income, such as health, dental, and life insurance paid for by the company or organization. *See benefits.*

benefit period In managed care and insurance, this is the period of time for which payments for benefits covered by a health plan or an insurance policy are available. The availability of certain benefits may be limited over a specified time period (e.g., two well-baby visits during a 1-year period or one set of glasses every 2 years in a vision plan). While the benefit period is usually defined by a set unit of time (e.g., 1 year), benefits may also be tied to a spell of illness. *See Medicare benefits; spell of illness.*

benefit proration A method of dividing health insurance benefits into subunits when multiple-item coverage is provided. *See also proration.*

benefits Under universal coverage and the National Health Security Program, these are the standard medical care insurance packages for all who qualify, which should be most Americans. Additions or alterations to the standard coverage package can enhance coverage but cannot make it less than the basic plan. *See benefit package.*

benefits, health Those outcomes or increases experienced in one's health status or quality of life that are related to health-care processes.

benefit year In health insurance, a 365-day period (which may or may not be a calendar year) during which certain benefits (such as health plan services or major medical payments) are provided. The 12-month period that an employer's organization uses to administer the employee's fringe benefits program. Each organization uses a set day or month for benefits to begin and end each year and for open enrollment periods. Some use a regular calendar year, others use a fiscal year, and still others use a season-related year such as one that starts in August or September (common for school, colleges, and universities).

benestressor Any occurrence, event, experience, life change, achievement, advancement, success, or recognition that is beneficial or positive and that causes stress but much less damage than distress or dystressors. *See stressor; dystressor.*

benign Not malignant; a tumor that does not metastasize.

bereavement 1. Loss of a loved one by death. 2. The act or process of mourning a loss or death.

bereavement care The multidimensional care provided to individuals who just lost a loved one. All dimensions of one's life are affected by the loss of a loved one. Thus, bereavement care can include counseling and psychotherapy; decision-making assistance in legal, financial, and social matters; and emotional, mental, spiritual, and physical care of the survivors.

best As used in consumerism and health-care cost containment, "best" means that services and care must go beyond helping consumers cope with costs, must contribute to setting standards for quality and disease prevention, can be synonymous with "appropriate" as used in health planning, and must reach past the mainstream to those persons traditionally neglected by the U.S. health-care system. *See also appropriate; appropriateness of care.*

best estimate In managed care, this is the final report of the utilization of health services and health-care providers, the cost of care, the resources used, and the health plan coverage; completed by assessing inpatient care, physician, and health plan data.

best evidence rule A legal rule whereby primary evidence of a fact, such as an original document, can be introduced, presented, or explained and is used before a copy or facsimile can be introduced or before testimony can be given concerning the fact or document.

Best's Report In health and other insurance, this is an annual financial report that presents a rating of the various companies, including financial status, underwriting results, and other pertinent data.

best value The most positive outcome, highest quality; a good result for the most reasonable cost.

beyond a reasonable doubt In criminal law, this is the amount, or level, of proof needed to convict a person of a crime.

BHCDA Bureau of Health Care Delivery and Assistance.

BHI *See Bureau of Health Insurance.*

BHPr Bureau of Health Professions.

bi- Prefix meaning "two."

BIA *See Bureau of Indian Affairs.*

bias 1. Preestablished or preacquired information or opinion that makes it difficult to be fair and impartial. 2. Preconceived opinion by a judge about persons that makes him or her inclined to lean to one side unfairly so as to have a preassessed judgment. 3. Prejudicial, slanted, or distorted opinions or beliefs. 4. In public health, biomedical, or epidemiological research design or practice, any effect that influences the outcome of research and causes the study procedures to depart from acceptable scientific methodology, thus affecting the actual findings and research results. In research, bias can occur in selection, sampling, reporting, participants, recall, research design, researcher attitudes, measurement, and other related variables. *See sample bias.*

bid To make an offer; an amount offered or proposed. To submit a proposal to participate in a project; to offer to do something specific for a certain amount of money of which the services or activities are laid out in detail.

bid bond Money presented in the form of a bond given to provide surety for a bid on a contract, thus assuring the seriousness of a bid.

bidders/offerers conference In health-care contracting and grants from the federal government, this is a meeting between the party presenting a proposal for a grant or contract or responding to a request for a proposal (RFP) and the appropriate governmental representatives. At such a meeting, questions about the work or research to be undertaken are presented and answers provided by the government representatives.

bilateral contract 1. An agreement wherein both parties have participated equally in the negotiations and both parties exchanged promises. 2. A two-sided agreement.

bilk 1. To deceive or defraud. 2. To get away without paying.

bill 1. A draft of a law presented to a legislature.

2. A written declaration, statement, or complaint, usually against someone who suffered because someone broke the law. Used in both criminal and civil law. 3. A financial statement sent to a patient itemizing money owed.

billed charge Under Medicare, this is the actual charge for a physician's services or a supplier's goods.

billed claims In managed care and medical insurance, these are the charges or costs a health plan member generates when using a managed-care plan and receiving health-care services that are submitted to the health plan or insurance carrier by the health-care provider.

billing/accounts receivable program As used in health-care finance and computerized business accounting systems using real-time interactive information systems, a software program that records patient charges, credits accounts, and prints bills, statements, and third-party claim forms. The program provides management and follow-up reports on demand. All detail is available on-line until the account balance is wiped out.

bill of costs An itemized statement of costs charged against the losing party in a legal action.

bill of credit A written request that credit be given to the bearer on the basis of the security of the requestor.

bill of exceptions A written statement of a party's objections to rulings, actions, and instructions made by a judge during a trial that forms the basis for an appeal.

bill of exchange A written document unconditionally ordering the receiver to pay a specific amount to a third person.

bill of indictment A written document presented to a grand jury that states the accusations of a crime. If this is proven to be factual, it is labeled a "true bill."

bill of lading 1. A cargo list. 2. A document provided by a shipping company that lists all goods or property for transport. The terms of the shipping agreement can also be stated in this document. It also is used to acknowledge receipt of the goods.

bill of parcels A list of items purchased, with the value of each listed on the invoice.

bill of particulars A detailed written statement of charges or pleadings of a plaintiff or prosecutor provided at the request of the defendant.

bill of patient's rights Legal and ethical principles utilized by health-care facilities that recognize the dignity and human rights of patients. The basic rights of patients are the right to be furnished with information on diagnosis, treatment, and prognosis and to participate in any and all decisions about their treatment and care. The bill allows for complaints to be registered and for corrective action to be taken. *See also patients' rights.*

bill of review A new lawsuit brought that requests that a court consider setting aside a prior decree.

binary code The language of the computer based on a 2-digit numeric system, represented by two distinct characters, usually 1 and 0.

binder 1. A written memorandum in contract law stating the most important items agreed on. 2. A temporary contract that is used until a formal policy of title insurance can be drawn up.

binding arbitration When the outcome of negotiations must be adhered to by both parties in the dispute.

binding authority The previous decisions of appellate courts that must be considered and followed by a judge when deciding a case. *See stare decisis.*

binding instruction Instructions to a jury that must be followed to arrive at a specified decision on the basis of whether the jury concludes certain facts to be true or false.

binding receipt A receipt given for a premium payment accompanying the application for insurance that, if the policy is approved, requires the company to make the policy effective from the date of the receipt.

binding review For Professional Review Organizations program purposes, this is a PRO review for which determinations are final and that affects payments by Title XVIII fiscal intermediaries and Title XIX state agencies.

bind over 1. A court order that the accused be held in custody pending a proceeding against him or her. He or she may post bond and be released. 2. To obligate an accused person to appear in court.

binomial distribution In biostatistics, this is the mathematical probability distribution that a certain number of successes (i.e., positive events) will occur in an arbitrary number of attempts.

bio- Prefix meaning "life."

bioavailability The extent and rate of absorption of a given drug, measured by the time-concentration curve for appearance of the administered drug in the blood. The concept is important in attempting to determine whether different drugs (e.g., generic as opposed to a brand name or, in some cases, different batches of the same brand-name drug) will produce the same therapeutic effect. The same drug made by two different manufacturers or different batches of the same drug made by the same manufacturer may demonstrate differing bioavailability. There is debate as to differences that are therapeutically significant. *See also maximum allowable cost program; antisubstitution laws; bioequivalence.*

biochemist A scientist specializing in the study of biological substances and processes that affect the function of the body or cause a physiological dysfunction within the body.

bioengineering A scientific specialty that studies the biological aspects of the body and applies related engineering principles to assist the human body and its physiological and anatomical functioning.

bioequivalence Describes drug preparations that have the same bioavailability. Such drugs are chemically equivalent, but preparations are not always bioequivalent. Bioequivalence is a function of bioavailability, and the terms are often used synonymously. Chemically equivalent drugs that are bioequivalent have the same treatment effect, although therapeutically equivalent preparations need not have either quality.

biofeedback An antianxiety or a body function control technique based on fundamental learning principles where the average person learns to make a certain response when he or she receives information related to a response or discovers that he or she is closer to the desired goal. Electronic monitoring is used to give the patient immediate and continual signals, or feedback, related to changes in bodily functions that one is not normally aware of, such as brain waves, blood pressure, and heart rate. Through control of the mind, the patient strives to learn control of various body parts and processes.

Biofeedback Society of America An interdisciplinary organization founded in 1969 interested in the techniques, application, and technology of biofeedback representing the fields of psychology, psychiatry, physical rehabilitation, dentistry, nursing, education, and others. These interdisciplinary professions are involved in the education, training, research, and application of biofeedback principles.

biological(s) This is any product, virus, serum, toxin, antitoxin or analogous product derived from living matter applicable to the prevention, treatment, or cure of disease or injuries in humans. Serums, substances, or drugs derived from plant and animal products. *See biologics.*

biological equivalents In medical care and drug and medicine selection for inclusion in a health plan's pharmacopoeia, those medicines, substances, or pharmaceutical preparations that are chemically similar to or the same as other drugs when administered in proper dosages and that will provide the same physiological or biological response or reaction and availability to the body for treatment as demonstrated by serum and blood tests, urine levels, etc.

biologics 1. Any virus, therapeutic serum, toxin, antitoxin, or analogous product of plant or animal origin used in the prevention, diagnosis, or treatment of disease and regulated by the Bureau of Biologics, a division of the Food and Drug Administration. 2. Biologics are usually derived from living microorganisms and cannot be synthesized or readily standardized by chemical or physical means. They tend to be chemically less stable than drugs, their safety cannot be as easily assured, and they are never as chemically pure as drugs.

biology The science of life and living organisms.

biomarker In environmental health and hazardous materials management, this is the use of data to measure a person's exposure or dose level to hazardous materials; provides confirmation and measures of the bioavailability of a contaminant (including continuous or intermittent exposures from all sources) and the process of the contaminant entering through any of the body's portals. Also called "biomonitoring." *See bioavailability.*

biomedical and consumer product safety Those measures taken to ensure that drugs, cosmetics, therapeutic devices, and all types of consumer products, including cleaning fluids, pesticides, and children's toys, are safe and appropriate for their intended use and are clearly labeled as to potential harm resulting from abuse or misuse. Two major subcategories are used: 1) drugs and medical devices and 2) hazardous substances and products.

biomedical engineer A person trained in engineering, applied physics, biochemistry, physiology, or medicine who utilizes engineering ideas and techniques in the development of new instruments, equipment processes, and systems for the medical care of patients and the improvement of health systems.

biomedical engineering A scientific specialty that studies the medical and biological aspects of the body and applies related engineering, physical science, and technological principles to assist in the medical, biological, physiological, and anatomical functioning of the body.

biomedical engineering, department of A department in a hospital or research facility that offers engineering services related to medical or biological activities.

biomedical engineering technologist/technician A person who assembles, repairs, and adapts medical equipment to assist biomedical engineers, physicians, and scientists in the delivery of health care.

biomedical equipment technologist/technician A person who tests, maintains, and repairs the variety of biomedical equipment used in healthcare facilities.

biomedical research Research concerned with human and animal biology and with disease and its prevention, diagnosis, and treatment.

biometry The application of mathematics, statistics, and research to biology; measuring the processes and functions related to living things.

bionics The science of the creation and function of electronic and mechanical devices or systems that operate similarly or in the same way as body parts or living organs.

biopsy The removal and examination of living tissue.

biostatistician A person with advanced training in the application of mathematics and statistics to research related to health care, biomedical concerns, medicine and health planning. This usually requires a masters or a doctoral degree in biostatistics, statistics, or mathematics. *See also health statistician.*

biostatistics The application of mathematical statistics and techniques to research information related to medicine, biomedical science, health and social problems, public health, vital statistics, and demographics.

birth certificate An official, legal public health document used to record the facts and details of live births. Basic data about the newborn and his or her parents are recorded, as are useful vital statistics and related information.

birth cohort In epidemiology and public health, this is a group of individuals who share the same birth year or who were born during a specific time period, allowing the study of certain characteristics of the group. *See cohort.*

birth control The intentional limiting of the number of children born, achieved by interfering with the conception process, controlling sexual activity, or using contraceptives. *See also family planning.*

birthing center A specialized labor and delivery unit; a freestanding outpatient labor and delivery facility used for normal deliveries and low-risk deliveries that would not require admission to a hospital. *See alternative birthing center.*

birthing room A comfortable, homelike room in a hospital or health facility used for both labor and delivery. Women are not moved to a surgical suite for delivery but have the baby in the homelike atmosphere. *See alternative birthing center.*

birth interval This is the time period between the termination/completion of one full-term pregnancy and the termination/completion of the next pregnancy.

birth rate 1. The rate at which babies are born in a specific population. 2. A formula used to determine the birth rate. The numerator is the total number of births in a population during a given period and the denominator the total number of person-years lived by the population during that same period per 1000 population. The latter is generally approximated by the size of the population at the midpoint of the period multiplied by the length of the period in years. The birth rate is usually stated per 1000 or 100,000. Like other rates in which the population at the period midpoint is used as the denominator of the fraction, this is sometimes called the "central birth rate." Where birth rate is used without qualification, the live birth rate is generally meant, and only live births appear in the numerator. The total birth rate, based on live births and late fetal deaths, is sometimes calculated. Legitimate birth rates and illegitimate birth rates (with legitimate and illegitimate births, respectively) are computed; and the illegitimacy ratio, or the number of illegitimate births per 1000 total births, is frequently used (see Appendix I). Some birth rates are restricted to births to women of a specific age, race, marital status, or geographic location or may use the entire population. *See also fertility rate; crude* *birth rate; age-specific birth rate*. The birth-rate formula follows:

$$\frac{\text{Number of live births to residents of a geographical area in 1 year}}{\text{Average or midyear population of a geographical area in 1 year}} \times 1{,}000$$

births The total number of children born in a health care facility during a certain period of time. Births do not include infants admitted just after birth or transferred from another hospital. When infants are born in a hospital, they are not included in admission and discharge statistics.

birth weight The actual weight of an infant at the moment of birth. Of concern to health care and public health are infants of low birth weight. Ultralow birth weight is below 1000 g; very low birth weight is below 1500 g; low birth weight is 2500 g or less; and small for gestational age is a birth weight below the 10th percentile. Another designation is large for gestational age, which is a birth weight in the 90th percentile, as compared to a normal birth weight, which is between the 10th and the 90th percentiles.

bit A binary digit and the smallest notation unit, usually a 0 or 1, in computer language.

bit-binary digit 1. In information management and/or computerized medical records, this is a single character in a binary number. 2. Each of the eight intersections making up a computer cell. *See magnetic core.*

black letter law Legal principles that are universally accepted by most judges.

black light Ultraviolet light radiation causing pigmentation of the skin.

black lung Common name for a chronic pneumoconiosis that is a severely debilitating lung disease caused by inhaling coal dust and found principally among coal miners. Certain medical benefits for the victims of the disease are available under Title IV of the federal Coal Mine Health and Safety Act of 1969 (P.L. 91-173) as amended by P.L. 92-303.

blanching Pressing a patient's fingernail to determine if there is an impairment in blood circulation to the limbs and fingers. The fingernail should turn white when momentarily pressed and then quickly return to its normal pink color if circulation is normal. If it is not normal, it may stay white. This test is used to ensure circulation to limbs and fingers when they are bound with bandages, casts, etc.

blank endorsement Signing a draft or check without specifying who can cash it.

blanket bond In health-care financing, a fidelity bond that provides uniform coverage for all employees.

blanket medical expense (coverage) A provision (usually included as an added feature of a policy primarily providing some other type of coverage such as loss of income insurance) that entitles the insured to collect, up to a maximum established in the policy, for all hospital and medical expenses incurred, without limitations on individual types of medical expenses.

blanket mortgage In health-care finance and/or construction, this is a provision for one mortgage to cover more than one property of the mortgagor (e.g., one mortgage may cover the addition of a hospital wing as well as a nursing home built adjacent to the hospital). This is also referred to as a "general mortgage" and covers both present and future real property.

blanket overhead rate In health-care finance/budgeting, this is a method of determining overhead and dividing or apportioning it to projects, services, or activities by using only one rate for the whole organization.

blanket policy 1. In managed care or insurance, this is to cover everything by one health-care plan or insurance policy. 2. A flexible insurance policy with broad coverage.

blended model One approach to the governance and management of health-care organizations that combines committee and corporate management model approaches.

blended rates In managed care, this is the use of mortality rates to determine premium rates for medium-sized group rates. A health plan's experience-based data and mortality rates are combined to determine the rates to be used in business decisions.

blinding *See blind studies.*

blind spot A term used in psychiatry to indicate an area of a person's personality of which he is totally unaware and is usually the result of repression to avoid painful emotions.

blind studies A research approach that is structured in such a manner as to prevent subjects and/or researchers from knowing which experimental subjects or control group subjects are included or excluded from the research treatment or intervention.

block In information management or computerized medical records, this is a set of things, such as words, characters, or digits, handled as a unit. *See also block diagram symbols.*

block diagram In information management and computerized medical records, this is a schematic chart that outlines the detailed sequence of operations to be performed in a particular computer application.

block diagram symbols In information management, computerized medical, or business records, symbols used in a block diagram to represent the basic instructions prepared for the computer. The terms "block" and "41 symbol" are used interchangeably.

block grants Grant funds made to local and state government units by the federal government. Although states are required to submit an annual plan explaining how such funds will be used, there is great flexibility in the distribution of grant money as long as the funds are used for acceptable purposes.

block policies In insurance, this is a special type of insurance that provides all-risk coverage to property subject to being moved from one location to another. This type of insurance is often applied to marine or floating property and could likewise be applied to certain specialized types of movable medical clinics.

blood bank A separate medical facility or medical unit that has the responsibility for blood procurement, processing, grouping, typing, and distribution. This facility provides a constant supply of blood, plasma, and blood components for use in hospitals, freestanding surgery centers, freestanding emergency rooms, or related health-care facilities. Some hospitals maintain their own blood banks, whereas others rely on outside facilities for their blood supply.

blood bank, commercial/proprietary A for-profit blood procurement organization that draws and prepares blood for distribution to health-care facilities; a private business that exists to make money from blood services by selling blood products to health-care organizations. *See blood services.*

blood bank, community A not-for-profit blood procurement organization that draws and prepares blood for distribution to health-care facilities and hospitals within the community. *See blood services.*

blood bank, hospital A special unit within a health-care facility that procures persons for blood donations and draws and prepares blood and its components for use within the health-care facility.

blood bank technologist A medical technologist working under the direction of a pathologist, physician, or laboratory director who prepares, collects, classifies, stores, and processes blood, including the separated components of whole blood. Other duties include detection and identification of antibodies in patient and donor bloods and selection and delivery of suitable blood for transfusion.

blood bank technology An allied health training program that prepares persons to work in blood banks under the supervision of a physician, microbiologist, pathologist, or lab director to collect, type, group, classify, store, and process blood. Blood is separated into its component parts, and testing is also learned to detect and identify antibodies and to determine if the blood is pure and usable for transfusion.

blood distribution The marketing and sale of blood and its components to hospitals and health-care facilities.

blood, outdated Donated blood that, because of its age, is no longer safe to use (i.e., blood that has been refrigerated for more than 21 days and is unsafe to use in transfusions).

blood pressure The pressure at which the heart pushes the blood as it pulsates through the arteries. The amount of pressure in the large arteries is assessed by the pulse wave felt on the outside of the body, which affects air pressure in a cuff on the arm, which in turn pushes mercury up a tube with pressure indicators on it. The pressure at the height of the heart's beat on both sides of the heart is used, with the left ventricle producing the systolic pressure and the right ventricle the diastolic pressure. Systolic average pressure is 120 mmHg, with abnormal pressure being above 140 mmHg; diastolic average pressure is 80 mmHg, and abnormal pressure is above 100 mmHg.

blood processing Once blood has been drawn, it is serologically tested, typed, and grouped. Some of the blood that is not used as whole blood is then processed so that its component parts (plasma and red blood cells) are removed. Whole blood or derivatives of the processed blood parts are prepared for distribution to hospitals.

blood replacement deposit A charge for the replacement of blood used by a patient while hospitalized in lieu of actually replenishing hospital blood supply.

blood repository A special unit within a health-care facility for storing blood or blood components by special arrangement with a blood bank. The hospital staff may be responsible for housekeeping chores and for maintaining a current supply.

blood services The array of blood acquisition, blood labs and testing, blood banking, and transfusion activities.

blood transfusion services Health-care services related to the transfusing and infusing of patients with blood or blood components (JCAHO for acute-care facilities).

blood usage review A function of a medical staff that involves the monitoring, evaluation, and quality improvement of the use of blood in health-care facilities. Preestablished standards are applied to health-care facilities to assess the quality of performance in blood use in providing health-care services (JCAHO for acute-care facilities).

blood, whole Blood that has been tested and typed but has not been processed to separate out its various components.

BLS Bureau of Labor Statistics (a division of the Department of Labor).

Blue Cross An independent, not-for-profit membership health insurance corporation providing protection against the costs of hospital care and, in some policies, protection against the costs of surgical and professional care. *See also Blue Cross Association (BCA); Blue Cross plan.*

Blue Cross Association (BCA) The national nonprofit organization to which the 70 Blue Cross plans in the United States voluntarily belong. BCA administers programs of licensure and approval for Blue Cross plans, provides specific services related to the writing and administering of health-care benefits across the country, and represents the Blue Cross plans in national affairs. Under contract with the Social Security Administration, BCA is an intermediary in the Medicare program for 77% of the participating providers (90% of the participating hospitals, 50% of the participating skilled nursing facilities, and 76% of the participating home health agencies). *See also Blue Shield plan.*

Blue Cross/Blue Shield A combined medical plan offered through a worker's place of employment that combines both hospital and physician coverage: Blue Cross covers hospital costs and Blue Shield physician costs.

Blue Cross plan A nonprofit, tax-exempt prepayment medical insurance organization providing coverage for health-care and related services. The individual plans should be distinguished from their national association, the Blue Cross Association. Historically, the plans were largely the creation of the hospital industry and were designed to provide hospitals with a stable source of revenues, although formal association between Blue Cross and the American Hospital Association ended in 1972. A Blue Cross plan must be a nonprofit community service organization with a governing body and a membership that includes a majority of public representatives. Most plans are regulated by state insurance commissioners under special enabling legislation. Plans are exempt from federal income taxes and, in most states, from state taxes (both property and premium). Unlike most private insurance companies, the plans usually provide service rather than indemnity benefits and often pay hospitals on the basis of reasonable costs rather than charges. There are 70 plans in the United States. *See also Blue Shield plan.*

Blue Shield An independent, not-for-profit membership health insurance association providing protection against the costs of physician services, surgery, and other items of medical care. Some policies also offer protection against the costs of hospital care. *See also Blue Shield plan.*

Blue Shield plan A nonprofit, tax-exempt medical insurance plan originally established in 1939 that provides coverage of physicians' services. The individual plans should be distinguished from the National Association of Blue Shield Plans. Blue Shield coverage is commonly sold in conjunction with Blue Cross coverage, although this is not always the case. The relationship between Blue Cross and Blue Shield plans has been a cooperative one, as the two organizations have a common board and a single management structure and are located in the same building. Blue Shield plans cover some 65 million Americans through their group and individual business plans. In addition, plan activities affect some 20 million persons through participation in various government programs, including Medicare (32 plans act as carriers under Part B), Medicaid, and CHAMPUS. Most states have enacted special enabling legislation for the Blue Shield plans. *See also Medical Indemnity of America, Inc.*

BNDD Bureau of Narcotics and Dangerous Drugs (a division of the Department of Justice).

BNDD number Former name of a number assigned to health care providers for the prescribing of narcotics and dangerous drugs. Currently a Drug Enforcement Administration (DEA) number is used.

board-and-care homes Long-term-care facilities that, for a monthly charge, provide minimal medical care (but mostly basic room and board as well as some protective care and supervision) on a 24-hour basis to aged or disabled persons. *See custodial care; personal care; supervisory care.*

board-and-care list In managed care, this is a listing of health plan members who currently reside in board-and-care facilities.

board certified Describes a physician or other health-care professional who has passed an examination given by a medical specialty board and has been certified by that board as a specialist in a specific area of medical practice. The examination cannot be taken until the board's eligibility requirements set by the specialty board have been met.

board-designated assets In health-care finance, these are special monies set aside by the board of directors for specific purposes or special projects.

board eligible Describes a physician or other health-care professional who is eligible for specialty board examination (including those who may have failed the examination if still eligible). Each of the specialty boards has requirements that must be met before the examination for specialty board certification can be taken. Usually this includes graduation from an approved school or an accredited program; approved training experience of specified type and length; and specified time in practice. The minimum time required after graduation from medical school to become board eligible is generally 3 to 5 years. Government and other types of health programs that define standards for specialists often accept board eligibility as equivalent to board certification, as the only difference is that the board-certified professional has passed an examination.

boarder A person housed in a health-care facility, such as a hospital or nursing home, who is not a patient staff member or physician but who may be a parent or spouse of a hospitalized individual and who stays to provide comfort and reassurance to the inpatient.

boarder census The head count of the number of nonpatients in a hospital who are receiving meals and sleeping accommodations.

boarding homes Organized or informal long-term-care facilities for the aged that provide room, board, and sometimes custodial care for a fee. The provision of medical supervision, social activities, or counseling is not normally included as it would be in a nursing home. In some states, boarding homes are not licensed as health facilities and may not be subject to any licensure.

board of commissioners Refers to the governing body of an organization, such as the Joint Commission on Accreditation of Healthcare Organizations, public utilities, or a county commission.

board of directors A group of people chosen to supervise business activities, select key employees, and plan for the future development of the health-care facility or enterprise. Members are usually elected because of their business ability, and it is not essential that they hold stock in the health-care organization. The board of directors also has legal power to take such actions as are necessary or proper to conduct the business activities of the hospital or health-care organization. It has the ultimate authority and is the highest level of governance of a health-care organization, has the legal control of the organization, and exists to ensure the continued existence of the organization.

board of directors, hospital A hospital governing board, also called a "governing board" or "board of trustees," that is usually elected by a community, a church, stockholders, etc., depending on ownership and tax status (for-profit or not-for-profit). A typical board of 5 to 15 members meets monthly, is governed by by-laws, and elects its own officers and chooses its own committees. The board chooses and appoints the administrator and staff physicians and makes major financial and administrative decisions beyond the usual day-to-day decisions delegated to the hospital administrator.

board of governors *See board of directors; board of directors, hospital.*

board of health A committee or board of citizens (including one physician), selected and appointed by elected and governing officials such as a mayor, county commissioners, or a governor to serve as an advisory and governing board to oversee administrative functions of the public health department and the community's health. Boards of health are usually comprised of 9 to 11 persons and often exist to represent a political constituency. Boards of health exist at both the local and the state levels and assume rule- and policymaking powers. Some efforts have been made to update these boards and their roles and may eventually be changed to public health councils. Such name and role changes have been recommended by the National Institutes of Health.

Board of Medical Quality Assurance A state-level agency that has as one of its roles to investigate medical quality complaints.

board of trustees *See board of directors, hospital.*

body contact–exploration maneuver A psychotherapy approach utilizing physical touching of others to gain awareness of feelings, sensations, and emotions created and aroused by the experience. A technique used in encounter groups.

body language The presentation of a person's thoughts and feelings by means of bodily activity, gestures, actions, or posture.

boilerplate 1. A general standardized form for a document. 2. In a contract, this is those sections and paragraphs of a general nature that do not deal with material specific to the contract.

BOMQA Board of Medical Quality Assurance.

bona fide (Lat.) 1. Genuine; without fraud. 2. In good faith. 3. Actual; real. 4. Honest; without deception.

bona fide occupational qualification Those qualifications of any employee of a health-care or other organization that are reasonably necessary or required for the position and for the normal operation of the organization. A justified business reason for employing the individual most suited for a position while still not discriminating against a group protected by Title VII of the 1964 Amendment of the Civil Rights Act; the burden of proof falls on the employing health-care organization.

bond 1. A written obligation with agreement to pay a specified amount of money once certain conditions are met. 2. A written agreement to do or not do something with an amount paid as security or bail. 3. A document used to show proof of a debt. 4. A binding agreement. 5. In health-care finance, a debt investment that legally represents a promise to repay borrowed money to the holder of the bond at a specific time and to pay interest to the holder of the bond at a specified rate until it is paid off.

bond certificate In health-care finance, this is a legal paper of proof of debt owed to the owner of the bond. This paper states the amount of the principal, the rate of interest, time payments of interest, and the maturity date.

bond discount In health-care finance, this is also referred to as "debt premium," or the amount of the selling price of a bond less the face value of the bond or other form of indebtedness.

bond penalty In health-care finance, the amount of money that the party who is liable for another's debts or defaults of obligations must pay for any loss as stated in the terms of a bond.

bond premium In health-care finance, this is also referred to as "debt premium," by which the selling price of a bond exceeds the value of the bond or other indebtedness.

bond ratings Alphabetical letters presented as grades indicating the quality of the bond. The ratings are based on earning records, size of the health-care organization, bond indebtedness, and the property value that serves as collateral for the bond.

bond yield In health-care finance, this is the annual rate of return that a bond is expected to earn.

book of original entry A journal or record in which an accounting action is first recorded.

book value 1. Proven assets minus liabilities. 2. The value of any assets as recorded on a hospital or health-care facility's records or accounting statement. 3. Net worth of the institution.

boot In information management and computers, this is the process of loading a program into the computer's memory.

borrowed servant In health-care law, this is an employee temporarily under the control of another (e.g., when a nurse employed by a health-care facility is "borrowed" by a surgeon in the operating room). The temporary master of the borrowed servant is responsible for the act of the borrowed servant under the doctrine of respondeat superior. *See respondeat superior.*

bottom-line test In human resource management activities for health-care or other organizations, this is an evaluation of the organization's overall employee selection processes to ascertain if the organization is meeting Equal Employment Opportunity Commission guidelines and to assure that the overall hiring and employment practices are not having an adverse effect on protected groups.

Boulwarism In labor relations, this is a negotiation strategy first developed by General Electric. The best offer is made to the union at the beginning of negotiations and is held firm unless an error in calculations can be found in the offer. The National Labor Relations Board and the federal courts have ruled this an unfair labor practice.

bounce-back form In hospitals and other health-care organizations, this is one approach to the suggestion box or suggestion/feedback form filled out by patients, residents, or clients.

bowel and bladder training Used in long-term-care settings and nursing homes, this is a program to assist persons who, as a result of stroke or senility, have lost the ability to control their bowel and bladder functions and have become incontinent. Retraining is used to help persons learn to control these functions and allow them to become self-sufficient by minimizing the problem of incontinence.

Box-Jenkins approach In managed care, this is a computer program time series analysis technique used to identify patient utilization patterns of the health plan in the past and then predict future utilization patterns.

boycott 1. To ban or discourage use of a product, business, or service. 2. To ban doing business with and to attempt to stop others from trading with a company or business. A primary boycott in labor law involves directly boycotting a union and the employer. A secondary boycott is banning the company from doing business with support companies.

BQA *See Bureau of Quality Assurance.*

Bradford frame A rectangular frame (3 × 7 ft), made from sturdy pipes, that has two strips of movable canvas stretched across it. It is used as a bed frame for patients with bone diseases (usually of the hip or spine) or with serious fractures. This frame allows immobilized patients to carry on bowel and urinary functions without moving or changing position.

Bradley training Husband-coached childbirth, developed over 30 years ago by Robert Bradley, an obstetrician. Oriented toward preparation for labor by doing what comes naturally, relaxing, and breathing deeply. Encourages the direct involvement of the expectant father.

bradylalia Abnormally slow speech, common in depression.

brainstorming A management and/or training method by which participants freely share their ideas on a problem, an issue, or a concern without question or criticism. Every idea suggested is accepted and is written on a blackboard as a serious possibility.

brainwashing 1. A method of manipulating human thought and behavior against the will of those involved. 2. A systematic effort of indoctrinating persons to a way of believing and thinking.

brain waves *See electroencephalogram.*

branding In health-care marketing, this is the process of developing brand-name loyalty, such as a patient wanting to use only a certain hospital, home health agency, or type of medication. Loyalty and association to a brand-name product or service.

brand name The registered trademark given to a specific drug product by its manufacturer, also known as a "trade name." There are no official rules governing the selection of brand names. According to the Pharmaceutical Manufacturers Association, the objective is to coin a name that is "useful, dignified, easily remembered, and individual or proprietary." Drugs are primarily advertised to practitioners by brand name. When a physician prescribes by brand name, antisubstitution laws in most states forbid the pharmacist from substituting either a brand-name or a generic equivalent made by a different manufacturer, although either may be less expensive than the drug prescribed. Some states have changed the laws to allow the use of a generic substitute.

breach 1. Failing to observe the terms of an agreement. 2. The breaking of a law or the violation of a duty.

breach of contract A legal principle describing the failure to perform or fulfill a promise or the terms of a contractual agreement.

breach of promise 1. Failing to keep one's word. 2. When one does not marry another after a promise was made to do so (an outdated principle).

breach of warranty The violation of any agreement or representation concerning the condition, content, or quality of a product but with no fraudulent misrepresentation.

break 1. To stop by force. 2. To overwhelm. 3. To disperse or scatter. 4. To intrude; to enter by force.

break-even financial status *See break-even point.*

break-even point 1. In health-care finance, this is the level where total monies equal total costs. The point where the income meets the total cost so that the organization neither loses nor makes money. Also referred to as "break-even financial status." 2. In managed care, when a health plan's or HMO's membership reaches a level where revenues from members' premiums match the total costs or are equal to the costs and expenses of operating the health plan with no losses from operations and no net financial gains.

breaking bulk 1. Illegally opening a bulk package and taking part of the contents or contaminating the contents. 2. An offense by a carrier in which part of the contents of a bulk package, box, or bale in shipment is removed or converted.

bribery 1. The act of offering or receiving rewards or items of value to influence a public official. 2. To receive a false judgment or an illegal performance.

bridge financing In health-care finance, this is a short-term interim loan.

brief 1. A legally written summary or brief statement. 2. A concise written statement prepared for a lawsuit explaining the case. A brief should contain a fact summary and a law summary and should demonstrate how the law applies to the facts. 3. A summary of a published opinion.

brief services *See also levels of service; services.*

bring suit 1. To start a lawsuit by filing the proper papers with the court. 2. To present a lawsuit in a court of law.

broad-form perils This is a special type of insurance endorsement on a fire insurance policy that includes extended coverage of perils and disasters and may include specific perils if those are listed and named in the policy. As the definition of perils is broader in this type of endorsement, it allows more coverage than specified policies.

broker 1. Any person who is paid to act as an agent to make bargains or enter into contracts. 2. One who deals in buying and selling money or notes. 3. An agent who sells health plans or insurance programs for more than one company. 4. In managed care, this is a licensed sale and service representative who handles health coverage for employees, generally working for a variety of insurance companies and health plans. *See broker, insurance.*

broker, insurance 1. One who writes insurance. 2. An insurance solicitor, licensed by the state, who does business with a variety of insurance companies and who represents the buyers of insurance rather than the companies even though paid commissions by the companies.

bronchogram An X ray of the bronchial tree using an iodized oil dye introduced into the body as a contrast medium.

bronchoscope A specialized lighted instrument used to visually examine the bronchi of the lungs.

bronchoscopy To visually examine the bronchi.

brown lung Common name for byssinosis. A chronic, disabling lung disease that is caused by long-term inhalation of cotton dust and that is prevalent among textile workers. Similar to but not the same as black lung. Federal benefits, such as those available for miners disabled by black lung, are not available for people with brown lung.

bruja (fem.); **brujo** (masc.) (Spanish) 1. Witch, sorcerer, magician. 2. One with cursing and healing powers.

BSN Bachelor of Science in Nursing.

buddy system In health-care organizations, this is a training and orientation approach where an experienced employee is assigned a new employee to train the new worker and help him or her adjust and get acquainted on the job.

budget 1. A detailed financial plan for carrying out a health service or hospital program in a specified period, usually a fiscal year. The budget typically accounts for all the program's proposed income for the year by source, by expenses, and by purpose, all based on management and operations assumptions. A process, based on assumptions, by which anticipated costs, profit, and operation parameters are determined for the coming year and are set forth in a set of documents that includes the agreements and decisions reached in the planning process. Revenue budgets must be developed before expense budgets are established. 2. Money provided for a particular purpose. 3. A plan or schedule of expenses. 4. An estimate of money needed over a certain time period. *See revenue.*

budget assumptions Statements of known facts, conditions, or issues on which budget decisions are made and budget monies allocated. A major part of the budget planning process is to state managerial conditions that influence the allocation of money to programs, departments, and projects. The budget planning process is incomplete without the statement of budget assumptions.

budget authority In the federal budget, authority provided by law to enter into obligations that will result in immediate or future outlays of government funds, except that it does not include the authority to ensure or guarantee the repayment of indebtedness incurred by another person or government. The basic forms of budget authority are appropriations, contract authority, and borrowing authority. Budget authority is classified by the timing of congressional action (current or permanent) or by the manner of determining the amount available (definite or indefinite).

budget committee In health-care finance, this is an organizationwide committee, often made up of department heads, charged with the responsibility for preparing the annual budget for the health-care organization, including activities such as writing assumptions, estimating operating expenses, determining the allocation of funds, and preparing proposed budget documents for approval by the administration and the governing board.

budget cycle 1. This is the period of time that granting agencies or foundations use as their fiscal year, or when they offer grants to applicants. 2. The fiscal year, or the time period of a budget; when a budget ends and a new budget begins.

budget, grant In grant proposals, this is a financial management plan for the project grant being submitted. Grant budgets can be written in one of two ways: as an "objective referenced" budget, in which each project or part of the project is itemized, or as a "line-item" budget, in which a cost is presented for various categories of expenses, such as travel, staff personnel, equipment, etc.

budget guidelines The use of key financial indicators to establish assumptions and rules for the budget process. The rules can be set forth by the administration and/or the governing board.

budgeting In health administration and healthcare financial management, this is the process of developing a formal plan of future operations expressed in quantitative and monetary terms and serving as a basis of measurement for subsequent control of operations. This involves the formulation and planning for a future set time period (usually 1 year) in monetary and numerical terms with a system of documentation and accountability, including anticipated outcomes and results expressed in monetary and numerical terms, such as revenue generated, expenses anticipated, personnel to be hired, equipment to be purchased, and capital expenditures.

budget variance The difference between actual costs incurred and the budget that has been adjusted to the real activity level.

burden of proceeding To be required to present evidence on a certain question in a lawsuit even before the other party is obligated to.

burden of proof 1. The need to prove an assertion or a disputed fact. 2. The legal principle used to determine which party must prove the facts.

bureaucracy 1. A large organization or administrative agency that has a hierarchical, or chain-of-command, organizational structure. 2. An organization with well-defined or specialized positions and responsibilities. The delegation of authority is usually downward, utilizing all levels. It is understood in administration that a bureaucracy, even in the United States, is not a democracy because of its hierarchical administrative structure. *See bureaucratic organization.*

bureaucratic organization A large organization where groups of individuals carry out administrative functions for the completion of the organization's mission. Work roles and different skills are brought together in one organization to obtain a single aim under a formal authoritative administrative structure. Most government organizations are bureaucratic organizations, as are large hospitals, universities, and other large private companies. *See bureaucracy.*

Bureau of Biologics A division of the U.S. Food and Drug Administration in charge of the control of such biological materials as serums, vaccines, antitoxins, antibiotics, toxins, blood plasma, etc.

Bureau of Drugs A division of the U.S. Food and Drug Administration in charge of the regulation of drugs. *See also Kefauver-Harris Amendment.*

Bureau of Health Facilities Financing, Compliance, and Conversion Bureau of Health Facilities (shortened name).

Bureau of Health Insurance (BHI) An agency within the Social Security Administration (SSA) that administers the Medicare program. The actual operation of the program is carried out through arrangements with intermediaries and carriers who operate under contract with BHI/SSA and receive all policy guidance from the bureau.

Bureau of Health Manpower *See Bureau of Health Professions.*

Bureau of Health Professions A component of the Health Resources Administration, Public Health Service, U.S. Department of Health and Human Services. The bureau supports development of the human resources needed to staff the U.S. health-care system. It is concerned with education of health professionals, credentialing of health-care personnel, and analysis of data to project needs for health professions personnel. Prior to March 18, 1980, the agency was known as the Bureau of Health Manpower.

Bureau of Indian Affairs (BIA) A division of the Department of Interior involved in the affairs of Native Americans and regulating their activities. The role of the Department of Interior and the BIA in regulating health and human services and activities of Native Americans has been greatly reduced and should decrease even more in the near future.

Bureau of Quality Assurance (BQA) A federal government agency within the Health Resources Administration that administers the Professional Review Organization program.

burn care A specialized form of care, providing emergency and advanced care to severely burned patients. Such care is more intense than the regular acute care found in most medical and nursing units in a hospital. Specialized beds and facilities are provided along with staff who have special training in treating burns. Severely burned patients are those with any of the following: 1) second-degree burns of more than 25% total body surface for adults or 20% total body surface area for children; 2) third-degree burns of more than 10% total body surface area; 3) any severe burns of the hands, face, eyes, ears, or feet; or 4) all inhalation injuries, electrical burns, complicated burn injuries involving fractures and other major traumas, and all other poor risk factors. Hospital beds must be set up and staffed in special units specifically designated for burn injuries.

burn care units A specialized treatment unit in a hospital that provides specialty inpatient care for severely burned patients recovering from several types and levels of burns: 1) second-degree burns of more than 25% total body surface area for adults or 20% total body surface area for children; 2) third-degree burns of more than 10% total body surface area; 3) severe burns of the face, eyes, ears, hands, or feet; and 4) burns to certain body parts or systems, such as electrical burns, inhalation burn injuries, or burns compounded by injuries such as fractures, internal injuries, or other high-risk injuries.

burned-out anergic schizophrenic A chronic form of schizophrenia. Symptoms include apathy and withdrawal with minimal psychotic symptoms but with persistent schizophrenic thought processes.

burnout A progressive condition found in many health care professionals in which adaptive energies are depleted by prolonged stress and exhaustion and that manifests itself as impairments within an individual's physical, mental, emotional, and behavioral functioning. This condition occurs over time, affects the totality of the body's defense mechanisms and adaptive capabilities, and is a consequence of work environment experiences, individual perceptions, and the individual's reaction to all these influences.

burn unit A special care unit in a hospital that provides specialized intensive care to burn patients. Not all hospitals have burn units, which are often found in level I trauma center hospitals.

business agent 1. An individual legally designated to carry out and make business decisions for the principle/organization (*see principle; agent; law of agency*). 2. In labor law, this is a full-time worker employed by the local union to help workers resolve their problems with management.

business insurance An insurance policy that provides benefits principally to a business (such as a hospital) rather than to an individual. It is issued to indemnify a business for the loss of services of a key employee or partner who becomes disabled.

business interruption insurance A special form of insurance providing continual income to cover payroll or loss of business income because of an interruption of business activity as a result of injury, loss, fire, or other peril.

business judgment rule If the executives of a health-care corporation (such as a hospital) make honest, wise, and careful decisions and stay within their powers, the courts will not interfere with the functions of the organization even if the results are not good.

business office This department, often found in health-care organizations (usually hospitals), is responsible for handling, compiling, and mailing patient bills and the forms and paperwork of the money-related activities of the organization. It also collects money from patient insurance companies, governmental bodies, and other types of third-party payers. The director of the business office ensures that financial records are properly maintained, budgets prepared, cost analysis reports completed, and payrolls efficiently handled.

business record exception In health law, this principle provides for an exception to the "hearsay exclusion rule." Thus, original routine records, such as medical and hospital business records used in transacting business, could be used as evidence in a trial.

business records 1. The main and supportive documents kept on administrative, accounting, financial, and related activities of a health-care facility. 2. "As evidence": administrative and management documents can be competent evidence if it is affirmed under oath that their identity and preparation is accurate, if they were prepared in the regular course of business and within a reasonable time of the business activity, and if the submission of the documents is justified as being important to the court. This applies not only to business office records but also to medical records as evidence, and medical records administrators may be asked to testify that medical records were kept in the usual and normal fashion and in the regular course of business.

business trust A company (such as a hospital) established as a trust and similar to a corporation.

business unionism In labor relations, this is when union representatives seek to improve benefits, wages, working conditions, hours, etc. for their union members through professional business approaches as opposed to striking or militant activities.

buy-back In human resources management, when an employee quits an organization and is then encouraged to return to employment at a higher salary, for a better position, or for other benefits. The employee is enticed back into employment, thus the term "buy-back."

buy-in The business arrangement used to purchase or acquire an interest in a medical group practice. This is possible only if the group is a corporation or partnership or is made into one of these legal structures.

bylaws 1. Subordinate laws or policies created by groups or corporations for policy and control of the membership and for the governance and operation of a facility. Such policies and bylaws are written, dated, and made available to all members of the governing body to ensure that they are operational, reviewed, and revised as necessary. These are the legal governing documents of the organization and are not easily changed. 2. The governance framework, such as laws, rules, or regulations adopted for the governing body of a facility that establishes the roles and responsibilities of the organization (JCAHO for acute care facilities). 3. In formal health-care meetings and hearings using parliamentary procedure, the rules of an organization that rank second in authority to the constitution or the founding basis for the organization and yet have more authority than standing rules. Bylaws may include the provisions of a constitution and set forth the policies and rules of governance of the board of trustees of a health-care organization.

bypass Refers to cardiovascular surgery where blockages in blood vessels are circumvented with external vessels.

byte In information management and computers, this is the smallest unit of information possible.

C

CA 1. Court of appeals. 2. Chronological age.
CABG Coronary artery bypass graft.
cacodemonomania When a person believes he or she is possessed by a devil or an evil spirit.
cafeteria benefit program A list of fringe benefits and services available to employees of health-care organizations.
cafeteria plan In human resources and employee benefits, this is a predetermined amount of benefit dollars allotted for employee benefits and services. Employees may choose different managed care, medical, life, and disability insurance–type policies and different levels of coverage and deductibles. If costs exceed the employer's contribution, employees must make up the difference out of their paychecks.
CAHEA *See Committee on Allied Health Education and Accreditation.*
CAHMO California Association of HMOs.
calendar year January 1 through December 31 of any given year. In managed care and insurance, this time period is used in connection with benefits incurred by health plan members or insurance expenses incurred by the insurance company for major medical, basic hospital coverage, surgical, and medical plans.
calendar year deductible In managed care or medical insurance, the deductible amount that applies to any eligible medical expense incurred by the enrollee in one calendar year.
California Employees Retirement System (CERS) A public employees' retirement fund that also runs a managed-care system.
California Relative Value Studies (CRVS) Procedure coding manual (numbering system) used by physicians to evaluate the level of difficulty of procedures used in patient care and/or payments. *See also relative value scale; procedure coding manual.*
call In health information management, this is the transfer of patient information from one part of a computer program to another, with the ability to return to the same place in the original program.
callable bond In health-care facility development and construction, this is a bond that the party issuing the bond has the right to pay off at a date earlier than the maturity date at the price specified in the original bond.
call period In health-care finance, this can be the term of a note or mortgage where the interest rate can be reestablished to meet current rates or where full payment of the note can be demanded as due.
CALPERS *See California Employees Retirement System.*
calumny Slander; false accusation of a crime.
CAMIS *See computer-assisted minimally invasive surgery.*
cancel 1. To void or draw a line across. 2. To make invalid; annul. 3. To end, abolish; to do away with; to stop.
cancellation Under the Uniform Commercial Code, this is the recision of a contract resulting from the other party's breach of contract.
cancellation clause A statement that allows the parties of an insurance contract, under certain and specified conditions, the right to terminate coverage offered by an insurance contract or legal contract.
cancer The number two cause of death in the United States, this is any growth or tumor that is diagnosed as malignant. Cancer is uncontrolled, unconstrained, and wild and unlimited cell growth that can easily spread throughout the body.
cancer registry A system of identifying and keeping data on cancerous tumors and factors common to patients with cancer. Hospitals use this system and then provide the information to a state or national system or network of hospitals or governmental agencies that in turn compile and retain the data for research and statistical purposes.
candy stripers Teenage volunteer workers in a health-care facility who are usually responsible to the auxiliary of that facility.
cannabis *See marijuana.*
canon A law, rule, or principle, generally related to the church.
canon law 1. Laws governing a church, especially where the religion is the society's laws. 2. English church laws or laws related to religion.
canons of construction Principles used to guide the legal interpretation or construction of written documents.
canons of ethics A system of ethics in use until 1969, when the Code of Professional Responsi-

bility, which delineates the ethical standards of the legal profession, was put into practice.

canons of judicial ethics Old rules of conduct for judges that are being replaced by the Code of Judicial Conduct.

CAP *See Community Action Program.*

capacity 1. Legal power to act; legal qualification or ability. 2. A measure of health-care services and their availability in a community; numbers of hospital beds or the utilization of certain health services in a community or region. The number of beds available within a region or hospital is one measure of the ability to treat inpatients. The number of patients that a home health agency can take care of, including providing the highest quality of care, is another way of measuring capacity of community-based health-care services. 3. The capacity of a hospital or a unit within a health-care facility can be assessed. The average daily census is divided by the average occupancy, which will provide the capacity. Another approach is to use hospital data to ascertain capacity; data used are operational bed complement, admissions, discharges, average daily census, average length of stay, bed days per year, patient days per year, occupancy ratio, turnover internal (vacant bed day per discharge), unused bed days per bed, and average hospital cycle. *See insufficient capacity criteria; accessibility; availability.*

CAPER Computer Assisted Pathology Encoding and Reporting System. A computerized medical reporting system written into the MUMPS system that serves as a comprehensive pathology information management system for hospitals. First used at Massachusetts General Hospital, it automatically labels each transaction with a patient number, consolidates information on different specimens from the same patient taken at different times, and provides immediate access to each specimen's analysis status. It is also used in research and for teaching. *See also MUMPS.*

capital In health-care finance, this is fixed or durable nonlabor inputs that are used in the production of goods or the delivery of services (e.g., the buildings, beds, and equipment that are used in the provision of hospital services). Capital goods are usually considered permanent and are thus distinguished from supplies and other nondurables. *See also capital depreciation; working capital.*

capital appreciation In health-care financial management, this is the rise in the price of a share of stock in, or in the total value of, an investment.

capital asset In health-care finance, this is depreciable property of a relatively permanent nature, such as land, equipment, or buildings, not held for sale in the regular course of business.

capital budgeting In health-care finance, this is the comprehensive process of generating, assessing, selecting, and following up on capital expenditures. The planning, allocation, and use of budget monies for capital items.

capital cost In health-care finance, this is money invested in the development of a new activity. These costs do not include costs of operations but include those costs incurred prior to the operation of the activity.

capital depreciation In health-care finance, this is the decline in value of capital assets over time with use. The rate and amount of depreciation is calculated in several ways (e.g., straight line, sum of the digits, declining balance), which often give very different results. Reimbursement of health services usually includes an amount intended to be equivalent to the capital depreciation experienced by the provider of the services in conjunction with their provision. *See also debt service; section 1122; funded.*

capital erosion In health-care finance and facility operations, this is when a health-care organization has failed to keep up with the need for revenue, renovated facilities, and upgraded equipment, technology, and capital assets. The cause may lie in inadequate earnings, poor planning, failure to meet financial requirements, poor decision making, poor financing strategies, and improper use of funded depreciation.

capital expenditure review (CER) Under the previous health systems agencies, this was a review of proposed capital expenditures of hospitals and/or other health facilities to determine whether the expenditures were necessary and appropriate. The review was conducted by a designated regulatory agency, such as a state health planning and development agency, and included a sanction attached to prevent or discourage unneeded expenditures. Some banks or money-lending institutions have used similar requirements in the process of approving certain capital loans to health-care organizations. *See also certificate of need; section 1122.*

capital expenditures In health-care finance, these are expenses and revenue outlays for health-care equipment, land, or facilities that exceed an expenditure minimum or that substantially change the services of a health-care facility; the cost of purchasing a capital asset. The determination is usually based on the previous 12-month period, and benefits received will be for a length of time greater than 1 year.

capital expense In health-care finance, this is a formula used to assess expenses on land, equipment, or buildings. (Formula: Interest plus depreciation divided by operating expenses minus interest minus depreciation multiplied by 100.)

capital facilities plan In health-care organization facilities development, this is an itemized list of the capital assets needed to be acquired, enhanced, or replaced based on a plan and a timetable. The dates on which the purchases are to occur are laid out, as is the type and source of fund for each. Such a plan helps to avoid capital erosion. *See capital erosion.*

capital financing In health-care finance, this is one approach to acquiring funds through loans or other financing approaches for the purchase of large or expensive equipment or for building construction or renovation.

capital gains In health-care finance, this is the money resulting from the sale of a piece of capital equipment or property, which is the difference between what it cost and what it was sold for, less allowable deductible expenses. Capital gains records are maintained for income tax purposes.

capital gains tax A tax placed on the profit made from selling stocks, property, or capital assets. Federal income tax on capital gains is at a lower rate than on regular earned income.

capital losses In health-care finance, loss of revenue realized from the sale of capital assets that are sold for less than their worth.

capital offenses Crimes punishable by death (e.g., murder and treason).

capital pass through In health-care finance under Medicare, this is a special capital purchase program allowing part of the cost of capital equipment, construction, or other capital assets to be financially passed on to Medicare and paid to the hospital under the prospective payment system (PPS).

capital rationing In health-care finance, this is an organizational or a policy constraint placed on the total amount or size of a capital investment during a specific time period.

capital stock 1. Stock issued by a corporation. 2. The assets or property of a corporation. 3. The value given to a corporation.

capital structure In health-care finance, this is the permanent long-term financial health and financing concerns of the health-care organization; the debt and equity structure of the health-care organization.

capitalization In health-care finance, this is a method of determining the value of property that is being used as income property. The value is determined by taking the annual net income, which is then discounted by using an acceptable rate of return used by buyers of comparable properties. If net income is $20,000 per year and has a rate of return of 10%, then the property would be worth $200,000.

capitalization rate In health-care finance, this is a discount rate used to determine the current value of a series of future cash receipts, often called a "discount rate."

capitalization ratio In health-care finance, this is when a moneylender or a bank favors certain hospitals whose capital (long-term debt plus fund balances) is owned by the hospital or community. This ratio recognizes the percentage of capital owned by the hospital by dividing fund balances by the total fund balances plus long-term debt. The capitalization ratio formula follows:

$$\frac{\text{Fund balance}}{\text{Fund balances} + \text{Long-term debt}} = \text{Capitalization ratio}$$

capitation In health-care finance and managed care, this is a method of payment for health services in which an individual or institutional provider is paid a fixed, per capita amount for each person served without regard to the actual number or nature of services provided to each person. A stipulated dollar amount established to cover the cost of health and medical care provided to each health plan member. Capitation, being a characteristic of managed care, is a set money amount received or paid out, usually under a contract, and is paid in advance on the basis of membership enrollments rather than on services delivered and is usually expressed in units of pmpm (per member per month). For example, a provider agrees to provide specified services to HMO members for a fixed, predetermined payment for a specific time period (usually 1 year), with no regard to how many times the member/patient uses the health-care service. A prepaid negotiated per capita rate that is contracted to be paid periodically by the carrier to the health-care provider and is usually paid monthly to the health-care provider, which renders all medical and health services provided for and listed in the contract. The amount paid is the same regardless of the type, level, or amount of medical care provided by the health-care provider. Any amount of medical care provided by the practitioner not in the contract is not paid for by the health plan or insurance. Either co-insurance, self-pay, or no payment at all is used to cover expenses. Treatment not listed in the health plan capitation contract in some cases is simply not provided if the condition does not threaten one's life or immediate health.

capitation fee Under managed-care programs, providers under HMO capitation contracts use this special payment structure, which is based on a fixed rate paid per enrollee and is contrasted with fee-for-service.

capitation grants A fixed payment received by an eligible school from the federal government for each student enrolled in a health professionals school authorized by the Comprehensive Health Manpower Training Act of 1971 (P.L. 92-157) and the Nurse Training Act of 1971 (P.L. 92-158) (Sections 770 and 810 of the PHS Act).

capitation payment Under managed-care programs, providers under HMO capitation contracts are paid a fixed amount per patient for a given time period regardless of the amount of services provided.

capitation rate In managed care, this is the amount of revenue paid to the health-care provider per enrollee per month for services to be provided at risk.

capitation tax A fixed rate of tax on each individual; referred to as a "head tax."

capricious Willful, wanton, and deliberate; purposefully allowed or done in an irrational manner.

captain of the ship In the operating room, the physician/surgeon is considered by law to have total responsibility and authority over all activities and personnel, much as would the "captain of the ship." In a real sense, surgery could not be conducted smoothly under any other organizational structure. In *McConnel v. Williams* (361 PA. 355, 65 A2d 243 [1949]), it is stated that "he is in the same charge of those who are present and assisting him as is the *captain of a ship* over all on board." In the captain-of-the-ship doctrine, the person in charge makes all the decisions and is ultimately responsible for all those under his or her supervision. *See also respondeat superior.*

captive insurance company In health-care finance and managed care, this is a special insurance company owned and operated by one or more corporations for the purpose of protecting corporation interests and assets by insuring the owners against loss or damage.

carcino- Prefix meaning "cancer."

cardiac Refers to the heart.

cardiac arrest The sudden and unexpected cessation of effective heart functioning. *See also myocardial infarction.*

cardiac care unit (CCU) An intensive care unit specializing in the provision of treatment and continuous monitoring of patients who suffer from cardiac disorders.

cardiac catheterization The medical procedure where a tube, called a catheter, is inserted into an artery or a vein and is then directed into the heart for diagnostic or treatment reasons.

cardiac catheterization service A medical service that examines the circulatory system by using catheterization procedures through a vein or an artery to reach the interior of the heart. *See also cardiac catheterization unit/laboratory.*

cardiac catheterization unit/laboratory A special unit that conducts diagnostic procedures for cardiac patients. Procedures include introducing a catheter into the interior of the heart through a vein or an artery or by the direct needle puncture technique.

cardiac intensive care A specialized level of patient care found in most hospitals. Treatment is provided by registered nurses who are specially trained to monitor and provide nursing care to patients who have had heart seizure, heart attacks, or open-heart surgery. Life support and treatment equipment for heart patients or patients with related life-threatening conditions that require close comprehensive monitoring, observation, and care is used.

cardiac intensive care unit A special treatment unit within a hospital that provides inpatient care at a higher and more intense level than standard medical/surgical units for persons who are recovering from heart conditions who are treated under physician's orders and treatment plans. The treatment unit is staffed with highly trained nursing personnel. The unit is equipped with special patient monitors and support equipment for seriously ill heart patients who are suffering from heart attacks, open-heart surgery, congestive heart failure, and other serious heart ailments. Similar units may include patients with myocardial infarction, pulmonary care, and heart transplantation recovery.

cardiac monitor A specialized graph or oscilloscope that measures and records the heart's function.

cardiac rehabilitation Therapy, treatment, counseling, patient education, physical therapy, occupational therapy, nutrition education and therapy, special exercise programs, stress management, etc. done to assist in restoration of health in victims of cardiac injury. Restorative activities are conducted after open-heart surgery, angioplasty, and acute myocardial infarction and in high-risk patients who have experienced an adverse cardiovascular event.

cardiac surveillance unit *See cardiac care unit.*

cardiac technician *See cardiology technician.*

cardio- Prefix meaning "heart."

cardiologists A physician with a specialty in the diagnosis and treatment of cardiovascular diseases and disorders.

cardiology services The variety of medical services providing for the diagnosis and treatment of patients with cardiovascular diseases and disorders.

cardiology technician An allied health professional trained to perform diagnostic cardiac testing under the supervision of a physician. Tests are noninvasive and may include electrocardiography, vector cardiography, stress testing, and echocardiography.

cardiopulmonary resuscitation (CPR) Administration of external artificial heart and lung action to the victim of an event of cardiac and/or respiratory arrest that includes two major resuscitation activities: artificial ventilation and closed-chest cardiac massage.

cardiopulmonary technician An allied health professional trained to perform a wide range of tests related to the functions of the heart/lung system. This individual assists in cardiac catheterization, cardiac resuscitation, and the treatment and rehabilitation of heart/lung patients, including their postoperative care and outpatient testing.

cardiopulmonary technology An allied health profession involved in the diagnosis, treatment, and testing of heart and lung functioning and related treatment and therapeutic services. This includes the operation of heart/lung machines for extracorporeal circulation, assisting in cardiac catheterization, cardiac resuscitation, and postoperative care and monitoring of heart/lung patients.

cardiovascular disease The number one cause of death in the United States, related to all conditions or illness resulting from disease states within the heart, arteries, veins, and all facets of the vascular system. Also a specialty of medicine in the branch of internal medicine that diagnoses and treats all diseases related to the heart, arteries, veins, and all other aspects of the vascular system.

cardiovascular perfusionist The allied health professional who operates the heart/lung machine during cardiopulmonary (heart-lung) bypass surgery performed to repair defects of the heart or large blood vessels. Specialized experience combined with advanced knowledge of anatomy, pathology, physiology, pharmacology, biochemistry, hematology, cardiology, and surgery are needed to recognize and deal with problems associated with the equipment, surgery, or patient's condition. Perfusionists may also be required to use the heart/lung machine to give anesthetics and other drugs on prescription and to control the body temperature of the patient. Perfusionists are employed by hospitals, surgeons, or professional health corporations. An umbrella term for cardiopulmonary technicians, cardiorespiratory technicians, cardiovascular technicians, and circulation technologists who perform the same general functions.

cardiovascular technician An allied health professional who assists in the testing and diagnosis of heart and circulatory system problems by operating the equipment used in making X rays, X-ray movies, and closed-circuit telecasts of the vascular and circulatory systems.

CARE Computerized Audit and Record Evaluation System. A medical records computerized record evaluation system.

care 1. Safekeeping, protection, or custody; watchful regard. 2. Attention or heed; to look after. In any health-care situation, a person must act with "reasonable care." 3. The attention, treatment, and assistance provided to patients by health-care providers, usually described by intensity, level, type, and amount provided.

care, ambulatory See ambulatory care.

CARE Coalition A special service used to identify problems of vulnerable elderly persons and to develop programs to meet their needs. The service often works closely with Area Agencies on Aging.

care, custody or control exclusion A phrase appearing in the insurance contract that is placed there in an attempt to reduce or eliminate liability for any property that is in the insured's care, custody, or control.

care, emergency See emergency care.

caregiver Any individual, professional or lay, who provides assistance, support, or care to a disabled or ill friend or relative. Lay caregivers are those with little or no formal health-care training who provide personal care and some medical care (under medical supervision) for an ill loved one.

caregiver markers and determinants In long-term care, seven factors of caregiving have been identified along with several elements that determine if the marker is active or needed. The seven markers with their determinants are as follows: 1) performing caregiving tasks; needs of the elder, role relationship, and perceived duty or obligation to provide care; 2) self-definition as a caregiver; doing caregiving tasks, role relationship, and role reversal; 3) performing personal care; needs of the elder, role relationship, and quality of interpersonal relationships; 4) seeking assistance and formal service use; needs of the elder, physical and psychological needs of the caregiver, perceptions of utility, and costs associated with use; 5) considering nursing home placement; physical needs of the elder and caregiver, psychological needs of the caregiver, and quality of the relationship; 6) nursing home placement; demographic characteristics of the elder, needs of the elder, needs of the caregiver, demands of caregiving, use of support services, and perceived obligation to provide care; and 7) termination of the caregiving role; death of the elder, recovery of the elder, and termination of the caregiving relationship. (By R. J. V. Montgomery, University of Kansas–Lawrence)

career development Those experiences and personal job and skill improvements that are undertaken by health-care professionals to advance their professional background and job effectiveness.

career goals Future health-care or health services positions one prepares for and strives to reach. Certain benchmarks, such as positions held or promotions achieved (e.g., a health administrator moving from an assistant administrator to a chief operating officer position and later to a hospital administrator position).

career path A sequential pattern of jobs that advances one toward his or her career goal and that forms one's career.

career plateau When a health-care worker is in a position that he or she does well but not well enough to be promoted yet not poorly enough to get demoted or terminated.

care, levels of See primary care; secondary care; tertiary care.

care plan A formal outline of activities, treatments, or procedures to be carried out by health-care personnel in a health-care facility on behalf of a patient. This plan is used to monitor and evaluate patient care and treatment needs and to assess patient progress. In direct patient care activities, this part of the medical record is a written set of activities that formally lays out the specific treatments, procedures, rehabilitative therapies, nursing care, medications, or other treatment activities required to assist the patient toward full recovery.

care, primary See primary care.

care, secondary See secondary care.

care team Under Medicare for home health care, this team includes the physician, pertinent members of the agency staff, the patient, and members of the family, all of whom assist in the health care of the patient.

care, tertiary See tertiary care.

carrier 1. A managed-care or insurance company that "carries" the insurance. Often referred to as "insurer," "underwriter," or "administrative agent." A type of financial company that determines risk to financial loss caused by insurance coverage (underwriter) and then administers various medical and life insurance plans and policies. The insurance company; the insurer; the managed-care health plan. 2. A commercial health insurer, a government agency, or a Blue Cross or Blue Shield plan that underwrites or administers programs that pay for health services. A carrier may, in some cases, provide services directly, but usually it administers claims submitted for or by its beneficiaries. 3. In public health and epidemiology, a person or an animal who is not ill but who harbors a disease and may or may not show the symptoms of the disease but can transmit it to others. A carrier contains, carries, spreads, or harbors an infectious organism. The infected person who harbors the disease-producing organism is absent of discernible clinical manifestation of the disease yet serves as a potential source of infection and disease transmission for other humans (or animals). The carrier condition can occur throughout the entire course of a disease or the course of the person's life and can be inapparent because the carrier may not be sick (called "healthy carriers"). Some carriers of certain diseases, such as Typhoid Mary, may be infected and can be carriers for their entire lives. Tuberculosis is another disease commonly known to have carriers, and some carriers can be cured of this condition. Typhoid Mary could have been cured by surgery (removal of the gallbladder was the treatment at the time), and if Mary had lived in modern times, antibiotics would be effectively used. Additionally, carriers have been found to have several different conditions or states in which they can be classified as carriers. Six types of carriers have been identified by the public health and medical fields: 1) active carrier: an individual who has been exposed to and harbors a disease-causing organism and has done so for some time even though recovered from the disease; 2) convalescent carrier: an individual who has been exposed to and harbors a disease-causing organism (pathogen) and is in the recovery phase of the course of the disease but is still infectious; 3) healthy carrier: an individual who has been exposed to and harbors a disease-causing organism (pathogen) but has not gotten ill or shown any of the symptoms of the disease. This could be referred to as a subclinical case; 4) incubatory carrier: an individual who has been exposed to and harbors a disease-causing organism (pathogen), is in the beginning stages of the disease, is showing symptoms, and has the ability to transmit the disease; this is the incubation period of the disease; 5) intermittent carrier: an individual who has been exposed to and harbors a disease-causing organism (pathogen) who can intermittently spread the disease or who can spread the disease at different periods or intervals; and 6) passive carrier: an individual who has been exposed to and harbors a disease-causing organism (pathogen) but has no signs or symptoms of the disease; same as a healthy carrier.

4. An organization employed to transport persons or property for hire, as in common carrier. In environmental health, trucks or trains are used to carry waste or hazardous materials and are usually specially approved carriers. *See also intermediary; third-party payer, Medicare; host.*

carrier replacement In insurance and managed care, this is where a single new or different insurance company steps in to take over the medical care coverage and contracts for a specific health-care provider or employer group while allowing for the consolidation of the employer group's risk and health-care utilization history and record.

carrier's lien The legal right to retain or hold items or property until all bills and costs have been paid.

carryback A tax law that allows the use of losses in the prior year on the current tax report to reduce taxes. Also referred to as "carryover."

carryback and carryforward The provision in tax law that allows a loss to be carried back to 3 previous years and forward to 5 succeeding years to offset operating income in each of those periods.

carryover *See carryback.*

cartel An association or a monopoly of companies doing the same or similar kinds of business. Often used to fix prices and control stocks.

case 1. A lawsuit; a dispute set for trial in a court. 2. Convincing evidence or grounds for a cause of action. 3. An appellate decision. 4. A specific disease or illness (or a combination of diseases) or mental, emotional, or social problems that are being studied, treated, and followed by a health-care provider. 5. In epidemiology, an individual in a study population, a subject, a person with a diagnosed disease, a medical record, a patient, or any person identified as having the disease being investigated.

casebook A published book of written judicial opinion and facts of legal cases. These books are used mostly in the teaching of law.

case comparison study *See case control study.*

case control study In epidemiology, this is a study in which groups of individuals are selected because they do (the cases) or do not (the controls) have the disease being studied. The groups are compared with respect to their past, existing, or future characteristics, which may prove relevant to the disease or disease causation to determine which of the characteristics differ and how they differ.

case fatality rate The number of persons getting a disease or condition who die from that disease or condition. The formula for case fatality rate follows:

$$\frac{\text{Number of deaths from a disease or condition in a specific time period}}{\text{Number of diagnosed cases of the disease or condition in the same time period}} \times 1,000$$

case fatality ratio The numbers of deaths from a specific disease in a certain period with the disease that occurred in that period. A ratio, rather than a rate, is sometimes figured because some deaths could be the result of episodes that began at an earlier time.

case history Information gathered on an individual, usually used in the practice of psychology, psychiatry, and medicine.

case history study *See case control study.*

case-in-chief The main evidence acquired for and presented by one party of a lawsuit (does not include evidence presented in opposition on the other party's side).

case incurred In managed care or health insurance, claims that originated, and for which the insurance company is liable, during a given period.

case law Law based on judicial decisions that set precedents for future cases; recorded judicial decisions.

case management 1. In long-term care, this is to design an appropriate package of services for needy persons, elderly, or those recently discharged from a hospital and to ensure that a delivery system is in place to provide the services. Case management involves coordinating those resources available to assist a client, purchasing services on the client's behalf, or authorizing expenditures. 2. In managed care, to identify health plan members who have special health-care needs. A plan is formulated, and actions are initiated and implemented that efficiently utilize health-care resources while achieving optimum patient outcome in the most cost-effective manner. The process utilizes health-care resources and professionals and is implemented to achieve the optimum patient outcome in the most cost-effective manner. Social service personnel are often the key professionals in developing case management plans. The coordination of medical care to patients to ensure that the appropriate type, level, and amount of services and care are delivered while containing costs of rendering care. 3. The primary care health-care provider coordinates medically necessary care and assures continuity of care for Medicaid enrollees. This responsibility includes referral; development of a treatment plan; consultation; ordering of therapy; admission to hospitals; follow-up care; prior approval of referred services; and locating, coordinating, and monitoring all standards of practice and periodicity schedules established for health plans. *See conservator; long-term-care case management.*

case management and channeling A service that helps link the patient being discharged from the hospital to various long-term-care or posthospitalization services or facilities to ensure continuity of care. This service provides patients with a discharge assessment, social service plan development, and follow-up monitoring.

case manager 1. A professional in the health or human service areas who works with patients, health-care providers, families, and third-party payers to coordinate, administer, and arrange for the least-costly set of services needed to take care of a needy or an elderly individual at home and/or in a community setting. 2. In health-care settings, this is a health-care professional who coordinates and manages health-care delivery by finding all services deemed necessary to provide the patient with a plan that is medically necessary, the most appropriate, and the least costly while ensuring succession of care and services usually done by social workers, nurses, or other human service personnel outside the acute-care setting. Case managers are usually nurses, social workers, or physicians who coordinate health services needed by patients with health-care providers, insurance companies, managed-care plans, and other health-care facilities, such as nursing homes, as well as community-based services, such as home health agencies or home-delivered meals, all done to ensure continuity of care and that appropriate medical care is provided, necessary, and cost-effective.

case method of study A teaching method used in some aspects of law school, business school, and health-care administration programs and in certain aspects of nursing and medical schools. Used as a teaching experience to present real-life or fictitious occurrences or situations to allow students to use their training and sharpen their analytical skills prior to actual experience.

case mix 1. The distribution and different types of patients cared for in a health-care facility. The age, type of patient, type of illness or injury, source of payment, acuity, severity of illness, intensity of care needed, utilization of services, types and amount of testing and treatment needed, and diagnosis-specific makeup of a health service or program's workload determine and affect the mix of patients in a hospital or other health-care facility. 2. The type and frequency of patient admissions reflecting the needs for different hospital resources. The types of patients as defined by diagnosis, disease, procedure, method of payment, age, and acuity treated in a hospital, nursing home, or other health-care facility. A case mix determination is achieved by counting and aggregating different types and groups of patients who share one or more types of characteristics. The frequency of hospital admissions and length of stay influenced by the intensity of care needed, the severity of illness, and the diagnosis reflect the different needs and use of the health-care resources in the hospital. 3. Case mix directly influences the length of stay, the intensity of care offered, and the cost and scope of the services provided by a hospital or other health program. In most health-care facilities, case mix varies slightly but generally remains fairly constant.

case mix complexity Describes the extreme diversity and variety of patients (illnesses) seen by hospitals or physicians. *See case mix index.*

case mix index (CMI) A single number that compares the overall complexity of the hospital's Medicare patients to the complexity of the average for all U.S. hospitals. The CMI is the amount by which the cost of treating the average Medicare patient in a hospital varies from the comparable cost for all hospitals. The higher the index, the more complex the institution's patient mix and the greater its Medicare payment, all other elements being equal. Numbers over 1.000 reflect a case mix more complex than the average. Most hospitals fall between .8000 and 1.200. The Health Care Financing Administration establishes the CMI for each hospital by evaluating a 20% sample of inpatient bills collected from each hospital and maintaining that information in the NEDPAR file, which has been classified into diagnosis-related groups (DRGs). Patients are classified by being assigned to one of several classes or categories, and each class or category is given a weight that is proportional to the average cost of treating each patient in that class or category. The case mix index formula follows:

$$\frac{\text{Proportion of patients falling into that class} + \text{Weight assigned to that class}}{\text{Total numbers in the patient class}}$$

case mix management 1. Coordinating and balancing facility resources with the types of patients being admitted to the health-care facility with regard to their effect on reimbursement from third-party payers. 2. In long-term-care and nursing home facilities, the attempt to acquire certain types of patients for that facility as the focus of the institution (e.g., a nursing home administrator may accept only private-pay patients).

case mix management information system The computer software and hardware used to access, analyze, and manage the case mix of a health-care facility or service.

case mix payment A system of reimbursement that takes into account the level of illness, disease, condition, method of payment, and common traits of each patient. Each patient is assessed at a standard time interval and is to be assured of receiving appropriate services to meet his or her needs. An average patient profile is developed for each health-care facility or unit. In long-term care, each facility is reimbursed on the average patient profile, and an average rate for all Medicaid residents in that facility is the basis for reimbursement.

case mix severity The extent or degree of illness found in different classes, categories, or types of patients, reflecting the level and type of care needed to treat and care for them, and the resulting additional costs required to care for the more ill patients. *See case severity.*

case mix system A computer software system that merges clinical data with financial information on a patient-by-patient basis, projecting the cost of treating a certain type of patient and diagnosis (DRG) as well as the charges of the physician, cost center, tests completed, clinical department, procedures, etc.

case of first impression *See impression, case of first.*

case referent study *See case control study.*

case severity It has been found that one of the best measures of case severity is ALOS (average length of stay) in the hospital. The longer the average length of stay, the greater the average severity of illness. Average length of stay can also be affected by other factors, such as the demand for hospital beds. The higher the occupancy rate, the shorter the ALOS. Following this logic, ALOS is adjusted to take out differences in pressure for beds (occupancy-corrected ALOS) by use of the following equation: $A^* = (00)$, where A^* is the ALOS corrected for differences in pressure for beds. Then the hospital's death rate is adjusted for differences in case severity by the following equation using the severity-adjusted death rate (SADR): $SADR = 100 \; DR. \; 0.94 \; (A^* - A^*)$. The SADR is the final measure of quality of medical care. *See Medicare case mix index; case mix index.*

cases treated The number of patients cared for by a health facility during a year. Inpatient discharges and outpatient visits can be combined into an aggregate weighted index of overall hospital output.

case summary In medical records, this is a clear and concise written review of the diagnosis, treatment, and prognosis of a patient and his or her condition. Included in the case summary are the patient's medical history related to the current condition, physical exam results, diagnostic and test findings, treatment and procedures, care plans, recommendations, and the health-care provider's clinical interpretations.

cash basis accounting In health-care finance, this is an accounting method that calculates income on the basis of receivables and deductible expenses (distinguished from accrual basis accounting).

cash budget In health-care finance and budgeting, this is a short-term financial planning tool. This financial statement is prepared on a month-by-month basis and includes cash receipts and disbursements anticipated to be received by the health-care organization during the coming year. This budget can assist in determining when surpluses are available and if some form of additional financing might be necessary.

cash cycle In health-care finance and budgeting, this is the time period between the delivery of services and the receipt of cash that was generated by the business transaction.

cash flow In health-care finance and budgeting, this is a measure of a health-care organization's liquidity that consists of profit plus depreciation less additional investment in working capital. Actual money taken in by a health-care organization—not what is owed but what is received and on hand. Cash outflows are also a part of the cash flow cycle.

cash flow/total debt ratio In health-care finance and budgeting, this is a leverage ratio used to monitor a health-care organization's ability to remain solvent and retire debt. The ratio is calculated by dividing cash flow (profit plus depreciation) by all debt (current liabilities plus long-term debt).

cash forecast (budget) In health-care finance and budgeting, this is an estimate of the amount of cash expected to be received in a given period of time, the amount to be spent, and the anticipated balance of cash to be left at the end of the budget period.

cash indemnity benefits In managed care and insurance, these are amounts of money paid to the owners of a medical insurance policy for care received. The treatment or care is verified by filing a claim with the insurance company. The cash can be sent to the insured person directly, or the money can be assigned to be paid to the health-care provider. The amount paid may or may not fully reimburse the enrollee/insured person for costs incurred.

cash operating fund In health-care finance, this is the amount of money usually maintained as unrestricted funds in the health-care facility's bank account for the operation of the facility. Money that is restricted by the donor to certain activities is accounted for in different, separate accounts from unrestricted operating funds.

cash payment option In managed care and health-care finance, this is a nonforfeiture option by which the policy owner receives the cash value of a policy in a single payment.

cash premium accounting system In managed care and health-care finance, this is an accounting approach used to inform the health-care plan's main office of the amount collected on each policy. The health-care plan updates the policy record to reflect the collections and then updates the main collection records.

cash surrender value The cash value of an insurance policy if surrendered to the insurance company that issued the policy (usually applies to life insurance). Also called "cash value."

cassette 1. In radiography, a lightproof box containing X-ray film used to take the X ray. The box contains special screens that fluoresce under the X rays and cause the lineage to appear on the film. 2. A small case containing film, magnetic tape, or videotape.

cast A mixture of plaster of paris (or gypsum) and water and stockinette that is placed around an injured or broken bone or body part to immobilize the injured part.

casualty Any injury caused by an accident.

casuistry A technique for solving cases of right and wrong on the basis of principles of ethics; subtle but evasive reasoning used to determine right from wrong or questions of duty.

CAT scanner *See computerized axial tomography.*

cata- Prefix meaning "down."

catalog In health-care information management, this is a listing of files on a computer disk.

cataract A lens of the eye that is no longer transparent. Its development is associated with the loss of blood supply to the lens caused by advanced age or abnormally high exposures to ultraviolet light.

catastrophe policy *See major medical.*

catastrophic anxiety Anxiety associated with organic brain syndrome. The patient is aware of his or her condition yet can do nothing about it or cannot accept it, which in turn causes overwhelming anxiety.

catastrophic care Advanced medical and nursing care services provided to patients on an inpatient basis for prolonged critical illnesses or injuries that are extremely costly to treat. Bills have been introduced into the U.S. Congress to help curtail the costs of such illnesses for which the average person cannot pay. Specialized medical insurance is available to cover such extensive and costly care. *See major medical.*

catastrophic illness Any illness that generates high costs and large expenses. Any sickness in which hospital and other inpatient costs exceed a certain percentage of annual net income, or the amount of such income in excess of public assistance levels, whichever sum is smaller.

catastrophic insurance Insurance against catastrophic illness. Also referred to as "major medical insurance." In managed-care and health-care finance, an alternative in insurance for a catastrophic event where a specified minimum number of claims results from a single occurrence (e.g., when two or more claims result from a major catastrophic event, such as an airplane crash, an earthquake, or a hurricane, where the reinsurer pays losses in excess of the plan's deductible). A reinsurer's liability is limited to a maximum amount per catastrophe. *See also catastrophic health insurance.*

catastrophic medical insurance Medical insurance that provides protection against the high cost of treating severe or lengthy illnesses or disabilities. Generally, such policies cover all, or a specified percentage of, medical expenses above a deductible amount. The deductible is paid out of pocket and is the responsibility of the insured or of another insurance policy up to a maximum limit of liability. There is usually no maximum amount of coverage under these plans; however, many include some co-insurance. *See also major medical; co-insurance.*

catatonia A mental state characterized by muscular rigidity and immobility, usually associated with the schizophrenic form of psychosis.

catchment area A geographic area defined and served by a health facility on the basis of such factors as population distribution, natural geographic boundaries, and transportation accessibility. The geographic area from which a managed-care plan or an HMO draws its clientele. All residents of the area needing the services of the program are usually eligible for them, although eligibility may also depend on such additional criteria as age or income. Residents of the area may or may not be limited to services other than those obtainable from the program. Used in mental health care to identify a geographical area that a mental health services facility includes or has responsibility for. *See also community psychiatry.*

categorical assistance Government financial assistance programs that have requirements other than financial need (e.g., Medicare, which is determined by age).

categorical grant Funds allocated by a grant that are restricted to certain areas of interest such as services for the elderly or for the training of minority students.

categorically needy Persons who are members of certain categories of groups eligible to receive public assistance and are economically needy. As used in Medicaid, this refers to a person who is aged, blind, disabled, or a member of a family with children under 18 (or 21, if in school) in which one parent is absent, incapacitated, or unemployed and, in addition, meets specified income and resource requirements that vary by state. In general, categorically needy individuals are persons receiving cash assistance under the AFDC or SSI program. In addition, a state may include additional specified groups, such as foster children, as categorically needy. A state may restrict its Medicaid coverage to this group or may cover additional persons who meet the categorical requirements as medically needy.

categorically related In the Medicaid program, the requirements (other than income and resources) that an individual must meet to be eligible for Medicaid benefits. Specifically, any individual eligible for Medicaid must fall into one of the four main categories of those who are eligible for welfare cash payments: aged, blind, disabled (as defined under the SSI program, Title XVI of the Social Security Act), or a member of a family with dependent children in which one parent is absent, incapacitated, or unemployed (as defined under the AFDC program, Title IV of the Social Security Act). After the determination is made that an individual is categorically related, income and resources tests are then applied to determine if the individual is poor enough to be eligible for assistance (categorically needy). As a result of this requirement, single persons and childless couples who are not aged, blind, or disabled and families headed by males in states that do not cover such groups under their AFDC programs cannot receive Medicaid coverage no matter how poor they are.

categorical program Originally, a health program that concerned itself with research, education, control, or treatment of only one or a few specific diseases but now more generally used for a program concerned with only part instead of all the population or health system. It is also used in a more general way to refer to any existing program that the federal government feels it should cease to support.

category Used in classification activities. Classification may have one or several types or levels under a single label. In epidemiological data analysis and in the tabulation of information or variables into contingency tables, categories are used to organize the information and data. *See contingency tables.*

catharsis A healthful and therapeutic release accomplished by bringing thoughts into awareness from the repressed area of the unconscious; the expression of repressed or pent-up emotions.

catheter 1. A plastic or rubber tube that is inserted into the bladder to allow the urine to flow out. 2. Any tube used to allow passage into a structure of the body for the purpose of injecting or withdrawing fluid.

catheterization The act of inserting a tube into a structure of the body for the purpose of injecting or withdrawing fluid. The insertion of a tube into the urinary tract to allow the outflow of urine. Catheterization can be done to other areas of the body (e.g., cardiac catheterization).

catheterize To participate in the act of inserting a catheter into a hollow of the body, usually the urinary tract, to allow fluid to pass from the organ via a plastic tube.

cathexis Conscious or unconscious attachment of emotions and significant thought to an idea or object.

cathode ray tube (CRT) An electronic vacuum tube containing a screen on which output data of a computer can be displayed in graphic form or by character representation. It depicts letters and numbers similar to the way images are projected on the tube of a television set. Cathode ray tubes also are used in cardiac monitors, CT scanners, and related technology.

causa (Lat.) Cause; purpose; motive; reason.

causal forecasting In health service delivery and health-care administration, this is the process of predicting the cause of utilization of health services on the basis of objective data as well as educated and experienced-based subjective judgments regarding the factors influencing utilization of health-care services.

causality In epidemiology, this is the process of studying a series of events leading to a disease outbreak in a community that involves developing a relationship of causes to effects that produces results; developing an association between a cause and the onset of disease, condition, injury, or death; developing a cause-effect relationship; relating causes to effects they produce. Dealing with cause-effect relationships to ascertain how different events or circumstances are related and relying on the concepts of "necessary" and "sufficient." *See cause; causation; necessary and sufficient cause.*

causa mortis (Lat.) In thinking about the cause of death or an approaching death.

causation In epidemiology and health promotion, this refers to those factors that contribute to disease or conditions in a population. Cause-effect association is used to study and determine how different events, exposures, or disease-causing situations relate to one another.

Several factors have been identified in disease causation: predisposing factors, enabling factors, precipitating factors, and reinforcing factors (see these terms in this dictionary). *See cause; causality; risk factors.*

cause 1. An action in court. 2. Legal procedures by which a party gains its claim, lawsuit, or case. 3. That which produces an effect. 4. Motive or reason enough; grounds for a case; producing an effect. 5. In epidemiology, something that, if prevented, removed, or eliminated, will prevent the occurrence of the event in question and/or, if permitted, introduced, or maintained, will be followed by the event in question. A necessary cause is a cause that must exist if a given event is to occur but may not itself result in the event. A sufficient cause is one that is inevitably followed by a given event or the existence of a given thing.

cause-effect relationships *See cause; causality; causation; association; necessary and sufficient cause.*

cause fatality rate The number of deaths from a certain disease or specific cause per 1000 or 10,000 reported cases of the same disease, condition, or disorder.

cause of action Having enough evidence and facts to support a lawsuit. All four aspects of a cause of action are required to be present or to exist: 1) a duty owed, 2) duty breached, 3) harm or damage done, and 4) proximate cause.

cause of death 1. In U.S. Public Health Service reporting of national mortality statistics, every death is attributed to one underlying condition on the basis of information reported on the death certificate and utilizing the international rules for selecting the underlying cause of death from the reported conditions.

cause of death, competing *See competing cause of death.*

cause-of-death ranking This ranking is based on a list of 72 selected causes of death. The list was adapted from one of the special lists for mortality tabulations recommended by the World Health Organization for use with the ICD-9. Two group titles—major cardiovascular diseases and symptoms, signs, and ill-defined conditions—are not ranked. In addition, category titles that begin with the word "other" are not ranked. The remaining category titles are ranked according to the number of deaths to determine the leading causes of death. When one of the titles that represents a subtotal is ranked (e.g., accidents and adverse effects), its component parts (in this case, motor vehicle accidents and all other accidents and adverse effects) are not ranked.

causes of death in the United States The U.S. Public Health Service, National Center for Health Statistics, reports the leading causes of death in the United States on a regular basis. The leading causes of death are listed in order of frequency, with the highest frequencies listed first, on the basis of the ICD-9-CM:

1. Diseases of the heart
2. Cerebrovascular disease (stroke)
3. Malignant neoplasms (cancer)
4. Chronic obstructive pulmonary diseases
5. Pneumonia and influenza
6. Tuberculosis
7. Chronic liver disease and cirrhosis
8. Diabetes mellitus
9. Accidents and adverse events
10. Motor vehicle accidents
11. Suicide
12. Homicide and legal intervention
13. Complications of pregnancy, childbirth, and puerperium
14. Malignant neoplasm of peritoneum and pleura
15. Coal worker's pneumoconiosis
16. Asbestosis
17. Silicosis

cause-specific death rate The number of deaths from a specific disease or cause in a specific period of time, usually 1 year, per 1000, 10,000 or 100,000 population and usually estimated in the middle of the year.

caveat (Lat.) Warning. A notice filed with the proper legal authorities ordering a named party to cease activities until the issue is heard in court.

caveat emptor (Lat.) Let the buyer beware. A term that suggests that the buyer is responsible to determine if goods that are bought are good or work properly.

caveat venditor (Lat.) Let the seller beware. A term that suggests that the seller is responsible for deficiencies in goods or products sold.

CBO Congressional Budget Office.

CC *See complicating and comorbid.*

CCA Circuit Court of Appeals.

CCC Council on Clinical Classifications.

CCEC Community Clinic/Emergency Center.

CCME Commission on Continuing Medical Education. *See also Coordinating Council on Medical Education.*

CCRC Continuing care retirement community. *See life care centers.*

CCRN Certified critical care nurse.

CCU See *cardiac care unit*.

CD See *certificate of deposit*.

CDC Centers for Disease Control. The name of this agency has changed to Centers for Disease Control and Prevention, but the acronym CDC is retained. See *Centers for Disease Control and Prevention*.

CE Continuing education.

cease and desist A legal order to discontinue, to stop, and to do no more; a directive to quit. An order from an administrative agency that is similar to an injunction.

cede 1. To assign. 2. To yield; to admit; to grant. 3. To give up or surrender. 4. To resign.

ceding insurance company A health-care organization seeking reinsurance. Also called a "direct writing company." See *reinsurance*.

CEI Continuing education inspector.

ceiling cap In health-care finance, this is the highest allowable cost payable by a state under the Medicaid program.

cell 1. A storage unit in a computer. 2. In biology, the structural and functional unit of an organism consisting of protoplasm, a nucleus, and a cell wall.

Celsius A metric system temperature scale in which zero degrees equals the freezing point of water and 100 degrees its boiling point. Also called "centigrade."

censor 1. To review, examine, eliminate, or stop; to put under censorship. 2. One who conducts censorship.

censorship 1. To censor; the act of censoring. 2. Denial of freedom of speech or freedom of the press. Not all censorship, however, is necessarily a violation of the First Amendment.

census 1. To estimate or assess. 2. In the United States, a total count of the population is conducted every 10 years. The census count is used for reapportionment as well as funding of social health programs that are based on populations, especially of underrepresented minorities. Public health issues such as sewage disposal, population density, and housing are ascertained through the questions asked in the census. 3. The total number of persons present as inpatients in a health-care facility or unit in a given period of time. 4. In managed care, a listing of subscribers and their dependents by sex and age that is submitted to health plans. See also *average daily census*.

census, average daily See *average daily census; midnight census*.

census, boarder The actual number of persons receiving food services in a hospital at a given time.

census days The total number of days of care rendered to inpatients by a health-care facility during a specific time period (usually 1 year).

census divisions The division of the United States and its territories into nine regions as determined by the U.S. Department of Commerce, Bureau of the Census.

census, inpatient The actual number of inpatients in the hospital receiving health-care services for a specified period of time.

Center for Healthcare Ethics A subsidiary of the St. Joseph Health System, this organization is to create programs and materials for recognizing, analyzing, and resolving ethical problems at the individual, institutional, and societal levels. It assists health-care organizations with their ethics committees, provides current information on ethical issues in health care, and improves the process by which ethical decisions are made. Headquartered in Orange, California, and publisher of the quarterly journal *Ethical Currents*.

Center for Research in Ambulatory Health Care Administration (CRAHCA) The research organization of the Medical Group Management Association. This charitable, scientific, and educational organization is devoted to the development of programs and services that contribute to the professional competence and personal growth of ambulatory health-care administrators. The center is funded through grants and contracts from private foundations, governmental agencies, and the private sector.

Centers for Disease Control and Prevention (CDC) A key organization within the Department of Health and Human Services serving as a focal point for disease control and prevention and public health activities. The center provides facilities and services for the investigation, prevention, and control of diseases; supports quarantine and other activities that prevent the introduction of communicable diseases from foreign countries; conducts research into the epidemiology, laboratory diagnosis, prevention, and treatment of infectious and other controllable diseases at the community level; provides grants for work on venereal disease, immunization against infectious diseases, and disease control programs; and sets standards for laboratories. Activities focus on improvement of the health-care system through emphasis on prevention and health education and through investigation, surveillance, and control operations, including training of state and local health workers in specific disease-control techniques or methodologies rather than through direct treatment.

centigrade A metric system temperature scale in which zero degrees equals the freezing point of water and 100 degrees its boiling point. Also called "Celsius."

central city The older, middle, first-established area of a city that once had fine buildings and homes but since has deteriorated, often resulting in old apartment buildings, hotels, and low-rent housing, thus attracting low-income, poor, and deprived persons. These circumstances in turn create many special social, crime, public health, and health-care delivery problems. *See metropolitan statistical area.*

centralized administration In health administration, this is an organizational structure approach that assists in understanding an organization's approach to the division of labor; the degree to which an organization resists delegating a large degree of authority, responsibility, and decision making. A centralized organization usually has a fairly tall organizational chart and is very bureaucratic in its organizational structure. *See decentralization.*

centralized services Those services of a hospital or major health-care organization, with diversified and community-based services, that are managed from the single main location to improve coordination, reduce costs, improve efficiency, provide continuous quality improvement, and provide managerial control.

centralized filing system A system of medical records maintenance in which all information is filed in one central location.

central location intercept In health-care research, this is a planning survey approach that conducts interviews using a sample of convenience by selecting people on the street or in a mall or shopping center to represent the opinion of those likely to be the recipients of a program being planned.

central medical supply *See central supply.*

central practice and review committee In managed care, this is a group of physicians who assemble to discuss medical issues, practice approaches, and policy issues.

central processing unit (CPU) A piece of computer hardware that supervises the transfer of stored data, controls math computations and logical decision making, and directs the action of input and output units.

central service department One of the ancillary or support service departments of a hospital that maintains an inventory of sterile goods and equipment for the hospital and that provides for the sterilization, distribution, and storage of the sterile equipment and supplies. Also referred to as "central supply."

central service technician An allied health worker who sterilizes, maintains, and inventories medical and surgical instruments and other hospital supplies.

central sterile supply *See central supply.*

central supply The service or department of a health-care facility that washes, sterilizes, and packages materials, equipment sheets, instruments, gowns, bandages, and dressings for use in the operating rooms or other parts of the hospital where sterile materials are required. Central supply may also distribute intravenous solutions.

central supply technology An allied health program that prepares persons to work in central supply departments in hospitals. The program trains persons to adjust, clean, sterilize, and assemble sterile hospital equipment, instruments, and supplies. This technologist is trained to follow set prescribed procedures and techniques in the handling and storing of instruments and supplies, including inspection, evaluation, and purchasing of equipment and materials. The technologist is also responsible for the distribution, receiving, and inventory of sterile equipment and supplies as well as controlling and handling contaminated items for reuse and resterilization.

central tendency 1. Average; middle. 2. Leaning to or tending to fall in the center, middle, or average part or area.

CEO *See chief executive officer.*

cephalo- Prefix meaning "head."

CER Continuing education reviewer. *See capital expenditure review.*

CERCLA *See Comprehensive Environmental Response, Compensation and Liability Act.*

cerebro- Prefix meaning "brain."

cerebrovascular accident (CVA) A blockage of the blood vessels serving the brain (usually the cerebrum), causing blood supply to be cut off from the tissue and resulting in tissue death. *See also stroke.*

certifiable Something that can be certified.

certificate 1. A printed or written document or statement; assurance or testimony that a formal requirement has been completed; a promise kept or qualification met. To attest to or to verify through the presentation of a special form or document stating the accomplishment. 2. In managed care or insurance, a document that is presented to each member indicating the type and amount of coverage and other contractual agreements and identifying the beneficiary.

certificate of authority (COA) An operating license issued by a state that authorizes a health maintenance organization to be established, become incorporated, and conduct business.

certificate of coverage (COC) In managed care, this is literature describing health plan benefits, guidelines, and coverage. This is required by state law and is to set forth in detail the coverage provided by a health plan or HMO under the contract or policy agreement issued to the employer group. Each employee/member is to receive a certificate.

certificate of deposit (CD) In health-care finance, this is a negotiable note issued by a bank or savings and loan company that earns interest. This indicates that the person or corporation named in the instrument has deposited a specified amount of money and that the interest and full amount is payable to the person making the note or its bearer.

certificate of insurance (COI) In managed care, this is a document delivered to the insured that summarizes the benefits and principal provisions of the group plan affecting the insured. In group insurance, a statement issued to a member of a group that certifies that an insurance contract covering the member has been written and that contains a summary of the terms applicable to that member.

certificate of need (CON) A certificate issued by a governmental health planning agency to an individual or organization proposing to construct or modify a health facility, offer a new or different health service, or incur a major financial expenditure. The CON recognizes that such a service or facility is actually necessary for those for whom it is intended. The CON requirement is meant to control expansion of facilities and services in the public interest by preventing excessive or duplicative development of facilities and services. CONs were developed and implemented by the former health systems agencies (former local planning bodies under P.L. 93-641), which required that recommendations be made to the state agencies regarding proposed institutional health services within their areas or state. Several states still maintain CON programs, which may be required for bank loans for new construction or new health facilities. CON is required and issued by some states for health-care franchises for new services and for new construction or renovation.

certificate of need controls Regulations intended to contain rising medical care costs.

certification A mechanism by which a nongovernmental agency or association (usually a professional association) grants recognition to an individual who has met certain predetermined qualifications specified by that agency or association. Such qualifications may include 1) graduation from an accredited or approved educational program, 2) acceptable performance on an examination, and/or 3) completion of a given amount of work experience. Certification is essentially synonymous with accreditation, except that certification is usually applied to individuals and accreditation to institutions. Because certification programs are generally nongovernmental, they do not exclude the uncertified from practice as do licensure programs.

certification by HCFA A statement by the Health Care Financing Administration (HCFA) that a health-care facility has been reviewed, is up to standards, and meets the conditions of participation in federal government health-care financial reimbursement programs such as Medicare and Medicaid.

certification for Medicaid A recommendation by a survey team attesting to the compliance of health-care providers and/or facilities with the conditions of participation and conditions of coverage as set forth for Medicaid participation by the Health Care Financing Administration of the Social Security Administration of the U.S. government.

certification for Medicare A recommendation by a survey team to the federal agency attesting to the compliance of health-care providers and/or facilities with the conditions of participation and conditions of coverage in Medicare as set forth by the Health Care Financing Administration of the Social Security Administration of the U.S. government.

certification of nursing homes Long-term-care facilities are certified for participation in financial reimbursement by the Medicare and/or Medicaid programs.

certified Possessing a certificate; meeting the requirement of certification; officially passed, approved, or vouched for. Passing off standards and evaluation procedures required of those wishing to possess a certificate.

certified environmental inspector (CEI) An entry-level public health and environmental health worker who inspects residential and commercial properties for compliance with health and safety regulations. Inspections include inspection of property and collecting data and information to present a comprehensive report to the client as to the health and safety status of the premises.

certified environmental reviewer (CER) The highest level of public health and environmental health worker who interprets, understands, and makes decisions on the basis of environmental data provided from CES and CEI workers in an environmental assessment report.

certified environmental specialist (CES) A public health and environmental health worker experienced in environmental professional work who can provide a range of environmental services. Two years of experience and passage of a certification exam are required for certification.

certified health education specialist (CHES) An individual trained and experienced in the field of health education who is credentialed in the field as a result of demonstrating knowledge and skill in health education in a competency-based set of criteria that has been established by the National Commission of Health Education Credentialing (NCHEC). *See National Commission of Health Education Credentialing; credentialism.*

certified home care program Most home health-care programs are associated with acute-care hospitals, or are freestanding visiting nursing associations, and receive reimbursement from various private insurance carriers and from Medicare and Medicaid. Home care is one of the health services of choice for discharged hospital patients because of reduced average length of stay. It is expected that, through nursing and rehabilitative services, recovery and the restoration of health will occur. Home care is available for persons of all ages, but a major portion of services is provided to elderly patients.

certified nurse aid program The original name of the certified nurse assistant program created by OBRA under Title 42 of the Code of Federal Regulations. Public Health Part 400 (Title 18, and 19). *See certified nurse assistant program.*

certified nurse assistant (CNA) An entry-level health-care worker who is one of the lowest level nursing care personnel working the health-care field. This person is certified and is most often utilized in long-term-care settings to carry out limited basic nursing functions under the direction of a registered nurse. This worker must have advanced nurse aid training, pass a test, and be certified by the state after meeting official requirements of the state licensing authority. This entry-level worker provides most of the nursing care provided in nursing home settings. They carry out nursing tasks delegated by LPN or RN personnel and usually include tasks such as bathing, feeding, toileting assistance, assisting with ambulation, bed making, helping residents transfer from beds to wheelchairs to toilets, taking pulses, blood pressure readings, respiration rates, temperatures, and collecting specimens. This person replaced the nurse aid, nursing assistant, or orderly in nursing homes and other long-term-care settings with the passage of OBRA law under Title XVIII (Medicare) of the Social Security Act.

certified nurse assistant program A specialized training program in long-term-care settings implemented to increase the level and quality of care to residents of nursing homes and other long-term-care facilities. This entry-level health-care worker is usually employed full time in a long-term-care facility and is required to meet certain minimal conceptual and theoretical learning requirements as well as demonstrate clinical skill competency. The training program is first approved by the state licensing authority and requires a combination of clinical skill training and classroom concepts and theoretical instruction. A supervised clinical experience, as well as a clinical skill competency exam, is required covering at least five clinical skill areas.

certified nurse midwife (CNM) An individual who is educated in the two disciplines of nursing and midwifery and who possesses evidence of certification according to the requirements of the American College of Nurse-Midwives. *See nurse midwife.*

certified professional in quality assurance (CPQA) In quality management, this is a person who has met the standards of, and has passed an examination for a credential in, quality assurance as determined by the National Association of Quality Assurance Professionals.

certified registered nurse anesthetist (CRNA) A graduate of an approved school of nursing who has first met state requirements and earned current registration by state licensing authorities as a registered nurse. The person then must graduate from an approved school of nurse anesthesia accredited by the Council on Accreditation of Educational Programs of Nurse Anesthetists, the nationally recognized accrediting body for schools of nurse anesthesia. While in this program, the student studies anatomy, physiology, biochemistry, pharmacology, and physics as they relate to anesthesia. The graduate must then show individual competency by passing a rigorous qualifying examination that makes the person eligible for certification by the Council on Certification of Nurse Anesthetists. To ensure the high-quality nursing and anesthesia care provided by a CRNA, a nurse anesthetist must be recertified every 2 years by the Council on Recertification of Nurse Anesthetists. This recertification is based on the fulfillment of continuing education requirements and other criteria. Due to their advanced education in the areas of respiratory and cardiopulmonary function, CRNAs often assist in the management and resuscitation of critical patients in intensive care, coronary care, and the emergency room.

certified respiratory therapy technician *See respiratory therapy technician.*

certified rural health clinic A facility that provides outpatient primary medical care and is eligible to receive Medicare and Medicaid reimbursement. "Rural" is designated by its location in a census-defined rural health manpower shortage area or medically underserved area and employment of a least one midlevel practitioner/physician extender (physician's assistant, nurse practitioner, or nurse midwife).

certified surgical technologist (CST) An allied health profession that requires members to meet the requirements of certification as set forth by the Liaison Council on Certification for Surgical Technologists, the certification board of the Association of Surgical Technologists.

certified trauma center An emergency care facility certified to provide emergency and specialized intensive care to critically ill and injured patients. Level I: a regional center that is capable of providing total care for every aspect of emergency medicine and injury treatment and that serves in a leadership role in trauma research, demonstration, and education; level II: a community center capable of providing emergency and injury care to all but the most severely injured patients who require highly specialized care (who are then referred to a level I trauma center; level III: a rural hospital with an emergency room that is capable of providing care to a large number of injury victims and can resuscitate and stabilize more severely injured patients so that they can be transported to higher-level trauma centers.

certify To attest to or to verify.

certiorari (Lat.) To make sure. A process that is similar to an appeal, wherein an appellate court, especially the U.S. Supreme Court, has the discretion to review a lower court's decision but is not required to do so.

cervico- Prefix meaning "neck."

CES Continuing education specialist.

cesarean section A surgical method of delivering a baby. When a medical or physical delivery complication does not allow the baby to come through the birth canal, the baby is surgically removed through the abdominal wall and uterus of the mother.

cession 1. To give something up. 2. To yield to force. 3. A voluntary surrender of property to a court or to creditors to avoid legal consequences. 4. Abandonment.

cesspool In environmental health and liquid waste management, this is the simplest form of primary treatment of sewage mostly found in rural areas. A large underground tank-type structure is constructed with a porous bottom and sides, often made of cinder blocks laid on their side, that lets the liquid wastewater filter into the surrounding ground while holding the solid waste. Periodically the tank must be cleaned out. If soil becomes clogged and is no longer porous, the tank is abandoned, closed, and filled in.

CEU *See continuing education unit.*

C.F.& I. or **C.I.F.** The price includes cost, freight, and insurance paid by the seller.

CFO *See chief financial officer.*

CFR *Code of Federal Regulations;* the publication containing federal administrative rules.

CHA Catholic Health Association of the United States. The name was changed from the Catholic Hospital Association.

chair The official presiding officer.

chairbound A patient or resident who is unable to get up and out of a chair without assistance or who is not ambulatory; restricted to a wheelchair. Also referred to as a "bed-chair patient."

chairside As used in the field of dentistry, the equivalent of "bedside."

challenge for cause A challenge of a prospective juror on the grounds of bias.

chamberlain An officer who is a treasurer.

champerty 1. An illegal agreement to accept a lawsuit of another person by buying or sharing the winnings of the suit. 2. Joint power or authority.

CHAMPUS A federally funded medical care program developed to provide health-care services and hospitalization coverage for dependents of former U.S. military and military personnel and dependents. *See Civilian Health and Medical Program of the Uniformed Services.*

CHAMPUS reform initiative The Department of Defense awards health plan contracts to care for retired military and their dependents. Under this program, enrollees may continue to use military treatment facilities or join a managed-care or an HMO plan. Claims for services or treatment are submitted to CHAMPUS claims administrative offices for reimbursement.

CHAMPVA *See Civilian Health and Medical Program of the Veterans Administration.*

change agents Those persons within a health-care organization who have the role of stimulating new and different managerial approaches or who influence or sway the actions of a group. Some are consultants, and some come from within the organization or group. A change agent's role can include diagnosing, planning, facilitating, and evaluating activities that assist in identifying issues or concerns and providing a means to deal with the issues.

change in parliamentary situation Relevant to formal health-care meetings or hearings, this is used to determine when a motion may be renewed or when the formal assembly might take a different position on a question in front of the assembly.

channels of infection The means through which infection enters the body. The usual channels are the respiratory tract, the digestive tract, or breaks in the exterior surfaces of the body.

CHAP Certified Hospital Admission Program. In managed care, some insurance companies use this program as a potential hospital utilization assessment program combining concurrent review and preadmission assessments used to determine medical necessity of hospital admission and length of stay.

chaplain A clergy member who performs religious functions and provides pastoral counseling to patients and their families in health-care settings.

chaplaincy service A service provided by some health-care facilities in the form of spiritual support and pastoral counseling for patients and families.

character 1. The sum of personality traits and modes of responses of an individual. 2. In computers, this is a single letter, number, or other symbol.

charge 1. To blame or accuse; to place liability on; to burden. 2. An injunction; an order. 3. A claim or an obligation. 4. The judge's instructions to a jury. 5. A formal accusation of a crime. 6. To take responsibility for. 7. The price or amount expected to be paid for services. *See also charges; costs.*

charge, covered In health-care finance, these are the charges for services provided to insured patients that are recognized as covered by the health insurance company.

charge, daily service In health-care finance, this is the actual amount a hospital charges for 1 day's stay in a hospital inpatient unit.

charge nurse 1. A registered or licensed practical (vocational) nurse in charge of a nursing unit (JCAHO accreditation of long-term-care facilities). 2. For Medicare certification purposes, a person who is 1) licensed by the state as a registered nurse or a practical (vocational) nurse. A practical nurse must be either a graduate of a state-approved school of practical (vocational) nursing or must have 2 years of appropriate experience following licensure by waiver as a practical (vocational) nurse. He or she must have achieved a satisfactory grade on a proficiency examination approved by the secretary or on a state licensure examination that the secretary finds at least equivalent to the proficiency examination, except that such determinations of proficiency shall not apply with respect to persons initially licensed by a state or seeking initial qualifications as a practical (vocational) nurse after December 31, 1977; 2) experienced in nursing service administration and supervision or who acquired such experience through formal staff development programs.

charge-based reimbursement The amount of money reimbursed to a hospital on the basis of the actual charges incurred during the hospital stay. *See cost-based reimbursement.*

charge-off 1. Writing off an item or money because of loss or depreciation. 2. In health-care finance, writing off the value of something in a health facility's records as a loss. When a debt becomes too difficult to collect or becomes a bad debt, it may be written off, or charged off. *See also bad debt.*

charge-out devices A file with cardboard ledgers that is filled out by one of the medical records staff to indicate the date and destination of a chart leaving the medical records department.

charges In health-care finance, prices assigned to units of medical service such as a visit to a physician or a day in a hospital. Charges for services may not be related to the actual costs of providing the services. Furthermore, the methods by which charges are related to costs vary substantially from service to service and institution to institution. Different third-party payers or managed-care programs may require different methods for determining either charges or costs. Charges for one service provided by an institution are often used to subsidize the costs of other services (cost shifting). Charges to one type or group of patients may also be used to subsidize the costs of providing services to other groups. *See also actual charge; allowable charge; cost shifting; customary charge; prevailing charge; reasonable charge; usual charge.*

charitable immunity A doctrine in use in a decreasing number of states that protects nonprofit or charitable hospitals and other health facilities from malpractice suits. This doctrine relies on and involves waiver of the patient's right to sue for negligence by accepting the charity; the basic unfairness, either assumed or stated, of applying a doctrine such as respondeat superior (which applies to commercial pursuits) to a nonprofit enterprise; and the increased financial demands on the assets of the charity that might result from adverse judgments. The following are exceptions to the rule of charitable immunity: a charity may be held liable for the negligence of an agent of the institution; a charity may be held liable to a stranger (e.g., one who is not a beneficiary); and, sometimes, a charity may be held liable only to the extent of its nontrust assets. The current trend is toward abolition of charitable immunity because the basis on which the doctrine was founded seems illogical and conflicting and deprives the injured of due process of law. Also, liability insurance is now more widely available than it was at the time the doctrine was put into use. *See also governmental immunity.*

charitable institution A nonprofit institution maintained by charity or public funds, usually for a specific reason or to benefit a specific group.

charitable trust Property, money, or real estate held by one party for the benefit of a hospital, school, nursing home, church, or charity.

charity allowance The reduced charge for health-care services for those who are indigent or medically indigent.

charity care 1. In hospital administration, these are patient charges that are not collectable because of the patient's inability to pay for health-care services received within the hospital. 2. The care given to patients by health-care providers when no payment is anticipated. Under the Hill-Burton Act, those hospitals that received Hill-Burton funds for hospital construction or renovation were required to give a certain amount of free care to those who needed it.

chart *See medical record.*

chart analysis The careful review and assessment of the entire medical record to identify gaps or missing information.

charter 1. Permission to start an organization; the document creating an organization. 2. Articles of incorporation and proper laws that are written into a legal instrument and give the right to incorporate. 3. A franchise. 4. To hire or lease a vehicle. 5. The contract used to create a lease.

chart of accounts In health-care finance and budgeting, this is a list of accounts and titles. Identified by numbers, a compilation of financial data concerned with the health-care organization's assets, liabilities, capital, revenue, and expenses.

chart-out guide A file, journal, or ledger used to record the date and name of the individual who has taken a medical record and the reason for its removal.

chattel Personal property other than land.

chattel mortgage In the development and construction of health facilities, a mortgage on personal money, items, or property.

chattel paper A legal document that shows a debt secured by collateral.

chattel, personal Any tangible personal article or personal property.

CHC Community health center.

CHD Coronary heart disease.

check-off In human resources management and labor union relations, this is a method through which union dues are directly collected from a worker's paycheck.

chemical dependency When an individual is addicted to and dependent on a legal or illegal drug, mind-altering substance, or alcohol to the point that he or she cannot function in society without it. Dependency can be physical, psychological, or both.

chemical dependency service 1. An inpatient or outpatient health-care service providing diagnosis and treatment for alcohol- or drug-dependent patients. 2. All therapies, supplies, facilities, and personnel needed in the diagnosis and treatment of alcoholism, substance abuse, and drug dependencies.

chemical equivalents Drug products from different sources that contain essentially identical amounts of the same active ingredients in identical dosages that meet existing physiochemical standards in official compendia and are therefore chemically indistinguishable. *See also bioequivalence.*

chemical name The exact description of the chemical structure of a drug based on the rules of chemical nomenclature. This description serves as a complete identification of the compound and is related to the chemical formula of the particular drug.

chemical restraints A drug used in a long-term-care or psychiatric facility to control behavior but in a manner that goes beyond the use recommended to treat a patient's psychiatric symptoms and medical care needs.

chemistry technologist A medical technologist working under the supervision of a pathologist, physician, or qualified scientist who performs qualitative and quantitative analyses of body fluids and exudates.

chemistry technology An allied health training program that trains persons to work under the supervision of a pathologist, physician, or scientist to perform chemical analyses of biochemical fluids and exudates and assist in providing information for diagnosis and treatment of disease.

chemo- Prefix meaning "drug" or "chemical."

chemoreceptor A specialized receptor that is sensitive to a chemical agent.

chemotherapy The therapeutic treatment of diseases or conditions through the use of chemical substances; sometimes used to identify treatment of infectious diseases or cancer with antimetabolites.

CHES *See certified health education specialist.*

CHESS Comprehensive Health Enhancement Support System. A consumer health promotion software program that uses e-mail sent to experts to acquire answers about health questions (developed by David Gustafson of the University of Wisconsin).

chief executive officer (CEO) The individual appointed and given authority by the governing body of a health-care organization to act in its behalf in overall administration. Synonymous job titles may include administrator, president, superintendent, director, executive director, and executive vice president.

chief executive officer exit conference A special meeting between accreditation surveyor(s) and hospital key personnel (e.g., the chief executive officer, chair of the governing body, nurse executive, president of the medical staff, chief operating officer) that is held at the conclusion of an on-site accreditation survey. The purpose of the meeting is to present findings of the accreditation survey, point out where significant compliance problems exist, clarify issues, and discuss the potential impact on the final accreditation decision of not meeting standards (JCAHO for acute-care hospital accreditation).

chief financial officer (CFO) The individual responsible for directing the overall financial management of an institution under the direction of the hospital administrator or chief executive officer. The CFO directs overall financial planning and analysis, accounting, budgeting, data processing, treasury functions, internal audits, and real estate and insurance activities for the health-care facility. He or she also plans, organizes, and analyzes accounting and statistical data with and for all departments of the institution and coordinates activities with third-party payers and managed-care programs.

chief of medical staff The formal director of the physicians on the medical staff at a community hospital. This is usually an elected position but may be appointed in a government hospital. *See chief of staff.*

chief of service A physician who is elected or appointed to serve as the administrative head or director of a clinical department within a hospital. Also called "chairman of services."

chief of staff A physician who has been appointed as the formal administrative head of the medical staff. *See chief of medical staff.*

chief operation officer (COO) That member of the top management team of a hospital or other major health-care organization responsible for the day-to-day detailed internal operation and management. The COO usually is directly responsible to the chief executive officer (CEO), is supportive of the CEO and directives from the board of directors, and carries out the decisions of the CEO and the management team.

child abuse *See battered child syndrome.*

Child Abuse Prevention and Treatment Act Created in response to the Baby Doe case, this law makes it an act of neglect to not treat life-threatening or correctable conditions in seriously ill children in hospitals. Amendments enacted in 1984 affected medical treatment decisions about seriously ill newborns by setting forth that any health-care provider withholding medically indicated treatment would be in violation of the law and held for child neglect (later referred to as "medical neglect"). A reporting process is also required by law.

childbearing age The age span of fertility for females. The U.S. Public Health Service, National Center for Health Statistics, uses the ages 15 through 44 years as the years of childbearing age or fertility; yet children as young as 8 and women in their 70s have also given birth. *See fecundity; fertility rate.*

childbirth center A freestanding or hospital-based facility providing prenatal labor, childbirth, and postnatal care, utilizing maternity care practices that embrace the concept of a family-centered and homelike atmosphere.

child care worker A social services worker who implements training programs and activities that provide therapeutic and preventive services for mentally ill and emotionally disturbed children. Specifically, the worker trains children in self-help skills through intensive group sessions involving structured daily activities and reinforcement of other therapeutic experiences.

Child Health Act A public law that amends the federal Social Security Act by authorizing funds for maternal and infant care and care for preschool and school-age children. Items covered include dental care, crippled children's services, family planning services, and money for training and research.

child-life worker *See recreational therapist.*

child neurology A medical subspecialty area of neurology that specializes in the assessment, treatment, and care of diseases and disorders of the nervous system and brain of children.

child psychiatrist, qualified According to JCAHO for psychiatric, alcoholism, and drug abuse facilities accreditation purposes, a doctor of medicine who specializes in the assessment and treatment of children and/or adolescents having psychiatric disorders. The individual shall have successfully completed training in a child psychiatry fellowship program approved by the Liaison Committee on Graduate Medical Education of the American Medical Association, or have been certified in child psychiatry by the American Board of Psychiatry and Neurology, or have documented equivalent education, training, and/or experience.

child-woman ratio A ratio of children under 5 years of age to women in the childbearing ages of 15 through 44 years. The ratio is of value to public health as it indicates the incidence of childbearing. Census data are used to determine this ratio. For undeveloped countries or those countries that do not have an accurate census or effective vital events registration system, the ratio provides a rough estimate of fertility. The number of children under 5 years of age is the numerator of the ratio, and the number of women ages 15 through 44 years the denominator.

CHIN *See community health information network.*

CHIP *See comprehensive health insurance plan.*

chiro- Prefix meaning "hand."

chiromancy Attempting to foretell future events through reading hands; fortune-telling by studying the palm of the hand; palmistry.

chiropodist *See podiatrist.*

chiropractic 1. The science and art that utilizes the inherent recuperative powers of the body and the relationship between the musculoskeletal structures and functions of the body, particularly of the spinal column and the nervous system, in the restoration and maintenance of health (American Chiropractic Association [ACA]). 2. The science and art that utilizes the inherent recuperative powers of the body and deals with the relationship between the nervous system and the spinal column, including its immediate articulations, and the role of this relationship in the restoration and maintenance of health (International Chiropractor's Association [ICA]).

chiropractor A practitioner of chiropractic. Treatment consists primarily of the adjustment or manipulation of parts of the body, especially the spinal column. Some chiropractors also use physiotherapy, nutritional supplementation, and other therapeutic modalities; radiography is used for diagnosis only. Operations, drugs, and immunizations are usually rejected as violations of the human body. Chiropractic was founded in 1895 by D.D. Palmer and by 1971 had grown to 19,151 practitioners with 36 active chiropractic colleges (requiring 4 years of post–high school education). Chiropractors are licensed by all states. Their services are covered in over half the state Medicaid programs.

CHMSA Critical health manpower shortage area.

CHN *See community health network.*

choate Complete.

choate lien 1. In the administration of buildings and equipment by a health-care organization, this is a complete lien. 2. A solid and legal lien; an enforceable lien in which both the lienor and the property under lien are definite and established.

choice-of-law A situation or a case where a court must choose between local laws and those of another jurisdiction that conflict.

cholangiogram An X ray of the biliary tract involving the injection of a dye.

cholecystogram An X ray of the gallbladder.

chore and homemaker services A support service that helps the elderly and handicapped live independently and avoid institutional care by providing household services such as shopping, cooking, and cleaning.

chose (French) Thing, article, personal property.

chose in action An article, debt, damages, money, or property wrongfully held by another party and recoverable by a legal action such as a lawsuit.

CHP (CHPa, CHPb) Comprehensive health planning. Agencies that preceded the former national system of health planning, which included health systems agencies. The "a" and "b" refer to state and local area groups, respectively.

CHPA Community health purchasing alliances.

Christian Science A religion that espouses a system of healing through faith, prayer, and the belief in faith over disease. The services of Christian Science are covered under some health insurance programs, including Medicare and, in some states, Medicaid, often with an exemption from standards applied by such programs to traditional medical providers.

chronic activity limitation In the assessment and identification of disability, individuals are classified into four categories on the basis of the extent of ability to do activities that may be limited by chronic conditions. A different set of criteria is used for different age and developmental levels. Because age causes activities to differ, preschool children, school-age children, housewives, workers, professionals, and others also differ in activity. The four categories are 1) persons unable to carry on major activity for their group, 2) persons limited in amount or kind of major activity performed, 3) persons not limited in major activity but otherwise limited, and 4) persons not limited in any activity.

chronic brain syndrome *See organic brain syndrome.*

chronic care The treatment of individuals who are ill with long-term noninfectious diseases, disorders, or conditions that require treatment over a long time period.

chronic condition 1. Any physical or mental illness or disorder of long duration (longer than 3 months) or of frequent recurrence. 2. An illness or disorder is considered chronic if it has lasted more than 3 months and is a type of disorder that ordinarily has a duration of more than 3 months such as diabetes, heart conditions, emphysema, or arthritis regardless of time of onset. *See chronic disease.*

chronic disease A disease that has one or more of the following characteristics: slow changes; permanent changes; not an acute phase; leaves a residual disability; caused by nonreversible pathological alteration; lasts longer than 3 months; requires special training of the patient for rehabilitation; or requires a long period of supervision, observation, or care and may require long-term care. *See also acute disease.*

chronic fatigue syndrome 1. An illness of unknown cause, thought to be possibly caused by the Herpes virus #6 or #7. Patients may have one or all of the following signs and symptoms of the illness: fatigue accompanied by nonrestorative sleep and worsened by exertion, weight gain, nausea, irritable bowel, chronic sore throat, fever and chills, sweats, muscle and joint pain, neck pain, bladder or prostate problems with frequent urination, low blood pressure, recurrent illness with flu-like symptoms, malaise, heat or cold intolerance, painful/swollen lymph nodes, systemic yeast or fungal infections, fungal infection of skin or nails, increased premenstrual syndrome (PMS) in women, low-grade fevers, fluid retention/swelling, subnormal body temperatures, severe allergies, and a large number of other possible symptoms. A single cure or treatment is unknown, and the disease often lasts 4 years or longer. A variety of treatments have been tried, and some work for some individuals but not for others. An early theory was that the immune system was sluggish—it is now thought that the immune system is overactive, which causes the fatigue. Some of the allopathic treatments have included antidepressants at various doses, nicotine patches, evening primrose oil, vitamin B-12, antiviral agents, and gamma globulin shots. 2. A collection of symptoms or signs by which persistent unexplained fatigue and a variety of other symptoms result, lasting more than 30 days.

chronic illness *See chronic disease.*

chronic maintenance dialysis Renal dialysis given on a regularly scheduled basis for end-stage renal disease patients who receive the treatment on an outpatient basis. Dialysis is conducted in relaxing settings to minimize pain and boredom related to the lengthy dialysis process.

chronic obstructive pulmonary disease services A provision for services providing for the treatment of disorders such as asthma, chronic bronchitis, and emphysema in which a persistent obstruction of bronchial airflow exists.

chrono- Prefix meaning "time."

chronobiology The field of study that deals with circadian rhythms or biorhythms.

chronohygiene The field of study and treatment that deals with health or medical problems related to changes in biorhythms and circadian rhythms that affect sleep patterns (e.g., shift work or jet lag).

CHSS *See cooperative health statistics system.*

Church of Christ Scientist The official name of the Christian Science religion. *See Christian Science.*

Church of Jesus Christ of Latter Day Saints A prominent religion with a health code that promotes a healthy lifestyle. Also called Mormons, devout members of the church adhere to the health code called the "Word of Wisdom," which states "That inasmuch as any man drinketh wine or strong drink among you behold it is not good . . . strong drinks are not for the belly, but for washing of your bodies . . . tobacco is not for the body, neither for the belly and is not good for man, but is an herb for bruises and all sick cattle, to be used with judgment and skill . . . hot drinks [coffee and tea] are not for the body or the belly . . . all wholesome herbs God hath ordained for the constitution, nature and use of man. . . . Every herb in the season thereof, every fruit in the season thereof; all these to be used with prudence and thanksgiving . . . flesh also of beasts and fowls of the air . . . [are] for the use of man with thanksgiving and nevertheless are use to be used sparingly" (Doctrine and Covenants, Section 89). Devout L.D.S. church members are known for having strong families, high standards, and long life expectancy and adhering to high moral values and unwavering commitment to their standards and to the principles of the gospel of Jesus Christ.

churning The practice of discharging a patient from a hospital and then readmitting the same patient to the same hospital for the same condition or spell of illness and then charging for the new admission. The rules on the Prospective Payment System have time and diagnostic restrictions imposed on payments and diagnoses to prevent this unethical practice.

Chux The brand name for a disposable pad that is soft on one side and waterproof on the other. It is used for incontinent patients or used under areas of the body that have drainage of body fluids.

circadian rhythm Repetition of certain rhythmic phenomena every 24 hours; biorhythms.

CircOlectric bed and Foster frame A device used to periodically alternate a patient between the prone and supine positions with little or no effort on the part of the patient.

circulating nurse A member of the operating

team whose purpose is to acquire and deliver surgical instruments and related items to the surgical team but who usually does not participate in the surgery.

circulation technologist *See cardiovascular perfusionist.*

circumstantial evidence Indirect proof used to infer a fact from certain occurrences. Possession of stolen drugs is circumstantial proof of a person being a thief.

citation 1. The final result of a health and safety investigation or inspection that has revealed a condition or circumstance to be in violation of regulations or standards. A written notification stating the nature of the violation, citing the standards violated, the time period in which they are to be corrected, and a possible fine or punishment. Violations of a regulation can be of a serious nature or can be minor enough to warrant only a notice. 2. Under OBRA regulations, an entry made on form HCFA-2567 that includes the prefix and data tag number, the deficiency, and the evidence to support the deficiency.

citations for serious violation Violation of a regulation that is of such magnitude and seriousness that it falls into a "serious" category and warrants that a monetary penalty be assessed.

cite 1. To summon. 2. To refer to. 3. To give legal notice. 4. To enjoin. 5. To name. 6. To prove through referring to a law.

city-county hospital *See hospital, city-county.*

civil action 1. Any legal action between two or more individuals or parties. 2. Any legal action that is not a criminal action.

Civilian Health and Medical Program of the Uniformed Services (CHAMPUS) A program administered by the Department of Defense, without premiums but with cost-sharing provisions, that pays for health care delivered by civilian health providers to dependents of active and retired military personnel, retired personnel, and dependents of deceased members of the military who died on active duty. This program protects those connected with the Army, Navy, Air Force, Marine Corps, commissioned corps of the Public Health Service, Coast Guard, and the National Oceanic and Atmospheric Administration.

Civilian Health and Medical Program of the Veterans Administration (CHAMPVA) A program administered by the Department of Defense for the Veterans Administration, without premiums but with cost-sharing provisions, that pays for health care delivered to dependents of totally disabled veterans who are eligible for retirement pay from a uniformed service.

civilian noninstitutionalized population According to the National Centers for Health Statistics, individuals who do not reside in institutions. Institutions include correctional institutions; detention homes and training schools for juvenile delinquents; homes for the aged; nursing homes; convalescent hospitals; homes for dependent children; homes and schools for the mentally and physically handicapped; homes for unwed mothers; psychiatric, tuberculosis, and chronic disease hospitals; and residential treatment centers.

civilian populations According to the National Centers for Health Statistics, for survey research purposes this excludes members of the armed forces. Families of members of the armed forces are considered a part of civilian populations.

civil law 1. Law that was developed under the Roman Empire and survived in most European countries except Great Britain. Roman civil law is based on codes and statutes and is distinguished from common law and case law. 2. In modern times and in countries that claim England as their mother country, legal proceedings not based on criminal law, statutes, codes or regulations, or military law. 3. Rules that regulate or control relationships between private parties rather than between private parties and governments. Also referred to as "private law."

civil malpractice Professional misconduct involving a criminal act. *See malpractice.*

civil rights All rights of U.S. citizens guaranteed by the U.S. and state constitutions.

Civil Rights Act of 1964 A law passed by the U.S. Congress making various forms of discrimination illegal.

civil service All government employees except elected officials and judges who are selected by a controlled, standardized method. Persons in military service are not considered civil service employees.

CJ Chief judge, chief justice.

claim 1. A statement or assertion of fact. 2. To demand; to call for; to urge; to assert; to insist. 3. A request to an insurance company by an insured person (or on the person's behalf by the provider of a service) for payment of benefits under a managed-care program or an insurance policy. 4. One's right to; to be entitled to. 5. In managed care, a demand for payment under a health plan, medical insurance policy, or contract based on an itemized statement of services from a hospital, physician, clinic, or other health-care provider. The claim creates a financial responsibility for payment by an insurance company for health-care services received by members covered by the health plan. The payment is set forth in a written request for payment in the form of a statement of services, treatments, and procedures rendered, usually in the form of numerical codes and the charges. On receipt of a claim by the carrier, the processing for payment of the claim is expected to occur within a reasonable time period.

claim accruals In managed care and medical insurance, this is a reserve established by the health plan, HMO, or preferred provider organization (PPO) for medical services provided to enrollees, for services rendered, and for accounts for services incurred but not reported or yet paid.

claim administration In managed care, medical insurance, or other insurance areas, the administrative unit responsible for processing claims. Claim examiners review claims submitted by policy owners or beneficiaries to verify the validity of the claims and to authorize payment of benefits to the appropriate individual. In a dispute over a claim, the examiner may be required to show evidence for the insurance company in court as to the reasons the claim was not honored.

claimant A person who files a claim, asserts a right, or applies for justice.

claim examiner The employee of a managed-care plan or medical insurance or other insurance company who is responsible for claims investigation, approving claims that are valid and denying claims that are invalid or fraudulent.

claim fluctuation reserve In managed care and medical insurance, this is a fund set aside and designed to predict and anticipate possible unfavorable, high-cost, and outlier claim outcomes, especially for small-group insurance or health plan coverage. With funds set aside in a reserve, health plans and insurance companies can risk offering small group premium rates to cover future time periods.

claim for relief 1. The first pleading in a complaint or lawsuit. 2. A summary statement that indicates that facts can be proven and that the plaintiff should have the court's support in the claim against the defendant.

claim frequency rate In managed care and medical insurance, this is the expected percentage of insured persons who will file claims. To determine the average cost of claims, actuaries must forecast the number of insured people who will become ill or injured or develop a medical condition, as well as the length of the illness, condition, or disability; the cost of hospital and physician care; and the differences in costs from one geographical region to another and from one economic cycle to the next.

claim lag schedules In managed care and medical insurance, these are reports used to trace the lag in time between the date the health care is rendered (when a claim is incurred) and when it is paid.

claim review A review process conducted by a panel of physicians and administrators employed by the managed-care plan or insurance carrier that determines the eligibility of a beneficiary or a provider, the appropriateness of medical services provided (including the cost and necessity of the services as stipulated by the health plan or insurance policy), and the amount to be paid under an insurance program. It includes the assessment of unusual claims that fall into the vague and unclear areas of claims processing, such as reconstructive/cosmetic procedures and research-related experimental and investigational treatments and procedures.

claims-incurred policy The conventional form of malpractice insurance that covers the insured for any claims arising from an incident that occurred or is alleged to have occurred during the policy period, regardless of when the claim is made. The only limiting factor is the statute of limitations, which varies from state to state. An alternative type of policy is the claims-made policy.

claims-made policy A form of malpractice insurance gaining increasing popularity wherein the insured is covered for any claim made, rather than for any injury that occurs, while the policy is in force. Claims made after the insurance lapses are not covered as they are by a claims-incurred policy. This type of policy was initially resisted by providers because of the nature of medical malpractice claims, which may arise several years after an injury occurs. A retired physician, for example, could be sued and not covered, unless special provisions are made to continue coverage beyond his or her years of practice. There are also retrospective problems for providers who switch from a conventional policy to a claims-made policy because the latter policy would not cover claims arising from events occurring during the years when the conventional policy was in effect. Insurers marketing such policies are now offering providers the opportunity to purchase insurance for both contingencies. *See also discovery rule.*

claims review A review of claims by governments, medical foundations, professional review organizations (PROs), insurers, or others responsible for payment to determine liability and amount of payment. This review may also determine the eligibility of the claimant or beneficiary and the eligibility of the provider of the benefit; that the benefit for which payment is claimed is covered; that the benefit is not payable under another policy; and that the benefit was necessary and of reasonable cost and quality.

claims status report A statement to the enrolled member of a health plan or medical insurance plan that explains action taken on each claim.

claims supplement forms In managed care, medical insurance, and other forms of insurance, this is a document or form used to request the release of a claim payment that is due because adequate supplemental information that justifies the claim release has been received.

class action suit A lawsuit filed in the name of all persons having a common concern regarding a defendant's action.

class-based reimbursement system Statewide rates are set for groups or facilities in a particular state on the basis of the history of the cost of care for an entire class or group of persons. The state may determine the group by geographic region, sizes, or the other characteristics of a population.

classification The process of giving order to facts, information, or data. Five constructs are used in the classification process: naturalness, exhaustiveness, usefulness, simplicity, and constructability.

classification of disease The categorization of diseases or conditions on the basis of different variables or factors. Classification can be based on time or duration such as acute versus chronic, source, or cause and effect. Other classification includes congenital and hereditary diseases, allergies and inflammatory diseases, degenerative or chronic diseases, metabolic diseases, and cancer/neoplastic diseases. The most commonly used classification is the World Health Organization's *International Classification of Disease* and ICD-9-CM. Psychiatric diseases are classified in the *Diagnostic and Statistical Manual IV* of the American Psychiatric Association.

classifying The process of coding similar types of data, such as medical record information.

Clayton Act A federal law, passed in 1914, that extended the Sherman Act, which prohibits monopolies, price control, and price fixing. One of the major antitrust laws.

clean 1. Free of disease-producing microorganisms. 2. No longer using drugs. 3. No longer breaking the law.

Clean Air Act The original act of 1976 refers to the discharge of pollutants from motor vehicles and industry into the atmosphere and into the ambient air outdoors. In 1970 the regulations empowered the Environmental Protection Agency (EPA) to protect the health and welfare of the public and was further empowered to set and review the National Ambient Air Quality Standards (NAAQS), which define maximum concentration of various pollutants allowable in the ambient air. The EPA identified ambient air quality standards for several agents or chemicals commonly found in air pollution, including ozone, sulfur dioxide, nitrogen dioxide, carbon monoxide, particulate matter, and lead. The Clean Air Act required the EPA to set the New Source Performance Standards (NSPS), which are allowable emission limits for various stationary sources of air pollution. The EPA also established the National Emission Standards for Hazardous Air pollutants (NESHAPs), which include arsenic, asbestos, benzene, beryllium, mercury, radionuclides, and vinyl chlorides. The threshold levels for these pollutants are those below which there should be no adverse effect on human health. In the 1980s the EPA recommended action for indoor levels of pollution; in the 1990s smoking was identified as a main source of indoor air pollution and harmful to human health.

clean hands 1. Being fair and honest in all dealings and matters. 2. Being honest in a request for equitable relief.

clean room A sterile room in a hospital. Any room with environmental controls configured in such a manner as to control infection and airflow. Bacteria and dust are prevented from coming in by air pressure and tight construction.

clean technique A technique that maintains a disease-free situation.

Clean Water Act In 1956 the Federal Water Pollution Act was passed, and the Clean Water Act reemphasized the importance of clean water to the public and the nation. The original aim of the Clean Water Act was to restore and maintain the chemical, physical, and biological integrity of the nation's waters. The Environmental Protection Agency (EPA) was given the responsibility for developing criteria for water quality standards, technology-based effluent limitation guidelines, pretreatment standards, new source performance standards, and a national permit program to control and regulate pollutant discharges into water sources. Individual states have the responsibility for their own water management programs and for setting and maintaining water quality standards. The Clean Water Act was passed in 1972 and has been amended in 1977, 1980, 1981, 1987, and 1995; tests for public drinking water supplies require analyses for 83 different chemicals and agents.

clear and convincing proof Strong evidence, but not as strong as "beyond a reasonable doubt."

clear and present danger A legal test used to decide whether what has been said is protected by the First Amendment. A statement may be punishable by law if it could lead to violence or if it weakens national safety and security.

clear title 1. In health-care facilities development, this is a property title that has no liens or any other legal claims against it. 2. A document stating that legal ownership is free from all restrictions and debts.

clemency Showing mercy, giving lenient treatment, or reducing the punishment for a criminal.

clergy A person ordained to a position in a church that authorizes the person to conduct religious services. *See also chaplain.*

clerk-of-the-works The hospital or health-care organization's own representative present at a construction site who ensures that the contractor carries out the construction of the building according to plans and specifications.

clerkship *See clinical clerkship.*

client A person who employs a professional for service. Patients in the mental health care system, especially those seen by psychologists, counselors, psychotherapists, and marriage and family therapists, are referred to as "clients."

climacteric Menopause.

clinic A facility or portion thereof used for diagnosis and treatment of outpatients. The term may include physicians' offices or medical group practices. It may be limited to facilities that serve poor or public patients or to facilities in which graduate or undergraduate medical education is conducted.

clinical 1. Pertaining to the course of a disease as observed by a physician, nurse, or other health-care provider. 2. The study, diagnosis, and treatment of diseases, disorders, conditions, or disabilities in patients as carried out in a formal health-care setting.

clinical algorithm The application of algorithms to medical record activities. This is a decision-making or systems analysis method that consists of a finite number of steps needed to solve a problem.

clinical anatomy An allied health science training requirement that includes describing the structure of the human body and the relationship of the body parts to the restoration and preservation of good health and medical treatment.

clinical animal technology An allied health training program that prepares persons to provide care and treatment to laboratory animals in hospitals, veterinary clinics, and research laboratories. These individuals are also educated in research and diagnosis procedures as prescribed and supervised by pathologists, physicians, and other qualified research scientists.

clinical biochemistry An educational program that trains professionals in the nature and chemical composition of the substances found in the makeup of the human body. Professionals in this area study, analyze, and test the substances of the human body to develop new medicines.

clinical chemist An individual who specializes in the study and analysis of chemical compounds used in clinical settings or in research.

clinical clerk A student serving an internship or clerkship in a medical school, dental school, or allied health program who receives controlled, supervised clinical training and practical clinical experience by working in a hospital or clinical setting. *See also clinical clerkship.*

clinical clerkship The internship or field experience required as part of an allied health profession educational curriculum conducted at the undergraduate level. This experience provides the student with supervised educational clinical experience in a health-care facility that has a formal affiliation agreement with a medical school, dental school, or school of health professions.

clinical criteria Guidelines, parameters, and limitations to the scope of practice and clinical activity for nurses and allied health professionals.

clinical dietitian, R.D. Registered Dietitian. A member of the health-care team who assesses patients' nutritional needs, develops and implements nutritional care plans, and evaluates and reports these results appropriately. When functioning in an organization that provides food service, the clinical dietitian cooperates and coordinates activities with those of the department's management team.

clinical engineer The person responsible for the adaptation, maintenance, and safe operation of hospital equipment and instruments.

clinical engineering department The department of a health-care facility that provides maintenance and repair of medical equipment and instruments.

clinical epidemiology Epidemiological activities that are practiced in hospitals, medical clinics, or public health clinics or that are performed in relation to definitive medical care activities to ascertain the cause-effect relationship of diseases or conditions for the purpose of instituting disease prevention and control measures.

clinical equivalents *See bioequivalence; therapeutic equivalents.*

clinical expectation An agreement or consensus among health-care providers as to the correct treatment or procedure that should be applied to a specific, recurring condition or circumstance of patient care.

clinical health sciences Those scientific disciplines devoted to the analysis of human body structures and functions and the procedures for the identification and classification of diseases and the treatment, restoration, and preservation of health.

clinical instructor A health-care professional who supervises the educational training of students in a clinical setting. This individual is considered a member of the faculty of a medical school, dental school, or school of allied health.

clinical investigator A biomedical scientist who is responsible for research involving patients in clinical settings, often under a research grant.

clinical laboratory A research and testing facility that conducts microbiological, bacteriological, biochemical, cytologic, hematologic, histologic, and serologic tests on tissue and other materials taken from the human body.

clinical laboratory aide An allied health worker who performs simple tasks in maintaining a clinical laboratory, including sterilization of equipment, maintaining supplies, and messenger services.

clinical laboratory assistant An allied health worker who performs routine clinical laboratory procedures under the supervision of laboratory technicians, physicians, pathologists, or biochemists.

clinical laboratory, hospital A facility serving a hospital that is equipped for the examination of material derived from the human body for the purpose of providing information to be used in the diagnosis, prevention, or treatment of disease for hospital patients; also called "medical laboratory" (JCAHO for acute-care facilities).

Clinical Laboratory Improvement Act (CLIA) Passed in 1967, this act affected 12,000 labs regulated under Medicare and Medicaid. Amendments were passed in 1988 and implemented in 1990 that affect up to 20,000 laboratories and are overseen by the Health Care Financing Administration, with the Public Health Service being responsible for blood bank operations and products. The CLIA, passed by Congress because of unethical laboratory practices by a portion of the operating labs, affects laboratories participating in interstate commerce as well as independent labs and sets forth conditions for participation in Medicare. Other areas affected by the 1988 amendments are proficiency testing requirements, cytology standards, personnel requirements, and access to care in the form of availability of lab services. Final review and published rules were published in 1992.

clinical laboratory services 1. The testing of specimens derived from the human body to aid in the diagnosis and treatment of physical diseases and other conditions that include but are not limited to hematology, chemistry, histology, and microbiology. 2. Entities that provide laboratory services and that are approved by Medicare as independent laboratories or hospitals.

clinical microbiology The study of the nature and properties of harmful microorganisms and of the disease processes they cause in humans.

clinical nurse practitioner A licensed nurse with advanced training, often at the masters degree level, in primary or specialized care who works as a physician extender by assuming advanced clinical responsibilities, including medical diagnosis and treatment under the supervision of a physician.

clinical nurse specialist A registered nurse with a graduate degree in a nursing specialty who may then practice, teach, supervise, or coordinate nursing care within that specialty.

clinical operations system Those provisions of health-care delivery found in a health-care organization that provide actual direct patient care services and that monitor patient care activities to ensure effective and quality care.

clinical pastoral counselor A clergy member who works in health-care settings with patients and their families to provide assistance in coping with temporary, chronic, or terminal illness.

clinical pathology The study and analysis of human disease. Pathology examines and tests the structural and functional changes resulting from the disease process. *See pathology; pathology, clinical.*

clinical patient Outpatients using the ambulatory services of a hospital or freestanding outpatient clinic.

clinical practice guideline development Four types of guidelines have been developed: 1) clinical practice guidelines that assist practitioner and patient decisions about appropriate health care for specific clinical circumstances; 2) medical review criteria that are used to assess the appropriateness of specific health-care decisions, services, and outcomes; 3) standards of quality that authoritatively state the minimum levels of acceptable performance or results, the excellent levels of performance or results, or the range of acceptable performance or results; and 4) performance measures (methods or instruments) that estimate or monitor the extent to which the actions of a health-care provider conform to the clinical practice guidelines, medical review criteria, and standards of quality. Eight attributes of good clinical practice are to be applied to the guidelines: 1) validity (the health and cost outcomes projected by the guidelines are met); 2) reliability/reproducibility (other experts produce the same statements and outcomes); 3) clinical applicability (clinical and scientific evidence that appropriately defined patient populations); 4) clinical flexibility (generally expected exceptions to recommendations were identified); 5) clarity (terms and procedures precisely defined); 6) multidisciplinary process (key groups participate on panels that develop guidelines and provide evidence); 7) scheduled review (guidelines reviewed to determine whether revisions are warranted because of new clinical evidence or changing professional consensus); and 8) documentation (participants, evidence used, assumptions, rationale, and analytical methods used should be meticulously documented and described). Developed by a committee of the Institute of Medicine (IOM) of the National Academy of Sciences, under the Omnibus Budget and Reconciliation Act of 1989 (P.L. 101-239), the Agency for Health Care Policy and Research (AHCPR) of the U.S. Department of Health And Human Services.

clinical preventive services Prevention that aims to delay or prevent the occurrence of injury or disease or its consequences. A three-tiered framework has been used to classify preventive services on the basis of the ultimate goal and the point along a disease process at which the preventive intervention is applied. The framework consists of: 1) primary preventive services, which are intended to prevent or delay the onset of disease or a health problem; 2) secondary preventive services, which are efforts to detect a disease or condition before it is clinically recognizable to avoid or delay its further progression; and 3) tertiary preventive services, which are attempts to reduce the impact of already existing disease on the quality of a person's life by maintaining and improving the ability to function. *See levels of prevention; levels of care.*

clinical privileges Permission granted to a staff physician or other health-care provider by a health-care facility's governing board to provide specified diagnostic, therapeutic, surgical, medical, treatment, procedures, and patient care services in the hospital and to render medical care in the granting institution within defined limits. Privileges are well-defined and determined by licensure, education, training, experience, skill, competence, ability, and judgment (JCAHO for acute-care facilities).

clinical privileges, delineation of The process of listing the specific clinical patient care, treatment, and medical procedure activities granted to a medical staff member by the hospital.

clinical psychologist A health professional specializing in the evaluation and treatment of mental and behavioral disorders. A clinical psychologist generally has a doctoral degree in psychology plus clinical training. Clinical psychologists are licensed by most states for independent professional practice, and their services are reimbursed by many health insurance and managed-care programs. They are not licensed to prescribe drugs.

clinical psychology services Mental health services provided by clinical psychologists or mental health therapists trained in clinical psychology. *See Council for the National Register of Health Service Providers in Psychology.*

clinicopathological conference (CPC) The presentation and discussion of a physical examination and diagnostic test results with the medical staff. A specialist or an expert then analyzes the findings and provides a diagnosis. On the basis of tissue examination and the opinions of the expert, the pathologist then reports the diagnosis to the proper authorities. Another scenario includes the presentation of a detailed case history of a patient to a clinical expert who discusses the case and then makes a diagnostic recommendation. The pathologist reports the findings and diagnosis on the basis of tissue examination and findings.

clinical outliers *See outliers.*

clinical record *See medical record.*

clinical resume A component of the medical record consisting of a concise recapitulation of the reason for hospitalization, course of treatment, procedures rendered while in the hospital, significant medical findings, the condition of the patient on discharge, and any specific instructions given to the patient and/or family related to treatment and recovery.

clinical support services 1. In a medical care setting, this is one or more health-care treatment units that consist of allied health specialties or clinical allied health professions that provide individual patient care under the orders of the attending physician and include units such as physical therapy, respiratory therapy, and occupational therapy. 2. In community health or public health, general community health services such as health promotion, health education, preventive medicine, well-child clinics, and immunization clinics with clinical activities conducted under the supervision of a physician.

clinical trail In biomedical research, this is a research design using the experimental design approach used to determine the efficacy of treatment procedures, biomedical devices, therapeutic substances, surgical procedures, etc. in both human and animal subjects.

clinic clerk An individual who performs routine clerical functions in an outpatient clinic, group practice, or a freestanding ambulatory care center.

clinic manager The administrator or chief executive officer of a clinic. *See also administrator, clinic; chief executive officer; health services administrator; medical group management.*

clinic patients 1. Those patients who are treated in public health clinics, government-administered clinics, or HMO clinics or who are regular patients in a medical group. 2. Outpatients who utilize hospital services, which are often less costly than inpatient care.

close corporation In health-care organization governance, this is a corporation in which the stock is held by a limited number of persons (usually family members) and not offered for public sale. Often refers to a corporation owned and operated primarily by a single family.

closed access In managed care, this is a type of health plan in which enrollees are required to select a primary care physician and to see that physician each visit as the gatekeeper until a referral is warranted. Any referral to a specialist within the health plan must come from the primary care physician. This organizational structure and utilization pattern is found in a staff, group, or network model–type HMO. Also referred to a "closed panel" or "gatekeeper model." *See closed panel; gatekeeper.*

closed claim In health-care law, this is an issue related to recovery from damages of a liability suit. The final decision of a court or an out-of-court settlement means that the final decision has been made and that the claim is closed.

closed contract 1. In managed-care and health plans, this is a special contract in which the terms of the contract constitute the complete agreement between the enrollee and the health plan company.

closed formulary A list of all drugs, name-brand and generic, that physicians select as the best drugs (providing the best therapeutic advantage while being the least expensive) on the basis of use, experience, literature reviews, and consultations. Patients using closed formulary drugs get them for reduced charges because they are bought in bulk. Drugs prescribed outside the closed formulary require the patient to pay full price. Often used in managed care and HMOs.

closed medical staff In hospital medical staff organization, this is one approach to medical staff structure that generally restricts most licensed physicians from joining the medical staff such as those on university faculties or HMOs.

closed panel In managed care, this is a health plan approach that contracts for physician services on an exclusive basis utilizing a selected list of physicians. Enrollees/members are not allowed to visit physicians outside of those listed in the contract. In the clinic owned by the HMO, or in a clinic staffed by physicians who belong to a medical group that only contracts with or works for that HMO, a primary care physician often serves as a gatekeeper and must be seen prior to any referral to a specialist. Used by staff or group model HMOs. *See closed access.*

closed panel group practice In managed care, this is a health-care or dental care plan in which beneficiaries are allowed to obtain care from those health-care providers or dentists who have agreed to be part of the prepayment plan.

closed shop A company or health-care institution where only members of a particular union may work in or do certain jobs; therefore, a worker must be a union member as a condition of employment. This is illegal under the National Labor Relations Act.

closed shop contract In health-care labor relations, this is a labor-management promissory agreement stipulating that only members of a certain union may be hired.

closed staff Those physicians approved by a hospital's governing board to admit patients and practice medicine in the hospital.

closed system activities A health-care administration and organization approach that assesses inputs, the internal functioning (process) of the organization to determine efficiency, and the effectiveness of the organization by comparing these to outcomes, standards, objectives, and expectations.

closed system model A health-care administration and organization internal assessment approach that assesses inputs, the internal functioning and processes, and outputs of the formal organization and then responds to external activities and occurrences in a predictable manner.

closely held *See close corporation.*

cloture 1. A formal closure. 2. The act of closing off a discussion or debate in a hearing. 3. A parliamentary procedure.

CLT Clinical laboratory technician (or technologist).

CLU Chartered life underwriter. A title issued to a life insurance agent who meets specific experience requirements and passes an exam as stipulated by the American Society of Chartered Life Underwriters.

cluster analysis In epidemiology research, this is the grouping of subjects, cases, observations, or variables into highly related statistical groupings.

clustering In epidemiology, this is the close grouping of subjects, cases, observations, or variables by disease, condition, time, place, or person characteristics; the aggregation of factors of disease causation or disease transmission; unusual disease states.

cluster sampling In epidemiology and biomedical research, this is a sampling approach used for approximating a random sample by aggregating individual cases into larger units or traits of observation that occur naturally as samples of convenience such as public schools, university classrooms, census tracts, senior citizen housing complexes, hospitals, and other institutions.

clyster An enema; a rectal injection; a pipe or syringe used for internal cleansing; to wash. *See lavement.*

CME Continuing medical education; comprehensive medical expense. *See continuing medical education.*

CMHC *See community mental health center.*

C/MHC Community/migrant health center.

CMI *See case mix index.*

CMP *See competitive medical plan.*

CMT Current medical terminology; a dictionary used in medical records that presents the terms of preferred use in medicine.

CNA *See certified nurse assistant.*

CNHS Committee for a National Health Service; Coalition for a National Health Service.

CNM *See certified nurse midwife.*

CNS Central nervous system.

COA *See certificate of authority.*

coaching In health-care administration, this is a management development mentoring approach where a midmanager is assigned to work with an experienced manager. The experienced manager guides, directs, mentors, encourages, and instructs the midmanager.

coalition An organized group of representatives that is supportive of a cause within a community and is jointly organized to pursue a common objective.

COB *See coordination of benefits.*

cobalt therapy service The provision of radioactive cobalt therapy for cancer patients done on an inpatient or outpatient basis.

COBOL Common business oriented language. A data processing language by which business data processing procedures can be precisely described in a standard form.

COBRA Consolidated Omnibus Budget Reconciliation Act of 1985. Legislation signed into law on April 7, 1985, that requires employers to offer insurance coverage for employees or dependents after they no longer have coverage because they are no longer employed. Coverage is offered from 18 months to a maximum of 36 months. Employees are allowed to purchase a continuation of their health care coverage under the medical insurance of the employer. One area of the law eases a Medicare recipient's ability to disenroll from an HMO with a Medicare risk contract.

COC *See certificate of coverage.*

code 1. A complete body or set of laws of a nation, state, city, county, etc. 2. A set of rules and regulations pertaining to a specific area or subject. 3. The compilation and arranging of laws in a systematic way. 4. The arranging and organization of statutes, regulations, and rules into books of law, as in the criminal code.

code blue Indicates a hospital emergency; usually announced over the public address system in the hospital to alert appropriate personnel who are prepared to respond to an emergency with crash carts and equipment, especially for heart and breathing resuscitation.

coded 1. When the medical record, DRG, procedure insurance code identification, and recording process have been completed. 2. When a patient has been responded to for a "code blue" call.

Code of Ethics for Hospital and Health Care Executives The administrator is held accountable for ethically conducting the business affairs of the institution within the policies adopted by the governing board (ACHE).

Code of Judicial Conduct Rules of conduct created specifically for judges, adopted by the American Bar Association and adhered to in many states.

Code of Professional Responsibility The specific ethical rules and regulations that govern the legal profession, developed by the American Bar Association.

codetermination In health-care administration, this is a form of participative management popularized in the former West Germany. Employees are given the right to have representatives vote on management decisions.

codification The collecting and organizing of laws on a certain subject into a complete set of laws.

codify 1. To arrange by numbers. 2. To arrange laws by areas, subjects, or topics. 3. To arrange diseases, treatments, or procedures by subject and assign numbers to them. *See also ICD-9-CM.*

coding 1. The organization of the principal and related diagnoses and treatment procedures into numerical designations, allowing for easy information retrieval and utilization. Coding is often a chore of medical records allied health professionals. 2. The writing of instructions for use by a computer, using symbols that are readable by the computer itself or to the assembler, compiler, or other language processor. *See medical record coding process.*

coercion Forcing someone to act against his or her own free will.

coercive In health-care administration, this is a human behavior that utilizes underhanded actions that bypass direct communication and interaction and preclude choice.

coffin A thick-walled lead container used to transport radioactive materials.

COG *See council of government.*

COGME Council on Graduate Medical Education.

cognition 1. The mental process of understanding, knowing, and being aware. 2. The process of being aware or of knowing; mental awareness rather than emotional response.

cognitive The process or mental state of comprehension, judgment, memory, and reasoning, contrasted with affective or emotional states.

cognitive impairment In mental health services, any limitation or relapse in the higher-level thinking and reasoning processes of the brain. It is more loosely used to mean loss of memory, reasoning, or orientation to time, place, and person and requires the patient to be supervised to protect them because they are a danger to themselves or others.

cognizable 1. Within the jurisdiction of the court or other tribunal. 2. Capable of being understood, known, or recognized.

cognizance 1. The hearing of a case in a court; authority to hear a case deal with a matter legally. 2. Judicial power to decide a matter; judicial decision; right to deal with a judicial matter.

cognovit 1. A written acknowledgment of one's liability or debt, especially one made by a defendant in a civil suit to avoid the expense of going to trial.

cohabitation Unmarried couples living together as if man and wife; not married and sharing a common abode, property, and all the rights and privileges of a married couple. *See common law marriage.*

coherent In laser technology as used in medical treatment, when all waves of light are spatially and temporarily in phase.

cohort 1. Those persons in a population who share a common characteristic, especially the same birth year or year of marriage. In demographics, all those persons born during a specified period. 2. A group of a population born during a particular time and birth period that can be followed as it successively passes through time periods and ages.

cohort analysis 1. In epidemiology, this is the analysis and tabulation of research findings using ages and/or the birth year of groups of people or other common characteristics. 2. The determining of the findings of data in different ages as they pass through time or the life span. 3. Assessment of morbidity or mortality rates by age in specific groups of people or cohorts in a specific time period or as followed through time.

cohort study In epidemiology, this is a research investigation in which a group (the cohort) is chosen for the presence of a specific characteristic, such as a common birth year, at or during a specified time and followed over time to observe the appearance of particular related characteristics, disorders, or problems. This has been referred to as a "panel study."

coida de la mollera (Spanish) Fallen fontanel. A disorder common only to and as described in Hispanic cultures.

co-insurance In medical insurance, this is a second insurance policy taken out by insured persons that is used to cover those areas of medical care not covered by the primary medical insurance policy. This cost-sharing approach to a managed-care plan or medical insurance policy provides that the insured will assume a portion or percentage of the costs of covered services or that it will be covered by another medical insurance policy or plan. The medical insurance policy usually provides that the insurer will reimburse a specified percentage (usually 80%) of all, or certain specified, covered medical expenses in excess of any deductible amounts payable by the insured. The insured is then liable for the remaining percentage of the costs until the maximum amount payable under the insurance policy, if any, is reached. 2. Insurance where the insured and the insurer carry the risk jointly. 3. Dividing the risk of medical care losses between the managed-care plan or insurance company and its enrollees. 4. A managed-care plan or medical insurance plan under which the insured and the insurer share hospital and medical expenses resulting from illness or injury. Sometimes used in major medical insurance plans. *See also cost sharing.*

COLA *See cost of living adjustment.*

cold turkey A common term for drug withdrawal, or the immediate cessation of the use of a substance that a person is addicted to (e.g., nicotine). Abrupt stoppage of drugs or smoking as a method to cease their use. Sometimes this results when the person is not able to get the drug. The term is based on a drug addict's description of the chills and consequent "gooseflesh" that is experienced when going through withdrawal.

co-linear In epidemiology or biomedical research, this is when two or more variables have a similar linear relationship with each other or with a common variable used for comparison.

collapsible corporation In health-care organization development, this is the creation of a corporation as a capital development project to sell the corporation. For example, hospital A and physician group B want to build a freestanding emergency center. Once it is built, instead of managing it and receiving the profits or selling the facility for a profit, hospital A and physician group B sell the corporation. The sale of the corporation is undertaken to qualify for a capital gains tax shelter; if it were sold as a facility, ordinary income tax would have to be paid on the profit. Federal tax laws regulate such transactions.

collateral 1. Additional; supplementary; complementary. 2. Property subject to a security interest. 3. Money or property put into security as a pledge to keep an obligation, as when taking out a loan.

collateral assurance A promise or guarantee on a deal made beyond a regular deed.

collateral attack Any effort to avoid a court's decision by requesting the case be heard in a different court or through different channels.

collateral estoppel An equitable doctrine that prevents a court from hearing a lawsuit involving issues that have already been determined in a different, prior proceeding.

collateral organization In health-care administration organizational development, this is when problems are dealt with across many units within the organization through committees, task forces, conferences, retreats, etc. with resolutions often required.

collateral source rule In health law, this is a litigation rule that restricts juries from considering the fact that the injured party (plaintiff) has been compensated from additional insurance sources not associated with the defendant/health-care provider. Even if a patient has had medical expenses covered, health-care providers can still be held to a malpractice lawsuit.

collection agency In health-care organization business office operations, this is a business or service contracted to collect overdue accounts receivable and bad debts. The services of a collection agency are usually utilized when all other internal means of collection have failed and after a specific amount of time has passed, as set by facility policy. A reliable collection agency is licensed and bonded and can furnish references from other facilities or businesses.

collection cycle (period) In health-care organization business office operations, this is the interval between the rendering of services, billing of the patient, and the receipt of payment.

collection report In health-care organization business office operations, this is a report prepared on a regular basis (monthly) that shows the total premiums collected, premiums paid in advance, and those overdue and uncollected.

collective bargaining In health-care organization labor relations, this is the principle that allows or requires employers to bargain with official union representatives about wages, hours, and other employment conditions.

collective bargaining agreement In health-care organization labor relations, this is the contract and promise made between a union and its employer as a result of employment negotiations.

collegial In health-care management, this is equal power, responsibility, and authority among peers or professionals.

collegiate school of nursing A department, division, or other administrative unit in a college or university that provides a program of education in professional nursing and allied subjects. This educational program may lead to the degree of bachelor of arts, bachelor of science, or bachelor of nursing or to an equivalent undergraduate degree. It may also lead to a graduate degree in nursing, including advanced training, if such program is accredited.

collimation In laser technology as used in medical treatment, this is the state in which all laser rays run parallel with each other within the bounds of a beam.

collusion Conspiracy; a secret agreement or promise between two parties involving fraud against a third party.

colon and rectal surgery A specialized medical and surgical field that involves the diagnosis and treatment of lower gastrointestinal tract disorders affecting the colon, rectum, and adjacent areas.

colonoscope A lighted optical instrument inserted into the colon and used to visually examine the interior of the colon.

colonoscopy The act of visually examining the interior of the colon with a lighted instrument.

color 1. A deceptive appearance that, while appearing to be one thing, represents another. Acting under color of law is an act that appears on the surface to be official but is not. 2. A sufficient warrant to cause action.

colorable 1. To cover or conceal; deceptive; false; counterfeit. 2. That which appears to be valid but is not.

colostomy A surgical opening where the colon has been opened to the outside body surface to allow for the outward passage of waste products into a specialized bag.

colostomy care The specialized care of a colostomy (the surgical diversion of the body's waste products through an artificial opening in the abdomen), including the care of the opening of the colon through the abdominal wall.

colposcope In medical care, this is a special endoscope used in the examination of a rape victim that magnifies injuries such as cuts or bruises that may have occurred during a sexual assault. It can be used to transmit images onto a color monitor in the medical care setting that can be preserved for use and transmission in the courtroom, even in distant locations via telemedicine.

COM Computerized output microfilm system. In health-care information management and medical and business office records management, this is the process of transforming computer information into microsize images on microfilm.

coma A level of unconsciousness with little or no detectable mental or physical responsiveness. *See consciousness.*

co-maker In health-care finance and business office operations, a second or third party who signs a negotiable instrument and is equally liable to the payment of the instrument.

combat fatigue Physical and mental reaction to the stresses of war, combat, or military duty.

combined acute-care/long-term-care facility *See combined facility.*

combined facility In health-care facility organization, this is a hospital with a nursing home wing that is attached to and is physically a part of the hospital and is under the direct administration of the hospital. The hospital administrator is usually required to also be a nursing home administrator. The nursing staff, housekeeping, central supply, laundry, food services, administrative services, and other services are commonly used and shared. Often this combined facility and shared support and ancillary services arrangement is found in rural locations, especially in the western United States.

combined ratio In health-care finance and business office operations, this is a method of determining the loss-expense ratio (the sum of the loss and expense ratios).

comity Politeness; civility; courtesy and respect.

command 1. In health-care management, this is to take charge of and direct; to give orders or assignments. 2. A word, mnemonic symbol, or character that instructs the computer to perform a predefined function.

command automatism A condition where a patient is open to the power of suggestion and follows it automatically.

commerce 1. The exchange of goods and products. 2. To deal in trade. 3. To carry on the trafficking of goods. 4. To have social intercourse.

commerce clause A clause in Article 1 of the U.S. Constitution that states that "commerce shall have the power . . . to regulate commerce with foreign nations, and among the several states . . . (Article 1, Section 8, Clause 3).

commerce power *See commerce clause.*

commercial disability insurance *See disability insurance.*

commercial health/medical insurance *See major medical.*

commercial paper In health-care finance, this is an unsecured short-term promissory note, used by large health-care organizations with an outstanding credit position, issued in denominations of $1 million or more. Interest rates are typically somewhat below the prime interest rate, and time of maturity can be up to 270 days and have a higher yield than other marketable securities.

commercial plan In managed care, this is the benefit package an insurance company or HMO offers to employers. This differs from a senior plan, which is available to persons over age 65 and not employed.

commercial term life insurance *See life insurance.*

commercial whole life insurance *See life insurance.*

commingle To mingle; mix together.

commission 1. Given the authority to perform certain tasks or exercise certain powers. 2. A written grant of authority that allows particular powers to be given by the government to one of its branches or to an individual or organization. 3. Committing a crime. 4. Authority to act for another person. 5. In insurance, the amount of money or premiums paid to an insurance agent, sales representative, or broker as compensation for services provided (a part of administrative expenses).

commissioner 1. One who has the authority to perform certain duties or acts. 2. The head of many public service boards or agencies. 3. The officer or chief in charge of agencies or branches of government.

Commission on Accreditation of the Council on Chiropractic Education (CCE) Recognized by the Council on Postsecondary Accreditation (COPA) as the formal accreditation body for programs leading to the doctor of chiropractic degree.

Commission on Heart Disease, Cancer and Stroke A special committee that recommends public health service guidelines at the federal level for dealing with, eliminating, or reducing the incidence of heart disease, cancer, stroke, and other chronic diseases. The recommendations of this commission influence legislation and grant authorizations for types of research needed at universities and medical schools related to any aspect of these disorders.

Commission on Professional and Hospital Activities (CPHA) A nonprofit, nongovernmental organization established in 1955 to collect, process, and distribute information and data on hospital use for management, evaluation, and research purposes. Two main programs of CPHA are the Professional Activity Study (PAS) and the Medical Audit Program (MAP). The system abstracts and classifies information from medical records in a standard way. A computer-accessible data library at CPHA is available, sponsored by the American College of Physicians, the American College of Surgeons, the American Hospital Association, and the Southwestern Michigan Hospital Council. *See also discharge abstract.*

commit 1. Lawful authority to send a person to a prison, reformatory, or asylum. 2. To do an act or crime. 3. To entrust; put into custody. 4. To offer or pledge services or obligations. 5. To consign a person to a mental hospital or psychiatric care facility.

commitment 1. The formal legal process of putting a person into the official care of another person or placing a person into a mental or psychiatric hospital. 2. A court order, ordering a person to a mental hospital or prison. 3. In health-care finance, a written agreement to make or insure a loan for a specified amount on specified terms. Often referred to as a "firm commitment."

committee A special group of people under one person's direction brought together for a special purpose, which may include tasks such as decision making, considering matters, taking action, and making reports on issues assigned to the group.

Committee on Allied Health Education and Accreditation (CAHEA) A nongovernmental agency that accredits educational programs for 26 allied health professions or occupations. The CAHEA encompasses a broad range of review and evaluation activities of educational programs in allied health on behalf of the American Medical Association and 46 collaborating organizations composed of allied health professional organizations, medical specialty societies, and other interest groups. As the final deliberative body for the assessment of compliance with established minimum acceptable standards for education in the allied health professions, the CAHEA formulates its accreditation decisions on the basis of recommendations received from 21 review committees that are sponsored by the collaborating organizations. Accrediting educational programs for the allied health professions began in 1933 through a cooperative agreement between the American Occupational Therapy Association and CAHEA's predecessor in accreditation, the Council on Medical Education of the American Medical Association. The growth in collaborative sponsorship for accreditation of allied health programs was moderate until the mid-1960s, when it accelerated. Recent changes in this committee's role and function occurred in 1993.

committee report A formal report by a congressional committee to the House of Representatives, Senate, or both concerning a proposed law or other matter. The report is a part of the legislative history and includes a summary of the proposed law, recommendations concerning its passage, and amendments and other relevant background information.

commode 1. A toilet. 2. A chairlike device with a hole in the seat and used as a portable toilet.

commodity An article or good that is produced, bought, or sold.

commodum ex injuria sua nemo habere debet (Lat.) A term meaning "no person should derive benefit from his own wrong."

common Usual; ordinary; regular; applying to many persons or things.

common law 1. Law made by judicial opinion or a judge's decisions; judge-made law. 2. Law that originated from English law derived from court decisions. 3. Case law, which is different from statutory law enacted by legislatures, by which a general body of legal principles is derived from usage, custom, and court decisions relating to governmental duties and security of individuals and their property. 4. Unwritten laws that are legally binding and are upheld by landmark or precedent cases rather than statutes or regulations.

common law action A civil lawsuit; a suit that is between private individuals and/or organizations.

common law crime An illegal act that could be legally dealt with under common law, as distinguished from crimes punishable under statutes. *See intentional torts.*

common law defenses In health law, these are defenses that can be used to defeat liability actions filed by employees in negligence cases. The three most common are contributory negligence, assumed risk, and fellow servant. *See also contributory negligence; fellow servant rule.*

common law marriage A couple living together as if married, holding themselves out publicly as if married and for a time period considered by law to be long enough to create a legal marriage. In many states, if a couple cohabitates for 7 years or longer, they are considered legally married.

common plan *See common scheme.*

common pleas Civil lawsuits between two private parties.

common scheme The planning or committing of two or more different crimes together.

common source epidemic Also called "common vehicle epidemic," this is an outbreak in which the event or exposure of a disease to a group of persons comes from a single agent, place, factor, or source that all persons in the group had a chance to encounter.

common stock 1. In health-care financial management, this is regular capital stock of a company or shares in a corporation that lack a definite dividend rate and are not preferred stock. The shareholders usually have voting rights at shareholders' meetings, depending on the amount of stock held. 2. Units of ownership in a corporation. Income from a stock is called a "dividend" and generally represents a share of stock of current profits and changes in the price of a share of stock.

common vehicle spread *See vehicle of disease; vehicle spread, common.*

communicable disease A sickness or pathogen that can be transmitted from person to person or from animal to man by fomites, vectors, water, air, food, unclean hands, animals, insects, or any other means; an infectious illness that is easily communicated between human and human or human and animal and that is caused by a specific infectious agent/pathogen or its toxic by-products. For an illness to be communicated, a susceptible host must be either directly or indirectly exposed and infected by an infected person animal, reservoir, plant, or other vehicle of infection. *See fomite; vectors; zoonosis; carrier.*

communicable period In epidemiology and infectious diseases, this is the time period in which an infectious agent or pathogen can be transmitted directly or indirectly from an infected person or animal to a susceptible person.

community 1. For public health purposes, this is a geopolitical unit, geographical region, town, city, or county for which a public health problem can be responded to. In certain areas, such as large metropolitan regions, it may be necessary to evaluate major "communities" in the area for variations in the incidence of each public health problem so that populations in greatest need of services can be specified and scarce resources effectively targeted. 2. A group of people, professions, or situations such as the medical community or the university community that have many commonalities. 3. According to JCAHO for accrediting purposes, the people, groups, agencies, or other facilities within the locality served by a long-term-care facility. 4. A group of geographically related units, organizations, or individuals that shares resources; a group of people with common values and mutual concern for the well-being of a group or an area.

community acquired infection A phrase used in health-care facilities indicating that a communicable disease as diagnosed in a patient was present prior to entering the health-care facility, thus coming from the community. *See infection; communicable disease; epidemiology.*

Community Action Program (CAP) An agency created by the Economic Opportunity Act in 1964 under President Lyndon B. Johnson's Great Society programs that provides federal monies to establish social service and health programs for special and needy populations. Programs created out of the CAP fund include those for drug rehabilitation, Head Start education programs, public television programs aimed at assisting the underserved minorities (e.g., *Sesame Street* and *The Electric Company*), elderly social service programs, neighborhood health centers, and family planning services. Health-related programs were supervised by the U.S. Public Health Service.

community agency In mental health, this is a private, nonprofit, state-assisted, community-based set of services for developmentally disabled individuals and the mentally retarded. Some states refer to such agencies as "regional centers."

community-at-large Includes all health-care providers, services and programs, and consumers in a geographical, regional, rural, or metropolitan area; the systems or services provided in these areas or the persons involved in the system or services.

community benefit standard In health-care finance with regard to the nonprofit tax status of a hospital or other nonprofit organization, the Internal Revenue Service lists several factors that should be considered in determining whether a hospital qualifies as a tax-exempt public charity: 1) Does the hospital have a governing board composed of prominent civic leaders rather than hospital administrators and physicians? 2) If the hospital is a part of a hospital system, do the minutes of the board meetings reflect corporate separateness? 3) Is the hospital's medical staff open to all qualified physicians in the area? 4) Does the hospital operate a full-time emergency department open to everyone regardless of ability to pay? 5) Does the hospital provide nonemergency care to everyone in the community who is able to pay, either privately or through third parties, including Medicare and Medicaid? (*IRS Audit Handbook*).

community counseling As a part of community mental health, this is the emotional and mental therapy conducted in a community mental health center to outpatients that emphasizes the total person and the entire social and emotional environment. *See community mental health.*

community development Those techniques, methods, and approaches used to organize and combine services, activities, and programs of the community to meet the needs of the target population and/or catchment area. Also included are attempts to combine different levels and types of funding sources to stimulate local initiatives and services by shared funding and effort and leadership efforts used to promote change at the local/grassroots level.

community development program A Native American health service program that emphasizes the methods as well as the goals of the community health representative program. The representative in this type of program strives to develop community organizations capable of identifying and solving health problems. The programs emphasize the community development approach to bring about a greater degree of self-determination by the community and a greater role by the entire community in the decisions made by outside agencies.

community dietitian, R.D. *See dietitian, clinical, R.D.*

community health 1. A term often used synonymously with "public health." Public health is only one aspect of community health, which includes a broad range and array of social, disease prevention, health promotion, and medical care activities. The array of community health activities includes social services; mental health services; aging services; nonprofit health and human service agencies; and private, voluntary health agencies and their community-based disease prevention and health promotion activities. Definitive care provided in the outpatient centers, day health-care programs, and related activities are all part of a community's health activities. 2. The health status of a community is influenced by educational levels, people's skill levels, socioeconomic status, employment/unemployment levels, availability of health care and disease prevention, public health measures, poverty, cultural and religious influences, moral state of the inhabitants, knowledge and practices of health-promoting behaviors, strength of the family unit, etc. *See continuum of care; healthy communities.*

Community Health Accreditation Program (CHAP) An accreditation program for home health agencies. CHAP is associated with the National League of Nursing (NLN). The accreditation process takes into account administrative outcomes, finance and accounting, planning, operations, service delivery, human resources, care outcomes, and overall evaluation.

community health care The accessibility, availability, acceptability, and capacity to deliver health care into a community; activities and programs intended to improve the health status of a specified community. The term is widely used and may be defined as being similar to public health or environmental health. It may also be considered synonymous with a community's ambulatory care, outpatient care capacity, and the availability of home health care. *See continuum of care.*

community health center An ambulatory health care program usually serving a catchment area with limited or nonexistent health services or a population with special health needs. Grant support for such centers was originally provided on a research and demonstration basis from the Community Action Program of the Office of Economic Opportunity. Subsequently, the funding authority for these projects shifted to Section 314(e) of the Public Health Service Act (now discontinued). Community health centers attempted to coordinate federal, state, and local resources into a single organization capable of delivering both health-care and related social services to a defined population. Other ambulatory centers have provided health services in areas of medical underservice supported with 314(e) funds, including family health centers and community health networks. The Health Revenue Sharing and Health Services Act of 1975 (P.L. 94-63), incorporating neighborhood health centers, family health centers, and community health networks under the single term of "community health centers," was defined in Section 330 of the PHS Act. Although such centers did not directly provide all types of health care, they arranged for all medical services needed by patients. *See also neighborhood health center.*

community health education 1. A process that bridges the gap between health information and health practices. Health education provides motivation to utilize health information and to keep oneself healthier by avoiding harmful behaviors and by activating beneficial habits and behaviors. Community health education includes the following activities: 1) inform people about health, illness, disability, and ways in which they can improve and protect their own health, including more efficient use of the health delivery system; 2) motivate people to cultivate more healthful practices; 3) help people learn the necessary skills and knowledge to adopt and maintain healthful behaviors and lifestyles; 4) foster teaching and communication skills in all those engaged in educating consumers about health; 5) advocate changes in the environment that facilitate healthful conditions and healthful behavior; 6) advocate social and political changes that facilitate healthful conditions and behavior; and 7) add to knowledge through research and evaluation concerning the most effective ways of achieving the previous objectives. 2. The application of a variety of methods resulting in the education and mobilization of community members in actions for resolving health issues and problems that affect the community. These methods include, but are not limited to, group process, mass media, communication, community organization, organization development, strategic planning, skills training, legislation, policymaking, and advocacy (Joint Committee on Health Education Terminology). *See also community public health educator; health education; community health promotion and protection.*

community health education empowerment The process of encouraging a community to take control of its own health education needs assessment, community educational diagnosis, planning, priority setting, and enabling activities as well as challenging and rallying the political and formal power structures to obtain support and resources to make a healthy community. Also referred to as "empowerment education."

community health educator A practitioner who is professionally prepared in the field of community/public health education and demonstrates competence in the planning, implementation, and evaluation of a broad range of health-promoting or health-enhancing programs for community groups (Joint Committee on Health Education Terminology).

community health information network (CHIN) 1. In health-care information management and computers, the sharing and merging of communication systems. CHINs allow the transmission of claims and clinical data to clear benefits and payments and to send administrative information and data while eliminating duplicative procedures. 2. Computerized patient records, data banks, data repositories, and various kinds of computer networks that are used as tools for building integrated health-care delivery systems. These computer networks and systems are the center of system-wide or community-based broad-scale processes and systems that emphasize and promote preventive care over medical care, treatment interventions, and inpatient care (developed at the CHIN National Center with the First Consulting Group, Long Beach, California).

community health network (CHN) A community (state, county, or city) health system that delivers medical care to the poor. Started by the Office of Economic Opportunity in the early 1970s, the program was transferred to the Department of Health and Human Services and has now become part of the community health center program. A CHN usually consisted of several centrally managed community or neighborhood health centers with necessary backup definitive health care.

community health promotion and protection A major subsystem of the health system that includes those services delivered to the community as a whole to improve or maintain their health status. Major service categories within community health promotion and protection include school health education, community health education, industry-based wellness programs, environmental health management, food protection, occupational health and safety, radiation safety, and biomedical and consumer product safety.

community health promotion and protection services Programs directed at the community level to improve the personal health behavior of community residents and to improve the quality of the environment, which affects health status. *See community health education; health promotion; health education; health protection.*

community health purchasing alliances Statewide medical insurance cooperatives for small-business owners in Florida. Eleven independent cooperatives have been formed and offer group purchasing advantages in buying less expensive insurance for businesses with 50 or fewer employees. This is a nongovernment, private effort. These cooperatives are passive in that they do not have power to negotiate bids with insurers, but the employer and employees do get to choose the coverage they want.

community health representative A paraprofessional health worker employed by Native American tribal governments to function as a liaison between the community and health resources. These health workers work closely with physicians, public health nurses, sanitarians, medical social workers, and other health team members to help improve the health conditions and health status of the group.

community health representative program A program of the Indian Health Service conducted on Native American reservations that emphasizes Native American involvement in community health. A product of the U.S. Public Health Services, it was developed to foster greater involvement of Native Americans in their own health programs and greater understanding between Native Americans and the Indian Health Service staff.

community health services 1. Programs or agencies that are related to health care and services of a population center such as a neighborhood, city, county, or other community structure and that provide services such as public health, environmental, social behavioral, mental health, education, aging programs, private nonprofit voluntary health agencies, etc. with the aim of preventing disease, promoting health, and assisting independent living, including support and rehabilitative services. Community health relates to the health of the public but is not limited to public health activities because it encompasses all community-based health and social services activities that affect the health of the community. 2. A field of health-care practice that encompasses the coordination of school health, public health, employee health, maternal and child health, environmental health activities, and personal health practices of families and individuals.

community health worker An individual who works in the community in cooperation with medical personnel and social workers to help the client and the health community locate and utilize available sources of assistance.

community hospital All nongovernmental, short-stay general hospitals established and organized to meet the inpatient medical care and treatment needs of a community or specific geographical area. Most are nonprofit organizations. In some definitions, units of a hospital available for public (Medicaid or welfare) patients are excluded. General services include general medicine; surgical; obstetrics and gynecology; eye, ear, nose, and throat; rehabilitation; orthopedic; children's services; and other specialties. The hospital may have rehabilitation units or a nursing home and still be classified as a community hospital provided that a majority of its patients are admitted to units where the average length of stay is less than 30 days. Since 1972, hospital units in prisons or university student health centers are no longer included in the category of community hospitals. *See hospital, community; hospital, general.*

community liaison program An Indian Health Service program that focuses on the liaison role of the community health representative but that, unlike the health liaison program, emphasizes the representative as a link between the community and all outside resources, whether health related or not. The representative in this type of program works with reservation, city, and county agencies to provide services in housing, education, employment assistance, and general welfare assistance and to direct health care.

community living center or facility A temporary living arrangement or halfway house that helps those recovering from mental illness, drug abuse, or alcohol abuse or former prisoners returning to the mainstream of the community.

community medicine The branch of medicine that concerns itself with community health-care delivery, public health, preventive medicine, or primary care to special populations. It also deals with assessing and evaluating needs and trends in disease and health-care delivery to specific groups or community populations. *See preventive medicine.*

community mental health This includes a commitment to preserving and enhancing the emotional well-being in a population or group, using proper treatment and therapy methods, through a multidisciplinary team of mental health workers to meet the array of emotional and mental health needs within a community while ensuring continuity of care with the same professionals or mental health team. Three levels of prevention common to public health and epidemiology are applied to mental well-being in a community context: 1) primary prevention includes efforts to halt or reduce the incidence of emotional and mental disorders within the community and avoid hospitalization, 2) secondary prevention reduces the duration and severity of the disorders and limits and reduces inpatient care, and 3) tertiary prevention limits mental and emotional impairment found in fully developed mental and emotional disorders with the aim of reducing hospital length of stay. *See community counseling.*

community mental health center (CMHC) 1. A facility that provides comprehensive ambulatory mental health services to individuals residing or employed in a defined catchment area (Community Mental Health Centers Act, Section 201). 2. A mental and emotional therapy and treatment facility that was at least partly supported by the Community Mental Health Centers Act of 1963 and made available comprehensive mental health services, including emergency and outpatient care, consultation, education, and hospitalization.

Community Mental Health Centers Act Section 201 of this law specified the psychiatric or mental health services to be provided and the requirements for the governance, organization, and operation of mental health centers. The CMHC Act provided for federal financial assistance for the construction, development, and initial operation of CMHCs and for the costs of their consultation and education services. *See also hospital, psychiatric.*

community organization The process of identifying the needs of the community and developing the services and resources essential to meeting those needs and of instituting cooperative and collaborative practices and attitudes at the local level.

community organization (for health) That process or method of health education by which the combined efforts of individuals and groups generate, mobilize, coordinate, and/or redistribute resources to meet unsolved or emergent health problems (Joint Committee on Health Education Terminology, 1973).

community-oriented administration A healthcare administration strategic planning approach used to identify the interests of the community and to explore ways a hospital can meet them.

community property Common or shared property acquired during the course of a marriage, regardless of who purchased it or in whose name it is listed.

community psychiatry *See community psychology.*

community psychology That branch of psychiatry or psychology concerned with the delivery of mental health care to a specified population, usually residents of a designated geographical area. Its purpose is the acceptance of continuing responsibility for all mental health needs of a community, including diagnosis, treatment, rehabilitation (often called tertiary prevention), and aftercare. Also included are early case-finding or secondary prevention, the promotion of mental health education, and the primary prevention of psychosocial disorders. The facility used to coordinate such services typically has been the community mental health center. *See community mental health center.*

community/public health educator A public health professional involved in teaching, community education, community health promotion, and the prevention of diseases, disability, injury, disorders, and death and who serves as a liaison, consultant, and disseminator of health information. This professional alerts community groups and individuals to changing patterns of diseases, health care, health hazards, and activities that will promote community health and safety and provide high levels of health status. *See health educator.*

community rating In managed care, this is a method of establishing premiums for medical insurance on the basis of the average cost of actual or anticipated health care used by all subscribers in a specific geographic area or industry. It does not vary for different groups or subgroups of subscribers or for such variables as the group's claims experience, age, sex, or health status. The HMO Act (Section 1302[8] of the PHS Act) defines community rating as a system of fixing rates of payments for health services that may be determined on a per person or per family basis "and may vary with the number of persons in a family, but must be equivalent for all individuals and for all families with similar composition." The intent of community rating is to spread the cost of illness evenly over all subscribers (the whole community) rather than charging the sick more than the healthy for health insurance; all enrollees in a health plan must pay the same amount of money for premiums. Some states have laws that allow the managed-care program to factor in differences for age, sex mix, and industry factors.

community rating system In managed care and HMOs, this is a system of fixing rates of payments for health services. Under this system, the rates of payments for health care may be determined on a per person or per family basis, depending on the number in the family, but are the same for family units of similar composition. Differential rates of payments may be established as follows: 1) rates may reflect differences in the marketing and administrative costs of collecting payments from individuals or families, small groups of members, or large groups of members; 2) rates may reflect the composition of the rates of payment in a systematic manner to accommodate group purchasing practices of various employers; and 3) rates may be established for members enrolled in an HMO pursuant to a contract with a governmental authority under Section 1079 or 1086 or Title 10 of the U.S. Code or any other governmental program for employees of states, political subdivisions of states, and other public entities.

community setting Settings where population- or group-based health services and education, rather than where personal health-care services or patient-related support services, are provided. Voluntary or public agencies or schools for health professions typically provide services in community settings. Health care or health promotion and disease prevention services and activities are provided where the people live and work rather than having them come to a health-care facility.

community trials In epidemiology research, this is a research project in which an entire community or subunit of a community receives a therapeutic intervention or treatment such as immunizations or fluoridation of drinking water supplies. A true experimental design approach may not be used (control groups may or may not be used) because it is almost impossible to identify controls because all persons receive the treatment.

commutation 1. An alteration; a change. 2. In criminal law, a reduction in sentence; changing a criminal's punishment to a less severe one.

commute 1. To stand in the place of another. 2. To reduce the sentence of a criminal. 3. Payment in kind or by compulsory duty.

comorbidity Coexisting diseases or illnesses. Relevant to prospective payment systems and diagnosis-related groups (DRGs), a preexisting condition that, because of its presence with a specific principal diagnosis, will affect the type and amount of treatment received and will thus cause the length of stay to increase. (Some studies have shown it to increase the length of stay by 1 day in 75% of the cases.) Also referred to as "substantial comorbidity."

compact An agreement or contract between two parties, usually between governments or nations.

company 1. To be a companion to or to accompany. 2. An organization established to do business. 3. A number of persons united for the same cause, purpose, or concern as a business; the members of a firm; a group of persons intent on fulfilling a common cause.

comparability provision A provision in Medicare that specifies that the reasonable charge for a service may not be higher than charges payable for comparable services insured under comparable circumstances by a carrier for its non-Medicare beneficiaries (see Section 1842[b][3][B] of the Social Security Act).

comparable worth In health-care administration personnel management, an administrative principle that jobs should be evaluated and salaries assigned by level and responsibility with entirely different jobs of equal responsibility and authority receiving equal pay. Individuals with widely different positions but of equal level, authority, and responsibility of equal value to the employer are paid the same.

comparative analysis In health-care finance, this is the comparison of a hospital's financial past performance with current performance and the organization's own goals and against competitors as well as industry standards.

comparative method A procedure used to estimate the construction replacement cost of a building by comparing the planned construction with the cost per square foot or cost per cubic foot of a similar existing building.

comparative negligence A legal principle by which "fault" on each side of a negligent act is measured and balanced by a judge or jury on the basis of the amount each party was at fault and contributed to the injury, with recovery and damages being determined by each party's share of the fault. In some states, this approach to measuring fault has replaced the less fair method of "contributory negligence." In cases where the negligent acts of the plaintiff and the defendant are compared, damages are determined by the degree of negligence of the defendant over and above that of the plaintiff. The degrees usually are "slight," "ordinary," or "gross." If negligence is concurrent and contributes to harm or injury, recovery is possible, but the plaintiff's damages are diminished proportionately as long as the plaintiff's fault is less than the defendant's and, if ordinary care was given, the injury could not have been avoided once it became apparent (*Rogers v. McKinley*, 48 Ga. App. 262, 172 S.E. 663, 664). This rule does not apply in some states but is a more common way of determining fault because it is the most fair. *See contributory negligence; fault.*

comparative statements In health-care finance, these are different financial statements that provide information on the same organization or institution for different times (usually for 2 successive years).

comparison groups In epidemiology and biomedical research, this is a form of control group that represents the study group or general population and is used as a comparison to the study group.

compelling state interest A concern serious or strong enough to result in the enactment of a law at the state level that justifiably limits a person's constitutional rights. The right to refuse medical treatment is a right held by all competent adults; however, this right has been be restricted to "a compelling state interest" such as preserving life, protecting minors, protecting innocent third parties, preventing suicide, and maintaining ethical integrity of the medical profession.

compendium A collection of information about drugs. Under the federal Food, Drug, and Cosmetic Act, standards for strength, quality, and purity of drugs are those that are set forth in one of the three official compendia: the *United States Pharmacopoeia*, the *Homeopathic Pharmacopoeia of the United States*, and the *National Formulary* (or any supplement to these). Since the mid-1960s, there has been a call for the FDA to publish a compendium of all marketed drugs to improve the amount and quality of information on drugs available to physicians or pharmacists. The compendium would consist of one or more volumes and would probably resemble an expanded version of the popular *Physician's Desk Reference*, a private compendium in which drug manufacturers purchase space and that does not provide information on all drugs. *See also formulary.*

compensating balances In health-care finance, this is cash revenue that is required to be deposited in a bank by a health-care organization as partial compensation for lending, lines of credit, or other banking privileges provided to a health-care organization.

compensation 1. The settlement of a debt. 2. A recovery payment for harm, damages, or loss. 3. In psychology, disguising an undesirable trait by exaggerating a positive, acceptable one; a mental mechanism by which a person substitutes one behavior for another, less acceptable one, believing it will help him or her to cope better in life.

compensatory damages Money or other forms of remuneration as a part of the recovery process given to a plaintiff who was a part of a negligence or malpractice lawsuit brought to remove damage, injury, unfair or unjust treatment, loss, or suffering. *See damages, compensatory; recovery.*

competence 1. Capacity equal to requirement. 2. Skill, education, training, and practice that produces a quality result.

competency An acceptable level of skill proficiency required to carry out an activity.

competency-based education An educational approach used in allied health, nursing, or medical education curriculum design. It focuses on learning outcomes and mastering skills and techniques, and students are required to demonstrate their level of mastery of a skill, technique, or activity. If the skills or techniques fall below predetermined levels, the instructor establishes learning experiences to help students achieve the skill. The learner can negotiate with the instructor to determine the learning activities needed to achieve the desired level of skill and to pass the competency test.

competent 1. Qualified or suitably capable; legally authorized and properly qualified; possessing the right or legal qualifications meeting all requirements. 2. Of sufficient mental capacity as required by law; mentally able to control one's life, take care of financial obligations, practice socially accepted behavior, and use reliable and controlled judgment and behavior so as not to be a danger to themselves or others.

competent court A court having lawful jurisdiction.

competent evidence In health law, this is proof or fact that is both relevant and proper.

competing cause of death As a cause of death becomes less common, other causes of death emerge and become the focus of compilers of health statistics and demographers. The new prominent cause of death is the competing cause.

competing risk Any risk factor that may have an outcome that is associated with other risk factors.

competition, managed *See managed competition.*

competitive analysis of health services In strategic health planning, this is the process of assessing the external environment in which a health-care organization or health system operates. The analysis assesses those organizations, services, or systems that offer the same or similar type of health services, the service area, target population, market niche they are trying to fill, the amount of threat and competition they pose, patient mix, threat of taking managed care and patients away, competitive position and threat each competitor holds, aggressiveness of the competitor, and strategic moves each might make.

competitive medical group plan In managed care, this is a type of prepaid, HMO-type organization created by the TEFRA Act of 1982 to facilitate the enrollment of Medicare beneficiaries into prepaid plans. These health plans are organized and financed much like HMOs but are not bound by the regulations and controls that dictate the structure and function of an HMO. *See TEFRA; HMOs; managed care; Medicare risk health maintenance organizations.*

competitive medical plan (CMP) 1. In managed care, this is a prepaid care plan that is not as limited or restricted as an HMO in benefits and the manner in which premiums are determined. 2. A Medicare designation that allows a health plan to obtain eligibility to participate in a Medicare risk contract. Qualifying as an official HMO and eligibility requirements are less restrictive than for HMOs. *See competitive medical group plan; Medicare risk health maintenance organizations.*

competitive positioning of health services In strategic health planning, this is the process of completing a competitive analysis and developing strategies and tactics used for organizational and financial positioning of the health service or health-care organization. The health service is positioned for current and future success with regard to types, level, amounts of programs and services, diversification of services, financial viability, survivability, marketing activity, program development needs, competitive advantage, and overall future dominance of health services in the field.

compiler In health information management, this is a program that translates common language or a computer language like BASIC into a lower-level machine language that the computer can recognize.

complainant 1. One who makes an official complaint or files a complaint in court. 2. A lawsuit seeking legal remedy in the courts. 3. A plaintiff in a lawsuit.

complaint 1. The initial document filed in a civil lawsuit. 2. A formal charge or accusation that includes a statement of the harm done to the plaintiff by the defendant and a request for remedial actions from the court.

complaint visit A visit to a health-care facility made by a survey team from a regulatory or licensing agency in response to a complaint received by the agency about the facility.

compliance 1. Yielding to a request; complying with wishes or demands. 2. Acting in a way that does not violate instructions; adhering to a prescribed treatment plan or therapeutic or preventive regimen; staying within the scope of practice. 3. To adhere to or fall within the scope of laws and regulations; to perform or act in a manner that does not violate rules, laws, regulations, or legal principles. 4. To act in accordance with standards (JCAHO for acute-care facilities). *See also patient compliance; scope of practice.*

complementary benefits Under Medicare, a nongroup agreement that allows an insurance intermediary like Blue Cross to pay the hospital deductible and co-insurance for Medicare beneficiaries.

complex A psychiatric term for a group of associated ideas that have a common emotional relation. These are viewed by some psychological theorists as unconscious and are believed to influence attitudes and associations.

complex treatment As used in medical insurance and managed care, this is radiation therapy and oncology treatment of malignant disease requiring complex field localization or use of beam-shaping devices (e.g., treatment of the eyelid; mantle fields in Hodgkin's disease) or treatment of two or more fields per region or two or more regions per day, massive single-dose treatment, or intracavitary therapy applied with general anesthesia.

compliance level In the accreditation process for hospitals, this is a measure of the extent to which a hospital acts in accordance with specified accreditation standards. Six levels have been set forth: 1) substantial, meaning the hospital consistently meets all major provisions of a specified standard with a score of 1; 2) significant, meaning the hospital meets most provisions of a standard with a score of 2; 3) partial, meaning the hospital meets some provisions of a standard with a score of 3; 4) minimal, meaning the hospital meets few of the provisions of a standard with a score of 4; 5) noncompliance, meaning the hospital fails to meet the provisions of a standard with a score of 5; and 6) not applicable, meaning the standard did not apply to the hospital, designated by "NA" (JCAHO for acute-care facilities).

complicating and comorbid In disease classification and diagnosis-related groups (DRGs), the Health Care Financing Administration in determining the severity of DRGs has developed three measures of severity of a medical case using the secondary diagnosis to a DRG to uniformly categorize the case as 1) noncomplicating or comorbid (non-CC), 2) complicating or comorbid (CC), and 3) major complicating or comorbid (MCC). Studies showed that a few DRGs with secondary diagnoses had higher use of resources when the patient lived and are placed in the MCC category; if the patient died and also had higher use of resources, the case is classified as CC. A secondary diagnosis is required to determine DRG assignment. The DRGs with secondary diagnoses mainly fall in the areas of circulatory disorders, certain cancer treatments and surgery, trauma and related surgical procedures, and HIV and related conditions.

complication A detrimental condition that arises during a hospital stay. The patient then requires more treatment, thus prolonging the length of stay in the hospital. This is any disease condition that worsens or arises from a hospital stay, is observed and treated in the hospital, and modifies the course of the patient's illness, treatment, and hospital stay. (Some studies have shown that a complication prolongs the length of stay by at least 1 day in approximately 75% of the cases.) *See comorbidity; iatrogenic.*

composite rate In managed care, this is a uniform premium rate that is applied to all subscribers to a health plan regardless of the number of dependents who are claimed to be eligible under the health plan. A group billing rate applied to all members in a specific employee group, regardless of whether enrolled as a single person or as a family. Common to large employer groups in which the members make a small premium payment or none at all.

composition 1. In health-care finance and business office management, a formal agreement that allows a creditor to accept as full payment less than the total amount owed. 2. A bankruptcy agreement where the person in debt agrees to pay the creditor's part of the money owed.

compound interest In health-care finance, the interest that is paid on the principal (or main debt) and on the unpaid interest.

compounding a felony Committing more than one crime during a felony violation.

comprehensive care Total, complete care and services provided beyond those offered by usual health insurance plans. Comprehensive care usually includes dental care, eye care, preventive care, and mental health services. This term is associated with managed-care prepaid group health plans, HMOs, Indian Health Services, and military health services.

comprehensive care facility A licensed health-care facility that provides a full range of health-care and support services, including but not limited to hotel services, board, laundry, nursing care, constant observation and attendance by nursing staff, personal care, social services, recreational therapy, rehabilitation, and administration of medications by a registered nurse under the supervision and responsibility of an attending physician.

Comprehensive Drug Abuse Prevention and Control Act of 1970 A law enacted by the U.S. Congress that controls and regulates controlled substances such as narcotics and other dangerous drugs that can be obtained only under prescriptions issued by properly licensed health-care providers.

Comprehensive Employment and Training Act of 1973 (CETA) Replaced by the Job Partnership Training Act, this program was designed to provide job training, employment, and job search assistance to less advantaged individuals.

Comprehensive Environmental Response, Compensation and Liability Act (CERCLA) Known as the "Superfund," the 1986 amendments to this act set forth procedures for reporting and controlling hazardous substances that have an environmental impact. The law imposes requirements for the use of protective equipment and procedures and requires a reporting system to the appropriate local, state, and federal government agencies. The design and operation of many manufacturing processes and waste disposal systems are also monitored and controlled. The law was enacted to assist in cleaning up contaminated sites by requiring those companies responsible for the environmental contamination or pollution to pay the cleanup costs.

comprehensive general liability A business insurance policy designed for various business liability situations and that usually covers operations of a physical plant and the premises of the health-care facility, product liability, activities of independent contractors, and day-to-day activities of the facility.

comprehensive geriatric assessment The diagnostic and evaluation services for elderly patients provided by geriatric, internal medicine, and family practice physicians to determine the short- and long-term health-care needs of the older adult. The elderly patient undergoes extensive evaluation of medical conditions, functional abilities, and mental health and emotional needs, and the findings are incorporated into a treatment plan that addresses family, social, and financial concerns and medical needs. *See activities of daily living; geriatric assessment center.*

comprehensive health care That amount and level of care intended to meet all health-care needs of a patient, including eye care, mental health care, dental care, inpatient, outpatient, home care, disease prevention, and health promotion.

comprehensive health-care delivery The process of providing and coordinating the continuum of health-care services for a predefined population. *See comprehensive care.*

Comprehensive Health Insurance Plan (CHIP) An approach to a national health insurance proposal.

comprehensive health planning The preparation of a plan for all health services and health-care delivery in a region, state, or nation that includes all kinds of health providers, health-care services, preventive services, and health promotion and protection activities through the use of data analysis. *See areawide comprehensive health planning agency; health systems agency; state health planning and development agency.*

comprehensive health planning agency (CHP) A former agency established to perform specified health-care planning functions under the Comprehensive Health Planning and Public Health Services Amendments of 1966 (P.L. 89-749). This law was later replaced by health systems agencies as a result of the implementation of the Health Planning and Resource Development Act of 1974 (P.L. 93-64 1), which was abolished in 1986. *See areawide comprehensive health planning agency; health systems agency.*

comprehensive major medical insurance A medical insurance policy designed to give the hospital and physician payment protection of both a basic and a major medical health insurance policy.

comprehensive outpatient rehabilitation facility A designation by the Health Care Financing Administration of the Social Security Administration for industrial rehabilitation centers that provides a complete range of physical therapy, occupational therapy, speech therapy, and related services for persons under workers' compensation insurance or individuals under the care of home health agencies who are treated on an outpatient basis. Injuries from sports, recreation, or non–work-related accidents or on-the-job adverse events could also be treated on an outpatient basis in an outpatient rehabilitation facility.

comprehensive quality management A variation on total quality management. *See total quality management; continuous quality improvement.*

comprehensive school health education The development, delivery, and evaluation of a planned curriculum, preschool through grade 12, with goals, objectives, content sequence, and specific classroom lessons including, but not limited to, the following major content areas: community health, consumer health, environmental health, family life, mental and emotional health, injury prevention and safety, nutrition, personal health, prevention and control of disease, and substance use and abuse.

comprehensive school health program An organized set of policies, procedures, and activities designed to protect and promote the health and well-being of students and staff of schools. The school health program traditionally included health services, healthful school environment, and health education. Also included, but not limited to these, are guidance and counseling, physical education, food services, social work, psychological services, and employee health promotion (Committee of American Public Health Association on Health Education Terminology).

comprehensive service *See levels of service; services.*

compress A sterile pad or cloth (sometimes medicated) that is applied to a wound or open sore.

compression of morbidity *See morbidity, compression of.*

comptroller *See controller.*

compulsion An uncontrollable impulse to do certain acts or behaviors repetitively. *See also obsession.*

compulsive personality A personality type characterized by overconscientiousness, controlling inhibition, inability to relax, and rigidity.

compulsory Used in connection with coverage under proposed national health insurance or other health insurance plans in which coverage must be offered or taken. A plan may be compulsory only for an employer (coverage must be offered to employees and a specified portion of the premium paid) or for individuals as well. Any universal public plan is necessarily compulsory in that the payment of taxes to support the plan is not optional with the individual.

compulsory process To force a person to appear in court by an official action.

computer An electronic machine that processes, analyzes, and stores large amounts of data. This machine can perform preprogrammed computations, word processing, and data analysis at high speeds and produce reports and retrieve information quickly, effectively, accurately, and economically.

computer assisted minimally invasive surgery (CAMIS) Surgery that utilizes a surgeon's wand containing infrared, ultrasound, and other anatomical sensors with a supercomputer interpreting and fusing sensor information instantly, generating a three-dimensional image on a cathode ray tube and helmet-mounted display in front of the surgeon's eyes. The technology is adapted from military fighter jet and helicopter pilots' helmet-mounted targeting display used in the cockpit for aiming weapons. The wand is inserted into cavities or organs of the body, and because the surgeon can see within the body, surgery can be conducted without making the usual large incisions.

Computer Assisted Pathology Encoding and Reporting System *See CAPER; MUMPS.*

computer conversion plan A plan developed for converting a manual record-keeping system to a computerized system.

computer interactive processing The operation of a computer or data processing system that allows for interaction between the operator and the computer by use of a keyboard or other input terminal.

computer program A plan or routine that allows the computer to solve problems. Software programs that run on computers carry out an array of health-care information processing and business activities.

computer system A data processing system consisting of hardware (computer terminals), software (the programs that run on the computer), and related pieces of equipment and documents that describe the function and operation of the hardware and the means to make the software run.

computer system design and resource allocation planning phase In planning for the implementation of a computer system in a health-care facility, the phase of the plan that sets forth the specifications needed in the computer hardware, software, staffing, space requirements, and other needed resources as determined by a feasibility and implementation study.

computer system development and conversion planning phase The actual implementation phase in setting up a computer system in a health-care facility: programs are written; software, hardware, and related equipment and materials are purchased; and the process of converting from a manual system to computer system is prepared.

computer system operation phase The phase of operations when the computer system is activated, debugged, made operational, and evaluated against predetermined plans and objectives.

computer system study A formal assessment of the computer needs in a health-care facility that includes feasibility studies, wiring access, the evaluation of hardware, software, space allocation, staffing, and related needs and costs.

computerized axial tomography (CAT) A noninvasive radiological diagnostic technique in which series of X rays are taken from several points around a single plane or level of the body. From these computerized X rays, a single, composite picture is developed by a computer. The scan represents a horizontal cross-section of the various tissues present at that level of the body. The machine used for this procedure is called an ACTA scanner. Another similar type of instrument for reconstructing cross-sectional planes of the body is an EMI scanner, now referred to as a CT scanner. CT scans are used extensively for studies of the brain and other body structures and organs.

computerized word processing system A specialized use of computers by medical records personnel, business office personnel, or other workers. The user types on a typewriter-like keyboard (information is input directly into a computer), and the results are shown on a cathode ray tube screen. The advantage of this approach for generating documents is that errors can easily be corrected, lines or blocks of text can be inserted into the document, the text materials can be proofread, and the document can be stored on a disk or diskette or other storage medium for later use. The document can be put back into the computer for editing, changes, or additions. Printed paper copies, called "hard copies," can quickly be produced.

computer tomography scanner (CT scanner) See *computerized axial tomography*.

con- Prefix meaning "with," "together," or "against."

CON See *certificate of need*.

concealment Hiding or withholding information or evidence.

concentration in employment When a higher proportion of employees in a protected class of worker is found in the health-care organization's labor market.

concentric diversification In strategic health planning, this is a growth tactic that involves adding new products or services that are similar to the organization's present products or services. The chosen tactic must lie within the organization's know-how, and they must have experience with the technology, product line, distribution, and customer base.

concessionary bargaining In labor relations in health-care organizations, this is when negotiations between management and the representatives of a health-care labor organization result in fewer employer-paid benefits or when wage concessions, such as a wage reduction, are agreed on.

conciliation 1. To win over and bring together. 2. To soothe two sides of an argument and bring them together to a compromise.

conclusion of fact A conclusion drawn or inference made from facts and evidence.

conclusion of law The application of facts to particular principles of law to reach a final decision.

conclusive 1. Finishing a matter; completing an inquiry; finishing a debate. 2. Not allowing further evidence. 3. Plain; visible; obvious; clear. 4. Ended; final; decisive; no longer refutable.

concordant As used in twin studies, this describes when both twins have a certain characteristic or trait common to each.

concur To unite in opinion; to agree. A concurring opinion is one in which two judges agree but for different reasons.

concurrent Having equal authority or jurisdiction.

concurrent analysis The ongoing quantitative and qualitative review of a patient's medical records during hospitalization.

concurrent certification *See admission certification.*

concurrent disinfection In epidemiology and medical care, a protective measure to contain and control the spread of an infectious disease by or through a patient who is infectious.

concurrently At the same time; to run together. In law, concurrently served sentences are prison terms that run at the same time.

concurrent resolution on the budget A resolution passed by both houses of Congress that requires the signature of the president. It sets forth, reaffirms, or revises the congressional budget for the U.S. government for a fiscal year. Two such resolutions must be completed each year; the first concurrent resolution by May 15 and the second by September 15.

concurrent review An assessment and analysis of the medical necessity of hospitalization or other health facility admissions on or shortly following admission and the periodic review of services provided during the course of treatment. The initial review usually assigns an appropriate length of stay to the admission (using DRG-specific criteria), which may also be reassessed periodically. Under managed care or standard health insurance, where concurrent review is required, payment for unneeded hospitalizations or services is usually denied. Concurrent review should be contrasted with a retrospective medical audit, which is done for quality purposes and does not relate to payment and claims review and which occurs after the hospitalization is over. Formerly applied to inpatient admissions, this review is also used in outpatient care, managed care, and other types of health-care settings to determine medical necessity, level of care, and appropriateness of services.

concurrent services In managed care, this refers to those health care services that are currently being provided to an enrolled member with other additional services.

condemn 1. To give a negative or adverse decision. 2. To blame; to sentence. 3. Found guilty of a criminal charge. 4. Official ruling that declares something unfit for use (this process is called "condemnation").

condition 1. Under health law, this is an uncertain future restriction or event that could create or destroy rights or obligations; a contract can have a condition written into it. 2. Anything required before performance or completion can be done; anything that could restrict or modify an occurrence; stipulations that may change or nullify a contract. 3. An illness, injury, disorder, disability, disease, or congenital malformation. 4. A health condition is a departure from a state of physical or mental well-being. Conditions, except impairments, are coded according to the ICD-9-CM. A general term of medicine and public health that includes any specific illness, injury, or impairment. When a population is surveyed by health interviews, to determine amounts and levels of conditions present in the population, respondents are asked to identify any conditions that caused certain types of impact associated with health such as a visit to a physician, diagnosis, treatment, or a day spent in bed. Respondents are also asked to read a list of chronic diseases and indicate which ones they or any family member have had. Two categories of conditions, based on duration, are acute and chronic. *See condition, acute; condition, chronic.*

condition, acute In the National Health Interview Survey, this is a disease or malady lasting less than 3 months and involving either a physician visit (medical attention) or restricted activity. *See condition; condition, chronic.*

condition, chronic Any illness or malady lasting 3 months or longer or the type of malady classified as chronic regardless of the time factor. The national nursing home survey uses a specific list of conditions classified as chronic that disregards time of onset.

conditional accreditation Under the accreditation process of JCAHO, the determination that substantial standards compliance deficiencies exist in a hospital. Corrections of shortcomings identified through the first survey must be completed and demonstrated in a follow-up survey 6 months after the initial survey.

conditional sales contract In health-care financing and management, this is a financing method used to purchase new equipment by paying for it in installments over periods of 1, 2, 3, or 5 years. Title to the equipment is retained by the financing institution until all payments are completed.

conditionally renewable A managed-care plan or medical insurance contract that allows the insured person to renew the contract to a predetermined and stated date or advanced age; to continue to insure an enrollee as long as the health plan continues to insure individuals in the same plan or the same state with the same kind of policy. The health plan or insurer has the option of declining renewal only under conditions specifically set forth in the insurance contract.

conditioning therapy *See behavior therapy.*

conditions of enrollment In managed care or medical insurance, those rules that determine eligibility for enrollment.

conditions of living In the assessment of the health status of individuals, especially the elderly, this is the combination of behavioral and environmental circumstances of an individual's life and health-related activities experienced on a daily basis.

conditions of participation (COP) 1. To make a determination related to whether a skilled nursing facility is eligible to participate in Medicare or Medicaid programs. Standards and various elements of performance are used to establish conditions. 2. Under Medicare, those conditions that a provider or supplier of services desiring to participate in the Medicare program is required to meet before participation is permitted. These conditions are specified in the statutes and regulations and include compliance with Title VI of the Civil Rights Act, signing an agreement to participate that is acceptable to the Secretary of Health and Human Services, meeting the definition of the particular institution or facility contained in the law, conforming with state and local laws, having an acceptable utilization review plan, and meeting appropriate Professional Review Organization requirements. Investigations to determine whether health-care facilities meet or continue to meet conditions of participation are made by the appropriate state health agency responsible for certifying that the conditions have been met and that the provider or supplier is eligible to participate. 3. Under the Omnibus Budget Reconciliation Act this is used interchangeably with "condition for coverage" when applied to suppliers and "level A requirements" when used for long-term-care facilities.

conference 1. A formal meeting where professionals gather to confer and share knowledge about their professional health-care area to stay current and learn new developments in their field. 2. In national lawmaking, a formal meeting of representatives of the House and Senate at which the differences between the two versions of a single piece of legislation or policy are resolved. Those chosen to conduct the conference are called "managers" and together form the conference committee. They jointly recommend a compromise version of the legislation, the text of which is the conference report. With the report is an explanation of how the differences were resolved (the equivalent of a committee report, called the "joint statement of managers"), which becomes part of the legislative history. Because the compromise version is different from those originally passed, the conference report must be enacted by both the House and the Senate before being sent for presidential signature.

confession 1. Acknowledgment of guilt; disclosing of fault or committing a crime. 2. A statement by a person that he or she is guilty of a crime; admission of wrongdoing.

confession and avoidance A form of pleading where a party confesses that the allegation made is true and then presents new material that renders the charges legally void.

confession of judgment When borrowing money, the borrower can sign a written promise that, should the borrower default on the loan, judgment may be entered against the borrower.

confidence interval In biomedical research and biostatistics, this is the range of values within which a known statistical probability should fall; the ability of a statistical test applied to research findings to show that there is a 90%, 95%, or 99% chance that the results are not caused by chance alone.

confidence limits In biomedical research and biostatistics, this is the range or band of values above and below a statistical confidence interval that shows the range of true values a probability might have.

confidential Private or secret information, practices, or procedures; information commonly held in privacy, including medical, financial, or other patient information obtained in the course of medical practice and information about the cost, quality, and nature of the practice of individual and institutional providers obtained through payment and regulation programs.

confidential communication Any communication that passes between persons in a fiduciary relationship who are obligated to not reveal the contents of the information.

confidential information Any statement made to a professional such as a psychologist, counselor, psychiatrist, physician, attorney, clergy, or others in confidence and with the understanding that the information should remain secret and not be shared with anyone.

confidentiality The ethical and professional requirement that a health-care provider not disclose information received from a client or patient (also called "privileged communication"). Some states do not legally recognize confidentiality and can require the health-care professional to divulge any information needed in a legal proceeding. *See fiduciary.*

confidentiality and disclosure policy A policy, overseen by the executive committee of the board of commissioners of JCAHO that requires 1) confidentiality of certain hospital information, including that obtained before, during, or following an accreditation survey; all materials that may contribute to the accreditation decision; standards compliance recommendations; and written staff analyses and Accreditation Committee minutes and agenda materials; and 2) the disclosure of certain hospital information, including that subject to public release, aggregate standards compliance data, and information subject to release to designated government agencies under specified circumstances (JCAHO for acute-care hospital accreditation).

confidentiality as a patient right A patient has the right, within the law, to personal and informational privacy, including the patient's medical record (JCAHO for acute-care hospital accreditation).

confidential relationship 1. A relationship where a client or patient has a right to receive a high level of trust from a physician, psychologist, counselor, lawyer, or other professional. 2. A relation in law that is created to prevent undue advantage being taken because unlimited confidential information is available to certain people; thus, a duty is created that requires an ultimate degree of good faith between the parties in all interactions and transactions. 3. Any legal relationship that is recognized and definite, requiring trust mid-confidence, where a fiduciary relationship legally exists. *See fiduciary.*

configuration The process of selecting hardware and software that will function together to make the computer system run.

confinement Any illness, disability, or injury that restricts the insured person, causing the person to stay at home or in the hospital. Many policies specify that coverage is provided only if the insured is medically confined, as determined by the health-care provider. An uninterrupted stay in a health-care facility for a defined period of time that is covered in a medical care policy.

confiscate 1. To seize by proper authority; to appropriate. 2. The taking of private property without payment.

conflict of interest A situation where business dealings can result in personal gain or where one's needs violate a duty owed to others. *See also substantial interest.*

conflict of laws 1. Contradiction and inconsistency in laws. 2. When a judge must choose between laws of more than one state or country that may apply to a case to make a decision.

conflict resolution In health-care management, this is a process of resolving differences, especially among employees or work units. All parties involved participate in and mutually accept decisions and work together toward an acceptable solution.

confounding variable In epidemiology and biomedical research, this is a factor that is known to be associated with the occurrence of a health or medical event that distorts research outcomes or influences the magnitude of the effect of the study and that is not equally distributed in a research population or in the controls.

confrontation The right of a defendant (usually through his or her lawyer) to see and cross-examine all witnesses to be used against the defendant.

confused When a person appears bewildered, makes inappropriate statements, or gives strange or incorrect answers to questions.

confusion 1. Failing to distinguish between two or more items or facts. 2. A merger or blending together. 3. To confound facts; intermingling.

confute To disprove or prove that a person or a statement is wrong, false, or invalid.

congenital Any condition, disorder, or defect prior to or at birth.

congenital anomaly Any abnormality present at birth with no regard as to cause.

congregate dining (nutrition programs) A nutritional service for the elderly that provides hot banquet-style meals in a center setting to provide proper nutrition, a balanced diet, nutrition education, and the benefit of social interaction.

congregate housing A group living arrangement, usually for the elderly, that promotes noninstitutionalized (nursing home) living. Residents are usually in good health but may need some social and medical support services and in some situations may share some common facilities such as meals and central living areas. Some individuals may be made eligible for additional supplemental security income (SSI) benefits.

Congressional budget The federal budget as set forth by Congress in a concurrent resolution on the budget. These resolutions include the appropriate level of total budget outlays and of total new budget authority; an estimate of budget outlays and new budget authority for each major functional category, contingencies, and undistributed intragovernmental transactions (on the basis of allocations of the appropriate level of total budget outlays and of total new budget authority); the amount, if any, of the surplus or deficit in the budget; the recommended level of federal revenues; and the appropriate level of the public debt.

Congressional Budget Office A key U.S. federal government agency that audits and provides analysis of various other governmental agencies, prepares analysis of various budget alternatives, and conducts studies for the U.S. Congress on all federal agencies and departments, including federal health and human services and agencies.

Congressional Record A daily publication that records the day-by-day proceedings of Congress.

conjoint medical staff The relationship between doctors and hospital administration assuming a close managerial affiliation. The requirements of a privileged medical staff are combined with a formal administrative plan for physician recruitment and ongoing medical staff participation in continuous quality improvement. *See medical staff.*

conjugal Related to marriage and the husband-wife relationship.

conjugal rights The sexual privileges of a husband-wife relationship.

conjugal room A room set aside in an institution such as a hospital, nursing home, or prison where a person may exercise his or her conjugal rights. *See conjugal rights.*

connecting up To put into evidence information or facts that have to "connect up" with other evidence to be relevant.

consanguinity Blood relationship.

conscience clause In health-care law, this is an element of law giving individuals, employees, or institutions the right to refuse to participate in an act or a treatment that is contrary to their moral or religious beliefs (e.g., participating in abortions).

consciousness A person's normal state of awareness.

consciousness, levels of Six suggested states of mental awareness: 1) alert: awake and oriented to time, place, people, weather, environment, and surroundings; 2) confused: awake but disoriented as to time, place, people, and surroundings; 3) somnolent: drowsy or sleepy when alone (when awake, the patient may be confused); 4) stuporous: difficult to arouse and may be combative, aggressive, or hostile at times; 5) semicomatose: very little spontaneous movement or motion unless strong attempts to arouse the patient are made; 6) comatose: the patient may or may not be responsive to painful stimuli, and no spontaneous movements are observable.

consent Permission, approval, or voluntary and active agreement. A patient has the right to be informed in decisions of his or her health, medical care, treatment, or surgery. Clear, concise explanation at the patient's level of understanding about his or her condition and all proposed procedures, treatments, risks, side effects, outcomes, probability of success, and recuperation are essential. *See also express consent; informed consent; implied consent.*

consent extension doctrine A patient's consent is limited to those treatments or procedures anticipated and planned for at the time consent is given. Any treatment or procedures beyond the original consent requires that a new consent form be signed for each treatment. If consent needs modification to remedy a condition that is discovered after the original consent is given, two options are considered: 1) Has the patient consented to remedying a condition rather than to a particular procedure? If so, no extension should be needed. 2) Does the signed consent form give the health-care provider broad enough latitude in treatment to cover the newly discovered condition? If not, a new consent form would be required (*McGuire v. Rix; Wells v. Van Nort; Cathemer v. Hunter; Kennedy v. Parrott*).

consent judgment An agreement by the parties to an action, entered into with the approval of the court.

consequential damages Losses or injuries that are a result of a wrongful act but are indirect or do not appear until later.

conservation In environmental health, this is avoiding waste of, and renewing when possible, human and natural resources; the protection, improvement, and use of natural resources according to principles that will ensure their highest economic or social benefits.

conservator Similar to a guardian, this is a person appointed by a court to take care of another person and all their legal and personal matters including finances, rights, medical consent, and the property of the conservatee.

consideration In health law, this is the material aspects or ramifications of a contract; any item of worth, value, or money given in a contractual agreement to complete the agreement; money, items of value, and monetary worth. *See also valuable consideration.*

consign 1. To give, send, or deliver; to entrust things over for transportation or sale while retaining ownership. 2. To leave in the custody of a third person. 3. To agree or consent to; to sign over to or to put in charge of.

consignment The act of entrustment or the document that entrusts an item to another person for sale while still retaining ownership.

console terminal A keyboard and cathode ray tube screen that allows for input into the computer system and for user interface with the system.

Consolidated Omnibus Budget Reconciliation Act of 1985 (COBRA) Signed into law in 1986, COBRA requires employers providing group benefits to workers to also provide medical insurance and other benefits to all qualified beneficiaries, with the right to elect to continue their coverage for a certain period of time after coverage terminates, usually because of job loss.

consolidation 1. In health law, treating separate lawsuits on the same subject and between the same persons as only one lawsuit. 2. Uniting separate things into one. 3. In health-care organization and corporate structure, to form a firm, combining two services into one; to formally combine two companies or institutions into a single legal entity with its own identity.

consortium 1. A partnership. 2. A joint effort on the part of institutions to organize for a common effort. 3. An organized partnership used to meet similar or common goals when a single organization lacks its own base or ability to be successful on its own. 4. The right of a spouse to receive the other's love and services.

conspiracy Persons joining together to plan and undertake an unlawful act.

constitution A document that provides guidelines, principles, and limitations of a governing body, government, or organization.

constitutional Consistent with the state or federal constitution and not in conflict with the basic laws of the state or nation.

constitutional law 1. The law that determines the organization, structure, functions, principles, and limitations of governments. 2. Laws created by federal, state, and/or provincial constitutions.

constitutional right Any and all rights guaranteed by the Constitution of the United States.

construct 1. A mental concept or process or the way an individual develops beliefs and values. Constructs screen one's differentiation of beliefs and elements in life. 2. In epidemiology or health promotion, this is a set of concepts with a causal explanation or theoretical framework representative of basic psychological or behavioral principles related to health or risk factors.

construction In health law, this is a judge's decision on the meaning of ambiguous words, determined by looking at the surrounding circumstances and relevant laws.

construction, cost of In health-care organization planning and development, this cost includes 1) the construction of new buildings; the expansion of existing buildings; and the acquisition, remodeling, replacement, renovation, major repair, or alteration of existing buildings, including architects' fees, but not including the cost of acquisition of land or offsite improvements; and 2) initial equipment of new buildings and of the expanded, remodeled, repaired, renovated, or altered part of existing buildings. This term does not include the construction or cost of construction of any facility that is to be used for sectarian instruction or as a place for religious worship.

construction loan In health-care finance and organization planning and development, this is a short-term or interim loan used for the financing of a construction project. The construction loan is usually followed by a long-term loan, called a "take out loan," which is given on completion of the construction or renovation.

construction management In health-care finance

and organization planning and development, the hiring of a professional construction consultant to coordinate and monitor a construction project. The consultant negotiates for competitive bids in purchasing materials, labor, and subcontractors. The consultant must keep costs down, keep the construction to a time schedule to meet completion dates, and monitor construction activities from start to finish.

constructive 1. A factor or incident that is legally true; established by legal interpretation. 2. Inferred; implied.

constructive discharge In health-care administration and personnel management, this is when an employee separates or resigns from work because of intentional imposition of unreasonable work conditions or when a situation forces the employee to resign when this person would not normally have resigned or quit.

construe To arrive at a meaning of a statute, contract, or statement by inference.

consul A person appointed by the government to reside in a foreign country to take charge of the needs, affairs, and interests of fellow citizens in the country.

consultant 1. Any professional who provides professional, expert, or technical advice or services as requested. 2. According to JCAHO, one who provides professional advice or services on request.

consultant, health care An independent professional who provides expert advice on health-care organization and management for hospitals or other health-care facilities.

consultant, hospital A health-care consultant who works with hospitals. *See consultant, health care.*

consultant, medical A health-care provider, usually a physician, who provides professional advice or services concerning a patient at the request of the attending physician.

consultation 1. The act of requesting advice from another provider, usually a specialist, regarding the diagnosis and/or treatment of a patient. Referral for consultation is distinguished from referral for services because responsibility for patient care is not usually delegated to the consultant. However, there can be frequent occasions when the consultant may subsequently 1) assume the patient's management in full or in part or 2) need to see the patient on a repetitive basis for the purpose of further evaluation and/or treatment in a continuing consultative capacity. Therefore, a referral may ensue after completion of a consultation, but such an event does not preclude the fact that the initial evaluation was a consultation. 2. A review of a patient's problems by a second practitioner such as a physician or other health-care provider and the rendering of an opinion and advice to the referring practitioner. In most instances, the review involves the independent examination of the patient by the consultant. The opinion and advice of the consultant are not usually binding on the referring health care provider (JCAHO for acute-care hospital accreditation). 3. Under Medicare managed care, the rendering of an opinion, advising on or prescribing treatment by telephone, and, when determined to be medically necessary jointly by the emergency and on-call specialty physicians, reviewing the patient's medical record and examining and treating the patient in person by a specialty physician who is qualified to give an opinion or render the necessary treatment to stabilize the patient. *See also referral.*

consultation and education services Programs and services required of each community mental health center (CMHC) by Section 201 of the CMHC Act. These consist of consultation with and education for the staffs of programs and institutions in the CMHC's community who are likely to be responsible for those with mental illness. Such services are specially subsidized by Section 204 of the CMHC Act because they are high-priority preventive care, are not usually reimbursed by the recipient institutions, and are not covered under medical insurance.

consultation in the accreditation process Advice given to hospital staff relating to hospital compliance with accreditation standards that are the subject of the accreditation survey (JCAHO for acute-care hospital accreditation).

consultation report The part of the medical record that consists of a written report of a physician asked to do an examination of a referred patient and that patient's medical records that sets forth the health-care provider's opinion, examination findings, and recommendations (JCAHO for acute-care hospital accreditation).

consulting medical staff Physicians on the medical staff of a hospital who provide consultation to other members of the medical staff on an on-call, yet continual, basis.

consumer 1. One who receives health services. Although all people at times consume health services, a consumer as the term is used in health legislation and programs is usually someone who is never a provider (i.e., is not associated in any direct or indirect way with the provision of health services). The distinction has become important in programs where a consumer majority on a governing body is required, as in community health centers and health agencies assisted under specific governmentally funded programs. 2. One who uses goods or services for his or her own use or needs rather than to use them for resale or to make other products to sell.

consumer awareness Being aware of defective or unsafe products or misleading information related to the consumption or use of products.

Consumer Credit The trade association created for the Insurers of Credit Insurance in life and health insurance.

consumer participation 1. The involvement of the layperson in learning about health-care services and health-care providers to make health services and programs more relevant to the needs of consumers. 2. The application of the principle of "involvement in teaming" intended to increase "provider" teaming and to make program plans more relevant to the needs perceived by consumers (Joint Committee on Health Education Terminology).

Consumer Price Index (CPI) An economic index prepared by the U.S. Bureau of Labor Statistics that measures the change in average prices of the goods and services purchased by urban wage earners and their families. The CPI is widely used as an indicator of changes in the cost of living, as a measure of inflation (and deflation, if any), and as a means for studying trends in prices of various goods and services. The CPI has several components that measure prices in different sectors of the economy. The medical care component provides trends in medical care charges on the basis of specific indicators of hospital, medical, dental, and drug prices. This component characteristically rises faster than the CPI itself; however, because the CPI measures charges, which are not always related to costs, the CPI may fail to accurately reflect changes in medical care costs.

consumer rights Provisions that ensure that consumers receive fair treatment and are not taken advantage of. Some of these rights include the right to be informed, the right to safety, the right to choose, and the right to be heard as well as the right to understand instructions, seek further information, understand performance claims, analyze alternatives, and look for recent or current developments in the consumer information field.

consummate To finish, complete, carry out an agreement, fulfill.

contact In epidemiology, this is the opportunity to acquire a disease or infection from a human or animal by close association or interaction.

contact, direct In epidemiology, this is a mode of disease transmission that occurs by direct touching or interaction between skin or mucous surfaces between an infected host and susceptible person such as kissing, sexual contact, or other physical touching.

contact, indirect In epidemiology, this is a mode of disease transmission where an infection is spread by vectors, fomites, or other vehicles of disease transmission.

contact, primary In epidemiology, this is the first, main, or direct interaction a susceptible individual has with a source of infectious disease.

contact, secondary In epidemiology, this is those persons exposed to a disease from contact with the primary contact/case; all persons getting ill after exposure to the primary contact.

contagion In epidemiology, this is the process of spreading disease by direct contact or through other mediums of transmission such as air, food, vehicles, vectors, or fomites.

contagious In epidemiology, this is those diseases that are transmitted by contact with an infected host or other vehicle of infection.

containment 1. In health-care delivery, this is the restricting and controlling of runaway spending on health care, termed "cost containment." *See cost containment*. 2. In epidemiology and public health, the control or limiting of the spread or eradication of infectious diseases at the community level. 3. In environmental health, the confinement of chemicals, substances, or radioactive materials in such a way that they are prevented from being dispersed into the environment or are released only at a specified rate. 4. In health and safety, the control of the expansion or propagation of accidental loss.

contaminants In environmental health, this is any physical, chemical, biological, or radiological substance or matter having an adverse effect on humans, animals, aquatic organisms, air, water, or soil.

contaminate To make unsanitary, unclean, or unsterile; to soil; to pollute.

contamination 1. Any unsanitary condition that results from contact with any object bearing unclean or pathogenic organisms; the presence of infectious agents or pathogens on the body, personal items, surgical instruments, materials or dressings, or food items such a milk, water, meat, or vegetables. 2. In environmental health, the presence of any unwanted biological, physical, chemical, or radiological substance or matter that has an adverse effect on air, water, or soil.

contemn 1. To scorn, slight, or despise. 2. To treat as despicable. 3. To reject or scorn with disdain.

contemner 1. One who despises or scorns; a person who contemns. 2. The person committing contempt of court; one guilty of contempt.

contempt This is the willful disregard for authority, whether judicial or legislative.

contest To argue against or oppose, as in a lawsuit.

contiguous area An area in close proximity to any health services delivery area based on travel time from a population center to the center of the point of service such a hospital or clinic.

continent 1. The ability of persons to be able to hold and control their bladder and bowel. 2. Refraining from sexual activity. *See incontinence.*

contingency fees Money paid for charges on the basis of future occurrences or on the results of services to be performed. Contingency fees are used by lawyers representing patients as plaintiffs in malpractice and negligence cases and are usually a set fraction (commonly a third) of any settlement awarded the patient. If no settlement is awarded, the lawyer is not paid. *See also New Jersey rule.*

contingency planning In strategic health planning, this is the process of assessing and anticipating changes in the health-care delivery system, health-care industry, governmental regulations, and medical care financing plus any reimbursement modifications, acquisitions, mergers, and adjustments in the competitive environment by making plans and developing strategies to account for any of these changes by having clear-cut and well thought out plans to deal with any events that might arise that will affect the position and viability of the health service or health-care organization.

contingency reserves 1. Reserves set aside by a managed-care plan or insurance company for unforeseen circumstances and expenses. 2. In health-care financial management and budgeting, liquid assets that are saved and not budgeted and may be used for emergency expenditures.

contingency table In epidemiology or health services research analysis, a method of tabulating data and findings with categories listed in the left column and the frequency of the response or occurrence listed in the right column, allowing for organization of the data and ease in entering into computer spreadsheets, calculation of numbers, statistical analysis, and the development of charts and graphs.

contingency tables A method of breaking data down into workable parts and pieces and organizing the information into categories and subcategories. Data are placed in a table in a logical organized manner by class and category using a horizontal (rows) and vertical (columns) organization approach to get rough counts and frequency counts and to apply descriptive statistics and advanced statistics to the data. The basic minimum parts of a contingency table are the "label," with "categories" placed on the left and "frequency" placed on the right, with the frequencies reflecting the data of the categories. This process is referred to as "tabulation."

contingent worker A person who works less than full time and thus does not receive any benefits such as medical insurance. This person also has low levels of income, less job security, and a low standard of living and cannot afford to pay for serious illness, high hospital and doctor bills, or medical insurance. Some definitions include persons who work less than 35 hours a week or less than 12 months a year. Also referred to as the "working poor," "near-poor," or "medically indigent." *See working poor; near-poor; medically indigent.*

continuance tables In managed care, this is a table that contains morbidity data indicating the distribution of claims according to the duration of illnesses and the amount of expense incurred by the claims.

continuation In managed care, this is when an enrollee in a health plan who would lose coverage because of the loss of employment or divorce is allowed to have continued coverage under certain conditions specified in the contract or allowed by law.

continued stay review Assessment and analysis of a patient's condition during a patient's hospitalization to determine the medical necessity and appropriateness of continuation of the patient's stay. It may also include assessment of the quality of care being provided. Occasionally used for similar review of patients in other health facilities. In the Medicare program, it is sometimes called "extended duration review." *See also concurrent review; medical review.*

continuing care retirement community *See life care centers.*

continuing education 1. Formal education obtained by a health professional after completing a degree and postgraduate training to improve or maintain the professional's competence. Some states require a specified number of hours of recognized continuing education per year as a condition of continued licensure for certain health professions. Usually the education is required to fulfill an externally imposed standard or to meet that standard within a specified minimum length of time. 2. Under JCAHO, education beyond initial professional preparation that is relevant to the type of patient care delivered in the hospital and that provides current knowledge relevant to an individual's field of practice and is related to findings from quality assessment and improvement activities.

continuing education unit (CEU) A standardized measure of educational activity in a continuing education program. A certain number of completed CEUs may be required of physicians, nurses, and other health personnel to assure continued licensure.

continuing medical education (CME) Postgraduate education provided for physicians to keep them current in their field of practice or to broaden their knowledge and understanding. Some hospitals require physicians on their staff to attend periodic medical education meetings. Some state medical societies require continuing medical education for continuance of membership, whereas some specialty boards require that a certain number of CME hours be taken for recertification. Some states require a certain number of CME hours to be completed for renewal of medical licenses.

continuing resolution Legislation enacted by Congress to provide budget authority for specific ongoing activities in a fiscal year in cases where the regular appropriation for such activities has not been enacted by the beginning of that fiscal year. This legislation usually specifies a maximum rate at which the agency may obligate funds on the basis of the rate of the prior year, the president's budget request, or an appropriation previously passed by either house of Congress.

continuing source epidemic In epidemiology, this is an outbreak of a disease that continues over long time periods that is indicative of a high prevalence of the disease because of the persistence of the source of the cause of the disease (the pathogen) in a population or environment.

continuity 1. A measure of health-care delivery; the degree of coordination present in the delivery of health-care services to each consumer. Continuity is a measure of the extent to which the health system interrelates and integrates the various services delivered to a consumer over time and in various settings. 2. Continued, complete, total care from one health-care practitioner or setting to another; succession of care.

continuity of care 1. Medical care that has succession of care and that proceeds across time and across different levels and places of care without interruption. 2. A component of patient care quality consisting of the degree to which the care needed by a patient is coordinated among practitioners and across organizations and time (JCAHO for acute-care hospital accreditation).

continuous improvement A health-care organization's ongoing effort toward more efficient and effective operation through better service to the customers.

continuous quality improvement (CQI) In health-care administration, this is the planned ongoing and enhancement of programs and services on a regular and continuing basis. It focuses on an organizational culture aimed at quality improvement through which "total quality management" operates and improves. This term reflects the efforts to continually evaluate and assess quality with efforts and commitment to improve management and health-care delivery systems of quality under a total quality management program. Continuous quality improvement is an ongoing effort on the part of all members and employees of a health services organization to meet the needs and expectations of its consumers by learning more about the activities, processes, and delivery of health services, management outcomes, and the interrelation of quality factors. The CQI process is accomplished by the cooperation and empowerment of workers and health-care providers to identify problems and improve quality of services and goods while reducing hassles, inefficiencies, and unnecessary complex approaches and policies. *See total quality management.*

continuous variable In epidemiology and biomedical research, any factor or element that can take on any value in a specified interval.

continuous wave In laser technology, this is the output of a laser that is operated in continuous mode rather than one that is pulsed.

continuum of care *See continuum of long-term care.*

continuum of long-term care A whole range of supportive health-care and social services available for the elderly who are fairly healthy that provide alternatives for, and prevent premature institutionalization of, those elderly whose needs demand institutional care or its equivalent. The continuum includes total independence, nutritional programs, transportation, social services, visitors' services, home health care, adult day care, respite care, residential care (group homes), personal care, institutional (nursing home) care, and hospice care.

contra (Lat.) Against; opposite.

contraband Imported or exported goods held in violation of law; prohibited goods.

contraception The prevention of fertilization of the ovum by the sperm by use of mechanical, chemical, behavioral, or other forms of fertility control.

contract 1. A binding promissory agreement between two or more competent parties that creates, modifies, or destroys a legal agreement to do or not do some act. *See also unilateral contract; bilateral contract; quasi-contract.* 2. In psychology, counseling, or psychiatry, a commitment by the patient or client to a specific course of action or change of behavior. 3. According to JCAHO for psychiatric, alcoholism, and drug abuse facilities accreditation purposes, a formal agreement with any organization, agency, or individual, approved by the governing body, that specifies the services, personnel, and/or space to be provided to, or on behalf of, the facility and the monies to be expended in exchange. 4. In managed care, a health plan agreement executed by an employer group for medical care and health services from a health plan; the legal agreement used to establish a health plan member's medical care coverage.

contract clause Article 1, Section 10, Clause 1, of the U.S. Constitution: "No State shall . . . pass any . . . law impairing the obligation of contracts. . . ."

contract count In managed care, this is the number of subscribers (excluding dependents) enrolled in a prepaid group health plan.

contract law That area of law that deals with promissory agreements between two or more parties, thus creating a legal relationship between the parties.

contract management General daily administration of a hospital by an outside management company or other organization under a formal contract. The management company reports directly to the board of trustees or owners of the hospital, which retains total legal responsibility and ownership.

contract physician A member of the medical staff of a hospital or other health facility who works on a contractual basis (full or part time) to provide health care and whose pay is determined by the terms of a contract. It may be on a fee basis or another predetermined arrangement.

contracted services Those services provided to a facility that are rendered by outside personnel contracted to that facility.

contract labor In health-care administration and human resources management, this includes those individuals who are hired through an outside, independent company who, for a fee, supply the health-care organization with human resources (workers).

contract managed hospitals *See contract management.*

contract mix In managed care, this is how health plan enrollees are distributed by dependency categories such as the percentage of single enrollees or double or family dependents. It is used in health plan contracts to assess types of enrollees and how they average out in a subscriber group agreements.

contractual adjustments In managed-care and health plans, this is a bookkeeping adjustment that reflects the uncollectable difference between set charges for services provided to those with health insurance and what is reimbursed by third-party payers.

contractual allowances In managed care, this is the difference between the amount billed or gross charges at previously established charges and the actual amounts received or due from third-party payers under their contractual agreements; similar to a trade discount.

contractual liability The liability one assumes as stipulated by a contract.

contract year In managed care, this is the time period from the effective date of the health policy or health plan agreement to the date of expiration.

contraindication To go against advice; recommended not for use. Any conditions that cause the use of a treatment or drug to be advised against. In the administration of drugs, some medications are recommended not to be administered under certain conditions or if certain other drugs are in use redundant.

contribution margin (marginal income) In health-care finance, this is revenue less variable costs. The contribution margin may be expressed on a per unit basis, as a total, or as a ratio.

contribution to surplus In health-care finance and managed care, this is the overattained funds that result from a health-care plan making more money than is needed to pay for the cost of providing insurance.

contributory benefit plans In health-care administration and personnel management, these are the fringe benefits that both employer and employee contribute to, including the cost of health-care plans, insurance, retirement, and other employer benefits.

contributory insurance A managed-care health plan or group insurance in which all or part of the premium is paid by the employee and whatever remains is paid by the employer or union. *See also enrollment period; noncontributory insurance.*

contributory negligence 1. A method used to determine fault. Negligence on the part of the plaintiff adds to or compounds the plaintiff's injury, which is assessed by a jury or judge. The negligence of one party, if established, will eliminate the liability of the second party; if the second party is 10% at fault, he or she is totally at fault. Comparative negligence is used more often, as it a much more fair way to determine fault. *See comparative negligence.*

contributory plan In managed care, this is a group insurance plan in which group members pay a portion of the medical insurance premium and the employer pays the rest. Contributory group plans have voluntary membership enrollment.

contributory program In managed care, this is one approach to payment for a premium of a health plan for an employer group in which part is paid by the employee and part by the employer or union.

control group In epidemiology or biomedical research, this is part of an experimental research design where the intervention treatment or factor being tested is deliberately omitted for a certain group called the "controls"; a comparison group for study consisting of individuals who were not exposed to the disease, condition, intervention, or procedure.

controllability The ability of Congress or the president to control budget outlays during a given fiscal year. "Uncontrollable" and "relatively uncontrollable" describe outlays and programs (such as Medicare) in which budget amounts cannot be increased or decreased without changes in existing substantive law.

controlled charges In health-care finance, this is the actual cost of providing health-care services plus a markup to cover the cost of indigent care, indirect costs, and a prompt-pay discount. This type of charge is limited to private pay because it is subject to certain limitations imposed by state, managed-care, third-party payers, and Medicare reimbursement systems.

controlled decentralized system In health information management, this is a record control system where all requisitions for records, filing procedures, and related record distribution and control processes are standardized so that all medical records are maintained at various locations within a health-care facility in an identical manner.

controlled (drugs) substances Those substances covered under the Federal Comprehensive Drug Abuse Prevention Control Act of 1970; those drugs (e.g., narcotics) regulated by the government.

Controlled Substances Act Comprehensive Drug Abuse Prevention Control Act of 1970. Passed to establish a system of control over drugs of abuse and narcotics. A classification of abused substances was developed and restriction on their use established. This law provided funds to develop programs related to drug addiction, treatment, rehabilitation, and public health education related to drugs and their effects on the individual and society.

controller The individual responsible for the financial and business affairs of an organization. This person may also serve as the chief financial officer. Also called "comptroller."

controls *See control group; controls, matched.*

controls, historical Cases or subjects of a research study that do not get the treatment but that are studied and compared with a disease or condition that occurred at a date different to and earlier than the current study. Selection of controls by this method is a bit faulty because they are not representative of the study group.

controls, hospital Cases or subjects of a research study that do not get the treatment but that are studied and come from clinical patients or from the medical records of a hospital. Selection of these controls by this method can cause selection bias.

controls, matched In epidemiology or biomedical research, cases or subjects of a research study that do not get the treatment but that are studied, are selected in a manner that ensures that the controls are similar to the subjects of the study, and are considered matched. Characteristics of the subjects can include age, race, gender, religion, education, occupation, and socioeconomic status and are used to match variables with research subjects.

controls, neighborhood In epidemiology or biomedical research, cases or subjects of a research study that do not get the treatment but that are studied and come from the same locality as the subjects of the study.

controls, siblings Family members, usually brothers and sisters, who are used in research studies for comparison with research subjects because of the potential for genetic comparison because of shared genetic makeup.

control selection In epidemiology or biomedical research, this is a sampling method used to increase the possibility of selecting samples with a preferred set of characteristics while still trying to retain credible and acceptable probability sampling methods.

controversy A dispute between interests of adverse parties.

controvert To dispute; contest; deny.

convalescence The continual and gradual recovery of a patient's health and strength after illness, injury, or surgery.

convalescent centers Facilities that provide care for convalescing patients for a short-term, intermediate, or long-term stay and that are generally licensed as either skilled or intermediate care facilities. The basic services include supportive and custodial care, medical supervision, rehabilitative programs, nursing services, special diets, and specialized medical services. Certain patients may be discharged once a certain level of health or rehabilitation is attained.

convalescent hospitals A term used in some states for a nursing home or skilled nursing facility. A convalescent hospital can provide intermediate and extended skilled care for young persons with extreme disability or for very ill elderly. When used synonymously with "nursing home," it is somewhat misleading because many patients do not convalesce but are provided skilled nursing care until death. A term used synonymously with "nursing home," "extended care facility," or "skilled nursing facility." *See convalescent centers.*

convene To officially open a formal meeting or hearing; to call a meeting to order.

convention A formal assembly of persons that is representative of a unit or profession or of an organization that gathers together to conduct a series of meetings.

conventional 1. Arising from or created by an agreement between persons, not by any legal arrangement. 2. The common or usual way of doing things; ordinary; acceptable.

conventional loan In health-care finance, a mortgage or deed of trust (not a government-backed loan) offered by a bank or money-lending institution.

conversion 1. An illegal act that deprives a person of the use of his own property (e.g., withholding a patient's personal belongings). 2. In managed care, a privilege given to a health plan enrollee that allows for medical coverage to be changed without having to demonstrate insurability. Most insurance master group contracts define the conditions of conversion. Conversion is made when the enrollee is no longer employed and thus no longer covered and can convert the policy on leaving the employee insurance group.

conversion plan In managed care, this is a benefit package available to all plan members on termination of group benefits.

conversion plan candidate In managed care, this is a terminated plan member who is interested in and eligible for a conversion plan. *See conversion plan.*

conversion privilege The right of an individual covered by a managed-care plan or group medical or dental insurance policy to continue coverage on an individual basis (paying the full premium) when terminating association with the insured group. In group health insurance, this allows the insured to change group insurance to some form of individual insurance without medical examination, usually on change of employment. Group insurance does not always offer a conversion privilege, but when it does the available individual insurance is generally not comparable in benefits or cost.

conviction 1. Having a firm belief. 2. Finding a person guilty of a crime.

COO *See chief operating officer.*

Cooperative Health Statistics System (CHSS) A program of the National Center for Health Statistics in which federal, state, and local governments cooperate in collecting health statistics so that data are collected by the agency best equipped to do so. When in full operation, the CHSS collects data in the following seven subject areas: health manpower (inventories and surveys), health facilities (inventories and surveys), hospital care, household interviews, ambulatory care, long-term care, and vital statistics. Legislative authority for the CHSS is found in Section 306(e) of the PHS Act.

cooperative hospitals 1. Under managed care, these are health-care facilities controlled by the users of the health-care services. These hospitals usually provide comprehensive care, have a prepayment system, and utilize group practice. Such prepaid comprehensive care programs are often referred to as HMOs. 2. A formal professional organization established to work on behalf of the members of the organization for specific purposes such as developing educational programs, conducting organizational meetings, and legislative advocacy.

coordinated The integration of the multidisciplinary services provided by patient care team members that meet the home health needs of the patient under Medicare.

coordinated care programs The governmental integration of managed-care programs that extends health care to all individuals and attempts to contain health care costs.

coordinated organizing In labor union activities, this is when two or more unions pool their resources to attempt to organize a targeted hospital or health-care organization.

Coordinated Transfer Application System (COTRANS) A system begun in 1970 by the American Association of Medical Colleges that evaluates U.S. citizens receiving undergraduate medical education outside the United States and that sponsors those it deems qualified to take part in one of the national board examinations. Students who take and pass the boards with this sponsorship may then apply to a U.S. medical school for completion of their training with advanced standing. Some students obtain such sponsorship from an individual school without using COTRANS.

Coordinating Council on Medical Education (CCME) A supervisory body established in 1972 to coordinate policy matters and accreditation at all levels of medical education. Among its organizational members are the American Medical Association, the American Board of Medical Specialties, the American Association of Medical Colleges, the American Hospital Association, and the Council of Medical Specialty Societies as well as public and federal members. *See also Liaison Committees on Medical Education and Graduate Medical Education.*

coordination The purposeful and planned process of assembling, synchronizing, and organizing differentiated work efforts or activities so that health-care personnel can function effectively and harmoniously in the attainment of the health-care organization's mission, goals, and objectives; the pulling together of all activities of the organization to make possible its effective and efficient functioning and ultimate overall organizational success. Characteristics of a well-coordinated organization are such that 1) each subsystem or department works in harmony with other organizational units, 2) each management unit knows its role and what tasks it must share and burden it must carry, 3) each management unit's work schedules are set up to meet the workload and organizational demands and the needs of the personnel, 4) continuous quality improvement is crucial in the organization's improvement and survival, and 5) thoughtfulness, good communication and listening skills, and the understanding of others' needs and positions are essential.

coordination of benefits (COB) In managed care and medical insurance, these are provisions used by insurers to avoid duplicate payment for losses insured by more than one carrier. This can also be the sharing of medical expenses through primary and secondary insurers to determine how charges and medical claims will be settled. For example, in benefits for medical costs arising from an automobile accident, an individual may be covered by both the automobile and the health insurance policies. A coordination of benefits or antiduplication clause in one of the policies will prevent double payment for the expenses by making one of the insurers the primary payer. There are standard rules for determining which of two or more plans, each having COB provisions, pays its benefits in full and which pays a sufficiently reduced benefit to prevent the claimant from making a profit.

coordination, types of In health-care administration, four types of coordination approaches have been identified: 1) *corrective coordination:* those coordinative activities that rectify an error or correct a dysfunction in an organizational system after it has occurred; 2) *preventive coordination:* those activities that aim to prevent the occurrence of anticipated problems of coordination or, at least, minimize the impact of anticipated problems; 3) *regulatory coordination:* those activities that aim to maintain existing health-care organization structural and functional arrangements; and 4) *promotive coordination:* those activities that attempt to improve the articulation of the various parts of a health-care organization.

COPA *See Council on Post Secondary Education.*

COP Conditions of participation. Under OBRA, this is an abbreviation that is also used interchangeably with "conditions for coverage" when applied to suppliers and "level A requirements" when used for long-term-care facilities. *See condition of participation.*

co-pay *See co-payment.*

co-payer *See co-payment; cost sharing; co-insurance; member co-payment.*

co-payment 1. A contract under which the insured party must pay a portion of the cost of professional services rendered. 2. In managed care, when a health plan member's share of charges for medical services is paid to the HMO or other provider at the time the care is given; a type of cost sharing whereby insured or covered persons pay a specified flat amount per unit of service or unit of time (e.g., $2 per visit, $10 per inpatient hospital day) and their insurer pays the rest of the cost. The amount paid does not vary with the cost of the service (unlike co-insurance, which is payment of some percentage of the cost). 3. An additional fee charged to a health plan member and paid directly by the member to the provider for services received under a health plan contract.

coping Using defense or mental mechanisms in a mentally healthy way to deal with or adapt to life and its constant state of change.

coping mechanisms *See mental mechanisms.*

coprolalia The use of vulgar or obscene language (characteristic in some cases of schizophrenia).

coprophagia Eating filth or feces.

coprophilia Excessive interest in filth or feces.

copyright An author's exclusive right over the publication, copying, and distribution of written or creative material protected by law.

coram (Lat.) Before; in the presence of.

coram nobis (Lat.) 1. In our presence 2. Calling the court's attention to errors of fact that were not brought out in a previous trial where a conviction resulted and that would constitute a valid defense.

coram non judice (Lat.) In a court of incompetent jurisdiction.

core services The essential and minimal services required by the American Hospital Association for membership. The minimum services include an organized medical staff, nursing services utilizing a registered nurse in supervision, pharmacy services, and an organized medical records system.

coronary Refers to the heart; the arteries that encircle the heart.

coronary care unit A special advanced-care unit in a hospital requiring highly skilled health-care providers, high levels of technology, and life-sustaining equipment to provide intensive care for patients with coronary disease. *See also special care unit.*

coroner A public official who investigates any violent, sudden, or unexplained death where there is suspicion of foul play.

coroner's jury A jury involved in investigating a death that is not the result of natural causes. The jury is usually called by a coroner when the death may have been caused by an act of crime.

corp. Abbreviation for *corporation.*

corporal punishment Physical punishment inflicted on an individual.

corporate United or combined into a legal organization; unified with or belonging to a corporation.

corporate bond In health-care finance, this is a bond payable by a corporation on a fixed date for a specified sum borrowed from bondholders. Interest is also payable at a fixed rate.

corporate liability *See liability, corporate; vicarious liability; respondeat superior.*

corporate model An organizational approach used in some hospitals and health-care organizations where the chief executive officer (CEO) assumes a powerful position, utilizing a centralized organizational structure that places the CEO at the top of a tall organizational chart.

corporate negligence doctrine In health law, this is the doctrine that holds a health-care facility or other corporation, rather than an employee, liable for a negligent act. *See respondeat superior; vicarious liability.*

corporate office The main executive office of a health-care organization, health-care and hospital system, or large corporate managed-care organization where major strategic plans and decisions are made.

corporate responsibility A joint responsibility commonly shared by the members of a group or an organization.

corporate strategy A health-care organization's long-term planning activity that includes a mission statement from which program directives flow, ensuring the accomplishment of the organization's mission; long-term tactics and planning, within set financial guidelines, using goals, objectives, and directives to ensure strong organizational positioning.

corporate veil The legal assumption that actions taken by a corporation are not considered to be a single action of one of its owners; thus, individuals cannot be held responsible for acts that occur in the corporation.

corporate wellness *See employee wellness; health promotion programs; worksite health promotion.*

corporation An organization that is created, established, and recognized by law as a legal entity, separate and distinct from its shareholders or promoters; a legal charter granting an organization certain legal privileges, rights, and liabilities similar to those of citizens.

corporeal 1. Having objective physical substance or material existence. 2. Bodily; affecting a body. 3. Able to visibly see or be perceived by sight.

corpus (Lat.) Body; a main body.

corpus delicti (Lat.) 1. The body of the crime. 2. The motive or reason for which a crime has been committed.

corpus juris (Lat.) Body of law; collection of laws. An encyclopedia of law, abbreviated as CJ or CJS (Corpus Juris Secundum).

corrective discipline In health-care administration and personnel management, this is an action taken against a worker when that worker has committed an infraction of a rule or policy. The action is taken to discourage future problems and to ensure that worker behavior complies with organizational policies or accreditation standards.

corrective point In health-care administration decision making, this is the point in time when a decision can be changed prior to the decision being implemented; when decisions can still be modified to change an outcome.

corrective therapist Provides medically prescribed programs of therapeutic exercise to physically and mentally ill patients to prevent muscular deconditioning and help attain resocialization. *See also recreational therapist; physical therapist; occupational therapist.*

corroborate To confirm with additional facts or evidence.

co-signer A person who signs a document in conjunction with another person, thus making that person legally responsible.

cosmetic procedures In medical care and managed care, these are treatments or surgical procedures that are conducted to improve personal appearance but that are not medically necessary or do not correct any physical or physiological functioning.

cosmetic surgery Any operation that improves appearance, except when required for the repair of accidental injury or for the improvement of the functioning of a malformed body member. Most medical insurance plans do not cover cosmetic surgery.

COSSMHO *See National Coalition of Hispanic Health and Human Services Organizations.*

cost 1. A measure of health-care delivery and services. 2. The total expense required for the provision of health services. 3. Actual expenses incurred for inputs; inpatient care including all direct and indirect expenses; direct costs such as staff salary, plant maintenance, equipment, supplies, utilities; indirect costs such as mortgages, loan repayment, and cost of capital. 4. A monetary value applied to an asset or service obtained by an expenditure of cash or a commitment to make a future expenditure of cash (encumbered).

cost accounting 1. A method of accounting in which information is assembled and recorded for all the costs incurred to carry on an activity or operation or to complete a unit of work or a specific job. 2. The accumulation and communication of historical and projected monetary information related to the financial position and operations of a health-care organization, all based on generally accepted accounting principles.

cost allocation In health-care finance, this is the distribution of funds to various departments or services of a health-care organization in an equitable proportion to meet expenses incurred in carrying out activities.

cost, allowable Charges recognized by a third-party payer that are incurred by health-care providers in the usual course of providing health-care services.

cost approach An appraisal method used in estimating the replacement cost of a structure, less depreciation, plus the value of the land.

cost-based reimbursement A method of payment of medical care programs by third parties (typically Blue Cross plans or government agencies) for services delivered to patients. In cost-related systems, the amount of the payment is based on the costs to the provider of delivering the service. The actual payment may be based on any one of several different formulas, such as full cost, full cost plus an additional percentage, allowable costs, or a fraction of costs. Other reimbursement schemes are based on the charges for the services delivered or on budgeted or anticipated costs for a future time period (prospective reimbursement). Medicare, Medicaid, and some Blue Cross plans reimburse hospitals on the basis of costs; most private insurance plans pay charges. Medicare reimburses acute-care hospitals according to diagnosis-related groups (DRGs) and a prospective payment reimbursement system. Other third-party payers are following Medicare's lead and moving from retrospective cost-based systems to prospective payment systems, capitation, and managed care.

cost-benefit In health-care financial management, this is a measure of the cost of an activity in relation to the benefit it yields, usually expressed as a ratio of dollars saved or gained for every dollar spent. *See cost-benefit analysis; cost-effectiveness.*

cost-benefit analysis A method of comparing the cost of a program, with its expected benefits expressed in dollars. For example, the cost of establishing an immunization service must be compared with the total cost of medical care that will no longer be necessary if more persons are immunized. Although there are exceptions, cost-benefit analysis generally excludes consideration of factors that cannot be ultimately measured in economic terms.

cost center An accounting device that attributes all related costs to some "center" within an institution, such as a department, service, or program (e.g., X ray or a hospital burn center). This contrasts with segregating costs by goods or services such as nursing, drugs, or laundry, regardless of which "center" incurred them.

cost containment The control of the overall cost of health-care services within the health-care delivery system. Costs are contained when the value of the resources committed to an activity are not considered excessive. Thus, the determination of cost containment is frequently subjective and depends on the specific geographic area of the activity and the measures used to determine fair or excessive costs.

cost contract In managed care, this is a formal agreement with Medicare and the Health Care Financing Administration that provides medical care services for health plan members over age 65 on the basis of reasonable cost or prudent buyer concepts. Under the contract, the designated health plan receives a lump sum payment on an interim basis, according to a capitated amount derived from an estimated annual budget from past treatment experiences that are audited at the end of each contract year to adjust final rates that the plan should be paid.

cost controls In managed care, this is a risk-sharing approach used to contain costs by HMOs. A risk pool of funds is developed as a buffer against unanticipated price changes or overutilization. When provider expenses come in over budget, the excesses can be shared by the health plan, the health-care provider drawing from the buffer account. Some health plans offer a system to share profits with providers, thus sharing both deficits and surpluses. Reinsurance is offered as protection against adverse patient selection and unexpected cases of catastrophic illnesses to share the risks common to managed care structures. Cost controls are based on capitation, workable premiums, rigid underwriting policies, risk sharing, concurrent review, effective management controls and authority, highly selective criteria for medical group selection, highly selective criteria for nonmedical group physician selection, well-developed and strict gatekeeper policies, restricted management costs, effective and efficient data collection and analysis, good use of data and information management, and a high focus on disease prevention and health promotion.

cost-effectiveness In health-care financial management, this is a measure of the cost of an activity in relation to its impact, based on the dollars per unit saved or the resulting outcome. This is done through a formal comparative analysis of the costs and accomplishments of a service as expressed in nonfinancial terms. *See cost-effectiveness analysis; cost-benefit; cost-benefit analysis.*

cost-effectiveness analysis In health-care finance, this is a method of comparing alternative ways to achieve a specific set of results. Comparison is based on the ratio of the cost of each alternative to its estimated future effects on objectives. Benefits and constraints are usually not expressed in dollars in a cost-effectiveness analysis.

cost finding In health-care finance, this is the process of comparing the allocation of the costs in non–revenue-producing department areas (cost centers) of a hospital to the revenue-producing centers on the basis of statistical data that measures the volume of services produced by each unit or cost center in relation to other centers. Also referred to as "step-down allocation." *See also cost center.*

cost of capital In health-care finance, this is the cost of money, including interest on debts and the cost of maintaining adequate owners' equity.

cost of care 1. The economic cost (including out-of-pocket and insurance coverage) of the health service being provided to the individual. 2. The total capital outlay for a unit of service.

cost of construction *See construction, cost of.*

cost of insurance The amount that a policyholder pays to the insurer minus benefits received. This should be distinguished from the rate for a given unit of insurance (e.g., $10 for a $1000 life insurance policy). Such costs are approximated by the loading or the ratio of amounts paid in benefits to income produced from premiums. *See also expense.*

cost of living adjustment (COLA) For Social Security beneficiaries, this is an automatic increase in benefits that reflects annual increases in the cost of living. If inflation and the cost of living were not considered, hundreds of thousands of beneficiaries, mainly the elderly and handicapped, would be forced into poverty.

cost of living index An indicator of the increase or decrease in the amount of money the average person needs to live based on monthly comparisons. This index is issued by the U.S. government. *See gross national product; gross domestic product.*

cost per case In health-care finance and hospital administration, this is the cost incurred by a hospital in treating a single patient.

cost per case management Under the Medicare Prospective Payment System (PPS), hospital administrators, as a cost control measure, monitor the cost of each type of case seen in the hospital to ensure that revenue will cover the cost of care and treatment.

cost per patient day In health-care finance and hospital administration, this is the cost of running a health-care facility divided by the number of inpatient days. Various adjustments in the cost figures are made to compare costs per patient day between health-care facilities.

cost plan That portion of a grant proposal that presents the plan for expending projected monies. This is the budget portion of a grant and provides more detail than a simple line item budget.

cost plus contract A contract that establishes the amount to be paid to a contractor plus a specified percentage of that price above the cost of services provided.

Cost Quality Management System (CQMS) An approach used to maintain quality and control costs in hospitals. Financial, clinical, patient/case, and diagnosis-related group (DRG) data are standardized and used to improve hospital operations and permit comparison among institutions and services by use of the data system.

cost, reasonable Generally, the amount a managed-care plan or third party using cost-based reimbursement will actually reimburse. Under

Medicare, reasonable costs are costs actually incurred in delivering health services, excluding any part of such incurred costs found to be unnecessary for the efficient delivery of needed health services (see Section 1861 of the Social Security Act). Medicare no longer reimburses for reasonable costs under the prospective payment system for acute-care hospitals and has moved away from reasonable cost reimbursement for other facilities or services. The lower end of the customary charge by a particular physician for a service and the prevailing charge by physicians in the geographic area for that service are considered and used in determining reasonable costs. Reimbursement is based on the lower of the reasonable and actual charges. Generally, the term is used for any charge payable by an insurance program, which is determined in a similar, but not necessarily identical, fashion.

cost reimbursement system In health-care financial management, this is a method of paying for medical costs determined by the actual costs of services rendered.

cost-related reimbursement See *cost-based reimbursement*.

cost reports The completed summary of financial data presented to the fiscal intermediary at the end of each cost-reporting period by the health-care facility. The information is used to calculate the total that Medicare will pay for services.

costs 1. Expenses incurred in a lawsuit that the court can order the opposing side to pay. 2. Expenses incurred in the provision of services or goods. Charges (the price of a service or amount billed to an individual or third party) may or may not be the same as, or based on, costs. Hospitals often charge more for a given service than it actually costs so they can recoup losses from providing other services where costs exceed feasible charges. Despite the terminology, cost control programs are often directed at controlling increases in charges rather than in real costs. *See also charges.*

cost sharing Provisions of a medical insurance policy that require the insured to pay some portion of covered medical expenses. Several forms of cost sharing are employed, including deductibles, co-insurance, and co-payments. A deductible is a set amount that a person must pay before any payment of benefits occurs. A co-payment is usually a fixed amount to be paid with each service. Co-insurance is payment of a set portion of the cost of each service. Cost sharing does not refer to or include the amounts paid in premiums for the coverage. The amount of the premium is directly related to the benefits provided and hence reflects the amount of cost sharing required. For a given set of benefits, premiums increase as cost-sharing requirements decrease. In addition to reducing premiums, cost sharing is used to control utilization of covered services, for example, by requiring a large co-payment for a service that is likely to be overused.

cost shifting The practice of increasing charges to reimbursement agencies such as commercial insurers, self insured employers, or private-pay patients when governmental third-party payers fail to pay full costs.

cost-to-charge ratio In health-care financial management, this is used to calculate a charge or cost of services or goods when incomplete charge or cost figures are available.

co-surgeons Under certain circumstances, two surgeons (usually with similar skills) may function simultaneously as primary surgeons performing distinct parts of a total surgical service (e.g., two surgeons simultaneously applying skin grafts to different parts of the body or two surgeons repairing different fractures in the same patient).

co-tenant 1. Two or more people sharing the same room or apartment. 2. One holding property by joint ownership.

COTRANS See *Coordinated Transfer Application System.*

Council for the National Register of Health Service Providers in Psychology The governing and policymaking body for the establishment and maintenance of a registry formed in 1974 by the American Board of Professional Psychology at the request of the board of directors of the American Psychological Association. Those included are certified and licensed psychologists who are trained and experienced in the delivery of preventive mental care, assessment, and therapeutic intervention services to individuals whose growth, adjustment, or functioning is impaired or is at high risk of impairment. The psychologist is a doctoral graduate from a regionally accredited educational institution with 2 years of supervised experience in psychology health services, one year of which is in an organized health service training program and the other in postdoctoral training. *See psychologist.*

council of governments (COG) A regional or multijurisdictional cooperative association of local governmental bodies of a state drawn together to develop a comprehensive approach to problems, receive federal grants, and coordinate services that affect the region as a whole. COGs are regional planning agencies established for the areawide review of projects and for the development of regional plans, including some health-related projects.

Council on Certification (Recertification) of Nurse Anesthetists The national professional organization that has the main role of certifying trained nurse anesthetists who have met the requirements set forth by the council.

Council on Clinical Classifications (CCC) A nonprofit organization established in 1975 for the purpose of reviewing and developing the International Classification of Disease of the World Health Organization. Representatives of most of the major physician and hospital organizations participated in the process. The final result is the ICD-9-CM for use in North America.

Council on Education for Public Health (CEPH) An independent agency recognized by the U.S. Department of Education and the Council on Postsecondary Accreditation to accredit schools of public health and certain graduate programs offered in educational settings other than schools of public health such as community health education, community health, or preventive medicine programs. The mission of CEPH is to enhance health in human populations through organized community effort and educational programs that prepare professional personnel to identify, prevent, and solve community health problems.

Council on Post Secondary Education (COPA) A private, nonprofit educational organization that evaluates and recognizes accrediting agencies in the health-care field.

counsel 1. A lawyer. 2. Professional advice.

counseling A process whereby a counselor or psychotherapist using knowledge of human behavior, communications, interviewing skills, behavior, rational thinking, etc. provides professional guidance or assistance to an individual, group, or family to help them deal with responsibilities and situations on the basis of interactions and relations with others. Counseling is done to guide the client toward effective decisions and acceptable behaviors, to set treatment goals, to cope with emotional pain and stress, and to function well in life's experiences. *See health counseling; psychotherapy; psychiatry; psychologist.*

counseling functions 1. Activities and services provided by counselors, psychologists, psychiatrists, marriage and family therapists, and psychotherapists. Some activities experienced in counseling and psychotherapy are guidance, reassurance, communication, release of emotional tension, orientation to reality, clarification of thinking, trust building, behavioral therapy, behavior modification, relationship problem solving, expression of emotions, dealing with unfinished emotional business, and developing emotional stability. 2. In health-care administration human resource management, advice giving, guidance, communication, employee personal and professional development, and orientation. *See health counseling; psychotherapy; psychiatry; psychologist.*

counseling services Therapy, guidance, and support provided to individuals and families to assist in solving family, interpersonal and personal problems, and conflict and emotional distress.

counselor A lawyer; one who provides counsel or advice.

count Charges in a criminal indictment or civil complaint.

counter To act in opposition to.

counterclaim An opposing claim used to offset an original complaint. In a civil lawsuit, a defendant presents a claim against the plaintiff. A counterclaim is usually related to the case at hand but is based on different charges than the plaintiff's original complaint.

counterfeit 1. Made without authority or right; forged copying or imitating without authority. 2. Passing off a false copy as an original.

counteroffer Return of an offer with another offer, or an offer made to offset an original offer that was not adequate or satisfactory.

countersign A second original signature used to approve or validate a document.

countersuit *See counterclaim.*

countertransference In mental health services, this is a process whereby the therapist's conscious or unconscious emotional reaction to his client is experienced. *See also transference.*

county hospital *See hospital, city county.*

County Organized Health System (COHS) "Look-a-Like" In health-care delivery systems and managed care in the county government and local public sectors, this is an entity established by a county board of supervisors (county commissioners) for administering locally developed managed-care programs for public health services. This could be an exclusive, managed-care program (as opposed to one developed and operated by the local government) plus a private HMO alternative, called a "local initiative." *See local initiative; two-fold program.*

coupon rate In health-care finance, this is the annual interest rate stated by a borrower and promised to be paid to a bondholder by the borrower.

course of employment In health-care administration, this is the activity that occurs during work hours in relationship to a person's employment activities.

court 1. The hall or chamber where law is practiced and justice is administered. 2. The assembling of persons and judges for hearing and trying cases. 3. Holding a judicial assembly.

court day The day that court is held.

courtesy medical staff Hospital medical staff privileges given on a temporary basis to physicians who are not official members of the hospital's medical staff. These physicians occasionally use the hospital as attending physicians or when providing consultation at the hospital.

court of appeals (CA) The middle-level court that hears and decides appeals from a trial court; in some states, it is the highest court.

court of claims A federal court that hears complaints against the U.S. government.

court of common pleas A court of original and general jurisdiction over civil suits between private parties; in some states it is called the "superior court" or "district court."

court of error A specialized court that has jurisdiction over cases that are alleged to have error.

court of last resort A court beyond which there is no further appeal to a higher court.

court of probate A court limited to the hearing of specialized problems such as wills and estates, problems of minors, or concerns of legally incompetent persons.

coutume (French) 1. Custom. 2. A close English equivalent for common law.

covenant An agreement that is written into a deed or other document promising performance or nonperformance of certain acts or fixing certain uses or nonuses for property.

cover 1. In insurance, to shelter, shield, or defend from harm or injury. 2. To protect, as in insurance "coverage." 3. To include or compensate for.

coverage 1. The guarantee against specific losses provided under the terms of an insurance policy. Frequently used interchangeably with the terms "benefits" or "protection." 2. In managed care, the percentage of a group, or population, served by a health plan or program. 3. As used in health services, an assessment of health services actually utilized as compared to the need for the health services; a rate formula expressed as a proportion in which the numerator reflects the number of services provided and the denominator the number of occurrences of the health services needed. The formula for coverage by health services follows:

$$\frac{\text{Actual number of patient encounters with a health care provider}}{\text{Expected number of encounters with health care provider within a given time frame for the same community or population}}$$

See also benefit.

covered charge In managed care or medical insurance, this is when a health plan member's medical care services are paid by third-party payers.

covered dependent cutoff In managed care, this is the point in time when a dependent child reaches the top age set forth in the health plan agreement when they are no longer eligible to use a health plan or are asked to prove full-time-student status, according to the terms of the health plan contract.

covered life *See lives; covered lives.*

covered lives In managed care, these are the numbers of individuals enrolled as members in a health plan or HMO. One enrolled member in a health plan is a "life," or "covered life." A measure of the size of a health plan is determined by the number of subscribers enrolled (e.g., a plan has 35,000 covered lives). *See lives.*

covered person In managed care and insurance, this is any individual who meets eligibility requirements for health plan coverage or medical insurance coverage, when premiums are paid as part of the worker's benefits, as set forth in the insurance policy or the employer group health plan agreement; an individual who has a medical insurance policy with the insurance carrier and is acknowledged as having medical care coverage benefits.

covered services In managed care, these are the services or benefits covered by a health plan as set forth in the terms of the employer group agreement. Also referred to as a "benefit package."

coverture The rights, conditions, and legal limitations or state of a married woman; the legal or liability status of a woman while married.

CPA Certified public accountant.

CPC *See clinicopathological conference.*

CPHA *See Commission on Professional and Hospital Activities.*

CPI *See consumer price index.*

CPQA Certified professional in quality assurance.

CPR Cardiopulmonary resuscitation; customary, prevailing, and reasonable charges; central practice and review committee.

CPT *See current procedural terminology.*

CPT-4 *Current Procedural Terminology, 4th Edition.*

CPU *See central processing unit.*

CQM Comprehensive quality management; a variation on total quality management.

CQMS *See cost quality management system.*

CQI *See continuous quality improvement.*

CRAHCA *See Center for Research in Ambulatory Health Care Administration.*

craft unions In labor activities in hospitals, those persons who work in maintenance and physical plant operations, such as carpenters or plumbers, and who often belong to labor organizations representing their craft or trade.

creaming *See skimming.*

credentialing 1. The process of privilege review. 2. The formal recognition of professional or technical competence that may include registration, certification, licensure, professional association membership, or the award of a degree in the field. Certification and licensure affect the supply of health manpower by controlling entrance into practice and influence the stability of the labor force by affecting geographic distribution, mobility, and retention of workers. Credentialing determines the quality of personnel by providing standards for evaluating competence and defines the scope of functions and use of personnel. 3. In managed care, when a health plan or HMO reviews and conducts an assessment of health-care providers who wish to participate as a provider in a health plan; the assessment is based on licensure, board status, malpractice coverage, and medical practice history. 4. The process of granting authorization by the governing body of a hospital to provide specific patient care and treatment services, within defined limits, on the basis of a health-care provider's license, education, training, experience, competence, health status, and judgment (JCAHO for acute-care hospitals).

credentialism 1. Where an agency, organization, or other entity requires a worker or professional to obtain a certain degree, certification, or license before the worker can practice a chosen profession. This action may be challenged by the courts if such a requirement is found unnecessary. 2. The exclusiveness and perpetuation of a profession or vocation by excluding all persons from the profession by creating licensure or certification requirements and not allowing people to work in the field unless the proper training, education, and testing is completed and they are properly certified or licensed.

credentials 1. Documents, licenses, and certificates issued as an indication of professional or technical competence. 2. One or more documents given to a person to show that the person has a right to the exercise of a certain position or authority (JCAHO for acute-care hospitals).

credentials committee A body of physicians and administrative personnel that reviews applications for medical staff membership.

credibility 1. Believability. 2. A method of measurement that demonstrates the degree to which an insurance company may rely on statistical observations in setting rates or in making rate revisions.

credible 1. Believable. 2. Ethically practicing a profession. 3. Reliable; reputable; trustworthy.

credit Confidence in another's ability and integrity to pay debts on the basis of goodwill and a favorable past record of payments.

credit insurance In health-care finance, this is a type of insurance issued as protection against bad debt; insurance that covers losses caused by a debtor's failure to pay accounts when due.

credit life A form of life insurance set up to pay the amount necessary to discharge a debt in the event the borrower dies.

creditor The one to whom a debt is owed and who has a legal right to collect what is owed.

credits The records of money owed or money paid out; the opposite of debits.

crimen falsie (Lat.) Falsehood of fraud used to interfere with the administration of justice. Such offenses include deceit, forgery, fraudulent alteration of a document, and perjury.

criminal 1. An act that violates law, morality, or a society's well-being; having to do with illegal or unlawful conduct. 2. One who has committed a crime; a person legally convicted of committing a crime.

criminal action The process of litigation through which a person charged with a criminal offense is brought to trial.

criminal forfeiture Property seized by a law enforcement agency because it was involved in a crime; for example, a purse can be seized because it was used to smuggle drugs out of a health-care facility, and an airplane can be seized because it was illegally used to fly narcotics across the border into the United States.

criminal law Statutes, laws, and regulations that deal with conduct offensive to the state or to society as a whole.

criminal malpractice Professional misconduct involving a criminal act or the breaking of criminal law.

crippled children's services programs Special service provided by the Child Health Act to identify, diagnose, and treat any child crippled or afflicted with a crippling condition. The Act established the Maternal and Child Health Program and the Crippled Children's Services Program. The purpose is to improve services for crippled children or for those who are suffering from conditions that eventually cripple and to provide facilities for diagnosis, hospitalization, and aftercare.

crisis of a fever The sudden reduction or passing of a fever.

criteria 1. Measures used to assess the performance characteristics (appropriateness and quality) of proposed or existing health system services; often used interchangeably with "guidelines." 2. Expected levels of achievement against which performance or care can be evaluated (JCAHO for acute-care hospitals).

criteria for survey eligibility Conditions necessary for hospitals to be surveyed for accreditation. The criteria address the structure, functions, and services of the hospital (JCAHO for acute-care hospitals).

criterion-referenced A clear description of a set of skills that are essential to the performance of a role and used in a test situation to determine an individual's status with respect to those skills.

critical care bed need formula In hospital administration, this is a formula used to determine the number of critical care beds needed per average population. A generalization is that .235 critical care beds are needed per 1000 population. Age and case mix will affect the ratio.

critical care nurse A registered nurse with advanced training and experience in a critical care unit who provides care to critically ill patients.

critical care physician Physicians who provide immediate treatment and relief of pain in persons who are seriously injured or critically ill. This physician may treat the sick or injured at the scene of an accident, during the transportation of a patient with a serious condition, or in a hospital critical care unit.

critical care services The care of critically ill patients in a variety of medical emergencies that require the constant attention of the physician such as cardiac arrest, shock, bleeding, respiratory failure, postoperative complications, or critically ill neonate. Critical care is usually, but not always, given in a unit within a hospital designed and designated as an intensive, advanced treatment or critical care area such as the coronary care, intensive care, respiratory care, or emergency care unit.

critical care unit A specially equipped and staffed intensive care, cardiac care, or post-emergency care unit.

critical incident In health-care administration human resources management, an evaluation method that requires a supervisor to use statements by employees that describe the extremely good and extremely poor work or job-related activity or employee behavior. The statements are referred to as "critical incidents" and are used in performance appraisals to assess employees.

critical management Documentation in the medical record of the minimal preventive and reactive procedures provided to a patient during a complication to verify that everything necessary to prevent the complication was provided or that when the complication occurred it was recognized in a timely fashion and was promptly diagnosed and appropriately treated.

CRNA *See certified registered nurse anesthetist.*

cross-claim Similar to a counterclaim, wherein one defendant makes a complaint against another defendant in the same lawsuit, usually seeking indemnification for any damages owed the plaintiff.

cross-examine To question a witness already questioned by the other party during a trial or hearing.

cross-infection 1. A patient contracting a second communicable disease while hospitalized for another condition or disease. 2. Infections acquired in a health-care facility or while under the care of a health-care provider or acquired from another patient or acquired from and during the course of treatment. *See nosocomial infection.*

crossover design In epidemiology or biomedical research, this is a research design that compares two or more treatments, interventions, or experiments in which treatment subjects change roles with controls. Controls become the treatment groups, and the treatment groups become the controls.

cross-product ratio *See odds ratio.*

cross-sectional study In epidemiology and biomedical research, this is a research design approach used to gather data at a single point in time. Surveys are often used when the point in time is relatively short. The presence or prevalence of a disease, condition, or state of health is locked in and studied at a point in time. The research findings are used to infer cause-and-effect relationships or may be used to determine the need for public health or health-care services.

cross-subsidization In health-care financial management, this is the process of using part of the higher-cost services income and reallocating part of it to a different cost center to balance the overall operation of the health-care facility. Rates for high revenue services or goods are adjusted to support low-revenue areas. *See cost shifting.*

cross-tolerance When a person addicted to one drug can delay withdrawal by taking another, similar drug from the same drug group (e.g., heroin can cause the same or similar effects of morphine).

crow-fly miles In rural health care, this is a term used to describe a straight-line shortest distance by air between two given points such as a hospital and clinic or a rural clinic and a level I trauma center hospital in a city.

CRT *See cathode ray tube.*

crude attack rate Crude attack rates are used in epidemiology to assess foodborne disease outbreaks or related epidemics. The formula for a crude attack rate is as follows:

$$\frac{\text{Number of persons ill with the disease}}{\text{Number of persons attending the event}} \times 1000$$

crude birth rate The number of live births in a specific period of time, usually a calendar year, per 1000, 10,000, or 100,000 population. The formula for the crude birth rate is as follows:

$$\frac{\text{Number of live births to residents in an area in a calendar year}}{\text{Average population in the area in the same year}} \times 1000$$

crude death rate The total number of deaths in a year divided by the average total population multiplied by a set part of the population such as 1000, 10,000, or 100,000. The formula for a crude death rate is as follows:

$$\frac{\text{Total deaths per year}}{\text{Average total population of that year}} \times 1000$$

CRVS *See California relative value studies.*

cryo- Prefix meaning "cold."

CSC Civil Service Commission; regulates federal employment.

CT *See computerized tomography.*

CT scanner *See computerized axial tomography.*

cui bono (Lat.) For whose best interest, for whose good; for what good, for what useful purpose or benefit.

culpable 1. Deserving blame. 2. One who is guilty. 3. One who is at fault; one who has done a wrongful act.

cultural shock The upset or disbelief that can occur when an individual moves from one social setting or culture to another.

culture 1. The cultivation of microorganisms, cells, or tissues in a special growth medium. 2. The belief and value system of a group or of a society; standards and beliefs with regard to judgments, rituals, and conduct that are passed from one generation to the next. 3. Ideas, traditions, customs, values, and practices that influence behavior, including health behavior and the beliefs of a group, society, or organization.

cum (Lat.) With.

cum onere (Lat.) Taken on with burdens. With burden.

cum testamento annexo (Lat.) With the will attached. A court-appointed administrator who supervises the property of a person who died without having appointed someone to legally take care of that property.

cumulative evidence In law, these are the facts and proof used to show what has already been proven.

cumulative incidence rate In epidemiology, this is that part of a disease-free population group that develops new cases of a disease within a specific time interval (numerator) compared to the population at risk within the same time interval (denominator); the cumulative observed proportions that fall ill within short time intervals within the identified overall time interval.

cumulative mortality rate In epidemiology, this is the proportion of a specific population experiencing death over a fixed time period.

curador (Spanish) Healer, physician, curer, surgeon. *See curandero.*

curandero (masc.), **curandera** (fem.) (Spanish) 1. Curer. 2. Quack. 3. Medical charlatan. 4. A folk healer of the Mexican-American culture viewed as a lay healer practicing by virtue of a gift from God. *See also bruja; curador.*

cure To heal through a system of medical treatment.

curettage In medical care, a curette is used to remove tissue or material from the wall of a cavity such as the uterus.

curette A spoon-shaped medical instrument used for removing tissue or material from a body cavity.

current assets In health-care finance, this is property that can be easily converted to cash in the normal course of operations or within 1 year. Cash, gross patient accounts receivable less allowances for bad debt, supplies, prepayments, and inventory make up current assets.

current liabilities The debts and costs that will come due and require payment from current assets within the coming year. Accounts payable, accrued expenses, and the current part of any long-term debt are current liabilities.

currently employed A public health and health services delivery–related principle that includes all persons over 18 years of age who reported that they have worked or presently have a job. Included in the definition are elements such as paid work as an employee of someone else, self-employed, or unpaid work on a family farm or in a family business. Persons temporarily absent from work but not terminated are currently employed. Excluded are persons with no definite employment but who work as needed, seasonal workers, and those not working or looking for work.

current portion of long-term debt In health-care finance, this is the portion due on a yearly basis, for the current year.

current position—long-term debt The amount to be repaid or that portion of the long-term debt due within 1 year of the date of the financial statement.

current procedural terminology (CPT) A system of terminology and coding developed by the American Medical Association that is used for describing, coding, and reporting medical services and procedures.

current ratio In health-care finance, this is current assets divided by current liabilities; a formula used to measure the current liquidity of a health-care organization, business, or facility. This liquidity ratio can be used by a hospital or other health-care organization to determine if it has working capital to meet short-term obligations. The current ratio formula is as follows:

$$\frac{\text{Current assets + balance of depreciation fund}}{\text{Current liabilities}}$$

current services budget A budget that projects estimated budget authority and outlays for the upcoming fiscal year on the basis of existing programs without policy changes at the same levels of service as the fiscal year in progress. The Congressional Budget and Impoundment Control Act of 1974 requires that the president submit a current services budget to Congress by November 10 of each year. To the extent mandated by existing law, estimates account for anticipated changes in economic conditions (unemployment or inflation), different caseloads, pay increases, and benefit changes.

current yield In health-care finance, the percentage of annual interest received on a bond compared to the price of that bond.

cursor An indicator on the cathode ray tube/TV screen of a computer showing one's present position on the screen.

cushion ratio In health-care finance, this is a method of assessment used to determine how serious a debt situation is with regard to annual debt service. The formula for debt ratio follows:

$$\frac{\text{Cash and investments + board-designated funds}}{\text{Maximum annual debt service}}$$

custodial care 1. In health-care delivery, this is the provision of board, room, and other personal assistance services, not including medical care, generally provided on a long-term basis. Such services are generally not paid for under private or public health insurance or medical care programs, except as incidental to the medical care that a hospital or nursing home inpatient receives. Care at this level is designed to meet the activities for daily living but does not require trained health care personnel. 2. Health services and nonmedical care services provided to a patient over long time periods that do not require constant medical attention but do require assistance with the activities of daily living. *See also boarding homes; supervisory care facility; personal care; activities of daily living.*

custodia legis (Lat.) 1. In the custody of the law. 2. Property taken by legal process.

custody Safekeeping, protection.

custom 1. Well-established, long-term practices. 2. Usual behavior and traditions of persons or businesses in a particular area. 3. Related to common law or unwritten law because it is a long-established standard practice, whereas common consent is backed by the force of the law; a legally relevant fact in some courts' decisions.

customary charges 1. In health-care finance, this is the fee or amount a health care provider usually expects as payment for services rendered from a majority of patients treated. Some insurance companies compile payment statistics on the average rate for services in a region or area and view this as an acceptable or usual charge made by most health-care providers serving the same socioeconomic geographic area. Under Medicare, before diagnosis-related groups (DRGs) this was the median charge used by a particular physician for specific treatment or service during a specified period of time. 2. The maximum amount a Medicare carrier will approve for payment for a particular service provided by a physician or health-care provider. The carrier computes the customary charge on the basis of the actual amount a physician charges for a specific service.

customary, prevailing, and reasonable charges In health-care finance under Medicare, this is a method used by insurance carriers of Medicare to determine the approved charge for a particular Part B service from a particular physician or health-care provider on the basis of the actual charge for the service, previous charges, and previous charges by peer physicians and health-care providers in the same area. In the absence of unusual medical treatments and services, prevailing charges are generally used. This is the maximum amount a Medicare carrier will approve for payment for a particular service provided by a physician or health-care provider and is generally equal to the lowest charge in an array of customary charges that is high enough to include 75% of all relevant customary charges. Reasonable charges are done on an individual physician basis by Medicare Part B carrier. In the absence of unusual treatment or procedures, this is the lowest of a health care provider's customary charge, prevailing charge, actual charge, or carrier's charge for a comparable service. *See customary charges.*

customers In health-care administration, especially hospitals, these are those who use the services of the organization, the entities on which the hospital relies, or units or services that are considered to be exchange partners. In hospitals, three major customers are generally identified: patient, physician, and third-party payers. For strategic planning, corporate culture, and organizational behavior purposes, employees are often recognized as a fourth customer.

cut-down day In measuring disability and chronic disease, this is a person who cuts down on work or activities for more than a half a day on usual tasks.

CVA *See cerebral vascular accident.*

CVP Central venous pressure.

cyanosis Bluish color in the skin and mucous membranes because of a lack of oxygen in the blood.

cybernetic As applied to health-care administration, this is an organizational behavior characteristic that promotes the setting of goals, measuring progress, and correcting problems to ensure continuous quality improvement throughout the organization with progress being made in all systems of the organization and as an organizational system as whole.

cyclicity In epidemiology, this is the occurrence and remission (cycling) of disease rates over a certain time period caused by influences of time, place, or person characteristics. Cyclicity is influenced most by the epidemiological concept of time, with season or time of year often an important variable.

cyclicity, seasonal In epidemiology, the upswing and downswing (cycling) of disease or illness occurrences as related to the seasons of the year, often with infectious diseases as a model. Some chronic diseases have acute periods that are cyclically based on seasons, as are some cultural and demographic factors such as marriage, births, suicide, and other forms of mortality. The peak of an outbreak may be seen in the winter and the low points of the cycle in midsummer, rising again in the winter to complete the cycle. Other diseases have the opposite cycle: mosquito-borne illness rates (e.g., malaria) peak in the summer and upper respiratory illness (e.g., the common cold) in the winter. This cycling process is observed epidemiologically over several seasons. Seasons are an aspect of the epidemiological factor of time.

cyclicity, secular Any long-term cycling of disease that exceeds 1 year is considered secular cyclicity; long-term cycling of disease incidence rates. Large interval swings as seen in the recurrence of pandemics of influenza is an example of secular cyclicity. Secular trends are an aspect of the epidemiological factor of time.

cyclothymic personality In mental health services, this is a personality disorder characterized by regular alternating periods of elation and depression, often not related to an experience or external circumstances.

cyto- Prefix meaning "cell."

cytologist A physician or medical technologist who specializes in the study and assessment of cells and their changes, especially those changes related to disease. *See also cytopathologist; cytotechnologist.*

cystoscope A lighted optical instrument used to visually examine the interior of the urinary bladder.

cystoscopy The examination of the urinary bladder with a cystoscope.

cytology lab A laboratory equipped and staffed to study human cells using electronic microscopes or other specialized equipment.

cytopathologist A scientist who specializes in the study of cellular changes in the human body as a result of disease, particularly cancer.

cytotechnologist A medical technologist whose specialty is the laboratory evaluation of cellular changes in the body resulting from disease, especially cancer. Cytotechnologists may also be involved in the supervision, administration, and teaching of other laboratory personnel in a cytology laboratory or department in a hospital, clinic, public health laboratory, or private laboratory. They work closely with and report information to a pathologist.

cytotechnology An allied health training program that prepares persons to stain, mount, screen, and slice tissues of the human body to determine such cell abnormalities as exfoliated cells, cancer, and other related abnormalities; works under the direction of a scientist or physician with specialization in physiology.

D

DA *See district attorney.*

daily inpatient census The number of persons present as inpatients at the time a census is taken, including those inpatients who were both admitted and discharged after the time of census taking on the previous day.

daily recap sheet The daily census count and summary of the total number of newborns, boarders, inpatients, outpatients, and deaths within a health-care facility.

daily service charge 1. The amount of money a hospital, nursing home, or other inpatient health-care facility charges for 1 day of stay in the facility. 2. The fee, usually a percentage of the fee due, added on to charges allowed on credit owed to the health-care facility or health-care provider by a former patient.

damage, faisant In health law, this is to cause damage; doing damage.

damages 1. Monetary awards granted by a court or hearing to a party or a person who has suffered harm, injury, or loss through the unlawful or negligent acts of others. 2. A plaintiff's legal claim for money; recompense for a legal wrongdoing. *See also recovery.*

damages, actual 1. In health law, these consist of any harm, loss, or injury that can quickly and easily be shown to have occurred or been sustained for which the injured party or person can recover damages or be compensated as a matter of equity or rightness. 2. Compensation amounting to the actual loss, harm, or damage sustained, incurred, or suffered. *See also damages, compensatory.*

damages, compensatory In health law, these are money or other remuneration awarded to a plaintiff to overcome damage, loss, or suffering.

damages, exemplary In health law, these are punitive damages; damages paid to the plaintiff in excess of actual losses in a tort action to serve as punishment.

damages, liquidated In health law, these are an established amount to be paid by the parties in a contract in the event of a default or breach by either side.

damages, nominal In health law, these are a recovery or award of a minimal amount, often $1, paid to the plaintiff, even though liability or malpractice has been proven in court.

damages, punitive In health law, these are money given beyond recovery that the defendant is required by the court to pay to the plaintiff. Unlike criminal law, tort law is not meant to have a punishment mechanism as part of it. However, punitive damages, having a punishing effect, are given to send a message to the health-care profession (in the case of medical malpractice) to discourage future misconduct or carelessness. Money given to the plaintiff is punitive to the defendant, goes beyond recovery, and is not a part of recovery or compensatory damages. *See damages, compensatory; recovery.*

damages, special In health law, these are damages arising from actual out-of-pocket expenses paid by a plaintiff in a personal injury action.

damages, treble *Treble* means "three times." In health law, this is when recovery provided by the court from damages is three times what the plaintiff is entitled to receive. This approach to recovery has a punitive damage effect and is often done to discourage professional misconduct.

damnatus (Lat.) Prohibited by law.

damnum (Lat.) Damage (singular).

damnum absque injuria (Lat.) Damage or loss for which there is no legal remedy; thus no civil action can be taken.

dance therapist In mental health services, this therapist applies the principles and techniques of dance to the rehabilitation of mentally ill, mentally retarded, or physically disabled patients. The dance therapist has a degree (a masters degree is required in some states) in dance therapy, including an approved clinical internship from an accredited college or university, or is a person registered or eligible for registration with the American Dance Therapy Association.

dance therapy An educational program that prepares persons to apply the principles and techniques of dance to the rehabilitation of physically and mentally ill patients.

D and C Dilation and curettage; surgically scraping the inside of the uterus.

dan et retiens nihil dat (Lat.) A person who gives and retains; one who gives nothing.

dangerous drugs *See Harrison Antinarcotic Act.*

dangerous instrumentality Tools, devices, instruments, items, or objects that are harmful in and of themselves or can be harmful by nature of the design (e.g., surgical instruments, knives, or guns).

dangerous per se An item dangerous in itself (e.g., gasoline, bottled oxygen, or drugs) that may cause harm without human cause.

dangerous to life or health Any condition that poses an immediate threat to life or health such as severe exposure to contaminants such as radioactive materials that have an adverse, delayed effect on one's health.

DAP A psychological test called "draw-a-person" that uses projective techniques.

Darling case A landmark case (*Darling v. Charleston Community Hospital* [211 N.E. 2nd 53, 111, 1965]) in which a trial court first allowed the Illinois Department of Public Health rules and regulations; the Charleston Community Hospital's bylaws, rules, and regulations; and the Joint Commission on Accreditation's Standards for Hospital Accreditation to be admitted as documentary evidence in a court of law. This allowed the jury to utilize and review these documents as evidence in determining the standard of care the hospital and staff used in caring for patients. The court ruled that the hospital failed to have an adequate number of professional nurses who were trained in recognizing the progressive gangrenous condition of a patient's fractured leg in a cast. It was further found that the physician in charge failed to get an orthopedic consultation, which was required by the medical staff bylaws.

data 1. Any or all facts, numbers, letters, or symbols. 2. The numerical findings of health, medical, and behavioral or social research; research information, numbers, or results of studies or experiments. 3. Basic elements of information that can be processed by a computer. 4. The collection of material or facts on which a discussion or an inference is based, such as indicator data used to identify processes or outcomes that may be improved (JCAHO for acute-care hospitals).

data bank A collection of data that is organized for rapid search and retrieval by computer.

database In epidemiology, public health, or biomedical research, this a computerized collection of information, statistics, or data that is accessible for research, developing epidemiological, public health or research reports, or planning health services.

data collection The gathering of information from one or more points to a central location for analysis and processing.

data collection network A system that collects, stores, and disseminates information by the use of a centralized computer. Information is entered into computer terminals at various locations within the health-care facility or its branches, satellites, or related institutions and agencies, all of which are linked to the central computer.

data entries All information or data that are entered into a medical record or business record through the use of a computer system.

data entry The process of inputting information into a computer system so that it may be processed and stored for retrieval.

data pattern An identifiable arrangement of data that suggests a systematic design or orderly formation relative to a data set; it may trigger further investigation of an indicator-monitored process or outcome (JCAHO for acute-care hospitals).

data phone A system that transmits computer language through telephone circuits. The transmitting end converts data from punched cards, punched tape, or magnetic tape into a transmission tone. The receiving end converts the tone into electrical pulses that enter a computer or other research, record, or business machines.

data processing 1. The transposing of crude information into a form that is usable and that can be analyzed and easily stored via computer. 2. The recording, classifying, summarizing, computing, transmitting, and storing of information; any hand or machine operation or combination of operations on information or numbers.

data security A method of protecting computerized information from unauthorized entry, modification, destruction, disclosure, or accidental modification or destruction. The protection can be accomplished in the software, electronic access, or the physical setup. Organizational policies and procedures can also be established for the protection of data.

data security administrator A medical records specialist who has knowledge, training, and skills in the security and protection of medical record information and related computerized medical record systems. This person's background is in medical records administration, computerized medical information handling, information science, and data security systems and is responsible for the supervision, maintenance, and protection of medical records and related information, either as a regular employee of a health-care facility or as a consultant. Verification of the person's expertise and trustworthiness by a recognized agency or authority is usually required, and in some cases the specialist may be bonded.

data set A set of standardized and uniformly defined and classified statistics that describes an element, episode, or aspect of health care (e.g., a hospital admission, ambulatory encounter, or a physician or hospital). Such data sets are used for evaluation, research, and similar purposes. *See also discharge abstract.*

data trend A key type of data pattern consisting of the general direction of data measurements (e.g., indicator rates), which may trigger further investigation of an indicator-monitored process or outcome (JCAHO for acute-care hospitals).

date of service In managed care and insurance, this is the month, day, and year that a medical care policy went into effect and medical services began being provided to a health plan member or an insurance policy holder.

DATTA *See Diagnostic and therapeutic technology assessment program.*

DAW Dispense as written. The instruction on a prescription from a physician to a pharmacist indicating that he or she should dispense a brand-name drug rather than a generic substitution.

day 1. According to the American Hospital Association and National Master Facility Inventory, days or inpatient days are the number of adult and pediatric days of care rendered during a reporting period. Days of care for newborns are excluded. 2. In public health and traffic safety, the time interval between sunrise and sunset, used when assessing motor vehicle accidents. *See also patient bed day; restricted activity day; bed disability day; work-loss day; school-loss day.*

day care 1. Care or treatment given in a health-care facility, usually for surgical procedures accomplished in 1 day; synonymous with "ambulatory surgery." 2. Care and babysitting of children for working parents. 3. Supervision, care, recreation, and food provided in the day for elderly people with working family members. *See adult day care; adult day health care.*

day-care center Special ambulatory services and treatment that meet the health-care needs of people to prevent their becoming residents in a health-care facility. *See also home health care.*

day-care services In mental health or developmental disability care, the comprehensive, coordinated sets of activities that provide personal care and other services outside the home and during part of the day to persons over 18 years of age. Services include social, emotional, creative, learning, physical, and recreational activities based on a care plan developed from the patient's evaluation. Day-care services provide supervised personal, training, counseling, occupational, and therapeutic recreational services, with the goal of improving the patient's independent living and effective use of leisure time.

day, certain A specific date or specified time in the near future.

day, charity Health-care services provided at no charge for a 24-hour period by a health-care facility; charges are waived because of the inability of the patient to pay.

day equivalents, inpatient Total number of inpatient days of service rendered; the volume of outpatient services equated to inpatient days of service for the same time period.

day health services 1. Programs offered on an outpatient or daytime basis only. 2. Health-care facilities that provide medical and health-care services to patients who regularly need them for a continual number of days in the daytime yet whose conditions do not require inpatient care or hospitalization.

day hospital A partial hospitalization in which a patient spends the daytime in the hospital and returns home at night.

day, inpatient bed count The number of beds available for use in a health-care facility during a 24-hour period.

day, inpatient services Health-care services that are provided by a health-care facility to a single person who is an inpatient for a 24-hour period of time.

day, occupied bed Hospital beds that have been assigned to patients admitted for inpatient care and the services offered to the patient between the assigned hours of census taking in 2 successive days. The discharge day is used in the census count only if the patient was admitted on the same day.

day, partial hospitalization Health-care services provided to an individual who was admitted for partial hospitalization in a 24-hour period.

day, patient *See day, inpatient services; patient days.*

day, resident Health-care services provided in a residential care facility in a 24-hour period.

days In health-care delivery, managed care, and insurance, this is a measure of the length of a hospital stay; the length of confinement to a health-care facility.

days, adjusted inpatient services The actual number of inpatient days of services rendered after extraneous variables are considered such as newborn care and outpatient care. *See also day equivalents, inpatient.*

days of care In the National Hospital Discharge Survey, this refers to the total number of patient days accumulated by patients at the time of discharge from nonfederal, short-stay hospitals during a reporting period. All days from and including the date of admission, but not including the date of discharge, are counted. *See patient bed days.*

days/one thousand (days/1000) *See bed days/1000.*

day treatment A specialized and intensive form of outpatient mental health service, less restrictive than inpatient care, through which the partially hospitalized patient receives treatment during work hours for up to 5 to 6 hours a day and returns to home or a halfway house.

DD *See developmental disability.*

DDS Doctor of Dentistry and Surgery; Doctor of Dental Surgery; Doctor of Dental Science. The degree designation given to dentists.

de (Lat.) Of, by, concerning, from.

DEA Drug Enforcement Administration.

DEA number Drug Enforcement Administration number. This is a number assigned by the DEA to health-care providers indicating that the person or facility is registered with the DEA to dispense controlled substances.

death 1. Permanent cessation of all vital functions; the end of life. Although a simple concept, the medical field has made it sometimes very difficult to define and measure. A consensus appears to be forming that death occurs when any measurable or identifiable brain functioning (electrical or any other kind) is absent for over 24 hours. 2. "Civil" death results in the loss of civil rights in some states; when a person is sentenced to life in prison. 3. "Presumptive," or legal, death results when an unexplained absence occurs for a length of time set by state law. *See also hospice; euthanasia.*

death certificate In public health, this is one form of vital statistics; a record of vital event of death as recorded and signed by a physician. This record is a key source of data giving name, date of death, sex, race, date of birth, military service, social security number, marital status, survivors, occupation, years in the occupation, education, place of residence including zip code, place of death, time factors related to cause of death, immediate cause of death and underlying cause of death set forth by the ICD-9-CM. Data from death certificates and the formal death reporting system provide a source for studying a variety of public health and epidemiological issues and events.

death from accident In public health and occupational health and safety, this is a death from a traumatic occurrence that is not caused by a disease, syndrome, or condition and that occurs within 1 year of the accident.

death instinct *See aggressive drive.*

death rate A public health measure derived by dividing the number of deaths in a population in a given period by the resident population to the middle of that period, expressed as the number of deaths per 1000 or 100,000 population. It may be restricted to deaths in specific age, race, sex, or geographic groups, or it may be related to the entire population.

death rate, disease-specific The number of disease-caused deaths (numerator) divided by a given population (denominator) for a given period of time and expressed in the number of deaths per 1000, 10,000, or 100,000.

death rate, fetal The number of deaths of fetuses (numerator) divided by the number of total births (fetal deaths and live births). The rate is expressed as fetal deaths per 1000 or 10,000 total births.

death rate, hospital The total number of deaths of inpatients (numerator) divided by the grand total of inpatients within the hospital (denominator) in a specified period of time per 100 or 1000.

death rate, hospital neonatal/hospital infant The total number of newborn deaths that occur in a hospital (numerator) divided by the total number of infant births (denominator) in the same hospital. This rate is expressed as a ratio and can be utilized for one hospital or a group of hospitals. The ratio used is the number of infant deaths per 100, 1000, or 10,000 total hospital births in a select time period per select population/hospital or hospitals.

death rate index A hospital-based statistic determined by dividing the number of deaths, excluding newborn deaths, by the number of admissions, excluding maternity admissions. The adjusted death rate index formula follows:

<u>Number of deaths excluding newborn deaths</u>
Number of admissions excluding
maternity admissions

death rate, infant The total number of deaths of infants (numerator) divided by the total number of children born in a select population (denominator) over a specified period of time. This rate is expressed as a ratio of infant deaths per 1000, 10,000, or 100,000 live infant births for the select population. *See infant mortality.*

death rate, maternal The total number of maternal deaths resulting from childbirth (numerator) divided by the total number of women going through childbirth in a select population (denominator) for a given period of time. This rate is expressed as a ratio of deaths of mothers who died from childbirth per 1000, 10,000, 100,000 population of total women going through childbirth for a select population. *See maternal mortality rate.*

death rate, maternal (hospital) The total number of maternal deaths occurring in a hospital that result from childbirth (numerator) divided by the population of total women who underwent childbirth (denominator) in a hospital per 1000 or 10,000. *See maternal mortality.*

death rate, neonatal The total number of newborn deaths (numerator) divided by the total births of infants in a select population (denominator) for a given period of time. This rate is expressed as a ratio of deaths of newborns times 1000, 10,000, or 100,000 for a select population in a given time period. *See neonatal mortality.*

death rate, neonatal (hospital) The number of newborn deaths in a hospital in the first 28 days of life in a given period of time (numerator) divided by the total number of newborns discharged in the same time period, both alive and dead (denominator), times 1000.

death rate, perinatal *See perinatal mortality.*

death rate, perinatal (hospital) Deaths of newborns surrounding birth in a hospital setting. The numerator includes deaths of fetuses in the hospital after the 28th week of gestation plus fetuses plus newborns dying in the hospital 1 week after delivery. The denominator includes the same deaths plus live births in the hospital in the same time period times 1000.

death rates The number of deaths reported in a period of time, usually in 1 year per 1000, 10,000, or 100,000 population. *See crude death rates.*

death rates, total The total number of deaths as compared to the total population per 1000, 10,000, or 100,000 population for a given period of time. *See also mortality; crude death rates.*

death registration area Established in 1900 with 10 states and the District of Columbia. The birth registration area was established in 1915, with the same 10 states and the District of Columbia, covering the entire United States since 1933. Puerto Rico, the U.S. Virgin Islands, and Guam are also now included in the statistical tabulations. These same areas were developed into death registration areas with death reporting requirements mandated.

debase To lower one's character, rank, or estimation.

de bene esse (Lat.) Conditionally. Referring to the appearance of a witness; the presentation of evidence. Depositions or evidence may be accepted de bene esse.

debenture In health-care finance, this is a certificate acknowledging a debt. An unsecured bond; a corporate bond that contains a promise to pay its debt to the bondholder, although it is not supported by security.

debit In health-care financial accounting, this is a sum of money owed and due; an amount owed as a debt. Opposite of "credits."

de bonis non (Lat.) Of the goods not taken care of. When a health-care administrator, especially in long-term care, has been selected to handle the property of a deceased person whose executor is no longer available or has died.

debt Goods, money, or services owed by one person to another; borrowed funds that must be repaid.

debt/assets ratio In health-care finance, this is a ratio that compares what a health-care organization owes to what it owns. The total debt should be less than half the total assets. An organization with a poor ratio will be less likely to get credit and loans from lending institutions. The debt/asset ratio formula follows:

$$\frac{\text{Total debt}}{\text{Total assets}} \times 100 = \text{Percentage}$$

debt capacity In health-care finance, this is the amount of money a health-care organization can borrow, as determined by its ability to generate revenue to pay off principal and interest.

debt capital In health-care financial management, this is the long-term debt divided by the fund balance plus long-term debt multiplied by 100. The debt capital formula follows:

$$\frac{\text{Long-term debt}}{\text{Fund balance + long-term debt}} \times 100 = \text{Percentage}$$

debt/equity ratio In health-care finance, this is a measure of a hospital's debt services as compared to the overall value of the health care organization (usually a hospital). A leverage ratio that is used most often by lenders to evaluate a hospital's capacity for debt service and solvency as it relates long-term debt to equity (i.e., a measure of the hospital's ability to meet its long-term financial obligations or needs). This ratio helps to determine how much a hospital relies on long-term debt to finance capital assets. A low ratio indicates that the hospital relies heavily on debt to finance capital assets. If the ratio is too high, lenders regard the hospital as a risk and will lend less money than is needed, lend it at high rates, or both. If a hospital has a high debt/equity ratio, it can still borrow money if it can show that it is capable of making the loan payments. The debt/equity ratio formula follows:

$$\frac{\text{Long-term debt}}{\text{Fund balance}} \times 100 = \text{Percentage}$$

debt for medical care In consumer-related medical care treatment, this is the money owed by a family to a medical care organization for bills incurred in the process of receiving medical treatment or therapy that was not covered by third-party payers.

debt/plant In health-care finance, this is long-term debt divided by net property (plant) and equipment. The debt/plant formula follows:

$$\frac{\text{Long-term debt}}{\text{Net property (plant) and equipment}} \times 100 = \text{Percentage}$$

debt ratio In health-care finance, this is the ratio of long-term debts to capital structure; total debt to total assets. The debt ratio shows relative risk.

debt service 1. In health-care financial management, this is the payment of matured interest and principal on debts; the cost of ending uncollectable old debts, including the principal amount needed, supplied, or accrued to meet payments and interest on the debt. 2. The cost of ending a debt during any given accounting period; the amount needed to meet principal and interest payments.

debt service coverage In health-care financial management, this is the net income divided by the maximum annual debt services of the organization.

debt service coverage ratio In health-care financial management, this is a measure that shows how many times a hospital's debt service requirements could be covered from existing cash flow. This ratio is affected adversely by declining profits, making it difficult for the organization to pay off debt and obtain credit at reasonable rates. A high debt service ratio is positive. This ratio is used by banks and lenders to determine a hospital's ability to meet long-term debts through revenue from operations. To obtain a high rating, 200% is usually needed for an "A+" rating, and a rating of 120% is the minimum coverage required for tax-exempt bond financing. The debt service coverage ratio formula follows:

$$\frac{\text{Net profit + depreciation + interest}}{\text{Principal + interest}} \times 100 = \text{Percentage}$$

debtee One to whom a debt is owed; a creditor.

debtor One owing a debt; the party who owes money or goods to another.

debug In health-care information management, this is the identification and correction of the source of errors in a computer program.

deceit Any untrue, deceiving, or false statement purposely made with intention of causing harm by fooling or misleading another party or person.

decentralization 1. In health administration, this is an administrative approach that assists in understanding an organization's approach to the division of labor; when a health-care organization develops and implements subunits and each manager is given a great deal of trust and autonomy in the responsibility, authority, and managerial decision making. A decentralized organization usually has a fairly flat organizational chart. 2. In health-care administration, the delegation of responsibility and authority to department heads; the giving of considerable autonomy in managerial decision making to division and department heads when reasonable and effective methods of evaluating performance, efficiency, and effectiveness, including cost control and profitability, are available.

decentralized filing system In health-care medical record administration, this is a systematic method of storing and retrieving files of information or medical records by locating them close to the source of their regular use.

decentralized services In health-care administration and health services delivery, this is providing services at locations removed from the hospital or central administration of the health-care organization. Decentralization empowers employees to be successful, to take on more responsibility, and to be efficient and effective. It also reduces costs and improves morale and problem solving at the level the problems occur.

decertification Under Medicare or Medicaid programs, this is the process of suspending or revoking a health-care facility's certification for participation in these federally sponsored programs.

decision 1. In health law, this is the formal result of the settlement of the dispute; a judge's resolution to a lawsuit. 2. In health-care administration, this is a management function that includes a process of resolving the direction in which to go regarding organizational or operational issues. Factors are interrelated in a complex manner and involve processes leading to a final culmination on the basis of a willingness to change or alter, if required, while considering long-term outcomes and effects. 3. In health promotion, a process of individually choosing health-enhancing activities or participating in behaviors that are risk factors to health such as tobacco or alcohol use.

decisional law Those laws determined by courts; decisions that rule from case results rather than from statutes. *See also case law; common law.*

decision analysis The use of a variety of decision-making approaches, including the use of decision techniques such as Pert charts, decision trees, fishbone models, and probability theory to determine the best or final alternatives in a series of choices. *See decision trees; fishbone charts; Pert charts.*

decision making 1. In health-care administration, this is a process whereby an administrator or manager, relying on past experience, insights and learnings, and rational psychological constructs, uses a process of identifying and considering the alternatives of a course of action appropriate and acceptable for the situation. The greatest possibilities of success for the issue at hand and for the overall operations of the health-care organization are considered. Four steps to decision making have been suggested: 1) define the issues to be analyzed that require a decision, 2) explore all practical alternative courses of action, 3) analyze positive and negative consequences or costs and benefits, and 4) assess possible benefits and problems with each alternative course of action and choose the best one. 2. The process utilized by an organization, community, or group to agree on a course of action, solution to an issue, or health services to be provided.

decision-making capacity The ability to make choices that reflect an understanding and appreciation of the nature and consequences of one's actions. A person is presumed to have the capacity to make health-care decisions unless the attending physician, together with family members, determines that the person is incapacitated or a court rules that the person is incompetent.

decision on the merits In health law, this is a decision reached and fully decided on an issue of a case so that no new or different lawsuits may be filed on the same issue by the same plaintiff.

decision-support technologies Any technology or scientific advancement used to support decision making such as computer decision-making models, algorithms, expert systems, Pert charting, pattern-recognition programs, or interactive information management software programs or databases.

decision symbol In health-care information management, this is a symbol denoting the need for verifying the existence or nonexistence of conditions or future actions.

decision tree A graphic representation of the alternatives available at each step in a series of choices, often answered "yes" or "no." Subsequent possible choices and outcomes are presented in a flow chart with branches, and a choice is presented at the end of each branch leading to two additional branches, providing a tool for decision analysis.

declaration 1. An unsworn statement. 2. A formal statement. 3. A public proclamation.

declaratory judgment A court decision outlining the rights and duties of the parties in a dispute that does not coerce any performance or payment of damages.

declining balance method of depreciation In health-care finance, this is a depreciation method determined by a fixed annual percentage of the balance of a loan or note; the amount remaining after deducting the amount of each yearly depreciation.

decreasing term A term life insurance policy where the amount of coverage decreases as the policy and the person grow older.

decree A judgment or order issued by a court or judge.

decree nisi In health law, this is a provisional decree set by the court that can become final at a specified law time, unless evidence is presented that shows why it should not become final.

decubitus care The treatment and attention paid to a decubitus ulcer once the pressure sore has occurred; treatment includes medication, dressing the sore, and repositioning the person by turning or rolling. It is important to reposition the patient frequently because this allows increased blood flow to the sore area.

decubitus ulcer A bedsore or pressure sore produced by the pressure of lying in one position for an extended period (a serious problem for bedridden long-term-care patients).

deductible 1. That which may be eliminated or subtracted such as subtracting items from income for tax purposes. 2. In medical insurance or managed care, the percentage of the total amount the insured person must pay from his or her own funds "out of pocket" as part of the care received or before policy benefits begin. Under federally qualified HMOs or some state HMO regulations, deductibles are not allowed. 3. Amount of loss or expense that must be incurred by an insured individual before an insurer will assume any liability for all or part of the remaining cost of covered services. Deductibles may be either fixed dollar amounts or the value of specified services (such as 2 days of hospital care or one physician visit). Deductibles are usually tied to some reference period over which they must be incurred (e.g., $100 per calendar year, benefit period, or spell of illness). Deductibles in existing policies are generally 1) static deductibles, which are fixed dollar amounts, and 2) dynamic deductibles, which are adjusted from time to time to reflect increasing medical prices. A third type is proposed in some national health insurance plans: a sliding-scale deductible, in which the deductible is related to income and increases as income increases.

deductible amount In Medicare policy, the amount of health-care charges for which the Medicare recipient is responsible; for hospital charges, an amount roughly equal to the cost of the first day's care; for physician or other Part B charges, an amount set annually by the government.

deductible carryover credit 1. In health-care financial management, managed care, and medical insurance, these are monies applied to the deductible portion of a health plan or medical care policy for the last 3 months of a calendar year that are used to meet the next year's deductibles. 2. The deductible part of a health-care policy for the previous year that may or may not have been paid for.

deductible liability insurance Coverage under which the insured agrees to pay up to a specified sum per claim toward the amount payable to the physician.

deductible ratio How much of a medical group or hospital's services can be delivered or sold at prices below the usual rate is of concern to a health-care provider organization when contracting a managed-care program. A discounted price can be determined by dividing the contractual allowances (the amount of the discount from regular charges) by the gross patient services revenue. The resulting deductible ratio is a percentage of gross revenue that the health-care organization will not receive as cash. The percentage is not of much value when viewed alone because it must be used as a part of the contractual decision-making process. The larger the percent of the contracted business, the less likely it is that the organization will make a profit. Under a managed-care program, the number of "lifes" in the pool of enrollees is also considered. The deductible ratio formula follows:

$$\frac{\text{Contractual allowances}}{\text{Gross patient service revenue}} \times 100 = \text{Percentage}$$

deduction 1. Reasoning from a known fact to an unknown. 2. Deducting; subtraction, such as items subtracted from income tax. 3. An abatement, as an amount deducted from a bill or charge.

deed A written paper defining an interest in real estate and/or its transfer to another party.

deed restrictions When a health-care organization purchases a piece of property from another party, the deed to the property may state limitations as to the use of the property, and these are conveyed to the new owner and all future owners.

deemed status An official designation given to a hospital by the Professional Review Organization (PRO) that indicates the hospital has met the PRO's effectiveness criteria for admissions review, continued stay review, and medical care assessment. This designation indicates that the hospital is eligible to participate in Medicare, Medicaid, and maternal and child health programs and indicates which services are acceptable for reimbursement by these programs.

de facto (Lat.) Actual, in fact. A situation that actually or factually exists, whether or not it is within the scope of law.

defalcation Defaulting; a failure to account for funds, not necessarily because of fraud or dishonesty; however, a suspicion that the money has been wrongfully used usually exists.

defamation 1. Slanderous speech. 2. Degrading, harmful, or slanderous written statements; malicious false statements made against another. 3. Injuring a person's character; injury to one's reputation by false and malicious utterances, including both libel and slander. *See also libel; slander.*

default 1. An omission or a failure to perform a duty that one is legally bound to perform. 2. Failure to take the required steps or follow the correct procedures in a court action. 3. Failure to perform or take care of a legal obligation; failure to follow court processes in a lawsuit.

default judgment 1. A decision from a judge or court against either party of a legal action for failure to follow due process, answer claims, present a defense, or appear in court. 2. A judgment against the defendant because of his or her failure to appear in court, reply to legal documents, or answer a plaintiff's complaint.

defeasible That which can be divested or revoked if some contingency occurs; being defeated, ended, or undone by future action.

defeasible fee A fee that may be no longer required because of the occurrence of some contingency.

defect 1. An imperfection; a flaw. 2. The lack of something required by law. 3. Less than adequate or acceptable. 4. The lack of legal principles that makes an action insufficient, inadequate, and not binding.

defendant In a court action, the person defending; the one against whom an action is brought in a civil or criminal case.

defendant in error In health law, this is when the party to a lawsuit who won the suit is now the adverse party when the losing party then seeks to have the judgment reversed in an appellate court by a writ of error; the appellee in an appeal of a judgment that the party had won in the trial court. *See also appellee.*

defense The facts, laws, and arguments presented by the defendant or the party against whom legal action is being taken.

defense mechanisms Learned behaviors, attitudes, or beliefs that are used by an individual to adjust to environment, stress, or challenging situations; unconscious or conscious processes used to cope with or provide relief from emotional conflict and anxiety. Several defense mechanisms that affect behavior are compensation, conversion, denial, displacement, dissociation, idealization, identification, incorporation, introjection, projection (blaming others), rationalization, reaction formation, regression, sublimation, substitution, and symbolization. *See also mental mechanisms.*

defensive medicine The excessive use of diagnostic tests by a physician, done more for protection against a malpractice suit or for insuring a good legal defense should a malpractice lawsuit occur than for justified medical reasons.

deference In health administration and assertiveness training, this is acting in a subservient manner as if one is less important than others who are more educated, powerful, experienced, or knowledgeable.

deferral of budget authority In the federal budget, any action or inaction of the executive branch, including the establishment of reserves under the Antideficiency Act, that temporarily withholds, delays, or effectively precludes the obligation or expenditure of budget authority. Under Section 1013 of the Congressional Budget and Impoundment Control Act of 1974, the president is required to report each proposed deferral to Congress in a special message. Deferrals may not extend beyond the end of a fiscal year and may be overturned by the passage of an impoundment resolution by either house of Congress. *See also recision.*

deferred compensation administrator In managed care, this is a special finance or insurance organization that provides administrative services through retirement planning administrators, third-party administrators, self-insured health plans, workers' compensation programs, claims administration, etc.

deferred payments Installment payments.

deficiency 1. A variation, usually a shortfall, from an expected level of performance or standard. 2. Under OBRA, an instance of noncompliance with a regulatory requirement. A deficiency may be cited if there are situations identified during the course of a survey of sufficient severity and or frequency that indicate an individual requirement is not met. If not in compliance, a citation may be issued according to the Code of Federal Regulations or Life Safety Codes. Specific and detailed regulations are cited as to the requirement that is not in compliance and are listed as "not met."

deficiency disease Any specific disease or pathological state, with characteristic clinical signs, that is related to an insufficient intake of energy or essential nutrients. It is usually of dietary origin and can often be prevented or cured by bringing the intake up to an adequate level of nutrition.

deficiency judgment 1. An action of foreclosure on a debt. 2. A decision by a court to cause a person to pay the difference between the amount gained by the creditor by selling property and the amount of the judgment.

deficit 1. A shortage. 2. Something missing, due, lacking, or being less than it should be. 3. When something is missing, due, or lacking; something being less than it should be.

deficit reduction targets The U.S. Congress must cut spending each year by a certain amount before the date and time of budgetary approval. If Congress fails to meet the targets, everything is cut across the board. Social Security surplus is considered part of the unified federal budget and is considered in meeting deficit reduction targets. If targets are not met, the cuts are in spending without the reserve factored in.

defined Regarding regulatory compliance under state or federal regulations, this means "explained in writing."

definitive 1. A final, conclusive, and complete settlement of a legal question. 2. Absolute; complete; final.

definitive care 1. Medical or dental care provided by a physician, dentist, or other health-care provider in a hospital, clinic, or medical environment, as opposed to emergency care at the site of an accident in the community. 2. Diagnosis and treatment.

deflation The decrease in the supply of money and credit. Prices drop, and the value of money is increased in relation to what it will buy; the opposite of inflation.

deforce To wrongfully withhold property from the rightful possessor.

DEFRA Deficit Reduction Act of 1984. A federal law passed to help prevent discrimination against elderly employees in medical insurance. Group health plans must be offered to the employee's dependents in the 65–69 age bracket even if the employees are not in that age bracket.

defraud To cheat; deceive; deprive by deception.

degree 1. The seriousness of an act or crime. 2. A step, level, or division. 3. A rank or diploma of recognition for educational attainment.

dehors (French) 1. Irrelevant to; foreign to; beyond; outside of. 2. Not contained within the record.

dehydration The lack of adequate fluid intake; a real concern in long-term-care facilities and children in poverty.

dei gratia (Lat.) By the grace of God.

deinstitutionalization The release of patients from health-care institutions to increase self-sufficiency, restore freedom, and reduce cost. Observed in long-term-care facilities but mostly in psychiatric institutions. Mental health care is continued in the community in outpatient centers, halfway houses, and community mental health centers, both public and private. Psychotropic drug use has assisted in this movement and outpatient treatment.

de jure (Lat.) 1. Rightful; legitimate; lawful; by law. 2. Often contrasted with "de facto." 3. Whether or not true in actual fact. An administrator may be the de jure head of a hospital while the governing board has the actual power.

del credere (Italian) One who works as an agent selling goods for another, with the buyer paying for the goods.

delectus personae (Lat.) The choice a person has; the legal right given to an original partner of a company, business, etc.; to approve or disapprove other partners.

delegate 1. One who is authorized to act for another; a person chosen to represent another person or a group. 2. To select a person to serve as a representative of someone in a position of authority or to give responsibility to. 3. To entrust authority and responsibility to another to act as one's agent. *See delegation.*

delegated hospital *See hospital, delegated.*

delegation 1. In health administration, this is the act of giving authority, responsibility, and accountability to another person. 2. In health-care administration, when an administrator, manager, or director commissions authority, decision making, power, and responsibility to a subordinate. The management process of empowering subordinates to be more responsible and effective as workers. 2. A group of delegates. 3. In the Professional Review Organization (PRO), the formal process by which a PRO, using an assessment of the willingness and capability of a hospital or other health program to effectively perform review functions, assigns a performance rating to that hospital or institution. The type and amount of delegation is agreed to in a written memorandum of understanding, signed by both the PRO and the hospital. The PRO monitors the performance of the review function that has been delegated and retains responsibility for the effectiveness of the review.

delegation of review An alternate method of performing peer reviews with the responsibility relinquished by the PRO to the hospital yet still conducted under PRO guidelines.

delegatory law In health law, this is a mandate stating that physician extenders, such as physician assistants, are allowed to practice whatever procedure, therapy, or treatment the supervising physician may see fit to delegate to the physician extender.

delete In managed-care and Medicare contracts under HCFA, this is to remove an enrollee from the health plan's Medicare program.

deleterious Harmful; injurious.

deliberate 1. To discuss carefully; to work through; to consider and discuss; carefully considered, planned, and thought out. 2. Premeditated, intentional; an act done on purpose.

delictum (Lat.) A wrongful, criminal, or tortious act.

delinquency 1. Failure; neglect; act of omission. 2. A violation of one's duty; misconduct. 3. Overdue monetary debts. 4. Failure to do what the law dictates.

delinquent 1. Overdue; unpaid. 2. Neglecting to do what the law or duty requires.

delirious Mental confusion; restlessness; incoherence.

delirium In mental health services, this is a mental disturbance characterized by restlessness, confusion, disorientation, bewilderment, agitation, and affective liability; associated with fear, hallucinations, and illusions.

delirium tremens An acute psychotic mental state that is caused by withdrawal from alcohol after a prolonged and severe period of drinking.

delivery room A medical and nursing unit in a hospital or freestanding emergency clinic for labor, delivery, and newborn resuscitation.

Delphi technique This is a research method that samples the opinions or preferences of experts, leaders, informants, participants, or those affected by the outcomes or recipients of a service whereby successive variables, factors, questions, or questionnaires are provided, and the results are ranked and value estimates assigned. The results are returned to the participants, and the process is repeated and summarized for further refinement. The process is repeated several times until an objective and useful level of refinement is reached that is the final result.

Delta Dental Plan The first multistate dental prepayment program, coordinated by the National Association of Dental Service Plans for the Northwest International Association of Machinists' Benefit Trust of Seattle.

delusion An idea with an irrational explanation that is maintained by a person despite logical argument, objective reasoning, contradictory evidence, or facts; clinging to an idea or belief that is not real.

demand 1. To seek what is due or claimed. 2. A valid claim that assumes that there is no doubt as to whom the claim belongs. 3. The claiming of a legal right as determined by the courts. 4. In health-care delivery, the amount of care a population would utilize if it were available, low cost, accessible, and acceptable. 5. From a health-care finance view, the amount and level of medical care that will be utilized at a set cost. The realized demand is the amount of medical care physically and actually utilized.

demand for care The amount of health-care service sought or needed by consumers in response to their perceived need for that service.

demand note A note expressly stating that something is payable on demand.

demand schedule In health economics, the varying amount of goods or services sought at varying prices, given constant income and other factors. Demand must be distinguished from utilization (the amount of services actually used) and need (for various reasons services are often sought that either the consumer or the provider feels are unneeded). *See also supply; elasticity of demand.*

demarketing This represents an effort by hospitals or health-care organizations to discourage certain market segments from using a service or to seek certain services elsewhere; the opposite of marketing.

demeanor Outward appearance and behavior; one's manner, conduct, or air. Not what a person utters but how he or she utters it; one's nonverbal actions and communications.

demedicalization The process by which the health-care community redefines and limits health-care consumers' expectations for medical care and its access. This also includes reforming unhealthy behaviors and social and personal attitudes regarding personal health considered outside the scope of medical care, by promoting preventive care and a health promotion perspective.

demencia (Spanish) The loss of one's mind; insanity; dementia.

dementia Organic loss of mental functioning.

dementia praecox An old term used to describe what is now clinically identified as schizophrenia.

de minis (Lat.) A writ of threats.

demise 1. Death. 2. Any lease. 3. A transfer or conveyance of property.

demographic characteristics A concise narrative and description of the characteristics of the total population of a state, region, county, city, etc.

demographics As used in public health, epidemiology, and related areas, this is the descriptive information about a population based on social and vital statistics as well as factual, objective information about groups of people used to predict health needs and use of health services; includes age, sex, race, income, education, occupation, socioeconomic status, place of residence, insurance coverage, medical status, stage in family life cycle, etc.

demographic segmentation The targeting or grouping of a part of a population by certain characteristics; grouping patients of a hospital or health plan according to selected statistical, social, and health traits.

demography The quantitative study of human populations and groups. The sociological statistical analysis and study of a region, population, or group; the study of population statistics and characteristics. Demographers study geographical distribution of people, death rates, birth rates, socioeconomic status, sex/gender, and age distributions to identify changes, developments, and structure of populations.

demonstration grants Grant money awarded by a foundation or governmental agency so that the recipient of the grant may demonstrate the effectiveness of a given approach or method. This type of grant may also be used to show how a research technique can be applied more widely or how groups in a select population can benefit from an approach originally designed for a different population or from an approach not previously tried.

demonstration model In health-care delivery, this is a trial or test approach to a new and different kind of health-care service, program, institution, or facility whereby provisions for administrative assessments are measured: flow of care, costs per units of service, rate assessments, feasibility of the service, goals/objectives, outcome results, efficiency, effectiveness, and satisfaction.

demonstrative evidence In health law, other than testimony; evidence physically shown or presented in court.

demotion In health-care administration human resource management, this is when a manager is moved down from one job level to a lower position with less pay, responsibility, and authority.

demur 1. To make or enter a demurrer. 2. To object formally to a pleading. 3. To delay or postpone.

demurrant One who demurs.

demurrer 1. A pleading for the dismissal of a lawsuit; a motion to dismiss a complaint because of failure to state a claim. 2. A legal pleading;

when the facts presented by one side of a case are not sound enough for a legal argument to stand up in court and thus should be dismissed.

denial 1. A contradiction of statements made by the opposing party. 2. A plea against the facts claimed by the other side of a suit. 3. Refusal; rejection. 4. Deprivation or withholding. 5. In psychology or psychiatry, a conscious or unconscious defense or mental mechanism by which an aspect of external reality is rejected or when experiences, behaviors, or actions are not accepted by the person. 6. In health-care finance, the rejection of payment by a fiscal intermediary.

denominator In epidemiology and descriptive statistics, this is the bottom half of a rate or ratio formula that represents the general aspects of the issue at hand or the general population of the study; the data on the general population or the population at risk is entered as the denominator.

de novo (Lat.) 1. Once again; starting anew. A writ "venire de novo" summons a jury for a second trial on a case set up for a new trial. 2. New from the start; for example, a trial de novo is a new trial ordered by a judge or by a court.

density sampling In epidemiology and biomedical research, this is a sampling method used in case control and longitudinal studies intended to reduce bias because of changing exposure patterns in the study population. Cases are selected only from incident cases within a set time period, and control subjects are also sampled and interviewed throughout the time period of the study rather than in a single time period; thus the controls are assessed just as the research subjects are.

dentacare A group dental plan whereby a fixed monthly payment is made to a group of dentists that guarantees care for enrolled subscribers.

dental appliance Any variety of orthodontic devices or structures used to move irregularly placed teeth into proper position; orthodontic devices.

dental assistant An individual who assists a dentist at the chairside in a dental operatory, performs reception and clerical functions, and carries out dental radiography and selected dental laboratory work. Dental assistants who have completed accredited educational programs are eligible for national certification examinations conducted by the Certifying Board of the American Dental Assistants Association. An accredited dental assistant program is usually conducted in a community college or vocational or technical school and must provide at least 1 year of academic training.

dental auxiliary Any of a number of assistants to a dental surgeon.

dental care, expenditures for See *expenditures for dental care*.

dental chart A diagram of the teeth on which clinical findings and results of examinations are recorded. The medical record of a dental patient. *See also medical record*.

dental engine The motor and associated equipment, such as continuous-cord belts over a pulley activated by a hand or foot switch, that controls the drill.

dental extender A dental hygienist or dental assistant who performs "expanded functions."

dental geriatrics The branch of dentistry treating dental-related disorders and diseases associated with advanced age.

dental health A state of complete normality and functional efficiency of the teeth and supporting structures of the surrounding parts of the oral cavity and the various structures related to mastication and the maxillofacial complex.

Dental Health Foundation A nonprofit organization headquartered in San Rafael, California, that assists local communities in developing programs that promote and protect sound dental health. The primary mission of the organization is to bring the latest findings in dental research to the general public, educators, and health practitioners, bridging the gap between current scientific knowledge and its application.

dental health services All services, diagnosis, treatment, and disease treatment designed or intended to promote, maintain, or restore dental health including educational, restoration, periodontic, oral surgery, preventive, and therapeutic services.

dental hygienist Oral health clinicians and educators who perform preventive and therapeutic services under the supervision of a dentist. Specific responsibilities vary, depending on state laws, but may include removing deposits and stains from patients' teeth, providing instructions for patient self-care, dietetic counseling, and applying decay-preventing fluoride treatments. Hygienists take medical and dental histories, expose and process dental radiographs, make impressions of teeth for study casts, and prepare other diagnostic aids for use by the dentist. In some states, they are permitted to administer local infiltration anesthesia; place and remove dams, matrices, and sutures; and place, carve, and polish restorations in teeth after the dentist prepares the cavity. These latter functions, along with a limited number of others, are called "expanded functions" and require extended training of the hygienist. Dental hygienists are licensed in all states. In addition, a few states have credentialing requirements for those dental hygienists who perform expanded functions. Graduation from an accredited program (except in Alabama) and licensing are required. The Commission on Accreditation for Dental and Dental Auxiliary Educational Programs established basic curriculum requirements and guidelines and accredits all approved dental hygiene programs. Individual states set requirements for licensing, but all states require passing a written and clinical examination.

dental insurance 1. A form of medical insurance that provides protection against the costs of diagnostic and preventive dental care, oral surgery, restorative procedures, and therapeutic dental care. 2. An insurance program that pays for all or part of outpatient dental care or may be part of a comprehensive prepaid group health plan. Accidental injury to teeth or dentistry performed only in a hospital setting is not considered a part of a dental insurance plan.

dental jurisprudence 1. Also referred to as "forensic dentistry," the area of law that encompasses dental knowledge and practice as found applicable to certain aspects of law. 2. Statutes and codes that control and limit the professional practice of dentistry.

dental laboratory technician *See dental technician.*

dental laboratory technologist Professionals trained to construct complete and partial dentures, make orthodontic appliances, fix bridgework and crowns, and perform other dental restorations and appliances as authorized by dentists.

dental public health An educational program that focuses on the formulation and development of preventive and curative dental health services.

dental service Hospital dental care provided for ambulatory patients and sometimes for inpatients. The dental staff is organized as part of the hospital's medical staff.

dental services (oral hygiene) According to JCAHO for long-term-care accreditation, services provided by a dentist that include, but are not necessarily limited to, annual oral examinations, routine and emergency dental care, and instruction to nursing personnel in routine oral hygiene.

dental technician An individual who makes complete and partial dentures, orthodontic appliances, bridgework, crowns, and other dental restorations and appliances as prescribed by dentists. Most dental technicians work in commercial dental laboratories; however, increasing numbers are employed by private dental practitioners and by federal, state, and private institutions. Traditionally, dental technicians have been trained on the job, but the current method of training is mainly through formal programs offered by 2-year, postsecondary educational institutions. On completion of an aggregate of 5 years in dental technology training and experience, technicians are eligible to apply for examination and certification by the National Board for Certification in Dental Laboratory Technology. *See also denturist.*

dental unit Equipment utilized in providing dental care such as a dental engine, operatory light, worktable, water, compressed air, cuspidor, and drills.

dental visit According to the National Interview Survey, a visit to a dentist's office for treatment or advice, including services by a technician or dental hygienist acting under the dentist's supervision. Services provided to hospital inpatients are not included.

Denti-Cal A dental health plan in California sponsored by both the federal and the state governments for people who are eligible for public assistance and for other low-income groups.

dentist 1. A professional who has earned a bachelors degree, completed premedical/dental course requirements, and graduated from an accredited dental school and who is licensed at the state level to practice dentistry (unless a foreign dental school graduate, who must meet different requirements). 2. Any individual who has received a Doctor of Dental Surgery (DDS) or Doctor of Dental Medicine (DDM) degree and is currently fully licensed to practice dentistry.

dentistry An educational program for the prevention, diagnosis, and treatment of diseases of the teeth and gums, including the replacement of missing teeth. Includes instruction in the principles and procedures of dental science and related supportive medical and science education.

dentistry, general The practice of all phases of dental care. A general dentist treats all members of the family and has generalized training to effectively treat all phases of dental disorders. Patients may be referred to specialists for extreme cases or specialized treatment.

denturist A dental technician who provides dentures for patients without benefit of a dentist's professional services. Denturists are rarely found in the United States, and their practice is illegal in many states. They are increasingly common in Canada, where provincial governments have proposed legalizing their practice. *See dental technician.*

deontology The study of acceptable behavior, duty, and ethics (e.g., patient and doctor relations and disclosure to patients).

department 1. A functional or administrative division of a hospital, health program, or government agency, also known as a program, division, or service. A department within a hospital or medical school is typically headed by a responsible individual (either a chairman or director), has its own budget, and admits its own patients but is not a separate legal entity. Departments are frequently organized by medical specialty such as pediatrics, radiology, or surgery. 2. For JCAHO accreditation purposes, an organizational unit of the hospital or the medical staff or a staff entity organized on administrative, functional, or disciplinary lines.

departmentation The structural framework of an organization that assigns authority. Departmentation has the advantage of improved coordination, empowerment of employees, delegation, and organizational responsibility because the end results can be readily identified and assigned. The major disadvantage, however, is the possible loss of central control. Four types of departmentation have been identified by management theorists: 1) functional departmentation: the grouping of activities according to a hospital's major tasks such as nursing, pharmacy, central supply, etc.; 2) process departmentation: the grouping of activities such as radiology around equipment and machinery; 3) territorial departmentation: the grouping of activities on the basis of geography; and 4) product departmentation: the grouping of activities on the basis of output.

Department of Corporations (DOC) A department within a state government that has the responsibility to regulate HMO and managed care.

Department of Health and Human Services (DHHS) The title for the former Department of Health, Education and Welfare. A cabinet-level department responsible for all national concerns related to personal and community health, including, but not limited to, services, research, program development, disease control, and prevention and regulations related to the health of, and services to, all people of the United States and its territories. *See U.S. Department of Health and Human Services.*

Department of Health, Education and Welfare (DHEW) The former name of the Department of Health and Human Services. *See Department of Health and Human Services.*

departmentalization *See departmentation.*

depecage (French) In a conflict of laws, when laws of different jurisdictions are used to determine the dispute or conflicts in a case that presents more than one issue.

dependence *See drug dependence.*

dependency The reliance on another for psychological, emotional, social, or financial support.

dependency needs In psychology, psychiatry, and mental health care, these are vital needs of love, affection, belonging, shelter, protection, security, food, and warmth. This may be the manifestation of a form of regression when such needs appear openly in adults.

dependency ratio The difference between the portion of the population who are self-supporting and the portion who are dependent (related to age distribution). The importance of dependent age segments of a population is viewed as to its importance to productively active age segments of a population. Three main age-groups are of concern: dependent children, active population, and dependent older adults. The numbers in each group influence the size of the ratio. One approach to determine who is included is to use all persons under age 15 plus all persons over age 65 (which may not be accurate in modern times because a high proportion of older persons are active, teens are not working, and many students are remaining dependent on parents until completing college; under age 18 and over age 70 may be more realistic ages to use in the ratio). The dependency ratio formula follows:

$$\frac{\text{Number of persons under age 15} + \text{number of persons 65 and over}}{\text{Number of persons 15 through 64 years of age}} \times 100$$

dependent An individual who relies on another individual for a significant portion of his or her support. In addition to the requirement for financial support, there is often a requirement for a blood relationship. The Internal Revenue Service (IRS) Code defines dependents for the purposes of tax deductions as any of the following, over half of whose support for the calendar year was received from the taxpayer: children (biological or adopted), grandchildren, or stepchildren; brothers and sisters, stepbrothers and stepsisters, or half brothers and half sisters; parents, grandparents, great grandparents, or stepparents; nephews and nieces; uncles and aunts; and in-laws (father, mother, son, daughter, brother, or sister) and nonrelatives living as members of the taxpayer's household. The IRS Code provides that if the support of a dependent was furnished by several persons, one may claim the dependency deduction if the others agree. In insurance and other programs the specific definition is quite variable and is often limited to the individual's spouse and children. 2. Under managed care, the spouse, dependent child, or other family member of an enrollee in a health plan as set forth by the health plan agreement.

dependent child In medical insurance, a natural or adopted child of the subscriber, under 23 years of age and unmarried, for whom the subscriber is allowed a tax exemption. This includes a physically handicapped or mentally retarded child regardless of age, provided the handicap existed before age 23, subject to verification.

dependent contract A conditional contract whereby one party does not have to perform on the contract until the other party does something that is required by the contract.

dependent nursing functions Medical care, treatment, and other patient care activities carried out by a nurse who is required to follow a physician's order.

dependents In managed care or other medical care benefit insurance programs, these are generally the spouse and children of an individual. Under some health plans or medical insurance or health programs, parents or other members of the family may be considered dependents such as elderly persons, foster children, or persons under guardianship. Anyone who depends on his or her family for finances, food, housing, clothing, and medical care is considered a dependent.

dependent variable In epidemiology or biomedical research, this is the research factor that is constant and stable and that does not change. The independent variable can be assessed by how much it changes the dependent variable. *See independent variable.*

deponent 1. One who testifies under oath. 2. One who gives sworn testimony out of court, as in a deposition.

depose 1. To testify under oath. 2. To unseat a person from public office. 3. To give sworn testimony out of court, as in a deposition.

deposition In the litigation process, the process of taking sworn testimony out of court. Written sworn testimony, made before a public officer for a court action, often provides answers to questions posed by an attorney. Depositions are used for the discovery of information or evidence for a trial and for the preservation of evidence for use in court.

deposits In health-care finance, the funds that have been set aside to insure a hospital's interest in business dealings or financial transactions.

depreciable life In health-care finance, this is the number of years that can be used to determine depreciation of an asset. The depreciation time line used is determined by the Internal Revenue Service.

depreciable property In health-care finance, for tax purposes, this is the determination of the longevity of property and how much the property has diminished in value over time, which can be deducted from income taxes. Vehicles, equipment, and the physical plant of a hospital are considered depreciable property; land is not.

depreciation In health-care finance, the allocation of capital costs to the period in which the assets purchased with those capital costs will be used. Although depreciation can be computed using many approaches, the most common is straight-line depreciation or the even distribution of capital costs throughout the life of the asset. *See also capital depreciation.*

depreciation expense In health-care finance, this is when an investment on a capital asset is set aside and then recovered during the useful life of the asset; that part of the original cost of capital assets allocated to a specific accounting period. Depreciation is included in a health-care facility's charge structure and is considered by third-party payers as an allowable cost.

depression In mental health services, psychology, and psychiatry, a mentally unhealthy state characterized by feelings of helplessness, hopelessness, extreme sadness and loneliness, low self-esteem associated with self-condemnation, psychomotor retardation, occasional agitation, withdrawal from interpersonal relations, sleep disturbance, and occasional desires to die. Insomnia and anorexia are also often noted.

derivative From another; owing its existence to something previous; being derived from; originating from another or common source.

derivative action A suit brought by a shareholder or stockholder on behalf of a corporation against a third party.

derivative evidence In health law, derived from evidence that is illegally gathered and so is not allowed in a trial.

dermatologist A physician who has completed a postgraduate residency, is board certified, and specializes in the diagnosis and treatment of diseases and disorders of the skin.

dermatology The study of the skin and its structures, functions, and diseases as well as treatments for its disorders.

dermatology technician One who prepares and administers materials that have been prescribed by a physician, usually a dermatologist, to cure or alleviate symptoms of skin problems.

dermatopathology A subspecialty of dermatology that focuses on the treatment of diseases of the skin.

derogate To impair; to partially repeal; to reduce.

descriptive statistics In epidemiology and health services research, this is the statistical presentation of data that describes events, services, charges, demographic data, and other pertinent numerical information using rates, ratios, percentages, or proportions. Often used in public health, epidemiology, and health-care facilities to demonstrate and quantify the operations, function, and management activities of the facility.

desertion Abandonment with no intention of either returning or reassuming one's responsibility.

DESI *See drug efficacy study implementation.*

designated mental health provider In managed care, this is a mental health practitioner or mental health center that is under agreement to evaluate, diagnose, and provide counseling, psychotherapy, and referrals for mental health, family relations, alcoholism, or other substance abuse problems.

Designated Service Plan A managed-care program for public employees of Utah that is unique because it has a major preventive care and health promotion approach that emphasizes wellness and consumer health education over medical treatment and surgical intervention. Implemented in 1993, it has a global fee system for high-volume outpatient and inpatient procedures with financial incentives to choose efficient, low-cost providers over expensive health-care providers. Health-care consumers are pushed to be active in helping beneficiaries identify and choose providers willing to reduce overall medical costs. Health-care providers are forced to compete for patients on the basis of price and quality.

desmoteric Pertaining to or caused within a prison; prison-associated injury or illness.

de son tort (Lat.) Of his own wrong. To take on a responsibility one has no right to assume whereby harm is done as a result of those actions.

destratification of the physician's role A position taken by some theorists in health-care reform to reduce the role and hierarchical status of the physician to one of less authority and to increase egalitarianism with the patient, members of the health-care team, and health-care administration.

destroy In contract law, this is the ending of contracts or other legal commitments or documents, not always by actual destruction but by rendering a document's legal effect useless. Destruction may be affected by obliterating the document, tearing it up (valid only with wills), or writing over it (i.e., "voiding" it).

desuetude Disuse; to cease use.

detail person A sales representative of a pharmaceutical manufacturer who promotes prescription drugs for use by physicians, dentists, and pharmacists. Such detailing includes personal presentations, advertising, and presenting drug samples and educational materials prepared by the manufacturers to professionals in their offices.

detainer 1. Unlawful holding or keeping of another's possessions, even if the possessions were originally being held for lawful reasons (e.g., withholding a patient's diamond ring, first lawfully kept for safekeeping, to ensure that the patient pays a bill). 2. Detaining a person against his or her will. 3. A legal document issued by the court to continue to hold a person who is already being held.

detection services Routine evaluation and screening of individuals without recognized symptoms for the purpose of identifying the individuals at risk who have certain diseases or conditions.

detention Detaining or confining a person against his or her will.

detention for questioning Holding a person in custody by the police for questioning without making a formal charge or arrest.

deter To discourage; to stop.

determinable 1. Liable to terminate if a predictable happening occurs. 2. To probably terminate; the potential to be ended. 3. Subject to being ended if a specific action occurs.

determinant In epidemiology, public health, and health promotion, this is any variable, experience, event, factor, trait, or characteristic that contributes to a change in the health status of an individual or a group.

determination The making of a final judgment or decision, this is usually done by a judge or other person such as an arbiter.

detinue 1. Possessions or property unlawfully held by another person. 2. To sue for damages for the wrongful holding or detention of personal property. 3. A court-ordered writ to regain property.

detoxification 1. To remove the toxic agents in alcohol or drugs from the body; treatment by use of medication, rest, fluids, medical care, and nursing care to reduce the toxic effect in drug-addicted persons. 2. According to JCAHO for psychiatric, alcoholism, and drug abuse facilities accreditation purposes, the systematic reduction of the amount of a toxic agent in the body or the elimination of a toxic agent from the body. *See also cold turkey; methadone.*

detriment 1. To cause injury, loss, or harm. 2. Giving up a right, resulting in harm or damage.

development 1. A person's capacity and skill in functioning related to size, learning, age, and growth, occurring mostly in childhood. Certain areas such as learning continue through the life span. 2. In health-care administration, fund-raising activities; activities of hospital or health-care organization foundations to raise money. 3. Used to refer to program planning, development, and implementation.

development and review of patient care policies In Medicare policy, a facility should have policies that are developed with the advice of a group of professional personnel, including one or more physicians and one or more registered nurses, to govern the skilled nursing care and related medical or other services it provides. There are also to be provisions for policy reviews from time to time, at least annually. *See also utilization review.*

development director A member of a health-care facility's administrative staff who is responsible for obtaining grants, bequests, or gifts and for conducting other fund-raising for the facility.

developmental disability (DD) A disability originating before age 18 that can be expected to continue indefinitely. It constitutes a substantial handicap to the disabled person's ability to function normally in society and is usually attributable to the following conditions: mental retardation, cerebral palsy, epilepsy, autism, or dyslexia.

developmental tasks Skills and behavior patterns learned during development that a person should be able to do by certain age levels.

devest *See divest.*

deviant 1. Differing from what is considered normal or average. 2. Unusual or abnormal behavior; carrying out behaviors that society disapproves of.

deviating insurer An insurance company that offers rates below those of competitors or that is promoted by organizations that are in a position to set rates.

deviation, statistical *See average deviation; standard deviation.*

device 1. According to the federal Food, Drug and Cosmetic Act, this is any instrument, apparatus, implement, machine, contrivance, implant, in vitro reagent, or other similar or related article including any component, part, or accessory that is recognized in the official *National Formulary* or the *U.S. Pharmacopoeia*. Any piece of equipment or technology intended for use in the diagnosis of disease or other conditions—or in the cure, mitigation, treatment, or prevention of disease in man or animals, or intended to affect the structure or any function of the body of man or animals—that does not achieve its primary purposes through chemical action within or on the body and that is not dependent on being metabolized for the achievement of its primary intended purpose. The Medical Device Amendment of 1976 expanded the definition to include anything intended for use in the diagnosis of conditions other than disease such as pregnancy and in vitro diagnosis products, including those previously regulated as drugs. 2. An item or piece of equipment used in medical care that is not a drug, defined by the Food, Drug, and Cosmetic Act as including instruments, apparatus, and contrivances, and their components, parts, and accessories intended for use in the diagnosis, cure, mitigation, treatment, or prevention of disease in man or animals or to affect the structure or any function of the body of man or animals. Among the products regulated as devices are crutches, bandages, wheelchairs, artificial heart valves, cardiac pacemakers, intrauterine devices, eyeglasses, hearing aids, and prostheses. The regulation of the marketing of devices assures that devices are safe and effective when properly used.

device user facility According to the Federal Drug Administration, this is a hospital, an ambulatory surgical facility, a nursing home, or an outpatient treatment facility that is not a physician's office and uses medical devices in diagnosis and treatment of patients.

devise That which can be given by a will; to transfer property by will.

devolution The transfer of a right or property by legal processes from one person to another.

DHEW Department of Health, Education and Welfare (the former name of the Department of Health and Human Services).

DHHS Department of Health and Human Services, the federal cabinet-level department concerned with and responsible for all aspects of public health, health care, health-care finance, national health status and related activities, and human services such as aging and welfare-type programs.

dia- Prefix meaning "complete" or "thorough."

diabetes A metabolic disorder characterized by excessive thirst and the production of large volumes of urine. Often refers to diabetes mellitus. *See diabetes mellitus; diabetes insipidus.*

diabetes insipidus A metabolic disorder characterized by producing large amounts of dilute urine and a constant thirst due to a deficiency of vasopressin, a pituitary hormone that regulates the levels of water allowed to remain in the blood or be passed off as urine.

diabetes mellitus A metabolic disorder in which carbohydrates and sugars are not oxidized by the body to produce energy because of a deficiency of the hormone insulin.

diagnose In the practice of medicine, this is the process of conducting a series of activities, assessments, procedures, and communication with a patient to examine and gather information on the medical status of a patient.

diagnosis 1. The art and science of determining the nature and cause of a disease and of differentiating among diseases. 2. A scientifically or medically acceptable term given to a complex of symptoms (disturbances of function or sensation of which the patient is aware), signs (disturbances that the physician or another individual can detect), and findings (detected by laboratory, X-ray, or other diagnostic procedures or responses to therapy) (JCAHO for acute-care hospitals). 3. In health education and health promotion, a behavioral or health factors identification process that indicates a public health need or that a health problem exists as determined by the status, frequency, occurrence, and distribution of the problem in a population. 4. The process of assessment, evaluation, and determination of possible or probable causes of risk factors associated with community-based medical or health needs or problems.

diagnosis, admitting The diagnosis of a physician at the time of admission of a patient to a hospital. The diagnosis may be vague at admission and revised once tests and advanced evaluations are completed.

diagnosis and treatment services In health-care delivery, these are services used for evaluating the health status of individuals and identifying diseases or conditions and the approaches, therapies, and treatments used to alleviate disease, ill health, pain, or symptoms of diseases or conditions.

diagnosis, behavioral health 1. Determining the behavior and psychosocial aspects of well-being or the contribution of behavior to a medical problem or prognosis. A behaviorally founded medical problem can be a symptom, an abnormal finding, or a threat to one's overall well-being or health status. 2. Assessing health status with regard to behavior and psychosocial matters. 3. Gathering behavior and psychosocial information needed for health services, program planning, and evaluation.

diagnosis, codable The diagnosis provided by a physician and used for placing the patient into a certain category by diagnosis-related group (DRG) and payment. The coded diagnosis is given a code number according to the ICD-9-CM and classified by a number from the DRGs. *See diagnosis code; diagnosis-related groups.*

diagnosis code The numerical classification of diseases, conditions, and injuries. The most common code adapted for use in the United States is the ICD-9-CM as compiled by the Commission on Professional Hospital Activities (CPHA). This provides a uniform system of recording statistical data covering health services.

diagnosis, discharge The diagnosis given to a patient at the time of discharge by the attending physician. The diagnosis is given a code number based on the ICD-9-CM and classified by a number from the diagnosis-related groups (DRGs). Under Medicare, a patient cannot be readmitted to the hospital under the discharge diagnosis for a designated time period (usually 2 weeks) and have the hospital receive payment care.

diagnosis, major That diagnosis most responsible for treatment, services received, resources used, and the length of stay. *See principal diagnosis.*

diagnosis, principal Under Medicare and the prospective payment system, this is the diagnosis-related group (DRG) used on the basis of the diagnosis established after study to be chiefly responsible for the hospitalization. Hospital payment is based on the DRG coded as the principal diagnosis.

diagnosis-related group (DRG) This is an approach to classifying a patient's disease or condition and treatment procedures in terms of the expected consumption of hospital resources; a method of identifying patients who have hospitalization and hospital resource consumption patterns that are similar and of classifying patients into a manageable number of diagnostic groups. Researchers from Yale University developed DRGs by using a large database of hospital records from New Jersey, Connecticut, and South Carolina. Clinicians classified the entire eighth edition of the ICDA-8 into broad, mutually exclusive, major diagnostic categories on the basis of three principles: 1) each category must be consistent in anatomical and physiopathological classification or in clinical management, 2) each category must have a sufficient number of patients to produce statistically meaningful patient populations, and 3) each category must cover the complete range of ICDA-8 codes without overlap. Length of stay became the independent variable used to determine the level of resource consumption. A computer program developed at Yale, called AUTOGRP, identified the categories that were medically meaningful groups on the basis of length of stay. The system adopted ICD-9-CM to utilize patient attributes, including principal diagnosis, secondary diagnoses, primary procedure, secondary procedures, age, and the presence or absence of psychiatric service. In the late stages of development using a clinical setting, all possible diagnoses identified in the ICD-9-CM system were classified into 23 major diagnostic category types on the basis of organ systems and then further organized into 467 distinct diagnostic groupings. After many trials, 470 DRGs became the standard, and the system was used on a national basis, first by Medicare to reduce hospital costs and reduce reimbursement to hospitals by encouraging the reduction of the length of stay of patients. (The motivation to develop DRGs was initially based on a Social Security amendment in 1983 that set a provision for a prospective payment system for hospitals' Medicare inpatient services. The cornerstone of the prospective payment system is the DRG system.) Some flexibility was built into the system. For example, DRG 468 is used when the principal diagnosis and principal operating room procedure are unrelated; DRG 469 is used when the principal diagnosis is correct but should not be the discharge diagnosis; and DRG 470 is for ungroupable diagnosis. All patients in the same DRG can be expected to have a set of clinical responses that will, on a statistical average, result in approximately equal use of a hospital's resources. *See also medically meaningful; ICD-9-CM; complicating and comorbid.*

diagnosis-related groups, measures of severity *See complicating and comorbid.*

diagnosis-related groups, pediatric modified Diagnosis-related groups (DRGs) for classification of diseases, illnesses, and medical conditions that affect only children. Developed by the National Association of Children's Hospitals and related institutions under research supported by the HCFA (Health Care Financing Administration), 100 DRGs were added to the Medicare list to accommodate children receiving care under federally supported programs paid under the Prospective Payment System; also used to ascertain a pediatric case mix and set cost structures.

diagnostic admission A physician admitting a patient to a hospital primarily for the performance of various lab and X-ray studies to establish a diagnosis.

diagnostic and other nonsurgical procedures These are procedures generally not considered to be surgery, including diagnostic endoscopy, radiography, radiotherapy and related therapies, physical medicine and rehabilitation, and other nonsurgical procedures. In 1989, a list of nonsurgical procedures was revised and published to include selected procedures previously classified as surgical procedures (National Center for Health Statistics, National Hospital Discharge Survey, 1989 annual summary).

Diagnostic and Statistical Manual of Mental Disorders (DSM) A standardized handbook for the classification of mental illnesses. Formulated by the American Psychiatric Association, it was first issued in 1952 (DSM-I). The second edition (DSM-II), issued in 1968, correlates closely with the World Health Organization's *International Classification of Diseases*. The third edition (DSM-III) was published in 1980 and revised in 1987, and the most recent edition (DSM-IV) was published in 1994.

Diagnostic and Therapeutic Technology Assessment Program (DATTA) The American Medical Association developed this medical technology evaluation program for the purpose of providing physicians with objective information about the effectiveness and appropriate use of the variety of medical technologies now available and those being developed.

diagnostic cost group (DCG) Under managed care and through the Health Care Financing Administration, this is an experimental program tested in HMOs and used to set HMO capitation rates. Patient care, history of hospitalization, and physician treatment and practice patterns are used to project future medical costs. Patients are placed in 1 of 8 categories on the basis of expenses incurred in treatment, with higher DCG values indicative of higher anticipated costs. Costs are weighted for each of the 8 categories based on age, sex, and welfare status.

diagnostic index A short form of a medical record used by physicians or clinics to record demographic information, time and date of visit and diagnosis, conditions, symptoms, or problems identified in patients.

diagnostic medical sonographer One who uses acoustic energy for diagnosis, research, and therapy; operates ultrasound equipment to obtain diagnostic results; and evaluates results for quality of technique.

diagnostic product Substances, chemicals, or agents used in patient testing and diagnosis.

diagnostic radioisotope facility A diagnostic unit in a hospital that uses radioactive isotopes to trace or detect abnormal or disease conditions in the body.

diagnostic radiology services 1. A special patient assessment service that detects the presence of physical diseases and other ill health conditions through the use of radiant energy. 2. According to the JCAHO, this is the delivery of care pertaining to the use of radiant energy for the diagnosis of disease. Standards are applied to evaluate a hospital's performance in providing diagnostic radiology services.

diagnostic-related group *See diagnosis-related group.*

diagnostics A set of procedures or methods used for the detection and isolation of a malfunction or mistake.

diagnostic services According to JCAHO for long-term-care accreditation, any service (e.g., laboratory or radiological) designed to assist the practitioner in establishing a diagnosis.

diagnostic studies Any test, X ray, CT scan, visual exam, or procedure ordered by a physician to assist in determining the seriousness, nature, and extent of a patient's pathological condition. Several types of tests are commonly conducted to assist a physician in disease or condition diagnosis: 1) bromosulphalein test (BSP—a dye is injected intravenously to study liver function; 2) culture (the growth of microorganisms on media from bodily sputum, urine, wound drainages, etc. under laboratory conditions); 3) urine tests. Additional tests include abdominal paracentesis, angiogram, bone marrow biopsy, barium enema, bronchoscopy, cholecystogram, colonoscopy, cystoscopy, electrocardiogram (EKG), electroencephalogram (EEG), gastroscopy, intravenous pyelogram (IVP), laryngoscopy, myelogram, opaque cystogram, pericardial aspiration, pneumoencephologram, proctoscopic examination, sigmoidoscopy, spinal tap or lumbar puncture, thoracentesis, and upper gastrointestinal (UGI) series. For definitions of individual diagnostic studies, consult a medical dictionary.

diagnostic X-ray services See *diagnostic radiology services*.

dialysis A process by which waste products and dissolved substances that have accumulated in the blood are removed from the blood of a patient by a special machine that uses a diffusion process: fluid in one compartment passes into a second compartment across a semipermeable membrane. Two types of dialysis are used: hemodialysis and peritoneal dialysis.

dialysis facility A special health care treatment unit that provides long-term maintenance dialysis.

dialysis technician One who operates and maintains renal dialysis equipment used in the treatment of patients with short- or long-term renal disorders or failures. This individual works under the direction of a physician, frequently an internal medicine specialist with a subspecialty in nephrology.

dialysis technology An educational program that prepares individuals to provide dialysis and intensive care to patients in a renal care unit, including the monitoring of the heart, renal dialysis therapy, respiratory therapy, isolation procedures, and adjustment and maintenance of dialysis equipment.

dialysis unit A hemodialysis unit in a hospital or other health-care facility used in the provision of long-term kidney dialysis. See *dialysis facility; hemodialysis unit*.

diastolic blood pressure The pressure of blood produced within the blood vessels when the ventricles of the heart relax.

dichotomous characteristic In the process of classifying disease, conditions, or other health phenomena, this is the placement of various traits into one of two categories using only two sets of classifications.

Dick-Read childbirth Based on the theory that fear is the main agent that produces pain during childbirth. Women in labor have pain, which increases fear and increases tension. The increased tension causes more pain. Breaking this self-defeating cycle includes slow abdominal breathing techniques and focusing on feelings and signals from the body during labor.

dicta (Lat.) Something a judge says that is not necessarily vital to the case; something said in passing. 2. Words in a written opinion not necessarily a part of the decision but a general comment.

dictionary A malevolent literary device used for confusing the uninformed and uneducated, adding to the unnecessary growth of language and straining student mental capacities and finances because of the high cost of books.

Dictionary of Occupational Titles (DOT) A federal publication that provides detailed job descriptions and job codes for most occupations in government and industry, including health care.

diener An orderly who assists a pathologist during an autopsy; one who is responsible for the equipment in and for managing a morgue.

diet manual An up-to-date, organized system for standardizing the ordering of diets and meals for patients.

diet, modified Changing a patient's normal diet to meet special nutritional requirements because of medical reasons. This can involve the inclusion of certain foods or nutrients and/or the exclusion of other foods and nutrients on the basis of disease or condition.

dietary A department in a health-care facility organized and administered to prepare and serve food to patients. The personnel in this department include dietitians who are responsible for special diets, dietary counseling of patients, and diet instructions.

dietary assessment The nutritional evaluation of patients or residents in health-care facilities based on dietary intake indicators, diagnosis, medical status, diseases, and conditions. Special diets are considered and individually developed. See *special diet*.

dietary services Activities related to providing nutritional, palatable, and well-balanced diets and attractive, nourishing meals in health-care facilities that meet the daily nutritional and/or special dietary needs of each patient or resident.

dietetic and nutritional services The selection and preparation of appropriate foods and the maintenance of equipment, sanitation, and cost control. Personnel provide nutritional education to individuals and groups and serve as nutritional consultants to health facilities and communities.

dietetic assistant One who writes menus following dietetic specifications, helps to ensure the coordination of food service to patients, orders supplies, maintains sanitation, and oversees the work of food service employees in health-care facilities.

dietetic educator, R.D. An individual responsible for planning the curriculum of the dietetic practitioner and who is responsible for the nutrition education of medical, nursing, dental, and allied health personnel. The dietetic educator may be employed in medical centers, universities, or colleges.

dietetics A profession concerned with the science and art of human nutritional care, an essential component of health science. It includes education on foods that will provide nutrients sufficient for health and during periods of illness throughout the life cycle and on management of group feeding.

dietetic service supervisor Under Medicare policy, this individual must be one of the following: 1) a qualified dietitian, 2) a graduate of a dietetic technician/assistant training program (correspondence or classroom) approved by the American Dietetic Association, 3) a graduate of a state-approved course that provided 90 or more hours of classroom instruction in food service supervision and experience as a supervisor in a health-care institution with consultation from a dietitian, or 4) an individual who has training and experience in food service supervision and management in the military service. *See also dietetic service supervisor, qualified.*

dietetic service supervisor, qualified For JCAHO accreditation of long-term-care facilities, an individual who is a qualified dietitian, a graduate of either an approved dietetic technician or dietetic assistant training program or a state-approved course in food service supervision, or an individual who has documented equivalent training and/or experience.

dietetic services The delivery of care pertaining to the provision of optimal nutrition and quality food service for patients. Standards are applied to evaluate a hospital's performance in providing dietetic services (JCAHO for accreditation purposes).

dietetic technician An individual who functions as a food service personnel in health-care facilities. Working with and under the direction of food service supervisors, dietetic assistants, and dietitians, this technician assists with the planning, implementation, and evaluation of food programs; teaches principles of nutrition; and provides dietary counseling. Where institutional policies permit, he or she may also train and supervise dietary aides.

dietitian 1. According to the American Dietetic Association, this is a professional responsible for the nutritional care of individuals and groups. This care includes the application of the science and art of human nutrition in helping people select and obtain food for the primary purpose of nourishing their bodies in health or disease throughout the life cycle. Being specially trained in applied nutrition and management of individuals in institutional and community settings, dietitians can be separated into 5 levels: administrative, clinical, community, research, and education. 2. For Medicare purposes, a person who is eligible for registration by the American Dietetic Association under its requirements and has a bachelors degree with major studies in food and nutrition, dietetics, or food service management; has 1 year of supervisory experience in the dietetic service of a health-care institution; and participates annually in continuing dietetic education. "R.D." is used in one's title to signify "registered dietitian." *See also dietitian, qualified.*

dietitian, administrative, R.D. A member of the management team whose objective is to provide optimal nutrition and quality food through the management of food service systems.

dietitian, clinical, R.D. A professional who applies the science and art of human nutrition to helping individuals and groups attain adequate nutrition. Diet prescription, food selection, and education and counseling of clients are the essential aspects of the clinical dietitian's service in hospitals, clinics, agencies, and community health programs.

dietitian, community, R.D. A member of the community health-care team who plans, organizes, coordinates, and evaluates the nutritional component of health-care services for a health agency or organization.

dietitian, consultant, R.D. A professional with experience in administrative or clinical dietetic practice who provides advice or services in nutritional care.

dietitian, qualified According to JCAHO for accreditation purposes, this is an individual who is registered by the Commission on Dietetic Registration of the American Dietetic Association or who has the documented equivalent in education, training, and/or experience and evidence of relevant continuing education.

dietitian, registered *See registered dietician.*

dietitian, research, R.D. A professional who evaluates and expands knowledge in nutrition, nutrition education, food management, food service, and the design of food equipment. The research dietitian is usually employed in a hospital or educational institution or may be involved in research in community health programs.

dietitian, teaching A dietitian who has advanced education, training, and experience and who plans and conducts nutrition and dietetic educational programs. *See also dietetic educator, R.D.*

difficult feats In school health and safety programs, these are activities in school programs that are by nature dangerous such as shop classes and athletics. Adequate instruction and warning should be directed to the student prior to performance in difficult feats or related course activities.

diffuse reflection In laser technology, this is any change in the spatial distribution of a laser beam's radiation when it is reflected by a surface.

diffusion In laser technology, this is any change in the spatial distribution of a laser beam's radiation when it is deviated in many directions by a surface or medium.

digital computer In health-care information management, this is a special computer that utilizes discrete data and logic processes on these data. This type of computer is contrasted with an analog computer. Using a number recording system, it works in units that can be counted. It is the computer most often used by hospital or health-care facility business offices for data processing.

dilatory 1. Intending to delay. 2. Delay used to gain time.

dilatory defense In medical malpractice and liability litigation, this is an approach used by the defense that avoids the merits of the case and attempts to delay the progress of the trial.

diligence Care; carefulness; caution; prudence.

dimunition 1. Where an error has occurred or a fact omitted from the record but is certified in a writ of error. 2. Decrease; a reduction.

diploma school A program that educates registered nurses or allied health professionals in a hospital setting or hospital-based school; a diploma is awarded by the hospital on completion of the program. Classroom and laboratory teaching may be given under an arrangement with a community college, but the students and clinical training are the responsibility of the hospital. No college-level degree is given. *See associate degree program; baccalaureate degree program.*

diploma school of nursing An accredited school affiliated with a hospital, a university, or an independent school that provides a program of education in professional nursing and allied subjects leading to a diploma or an equivalent, indicating that such a program has been satisfactorily completed. *See diploma school.*

diplomate One who has a diploma; sometimes used to describe a board-certified physician because a diploma is given with certification.

dipsomania An abnormal craving for alcohol; an uncontrollable impulse to become intoxicated.

direct care provider A health-care provider who delivers care and treatment directly to the patient and is the attending physician or physician extender.

direct cause The determination that an act was the actual cause of harm, injury, or damage. *See also proximate cause.*

direct contracting In managed care, this is where employer groups or business coalitions make formal health plan agreements directly with health-care providers for medical and health services without an HMO- or a PPO-type intermediary, enabling the employer group to stipulate specific services preferred by the employees/members. ERISA guidelines are followed.

direct cost In health-care finance, this is the cost of resources devoted solely to the operation of a specific activity. These costs do not include the distribution of costs to a cost center that are not specifically attributable to that cost center. *See also indirect cost.*

direct distribution In health-care financial management, this is a cost-finding approach where expenses are allocated directly to the health-care facility's cost centers.

directed verdict 1. In the litigation process of a trial, this is when the judge takes the judgment responsibility away from the jury by telling them what decision they must reach. 2. A verdict rendered by the court when the evidence is overwhelming for one party.

direct evidence In health law, these are facts showing proof or establishing factual material about an issue without the need for other facts.

direct examination In the litigation process of a trial or a health law hearing, this is the opportunity to have the first examination of a witness. Courtroom procedure allows the side that called the witness to do the first questioning.

directing 1. In health-care administration, this is one of several functions of administrators to put planning functions and activities into action, including issuing orders, instructions, and assignments that assist subordinates in understanding what is expected of them on the job. 2. The guidance and supervision of workers toward attainment of department and organizational goals and objectives. Directing is accomplished through communicating, giving orders, setting forth work tasks, organizing, leading, motivating, and ensuring that work takes place. *See functions of a manager.*

direction For JCAHO accreditation purposes, authoritative policy or procedural guidance for the accomplishment of a function or activity.

direct loss A property and economic loss covered by insurance and directly related to an unbroken chain of events leading from a peril.

direct method In health-care information management, this is an outdated method of recording research, business or medical records, or pharmacy input data onto cards or tape by punching holes directly into the cards or tape by means of a card- or tape-punching machine. Direct computer input is now by keyboard, handwriting pads, scanners, and voice.

direct nursing activities Any treatment or care activities provided by a nurse.

director A person who directs, controls, supervises, or manages an organization or component thereof (JCAHO).

director of education In hospital or health-care organization management, this is an individual qualified in educational programming who is responsible for coordinating, planning, and implementing staff development and employee training and facility orientation.

director of medical affairs This is the physician designated by the governing board to manage and be responsible for the formally organized medical staff of a hospital. Also referred to as "chief of medicine," "chief of staff," or "director of the medical staff."

director of medical education In hospital or other health-care organizations, this is an individual qualified in educational programming who may be a physician or other qualified personnel and who is responsible for coordinating, planning, and implementing continuing medical education (CME) for physicians.

director of nursing According to JCAHO for long-term-care accreditation, a registered professional nurse who is responsible for the full-time direct supervision of the nursing services and who is currently licensed by the state in which he or she is practicing. This person should have training and/or experience in rehabilitative, psychiatric, and/or gerontological nursing and 1 year or more of additional education and/or experience in nursing service administration. He or she must attend continuing education programs at least annually.

director of nursing services For Medicare purposes, a registered nurse who is licensed by the state in which he or she is practicing, has 1 year of additional education or experience in nursing service administration, has additional education or experience in such areas as rehabilitative or geriatric nursing, and participates annually in continuing nursing education.

director of staff development Also referred to as "director of inservice training" or "director of education." *See director of education.*

director of volunteer services. A person qualified in working with volunteer programs, this employee of the health-care organization manages this ancillary department of the health facility. The director is responsible for coordinating, supervising, planning, and implementing all volunteer-related activities.

directory In health-care information management, a table containing the names of, and pointers to, files that are stored in a mass-storage volume such as a hard disk tape.

direct patient care support services Services that lend assistance to the prevention, diagnosis, and treatment of disease, other illnesses, or conditions and to the restoration or habilitation of the ill or disabled.

direct patient data The facts relevant to a particular patient, including remarks and behaviors observed by health-care providers and recorded in the medical record.

direct reimbursement In health-care finance, this is when a patient or health plan pays the health-care practitioner directly for providing health-care services.

direct tax A tax that is directly paid to the government (e.g., income tax).

direct writer When an insurance company or managed-care program bypasses independent insurance agents and coverage is offered directly to employees through salaried or commissioned employees who work for the health plan or insurance company as controlled agents; sometimes referred to as "exclusive agents" or "captive agents."

disabilities, degree of Four categories of disability have been developed: temporary total, temporary partial permanent, permanent partial, and permanent total. Temporary total disability is when an injured worker is temporarily incapable of gainful employment and has a good prospect of improving and returning to work with no or only partial disability. Temporary partial permanent assumes that the worker's condition has stabilized and is expected to improve, and that he or she can return to work at some time under light duty or part-time work. Permanent partial disability means that an injured worker, after using medical and rehabilitative services, has recovered as much as possible yet falls short of full recovery and will always suffer a partial disability. Several perspectives are considered at this level: whole-person, wage loss, and loss of wage-earning capacity theory. Finally, permanent total disability is when, after medical and rehabilitative services, the chance of full recovery does not exist and disability is such that the individual is not able to work.

disability 1. Any physical, mental, or social limitation of an individual as compared with other individuals of similar age, sex, and occupation. Frequently refers to limitation of the usual or major activities, most commonly vocational. There are varying kinds (functional, vocational, learning), degrees (partial, total), and duration (temporary, permanent) of disability. Benefits are often only available for specific disabilities such as total and permanent (the requirement for Social Security and Medicare). 2. The absence of adequate or competent physical or mental functioning that has a negative or diminishing effect on earning ability. 3. The lack of legal capability to do an act. 4. A condition that renders an insured person incapable of performing one or more of the duties required by his or her regular occupation. 5. A restriction in the ability to perform essential components of everyday living, such as personal hygiene or moving about (ICIDH). *See also rehabilitation; impairment; handicapped.*

disability day 1. The number of active days that are lost by a worker because of accident or illness. 2. The National Health Interview Survey has identified several types of days on which a person's usual activity is reduced because of illness or injury (reported for the 2-week period preceding the week of the interview). Short-term disability days are not mutually exclusive categories. *See bed disability days; cut-down day; restricted activity day; patient bed day; school-loss day; work-loss day; activities of daily living.*

disability income insurance A medical insurance that provides periodic payments to replace the usual income of a person who is unable to work as a result of illness, disease, or injury.

disability insurance Compensation paid to the employee for lost income and medical expenses because of limitation of usual or major activities resulting from injury or illness. The different payment approaches are as follows: 1) commercial group disability: coverage for a group of persons, such as that provided by an employer; 2) commercial individual disability: coverage for a single person usually purchased by or for that person; 3) workers' compensation: compensation for lost income and medical expenses resulting from diseases or injuries experienced through employment; 4) Social Security benefits: compensation for lost income for persons who have paid into Social Security for physical or mental ability following at least 12 months of disability.

disabling injury Any injury causing death, permanent disability, or any degree of temporary total disability beyond the day of the adverse event.

disaffirm 1. To refuse to adhere to. 2. To set aside; repudiate; take back consent; refusing to abide by a former agreement.

disallow To deny or refuse.

disaster drill A large-scale, planned, simulated disaster that is conducted in such manner as to promote realism to the event; a practice test used to assess a hospital's or community's disaster plan and determine the true level of readiness for a disaster. Conducted periodically, these practice drills help train personnel, assess effectiveness and efficiency in response, and discover shortcomings to improve the disaster plan and related activities in preparation for the real event.

disaster plan A plan that specifies employee, nursing, and medical staff responsibilities in a situation where a hospital responds to a disaster in a community and receives massive numbers of casualties. This is also a formal plan for possible crises in the hospital such as a power outage, telephone outage, water shortage, fire, terrorist act, hostage crisis, or strike. The plan details actions needed for coordinating the response of a hospital to any disaster inside or outside the hospital and requiring hospital support, including coordination with fire departments, police, the Red Cross, and other hospitals in the area. All hospitals accredited by JCAHO are required to have disaster plans. Also referred to as "disaster preparedness plans."

disaster plan, external A disaster preparedness plan focusing on all disaster-related activities that are community based and would occur outside a hospital. This plan is required of all accredited hospitals to plan and coordinate all activities surrounding a disaster within the community or region, including interacting with community disaster groups, fire departments, police and sheriff's departments, the Red Cross, and other hospitals in the region.

disaster plan, internal A disaster preparedness plan focusing on all disaster-related activities that would occur inside a hospital, including identifying who is responsible for what actions, how personnel are to respond, what they are to do, and what actions each area of the hospital is responsible for.

disaster preparedness plan *See disaster plans.*

disbursement Payment of money to cover a debt of expense; payment of a bill by the hospital's business office.

discharge 1. Release; dismiss. 2. To do or perform a duty. 3. To end a contractual obligation. 4. The formal discharge of a patient from the care of a health-care provider or health-care facility. 5. According to JCAHO for psychiatric, alcoholism, and drug abuse facilities accreditation purposes, the point at which the patient's active involvement with a facility is terminated and the facility no longer maintains active responsibility for the patient. 6. To separate an employee from work; he or she is removed from the payroll if the employee has been allowed due process, unless certain serious acts are committed. Violations of safety regulations, certain standards of behavior, or unsatisfactory performance are some of the issues for which an employee is at fault and may be justifiable reasons for discharge. *See discharge planning; hospital discharge.*

discharge abstract A summary description of an admission prepared on a patient's discharge from a hospital or other health facility. The abstract records include data about the patient's stay in the hospital such as diagnoses, treatments, procedures and services received, length of stay, source of payment, and demographic information. The information is usually obtained from the patient's medical record and abstracted in standard, coded form. *See also uniform hospital discharge data set.*

discharge against medical advice (AMA) This is not a true discharge because the patient leaves against the will of the health-care providers and on their own and thus are not discharged. This is recorded in the medical record as AMA: discharged (left) against medical advice.

discharge analysis The gathering of information about discharged patients to assess the professional and health-care services provided while the patient was hospitalized.

discharge by (due to) death This is recorded in the medical record only if the death occurred after the patient was admitted to the hospital.

discharge by transfer When a patient is transferred out of a hospital to another facility, with care and treatment being transferred to the receiving health-care facility. Medicare policy governs payment on such transfers as to which facility receives how much.

discharge coordinator A social services worker in a health-care facility who identifies and arranges for support and aftercare services offered by community agencies for patients who are being released from the health-care facility and who need continual care on either a short- or a long-term basis.

discharge, hospital *See discharge; hospital discharge.*

discharge, inpatient The formal release of a patient from a hospital who no longer needs hospital care, determined and directed by the attending physician, including discharges against medical advice, by death, or by transfer.

discharge, outpatient The release from formal care of a patient from the hospital outpatient service.

discharge patient days The total number of days each discharged patient spent in the health-care facility. *See also patient days.*

discharge planner The person who is responsible for planning and coordinating all discharges from the hospital. This person is often a qualified social worker or registered nurse and works in the department of social services.

discharge planning 1. A part of patient management, continuity of care, and medical/nursing care plans. Planning for the patient release begins when a patient is admitted for treatment and provides the patient with the proper segments of care found in the health care continuum and with the coordination of various services necessary to achieve a successful release from care, including a place to go on discharge. 2. The process of preparing a patient for another level of care and arranging the patient's release from the current health-care setting. 3. In managed care, the coordination of the succession of care with institutional discharge planners. This provides health plan coverage information and assists in acquiring aftercare and home health services, including durable home-care equipment necessary for the patient to survive in a nonmedical situation/environment.

discharges and deaths The actual number of inpatients leaving a health-care facility in a certain period of time. This usually does not include newborns.

discharge status The disposition of the patient on discharge; how the patient left the health-care facility and to what destination such as to another hospital, nursing home, or the patient's own home.

discharge summary A synopsis of a patient's hospital stay that records the principal diagnosis and other diagnostic findings; principal procedures; treatments; patient's response to treatment; and recommendations for aftercare, follow-up, and continual care on release from the hospital. This is prepared by the attending physician when the patient is released from the health-care facility.

discharge transfer The transfer and formal discharge of a patient from one inpatient health-care facility to another to continue inpatient treatment.

disciplinary rules 1. Acts or performances a lawyer is not allowed to do. 2. A part of a code of professional responsibility.

discipline In health-care administration, this is a management action taken to encourage compliance with organization policies, rules, and standards.

disclaimer 1. A denial of facts in question. 2. Rejection; repudiation of right, interest, or responsibility.

disclose To reveal.

disclosure 1. Revelation. 2. That which is disclosed, told, or revealed. 3. The impartation of secret information.

disclosure of ownership Under Medicare policy for skilled nursing facilities, a facility must supply full and complete information on the following: 1) the identity of each person who has any direct or indirect ownership interest of 10% or more in the facility or who is the owner (in whole or in part) of any mortgage, deed of trust, note, or other obligation secured (in whole or in part) by the facility or any of its property or assets; 2) if the facility is organized as a corporation, the identity of each officer and director of the corporation; and 3) if the facility is organized as a partnership, the identity of each partner. Any changes that would affect the current accuracy of the information are also required to be supplied.

disclosure report This is an annual report provided to a government commission by individual health facilities regarding each facility's costs and operations.

discontinuance Dismissal.

discordant 1. Disagreeing; being at variance; incongruous, contradictory. 2. As used in epidemiology and biomedical and psychological research using matched-pair case control/longitudinal studies, when one of the mates of matched cases is exposed to a disease or risk factor that is different for the matched mate. 3. In twin studies, when one identical twin manifests certain traits that the mated twin does not. By this process insights are gained about health effects of exposures to environmental or behavioral risk factors.

discount 1. To lower the price. 2. To prove untrue.

discount fee-for-service In managed care, health-care providers' services are offered as fee-for-service but often at a rate that is less than the going rate or the usual and customary fee.

discounting In health-care finance, this is the process of determining the present value of future cash flows; the opposite of compounding.

discounting of accounts receivable In health-care finance, this is a short-term financing arrangement in which accounts receivable are used to secure the loan. Revenue owed to the organization is not collected but is used as collateral for a loan. Also referred to as "pledging of accounts receivable."

discount rate Interest rate used to discount future cash flows to their present value; cash flow is reduced to determine the present value.

discovery 1. In health law and the litigation process, this is the formal display, sharing, inspection, review, discussion, and exchange of facts, evidence, and information between the various parties to a legal action or a lawsuit. 2. The process by which opposing parties obtain information from one another through adverse examination interrogatories, depositions, and inspections of pertinent documents. A major important requirement of the pretrial litigation process in which both the plaintiff and defendant must participate.

discovery period 1. In health-care law, this is the time span in the litigation process during which discovery is in effect. 2. In managed care and medical insurance, the period of time after the termination or expiration of a health plan or insurance policy during which the enrollee may report a condition that needed treatment during the time the policy was in effect.

discovery rule A rule in some jurisdictions by which the statute of limitations does not commence until the wrongful act is discovered or, with reasonable diligence, should have been discovered. The statute of limitations is the period of time, ordinarily beginning with the wrongful act, during which an injured party may sue for recovery of damages arising from the act. Some states have adopted statutory rules in malpractice cases that impose double time limits during which an action for malpractice may be brought. Typically these statutes require that the action be filed within a limited time after its discovery and within a limited time from the date the negligent act occurred.

discrete Separate; individual.

discrimination 1. To make or observe a difference. 2. Illegally and unfairly treating people differently on the basis of race, religion, sex, or age.

disease Means "without ease"; an abnormal state in which the body is not capable of responding to or carrying on its required functions; a failure of the adaptive mechanisms of an organism to counteract adequately, normally, or appropriately the stimuli and stresses that affect it, resulting in a disturbance in the function of structure of some part of the organism. Disease is multifactorial and may be prevented or treated by changing some or all of the disease-causing factors. Variations in the seriousness, effect, and extent of diseases are often classified into three levels: 1) acute: relatively severe and of short duration, 2) chronic: various levels of severity that are of long and continuous duration, and 3) subacute: intermediate in severity and duration. Disease can be caused by organisms called pathogens, nutritional deficiencies, physical agents (e.g., heat, cold, blows from objects), chemicals, birth defects, degeneration, and neoplasms. Disease can be communicable (easily spread from person to person such as measles) or noncommunicable (occurs in a person but is not easily spread from person to person such as cancer). Being largely socially defined, disease is a very elusive and difficult concept to define. Thus criminality and drug dependence presently tend to be seen as diseases, when they were previously considered to be moral or legal problems. *See acute disease; causation; chronic disease; epidemiology; health; injury; illness; pathogen; subacute.*

disease and operation index An index of diseases, disorders, diagnoses, and procedures categorized by a number for index purposes. *See also ICD-9-CM.*

disease code manual A listing of diseases by code according to the hospital adaptation of the *International Classification of Diseases*. *See ICD-9-CM.*

disease frequency *See morbidity; prevalence; period prevalence; point prevalence.*

disease, preclinical The state of disease in which an infected susceptible person has not shown the signs or symptoms of the disease because they have not yet developed.

disease, subclinical A disease that is detected first by tests because the infected susceptible person has not yet developed any signs or symptoms of the disease.

disengage From a social and gerontological perspective, this is when elderly persons choose to become removed from social contacts and alienate and disassociate themselves from social interactions.

disenfranchise To take away one's rights, particularly one's right to vote; to remove one's authority, power, respect, or position.

disenrollment In managed care or medical insurance, this is the process of terminating coverage. This is not an enrollee quitting because of loss of work or voluntarily terminating with the health plan but the health plan terminating a member's coverage against his or her will. Serious offenses are required under law for such an action, including fraud, abuse, nonpayment of premium, or inability to comply with recommended treatment.

dishonor 1. To refuse to accept. 2. To fail to respect a legal obligation.

disinfectant Any substance, method, or agent used to kill disease-producing microorganisms existing outside the body. Several approaches to killing pathogens and disease-producing agents are used, including heat for sterilization and incineration. Sunlight and chemical substances and agents are the most commonly used approaches. The chemical agents phenol, chlorine, and carbolic acid are standards to which other agents are compared.

disinfection To render pathogens harmless through the use of heat, antiseptics, antibacterial agents, chemicals, etc.

disinfection, concurrent This is an approach to disease and infection control that applies any disinfective measure, agent, or chemical as soon as possible after the infection is caused or discovered.

disinfection, terminal This is an approach to disease and infection control that applies any disinfective measure, agent, or chemical to surgery suites, patient rooms, recovery rooms, or other places contaminated by patient exposure after the patient has been removed. If the risk of exposure is high because of recent treatment of a highly communicable disease, steam sterilization or incineration of bedding may also be used.

disinfestation In public health, this is the application of any process, agent, or chemical to kill, destroy, or remove insects, rodents, or other pests from a person's body, bedding, clothing, or living environment or from animals.

disinhibition Withdrawal of or lack of inhibition. Some drugs and alcohol can remove inhibitions. In psychiatry, disinhibition leads to the freedom to act on one's own needs rather than to submit to the demands of others or adhere to the expectations of law or society.

disinter To exhume; to take out of the grave.

disinterested 1. Having no personal interest or opportunity for personal gain; indifferent. 2. Impartial; an unbiased opinion. 3. Having no vested interests.

disjunctive allegation Two mutually exclusive yet alternative charges.

disk set storage A storage device used with computerized medical records or insurance forms that permits the use of interchangeable disk sets or packs.

dismemberment The loss of a limb or one's sight.

dismissal 1. A court order that removes a suit from litigation. 2. In health-care administration and human resource management, this is the ultimate disciplinary act against an employee because it forces a separation of the worker from the organization and removal from the payroll.

dismissal with prejudice A final decision on an action that bars the right to bring any other action on the same cause.

dismissal without prejudice Dismissal of an action that does not bar subsequent action on the same concern.

disorder Any pathological state or condition of the body or mental status.

disorientation To lose one's orientation and sense of direction. Inability to judge time, space, and personal relations. This can occur in most acute and chronic brain disorders.

disparagement 1. Anything that degrades, disgraces, or detracts. 2. Discrediting or belittling something or someone.

disparate impact In human resource management, this is when the act or decision of a health-care manager results in having a different effect on one or more protected groups or classes.

disparate treatment In human resource management, this is when the act or decision of a health-care manager results in members of a protected class receiving unequal treatment.

dispensary 1. A place where medicines are dispensed. 2. A treatment facility similar to an outpatient clinic where free primary care is delivered and medications are provided to patients.

dispense To prepare and fill a prescription for a drug or medication under the order of a physician.

dispensing fee A fee charged by a pharmacist for filling a prescription, being one of two ways that pharmacists charge for the service of filling a prescription, the other being a standard percentage markup on the acquisition cost of the drug involved. A dispensing fee is the same for all prescriptions, thus representing a larger markup on the cost of an inexpensive drug or a small prescription than on an expensive drug or a large prescription. However, it reflects the fact that a pharmacist's service is the same regardless of the cost of the drug. Some pharmacists combine the two approaches, using a percentage markup with a minimum fee.

dispensing optician A technologist who makes and fits glasses or lenses prescribed by ophthalmologists or optometrists. Opticians measure facial contours and assist in frame and lens selection. Optical laboratory technicians grind lenses according to prescription. Some opticians grind lenses and adjust and fit the type to the customer. A 2-year associate degree in ophthalmic dispensing or 3 to 4 years of on-the-job training in an apprenticeship program can also qualify individuals for this field. Additional training is necessary to fit contact lenses.

displacement A defense or mental mechanism in which an emotion or experience is transferred from its original object to another object.

display A television-like screen called a cathode ray tube (CRT) that displays information on a screen in pictorial form, such as on a cardiac monitor, CT scanner, or computer.

disposable earnings One's total pay less deductions.

disposition 1. A final settlement decision, resulting from a court's judgment. 2. In psychiatry, a person's inclinations as determined by his mood.

disposition of motion In formal health-care meetings or hearings, to act on a motion by voting on it, referring it to a committee, postponing it, or removing the motion from the discussion and consideration of the assembly in any other way that is acceptable under parliamentary procedure.

dispositive facts Truth and objective information that clarifies and settles legal issues.

dispossession Wrongfully ousted; removing a person from his or her property by force, deception, or illicit use of the law.

dispute 1. To debate or argue. 2. A disagreement between two parties. 3. To doubt; to question the truth of a matter.

disqualify 1. To make ineligible. 2. To make disabled or unfit. 3. To declare unqualified.

disseisin The wrongful dispossession of the property of the rightful owner.

dissemble 1. To conceal. 2. To disguise the appearance of.

dissentiente (Lat.) Dissenting.

dissenting opinion A judge's formally recorded disagreement with the majority decision of a lawsuit.

dissociation A defense or mental mechanism through which one's emotions are separated and detached from an idea, a situation, or an object.

dissociative reaction In mental health services, this is a breakdown in mental functioning, possibly a defensive response to psychological stressors that may be too overwhelming to cope with; not to be confused with a dissociative disorder (multiple personalities).

dissolution To dissolve or terminate; to end.

dissolution of marriage The legal termination of a marriage, except for annulments. *See divorce.*

dissolve Terminate; end; cancel or do away with.

distinct part In long-term-care administration, this is an identifiable unit accommodating beds that includes but is not limited to contiguous rooms or a wing, floor, or building that is approved for a specific purpose.

disto- Prefix meaning "far."

distortion False presentation of reality.

distrain To unlawfully or legally seize another person's personal property; to seize goods or property.

distress 1. The seizure of property or goods, without legal process, from a wrongdoer to procure payment. The seizing of personal property to force the payment of taxes. 2. Suffering of the mind; worry; anguish; emotional response to a negative experience.

distressed hospital Health-care facilities that are not doing well administratively or financially and that exhibit adverse changes in profit margins, low admissions, and low occupancy rates.

distribution *See normal distribution.*

distribution system In hospital materials management and central supply activities, this is the action of processing orders and delivering supplies, equipment, and materials to the proper place of need and usage within the hospital.

distributive justice In health-care delivery, access to care, and health-care rationing, this is a theoretical approach that describes how all persons are to share a limited or finite resource; to decide who receives health-care services and who does not and the justification for being excluded.

distributive law The legal authority for the distribution of funds and services by government agencies or bodies. Deals with the allocation of monies and services by government health agencies.

district A subdivision that includes different geographical areas, created for judicial, political, or administrative purposes. *See also hospital district.*

district attorney (DA) The head criminal prosecuting lawyer of a federal or state district. County or city attorneys are also equivalent to a district attorney.

district court Trial courts of the United States or low-level state courts.

diuretic Any drug that promotes excretion of urine.

divergence In laser technology, this is the increase in diameter of a laser beam over distance from the exit aperture.

divers Many or several; different.

diversification In health-care administration, this is an organizational structure and management approach whereby the top management team positions the health-care organization to competitively offer the types and amounts of services necessary for the survival and growth of the organization. Two key positioning approaches often used are horizontal integration and vertical integration. Diversification is the opposite of specialization. Concentration, specialization, and diversification approaches are compared and considered. Two common diversification approaches are 1) concentric, which uses lines of business common to the health-care organization and those that fit with common service usage, technology distribution channels, methods of operation, and management team know-how, and 2) conglomerate diversification, which is unrelated, true diversification and may lack a good organizational fit but is a good business venture. *See horizontal integration; vertical integration.*

diversion 1. Turning aside. 2. To divert; to refocus attention. 3. The placement of criminals or juvenile delinquents in special rehabilitation programs rather than in jail.

diversity of citizenship A constitutional doctrine that requires the parties on opposing sides in a lawsuit to reside in different states as a prerequisite to the federal courts taking jurisdiction.

divest To strip or dispossess; to take away; to deprive someone of authority, property, a right, or title. Also called "devest."

divestiture strategies In health-care administration, when a line of business or health service loses its appeal or lacks adequate utilization, the health-care organization may wish to divest it. Several divesting approaches include 1) forming a new and separate company, 2) combining the service with a closely related program, 3) attach it to a highly successful program as a side attraction, 4) sell the service to a more appropriate organization with a better fit, or 5) simply close it down.

dividend 1. A policyholder's share in the divisible surplus funds of an insurance company apportioned for distribution that may take the form of a refund of part of the premium on the insured's policy. 2. A share of profits or property of a corporation that is distributed to its stockholders.

division In formal meetings using parliamentary procedures, this is a call for a second count of a vote. Any committee or board member, once a vote count has been announced and it is not definite (especially after a voice vote), can call for division. Any member can call for "division" without formal recognition.

division and region Under the U.S. Bureau of the Census, the 50 states in the United States, plus the District of Columbia, are grouped for statistical purposes into 9 divisions within 4 regions.

division directive An order, statement of desired outcome, or expectation of subordinates at or below the division level; an intermediate-level order or outcome derived from organizational, department, and operating objectives, given at the division level within a large health-care organization.

division of assembly A method of taking a vote by having the voting members of the assembly rise to be counted to verify a voice vote.

Division of Emergency Medical Services A subagency of the U.S. Health Service Administration that administers programs at state and local levels that are supported by federal grants to develop local emergency medical care programs.

Division of Health Professions Analysis A federal agency that has the concern and responsibility of promoting and assessing the allied health professions.

Division of Manpower Training Support A federal agency that has the concern and responsibility of promoting, funding, evaluating, and training allied health professions.

divorce Legally ending a marriage by a court order. Also called "dissolution of marriage."

DMA Direct memory access. In health-care information management, this is a process whereby information can be transferred to a main memory from a computer terminal without going through the central processor of the main computer.

DME *See durable medical equipment; director of medical education.*

DMF Decayed, missing, and filled teeth. In public health dentistry and dental epidemiology, uppercase letters refer to permanent teeth and lowercase letters to temporary (baby) teeth.

DMS Diagnostic medical sonographer.

DNA Deoxyribonucleic acid. The genetic matter contained in most living organisms that is responsible for the control of heredity.

DNAR Do not attempt resuscitation.

DNR *See do not resuscitate order*

DO Doctor of Osteopathic Medicine. *See osteopathic medicine, doctor of.*

docket A calendar or agenda of scheduled court proceedings, usually prepared by a clerk of the court.

doctor Usually used synonymously with physician. Used as a title for any person possessing a doctoral degree, including the following: PhD, MD, DrPh, HSD, DHSci, EdD, DA, DBA, DPA, and DSci.

Doctor of Dental Surgery (or Science) (DDS) An individual who has earned a medical degree in dentistry from a graduate school of dentistry.

Doctor of Medicine (MD) An individual who has earned a medical degree from a graduate school of medicine.

Doctor of Osteopathic Medicine (DO) An individual who has earned a medical degree from a graduate school of osteopathic medicine.

doctor-patient relationship 1. The confidential interaction between one who is ill (patient) and the professional who is selected to treat or cure a disease or condition (a physician). 2. A legal and fiduciary relationship between a healthcare provider and client/patient that includes the protection of privacy and confidential matters disclosed in this somewhat sacred relationship. *See fiduciary.*

doctrine A common law principle or policy followed by the legal system.

document A written legal paper or a printed record such as a contract, medical record, or X ray.

document of title 1. A written record used in business as proof of a right to possess goods. 2. A bill of lading; a receipt.

documentary evidence Written evidence; important written information that could be used to prove certain facts or have important legal meaning.

documentation The process of recording information in the medical record and other source documents (JCAHO for acute-care hospitals).

documentation, quality of *See quality of documentation.*

doing business 1. The continuous management of business within a jurisdiction that renders the business subject to the jurisdiction of the local courts for tax, liability, or other legal actions. 2. Carrying on business for profit within a state so that another person could sue if necessary. 3. The ability of the state to tax an organization and hold it legally responsible for its business transactions.

Dole Foundation for the Employment of People with Disabilities A nonprofit foundation established by former Senator Robert Dole that offers grants to nonprofit community-based organizations for innovative programs in job training, skill development, and job placement for people who are handicapped or suffering from some form of disability.

domain Ownership or control; ultimate ownership.

domestic 1. Belonging or relating to home, state, or country. 2. Pertaining to one's place of residence.

domestic corporation A corporation created and incorporated under state law, as opposed to a foreign corporation.

domestic insurer An insurance company incorporated to do business in certain states that recognize it as an acceptable insurer.

domicile 1. A person's permanent official and legal residence or home. 2. Residing within a jurisdiction with no present intention to live elsewhere.

domiciliary Relating to one's domicile, or permanent home.

domiciliary facility A residential living facility for people in need of personal care such as nutritional assistance, outpatient care, hygiene assistance, and help with medication but not extensive medical care services. Some Veterans Administration hospitals have domiciliary facilities adjacent to them.

dominant Having rights, responsibility, or control over another.

dominant cause *See proximate cause.*

dominion Control, domination, ownership, or power over people, positions, property, or land.

domitae naturae (Lat.) Domestic animals. Animals that are generally tame and occasionally wander at large. Opposite of ferae naturae.

donated services Volunteer services provided by physicians or other personnel without pay. The monetary value of time spent in free or volunteer work.

donatio causa mortis (Lat.) See causa mortis.

donatio inter vivos (Lat.) A gift between living persons.

donative Related to old canon law, a donation or benefit given; a gift. A donative trust is a gift given to another person.

donee One to whom a gift or grant is made or power given.

donor A person giving a grant, gift, or power to another.

donor, blood One who gives blood through a blood service for use in medical care.

donor, organ An individual who gives written permission to have organs removed from his or her body for use by another person through transplant surgery. This can occur when the donor is still alive and healthy, or the organ can be removed on that person's death with written consent.

donor, professional blood An individual who donates blood to a blood bank for payment.

donor, replacement blood When blood is donated to a hospital in the name of a particular patient, reducing the need for blood from the facility's blood bank. This, in turn, reduces the cost of the patient's hospital bill.

donor, tissue An individual who donates body tissues or organs for use in a transplant operation in another human being.

donor, voluntary blood A blood donor who gives blood without receiving payment for the donation.

do not code An order written in the medical record giving all health-care personnel a mandate to not resuscitate the patient.

do not resuscitate order (DNR) An order entered into a patient's medical record by the attending physician that respects a patient's request to die by not intervening with cardiac stimulation.

dormant Sleeping, latent, inactive, silent, or concealed.

dormant partner Silent partner.

DOS Date of services.

dosage The control of the number, amount, size, and frequency of a dose.

dose 1. The amount of a substance, drug, or agent to be given in one administration. 2. In environmental health, the amounts of substances penetrating the exchange boundaries of organisms after contact. Doses are calculated from the intake and absorption efficiency of organisms and usually are expressed as the mass of a substance absorbed into the body per unit body weight per unit time. In radiation, this term denotes the quantity of radiation or energy absorbed in a specified mass.

dose, booster A quantity of vaccine given to a person at a predetermined time interval after a primary dose has been given. It is usually a smaller amount and works to extend the immune response of the primary dose.

dose, fatal A quantity or amount of a substance that can cause death.

dose, lethal The amount of a drug, substance, or agent that is large enough to cause death.

dose limit The value or quantity of a substance that must not be exceeded (e.g., radiation exposure).

dose rate The dose delivered or administered in a specified period of time or frequency.

dose-response evaluation In environmental health, this is the process of quantitatively evaluating the toxicity information and characterizing the relationship between the dose of the contaminant administered or received and the incidence of adverse health effects in the exposed population. From the quantitative dose-response relationship, toxicity values are derived that are used in the risk characterization step to estimate the likelihood of adverse effects occurring in humans at different exposure levels. *See dose-response relationship.*

dose-response relationship 1. In biomedical research, this is used in drug research clinical trials to determine the levels at which a substance produces an effect from either increasing or decreasing the amount and what effect the change has on the health status of the subject. 2. In health promotion, the increases in outcome measures associated with disease prevention and risk factor intervention efforts, often using levels of expended resources as the measure. *See dose-response evaluation.*

dose-response study In biomedical research, this is a study that ascertains how the risk of a drug or specified substance or event increases with the amount of exposure to the causative agent or risk factor.

dose, skin The amount or quantity of radiation at the skin level, including primary and backscatter radiation.

dose, tolerance The greatest amount of a drug, substance, or agent that can be safely administered to a patient without any risk of harm.

dose upper bounds In environmental health, this is the levels of exposure to a substance established by a competent authority to constrain the optimization of protection for a given source or source type.

dosimetery The theory and application of the principles and techniques involved in measuring and recording doses.

DOT Department of Transportation. *See also Directory of Occupational Titles.*

double-blind studies (trials, technique) In biomedical research, this is an approach used in drug studies or other medical procedures in which both subjects and investigators are unaware of who is actually getting what treatment. As long as good sampling procedures are used, the method is one of several ways of eliminating bias (conscious or unconscious) in both subjects and investigators. Classically used in drug studies, the method involves the use of a "look-a-like" placebo. In "triple blind" studies, the people analyzing the data, as well as the investigator, subjects, and controls, are unaware of the treatment or intervention used.

double distribution In health-care finance, this is when the general service cost center costs are first distributed to the appropriate general service centers, and the final distribution is to end-cost centers.

double entry 1. In health-care financial management and accounting, this is a bookkeeping method that records every transaction made. 2. A system of accounting that requires that for every entry there be a debit and a credit.

double indemnity Insurance that pays off double the amount if certain events occur. A policy provision usually associated with death that doubles the payments of certain benefits when certain kinds of accidents occur.

double insurance A person holding life or health insurance from two or more companies that cover the same risk. It may be illegal according to the insurance contracts to collect the total benefit from more than one company.

double jeopardy In criminal law, this is to be prosecuted twice for the same crime; prohibited by the U.S. Constitution.

doubt To have strong disbelief, mistrust, or uncertainty about the proof of facts; to fluctuate or appear uncertain about the truth or the facts.

Dow Jones Industrial Average The most widely recognized stock market system, used as a benchmark to which all others compare their investments. Originally established in the 1800s as a gauge of the U.S. stock market, it is based on changes in the prices of the 30 largest companies. It is no longer based on industrial business but includes food services, retail, and health and medically related organizations.

down payment A large sum of money paid at the time of purchase for an item that is to be paid off in installment payments.

downsizing In health-care administration, this is taking the steps necessary to reduce the number of beds, employees, expenses, and operations of a health-care organization to better position it and to adjust to a diminishing demand for service while ensuring the survival of the organization.

downstream holding company In health-care organizational structuring, this is an organizational arrangement whereby a parent company establishes a holding company, and the holding company establishes subsidiary firms, leaving the parent company free and unaffiliated.

downtime The period of time that a computer and its associated equipment is shut down for repair or maintenance or because of malfunction.

DP Doctorate of Podiatry.

DPhar Doctorate of Pharmacy.

DPH (or DrPH) Doctorate of Public Health.

DPT A triple antigen immunization vaccine containing diphtheria, pertussis, and tetanus. *See also diphtheria; pertussis; tetanus.*

DPW Department of Public Welfare.

DR *See diagnostic radiology services.*

Draconian law Related to the Athenian lawgiver Draco's (7th c. B.C.) code of laws that is especially cruel, harsh, severe, and rigorous.

draft 1. The first writing; a sketch. 2. A bill of exchange; a check.

drainage bag A plastic bag used to collect urine from a catheter in persons who are incontinent. Used mainly in long-term-care, nursing homes, and home health settings.

dramshop exclusion An exclusion clause in liability insurance policies that relates to the distribution of alcoholic beverages by an organization or facility.

draw 1. To write a check; to take money out of an account. 2. To create a legal document. 3. To take out of one's body, as to draw blood.

drawee In health-care finance, this is the person on whom a bill of exchange, order, or draft is drawn and who is expected to pay the bill for the amount presented.

drawer In health-care finance, this is the person drawing or preparing a bill of exchange, draft, or order or one who signs the draft or order.

drawing tests Any psychological projective test that asks the subject to draw objects such as people, trees, and houses. The tests are used to assess their attitudes, feelings, and perceptions.

draw sheet A bed sheet that is purposely shortened. It is placed over the bottom sheet and covers the area between the chest and the knees of the patient to protect the mattress and lower sheet while helping to keep the patient dry and comfortable.

drayman One who transports goods.

dread Anxiety related to or created by fear of a specific danger.

dread disease insurance *See specified disease insurance.*

dread disease policy In managed care and medical insurance, this is a form of insurance that provides benefits to the policyholder or health plan member for care and treatment of certain serious, debilitating, or life-threatening diseases as set forth in the policy or benefit package.

dread disease rider A clause added to a health insurance policy that provides supplemental benefits for certain conditions, diseases, or disorders.

dressing The sterile, clean, bandaging material used to directly cover and protect a wound to help control bleeding.

DRG *See diagnosis-related group.*

DRG coordinator A hospital employee assigned the responsibility of overseeing the activities of the Medicare Prospective Payment System within the hospital. This person verifies as soon as possible the best and appropriate DRG for each Medicare admission, tracks length of stay, informs the attending physician of average length of stay and costs, assists in case mix analysis and discharge planning, and reviews Medicare readmissions.

DRG cost weight Each diagnosis-related group is given a number and weighted for average cost, resource use, and length of stay on the basis of averages for the region in which the hospital is located. Medicare's average cost is multiplied by the DRG cost weight, providing the price assigned to the DRG being reviewed.

DRG enhancer In health information management systems, a software computer program that works with Medicare's medical billing data to select the DRG category with the most severity, providing the hospital with the best financial return.

DRG inlier Patients who fall within the DRG classification and categorization system. *See also trim points.*

DRG measures of severity *See complicating and comorbid.*

DRG mix A case mix system that identifies by DRG the various types of treatments a hospital provides. *See case mix.*

DRG outlier Under Medicare, these are hospital-based patient cases with unusually high or low resource use and length of stay. Atypical hospital cases that have either an extremely long length of stay or extraordinarily high costs when compared to most discharges classified in the same DRG. *See diagnosis-related group.*

DRG rate A fixed amount of money for which a DRG is to be reimbursed on the basis of the average of all patients in that DRG in the base year and adjusted for inflation, economic factors, and bad debts.

Drinker respirator In medical care, this is a special device that allows the controlled automatic breathing in a patient who suffers paralysis of the breathing muscles.

drip In medical care, this is the slow, continuous administration of a liquid via an intravenous line.

drip, Murphy In medical care, this is the slow, continuous administration of saline solution into the rectum.

Dr.P.H. Doctorate in Public Health.

droit (French) Right; justice; law.

drug 1. Any substance intended for use in the diagnosis, cure, mitigation, treatment, or prevention of disease or intended to affect the structure or function of the body (not including food) or components of these substances. These substances are recognized in the official *U.S. Pharmacopoeia*, the official *U.S. Homeopathic Pharmacopoeia*, and the official *National Formulary*. 2. Any chemical compound that may be used on or administered to persons as an aid in the diagnosis, treatment, or prevention of disease or other abnormal condition (JCAHO for acute-care hospitals). *See device and biologic; safe and effective; compendium and formulary; over-the-counter and prescription; labeling and package insert.*

drug abuse Persistent or sporadic drug use, inconsistent with or unrelated to acceptable medical or cultural practice. Drug abuse may involve excessive use of a drug, unnecessary use (thus incorporating recreational use), drug dependence, or illegal use. *See also alcoholism.*

drug addiction Generally synonymous with "drug dependence" but not necessarily synonymous with "drug abuse."

drug administration 1. For Medicare purposes, an act in which a single dose of a prescribed drug or biological is given to a patient by an authorized person in accordance with all laws and regulations governing such acts. The complete act of administration entails removing an individual dose from a previously dispensed, properly labeled container (including a unit dose container); verifying it with the physician's orders; giving the individual dose to the proper patient; and promptly recording the time and dose given. 2. For JCAHO accreditation purposes, the act in which a single dose of an identified drug is given to a patient.

drug allergies A state of hypersensitivity induced by exposure to a particular drug antigen, resulting in harmful immunologic reactions (e.g., penicillin drug allergy) on subsequent drug exposures (JCAHO for acute-care hospitals).

drug categories The Comprehensive Drug Abuse Prevention and Control Act of 1970 places controlled substances into the following categories: opiates, barbiturates, tranquilizers, stimulants, hallucinogens, and marijuana. *See also schedule of controlled substances.*

drug compendium *See compendium.*

drug dependence A state, emotional as well as physical, resulting from the interaction between a person and a drug, characterized by responses that always include a compulsion to take the drug on a continuous or periodic basis. Tolerance for the drug may or may not be present. A person may be dependent on more than one drug. Dependence characteristics will vary with the substance involved, and this must be made clear by designating the particular type of drug dependence in each specific case (e.g., drug dependence on narcotics, cannabis, barbiturates, or amphetamines).

drug dispensing 1. For JCAHO accreditation purposes, the issuance of one or more doses of a prescribed medication in containers that are correctly labeled to indicate the name of the patient, the contents of the container, and all other vital information needed to facilitate correct patient usage and drug administration. 2. Under Medicare, an act entailing the interpretation of an order for a drug or biological and the proper selection, measuring, labeling, packaging, and issuance of the drug or biological for a patient or for a service unit of the facility.

drug efficacy study implementation (DESI) The plan of the Food and Drug Administration for implementing the evaluations and recommendations of the Drug Efficacy Study Group of the National Academy of Science and the National Research Council regarding the effectiveness of drugs marketed prior to 1962 under approved new drug applications. The Drug Efficacy Study was undertaken in 1966 to evaluate the drugs the FDA had approved as safe prior to 1962, when Congress first required that drugs also be proven effective before marketing. The Drug Efficacy Study Group evaluated nearly 4000 individual drug products, finding many of them ineffective or of only possible or probable effectiveness. The FDA is still in the process of implementing those judgments by removing some of the drugs from the market.

drug error A medication error, with the drug already given to a patient.

drug formulary In managed-care health plans and HMOs, this is a list of drugs, medicines, and medical care treatment substances that has been reviewed and approved for use and that is expected to be adhered to by the health plans under a managed-care contract and are to be dispensed by the HMO's pharmacy or participating pharmacies to the health plan members. Drugs not on the list are not covered by the health plan. All drugs are reviewed, and changes to the list are made periodically. Physicians who are participants in the health plan are often involved in the development and review of the formulary. Generic drugs or the least expensive ones with the same formula, equivalency, or treatment outcomes are used. *See formulary.*

Drug Free Workplace Act of 1988 Federal legislation passed to require all organizations applying for federal grants to certify that a good faith effort will be made to provide a drug-free workplace.

druggist One who operates a drugstore. Sometimes considered synonymous with "pharmacist" but not always limited to people with a pharmacy degree (or even to operators of drugstores in which prescription drugs are dispensed) and usually applied only to pharmacists who operate or work in drugstores.

drug habituation Generally synonymous with "drug dependence" or "addiction" and sometimes used to mean "psychological drug dependence"; often wrongly assumed to be synonymous with "drug abuse."

drug history In medical care, this is a delineation of the drugs used by a patient, including prescribed and unprescribed drugs and alcohol. A drug history includes, but is not necessarily limited to, the following: drugs used in the past; drugs used recently, especially within the preceding 48 hours; drugs of preference; frequency with which each drug is used; route of administration of each drug; drugs used in combination; dosages used; year of first use of each drug; previous occurrences of overdose, withdrawal, or adverse drug reactions; and history of previous treatment received for alcohol or drug abuse.

drug holiday Discontinuation of the administration of a drug to patients or residents in long-term care for a period of time to evaluate and determine baseline need, the behavioral effects of drugs, the correct dosage of psychoactive drugs, and interactions with other drugs and their side effects.

drug incompatibilities In medical care, this is when one medication has a negative reaction with another medication or causes an interference with its normal action.

drug information services A health-care provider drug information service that provides information about drugs and medications and their actions, properties, effects, dosage, contraindications, and drug interactions.

drug insurance In managed care and medical insurance, this is a form of insurance that pays for all or part of the cost of prescribed medications. Some major medical plans pay only for prescribed medications for a specified illness and/or only when a deductible has been met.

drug interaction The effects or reaction of two or more drugs taken simultaneously. Often the effect is different than if either drug was taken alone. The interaction of two drugs may have a potentiating and/or additive effect with possible serious side effects resulting. *See also synergistic effect.*

drug list A list of pharmaceuticals and substances kept in stock on a regular basis in a hospital pharmacy. *See drug formulary; formulary.*

drug maintenance list Also referred to as the "additional drug benefit list." *See additional drug benefit list.*

drug monograph A rule that prescribes for a drug or class of related drugs the kinds and amounts of ingredients it may contain; the conditions for which it may be offered; and directions for use, warnings, and other information that its labeling must bear. Drug monographs established by the FDA state conditions under which drugs may be marketed as safe and effective (not adulterated or misbranded) and thus without an approved new drug application.

drug prescription A formal order written to a pharmacist to have a medication order filled for a patient. The order is written by a physician, dentist, or other health-care provider authorized by law to prescribe medications.

drug price review (DPR) In medical care and managed care, this is the process of updating drug prices on a monthly basis on the basis of average wholesale prices set by the *American Druggist Blue Book* (*ADBB*). The maximum prices for each drug are set.

drug room A room that is specially maintained in a hospital, nursing home, or other long-term-care facility for the sole purpose of housing a limited supply of drugs that are to be dispensed by a registered nurse to the patients or residents. This room has specific drugs prescribed for the patients who are being served and is not a pharmacy.

drugs and biologicals Substances found favorable to be included, or approved for inclusion, in the *U.S. Pharmacopoeia*, the *National Formulary*, the *U.S. Homeopathic Pharmacopoeia*, or *New Drugs or Accepted Dental Remedies* or as approved by the pharmacy and drug therapeutics committee of the medical staff of a hospital.

drugs, expenditures for *See expenditures for drugs.*

drug therapy The use of drugs to treat physical and mental illness. Also referred to as "chemotherapy." *See also maintenance drug therapy.*

drug utilization review (DUR) In managed care and medical care, this is the assessment and analysis of drug prescribing patterns by health-care providers to determine drug use, appropriateness of use, therapeutic results and outcomes, and appropriateness in prescribing patterns.

drug utilization/usage evaluation A hospital medical staff responsibility done in cooperation with other relevant departments/services that entails monitoring, evaluating, and improving the quality of prophylactic, therapeutic, and empiric use of drugs in the hospital. Standards of drug use are applied to evaluate a hospital's performance in assessing the quality of its drug usage (JCAHO for acute-care hospitals).

DSM *See Diagnostic and Statistical Manual of Mental Disorders.*

DSM-I Abbreviation for the first edition of the American Psychiatric Association's *Diagnostic and Statistical Manual of Mental Disorders* (1952).

DSM-II Abbreviation for the second edition of the *Diagnostic and Statistical Manual of Mental Disorders* (1968).

DSM-III Abbreviation for the third edition of the *Diagnostic and Statistical Manual of Mental Disorders* (1980).

DSM-IIIR Abbreviation for the third edition, revised, of the *Diagnostic and Statistical Manual of Mental Disorders* (1987).

DSM-IV Abbreviation for the fourth edition of the *Diagnostic and Statistical Manual of Mental Disorders* (1994).

DSRF Debt service reserve fund.

DT *See dietetic technician.*

dual capacity A legal principle that allows an employee to sue his or her employer over an injury that occurred on the job that was covered by workers' compensation or one that was incurred during treatment in a health-care facility from negligent treatment by a health-care provider, who can also be sued for malpractice.

dual choice (dual option) In managed care, these are provisions of federal legislation that require employers to give their employees the option to enroll in a local health maintenance organization or in the conventional employer-sponsored health insurance program; the practice of giving people a choice of more than one health insurance or health program to pay for or provide their health services (required by the HMO Act, P.L. 93-222, of employers with respect to qualified HMOs [Section 1310 of the Public Health Service Act]).

dual coverage An insurance plan under which the insured has coverage by more than one carrier.

duality of interest When persons in decision-making or administrative positions have personal, vested, or outside interests that could affect their decisions; usually a concern for persons serving on boards, committees of health systems agencies, or related regulatory agencies. *See conflict of interest.*

dually certified facility A health-care institution that has been approved by a state agency to provide two levels or kinds of care; nursing homes that have been approved by the appropriate state agency to provide two levels of care (e.g., skilled and intermediate care) in all areas of the facility.

dubitante (Lat.) Doubting. A term fixed to a judge's name in court reports, indicating that he doubts the correctness of the decision.

duces tecum (Lat.) Bring with you. In law, this is a subpoena requiring a person summoned to court to bring certain documents or evidence to court. A physician may be required to bring medical records or X rays to court to be used as evidence.

due 1. Suitable; proper; usual; regular; sufficient or reasonable. "Due care" is ordinary or expected care that is at the level sufficient for the situation. 2. Payable, owed, and already matured, as in a "note is due."

due care In health law, this is that amount or degree of care that would be exercised by an ordinary person in the same situation. *See also reasonable man; ordinary person; negligence.*

due date 1. In health-care finance, this is the day a debt must be paid; the date that something is due or is to arrive. 2. In medical care, the date that the physician calculates that a pregnant women is due to deliver her baby.

due notice Reasonable or sufficient notice.

due process 1. The right to proper litigation procedures in the event that a legal action occurs, such as a right to a hearing or a fair trial. The due process clause of the U.S. Constitution provides that no person shall be deprived of life, liberty, or property without due process of law, including the right to a trial by jury. A person should have enough advance notice and a chance to present his or her side of a legal complaint. 2. In human resource management, rules and procedures that are established and followed so that employees have an opportunity to respond to charges made against them or over termination from a job.

due-to/from-other funds In health-care finance, an asset or liability that is owed or due from the operating fund to another internal health-care facility fund; a method of internal borrowing from one internal account to put funds in another internal account, which is then owed back to that account; an interfund transaction.

DUI Driving under the influence. Some states use this abbreviation to identify persons who drive while drunk and who are arrested. Other states use DWI ("driving while intoxicated").

dum fervet opus (Lat.) In the heat of the action.

dummy Fake; sham; set up as real; a front.

dummy corporation A corporation that meets legal requirements but is really acting as a vehicle of, or is secretly controlled by, another corporation.

dumping In health services delivery, this is a slang term that refers to a hospital refusing to accept certain types of patients who have no medical insurance coverage and then sending them to county hospitals or other health-care facilities that will provide free care, thus "dumping" the patients on the county- or state-supported hospitals. Laws have been enacted that prevent dumping to prohibit the transfer of patients if such a transfer cannot be medically justified.

dun 1. To urge or demand payment. 2. To loudly, persistently, and insistently demand payment of a debt. Literal meaning is "with a loud noise."

Dun & Bradstreet Established in 1930 to continue a business that was started in 1841, it provides credit, marketing, training, consulting, and business information about all established businesses for a fee.

duo- Prefix meaning "two."

duplicate coverage inquiry (DCI) In managed care and medical insurance, this is a request to an insurance carrier or managed-care company from another insurance carrier or managed-care company to inquire about an enrollee or policyholder to determine if other coverage exists so that benefits can be coordinated.

duplication of benefits Occurs when a person covered under more than one medical or accident insurance policy collects, or may collect, payments for the same hospital or medical expenses from more than one insurer. Individual health insurance policies, under state laws, sometimes include antiduplication clauses. Because the limitation does not apply to group insurance, it usually does contain such clauses, especially in major medical policies. However, most states will not allow group policies to apply such clauses to individual insurance. Where duplication does exist with a group antiduplication clause, the group insurer responsible for paying the benefits first is the primary payer. Also referred to as "multiple coverage." *See also coordination of benefits.*

durable medical equipment Generally, equipment purchased by a health-care facility that has the following dimensions: nondisposable, has a life expectancy of more than 1 year, is priced over $300, is a nonpatient charge, and is reusable by the hospital. This definition varies from facility to facility and region to region in the United States.

durable power of attorney for health care In 1983, California enacted the first statute in the United States allowing a person to appoint an agent for health-care decision making when the person lost decision-making capacity. By completing a document known as "Durable Power of Attorney for Health Care," an adult of legal age can appoint another person to make health-care decisions if the person signing it later becomes mentally incapacitated. Preferences regarding medical treatment and/or life-sustaining procedures can be chosen or stated and are to be followed if medical circumstances require it. This is also referred to as an "advanced directive," which is established in conformance with state statutory law (California passed such a law, and other states passed similar laws) by which an individual may appoint someone else as their agent or attorney-in-fact to make health-care decisions in the event the individual becomes unable to make such decisions. Also included may be specific instructions regarding which health-care treatment(s) should be utilized in the event of incapacity. *See advanced directive; Patient Self-Determination Act; living will.*

duration 1. In health-care administration, this is the time period through which a decision is effective and through which utilization patterns attest to the success of the decision. 2. In epidemiology, a time element for the length of an epidemic or the course of a disease or condition.

duration of visit The time the physician spends in face-to-face contact with the patient, not including time the patient spent waiting to see the physician or receiving care from someone other than the physician without the presence of the physician or time the physician spent reviewing patient information. In cases where the patient received care from a member of the physician's staff and did not see the physician during the visit, the duration of visit is recorded as zero minutes.

duress Coercion; threats; pressure or force put on a person to do what he or she would not otherwise do, such as commit a misdemeanor.

Durham Rule A test for criminal responsibility based on the concept of "irresistible impulse." If it is shown that a defendant was diseased and had a defective mental state when he or she committed a crime and that the crime was due to the mental state, the Durham Rule maintains that the defendant cannot be held criminally responsible.

duty 1. Any moral or legal obligation to another person. 2. Conduct owed to a person or patient, especially if he or she has a right to expect something from another person; therefore it is ensured that the expectation is carried out in a competent manner. 3. Any obligation, moral or ethical, to perform or follow a specific order of conduct.

DVM Doctor of Veterinary Medicine. *See veterinarian.*

DWI 1. Driving while intoxicated. 2. Died without issue; childless.

Dx Diagnosis.

Dyer Act A federal law passed in 1919 making it an offense to take a stolen motor vehicle across a state line.

dying declaration Words of a dying person about a crime. Under usual conditions, such testimony is not considered good evidence, but words of a dying person are usually allowed or believed.

dys- Prefix meaning "bad," "malicious," "hard," "painful," or "difficult."

dysfunctional Unable to function or operate in a normal manner; abnormal or impaired function of a body part, organ, mind, or behavior; a behavior or emotional response that limits or restricts normal process, actions, activity, or functioning.

dyslexia Impaired ability to comprehend or understand the written word (not related to one's intelligence level).

dysphagia Difficulty in or inability to swallow.

dyssocial behavior Behavior that is marginally criminal such as sadism, racketeering, prostitution, and illegal gambling. Also known as "sociopathic" behavior. *See also antisocial personality.*

dystressor Any occurrence, event, experience, life change, loss, difficulty, or pain that causes mental or emotional upset, physiological changes, or wear and tear on the body or any deviation from positive conditions that causes stress and to which a person cannot easily adapt, cope, or adjust.

E

EAA *See Environmental Assessment Association.*

EACH Essential access community hospital. *See eaches/peaches.*

eaches/peaches A rural health services delivery approach where *eaches* (essential assess community hospital) and *peaches* (rural primary care hospital) some regulatory allowance is given to some rural hospitals in California, Colorado, Kansas, New York, North Carolina, South Dakota, and West Virginia, allowing them to convert the focus of hospital services from acute care to primary care. The small rural essential access community hospital is formally linked to a larger, rural primary care hospital that provides emergency and medical care backup and accepts all transfer patients. Physician staff privileges are granted at both hospitals.

EAP *See employee assistance program.*

Early and Periodic Screening, Diagnosis, and Treatment (EPSDT) A Medicaid program mandated as law. Section 1905(a)(4)(B) of the Social Security Act required that by July 1, 1969, all states have in effect a program for eligible children under age 21 that determines their physical or mental defects and provides health care, treatment, and other measures to correct or ameliorate defects and chronic conditions discovered thereby, as may be provided in regulations. State programs not only pay for services but also include an active outreach component that brings eligible persons into care so that they can be screened and, if necessary, assisted in obtaining appropriate treatment. EPSDT should refer only to those programs that have all these elements.

early prenatal care The provision for nutritional, health, and medical care beginning in the first part of the first trimester of pregnancy, including avoiding taking medications, illegal drugs, alcohol, or any substance that might have a potential to injure the fetus if ingested.

early retirement A health administration and gerontological issue, this is when a person elects to or is forced to retire from work or his or her profession or when an employer demands retirement before one's normal retirement age, which is 70 years of age in organizations under governmental control or influence.

earned income Monetary gain derived from work or services rendered, usually on the individual worker basis and distinguished from other kinds of income, such as income from the health facility or business activities.

earned income tax credit In tax law, this is a tax credit to low-income wage earners to offset the regressive burden of the payroll tax on poor workers. Wage earners may receive a cash refund even when there is no equivalent income tax liability and is currently offered only to those with dependent children.

earnest money In health-care finance, this is an amount paid by a buyer to hold or bind a seller to a deal or to the terms of an agreement; a deposit to show a buyer's good faith.

earnings record Under Social Security, this is a record maintained by the Social Security Administration of the amounts earned by each person for whom Social Security taxes were paid.

earnings test In health-care finance, this is a formula used to determine and assess retirement benefits in which payments are reduced according to one's current earnings as determined by a preestablished schedule.

ear, nose, and throat (ENT) A medical specialty in which a physician completes a residency and becomes board certified in the diagnosis and treatment of diseases and disorders of the ear, nose, and throat. Also referred to as "otolaryngology."

EBCDIC Extended binary-coded decimal interchange code. In health-care information management computer languages, an 8-bit alphanumeric character set.

EBD Employee benefits division. The benefits sections of a health plan.

E-book In epidemiology, this is an observation research recording method used in studies in primary care or clinical settings. The physician records each patient encounter and arranges the encounter book by diagnostic category, condition, or medical problem seen, making it easy to tabulate the number of patient encounters and the number of times each patient is examined or seen in a given time period.

EBR Employee benefits representative.

EBT Examination before trial. In health-care law and the litigation process, this is a part of the discovery process. *See also deposition; discovery.*

ECF *See extended care facility.*

ECFMG *See Educational Commission for Foreign Medical Graduates.*

ECG *See electrocardiogram.*

ECH Extended care hospital. *See extended care facility.*

echo- Prefix meaning "sound."

echocardiography An ultrasound diagnostic method using an echo or other sound-reflecting technique to determine the presence or absence of fluid in the sac surrounding the heart or the position and motion of the heart walls.

echoencephalography An ultrasound diagnostic method in which sound waves are beamed through the skull and echoes recorded graphically to determine any change in brain structure.

echogram The visual record made from ultrasound waves by echography.

echography The use of ultrasound or ultrasonic sound waves as a diagnostic method. These waves are beamed at the tissue to be diagnosed and the echoes recorded on a graph or oscilloscope, which helps determine density, structure, etc. *See also ultrasonography.*

E code A section in volume 1 of the ICD-9-CM coding manual that permits classification for environmental events, accidents, circumstances, or conditions that cause injury, poisoning, or other adverse effects. Codes from this section are used to augment codes from the main section of volume 1, providing more detailed codes for a medical condition. *See also ICD-9-CM; V code.*

ecological correlation In epidemiological studies and analysis, this is when populations units are studied and statistical correlations are conducted.

ecological fallacy Any mistake in statistical or epidemiological inference; erroneous assumptions that two things are associated (i.e., that one must be caused by the other). *See also Hawthorn's effect; halo effect.*

ecology The study of man's relationship with the environment; the relationship of organisms to each other in similar environments as well as to other organisms contributing to various aspects of the same environment.

economic characteristics The economic condition of the state and its residents.

economic cost In health-care finance, this is the full expense of operating a health-care organization or facility, including both tangible and intangible costs.

economic credentialing In hospital administration, this is a medical staff assessment process that measures the potential physicians have for making money for the hospital or for costing the hospital money on the basis of the type of patient admitted and the specialty of the physician. This is an approach to medical staff selection for a hospital that evaluates a physician's or specialist's use of hospital resources and the costs of providing care to patients within the hospital. It is illegal to use such an approach in reviewing and selecting potential medical staff members; however it is not illegal to consider these factors when considering dismissal from a medical staff.

economic feasibility An assessment of a health-care organization or service's potential for success based on factors such as cost of construction, equipment, services, revenue sources, and population economic indicators.

economic issues or constraints Those economic aspects that might hinder the implementation of a health systems plan.

economic life The period of time that an improvement to the physical plant of a health-care facility or piece of equipment will continue to produce an income or profit, usually shorter than the physical life of the facility or equipment.

economic nonproductive years Of concern to gerontology and health-care economics, these are the years outside the work life span for individuals under 18 years of age and in the retirement years. The nonproductive years listed are misleading because some older Americans continue to work for wages into retirement age, and most teenagers also have earnings.

Economic Opportunity Act of 1969 *See Community Action Program.*

economic order quantity In materials management, the best mix of cost and amount of inventory or supplies to be ordered when the inventory is reduced to a level that requires replenishment.

economic productive years Traditionally the legal, or traditional, work period of 18 to 65 years of age; now ages 18 to 70.

economics of scale The increase in cost-effectiveness of a health service that is directly attributed to the increased efficiency of a large-scale operation; increase in cost efficiency that is directly correlated to increase in size. When a health care organization's total costs decrease as the size of operations increases. *See economies of scale.*

economics outcomes In health-care finance, this is the monetary results of care provided by a hospital or health care organization as measured by costs, earnings, losses, and savings.

Economic Stabilization Program (ESP) A federal program established to control wages and prices. On August 15, 1971, all wages and prices were frozen for a period of 90 days. During that period, a system of wage and price controls was implemented. Controls continued with periodic changes until their legislative authority ultimately expired in April 1974. Wages and prices in the health-care industry were controlled through a specialized series of regulations. For the 32½ months the controls were in effect, that was the only period in which medical care price increases slowed markedly since the enactment of Medicare and Medicaid; increases in medical care prices were limited to 4.3%.

economies of scale 1. Cost savings resulting from aggregation of resources and/or mass production, in particular, the decreases in average cost when all factors of production are expanded proportionately. Sometimes refers to savings achieved when underused resources are used more efficiently. 2. The point in efficiency, effectiveness, or growth of a health-care service where each additional element of service costs less to offer or produce; the point where larger size or bulk purchasing is less costly and reduces the costs of operations. Also referred to as "economy of scale." *See economics of scale.*

ECT *See electroconvulsive therapy.*

ECU *See extended care unit.*

ED *See emergency department.*

EDC *See expected date of confinement.*

edentulous Without teeth.

EDI *See electronic data interchange.*

edict An official public order announced or proclaimed by a public official or head of state.

editor In health-care information management, this is a computer program that interacts with the user at a terminal to enter or edit information in the computer when commanded to do so.

EDP *See electronic data processing.*

education In public health, epidemiology research, and demographic information, this is the number of years of formal schooling obtained in accredited schools offering diplomas or degrees that individual adults in the survey population have completed.

education department A department in larger health-care facilities responsible for planning and providing staff development programs including orientations, continuing education, on-the-job training, and patient- and community-oriented educational programs.

education director The individual responsible for the management of the education department in a health-care facility or agency. This person coordinates and manages the employee orientation, continuing education, and on-the-job training that the department provides.

education, in-service *See in-service education.*

Education Resources Information Center (ERIC) A national computerized clearinghouse of information and materials related to education, including health-care issues and health education programs.

Educational Commission for Foreign Medical Graduates (ECFMG) An organization sponsored by the American Medical Association, the American Hospital Association, the American Association of Medical Colleges, the Association for Hospital Medical Education, and the Federation of State Medical Boards of the United States. It operates a program of educating, testing, and evaluating foreign medical graduates (FMGs) who seek internships and residencies in the United States. The ECFMG was formed in 1974 through a merger of the Educational Council for Foreign Medical Graduates with the Commission for Foreign Medical Graduates. Certification for these students is granted by the ECFMG after receiving documentation of their education and after the student passes an examination of medical competence and comprehension of spoken English. Such certification is necessary for full licensure of FMGs in 47 states and territories. *See also Federation Licensing Examination.*

educational diagnosis As used in health education and health promotion, this is the determination, assessment, and delineation of causes of disease, conditions, injuries, or risk factors that predispose, allow, and reinforce certain unhealthy behaviors that can be changed by educational intervention and learning or behavior modification.

educational evaluation As used in health education and health promotion, this is the comparison of some combination of predisposing, enabling, and reinforcing factors regarded as causes of unhealthy behavior of concern to preset standards or objectives.

educational therapist A person who instructs mentally ill, mentally retarded, or disabled patients in academic subjects to further their medical and mental recovery and prevent mental deterioration.

educational tool In health education and training, this is any method or material designed to enhance learning and teaching by affecting the senses of the learner.

EECP *See enhanced external counterpulsation.*

EEG *See electroencephalogram.*

EENT *See eye, ear, nose, and throat.*

EEO Equal employment opportunity. *See Equal Employment Opportunity Commission.*

EEOC *See Equal Employment Opportunity Commission.*

effect 1. The power to produce results. 2. Operative or in force. 3. To produce. 4. A result; to begin or to show results.

effective date In managed care and medical insurance, the date on which a medical care insurance policy or health plan goes into effect, making benefits available; the exact time medical coverage from a health plan as set forth in the group subscriber agreement begins.

effective dose equivalent In drug testing and environmental health, this is the summation of the products of the dose equivalent received by specified tissues of the body and a tissue-specific weighting factor. This sum is a risk-equivalent value and is used to estimate the health effects of the exposed individual.

effectiveness 1. In health-care administration, this is the extent to which an intended managerial effect or benefit is achieved under optimal conditions; how well managerial operations are successful and how completed goals and objectives produce the desired outcome. 2. In therapeutics, treatments, and medications, the degree to which diagnostic, preventive, therapeutic, or other actions achieve the intended result. Effectiveness requires a consideration of outcomes but does not require consideration of the cost of the action. Although the federal Food, Drug, and Cosmetic Act requires prior demonstration of effectiveness for most drugs marketed for human use, no similar requirement exists for most other medical actions paid for or regulated under federal or state law. Usually synonymous with "efficacy" in common use. *See also quality; efficiency; safety.*

effects Personal property; one's personal belongings.

effects modifier In epidemiology, this is any condition or factor of a study that changes the effect of causality; observed differences in measures of association. *See causality, association; risk analysis; confounding variable.*

efferent Moving away from the center.

efficacy 1. The results of actions undertaken under ideal circumstances or results under usual or normal circumstances. Actions can be efficacious and effective or efficacious and ineffective but not the reverse. 2. In health promotion, the ability of an intervention to show that it can be beneficial in those exposed to it. 3. In health services, the extent to which benefits to patients are achievable under ideal conditions.

efficiency 1. The quality of an output achieved for a given level of input while conserving resources; the relationship between the quantity of inputs used in the production of health services and the quantity of outputs produced. Efficiency has three components: input productivity (technical efficiency), input mix (economic efficiency), and the scale of operation. Efficiency is usually measured by indicators such as output per man-hour or cost per unit of output. 2. In health-care administration, the amount of waste reduced, resources used wisely and conserved, quality and quantity of work produced, and/or units of services realized as compared to the amount of effort, cost, manpower, and time spent; a measure of resources consumed (e.g., time, labor, and material) in relation to the effects produced or the outputs experienced.

effluent 1. Flowing out, flowing forth. Something that flows forth, such as sewage out of a pipe. 2. In public health, the outflow of a sewer, storage tank, pipe, canal, or channel that causes pollution. Wastewater (treated or untreated) that flows out of a treatment plant, sewer, or industrial discharge pipe or ditch. Generally refers to waters discharged into surface waters. 3. In environmental health, treated or untreated air emissions or liquid discharges. Airborne or liquid wastes deliberately discharged without treatment and effluent controls. Solid waste, waste for shipment off-site, and wastes that are contained or stored are not included.

effluent limitations In environmental health, these are restrictions on quantities, rates, and concentrations of chemical, physical, biological, and other constituents of waste water discharges that are discharged from point sources into surface waters.

effluent monitoring In environmental health, this is the collection and analysis of samples, or measurements of liquid or gaseous effluents, for the purpose of characterizing and quantifying contaminants, assessing radiation exposure to the public, providing a means to control effluents at or near the point of discharge, and demonstrating compliance with applicable standards and permit requirements.

e.g. (Lat.) Exempli gratia. Used in writing, meaning "for example."

ego (Lat.) The self. In psychoanalytic theory, the ego, id, and superego are the three parts of the psychic apparatus. The ego represents certain mental mechanisms and serves to mediate between the demands of primitive instinctual drives (the id), internalized parental and social prohibitions (the superego), and reality.

egomania Serious or pathological self-centeredness or self-preoccupation.

egregious Negatively exceptional; known for negative qualities; infamous.

EHIP See *employee health insurance plan*.

EHL Electrohydraulic lithotripsy. See *lithotripsy*.

EHSDS See *Experimental Health Service Delivery System*.

EIS See *Epidemic Intelligence Service*.

ejusdem generis (Lat.) Of the same kind of class or type.

EKG See *electrocardiogram*.

elasticity of demand A measure of the sensitivity of demand for a product or service to changes in its price (price elasticity) or the income of those demanding the product or service (income elasticity).

elder abuse Taking unfair advantage of vulnerable older adults to the point of exploitation and/or doing emotional, mental, and physical harm. The Select Committee on Aging set forth six categories of elder abuse: physical abuse, negligence, financial exploitation, psychological abuse, violation of rights, and self-neglect.

elder care Nursing and health care of older adults at home by family or friends.

el doctor (Spanish) Physician. See also *medico*.

elective 1. Optional; any need, want, or demand that can be met at a later time. 2. Any treatment, therapy, or health care service that is advisable but can be delayed without substantial risk to the patient and is not immediately necessary and does not jeopardize health or life.

elective benefit In managed care or insurance, this is a benefit payable in lieu of another. For example, a lump sum benefit may be allowed for specified injuries in lieu of a weekly or monthly indemnity.

elective surgery Surgery or a procedure that need not be performed on an emergency basis because reasonable delays will not affect the outcome or surgical results in an unfavorable way. Any procedure or surgery that can be performed at a convenient time.

electro- Prefix meaning "electricity."

electroanesthesia Anesthesia by use of electric current passed through tissue.

electrocardiogram (ECG or **EKG)** A tracing of the heart muscle's electrical impulses recorded at the body surface; a medical test used to measure the electrical activity of the heart and for diagnosis.

electrocardiograph An electronic device that measures and records the heart's impulses on a graph called an electrocardiogram.

electrocardiographic effect Changes in the electrical activity of the heart, usually caused by the effect of drugs.

electrocardiographic technician/technologist A person who maintains and operates electrocardiographic machines in clinical settings or private offices. This technician also may conduct other tests such as vectorcardiograms and phonocardiograms, schedule appointments, and maintain EKG files, depending on the healthcare setting. The data generated by the electrocardiogram are supplied by the technician to the physician, usually an internist or cardiologist, to diagnose, treat, or monitor change in a patient's heart over time.

electrocardiographic technology An educational program that prepares persons to operate and make minor repairs on electrocardiographic equipment.

electrocardiography services The EKG or ECG technician assists in recording the electrical impulses produced by the heart muscles. The graph recordings are reviewed and interpreted by a physician, usually a cardiologist, to assess heart conditions.

electrocautery In medical care, this is the destruction of tissue for medical reasons by the use of a hot needle or snare that is inserted into warts, polyps, or other tumorous growths to burn them off.

electroconvulsive therapy (ECT) 1. A psychiatric

treatment procedure primarily used to treat depression. Electric current is passed through the brain to induce unconsciousness or convulsive seizures, which may reduce or eliminate depression. 2. According to JCAHO for psychiatric, alcoholism, and drug abuse facilities accreditation purposes, a form of somatic treatment in which electrical current is applied to the brain, producing uncoordinated muscle contraction in a convulsive manner.

electroencephalogram (EEG) In medical care, this is a tracing-type recording obtained from attaching electrodes to the skull. From the electrical activity of nerve cells in the brain, a record is made on either a paper graph or an oscilloscope.

electroencephalograph In medical care, this is an electrical instrument that records the electrical activity of the brain on a graph called an electroencephalogram with a record of the exam made on a paper graph or oscilloscope.

electroencephalographic technician The EEG technician operates and helps maintain encephalographs, which record tracings of the brain's electrical activity. Depending on the health-care setting, the EEG technician usually schedules appointments, assists the physician, and maintains EEG patient medical records.

electroencephalographic technology An educational program that prepares a person to operate and make minor repairs on electroencephalographic equipment.

electroencephalography An EEG technician uses an electroencephalograph to record a patient's brain waves. Electrodes are attached to the patient's head, recordings are made, and the results are interpreted by a physician. Tracings obtained from the electroencephalograph are used by physicians, usually neurologists, to diagnose and monitor the progress of such disorders as epilepsy, tumors, cerebral vascular strokes, and head injuries. The use of EEGs in determining the cessation of brain function has also made this procedure important in vital organ (heart, kidney, liver) transplant operations.

electrohydraulic lithotripsy (EHL) *See lithotripsy; lithotripter.*

electromagnetic radiation A therapeutic type of radiation that has electric and magnetic components that oscillate perpendicular to each other.

electromyogram (EMG) A recording of the electrical activity of the muscles.

electromyographic technician An individual who assists physicians in recording and analyzing bioelectric potentials originating in muscle tissue. This information is used to diagnose and monitor various disease processes. The electromyographic technician operates and helps maintain the various electronic equipment used to gather this information and assists in patient care and record keeping.

electroneurodiagnostic technologist (ENDT) An allied health professional who assists neurologists in the diagnostic testing of patients.

electronic calendar In health-care information management and computers, this is a software program used in maintaining an accurate schedule and as a reminder of important events such as meetings and deadlines.

electronic data interchange (EDI) In health information management and computers, this is an interactive processing concept that is highly automated for producing, purchasing, invoicing, billing, and order-delivery confirmation directly through computer linkages. More than a software system and an order-delivery system, this is an electronic, automated, interactive process whereby health-care organizations can shop, buy, order, receive confirmations, pay, and control inventories through one automated system connected with all manufacturers, distributors, and buying groups.

electronic data processing (EDP) In health information management and computers, the accumulation, analysis, and processing of data through electronic computers.

electronic fetal monitoring In medical care, this is the attachment of electrodes to the abdomen of a woman in the late stages of pregnancy to continuously monitor the fetal heart rate and uterine contractions. An internal amniotic fluid catheter and pressure transducer are also used to detect abnormal fetal cardiac patterns during labor and delivery.

electronic filing In health-care information management, this is the use of computers to store and retrieve information. Documents and messages are filed in electronic memory the same way an individual would file paper documents in a file cabinet.

electronic mail In health-care information management, this is a software/hardware interactive computer system that sends, receives, and stores messages on other persons' computers through a computer communications network linked to all systems users. Commonly referred to as "e-mail."

eleemosynary 1. Charitable, relating to or given by charity; gratuitous, free. 2. A hospital or other organization that receives or is supported by charity.

element 1. The first and most fundamental principal or part; a basic part. 2. In health facilities regulation, these are the regulatory certification requirements that explicate standards and conditions of participation.

elephant policy In insurance, this is a slang term indicating that benefits are difficult to collect. It is based on the concept that one must be run over by an elephant before receiving benefits from the policy. Also referred to as a "trolley car policy" for the same reason. *See trolley car policy.*

elevator 1. In orthopedic injury care, this is a device used to raise a broken bone of the skull or cheek. 2. In dentistry, a plier- or lever-like device that lifts a tooth up and out of its socket during extraction.

eligibility Meeting minimum guidelines, usually income and monetary levels, established by government agencies, services, or programs to participate in the program or service; meeting requirements, guidelines, qualifying criteria, or regulations to participate.

eligibility date In managed care, this is the exact day of the week or month on which an employee or his or her dependents can begin to use medical coverage of a health plan under the group subscriber agreement.

eligibility, home health care For Medicare coverage, two major criteria must be substantiated for eligibility: 1) the patient must be homebound and 2) the patient must be homebound because of medical necessity. Both criteria must be met to meet Medicare requirements. *See also homebound.*

eligibility, Medicaid To be eligible for benefits under Medicaid, an individual must meet the minimum guidelines that are established by each state as directed by federal guidelines. Usually anyone who qualifies for the following four federal programs is also eligible for Medicaid: Aid to the Blind, Aid to the Permanently and Totally Disabled, Old Age Assistance, and Aid to Families with Dependent Children. States may optionally provide for those categorized as medically needy who earn incomes too large to meet public assistance eligibility but do not have sufficient income to pay medical bills. *See indigent.*

eligibility period 1. In managed care, this is the time during which potential members may enroll in group life or health insurance programs without providing evidence of insurability. 2. The time period under a major medical health insurance policy during which reimbursable expenses can be accrued.

eligible Legally qualified; worthy of receiving; meeting legal requirements of government assistance programs such as Medicaid; capable or qualified to participate. *See eligibility, Medicaid.*

eligible dependent In managed care and medical insurance, this is any member of the worker's family or anyone who relies on the worker for their subsistence and qualifies as a dependent set forth by the health plan agreement and for whom the premium is paid.

eligible employee In managed care and medical insurance, this is any worker who has paid the premium or had it paid for and has met the requirements for medical care coverage under a group employer contract or health plan agreement. Usually the requirements are that the worker be a permanent full-time employee working 35 or more hours per week and 40 hours or more per 2-week pay period.

eligible expenses In managed care and medical insurance, any worker who meets the qualification requirements set forth in the employer group contract or health plan agreement.

elimination period 1. In managed care, these are the first days of confinement caused by illness or injury not covered by the health plan or the medical insurance policy. 2. In disability insurance, the period of time between the onset of a disability and the start of a disability income when no indemnities/benefits are payable.

ELISA *See enzyme-linked immunosorbent assay.*

elixir A liquid preparation usually containing alcohol, glycerin, or syrup used as a medium or vehicle to carry medicine or drugs.

emancipated No longer under the control of another. *See emancipation.*

emancipation Removal of control or influence; setting free. A young adult (teenager) can become emancipated when he or she is mature enough and shows enough self-responsibility that parents have no further control over or parental duties to them. A teenager who can prove total self-sufficiency, self-responsibility, and self-reliance (e.g., maintaining a job, attending and finishing school, paying rent, being financially self-reliant, and not being in trouble with the law) can apply to the courts for emancipation from his or her parents according to state and local laws.

embalming The process of preserving dead bodies using chemical compounds, usually formaldehyde, to delay putrefaction.

embezzlement In criminal law, this is the fraudulent appropriation of money or goods entrusted to one's care by another.

embracery Attempted corruption of a juror; jury fixing.

EMCRO *See Experimental Medical Care Review Organization.*

emergency 1. A sudden and unexpected illness or injury; any sudden and immediate threat to life or health; a demand that must be met immediately; a situation that requires immediate care to prevent death, serious injury, illness, disability, deformity, or death. 2. Any condition requiring first aid and/or immediate medical attention; any condition that in the opinion of an individual or his or her family warrants medical attention from a health-care provider or health-care facility that provides emergency medical care to the public. *See first aid.*

emergency admission When a sick or injured patient is brought into a definitive care medical environment for emergency care or surgery that needs to be cared for or treated immediately, as compared to elective admission or elective surgery, which can be delayed without harm to the patient's health.

emergency care Treatment and care for patients with severe, life-threatening, or potentially disabling conditions, injuries, or illnesses that require intervention within minutes or hours. Most hospitals and services providing emergency care also provide care for many conditions that providers would not consider emergencies, suggesting that consumers define the term almost synonymously with "primary care" and use such programs as screening clinics. *See also emergency medical service system.*

emergency center, freestanding A non–hospital-based, community-based emergency room, conveniently located in a community or area for the purpose of decreasing travel time to emergency care and to serve as an outpatient facility for minor medical emergencies. Such a facility helps increase the availability, accessibility, and distribution of emergency and some outpatient health-care services. Major emergencies may or may not be treated in this type of facility depending on the sophistication of center equipment and staffing.

emergency department A unit found in most major hospitals that operates on a 24-hour basis and is organized to provide for unscheduled emergency care and/or outpatient services to those requiring immediate medical attention.

emergency department admission 1. Usually, any patient being admitted through the emergency room prior to normal business hours for surgery and in need of preoperative preparations or testing. These procedures or tests may be conducted in the emergency room just prior to surgery, especially if it is an early morning surgery and the facility is operating on a limited night shift staff with no other personnel available to make the preparations. 2. This can also refer to any patient seen first in the emergency room for treatment and then admitted to the hospital for further treatment or observation.

emergency department outpatient visit A provision available in some hospital emergency rooms where minor nonemergency health-care needs are treated and the patient is not admitted to the hospital; an outpatient clinic visit administratively provided through the emergency room.

emergency department visit The admission of a patient to the emergency room of a hospital for treatment of seriously acute illnesses or injuries. Once the patient is stabilized, he or she either is admitted to the hospital for further treatment or observation or is discharged.

emergency/disaster science An educational program that trains individuals in the methods and techniques of providing emergency health-care services and treatment within the community, especially after a major disaster in the community, outside an emergency unit or hospital.

emergency hospital services A hospital-based service or department that provides immediate emergency care on a 24-hour basis for acutely ill or injured patients and for some patients who may not be acutely ill. Some hospitals may have their own ambulance service to augment the hospital emergency services. Emergency medicine is a fairly new medical specialty, and some hospitals contract emergency services out to a group of emergency physicians.

emergency kit According to JCAHO for psychiatric, alcoholism, and drug abuse facilities accreditation purposes, a kit that includes the medical supplies and pharmaceutical agents required during an emergency. In compiling emergency kits, staff should consider the patient's needs for psychotropic, anticholinergic, and adrenalin agents.

emergency medical condition Under the Consolidated Omnibus Budget Reconciliation Act of 1985 (COBRA), this is any medical condition manifesting itself by acute symptoms of sufficient severity (including severe pain) that the absence of immediate medical attention could reasonably be expected to result in placing the patient's health in serious jeopardy, serious impairment to bodily functions, or serious dysfunction of any bodily organ or part.

emergency medical services (EMS) The provision and organization of medical services, ambulance transportation, and personnel trained in emergency medical and paramedical techniques for the treatment of trauma, injuries, serious illnesses, and other medical emergencies in the community.

emergency medical services board A state agency and licensing body that is responsible for licensing emergency medical technicians and paramedics, sets standards for ambulances and freestanding emergency centers, and provides coordination and oversight for all emergency medical services for the state.

emergency medical services system (EMSS) An integrated system of appropriate health manpower, facilities, and equipment that provides all necessary emergency care in a defined geographic area. The development of such systems is federally assisted under the Emergency Medical Services Systems Act of 1973 (P.L. 93-154), which defines the necessary components of the system (Sections 1201 and 1206 of the PHS Act). One characteristic of such a system is a central communications facility that uses the universal emergency telephone number, 911, and that has direct communications with all parts of the system with planned dispatching of cases to properly categorized facilities.

Emergency Medical Services System Act of 1973 Congress mandated through this act (P.L. 93-154) that the provision of emergency medical care utilize a systems approach. The 15 elements of an emergency medical system are 1) enough manpower to provide 24-hour care, 2) adequate training programs for all levels of EMS care on a regional level, 3) an emergency medical communication system, 4) transportation capabilities available at a regional level, 5) the development of specialized emergency facilities, 6) advancement of critical care units, 7) integration of EMS with public safety agencies, 8) consumer participation, 9) a guarantee of accessibility of care, 10) continuity in transfer of patients, 11) standardization of medical records, 12) advancement of consumer education, 13) ongoing review and evaluation, 14) linkage to disaster programs, and 15) the creation of regional and interregional mutual aid agreements.

emergency medical technician (EMT) As part of the emergency medical team, this individual responds to and provides immediate care to the critically ill or injured and transports them to medical facilities. The EMT determines the nature and extent of illness or injury and establishes either first-aid procedures to be followed or the need for additional assistance. EMTs administer prescribed first-aid treatment at the site of the emergency or in specially equipped vehicles. They communicate with professional medical personnel at emergency treatment facilities to obtain instructions regarding further treatment and to arrange for reception of victims at the treatment facility. *See also paramedic.*

emergency medical technician, advanced *See emergency medical technician, intermediate (IEMT or EMT-II).*

emergency medical technician, intermediate (IEMT or EMT-II) Many states have different levels or designations of emergency medical technicians and ways of differentiating levels of expertise and training. This level is more advanced than an EMT and less qualified than a paramedic. Under the direction of a physician, this level of emergency medical technician can administer certain advanced medical interventions such as giving injections and starting IVs.

emergency medical technology, ambulance An educational program that prepares persons to function in emergencies such as treating cardiopulmonary problems using cardiac resuscitation and emergency equipment such as airways, splints, bandages, and dressings and managing emergencies such as exposure to heat or cold, automobile accidents, industrial accidents, and all injuries caused by other accidents. This is the lowest level of emergency care professional training program.

emergency medical technology, paramedic An educational program that prepares persons to function in serious emergency situations and to provide prehospital emergency care, including cardiac field care, starting and using IVs, and giving injections. The training includes knowledge about acute care and the critical differences in physiology, pathophysiology, or clinical symptoms so that appropriate emergency assessment and treatment can be provided and the necessary information communicated to a responsible and responding emergency physician at an emergency room or emergency center. The program was created by the U.S. Department of Transportation and requires the completion of a 15-module program or its equivalent. *See also paramedic.*

emergency medicine A medical specialty that trains physicians in the most current procedures and treatments in the care of medical emergencies. Care is usually provided in a hospital setting or freestanding emergency care center. The training usually involves a residency or specialty field training and also prepares the emergency physician to be in charge of the associated field emergency care personnel.

emergency patients Outpatients who are acutely ill or injured and who use or are brought to a hospital emergency room or a freestanding emergency center for emergency treatment.

emergency physician *See emergency medicine.*

Emergency Planning and Community Right-to-Know Act This act requires each state to appoint a state emergency response commission. Every state must be divided into emergency response planning districts, each with a local emergency planning commission (LEPC). Each commission is to be composed of elected officials, law enforcement, civil defense, firefighting organizations, first aid, health-care providers, hospitals, environmental health, transportation, community groups, media, and companies that manufacture or store chemicals.

emergency preparedness plan A component of a hospital's safety management program designed to manage the consequences of natural disasters or other emergencies that disrupt the hospital's ability to provide care and treatment (JCAHO for acute-care hospitals).

emergency response program (ERP) Legally established to be an ongoing program and maintained in a readiness state, this regionally based emergency response system is required to have nine elements: 1) administration, 2) emergency response organization, 3) emergency response training and retraining, 4) emergency response facilities and equipment, 5) emergency plan implementing procedures, 6) coordination with off-site agencies, 7) drills and exercises, 8) communications, and 9) hazard evaluation.

emergency response system In the care of the elderly, this is an organized and coordinated electronic communication system that permits older adults to live alone and frail persons to easily call for help. Such systems use portable call buttons that alert a central communications center. Devices that attach to the body can also be activated by a change in the pulse or respiratory rate. Long-term-care facilities, home health agencies, and senior housing projects may also use such response systems.

emergency response team A community-based response organization trained and prepared to handle firefighting, medical emergencies, spill cleanups, disasters, rescues, and a variety of other related duties.

emergency response time *See response time.*

emergency room (ER) *See emergency department.*

emergency services 1. Programs or departments established and organized for the purpose of administering services to meet emergency or disaster situations. Such services are coordinated with sheriff, police, and fire departments and other community response systems to render temporary medical help by responding to, evaluating, and assisting in emergency situations and transporting sick or injured persons to definitive care centers such as a hospital emergency room. Ambulances (public or privately held) and the emergency response/disaster section of the Red Cross are examples of emergency services. 2. The delivery of emergency care to patients. Standards are applied to evaluate a hospital's performance in providing emergency care (JCAHO for acute-care hospitals). 3. Under Medicaid, this is health services required for the alleviation of severe pain or immediate diagnosis and treatment of unforeseen medical conditions that, if not immediately diagnosed and treated, could lead to disability or death.

emergency services, levels of care (IV) A classification system based on specific and general requirements that describes the capability of a hospital to provide a range of emergency services for patients who need them. For example, a hospital with level I emergency services offers comprehensive emergency care 24 hours a day, at least one physician experienced in emergency care on duty in the emergency care area, and in-hospital physician coverage by members of the medical staff or senior-level residents for at least medical, surgical, orthopedic, obstetric/gynocologic, pediatric, and anesthesia services (JCAHO for acute-care hospitals).

emergency surgery Serious injuries, illnesses, and life-threatening cases admitted to a hospital emergency room or being treated in a hospital or surgical center that must be immediately treated surgically. Delayed treatment may result in serious impairment of the patient's health or possibly result in death.

emergency, true Any serious clinical condition requiring immediate medical care to survive or immediate treatment for serious injury. After testing, diagnosis, and observation, the patient may be released or admitted to the hospital for further treatment and observation.

emergi-center See *freestanding emergency center*.

EMG See *electromyogram*.

eminent domain The government's right to take private property for public use on payment or compensation for it.

emission standards In environmental health, this is the maximum amount of a pollutant allowed to be discharged from a single source. See *effluent*.

emotional deprivation Lack of sufficient and appropriate interpersonal relations and love, especially in the early developmental years. Separation from one's mother or a child experiencing poor mothering, neglect, and abuse can contribute to emotional problems because of lack of love.

emotional distress In health law, this term is used in a legal medical context to describe emotional trauma for which courts have awarded recovery money when included as part of malpractice suits. Recovery is rarely awarded by itself for emotional distress. A third-party witness to a distressing event may claim emotional distress, but this concept is difficult to measure and to assess objectively. See *stress, recovery*.

emotional support Encouragement, hope, and inspiration given to patients who are ill, injured, recovering, or disabled.

empacho (Spanish) A disease occurring mostly in children that is characterized by a swollen abdomen as a result of an intestinal blockage; surfeit, indigestion.

empirical Based on or relying on observation, experiment, or research.

empirical research Scientific research using the utmost scientific controls and objective observations and experiments and employing only recognized and accepted research designs, sampling procedures, statistical analyses, and ethical reporting practices.

employee An individual who is formally hired by and works for another person or an organization for pay and draws benefits. An employee agrees to give up personal time, space (location), and personal control and to put forth effort in exchange for pay.

employee assistance program (EAP) When groups of workers or companies help employees overcome personal problems by setting up programs related to counseling, drug, alcohol, family, stress, emotional problems, and helth promotion and wellness for smoking, weight loss, health counseling, physical fitness, health screening, and health education.

employee benefit program In health administration and human resource management, these are workers' benefits provided by the employer and not included in the employee's gross salary. Medical insurance, disability income, retirement, and life insurance, paid for all or in part by the employer, may be provided.

employee benefits Nonpayroll expenses; the extra cost-related factors that offset employee salaries, including amounts paid by the employer that are not included in the gross salary. Such payments are usually considered fringe benefits and, although not paid directly to employees, are a part of the cost of salaries and benefits and include group medical or life insurance, contributions to employee retirement, professional fees, educational benefits, etc.

employee contribution In managed care, this is the amount of money the worker pays toward the premium for medical care insurance or health plan coverage; that part of a medical care insurance premium the worker must pay, with the rest paid by the employer. See *employer contribution*.

employee handbook A document developed by the human resource department of a healthcare organization explaining key benefits, policies, rules, and information about the organization.

employee health (medical) benefit plan A benefit package plan made available for workers of companies and organizations that includes a managed-care plan choice for the worker and dependents.

employee health insurance plan (EHIP) One of the three parts of a national health insurance proposal.

employee health services Health-care services provided to workers of major organizations or hospitals that can include such services as pre-employment screening programs, primary care, some secondary care services and treatment, emergency care, health education, and health promotion activities but that do not replace the primary care physician.

Employee Polygraph Protection Act A federal law prohibiting the use of polygraphs in private industries such as hospitals, HMOs, or other health-care organizations. The act forbids the employer from directly or indirectly requiring, requesting, or causing any employee or prospective employee to take or submit to a lie detector test. Restrictions also cover the use of information regarding results of such a test and the taking of adverse employment action against any employee who refuses, declines, or fails to take a lie detector test.

Employee Retirement Income Security Act of 1974 (ERISA) A federal law (P.L. 93-406) affecting the financial position of employees covered by a retirement plan. The act prescribes minimum federal standards for funding, participation, vesting, termination, and disclosure responsibility of fiduciary and tax treatment of private retirement plans. A provision of the act allows self-funded health plans to avoid paying premium taxes or complying with state-mandated benefits. An explanation of benefits (EOB) is to be provided to each plan member in the event of a claim denial, explaining why a claim was denied and informing the member of his or her rights of appeal. *See also Pension Reform Act of 1974.*

employee stock ownership plan (ESOP) An approach to the ownership of an organization such as a hospital through an incentive structure in which a company contributes money to a trust fund used to purchase shares of the company's own stock for the workers. At the end of each fiscal year, the organization contributes to a trust fund on the basis of a percentage of each employee's annual salary.

employee wellness and health promotion programs A preventive health-care service provided by companies either at the worksite or at an adjacent location that is aimed at preventing illness and injury and also boosting employee morale and job satisfaction. Health screening, assessment, behavioral health, health counseling, rehabilitation, physical fitness, and health education activities are utilized to establish a preventive care and health promotion perspective in the participants. Some companies establish these programs simply as an employee benefit, whereas others are created to reduce physician hospital visits and health care costs. Worksite health promotion increases health status and decreases the costs of employee medical insurance premiums, resulting in tremendous savings to the company. *See worksite health promotion.*

employer A person or organization who selects employees; pays their salaries and worker benefits; retains power over workers' time, location of work, and dismissal; and directs their conduct during working hours.

employer contribution In managed care and medical insurance, this is the amount of money that the company, organization, or business pays toward the premium of a health plan or medical insurance for the worker. The amount is based on a variety of factors such as percentage, employment status, contracts negotiated by unions, and family status. *See employee contribution.*

employer eligibility requirements In managed care, these are the conditions of employment set by the organization/employer that must be met by all employees to be eligible for group health coverage.

employer mandate According to National Health Security programs and universal coverage and required by federal law, small businesses must purchase as much as 80% or more of the health-care benefits for their workers to guarantee medical care insurance coverage for all workers in the United States.

employment at will The circumstance under which most workers accept a position with a hospital or other health-care organization; a worker freely accepting a job without a personal employment contract or a union contract.

employment freeze This is when a hospital or health-care organization halts all hiring of workers, usually because of low occupancy rates or financial difficulties.

employment function In health-care administration and human resource management, these are the personnel functions of recruiting, selecting, and hiring new employees.

employment interview In health-care administration and human resource management, this is the type of interview that furnishes an administrator and a job applicant the opportunity to determine if the candidate is qualified and suited for a position and if the job is suited for the candidate.

employment references In health-care administration and human resource management, these are recommendations and assessments of a worker from past employers or others who know the candidate; used to assist in hiring decisions.

employment-related insurance In managed care, this is group medical insurance obtained through employers or labor unions, whether or not the employer pays any or all of the premium.

employment tests In health administration and human resource management, assessment, and evaluation, instruments used to assess aptitude and interest and to match applicants to jobs.

emporiatrics A subspecialty of medicine specializing in treating conditions or illnesses associated with travel or travelers.

empowerment In health-care administration, this is the use of management knowledge and approaches to influence working conditions and organization policies as applied to mid- and lower-level managers and employees; the delegation of authority and responsibility to those under one's charge, motivating them to be more productive, effective, and efficient on the job. *See community health education empowerment.*

emptor (Lat.) A buyer; a purchaser.

EMS Emergency medical services.

EMSS *See emergency medical services system.*

EMT *See emergency medical technician.*

EMT-A Emergency medical technician, ambulance. A designation given to those who successfully complete the 80-hour course as set forth by the U.S. Department of Transportation. These allied health-care professionals work in ambulances and are usually the first medically trained personnel to arrive at the scene of an accident or serious illness. Most states require EMTs to be certified. *See also emergency medical technician.*

EMT-I Emergency medical technician, intermediate. These are emergency medical technicians who have completed advanced training in life support that includes advanced field cardiac treatment, IV training, and injections. This level of training is greater than that of EMTs and less than that of paramedics. Some states offer certification at this level. *See also emergency medical technician, intermediate.*

EMT-P Emergency medical technician, paramedic. These are emergency medical technicians who have completed advanced training in life support beyond that of EMT-A and EMT-I. The required training includes a 15-module program, and most are state certified. *See also emergency medical technology, paramedic.*

emulation In health information management and computers, when one software computer program causes a computer to respond to another computer and its software.

emulator In health information management and computers, when a computer hardware device permits a software program to be run on a different type of computer than it was written for.

en (French, Spanish) In.

enable To give authority, power, or opportunity to act.

enabling clause The portion of a law that provides officials with the power to put a statute into effect and to enforce it.

enabling factors In health promotion and health education planning, these are any environmental factors, skills, or resources required to attain the desired health behavior.

enabling statute A law that provides power to a public official or public office.

enact 1. To make into. 2. To put a law into effect. 3. To establish a law; to decree.

encapsulation suit In environmental health and hazardous waste management, this is protective clothing used in hazardous waste situations. For maximum respirator and skin protection, the Environmental Protection Agency requires "level A" protective equipment for worst-case scenarios. This type of suit protects the worker and respiratory systems from hazardous materials or fumes. Three factors are considered when selecting this type of protective garment: 1) chemical resistance, 2) integration of suit with respiratory protection equipment, and 3) accessories and options for special circumstances.

en banc (Lat.) On the bench; With all judges sitting in the court. *See also in banco.*

enceinte (French) Pregnant.

encoding The use of specific signs and symbols to communicate a message.

encopresis Involuntary passage of feces, usually during sleep.

encounter 1. A contact between a patient and health professional in which care is given; a face-to-face interaction between the health-care provider and the member of a health plan during which medical and health services are rendered. Some definitions exclude both telephone contacts or home visits. 2. Under Medicaid managed care programs, a record of a medically related service (or visit) rendered by a provider to a beneficiary who is enrolled in a "local initiative" during the time of service. It includes, but is not limited to, all the services for which the contractor incurred a financial liability.

encounters per member per year In managed care, this is the number of face-to-face interactions between the health-care provider and the members of a health plan whereby medical and health services are rendered on a yearly basis. The formula for encounters per member per year follows:

$$\frac{\text{Total number of encounters per year}}{\text{Total number of members per year}}$$

encroach 1. To gradually intrude; to advance beyond acceptable or prescribed limits. 2. The extending of one's rights over another person's rights. 3. To go beyond customary limits; inroads beyond proper or original limits.

encumber 1. To hold back an action. 2. To burden and load down with claims or debts.

encumbrance In law, this is to put a claim or lien on an estate; a claim or lien against property.

endocrine A part of anatomy and physiology that refers to the organs of the body that produce secretions in the body.

endocrinologist This is a physician who has completed a residency and is board certified and specializes in the treatment of the organs of the body that produce internal secretions and related serums and biochemicals.

endocrinology In medicine, this is the specialty of medicine dealing with organs of internal secretion.

endemic In epidemiology and public health, this is a disease or disorder that is native or restricted to a particular area; the usual presence of disease or disorder observed in a given area and a given population.

endemic disease In epidemiology and public health, this is a persistent and constant presence of a disease within a given geographical area or population group; the usual level of prevalence of a disease in a population in a particular area.

endodontics The specialty in dentistry that studies the etiology, diagnosis, prevention, and treatment of conditions of the teeth that affect the dental pulp and other periodontal tissues, including pulp canal and root canal therapy and surgery.

endogenous 1. Coming from within. 2. Derived from within the body.

endorsement 1. The recognition by one state, of the license of another state, when the qualifications and standards required by the original licensing state are equivalent to or more stringent than those of the endorsing state. 2. In managed care or medical insurance, this is a provision added to a subscriber contract that widens the scope of coverage; modified rider.

endoscope In medical care, this is an instrument used to visually examine the interior of the body. For example, a proctoscope is used to visually examine the rectum and sigmoid colon.

endostomy therapist *See enterostomal therapist.*

endowment funds A fund, usually consisting of donations, established for a public nonprofit institution such as a hospital; a special fund established by a nonprofit health organization to accept monetary contributions from private sources. Only the interest from the contributions is allowed to be used to support operations or make purchases.

endpoint 1. The final recovery from a long-term illness; recovery from an acute illness. 2. Death from a long-term illness or injury. 3. In epidemiology, this is the final result from some exposure with either a positive or a negative result. Used in causation assessment, exposure-endpoint associations suggest that a risk relationship must exist for a cause-effect relationship to be established, but a sequence of events may be lacking and a scientific and rational connection may not exist.

ENDT *See electroneurodiagnostic technologist.*

energy In laser technology, this is the output from pulsed lasers that is generally expressed in joules or watt seconds.

enfranchise To make free; to naturalize; to allow political privileges.

engage 1. To promise or pledge. 2. Take part in; to be involved in; to encounter.

engineer, administrative *See engineer, chief (plant).*

engineer, chief (plant) An engineering professional working in a health-care facility who is responsible for overall day-to-day management of the facility's physical plant, physical environment, equipment, physical systems, grounds, maintenance, and general repair. Also referred to as the "administrative engineer" or "hospital engineer."

engineer, clinical An individual trained in health-care equipment and devices, working in a health-care facility's engineering department, who is responsible for the maintenance and safe use of the facility's instruments, electronic and mechanical devices, and equipment used in patient care treatment.

engineer, hospital *See engineer, chief (plant).*

engineer, industrial An individual trained in industrial engineering, working in a health-care facility's engineering department, who is responsible for the maintenance, improvement, and safe use of nonclinical equipment and electronic and mechanical devices in the facility. This engineering professional may also be responsible for assisting the health-care institution's administration in the management of material and human resources related to engineering activities. *See also engineer, chief (plant).*

engineering and maintenance department The special division in a health-care facility responsible for providing upkeep of the physical plant, especially for its major systems (electrical, heating, ventilation, air conditioning, water, telephone) and clinical equipment and devices. Emergency systems (emergency lighting, electrical services, and equipment) are also the responsibility of this department.

engineering controls In hospital or clinic sanitation and safety against blood pathogens, this is a means of controlling sharps disposal containers and self-sheathing needles that isolate or remove blood-borne pathogen hazards from the workplace.

en gros (Lat.) 1. In gross amounts. 2. Wholesale. 3. To buy in bulk or by the gross.

engross Make a final or official copy of a document.

enhanced external counterpulsation An alternative medicine treatment in which a patient has the lower part of the body encased in a suit that is pumped up, causing the blood in the extremities to be pumped from the legs up to the heart; this may open up new coronary blood vessels when a patient is experiencing a heart attack caused by plugged coronary arteries.

enhancement To augment; to make higher; increasing or making larger; to make greater or better.

enjoin 1. To forbid; to prohibit; to stop by injunction; to command or require. 2. A court order to stop a person from doing something. 3. Directing a person or persons to refrain from doing certain acts or to begin doing some acts.

enroll In managed care, this is to agree to participate in a contract for benefits from a health plan, insurance company, health maintenance organization, or other managed-care program. A person who enrolls is an enrollee, member, or subscriber. The number of people and their dependents who join a managed-care program constitutes its enrollment. *See also open enrollment.*

enrolled bill A bill that is going through the proper legislative process.

enrolled member In managed care, this is a subscriber, spouse, or dependent who has been accepted for medical care under a health plan or medical insurance program by completing the proper application, meeting eligibility criteria, and making the necessary payments.

enrollee 1. One who is enrolled; a member; a subscriber. An individual, dependent, or worker who is a paid subscriber of a health plan. 2. In managed care, this is an individual and/or a dependent who is eligible for and entitled to receive a specific set of medical care services from a health plan. Prepayment is usually a requirement of health plan enrollment. 3. Under Medicaid, this is one who is enrolled in a health plan under contract with the state Medicaid program.

enrollment 1. In managed care, this is the process by which a health plan signs up individuals or employee groups as members. 2. The number of members in a managed-care program; the numbers of enrollees assigned to certain health-care providers (physicians, hospitals, and medical groups) under a contract with a health plan. 3. The method that enables individuals, family members, and dependents to become eligible for medical insurance or benefits of a health plan. Two types of enrollment are available: 1) group: becoming a health plan member through an organization, usually a large employer covered by one plan, and 2) non-group: becoming a health plan member by direct purchase of a single policy covering an individual, dependents, or family members from an insurance company or agent, which can include the conversions of insurance over from a group. 4. In managed care, the process of converting an employer group into HMO members; the total number of members of an HMO at a given point in time; total health plan membership entitled to medical care coverage.

enrollment period In managed care, medical insurance, or other insurance, this is the period during which individuals may enroll or change benefits. Most contributory group insurance has an annual enrollment period when members of the group may elect to begin contributing and become covered. Under Medicare there are two types of enrollment periods: 1) supplementary medical insurance initial enrollment period (7 months beginning 3 months before and ending 3 months after the month a person first becomes eligible, usually by turning age 65) and 2) general enrollment period (the first 3 months of each year). *See also open enrollment.*

enrollment protection In managed care, this is a practice used in health plans to protect its contracted medical groups from partial or total losses incurred for health-care provider services, above a specified dollar amount, while caring for the health plan members.

ENT *See ear, nose, and throat.*

enter 1. To introduce; to admit. 2. To put in writing. 3. To file. 4. To go into; to become a part of; to formally write in the court record.

enteric coated A special coating used on tablets and capsules that delays the release of the drug until it is in the intestines.

enteric transmission In epidemiology, this is one of several modes of disease transmission whereby pathogens found in feces are ingested by susceptible individuals, usually through fecally contaminated hands, food, or water. *See modes of transmission.*

entering judgment In litigation and the legal process, at the end of a formal courtroom trial, the formal recording of a court's final decision in the court's permanent records.

enterostomal therapist An allied health care professional, usually a nurse, who is trained or accredited to provide treatment, maintenance, and therapy for a wound created by a stoma and its drainage.

enterprise liability In health-care law, this is the controlling of medical malpractice insurance premiums by a central controlling organization or a government agency.

entirety All; completely; a whole.

entitle 1. To give a title to; to be honored by a title. 2. To give claim to. 3. The right to something once legal requirements are met.

entitled Under Medicare, one who has established eligibility for Medicare benefits. Any elderly person 65 years or older must apply with the Social Security Administration before being entitled to benefits. In cases where the person failed to establish eligibility by age 65, benefits may be made retroactive, but not to exceed 1 year. Protection begins at age 65 but has been interpreted to begin on the first calendar day of the month in which the person becomes 65. Dependents and survivors of the deceased may qualify for benefits as well. Aliens who have met certain resident requirements may also qualify. *See also eligibility; medical eligibility.*

entitlement authority In the federal budget, legislation requires the payment of benefits or entitlements to any person or government meeting the requirements established by such law. Mandatory entitlements include Social Security benefits and veterans' pensions. Section 401 of the Congressional Budget and Impoundment Control Act of 1974 placed restrictions on the enactment of new entitlement authority. *See entitlements, mandatory.*

entitlement programs Under Social Security, this is a public trust into which all participants pay and are guaranteed a minimum income in old age or disability. This is not welfare because it is open to all who contribute.

entitlements, mandatory Under Social Security benefits and veterans' pensions and Section 401 of the Congressional Budget and Impoundment Control Act of 1974, eligible individuals have the right to participate in these programs; however, restrictions have been placed on the enactment of new entitlement authority. *See entitlement authority.*

entity 1. An existence; a real item.

enteral Pertaining to; into the small intestine.

entrapment In law, this is an act by a law enforcement officer or agency that induces a person to commit a crime that the person would otherwise not have done.

entrepreneur One who organizes a business undertaking and assumes risks for the sake of profit. An individual who has much creative business ambition and wherewithal and plays a leading, creative role in developing and organizing the implementation of a new business or enterprise. Often referred to as a "small-business owner."

entrepreneurship The creative risk-taking, adventurous spirit needed in developing new enterprises; the activities of an individual who creates, organizes, implements, and ensures success of a business or an organization that does not already exist. Characteristics that develop entrepreneurship are drive, mental ability, human relations skills, communications, and technical knowledge.

entrust To deliver something to another with a mutual understanding as to its use and the belief that the understanding will be honored. *See also intrust.*

entry-level health educator The level of training, knowledge, skill, and experience in health curriculum content, diseases and preventive care, health behavior, and educational approaches and methods at which an individual is capable of performing an educational role in health matters. The skills and knowledge necessary to perform in the entry-level health education role are obtained through successful completion of a bachelors degree program at an accredited university or college with a major in health education or an equivalent area. Also referred to as "health education associate" in some publicly supported programs. *See also health educator; health education; health promotion.*

entry, writ of A written order from a court to recover real property wrongfully withheld or taken.

enure 1. To take effect. 2. To a person's advantage. *See also inure.*

enuresis Bed-wetting.

envidia (Spanish) 1. Envy; a grudge; emulation. 2. An emotional disorder existing among the Mexican American culture, caused by fear and anger, that is based on the natural, emotional, and supernatural.

environment 1. Any or all aspects, conditions, or elements that make up an organism's surroundings and that influence its growth, development, survival, and behavior; all external conditions affecting the life, development, and survival of an organism. 2. The totality of biological, social, behavioral, and physical circumstances that help define the quality of life, health, and lifestyle goals. 3. As used in epidemiology, external factors and surroundings in which pathogens find harborage and subsistence or those factors that contribute to, affect, or influence the transmission of a disease, the course of a disease, or an epidemic.

environmental assessment In health-care administration and strategic planning, this is the observation, surveillance, and identification of changes in the operations, competition, and interactions of the health services in the community, with particular concern being focused on how these changes affect occupancy rates, admissions, customers/patients, physicians, managed-care plans, competitors, and the health-care organization.

Environmental Assessment Association (EAA) An international organization of professionals that provides environmental information to a wide constituency. The EAA awards two professional designations to qualified individuals in the real estate and environmental industries: CE (certified environmental inspector) and CER (certified environmental reviewer). An advanced designation, the CES (certified environmental specialist), is also offered. *See certified environmental inspector; certified environmental reviewer; certified environmental specialist.*

environmental diagnosis A systematic assessment of risk factors to individual and community health found in the social and physical domains that interact with behavior and affect health and quality of life.

environmental epidemiology The study of ecological factors that influence the distribution and determinants of disease in human populations; the study of ecological effects on the health of populations based on the physical, biological, and chemical factors in the external surroundings; the examination of specific populations exposed to different environmentally founded risk factors that seeks to clarify cause-effect and association relationships among physical, biological, and chemical factors and the health of the population.

environmental factor 1. An element or component of the biological, social, or physical aspects surrounding one's living activities that is determined by an environmental diagnosis and is shown to be causally linked to health, lifestyle, or quality-of-life goals. 2. An element in accident causation related to the way the workplace directly or indirectly contributes to accidents. Contributing factors include physical, chemical, biological, and ergonomic conditions.

environmental factors affecting the health of the residents A description of the environment in which individuals operate, live, or function and how it affects health.

environmental health The process of health hazard identification, detection, management, and control. Practitioners in this field are referred to as "sanitarians" or "environmentalists." Environmental health personnel are involved in inspections and regulatory activities and oversee the interpretation and enforcement of regulations and laws related to public health and safety. Public agencies monitor money aspects of the external environment, including air and water pollution, liquid waste management, solid waste management, food and milk surveillance, and institutional and eating establishment sanitation.

Environmental Health Association *See National Environmental Health Association.*

environmental health engineer This environmental health professional applies engineering principles to the control, elimination, and prevention of environmental hazards such as air pollution, water pollution, solids pollution, and noise pollution. Also referred to as a "sanitary engineer."

environmental health technician Having completed training at the associate degree level, the technician assists in the survey of environmental hazards and performs technical duties under professional supervision in many areas of environmental health such as pollution control, radiation protection, and sanitation protection. Also referred to as a "sanitary technician."

Environmental Protection Agency *See U.S Environmental Protection Agency.*

environmental quality management Those measures taken to protect the community from environmental hazards causing or contributing to disease, illness, injury, or death. Environmental hazards include air, water, and noise pollution; milk and food protection; solid waste disposal; housing and residential hazards control; vector control; recreational area hazards control; highway and traffic safety; and hazards related specifically to unsafe residential and community living.

environmental services Those public health and environmental health activities and processes that inspect, evaluate, and gather data for use in the design, operation, and control of systems for prevention and elimination of environmental hazards.

environmental services department A support service unit in a health-care facility that provides safety and sanitary services by controlling and monitoring liquid wastes, radiation materials, and solid waste and by controlling infection in the health-care facility. *See also environmental services.*

environmentalist A professional who plans, develops, inspects, enforces regulations and laws, and implements standards and systems to improve the quality of air, water, food, shelter, and other environmental factors in the community or industrial settings. This professional also manages comprehensive environmental health programs and promotes public awareness of the need to prevent and eliminate environmental health hazards. This person serves as a public health or environmental health "policeman." Also referred to as a "sanitarian." *See sanitarian.*

enzyme-linked immunosorbent assay (ELISA) An AIDS diagnostic test.

EO *See executive order.*

EOB Explanation of Benefits Statement. In managed care, this is a statement presented or mailed to health plan members explaining why a claim was or was not covered or paid.

EOC Evidence of Coverage. In managed care, this is the legally contractual document presented to health plan members that sets forth the terms of benefits and coverage.

EOMB Explanation of Medicare Benefits.

eo nomine (Lat.) Under that name.

EP Emergency physician.

EPA Environmental Protection Agency. *See U.S Environmental Protection Agency.*

EPCRA *See Emergency Planning and Community Right-to-Know Act.*

epidemic In public health and epidemiology, this is the widespread outbreak of a disease affecting significant numbers of persons in a specific population at any time; the high occurrence and large number of cases of a disease in many people, in a single community or relatively small area, in a specific, short time period.

Epidemic Intelligence Service (EIS) A special program of the Centers for Disease Control and Prevention that provides quality, comprehensive epidemiologic assistance in the investigation and prevention of public health problems wherever and whenever they arise. This is also a unique 2-year postgraduate program of service and on-the-job training for health professionals interested in the practice of epidemiology. Since 1951, thousands of EIS officers have responded to the call for epidemiologic assistance throughout the United States and the world. The EIS training involves epidemiologic investigations, research and public health surveillance, assisting state health departments in epidemiologic investigations, disseminating public health information, and giving presentations at national medical and public health conferences.

epidemiologic Pertaining to epidemiology; related to or referring to epidemiology.

epidemiological Pertaining to epidemiology; related to or referring to epidemiology or the process of epidemiology.

epidemiological autopsy *See autopsy, epidemiological.*

epidemiological diagnosis Assessing, testing, evaluating, and determining the extent, distribution, and causes of diseases, disorders, conditions, injuries, or deaths in a defined community or population.

epidemiologic reasoning A scientific process used in the determination of association between exposure to a disease, substance, chemical, or other risk factor and its endpoint (the formulation of causation relationships and the testing of hypotheses).

epidemiologist A highly trained health professional who studies the incidence, prevalence, spread, prevention, and control of disease in populations. These health professionals use observational methods, surveys, investigative approaches, statistical analyses, and data-gathering techniques to aid in the investigation of diseases or conditions that affect populations and the development of disease prevention and control methods and measures. As public health professionals, they usually have a masters degree (MS or MPH) or a doctoral degree such as a Doctor of Public Health (DrPH) or a PhD in health science or related academic areas, or are medical doctors with training in epidemiology or preventive medicine who work for universities, government health agencies, nonprofit health organizations, the military, or private industry.

epidemiologist, hospital A health professional who is responsible for the administration of a hospital's infection control program and related activities.

epidemiologist, medical A physician who studies and analyzes the occurrence of diseases in a specified population.

epidemiology The study of the nature, cause, control, and determinants of the frequency and distribution of diseases, conditions, injury, disability, and death in human populations. This involves characterizing the distribution in terms of age, sex, race, education, marital status, socioeconomic status, occupation, etc.; explaining the distribution of a disease or health problem in terms of time, place, and person (causal factors); and assessing and explaining the impact of control measures, clinical intervention, and health services on diseases and other problems. The epidemiology of a disease is the description of its presence in a population and the factors controlling its presence or absence. *See also incidence; prevalence; morbidity; mortality.*

epidemiology, analytic In epidemiology, this is a research perspective that tests hypotheses and the association between causative factors and disease. Retrospective, cohort, cross-sectional, prevalence, and prospective study designs are types of analytic studies used in epidemiology.

epidemiology, descriptive General observations about diseases, conditions, injuries, or death in populations through the use of characteristics such as age, sex, race, education, occupation, religion, and socioeconomic status as well as "time," "place," and "person," which are analyzed by rates, ratios, percentages, and proportions.

epidemiology triangle A graphic presentation of four factors that are foundational to the field of epidemiology. Three factors are locataed at each point of the triangle: environment, host, and agent. The fourth element, time, is located in the middle. The triangle is a model that shows the interactions and interdependence of the four elements in the investigation of diseases.

epidemiology triangle, advanced The basic concepts of the epidemiology triangle have been applied to create an advanced model in which causative factors replace agent, groups, or populations; their characteristics replace host; and environment, behavior, culture, physiological factors, and ecological elements replace environment. Time is found in the center of the triangle. The same interactive and interrelatedness of the four elements remain. The advanced model has been developed to more closely reflect current source and types of disease causation of modern times, which often involves behavior, lifestyle, risk factor exposure, occupational exposure, or chronic disease.

episode of care The continuous stay of a person as an inpatient in a health-care facility; identifies the sequence of care that is one measure of health-care services provided.

episode of illness Spell of illness; the course of a disease or an illness from onset to its endpoint.

episodes of persons injured In emergency care and health-care delivery, this is each time a person is involved in an accident or a violent act resulting in injury to the point of needing medical attention that results in at least half a day of restricted activity. This is not equivalent to the number of accidents because an accident may involve no injury or multiple injuries or a person may have more than one injury per accident (nonaccidental violence can also cause injury).

epizootic In epidemiology, this is an epidemic in animal populations that has the potential to affect humans.

EPO *See exclusive provider organization.*

eponyms Diseases or syndromes named for or after persons.

epornithic In epidemiology, this is an epidemic of zoonotic diseases in bird populations that has the potential to affect or threaten the health of humans.

EPSDT *See early and periodic screening, diagnosis, and treatment.*

Equal Opportunity and Full Employment Act of 1976 A law that states that all persons have the right to equal employment opportunities and that the free exercise of this right is available to every American irrespective of sex, age, race, color, religion, or national origin, with no unequal conditions for women, older people, or children.

equal employment opportunity In health administration and human resource management, the law that all individuals have an equal chance to succeed on the job and advance on the basis of merit and ability without discrimination (decisions to hire made on the basis of factors unrelated to job performance such as age, race, religion, or national origin). The law applies to all employers who employ over 15 workers.

Equal Employment Opportunity Act of 1972 Used to strengthen the role of the Equal Employment Opportunity Commission by amending the Civil Rights Act of 1964, empowering the EEOC to initiate court action against noncomplying organizations.

Equal Employment Opportunity Commission (EEOC) A federal agency of the United States created in 1964 to enforce Title VII of the Civil Rights Act and end discrimination in employment on the basis of race, color, religion, sex, or national origin and to promote programs that make equal employment opportunity a reality. The commission reviews charges of discrimination and investigates accordingly. If necessary, the commission attempts to remedy noncompliance through conciliation, conference, persuasion, and, if necessary, appropriate legal action.

Equal Pay Act of 1963 A federal law that prohibits discrimination in pay because of a person's gender.

equal protection of laws A constitutional requirement that requires the government to treat people equally. It is restricted from setting up illegal categories to justify unfair treatment based on race, religion, age, or national origin.

equipment management A component of a hospital's plant, technology, and safety management program designed to assess and control the clinical and physical risks of fixed and portable equipment used for the diagnosis, treatment, monitoring, and care of patients and of other fixed and portable electrically powered equipment.

equitable Just, reasonable, fair, honest, right; having equity.

equities In health-care financial management, these are the common stock, preferred stock, options to buy stock, and other forms of ownership of a business or company; any asset that has assessable worth that can be added to the financial statement.

equity 1. Fair treatment. 2. When the law is lacking or does not cover an issue, then fairness is used to make the judgment; a court's power to use fairness to make a judgment when specific laws do not cover the situation. 3. Fairness; moral justness; fairness in a particular situation. 4. The owner's net value in property.

equity court In the litigation and legal process, this is a special court that ministers justice according to a sense of fairness.

equity financing ratio In health-care finance, this is a leverage ratio that indicates the importance of equity in financing assets. A high ratio means that the hospital tends to use profit and gifts to pay for assets; a low ratio means that the hospital tends to rely on debt. Lenders are more likely to provide loans at a favorable interest rate to a hospital that has a high ratio because it is more likely to be able to pay long-term debts. The equity financing ratio formula follows:

$$\frac{\text{Fund balances (equity)}}{\text{Total assets}} \times 100 = \text{Percentage}$$

equivalency testing An evaluation process that compares an individual's knowledge, experience, and skill, however acquired, with the knowledge, experience, and skill acquired by formal education training. Successful completion of equivalency tests may be used to obtain course credits toward an academic degree without taking courses or a license that requires academic training. *See also proficiency testing.*

ER Emergency room. *See emergency hospital services.*

-er Suffix meaning "one who."

eradication of disease In public health and medical care, this is the removal of disease from a population or geographical area; halting the transmission of a disease or condition; removal of infectious agents or pathogens from infecting humans or animals.

ergo (Lat.) Therefore.

ergonomics 1. Human factors engineering; assessment of work and machines for ease of use and how well they fit the physical structure of humans. 2. The study of physical, biological, and technical relationships between worker physical attributes and the physical demands of jobs and equipment. 3. The assessment of a person's fit with machines with the objective of reducing physical strain and mental stress to reduce on-the-job injury, improve quality of work life, and increase productivity.

ERIC *See Educational Resources Information Center.*

ERISA *See Employee Retirement Income Security Act.*

erogenous Sexually sensitive to touch.

erotomania Unhealthy preoccupation with sexual activities or fantasies.

erratum (Lat.) Mistake.

error 1. In malpractice litigation, a serious enough mistake to entitle the losing party to have the case reviewed by an appellate court. 2. A mistake made by a judge in the litigation process, either in fact or in law. 3. A mistake in judgment. 4. An opinion that is or was wrong. 5. In computers, any discrepancy between a computed, observed, or measured quantity and the true, specified, or theoretically correct value or condition. 7. In epidemiology or health services research, a false result of a study; stating that something is true when it is not (type I error, or rejecting a null hypothesis) or that something is false when it is true (type II error, or accepting a null hypothesis).

error of central tendency In health administration and human resource management, this is a human response by a manager who evaluates an employee's performance as neither good nor poor and rates all employees as average, even when some workers have performed exceptionally well and others poorly.

errors and omissions insurance (E & O) A type of insurance that relates to the liability of professional health-care providers for malpractice protection.

escalator clause A contract clause that allows rent or prices to be raised as costs, expenses, inflation, or shortages increase.

escheat The taking over of property by the state because of abandonment or lack of ownership.

Escobedo Rule In law, this is the case that resulted in the ruling that a suspect must be warned of the right to remain silent and the right to an attorney; similar to the Miranda rule (*Escobedo v. Illinois,* 378 U.S. 478 [1964]).

escrow 1. In health-care finance, this is to trust a document or money to a third party to be delivered to the benefited party on satisfaction of certain specified conditions or agreements. 2. The condition of being ineffective until certain conditions are met. For example, in the purchase of property, money is prepaid into a special account and the holder of the account pays insurance and tax bills out of the account as needed.

ESOP *See employee stock ownership plan.*

ESP *See Economic Stabilization Program.*

espanto (Spanish) A disorder in which the individual is frightened by what he or she claims to be supernatural spirits or events.

esq. Esquire (usually a title given to lawyers).

ESRD End-stage renal disease.

essay appraisal In health administration and human resource management, this is one form of performance appraisal in which managers or supervisors write a handwritten report on each of their subordinates, assessing qualities such as job performance, strengths, areas of need in professional and personal development, meeting work objectives, work accomplishments, and potential for promotion.

essential access community hospital (EACH, or "eaches") A specially designated type of rural hospital created by Public Law 101-239 and limited to California, Colorado, Kansas, New York, North Carolina, South Dakota, and West Virginia that allowed them to convert the focus of hospital services from acute care to primary care. The hospital must be in a rural area, agree to accept payments from a rural primary care hospital (RPCH, or "peach"), be reimbursed as a sole community hospital by Medicare, and have at least 75 beds that provide backup to RPCHs, an organized patient referral network. Approved hospitals are designated for Medicare's payment rules for sole community hospitals. *See eaches/peaches.*

establish 1. To appoint. 2. To demonstrate or prove; to prove a point. 3. To set up, organize or create. 4. To set a precedent.

established name The formal identification given to a drug or pharmaceutical product by the U.S. Adopted Names Council (USAN). This name is usually shorter and simpler than the chemical name and is the one most commonly used in the scientific literature. It is the name by which most physicians and pharmacists learn about a particular drug product (e.g., penicillin, a well-known antibiotic). Also known as the generic name or official name. An established name for drugs is required by Section 502(e) of the federal Food, Drug, and Cosmetic Act.

established patient A patient known to the physician and/or whose records are readily available in a managed-care program.

establishment clause The First Amendment of the U.S. Constitution guarantees that "Congress shall make no law respecting an establishment of religion. . . ."

estop To bar, preclude, or prevent.

estoppel 1. To bar or prevent. 2. A statement or admission that prevents the person making it from producing evidence to the contrary.

estoppel by judgment Being barred from raising an issue against a person in court because a judge had already decided the issue.

estoppel certificate A written statement by a mortgage company about the amount due on a mortgage on a particular date.

estro- Prefix meaning "female."

ESWL *See extracorporeal shock wave lithotripsy.*

ethical drug A prescription drug that is advertised only to physicians and other prescribing health professionals. Drug manufacturers that only make or primarily manufacture such drugs are referred to as the "ethical drug industry."

ethical malpractice Any professional misconduct or negligence that is considered improper or immoral by the entire profession. *See also malpractice.*

ethics A system of morals, expectations, and behaviors for all professionals, especially health-care providers; professional standards of conduct.

ethics committee In hospital administration, this is a committee made up of representatives from hospital administration, medical staff, nursing, clergy, social services, and other allied health professionals and personnel that is formed to consider biomedical ethical issues and medical decision processes on issues related to the care of patients and cases that present ethical problems.

ethnic Relating to cultures, races, or groups of people with similar traits and customs that are unique.

ethnoscience The systematic approach to the study of the customs of a designated race or group to obtain accurate data regarding behavior, beliefs, perceptions, values, and interpretations of life.

etio- Prefix meaning "cause."

etiology 1. In epidemiology and medicine, this is the study of the causes of disease; the first part of the natural history of a disease. 2. The science of causes or origins; the study of beginnings or causation. *See cause; causation.*

et non (Lat.) And not. In the litigation process, this is a phrase used in pleading, or introducing negative arguments.

et ux (Lat.) Et uxor. And wife.

et vir (Lat.) And husband.

EUOAIHC Excessive use of acronyms in health care.

euphoria An exaggerated feeling of well-being that is inappropriate for the actual experience at hand, often associated with opiate, amphetamine, and alcohol abuse.

eustress Positive stress or stress reactions; euphoria. *See also benestressor; dystressor; stress; distress.*

euthanasia 1. Mercy killing. 2. Painlessly putting a person to death who suffers from painful and incurable disease. 3. The act or practice of killing individuals (active approach) or allowing them to die without giving all possible treatment for their disease (passive approach), because they are hopelessly sick or injured, for reasons of mercy. *See also hospice; death.*

evaluation 1. The process of determining the degree to which an objective of a program or procedure has be completed or met; a review of the goals and objectives and establishing the criteria used to measure the degree of success; an assessment of actions and results measured against a norm or standard to select alternatives for the future. 2. The comparison of an objective of interest against a standard of acceptability. 3. To determine the worth of or to appraise, as in the "evaluation" of hospital performance (JCAHO for acute-care hospitals). 4. In health promotion and health education, determining the extent to which goals and objectives have been met and whether health promotion program inputs are causally related to outputs; determining how health promotion and health education activities are carried out to achieve goals.

evaluation interviews In health administration and human resource management, this is a performance appraisal meeting between a manager and an employee intended to provide feedback about past performance and to set objectives for future job performance.

evaluation of care In the provision of medical care, this is the assessment of the extent to which the care of a patient meets recognized standards of care. *See quality of care.*

evaluation program In health promotion, this is an essential part of a comprehensive health promotion activity that assesses objectives, processes, and outcomes to determine levels of success and improve future health promotion services.

Evans' Postulates (Epidemiological) To explain disease causation and association and to assist epidemiologists in epidemiologic investigation, Alfred Evans revised Henle's and Kock's epidemiological postulates. Below is a summary of the 10 postulates suggested by Evans: 1) The prevalence of a disease should be higher in those exposed to the cause than in controls not exposed. 2) The exposure to the cause of disease should be more frequent among those with the disease than in controls without the disease when risk factors are held constant. 3) The incidence of a disease should be higher in those exposed to the cause than in those not exposed, as shown in prospective studies. 4) The disease should follow exposure to a causative agent with a distribution of incubation periods on a bell-shaped curve. 5) A range of host responses should follow exposure to an agent, ranging from mild to severe. 6) A measurable host response following exposure to a cause should have a high probability of symptoms appearing in those lacking protection before exposure to the cause. 7) Experimental reproduction of the disease should occur more frequently in animals or humans exposed to the cause than in those not exposed. 8) Elimination of the cause should decrease the incidence of the disease. 9) Prevention or modification of the host's response on exposure to the cause should decrease or eliminate the disease. 10) All of the relationships should make biological and epidemiological sense (Source: *Yale Journal of Biological Medicine* 49 [1976]: 175–95). *See Henle's and Kock's postulates; Kock's postulates.*

evasion 1. Artful avoidance; to avoid duty or a question by cleverness or deceit. 2. The act of not facing up to something or of avoiding it.

evasive The act of avoiding duty or questions by avoiding the issue; cleverness or deceit.

eviction A landlord, hospital, nursing home, or other institution removing a tenant from the property either by taking direct action, using force if needed, or going to court to get an order for removal.

evidence 1. Information, facts, observation, objects, recollections, papers, medical records, X rays, or other documents, records, or forms presented at a trial or hearing. 2. Any facts, information, or testimony that might be used in a trial to prove the alleged claims. 3. Under OBRA and nursing home regulation, the integral part of a citation against a facility that begins with a statement identifying the noncompliance or deficiency and sets forth relevant findings that substantiate the failure to comply with regulations.

evidence law The rules and principles controlling the testimony or documents that can be admitted or accepted as proof in a trial.

evidence of coverage *See certificate of coverage; evidence of insurability.*

evidence of insurability 1. In managed care, this is the presentation of proof by a member who is eligible for enrollment in a health plan or medical insurance; the completion of an application form as proof of eligibility to be a member of a health plan and receive medical care benefits. 2. Any statement or proof of a person's physical condition (such as a medical exam) or occupation affecting his or her acceptability for insurance coverage. Formal forms that ask eligibility questions are often required to be filled out and presented to the insurance company to establish if the candidate meets the guidelines for insurance coverage. This is often required of applicants who do not enroll during open enrollment periods and who later apply for coverage. It also applies for persons who request extra coverage under a group life insurance program. Also referred to as "evidence of good health." *See health coverage; medical care coverage.*

evidentiary fact A fact that is learned from evidence.

ex- Prefix meaning "out."

ex (Lat.) Forth, out of, away from; no longer; from; thoroughly; because of, by; with; appears as if.

ex aequitate (Lat.) From or in equity.

examination The act of searching, or inquiring for, facts or truth; questioning a witness in court.

examine To inspect, scrutinize, investigate, and question.

examiner A physician appointed by the medical director of a life or health insurer to examine applicants prior to purchasing a policy.

except To eliminate or omit from consideration; to make an exception of; to take exception to, to exclude; to object to.

excepted period The time after the beginning date of a policy during which benefits are not payable. Also referred to as the "waiting period."

exception In legal proceedings and the litigation process, this is a formal disagreement with a judge's ruling. A statement that the lawyer does not agree with the judge's decision and will save the objections until later.

excess margin In health-care finance, this is the level of profitability or the overattained income. The excess margin formula follows:

$$\frac{\text{Excess income}}{\text{Total operating revenue + net nonoperating revenue}}$$

exchange 1. In health administration, this is a mutually agreeable or reciprocal interaction or assistance that occurs when both parties benefit from it. 2. A relationship between a health-care organization and its management environment such as employment, services to patients, gifts and donations, and provider interactions.

exchange partners In health administration, this is the companies, organizations, and healthcare providers who participate with and assist hospitals in their operations.

excise tax A single-stage commodity tax such as a tax levied on a commodity only once as it passes through the production process to the final consumer. An excise tax is narrowly based, and legislation specifies precisely which products are taxed as well as the tax rate. Excise taxes are commonly assessed on automobiles, cigarettes, liquor, or gasoline and are sometimes levied in an effort to discourage the use of the product being taxed. Revenues from such taxes may also be set aside from general revenues and used for a purpose related to the taxed product. For example, an excise tax on cigarettes might discourage smoking by raising the cost of tobacco products, and revenues from tobacco sales might be used to fund cancer screening programs and health education smoking prevention programs.

exclusionary clause In contract law, this is a part of a contract that restricts the legal remedies for one side if the contract is broken.

exclusionary rule In law and the litigaion process, this is a rule that keeps relevant but illegally obtained evidence out of a trial. The exclusionary rule often means that illegal evidence may not be used in a trial.

exclusions Specific hazards, perils, or conditions listed in an insurance or medical care coverage policy for which the policy will not provide benefits or coverage payments. Common exclusions include preexisting conditions such as heart disease, diabetes, hypertension, or a pregnancy that began before the policy was in effect. Because of such exclusions, persons who have a serious condition or disease are often unable to secure insurance coverage either for the particular disease or in general. Sometimes these conditions are excluded only for a defined period after coverage begins, such as 9 months for pregnancy or 1 year for all exclusions. Exclusions are often permanent in individual health insurance, temporary for small groups in group insurance, and uncommon for large groups capable of absorbing the extra risk involved. Other common exclusions are self-inflicted injuries, combat injuries, plastic surgery for cosmetic reasons, and on-the-job injuries covered by workers' compensation.

exclusions and limitations In medical care insurance, managed-care health plans, and health services, supplies, or benefits, these are factors, issues, conditions, or concerns that are excluded from or limited in an agreement or health plan contract; those specific conditions, services, or circumstances set forth in a health plan agreement or medical care policy that will not be covered.

exclusive 1. Limited; sole; one only. 2. Excluding or shutting out others; keeping out everything except what was called for or specified.

exclusive dealing In health-care administration, this is purchasing supplies or services from only one supplier to the exclusion of other suppliers in an unfair manner, which may violate antitrust laws.

exclusive HIPC See HIPC, exclusive.

exclusive jurisdiction A jurisdiction of one court to the exclusion of all other courts.

exclusive provider organization (EPO) In managed care, this identifies an HMO-type arrangement that is similar to a preferred provider organization because it relates to the agreement between parties (employee, member) and the contracted health-care provider's reimbursement. A subscriber in an EPO health plan must receive medical care exclusively from the health-care provider chosen by the health plan. Any care provided outside the health plan is the financial responsibility of the member. Patients are allowed to go outside of the provider network but then must pay for these medical expenses. What makes the organization exclusive is that enrollees are required to stay within the network of contracted health-care providers. Capitation is usually not used in EPOs. The full, self-contained HMO/staff model approach is an EPO model.

ex colore officii (Lat.) By color of office. An erroneous assumption of a right to perform an act by authority of one's office, status, or position.

ex contractu (Lat.) From a contract. One of the two sources of obligations and causes of action. See ex delicto; cause of action; contract.

excreta Feces; urine; waste products eliminated by the body.

exculpate 1. To find fault with; blame. 2. To clear from a charge; to prove guiltless; to provide an excuse or justification; to excuse; to free from blame or guilt.

exculpatory 1. To exculpate. 2. Excusing blame or actions; diminishing or extinguishing guilt or blame.

exculpatory clause A provision or stipulation in a document by which one party is relieved of responsibility or has the burden removed for things that go wrong or for losses incurred.

excuse 1. An explanation of justification for an act. 2. A plea offered in defense of one's unintentional act or conduct. 3. A false or pretended reason for one's acts.

ex delicto (Lat.) From a tort. One of the two sources of obligations or causes of action. See also ex contractu; cause of action; tort; malpractice.

execute 1. To fulfill; to put into effect to complete; make valid. 2. To carry out; to perform all necessary formalities. 3. To make valid by signing and delivering a document. 4. In computers, to carry out an instruction or to run a software program on the computer.

execution 1. Making a document valid. 2. Carrying out or completing; carrying into effect. 3. Putting someone to death.

execution sale A sale made under proper court authority following a levy on property of a debtor.

executive 1. The branch of government empowered to carry out and administer the laws. 2. The administrative branch. 3. A high-level administrator or official in a branch of the top levels of government or as found in a hospital, company, or other organization; one of the top administrators of a health-care organization. 4. Pertaining to the top office of an organization; any order, policy, rule, or expectation that comes from the top officers or administrators of an organization or their office.

executive committee 1. In health-care administration, this is an administrative group or body made up of the chiefs of departments and service, elected members of the staff, and other administrative officers that is often the major decision-making body for the medical staff. 2. In a health-care organization's board of directors, this is a select group of decision makers consisting of the board leadership (president, vice president, secretary/treasurer, and possibly elected members) that deals with the general business, policy, personnel actions, and functions of the board.

executive committee of the medical staff A group of physicians usually selected by election or appointment from the medical staff of a health-care facility that has the responsibility and authority to act for the medical staff during those periods between formal medical staff meetings.

executive departments The administrative areas within the federal government that ultimately report to the president of the United States and that make up the Cabinet.

executive director (officer) The head administrator or chief executive officer of a health-care facility, organization, or agency. *See also administrator; chief executive officer; health services administrator.*

executive order (EO) 1. A law or policy issued by the chief officer of an organization. 2. A law set forth by the president or a governor that need not be passed by the legislature or by Congress. 3. Decrees that apply to government agencies or contractors under the executive branches of the federal government.

executive search firm In health-care administration, this is an employment agency that assists hospitals and health-care organizations to locate and place executives and upper-middle managers in professional jobs.

executive session In health-care organization governance, this is a meeting by members of the governing board of the organization that is closed to the general public and open only to the executive committee members, their staff, and other invited guests. Sometimes synonymous with "markup," especially in the House of Representatives, where markups are now rarely held in private.

executive vice president In some major organizations and large health-care facilities, this is the manager responsible for the day-to-day operation of the organization or institution, often called the "chief operating officer" (COO). The executive vice president works under the direction of a president. In some facilities, the president may be a physician who serves essentially as a statesman for the hospital and a liaison for the community. The executive vice president usually holds a masters degree in health-care administration and operates and manages the health-care facility.

executor, executrix One with authority; one who is designated to administer and settle an estate.

executory That which has yet to be performed; still to be carried out; incomplete.

exemplary damages *See damages, exemplary; punitive damages.*

exemplification An official transcript of a public document used as evidence.

exempli gratia (Lat.) For the sake of example; for example. Abbreviated "e.g."

exemption To be free from service, burden, or tax.

exemption, certificate of In health planning and health delivery access, this is a written order from the state health department or its responsible agency that exempts a health-care organization from a certificate of need. *See certificate of need.*

exercise physiologist An individual who works with clinicians in hospitals with rehabilitation programs to provide exercise stress testing and cardiovascular rehabilitation for patients. This person may have a bachelors, masters, or doctoral degree in exercise physiology, physical therapy, or a related field.

ex gratia (Lat.) By grace; gratuitous.

exhibit 1. Any object or document offered to a court as evidence. 2. To administer a drug or other treatment as a cure or remedy.

exhume 1. To disinter; dig out of the ground or unbury. 2. To disclose or reveal.

exigency A situation requiring immediate aid or attention.

exit interview In health administration and human resource management, this is a meeting conducted between an employee who quit or is terminated and a manager to explore the departing worker's views of the organization and his or her work experience.

ex necessitate (Lat.) By necessity.

ex officio 1. By the power of office. 2. According to JCAHO, it is a position by virtue or because of an office, with no reference to specific voting power. When a person is an ex officio member of a board or committee, he or she is allowed to attend and listen to all proceedings but has no say, input, or vote.

exoneration 1. To unburden; to relieve or take away a charge or obligation. 2. Clearing a crime, a harm done, or wrongdoing.

expanded functions Dental care clinical procedures, formerly only performed by dentists, that dental hygienists now perform according to state laws. These functions vary from state to state, from the delivery of local anesthesia to root planing, curettage, and packing amalgams.

expanded functions training program An educational program with the objective of educating individuals to assist in the provision of dental care under the supervision of a dentist.

expansionist diagnosis A diagnostic approach that seeks to explain the causes of diseases or conditions beyond immediate or obvious test results or standard diagnostic approaches. *See reductionist diagnosis.*

expectancy theory In health-care administration, this is a theory of management and motivation based on successful performance, which is influenced by the expectations of both the management and the worker. The worker must feel that he or she can accomplish what is requested, that a reward or recognition will result, and that management will value the performance.

expectant 1. A woman who is "with child" and soon to have a baby; pregnant. 2. One taking an exception during a legal hearing or proceeding such as in a malpractice hearing or trial.

expectant right A right that is contingent on a set of circumstances that can occur in the future.

expected claims In managed care, these are the anticipated or projected levels of utilization and the amount of claims that will be generated for an employer group or a population of a health plan. Also referred to as the "desired loss ratio" or "break-even point" (based on projected premium income) or as an "experience rating."

expected date of confinement (EDC) Expected date of the birth of a baby.

expected morbidity In epidemiology, this is the expected incidence of sickness or injury within a given population during a given period of time as shown in a morbidity table. *See morbidity; disease.*

expected mortality In epidemiology, this is the expected incidence of death within a given group during a given time period as shown in a mortality table. *See mortality; death.*

expected return In managed care and health finance, this is the rate of interest and/or financial gain anticipated from an investment; the mean value of the probability distribution of possible financial return.

expedite To facilitate; to hasten.

expedited arbitration In health law, this is an attempt to move the arbitration process forward as rapidly as possible. Arbitrators must be available on short notice and be able to render quick decisions at the conclusion of the hearing.

expediter One who expedites; the individual responsible for assuring the completion of an activity in a timely manner.

expenditures 1. Costs of medical care that have a monetary value attached that the consumer pays out-of-pocket or through a third-party payer who pays on the patient's behalf. 2. Under Medicaid, an amount paid by a state for the medical expenses covered for eligible participants.

expenditures for dental care Charges by a dentist for services and those of the staff, including dental assistants and hygienists, laboratory services, dental manufacturers products, and materials such as dental appliances and braces.

expenditures for drugs Charges to patients for medications or substances prescribed by a physician that are purchased directly by the consumer from a pharmacy. Also included are nonprescribed over-the-counter-drugs taken to treat medical problems.

expenditures for hospital care Charges by an acute-care health-care facility for inpatient and outpatient care. Inpatient care charges include but are not limited to meals and nutrition services, hotel services, emergency room fees, laboratory fees, drugs and medications, X rays, treatment procedures, therapies and rehabilitation, testing and diagnostic services, and operating and delivery room fees. Outpatient care charges exclude hotel charges, meals, and nutrition services but also include outpatient clinic and surgery suites and emergency room fees.

expenditures for medical care, other All charges and fees for nonphysician providers such as private duty nurses, physical therapists, occupational therapists, psychologists, counselors, psychotherapists, speech pathologists, audiologists, and chiropractors. Other expenditures are appliances and prostheses such as eyeglasses, hearing aids, crutches, braces, artificial limbs, wheelchairs, orthopedic shoes, vaporizers, special beds and chairs, and pads.

expenditures for physician care Charges by a physician in both inpatient and outpatient settings for all treatments, procedures, diagnostic procedures, tests, X rays, medications, therapies, and medical care. The main areas of charges are surgery and all cutting procedures, circumcisions, suturing, setting of fractures and dislocations, preoperative and postoperative care, consultations, assistance from physician extenders, assistant surgeons, anesthesiologists, and assessing and reading certain tests, X rays, or diagnostic procedures.

expenditures for physician care, inpatient The costs and charges for inpatient surgery and all physician care delivered to a patient who is an inpatient in a hospital; excluded are the charges for anesthesiology, pathology, radiography, and emergency care by hospital salaried or contract physicians, which are billed separately. Obstetrical and perinatal care, covered under outpatient physician charges, are also billed separately.

expenditures for physician care, outpatient The costs and charges for outpatient care and all physician care delivered to a patient who is an outpatient or clinic patient and all care delivered outside the hospital. Obstetric care, including labor and delivery, is a part of physician outpatient fees.

expenditures, free Costs of medical goods and services provided to patients that are not charged to the patient or the medical insurance carrier. *See expenditures.*

expenditures, nonfree *See expenditures.*

expenditure per live birth All charges and fees connected with live births in a hospital, including labor, delivery, and aftercare for the mother and pediatric and nursery care for the infant. Charges also include circumcision, special care, drugs, and tests connected with labor, delivery, and infant care.

expense 1. In health-care finance, this is money paid for needed goods or services. 2. In managed care, the cost an insurance company or health plan experiences in conducting its business other than the payment of losses, including acquisition and administrative costs. 3. In hospitals, all costs of doing business for an accounting reporting period. Payroll expenses include all salaries and wages except those paid to medical and dental residents and interns, administrative residents, student nurses, and other trainees.

expense budgets In health administration and health-care finance, these are detailed plans on the allocation of monies used to carry on operations and how the funds are distributed to certain programs, departments, or services within a health-care facility or organization.

expenses, labor-related In health-care finance, these are payroll expenditures plus employee benefits; all personnel costs.

expenses, non–labor-related In health-care finance, these are all expenditures and costs of doing business, except payroll.

expenses, payroll In health-care finance, these are costs for salaries and wages except those paid to interns, residents, and trainees. Consulting fees, honoraria, professional fees, and salary expenditures are not included and are considered nonpayroll items; thus they are included in total expenses.

expenses per adjusted patient day *See adjusted expenses per inpatient day.*

expenses per inpatient day In health-care finance, this includes all costs incurred for all inpatient care. The formula for expenses per inpatient day follows:

$$\frac{\text{Total expenses}}{\text{Number of inpatient days during a specific time period}}$$

experience rating In health-care finance, this is a method of establishing premiums for medical insurance from a company's own experience. The premium is determined by the average cost of an act or anticipated health care used by various groups, subgroups, or subscribers; this varies with the health experience of groups and subgroups and with such variables as age, sex, or health status. It is the most common method of establishing premiums for medical insurance in private programs; rates are set for the policy year by evaluating previous claims and relying on past experience with a certain employer group or population of enrollees. *See community rating; expected claims.*

experience rating refund In managed care, this is the paying back of a premium to a policyholder or health plan member of a nonparticipating group if that group's health-care utilization or costs were better than anticipated when the premiums for the health plan were originally set. Also referred to as "retroactive rate reduction."

experiential learning In health education, this is an educational method and learning approach that allows the learner to gain knowledge and experience by participating in an actual experience that is structured so that it closely resembles the real experience. Some examples are field experiences, internships, and simulators.

experiment A research tool using a set of procedures and scientific rules of evidence applied to a hypothesis or question to determine if it is correct or incorrect.

experimental design An approach in biomedical research that randomly assigns a group of research subjects to one of two groups. One group becomes the study group and the other the control group. The study group receives a set of treatments or procedures, and the control receives none. Conditions are kept the same for both groups, and, after the treatment is completed, the outcomes of both groups are compared.

experimental epidemiology Also referred to as "community trials" or "randomized controlled trials" and often used to refer to animal research studies. *See experimental design.*

experimental group In biomedical research using an experimental design, the group to which the treatment under study is administered. *See control group; experimental design.*

Experimental Health Service Delivery System (EHSDS) A system developed by general health services research authorities under a program supported by the Health Services and Mental Health Administration that develops, tests, and evaluates the organization and operation of coordinated, community-wide health service management systems in various kinds and sizes of communities. The EHSDS sought to improve access to services, moderate costs, and improve quality.

experimental, investigational, and unproven procedures In managed care and medical care activities, this is any treatment, procedure, surgery, devices, therapy, or curative activity, including those used in alcohol and drug treatment, substance abuse therapy, and psychiatric or psychological services, that are determined by the health plan or medical insurance carrier to not be generally accepted. It is acceptable for use if informed health-care providers in the United States believe it to be effective in treating the condition, disease, diagnosis, or disorder for which it has been used or is proposed to be used or if the treatment has been proven by scientific research, clinical trials, or other evidence to be effective.

Experimental Medical Care Review Organization (EMCRO) An organization assisted by a program initiated in 1970 by the National Center for Health Services Research and Development (now NCHSR). The program, a forerunner to PSRO (which then became the PRO program), was set up to help create formal organizations and procedures for reviewing the quality and use of medical care in hospitals, nursing homes, and clinics throughout a defined community. The use of explicit criteria and standard definitions were required of all EMCROs; the approach to organizing the review was determined by the individual organization. Ten such organizations were initially supported. The program was phased out after enactment of the PSRO (now PRO) program. *See peer review; peer review organizations.*

expert witness In health law and malpractice litigation, this is a person possessing particular knowledge, expertise, or experience who is called on to present specialized information and to draw professional conclusions on the basis of facts relevant to a case, usually in legal hearings or a court of law, such as a malpractice lawsuit.

expire 1. The medical community's euphemism for death or "to die." 2. To close or conclude something that is renewable such as a driver's license. 3. To give off, breathe out.

explanation of benefits In health-care finance and under Medicare or Medicaid, this is a recap sheet that accompanies a Medicare or Medicaid check and shows the breakdown and explanation of payment on a claim.

explosive personality A personality disorder in which a person shows extreme anger and hostility.

exponential smoothing In health administration, this is a forecasting method used to adjust forecasts of facility utilization. The discrepancy between a recent forecast and actual utilization for that period is done by adjusting actual utilization data and is used to develop future forecasts.

expository statute A law that explains the meaning of a previously enacted law.

ex post facto (Lat.) After the fact.

exposure 1. In environmental health, this is any contact of an organism with a chemical or physical agent, as quantified by the amount of the agent available for absorption at the exchange boundaries of the body such as skin, eyes, or lungs. 2. The amount of pollutant or radiation present in the environment that poses a health threat to humans or animals. 3. In X-ray or laser technology, the product of an irradiance and its duration. 4. In health administration, a career advancement process whereby a manager or potential manager becomes known to those who decide on promotions, transfers, and other career opportunities.

exposure assessment In environmental health, this is the determination or qualitative or quantitative estimation of the magnitude, frequency, duration, and route of exposures to a harmful chemical or physical agent.

exposure control plan In infection control and AIDS protection, this is a plan that contains several elements, including communication of hazards to employees, a list of all tasks and procedures that have occupational exposure risks and are performed by employees, procedures for evaluating circumstances surrounding exposure incidents, and plans for hepatitis B vaccination and postexposure evaluation and follow-up. The plan must be periodically reviewed and updated and made available to all employees.

exposure determination In infection control and AIDS protection, this is when each employer identifies all tasks and job classifications that are at risk of occupational exposure.

exposure event In environmental health, this is an incident of contact with a chemical or physical agent as defined by time and the number of exposures in the incident.

exposure incident In infection control and AIDS protection, this is a specific procedure or measures taken to protect the eyes, mouth, other mucous membrane nonintact skin, parenteral contact with blood, or other potentially infectious materials encountered in the performance of duties of health-care providers.

exposure point In environmental health, this is the point of contact between an organism and a chemical or physical agent.

exposure rate In environmental health, this is the increment of exposure in a specified time period.

exposure ratio In a case control study, this is the ratio of rates at which subjects and controls are exposed to risk factors.

exposure route In environmental health, this is the way a chemical or physical agent comes into contact with an organism such as ingestion, inhalation, or dermal contact.

express 1. Clear, direct, or actual. 2. Unambiguous; definite; stated explicitly.

express assumpsit An undertaking to perform some act, manifested in unmistakable terms.

express consent In health law, this is any consent that is given directly, orally or in writing. Express consent is positive, honest, direct, informed, and unequivocal; no inference or implication to its meaning (*Pacific Nat. Agricultural Credit Corp. v. Hagerman*, 40 N.M. 11 6, P.2d 667, 670).

expressio unius est exclusio alterius (Lat.) The expression of one thing rules out the other. A rule often put into effect for interpreting documents.

express trust In health law, this is a trust created by express intent and terms of the settler, as opposed to an implied trust.

expropriation The taking of private property for public use.

expunge 1. In formal health-care meetings and hearings, a parliamentary procedure that deletes a motion or resolution from the minutes. 2. To strike out or blot out; to wipe off the books.

ex relatione (Lat.) Upon relation. For example, when a case is titled "State ex rel. *Doe v. Roe*," it means that the state is to file a lawsuit under the title of *Doe v. Roe*.

ex tempore (Lat.) Without preparation.

extended benefits In managed care or medical insurance coverage, this is a supplement to either a basic hospital plan or a basic hospital surgical-medical plan that may include diagnostic, X-ray, and laboratory examinations on an outpatient basis.

extended care Treatment and nursing care provided in a nursing or convalescent home, as opposed to care provided in a residence or hospital. *See nursing home; long-term-care; extended care facility.*

extended care benefits Insurance coverage for residents in a skilled nursing facility that is approved by Medicare. The continued use of the term "extended care facility benefits" is a kind of shorthand that refers to the benefit limitations on skilled nursing facility care under Medicare.

extended care facility (ECF) 1. A medical care institution used for treatment of a patient who has been discharged from a hospital yet still needs further specialized and continued care. 2. Previously used in Medicare to mean a skilled nursing facility that qualified for participation in Medicare. In 1972, the law was amended to use the more generic term "skilled nursing facility" for both Medicare and Medicaid. Medicare coverage is limited to 100 days of posthospital extended care service during any spell of illness; thus Medicare coverage in a skilled nursing facility is limited in duration, must follow a hospital stay, and must be for services related to the cause of the hospital stay. These conditions do not apply to skilled nursing facility benefits under Medicaid.

extended care services As used in Medicare, services in a skilled nursing facility that are provided for a limited duration (up to 100 days in a spell of illness) after a hospital stay for the same condition as the hospital stay. As defined under Medicare, items or services furnished to an inpatient of a skilled nursing facility include nursing care provided or supervised by a registered professional nurse; bed and board associated with the nursing care; physical, occupational, or speech therapy furnished by the skilled nursing facility or by others under arrangements with the facility; medical social services; such drugs, biologicals, supplies, appliances, and equipment as ordinarily used in care and treatment in the skilled nursing facility; medical services provided by an intern or resident of a hospital with which the facility has a transfer agreement; and other services necessary to the health of patients.

extended care unit A long-term-care unit located within a hospital or acute-care facility; a skilled nursing facility attached to and under the control of a hospital. These are referred to as "combination facilities," "hospital-nursing home combinations," or "transitional care units." *See also nursing homes; convalescent centers; skilled nursing facility; transitional care.*

extended coverage In managed care and medical insurance, this is the provision of care set forth in certain medical care and hospitalization policies, usually group policies, that allows the insured to receive certain benefits for specified losses sustained after termination of coverage (e.g., maternity expense benefits incurred for a pregnancy in progress at the time of the insured's termination).

extended coverage endorsement A special type of liability insurance policy added to a basic fire insurance policy to cover losses from perilous events such as tornadoes, wind, hail, explosions, riots, or other perils.

extended duration review *See continued stay review.*

extended family Includes the central or nuclear family and other relatives such as uncles, aunts, grandparents, and cousins.

extended service *See levels of service.*

extended survey In epidemiology or health-care research, this is a comprehensive survey that requires the surveyor to assess all conditions, standards, and elements of the study carefully and to interview a large number of subjects/participants; can be a longitudinal survey. *See longitudinal survey.*

extension 1. An agreed-on postponement of a planned legal proceeding. 2. A lengthening of time; allowing more time to pay a bill, pay off a loan, or meet a contract.

extension of benefits In managed care or medical insurance, this is when a medical care insurance policy is extended past the termination date of the policy for workers who are not actively at work or for dependents who are under care or hospitalized past the date the policy expires. Often the extended coverage is allowed only for the disease or disorder that has caused the disability and continues only until the worker returns to work. COBRA regulations now control similar circumstances. *See COBRA.*

extension service An educational branch of land-grant universities, operated at the county level, that provides youth programs, information services, and community education activities such as nutrition and health education programs. The formal title is the Cooperative Extension Service.

extent of deficient practice In long-term care, under OBRA, this is the frequency with which a long-term-care health care facility records or conducts regulatory deficiencies.

extenuate To reduce; to mitigate; to diminish; to underrate or lessen.

extenuating circumstances Situations, occurrences, or facts that tend to diminish the severity of a crime and its punishment. Situations that cause an occurrence to diminish or lessen in its importance.

extern According to JCAHO, this is a student in a recognized medical or dental school who is employed by a hospital to perform specific educational and supervised duties with the approval of the dean of the school. *See also internship.*

external assessment In strategic health planning, this is the evaluation of the political and competitive climate in the organization's service area that will have future effects on the organization. A formal process of conducting an evaluation of the climate of threat, loss of competitive position, emerging competitors, the effect of governmental policy, changes occurring in the type or approaches to funding or payment of medical care services, and changes in health-care financing structures; generally ascertaining any changes or threats in the community or government policies that will be detrimental (or beneficial) to the organization.

external audit In health administration and health financial care management, this is the process of hiring a professional auditor or audit team from an accounting firm that is not associated with the organization to conduct accounting and financial audits of the organization's accounting books and journals for the administrator and board of directors.

external disaster According to JCAHO for psychiatry, alcoholism, and drug abuse facilities accreditation purposes, a catastrophe that occurs outside the facility and for which the facility, on the basis of its size, staff, and resources, must be prepared to serve the community.

external evaluation *See external assessment.*

externality 1. In health-care finance, this is something resulting from an encounter between a consumer and provider that confers benefits or imposes costs on others and is not considered in making the transaction (its value, the external cost, not being reflected in any charge for the transaction). 2. In health, an externality of immunizations is the protection that they give the unimmunized because that protection is not considered when an individual immunization is obtained or priced.

external reporting In health-care finance, this is the reporting of financial activities to stockholders and the public.

external storage In health-care information management, this is an information storage medium other than the main memory of the computer such as a hard disk, floppy disk, diskette, or tape.

external validity In epidemiology and biomedical research, this is the assurance that the results of a research study can be generalized to the general populations or at least to other similar settings and populations.

externship An educational training experience that occurs outside or external to the mother educational institution. An example is a radiologic technologist student going into a hospital to gain practical experience taking X rays and learning related work. *See also internship.*

extinguishment 1. To put an end to; to nullify. 2. The ending or stopping of a right, authority, or power. 3. To wipe out or end, such as ending a contract or a vested interest.

extort 1. Misuse of authority to obtain something. 2. To compel; coerce (e.g., to force a confession by depriving a person of food); to get something by illegal threats of harm.

extortion The illegal forceful taking of money by use of threats, force, or misuse of public office; blackmail or the selling of protection.

extra cash policy An insurance policy that pays cash benefits to hospitalized individuals in fixed amounts unrelated to the individual's medical expenses or income. Such policies are usually sold to individuals separately from whatever other health insurance they have and typically have high loadings.

extracorporeal shock wave lithotripsy (ESWL) A medical application using shock waves generated outside of the body by an underwater "spark plug" to pulverize urinary stones into the size of grains of sand. Often referred to as a "lithotripter." *See also lithotripter.*

extracorporeal technologist *See cardiovascular perfusionist.*

extra expense insurance A type of property insurance utilized by some health facilities to cover extra expenditures caused by the interruption of business and patient flow. Such a policy pays if the facility does not close down and continues to provide health-care services in an alternative facility; however, the health-care facility has to pay higher-than-usual insurance costs. The policy also pays if there are freight losses from a shipping peril.

extradition The act of turning a person over to another state when the individual is wanted by the second state for a criminal charge and trial.

extrajudicial Unconnected with the business of the court or the litigation system.

extrajudicial confession A confession made out of court.

extra judicum (Lat.) Out of court; beyond jurisdiction.

extraordinary remedy Actions a court will take if necessary, including habeas corpus and mandamus.

extra percentage tables method In managed care and insurance, this is a common rate plan practice for setting rates for substandard risks. Under this method, each substandard risk class is charged a premium rate that is a certain percentage above standard rates.

extrapolation In health care administration or epidemiology, this is a forecasting approach based on past experience and past rates that uses statistical and graphical methods to identify patterns of performance or to provide an extension and projection of rates of change or utilization into the future.

extremis (Lat.) Last illness.

extrinsic evidence Facts drawn from outside a contract or document in question.

eye, ear, nose, and throat (EENT) A medical field specializing in the diagnosis and treatment of diseases and disorders of the head and neck that focuses on the eye, ear, nose, and throat. Some hospitals have special units specially staffed and equipped for the treatment of EENT diseases and disorders and are directed by physicians with training in otolaryngology or ophthalmology. *See also ear, nose, and throat; ophthalmologist.*

eyewitness 1. One who saw an illegal act occur; someone with firsthand knowledge of an act. 2. Someone who can testify as to what was seen, heard, or witnessed.

F

FAAN Fellow in the American Academy of Nursing. *See Appendix II.*

face of instrument In health law, this is the factual information in a document or note without extrinsic facts added to or allowed in the interpretation of the document; the acceptance of a document's language without modification, interpretation, or explanation. *See also four corners.*

FACEP Fellow in the American College of Emergency Physicians. *See Appendix II.*

face sheet The top document of a record; the first page of a medical record that includes the physician's diagnosis and attests to the conditions and procedures used in obtaining reimbursement from Medicare and Medicaid.

face value In health-care finance, this is the actual and obvious worth of a monetary instrument, item, or note as determined by the language used in it; the amount written on a financial document.

FACHA Fellow of the American College of Hospital Administrators (no longer used). *See FACHE.*

FACHE Fellow in the American College of Healthcare Executives. *See Appendix II; see also American College of Healthcare Executives.*

facilitator 1. An individual who leads a group or conducts specialized meetings or training. This leader goes beyond teaching to include motivating and stimulating individuals to participate and interact in group exercises and problem solving and to contribute to the function of the group process. 2. In quality circles or focus groups in health-care organizations, person who organizes and leads the interactions of these groups.

facilities 1. Buildings, including physical plant, equipment, and supplies, necessary in the provision of health services. 2. Hospitals, nursing homes, and ambulatory care centers. The offices of individual practitioners are usually not included. 3. According to JCAHO accreditation guidelines, facilities are building(s), equipment, and supplies necessary for the implementation of medical services by personnel. *See also health facilities; primary care facilities.*

facility Any health-care institution consisting of a large physical plant and building structure or several buildings such as a hospital, nursing home, convalescent hospital, or large clinic. Compared with a service or program, these can operate without a large building. *See also health facilities; primary care facilities.*

FACPE Fellow of the American College of Physician Executives. *See Appendix II.*

facsimile An exact copy.

facsimile transmission (FAX) An electronic communication system and its accompanying devices that generates an exact copy (usually a Xerox-type copy) of a document sent electronically from one location to another. A hard copy of the document can be sent from the sender to the receiver who receives a hard copy. An electronic/computer version of the document can also be sent, and the receiver receives a printed hard copy of the document.

fact 1. An act, actual event, or occurrence that took place; an actual happening. 2. Something that exists and is real; not what should be but what is or has been; that which has taken place. 3. In health law, a physical object, event, or circumstance as it actually occurred at the time of the incident.

facta sunt potentiora verbis (Lat.) Facts or deeds are stronger than words.

factor 1. In epidemiology and health promotion, this is an agent, behavior, or substance that can lead to a diseased state or that is detrimental to one's health or the health status of a population; referred to as a "risk factor." 2. A broker; a commercial agent or servant utilized to sell goods entrusted to that agent by a principal or master; a person who is provided with goods or items of value for the express purpose of marketing and selling them and who receives a commission for such activities. *See risk factor.*

factor comparison method In health administration and human resource management, this is a form of job evaluation that allocates the monetary (wage, budget) part of the tasks of each job to key factors of the job, providing an evaluation of the job and how it contributes to the overall budgetary plan and mission of the organization.

factored rating *See adjusted community rating.*

factoring In health-care financial management, this is the practice of one individual or organization selling its accounts receivable (unpaid bills) to a second party at a discount. The latter organization, called the "factor," usually assumes full risk of loss if the accounts prove uncollectable. In health services delivery, the expression generally refers to a hospital's or physician's sale of unpaid bills to a collection agent. Factoring has sometimes been used in Medicaid because of the delays that hospitals and physicians experience collecting from the state Medicaid agency. In such cases where factoring is used to improve cash flow, this service is viewed as worth the discount of the amount received by the provider. Because factoring is subject to fraud and abuse, Congress has sought to prohibit some of its uses.

factory mutual A mutual insurer specializing in major risks in the area of loss prevention.

fact situation In health law, a summary of the facts of a case or dispute without any legal conclusions drawn or interpretations or comments made.

factum (Lat.) Act; fact; a central fact or an act, as distinguished from a legal concern on which a question focuses or that can change a question.

facultative-obligatory reinsurance treaty (fac-ob) In managed care and insurance, this is a special agreement that combines the features of automatic and facultative treaties. The assigning company chooses only selected risks that it submits to the reinsurer, without input from or underwriting papers being completed by the reinsurer, rather than all the risks as would be found in an automatic treaty. The reinsurer is obligated to accept the submitted risks unless it does not have the retention capacity to cover the risks submitted.

facultative reinsurance Specific insurance coverage arranged for each separate exposure of risk. *See also treaty, reinsurance.*

facultative reinsurance treaty In managed care and insurance, this is a special agreement whereby a health plan or company submits only those risks for which it wants reinsurance and the reinsurer makes decisions on the reinsurance of each risk.

faculty practice plan The rules and policies of medical practice and reimbursement for physicians on the faculty of medical schools. *See medical practice plan.*

failure 1. Inadequate performance; abandonment or defeat. 2. Lack or deficiency. 3. An unsuccessful attempt or neglect of duty.

failure of consideration In contract law, this is something of value that completes a contract that is given and accepted but has lost its worth or diminishes in value or is not complete; consideration that was once good but that has become worthless or no longer exists, either all or in part. A want for or lack of consideration; a contractual obligation unperformed. *See also consideration.*

failure of evidence In health law, this is the inability to offer proof or to establish the necessary facts related to an issue.

failure of good behavior Acts that are against recognized standards of conduct, morality, and propriety and that can be sufficient reason for termination of employees in some jobs, occupation, or organizations.

failure of issue How a will or deed is viewed in the event the person making it has no surviving children or is childless.

failure to cooperate Any intentional fraudulent changes in, or variations of, statements given before or at a trial.

failure to look Failing to see an object, item, or event that was obvious, clear, and within the range of normal perception or vision by any ordinary person. In health law, this could be linked to negligence or malpractice.

failure to perform In contract law, this is when reciprocal promises have been made and a person has not fulfilled those promises, which is viewed as a refusal to perform unless it is based on a previous condition or circumstance; in a contract, the failure of one party to fulfill the promises, agreements, or actions of the contract.

Fair Allowance Reimbursement Effort (FARE) A Blue Cross/Blue Shield of Arizona reimbursement system that provides an adequate level of reimbursement to providers and at the same time moderates the rate premium increases for health insurance subscribers. Beginning November 1, 1983, Blue Cross/Blue Shield of Arizona initiated this new system to reimburse hospitals for charges incurred by policyholders. FARE reimbursements are determined by diagnosis-related groups (DRGs). FARE takes into account some cost differentials such as extensive equipment for treating intensive illnesses or accidents. These variances are determined by an index developed by consultants from Arizona State University. *See diagnosis-related group.*

fair and impartial trial In constitutional law, this is safeguarding an accused person's constitutional rights by providing a trial and one appeal and related rights as guaranteed by the U.S. Constitution.

fair and reasonable compensation Payment of full compensation; payment of the "going rate" for goods or services; the average rate paid; the rate that two parties agree is acceptable for an item or a transaction.

fair comment Under libel law and the First Amendment, the right to comment on the conduct of public figures or officials without being held liable for defamation of character, slander, or libel, providing that the statements are made with an honest belief that they are true, even though they may be inaccurate.

fair damages In health law, torts, and the litigation process, this is recovery from a medical malpractice or liability lawsuit that is beyond nominal damages so as to compensate for injury, harm, or damages suffered. *See recovery.*

fair employment practices State and local laws that prohibit an employer from discrimination in employment against protected classes.

fair hearing 1. In health law, this is a trial-like decision-making-process hearing that is used when a party appeals an administrative policy or decision. The hearing does not have to use full trial rules or procedures but attempts to be fair because authority is fairly exercised, and accepted procedures and rules are used. 2. Under Medicare, an opportunity to be heard, as in judicial proceedings, on request from a Medicare beneficiary when a request for Part B payment is denied or not acted on within a reasonable length of time, provided the amount in controversy is over $100. The hearing is conducted by an impartial party, and the decision of the hearing officer is final.

fair knowledge and skill Health-care providers are expected to attain a reasonable level of knowledge, understanding, and skill in their area of expertise to perform competently and effectively. *See also reasonable man (person); standard of care.*

Fair Labor Standards Act of 1938 (FLSA) A comprehensive federal law affecting compensation of employees that sets minimum wage, overtime pay, equal pay, child labor, and recordkeeping.

fair persuasion Argument, debate, or convincing conversation addressed to a patient without threat of physical harm, financial loss, or persistent molestation, harassment, or misrepresentation.

fair use In copyright law, this is the limited use of a copyrighted item that does not infringe on the copyright or commit plagiarism.

faith Confidence, trust, belief; unquestioning belief, reliable trust.

faith cure A religious approach to healing through prayer, spiritual confidence, and the laying on of hands.

faith healer A person or member of a religious group who assists in the curing of disease through prayer and/or the laying on of hands. Also referred to as a "faith curer."

false Untrue; fake; unreal; phony; wrong.

false arrest In criminal and tort law, this is the unlawful restraint or deprivation of one's liberty and wrongful accusation of a crime or wrongdoing; a tort.

false imprisonment 1. In tort and constitutional law, this is to hold a person against his or her will. A lawsuit can be filed to recover damages even if no physical damage occurs. 2. In health law, unlawfully detaining, restraining, or constraining a person; a tort.

false negative In epidemiology or medical testing, this is when a person is diagnosed as not having a disease or condition when in fact he or she does have the disease or condition. *See also false positive; sensitivity; specificity.*

false positive In epidemiology or medical testing, this is when a person is wrongly diagnosed as having a disease or condition when in fact he or she does not have it. In medical screening or other diagnostic procedures, it is important to know the number of both false positives and false negatives the procedure produces under normal use to know the effectiveness of a test. *See also sensitivity; specificity; false negative.*

false pretense A lie used to cheat a person out of money, property, or an item of value; deceit through the use of fake or untrue information, credentials, documents, or purpose. This can be a crime in most states.

falsus in uno (Lat.) In one false part. In legal hearings or trails, if a jury believes that one part of what a witness says is deliberately false, it may disregard all of the testimony as false.

family 1. A group of people living in one household related by blood, marriage, or other legal arrangement. A small family is defined as one to three members, a medium family is four to five members, and a large family is six or more members. 2. For U.S. Census purposes, a group of two or more persons related by blood, marriage, or adoption living together in the same household, or anyone else living in the same house such as a roommate, boarder, foster child, or live-in housekeeper, is considered a family. 3. For insurance purposes, this is an individual and his or her dependents. 4. According to the findings of several research studies and from scientific observations, a model healthy family exhibits the following 20 traits: 1) family rules that give values and direction but are not overly restricting, 2) support, 3) respect, 4) trust, 5) both husband wife present in the home, 6) sense of humor, 7) balanced interaction, 8) shared leisure time, 9) shared responsibility, 10) strong sense of right and wrong, 11) rituals and traditions, 12) shared religion, 13) privacy rights, 14) service, 15) admitting problems, 16) communication, 17) spouses support each other's decisions and do not undermine the position or respect of the other, 18) shared meals, 19) regular family meetings/time together, and 20) restriction of teasing, fighting, and violence, with parents not fighting in front of children.

family and community services Educational and instructional programs addressing the social, cultural, psychological, and technological influences on the family in a changing society, focusing on the family organization and structure and its support services.

family birth center Also referred to as ''birthing centers,'' this is a labor and delivery unit in a hospital that provides a family-focused healthcare environment where mothers having a normal pregnancy can deliver their babies in a homelike environment and still be in a definitive care environment with backup emergency care readily available.

family care home (FCH) An informal health-care environment, often in a neighborhood residential family homelike setting where a limited number of persons (usually elderly) reside and are cared for by an informal caregiver. Some states limit the number of persons that can stay in this type of home (e.g., less than six individuals). More persons than the stated number would require that the home be approved and licensed as a health-care–type facility (board, care, or nursing home) by the appropriate governmental agencies.

family centered maternity and newborn care A specialized type of health care designed to help a family adapt to the physical and psychosocial needs of a healthy newborn child.

family dependent In managed care and medical insurance, this is when a person is enrolled in a health plan and can receive medical care services under the employer group contract or insurance agreement if he or she is: 1) the member's spouse; 2) an unmarried dependent child, including legal stepchildren or adopted children of either the spouse or the member; and 3) residing in the principal place of residence unless other arrangements have been made with the health plan. The definition of a dependent or a family dependent is usually stipulated in the health plan agreement or insurance contract.

family expense policy In managed care and insurance, this is a health plan policy that insures both the policyholder and immediate dependents.

family ganging In health-care delivery, this is the practice of requiring, requesting, or encouraging a patient to return for care with the whole family, even if the rest of the family does not need care. With the entire family coming for health care, the health service can charge the patient's third-party payer for care provided to each member of the family. The practice and term originated in and is most common to Medicaid mills, which frequently request that the mother of a sick child bring in all her children for care whether they need it or not. From the payment perspective this seems a questionable activity, but from a preventive care perspective it is acceptable because disease can be stopped from spreading among family members.

family health The family is the basic influence on the health and health behavior of its members and has the ability to mobilize and enhance (or diminish) the health status of its members. Family health is multidimensional and must have positive inputs into seven dimensions: 1) biological/physical, 2) social, 3) emotional, 4) mental, 5) values/spiritual/morals, 6) security/stability, and 7) occupation/education. The family is the central unit for teaching and developing a culture of good health practices, behaviors, activities, perceptions, and lore. A healthy family needs to have both parents present and an emotionally stable setting with a strong value system that allows the family as a whole, and all individuals, to be enhanced in each of the seven dimensions. A stable family unit teaches and influences each family member on health practices, how to use and avoid needing the health-care system, diet and nutritional practices, attitudes about exercise and fitness, personal health practices and health maintenance, coping skills and meeting the demands of society, attitudes about sick role behavior, attitudes about self-care and home nursing, strong positive values and morals, emotional well-being and socialization, meeting the need for intimacy and security, concern for the environment, dealing with the demands of society, consumerism in purchasing, and the use of health products. *See family; nuclear family.*

family income Total money before taxes generated by all members of the family in a year. Income is considered from all sources, including wages, salaries, small business, tips, farm, professional trade, pensions, rents, welfare, unemployment compensation, alimony, contributions from friends and relatives, dividends, interest, and other sources. In-kind income (e.g., free rent) is excluded.

family income, poverty level The Bureau of Labor Statistics periodically sets the income poverty level for families according to inflation and family size and adjusted for each additional family member up to seven or more members.

family income policy A type of life insurance that combines decreasing term with ordinary life.

family member In managed care and medical insurance, a spouse or any eligible children of the subscriber who have been enrolled by the subscriber.

family numbering A practice in medical record keeping that assigns the family a number and each member a separate subnumber.

family physician A medical doctor who assumes ongoing responsibility for the health care of all members of a family regardless of age. Previously viewed as a low-level generalist, such physicians are highly trained specialists whose skills include treating the total person and family with general medicine, psychiatry, pediatrics, geriatrics, internal medicine, some surgery, obstetrics, and gynecology. *See family practice; family practitioner.*

family planning The use of a wide range of fertility regulation methods that help individuals or couples avoid unwanted births, plan a pregnancy, control the number of children born, regulate the intervals between pregnancies, and control the time at which births occur in relation to the age of parents. Its components include birth planning, use of contraception, dispensing birth control substances, materials and devices, management of infertility, sex education, and genetic counseling. Family planning has replaced the term "birth control," which is only one aspect of family planning.

family planning services Education, materials, exams, and birth control methods made available to patients in a clinic setting that aid in birth planning, birth control dispensing, and child spacing. *See family planning.*

family practice A medical specialty that actually encompasses several subspecialties. It has replaced the old general practitioner and has been enhanced by in-depth training. Those who complete the family practice residency become extremely well trained generalist physicians. A 3-year residency is required to provide well-developed, broadly trained physicians. The residency includes rotations in psychiatry, pediatrics, internal medicine, geriatrics, and obstetrics and gynecology. The training stresses prevention, diagnosis, and treatment of diseases, injuries, and illness that are common to the family and the general population. Family practice is practiced by doctors of medicine and by doctors of osteopathy.

family practice service A medical care provider or clinic that provides general medical care to all members of a family regardless of age.

family practitioner A physician who assumes continuing responsibility for supervising the health and coordinating the care of all members of a family regardless of age. Such physicians are highly trained specialists whose special skills include medical manager, advocate, educator, and counselor for their patients. Most family practitioners are specialists, having completed certification and residency in family practice medicine or osteopathic medicine, and may be assisted by physician assistants or nurse practitioners. *See also personal physician; primary care; general practitioner.*

family rate In managed care, this is a monthly rate that a health plan charges an employer to insure both the employee and his or her immediate dependents such as spouse and children.

family services An educational or instructional program that trains people to utilize home economics and the protective and preventive services that are provided by governmental and public agencies.

family style As used in dietary services in healthcare facilities, this is the process of serving nutritious meals to residents or patients without special diets, in a manner found in a family setting, by letting them serve themselves from bowls on the table.

FARE *See Fair Allowance Reimbursement Effort.*

farmer's lung A lung disorder resulting from occupational exposure to fungal spores that grow in hay stored prior to proper drying. An acute form of the disease is reversible, but the chronic form can cause irreversible restricted lung capacity.

FAS Fetal alcohol syndrome.

fas (Lat.) Right; justice.

fast 1. To abstain from food for a long period of time. 2. Secured or held firmly.

fastigium The highest point of a disease or fever.

fast track or tracking 1. In health-care facility construction, this is a construction development method whereby time is saved by providing an overlap of design and construction activities. This procedure requires the bidding of the project in phased bid packages so that, as portions of the design are completed, portions are put out to bid according to a predetermined schedule; synonymous with "phased construction." 2. Treating patients in the emergency room (ER) by using it as a primary care entrance into the health-care system, providing low fees and ongoing basic primary care in the ER. This competes with primary care private practice physicians. 3. In health administration, pushing ambitious, sharp, bright, young administrators who have great potential up through the ranks of a large organization, grooming them for top management positions. This is often found in family-owned businesses and is used to prepare younger family members for top management positions.

fatal 1. Ending in death; capable of causing death; causing death. 2. A serious mistake in a legal procedure that could unfairly hurt the party who complains about it. 3. An error in the legal process that could result in a new trial or a default.

fatal accidents In public health and health and safety management, these are all accidents that result in one or more deaths within 1 year.

fatality ratio See case fatality ratio.

fault 1. Guilty of an improper act, mistake, or error; negligence; lack of care; failure to perform duty. 2. A defect or imperfection. 3. In health law and medical malpractice litigation, a wrongful act, omission, or breach of duty and the determining or fixing of blame; to blame. See also negligence.

favorableness A leadership concept of organizational behavior and management that relates to the extent or degree of effectiveness of a leader on the basis of group atmosphere, the structure of the work tasks, and the leader's authority and power.

favorable selection See skimming.

favored nations discount In managed care and medical insurance, this is a contractual agreement between a health-care provider and a third-party payer. According to the contract, the third-party payer will automatically get the best discounts provided to any other third-party payers.

FAX See facsimile transmission.

FDA See Food and Drug Administration.

fear Unpleasurable or painful perceptions and/or feelings with accompanying psychophysiological response to a real or perceived threat or danger that, if not solved, can cause stress or anxiety or can lead to problem-solving behavior and approaches. See also anxiety.

feasance To perform an obligation; to carry out an obligation or duty; to put a condition into effect.

feasibility analysis In medical records, the process of examining, identifying, and ranking various solutions to problems encountered. The validity of storage methods; the use of hardware, software, and staffing; and a cost analysis of the variables are measured.

FEC Freestanding emergency center. See emergency center, freestanding.

fecal impaction A mass of hardened, mostly dry feces packed into the folds of the rectum, usually in senile patients as found in long-term-care facilities. Also called "impacted stool." See impaction.

feces The solid waste discharged by the large intestine. Also referred to as the "stool."

fecundity In public health and epidemiology, this is the ability of females to have babies; the physiological capability to produce offspring, as opposed to infertility. See childbearing years.

federal 1. Having to do with the major central government. 2. Created and supported by a central authority in common affairs such as the federal government of the United States.

federal crime insurance A special type of insurance offered by the federal government that covers burglary and theft.

Federal Employees Health Benefits Program (FEHBP) The group health insurance program for federal employees; the largest employer-sponsored contributory health insurance program in the world. It was established under

Federal Employees Health Benefits Act of 1959 (P.L. 86-382 codified in Chapter 89, title V, U.S. Code) and began operation in July 1960 and is administered by the U.S. Civil Service Commission. Every employee may choose between two government-wide plans: a service benefit plan administered by Blue Cross/Blue Shield and an indemnity benefit plan offered by the insurance industry through the Aetna Life Insurance Company. In addition to these two plans, 15 or more employee organizations offer indemnity-type plans to their members. Prepaid group practice plans are also available to employees residing in certain geographic areas.

Federal Financial Participation The revenue provided to states from U.S. governmental agencies for specified health or medical programs as a match to proper state expenditures (e.g., a monetary match provided to Medicaid to assist in contracted managed-care plans).

Federal Health Insurance Plan (FHIP) One of three health insurance proposals for national health insurance, or the Health Security Program. Also called the Comprehensive Health Insurance Plan.

federal hospital *See hospital, federal.*

federalism Rules, constitutions, or principles of a central controlling government.

federalist One who works for or supports a central controlling government.

federal judicial districts The United States is divided into several major divisions that are under the jurisdiction of a single federal court of appeals. The federal district courts review regulations and establish precedents that the governmental agencies follow, if made a part of the original law through legislative action by the U.S. Congress.

Federally Qualified Health Centers (FQHC's) Programs operating directly under the Bureau of Primary Health Care (BPHC), which is within the Health Resources and Services Administration of the U.S. Dept. of Health and Human Services. Community Health Centers, Migrant Health Centers, Health Care for the Homeless, and Public Housing grantees are automatically eligible for a cost-based reimbursement rate from Medicare and Medicaid, under the Federally Qualified Health Center (FQHC) program. The BPHC also reviews applications from centers seeking to qualify as FQHC "Look-Alikes" because they meet the statuatory requirements for these programs but do not receive grant funding. Over 100 organizations have been recommended to the Health Care Financing Administration, and as a result receive the benefits of cost-based reimbursement along with BPHC programs.

federally qualified HMO 1. In managed care, this is when an HMO meets certain federally stipulated provisions aimed at protecting consumers, such as providing a comprehensive set of services, ensuring financial solvency, and monitoring the quality of care. To become qualified, the HMO must apply to the federal Office of Prepaid Health Care of the Health Care Financing Administration (HCFA) and fulfill the requirements, amendments, and regulations of the HMO Act. Section 1301 of the HMO Act governs federal qualification and includes such requirements as basic and supplement services and capitation rate settings.

Federal Mediation and Conciliation Service (FMCS) fee-for-service An agency created by the Labor Management Relations Act of 1947 to help labor and management negotiate and resolve impasses peacefully through mediation without resorting to strikes.

federal qualification In managed care, this is a designation made by the Health Care Financing Administration (HCFA), after conducting an extensive evaluation process of a health plan's entire method of doing business, including its documents, policies, contracts, facilities, clinics, and delivery system. On compliance with the regulatory requirements, which are more stringent than the state laws, the organization is eligible to apply for federal loans and grants. Larger employers also must make managed-care plans locally available to their employees if requested.

federal question(s) A legal issue concerned with the U.S. Constitution or any statute enacted by the U.S. Congress; cases or disputes directly involving the U.S. Constitution or U.S. statutes.

Federal Register An official, daily publication of the federal government that makes available to the public proposed and final rules, legal notices, and similar proclamations, orders, and documents having general applicability and legal effect. The *Federal Register* publishes material from all federal agencies.

federal safety standards Safety rules set by federal agencies that any organization receiving federal funds must comply with. State safety regulations that are as stringent or stronger may be used.

Federal Tort Claims Act Passed in 1946, this act (28 U.S.C.A. Sec. 1346 [b] [Supp. 1988]) waived the sovereign immunity of the federal government and allowed an injured party to sue the U.S. government. Prior to this act, if a patient of a federal health-care facility, under the care of a federally employed health-care provider, was harmed while receiving health care, any action against the employee had to be entered as a bill into the legislative process of the U.S. Congress so that money could be appropriated to pay the claim. Now federal employees can be sued for causing harm or injury to citizens, as can the agency they work for, if circumstances dictate legal action. Governmental immunity has been reduced and in some cases eliminated by this act.

Federal Toxic Substance Control Act (TSCA) Enacted in 1976 by the U.S. Congress to prevent the environment from becoming a laboratory from which harmful effects of chemicals are discovered. Designed to control new chemicals, the act requires manufacturers to test new chemicals and give a 90-day notice to the EPA of new chemical to be manufactured. *See premanufacture notification.*

Federal Trade Commission (FTC) Created in 1914 by the Federal Trade Commission Act, this federal agency has jurisdiction over unfair, unsafe, and deceptive trade practices including medical quackery and antitrust areas.

federation A formal organization, league, or government united in a central power for a common goal or purpose.

Federation of American Health Systems A national trade association of the investor-owned hospitals and for-profit health-care systems industry. Located in Washington, D.C., it represents about 1400 hospitals and 65 organizations that own and operate hospitals, nursing homes, or clinics. Organizational officials lobby in Congress and are spokesmen for the industry, media, academia, and the public on issues related to investor-owned hospitals and health care.

Federation Licensing Examination (FLEX) A standardized licensure test for physicians developed by the U.S. Federation of State Medical Boards for potential use on a nationwide basis. Forty-eight states use the FLEX test for licensure, although scores required for licensure vary. The FLEX exam covers test materials developed by the National Board of Medical Examiners. *See also national board examinations.*

Federation of State Medical Boards A national association whose members serve on medical boards for the states and territories of the United States. The association provides a forum for the discussion of issues facing medical boards, licensing of physicians, and standardization of activities, testing procedures, disciplinary issues, ethical issues, etc.

feds Slang for any government agency or federal government employee.

fee Payment for professional services; a charge for service rendered.

feedback 1. In health administration and systems management, this is the ongoing assessment of effectiveness, efficiency, and any shortcomings that are communicated back to the source or original input to the process. 2. A positive or negative response to a system's output for the purpose of influencing a process. 3. Information directed back to the beginning or to selected parts of a process, project, or program, providing an assessment and evaluation that aids in improving quality or control. 4. In communication, the response. 5. In organizational behavior and management, gaining input and knowledge about job function and job performance by receiving information back from the job itself or the employees.

fee-for-service 1. A method of charging patients for medical care services or treatment whereby a physician or other practitioner bills the insurance company or the patient for each patient encounter, treatment, or service rendered. In the past this has been the usual method of seeking payment by most physicians, especially in solo or small-group practice. Self-pay by the patient is also usually directly for services rendered, tests, and other services. Under a fee-for-service payment system, if expenditures increase, the fees themselves increase; that is, if more units of service are billed or more expensive services are substituted for less expensive ones, the high costs are reflected in the bill sent to the insurance company or the patient. This system contrasts with salary, per capita, capitation, or prepayment systems, in which the payment for each patient encounter does not change with the number of services used, or even if none are used. The fee-for-service system has been generally used by physicians, dentists, psychologists, counselors, podiatrists, optometrists, and other solo practitioners or group practitioners; a number of other practitioners, such as physical therapists and physician assistants, have sought reimbursement on a fee-for-service basis. Nearly all fee-for-service charges are paid at the time of service or retrospectively. 2. A method of reimbursement based on payment for specific services rendered to a patient. Payment may be made by an insurance carrier. 3. Under national health security programs and universal coverage, the traditional method of paying for health care, whereby the patient pays the doctor, and the patient is later reimbursed by the insurance company after the receipts and claims are submitted. Also known as an "indemnity insurance payment system." *See also fee schedule; fractionation; capitation.*

fee-for-service contract In managed care or other health-care contracted services, this is a financial management arrangement whereby the health plan or insurance company pays back the health-care provider directly; the amount reimbursed is dependent on the "going rate" of charges.

fee-for-service reimbursement In managed care and medical insurance, this is the traditional manner of payment for medical care services by which health-care providers receive a payment that does not exceed their billed amount for each unit of service provided.

fee-for-services equivalency In health-care delivery and health-care finance, this is a quantitative measure of the difference between the fees a health-care provider receives for services rendered from the several types of reimbursement systems (prospective payment system, capitation, or contracted care) and what is usually charged.

fee maximum In health-care finance, this is the highest amount of fees the health-care provider can be paid for any medical care service or treatment provided to health plan members under the terms of a specific health plan agreement. Also called "fee max." *See maximum allowable cost.*

fee schedule In managed care and medical insurance, this is a list of and the charges for each health- and medical care service or treatment available; a listing of established allowances for specified medical or dental procedures. It usually represents either a physician's or a third party's standard or maximum charges for the listed procedures. *See also relative value scale.*

fee schedule, physician services An extensive list of services, treatments, and procedures usually offered by physicians, each of which has an assigned monetary amount that represents the payment approved by a given insurance plan or health plan.

fee screen In the Social Security Administration, the customary, prevailing, and reasonable charge amounts established for physician services by the carrier at the beginning of each fiscal year. It implies that charges (or fees) in excess of these computed rates are "screened out" and that the payment to the physician by the carrier is less than the actual charge. Synonymous with "prevailing charges" or "prevailings."

fee splitting An unethical practice by a physician, surgeon, or consultant that returns part of the referral fee back to the referring physician for making the referral.

FEHBP *See Federal Employees Health Benefits Program.*

fellow 1. Those individuals in a profession with top rank or position; a member of a professional or esteemed society such as the American College of Healthcare Executives, who is granted a special status in that organization after meeting specific standards and strict qualifications such as having a certain number of years in the profession, passing rigorous exams, or completing professional activities such as publishing articles in professionally reviewed journals. Once all the criteria have been met, the member is in good standing and is elevated to the rank of "fellow" and can use initials such as FACHE behind his or her title to indicate advanced professional advancement and performance. 2. A colleague in a profession. *See Appendix II.*

fellow (mid- or post-residency) A graduate of a medical, osteopathic, or dental school or a health-care administration program who has had an advanced period of graduate training and is in a fellowship program in a subspecialty or clinical research program.

fellow servant rule An employer is responsible for injuries inflicted by one employee on another if the employees were carefully chosen or if proper care was exercised to avoid the mishap.

fellowship 1. Being an associate. A mutual association of professional persons on an equal basis who have the same occupations or interests. 2. A special position of advanced training accompanied by an honorarium, stipend, salary, or endowment of money to provide support of a graduate student in a college, university, or health-care institution for advanced training and experience; the rank of a fellow in a university or health-care facility.

felon In criminal law, one who commits a felony or has been convicted of committing a felony.

felony In criminal law, this is a crime for which a person can be sent to state prison. Such a crime is determined by the degree of seriousness of the crime committed and varies from state to state.

felony murder In criminal law, this is a homicide committed during a felony attempt.

felony murder rule An accidental killing during the act of committing a felony may result in the death being ruled as a murder.

feme covert A married woman; used to describe the legal disabilities of a married woman.

feme sole A single woman, including one previously married.

fertile Capable of reproducing; a female's ability to have a child and a male's ability to complete conception.

fertility drug A chemical substance, when taken by an individual, that enhances the possibility of pregnancy.

fertility rate In public health and epidemiology, this is a measure of the crude fertility rate of a population, state, or country. A fertility rate is computed by dividing total live births occurring in 1 calendar year by the midyear population of women aged 15 to 44. Some sources suggest the age range of 14 to 49 years be used. The fertility rate formula follows:

$$\frac{\text{Total live births in 1 calendar year}}{\text{Total midyear population of women aged 15 to 44 for the same time period}} \times 1000$$

See fecundity; childbearing years.

fertility rate, completed In public health and epidemiology, this is the sum of the central birth rates over all ages of childbearing (14–49 years) for a given birth cohort; the same as the fertility rate, but the numerator and denominator are restricted to a cohort characteristic such as the same birth year.

fertility rate, general In public health and epidemiology, this is a better and more refined assessment of fertility preferred over a crude fertility rate. The numerator is the number of live births for the population group or geographic unit for 1 year. The denominator is restricted to all females of childbearing age (15–44 years), with some agencies using 15 through 49 years. The general fertility rate formula follows:

$$\frac{\text{Number of live births in a geographical area or a population during 1 year}}{\text{Midyear female population ages 15–44 for same area and same year}} \times 1000$$

fetal alcohol syndrome (FAS) Characterized by birth defects in babies born to mothers who have consumed alcohol excessively throughout a pregnancy and just prior to delivery.

fetal death In public health, epidemiology, and medical care, this is the complete expulsion or extraction from the mother of a nonliving product of human conception regardless of the duration of pregnancy. The death is indicated by the fact that after such expulsion or extraction, the fetus does not breathe or show any evidence of life. In most states, the death of a fetus 20 weeks or older in the gestational age must be registered with the local registrar (W.H.O. and California Administrative Code, Title 17, Chapter 1, Article 3). *See live birth; infant mortality.*

fetal death rate In public health and epidemiology, this is the number of fetal deaths with stated or presumed gestation of 20 weeks or more per 1000 live births plus fetal deaths (all births). The fetal death rate formula follows:

$$\frac{\text{Total number of fetal deaths of 20 weeks gestation or more in a specific time period}}{\text{Total live births + all fetal deaths for same time period}} \times 1000$$

fetal heart monitor In medical care, this is a specialized electronic instrument with highly sensitive sensors that are attached to the outside of a mother's stomach in the last hours of labor. The sensors detect fetal heartbeat activity and record it on a graph and/or an oscilloscope. The physician can then determine if the baby is in distress or is healthy.

fetal mortality ratio The annual number of fetal deaths as a proportion of the annual number of live births.

fetishism Achieving sexual excitement from an inanimate object (e.g., underwear) that has a sexual implication; a deviant form of sexual behavior.

feto-infant mortality rate In public health and epidemiology, the number of fetal deaths with stated or presumed gestation of 28 weeks or more plus the number of infant deaths per 1000 live births plus late fetal deaths. The feto-infant mortality rate formula follows:

$$\frac{\text{Total number of fetal deaths of 28 weeks gestation or more + all infant deaths in a specific time period}}{\text{Total live births + all late fetal deaths for same time period}} \times 1000$$

fetus The unborn developing baby from the third month (18 weeks) of pregnancy until birth. Under 18 weeks the unborn baby is referred to as an "embryo."

fever A rise in the body temperature above the normal temperature of 98.6° F or 37° C (oral temperature). Also referred to as "pyrexia."

ff. (abbr.) Following (pages).

FFS *See fee-for-service.*

FHIP *See Federal Health Insurance Plan.*

fiat (Lat.) Meaning "let it be done"; a command or directive given by legal authority.

FICA Federal Insurance Contributions Act; the Social Security tax that is prepaid to the Social Security Administration from the money withheld from one's paycheck. This money is added to the national Social Security Fund, which in turn provides revenue for various Social Security programs, including Medicare.

fiction, legal *See legal fiction.*

fictitious Fake; false; not real; made up; imaginary; counterfeit; not genuine.

fidelity bonding In health administration and health-care financial management, these are bonds used for the protection of the principal (employer) against loss caused by dishonesty or theft by the employees.

fides (Lat.) Faith; "bona fides" means "good faith"; "mala fides" means "bad faith."

fiduciary 1. Relating to or founded on trust or confidence; any relationship based on trust and confidence; a relationship and commitment between two persons in which one person acts for another in a position of trust 2. In health law, this is the obligation of an individual or organization to act in a confidential manner on behalf of another person in matters that affect the other person or organization. Such relationships may include physician-patient, psychologist-client, parent-child, attorney-client, and others. *See also trust; trustee.*

fiduciary interest A relationship in which an individual or members of an organization have an obligation to act on behalf of patients or clients and their interests.

fiduciary relationship *See fiduciary.*

field A specific or designated area of a computerized record that is used for a special category of data.

field experience An educationally controlled on-the-job training experience for students established through the cooperation of a college or university and health agencies, health facilities, and institutions for the students to gain practical career-related experience. *See also internship; externship; residency; administrative residency.*

field experiment In epidemiology, health administration organizational behavior, or related research, this is a research experiment in which independent variables are deliberately maximized. Researchers study workers (the subjects) under usual conditions to determine how they react to new approaches, services, changes, or programs.

field force In managed care and insurance, this is the insurance company employees who work for the insurance company or health plan in the community and closely with the clients or health-care providers.

field review method In health administration and human resources management, this is when personnel from the human resources department, trained in employee evaluation and performance appraisal, go out into the health-care organization or facility to assist supervisors with performance appraisals and employee ratings. The evaluation form or performance appraisal form is filled out under the direction of the supervisor.

field study 1. Research approaches based in an institution, a hospital, or an agency (or, in the case of epidemiological studies, a community or population) under investigation that utilize a systematic observation of variables or people functioning in real-world activities or settings. 2. Another term for "field experience." *See also field experience; internship; externship; residency.*

field underwriting In managed care and insurance, this is the first step in risk analysis and selection. An agent gathers, screens, and analyzes vital information about prospective participants in a health plan or medical insurance program by obtaining pertinent information about the company, employer group, or clientele to be insured and reports the information and findings to the home office underwriter so that underwriting decisions can be made.

FIFO *See first in, first out.*

fifth pathway In medical and physician education, a method that an individual who obtains all or part of his or her undergraduate medical education abroad can enter graduate medical education in the United States. The fifth pathway provides a period of supervised clinical training to students who obtained their premedical education in the United States, received undergraduate medical education abroad, and passed a screening examination approved by the CCHE. When these students successfully complete a year of clinical training sponsored by a U.S. medical school, they then become eligible for an internship or a residency approved by the American Medical Association.

fifty one fifty (5150) A term, based on the criminal code of a state, to indicate the commitment of a patient to a psychiatric ward by police or the medical staff of a psychiatric facility if the patient is determined to be a danger to him- or herself or others. Some states have different terms or numbers for the same commitment procedure.

file In health information management, this is a logical collection of data treated as one unit. Data or information occupying one or more blocks of space on a storage media such as a disk or tape and identified by file name.

file maintenance In health information management, this is the updating of storage media and files by adding, changing, or deleting files.

file name In health information management, this is the alphanumeric name assigned to a file for identification. A file name has a fixed maximum length that is related to the computer system.

file specification In health information management, this is a special label that uniquely identifies a computer file, usually consisting of three components: 1) identification of the volume on which the file is stored, 2) a file name, and 3) a file type.

file-structured device In health information management, this is a tape, hard disk, or diskette on which files are stored. A directory of the files is maintained, and the data or information is stored and organized in files on disk.

filiation proceeding A paternity suit. *See paternity suit.*

filibustering In parliamentary procedure, this is the process of speaking for the purpose of keeping control of the time and preventing the opposition from getting a chance to speak by consuming the allotted time for a motion to be made and passed.

film badge A piece of photographic film worn as a badge. The badge darkens when exposed to nuclear radiation, and radiation exposure levels can be checked by inspecting the film. Such badges are worn by nuclear workers, radiologists, radiological technologists, or anyone working with radiation.

FIM *See functional improvement measures.*

final argument In health law and litigation, this is the final statement presented to the jury in a trial that shows how the attorney perceives the facts and how he or she thinks law, fairness, and justice apply to the facts.

final decision 1. In health law and litigation, this is the last decision in a trial court on which an appeal can be based. 2. In a court of appeals, the last decision from which there are no more appeals.

final disposition 1. A final judgment before a court. 2. A final decision establishing the rights and obligations of the parties involved in a dispute or action.

final product In health-care delivery, this is the endpoint of any set of clinical services or course of treatment; the outcome of the process of delivering health care to a patient by a health-care provider.

finance committee A committee of a board of directors of a health-care organization responsible for determining the board's financial status, policies, and plans for issues such as investments, loans, lines of credit, and removing debt.

finance system That part of a health-care organization's structure and organizational management that collects, manages, and analyzes the revenue and monetary accounting activities of the organization. Parts of the system include budgetary planning, accounting, record keeping, proper use of resources, contracting, third-party payer management, and maintaining an information management system for input, control, use, and analysis of revenue and output of funds and financial reports.

financial analysis In health-care financial management, this is the process of evaluating all accounting, budgeting, and financial records of the health-care organization to determine profitability and financial stability.

financial director In health administration, this is the administrator (usually an assistant administrator or vice president) of a health-care facility who is responsible for the financial affairs of the facility.

financial feasibility In health-care financial management, this is the evaluation of a proposed health-care service in terms of its ability to be financially solvent and make a profit. The analysis of the financial feasibility of new services is measured by matching the reasonable revenues to be received to the costs of the activities.

financial statement In health-care finance, this is a report of the financial condition of a health-care organization. A balance sheet and income and expense statement are the main parts of the report, which discloses the financial health or shortfalls of the organization.

financial structure In health-care finance, this is the entire "right hand" of the balance sheet that presents and discloses the manner in which the health-care organization is financed.

financial viability In health-care finance, this is when a health-care organization is operated in an efficient and effective manner and makes an overattainment of funds compared to expenses, ensuring that the hospital can continue to operate successfully in the future.

financing In health-care finance, these are the methods of gaining, and the sources of, revenue in health services. Modes of financing include third-party payers, public grants, contracts with managed care, government contracts, direct public/government payment for service, philanthropic grants and payments for service, loans, bonds, and self-pay.

finder's fee A fee paid to a person for finding business or referring business to another person.

finding 1. A determination of a question of fact; the results of a research study. 2. A decision about evidence. 3. A conclusion of law. 4. Under the Omnibus Budget Reconciliation Act (OBRA), information about practices or procedures discovered during a survey of a health-care facility and how it compares to required standards and regulations. 4. The results of medical testing and the information made available to the physician about a patient from blood tests, allergy testing, X rays, MRI, EEG, EKG, and CT scans and other diagnostic procedures.

fire partition or wall For JCAHO long-term-care accreditation purposes, a wall or barrier constructed to resist the passage of both fire and smoke for a minimum of 2 hours. Such walls are required to separate patient-occupied areas from other areas or to separate conforming and nonconforming structures.

firm offer A written offer or agreement between two parties that will be held open for a certain period of time.

firmware In health information management, this is software that is embedded in the hardware of a computer to accomplish frequently repeated tasks requiring extreme accuracy in the output. Also referred to as a "microde."

first aid The immediate emergency care and treatment given to a person who has been injured or has become suddenly ill. It includes self-help and home emergency care. Words of comfort, encouragement, evidence of willingness to help, and the promotion of confidence and air of competence also are essential. Emergency care is given until advanced and complete medical care is provided.

first-dollar coverage In managed care and medical insurance, this is coverage under a health plan or a medical insurance policy that begins with the first dollar of expense incurred by the insured for the covered benefits. The third-party payer pays the consumer's entire medical bill, including the first dollar. Such coverage, therefore, has no deductibles but may have co-payments or co-insurance. *See also last dollar coverage.*

first impression, case of In health law, a case presenting a question of law never considered previously and for which no precedent has been set.

first in, first out (FIFO) In health administration, this is an inventory method whereby the items received first are used first, thus keeping all inventory stock fresh or current.

first intention healing In medical care, this is the primary (or first) healing that occurs in an injury or wound when the tissues have been closed or pulled together.

first-line supervisor In health administration, this is a midmanager position directly under department heads on an organizational chart in a traditional hospital or health-care organization. *See also front-line supervisor.*

first-listed diagnosis In medical care, this is the diagnosis of the physician written on the face sheet of the medical record as the primary diagnosis (written at the top, or first).

first party In health-care financial reimbursement, this is the patient, often using self-pay. Also referred to as a "first-party payer" or "reimbursement."

first responder An individual trained in emergency medical care who is the first to arrive at the scene of a medical emergency and is capable of rendering basic life support.

first-surplus treaty An insurance agreement whereby the granting company accepts a certain amount of risk and the other party the remaining amount.

first-year commission In insurance, this is an amount paid to an insurance agent according to the policy's first annual premium amount.

fiscal Pertaining to financial matters and time periods or budget periods. *See also fiscal year.*

fiscal agent 1. An agent or insurance company that processes claims and issues payment for state or federal health insurance agencies or other insurance companies. 2. A contractor who is responsible for processing claims for health-care services provided by health-care practitioners and institutions to Title XVIII beneficiaries or Title XIX recipients. Title XVIII fiscal agents are known specifically as "intermediaries" and "carriers."

fiscal court A term for a county board of supervisors or county commissioners in some states in the southern and eastern United States.

fiscal intermediary A contractor that processes and pays provider claims on behalf of a state Medicaid agency. Fiscal intermediaries are rarely at risk and serve as administrative units for the state, handling the payment of bills. Fiscal intermediaries may be insurance companies, management firms, or other private contractors. *See also intermediary.*

fiscal management 1. The directing, controlling, administering, and planning of activities related to financial matters. 2. According to JCAHO for psychiatric, alcoholism, and drug abuse facilities accreditation purposes, procedures that control a facility's overall financial and general operations such as cost accounting, program budgeting, materials purchasing, and patient billing.

fiscal period *See fiscal; fiscal year.*

fiscal year (FY) Any 12-month period for which annual accounts are kept or budgets allocated. In some organizations, it may be the same as the calendar year; other organizations may use different year periods such as July 1–June 30 or September 1–August 31. The federal government's fiscal year was changed from July 1–June 30 to October 1–September 30 in 1976.

fishing expedition 1. In health law, this is using the court to question a witness to uncover information that is suspected but has not been brought out or proven; using a court to get information that is not actually part of a lawsuit. 2. Irrelevant questioning of a witness. 3. A broad and probing use of the legal discovery process.

fitness center This is a special facility that promotes health by providing exercise, health, and physical testing and evaluation programs and exercise and fitness activities to the community and/or organization employees. *See health promotion.*

fitness program A preventive care activity that achieves and maintains a high-level state of physical well-being, contributing to a high personal health status in individuals.

five-star rating system *See JCAHO five-star rating system.*

fixed assets In health-care financial management, these are tangible items (e.g., land, buildings, equipment, machines, or vehicles) that are essential to the operation of a health-care organization and to which a dollar value can be fixed.

fixed assets financing ratio A ratio used by lenders to examine the relationship of long-term debt to net fixed assets. A ratio that indicates the proportion of assets such as property, physical plant, and equipment that is financed by long-term debt and informs a bank or lender of the proportion of the assets that are actually backing any proposed new loan. The fixed assets financing ratio formula follows:

$$\frac{\text{Long-term debt}}{\text{Net fixed assets}} \times 100 = \text{Percentage}$$

fixed charges In health-care financial management, these are set fees, costs, or expenses; costs that do not vary with output levels.

fixed costs In health-care financial management, these are costs that are constantly incurred regardless of the volume of income or business and that do not vary with utilization rates (e.g., rent, leases, and utilities). Also called "constant costs."

fix the time for the next meeting In formal or official health-care organization meetings using parliamentary procedure, this is a statement of the highest privileged motion. This motion is in order at any time, and often this motion is used to set a meeting time if different than the regular meeting time.

flagrante delicto (Lat.) In the act of committing a crime.

flat extra premium method In managed care and insurance, this is a method for rating substandard risks that is used when extra risks are considered to be constant. The underwriter assesses a specific extra premium for each $1000 of insurance.

flat maternity In managed care and medical insurance, this is a single inclusive maternity benefit for all charges incurred as a result of pregnancy, childbirth, and complications arising from the maternity process. A limit (e.g., $1500) may be applied per pregnancy or per year. *See also switch maternity; swap maternity.*

flat schedule In managed care and insurance, this is a type of policy structure in group insurance that insures everyone for the same benefits regardless of salary, position, or circumstances. Also called a "flexplan."

FLEX *See Federation Licensing Examination.*

flexible benefit plan In managed care, this is a health plan that offers employees a choice among a number of alternative benefits during each year's open enrollment period, allowing members to tailor their benefits to their specific needs. Also referred to as a "flexplan." *See flexplan.*

flexible budgeting In health-care financial management, this is a revenue planning and allocation method that uses the concept of fixed and variable costs and is adjusted for actual level of operations.

flexible spending account (FSA) In health-care financial management, this is money set aside by an employer; pretax funds allotted to employee benefits for medical, dental, retirement, legal assistance, or insurance.

Flexner Report The results of a 1910 survey of all U.S. and Canadian medical schools commissioned by the Carnegie Foundation and undertaken by Abraham Flexner, Dean of Education at Johns Hopkins University. In evaluating medical education, the report found the quality of education inconsistent and below acceptable standards in many, if not most, medical schools. Subsequent to this report, over half the medical schools were closed permanently. Flexner recommended a medical education curriculum founded in the hard sciences that is still the foundation of medical education and many allied health clinical training programs today. A year of physics, biological sciences, and chemistry is required for medical schools, dental schools, and most high-level allied health and nursing programs that also followed the Flexner model. The educational findings were implemented in the Medical School at Johns Hopkins University and were to provide a basis for a model for all medical school education.

flexplan In managed care and insurance, this is a system for managing insurance expenditures. By law these plans are for employees only. Employees have their part of the insurance paid with pretax dollars, the amount of the premium deducted each month from the employee's paycheck and held in a premium conversion account. The salaries are lower, and both employees and employers pay less taxes.

flextime In health administration and human resource management, this is an employee scheduling approach that allows workers to choose the times of the day or week that they wish to work. It is an innovative approach that sets aside rigid starting and quitting times. Employees are allowed to begin and end work at times agreed on by the supervisor and the worker. This scheduling approach has been used to reduce absenteeism and turnover and to increase job satisfaction.

flexyear In health administration and human resource management, this is an employee scheduling approach that allows workers to be off the job for part of the year. Usually 2000 hours of work (a year's time) obligation is fulfilled.

floating capital In health-care financial management, these are financial resources available to meet current or due expenses that are not tied up in equipment or the physical plant.

float nurse In a hospital, nursing home, or other health-care facility or agency, this is when a nurse who is available for assignment to whatever department or agency has a nursing personnel need either because of personnel shortage or because of increased need.

float pool In a hospital, nursing home, or other health-care facility or agency, a group of nurses or allied health professionals who are available for assignment to duty on an ad hoc basis. They are available to fill in during vacations, absences, or peak periods of heavy workloads.

floor In parliamentary procedure, when a person is formally recognized by the chairman, is given the privilege to speak, and is the only one allowed to do so.

floppy disk In health information management and computers, this is a disk made of a metal-coated flexible plastic sealed in a protective envelope that functions somewhat like magnetic tape. It is used as a storage device for computerized information.

flora (microflora) Microorganisms in the intestine that are essential for digestion and normal physiological functioning.

flow A quantity of activity occurring in a given time or duration (e.g., the number of patients treated in an outpatient center in a certain time period).

flow chart In health administration and health planning, this is a diagram used to show organizational structure, staffing procedure, or steps in a process; in computers, the sequence of data processing operations.

flow chart symbol A symbol used to represent operations, direction, data flow, or equipment in a problem.

flow line A line representing a connecting path between symbols on a flow chart.

fluorescein angiography In medical care, this is a photographic technique formulated by Novotney and Alvis in 1961 that uses injection of an intravenous bolus of sodium fluorescein followed by a rapid sequence of photographs of the vasculature of the retinal areas as the dye enters the vascular system.

fluoridation The addition of small, controlled amounts of fluoride to public water supplies for the purpose of reducing the incidence of dental cavities in the population using the water.

fluoroscope In medical care, this is a diagnostic device that aids a physician in viewing the internal condition of the human body. An X ray image is viewed directly as the X rays pass through the body of the patient. The X rays are projected onto a special screen instead of X-ray film, and the viewer can see the movement of body organs or the movement of radiopaque materials as they pass through the organs and vessels of the body. Permanent films can also be taken if needed.

fluoroscopy In medical care, this is a radiologic or diagnostic study using a fluorescent screen rather than the X-ray type.

FMC *See Foundation for Medical Care.*

FMG *See foreign medical graduate.*

FmHA Farmers Home Administration of the U.S. Department of Agriculture.

FNP Family nurse practitioner.

FOB *See free on board.*

focal length In laser technology, this is the distance measured in millimeters between the focal lens and the site on the body of the treatment or incision.

focal point In laser and X-ray technology, this is the point at which the beam converges or from which it diverges.

focus 1. The point of convergence of light rays, sound waves, or laser beams. 2. The principal site of an infection. 3. The emphasis of treatment or therapy.

focused audit A medical care review process that identifies a problem and then seeks to correct it. *See also focused review.*

focused review A review process in medical records whereby cases are identified by the medical record data system as being "questionable" in effectively utilizing resources. This process assists utilization review programs in avoiding review areas that have shown consistent or effective utilization of services or in selecting out utilization problem areas.

focused survey *See accreditation survey.*

focus groups In health-care organization strategic marketing and research, used to gather opinions or obtain information from persons affected by some experience. The nature of focus groups usually is more subjective in the process and is then made objective in the analysis. An average of 10 to 12 persons who are consumers or potential consumers of a health service are asked to participate in a session; 3 to 15 different focus groups are held with new participants each time. Five or six well-developed questions are used for every session. Each session is videotaped. When all the focus groups are completed, the researcher reviews the tapes, makes a grid of comments, and develops an objective, quantified database from them. The goal is testing the perception and receptivity of a target population to an idea with recurring comments, trends, problems, and concerns noted and indicated in the grid, which becomes the database and shows the trends.

follow-up visit 1. In health-care delivery, this is a brief return visit to a health-care provider by a patient to determine if treatment has progressed and healing has occurred. 2. In the assessment of health-care facilities for quality or compliance with regulations, a return site visit made by a survey team or a representative within 90 days of the end of the annual survey to determine if progress has been made on correcting violations found by the survey.

fomite In epidemiology, this is any inanimate object or article of clothing or material that carries, spreads, or harbors pathogens and is capable of transmitting disease.

Food and Drug Administration (FDA) An agency of the Department of Health and Human Services that protects the public against poisoning, contamination, or any other health hazards in foods, food substances, or food additives. This agency also ensures the safety and effectiveness of drugs and drug substances. The FDA has six subagencies: 1) foods, 2) drugs, 3) biologics, 4) radiological health, 5) medical and diagnostic products, and 6) veterinary medicine.

food-borne In epidemiology, these are diseases that multiply in, and are usually spread by, foodstuffs or substances.

food-borne illness In epidemiology, these are symptoms of diseases caused by contaminated food and drink that can be of two types: 1) delayed onset (food-borne infections) and 2) abrupt occurrences in nature (food-borne intoxication).

food-borne infections In epidemiology and infection control, these are illnesses caused by foodstuffs or drink containing pathogenic organisms such as harmful bacteria, viruses, and protozoa. Symptoms of the onset of food poisoning are often delayed because of the growth process of organisms after ingestion.

food-borne intoxications In epidemiology, these are toxins that are found in and transmitted by foodstuffs and drink. Sources of toxins in food are bacteria, poisonous plants, animals, and chemicals. Toxins can be the by-products of bacteria or can be directly toxic substances.

food-borne transmission In epidemiology, this is the spread of disease by food substances. Consumable foodstuffs are the medium for pathogen growth and the spread of diseases, often contaminated by those who prepare or serve it. *See food-specific attack rates; attack rates; waterborne transmission.*

food poisoning The eating of food products contaminated by microorganisms or toxins from bacteria or insecticide residues. The most common bacterial food poisonings are *salmonella, staphylococcus, clostridium welchii,* and *clostridium botulinum* (botulism).

food protection Public health and epidemiological measures taken to ensure wholesome and clean food that is free from unsafe bacteria and chemical contamination, natural or added deleterious substances, and decomposition during production, processing, packaging, distribution, storage, preparation, and service. Labels on marked foods must comply with established nutritional quality and packaging identification guidelines. The three major food protection components are sanitation, safety, and nutritional quality.

food service administration The management and organizational activities related to the preparation and serving of nutritional food in hospitals, long-term-care facilities, or other healthcare institutions. Personnel include dietitians, cooks, and other food service providers. Food services activities are coordinated with the special dietary needs of patients. Some health-care facilities also provide food services for employees or families or prepare food for support services such as home-delivered meals for homebound persons.

food service administrator or manager Individuals in midmanagement positions in health-care facilities, long-term-care facilities, and hospitals who, depending on the size and type of facility, usually report to the assistant administrator, the vice president in charge of food services, or the administrator. Administrative activities of this position include, but are not limited to, usual management and administrative activities, budgeting, providing adequate food and goods control, and maintaining proper records for meal counts, scheduling, costs, and employee time activities. Planning menus, making and maintaining a standardized set of recipes, following up by visits to floors, and supervising food production are also the responsibility of the food service administrator, though these are often done by others such as dietitians.

food services In health-care facilities, this is the provision of food, drinks, meals, and dietary and nutritional services to patients and, in hospitals, to staff and visitors.

food services department The section of a health-care facility responsible for food acquisition, preparation, and service to patients, employees, and visitors and nutrition education for patients, health-care providers, and the public.

food service systems management An array of

administrative, personnel, purchasing, and production components utilized in receiving, preparing, and serving foodstuffs as a systematic, purposeful activity that includes the planning, organizing, directing, supervision, coordinating, and controlling of all activities related to food acquisition, preparation, and service.

food service workers Personnel who are the employees in the food services of hospital, nursing homes, or other health-care facilities and perform the functions of the dietary service such as preparing and cooking food, serving the food, washing dishes, and making the kitchen and food service area clean and sanitary.

food-specific attack rate In epidemiology, this is a detailed attack rate that ascertains whether a statistical association exists between the ingestion of a specific foodstuff at a specific event, location, and time period to determine if it is related to a certain disease. Those who ate certain foods are compared to those who had not eaten the food. The food-specific attack rate formula follows:

$$\frac{\text{Number of persons who ate a specific food and became ill}}{\text{Total number of persons who ate the specific food}} \times 100$$

See attack rate; crude attack rate.

footboard A board placed at the foot of a bed so that a patient can brace his or her feet against it.

forbearance 1. A delay in enforcing rights. 2. Refraining from action on a case.

force 1. Compel; a binding power. 2. Unlawful violence. 3. To strengthen power, authority, or validity.

forced choice method In health administration and human resource management, this is an employee performance appraisal approach that requires the supervisor or rater to choose the most descriptive statement in each pair of preprepared statements about the work performance of the worker being evaluated.

forced sale A sale of goods or property made by a court order to pay off a judgment.

force majeure (French) Major force; superior power or force; a strong force that is difficult to resist.

forceps In medical care, this is any surgical instrument with two handles and two grasping surfaces that are attached and articulate in the middle; used to handle sterile supplies or to compress or grasp tissues.

forecast In strategic health planning and healthcare administration, this is predicting a healthcare organization's future direction and needs; reasonable estimates of future position, direction, growth, competition, and organizational need based on the assessment of present resources, finances, and circumstances projected into the future that help make decisions about anticipated change or the direction of the industry. *See exponential smoothing.*

forecasting In health administration, this is the process of planning and projecting for growth, development, capital development and retention, physical plant maintenance needs and the replacement of fixed assets, and organization profitability and stability.

foreclosure In health-care finance, this is forcing the payment of a debt through seizing and selling property or security for a debt, usually related to a mortgage and real estate.

foreign corporation Any organization or corporation not legally incorporated in the United States. Referred to as an "alien corporation" (the opposite of a domestic corporation).

foreign jurisdiction A jurisdiction of a court other than the one in which a court normally sits.

foreign medical graduate (FMG) A physician who graduated from a medical school outside the United States (and usually Canada). Citizens of the United States who attend medical school outside the country are classified as foreign medical graduates (sometimes distinguished as USFMGs), just as are foreign-born persons who are not trained in a medical school in this country. The term is occasionally defined as, and is nearly synonymous with, any graduate of a school not accredited by the Liaison Committee on Medical Education (LCME). *See also COTRANS; ECFMG; fifth pathway; J visa; labor certification; schedule A.*

forensic Having to do with law. The legal aspects of a profession, other than those of the actual legal profession, such as forensic psychiatry or forensic pathology; the legal philosophical aspects of a profession.

forensic dentistry *See dental jurisprudence.*

forensic medicine Medical knowledge related to law and to the solving of legal issues in health care and medicine.

forensic pathologist A medical doctor who specializes in the legal ramifications of an unnatural death, often a coroner or one who works with a coroner and investigates unnatural or suspicious deaths by conducting autopsies, tests, and other medical modalities.

forensic psychiatry The branch of psychiatry concerned with the legal aspects of mental illness, psychiatric problems, and mental health care.

foreseeability, doctrine of 1. In health law and negligence, this is the responsibility and liability of an individual to know about potential natural and proximate results of any act to another person to whom a duty is owed. 2. What a prudent, careful, ordinary, and thoughtful person under similar circumstances, with similar training and skills, would expect or predict to happen or would do. 3. Alertness to possible future hazards that could exist in a certain behavior, event, or act.

forfeit 1. To lose or give up. 2. To lose a right as a result of some fault, crime, or error. 3. Being negligent in a duty; breach of contract.

forgery 1. Making a fake or fraudulent document. 2. Intent to commit fraud by fabricating or altering a record or signature.

formal party In health law, this is to be involved in a lawsuit in name only; having no interest in a legal proceeding but named in it.

format In health information management and computers, this is the preparation of a disk or floppy diskette by the computer so that it can be used by the computer to save and store information. Disks and diskettes must be formatted before the computer can store information on them. The computer puts a magnetic charge on the surface of the diskettes so that they can systematically store information.

formative evaluation In health promotion and health services, any combination of measurement obtained and judgments made before or during the implementation of materials, methods, activities, or programs to control, ensure, or improve the quality of performance or delivery. Measurement during the program implementation is called "process evaluation." *See evaluation; process evaluation.*

format of record The systematic purposeful arrangement of a form or the special organization of forms in a permanent file. The arrangement directs the type of entries to be made, the method of entry, and how those entries will be used in the future.

former smoker Any person who has smoked at least 100 cigarettes in a single time span during his or her entire life but who reports smoking no cigarettes at the present time.

formication The sensation of ants running over the skin, commonly experienced in delirium tremens and cocainism.

forms 1007/1008 In health-care finance under the Prospective Payment System under Medicare, these are special documents used to calculate adjustments to base-yearly Medicare costs for a hospital.

forms of action 1. In health law, this is the special and technical way each type of lawsuit is formally filed. 2. Classes or types of private or common law related to personal actions.

formula grant A grant of federal funds, usually given to states but sometimes to other governmental units or private organizations. The funds, as authorized by law, are usually for specified purposes, and the amount of the grant is often determined by a formula that divides the total funds available among the eligible recipients according to factors such as the number of recipients and average income of the population to be served.

formulary 1. A listing of drugs, usually by their generic names. A formulary is intended to include a sufficient range of medicines that enables physicians or dentists to prescribe medically appropriate treatment for all reasonably common illnesses. A hospital formulary normally lists all the drugs routinely stocked by the hospital pharmacy. Substitution of a chemically equivalent drug for a brand-name drug (generic) in filling a prescription in the formulary is often permitted. A formulary may also be used to list drugs for which a third party will or will not pay or drugs that are considered appropriate for treating specified illnesses. 2. According to JCAHO for psychiatric, alcoholism, and drug abuse facilities accreditation purposes, a catalog of the pharmaceuticals approved for use in a facility. A formulary lists the names of the drugs and information regarding dosage, contraindications, and unit dispensing size. 3. In managed care, a list of drugs selected by a health plan as the only drugs the health plan will offer or cover. Often included are generic drugs that have been found safe, efficacious, and cost-effective, but excluded are expensive brand-name drugs for which there are less expensive, equally safe, effective substitutes. *See also compendium; National Formulary.*

for-profit Any business or health-care organiza-

tion that has a tax status of doing business with the intent of making money. Excess income is distributed to the owners or stockholders. *See nonprofit organization.*

for-profit hospital *See hospital, proprietary; for-profit; nonprofit.*

forswear 1. To falsely swear to; similar to perjury. 2. To make an oath to or to swear to; that which a person knows is untrue or false.

forthwith Immediately or as soon as possible.

FORTRAN A computer language that was developed as a scientific problem-oriented language using mathematical operations in a familiar form.

fortuitous By chance; an accidental occurrence.

forum (Lat.) 1. A court; the court in which an action is heard. 2. A formal professional meeting for the discussion of matters concerning health-care delivery and administration.

forum non conveniens (Lat.) Court of inconvenience. A court may refuse to hear a case if it is believed that hearing it might cause an undue hardship to the defendant. This assumes that there is a competent jurisdiction where the case may be heard.

forward funding When an agency or organization obligates or sets funds aside in the same year for anticipated needs in subsequent fiscal years. *See also advance appropriation.*

foster care Individuals taken into a family situation and provided the same subsistence, privileges, emotional support, and social acceptance as a regular member of the family. Children, youth, and the elderly are most often the participants in these programs.

foster care homes Special long-term-care arrangements or homes that provide personal or supervisory (custodial) care to children, youth, or the elderly. Such living arrangements are usually certified by a county or state agency. *See foster care.*

Foundation for Health Services Research A nonprofit educational and scientific organization designed to aid the field of health services research. It provides a resource center and serves as a source of information and expertise in health services, policy and administrative research issues, and educational activities.

Foundation for Medical Care (FMC) A nonprofit organization of physicians, sponsored by a state or local medical society or association, that is concerned with the development and delivery of medical services and the cost of health care. Some FMCs contract with the government and private health insurers to provide medical services for a targeted or designated population at a predetermined cost and perform various utilization review activities. *See also medical foundation.*

four corners 1. All information in a document, excluding all other related material not in the document; completeness of a document. 2. The face of a written document. 3. The examination, writing, and construction of the document as a whole. *See also face of instrument.*

fourth-party payer The business, organization, or industry that purchases medical, dental, long-term-care, or other insurance for its employees, as compared to third-party payers, which are the managed-care programs or insurance companies that pay for the medical care to health-care providers.

Fowler's position A semi-lying, bed-sitting position in which the head of the bed is raised and the patient's knees are elevated.

FP Family practitioner.

FQHC *See Federally Qualified Health Centers.*

FR Federal register.

fractionation In health-care financial management, this is a billing practice used by health care facilities whereby charges are made separately for several services or components of a service that were previously subject to a single charge. The usual effect is an increase in the total bill. The practice is a common response to the limiting of increases in regular or general charges.

fracture board A board placed under the mattress of a bed to provide added support.

franchise 1. A right or special privilege granted by a government or a corporation; the limit or jurisdiction of a privilege. 2. A special privilege granted by the government to a corporation to operate a regulated monopoly-type business and to use trade names to market the product or service. 3. An insurance deductible where there is no liability on the insurer's part unless loss exceeds a predetermined amount and full liability occurs after the stated amount.

franchise insurance A form of insurance that issues individual policies to the employees of a common employer or the members of an association under an arrangement by which the employer or association agrees to collect the premiums and remit them to the insurer.

frank Freely speaking or admitting; free.

franking privilege The right to send materials or mail through the U.S. Postal Service without paying postage.

fraternal benefit societies Community organizations such as religious groups, ethnic groups, clubs, and fraternities that provide insurance benefits to their members or pay for health care directly to hospitals or nursing homes.

fraternal insurance An insurance cooperative provided by social organizations for their members.

fraud 1. Something done or said to deceive. 2. An act of deceit, deception, or trickery. 3. Intentional misrepresentation by either providers or consumers to obtain services or payments or to claim program eligibility. Fraud may include receipt of services that are obtained through deliberate misrepresentation of need or eligibility, providing false information concerning costs or conditions to obtain reimbursement or certification, or claim payment for services that were never delivered. Fraud is illegal and carries a penalty when proven, and damages may be recovered through a lawsuit. *See also abuse.*

frauds, statute of Statutes patterned after an English law (statute) of 1677 that required certain instruments and sales of some goods to be in writing to avoid fraud and perjury.

fraudulent Cheating; deceitful; under false pretense.

fraudulent concealment Hiding or suppressing a fact or circumstances that a party to a lawsuit is legally or morally bound to provide or disclose.

fraudulent conveyance The illegal transfer of property to a third party to cheat the rightful owner out of the property.

FRCP Federal Rules of Civil Procedure.

free clinics Neighborhood clinics or health services that provide medical services in relatively informal settings to students, transient youth, and population groups that cannot afford to pay for care. In some clinics, care is given free or at nominal charge mainly by volunteer staffs. Some types of medical care and preventive care offered by public health departments are well-baby, prenatal, and immunization clinics.

freedom of choice options In managed care and health maintenance organizations, this is an arrangement under which members can choose physicians who are outside the panel of participating doctors, if the patient needs to do so. Usually additional payment by the member is required.

freedom of speech A constitutional right guaranteed by the First Amendment that allows the freedom to speak as long as it does not interfere with or infringe on others' rights.

free enterprise As applied to health services, this is the commitment of the United States and its economic approach to supporting the medical profession by having competitive fee-for-service private practice or privately owned health facilities such as hospitals, clinics, and nursing homes.

free exercise clause The First Amendment of the U.S. Constitution guarantees that "Congress shall make no law . . . prohibiting the free exercise of religion, speech. . . ."

free-fall advertisements In health-care marketing, these are preprinted ads commonly inserted loosely in newspapers or magazines.

free noncontractual patient A patient for whom a facility, physician, or clinic agrees to provide facilities and services for which no bill is rendered. *See charity care; bad debt.*

free on board (FOB) Goods ready for shipment that are to be loaded without expense or charge.

freestanding In health-care delivery, this is any service, agency, or facility that is not physically a part of a larger health care facility.

freestanding ambulatory surgery centers *See surgi-center; outpatient, ambulatory surgery centers; ambulatory surgery; outpatient surgery services; outpatient services.*

freestanding emergency center *See emergency center, freestanding.*

freestanding emergency medical service center *See emergency center, freestanding.*

freestanding facilities Any health-care facility that is not physically, administratively, or financially connected to a hospital such as freestanding emergency centers and freestanding surgery centers.

freestanding outpatient surgical center *See surgi-center; outpatient, ambulatory surgery centers; ambulatory surgery; outpatient surgery services; outpatient services.*

freestanding psychiatric outpatient clinics Ambulatory mental health services provided by psychologists, counselors, psychotherapists, and psychiatrists to outpatients on either a regular or an emergency basis. The medical aspects of the services are assumed by a psychiatrist.

freestanding surgery centers *See surgi-center.*

freestanding support setting A place, such as a

pharmacy, that provides health services supporting the delivery of personal health-care services but does not provide direct patient care. It is also not a component of an organization that delivers personal health-care services in another setting such as medical labs, dental labs, pharmacies, blood banks, or tissue banks.

frequency 1. In health-care delivery and utilization of health-care services, this is the number of times a patient sought medical care services; the number of times a health service was provided or was used. 2. In the inspection and survey of long-term-care facilities to determine compliance with regulations, this is the incidence or extent of the occurrence of an identified situation in the facility. The situation can affect a single resident or several residents within a given facility.

frequency distribution In epidemiology and biomedical research, this is a table used in the organization of data and the statistical analysis of data that shows the number of observations in a group or category (e.g., the numbers of persons with a specific disease in certain age-groups). *See contingency table.*

friendly fire In health and safety of health-care facilities, this is a fire that does not spread to any area beyond the boiler, stove, or other place designed to contain the fire.

friendly suit In health law, a legal proceeding initiated by a friendly agreement; a lawsuit used to settle a point of law affecting opposing parties who are friendly.

friendly takeover In health-care finance and organizational development, this is a corporate acquisition approach by an organization interested in acquiring another company. The interested company makes an offer to purchase the company, and both sides negotiate and agree on a purchase price. The board of directors of the targeted company must approve the deal and, if publicly held, make a public announcement to stockholders that the offer has been accepted.

friendly visitor service A long-term-care service that decreases the social isolation of the elderly through regular in-home visits by volunteers, friends, or professionals on a prearranged and regular basis. These visits provide companionship, transportation, shopping, or medical care access assistance and maintain the elderly person's well-being, reducing the risk of being institutionalized.

fringe benefits Special programs provided to employees over and above wages or salary. These are extra compensation (not necessarily in the form of money) and can include but are not limited to vacation, retirement, health insurance, life insurance, and employee discounts. Some organizations refer to these extra compensations as "employee-related expenses" or "employee-related costs."

frolic An act by an employee or health-care provider that has nothing to do with what he or she is employed to do.

frontier counties In rural health-care delivery, these are counties within various states, especially midwestern and western states, that have a population density of six or fewer persons per square mile.

front-line supervisor The lowest midmanagement position, just above the front-line workers on an organizational chart in a traditional hospital or health-care organization. *See also first-line supervisor.*

FRSH Fellow in the Royal Society of Health. For those accepted as fellows, these initials can appear as part of their professional titles. *See Appendix II.*

fructus industriales (Lat.) Industrial fruits; products of labor and industry (i.e., drugs produced by pharmaceutical manufacturers); opposed to "fructus naturales," the products of nature such as minerals or vegetables.

frustration of contract In contract law, this is when the chance for completing an agreement has become impossible because of a change that is not the fault of the persons establishing the contract.

FSA Flexible spending account.

FSOP Freestanding surgical outpatient facility.

FTC Federal Trade Commission; the federal agency that enforces prohibitions against unfair competition and unfair or deceptive acts and trade practices.

FTCA Federal Tort Claim Act.

FTE *See full-time equivalent.*

fugues A state in which a person unconsciously wanders about performing involuntary acts. *See also ambulatory automatism.*

full costs In health-care financial management, these are the total costs incurred in providing a service, accomplishing an activity, or completing a program.

full disclosure In health-care financial management, this is a procedure that requires all significant information on the financial position and operation of a health-care facility to be presented in the financial statements.

full faith and credit 1. The recognition and acceptance of laws and cases from other states when appropriate. 2. A judgment rendered in a foreign jurisdiction that has the same effect, obligation, and force in other states as it has in the state where it originated, as provided by the U.S. Constitution (Article IV, Section 1).

full financial requirements In health-care administration, especially hospital and nursing home administration, this is the process of identifying and managing those resources needed to meet current operating needs as well as having sufficient resources to permit replacement of the physical plant when appropriate and to allow for changing community health and patient needs, education, research, and other factors that affect the facility's delivery of quality health-care services.

full-time equivalent (FTE) The number of employees who work for or provide service to a hospital or other facility during a specific period. One person working full time for a full year equals 1.0 FTE; a person working full time for a 6-month period equals .50 FTE, and a person working half time for a full year also equals .50 FTE. *See staffing ratio.*

full-time staff Physicians and other health-care professionals or support personnel who work full-time in a health-care facility are paid by that facility. They are distinguished from the visiting staff, who are physicians or allied health-care providers in private practice earning their livelihood through fees for services not employed by the health-care facility.

fully delegated hospital *See delegate hospital.*

fully insured workers Under Social Security and Medicare, employees who have contributed 40 quarters, or 10 years, to the Social Security system.

function 1. A collection of related activities that must be performed to fulfill an area of responsibility. 2. A specific or special duty or performance required of a professional in the course of his work; normal or expected action. 3. Goal-directed interrelated series of processes such as quality assessment and improvement functions.

functional administration In health-care administration, this is the traditional operations management aspect of administering a hospital or nursing home that ensure that all systems are working and interacting in an efficient and effective manner.

functional age A measure of one's age as determined by ability and capacities rather than chronological age.

functional authority In health administration, this is empowering the staff to become experts in their own areas and to make decisions in specified circumstances that previously were reserved for mid- to upper-level management.

functional classification In the federal budget, a means of presenting budget authority, outlay, and tax expenditure data in terms of the principal purposes that federal programs are intended to serve. Each specific account is generally placed in the single function (e.g., national defense or health and human services) that best represents its major purpose, regardless of the agency administering the program. The Congressional Budget and Impoundment Control Act of 1974 requires Congress to estimate outlays, budget authority, and tax expenditures for each function. Functions are subdivided into narrower categories called "subfunctions."

functional cost analysis When managed-care programs, hospitals, public health departments, or other health-care services use data from other similar organizations as a cost control planning tool. Health-care administrators can compare the costs of specific organizational operations such a recruiting, manpower needs, materials, fees, revenue, and budgets by averaging the costs of other similar organizations of the same size.

functional dependence In long-term-care, rehabilitation, and disability assessment, this is the inability to attend to one's own needs, including the basic activities of daily living. Dependence may result from changes that accompany natural aging or from a disease or related pathological condition.

functional evaluation In health administration, this is a study of the internal operations of a department that examines locations and adequacies of the administrative unit including inter- and intradepartmental relationships and how they affect current utilization of space or their future needs.

functional illiterate One who is not able to read at the level needed to exist and function properly in a complex society.

functional impairment In long-term-care, rehabilitation, and disability assessment, this is the inability to perform basic self-care functions such as eating, dressing, bathing, or the basic activities of daily living such as homemaking, cooking, shopping, cleaning, and washing clothes because of physical, mental, or emotional limitations or disabilities. *See activities of daily living; functional dependence.*

functional improvement measures (FIM) In medical care, rehabilitation, and outcome measures, this is the percentage of patients who reach a level of activity that requires minimal assistance in performing activities of daily living, mobility, locomotion, cognitive functioning, and independent living on discharge. The self-care component measures tasks include the following: eating: ability to bring food to the mouth and successfully swallow; grooming: ability to brush hair and teeth and apply make-up and/or shave; bathing: ability to set up bathing articles and wash body, including shampooing hair and dressing upper body; dressing upper body: ability to get clothing from closet and put on oneself; dressing lower body: ability to get clothing from drawer/closet and put on oneself; toileting: ability to transfer to and from a toilet and manage clothing and hygiene; transfer (bed, chair, wheelchair): ability to transfer from one to another surface; toilet transfer: ability to transfer from a bed, chair, or wheelchair to a toilet; bathing transfer: ability to transfer from a bed, chair, or wheelchair to a tub or shower; walk: ability to ambulate on a solid surface approximately 13 to 30 feet; and stairs: ability to ambulate up and down approximately a five-step staircase. Functional improvement measures are given function values: 7.0 = complete independence (timely and safely); 6.0 = modified independence (devise); 5.5 = stand by assist (hands off); 5.0 = supervision; 4.5 = contact guard; 4.0 minimal assist (subject = 75%); 3.5 moderate/minimum assist; 3.0 = moderate assist (subject = 50%; 2.5 = maximum/moderate assist; 2.0 = maximum assist (subject = 25%); 1.5 = dependent/maximum assist; 1.0 = total assist (subject = 0%).

functional maintenance services Equivalent to rehabilitation services (JCAHO).

functional obsolescence The need to replace or upgrade equipment or facilities because they have become inefficient or outdated since the original purchase or construction.

functions of a manager In health administration, these are the activities that a health-care manager usually performs and is expected to be accomplished in. The traditional functions are often considered to be planning, organizing, directing, and coordinating. Sometimes included are controlling, supervising, staffing, communicating, and commanding. Henri Fayol (1910) suggested five functions of a manager, referred to as POC$_3$: planning, organizing, controlling, coordinating, and commanding. A more recent set of functions of a manager uses a PRINCESS acronym: planning, representing, investigating (problem solving), negotiating, coordinating, evaluating, supervising, and staffing (Source: Carroll and Gillen in *Academy of Management Review*, vol. 12, no. 1, 1987).

fund 1. In health-care finance, this is any sum of money kept available for use on demand; a collection of money allocated for a specific use. 2. Having a store or stock of something.

fund accounting In health-care financial management, this is a system of accounting that separates a health-care organization's resources, obligations, and capital balances into logical account groups according to administrative requirements and legal restrictions. Each separate account group is a subordinate accounting fund, created and maintained in that manner.

fund balance In health-care financial management, this is the amount of money that a health-care facility has left over in assets after income and expenses have been designated; equivalent to net worth as shown on a balance sheet.

fund, board-designated In health-care financial management, this is the money set aside by the governing board of a health-care facility for specified projects or purposes.

funded In managed care or medical insurance, having sufficient funds to meet future liabilities; can also refer to trust funds for social insurance programs. Capital depreciation is said to be funded if the amounts included in an institution's reimbursements for capital depreciation are set aside in a fund used for capital purposes rather than being spent on current operating costs. Few third-party payers that reimburse capital depreciation require that it be funded as a condition of reimbursement.

funded debt Long-term debt.

funded depreciation In health-care financial management, this is budgeted money that is set aside to cover the cost of replacing equipment and other fixed assets.

funded plan In health-care financial and human resource management, this is when an employer is required to accumulate monies in advance from the employee to ensure that the organization's contribution plans (e.g., medical and dental insurance and interest) will cover its obligation.

funded retirement plans In health-care financial and human resource management, this is when a employer is required to set aside monies to ensure that the organization has the ability to meet future retiree payment requirements.

fund, endowment In health-care financial management, this is an account established by a person donating money or gifts to be spent for a specified purpose or used at the discretion of the governing board. Often it is only the interest that is spent, whereas the principal is maintained in a bank or an investment, earning dividends or drawing interest. *See endowment.*

fund, general In health-care financial management, these are the monies set aside for use at the discretion of administration.

funding level In managed care and medical care insurance, this is the amount of money required to finance a health service or medical care delivery program. Premium rates and projected utilization influence a health plan's anticipated level of financial outlay or support needed. In self-funded plans, this is the amount needed for the cost of treatment, claims, and fees plus all other insurance risk considerations (e.g., stop-loss insurance).

funding method In managed care and medical care insurance, this is the means by which employers fund the employee medical care benefit plan. Risk is shifted from the employer to the insurance carrier in non-self-funded plans. The most common methods used are prospective premium payment/retrospective premium payments, refunding products, shared risk arrangements, and self-funded medical care coverage programs.

fund, permanent In health-care financial management, this is an endowment fund whereby the principal is maintained in the account and is used to generate interest or dividends that are then used for the operation of the organization. *See also fund, endowment.*

fund-raising The soliciting of gifts, money, and other donations for a hospital or health-care facility. In some health-care facilities, this is a permanent or temporary department and often a top administrative position, with some health-care facilities expanding the role to include marketing activities. Also referred to as "development," "hospital development," or the "foundation."

fund, sinking In health-care finance, this is a special fund that sets money aside in a special account to pay off financial obligations or debt.

funds, restricted In health-care financial management, these are monies that can be used only for specified purposes. Often these funds are donated to the health-care facility for use in specified ways.

funds, specific-purpose In health-care financial management, this is a special account established by or for a person who donated the money to a health-care facility. The principal and income can be used only for designated purposes.

funds, unrestricted In health-care financial management, this is money that can be used by a health-care facility at the discretion of the administration or the governing body.

fungible goods Goods that are uniform; one unit is equivalent to any other of the same product (e.g., 1 liter of plasma is interchangeable with another).

futures 1. Speculative transactions. 2. For delivery at a future time. 3. In contract law, an agreement made to buy or sell at a set price and by a certain date.

FY Fiscal year. *See fiscal year.*

G

gainful Profit producing; advancing oneself; productive activities.

gainsharing In health administration, this is the process of matching improvements in a hospital or health-care organization by sharing the benefits of the gain realized with the employees.

GANTT chart A health planning and time line project management, a tool utilizing a sliding bar technique as the control mechanism to provide a quick pictorial representation of separate projects and their respective time frames. One bar represents each project with two parts: the top portion of the bar (actually a separate smaller bar) indicates the work completed or the actual progress of the project, and the bottom bar is the projected and anticipated, planned part. The top bar may be further subdivided into activities to be accomplished and as many bars developed as needed. The status of various projects is easily ascertained by a quick glance at the bar chart.

GAO General Accounting Office; the office that assists the U.S. Congress in financial matters and conducts investigations and studies on issues related to budgets and expenditure of money.

garnishment 1. A legal proceeding through which a person's wages are withheld and given to the person to whom a debt is owed. 2. A legal notice to hold a defendant's property until a lawsuit is settled; property or money legally held until related legal matters are settled. The money may be given to the party it is owed to on the decision of the court or completion of the legal process.

GAS See *general adaptation syndrome*.

gastric- Pertaining to the stomach.

gastric decompression In medical care, this is the aspiration or removal of gastric contents, fluids, or gas using a syringe or suction machine.

gastric gavage In medical care, this is a method of artificial feeding using gastric intubation.

gastric intubation In medical care, this is to insert a tube into the stomach for therapeutic or diagnostic purposes.

gastric lavage In medical care, this is to administer and then siphon back a liquid or solution through a catheter that has been introduced into the stomach.

gastroenterologist A physician who specializes in the diagnosis and treatment of diseases and conditions of the stomach, intestines, and digestive tract.

gastroenterology An internal medicine specialty area that requires the completion of a postgraduate medical residency and board certification for the physician to conduct diagnosis and treatment of diseases, disorders, and conditions of the digestive system and gastrointestinal tract.

gastroscope In medical care, this is a lighted endoscope that visually examines the internal aspects of the stomach.

gastroscopy In medical care, this is the examination of the stomach with an endoscope or gastroscope.

gatekeeper In managed care, this is a primary care physician who has the main responsibility for enrollees' medical care and costs and who must ascertain and authorize all needed medical services to keep costs reduced such as admission to a hospital, testing and diagnostic assessments, consultations, and referral to specialists. This primary care physician is also the one who authorizes expenditures for external medical services. To see a specialist, the patient must be referred by the primary care physician. Primary care physician gatekeepers are usually family practitioners, pediatricians, geriatricians, some areas of internal medicine, and in some cases obstetrics and psychiatry. In managed care, physician's extenders such as physicians assistants and nurse practitioners also function as gatekeepers. See *gatekeeper model*.

gatekeeper model In managed care, this is an approach to health plan utilization and management control whereby a primary care physician or related health-care provider is the initial patient contact for all basic medical care and must be seen for referrals to specialists or other therapists or therapy situations. This model controls the unnecessary use of specialists and helps conserve resources, reduce costs and utilization, and maximize the primary care practitioner's role. Also referred to as "closed panel" or "closed access" model.

gauss A measure of strength or power in radiation-related technology; a unit of intensity of a magnetic flux. Named after Johann Karl F. Gauss, a German physicist (1777–1855).

gaussian curve In laser technology as used in medical treatment, this is a cross-section of the radiant power density of a laser beam.

gauss line In magnetic resonance imaging (MRI), this is the magnetic strength of the MRI magnet as measured from the center outward. The center of the circular magnet is the strongest point of the magnetic field and dissipates rapidly as the field moves outward from the center (e.g., an MRI might have a 1.5 gauss as measured in the center).

gavage In medical care, this is a method of artificial feeding through a tube inserted into the stomach.

GB Governing body.

GDP *See gross domestic product; gross national product.*

Geiger counter A gas-filled electrical instrument that counts the presence of atomic particles or rays in the air or surrounding environment.

genealogy As used in epidemiology, this is the use of family trees to assist in investigating diseases retrospectively from a kinship historical perspective. Through the use of family trees, family group sheets, and past family generations and kinship, genealogy is used to study genetically transmitted conditions and chronic and communicable diseases.

General Accounting Office A federal agency that is the consultative, investigative, and auditing arm of the U.S. government, including matters related to Medicare, Medicaid, the Health Care Financing Administration, and other federal health agencies and programs.

general adaptation syndrome (GAS) The body's general response to, or a means of coping with, stress.

general administrative expense budget In health administration and budget planning, the usual administration and operating expenses of a hospital, medical group, clinic, or other health-care organization but not those included in the benefits budget or other special budgets.

general administrative expenses In health administration and budget planning, these are the office supplies and materials, office equipment purchases, building maintenance, rent, and salaries of administrative staff.

general agent In managed care and insurance, this is an individual in charge of a field office under a general agency structure. This person is an independent entrepreneur who is under contract to the insurance company, and the insurance company's control over the general agent limited by the contract with the insurance company.

general consent In health law, this is a form of patient consent generally used on admission to a hospital to remove the possibility of liability or lawsuit coming from a patient. General consent forms have not held up well in court because informed consent is most often required and a broad or blanket approach consent not legally acceptable. *See also consent; informed consent.*

general denial In health law and the litigation process, this is used in a pleading to deny every allegation set forth in a legal complaint.

general duty nurse A registered nurse or a licensed practical nurse on the staff of a health-care facility who provides general nursing care in a medical or nursing care unit.

general enrollment period 1. In managed care, this is the time span or window of time in which a potential health plan enrollee or an employee group member has the right to enroll in a health plan or HMO. 2. Under Medicare, this is from January 1 to March 31 of each year when anyone eligible for Part B can enroll.

general execution In the litigation process and under procedural law, this is a court order to seize a defendant's personal property to pay off a judgment brought against the defendant.

general fertility rate *See fertility rate, general.*

general fund In health-care finance, these are monies retained in a special account for use at the discretion of the chief executive officer and/or the board of trustees for the day-to-day operation of the institution; money not yet allocated or budgeted for departments or projects of the health-care facility.

general hospital An acute-care facility that provides both diagnostic and treatment services for patients with a variety of medical conditions (surgical and nonsurgical). According to the World Health Organization, these health-care facilities provide medical and nursing care for more than one category of medical discipline (e.g., general medicine, specialized medicine, general surgery, specialized surgery, and obstetrics). Excluded are rural and small hospitals that provide a limited range of care. *See hospital.*

general issue An answer to a complaint. *See also general denial.*

general jurisdiction A court's ability to rule over any controversy that may be brought before it within the legal bounds of a person's rights or the court's responsibility, authorization, or geographical boundaries.

general ledger In health-care finance and general accounting, this is a record book that records the transactions of business as they occur; a collection of the various accounts of business activities used to classify transactions and determine their cumulative effect on the accounts.

general ledger transactions In health-care finance and general accounting, these are financial transactions that are internal exchanges rather than external and deal with resources that are considerably longer than one budget or accounting cycle.

generally accepted accounting principles In health-care finance and general accounting, these are the prominent rules and procedures used in accounting practice hospitals and health-care organizations, as set by the Accounting Principles Board and the Financial Accounting Standards Board, including both general guidelines and the detailed practices and procedures.

generally recognized as effective (GRAE) In the assessment of new pharmaceutical preparations, this is one of the conditions that a drug must fulfill for it not to be considered a new drug and thus not be subject to the premarket approval requirements of the federal Food, Drug, and Cosmetic Act. To be so recognized, the drug must be evaluated as effective by "experts qualified by scientific training and experience to evaluate the safety and effectiveness of drugs" and have been "used to a material extent or for a material time." The FDA makes the determination subject to judicial reversal if its determination is arbitrary or capricious. The Supreme Court has held that for a drug to be approved as effective, its sponsor must supply the FDA with the same kind of evidence consisting of adequate and well-controlled investigations by qualified experts that the law requires. *See also generally recognized as safe.*

generally recognized as safe (GRAS) A condition that a drug must fulfill for it not to be considered a new drug; likewise, a food must fulfill this condition if it is not to be considered a food additive. Such a drug need not be submitted to premarket approval procedures prescribed in the federal Food, Drug, and Cosmetic Act for new drugs. General recognition of the safety of a drug must be "among experts qualified by scientific training and experience to evaluate the safety and effectiveness of drugs"; to acquire the general recognition of safety and effectiveness, a drug must be "used to a material extent or for a material time."

general medical and surgical unit In hospital administration and nursing care, this is a special floor or area of a hospital set up and staffed to provide acute medical and nursing care to patients after surgery or while under the care of the attending physician who do not require specialized treatment. The health care is based on the orders of a physician and a treatment and nursing care plan. Beds must be set up and staffed in a specified and designated unit for this service.

general medical services In hospital administration and medical care, this is the diagnosis and treatment of nonemergency physical diseases and other conditions or their symptoms by techniques distinct from those used in obstetric, surgical, diagnostic, and therapeutic radiology and clinical laboratory services.

general obligation In health-care financial management, this is a bond secured by pledge of the issuer's full faith, credit, and taxing power.

general obligation bond In health-care financial management, this is a government bond backed by the taxes of a government unit that issues them.

general paresis Organic brain syndrome caused by a chronic syphilitic infection.

general partner In the legal structure of organizations, this is a member of a partnership who has the authority to bind the partnership and share the profits and who has unlimited liability for the losses. A partnership must have at least one general partner and may in fact have more than one general partner as well as limited partners.

general power of appointment 1. Authority by which a person in a position of authority or power appoints anyone he or she chooses. 2. The authority given by a testator to a third person to dispose of the testator's estate.

general practice The delivery of a wide range of primary care medical services, including diagnosis and treatment by a physician or physician extender. *See family practice; general practitioner.*

general practitioner (GP) A practicing physician who is a generalist and a primary care physician and who does not specialize in any particular field of medicine. The GP has been replaced by family practice physicians and physician assistants. A family physician is trained in general practice, is subject to specialty board examination in the care of families, and is a primary care practitioner. Older GP physicians were allowed to qualify for the family practice designation through the demonstration of competence and through examination, thus being recognized in the higher-level specialty area. In 1973 the family practice specialty was approved and implemented, making the GP outmoded.

general revenue Government revenues raised without regard to any specific purpose for which they might be used. Federal general revenues come principally from personal and corporate income taxes and some excise taxes. State general revenues come primarily from personal income and sales taxes.

general surgery In medical practice, this is the branch of surgery comprised of generalists who do mostly basic and general secondary-care-level surgical procedures. Surgical treatments excluded are the highly complex and tertiary-level surgical specialty areas such as the brain, hand, heart, orthopedic, and cardiovascular.

general verdict In the litigation and trial process, this is a verdict by a jury without elaboration on the specific facts of the case.

general writing mutual An insurance company that is a mutual insurer and that does not specialize in any particular type, level, or class of risk.

generation effect In epidemiology, this is the same as a cohort effect; the differences seen in the health status of various birth cohorts exposed to different causes (environmental or social factors) as time passes. Each separate birth cohort as it passes through the life span is exposed to different risk factors and unique social and environmental exposures, making the exposures and health status of each birth cohort unique.

generational equity In aging policy and Social Security, this is a structure for making policy choices about fairness in the use of Social Security funds as compared to those who make contributions to the program. One approach blames the difficulties on the baby-boomer generation and poor children on the cost of the entitlement programs for the aged. This develops fairness in the contributions and future availability of Social Security funds as generations move through the life span.

generational inversion In gerontology and aging policy, this is used to describe family circumstances in which an elderly parent is a social, financial, physical, emotional or psychological dependent on his or her children for support and assistance.

generation time In epidemiology and infection control, this is a time interval between the exposure of an infectious agent to a host and a complete state of infection. On transmission of a disease, the interval between infection and the onset of signs of the disease in each new case in a population is referred to as the "generation time," or the time it takes for the disease to develop.

generic Characteristic of the whole; representative in quality of any product of the same line. In health-care delivery and especially in managed-care pharmaceuticals, this is a prescription drug that is prescribed by its chemical formulary instead of its trade or market name. Generic drugs are usually less costly than brand-name drugs.

generic drug 1. A chemically equivalent copy of a medicine, designed from a brand-name drug that has an expired patent and referred to as a generic drug. 2. Any substance that is generic is typically less expensive and sold under a common or generic name for that drug instead of the brand name. Also referred to as "generic equivalents."

generic equivalents Drug products with the same active chemical ingredients sold under a generic name and often sold under different brand names. Generic equivalents are often assumed to be, but are not necessarily, therapeutic equivalents.

generic name The established, official, or nonproprietary name by which a drug is known as an isolated substance regardless of its manufacturer. Each drug is licensed under a generic name and also may be given a brand name by its manufacturer. The generic name is assigned by the U.S. Adopted Names Council (USAN), a private group of representatives of the American Medical Association, the American Pharmaceutical Association, the U.S. Pharmacopeia, the Food and Drug Administration, and one public member. *See also maximum allowable cost program; antisubstitution law.*

generic screen 1. Any health-care condition that affects a patient or his or her care; activities, procedures, conditions, or other variables that might identify problems in health-care delivery. 2. In the medical care review process, questions that are asked about underlying deficiencies in the delivery of patient care that may cause a problem to surface on a regular basis.

genetic assistant An individual who works with a genetics counselor in providing services to patients. He or she obtains complete genetic case histories from patients and families with inherited diseases or birth defects.

genetic counseling *See genetic counseling service.*

genetic counseling service A patient education or health counseling service that provides information and counseling to prospective parents concerned with their genetic makeup and the possibility of transmitting genetic defects to their offspring. A well-equipped laboratory for assessing tests, genetic serums, and tissues and a qualified physician are necessary to advise parents and prospective parents on potential problems in cases of genetic defects. Clinic services usually include antenatal diagnosis using amniocentesis, chorionic villi sampling, fetal blood sampling, ultrasound evaluation, and MRI.

genetic counselor A person trained to offer coordinated and supportive care to the patient with potential or actual genetic disease and to counsel patients concerning the origin, transmission, and development of hereditary characteristics that have a relationship to birth abnormalities. The genetic counselor obtains a complete genetic history from patients and families with inherited diseases or birth defects and counsels them about the probability of transmitting these characteristics to their offspring.

genetic disease Conditions or disorders that result from a defect in the person's genetic makeup and are set at the instance of fertilization.

genetic drift As used in epidemiology, these are changes and fluctuations seen in certain genetic traits, changes, or manifestations of genetic disorders in small populations.

genetic linkage Arrangement and location of genes on chromosomes from each parent. When two genes are fairly closely aligned from each parent, the trait tends to be inherited together.

genetic penetrance As used in epidemiology, this is the frequency of genetic effects or defects in a population or group.

geographical maldistribution In health-care delivery, this refers to the uneven access and availability of health-care providers, mostly hospitals and physicians, because of the location of practice or service. Major hospitals with tertiary care and level I trauma care are located in metropolitan areas, as are most physicians and specialists. Rural areas suffer from a lack of physicians and medical services.

geographical pathology In epidemiology, this is a manifestation of variations in morbidity and mortality in different countries, regions, or areas. Comparative studies of different countries or areas often have the aim of demonstrating variation in diseases caused by or related to the differences in topography, climate, natural boundaries, elevation, ecological elements, and environment; a place-related issue of epidemiological investigations.

geographic areas In the United States, the Census Bureau and some other federal health agencies have grouped the 50 states and the District of Columbia into four regions: Northeast, North-central, South, and West. These are further subdivided into nine divisions.

geographic characteristics 1. A description of the topography of the state and its relationship to health and health care. 2. In epidemiology, an element of "place" that can influence the spread or control of diseases in populations.

geographic divisions and regions *See geographic areas.*

geographic practice cost index (GPCI) In Medicare, this is an index used by some researchers to examine differences in physician practice patterns and costs across geographic areas. The index is based on per unit cost.

geometric mean In epidemiology and analysis of data, this is the calculation of logarithms of positive values; arithmetic means are calculated for the positive values and are changed back by taking the antilogarithm.

geriatric Pertaining to the medical care and medical aspects of growing old, the aging process, and diseases of old age; that part of medicine that deals with aging and the elderly. *See gerontology.*

geriatric acute care unit A special service found in a hospital that provides primary acute care to older adult patients. Care is provided by a multidisciplinary team trained in gerontology and geriatrics. Special needs of the older patient are taken into account, including clinic design and structural accommodations, scheduling, and time with the patient.

geriatric aide In health-care delivery, this is an individual who, under the supervision of a nurse, performs tasks related to nursing and personal care for elderly patients.

geriatric assessment As used in the delivery of medical care services, this is an interdisciplinary diagnostic process that quantifies health status, medical problems, and the psychosocial and functional capabilities of the older adult patient for the purpose of developing a comprehensive therapy plan, case management, continuity of care, and follow-up.

geriatric assessment unit A health-care delivery approach for older adult patients that is often found in a hospital setting, providing the patient with an extensive and thorough medical exam and patient evaluation by geriatricians, geriatric nurse practitioners, geriatric social workers, discharge planners, and case managers. The thorough evaluation is done with the goal of identifying remediable conditions, simplifying treatment regimens, assessing activities of daily living, and evaluating social, domestic, and mental functioning with treatment plans developed to maximize functioning in all dimensions of an individual.

geriatric care worker An individual who works in skilled nursing facilities, especially ones providing care to infirm, elderly patients. He or she administers to the various social needs of the elderly patient in an institutional setting.

geriatric clinics In health-care delivery, these are special medical and surgical services for older adults only. These provide primary care, treating mostly chronic conditions such as heart problems, arthritis, and foot problems.

geriatrician A physician who specializes in the diagnosis and treatment of diseases and disorders that are prevalent in older persons that may be a result of the aging process. A board-certified specialty is available in geriatrics, and a geriatrician must be board certified in this specialty.

geriatrics A medical specialty that deals with the aged and the diseases, conditions, disorders, and medical and health problems of older adults.

Geri-chair A special wheelchair so constructed that it cannot be self-propelled.

germane Native to; related; appropriate; pertinent.

germicide Any agent or substance that kills pathogenic microorganisms.

gerodontics The branch of dentistry dealing with diagnosis, treatment, and research of dental disorders and conditions peculiar to elderly persons. *See also dental geriatrics; geriatrics; gerontology.*

gerontocracy A political situation whereby the elderly citizens constitute the political ruling group by virtue of their age, wisdom, loyalty, and dedication to the country.

gerontologist A scientist with advanced training and a degree or certificate in gerontology who studies, researches, and advances the issues and causes of the social, mental, biological, and health aspects of the aging process and old age. *See geriatrics.*

gerontology The health, sociological, psychological, and biological study of aging; social and health aspects of growing old.

gerontology, preventive The health education, promotion, and protection of the elderly that helps prevent, avoid, or minimize illness, conditions, and disability in older adults.

geropsychiatry A branch of psychiatry that deals with mental health problems of being old or growing old.

gerrymandering 1. The purposeful changing of political boundaries or districts to assure one political party continued majority control of a legislature. 2. In hospital administration, the dividing of responsibilities to take executive power and responsibility away from the administrator. This is done by the governing board when it wishes to take or retain direct control and policy responsibility, either because the board feels that it can run the hospital better than the administrator or because the administrator has been incompetent and ineffective. The result is usually that the administrator's responsibilities are limited to the housekeeping and hotel functions only, and amounts of money that he or she can spend without the board's permission are limited to small sums. A business manager may be appointed to be responsible for the financial aspects of the hospital, reporting directly to the treasurer of the governing board. A large number of committees can be appointed to cover every hospital function and take over executive functions. These acts put hospital responsibilities on the governing board, and thus its members effectively become not only the board but also the executives of the hospital.

gestalt (German) A specific, existing, concrete, and organized entity with definite shape or form; whole or wholeness.

gestalten (German) Common and familiar objects as perceived in one's mind as a whole.

gestalt psychology A psychological theory that studies natural configurations and patterns learned from direct experience. It does not search for mental elements, and it discounts the stimulus-and-response theories. It emphasizes perceptual wholeness and suggests that behavior takes place in an environment full of organized stresses and strains.

gestalt therapy In mental health services, this is a type of psychotherapy that emphasizes the treatment of the person as a physical, mental, and emotional whole and considers his or her perceptual configuration and interrelationships with people and the environment.

gestation For public health survey and research purposes, the length of time that a pregnancy lasts, beginning with the first day of the last normal menstrual period and ending with the day of birth.

gestational age The age of a fetus since conception. Often conception is unknown, so it is measured from the first day of the last normal menstrual period and is the days or weeks of age of the fetus.

GHAA See Group Health Association of America.

GI See gastroenterology.

gift-over A gift, made from person A to person B for life, that is then given to person C.

GIGO Garbage in, garbage out; an expression used by computer specialists referring to the fact that if incorrect input or information (garbage) is entered into a computer, then the resulting output will also be incorrect and useless (garbage).

glossolalia Terminology or jargon that is not understandable.

GME Graduate medical education.

GMENAC Graduate Medical Education National Advisory Committee.

gnoso- Prefix meaning "knowledge."

GNP See gross national product.

goal 1. General statements of aims and general outcomes that are achieved by the specific activities of the objectives; overall expected results, aims, or conditions that take time to achieve; a specified state to be achieved that is broad in scope and provides guidance in establishing objectives. General aims of an organization are more specific than mission statements and less specific than objectives. Goals differ from objectives by lacking deadlines and by being long range rather than short range. Goals are used to accomplish the mission of an organization, whereas outcome objectives are used to accomplish goals. 2. The highest attainable health status and the optimum health system performance technically achievable and consistent with community ideals. 3. In public health planning, a quantified statement of a desired future state or condition (e.g., an infant mortality of less than 20 per 1000 live births or a physician-to-population ratio greater than 4 per 1000. 4. According to JCAHO for psychiatric, alcoholism, and drug abuse facilities accreditation purposes, an expected result or condition that takes time to achieve, is specified in a statement of relatively broad scope, and provides guidance in establishing intermediate objectives directed toward its attainment.

goal level In health planning, this is the quantitative level of a particular health status indicator that is specified in a goal to express the desired level of goal achievement.

goal-need analysis In health planning, the second major phase of the plan development process. It begins with a review of the health status and health system reference projection and ends with the establishment of objectives and priorities.

goal setting In health service delivery, this consists of defining the highest attainable levels of quality and excellence to which a community may reasonably aspire. Because health status and health system goals are expressed quantitatively wherever possible, the gap between projected indicator levels (from the reference projection) and the desired, or goal, level can be calculated. This gap represents either a health status improvement need or a health system need.

going bare In health law and medical malpractice, this is when a health-care provider practices without malpractice coverage or professional liability insurance.

golden parachute In health-care administration, this is an employment contract for continued compensation and benefits of the chief executive officer or other top managers should they be discharged before the end of their contracts or be displaced by a merger or acquisition so that they may have continued income and benefits for a period of time.

Gompertz' Law In public health and epidemiology, this is used to describe the relationship of deaths in a population to age. Death rates are high during the first year of life, drop to their lowest level after 1 year of life and into childhood, and slowly increase into old age. After age 40 the increase in death rates tends to be logarithmic into old age. These survival curves were first noted by Benjamin Gompertz in England in the 1800s.

good 1. Valid. 2. Lawfully sufficient, collectible. 3. Legal.

good cause With justification; to have a sufficient legal reason; not arbitrary.

good consideration 1. Natural duty. 2. Consideration of love and affection. 3. In contract law, this is when the parties to a contract determine that the items of value used to complete a contract have high levels of worth and value, making the contractual agreement legally sound.

good distribution of risk In managed care and group insurance, a large number of healthy members in a health plan's membership offsets the claims of the unhealthy members, thus reducing the risk of losing money on the contract.

good faith Honest; having standards of fair dealing. In health law, this is the mental state of an individual having no malice intent. A health professional or health administrator conducting business dealings in an honest and fair manner without any ulterior motive.

Good Samaritan Act A law in most states that protects physicians, nurses, and citizens who render first aid to an injured person at the site of an accident or in an emergency situation. *See also Good Samaritan statutes; Good Samaritan Doctrine.*

Good Samaritan Doctrine When giving first aid to an injured person in an emergency, a person or health-care provider may not be held liable for any harm caused to an injured person in the act of providing first aid if difficult and primitive conditions are present at the scene of an accident.

Good Samaritan statutes Laws that create immunity from liability so that health-care providers and, in some states, laypersons will be more willing to render first aid in an emergency. These statutes protect those who render first aid in an emergency situation from any civil redress, lawsuit, and compensation to the injured. It provides limited protection (even if harm results) if the caregiver acted in good faith and as a reasonable and prudent person.

goods Personal belongings; personal property; merchandise, freight, wares.

goodwill 1. In health-care finance and health-care organization, this is the price set above the selling price on the basis of the good name and reputation of an organization, patient base, and referrals. 2. The free care given away by a health-care organization.

gork Originally an acronym for "God only really knows," used by hospital house staff to describe diseases or conditions that are so mysterious they defy diagnosis. It has also been used in a negative manner to describe patients who are comatose and likely to remain so.

governance The controlling or directing of an organization through a group of persons chosen to serve as a governing body; the board of directors or trustees.

governance system The part of a health-care organization that monitors the external health-care environment; determines and chooses the best alternatives, services, organizational changes, and approaches; and negotiates the implementation of decisions with staff and community organizations and professionals.

governing board A group of representative people who make important final decisions, direct, rule, manage, and administer policy and rules over a company or corporation such as a hospital, nursing home, or HMO. Also referred to as "board of directors" or "board of trustees." *See also board of directors.*

governing body 1. In community health agencies and programs funded by federal grants or contracts, this is an assembly of persons that is legally constituted and required to be comprised of 50% health-care consumers and 50% providers. 2. According to JCAHO for long-term-care accreditation, the individual, group, or governmental agency that has the ultimate responsibility and authority for the operation of the facility. 3. In a hospital, the individual(s) or group that has ultimate authority and responsibility for establishing policy, maintaining quality patient care, and providing for organizational management and planning. Standards are applied to evaluate the performance of a hospital's governing body (JCAHO for acute-care facilities). *See also board of directors.*

governing body and management For Medicare purposes, a skilled nursing facility should have an effective governing body, or designated persons so functioning, with full legal authority and responsibility for the operation of the facility. The governing body adopts and enforces rules and regulations relative to the health care and safety of patients, the protection of their personal and property rights, and the general operation of the facility. The governing body develops a written institutional plan that reflects the operating budget and capital expenditures plan.

governing body bylaws Rules that establish the roles and responsibilities of the governing body (JCAHO for acute-care facilities.)

governmental function Duties imposed on governmental health agencies as a corporate subdivision of the state.

governmental hospitals Acute-care institutions or long-term-care facilities that are owned and operated by city, county, state, or federal governments.

governmental immunity In health law and medical malpractice, this is a doctrine that provides, despite the general proposition that a negligent act gives rise to tort liability for that act, that the government, subject to certain qualifications, cannot be sued for the negligent acts of its officers, agents, or employees unless it consents to such a suit. This concept of governmental immunity originated in ancient common law doctrine, and the principle has been firmly established that a state cannot be sued without its consent. It is also based on the historic concept of the "Divine Right of Kings," which maintains that the king is the source of all power and law and cannot do wrong. However, the negligent individual can still be held liable for his or her own acts. As with charitable immunity, the trend is toward an increasing willingness of the courts to impose liability as the states and the federal government enact statutes to waive their immunity in tort suits. Governments can be sued according to the Federal Tort Claims Act and other tort reforms at the state level that vary from state to state. *See Federal Tort Claims Act.*

government business In health-care administration strategic planning, this is a growth strategy of being certified for a government program or contracts for health services. This is a way to develop advanced technical capabilities and special programs. Long-term contracts, low profits, red tape, standards, requirements, and bureaucratic imposition are to be expected.

government de factor The actual government in power.

government de jure The rightful government.

government, federal hospitals Acute-care medical care facilities controlled by an agency or department of the federal government, usually military, public health service, Indian health service, or prison hospitals.

government hospitals Acute-care or long-term-care medical facilities under the ownership or control of federal, state, or local governments (city or county). Local government hospitals are usually community or general hospitals. Local governments often administer long-term-care facilities/convalescent hospitals as well. State hospitals are usually teaching, specialty, or psychiatric facilities. *See government, federal hospitals.*

government instrumentality doctrine A law stating that any organization run by a branch of the government cannot be taxed.

GP *See general practitioner.*

GPCI Geographic Practice Cost Index.

grace period In managed care and insurance, this is a specified period after a premium payment is due in which an insurance policyholder may still make a payment. During this period of time, the protection and coverage of the insurance policy continues and will do so if the premium is paid.

gradient of infection In epidemiology and infection control, this is a continuum of infection whereby the host has a different response to the presence of a pathogen, ranging from no signs or an inapparent infection to serious illness or death from the disease.

graduated lease In health administration materials and equipment management, this is a special lease that calls for varying rental charges, usually according to a periodic appraisal or the passage of time.

graduate medical education Medical education taken after and beyond the receipt of the MD or equivalent degree, including the education received as an intern, resident, or fellow. This is contrasted with general education, whereas graduate education refers to graduate school education leading to a masters, doctoral, or equivalent degree (called undergraduate medical education in medicine). It is usually limited to education such as a residency, which is required for specialty board certification and usually includes supervised practice, research, and teaching.

graduate nurse One who has graduated from a nursing program but has not yet passed the registry exam and thus is not a registered nurse (RN) and cannot practice as a nurse.

graduate training program, bilateral Medical education programs conducted in a medical school department and a separate teaching hospital or medical education experience in the same clinical services but in two different hospitals where there is no medical school involvement.

graduate training program, independent A program that operates with no relationship to a medical school for graduate training. The hospital administration and medical staff determine the number of house officers to be trained, select the candidates, and supervise the training programs.

graduate training program, integrated A program designed by medical school academic department staff that determines the number of house staff in the clinical services in two or more hospitals. Residents rotate from hospital to hospital. The hospital may pay the house officer salaries directly or pay the salary amounts into a central fund that is usually administered by a medical school department.

graduate year one In medical education, a resident medical student who has completed the formal 4 years of medical school and is in the first year of advanced specialty training; a first-year resident or one doing his or her first-year residency.

GRAE *See generally recognized as effective.*

-gram Suffix meaning "record."

grandfather clause Used in licensing and certification actions, this is an exception to a newly developed law or regulation that allows those already practicing in a profession to continue to do so (otherwise they would be stopped by newly passed legal restrictions). This is one aspect of a new law that provides an exception to certain individuals, especially those who have been in the profession for years, when a new law or conditions for a person entering a field or profession require minimum education and standards for licensing or certification. It would be unrealistic to demand that persons already successfully working in a field quit or return to school for training, so they are allowed licensure or certification without testing or obtaining the new educational requirements. A grandfather clause has time limitations written into it, and the open enrollment period lapses after a certain time.

grandfather provision 1. A clause or provision of law that permits continued eligibility or coverage for individuals or organizations receiving program benefits despite a change in the law that would otherwise make them ineligible. 2. A clause that exempts a person, an organization, or a thing from a change in law that would otherwise affect it. For example, the federal Food, Drug and Cosmetic Act exempts certain drugs from premarket approval requirements on the basis of their longstanding use.

grand jury In the litigation process, this is a special jury put together to determine whether there is sufficient evidence to prove that a crime has been committed and to justify bringing charges and a case to trial. A separate jury is later called to try the case. The grand jury consists of a greater number of members than the trial jury (petit, or small, jury) and is used in criminal cases. The members are sworn in by the court and listen to evidence presented by the prosecuting attorney but do not determine guilt. After hearing state's evidence, and if enough reasonable and probable cause exists to believe a crime has been committed, arrests are made and a trial is held; the grand jury issues a "bill of indictment" if there is a case.

grand larceny In criminal law, this is the theft of property that is valued at more than a specified dollar amount constituting a felony.

grand rounds In a medical school or teaching hospital, this is the weekly review and discussion of clinical cases or didactic presentations on clinical subjects to all the hospital medical staff for educational purposes.

grant 1. To provide money for special purposes. 2. To give; convey; bestow or confer a gift. 3. A subsidy. 4. A document written as an application and request for money. Money is provided to hospitals, health-care organizations, health services, medical schools, schools of public health or universities, or other nonprofit organizations to provide financial support for an activity such as a demonstration project, a new service, or research. Grants are often given by government agencies at the state level and by federal departments and agencies who issue requests for proposals (RFPs) on a regular basis, causing competition for funds. Foundations and philanthropists also grant funds for which much competition exists.

grantee The person or organization to whom a grant is made.

grantor The organization or person making a grant.

grapevine communication The informal communication process common to hospitals or other closely knit organizations that arises from close social interaction of the employees in the organization.

-graph Suffix meaning "record" or "instrument for recording."

graphic rating scales In health administration and human resources management, this is a performance appraisal approach that uses an array of worker traits and characteristics that relate to job performance and usually incorporates a five-point rating scale, rating each trait from poor to excellent. The preferred approach is to have the form made out by a supervisor in a conference with the worker (it is also recommended that the worker fill out the form as a self-evaluation prior to the conference.) The traits should be objective, measurable, and related to worker performance, not to subjective traits and personality assessments. A space should be left for comments and objective setting.

-graphy Suffix meaning "process of recording."

GRAS *See generally recognized as safe.*

gratuitous Freely given without stipulation or consideration; voluntary; given or done without payment.

gratuitous guest A person riding in a vehicle (such as a bus or an ambulance) without payment but with permission and knowledge of the operator (e.g., a loved one accompanying an injured family member in an ambulance).

gratuitous licensee A visitor who is not a trespasser (i.e., visitors in a hospital); a nonbusiness visitor.

gratuitous transfer A free transfer made without payments, limitation, or consideration.

gravamen In health law and the litigation process, this is the foundation, basis, main parts, or essence of a legal complaint.

gravidity In medical care, this is the total number of pregnancies a female has experienced regardless of the outcome.

greatest economic need In aging services, this is an older adult whose monthly income is at or below Supplemental Security Income (SSI)/SSP benefit level.

greatest social need In aging services, this is an older adult who has two or more of the following characteristics: 1) handicapped, 2) language/communication barrier, 3) lives alone, or 4) is age 75 years or older.

grief Extreme sadness appropriate to an actual loss; emotional or mental suffering caused by loss and bereavement.

grievance 1. In health administration and human resource management, this is an employee's written or oral complaint about working conditions or situations or a dissatisfaction with co-workers or superiors. 2. In managed care, a formal request by health plan members for review of a supplemental benefit offered through their own health-care plans or for a special medical concern not covered by the health plan; a complaint or disenrollment request filed by an enrollee or provider.

grievance procedure 1. In health administration and human resource management, this is a special administrative procedure or policy establishing a proper and accepted way of dealing with employment problems or for hearing complaints between employees and employers. 2. In managed care, the process by which a health plan enrollee or participating provider can register complaints and seek solutions or remedies.

Griggs v. Duke Power Company A case heard by the U.S. Supreme Court that determined that when an employment criterion disproportionately discriminates against a protected class, the employer is required to demonstrate how the criterion is job related.

gross 1. Total amount. 2. Great. 3. Flagrant or shameful.

gross autopsy rate The ratio of all inpatient autopsies to all inpatient deaths for a given period of time. *See also autopsy rate.*

gross death rate (group or shelter home) The ratio of deaths to the total number of persons living in a group or shelter home during a given period. The gross death rate formula follows:

$$\frac{\text{Total number of deaths for the time period}}{\text{Total number of persons in the home for time period}} = \frac{20 \times 100}{120} = 16.7\% \text{ (GDR)}$$

See also death rates.

gross death rate (nursing home) The ratio of deaths to the total number of discharges from a nursing home facility during a given period of time. The gross death rate formula follows:

$$\frac{\text{Total number of deaths for the time period}}{\text{Total number of patients discharged for time period}} = \frac{20 \times 100}{200} = 10\% \text{ (GDR)}$$

See also death rates.

gross domestic product (GDP) This is the gross national product (GNP) plus an adjustment (typically small) for the value of productive services performed domestically by foreign subjects minus the value of productive services performed abroad by nationals. The GDP measures all the goods and services produced by workers and capital located in the United States regardless of ownership and is shown as percentage change from quarter to quarter. *See gross national product.*

gross earning form A special type of insurance covering business interruption; coverage is based on the gross earnings of the business.

gross income All money and income; expenses and cost included in the total amount of income. *See also net income.*

gross lease In health-care financial management, any lease that requires the lessor to pay all or most of the expenses of the leased equipment or property, including items such as taxes, insurance, maintenance, and utilities.

gross national product (GNP) The overall value of all goods and services produced by the nation's economy for a selected period of time, usually 1 year; the most comprehensive measure of a nation's total output of goods and services. It is the dollar value in current prices of all goods and services produced for sale plus the estimated value of certain imputed outputs based on goods and services that are neither bought nor sold. The GNP is the sum of 1) consumption expenditures by both individuals and nonprofit organizations plus certain imputed values; 2) business investment in equipment, inventories, and new construction; 3) federal, state and local government purchases of goods and services; and 4) the sale of goods and services abroad minus purchases from abroad. A related concept is the gross domestic product. *See gross domestic product.*

gross negligence In health law, this is the performance of expected duties in a reckless manner, having no concern or regard for the consequences of the act; willful and wanton disregard for the rights or the care of others; the want of a level of care that a prudent health care provider would provide if personal health or property were the concern. Such negligence is shown by the reckless disregard of another's life, limb, happiness, or health or ignoring the safety of persons who are exposed to dangerous circumstances; indifference to one's legal duty, but not an intentional wrong. Gross negligence occurs when a person knows the results of his or her acts but is wanton and indifferent to the results, although he or she did not intentionally perform the acts to purposefully cause harm.

gross operating revenue The total amount of money in all areas of operating revenue accounts prior to any money being removed for allowances or adjustments.

gross patient revenue In health-care finance, this is the income from regular inpatient services and income from outpatient services; the full amount of revenue from all services rendered to all patients, including all payments received by the health-care organization or facility from self-pay patients, third-party payers, government payment programs, or other sources of payment.

gross premium 1. In health administration and insurance, this the total charge for insurance policies utilized by health-care facilities that includes anticipated cost of losses, overhead, and profit; the amount that the health-care organization/policyowner pays for all insurance, including net premium plus the loading factors.

gross reproduction rate In public health and epidemiology, this is the average number of female live births to women no older than age 50 based on a constant fertility rate. *See net reproduction rate.*

gross revenues In health-care finance, this is the sum of all charges in a specific time period. *See gross patient revenue.*

gross weight A total weight, including the weight of containers.

ground rules In health insurance, the basic and introductory material provided in the procedure coding manual to help with the filing of insurance claims by the health-care provider, including general information and instructions, special services and modifiers, and codes for services and procedures.

grounds Basic facts; the foundation or points of a case or dispute. The basic reason for a cause of action.

ground state In laser technology, this is when all electrons are in orbits closest to the nucleus, which is a very low energy point of the atom and the laser beam used in treatment or diagnosis.

groundwater In environmental health and safe water management, this is the supply of fresh water found beneath the earth's surface, usually in aquifers that supply wells and springs. This is a major source of drinking water and must be protected from pollutants. Major sources of pollution include leaching agricultural or industrial chemicals and wastes, leachate from landfills, leaking underground storage tanks such as gasoline tanks, sewers, industrial solvents, and crop spraying with chemicals.

groundwater resources In environmental health and safe water management, this is water in saturated zones or strata beneath the surface of land or water and rocks or sediments through which groundwater moves, including groundwater resources that meet the definition of drinking water supplies.

groundwater, significant source of *See significant source of groundwater.*

groundwater, special source In environmental health and safe water management, these are those classes of water from ground sources that are to be restricted and protected. Class 1 groundwaters are 1) within the controlled area encompassing a disposal system or are less than 5 kilometers beyond the controlled area, 2) supplying drinking water for thousands of persons within an area planned for detailed characterization as a potential disposal site, and 3) are irreplaceable in that no reasonable alternative source of drinking water is available to that population. *See site characterization.*

group In managed care, this is a body of subscribers eligible for group insurance by virtue of some common identifying attribute (e.g., common employment by an employer) or membership in a union, association, or other organization. A large number of eligible persons who group together as a single entity to be eligible for group rates and price breaks for having larger numbers in a purchasing cooperative arrangement. Groups considered for insurance are usually larger than nine persons.

group agreement In managed care and medical insurance, this is a method of providing medical coverage under one master plan for a number of individuals comprising a group by virtue of employment or other associations.

group annuity An annuity covering all the employees of a health-care organization such as that in a private group retirement plan.

group certificate In managed care, this is a special document given to each member of a group health program to show the benefits provided under the group plan's contract. It is issued to the employer or other insured person.

group contract A contract made with an employer that covers a group of persons. In managed care, this is a health plan agreement, signed by the health plan and the employer group, that sets forth benefits, exclusions, and conditions between the health plan and the enrolling group.

group dining In long-term care and health and social services for the elderly, this is a nutrition program with a congregate approach that provides nutritious noontime meals and social activities for older persons at senior centers, churches, or schools. Transportation may be offered to bring the elders to and from the center. Officially called "congregate dining."

grouper In health information management, this is a computer program using medical abstract data that automatically assigns a DRG to a patient on the basis of principal diagnosis, procedures, other diagnoses, discharge status, age, and a "decision tree" of the uniqueness of the DRG.

Group Health Association of America (GHAA) Founded in 1959 to assist and represent health maintenance organizations, the GHAA interacts with HMO plan personnel and is familiar with their management needs.

group health plans In managed care, those health care services and facilities that are comprehensive, prepaid HMO health-care services providing health care to members who have enrolled in and prepaid for health and medical services. Many group health plans charge a small additional fee. Drugs and other healthcare items and services are usually provided at a reduced cost. *See also prepaid group practice plan; health maintenance organization.*

group insurance Any managed care or insurance plan by which a number of employees (and their dependents) or members of a similar homogeneous group are insured under a single policy. The plan is issued to their employer or the group with individual certificates of insurance given to each insured individual or family. Individual employees may be insured automatically by virtue of employment, only on meeting certain conditions (employment for over 1 month) or only when they elect to be insured (usually requiring a contribution to the cost of the insurance). Group health insurance is usually experience rated and less expensive for the insured than comparable individual insurance (partly because an employed population is generally healthier than the general population and partly because of lower administrative costs, especially in marketing and billing). Note that the policyholder or insured is the employer, not the employee. *See also contributory insurance.*

group legal services Legal aid given to members of an organization or employees of a company. It is prepaid on a group basis, similar to prepaid medical insurance.

group life insurance A term life insurance program offered as a group policy benefit for the employees of a health-care organization.

group model 1. In managed care, this is one approach to a health maintenance organization (HMO). The HMO contracts with a group of physicians who is paid a set amount per patient to provide a specified range of services. The physician group determines compensation, costs, and other contractual issues. 2. A health plan model involving contracts with physicians organized as a partnership, professional corporation, or other legal association. The health plan compensates the medical group for contracted services as a negotiated rate, and that group is responsible for compensating its physicians and contracting with hospitals for care of the patients.

group model health maintenance organization (HMO) 1. In managed care, this is one approach to an HMO that is self-directed, controlled, and staffed by the physician of a group practice who may or may not have ownership of the HMO. 2. A health delivery approach that involves contracts with health-care providers organized as an HMO corporation or partnership containing all the elements, regulations, and mandates of a federal or state HMO using the group model.

group model HMO *See group model; group model health maintenance organization.*

group practice 1. A formal association of three or more physicians or other health professionals who share expenses, facilities, staff and diagnostic equipment, lab, information management systems, and administrative overhead. 2. A group of health-care providers who provide services to patients; the income from medical practice is pooled and redistributed to the members of the group according to a prearranged plan (often, but not necessarily, through a partnership). This formal association of physicians provides specialty care or comprehensive general and primary care to patients on an ambulatory and outpatient basis. Multispecialty groups offer advantages to the patient by providing several kinds of services on an integrated basis. Groups vary in size, medical specialty composition, and financial arrangements. *See also solo practice; private practice; prepaid group practice.*

group practice, multispecialty In medical group management, this is an organized business approach providing several kinds of medical and clinical services in different specialties. Physicians from various specialties including family practice, general surgery, and internal medicine are considered minimal for a multispecialty practice. Other specialties include psychotherapists and psychologists.

group practice, prepaid *See prepaid group practice.*

group practice, single-specialty In medical group management, this is an organized business approach to running a clinic for physicians, dentists, or other health-care providers, all within the same medical specialty.

group process The application of educational and communication principles in group situations designed to facilitate problem solving and decision making through mutual stimulation of creative and critical thinking or to increase the credibility and attractiveness of recommended health practices (Joint Committee on Health Education Terminology, 1973).

group psychotherapy In mental health services, this is a type of psychiatric or psychological treatment involving several patients participating together in therapy. One or two psychotherapists facilitate emotional and rational cognitive interactions in the members of the group to change maladaptive behavior in each member.

group purchasing In health-care administration, this is when health-care organizations work together in a shared services arrangement to increase purchasing power and lower costs by bulk purchasing.

group representative In managed care and insurance, this is an employee of the insurance company who deals with the distribution of group insurance products by finding prospects, designing proposals, installing the new plans or policies, and renegotiating policies and health plans on renewal.

group role In organizational behavior in health-care organizations, this is a set of behaviors or posture assumed by employees as part of the social interaction of the group as a whole. The behavior of individuals and how they respond and interact with other co-workers.

group service agreement In managed care, this is the contract document between a health plan and an employer or a union that negotiates benefit packages for workers.

group solidarity The presentation of a unified front, indicating that a group of employees, union members, or other groups are in total agreement.

group subscriber agreement In managed care, this is an agreement between a health plan and the employer group (subscriber group) that defines the terms and conditions of the health coverage to be provided by the health plan.

group termination In managed care, this is when an employer (work group) ceases participation in a group medical care benefit program and the employees are no longer covered under a health plan.

groupthink In health administration and organizational behavior, this is the unproductive and inefficient group problem solving that occurs when all members give in to group social pressure and go along with poor, wrong, or ineffective decisions, resulting in loss of time, revenue, and resources and even the demise of an organization.

growth 1. A normal or natural increase in weight and height; normal increase in physical size. 2. The multiplication and proliferation of cells. 3. In health services, the continual success, development, and advancement of a health-care organization in both size and financial stature.

growth rate of population 1. The natural rate of increase. 2. The difference between crude birth rates and crude death rates. 3. In public health and epidemiology, the rate of increase in the population of a city, county, region, state, or country, excluding migration, taking into consideration the addition of newborns and subtracts deaths. The growth rate of population formula follows:

$$\frac{\text{Live births during the year} - \text{deaths during the year}}{\text{Midyear population}} \times 1000$$

growth stocks In health-care finance, these are stocks offered on the stock market that are believed to have strong potential for better-than-market-average increases in worth because of expected higher earnings and faster expansion of the company or product area. Such stocks involve a greater risk than some other forms of stock.

growth strategy In health-care strategic planning, this is the effect that expansion of a health-care organization or services of a hospital will have on the organization with regard to profitability, competitive position (niche and market share), innovative services, acceptability of the services, accessibility, cash flow, and revenue. Expanded market position and expanded capacity of service are two goals of growth.

GSA General Services Administration; the federal agency that manages the property of the U.S. government.

guarantee A promise (sometimes incorporated into a contract) that goods are of a certain high quality, will be fixed if broken, and will last for a certain time period.

guaranteed annual wage In health administration, human resources management, and labor relations, workers are ensured to receive a minimum amount of work and a certain level of pay during the course of a year.

guaranteed continuable *See guaranteed renewable.*

guaranteed-issue basis In insurance and managed care, this is a type of contract and/or conditions of a policy that cannot refuse an applicant; a direct response insurance product.

guaranteed renewable In managed care and insurance, this is a health plan contract that allows an insured person to continue the right to keep a health plan or insurance policy in force by paying the premiums, during which period the insurer has no right to make any unilateral changes in any provision of the contract; an agreement to continue a health plan or insurance policy up to a certain age or for life, as long as the premium is paid; premium rates are maintained, unless the class of enrollment one belongs to has a rate increase. Premiums may not be changed for an individual but only for classes or groups.

guardian 1. One who has the legal right and duty to take care of another person because that person legally cannot take care of himself or herself (e.g., a child or an elderly person). A legally competent person appointed by the court to take care of the less-than-competent person, the person's property, or both. 2. For JCAHO long-term-care accreditation, an individual who has legal authority to act on behalf of another individual. 3. According to JCAHO for psychiatric, alcoholism, and drug abuse facilities accreditation purposes, a parent trustee, committee, conservator, or other person or agency empowered by law to act on behalf of, or have responsibility for, an applicant or patient. *See conservator.*

guardian at litem A lawyer, appointed by a court to handle the interests of another person, usually a minor or other person under legal disability, during the process of a lawsuit in which the person is involved.

guest bed service In hospitals, this is a bed provided by a hospital to accommodate a patient's family member, relative, or guardian, especially pediatric patients; hotel services for a patient's family or relatives.

guest statute In some states, a law providing that a person who rides as a guest in another person's car cannot sue the driver if there is an accident, unless it involved more than ordinary negligence.

guideline, practice In medical care and hospital accreditation, this is a tool of standardized specifications for care of a typical patient in the typical situation, developed through a formal process that incorporates the best scientific evidence of effectiveness with expert opinion. Synonymous with clinical criteria, parameter (practice parameter), protocol, review criteria, preferred practice pattern, and guideline (JCAHO for acute-care facilities).

guidelines General directions, criteria, or policy. A standard, principle, or instructions by which a judgment can be made, a policy determined, an action taken, or a grant application filled out.

guideline, scoring In hospital accreditation, this is an instrument used to assist the hospital in its efforts to comply with quality standards and to determine degree of compliance with a set of quality evaluation standards. Scoring guidelines are described in the *Accreditation Manual for Hospitals,* Volume 2 (JCAHO for acute-care facilities).

guilt 1. The act of having done wrong. 2. In law, this is having done a wrong or a crime, usually with intent; having a crime and wrong proven with punishment imposed. 3. Shame; the painful, emotional feeling associated with the violation of one's value system or a transgression of moral/ethical beliefs. 4. In psychiatric and psychological constructs, this is an emotional state filled with self-reproach and the feeling of a need for punishment. Guilt can provide normal psychological and social functions and useful and moral constraints; excessive guilt can cause depression. A lack of guilt can result in antisocial or amoral behavior. As a motivation factor, some amount of guilt can be productive and helpful in directing moral behavior.

guilty 1. Deserving of blame. 2. One responsible for doing harm or committing a crime. 3. Proven to have committed a crime or a civil wrong; the opposite of being innocent.

gyneco- Prefix meaning "female."

gynecological conditions Diseases or disorders peculiar to females, the reproductive process, and their reproductive organs.

gynecologist A medical specialty requiring the completion of a postgraduate medical residency and board certification for the physician to conduct diagnosis and treatment of diseases, disorders, and conditions of the female reproductive system. This physician often has a second area of specialization in obstetrics and is referred to as a "specialist in obstetrics/gynecology."

gynecology The branch of medicine that deals with the female reproductive system and associated conditions, diseases, and processes.

H

H&P History and physical exam.

HA (Lat.) Hoc anno. In this year.

habeas corpus (Lat.) You have the body. In law, this is a court order to secure the release of a person who is being held unlawfully. The principle implies neither guilt nor innocence but addresses the issue of due process: it is unlawful to detain a person without evidence or being charged with a crime.

habilitation *See rehabilitation.*

habilitation and rehabilitation services Healthcare services provided to restore the health, independence, and mobility of ill and disabled individuals or to assist the developmentally disabled in achieving the fullest physical, mental, social, vocational, and economic usefulness that they are capable of. Included in these services are the medical evaluation of needs; design, management, evaluation of habilitation or rehabilitation programs; therapeutic techniques from physical, occupational, and recreational therapy; prosthetic/orthotic services; speech therapy; audiology; and psychological and social therapies. *See also rehabilitation.*

habitability The legal principle that requires a rented place or residence or apartment be fit to live in; a public health concern in that rented property should be free of rodents, insects, the trash and garbage that would attract them, and any unsanitary conditions.

habitual 1. On a regular basis. 2. Something done so often that it is done by habit, not by chance; occurring more than just occasionally; doing a behavior so frequently that it occurs by compulsion rather than by chance.

habitual intemperance Continual drunkenness that interferes with family life or employment. It can be grounds for divorce in many states. In some states, drug addiction falls under this rule.

habituation In mental health, this is when an individual has developed a pattern of behavior in his or her lifestyle that is so ingrained that it is done without thought but does not necessarily involve physical or psychological dependence. *See drug habituation; drug abuse; drug dependence.*

HAC Health Advisory Council; a former local advisory council to the now-defunct health systems agencies. In some areas these were called "subarea advisory councils."

half-life In environmental health and chemical and radiation safety, this is a measure of strength that is used to classify the rate of decay of radioisotopes or chemicals according to the time it takes them to lose half their strength or intensity; the time required for a pollutant to lose half its effect on the environment.

halfway house 1. In mental health-care or substance abuse rehabilitation, this is a community-based facility (house) for patients with mental, behavioral, or emotional problems who no longer need the full facilities of a mental hospital but are not yet ready to go out on their own or live by themselves in their own private housing. 2. A nonmedical transitional residential living facility developed by, and under the direction of, public or nonprofit organizations that provides room, board, and assistance to mentally or physically handicapped persons trying to make the transition to independent living back into the community. They share living facilities and are under the supervision of a counselor or social worker. Supervised living, supportive, rehabilitative, group therapy, and other services are often a part of this transitional living arrangement. 3. The term is also used to describe minimum security penal institutions.

hallucination A false experience or an experience that exists only in one's mind. It can be brought on by emotional factors or by drugs or alcohol. Common hallucinations involve sights, sounds, and tastes, but a reaction by any of the senses is possible.

hallucinogen Any drug that causes distortion of one's emotions, perceptions, or sensations; any substance that causes hallucinations.

halo effect 1. A positive response or effect in a patient brought on by the manner, attention, and caring attitude of a health-care provider; positive reactions in a patient during a medical encounter regardless of what medical procedures or services the encounter actually involves. 2. In health administration and human resources management, this is when an employee is given an unjustified high performance appraisal by a boss who likes the worker; a tendency to rate workers high on work performance because all are seen as good employees. *See also Hawthorne effect; placebo.*

halt symbol In health-care information management and computers, this is a symbol that stops a computer when a job is completed.

hand feeding In long-term-care facilities, this is the process of feeding a patient who is unable to feed him- or herself.

handicap A limitation on the fulfillment of a role that is normal for most individuals; a disadvantage resulting from a physical or mental impairment or disability that limits or prevents the fulfillment of a role that is normal for most individuals. A handicap is the consequence of disability. A disability is a consequence of an impairment, which does not necessarily lead to disabilities, nor do disabilities necessarily lead to handicaps. Handicaps and disabilities are frequently permanent conditions (e.g., paraplegia due to a polio infection). *See impairment; disability.*

handicapped Under the Rehabilitation Act of 1973, any physical or mental condition limiting a person from life's nominal activities. Individuals with handicaps under this act do not include those engaging in the illegal use of drugs. Persons who have successfully completed supervised drug rehabilitation and no longer engage in illegal drug use are not excluded. *See American's with Disability Act.*

hand over hand As used in rehabilitation activities, this is assisting a patient or client through activities by the therapist placing his or her hand over the patient's hand to guide them through the task.

handrails Common to long-term-care facilities or rehabilitation centers, these are bars and railings that have been installed beside bathtubs, showers, and toilets and along walls to assist and steady the patient in carrying on activities in the facility. Regulations set forth the type, height, and location of hand rails in long-term-care facilities.

HANES Health and Nutrition Examination Survey.

Hantavirus Also called the Four-Corners Disease, a virus first discovered on the Navajo reservation near where the four corners of Arizona, New Mexico, Colorado, and Utah meet. In epidemiology and public health disease control, this new virus is often fatal and is transmitted by the dry urine, saliva, and feces (or dust thereof) of the deer mouse and other rodents. The virus causes fever, headache, muscle aches, breathing difficulty, bleeding, kidney failure, and shock. The disease has been found in many western states and other states in the United States.

haphazard sample In epidemiology and health services research, this is the process of choosing subjects for a research study with no regard to proper sampling approaches, research design, or considering whether the subjects are representative of the study population. Because this approach is usually a sample of convenience or accessibility, it limits the researcher's ability to apply the findings to a general population.

haplology In mental health care, this is a disorder characterized by such rapid speech that syllables are left out. Certain manias and schizophrenic conditions exhibit this symptom.

harass To badger; to trouble or bother; to disturb persistently; to weary; to fatigue.

harbor 1. To feed and shelter; conceal, keep, or detain a person for illegal purposes. 2. To hide something. 3. To keep a person from law enforcement officers. 4. In epidemiology, this means to possess a disease or pathogen within one's body, as a carrier of a disease does. 5. In psychology and mental health, this is to cling to and retain strong emotional states or beliefs, such as anger toward another person, that create stress and deter from a positive mental health status. *See carrier, host.*

hard case 1. In health law, this is a case in which fairness requires a loose interpretation of legal principles because of difficulties and problems experienced by the party of the case. 2. In health-care social services and financial management, this is a situation in which a patient is having serious financial problems and cannot afford to pay for health-care services and is assisted by personnel from the social services department in acquiring financial assistance from outside sources. Also called "hardship case."

hard disk In health-care information management systems and computers, this is a disk made of hard metal sealed into a cartridge and used to store data and information; a large information storage computer hardware device.

hard money In health-care finance, this is income or revenue from predictable and dependable sources such as self-pay or third-party payers or government payment sources that are used to run a program, an organization, or an institution; revenue from an assured and ongoing source. This money will flow regularly into an organization or a program on a continuous and dependable basis. Sources of hard money usually are insurance payments, state government sources, local government sources, or fees for services rendered. *See also soft money.*

hardship case *See hard case.*

hardware 1. In health-care information management, this is the equipment and materials that make up a data processing system. 2. In media and telecommunications, the machinery and equipment such as projectors and videotape machines (software items are played or used on the hardware). *See also software.*

harm In health law, this is any injury, wrong, or damage done to either a person, a person's rights, or property that warrants legal consideration.

harmless error In law and the litigation process, this is an error of a lower court that has little effect on an appellant's basic rights or on the decision or the merits of the case. This error does not merit a review or reversal of a judgment.

Harris flush In medical care, this is irrigation of the lower bowel to promote the expulsion of gas from the intestines. This is used with postoperative patients whose intestinal tracts are not functioning properly and need assistance in re-establishing normal peristalsis.

Harrison Antinarcotic Act A law established by the U.S. government that restricts the use and distribution of dangerous drugs. Drugs controlled by this law include opiates and their derivatives such as morphine and heroin, many stimulants such as amphetamines and cocaine, and hallucinogens such as LSD and marijuana. This law also provides certain limitations and requirements for writing prescriptions for the drugs controlled by this act. *See also schedule of controlled substances.*

has the floor In formal health-care meetings using parliamentary procedure, when a member of a committee or board has been recognized by the chair. When recognized, this person should not be interrupted but may yield the opportunity for others to speak (give them the floor).

Hawthorne effect A reactive but beneficial effect patients experience during an encounter with a health-care provider, health program, or other part of the health system that is independent of the medical content of the encounter because the patients respond in a positive manner to the attention afforded them. The Hawthorne effect is similar to the placebo effect but is not intentionally obtained and is the effect of the encounter with a provider or program on the patient rather than the treatment. The effect may be changed by altering the provider or program (e.g., by painting a clinic or changing its appointments system). Because health services research usually changes the services being studied, the resulting change in the Hawthorne effect may well confound the results of the research. The name comes from historical classic industrial management experiments on the effect of altering light in the workers' environment, resulting in a change in work performance and productivity at the Hawthorne plant of the Western Electric Company. *See also halo effect; placebo.*

hazard 1. A situation or event that introduces or increases the probability of property loss arising from a peril. External hazards are winds, earthquakes, and tornadoes, and in the health-care facility they include fire, slippery floors, and unsanitary conditions. 2. In environmental health and occupational health and safety, this is any existing or potential condition in the workplace that can result in death, injury, or property damage or loss. A condition does not have to presently exist to constitute a hazard and may result from independent negligence in the workplace where one event or circumstance interacts with others, resulting in a bad outcome.

hazard analysis 1. In environmental health and occupational health and safety, these are the functions, steps, and criteria for designing and planning work that identify hazards and residual risks and provide both measures to reduce probability and severity potentials and alternative methods of further control. 2. The procedures involved are 1) identification of potential sources of release of hazardous materials from fixed facilities or transportation accidents, 2) determination of the vulnerability of a geographical area to a release of hazardous materials, and 3) comparison of hazards to determine which present greater or lesser risks to a community (EPA).

hazard categories In environmental health and occupational health and safety, the classification is as follows: 1) immediate (acute) health hazard: highly toxic, toxic, irritant, sensitizer, corrosive, and other hazardous chemicals that cause an adverse effect to a target organ that usually occurs rapidly as a result of short-term exposure and is of short duration; 2) delayed (chronic) health hazard: carcinogens and other hazardous chemicals that cause an adverse effect to a target organ and that generally occurs as a result of long-term exposure and is of long duration; 3) fire hazard: flammable and combustible liquid, pyrophoric, and oxidizers; and 4) sudden release of pressure: explosive and compressed gas. *See hazardous waste characteristics; hazard classification.*

hazard classifications In environmental health and occupational health and safety, the three alphabetical designations to classify hazards: class A: potential for permanent disability, loss of life or body part, or extensive loss of structure, equipment, material, or property; class B: potential of serious injury or illness resulting in temporary disability or property damage that is disruptive; class C: potential for minor injury or illness or nondisruptive property damage. *See hazardous waste characteristics; hazard categories.*

hazard control program The program must be supported by the top-level administration of the health-care organization and carried out by department heads, supervisors, and employees who make certain that materials, chemicals, biohazards, equipment, and machines are hazard free through proper maintenance and design and that adequate safety and protection measures are in place. Accident and injury investigation trends must be followed and measures taken to correct or prevent them. Proper policies and procedures and a system to ensure that they are followed must be established, especially for those activities regarded as dangerous.

hazardous air pollutants In environmental health, these are air pollutants that are not covered by ambient air quality standards but that may, as defined in the Clean Air Act, be reasonably expected to cause or contribute to irreversible illness or death. Such pollutants include asbestos, beryllium, mercury, benzene, coke oven emissions, radionuclides, and vinyl chloride.

hazardous analysis In environmental health and occupational health and safety, this is an information processing approach that assesses data regarding hazards and safety failure. By locating hazards that are most probable and that have the potential for the severest consequences, effective control measures can be implemented. The analysis uncovers hazards that have been overlooked; locates hazards that have developed after a particular process, operation, or task; indicates qualification prerequisites to safe and productive work processes; and identifies situational hazards in facilities, equipment, tools, operations, and materials.

Hazardous and Solid Waste Amendments (HSWA) In 1976 the Resource Conservation and Recovery Act (RCRA) was passed. In 1984 the U.S. Congress reauthorized the RCRA as the Hazardous and Solid Waste Amendments, providing comprehensive federal and state hazardous waste management and requiring industries to identify all hazardous wastes, toxicity, persistence, degradability, potential for accumulation in tissues, and other characteristics of waste materials. Performance standards and a permit system were established for operators of hazardous waste treatment, storage, and disposal facilities. Corrective action is to be taken at hazardous waste sites with problems, including underground storage tanks for petroleum products and other hazardous substances. The EPA has issued technical standards for the release, prevention, and corrective action for all tanks.

hazardous area In JCAHO long-term-care facilities accreditation, a room that contains combustible or flammable materials of such a nature as to increase the potential hazards of a fire. Hazardous areas include kitchens with commercial cooking ranges, maintenance and repair shops, handicraft and gift shops, and boiler rooms. They also include rooms used to store combustible supplies, flammable gases or liquids, or oxidizing agents in significant quantities.

hazardous chemicals 1. In environmental health and safety, these are any food, food or color additive, drug, or cosmetic regulated by the Food and Drug Administration. 2. Any substance present as a solid in any manufactured item to the extent that exposure to the substance does not occur under normal conditions of use. 3. Any substance used for personal, family, or household purposes or present in the same form or concentration as a product packaged for distribution and use by the general public. 4. Any substance used in a research laboratory, hospital, or other medical facility under the direct supervision of a technically qualified individual. 5. Any substance that is used in routine agricultural operations or that is a fertilizer held for sale by a retailer to a customer.

hazardous materials 1. In environmental health, these are any substances or materials, including hazardous substances, that have been determined to be capable of posing an unreasonable risk to health, safety, and property when transported in commerce. 2. In hospitals, clinics, or research facilities, radioactive or chemical substances that are dangerous to humans and for which policies and hazardous materials plans and procedures are developed.

hazardous materials emergency In environmental health, these are conditions, circumstances, or potential situations that could result in the accidental release or loss of control of radioactive or toxic materials.

hazardous materials emergency plans Hospitals, clinics, and research facilities are required to prepare community-level hazardous materials plans similar to disaster preparedness plans that detail plans for dealing with any hazardous material emergency.

hazardous materials response team In environmental health, the HAZMAT team is an organized group of employees, designated by an employer, who are expected to handle and control actual or potential leaks or spills of hazardous substances for the purpose of stabilizing the incident. HAZMAT teams may be a part of a fire department or brigade.

hazardous procedures According to JCAHO for psychiatric, alcoholism, and drug abuse facilities accreditation purposes, procedures that place the patient at physical or psychological risk.

hazardous ranking system (HRS) In environmental health and hazardous waste, this is the principal screening tool of the EPA that evaluates risks to public health and the environment associated with abandoned or uncontrolled hazardous waste sites. The HRS calculates a score according to the potential of hazardous substances to spread from the site through the air, surface water, or groundwater and to other factors such as closeness of nearby populations. The score is the primary factor in deciding if the site should be on the National Priorities List and, if so, what ranking it should have compared to other sites on the list.

hazardous substances 1. In environmental health, these are materials that pose a threat to human health and/or the environment. Typical hazardous substances are toxic, corrosive, ignitable, explosive, or chemically reactive. 2. Any chemical, material, or substance designated by the EPA to be hazardous if spilled in the waters of the United States or if otherwise emitted to the environment.

hazardous waste 1. In environmental health, this is any combination of waste that, because of its quantity, concentration, or physical, chemical, and infectious characteristics, may cause or significantly contribute to an increase in mortality or serious irreversible or incapacitating reversible illnesses or pose a substantial present or potential hazard to human health or the environment when improperly treated, stored, transported, disposed of, or otherwise managed. It must possess at least one of the four characteristics of hazardous waste characteristics: ignitability, corrosivity, reactivity, and toxicity. 2. In health-care facilities and health-care delivery, these are leftover tissue or bioproducts from health care that are dangerous to humans and the environment. In hospitals, hazardous waste includes radioactive waste; chemicals; toxic substances; drugs; human remains; infectious waste products such as tissue, blood, and used surgical sponges and needles; other biological waste products; and any infectious material that can transmit disease or cause disease or injury. *See hazardous substances; hazardous materials; infectious waste.*

hazardous waste characteristics In environmental health and occupational health and safety, there are four determining categories: ignitability, corrosivity, reactivity, and toxicity. *See hazardous waste.*

hazardous waste discharge In environmental health and occupational health and safety, an accidental or intentional spilling, leaking, pumping, pouring, emitting, emptying, or dumping of hazardous waste into or on any land or water.

hazardous waste facilities In environmental health, all controlled land, structures, or other appurtenances and improvements on the land used for treating, storing, or disposing of hazardous waste. A facility may consist of several treatment, storage, or disposal operational units such as landfills or surface impoundments.

hazardous waste management In environmental health, the systematic control of the collection, source separation, storage, transportation, processing, treatment, recovery, and disposal of hazardous wastes.

hazard quotient In environmental health and occupational health and safety, the ratio of a single substance exposure level over a specified time period to a reference dose for that substance derived from a similar exposure period.

hazard surveillance program In JCAHO long-term-care facilities accreditation, a program involving routine periodic surveys by personnel or staff to identify unsafe conditions or practices occurring at the facility.

HAZMAT Abbreviation for "hazardous materials."

HAZMAT team *See hazardous materials response team.*

HAZRAP Hazardous Waste Remedial Actions Program.

HB House bill; a bill introduced in the House of Representatives to become law.

HCC *See health-care corporation.*

HCFA *See Health Care Financing Administration.*

HCFA 1500 In health-care finance, a universal form developed by the Health Care Financing Administration (HCFA) for health-care providers to use in billing for professional services to intermediaries or carriers.

HCFA 2567 Under the Omnibus Budget Reconciliation Act, a statement of deficiencies and a plan for making corrections; the official document on which citations are recorded.

HCFA common procedural coding system (HCPCS) In health-care finance, the Health Care Financing Administration (HCFA) developed a five-digit code system with the first digit being a letter, followed by four numbers. Codes W–Z are local codes, and A–V are federal/national codes. The HCPCS is a list of procedures, supplies, therapies, and procedures offered by health-care providers. Current procedural terminology codes (CPT), alphanumeric codes, and common alphanumeric codes are included in the HCPCS. The HCFA created the codes for national use as a supplement to CPT codes. Certain physician services and nonphysician services such as ambulance use, durable medical equipment, physical therapy, and occupational therapy are not usually included in CPT codes. Medicare carriers develop codes for use in local areas to supplement the HCFA federal-level codes.

HCFA rate cell verification Under Medicare, the procedure by which the Health Care Financing Administration (HCFA) assigns all Medicare beneficiaries to a certain capitation rate. The verification process involves confirming the criteria that HCFA uses to assign the beneficiaries to rate cells such as sex, age, economic status, and geographical location.

HCPCS Heath Care Common Procedure Coding System.

HCQIA Health Care Quality Improvement Act.

head nurse A registered nurse who is the responsible administrative agent of a nursing unit in a hospital or nursing home. This person is responsible for all activities of the unit 7 days a week and 24 hours a day.

head of family The person who is financially and morally responsible for, and is the support of, a family or group of related persons who all live together. *See family; family health.*

health Defined by the World Health Organization as "a state of complete physical, mental, and social well-being and not merely the absence of disease or infirmity." Health science and public health professionals recognize that health has many dimensions (physiological, emotional, spiritual/value, social, mental, the absence of pathological conditions, and a perceived sense of well-being) and is often culturally defined. The relative importance of various levels of health status and perceived sense of well-being will differ depending on the cultural milieu, family, health belief system, social environment, and the role of the individual in that culture. Most attempts at the measurement of health have taken a negative approach in that the degree of ill health is assessed in terms of morbidity and mortality, implying that health is the absence of these factors. In general, the detection of changes in health status is easier than the definition and measurement of an absolute level of well-being. Terms and phrases used to describe health include well-being, lifestyle, quality of life, absence of disease or abnormality, more than biological well-being and fitness, absence of mortality, morbidity, disability and distress, and how well one operates effectively within particular circumstances of one's heredity and environment.

health administration 1. The operation and management of health-care organizations, including hospitals, medical groups, clinics, managed-care plans, public health agencies, and long-term-care facilities. Tasks and activities include financial and budgetary control, personnel and human resource management, governing board relations, medical staff management and physician relations, nursing services and patient care administration, materials and central supply control, public relations and marketing, long-range and strategic planning, training of personnel, communications, physical plant management, and planning day-to-day operations. 2. A generic term for the work and employment activities of a broad range of administration professionals who work in health-care organizations such as hospital administrators; medical group managers; some managers in managed-care organizations; health planners and policy analysts in federal, state, regional, and local agencies; clinic administrators; and administrators of public health agencies, health maintenance organizations, and long-term-care facilities. 3. The management of resources, personnel, procedures, policies, and systems that operate in a health-care organization or facility to meet the needs and demands placed on the health-care system.

health administrator 1. Individuals trained and experienced in health care administration, usually possessing a college degree in health administration at the bachelors and/or masters degree level. Health administrators are involved in planning, coordinating, evaluating, and directing the facilities, services, programs, personnel, resources, and procedures necessary to provide health and medical care services. Administrators work in hospitals, rehabilitation centers, ambulatory health-care centers, group practice plans, health maintenance organizations, voluntary health agencies, state and local health departments, home health agencies, nursing homes, and health services or agencies. Health administrators are also employed by managed-care organizations, private health insurance firms, and research agencies to design, implement, and evaluate health programs. Administrators may also teach or conduct research in educational programs that train health service administrators at both graduate and undergraduate levels. Some positions in government service utilize health administrators in areas such as health manpower, health statistics, health services research, health planning, program evaluation, and program planning. 2. Planning, organizing, directing, controlling, and coordinating the resources procedures by which the needs and demands for health and medical care and a healthful environment are converted to specific services for individual clients, organizations, and communities. *See Commission of Education for Health Administration.*

health advising In health promotion, the process of informing, directing, educating, and assisting individuals, families, groups, or workers in making decisions and solving problems related to individual health and well-being.

health advocacy Patient advocacy by an allied health professional called a "patient representative." *See patient representative.*

Health Aide Program Characterizes the role of the health representative who assists specific Indian Health Service personnel in both clinical and field health programs. Health representatives in programs of this type work closely with physicians, public health nurses, sanitarians, medical social workers, and other health team members.

health alliance According to the National Health Security program under the *Clinton Health Proposal*, these were once called Health Care Purchasing Cooperatives (HIPC). These are large purchasing and pooling organizations that would be regulated and operated much like a public utilities commission and would coordinate and monitor managed-care organizations' health plans and health-care delivery systems, all developed as a component of managed competition. These are state-, community-, or company-based purchasing pools that approve health plans and administer federal subsidies for low-income families and low-wage businesses. Regional health alliances enroll almost all people in a geographical area and would publish report cards on each health plan. Many analysts believe the government's approach to facilitating managed-care programs (providing access to health care for all citizens of the United States) would increase administrative costs. Each alliance would provide a menu of providers and fees for services and certify HMOs, PPOs, and IPAs. Each alliance would offer a least one traditional plan in which people could see any doctor they choose. The federal government would mandate the benefit package, which would be comprehensive and provide universal coverage. Budgets would be set by states, and new standards, malpractice reform, and fraud and abuse control would be implemented to help reduce cost. Small businesses would receive subsidies, with caps placed on small business and employees. A safety net of providers, especially in the inner cities and for rural hospitals, would also be provided. Medicare would continue to provide individual choices of providers. The health alliance would hold annual enrollment periods, allow a choice of health plans, set baseline rates, and communicate options to the public such as information and evaluation reports on each health plan. Health alliance would collect premiums from employers and individuals and distribute the premiums to the health plans on the basis of enrollment. *See HIPC, exclusive; national health board; managed competition.*

Health and Human Services, Department of *See Department of Health and Human Services.*

health and medical care system The combination of institutions, facilities, agencies, services, and resources that work interactively to help achieve the delivery of health-care services, medical services, community and public health services, health-related social services, mental health services, and home health-care and personal care services on a preventive, acute-care, or long-term-care basis. From a government bureaucratic and policy perspective, the health-care system appears to be a nonsystem; however, from a consumer perspective, the health-care system, as put together by consensus according to individual need, creates an effective system that meets individual patient or family needs.

health and safety studies In environmental health and occupational health and safety, investigations of any effect of a chemical substance or mixture on health, the environment, or both, including underlying data and epidemiological studies; studies of occupational exposure to a chemical substance or mixture; toxicological, clinical, and ecological studies on a chemical substance or mixture; and any test performed pursuant to the Toxic Substance Control Act.

health appraisal clinic A health promotion or preventive care clinic located in a managed-care program, HMO, hospital, or freestanding clinic that offers health screening, including multiphase health testing and health risk appraisal. *See also health risk appraisal.*

health behavior Any activity, act, or lifestyle undertaken by an individual that will enhance health status, prevent disease, or detect any condition, disorder, or disease that is not clearly obvious or is asymptomatic. Health behavior includes self-care, health activation such as starting an exercise or weight-loss program or getting immunizations, adhering to health education knowledge, or visiting a physician or clinic to obtain preventive care, diagnosis, or treatment within the health-care system. *See health maintenance behaviors; health seeking behaviors.*

health benefits package In managed care, the services, treatments, therapies, and products offered by a health plan to its members.

health belief model 1. A theoretical foundation of the fields of preventive medicine, health education, and health promotion based on the convictions held by an individual. A systematic method of reviewing one's beliefs, values, and expectations in terms of health status, health behaviors, health practice, and utilization of the health-care system based on a composite of theories that predicts a person's willingness to accept or reject healthy lifestyle behaviors, seek medical help, or participate in preventive care and detection activities. 2. A paradigm that predicts and explains health behavior on the basis of value-expectancy theory, in which an individual bases decisions about health on a cost-benefit analysis and risk assessment of choices and alternatives, according to 1) believing his or her health is at risk, 2) a sense of the potential seriousness of the disease or condition or the risk factors that contribute to it, 3) feeling vulnerable to the disease and believing that the benefits of avoiding it outweigh the costs or inconvenience of getting it, and 4) perceiving a meaningful enough outcome to motivate a response.

health card An identification card, similar to a credit card, suggested for use in several national health insurance programs that would be issued to each covered individual or family unit in the United States. This card would be presented at the time services are rendered in lieu of any cash payment. The individual could subsequently receive a bill for any cost sharing not covered. Health cards could simplify eligibility determination, billing, accounting, and the study of use of services. The idea presents interesting confidentiality problems, particularly under the Federal Credit Disclosure Act. *See health security card.*

health care 1. Services, diagnoses, therapies, and treatments provided by health-care providers for the restoration or preservation of health, aimed at relieving pain, providing comfort, and maintaining health; the prevention of illness and the treatment of injury, illness, disability, and disorders for the purpose of healing and rehabilitating the sick. 2. The process of enabling people to increase control over and improve health (WHO). 3. The two levels of health care are 1) public health, where preventive care, health promotion, and protection of groups and populations are provided, and 2) individual consumer, where the opportunity is provided to practice self-care or to arrange an encounter with individual primary care physicians, specialists, or other practitioners and to utilize referrals, health-care facilities, diagnostic facilities, rehabilitation centers, long-term care, and home health care.

health-care administration 1. An educational and instructional program at the graduate and undergraduate levels that provides a generalist background and skills in all aspects of management and operations of health-care organizations and for training individuals to work in the administrative aspects of a variety of health-care organizations. Such programs provide and teach the constructs, concepts, principles, approaches, methods, and procedures of planning, organizing, coordinating, and controlling a hospital, health-care facility, managed-care plan or other health-care organization, health service, or agency. Practical and experiential training is often provided to students through an administrative residency or internship in a health-care organization as part of the requirements for a degree in health-care administration. It is also referred to as health administration, health services administration, and health-care management. Degrees offered in health-care administration at the graduate level have a variety of labels, the most common being the MHA (masters of health administration), MSHSA, (masters in health services administration), MSHCA (masters in health-care administration), and MPH (masters of public health in health-care administration). Other degrees less recognized and less commonly found are MPA (masters of public administration with an emphasis in health services administration), MBA (masters of business administration with an emphasis in health-care management), or a generic MA or MS with an emphasis in health administration. 2. A generic term for the overall management and operation of a health-care facility or health-care organization. The management of all facets of a health-care organization, including planning, organizing, controlling, coordinating, commanding, and communicating with and supervising all personnel, systems, structures, functions, activities, and responsibilities in the provision of providing health services, supportive and ancillary services, and related health-care programs to patients. *See health administration.*

health care administrator The chief executive officer of a health-care facility, agency, hospital, or any health organization offering health-care services. *See also health services administrator; health administration.*

health-care advertising *See advertising, health-care.*

health-care coalition In health-care delivery, this is a grouping of health-care providers, businesses, government agencies, and consumers to increase access and reduce health-care costs.

health-care consultants As recognized by the American Association of Healthcare Consultants, this is an individual who consults for hospitals, medical groups, and other health-care organizations. Several specialty areas are recognized: facilities programming and planning, finance, human resources management, information management systems, organization and management, and strategic planning and marketing.

health-care corporation (HCC) An organization proposed by the American Hospital Association in a national health insurance proposal that would assume overall management responsibility for providing all needed personal health services in a defined catchment area.

health-care delivery The process of getting health-care services to the community; the coordination and provision of health care through a set of separate but related health-care services to persons or families in need of such services. *See also accessibility; acceptability; availability; health-care system; geographical maldistribution.*

health-care delivery system *See health systems.*

health-care district (authority) *See hospital district.*

health-care economics *See health economics.*

Health Care EDI (electronic data interchange) Association A professional society that establishes electronic data interchange with the health-care industry as a common utility. The goal is to identify and address EDI applications; ensure provider access to the utility for conducting business electronically with all suppliers; support standardized technology, including hardware, software, and communication links to ensure standardization; facilitate cost controls; and speed implementation of the EDI utility. The association membership is of multi-hospital groups and other health-care provider groups and their trading partners.

Health Care Financing Administration (HCFA) 1. A federal agency under the Department of Health and Human Services, Social Security Administration, that administers the Medicare and Medicaid programs and Medicare's Peer Review Organization (PRO) and Quality Review Organizations (QRO), which focus on the regulations and policies relating to payments for health care. 2. In managed care, this federal agency oversees all aspects of financing and regulation for the Medicare program, including the Medicare Risk program, which contracts with local HMOs.

Health Care Financing Administration (HCFA) rate cell verification *See HCFA rate cell verification.*

Healthcare Financial Management Association (HFMA) A national professional association for financial management professionals who hold the position of chief executive officer, chief financial officer, controller, patient accounts manager, accountant, and consultant and are employed by hospitals, long-term-care facilities, public accounting and consulting firms, insurance companies, government agencies, and other organizations. The organization offers educational programming and networking opportunities and communicates timely news and information on key issues and technical data. The HFMA represents membership to health-care policymakers in government to influence policy decisions.

Healthcare Forum Formerly the Association of Western Hospitals, this is a national health-care administration professional association that seeks to improve the quality of health-care delivery by providing leaders and managers with innovative, future-oriented education and information designed to enhance both individual and organizational performance. Headquartered in San Francisco, this organization is a network of health-care managers and leaders who share their varied points of view. The organization's key publication is *Healthcare Forum*.

health-care institution A health-care service or facility having a physical plant, facilities, personnel, and qualified health-care providers to conduct medical and health-care services.

health-care management The process of coordinating and administering all the operations and activities in a health-care facility to accomplish the predetermined goals and objectives. *See health administration.*

health-care management (administration) content competencies The basic and essential knowledge, understanding, and skills necessary for the administration of health-care facilities or agencies.

health-care management (administration) process competencies The basic and essential use of cognitive skills in the process of managerial analysis, synthesis, and the use of data and information in decision-making and other problem-solving activities.

health-care marketing *See marketing, health-care.*

health-care organization A generic term used to describe many types of organizations that provide health-care services (JCAHO). Any hospital, medical group, health maintenance organization, IPA, PPO, multifacility and/or services health-care system, or other organization that exists for the purpose of providing health-care services.

health-care planning The processes involved in developing alternative ways of achieving health goals and related political and societal expectations; a process of looking at future implications of health-care services that involves the identification of the consequences of each alternative or approach to health-care delivery and guides decision makers in their choices concerning expenditure of resources. *See also health planning; strategic planning.*

health-care portability In health-care delivery, this is the structure, system, or process of getting health care to the people where it is needed.

health-care practitioners 1. All persons who work as health-care providers, including physicians, physician assistants, nurse practitioners, dentists, and podiatrists. 2. Under Medicare and Medicaid, allied health-care providers who are not medical or osteopathic physicians, who have met state and federal practice requirements, and who are actively involved in the delivery of patient care or services that are paid for under Title XVII or XIX are considered to be health-care practitioners.

health-care provider distribution A plan suggested by the Clinton administration to influence medical schools to produce more primary care physician and family practice physicians and fewer specialists and to get physicians to practice more in rural areas. *See geographical maldistribution.*

health-care proxy *See living will; patient self-determination act.*

Health Care Purchasing Cooperative (HIPC) *See health alliances.*

Health Care Quality Improvement Act (HCQIA) A public law (42 U.S.C. Secs. 11101–11152) passed in 1986 that gives physicians and hospitals certain protection from lawsuits with provisions for peer review and the establishment of a national clearinghouse of information on disciplinary actions taken and malpractice lawsuits against physicians; thus, the National Practitioners Data Bank was formed.

health-care reform Anticipated changes in the nation's health-care delivery system with an aim of universal coverage and a national health security system. Models, policies, public forums of discussion, committees and task forces, proposals from associations, government agencies, private industry, government-directed committees, and private ad hoc groups all suggest different focuses and directions of emphasis and restructuring of payment and delivery approaches to reduce costs and still provide medical coverage and access for all who do not have access to health care.

Health Care Reform Taskforce A group of 400 to 500 government employees and consultants from the private sector, representing all facets of the U.S. health industry and health-care delivery system, including 20 senior Cabinet and White House officers, directed by Hillary Rodham Clinton, wife of William Clinton, President of the United States. The task force members are professionals from government health and financing agencies, politicians, professionals from the health-care industry and health-care associations, academicians, and health-care delivery experts who provided input regarding the restructuring of health care. This group developed the "Clinton Plan" for reforming the health-care system in the United States and providing universal coverage for all U.S. citizens. Managed competition would ensure access and universal medical care coverage of health care for all citizens, turning the current health-care system into a national health plan. A single-payer system was also part of the discussion. *See health alliance; universal coverage; managed competition; National Health Board.*

health-care system 1. The interactive network of health-care services, programs, agencies, facilities, and practitioners providing preventive care, health education and promotion activities, and definitive care at the primary, secondary, and tertiary care levels in hospitals and clinics, long-term care, and emergency and intensive care in hospitals. Physicians and other health-care providers and personnel who provide services as well as the facilities and resources that support them in the delivery and provision of health services are also included. Other services are administrative functions, communications, financial activities, and other support services. From a government bureaucratic and policy perspective, the health-care system appears to be a nonsystem; however, from the consumer perspective, the health-care system as put together by each individual creates an effective system that meets the medical needs of individual patients or families. 2. A multihospital, multiservice corporate health-care organization that owns and/or manages a range of types of health facilities and/or health-related services or subsidiaries as well as non–health-related facilities. *See continuum of care; health-care delivery.*

health-care system goals and objectives A description of the desired state of health services that are provided for the people of a state to improve the citizen's health status.

health-care team A group of health-care professionals who provide coordinated services to achieve optimal health care of the client. *See also health team.*

health-care technology The pharmaceuticals, substances, materials, equipment, electronic devices, mechanical devices, instruments, and procedures that have a role in clinical applications, diagnosis, and treatment.

health-care universality In health-care delivery and health-care financing, this means that comprehensive health care is accessible and available to all citizens.

health continuum In health services, this is a line that delineates high health status on one end supported by public health, health promotion, and preventive care and extreme illness and death at the other end supported by definitive medical care. In the middle are the various levels of health services and medical care such as health activation, health education, behavior change, long-term care, home health care, hospitals, and hospice care. Preventive care and health promotion are integrated throughout the entire continuum on the basis of three levels of prevention. *See levels of prevention.*

health coverage In managed care or medical insurance, this is the medical insurance protection in the form of payment by a health plan or insurance carrier for medical services rendered and products for members who are sick or injured. Medical treatment, therapy, procedures, and products include medical care, dental care, vision care, long-term and short-term disability, and in some programs death benefits. The term "health coverage" is misleading because it is really medical care coverage, with preventive care and health promotion receiving minimal support.

health-directed behavior In health promotion, this is a deliberated and conscious pursuit by individuals to maintain good health practices and to begin new health behaviors that will improve health.

health economics 1. A specialized area of health-care administration and health policy that studies and analyzes the financial, business, and social behavior aspects of supply and demand; the resulting economic, social, and financial implications of health-care delivery; and their impact on the health services and health status of a target population. 2. A subarea of the field of economics concerned with the distribution of health-care resources, costs of health care, health-care delivery, and the supply-and-demand aspects of health administration and medical care delivery.

health economist A health-care administration/policy professional who studies and analyzes the financial and business aspects of health-care delivery supply and demand and the effects that economic changes have on the service delivery and financial resources of a health-care system.

health education 1. An educational process using medical and scientific knowledge to increase the ability of people to make informed decisions affecting personal, family, and community well-being. Health education processes create 1) awareness of good health practices, 2) maintenance of good health practices and health status, 3) prevention that depends on awareness and maintenance essential to preventing the acquisition of new negative risk-taking behaviors, 4) behavior change that reduces risk factors to positive health practices, and 5) bridging the gap between scientific knowledge and the consumer. Health education is ultimately dependent on the motivation aspects of each individual to ensure that all the above are used to enhance health status. Health education is comprised of activities that 1) inform and educate people about health, preventive care, illness, disability, and ways in which they can improve and protect their own health, including more efficient use of the delivery system; 2) motivate people to want to change to more healthful practices; 3) help people learn the necessary skills to adopt and maintain healthful practices and lifestyles; 4) foster teaching and communication skills in all those engaged in teaching consumers about health; 5) advocate changes in the environment that facilitate healthful conditions and healthful behavior; and 6) add to knowledge via research and evaluation concerning the most effective ways of achieving the above objectives. 2. Any combination of learning or behavior change experiences designed to predispose, enable, and reinforce behaviors conducive to the health of individuals, groups, populations, or communities. 3. An education and learning process whereby individuals, populations, or communities learn to make informed decisions about issues related to health, disease, and health care. Scheduled and planned activities are used to assist the target population in making decisions toward a healthy lifestyle. 4. A learning process that empowers individuals to make informed decisions affecting their personal, physical, medical, behavioral, mental, socioeconomic, emotional, and spiritual health.

health education administrator A professional health educator who has the authority and responsibility for the management and coordination of all health education policies, activities, and resources within a particular setting or circumstance (Joint Committee on Health Education Terminology).

health education associate *See entry-level health educator.*

health education coordinator A professional health educator who is responsible for the management and coordination of all health education policies, activities, and resources within a particular setting or circumstance (Joint Committee on Health Education Terminology).

health education field A multidisciplinary practice that is concerned with designing, implementing, and evaluating educational programs enabling individuals, families, groups, organizations, and communities to play active roles in achieving, protecting, and sustaining health (Joint Committee on Health Education Terminology).

health education of the public A process designed for the improvement and maintenance of health directed to the general population, as contrasted with education for the preparation of a health professional (Joint Committee on Health Education Terminology).

health education process A continuum of learning that enables people, as individuals and as members of social structures, to voluntarily make decisions, modify behaviors, and change social conditions in ways that are health enhancing.

health education program 1. A planned and organized series of health education activities or procedures implemented with 1) an educational specialist assigned the primary responsibility, 2) a budget, 3) an integrated set of objectives sufficiently detailed to allow evaluation, and 4) administrative support. 2. A planned combination of activities developed with the involvement of specific populations on the basis of a needs assessment, sound principles of education, and periodic evaluation using a clear set of goals and objectives (Joint Committee on Health Education Terminology).

health education resources All the assets, both human and material, that may be enlisted in the school or community to enrich the health education experiences of individuals and groups (Joint Committee on Health Education Terminology).

health education services Instruction and learner activities about health directed toward informing, educating, and motivating the public to adopt personal lifestyles and nutritional practices that will promote optimal health, minimize health risks, and make appropriate use of health-care services in the community. Health education services goals include the transfer of knowledge and information and motivation toward positive health behavior. *See community health promotion and protection services.*

health education settings The variety of physical settings in which health educators may be working.

health educator 1. A practitioner who is professionally prepared in the field of health education, demonstrates competence in both theory and practice, and accepts responsibility to advance the aims of the health education profession (Joint Committee on Health Education Terminology). 2. An individual prepared to assist others in making informed decisions regarding matters affecting their personal health and that of others. *See also entry-level health educator.*

health educator, entry-level *See entry-level health educator.*

health educator, entry-level competencies All health educators, to practice at a well-trained and competent level, must have the following minimal competencies: 1) Assessing individual and community needs for health education by obtaining health-related data about social and cultural environments, growth and development factors, needs, and interests; distinguishing between behaviors that foster and those that hinder well-being; and inferring needs for health education on the basis of obtained data. 2) Planning effective health education programs by recruiting community organizations, resource people, and potential participants for support and assistance in program planning; developing a logical scope and sequence plan for a health education program; formulating appropriate and measurable program objectives; and designing educational programs consistent with specified program objectives. 3) Implementing health education programs by exhibiting competence in carrying out planned educational programs; identifying enabling objectives needed to implement instructional programs in specified settings; selecting methods and media best suited to implement program plans for specific learners; and monitoring educational programs, adjusting objectives and activities as necessary. 4) Evaluating the effectiveness of health education programs by developing plans to assess achievement of program objectives; carrying out evaluation plans; interpreting results of program evaluations; and identifying implications from findings for future program planning. 5) Coordinating the provision of health education services by developing a plan for coordinating health education services; facilitating cooperation between and among levels of program personnel; formulating practical modes of collaboration among health agencies and organizations; and organizing in-service training programs for teachers, volunteers, and other interested personnel.

6) Acting as a resource person in health education by utilizing computerized health information retrieval systems effectively; establishing effective consultative relationships with those requesting assistance in solving health-related problems; interpreting and responding to requests for health information; and selecting effective educational resource materials for dissemination. 7) Communicating health and health education needs, concerns, and resources by interpreting concepts, purposes, and theories of health education; predicting the impact of societal value systems on health education programs; selecting a variety of communication methods and techniques in providing health information; and fostering communication between health-care providers and consumers (Joint Committee on Health Education Terminology).

health enhancement In health promotion, this is one aim of health promotion programs and activities: to motivate and assist individuals and groups to reach a high level of wellness beyond that of the absence of disease or infirmity.

health evaluation 1. In health promotion and preventive care, this is the comparison of health status and conditions against a previously established standard of acceptable health status. 2. The use of medical tests and health screening exams, processes, and instruments.

health facilities All the buildings, physical plant, and structures used in the provision of health services. Usually limited to buildings or centers (e.g., hospitals and nursing homes) built for the purpose of providing medical care and usually not including places such as an office building that houses a physician's office. Synonymous with "institution." *See also bed; boarding homes; capital; capital depreciation; certificate of need; clinic, Hill-Burton; inpatient; institutional health services; institutional licensure; JCAHO; length of stay; Life Safety Code; modernization; outpatient; per diem cost; proprietary hospital.*

health facility licensing agency A branch of state government that, through state statutes, is granted legal authority to establish and enforce regulations and standards regarding the function and operation of health-care facilities.

health fair In health promotion and health education, this is an organized community-based health screening and health education event that screens well people for potential or hidden diseases and conditions as well as risk factors and behaviors that place the individual's health in jeopardy. Various screening efforts such as taking blood pressures, chest X rays, cholesterol blood tests, computerized nutritional and lifestyle assessments, fitness assessments, physician referrals, health education, and health counseling are performed. Multiphasic screening, computer stations, and health-enhancing exhibits set up in shopping malls, hospitals, universities and colleges, senior citizens centers, and other strategic places to access large populations of well people.

health field concept In health promotion and health education, these are the factors of the world that influence health status as found in the environment, biology, behavior, social sciences, and health-care delivery.

health for all A level of health that enables people to lead economically and socially productive lives (a strategy of WHO).

healthful environment The promotion and maintenance of safe and appropriate surroundings, organization of day-by-day experiences, and planned teaming procedures to influence favorable emotional, physical, and social health (Joint Committee on Health Education Terminology).

healthful school environment An aspect of a comprehensive school health program that includes a congenial faculty and staff; good student relationships; a clean and sanitary physical plant of adequate size; safe location; plant construction that meets OSHA standards; regulations and standards for sanitation, safety, lighting, noise and acoustics, heating, and ventilation; adequate maintenance of the facilities; quality food services; safe and effective bus services and operation; and support of the school administration.

health gap In public health and health-care delivery, these are those persons who lack access to services or who lack eligibility and cannot receive health services.

health hazard appraisal *See health risk appraisal.*

health hazards In environmental health and occupational health and safety, this is a chemical, mixture of chemicals, or a pathogen for which there is statistically significant evidence based on at least one study conducted in accordance with established scientific principles that acute or chronic health effects may occur in exposed employees. Also included are chemicals or substances that are carcinogens, toxic or highly toxic agents, reproductive toxins, irritants, corrosives, sensitizers, hepatotoxins, nephrotoxins, neurotoxins, agents that act on the hematopoietic system, and agents that damage the eyes, lungs, skin or mucous membranes. It also includes stress caused by temperature extremes.

health history 1. In the delivery of health care and the practice of medicine, this is the family and personal experiences with diseases, injuries, illnesses, and the lifetime medical background of patients. 2. In managed care, the form used by health plans to obtain the family and personal disease, injury, illness, and medical backgrounds of potential health plan members. *See medical history; evidence of insurability.*

health index In epidemiology, this is a numerical system of assessing and comparing health status with numerical values assigned to various health status indicators of a group, population, or community that are placed in formulas for assessment and analysis.

health indicator *See health status indicator.*

health information 1. In health promotion and education, this is the content of communications based on data derived from systematic and scientific methods relating to health issues, policies, programs, services, and other aspects of individual and public health that can be used for informing various populations and in planning health education activities (Joint Committee on Health Education Terminology). 2. Any facts, findings, or data that affect or pertain to the physical, mental, social, or emotional well-being of individuals or groups of individuals (Joint Committee on Health Education Terminology).

health institution administration *See health-care administration; health-care management.*

health instruction Usually refers to the teaching of personal health and other health content areas in a school setting. Also referred to as "school health education." *See health education.*

health insurance 1. All types of insurance coverage that pays for the cost of hospital and medical care; in reality it is not "health" insurance because it is actually insurance against medical care costs. In some cases, a person is reimbursed for lost income arising from illness or injury. Also known as "medical insurance," "accident and health insurance," and "disability income insurance." 2. Insurance against loss caused by disease or accidental bodily injury. Such insurance usually covers some of the medical costs of treating a disease or injury, may cover other losses (such as loss of present or future earnings), and may be individual or group insurance.

Health Insurance Association of America (HIAA) The national professional organization for companies involved with managed care and health plan insurance; also writes medical care and hospitalization insurance.

health insurance benefits In managed care and medical insurance, these are any benefits paid by a health plan or insurance carrier that are for the payment of care rendered by health-care providers.

Health Insurance Benefits Advisory Council (HIBAC) An advisory council to the Department of Health and Human Services. Pursuant to Section 1867 of the Social Security Act and as detailed in its charter, the council provides advice and recommendations on matters of general policy in the administration of Medicare and Medicaid. This role was reaffirmed after HHS review, and the council was rechartered on December 13, 1974, to continue the provision of such advice for 2 additional years. The HIBAC consists of 19 nongovernmental experts in health-related fields who are selected by the Secretary of Health and hold office for 4-year terms. In recognition of the broad impact of Medicare and Medicaid on health-care delivery throughout the country, the management and staff support for the council has been transferred to the Office of the Assistant Secretary for Health. This enables information on policy issues to be more directly channeled to the council and to provide the Assistant Secretary of Health with ready access to and analysis of HIBAC issues.

health insurance claim number (HIC) An identification number assigned to a Medicare beneficiary; a seven- or nine-digit number, which may be the social security number, with an alpha prefix or suffix. The number must appear on all documents related to a beneficiary.

Health Insurance Counseling and Advocacy Program (HICAP) A community-based agency or service offered to the elderly that offers an objective assessment of medical insurance, coinsurance, and Medigap insurance that is compared to Medicare coverage to discover unneeded overlaps of coverage and gaps in insurance where coverage is lacking. Advice is offered on types and amounts of insurance needed without suggesting any company or agency.

Health Insurance for the Aged and Disabled The social insurance program authorized by Title XVIII of the Social Security Act and known as Medicare.

Health Insurance Plan of California (HIPC) A cooperative group insurance purchasing alliance created to serve small business from 5 to 50 employees. Created by the California state legislature, it defines coverage, negotiates premium rates, and oversees all health plans. The Major Risk Medical Insurance Board was developed to implement the HIPC and negotiate with insurance carriers in six different cost-of-living areas established across the state of California. A report card is to be issued for each health plan for the consumer. Most major insurance carriers participate and cooperate in the HIPC.

health interview survey An information-collecting system used by the U.S. Public Health Service for gathering data on health-related issues. On a periodic or special care basis, interviewers from the Public Health Service visit homes in the United States to interview residents about illness, abnormal conditions, disabilities, and utilization of health services.

health law Often associated with medical malpractice, this is a much broader area of law that is emerging and being recognized as a separate area of law embracing and accommodating all aspects of medical care, public health, environmental health, health-care delivery, medical practice, nursing and allied health practice, licensing, medical facilities and health-care organization liability, and mental health care that are influenced and controlled by some aspect of the formally recognized areas of law, most often tort law, negligence, malpractice, intentional torts, statutes and codes, administrative law and regulations, liability, patients' rights, right to treatment, contracts, corporate law, and civil and common law.

Health Liaison Program A program that emphasizes the liaison role of the community health representative (CHR) as a link primarily between the community and the health resources such as the Indian Health Service, county medical agencies, medical welfare programs, and local voluntary medical agencies. *See also community health representative.*

health literacy In health education and health promotion, this is the capacity of an individual to obtain, interpret, and understand basic health information and services and use such information and services in ways that are health enhancing (Joint Committee on Health Education Terminology).

health maintenance Preventive, diagnostic, curative, and restorative health services available to a client, group, or community; health education and health promotion efforts done to retain and preserve an individual's health status.

health maintenance behavior 1. Keeping those good health practices that an individual already has that are active and effective in influencing his or her health status. 2. The influence of social and family systems on an individual's health practices such as not participating in negative health practices (e.g., smoking or using alcohol or drugs), eating a nutritious diet, exercising, having a healthy lifestyle, and retaining a high level of wellness.

health maintenance organization (HMO) 1. A prepaid health plan that provides comprehensive health-care services for a specified group or members at a fixed cost or through prepaid periodic payments. It has four essential features: 1) an organized system for providing health care in a geographic area that accepts the responsibility to provide or otherwise ensure the delivery of health care, 2) an agreed-on set of basic and supplemental health maintenance and treatment services, 3) a voluntarily enrolled group of persons, and 4) the HMO is reimbursed through a predetermined, fixed, periodic prepayment made by or on behalf of each person or family unit enrolled in the HMO without regard to the amounts of actual services provided (from the report of the Committee on Interstate and Foreign Commerce on the HMO Act of 1973 [P.L. 93222] and also Section 1301 of the PHS Act.) The HMO must employ or contract with health-care providers who undertake a continuing responsibility to provide services to its enrollees. Preventive care and health promotion are major components of HMOs. The prototype HMO is the Kaiser-Permanente system, a prepaid group practice located on the West Coast. HMOs are of public policy interest because the prototypes have demonstrated the potential for providing high-quality medical services for less money than the rest of the medical system. Specifically, rates of hospitalization and surgery are considerably less in HMOs than those found outside such prepaid groups, although some experts suspect that earlier care, skimping, or skimming explain this difference. 2. Any organization that provides a wide range of medical care services for a specified group of enrollees at fixed period payment. *See also prepaid health plan; individual practice association; group practice; group health plans.*

health maintenance organization, group An HMO that delivers health services through a physician group controlled by the HMO unit or that contracts with one or more independent group practices to provide health services. *See also prepaid health plan; individual practice association; group practice; group health plans.*

health maintenance organization, nursing *See HMO, nursing.*

health maintenance organization, open-ended *See point-of-service health plan.*

health maintenance organization, social *See social health maintenance organization.*

health manpower In health administration and delivery of health-care services, these are all personnel employed in health-related professions and involved in the provision of health services as individual practitioners or employees of health-care institutions and programs. They may or may not be professionally trained or subject to public regulation. Facilities and manpower are the principal health resources needed to provide health services.

Health Manpower Education Initiative Award (HMEIA) A grant or contract under section 774 of the PHS Act (added by the Comprehensive Health Manpower Training Act of 1971 [P.L. 92-157]) that authorizes awards to health or educational entities for health manpower programs that improve the distribution, supply, quality, utilization, and efficiency of health personnel and the health services delivery system. Support has been provided for the development of area health education centers, the training of physician assistants, and the identification and encouragement of disadvantaged students with a potential for training in the health professions.

health manpower plan An assessment and projection of need for health-care personnel in all health occupations and practitioner areas that focuses on the health manpower needs of a state, region, county, or city.

health manpower shortage area (HMSA) The geographical areas, population groups, and facilities designated by the federal government as having shortages of health personnel. These areas are designated for primary care, dental, and psychiatric personnel and are determined primarily by population-to-practitioner ratios.

health manpower shortage area placement opportunity list A list of the most needy health manpower shortage areas used by the National Health Service Corps in the placement of volunteer and obligated personnel.

health of the public A program to assist academic health centers in identifying strategies that help solve health problems at the community level and fulfill their missions as public trusts. Strategies were developed to reform medical education curriculum toward prevention programs in the community and lead academic health centers to confront problems such as the high cost of care, the unfavorable distribution of physicians, and substandard quality of care (funded by Robert Wood Johnson Foundation grants).

Health Online In health information management, this is a national, direct-access computer service started by Kaiser & Associates, a consulting firm in Denver, in association with Healthcare Forum, a hospital association headquartered in San Francisco. Using a mouse/cursor interface with a pictorial representation of a community, the individual can access information from the graphic representation of the Library, Town Hall, Post Office, Professional Building, and Emporium. Similar to America Online and CompuServe, items such as e-mail, health-care bulletin boards, health-care literature and journal articles, databases, and other health-care-delivery–related data and information can be accessed on Health Online.

health outcomes 1. In health promotion and health education planning, any change in health status of a group or population resulting from any health promotion or health care utilized, as measured at one point in time. Any characteristic of a patient or a population as a measure of health status resulting from health promotion or health care provided. 2. A cross-sectional epidemiological study of health concerns or health status. 3. The results of health care as measured by health status or quality of life.

health physicist An individual trained at least at the baccalaureate level who directs research and training and monitors programs that protect hospital patients and laboratory personnel from radiation hazards, inspects and evaluates standards and decontamination and hazardous waste procedures, and develops new methods to safeguard humans and the environment against unnecessary radiation exposure.

health physics A term used to describe the branch of radiological science that deals with the protection of personnel from harmful effects of ionizing radiation.

health physics technician An individual trained to monitor radiation levels, give instruction in radiation safety, label radioactive materials, and assist the health physicist in conducting experimental studies in radiation.

health plan 1. Any managed-care health service or health-care delivery and medical care program such as health maintenance organizations, preferred provider organizations, and independent practice associations. 2. The formal document and process that determines the plan of future delivery of health and medical care services for a community, region, state, or health-care organization or medical care system.

Health Plan Employer Data and Information Set (HEDIS) In managed care, this is a measure of health plan quality that was developed by a consortium of 17 group and staff models of HMOs and four large employer groups and insurance benefits consultants. The consortium identified several major sections used to measure health plans, including quality, access, patient satisfaction, membership, utilization, and finance and management activities. The quality section measures performance in the delivery of selected services in preventive medicine, prenatal care, acute and chronic diseases, and mental health care. The indicators are preventive medicine, childhood immunizations, cholesterol screening, mammography screening, cervical cancer screening, prenatal care, low birth weight, prenatal care in the first trimester, acute and chronic diseases, inpatient admissions for asthmatics, diabetic retinal examinations, mental health, and patients receiving ambulatory follow-up visits after hospitalization for a major affective disorder. The access and patient satisfaction sections measure a health plan's performance in providing its members with appropriate access to health care and in satisfying members. The measures are access, percentages of members between ages 23 and 39 and 40 and 64 who have visited the plan in the previous 3 years, number and percentage of primary care physicians accepting new patients, provision of plan access standards for various types of visits, and, for telephone response satisfaction, the percentage of members who indicated they are "satisfied" with the health plan. The membership and utilization sections measure performance in membership, stability, and resource allocation. The measures are enrollment and disenrollment figures, frequency and average cost of nine common diagnosis-related group (DRG) categories, frequency of seven selected high-cost procedures; inpatient utilization rates for general acute or hospital care (including surgery, maternity, and newborns); ambulatory care utilization rates (including outpatient visits, emergency room visits, and ambulatory surgery or procedures); inpatient utilization rates for nonacute care in nursing homes, rehabilitation facilities, hospices, transitional facilities, and respite facilities; total newborn deliveries (including subdivisions for vaginal births and cesarean sections); length of stay for well and complex newborns; mental health treatment in inpatient, day/night, and outpatient locations; readmission rates for major affective disorders; chemical dependency treatment in inpatient, day/night, and outpatient locations; and average costs and number of prescription drugs per members. The financial section measures financial stability using 14 indicators that encompass financial performance, liquidity, efficiency, and compliance with statutory requirements and premium trends. The remaining section uses written measures of recredentialing, utilization review, value, and accountability (Group Health Association of America).

health planner A health-care administration professional, trained or experienced in health planning methods, who is responsible for planning the administrative and health-care delivery needs of a hospital, target population, specialized health service, or health-care delivery system. This person may work in a state health planning agency, public health department, hospital, HMO, or other health-care organization.

health planning 1. A process that establishes desired future levels for health status and health system performance, designs and selects among alternative actions aimed at modifying the health system so that these levels conform to desired levels, and suggests steps for implementation of the recommended actions. 2. Planning concerned with improving health undertaken either comprehensively for a whole community or for a particular situation of health service or health program. Some definitions clearly include all activities undertaken for the purpose of improving health (e.g., education, traffic, and environmental control and nutrition), whereas others are limited to conventional health services and programs, public health, or personal health services. *See also goal; objective; state health planning and development agency; health systems agency.*

health planning agency *See health systems agency; comprehensive health planning agency; state health planning and development agency.*

health policies The course of action selected to guide and determine present and future decisions affecting the health status of the nation or a state, region, or area.

Health Policy Agenda for the American People A set of proposals for improving health and health care in America, developed in 1987 by a task force representing nearly all the leading health and medical societies and associations, spearheaded by the American Medical Association. A summary of recommendations was published in 1987 in the *Journal of the American Medical Association.*

health practitioner Any properly trained person who provides clinical health-care services to patients, including physicians, podiatrists, dentists, physician assistants, and nurse practitioners.

health professional *See professional.*

health promotion 1. The science and art of helping people change their lifestyles toward a state of optimal health. Lifestyle change can be facilitated through a combination of efforts that enhance awareness, change behavior, and create environments that support good health practices. Of the three, supportive environments will probably have the greatest effect in producing lasting changes (M. P. O'Donnell, *American Journal of Health Promotion*). 2. Preventive care and health education activities that focus on improving quality of life and well-being through increasing awareness, challenging former approaches to preventive medicine, influencing values, and providing informed choices about health behavior with the aim of maximizing optimum health status. 3. Any combination of health education and related organizational, political, and economic interventions designed to facilitate behavioral and environmental adaptations that will improve or protect health. (L. Green) 4. Behavioral modification programs intended to modify lifestyles and habits to promote better health. *See health; health education; health counseling; behavior change.*

health promotion and disease prevention The aggregate of all purposeful activities designed to improve personal and public health through a combination of strategies, including the competent implementation of behavioral change strategies, health education, health protection measures, risk factor detection, health enhancement, and health maintenance (Joint Committee on Health Education Terminology).

health protection In public health, environmental health, and health services delivery, this focuses on the environmental determinants of health that include the constant evaluation and/or regulation of all factors that, if not regulated, could lead to disease or death. Examples include monitoring water and milk supplies; ensuring that food is not contaminated; keeping hospitals, health-care facilities, and eating establishments sanitary; and controlling radiation control.

health psychology 1. A relatively new discipline, recognized by the American Psychological Association, that crosses several disciplines, embracing psychosomatic medicine, behavioral medicine, behavioral health, health education, health promotion, health counseling, medical anthropology, medical sociology, and the basics of various aspects of preventive medicine and psychology. This discipline includes the study, research, intervention, application, and teaching of psychological factors relating to physical health, illness, and treatment at the individual, group, and community levels. 2. An application of educational, scientific, and professional contributions of the discipline of psychology to the promotion and maintenance of health, the prevention and treatment of illness, the identification of etiologic and diagnostic correlates of health, illness and related dysfunction, and the analysis and improvement of the health-care system and health policy formation.

health purchasing alliance *See health alliances.*

health quackery The promotion, marketing, and commercialization of unproven, questionable, and potentially dangerous health products, devices, treatments, cures, or procedures. Marketing and promotion are based on deception, omission of adverse reactions, and information on safety and effectiveness of the products or cure. Fraud, intentional perversion of truth for gain, practicing medicine without a license, and deception in the name of promoting health are also quackery activities.

health record A patient's medical record; a document used by health-care providers to account for all activities done with or to a patient during medical treatment that contains information concerning medical status, diagnoses, treatments, procedures, and doctor and nursing observations of an inpatient's recovery in a health-care facility. It also provides a history of a patient's medical experiences and can be used as a legal document, a source of research information, or a financial billing verification.

health record analyst Also referred to as a "medical record analyst," this individual is trained in the technical aspects of medical record administration and analyzes information and data found in medical records. The data are used by hospital administration, public health researchers, epidemiologists, and health services researchers. Data are abstracted from the medical record for input into a health information management system via computer. Analysis requires interpretation and assessment. *See registered records administrator.*

health-related behavior In health promotion, these are activities that an individual participates in that may only indirectly improve health but that have positive health outcomes. Actions by individuals that reduce participation in or exposure to risk factors, enhancing one's health status and disease prevention.

health-related services Health and medical programs and activities that are external to direct medical care delivery and treatment by a physician yet contribute substantially to the well-being of patients. These include preventive services, health education, and protective and social services.

health resources Personnel, monetary, or material resources involved in the provision of health care and services. These resources, available or used, can be measured and described for a health service area, a population, a health-care facility, an institution, a managed-care program, or an individual program or service.

Health Resources and Services Administration (HRSA) A federal governmental agency of the Department of Health and Human Services that consists of the Bureau of Health Professions, which does, among other tasks, physician supply projections and nursing supply estimates.

health risk appraisal A health promotion/preventive medicine tool that seeks to identify and reduce major risks to continued good health. A questionnaire is filled out, and tests such as blood analyses are conducted. The purpose of such an appraisal is to determine health risks and assist in lifestyle changes or to develop a treatment program. An appraisal provides answers to the following questions: 1) What are the major causes of death for people in my age, race, and sex grouping? 2) How do my risks of dying in the next 10 years compare to the average? 3) What can I do to reduce my risks?

health risk assessment *See health risk appraisal.*

health science 1. An educational degree program at the undergraduate and graduate level in health education or health promotion, community or public health, community health education, health and safety education, drug and alcohol education, school health education, occupational health and safety, and related areas. Course work provides a general background and covers a continuum of topics and supportive subjects related to medicine, biological sciences, public health, psychology, behavioral sciences, education, and health services. 2. A term used in a general sense to embrace any or all aspects of health-related activity, career areas, or service.

health science administration *See health administration.*

health science educator Synonymous with "school health educator." Also used in life sciences, medicine, or allied professions to denote instructors who prepare various health professionals or teach other than applied science (Joint Committee on Health Education Terminology).

health science instruction *See health instruction; health science; health science educator.*

health screening A process used by health-care organizations, managed-care programs, or public health that determines a potential group's level of risk by assessing and testing the health status of each person or group of employees.

health security card An identification card, similar to a credit card, that would have been used under the "Clinton Plan" for a National Health Security program called the American Health-care System, issued to each covered individual or family unit. This card would be presented at the time that services are rendered in lieu of cash payment. The individual could subsequently receive a bill for any cost sharing not covered under the insurance plan. Health cards simplify eligibility determination, billing, medical records, insurance claims, accounting, and the study of use of services.

Health Security Commission (HSC) Under some universal coverage and managed competition proposals, a federal agency that would be established to guide, oversee, and facilitate transition to the new, universal coverage system. It would also recommend to the U.S. Congress such items as budgetary changes, health plan benefits, approaches to standardization, setting standards, and agreements with states (Jackson Hole Group).

Health Security Program The title given the national universal coverage medical care plan or national health insurance program of the federal government.

health service area A geographic area appropriate for the effective planning and development of health services. In the former health system agency, Section 1511 of the PHS Act required that health service areas be delineated throughout the United States. The state governors designated areas according to geography, political boundaries, population, and health resources and coordinated with areas defined for other purposes, as required by law. *See catchment area; locality.*

health service plans Plans of state agencies that address the provision of health services to the residents of a state.

health services 1. Medical, health promotion, and preventive care activities related to the diagnosis, treatment, therapy, and rehabilitation of patients; activities that affect the recovery, health status, and well-being of patients, including the provision of acute-care treatment, chronic disease care, long-term care, home care, community health, public health, health promotion, and preventive care activities. All medical and health services that promote and protect the health status of populations. All health- or medical care organizations, agencies, facilities, institutions, centers, programs, and activities that serve, support, or deliver treatment, therapy, disease prevention, or health promotion services to individuals, communities, or targeted populations. 2. In managed care, services or activities covered by a health plan agreement. *See also health administration; health science.*

health services administration A broader generic term for "health-care administration" that goes beyond hospital and nursing home administration to include the management, operation, and general administration of all medical care and health services such as community-based health-related programs, services, and agencies and all health-care facilities, institutions, and organizations. The functions of the health administrator are similar for all organizations but are specifically applied to each health-care setting or service. *See health administration; health-care administration; management.*

health services administrator Health administrators who occupy middle- and top-level management positions in a variety of health-care organizations and settings such as hospitals, public and private health agencies, managed-care programs, social service agencies, and government health agencies. Minimum education at the baccalaureate level is required, and a masters degree in health administration is preferred. Those who serve as administrators include chief executives who have major responsibilities in policy formation, operations managers who direct the internal operations of a health organization, and staff specialists such as health planners, systems analysts, or fiscal experts. Administrator functions are broadly based and include planning, organizing, staffing, budgeting, directing, and coordinating all phases of health-care and health services delivery. *See also health administration.*

health services and supplies expenditures In health-care financial management at the national level, this is the outlay of revenue for goods and services relating directly to patient care plus expenses for administering medical insurance programs and government public health activities. This category is equivalent to total national health expenditures minus expenditures for research and construction.

health services research Scientific studies concerned with the organization and structure, cost and financing, delivery and effectiveness, access and utilization, manpower needs and utilization, administration, or other nonmedical aspects of health services. It utilizes constructs and theories from management, organizational behavior, psychology, social psychology, sociology, anthropology, economics, and epidemiology. Input, structure, process, output, and outcome are often considered in the research.

Health Services Research and Development Service (HSR&D) A Department of Veteran Affairs (VA) program that supports a broad range of research in areas such as cost-effectiveness, clinical decision making, and innovative health-care delivery models. The legislative order that created the HSR&D program was created in 1976 to carry out a more effective Department of Medicine and Surgery of the VA to contribute to the nation's knowledge about disease and disability. The VA administrator was mandated to carry out a program of medical research, including health-care services research.

Health Standards Board In managed competition, national health insurance proposals, and health-care reform proposals, this is a powerful regulation and adjudication board at the national level that sets forth uniform effective health benefits that could be eligible for revenue/tax support and inclusion as a benefit. This board could also be used to assess new technologies and research efforts. *See National Health Board.*

Health Standards Quality Bureau A division of the Health Care Financing Administration of the U.S. Department of Health and Human Services.

health state A measured level of health as assessed by specific criteria or variables of an individual or population at a specific point in time. *See health status.*

health statistician A professional who uses statistical theory, techniques, and methods to determine useful measurements or meaningful relationships of information relating to health, health care, health services, delivery, or disease. Also referred to as a "biostatistician."

health statistics 1. Also referred to as "biostatistics," this is the use of inferential statistics to assess and analyze the data of biomedical and health services and public health research. Data from specific research approaches using acceptable research designs and sampling approaches are analyzed using probability statistics. 2. In public health and epidemiology, this is the use of vital, morbidity, mortality, and other descriptive statistics to determine health status of populations and the need for health services, health promotion, preventive care, and disease prevention and control.

health status The state of health of a specified individual, group, or population (e.g., a city, county, state, HMO, or work organization). Health status may be measured with people's subjective assessments of their own health or with one or more objective health status indicators of mortality and morbidity in the population such as longevity, maternal and infant mortality, and the incidence or prevalence of major diseases (communicable, coronary, malignant, or nutritional). Although these are measures of disease status, they must be used as proxies in the absence of measures of either objective or subjective health. Health status is the proper outcome measure for the effectiveness of the specific population's medical care system, although attempts to relate variations in health status and the effects of available medical care have proven difficult and generally unsuccessful. It cannot be measured with data from available health resources or services (such as physician-to-population ratios), which in this context would be process measures. *See also vital statistics; National Health Survey; health risk appraisal; activities of daily living.*

health status and health system assessment The part of health plan development processes involving the selection of health status and health system indicators, collection (or estimation) of past and current data for the selected indicators, and a reference projection of how those indicators will change over a 5- to 10-year period if there are no changes in current plans or programs. Assessment is the first major phase of activities in plan development and ends just prior to the selection of goals.

health status goals and objectives In health planning and health services delivery, statements that specify in quantitative and qualitative terms the desired achievement in the personal health of a population and the time frame for this achievement.

health status index In epidemiology, health promotion, and health services delivery, this is a set of measures assigned a numerical system and magnitude that detect health status changes on a short-term basis in a group or population. Measurements often include physical fitness, physiological functioning, disease, risk factor exposure, emotional well-being, lifestyle, and behavior.

health status indicator As used in epidemiology, health promotion, health planning, and health services delivery, these are quantitative measures used to reflect the health status of a community, population, state, or country. These general measures can indicate the quality of health-care delivery or public health service by reflecting levels of disease, death, longevity, and functional ability or measures of conditions or disorders that comprise or account for dysfunction, disability, or mortality. The most common health status indicators are infant mortality, maternal mortality, perinatal death rates, fetal death rates, life expectancy, fertility rates, mortality rates, and morbidity rates (incidence or prevalence of major diseases such as communicable, coronary, malignant, or nutritional).

health status of the residents A description of the wellness level among residents of a geographical or political area at a particular point in time. It should represent the current health of the citizens, the factors affecting their health, and the existing health delivery system; also applied to assessing the level of wellness of residents in long-term-care or psychiatric facilities.

health status priorities The ranking of desired changes in the personal health of a population according to the amenability to intervention.

health survey A system for studying or interviewing a group or population to assess the population's health status, the conditions influencing or influenced by its health, and the health services and medical care available to and used by that population. *See also National Health Survey.*

health system All the services, functions, programs, financing mechanisms, and resources in a geographic area that are intended to deliver medical care and provide preventive care services and health promotion activities to affect the state of health of the population. The health system may include community health promotion and protection, personal health care, and health system–enabling services. Three components of a health system are recognized: 1) characteristics of the health system: cost, availability, accessibility, continuity, acceptability, quality, and capacity; 2) health system services: community health protection, health promotion, preventive care, detection services, diagnosis and treatment services, habilitation and rehabilitation services, and maintenance and support services; and 3) health system setting: community, home, mobile, ambulatory, short-stay, long-term care, and freestanding.

health system–enabling services In health-care delivery, these are the organized activities that deliver health services; all major subsystems of the overall health system, including services provided by various governmental and nongovernmental agencies, that ensure the availability, accessibility, and acceptability of quality health services in the most cost-effective manner possible. Major categories in health system–enabling services are health planning, resources development, financing mechanisms, regulation, research, financial management, and organization and function of health services.

health system indicator In health planning and health services delivery, this is a measure of how well the health system is performing. Health system indicators usually measure broad, general characteristics of health system services such as availability, accessibility, acceptability, capacity, quality, continuity, and cost-effectiveness.

health systems agency (HSA) Health planning and resources development agencies that existed from 1976 to 1986, mandated by the National Health Planning and Resources Development Act of 1974 (P.L. 93-641), which required the designation of an HSA in each of the health service areas in the United States. The HSAs were nonprofit private corporations, public regional planning bodies, or single units of local government and performed the health planning and resources development functions listed in Section 1513 of the PHS Act. The legal structure, size, composition, and operation of HSAs were specified in Section 1512 of the Act. Functions of the HSA included preparation of a health system plan (HSP) and an annual implementation plan (AIP), the issuance of grants and contracts, the review and approval or disapproval of proposed uses of a wide range of federal funds in the agency's health service area, the review of proposed new and existing institutional health services, and the making of recommendations to state health planning and development agencies. The HSAs replaced areawide comprehensive agencies but health planning had greater duties and regulatory powers. *See also comprehensive health planning.*

health systems analyst A health-care administration professional who utilizes the methods and techniques of behavioral sciences, business management, and human material resources management to assist health-care facilities in effective and efficient administration and management of their material, financial, and personnel resources.

health system services In health planning and health services delivery, these are activities that utilize health resources primarily to contribute to the improvement or protection of the health status of the population or the environment.

health system settings In health planning and health services delivery, these are sites in which health resources are utilized to deliver health system services.

health systems plan (HSP) A long-range health plan, prepared by former health systems agencies for health service areas, that specified the health goals considered appropriate by the agency for an area. The HSPs followed national guidelines issued by the Department of Health and Human Services and studied the characteristics, resources, and special needs of the health service area. Section 1513 of the Public Health Service Act required and specified the nature of an HSP. *See also Annual Implementation Plan.*

health systems plan facilities component That portion of a health systems plan (HSP) that was concerned with health-care facilities; that segment of the HSP describing the existing health facilities in a state.

health systems priorities In health planning and health services delivery, the ranking of desired changes in characteristics of health delivery mechanisms according to importance and amenability to intervention.

health team An organized group of health-care practitioners and other allied health personnel with various skills, training, and professional backgrounds who cooperatively plan and provide health-care services designed to provide individuals with diagnosis and treatment and assist in the restoration of health. *See health-care team.*

healthy cities Originally derived by the World Health Organization in 1986, this is the recognition that health and well-being are interconnected with social, cultural, physical, economic, and other factors; involves community-wide participation and collaboration in defining and meeting needs to improve health and the quality of life and intersector responsibility for developing locally relevant solutions. *See healthy communities.*

healthy communities The application of health promotion at the local level that focuses on local governments' role in creating the conditions within the community that enhance health, including equity in health and health care, sustainable development of health in the community, participation and citizen involvement, empowerment of citizens through self-care, medical care at the personal level, affordable and reasonable costs for organized medical care and treatment, a well-organized approach and governmental support, and long-term commitment in the development, implementation, and sustainability of a high-level health status. Nonmedical factors that contribute to the health of a community are unemployment, socioeconomic status, education, skills and training, crime, homicide rates, violence, integrity of family structure, morality, and value systems. *See healthy cities.*

healthy lifestyle A set of health-enhancing behaviors shaped by internally consistent values, attitudes, beliefs, and external social and cultural forces (Joint Committee on Health Education Terminology).

healthy worker effect In health promotion, this is when workers or employee groups tend to have a lower mortality rate than the general population. Workers tend to be healthier than persons who do not work. The unemployed are more likely to be unhealthy, and those who have a life-shortening condition are more likely to be unemployed. To be able to work, one has to be healthy, and thus workers are more likely to be healthy.

hearing A court or trial-like proceeding that takes place in a legislative body or an administrative agency and is held in a court-like manner.

hearing body In certificate of need (CON) hearings, this is the governing body or executive committee that has a majority of members present that acts as the hearing body for a CON and conducts public hearings on applications and makes recommendations to the state office that regulates health care. It is not applicable in all states because not all states have CON laws (HSAs ended in 1986).

hearing examiner (or hearing officer) A judgelike official who directs hearings. Also known as a "hearing officer."

hearsay Secondhand evidence; evidence or facts not from or based on personal knowledge of a witness but based on information from other persons.

hearsay evidence In health law, these are statements used as evidence that are not from the personal knowledge of the witness.

hearsay exception In health law, certain evidence based on hearsay can be admitted in a trial if it falls under the special evidence rule that provides for an exception. Hearsay exceptions are determined by the probability that under the circumstances the evidence is accurate.

hearsay rule In health law, this is a rule of evidence law restricting the admission of evidence that is not the personal knowledge of a witness. Hearsay evidence is allowed only under certain situations and is governed by strict rules.

heart attack See *cardiac arrest; myocardial infarction.*

Heart-Balm Act State laws that eliminate or restrict civil lawsuits for breach of promise to marry.

heart-lung machine In hospital operations and patient care, an advanced technology device that substitutes for a patient's heart and lungs during open-heart surgery and other surgery involving the heart, lungs, and sometimes the liver. The patient's blood is circulated through this machine, bypassing the heart. The machine supplies oxygen to the blood and replaces the pumping action of the heart.

heat of passion 1. A state of violent, uncontrollable, and provoked anger. 2. A court-determined state of mind that may reduce a charge from murder to manslaughter.

heavy-care patients 1. Individuals with illnesses, conditions, or disabilities in a nursing home or who are under home health care and need high levels of care and highly technologically assisted care. These patients are more common in nursing homes or home health agencies because Medicare's Prospective Payment System provides incentives for the early discharge of elderly patients from hospitals. 2. Under Medicaid, this is a patient who has been approved for acute administrative days of care and whose medical and nursing needs exceed the level of care available in skilled nursing and intermediate-care facilities in the community.

heavy-care residents Individuals who are long-term-stay patients in nursing homes and require extensive attention for medical and nursing care and extra assistance for activities of daily living. The bed-fast, chair-fast, and severely demented residents who require more care and attention than the average long-term-care patient. Patients of long-term-care facilities are referred to as "residents" instead of "patients." See *heavy-care patients.*

heavy metals In environmental health, these are metallic elements with high atomic weights such as mercury, lead, chromium, cadmium, and arsenic, which can damage living organisms and tissue, especially in humans, even at low concentrations, and tend to accumulate in the body and the food chain.

hebdomadal mortality rate In epidemiology and public health, this is a mortality rate used to assess deaths in the first week of life; the denominator is the number of live births in a 1-year period and the numerator the number of deaths in the first week of life for the same time period per 1000.

hebephrenia A type of schizophrenia characterized by shallow, inappropriate emotions and unpredictable, childish behavior and mannerisms. Delusions may also be present.

HEDIS See *Health Plan Employer Data and Information Set.*

hedonism Seeking pleasure and avoiding pain.

heed To regard with care; to give careful notice; to pay close attention to; to take special care; to consider.

heedily Cautiously.

heedless Inattentive; unmindful; careless.

held Decided in court; a final decision of a court.

HelP The Health Plan Store; an alternative to HIPCs and health alliances, as proposed in different universal coverage proposals, that would be local, large alliances of health-care delivery organizations and services such as hospitals, medical groups, and health plans forming managed-care organizations so that employer groups could purchase medical care coverage from a single, full-service provider.

help-seeking behavior When an individual is motivated by symptoms of a disease, disorder, condition, or unusual occurrence to contact or visit a health-care provider. Once symptoms of a disease or condition occur, the several choices available to the individual are self-care and self-medication, ignoring the symptoms, consulting family and friends, visiting a folk healer, or going to a qualified health-care provider.

hematocrit In medical care and clinical testing, this is the amounts of plasma and corpuscles in the blood.

hematologist A physician who specializes in the study, diagnosis, and treatment of blood, bone marrow, and blood-forming organs and their physiology and biochemistry; a branch of internal medicine.

hematology laboratory A specialized lab within or serving a health care facility that examines and tests blood and its various components.

hematology pathology A physician who specializes in the study, diagnosis, and treatment of diseases and conditions of the blood, bone marrow, and blood-forming organs and their physiology and biochemistry; a branch of pathology.

hematology technologist A medical technologist who works in a hospital under the supervision of a hematologist or laboratory director and performs quantitative and qualitative tests on cellular and plasma components of blood for use in the diagnosis and treatment of disease.

hematology technology An educational program that prepares individuals to work in a hematology lab under the supervision of a qualified director, performing quantitative and qualitative, serological, and coagulation tests on cellular and plasma components of blood for use in the diagnosis and treatment of disease.

hemiplegia Paralysis of one side of the body, usually the result of a cerebral vascular accident (stroke). Because some of the nerve cells of the brain have been damaged and cannot function, the part of the body controlled by the damaged tissue cannot function. There may also be loss of sensation and motor ability. The severity of loss in either of these areas will vary with individual patients.

hemodialysis In medical care, this is a blood treatment process whereby a patient's blood is passed through a machine and its membranes and tubes. Only certain parts of the blood pass through the membranes, thus filtering out waste products, toxic substances, and harmful products that the body normally eliminates; the remaining clean blood is returned to the body. The process functions much like normal kidneys do.

hemodialysis technician A qualified person, usually a nurse, who is trained to assist patients with kidney diseases and disorders, including the operation of an artificial kidney machine.

hemodialysis unit A medical and nursing unit, either in a hospital or a freestanding health facility, that is equipped, staffed, and maintained for the treatment and therapeutic assistance of patients with kidney diseases or disorders. Services may be rendered on an inpatient or outpatient basis. *See also renal dialysis.*

hemostat In medical care, this is a surgical clamp that stops the flow of blood from blood vessels. *See also Kelly forceps.*

henceforth From this time forward; now and in the future; from now on.

Henle-Koch postulates *See Koch postulates.*

herb A plant that is valued for its medicinal, drug, savory, or aromatic qualities.

herbalist A healer who uses herbs for treatment; an herb doctor; one who prescribes herbs to heal illnesses and restore health.

hereafter In the future; in the time to come; following this.

herein In this document.

hereinabove Before this.

hereto To this.

heretofore Before, or in times past.

herewith In this, or with this.

hermeneutics The science or art of interpretation, especially of legal documents.

heroin An addicting opiate drug most commonly used by narcotics addicts.

heuristic managerial decision making In healthcare administration, this is a theoretical management construct meaning to help to discover or learn; designating methods of education or decision making empirically, using "rules of thumb" to find solutions or managerial answers. A method of empirical decision making in education programs or computer software systems.

HEW The former U.S. Department of Health, Education and Welfare; renamed the Department of Health and Human Services. *See Department of Health and Human Services.*

hex A jinx; a supernatural spell imposed through witchcraft.

HHA *See home health agency.*

HHS *See Department of Health and Human Services.*

HIAA Health Insurance Association of America.

HIBAC *See Health Insurance Benefits Advisory Council.*

HIC *See health insurance claim number.*

HICAP *See Health Insurance Counseling and Advocacy Program.*

H-ICDA *See Hospital International Classification of Diseases, Adapted for Use in the United States.*

hierarchical data system In health-care informational management, this is a structured automated data retrieval system for automated data that uses a prearranged set of retrieval categories or definitions.

hierarchy In health administration and organizational structure, this is the ranking of employees and administrative personnel by levels, usually with more personnel at the bottom and gradually fewer at the top. Most bureaucracies and many health-care organizations are arranged this way.

highest practicable level of care Under the Omnibus Budget Reconciliation Act (OBRA), this is the requirement that each resident of a long-term-care facility receive the necessary care and services to attain or maintain the highest practicable physical, mental, and psychosocial well-being in accordance with a comprehensive assessment and treatment care plan. The facility must ensure that a resident's abilities in activities of daily living do not diminish unless the circumstances of the individual's clinical condition demonstrate that diminution is unavoidable. *See activities of daily living; treatment plan.*

high hazard area In JCAHO long-term-care facilities accreditation, this is a room in which combustible and flammable supplies are stored in such a manner as to increase the hazard potential. These areas include paint shops and soiled linen and trash collection rooms.

high-level language In health-care information management and computers, this is a language used to program computers whose messages must be translated into a machine language to run in the computer. High-level languages such as BASIC and COBOL will not run directly in a computer but must be converted to a machine language that the computer recognizes.

high option In the Federal Employees Health Benefits Plan and some other insurance policies, one of two or more levels of insurance that may be chosen by the subscriber. The benefits covered are essentially the same, except that the high option provides lower deductibles and other cost-sharing requirements and more generous time or quantity limits than the low option. The premium for the high option is higher than the low option to reflect the more generous coverage.

high-risk nursery In a hospital, this is an intensive care unit for newborns who have complications and are at risk of illness or death.

high-technology services In long-term care, this describes the high levels of care and advanced services such as cardiac monitoring, oxygen services, nutrition feeding, catheters, respiratory therapy, and rehabilitation. *See heavy-care patients.*

Hill-Burton The legislation and programs authorized by federal legislation for support of construction and modernization of hospitals and other health facilities, beginning with the Hospital Survey and Construction Act of 1946 (P.L. 79725). The original law provided for surveying state medical care delivery needs, developing plans for construction of hospitals and public health centers, and assisting in construction and equipping facilities. Until the late 1960s, new amendments expanded the program in dollar amounts and scope. Later, Congress sought to restructure the law to support outpatient facilities, facilities to serve areas deficient in health services, and training facilities for health and allied health professions. Under the National Health Planning and Resources Development Act of 1974 (P.L. 93-641), the Hill-Burton program began to be administered by state health planning and development agencies to acquire grants, loans, or loan guarantees for the modernization of health facilities, the construction of outpatient health facilities and of inpatient facilities in areas that have experienced recent rapid population growth, and the conversion of existing medical facilities for the provision of new health services. At the end of the program, Hill-Burton hospitals were required to pay the community back by providing a certain percentage of free care to the needy within their community according to the amount of funds, grants, or loans the facility received. Hill-Burton activity has now ceased.

HIPC Health Insurance Purchasing Cooperative. *See Health Insurance Plan of California; health alliance.*

HIPC Exclusive In national health insurance programs and health-care reform, this is a part of a health alliance proposal that is dominated by the larger and controlling insurance companies, carriers, or health plans. *See health alliance.*

hip-pinning A surgical procedure, common in elderly patients, that is used to repair a broken hip.

Hippocrates A famous Greek physician of the late 5th century B.C. who is regarded as the "father of medicine."

Hippocratic Oath The text of the oath is as follows: "I swear by Apollo the physician, by Aesculapius, Hygeia, and Panacea, and I take to witness all the gods, all the goddesses, to keep according to my ability and my judgment the following Oath: 'To consider dear to me as my parents him who taught me this art; to live in common with him and if necessary to share my goods with him; to look upon his children as my own brothers, to teach them this art if they so desire without fee or written promise; to impart to my sons and the sons of the master who taught me and the disciples who have enrolled themselves and have agreed to the rules of the profession, but to these alone, the precepts and the instruction. I will prescribe regimen for the good of my patients according to my ability and my judgment and never do harm to anyone. To please no one will I prescribe a deadly drug, nor give advice which may cause his death. Nor will I give any woman a pessary to procure abortion. But I will preserve the purity of my life and my art. I will not cut for stone, even for patients in whom the disease is manifest; I will leave this operation to be performed by practitioners (specialists in this art). In every house where I come I will enter only for the good of my patients, keeping myself far from all intentional ill-doing and all seduction, and especially from the pleasures of love with women or with men, be they free or slaves. All that may come to my knowledge in the exercise of my profession or outside of my profession or in daily commerce with men, which ought not be spread abroad, I will keep secret and will never reveal. If I keep this oath faithfully, may I enjoy life and practice my art, respected by all men and in all times; but if I swerve from it or violate it, may the reverse be my lot.' "

Hippocratic theory of bodily humors According to Hippocrates, humors are blood, phlegm, black bile, and yellow bile, which vary in both temperature and moistness. Health is a state of balance among the four humors and is evidenced by a somewhat warm, wet body. Sickness is believed to be a result of a humoral imbalance that causes the body to become excessively dry, cold, hot, wet, or a combination of these. Herbs, food, and medications are also classified as wet or dry, hot or cold. To restore balance to the body, a "cold" disease is treated by administering "hot" foods, herbs, or medications. In folk medicine practice, the hot-cold (caliente-frio) application has been a somewhat useful system of diagnosis and treatment.

hirsutism Abnormal hairiness.

HIS Hospital (or Health) Information Systems.

histogram As used in developing epidemiological reports, this is a graph that is similar to a line graph except that it uses vertical bars to indicate levels or points.

histologic technician (technologist) An individual who works under the supervision of a pathologist or other qualified physician and sections, stains, and mounts human or animal tissues and fluid for microscopic study. One year of training is required, and skills are primarily technical; tissue evaluation and screening are not involved at this level. *See medical technologist.*

histologist A microbiologist or pathologist who specializes in the preparation, study, and examination of tissues and cells.

histology The study of the anatomy and physiology of tissues and cells through the use of various types and kinds of microscopes. Cytology is a subarea of histology that studies individual cells.

histopathologist A physician whose specialty involves preparing, examining, and testing for changes in tissues and cells as an indication of disease.

histopathology laboratory A laboratory in a hospital or special unit such as a public health lab in which tissue and cells are prepared and examined for disease by a pathologist or microbiologist.

historical cohort study In epidemiology, this is a research study design that uses data from medical records, vital statistic records, or other data sources to evaluate persons with the same birth year and similar characteristics from which epidemiological events of the past are reconstructed and analyzed.

historical comparison In health-care finance and budgeting, a method of managerial control used to help a health-care organization evaluate operating expenses by comparing the organization's current performance with performances in previous years.

historical study *See retrospective study; cohort study.*

histotechnologist One who conducts microscopic study of human and animal tissue for diagnostic, research, or teaching purposes, serves in a supervisory capacity to the histologic technician, and may perform preliminary tissue evaluation and screening prior to tissue examination by the pathologist. This position requires a baccalaureate degree. Also called a "histologic technologist."

hitherto Of the past; in the past.

HIV Human immunodeficiency virus.

HIV infection codes Beginning with data for 1987, ICD-9-CM-type codes (*042, *043, *044) were developed for classifying and coding human immunodeficiency virus (HIV) infection, formerly referred to as human T-cell lymphotropic virus-III/lymphadenopathy-associated virus (HTLV-III/LAV) infection.

HIV testing A health-care service that performs blood and laboratory testing to detect the presence of or exposure to the HIV.

HMEIA See *health manpower education initiative award*.

HMO See *health maintenance organization*.

HMO, nursing The first nursing health maintenance organization was developed in Arizona as a division of St. Mary's Hospital. The HMO was formed to provide nursing services to senior citizens enrolled in Medicare under senior risk contract programs. The average length of stay was decreased because of good case management. Nurse case managers oversee patient care and ensure that the most economical care and approaches are used for inpatient and outpatient care. Community services and home health care are also arranged. Case managers monitor patients on a regular basis and can observe when a chronic condition becomes acute so that it can be treated quickly.

HMO revenue distribution Under managed care, this deals with how HMOs receive revenue from insurance premiums charged to the employer or individual subscriber. The HMO spends the revenue on administrative costs, marketing, physician, hospital and other direct patient care services and reinsurance. Each medical group accepts specific contracts on the basis of contract negotiation that may differ in service and responsibility.

HMSA Health manpower shortage area.

Hobson's choice 1. Choosing between two or more objectionable or devastating choices. 2. Freedom to choose when no meaningful choice exists, such as having a breast removed because of cancer or not having it removed and eventually dying of cancer.

hoc (Lat.) This.

Hogben number As used in epidemiology, medical records, or research, this is an identification number system developed by Lancelot Hogben, an English mathematician. The system uses a sequence of digits as labels for birthdate, sex, birthplace, and other identifying factors of value.

hold 1. To retain or detain. 2. To have in safekeeping. 3. To own something lawfully. 4. To decide; a final decision of a court. 5. To conduct or take place; to hold a hearing. 6. To bind by contract.

holder 1. One who holds. 2. A person with legal authority to detain or hold something. 3. One legally possessing a negotiable instrument. 4. The legal owner of an item.

holder in due course An individual who has or obtains a negotiable instrument in good faith and without knowledge or any information that the instrument is bad or overdue.

hold harmless 1. In law, this is to promise to cover any claims that could arise against another party. 2. A provision of law that prevents a governmental entity, institution, or other party from suffering additional expenses or loss of benefits as a result of a change in a statute or regulations. Without such a provision, the entity or institution would be responsible for expenses not previously anticipated because of an expanded caseload, more generous coverage provisions, or both. On the other hand, the use of "hold harmless" provisions often creates substantial confusion, heterogeneity, and inequity in eligibility, coverage, and responsibilities under a statute. 3. In insurance, a provision offering the insured protection in disputes between the insurer and the provider of a covered service.

holding 1. In health law, this is a ruling on the admissibility of evidence or issues raised during a trial. 2. Ownership of stocks or shares.

holding company A company created to control, or to have a dominant interest in, other companies by owning or controlling their stock or creating a tax shelter; an incorporated company that is in control of or that influences the management of one or more other services, organizations, or companies by virtue of ownership and its administrative right to appoint administrators in the subordinate companies.

hold over 1. To keep possession after the period of agreement ends. 2. To stay in office after the term of office has ended.

holism A theory of healing, health promotion, preventive medicine, or therapy that views the body as a whole, or as the sum of its parts. In health, the whole person (physical, social, mental, spiritual, and emotional parts) must be treated as having equal importance. *See also wholistic.*

holistic Relating to organic or functional relationships between parts and wholes; the study of the totality of the individual, including the psychological, physiological, values, and social characteristics. *See also wholistic.*

holistic health An approach to health that views a person as needing to be healthy in all dimensions of life. Thus the physiological aspects are not the only ones considered; the mental, emotional, spiritual, values, environmental, behavioral, and social aspects that constitute the "totality" of a person must also be considered and must be in harmony to achieve optimum health. *See also wholistic.*

holistic health care A multidisciplinary, multifaceted approach to health care in which all dimensions of a person are treated or at least considered in the treatment process. Unconventional and nontraditional approaches to treatment are accepted and utilized if they work and benefit the patient. Although traditional approaches to medicine are used, its rigid approach to treatment is not allowed to limit the treatment process. *See also wholistic.*

holo- The prefix meaning "whole" or "all."

holoendemic In epidemiology and public health, this is when a disease has a high level of prevalence in a population at an early age in life, affecting most of the children in a population, and then levels off later in life, so that the adult population shows stronger evidence of having had the disease than the children. Malaria is a classic example of a holoendemic disease.

holograph A handwritten and signed legal document; a document written entirely in the hand of the person who executed it and signed it (usually a will).

holographic will A handwritten will by the individual or testator.

home accident In public health and accident classification, this is an injury or property damage that occurs either inside or outside a person's place of residence, which can be the person's own place of living or any other home in which a person may be injured.

home- and community-based care (HCBC) Under one national health-care initiative, this is a cost containment program designed to provide care for severely disabled people of all ages in the home or in community-based clinics to help them avoid institutional care. Each state would be allowed to choose from a menu of services and may include or exclude various aspects of long-term care. Long-term-care benefits are not a universal entitlement but are determined by disability criteria for eligibility.

homebound This is a vague term that is open to interpretation, but under Medicare and health insurance programs and when referring to home health care, it generally means that a patient is unable to leave home or requires exceptional effort to do so. If the patient does in fact leave home, he or she could still be considered homebound if the absences are infrequent, of short duration, for the purpose of receiving medical treatment, or for occasional supportive personal care (e.g., a barber or beautician). The nature of the absences must not indicate that the patient has the capacity to obtain the health care provided outside rather than in the home.

home care Helping an ill or disabled person with such activities as bathing, housekeeping, meal preparation, transportation, and financial matters. It is related to, but may be considered distinct from, home health care, which is the provision of medical, social, and supportive services or other care in the patient's home by nurses, therapists, social workers, physicians, and other caregivers with the intent of maintaining independent functioning and avoiding institutionalization.

home care department According to JCAHO for accreditation purposes, a formally structured organizational unit of the hospital that is designed to coordinate the effective provision of physician-directed nursing and other therapeutic health-care services in the patient's residence and that provides at least one therapeutic service directly.

home-delivered meals *See home-delivered meal services; Meals-on-Wheels.*

home-delivered meal services A service provided by an Area Agency on Aging facility or other health or social service agency that offers nutritious meals to homebound people, the elderly, or others who cannot cook for themselves, resulting in a good diet and healthy nutritional intake.

home economics A professional educational program of activities in the home, ranging from cooking and homemaking to health and nutrition. The program trains persons to work in schools, agencies, or businesses and describes the relationship between the physical, social, emotional, and intellectual environment in the home and family and the health, emotional, and mental development of individuals and families. Dietitian and nutrition training programs are often housed in this academic area.

home health agency (HHA) 1. An organization, public agency, nonprofit organization, or private company that is licensed, certified, or accredited to provide nursing, medical, therapy, and health services to patients in their own homes. To be certified under Medicare, an agency must provide skilled nursing services and at least one additional therapeutic service (physical, speech, or occupational therapy; medical social services; or home health aide services) in the home. Services are determined by and adapted to the health needs of individuals and families in all age-groups, diagnostic categories, and economic situations. These services must be ordered by a licensed physician or a physician who is federally employed. Direct reassessments followed by renewal of orders are mandatory. Standards are established and required by state law to be followed to ensure the health and safety of the home-treated patient. 2. In managed care, these are home care organizations or private companies that are licensed, certified, or accredited to provide nursing, medical, and health services to patients in their own homes. Patients must be members under contract with and approved by a health plan to receive care, treatment, and services.

home health aide A specially trained paraprofessional who helps public health nurses, home health nurses, and other health-care providers with bedside care of patients in their own homes.

home health aide services A home health program providing care in the patient's home under the supervision of a registered nurse in accordance with a treatment plan that includes a range of care provided by an individual who is certified in those skills needed to care for the chronically ill, aged, or disabled.

home health care 1. An essential component of comprehensive health care that includes skilled medical and nursing care and supportive services necessary to maintain a person in his or her place of residence. Services are planned and coordinated to promote, maintain, or restore health or to minimize the effects of illness or disability. Health services are rendered to an individual as needed in the home. The services may be provided by a visiting nurse association (VNA), home health agency, hospital, or other organized community group. The care can be quite specialized or comprehensive (nursing services, speech, physical, occupational and rehabilitation therapy, homemaker services, and social services). Under Medicare, home-based medical and nursing services must be provided by a home health agency. Under Medicaid, states have the right to restrict coverage of home health care to services provided by home health agencies. Under managed care, home health care is provided in a patient's home as a cost containment method for patients who do not need extensive treatment in a hospital or nursing home. 2. From the medical care delivery perspective, this is the provision of nursing care; social work; therapies such as diet, occupational, physical, psychological, and speech; vocational and social services; and homemaker-health aide services. These are provided at home as an extension of the physician's therapeutic responsibility. At the physician's request and under his or her medical direction, the personnel who provide these home health-care services operate as a team in assembling and developing the home health-care plan (AMA).

home health-care eligibility See *eligibility, home health-care.*

home health care, intensive Specialized health care provided in the home for persons with serious yet short-term medical conditions who are not sufficiently ill to require institutionalization.

home health care, intermediate Health care provided in the home by nurses under the supervision of a physician to patients whose medical condition is stable and whose recovery is occurring in a predictable manner.

home health care, maintenance Health care provided in the home by nurses and other health-care providers under the supervision of a physician to a patient whose medical condition is stable or who has a chronic disease requiring personal care, supportive services and intermittent therapy, nursing care, and medication supervision.

home health-care program, hospital-based A home health agency that is either a subdivision of a hospital or sponsored by it; the program functions outside the hospital and is staffed and managed by hospital personnel.

home health services 1. An array of services provided separately or in combination with other treatment regimens to individuals and families in their place of residence or in ambulatory care settings for the purpose of preventing disease and the restoration of health. Services appropriate to the needs of the individual and his or her family are planned, coordinated, and made available by an organized health agency through the use of agency employed staff, contractual arrangements, or a combination of administrative patterns. Medical services are primarily provided by the individual's private or clinic physician, although in some instances agencies will employ or contract for physician's services. 2. Health services that can be safely and effectively rendered in the patient's home or place of residence on an intermittent basis. Home health services include skilled nursing services and at least one of the following services: physical, respiratory, occupational, or speech therapy; medical social work; and home health aide. *See also home health care; home health agency.*

home life care Another term for "home health supportive services" where an individual is assisted in independent living by having homemakers and home aides assist in the activities of daily living provided to the individual in his or her home; excludes nursing, therapy, and medical care.

homelike Medical, hospital, or health-care facilities that are purposely arranged to provide surroundings that are pleasant and as one finds in a private home (e.g., birthing rooms or exclusive patient care rooms usually reserved for dignitaries).

homemaker aide An individual who works under the professional supervision of appropriate health professionals or social workers and assists elderly, ill, or disabled persons with meals, shopping, household chores, bathing, and other daily living needs, both physical and emotional.

homemaker services Nonmedical support services (e.g., food preparation, housekeeping, bathing, and shopping) given to a homebound individual who is unable to perform these tasks for him- or herself. Such services are not covered under the Medicare and Medicaid programs or most other health insurance programs but may be included in the social service programs developed by the states under Title XX of the Social Security Act. Homemaker services are intended to preserve independent living and normal family life for the aged, disabled, sick, or convalescent. *See also alternatives to long-term institutional care.*

home management training Supportive long-term-care services provided in the home that provide training in activities related to the use of adaptive devices. Such services allow the individual to perform daily functions within the home setting.

homeo- A prefix denoting "like," "similar."

Homeopathic Pharmacopeia of the U.S. One of the three official compendia in the United States that is recognized by the federal Food, Drug, and Cosmetic Act.

homeopathy A system of medicine expounded by Samuel Hahnemann based on the simple phenomenon (similia sinilibus curantur), using principles set forth by Hippocrates, especially those related to the notion that disease may be cured by the means that caused the symptoms in healthy people. This approach to curing illness tries to restore the self-healing potential of the organism, working with the lowest doses capable of provoking a reaction in the organism. Diagnosis of the person uses the limited symptomatology of allopathic medicine extended into such realms as constitution, mental, functioning, reactions to food, and changes in temperature. Cure of disease is said to be effected by minute doses of drugs that produce the same signs and symptoms in a healthy person. This is said to stimulate bodily defenses against the signs and symptoms. Theoretical bases for this curative approach are limited in effectiveness and not completely founded in known biomedical science or sound research findings, even though some interesting and positive results have been seen. This system of medicine is in limited practice in the United States. *See also osteopathy; allopathy.*

homeostasis 1. The maintenance of a constant balance in bodily processes to continue optimal functioning. 2. In physiology or biology, this is a state of physiological equilibrium produced by a balance of functions and chemical actions in the body that gravitate toward stable equilibrium between all internal elements, organs, systems, and functions.

home plan A term used by some managed-care plans to identify the health plan that provides coverage for a subscriber. *See also host plan.*

home repair, adaptation, renovation A social service, especially for the elderly and disabled, that provides for structural repairs and modifications to homes when the repairs are necessary for safety or when special adaptations are required because of a disability. For example, minor modifications to the home can easily be made to accommodate a wheelchair, thus increasing the disabled person's mobility.

home rule Local government, self-governing.

home services system Under managed care or insurance, this is a marketing system that uses commissioned agents to sell policies and provide service only to an insurer's policyowners in a specified area.

home setting A person's usual or temporary place of residence (except where such place of residence is the health care institution) with the result that the patient does not travel to receive services.

homes for the aged Institutions, ranging from skilled nursing facilities to private homes, that offer custodial care. The most basic services a custodial care home usually provides are clean, well-maintained rooms; good meals; assistance in personal care; some recreational programs; a courteous, concerned, and pleasant staff; and a system for emergency treatment.

hometown medical and dental care In the Veterans Administration health-care program, outpatient medical or dental treatment paid for by the program and provided to eligible veterans in their own communities by VA-approved doctors or dentists of their own choice. Such treatment is furnished when the care cannot be given by VA clinic facilities or when the health of the patient or distance to be traveled gives sufficient justification.

home visit See *housecall; visit; home health care; home health services.*

homicide A general term for the taking of a life; the killing of a human being; a general term for murder (but not always a crime).

homogeneous Those that are the same; similar or like background or characteristics.

Hon. Abbreviation for "honorable," a title used to address a judge.

honesty Forthrightness of conduct and uprightness of character; truthfulness.

honor 1. To accept and pay when due. 2. To accept or pay a negotiable instrument; to honor a check. 3. Integrity, credibility, uprightness.

honorary staff Physicians and other related health-care providers who are recognized for their outstanding contribution to patient care, professional activities, and long and loyal service to the health-care facility.

horizontal diversification In health administration and strategic planning, this is a growth strategy that adds new products or services to a health-care organization's overall organizational structure, often through the purchase of or merger with related services or facilities such as purchasing a long-term-care facility or home health agency.

horizontal exit In JCAHO long-term-care facilities accreditation, an exit that leads from one area of refuge from fire and smoke on a given floor of a building to another area of refuge on the same floor of the building or at the same level in an adjoining building. Both areas of refuge must be of sufficient size to accommodate the number of people expected to occupy both areas at any given time, and both areas must be separated by a fire partition extending from the top of the building to the floor that provides exit to the outside.

horizontal integration In strategic planning for health-care organizations, providing the same type of service such as having two hospitals, surgical centers, or clinics.

hornbook A book on the basic principles of one subject of law; a basic book or primer on law.

Hoshin planning In health administration and quality management, a quality management and planning system that allows the health-care organization to organize, implement, and administer all aspects and functions within the organization so that it moves toward an increase in quality, efficiency, and effectiveness in health services delivery, support services, and management activities. The guiding principles are participation by all managers, individual initiative and responsibility, and focusing on root causes, quality, vision, and process. Steps to be taken are developing an organizational vision, identifying gaps, determining organizational need for quality management development, and fulfilling needs of the organization using the following steps: 1) vertical alignment, 2) disciplined process, 3) fact-based participative measures, 4) capability assessment according to goals and means, and 5) key objectives consistently achieved.

hospice A program providing palliative and supportive care for terminally ill patients and their families directly, on a consulting basis with the patient's physician, or with another community agency such as a visiting nurse association; helping people die with as little discomfort and as much serenity as possible. Originally, a hospice was a medieval way station where crusaders could be replenished, refreshed, and cared for. Today it is used for an organized program of care for people going through life's last station. The whole family is considered the unit of care, and care extends through the mourning process. Emphasis is placed on symptom control, medical relief of pain, and preparation for, and support before and after, death. Hospices originated in England and are prevalent in the United States.

hospice care Specialized health care provided to a dying person that is supportive in nature; thus the health and nursing care offered is based on the acceptance of death. A holistic approach to the dying patient is provided, and the patient's family is offered legal, financial, spiritual, emotional, and social counseling. Hospice care is offered in the home, in specially designated areas of long-term-care facilities, in hospitals, and in special separate facilities provided solely for the treatment of the dying patient (including AIDS patients).

hospital 1. According to the American Hospital Association and National Master Facility Inventory of the U.S. Public Health Service, this is an institution licensed as a hospital that provides diagnostic and therapeutic patient care services for medical conditions and has at least six beds, an organized physician staff, and continuous nursing services under the supervision of registered nurses with a length of stay of less than 30 days. The World Health Organization considers a facility or institution a hospital if it is permanently staffed by at least one physician, offers inpatient accommodation, and provides active medical and nursing care. Hospitals may be classified by type of service, ownership, and length of stay. 2. A facility with at least six beds, licensed by the state as a hospital or that is operated as a hospital by a federal or state agency and is therefore not subject to state or local licensing laws. 3. An institution whose primary function is to provide inpatient services, diagnostic and therapeutic, for a variety of medical conditions, both surgical and nonsurgical. In addition, most hospitals provide outpatient services, particularly emergency care. Hospitals are classified by length of stay (short term or long term), teaching or nonteaching, type of service (e.g., psychiatric, tuberculosis, general, maternity, children's, or ear, nose, and throat), and control (federal, state, or local government; for-profit [proprietary] or nonprofit). The hospital system is dominated by the short-term, general, nonprofit community hospital often called a "voluntary hospital." *See hospital, acute-care.*

hospital, accredited The status given to a hospital by the Joint Commission on Accreditation of Hospitals (JCAHO) indicating that the hospital meets the criteria and standards set forth by JCAHO. This status is granted to the hospital after the inspection team has assessed the hospital for its quality of care, nursing and healthcare administration, environmental health and safety, maintenance and housekeeping, and governance and organization.

hospital acquired infection *See nosocomial infection; iatrogenic illness.*

hospital, acute-care 1. A short-stay hospital with an average length of stay of less than 30 days (AHA). 2. For PSRO program purposes, a health-care institution or distinct part of a health-care institution providing health-care services in the PRO area, as defined in Section 1861(e)–(g) of the Social Security Act, except that the institution shall not be a Christian Science sanatorium as operated, listed, and certified by the First Church of Christ Scientist, Boston. The PRO only gathers data health-care institutions in which the average patient stay is less than 30 days.

hospital administrator A highly skilled and well-educated individual who is the chief executive officer or president of a licensed hospital, responsible for the overall management and operations of the facility, leads the hospital's management team, and is appointed by the board of directors as the legally responsible administrator of the hospital and its medical staff, facilities, and operations. *See health administrator; health-care administrator.*

hospital admissions Overnight short-term stays, surgery, or other arrangements or types of care where the patient is formally admitted as an inpatient. Obstetrical "admits" are counted as one admission, but the delivery of the child is not counted as an admission. If the infant remains in the hospital on the discharge of the mother, the infant is then admitted.

hospital, affiliated A hospital that has a contractual or other formal agreement with a medical school, nursing school, or school of allied health professions to accept their students for clinical training.

hospital affiliation In managed care, this is a formal agreement or contract between a hospital and a health plan that provides inpatient care for health plan members under the benefits of the managed-care health plan.

hospital alliances In health finance, this a cooperative of inpatient acute-care medical facilities that have joined together to take advantage of group purchasing and improve competitive positioning and the sharing of services to save money and reduce costs.

hospital autopsy rate, adjusted The ratio of autopsies actually performed compared to the number of bodies available for autopsy in a hospital's morgue.

hospital auxiliary A volunteer organization established to carry on volunteer services within the hospital and in the community representing the hospital.

hospital-based facility A long-term-care or extended care unit that is a separate designated area of a hospital certified by the state to provide skilled nursing care or intermediate care. Referred to as a "transitional unit" or an "extended care facility."

hospital-based physician A physician who spends most of his or her practice in one or more hospitals, seeing and treating patients, instead of working in an office setting. Such physicians sometimes have special financial arrangements with the hospital (salary or percentage of fees collected) and may be associated with a teaching hospital situation. Also included are directors of medical education, pathologists, anesthesiologists, radiologists, and physicians who staff emergency rooms and outpatient departments. In some states, laws prohibit physicians from being employed by hospitals unless they are in the specialties listed above.

hospital-based specialists Physicians who provide consultative services or otherwise assist the attending physicians in the hospital setting; these specialists include such hospital-based physicians as pathologists, radiologists, and anesthesiologists.

hospital beds 1. The average number of beds, cribs, and pediatric bassinets (excluding bassinets for newborn babies) that are regularly maintained and used for inpatients in an acute-care health-care facility during a certain time period, usually 1 year. 2. A basic measure of the size of a hospital, determined by the physical plant/construction size and structure and the facility being licensed for a certain number of beds. Each inpatient admission requiring a bed as a hospital admission usually also means an overnight stay and that the person is ill enough to require a bed. Hospitals have no accommodations for patients unless assigned a bed. See *bed(s); bed, hospital; bed, inpatient.*

hospital benefits Medical insurance or managed-care plans offered as employee benefits that are provided to workers and their dependents under an insurance policy or health plan to cover hospital charges incurred because of an illness or injury.

hospital board See governing body; governing board; board of directors; board of directors, hospital.

hospital care, expenditures for See *expenditures for hospital care.*

hospital, certified The acceptance of a hospital to participate as a provider under Title XVIII of the Social Security Act (Medicare) by meeting the standards for participation as set forth by the U.S. Department of Health and Human Services.

hospital cesarean section rate The number of cesarean sections (C-sections) performed in a hospital or surgical center, as compared with the total number of deliveries in the same health-care facility with multiple births counted as a single delivery. The numerator is the number of C-sections and the denominator the total number of deliveries in the same time period, usually 1 year, multiplied by 1000. The hospital C-section rate formula follows:

$$\frac{\text{Number of C-sections performed in a given time period}}{\text{Total number of deliveries in the same time period}} \times 1000$$

hospital chain See *multi-institutional organization; multihospital system.*

hospital, chronic disease A long-term-care hospital that provides intensive medical and skilled nursing services to persons with long-term diseases and disorders who need a higher level of health care than is available in a nursing home or convalescent center.

hospital, city A hospital administered, financed, and controlled by a municipal government and managed by an appointed board of consumers and citizens. Such hospitals primarily serve the indigent, and some provide care for both indigent and paying patients.

hospital, city-county A hospital that is jointly financed and controlled by municipal and county governments, often serving mostly indigent patients. *See also hospital, county.*

hospital, closed staff In hospital administration and medical staff management, this is the process of developing a formal plan that sets forth the parameters for types of physicians and specialties needed and the size of the medical staff. Physicians can join the medical staff of a hospital under such a management plan only if they meet the defining criteria.

hospital, community An independent nonprofit hospital corporation governed by citizens interested in establishing and providing hospital care for their community. These are nonprofit corporations that have elected boards of trustees. All nonfederal short-stay hospitals as classified by the American Hospital Association offer some of the following services: general medical and surgical; obstetrics and gynecology; eye, ear, nose, and throat; rehabilitation; orthopedic or other specialty; children's general; children's eye, ear, nose, and throat; children's rehabilitation; and children's orthopedic or other specialty. *See community hospital.*

hospital computer system In health-care information management systems, this is a data processing and communications system configured, adapted, and set up in a hospital to provide on-line computer processing with interactive computer capability. Patient data and medical records data can be entered or retrieved within the hospital and can be linked to physician offices, outpatient or freestanding facilities, and service areas in the hospital such as pharmacy, labs, and business offices.

hospital control In managed care, this is an incentive program by health plans that encourages the health-care provider to control the costs of certain services, similar to a hospital incentive pool or shared risk pool. When actual incurred costs are favorable, compared to a predetermined budget, the savings are shared with the physician group or IPA. Conversely, when actual incurred costs exceed the budget, the physician group or IPA shares in the cost overrun. This approach limits rewards, and risks are usually set to moderate extraordinary fluctuations in the process of providing care.

hospital cooperative *See cooperative hospitals; alliance.*

hospital corner Used by hospitals and other health-care facility housekeeping staff, this is a way to neatly fold the corners of the blankets and sheets in a triangle shape to tuck in blankets and sheets with the bottom corners folded over on each other so they do not easily come undone. *See mitered corner.*

hospital, county A hospital under the administration of a county board of supervisors or a county commission, supported in part by county tax funds. The hospital administrator reports to the county board of supervisors or commission. Large urban county hospitals provide care for the indigent and medically indigent. Smaller, rural hospitals provide care for both private and indigent patients and serve as general community hospitals.

hospital customer In hospital marketing and strategic planning, these are the patient, the physicians on the medical staff with admitting privileges, and those paying for the care (third-party payers). Some health-care marketing professionals suggest that hospital employees also be considered a customer.

hospital, day *See day hospital.*

hospital day(s) 1. In managed care and hospital administration, this is a measurement of the number of days of hospital care that health plan members use in a specific time period, usually reported as a rate such as days per 1000 members per year. Also referred to as "bed days." 2. The day on which a person is admitted to a hospital is counted as a hospital day only when the patient stays overnight; a patient who enters the hospital in the afternoon and is discharged the next day at noon or later is counted as having 2 hospital days. The formula for hospital days follows:

$$\frac{\text{Total number of days spent in a hospital by members of a population or health plan}}{\text{Total population}} \times 1000$$

3. In public health surveys or the assessment of health-care delivery, this is the total number of days spent in short-term hospitals during the survey year; only those days actually occurring during the survey year are included in the data. *See also bed, occupied; patient days; bed, occupancy; occupancy rate.*

hospital days during the year In public health surveys or the assessment of health-care delivery, this is the total number for all hospital episodes in the 12-month period prior to the interview week. Episodes that overlap the beginning and end of the 12-month period are subdivided so that only those days falling within the period are included.

hospital days per admission In public health surveys or the assessment of health-care delivery, this is the total number of days spent in short-term hospitals during the survey year for all stays regardless of when they began or ended, divided by the number of admissions during the year. The denominator excludes admissions that started prior to the survey year and extend into the survey year but includes admissions that extended into the year following the survey year. For terminated pregnancies, it includes all admission and days regardless of when they occurred.

hospital, deemed Under Professional Review Organization (PRO), this a hospital that has been given the responsibility and authority to carry out its own review functions such as admission, continued stay, length of stay, and medical care evaluation.

hospital, delegated A hospital that has met the standards and criteria of the Professional Review Organization (PRO) in providing three review functions: 1) medical/nursing care evaluation, 2) admissions, and 3) length of stay/continued stay. These are used to determine which services are appropriate for payment under the Prospective Payment System of Medicare, Medicaid, and Maternal and Child Health programs.

hospital discharge 1. The formal release of a patient from any type of hospital, under the direction of and orders from the attending physician. 2. The completion of any continuous period of stay of one night or more in a hospital as an inpatient, except for the period of stay of a well, newborn infant. 3. The formal release of an inpatient by a hospital such as the termination of the period of hospitalization by death or disposition to a place of residence, nursing home, or another hospital, with newborn infants excluded. 4. In public health surveys or the assessment of health-care delivery, this is when a hospital discharge is recorded in a survey whenever a member of a household is reported to have been discharged from a hospital in a 12-month period prior to the interview.

hospital discharge abstract system In medical records of hospitals, HMOs, or clinics, a summary of the diagnoses, conditions, procedures, and prognosis of each admission and discharge of patients. The abstract is used as a source of data for health services research, hospital administration, and some epidemiological studies. These data include information such as length of stay, primary and secondary diagnosis, procedures and surgical operations, specific hospital diagnostic and treatment services received, and outcomes of the course of treatment including death or discharge status. *See discharge abstract.*

hospital, disproportionate share Under Medicare, this is a designation given to a hospital serving a higher-than-average proportion of low-income populations.

hospital district A geographic area created and controlled by a political subdivision of a state, county, or city for the purpose of establishing and maintaining hospitals and health-care institutions for the citizens of that political subdivision. The hospitals and health-care facilities are organized on a regional basis similar to school districts. Hospital districts are governmental subdivisions established for the purpose of supporting and administering hospitals through the power of taxation of the population in the district; tax funds are turned directly over to the hospital. The hospitals are governed by a board of directors consisting of local citizens elected by the district residents, making the district independent of city, county, or state government. This is a less common form of health-care organization, except in a few states such as Texas and California. Also referred to as "health care districts" or "health care authorities."

hospital emergency department The facilities and services found in acute-care hospitals that provide for the management of outpatients who come to the hospital for treatment of conditions considered by the patient or his or her representative to require immediate medical care in the hospital environment. The term is synonymous with "emergency room," "accident room," and "casualty room."

hospital engineer In hospital plant operations, this is sometimes used as the title for the individual in charge of physical plant maintenance and operations.

hospital episode In public health surveys or the assessment of health-care delivery, this is any continuous period of stay of one night or more in a hospital as an inpatient, except the period of stay of a well, newborn infant. A hospital episode is recorded for a family member whenever any part of a hospital stay is included in the 12-month period prior to the survey.

hospital expense insurance Medical insurance protection against the costs of only the hospital care resulting from the illness or injury.

hospital experimental payment program (HEP) A program in the Rochester, New York, area that began in 1980 when a group of hospitals voluntarily signed a contract for a new healthcare financing system. The system provided for local administration and control over a community-wide cap on all hospital patient care revenues. The program covered two counties of approximately 760,000 people and nine hospitals. The HEP program had four goals: 1) cost containment should be more effective through incentives than through punishment and sanctions, 2) hospitals should be paid for their output rather than the input expended to create the output, 3) hospitals should be held accountable only for the cost increases within their control, and 4) hospitals should be able to project their revenue in advance and budget accordingly. Top-down budgeting and the development of spending priorities are used to ensure the success of the program.

hospital fatality ratio See *case fatality ratio*.

hospital, federal An acute-care health-care facility funded and administered by a department of the U.S. government. See also *government hospitals; Indian Health Service; Public Health Service; military hospitals; Veterans Administration hospitals*.

hospital fetal death The death of an unborn child prior to being removed from the mother's womb that occurs in the hospital with no consideration for the status or duration of the pregnancy. Death is determined, once the fetus is expelled or extracted from the mother, by the lack of breathing, heartbeat, or pulsation of the umbilical cord or by a failure to move or cry (or other signs of life).

hospital, for-profit Private or publicly owned corporations that own hospitals that are basically of the community or general hospital type. The corporations distribute profits and dividends to individual investors and owners. Also referred to as "investor-owned hospitals." See *hospital, proprietary (for-profit); hospital, investor-owned*.

hospital, general 1. A full-service medical care institution that provides diagnosis and treatment, both surgical and nonsurgical, for inpatients who have any of a variety of medical conditions. Its components include but are not limited to an organized medical staff, medical care treatment services and facilities, inpatient beds, a full range of medical services, testing and therapy at the secondary and tertiary levels, continuous nursing services, an administrator to whom the governing authority has delegated the full-time responsibility for the operation, an organized administrative team and management structure, patients admitted on the medical authority of the medical staff, a medical record maintained for each patient, pharmacy services maintained in or by the institution and supervised by a licensed pharmacist, diagnostic and X-ray services, clinical laboratory services, anatomical pathology services, operating room services, and food service, all for the care of a complete range and type of patients and all other support and ancillary services needed. 2. The World Health Organization's definition states that this facility provides medical and nursing care for more than one category of medical discipline (e.g., general medicine, specialized medicine, general surgery, specialized surgery, and obstetrics); excluded are hospitals having a limited range of care such as small hospitals in rural areas, nursing homes, convalescent hospitals, psychiatric hospitals, or other specialty hospitals.

hospital hotel A facility that is a cross between an outpatient and an acute-care facility with a homelike or traditional hotel atmosphere but that is connected to the hospital as a low-cost alternative to traditional inpatient care, especially for long-term recovering patients. See *medical hotel/hospital*.

hospital information system (HIS) Computers and related equipment and hardwired networks allowing integrated and interactive use throughout the entire hospital, developed to assist in administration, medical records, patient care, financial data, communication and information sharing, research, outcome studies, and other informational needs.

hospital inpatient An individual admitted to a hospital and provided with room, bed, board, and nursing services in a medical or nursing unit within a hospital for the minimum of an overnight stay. See also *inpatient*.

hospital inpatient autopsy The postmortem examination of the body of a patient who died during hospitalization as an inpatient, conducted by a hospital pathologist or physician to assist in understanding the cause of death.

hospital inpatient services reimbursement Under Medicaid, this is a method of determining charges to Medicaid patients in some states, where the charge is the lesser of the following: the customary charge, allowable cost, or all-inclusive rate per discharge.

hospital insurance A form of medical insurance designed to pay all or part of the hospital bill from an inpatient stay for an insured person. The hospital bills paid by the insurance include only those bills submitted by the hospital and exclude the bills of doctors and private-duty nurses, home health agencies, or outside therapists. Flat-rate insurance that pays a set amount for each day the person is hospitalized is considered hospital insurance, as are major medical, Medicare Part A, and CHAMPUS.

Hospital Insurance Program Also known as Part A, the compulsory portion of Medicare that automatically enrolls all persons aged 65 and over who are entitled to benefits under the Old Age, Survivors, Disability and Health Insurance Program (OASHDI) administered by the Social Security Administration, railroad retirement, persons under 65 who have been eligible for disability for over 2 years, and insured workers (and their dependents) requiring renal dialysis or kidney transplantation. After various cost-sharing requirements are met, the program pays for inpatient hospital care and care in skilled nursing facilities and home health agencies following a period of hospitalization. The program is financed from a separate trust fund funded with a contributory tax (payroll tax) levied on employers, employees, and the self-employed. Under the program each hospital nominates an intermediary that reviews and pays claims to that hospital under the Prospective Payment System.

Hospital International Classification of Diseases, Adapted for Use in the United States (H-ICDA) *See International Classification of Diseases, Adapted for Use in the United States.*

hospital, investor-owned A hospital in a system or chain of hospitals owned by a corporation. The corporation also provides management contracts to other hospitals. Some are not-for-profit corporations, and others are private, for-profit entities that provide stock for public sale.

hospitalization 1. Admission of persons to a hospital as inpatients for treatment or therapy. 2. The course of treatment and length of stay of an inpatient in a hospital.

hospitalization insurance A medical insurance policy that pays inpatient care for hospital room, board, nursing services, lab fees, operating room expenses, medications, therapies, treatments, and expenses directly related to the recovery of the patient as an inpatient within a hospital. *See also hospital insurance; hospital-medical insurance.*

hospital, licensed An acute-care health-care facility that is allowed the legal right to operate as a hospital as long as the required fee is paid, licensing requirements are met, and it continues to be administered as a hospital within the laws and regulations of the state granting the license.

hospital live birth The delivery of a live fetus from its mother with such life signs as breathing, heartbeat, pulsation of umbilical cord, and movement and crying responses.

hospital, long-term Health-care facilities where more than half the patients are admitted to units with an average length of stay of 30 days or more; also, state hospitals providing institutional care of the mentally ill, blind, deaf, and retarded and those with tuberculosis. These hospitals are administered by departments, boards, or administrative agencies of state governments such as a department of health and welfare or health services. The state operates psychiatric hospitals; schools for the blind, deaf, and mentally retarded; and infirmaries or hospitals in or supportive of reform schools, detention centers, and prisons.

hospital marketing As support to hospital administration, this is the process of utilizing basic marketing analysis, planning, implementation activities that apply to and are unique to hospitals (e.g., identification of the customers of the hospital), target audiences, and entities that are influenced to enhance the hospital's competitive position and role in the community.

hospital medical care hotel *See hospital hotel.*

hospital-medical insurance Medical care cost protection that provides benefits toward the cost of paying for any or all health-care services normally covered under various medical and hospital insurance plans.

hospital, municipal *See hospital, city; hospital, city-county.*

hospital, night An acute-care health-care facility that provides personal and nursing care services in the evening and nighttime to patients who are not in need of health care on a 24-hour basis yet who require part-time continuous inpatient care. These individuals cannot live 24 hours a day at home independent of nursing and medical care.

hospital, nondelegated A hospital that has failed to meet the criteria and standards set forth by the Professional Review Organization (PRO). *See also hospital, delegated.*

hospital, nonfederal Government hospitals administered by state or local governments.

hospital, nonprofit (not-for-profit) A hospital that has a legal and Internal Revenue Service tax status as a nonprofit organization, exempting it from paying income taxes and property taxes. To survive, any not-for-profit facility must achieve an overattainment of funds to improve the facilities, purchase new equipment, make additions to the physical plant, give employees raises, etc.; thus excess funds are turned back into the hospital to be used for its improvement and growth. A for-profit hospital, on the other hand, turns a portion of its excess money over to investors, stockholders, or owners as profits and dividends.

hospital nursing care In hospital patient care and nursing administration, this is the management of a 7-day, 24-hour-a-day operation of delivering bedside supervised nursing care to inpatients in acute-care hospitals by registered nurses and licensed vocational nurses or by licensed practical nurses supported by nursing assistants and ward clerks.

hospital, open-staff In hospital administration and medical staff management, this is when no formal management system is in place for restricting or assessing types and kinds of physicians or specialties the hospital needs or wants. If physicians meet the criterion for practice in their specialty areas, they are allowed to admit patients and to practice at the hospital.

hospital, osteopathic An acute-care short-stay medical care facility that is a full-service general or community hospital staffed by osteopathic physicians (DO) who practice the specialized aspects of osteopathic medicine and provide most aspects of allopathic medical care. *See osteopathic medicine; hospital, community; hospital, general.*

hospital, partially delegated A hospital that has been recognized as meeting one or two, but not all three, of the criteria and standards set forth by the Professional Review Organization (PRO). *See also hospital, delegated.*

hospital patient A person receiving hospital-based medical and nursing care and therapeutic and treatment services that the health-care facility and its health-care providers are responsible for. *See also hospital inpatient; inpatient.*

hospital, private Any nongovernmental hospital, either proprietary or nonprofit.

hospital privileges *See staff privilege.*

hospital, proprietary (for-profit) A hospital owned by one individual owner or a group (of physicians or other investors) as a partnership or corporation. Usually such hospitals are used for the care of physicians' own patients or are referred by other physicians who are part owners or stockholders. Profits in this type of hospital are turned over to stockholders or the owners. Under Internal Revenue Service and local tax codes, this type of ownership requires the legal owners to pay income and property taxes.

hospital, psychiatric 1. A long-term-care institution that offers diagnostic and treatment services for patients who have psychiatric-related illness and that provides or arranges for clinical laboratory services; diagnostic X-ray services; psychiatric, psychological, and social work services; and electroencephalograph services. It also makes formal arrangements for transfer to general hospitals as needed for services not available in-house (American Hospital Association). 2. A long-term-care health-care facility that provides a range of services including psychiatric and psychological evaluations, diagnoses, crisis intervention, counseling, and other therapies to patients on either an inpatient or an outpatient basis. *See also community mental health center.*

hospital, publicly owned A corporate-owned hospital that holds out to the public the opportunity to own shares in the hospital. *See hospital, investor-owned.*

hospital record Referred to as a medical record or chart, this is written documentation of all health-care services, treatments, procedures, or activities provided to a person on an inpatient or outpatient basis. For inpatients, this is a detailed written account of the activities of the stay in the health-care facility from the time of admission to the time of discharge. The document identifies dates, medical or nursing unit, physical location of the patient, names of health-care providers, progress of care, principal diagnoses, secondary diagnoses and procedures, medications, therapies, treatments, behavioral observations, etc.

hospital, registered A hospital that is recognized by the American Hospital Association as having the essential specific characteristics of a hospital (American Hospital Association). *See hospital; hospital, general.*

hospital, rehabilitation A long-term-care healthcare facility that uses medical, physical therapy, psychiatric/psychological, occupational therapy, social, educational, and vocational measures to assist patients on an inpatient basis in the recovery from serious injury or illness. *See also rehabilitation facility.*

hospital, rehabilitation and chronic disease A long-term-care institution that provides diagnostic and treatment services to handicapped and disabled individuals requiring restorative and adjustive services. This facility also provides or arranges for diagnostic X-ray services, clinical laboratory services, operating room services, physical therapy, occupational therapy, psychological and social work services, and educational and vocational services. It also makes formal arrangements for transfer to general hospitals as needed for services not available in-house (American Hospital Association).

hospital, satellite A secondary health-care facility that is supportive of or complimentary to a central hospital or facility and that provides health services close to the workplace or home; a branch of the main hospital.

hospital satellite network In continuing education for nurses and continuing medical education, this is a television network system serving all hospitals that subscribe to the system, providing continuing education programming, informational services, and specialized reports.

hospital, self-insured A hospital that has enough money in savings or a reserve of funds that it is not required to purchase insurance. Under such circumstances, a hospital develops a special fund to cover any liability or lawsuit that might arise. Another approach sets aside a fund up to a certain amount, and then the hospital purchases liability insurance to cover lawsuits over that amount. For example, $1 million is kept in the liability fund, and insurance is secured for any lawsuits exceeding $1 million.

hospital service charge The price per day for inpatient care in an acute-care facility, usually including hotel services, food services, nursing care, operating room and materials, overhead, administration, diagnostic and therapy services, and any services used by the patient, including all ancillary charges such as lab tests and X rays.

hospital, short-stay Acute-care facilities that have the average length of stay of less than 30 days and in which the type of services provided are general; maternity; eye, ear, nose, and throat; children's or osteopathic; and medical and nursing care.

hospital, short-term Acute-care facilities in which more than half the patients are admitted to units with an average length of stay of less than 30 days. *See short-term hospital; hospital, acute-care.*

hospital, sole community *See sole community hospital.*

hospital, special An acute-care facility that has the primary function of providing diagnostic and treatment services for patients who have specified medical conditions, both surgical and nonsurgical, or who have specific diseases or are from special populations such as children. Also provided are diagnostic and treatment services for specified medical conditions for which medical services are provided, and these services must be maintained in the institution with suitable facilities and staff. If such conditions do not normally require diagnostic X-ray, laboratory, or operating room services, and if any such services are not maintained in the institution, written arrangements are made to make such services available to patients requiring them (American Hospital Association).

hospital, specialty Inpatient medical care facilities such as psychiatric, tuberculosis, chronic disease, rehabilitation, maternity, and substance abuse and alcohol facilities that provide a particular type of care or services to a majority of the admitted patients.

hospital-sponsored ambulatory care services According to JCAHO for accreditation purposes, this is the delivery of care pertaining to nonemergency, adult, adolescent, and pediatric ambulatory encounters, whether performed through the clinical departments of the hospital or an organized ambulatory program, regardless of the physical location of such services (within the hospital, on its campus, or at off-campus satellite facilities). Hospital-sponsored ambulatory care services are provided by one or more organizational units (or components thereof) of the hospital under the responsibility of the governing body; they do not include individual diagnostic studies performed by the hospital as a service or services provided by practitioners in their office through written agreement. Standards are applied to evaluate a hospital's performance in providing ambulatory care services. *See also ambulatory care; ambulatory setting.*

hospital, state A term commonly used to refer to mental hospitals, as most all mental hospitals in the past were administered by state government. More correctly, this describes any hospital operated by state government but excludes state-funded state university medical school teaching hospitals. Most state hospitals are specialty hospitals (e.g., psychiatric, developmental disabilities, or children's).

hospital statistics 1. Data and information about the functioning, and operational effectiveness, of a hospital. 2. Data from hospital medical records and patient care information that assist administrators in the management of the hospital. 3. The title of an annual publication of the American Hospital Association, presenting information and data about hospitals in the United States.

hospital, teaching *See teaching hospital.*

hospital types The American Hospital Association designates five major type of hospitals: general, special, rehabilitation, chronic disease, and osteopathic. *See hospital, general; hospital, special; hospital, rehabilitation; hospital, chronic disease; hospital, osteopathic.*

hospital, university A hospital that is affiliated with or owned by a university medical school for teaching purposes and the education and training of physicians.

hospital, voluntary A nongovernmental health-care facility established by a community, church, religious order, or other nonprofit group that is autonomous from any other health-care organization and is self-sufficient. *See also community hospital; hospital, nonprofit.*

host 1. In epidemiology, this is any live organism such as a human or an animal that provides harborage, nutrients, and subsistence for another organism, usually a pathogen, such as a parasite or an infectious agent such as a bacteria or virus; an individual who harbors a disease. 2. As used in epidemiology, this is one dimension of the epidemiology triangle. *See epidemiology triangle.*

host, definitive *See host, primary.*

hostile fire In health and safety of health-care facilities, any fire that occurs outside its normal confines.

hostile witness In health law, this a person who observed an act who has an obvious prejudice and hostility toward the party who identified him or her. *See also adverse witness.*

host, intermediate *See host, secondary.*

host plan A term used by some managed-care plans to identify the health plan in the geographical area where services are provided to a subscriber who is a member of another managed-care plan.

host, primary In epidemiology and infection control, this is an organism in which a parasite finds harborage and attains maturity or passes through its developmental or sexual stages. Also referred to as a "definitive host."

host, secondary In epidemiology and infection control, this is an organism in which a parasite finds harborage and is in its larval or asexual stage. Also referred to as an "intermediate host."

hot and cold applications In medical care and therapy, this is any hot or cold packs that are applied to an area of a patient's body to cause a change in temperature in the tissue for a therapeutic purpose.

hot cargo clause In health-care labor relations, this is used in a contract between an employer and a union stating that the employer will not allow anyone to handle materials manufactured or transferred by an organization or body with whom there is a labor dispute.

hotel hospital *See medical hotel/hospital; hospital hotel.*

hotline A crisis telephone service used to provide assistance for people in distress or need of help (e.g., suicide prevention) and staffed by trained laypeople and by professionals in advisory or back-up roles. Most hotlines operate 24 hours a day, 7 days a week. Also called a "crisis line."

hot-stove rule In health administration and human resource management, this is a behavior modification notion held by some regarding how to deal with discipline problems. It requires that any disciplinary action have the same type of result as a person would get by touching a hot stove. Discipline should be with warning and be immediate, consistent, and impersonal.

housebreaking Breaking in to and entering a hospital, health-care facility, or other building or house to commit a crime; it is called "burglary" if done after dark.

housecall A visit by a physician or other health-care provider to a patient's home.

household A group of related people or family living together. *See family; family health.*

household survey (household interview survey) In health services or epidemiology research, this is the process of collecting data and information from a household chosen by an acceptable research sampling process. Interviewers visit the household and give a survey to an individual, the family, or those present in the dwelling. In some cases trained interviewers also record observations made while at the dwelling.

household work A support service offered to the disabled or handicapped that provides assistance in the performance of activities related to routine household maintenance and related activities.

housekeeping An ancillary department in a health-care facility that provides custodial and related support services and is responsible for cleaning, changing linen, trash disposal, etc.

housekeeping aide An individual who cleans and does custodial services in the physical plant of a health-care facility and works under the direction of the housekeeping supervisor.

housekeeping director The individual who is responsible for the coordination, monitoring, and day-to-day administration of a health-care facility's housekeeping program while ensuring that the housekeeping activities meet quality standards and predetermined work procedures and criteria.

housekeeping services In health-care facilities, this includes maintenance and custodial services necessary to maintain a safe and clean environment. Services provided include changing linen on beds and cleaning equipment, patient rooms, restrooms, nursing units, treatment and therapy areas, administrative and public areas, and the general internal and external areas of the hospital or nursing home's physical plant to ensure a high level of cleanliness, sanitation, and safety and the effective functioning and attractiveness of the facility.

housekeeping supervisor A midmanagement employee in the housekeeping department of a health-care facility who ensures that the daily housekeeping duties and activities in the facility are carried out.

house officer A medical, osteopathic, or dental school graduate who is an intern, a resident, or a fellow in a program of clinical training, service, and research in a health-care facility or hospital.

house order Policies, procedures, and rules passed by the medical staff that require (or in some cases prohibit) the performance of certain tests and/or procedures on all patients admitted to the hospital. Also referred to as a "standing order."

house organ In a hospital or other health-care organization, this is a newsletter, bulletin, or magazine directed at employees and published internally by the organization.

housestaff 1. Generally, the physician staff in training at a hospital, principally comprised of the hospital's interns, residents, and fellows. Members of the housestaff are called "house officers"; occasionally applies also to physicians salaried by a hospital who are not receiving any graduate medical education. 2. According to JCAHO for hospital accreditation purposes, individuals (licensed as appropriate) who are graduates of medical, dental, osteopathic, or podiatry schools who are appointed to a hospital professional graduate training program that is approved by a nationally recognized accrediting body approved by the Commissioner of Education. These individuals participate in patient care under the direction of licensed practitioners of the pertinent clinical disciplines who have clinical privileges in the hospital and are members of, or affiliated with, the medical staff.

Hoyer lift A portable and movable lift that utilizes a sling to lift handicapped or aged persons into and out of bathtubs or whirlpools.

HPPC Health Plan Purchasing Cooperative. *See health alliance.*

HR House of Representatives.

HRA Health Resources Administration; Health Record Analyst.

HRG Health research group.

HRSA Health Resources and Services Administration.

HSA *See health systems agency.*

HSP *See health systems plan.*

HSQB Health Standards Quality Bureau; a division of the U.S. Department of Health and Human Services, Health Care Financing Administration.

HSR&D *Health Services Research and Development Service.*

HSWA *See Hazardous and Solid Waste Amendments.*

HUD U.S. Department of Housing and Urban Development; the U.S. cabinet-level department that coordinates federal housing and land use policy and funds housing construction through a variety of programs.

human capital The stock of knowledge, abilities, and skills held by individuals that enables the flow of health services produced by trained individual health professionals.

human environment A comprehensive approach to all natural and physical aspects of ecological living and the relationship of people with ecological factors, including all economic or social effects. When an environmental impact statement is prepared and economic or social and natural or physical environmental effects are interrelated, then the environmental impact statement will discuss all these effects on the human environment.

human factors The biomedical, psychological, and workplace environment and engineering consideration pertaining to people in human-to-machine systems. Some of these considerations are the allocation of functions, task analysis, human reliability, training requirements, job performance aiding, personnel qualification and selection, staffing requirements, procedures, organizational effectiveness, and workplace environmental conditions.

human immunodeficiency virus (HIV) The virus that causes AIDS (acquired immunodeficiency syndrome).

humanism The interest a person has in, or one's devotion to, human welfare.

humanistic Being sensitive to a person's health, social, mental, emotional, spiritual, cultural, and economic needs by treating that person with fairness, kindness, and understanding while viewing that person as good, capable, worthwhile, and positive.

humanistic medicine A medical practice perspective that respects and incorporates the concept that the patient is more than his or her disease and that the professional health-care provider is more than a scientifically trained mind using technical skills. Both health-care provider and patient are whole human beings interacting in the healing process and effort. A person is more than his or her body; a person is unique and has an interdependent relationship of body, mind, emotions, culture, and spirit. The professional seeks to assist the patient in taking and fulfilling self-responsibility. Health and disease are not matters of the moment but have an intricate past, present, and future. Physical disease, pain, suffering, aging, and even death can frequently be valuable, meaningful events in an individual's life, and effective practice requires not just conventional skills but also effective development and use of human qualities such as intuition, inventiveness, and empathy; a wholistic view that considers the emotional and spiritual aspects and is not focused only on the physical body and its physiological processes. *See wholistic health.*

humanistic psychology A somewhat recent development in the field of psychology, this is a combination of existential, cognitive, and traditional psychology. Humanistic psychology believes that the individual is basically good, is capable of healing oneself, and is worthwhile. It stresses the positive aspects of life and personal growth while maximizing one's abilities, self-worth, self-responsibility, and capacity for choice.

human resources In health administration, these are professional employees, skilled, semiskilled, and unskilled workers who are ready, willing, and able to use their time, effort, and skills and to practice their profession for, work for, and contribute to the mission and goals of the health-care organization.

human resources committee In health administration, these are interdepartmental committees that develop company policies, rules, and procedures pertaining to the hiring, training, retention, promotion, advancement, and dismissal of the health-care organization's employees. This group reviews and makes recommendations on compensation plans, salary scales, benefits, and retirement programs.

human resources department In health administration, this is the administrative unit responsible for all matters related to the company's employees. The department director and its employees formulate policy with respect to hiring, training, and dismissal of workers; follow guidelines on compensation, recruitment, hiring practices, and performance reviews; and ensures compliance with federal and state employment regulations and law. The employees of this department administer employee benefit plans such as medical insurance, life insurance, retirement plans, training and tuition refund plans, and other benefits. Also called the "personnel department."

human resources developer An individual responsible for staff development, in-service education, continuing education, orientation, and related work development activities. *See also education director.*

human resources development The process of increasing knowledge, skills, abilities, and capacities and of training all employees in a health-care organization.

human resources director The individual who is usually responsible for all personnel activities including recruitment, interviewing, and payroll. In some facilities, staff development and education fall under this department. Synonymous with "director of personnel."

human resources forecasts In health administration and personnel management, this is management's prediction of the hospital's or health-care organization's future need or demand for employees in professional, skilled, and unskilled areas. *See human resources planning.*

human resources planning In health administration, this is the process of determining the number of professional, skilled, semiskilled, and unskilled personnel needed to maintain efficient operation of the health-care organization now and in the future. Primarily two broad functions are done: forecasting the company's need for qualified workers and determining the number of qualified personnel who are now available or will be needed in the future to fill anticipated positions.

human resources system In health administration, this is the part of a health-care organization that recruits and supports the organization's employees, volunteers, and physicians.

human services/mental health technologist A health-care professional with a minimum education at the associate degree level; employs skills as a generalist on the basis of knowledge of human behavior and social and emotional problems in settings providing mental health and social rehabilitation services; employs a holistic, noncustodial approach to the individual, treating the symptomatic and causative elements that affect the individual's ability to respond to his or her environment. Also referred to as a "psych-tech." *See psychiatric technician.*

human subject research According to JCAHO for psychiatric, alcoholism, and drug abuse facilities accreditation purposes, the use of patients receiving services in the systematic study, observation, or evaluation of factors related to the prevention, assessment, treatment, and understanding of an illness. This involves all behavioral and medical experimental research that involves human beings as experimental subjects.

hung jury In the litigation and trial-by-jury process, this is the inability of a jury to reach a verdict, or decision.

husband abuse *See spousal abuse.*

hydrocollater A health-care therapy and treatment assistance device and process consisting of a wax bath that keeps wax only hot enough to be a liquid. It provides heat to the wax at a temperature that helps bodily tissue heal or relieves pain but does not burn a hand or other body part on immersion. The hot wax provides a lasting, penetrating heat to the body part and provides therapeutic results, especially for persons suffering arthritis in the joints of the hands or feet.

hygiene The care, upkeep, and maintenance of one's physical body and person; personal health. An antiquated term for the science of health and its preservation, it now refers more to the maintenance aspects of personal health.

hygiene factors In health administration and organizational behavior theory, these are administrative or managerial elements or activities needed to provide maintenance and stability to an organization. The term "hygiene," meaning "maintenance to the body," is applied to organizations. The concept, developed by Frederick Herzberg, Ph.D. (an international management consultant), is based on the notion that many managers use maintenance factors to try to motivate employees, which then cause job dissatisfaction. Motivation is caused or allowed by motivation factors, not hygiene factors. The hygiene factors identified by Herzberg are status, job security, pay/salary, company policies, relationships with the supervisor, working conditions, fringe benefits, and interpersonal relations. *See motivation.*

hyper- Prefix meaning "above" or "up."

hyperactivity Increased muscular activity; a disturbance found in children that is manifested by constant restlessness and rapid movements.

hyperalgesia Unusual sensitivity to pain.

hyperalimentation The long-term administration of nutrients intravenously to patients.

hyperbaric chamber A specialized treatment room designed to house and provide to patients air consisting of pure oxygen and compressed air. The compressed air is introduced into the sealed chamber to raise the atmospheric pressure several times above normal, and the patient is given pure oxygen.

hyperendemic In epidemiology and public health, this is when a disease is constantly present at a high level of prevalence and equally affects all persons in a population, community, or institution.

hyperkinesis *See hyperactivity.*

hyperorexia Extreme hunger.

hyperpragia Excessive thinking, self-talk, and mental activity. It is often a part of the manic phase of manic-depressive illness.

hypersensitivity An acute response by the body to a foreign substance, drug, food, etc.

hypertension Persistently high arterial blood pressure. It may have no known cause, or it can be associated with other diseases, intake of certain drugs, salt, being overweight, lack of fitness, and stress.

hypnosis Using techniques of suggestibility to alter the consciousness of another. The subject responds with a high degree of suggestibility, both mental and physical, during the trancelike state.

hypnotic A drug used for the sole purpose of producing sleep.

hypo- Prefix meaning "below" or "under."

hypothesis A supposition used to explain phenomena; a theory, an assumption, or a calculated guess; a research question; the projected results of a research study.

hypothetical question In epidemiology or health law, this is combining a group of facts in such a manner as to create a logical situation or question that has not been shown to be true. In health law situations, hypothetical questions are often asked of expert witnesses to elicit an opinion based on facts that the expert does not personally know but that the examining attorney hopes to prove.

I

IADL *See Instrumental Activities of Daily Living Scale.*

iatro- Prefix meaning "physician" or "physician caused."

iatrogenesis A secondary illness, injury, infection, or disease produced inadvertently as a result of treatment by a physician or other healthcare provider for some other disorder or illness.

iatrogenic Resulting from the activity of a physician; physician produced. Originally applied to disorders induced in the patient by autosuggestion based on the physician's examination, manner, or discussion, it is now applied to any condition in a patient occurring as a result of treatment by a physician or surgeon such as a drug reaction or secondary infection.

iatrogenic illness Any illness or condition that was unintentional, precipitated, or secondarily induced by a health-care procedure or treatment. Also referred to as "iatrogenic disease."

ibid. (Lat.) From the same place.

IBNR *See incurred but not reported.*

IC *See infection control.*

ICCS *See International Classification of Clinical Services.*

ICD International Classification of Diseases.

ICDA *See International Classification of Diseases, Adapted for Use in the United States.*

ICDA-8 *International Classification of Diseases, Adapted for Use in the United States, 8th Revision;* in use from 1968 to 1979 and, for the first time, provided for the coding of hospital, diagnostic, and morbidity data.

ICD-9 *International Classification of Diseases, 9th Revision;* published by the World Health Organization and used by state health departments and the U.S. Public Health Service in coding causes of death and preparing mortality data and statistics.

ICD-9 Classification of Procedures in Medicine The former classification system used to code procedures used in medicine; replaced by the *ICD-9-CM Procedures Manual.*

ICD-9-CM *See International Classification of Diseases, 9th Revision, Clinical Modification.*

ICD-9-CM Diseases Alphabetical Index Volume 2 of the ICD-9-CM manuals containing many diagnostic terms that do not appear in the first volume plus an index to diseases and injuries, a table of drugs and chemicals, an index to external causes of injuries and poisoning, and a table of neoplasms.

ICD-9-CM Procedures Volume 3 of the ICD-9-CM set of manuals. In the past, surgical procedures were not a part of the ICD. This volume, containing surgical, investigative, and therapeutic procedures, is published separately from the ICD-9-CM manual. This part of the system is a modification of WHO's *Fascicle V,* "Surgical Procedures," which has been in use since 1962. For coding purposes it uses a numerical two-digit number plus a decimal system, whereas the ICD-9-CM system uses a three-digit number plus a one- or two-decimal system.

ICD-10-CM *International Classification of Diseases, 10th Revision, Clinical Modification.*

iceberg phenomenon In epidemiology and public health, this is the disease level existing in a community or population that has avoided detection by diagnostic efforts and disease surveillance activities, so a portion remains out of view of public health professionals, yet the disease continues within the population; the portion of the disease that is under the surface, outside of detection, and often not attended to medically, not accurately diagnosed, or, if detected, not reported. The limited number of cases of diagnosed and reported disease would be the tip of the iceberg observed above the surface of the water.

ICF *See intermediate care facility.*

ICF/MR *See intermediate care facility for the mentally retarded.*

ICHPPC International Classification of Health Problems in Primary Care.

ICIDH International Classification of Impairments, Disabilities and Handicaps. *See impairment.*

ICP *See interdisciplinary care plan.*

ICP-MA *See inductive coupled plasma-mass spectrometer.*

ICRC Infant care review committee.

ICS *See Incident Command System.*

ICT *See insulin coma therapy.*

ICU *See intensive care unit.*

id In psychiatry, according to psychoanalytic theory, this is the unconscious part of the person that controls primitive desires and urges.

idealization In mental health, this is a mental mechanism where self-confidence is carried to an unrealistic level. One is blind to one's own faults, mistakes, and shortcomings and may wrongly see another person as being perfect.

ideational shield In mental health, this is an intellectual and rational defense against anxiety that could be caused by being subjected to criticism and rejection.

idee fixe In psychiatry/psychology, this is a recurring idea associated with obsessional states.

idem (Lat.) Exactly alike or the same.

identifiable medical services In managed care and health insurance, these are services that are provided prior to or during a surgical procedure or in the postoperative period (e.g., diabetic management, operative monitoring of cardiac or brain conditions, management of postoperative electrolyte imbalance, prolonged patient or family counseling, and psychological support).

identification In mental health, this is a mental mechanism that is a form of hero worship; to feel, act, and wish to be another person or like them; identifying with and having excessive admiration for someone who is looked up to.

identification card In managed care, this is a card issued by a health plan or health maintenance organization to each enrollee, identifying the person as being eligible to receive coverage for services. Also referred to as a "health card." *See health card.*

identification number 1. In managed care or insurance, this is a subscriber's six- or nine-digit number used on the medical record and to verify membership. Also called the "agreement number." A national identification card and number have been proposed for all U.S. citizens for the purpose of accessing health-care services. 2. An unduplicated number given to each person, such as a Social Security number. *See health card.*

identification with the aggressor In psychology/psychiatry and mental health, this is when a person creates, dwells on, and incorporates within him- or herself the behaviors of a person from the outside world who is a source of anger and frustration.

identity crisis In psychology/psychiatry and mental health, this is a loss of the sense of one's self and an inability to accept the role expected by society; characterized by isolation, withdrawal, extremism, rebelliousness, and negativism.

idiopathic 1. Without known cause. 2. Disease that originates in itself.

idiosyncratic effect 1. In medical care, an unusual and unexpected effect from a medication where abnormal and unpredictable symptoms occur. 2. In health administration, this is any unusual approach to management or human behavior in the workplace.

idiot In psychology/psychiatry and mental health services, this is an obsolete term formerly used to distinguish a level or degree of mental retardation in a retarded individual; a former classification of mental deficiency used to describe a person with an IQ of less than 25; a person mentally equal to a child less than 2 years of age; the lowest classification of mental retardation below moron and imbecile. *See imbecile; moron; mental retardation.*

idiot-savant A retarded person able to perform mental feats unusual for his or her capability such as solving complicated puzzles or calculations or playing the piano.

i.e. (Lat.) Id est. That is.

IEMT Intermediate emergency medical technician. *See EMT-1; emergency medical technician.*

ignominy Dishonor; public disgrace.

ignorantia legis non excusat (Lat.) Ignorance of the law is no excuse.

IHCA *See individual health-care account.*

IHS *See Indian Health Service.*

IIPP Injury and illness prevention program.

illegal Against the law; contrary to the law; illicit.

illegitimate 1. Not logical; an incorrect deduction. 2. Not having any legal authorization. 3. Bastard; a child born to parents who are not legally married. 4. Actions that are against the law; unlawful; contrary to law. 5. Actions not in keeping with accepted behavior or use.

illicit Unauthorized, unlawful; against; prohibited, illegal; not allowed by law.

illness Abnormal signs, symptoms, or conditions in the human body; the loss of vigor or energy; weakness; malfunction of normal body processes caused by a pathogen, agent, physical exposure, chemical, or other factors; physically feeling incapable of carrying on life's daily activities; the opposite of total well-being or optimum health usually used synonymously with "disease"; is present when an individual perceives him- or herself as not feeling healthy and disease is present, as identified by objective criteria such as signs, symptoms, clinical testing, and identification of a pathogen or disease-causing agent through laboratory tests; being sick or diseased.

illness behavior 1. Any activity undertaken by a person who experiences the signs and symptoms of disease, including self-care and treatment, seeking folk remedies, or definitive allopathic care; the response taken by a sick person to obtain a diagnosis and a determination of one's health status by a health-care provider to discover and obtain a suitable remedy, therapy, or treatment. 2. The sick role or sick role behavior, which means the patient is freed from normal social or work obligations and will assume behaviors to try to get well and to seek and cooperate with health-care providers to recover. Some individuals adapt sick role behavior to get sympathy, avoid work or school, or get out of obligations, as the sick role is one acceptable social behavior that allows one to be excused from responsibilities. *See health behavior; malingering; sick role.*

illness perils In managed care and medical insurance, this is used by underwriters to evaluate the type and degree of peril represented by a particular lifestyle or occupation. In some occupations workers are exposed to dust, poisons, extreme temperatures, dampness, etc., which affect and increase the risk of illness occurring. *See perils.*

illuminism A hallucination in which the patient carries on conversations with imaginary supernatural creatures.

illusion Any false mental picture; unreal perception and misinterpretation of an occurrence.

illusory Deceptive; having false appearances.

illusory promise In health law, this is an agreement having the appearance of a promise or contract and is contingent on the intent of the promisor. Usually this is not a contract and is not legally binding.

imaging In medical care and the diagnosis and assessment aspects of health-care delivery, this is a general term used to identify the process of making pictures of the internal parts of the body for diagnosis and evaluation purposes. This is also the title of the department in a hospital that does X rays, computed tomography (CT) scans, magnetic resonance imaging (MRI), ultrasound, and positron emission tomography (PET) and single photon emission tomography (SPET) scans. Also referred to as "radiology" in some hospitals or clinics, but the more modern title is "medical imaging department."

imbecile In psychology/psychiatry and mental health, this is an obsolete term used to distinguish a level or degree of mental retardation in a retarded individual; a former classification of mental deficiency used to describe a person with an IQ ranging from 25 to 50; a person mentally equal to a child between the ages of 3 and 8; the middle classification of mental retardation between moron and idiot. *See idiot; moron; mental retardation.*

IMC *See indigent medical care.*

imitation Following, mimicking, or copying the behaviors, activities, and values of another person, product, or organization. In health administration, this is referred to as a "me-too product."

immediate cause 1. In health law, this is the final cause or event that resulted in injury, harm, or danger without any further related events. 2. As used in occupational health and safety, these are practices or conditions that physically cause an accident or incident at a specific time and place. *See also proximate cause.*

immediate (acute) health hazards In environmental health and occupational health and safety, this includes "highly toxic," "toxic," "irritant," "sensitizer," and "corrosive" and other hazardous chemicals that cause an adverse effect to a target bodily organ. The effect generally occurs rapidly as a result of short-term exposure and is of short duration.

immediate issue A child or children.

immediately dangerous to life and health In environmental health and occupational health and safety, this is the maximum level to which a healthy individual can be exposed to a chemical for 30 minutes and escape without suffering irreversible health effects or impairing symptoms; used as a level of concern.

immediately dangerous to life and health values In environmental health and occupational health and safety, this is a condition that either poses an immediate threat to life and health or is a threat of severe exposure to contaminants such as radioactive materials, which may have an adverse delayed effect on health.

immediate pending question In formal health-care meetings or hearings using parliamentary procedures, when several "questions" are pending before the assembly and the assembly must deal with the most recently proposed question first and make a decision on the one presented last, which is the immediate pending question.

immigration and naturalization records Hospitals, medical groups, nursing homes, and other health-care organizations that serve as employers are required to maintain records that show that an alien has legally entered the United

States or has become a citizen as set forth by the Department of State and the Department of the Interior.

Immigration Reform and Control Act of 1986 Hospitals, medical groups, nursing homes, and other health-care organizations that serve as employers are required to screen potential employees for unauthorized aliens. Employment verification systems, recordkeeping, and a good-faith effort must be demonstrated to show compliance with this law.

imminent Impending, likely to occur without delay; about to happen, threatening to occur.

imminent and substantial endangerment As used in environmental health, this is a qualifying condition given to any solid or hazardous waste that, when applied, allows the EPA to take necessary actions to protect the health of the public and the environment. This action may include but is not limited to restraining any person from handling, storage, treatment, transportation, or disposal of solid or hazardous wastes that meet this condition. This test for imminent and substantial endangerment places a heavy burden of proof on the EPA and limits the EPA's authority to address disposal site problems.

imminent danger 1. In occupational health and safety and risk management activities in hospitals, nursing homes, or other health-care facilities, this is a situation that is likely to lead to death or serious injury if allowed to continue. 2. In environmental health and occupational health and safety, this is any condition or practice that is such that a hazard exists that could reasonably be expected to cause death or serious physical harm to employees (permanent or prolonged impairment of the body or temporary disablement requiring hospitalization) unless immediate actions are taken to mitigate the effects of the hazard and/or remove employees from the hazard.

imminent hazard In environmental health and occupational health and safety, these are situations that exist when the continued use of a pesticide during the time required for cancellation proceeding would be likely to result in unreasonable adverse effects on the environment or will involve unreasonable hazard to the survival of a species declared endangered or threatened.

immobility Restricted movement of a patient; a patient unable to move about or walk.

immobilization 1. The rendering of a limb, injured part of the body, or the total body immobile by applying a splint, cast, or weights. 2. Strapping down or securing a patient to a stretcher or ambulance bed for transportation to a hospital, nursing home, or other health-care facility. 3. Restraint or restriction of a hostile or violent person through physical devices or drugs. *See restraints.*

immunity 1. Freedom from obligation; exempt from duty; freedom from duty as required by law. 2. In health law, this is freedom from prosecution on items about which testimony has been given. 3. Resistance to or protection from a disease. 4. When government boards or agencies are exempt from duties generally required of others.

immunity, acquired In epidemiology, this is a level of resistance to certain disease-causing pathogens in a host caused by being exposed to a mild case of the naturally occurring pathogen, which stimulates the immune system to recognize and fight off the disease should it occur.

immunity, active In epidemiology, this is a level of resistance to certain disease-causing pathogens in a host caused by being exposed to a stimulus by an antigen such as a vaccine or other agent, which causes the host to create an antibody against that pathogen.

immunity, natural In epidemiology, this is the resistance to certain disease-causing pathogens in a host caused by being born with the natural resistance or its being inherent in certain species.

immunity, passive In epidemiology, this is a level of resistance to certain disease-causing pathogens in a host caused by a vaccine developed in another host and then given to individuals to create immunity. Babies can also obtain immunity from their mothers or by the administration of artificially developed antibody-containing serums or immune globulin.

immunity, specific In epidemiology, this is a level of resistance to specific disease-causing pathogens in a host caused by the host responding to a specific vaccine or a natural infection of certain specific diseases.

immunization In epidemiology, medical care, and public health, this is the process by which a person becomes resistant or immune to a pathogenic organism or harmful agent through protection acquired by the administration of a vaccine, a live but weakened strain, a killed strain of the disease, a closely associated disease, or an inactivated toxin.

immuno- Prefix meaning "safe."

immunology A medical specialty that studies the process and function of the body's resistance to disease, how it produces protection from microorganisms, and the body's sensitivity to diseases and allergies.

immunosuppressent drugs Pharmaceutical preparations given to a patient to control the immune system to keep it from damaging a transplanted organ or from causing damage to normal tissue in an autoimmune disease.

IMO *See integrated multiple option.*

impact In health-care delivery or administration, this is the observable result or effect of an administrative decision or the effectiveness of a service or program; effects and observations on planning, implementation, and management activities and how well they lead to meeting the objectives and outcomes of the service.

impacted stool *See impaction; fecal impaction.*

impact evaluation In health promotion and health-care delivery activities, this is the assessment of the effects of programs on the intermediate objectives and the changes observed on the predisposing, enabling, and reinforcing factors as well as behavioral and environmental changes. Behavioral outcomes and program quality are also assessed.

impaction A condition often found in some older long-term-care patients of mostly dry, hardened, and lodged feces in the rectum. Also referred to as "impacted stool" or "fecal impaction." *See fecal impaction.*

impact objectives In health promotion and health-care delivery activities, this is the assessment of outcomes expected in a service or project as determined by the level of participation and the effect the program had on the participants.

impair To diminish in acceptance or quality; to hinder; to lessen one's power; to make worse, lessen, or otherwise limit.

impaired Any condition that limits professionals from functioning effectively and safely in their profession such as being under the influence of alcohol or drugs. Physical handicaps, mental and emotional illness, or behavioral problems can also limit the ability to function in a profession.

impaired physician A medical doctor who is not capable of safely and adequately performing required duties because of alcohol or drug addiction or some other physical or mental limitation, disease, or disorder.

impairment 1. Any loss or abnormality of psychological, physiological, or anatomical structure or function (International Classification of Impairments, Disabilities and Handicaps [ICIDH]); dysfunctional behavior; a physical or mental abnormality that can be identified and diagnosed. 2. A chronic or permanent defect, usually static in nature, resulting from a disease, disorder, injury, or congenital malformation. It represents a disease in the sense organs or musculoskeletal system and/or the loss of ability to perform various functions. 3. According to the ICIDH, two types of impairments are listed: 1) disability: a restriction in the ability to perform essential components of everyday living such as personal hygiene or moving about and 2) handicap: a limitation on the fulfillment of a role that is normal for that individual and is a consequence of a disability, which is a consequence of an impairment. Impairments do not necessarily lead to disabilities, nor do disabilities necessarily lead to handicaps and are not necessarily permanent. *See handicapped; disability; activities of daily living.*

impairment rider In managed care and insurance, this is an attachment to a medical insurance policy or health plan that limits coverage or excludes coverage for certain handicaps or disabilities. *See impairment.*

impanel The selection and retaining of jurors for a trial.

impeach 1. To remove a public official from office for misconduct 2. To establish the untruthfulness of a witness and cause that witness to lose credibility.

impeachment The removal of an official from public office such as a governor, judge, or president.

impediment 1. A disability. 2. A restriction to making a legal contract.

impertinence 1. Irrelevant. 2. Not pertinent to the trial or issue at hand. 3. Without relationship to the matter. 4. Proof or evidence presented that is not relevant to the issue.

implant In the process of patient care, this is to surgically attach or replace an organ of the body with a substitute organ, tissue, or mechanical or electronic device; mainly refers to surgically placing devices in the body to aid in its functioning.

implead In law, this is to bring a third party into a lawsuit; to accuse; to bring suit; to sue at law.

implementation 1. In health planning, healthcare delivery, or health promotion, this is the act of converting planning, goals, and objectives into action through administrative structure, management activities, policies, procedures, regulations, and organizational actions of new programs or health services. 2. In environmental health and occupational health and safety, the *Management Oversight and Risk Tree* is used to analyze whether the overall program should represent the intended fulfillment of a policy statement. If problems are encountered in carrying out a policy, the concerns are relayed back to the policymakers. The process should be a continuous, balanced effort designed to correct systemic failures and generally should be proactive rather than reactive. A program implementation process can include management and personnel responsibilities, information flow, directives, budgeting, delays, accountability, and all management activities necessary for its success.

implementation plan 1. The organized and purposeful administrative actions necessary to bring goals and objectives into action, resulting in a health service or program being established and brought to full successful operation. The process by which a health-care organization, health service, or other health agency accomplishes the recommendations in its plan. Plan implementation utilizes a combination of methods including advocacy, financial assistance, personnel, technical assistance to providers, administrative structure, controls, and feedback. 2. In environmental health and occupational health and safety, this is a concise description of the approach, resources, and time period planned for implementing orders that require such plans on a site-wide basis. The plan includes a description of the execution of environmental protection, safety, and health responsibilities and authorities by the filed organization and proposed generic exemptions. 3. In environmental health, this is a written record of the results of the scoping process and outline of the procedures by which an environmental impact statement is prepared on the basis of governmental guidelines.

implicit In health services delivery, epidemiology, and public health, this refers to issues, factors, or constructs that are built into or are a natural part of an event or outcome, even if not clearly stated.

implied 1. Suggested, expected, or understood but not actually expressed. 2. Known indirectly; assumed to be known. 3. Obvious because of the facts.

implied consent In health law, this is the process of proceeding to treat someone, assuming that consent to do so would be forthcoming, usually in an emergency with a minor patient or an unconscious person who has not provided written or orally agreed-on consent for the treatment. Consent is derived by acts, signs, behaviors, facts, inaction, or silence or any action that causes the health-care provider to assume that consent would be or has been given or, if they could give consent, that they would give express written consent under the circumstances. Implied consent relies on the inference by a patient's actions or the medical circumstances that consent is granted for medical care or treatment about to transpire even without explicit oral or written consent. It is assumed that the average, usual, ordinary person under the same or similar medical circumstance or emergency situation would give consent to treatment, surgery, or the needed medical procedure. Physicians often rely on implied consent in emergency situations or with unconscious persons. *See also informed consent; express consent.*

implied contract In contract law, this is a contract not created by an expressed or written agreement but one that may legally be deduced from assumptions, actions, circumstances of a transaction, and/or the relationship of the parties.

implied remedy A lawsuit brought to protect a constitutional right. A right being violated shows that a remedy through a lawsuit is justified.

implied trust A trust that is inferred from circumstances rather than expressed in writing.

implied warranty A legal inference of quality when something is sold by a merchant.

imposed consent In health law, this is an involuntary submission to treatment as authorized by law. Some public health statutes allow the state to require that children be inoculated or immunized against specific diseases prior to being allowed to enter school; thus consent is not an issue. Adults may also be required to have certain vaccinations prior to embarking on foreign travel or returning to the United States. In some states, teachers must be immunized against certain diseases such as tuberculosis prior to being allowed in the classroom.

imposibilium nulla obligatio est (Lat.) There is no obligation to do the impossible.

impossibility of contract completion *See impossible.*

impossible 1. Not capable of happening or being completed. 2. That which cannot be finished. 3. A contract is not binding and is an impossibility if it objectively cannot possibly be completed.

imposts Taxes; usually duty on goods or import taxes; any tax imposed by proper authority or power.

impound 1. To take into legal custody. 2. To legally seize, secure, or take an item into custody until any legal disputes about it are decided.

impoundment In the federal budget, any executive branch action or inaction that precludes the obligation or expenditure of budget authority provided by Congress. An impoundment resolution is a resolution of the House of Representatives or the Senate that expresses its disapproval of a proposed deferral of budget authority set forth in a special message ordinarily transmitted by the president. Passage of an impoundment resolution by either house of Congress has the effect of overturning the proposed deferral and requires that such budget authority be made available for obligation.

impression, case of first A dispute involving a new question, never dealt with before by the courts and lacking precedent.

imprimatur (Lat.) Let it be printed.

improper venue In health law and the litigation process, this is a wrongly selected or incorrectly designated city, county, or area to hear a case in court. It has nothing to do with a court's jurisdiction but only the location of a court. *See also venue.*

improved risk In insurance risk assessment, this is evidence of compliance with certain questionable areas that pose an insurance risk such as fire protection and loss prevention standards.

improvident Lacking foresight.

improvidently Diminishing the effectiveness of a court.

impugn To refute; to show as untrue; to oppose; to challenge.

imputed 1. To be accountable for. 2. A fact one should know even if one does not know it.

imputed knowledge In health law, this is when a health-care provider or worker has a duty to know certain available facts. Knowledge may be imputed to a person, who will be legally held accountable for it as if the facts were known.

imputed negligence If a physician is negligent and a registered nurse is responsible for carrying out the physician's orders or actions, the physician's negligence is imputed, carried over, or attributed to the registered nurse.

imputed notice In health law, if a physician or other health-care provider is given notice of a court appearance or a fact or a lawsuit, and the physician or health-care provider is a nurse's agent, master, or manager, then notice to the physician can be imputed as notice to the nurse.

IMR Institution for mentally retarded.

IMU Index of Medical Underservice.

inactive facilities In environmental health, this is any area where a hazardous substance has been deposited, stored, disposed of, or placed such as a building, structure, installation, equipment, pipe or pipeline (sewer pipe), well, pit, pond, lagoon, landfill, or ditch. Excluded are areas with a permit to serve as a solid waste disposal site.

inadequate personality Emotional and physical instability where a person is unable to cope with the normal demands of life.

inadmissible Facts or items that cannot be admitted into evidence in a trial.

inadvertence 1. Lack of attention. 2. Carelessness. 3. A mistake or oversight; an act that could lead to liability, negligence, or a malpractice lawsuit.

inalienable Cannot be given away, taken away, bought, transferred, or sold. Constitutional rights are inalienable and cannot be taken away.

inapparent infection In epidemiology and infection control, this is when a host has a disease without the obvious signs or symptoms of the disease. Carriers can have inapparent infections, and, because of the lack of the signs of the disease, the disease is easily transmitted to others.

inappropriate affect 1. In psychology/psychiatry and mental health, this is when emotions and behavior are not congruent or are out of harmony with ideas and thought processes. 2. Having emotions not appropriate for the situation.

in articulo mortis (Lat.) At the point of death.

inattentive Lacking the ability to concentrate or focus one's thoughts on a specific idea or object.

in banco (Lat.) On the bench. Court proceedings before a9l1l the judges of the court, as opposed to proceedings at nisi prius, which is with only a single judge and a jury.

inc. Abbreviation for "incorporated."

in camera (Lat.) In chambers. A hearing or court in session held in the judge's private office.

incapacity The lack of the legal ability or power to do something; an injury serious enough to prevent working.

incarceration 1. Confinement. 2. Shut in. 3. Imprisonment.

inception Beginning; commencement.

inchoate 1. Not completed; unfinished. 2. An incomplete or invalid document; a partial legal document or part thereof, thus lacking completeness.

incentive A reward given as a result of a desired or an expected behavior; money or other tangible assets offered and used to influence behavior toward an expected outcome or result.

incentive reimbursement In financial management, this is a payment scheme that not only provides for the direct payment for health services rendered but also includes an added financial reward if certain conditions are met. The purpose of such an arrangement is to promote increased efficiency and contain costs with an increase in quality of care.

incentive systems 1. In human resource management, this is a reward for performance at work. An employee is paid an additional sum of money for performance above and beyond the usual. 2. When compensation is linked with performance by paying workers for outcomes or certain levels of results achieved instead of being based on hours worked or a salary.

incidence 1. In epidemiology, this is the occurrence of the number of illnesses or the general increase of cases of disease in a community or population as a measure of morbidity; the number of new cases of a disease, infection, condition, or some other illness or malady having an onset during a prescribed period of time in relation to the unit of population in which it occurs. It measures morbidity and related events as they happen over a specific period of time. This is also the number of new cases of mumps occurring in a school during a month in relation to the pupils enrolled in the school. Usually it focuses only on the number of new cases or the overall increase of the disease in the population. The incidence of common colds is high relative to their prevalence. 2. In health economics, the distribution of a tax among groups, usually income groups, in the population. Nominal incidence is the distribution mandated by law, such as a specified division of a payroll tax between employers and employees. Ultimate incidence is the distribution after the income effects of the tax are allowed for. For example, most economists feel that the employer's share of a payroll tax is ultimately borne by the employees in lower wages or consumers in higher prices. *See incidence rate; prevalence; prevalence rate.*

incidence density In epidemiology, as a measure of morbidity, this is the number of new cases of a disease that occur in a certain population as assessed by a limited time factor. Controls of the study are selected at the same time as cases, allowing them to become cases before the study is completed if they are infected when selected. *See force of morbidity.*

incidence-density ratio In epidemiology, as a measure of morbidity, this is the calculation of the ratio of two separate incidence densities. Also related to rate ratio.

incidence of conditions The number of cases that had their onset during a specified period of time. A person may have more than one acute condition during a period of time or may have the same condition twice or more (e.g., a headache). Ordinarily, however, a chronic condition can begin only one time during the specified time period.

incidence rate In epidemiology, this is a measure of the frequency of the occurrence of a communicable disease, chronic disease, condition, injury, or other malady or disorder in a group or population based on the number of new cases that have occurred in a specific time period, usually 1 year. The incidence rate is obtained by dividing the number of new cases (numerator) by the midyear population (denominator) and multiplying the results by 1000, 10,000, or 100,000, which constitutes a rate. The incidence rate formula follows:

$$\frac{\text{Number of new cases of a disease in a specific time period}}{\text{Total population of the group affected by the disease in the same time period}} \times 1000$$

See morbidity; attack rate; rate; cause-specific death rate; mortality rate. See also Appendix I.

incidence rate, lost workday cases In occupational health and safety, lost workday cases is the number of lost workday cases multiplied by 200,000 divided by total hours worked.

incidence rate, LWD (lost workday) In occupational health and safety, these are the total lost workdays (WDL) resulting from the days away and days restricted (WLDR). The LWD incidence rate formula follows:

$$\frac{(WDL + WLDR) \times 200{,}000}{\text{Total hours worked}}$$

incidence rate, occupational health and safety As used in occupational health and safety and as set forth by the Occupational Safety and Health Administration (OSHA), this is based on the exposure of 100 full-time workers using 200,000 employee-hours as the equivalent (100 employees working 40 hours per week for 50 weeks per year). An incidence rate is computed for each classification of cases or days lost on the basis of what number is put in the numerator of the incidence formula. The denominator of the formula should be the total number of hours worked by all employees during the same time period as that covered by the number of cases in the numerator. Rate formulas used for occupational health and safety incidence rates follow:

Occupational health and safety incidence rate formula no. 1:

$$\frac{\text{Number of injuries and illness} \times 200{,}000}{\text{Total hours worked by all employees during same time period}}$$

Occupational health and safety incidence rate formula no. 2:

$$\frac{\text{Number of lost work days} \times 200{,}000}{\text{Total hours worked by all employees during same time period}}$$

incidence rate, total recordable cases (TRC) The number of recordable injuries and illness per 200,000 total hours worked by all employees during the period covered. The 200,000 hours worked are equivalent to 100 full-time workers at 40 hours per week for 50 weeks. The formula follows:

$$TRC = \frac{\text{Number of recordable injuries and illness} \times 200{,}000}{\text{Total hours worked}}$$

incidence rate, workdays lost (WDL) The number of recordable days away from work per 200,000 total hours worked by all employees during the period covered. The formula follows:

$$WDL = \frac{\text{Number of workdays lost} \times 200{,}000}{\text{Total hours worked}}$$

incidence rate, workdays lost restriction (WDLR) The total number of days away from work because of restriction per 200,000 total hours worked by all employees during the period covered. The formula follows:

$$WDLR = \frac{\text{Number of workdays restricted} \times 200{,}000}{\text{Total hours worked}}$$

incident According to JCAHO for accreditation of long-term-care facilities, an action or occurrence of minor significance that caused some harm or problem or had a potential to do so. Any action or event that does not comply with a health-care facility's policies or standards. Any event in a hospital or other health-care facility by or to a patient, visitor, or employee that is harmful, that may result in injury, that results in unexpected outcome, or that could cause liability. An incident report form is filled out for each incident to create a record of the event. See *incident report*.

incidental Occurring in connection with something else or depending on something else more important.

incidental motions In formal health-care organization meetings, these are the motions that are occasionally stimulated by the carrying on of business of the assembly and that are presented and acted on.

Incident Command System (ICS) A regional or metropolitan disaster emergency system that coordinates and activates the appropriate disaster responder or service such as the fire department, paramedics, or police. Some cities or regions use a 911 dialing system, which contacts a command post system and then notifies the appropriate service to respond.

incident form See *incident report*.

incident report 1. In hospital administration, this is a written report of any event or occurrence that could result in liability and a lawsuit. 2. According to JCAHO for accreditation of long-term-care facilities, a written report by either a patient or a staff member that documents any unusual problem, incident, or other situation for which the patient or staff member wishes to have follow-up action taken by appropriate administrative or supervisory personnel. 3. According to JCAHO for psychiatric, alcoholism, and drug abuse facilities accreditation purposes, this is the documentation of events or actions that are likely to lead to adverse effects and/or that vary from established policies and procedures pertaining to patient care.

incident to Belonging to, a part of; dependent on some other thing.

incineration 1. In environmental health, this is a controlled combustible process for burning solid, liquid, or gaseous combustible waste to gases and to residue that contains little or no combustible material. Waste is reduced in both density and volume and is used to economically reduce and sterilize solid waste. When waste is converted to ash, it is sterile, contains few combustible materials and gases, and consists mainly of metals, water, vapor, oxygen, and carbon dioxide, which are released into the air. Hospitals have used incineration to dispose of biohazardous wastes and reduce the volume of solid waste placed in landfills. 2. According to the EPA, this is a treatment technology that uses combustion to destroy organic constituents and reduce the volume of wastes; the burning of certain types of solid, liquid, or gaseous materials; a treatment technology involving destruction of waste by controlled burning at high temperatures. *See incinerators.*

incineration vessels In environmental health, these are boats or trucks that carry hazardous substances for the purpose of incineration as long as the residues are kept on board and contained from spilling into the environment.

incinerators In environmental health, these are furnaces used in the process of burning solid waste for the primary purpose of reducing the volume of waste by removing the combustible matter. These technologically advanced burning facilities, equipment, and devices use controlled flame combustion to thermally degrade all forms of combustible solid waste, infectious waste, and pollutants such as PCBs. Rotary kilns, liquid injection, cement kilns, and high-temperature boilers are some of the approaches used in incinerators. *See incineration.*

incised wound A cut that is smoothly and cleanly made, usually by a knife, metal edge, glass, or other very sharp object.

incision In medical care, this is a surgical cut done with extremely sharp, sterile surgical cutting tools.

incite Provoke; encourage; stir up; cause, create, or start something.

incoherence Disconnected, illogical, and incomprehensible communication.

income The return, often measured in money, from one's business, labor, or capital invested. Welfare programs attempt to distinguish earned income (wages or net earnings from employment) and unearned income (support or maintenance furnished in kind or cash; annuities, pensions, retirements, or disability benefits; prizes, gifts, and awards; proceeds from insurance policies; support and alimony payments; inheritances; and rents, dividends, interest, and royalties). Note that fringe benefits of employment (such as the employer's contribution to the cost of health insurance) are often not considered income for tax purposes, thus enhancing their real value (and creating, e.g., an indirect federal subsidy of group health insurance). *See also resources.*

income adjusted for family size In health services delivery and public health, this is using family income within family size categories to establish the poverty line for eligibility for health and social programs.

income and expense statement *See profit and loss statement.*

income approach In health-care finance and accounting, this is an appraisal method used to determine the value of rental or lease property by using the estimated net income over the life of the equipment or property, discounted to determine its current value.

income averaging Reducing taxes by showing that income in prior years was far lower than the present income and thus that one should pay taxes on the average income for previous years.

income distribution plan A finance program that establishes how income will be paid to its recipients. Various factors of a distribution plan include 1) equal distribution, 2) production incentive, 3) seniority, 4) administrative functions, 5) developmental activities, 6) outside income, 7) length of service, and 8) new members. Income distribution plans that include production incentives are more widely used.

income of family In public health, social services, and health services delivery, each family member is classified according to the total income of the family of which he or she is a member. Included in the family unit are all persons in the household and all persons related to each other by blood, marriage, or adoption. The total of all income received by members of the family from all sources in the preceding year constitutes family income.

income statement In health-care finance, this is an accounting report or financial statement that evaluates operating performance by comparing financial gains with incurred costs over a given period of time. A report on the profitability of a health-care organization, summarizing the income and expense during a specific time period. Also referred to as a "profit and loss statement." *See profit and loss statement.*

income tax Taxation on profits from business, work, or investments.

incommunicado Cut off from communication (e.g., a prisoner who is kept from communicating with his or her attorney, family, friends, or others outside the jail or prison).

incompatibility Incapable of legally existing together.

incompatible wastes In environmental health, these are hazardous wastes that are unsuitable for placement in a particular device or facility because they may cause corrosion or decay of containment materials or, if commingled with another waste or material under uncontrolled conditions, might produce heat or violent reactions, toxic dusts, mists, fumes, or gases.

incompetence 1. A psychiatric legal term suggesting that perceptions and thought processes are not totally adequate to make sound judgments or good decisions. A person may be confused, which may lead to abnormal behavior or harm to the person or others; mentally incompetent. 2. In health administration, this is not performing up to the skill and knowledge level expected for the position and level of responsibility. *See insanity.*

incompetency 1. Lack of a legal right to do something. 2. Lacking the mental ability to take charge of and manage one's own affairs; confused. 3. Inability to perform and do something that is normally expected.

incompetent One who is unfit to do a job because of morality, insanity, a mental deficiency, or some other disabling reason; not legally qualified; inability to make decisions; lacking competence. *See also incompetence; insanity; mentally incompetent.*

incompetent evidence In health law, this is evidence lacking in facts and thus may not be admitted into a legal proceeding.

inconsistent 1. Lacking consistency and predictability. 2. Contradictory. 3. Not dependable.

incontinence In medical care, this is the loss of control of bowel, bladder, or both. Some of the common causes of incontinence are spinal cord injury, disease, infection, loss of sphincter (muscle) power, loss of bladder tone, disorientation caused by drugs, or lack of interest on the part of the patient or nursing assistants in maintaining or establishing control.

incontinent 1. Not capable of restraining oneself. 2. Not capable of holding back or restraining a natural bodily discharge such as urine or feces. 3. Not capable of restraining one's passions or appetites for indulgences such as food or sex.

inconvenience 1. Posing a minor hardship. 2. From a trivial to a serious injustice.

incorporate The process of formally and legally creating a corporation.

incorporated In law, this is the process of filing all appropriate legal documents to create a legal entity for a company under the articles of incorporation of the state, taking the legal responsibility off the individual owners and placing it on the company. For example, in the case of a lawsuit, once incorporated, the incorporated company is sued, not the owners. It is designated by "Inc."

incorporeal Without bodily existence.

incorporeal hereditament Something intangible yet capable of being inherited.

increment 1. A step-by-step gain or increase. 2. The process of adding to something. 3. A step upward.

incremental cost In health-care finance, this is the difference between the total cash outlay needed to operate the health-care organization if a planned action is taken, the outlay of revenue required for any alternative action that the organization will accept if the plan is rejected.

incriminate To expose facts or information about oneself or another that would lead to being charged with a crime.

incriminatory Showing guilt of committing a crime.

incubation In epidemiology and microbiology, this is the growth of microorganisms by placing them on a nutrient-rich growth medium and then placing it in a favorable, heated environment in which microorganisms flourish; the growing of microorganisms; the time period of growth of microorganisms.

incubation period In epidemiology and infection control, this is the time it takes for the growth of a pathogen; the time between the pathogen entering into a medium (e.g., a human body) that is conducive to growth and the onset of the symptoms of the infection; the interval between the invasion of a host by an infectious agent and the first appearance of symptoms of the disease. In a vector, this is the interval between the time the pathogen enters into the vector and the time it becomes infective.

incubator 1. A small self-contained bed and protection unit that produces controlled levels of heat in which premature babies are kept for a period of time right after birth. 2. A storage unit that produces controllable levels of heat used in microbiology or medical labs to grow microorganisms.

inculpatory In health law, this is to accuse; to establish or fix blame or guilt.

incumbent One who presently occupies a public office.

incur 1. Acquire; get; to obtain or inherit something bad. 2. In managed care or medical insurance, this is to become liable for a loss, claim, or expense. Cases or losses incurred are those occurring within a fixed period for which an insurance or health plan becomes liable whether or not they are reported, adjusted, and paid.

incurred but not reported (IBNR) In managed care, this is the amount of money a health plan is to accrue for medical care expenses that have occurred but not yet been turned into the health plan or carrier; a calculation made by the finance department of a health plan for claims not yet sent in for payment; the expenses for the delivery of health care that the authorized health plan has not captured and for which claims have not yet been reported.

incurred claims In managed care, these are services that have been rendered to health plan members and billed to the health plan as a claim for services rendered.

incurred losses In health-care financial management, these are losses that have happened, including amounts paid and reserved for future payments.

IND *See investigational new drug.*

indecent Offensive to the morality of the public or society.

indefeasible A right that cannot be revoked or taken away; that which cannot be voided.

indemnified Made whole again; reimbursed; the beneficiary getting the money or benefits of an insurance policy.

indemnify In insurance, this is to compensate or reimburse a person who has suffered a loss or damages.

indemnity In insurance, this is to pay off or to compensate a person for losses of a limited or particular type or occurrence on the basis of an insurance policy, agreement, or contract; insurance benefits in the form of cash payments rather than services; money to be paid on life insurance to a beneficiary or the health-care benefits to be received under medical care insurance or a health plan. In managed care or medical insurance programs using a cost-based reimbursement based on charges for treatment, the health plan pays for the medical care for members covered by the premium, and a direct payment or indemnity may not occur but still theoretically exists. This is the money given to a beneficiary for benefits provided in an insurance policy to the member; benefits paid in a predetermined amount in the event of a covered loss occurs.

indemnity benefits Under managed care or medical insurance policies, these are benefits in the form of cash payments rather than services. The indemnity insurance contract usually defines the maximum amounts that will be paid for the covered services. In most cases, after the provider of service has billed the patient in the usual way, the insured person submits to the insurance company proof that the bills have been paid and is then reimbursed by the company in the amount of the covered costs, the insured person making up the difference. In some cases, the provider of service may complete the necessary forms and submit them to the insurance company directly for reimbursement, billing the patient for costs that are not covered. Indemnity benefits are contrasted with service benefits.

indemnity plan In health-care finance, this is a fee-for-service financing approach that is the most attractive and also the most expensive approach. Employees are allowed to choose their own physicians. Once deductibles or co-insurance are paid, insurers reimburse doctors and hospitals for up to 80%. The consumers pay the remainder, and premiums are raised to cover the shortfalls and cost increases. This is also a health plan that compensates for illness, injury, or loss at a rate determined by the insurance contract on the basis of the customary or reasonable fee-for-service.

indenture In health administration real estate management, this is a deed to which two or more persons are signatories and parties.

independent contractor A separate contractor hired to do a particular piece of work using one's own skills and working under one's own control. Some health-care facilities or services hire therapists or specialized physicians as independent contractors to provide certain specified services, treatments, therapies, or procedures.

independent living In gerontology, this is when elderly persons with some limiting diseases, conditions, or disabilities maintain the ability to continue living in their own homes or apartments while avoiding institutionalization or nursing home placement. This is living alone or at one's normal place of living while maintaining self-sufficiency, even if it requires some supportive services such as participation in delivered meals programs, transportation programs, or housekeeping and chore services.

independent living centers Condominiums or high-rise apartments that accommodate only the healthy or semihealthy elderly. Health and social support services are available to allow them to continue living on their own, and medical care is arranged if needed.

independent living project A health and social support service system providing services to the elderly or handicapped to help them continue living on their own in their own homes. These programs provide hot meals brought to the home and assistance in shopping and homemaking, thus avoiding institutionalization and allowing these individuals to continue living in their own homes with the freedom and dignity of any other healthy person.

independent medical evaluation For Medicare purposes, a policy that a hospital or skilled nursing facility must adopt that provides for at least an annual independent review and audit of the patients' medical care and of their continued need for skilled nursing care.

independent physician association (IPA) In managed care, this is when a health plan contracts with physicians who see enrollees of the prepaid health plan and also see their own patients and maintain their own private practice, receiving self-pay and standard medical insurance reimbursement as well. *See individual practice association (IPA).*

independent practice association (IPA) These are managed-care plans that provide medical care for an annual premium and that pay affiliated physicians on a capitated or fee-for-service basis. *See independent physician association; individual practice association (IPA).*

independent practitioner *See practitioner.*

independent practitioner organization (IPO) In managed care, this is an organization of physicians and other health-care providers that contracts with health plans for a whole range of services. The difference is that an IPO may contract with multiple types of health plans and does not assume risk instead of contracting with an HMO, which may have a risk structure. This is similar to an IPA.

independent professional review (IPR) Another name for medical review required by Medicaid for inpatients in long-term-care facilities.

independent safety review In occupational health and safety, this is when personnel who are either financially or organizationally removed from the business, company, or organization are used to conduct a primary safety analysis.

independent variable In epidemiology, health services, or biomedical research, this is any measurable research activity used as the basis for predicting or determining outcomes; those factors that influence events and outcomes; the factors that cause change or those variables of research from which changes are observed; the causes of variation in research results; factors that are observed to influence the events of research or that cause variation in the outcomes of certain aspects of a research design. *See dependent variable; intermediate variable.*

indeterminate An indefinite time period; when an exact time period is not set; when results or findings are unclear.

indexation In health administration and human resource management, this is the estimation of future employment needs by matching employment growth with a previously established standardized index.

index case In epidemiology, this is the very first case of a communicable disease identified in a group, community, or school in an outbreak of a disease; the first case of a disease identified by the epidemiologist in a population.

indexed A process that adjusts amounts of benefits in proportion to changes in an index (e.g., Social Security payments are indexed to, or adjusted to reflect changes in, the Consumer Price Index); some proposed managed competition (national health insurance/universal coverage) plans to index premiums, cost sharing, catastrophic thresholds, income levels, or reimbursement rates to the CPI.

index group In epidemiology, this is the group of persons who are under investigation. For example, in a cohort study this is the exposed group, and in a case control study it is the cases with the disease. This is also the group receiving the treatment.

indexing In health-care finance, this is a procedure for using a formula with a fixed payment or rate of return to compensate for the devaluation caused by inflation.

index of medical underservice (IMU) In healthcare delivery, this is the sum of weighted values of four indicators of unmet health-care needs in an area (infant mortality rate, the population 65 years and older, percentage of population in poverty, ratio of population to primary care physicians) and is used to determine the status as a medically underserved area. Values of IMU range from 0 to 100, with lower scores indicating increasing medical underservice.

Indian governing bodies The politically elected governing board of tribes, bands, or groups of Native Americans (American Indians) subject to the jurisdiction of the United States and recognized by the United States as possessing power of self-government.

Indian Health Service (IHS) A bureau of the U.S. Department of Health and Human Services that is responsible for delivering public health and medical services to American Indians throughout the country. The federal government has variable but direct and permanent legal obligations to provide health services to most American Indian peoples because of agreements in treaties written with the Indian nations in the last two centuries. The Indian Health Service is responsible for trying to fulfill these obligations within very severe budgetary restrictions.

Indian tribes According to the Resource Conservation and Recovery Act, Native American (American Indian) tribes, bands, nations, or other organized groups or communities, including any Alaska Native regional or village corporations, that are recognized as eligible for the special programs and services provided by the United States to Native Americans and having a federally recognized governing body carrying out substantial governmental duties and powers over defined areas; also tribes or bands recognized by the Alaska Native Claims Settlement Act.

indicated In the process of delivering health care, this term is used by a practicing physician indicating that a certain treatment should be done on the basis of signs, symptoms, tests, and diagnosis. A certain procedure, therapy, or treatment is called for or is required to reduce the injury or to cure the illness or condition on the basis of certain criteria or findings.

indication In the process of delivering health care, this term is used by health-care providers to describe the results of preliminary observations of injury or illness in patients, suggesting that certain types of tests or exams be conducted or treatments applied.

indicator 1. A quantitative measure chosen to reflect the status of an organization, service, program, community, or population or to represent how well a health system is performing; the data or mechanisms through which the level, condition of, or change in a community's health or in a health system's performance are judged. 2. According to JCAHO, this is a measurement tool used to monitor the quality of important governance, management, clinical, and support functions and processes of a health-care organization.

indicia 1. Signs; circumstances. 2. A fact that is probable but not certain, as shown by some indication or circumstance.

indictment A legal, formal accusation of crime made by a grand jury.

indigent A person of poverty status; a poor person; a person without property or money. As defined by governmental programs, these are persons whose income and resources fall below a set level. *See also medically indigent; poverty.*

indigent medical care (IMC) Medical care provided to patients who meet a definition of poverty and/or qualify for Medicaid or other programs for the poverty stricken; care provided for those who have an inability to pay for the medical care rendered. *See medically indigent.*

indigent patient A patient who has limited financial resources and is unable to pay for health-care services, treatment, therapy, procedures, or hospitalization. *See also medically indigent; poverty.*

indirect cost 1. In health administration, this is an assessment of cost as provided by office space, heat, lighting, office equipment. security, etc. 2. In health-care financial management, this is a cost that cannot be identified directly with a particular activity, service, or product of the program experiencing the cost. Indirect costs are usually apportioned among the program's services in proportion to each service's share of direct costs and are allocated to patient care areas on the basis of some statistical factor or unit of services indicator.

indirect evidence In health law, this is circumstantial evidence; evidence from facts that are not obvious or easily observed.

indirect loss Any loss or damage that is related to a peril or disaster yet was not directly caused by it.

indirect patient data Scanty information gained from a patient that must be interpreted and about which some assumptions must be made.

indirect provider An individual health-care practitioner or a health-care organization with less than a direct involvement or interest in the delivery of health-care services; a secondary-level provider that participates in rendering health services.

indirect reimbursement In managed care, this is where a health-care practitioner is reimbursed for his or her services but only through a physician or health-care organization, not directly.

indispensable party In health law, this is a person or group of people who have a vested interest in the outcome of a lawsuit; thus a final decision cannot be made unless they are formally included in the lawsuit.

individual care plan A part of the patient medical record that documents all aspects of care provided by each health-care provider. This record pulls the various portions of information on a patient's treatment and care activity together to develop a coordinated plan to give continuity and direction to further or future treatment. *See also care plan.*

individual enrollment period In Medicare, this is the time, running from 3 months before one's sixty-fifth birthday to 3 months after, during which time one can enroll in Part B of Medicare without a premium increase for delayed enrollment.

individual generation sites In environmental health, these are sites on or at which one or more hazardous wastes are generated. Individual generation sites usually are large manufacturing plants and may have one or more sources of hazardous waste but are considered single or individual if the sites or properties are contiguous. Other, smaller sites such as small private businesses, small manufacturing operations with painting done in the ambient air, restaurants spewing smoke and particulate matter into the ambient air, large dairy farms, and stockyards with cows are now considered individual generation sites, as are many other small plants and businesses, including hospitals.

individual health-care account (IHCA) One approach to health-care financing based on the principle of giving individuals or small businesses who establish and maintain IHCAs a tax advantage.

individual health insurance Medical insurance covering an individual (and usually dependents) rather than a group such as an employer group. Individual insurance usually offers indemnity benefits and has higher loadings than group insurance agreements.

individual health protection services Individual education, routine examination, and the use of drugs, substances, or devices to render an individual protected against disease and promote his or her optimum health.

individual insurance Insurance policies that provide protection to the policyholder and/or his or her family (as distinct from group insurance). Sometimes called "personal insurance."

individual practice *See solo practice.*

individual practice association (IPA) 1. In managed care, this is a health plan, usually an HMO, that contracts directly with physicians in independent practice, with one or more associations of physicians in independent practice, or with multispecialty group practices. 2. A partnership, corporation, association, or other legal entity that has entered into an arrangement for the provision of services with persons who are licensed to practice medicine, osteopathy, dentistry, or other allied health professions. Under this arrangement, health-care providers render their professional services in accordance with a compensation agreement or contract established by the insurance carrier or a health plan. To the extent feasible, such persons use such additional professional, allied health professions, and other health personnel as are available and appropriate 1) for the effective and efficient delivery of the services; 2) for the sharing by such persons of medical and other records; equipment; and professional, technical, and administrative staff; and 3) for the arrangement and encouragement of the continuing education of such persons in the field of clinical medicine and related areas. The term originated and is defined in the Health Maintenance Organization Act of 1973 (P.L. 93-222, Section 1302-5).

Individual practice associations are one source of professional services for HMOs and are modeled after medical foundations. *See also individual practice plan; health maintenance organization; managed care; independent physician association; independent practice association.*

individual practice plan Usually synonymous with "medical foundation," this is sometimes used to refer specifically to a managed-care plan or health maintenance organization that obtains its professional services from an individual practice association.

Individual Responsibility Program (IRP) A private medical relationship entered into by a patient and a physician. The doctor undertakes to provide the patient with the best medical services possible, and the patient assumes the responsibility of compensating the physician for his or her efforts.

individual retirement accounts (IRAs) Special savings accounts available in the United States that enable a person to save money for retirement on a tax-deferred basis; an employee benefit sometimes offered to employees of health-care organizations.

individual therapy In mental health services, this is a form of psychotherapy where a professional psychotherapist treats only one patient at a time. *See also group psychotherapy; psychotherapy.*

indoor air In environmental health, the breathing air inside a habitable structure or conveyance.

indoor air pollution In environmental health, this is any chemical, particulate matter, smoke (including cigarette and tobacco smoke), physical, chemical or biological contaminants, or other pollutants in the air inside of buildings occupied and used on a regular basis by humans.

indoor climate In environmental health, this is the temperature, humidity, lighting, and noise levels in a habitable structure or conveyance. Indoor climate can affect indoor air pollution.

indorse The signing of a name on the back of a document such as a check whereby the property or money of the name written is given to another; to sign a paper or document; to legally sign over to another party.

indorsement 1. The actual process of signing a negotiable instrument or document. 2. To support, reinforce, or back up a cause.

indorso (Lat.) On the back.

induced radioactivity In environmental health, this is any radioactivity produced within materials by nuclear reactions. It is created when stable substances are bombarded by ionizing radiation.

inducement 1. Convincing another person to enter into a proposition or to get involved in a situation. 2. In health law and the litigation process, this is when a case is in the pleading stage, in which an explanatory introduction is given about the complaint allegations. 3. A motive or reason for something happening.

induction period In epidemiology, this is the time period required for a specific pathogenic organism or agent to cause a disease; the time from the infection or causal action to the onset of the disease. *See incubation period.*

inductive coupled plasma-mass spectrometer A plasma-powered computer-controlled, solid-state, water-cooled RF generator spectrometer.

industrial democracy In health administration, this is a term that is sometimes used to refer to the management process of giving employees a larger voice in making work-related decisions affecting them.

industrial engineer An individual with experience and training in public health and health-care services who works as a plant engineer in a hospital or for a public health department and is responsible for the maintenance, improvement, and safe operation of nonclinical equipment.

industrial engineering As used in health-care facilities, this is the design of an environment that assists in the delivery of health care, including the installation and use of technology and equipment as well as the maintenance and upgrading of technological systems to adjust, modify, and integrate people with equipment and materials.

industrial health services Health services provided by physicians, dentists, nurses, or other health personnel in an industrial setting for the appraisal, protection, emergency care, and treatment of minor medical problems and health promotion, all done to or for employees while on the job. "Occupational health services" is now the preferred term.

industrial hygiene The science and art devoted to the recognition, evaluation, and control of environmental factors or stresses arising in or from the workplace that may cause sickness, impaired health and well-being, or significant discomfort and inefficiency among workers or those with whom they come into contact.

2. Control of environmental health hazards that occur in the workplace. 3. A component of an industrial health program that concerns itself with loss control and accident prevention as found in health-care institutions.

industrial hygienist Conducts programs in industry to measure and help control, eliminate, and prevent occupational hazards and diseases.

industrial life insurance One form of formerly used life insurance that used a face amount of $2000 or less with a weekly or biweekly or monthly premium payment schedule and the collection of premiums at the policyowner's home by an agent. Also referred to as "debit insurance."

industrial quality management systems (QM) In quality management activities of a health-care organization, this approach stresses total organizational involvement, meeting the expectations of the customer, and process improvement as keys to quality health services.

industrial medicine A medical specialty concerned with injury, illness, diseases, and preventive medicine issues of employees on work sites. It focuses on the prevention of disease, injury, and debilitating conditions that occur in industrial settings and various occupations rather than trying to create optimal health and social adjustment within the industry. *See also occupational medicine.*

industrial place In health and safety, this refers to places of industrial accidents, including locations such as factory buildings, railway yards, warehouses, workshops, loading platforms of factories, distribution centers or stores, construction yards, projects, and buildings undergoing remodeling. Accidents during home remodeling are considered a home accident.

industrial union In labor management, this is when labor organizations seek to include all an employer's eligible workers in one union regardless of whether or not they are skilled, semiskilled, or unskilled.

industry median In health-care delivery, this refers to the point at which 50% of all medical care facilities have financial, quality, employment, or other measurable values above that figure and 50% have values below this level.

industry standard Any standard that is commonly used and accepted as the norm by the majority of persons within the industry.

ineluctable Inevitable; not to be avoided.

inert ingredients In environmental health, these are innocuous materials used as carrier materials in chemical compounds. In pesticide components, these are substances such as solvents, carriers, and surfactants that are not active ingredients against the target pests. In pharmaceuticals, these are the nonactive substances used to form pills.

in esse (Lat.) In being; existing.

in evidence In law and the litigation process, this is proof, facts, or items presented and accepted in a trial as evidence.

in extremis (Lat.) In the final illness before death.

infamy Loss of one's reputation caused by conviction of a major crime.

infant 1. A person under the age of majority. 2. A very young child. 3. A minor.

infant death All deaths occurring during the first year of life; deaths from birth to age 1.

infant mortality The death rate of live-born children who have not reached their first birthday. The number of infant deaths during a year per 1000 live births reported in 1 year. The infant mortality rate is the most commonly used measure of health status. One of the key health status indicators, infant mortality, varies among countries, partly because the definition is somewhat variable and reporting does not follow standardized approaches. This is also death in the first year of life. *See also neonatal mortality; perinatal mortality; maternal mortality; health status indicator.*

infant mortality rate Live-born children who have died within their first year of life and expressed as the number of deaths in 1 year per 1000 live births. The infant mortality rate formula follows:

$$\frac{\text{Number of deaths in a year of infants of less than 1 year of age}}{\text{Number of live births in the same year}} \times 1000$$

infarct Death of heart muscle in a localized area usually caused by an obstructed artery in the heart.

infectibility In epidemiology and infection control, this is the susceptibility of the host; the ability of the host to get a disease.

infection 1. The invasion of an organism (the human body) by pathogenic organisms, including the growth and spread of the disease-producing microorganisms and the effect on and reaction of the body to their presence. The effects of pathogens (bacteria, viruses, or parasites) or their by-products such as toxins, pus, tissue damage, and systemic involvement. 2. An illness produced by an infectious agent (JCAHO).

infection, community-acquired As used in infection control in hospitals or other inpatient facilities, this is any communicable disease acquired before admission to a facility, even though the signs and symptoms of the disease do not show until after admission.

infection control In a hospital or nursing home, these are the policies and procedures developed for the surveillance, prevention, and control of the transmission of communicable diseases and of sanitation and sterilization practices. All patient care and support departments and services are under surveillance and control. Standards are applied to evaluate the quality of an infection control program (JCAHO).

infection control committee The Joint Commission on Accreditation of Healthcare Organizations (JCAHO) and the American Hospital Association have recommended the organization of a multidisciplinary infection control committee that is responsible for the investigation, control, and prevention of infections and the transmission of diseases within each hospital. The committee is made up of representatives from at least the medical staff, nursing, administration, and persons directly responsible for the management of infection surveillance, prevention, and control and develops policies that are to follow these guidelines: all hospitals and other health-care facilities shall establish a committee on infection control; the committee shall meet regularly (monthly or bimonthly) and at special times as the need arises; and the committee should include an infection control coordinator, a hospital administrative person, and persons from the departments of internal medicine, surgery, pathology, and nursing. Small hospitals and nursing homes must develop some form of disease surveillance program. If it is not feasible for smaller institutions to employ a full-time infection control coordinator, they may meet the requirement in several ways: 1) private qualified consultants in infection control practices, 2) infection control coordinators of large health-care facilities serving as consultants, and 3) interhospital infection control committees.

infection control, director of The individual, usually a nurse, who is responsible for the surveillance and control of communicable diseases within a health-care facility.

infection control nurse A registered nurse in charge of the prevention, surveillance, and control of the spread of infections and microorganisms within a health-care facility.

infection, cross *See nosocomial infection.*

infection, gradient of In epidemiology and infection control, this is the response of the host to a pathogenic organism; the progress of the disease and the signs and symptoms of an illness observed in the host; the amount and level of response of the host or organism to the infectious agent.

infection, hospital-acquired *See nosocomial infection.*

infection, latent period of In epidemiology and infection control, this is the period of time between the introduction of the pathogen into the organism and its first excretion of a toxin or other by-product.

infection, postoperative Any infection acquired in a health-care facility caused by a surgical operation; a nosocomial infection.

infection rate risk *See nosocomial infection rate.*

infection rate stratification *See nosocomial infection rate.*

infection, subclinical An inapparent infection; the lack of signs or symptoms in the host. *See carrier; inapparent infection.*

infectious agent In epidemiology and medical care, this is any microorganism or pathogen capable of producing infectious disease through a host or an environmental condition favorable to the transmission of the pathogenic organism.

infectious disease A disease caused by the invasion and multiplication of microorganisms in body tissues, especially those that cause local cellular injury; illnesses caused by organisms that destroy living cells and have a rapid onset. Also referred to as a "communicable disease." *See communicable disease.*

infectiousness In epidemiology and infection control, this is the ease with which a disease is transmitted to and received by the host; the mode of transmission, characteristics of the organism, incubation period, and virulence influence; the infectiousness of a pathogen.

infectious waste In environmental health and hazardous waste management, these are the equipment, instruments, needles, utensils, and any fomites of a disposable nature from the treatment of patients or from the rooms of patients who are suspected to have or who have been diagnosed as having a communicable disease and must therefore be isolated as required by health agencies. 2. Laboratory wastes such as pathological specimens (i.e., tissue, blood elements, excreta and secretions from patients or laboratory animals, and disposable fomites or any substance that may harbor or transmit pathogenic organisms). 3. Surgical operating room, outpatient surgery, outpatient areas, emergency room pathological specimens, and disposable fomites that are biohazards.

infectivity In epidemiology and infection control, this is the ability of a pathogenic organism to enter, survive, multiply, and produce illness in the host.

inference To show a fact or circumstance to probably be true through reasoning based on other proven facts or propositions.

inferential statistics An area of statistics that deals with various types of mathematical probability statistical formulas that are applied to parametric and nonparametric data to determine probability and correlations of variables to arrive at the results of medical and health-care research data and to present them as meaningful findings.

inferior court In law and the litigation processes, this is any lower court; a court with limited or special responsibilities and jurisdictions.

infertility The physiological inability of either a male or a female to reproduce offspring. In public health and demographics, this is mostly a concern of whether females in a population are capable of bearing or not bearing children. *See fertility rate.*

infestation In medical care and epidemiology, this is the invasion of an individual's body by parasites, worms, mites, or ticks.

infirm Ill; feeble; weak; suffering from a disease.

infirmary A term more commonly used in the past for a health-care facility, hospital, or institution where sick or infirm patients are housed or treated.

infirmity 1. An ailment or disease of character substantial enough to cause an insurer not to issue a policy. 2. An unsound or unhealthy state of one's body; feebleness. 3. A defect or moral weakness.

inflammation The reddening, heating, swelling, and pain that accompanies injured or infected tissue.

inflation The condition of rising prices; the increased amount of money needed to offset reduced purchasing power; price increases that do not reflect improvements in quality or quantity. A gallon of milk does not have any more volume nor is of any better quality than it was in years past but costs much more.

inflow In health-care delivery, the number of people who are not regular residents of a defined service yet obtain care from health-care providers in that same area.

influence In health administration, the ability to impact, change, or direct an organization, a program, or a service and its success; controlling resources to motivate or change an outcome or a behavior.

influents In environmental health, this is the water, wastewater, or other liquid flowing into a reservoir basin or treatment plant.

informal consideration In formal health-care meetings and hearings using parliamentary procedures, this is a method of reviewing a "question" without observing all the formal rules for debating the question.

informa pauperis (Lat.) As a pauper. In legal proceedings, this is allowing a person to have subpoenas issued and have counsel provided without having to pay any legal fees because of poverty.

information Transforming, processing, and analyzing data and other facts into an understandable, meaningful form.

information activity list A record kept on a patient's chart that provides information on, for example, the activity of a patient's record and how often it is requested or copied.

information areas Specific areas that must be addressed in a certificate of need application and sequentially reviewed within the health systems agency hearing and review framework.

information center In health information management, this is a department within a hospital or other health-care organization established to increase productivity of the various functional areas using computer facilities by providing training, technical assistance, end-user software applications, and internal consultant functions.

information processing system In health-care information management and computers, this is the procedure of determining, classifying, assessing, sorting, recording, summarizing, communicating, and storing information.

information services In health-care information management and computers, this is the department that supports the development and integration of information systems and supplies information to those who use it within the organization.

information synthesis In epidemiology, this is the process of systematically identifying, compiling, and analyzing scientific findings and information. Delphi techniques, meta-analysis, and quantitative synthesis are some of the methods used to synthesize the information.

information system(s) 1. In health-care information management and computers, this is an automated process of capturing, transmitting, and recording data, facts, and information that are made accessible to administration, planners, and selected individuals who might use the information or the organization as a whole. The procedures, approaches, methods, organization structure, and hardware and software used to file and retrieve information for planning and decision making. 2. In public health and epidemiology, this is the vital and health statistics data used to develop information about health services, health resources, health promotion programs, etc. to improve and develop health-care and public health programs essential to meeting the needs of the community and to increase quality of life and health status.

information systems department In health-care information management and computers, this is an administrative unit of a health-care organization, health plan, or insurance company responsible for developing and maintaining the computer system within the organization. Included in this responsibility are data processing, word processing, forms processing, data analysis, and office automation systems. Assistance to other departments in the purchase, development, maintenance, and administration of software and hardware systems is provided. This administrative unit tends to tasks such as maintaining records in computerized files, developing and maintaining data banks, preparing financial statements, and conducting analysis of various computer procedures and systems of the organizations.

information systems director In health-care information management and computers, this is the individual responsible for the management of computer services and data processing in a health-care facility.

informed consent 1. In health law, this is an agreement between a physician and a patient that allows a treatment procedure to take place (e.g., surgery) on the basis of a full disclosure of facts and options (including the one to do nothing) to the patient so that he or she can make an informed decision and decide whether to proceed. Informed consent must be competent, without coercion, and given freely, willfully, and voluntarily while explained at a level where the patient can fully understand the procedures and all alternatives. 2. A legal doctrine that requires that no diagnosis, treatment, or therapeutic procedure be performed on a patient who has not been informed in clear, understandable terms of the risks, dangers, and alternatives prior to giving consent. Unless a patient is given clear, understandable, and adequate information, informed consent lacks the element of being informed, has not been completed, and may not be valid. If the patient is a minor or is incapable of understanding or communicating, such consent must be obtained from a close adult relative, preferably a parent or legal guardian. Informed consent can be given only by the one receiving the treatment or procedure (as long as he or she is legally competent). Legally, a spouse cannot give consent for his or her mate, but parents must give it for minor children until they reach the age of majority or can demonstrate competence to exercise informed consent.

in foro conscientiae (Lat.) In the forum of the conscience. From a moral point of view.

infra- Prefix meaning "below" or "inferior."

infra (Lat.) Below; within; beneath or under.

infraction A breach or violation of a law, duty, or contract.

infrared heat In medical care and therapy, this is a radiant type of heat used to penetrate body tissues by using infrared rays, heat lamps, and incandescent light bulbs for therapeutic reasons.

infringement 1. A violation of a right. 2. The illicit or unauthorized using, selling, manufacturing, or distributing of something protected by law. 3. Encroachment.

ingestion In medical care and occupational health, this is the intake of a substance or material into the body by way of the gastrointestinal system.

ingestion exposure pathways In environmental health and occupational health, these are the pathways in which exposure occurs after ingestion of contaminated water or foods such as milk, fresh vegetables, or aquatic foodstuffs.

ingress The act of entering a structure or area through a point of access.

ingrossing Making a document in its final, official form by producing a perfect copy.

in haec verba (Lat.) In these words. By these words.

inhalation In environmental health, this is the intake of microscopic material or substances such as dusts, gases, mists, or vapors by way of the respiratory system.

inhalation LC 50 A concentration of a substance expressed as milligrams per liter of air or parts per million parts of air. This is lethal to 50% of the test population of animals under test conditions.

inhalation therapist A respiratory technologist trained in specialized therapies and treatments used to care for patients with respiratory problems. *See respiratory therapist; respiratory therapy; respiratory disease.*

Inhalation Toxicology Research Institute Established in 1960, ITRI's primary mission is to assess adverse human health effects associated with commercial energy technologies. The institute investigates the degree to which the inhalation of by-products of energy technologies (e.g., fugitive or operating emissions) may harm the health of operators or the general public.

inhalation therapy An allied health educational program that trains persons to work with various types of aerosol inhalants and mechanical respiratory equipment.

inhalation therapy services The administration of oxygen and therapeutic gases and mists to patients by an inhalation therapist under the direction of the physician.

inherent 1. Built in; a part of the item itself. 2. Derived and inseparable from. *See also inherently dangerous.*

inherently dangerous An object that has, in itself, the potential for causing harm, injury, or destruction and against which precautions must be taken. *See also dangerous per se.*

inherent vice A basic defect.

inhibition The abnormal suppression or depression of a normal function or behavior (e.g., sexual desire).

in-house Taking place or generated within the hospital or other health-care organization.

in-house complaint procedures In health administration and human resource management, this is the process developed for and used by employees to register complaints about any aspect of an organization and/or its administration.

in invitum (Lat.) 1. Against the unwilling. 2. Initiating proceedings against an unwilling, nonconsenting party.

initialize In health-care information management and computers, this is using separate computer terminals to set switches or computer program addresses in software programs counters, which are the starting values activated at prescribed points to assist in the execution of the program. This is also the formatting of a disk, diskette, or tape to accept and receive data and information.

initiative 1. A motivation, power, or driving force from within. 2. The power of the people to enact laws by voting.

injection In medical care, this the administration of medicine or nutrients directly into the muscle tissue by inserting a hollow needle into the muscle and pushing the medicine directly into the muscle itself. Referred to as "IM" or "intramuscular injection."

injunction A court order prohibiting a person from performing some act (a preventive injunction) or demanding that a person begin to perform some act (mandatory injunction). An injunction may be preliminary or temporary until the charge can be fully heard in court or the dispute passes. It can become permanent or final once the case has been decided.

injunctive relief Redress for a wrong done through an injunction against the party causing the harm.

injure 1. To hurt or harm. 2. To violate the legal rights of another person.

injurious falsehood In law, this is a false or untrue statement that leads to intentional harm (even if it is not a defamation of character) for which a lawsuit may be initiated.

injury 1. Any physical harm or damage experienced in one's body as a result of any mechanical, chemical, thermal, or environmental energy that exceeds the body's tissue tolerance. 2. In health law, this is any wrong, harm, or damage done to a person's rights, body, reputation, or property. 3. Traumatic (in insurance) or iatrogenic (in malpractice) damage to the body, of external origin, unexpected and undesigned by the injured person.

injury condition Any number of experiences or events and their results that are classified according to the nature-of-injury code numbers (800–999) in the ICD codes. In addition to fractures, lacerations, contusions, and burns, poisonings and impairments caused by accidents or nonaccidental violence are included. A person may sustain more than one injury in a single accident (e.g., a broken leg and scalp laceration from one accidental event), so that the number of injury conditions may exceed the number of accidents or the number of persons injured. In public health and health services statistics, only injuries that involve medical attendance or at least a half day of restricted activity are tracked and recorded.

injury independent of all other means An injury resulting from an accident, provided that the accident was not caused by an illness.

in kind 1. In grants or requests for funding from governmental agencies, a dollar value given to office space, desks, office machines, vehicles, etc. to be used as matching funds to acquire a grant. 2. A closely similar but not identical object. 3. In law, to restore or provide the protection of the law to a situation.

inlier An illness or disorder of a hospital inpatient that falls within DRG criteria.

in litem (Lat.) For a lawsuit.

in loco parentis (Lat.) In place of the parent. A legal principle, meaning acting as a parent for protective, legal matters, care, supervision, and discipline of a child.

in medias res (Lat.) 1. In the middle of the thing. 2. To the heart of the matter; without introduction.

inner liners In environmental health, these are continuous layers of material placed inside tanks or containers that protect the construction materials of the tanks or containers from the contained waste or reagents used to treat waste.

innocent Not guilty; not involved with or responsible for an act or harm done or a crime; without knowledge of legal problems involved.

innovation adoption curve In health-care facility planning and the implementation of new technology or in health administration, this is a forecasting process that observes historical patterns of the gradual adoption of new technology or new managerial approaches or methods through which it is observed that slow early acceptance or growth and is followed by a period of rapid growth before leveling off to little or no growth.

innovative quality management The process of incorporating all new and modern approaches and technology such as computer software systems, expert systems, data processing, and behavioral techniques into a quality management program.

inocula In environmental health, this is the bacteria placed in compost to start biological action; a medium containing organisms that are introduced into cultures or living organisms.

inoculation To inject a substance into an organism; to get a dose of a substance through an injection. A mosquito can give an inoculation of a disease, or a nurse can give an inoculation of a vaccine against a disease.

inoperative 1. Not presently in effect. 2. Not active or effective.

in order In formal health-care meetings or hearings using parliamentary procedure, when a procedure, motion, question, voting, or a person's right to speak is done within the rules of parliamentary procedure.

inorganic Having no organic origin; used to describe acids or compounds that do not contain carbon.

inorganic chemicals In environmental health, this is any chemical substance of mineral origin not of basic carbon structure.

in pais (French) 1. In the country. The legal meaning is "not in a court or on a record." 2. An act done informally.

in pari delicto (Lat.) In equal fault; equally to blame; having an equal portion of the fault.

inpatient 1. A bed patient formally admitted to a hospital or skilled nursing facility who requires routine or specialized health-care services. 2. A patient who has been admitted at least overnight to a hospital or other health facility (which is responsible for his or her room and board) for the purpose of receiving nursing care, tests, treatment, or other health services. 3. Patient care services rendered in a hospital to a patient who has been admitted for treatment or services and stays at least overnight. *See inpatient care.*

inpatient admission The official acceptance of person as an inpatient by a health-care facility under the supervision of an attending physician. The patient is provided with hotel-type services, including room and board, housekeeping, nursing care, and routine treatment and therapy on a 24-hour basis in a medical or nursing care unit, all under the supervision of the patient's attending physician, who does the admission.

inpatient, ambulatory Any patient in a health-care facility who is of independent walking status as opposed to being wheelchair bound or bedfast. *See also bed-chair patient; ambulatory.*

inpatient bed count The total number of officially designated beds at any given time in a health-care facility for inpatient stays, whether occupied or unused.

inpatient bed occupancy ratio The ratio of inpatient service days to inpatient bed count for a given period of time; percentage of occupancy; the proportion of occupied inpatient beds. *See day; inpatient services.*

inpatient care Services provided to a patient who has been admitted and registered as a bed patient and has at least an overnight stay in a hospital, nursing home, or other medical or psychiatric institution to receive treatment, therapy, nursing services, or other medical services or to recover from an illness or injury.

inpatient care episodes In public health and health service delivery surveys, this is the number of residents as inpatients in facilities at the beginning of the year plus the total additions to those facilities during the year. Total additions during the year include new admissions and readmissions. It counts admissions rather than persons, so the same individual may be counted more than once. If the same person is admitted more than once to a particular facility during the year, that person is counted as many times as admitted. If the same person is admitted to two or more different organizations during the year, that person is counted as an admission for each organization.

inpatient care unit A medical or nursing care unit in a health-care facility staffed and equipped to provide inpatient health-care services and treatment and occupied according to diagnosis, disorder, or medical characteristics of the patients.

inpatient care, unit-mixed A general medical or nursing care unit in a health-care facility that receives most patients regardless of their disease, disorder, or treatment needs.

inpatient census The total number of persons who are inpatients in a health-care facility at a given time.

inpatient day equivalents The total number of days of inpatient care plus an estimated volume of outpatient services, which is expressed in units equivalent to an inpatient day in terms of level of effort. This is achieved by multiplying the number of outpatient visits by the ratio of outpatient revenue per outpatient visit to inpatient revenue per inpatient day and then adding the total (the number of patient days resulting from outpatient services) to the number of patient days.

inpatient day expenses *See expenses per inpatient day.*

inpatient days The total number of patient days, including adult and pediatric days of health-care services and excluding newborns, provided in a given time period. *See also patient days; days; inpatient services.*

inpatient days, adjusted *See inpatient day equivalents.*

inpatient discharge The formal release of a person from inpatient care by the health-care facility. *See also discharge.*

inpatient hospital care Health-care services, therapies, or treatments provided in an acute-care health-care facility to an individual who has been formally admitted and registered as a bed patient who must have the minimum of an overnight stay.

inpatient, pediatric Persons accepted for care in a health-care facility who are not newborns and who have not attained the age of majority. *See also age of majority.*

inpatient programs According to JCAHO for psychiatric, alcoholism, and drug abuse facilities accreditation purposes, programs that provide services to persons who require an intensity of care that warrants 24-hour supervision in a hospital or other suitably equipped setting. Such programs are usually located in facilities classified as institutional occupancies in Chapter 10 of the 1973 edition of the Life Safety Code (NFPA 101).

in perpetuo (Lat.) In perpetuity. Forever.

in personam (Lat.) The bringing of a legal action or lawsuit to enforce rights against another person but not against society as a whole.

input 1. To put data into a computer to be processed. 2. To transfer computer data from an external to an internal storage unit.

input and output symbol A symbol used in computers to identify either input or output functions.

input measure A measure of the quality of services based on the number, type, and quality of resources used in the production of the services. Medical services are often evaluated by measuring proxies such as the education and training level of the provider, the reputation and accreditation of the institution, the number of health personnel involved, and the number of dollars spent. Input measures are generally recognized as inferior to process and outcome measures because they are indirect measures of quality and do not consider the actual results, or outcomes, of services. They are still often used because they are easily obtainable. *See also output measure.*

input measurement In health services delivery, this is the examination of resources, activities, or tools used to provide a health-care service to determine the quality of services provided.

input media In health-care information management and computers, these are the forms on which data are recorded.

input-output device In health information management and computers, this is a device attached to a computer that makes it possible to put information and data into the computer and to retrieve them.

inquest An official inquiry; a coroner's hearing into the cause of a person's death, especially when the death was caused by violence or the cause was suspicious.

inquisitorial system The process by which a judge finds facts to represent the state's interest in a trial. It is the opposite of the adversary system used in U.S. trial courts.

in re (Lat.) Concerning; in the matter of. A title used in judicial proceedings in which there are no opponents but an item of concern requiring a court's attention; commonly used in appellate case titles (e.g., In re Karen Quinlan).

in rem (Lat.) Judgment. A judgment against the property within a court's jurisdiction. A judgment in rem can be enforced against any person controlling the object of the judgment.

irrevocable beneficiary In insurance, this is when a beneficiary of an insurance policy who has rights to the proceeds of a life insurance policy cannot be canceled by the policy owner unless the beneficiary consents.

insane A legal term for mentally incompetent; a danger to oneself or to others. *See insanity.*

insanity 1. A legal term with medical psychiatric implications, but not a medical term, that refers to the state of an individual who is incapable of managing or controlling his or her life, taking care of finances, practicing socially acceptable behavior, and distinguishing right from wrong according to society's rules and laws. A person can be judged legally incompetent if that person's judgment and behaviors are so unreliable and uncontrollable as to cause that person to be a danger to him- or herself or others. A person determined insane can be committed to a mental hospital or a psychiatric ward of a hospital for observation, therapy, and treatment. *See incompetent; mentally incompetent.*

insecticides In environmental health, these are chemical compounds (pesticides) that are used specifically to kill or control the growth of insects.

insecurity In mental health, these are feelings of helplessness and inadequacy; unable to comfortably face anxieties about one's place in life, future, goals, and relationships.

insecurity clause In contract law, this is a clause in a contract purposefully included so that a creditor can cause a debt to come due if there is reason to believe that it is necessary.

in-service education Staff development and training activities conducted in health-care facilities for personnel; considered a form of continuing education.

in-service education department The administrative unit of a health-care facility responsible for planning, coordinating, arranging, and conducting in-service training activities and ensuring that all documentation and certification paperwork is completed in a timely manner.

inside directors In health-care organization governance and administration, this is when a member of the board of directors holds a position in the health-care organization as well as the position on the board.

insight 1. Becoming aware of and having an understanding of one's own emotional, psychological, and maladaptive behavior. Two types of insight are possible: 1) intellectual insight: knowledge and awareness without any change of behavior, and 2) emotional insight: knowledge and understanding of one's own feelings, values, and behavior, providing positive changes in personality and behavior. 2. Self-understanding. 3. The extent to which one understands the mechanisms of one's attitudes and behavior; acceptance by a patient that he or she is ill or well.

in situ In the existing or original location.

in solido (Lat.) As a whole; for the whole. When two or more parties are in solido, each party is liable for the entire payment.

insolvency The inability of a person to pay debts as they become due.

insolvency funds The creation of funds, by state law, to guarantee the payment of bills of insolvent insurers.

insolvent A person who cannot pay debts or any health-care organization that has assets less than its liabilities.

in specie (Lat.) 1. In the same way. 2. A specific, similar, or same act.

inspection In health law and the litigation process, this is a part of discovery; the right to see, review, question, and copy the opposing party's documents to view their information and case and to gather evidence for their side of the case to be presented later in court.

inspection and maintenance In environmental health, these are activities used to ensure proper emissions-related operation of mobile sources of air pollutants, particularly automobile emissions; also applies to wastewater treatment plants and other antipollution facilities and processes.

inspection of care In long-term care, this is a program of medical review and evaluation done by one or more medical review teams that are composed of physicians, registered nurses, allied health professionals, and social services personnel who assess nursing home care to determine the care being provided; the adequacy of services available needed to meet the health needs of, and to promote maximum well-being in, the residents; the necessity and desirability of continued placement of patients in the nursing home; and the feasibility of meeting health-care needs of nursing home residents through alternative institutional or noninstitutional services.

inspection report *See investigative consumer report.*

inspections Deliberate, systematic scrutiny or examination of activities or projects; thorough, close, critical examination; checking or testing against established standards.

installation In managed care and medical insurance, this is all activities that take place to institute an insurance program from the time the interested group agrees to purchase a group insurance policy to the time the policy goes into effect.

installment 1. Any part or partial payment of a debt on a regular basis. 2. To be placed into an office. 3. Parts appearing at intervals.

instant case The present case at hand; the case being discussed.

instantaneous incidence rate Similar to force of morbidity. *See incidence rate; force of morbidity.*

interaction In epidemiology, this is a factor of causation or causality where interdependent actions of two difference causes produce an effect; the results of outputs and the differences in effects of one or several factors compared to the level of output observed that rely on the actions or reactivity of the first factor(s).

intermediate variable In epidemiology, this is a factor, element, or action observed to occur between the independent and dependent variables. *See independent variable.*

instigate 1. To incite; to provoke into action; abet. 2. To prompt or to urge on.

institution 1. A health-care facility. 2. A public or private organization such as a hospital, nursing home, prison, college, or church. 3. The starting of a process. 4. A basic system of laws. 5. The act of establishing new rules or laws.

institutional advertising In hospitals or managed care, this approach promotes the image of the organization instead of marketing specific services or programs.

institutional health services Health services delivered on an inpatient basis in hospitals, nursing homes, or other inpatient institutions and by a self-contained staff model health maintenance organization; may also refer to services delivered on an outpatient basis by departments or other organizational units of or sponsored by such institutions. The now defunct National Health Planning and Resources Development Act of 1974 (P.L. 93-641, Section 1531[5]), defined them as services and facilities subject to Section 1122 review, which required that all institutions be subject to a certificate of need review and periodic review for appropriateness. Some states still require a certificate of need for new institutional health services.

institutional licensure A proposed licensure system (not presently in use in any state) under which medical care institutions would be generally licensed by the state and would then be free to hire and use personnel as they saw fit whether or not they met the usual, individual licensure requirements. Under this system, formal education would become only one of many criteria used in assigning employees to particular positions. Institutional licensure is a suggested remedy to the alleged rigidities of the individual personnel licensing and certification programs presently in use in the health field. Other criteria could include job experience and in-service training. Arguments in favor of this practice are that it would allow increased job mobility in the health-care field and greater institutional efficiency. It would perhaps also foster teamwork and require only one licensing body at the state level rather than the many health licensing agencies presently functioning in each state. Such a system would not end the need for separate licensure of independent practitioners.

institutional neurosis In mental health services, this is a form of psychological railroading characterized by an erosion of individual personality traits, increased dependency, and emotional distance, all as a result of institutionalization; a failure of the staff to treat the elderly or mentally ill humanely and with appropriate respect and to offer them a good sense of reality.

institutional planning 1. In the administration of a health-care facility, this is a continuous cycle of events that includes preparatory organization looking at future events, the development of strategies and plans, and the development of methods for the implementation and evaluation of the new cycle of planning. This provides for a logical and planned direction and focus to the various activities. 2. For Medicare purposes, a plan that provides for an annual operating budget that includes all anticipated income and expenses related to items that would be considered income and expense items under generally accepted accounting principles. It also provides for a capital expenditures plan for at least a 3-year period that includes and identifies in detail the anticipated sources of financing for, and the objectives of each anticipated expenditure in excess of a certain amount ($100,000) related to the acquisition and improvement of, land, buildings and equipment, and the replacement, modernization, and expansion of the buildings and equipment that would be considered capital items under generally accepted accounting principles. Review and updating is done at least annually and is prepared under the direction of the governing body of the institution by a committee consisting of representatives of the governing body, the administrative staff, and the organized medical staff (if any) of the institution.

Institutional Review Board (IRB) A committee of clinicians such as physicians, nurses, and therapists in a hospital concerned with patient safety, research activities, cancer, treatment, new kinds of surgery, new technology and equipment, etc.

institutional solid waste In environmental health, these are solid wastes generated by educational, health, correctional, or other institutional facilities.

institution for mental diseases Under Medicaid, this is an institution that is primarily engaged in providing diagnosis, treatment, or care of persons with mental diseases; long-term-care inpatient psychiatric facilities such as state hospitals or private mental hospitals that treat severe psychiatric illnesses and often treat substance abuse, alcoholism, and adolescent behavioral and emotional problems on a short-term inpatient basis.

instruction 1. The process of giving knowledge; learning of information; teaching or facilitating the learning process. 2. In computers, a coded command that tells the computer what to do. 3. In health-care administration, this is an activity of management or supervision where a worker is given or taught a set of procedures to follow and directed to do them and complete a job or task.

instructions In a legal context, these are the rules and directions provided by a judge to a jury explaining procedures, expectations, burden of proof, questions to be considered, and issues to be decided.

instrument 1. A legal written document or paper. 2. A questionnaire used in research; a form, questionnaire, or information-gathering tool.

instrumental activities of daily living (IADL) In long-term care and home health care, these are home management and independent living activities such as preparing meals, cleaning, using a telephone, doing laundry, managing money, light housework, heavy housework, shopping, and obtaining transportation. *See activities of daily living.*

instrumentality In health-care administration and organizational structuring, this is a legal situation created when a minor corporation is completely controlled by another, major corporation.

insufficiency In legal proceedings, and specifically in an equity pleading, an answer that fails to reply to the allegations of a complaint.

insufficient-capacity criteria In health-care delivery, these are factors or elements used to determine if primary care services are lacking as well as the inability of individuals to obtain healthcare services in a timely fashion, including unusually long waiting times and lack of enough primary care practitioners in a certain area. *See capacity; accessibility; availability.*

insulin coma therapy (ICT) A form of shock treatment therapy that uses large amounts of insulin to induce a coma in depressed or schizophrenic patients; no longer widely used. *See also electroconvulsive therapy.*

insurable interest 1. A financial interest in a person, organization, goods, or items. 2. An insurance contract must include an insurable interest or activity. If a person suffers a property or financial loss if an item is lost or destroyed or if a person dies, an insurable interest exists.

insurable risk In managed care and insurance, this is a risk that has the following attributes: it is one of a large homogeneous group of similar risks, the loss produced by the risk is definable and quantifiable, the occurrence of loss in individual cases is accidental or fortuitous, the potential loss is large enough to cause hardship, the cost of insuring is economically feasible, the chance of loss is calculable, and it is sufficiently unlikely that loss will occur in many individual cases at the same time.

insurance Protection by written contract, agreement, or policy against the financial hazards or loss of specified events. The contractual relationship that exists when one party, for a consideration, agrees to reimburse another for loss to a person or thing caused by designated contingencies. The first party is the insurer, the second is the insured, the contract is the insurance policy, the consideration is the premium, the person or thing is the risk, and the contingency is the hazard or peril. Generally, this is a formal social device for reducing the risk of losses for individuals by spreading the risk over groups. Insurance characteristically but not necessarily involves equitable contributions by the insured, the pooling of risks, and the transfer of risks by contract. Insurance may be offered on either a profit or a nonprofit basis to groups or individuals. The term is also used to indicate coverage by insurance. *See also social insurance; prepayment.*

insurance, catastrophic *See catastrophic insurance.*

insurance categories A variety of types of medical insurance policies, plans, and sources (companies) exist, both private and government supported, and are in a constant process of change. Government-supported insurance categories are Medicare, Medicaid, the Civilian Health and Medical Program of the Uniformed Services (CHAMPUS), the Civilian Health and Medical Program of the Veterans Administration (CHAMPVA), the Veterans Administration, the Indian Health Service, and military and federal government employees' health services and public assistance programs at the county or city level. Categories of private insurance include traditional private insurance companies such as Blue Cross and Blue Shield and Mutual of Omaha. Examples of health maintenance organizations that provide their own clinical and hospital services are Kaiser Permanente and Family Health Plan. Examples of those without clinics that contract for services of physicians and hospitals are IPAs, IPOs, and PPOs such as Aetna Health Plans and Health Net.

insurance clause The clause that indicates who the parties are to a health or other insurance contract; sets forth the type of losses, benefits, or services covered; and defines the benefits to be paid.

insurance clerk An individual who works in a hospital, medical group, clinic, or other healthcare facility who is trained to compute health and medical insurance benefits and to maintain records and documents on these benefits. *See also patient service representative.*

insurance commissioner This is the state official charged with the enforcement of laws pertaining to insurance in the respective states. The commissioner's title, status in government, and responsibilities differ somewhat from state to state, but all states have an official with such responsibilities regardless of title.

insurance company In managed care, medical insurance, or other insurance, this is any corporation primarily engaged in the business of furnishing insurance coverage and protection to consumers.

insurance, out of area In managed care, this is when traditional medical insurance is purchased by a health plan to pay for care for enrollees when enrollees are temporarily living away from their usual residence and away from hospitals and physicians of the health plan or its own clinics and facilities.

insurance pool An organization of insurers or reinsurers through which particular types of risk are shared or pooled. The risk of high loss by any particular insurance company is transferred to the group as a whole (the insurance pool) with premiums, losses, and expenses shared in agreed-on amounts. The advantage of a pool is that the size of expected losses can be predicted for the pool with much more certainty than for any individual party to it. Pooling arrangements are often used for catastrophic coverage or for certain high-risk populations such as the disabled. Pooling may also be done within a single company by pooling the risks insured under various different policies so that high losses incurred by one policy are shared with others. *See also assigned risk.*

insurance service office (ISO) A national level insurance rate-setting body for liability insurers. This organization promotes rates that serve as the basis for individual rates used by its member organizations.

insured In insurance, this is the individual or organization protected in case of loss under the terms of an insurance policy and who may or may not pay the premium. The insured is not necessarily the one at risk but the one who is protected from accident, sickness, or other risks. In group insurance, the employer is the insured, and the employees are the risks. This is also any individual covered by any type of medical insurance or health plan. Dependents are the insured and do not pay the premium yet are the risks.

insured family This is where one or more members of a family unit are covered by some type of private health plan or medical insurance.

insured services In managed care, this is when the health-care provider renders special procedures or tests performed on a health plan patient that are not considered part of the services to be covered under the normal capitation payment. The health-care provider thus has to send a bill for the special services at an agreed-on price.

insurer 1. The organization, agent, or company that provides and writes insurance. The party to an insurance policy who contracts to pay losses or render services. Also called the "carrier," the "company," the "insurance company," or the "entity." 3. In managed care, these are organizations that provide reimbursement for the cost of providing health care in return for premiums.

insurer-administered group insurance plan In managed care and insurance, this is the part of an insurance company performing the administrative work for a health plan such as computing premium amounts due or mailing monthly statements to policyholders.

insuring clause In insurance, this is a clause in an insurance policy that sets forth the type of loss being covered by the policy and the parties to the insurance contract.

intake 1. According to JCAHO for psychiatric, alcoholism, and drug abuse facilities accreditation purposes, the administrative and assessment process for admission to a program. 2. In environmental health, this is a measure of exposure expressed as the mass of a substance in contact with the exchange boundary per unit of body weight per unit of time (e.g., mg/Kg/day). Also called the "normalized exposure rate." This is also the amount of radioactive material taken into the body by inhalation absorption through the skin, by ingestion, or through wounds.

intangible Rights rather than physical properties; that which has no physical quality.

intangibles Things that have no physical properties, such as rights, rather than objects: bank accounts, patents, copyrights, etc.

integrated To complete; combined together into one; made whole.

integrated agreement In contract law, an agreement made in a document as to the final and complete explanation of the agreement. This written document is labeled the "integration."

integrated information system In health-care information management, this is a set of two or more information systems such as computer networks established to provide quick and continued access to one another.

integrated multiple option In managed care, this is a combined insurance or health plan product offered to employers that integrates certain administrative and/or financial results between managed-care plan/HMO products and the traditional indemnity (IPA and PPO products).

integrated pest management In environmental health, this is a mixture of pesticide and nonpesticide methods to control pests.

integrating services In health services delivery, this is the coordination of services in a continuum to provide the maximum efficiency and utilization while minimizing duplication and cost.

integration 1. In contract law, a document accepted by both parties as final. 2. The process of making whole or complete. 3. Bring together. 4. In a social, educational, and employment context, this the balancing of ratios of races giving all races equal treatment. 5. In health administration, this is the process of achieving unity of effort among various subsystems of a hospital or health-care organization in the accomplishment of the organization's tasks. *See also integrated; horizontal integration; vertical integration; diversification.*

intelligence Capacity for understanding, recalling, and integrating what one has learned and using it in new situations; ability of the mind, specifically, the ability to make good and rational judgments on the basis of memory, imagination, reasoning, and perception and the ability to distinguish and recall.

intelligence tests Standardized psychological tests designed to measure an individual's general intellectual ability in an academic sense and compare it with demonstrated average results of a multitude of other persons who have taken the tests whose results have been compiled and analyzed. The Wechsler and the Stanford-Binet, two of the most common tests, use a score of 100 as an average IQ. Also referred to as "IQ tests."

intelligent terminal In health-care information management and computers, this is a computer terminal that is programmable, has its own central processing unit (which can perform certain levels of data and information processing and can check spelling), validates and edits certain programs, and performs certain operations independent of a mainframe or desktop computer.

intensity of service In health-care delivery, this is the quantities of services provided to patients in a hospital or some other identifiable inpatient setting. Intensity can be expressed in terms of a weighted index of services provided or in terms of a set of statistics indicating the average number of laboratory tests, surgical procedures, X rays, etc. provided per patient or per patient day. Intensity is a function of the type of program and its case mix.

intensity, severity, and discharge screening criteria (ISD) In quality assurance and utilization review activities, ISD addresses the medical necessity of treatment and hospitalization in terms of the severity of the patient's condition, the intensity of treatment the patient receives, and indications that the patient can be discharged safely. Three factors are considered in ISD: 1) the intensity of services are those diagnostic and therapeutic services that can be provided only in a hospital setting; 2) the severity of illness is determined by the clinical factors that can objectively determine how severe an illness is; and 3) discharge screening is done to ascertain the stability of the patient and his or her readiness for discharge from the hospital. These factors are of primary importance to the continued management of DRGs and the concern for patient care and health status resulting from the trend for shorter lengths of stay.

intensive care Medical treatment in excess of the usual care and treatment provided on an inpatient basis in an intensive care unit (ICU) or critical care unit (CCU) in a hospital. This level of care, the highest available, is provided to inpatients who have a high level of severity in their conditions; who suffer from trauma or surgery or who are seriously or critically ill; and who need intense, specialized care by physicians and specially trained nurses who operate monitoring and treatment equipment.

intensive care, cardiac care unit A medical and nursing care unit providing highly specialized care and staffed with highly trained nursing personnel who operate and monitor specialized equipment for patients with myocardial infarction, pulmonary problems, organ transplant, open-heart surgery, or other heart-related life-threatening conditions requiring comprehensive care, observation, and monitoring based on a physician's orders and nursing care plans. Beds and equipment must be set up and staffed in a unit specifically designated for health and pulmonary patients.

intensive care, medical A specialized medical and nursing unit that provides highly specialized care to nonsurgical patients. The unit is staffed with highly trained health personnel who monitor and treat patients with a variety of injuries and illnesses requiring advanced care.

intensive care, mixed A medical and nursing care unit providing advanced, highly specialized care to medical, surgical, trauma, psychiatric, and general patients. This is similar to the intensive care unit for cardiac care, but it accepts any patient needing advanced treatment by specially trained health-care providers in a specially equipped health-care unit where there can be close monitoring, comprehensive observation, and care. Beds and equipment must be set up and staffed in a unit specifically designated as a mixed unit.

intensive care, neonatal (NICU) A medical and nursing care unit providing advanced and highly specialized care to newborn infants. The unit is specifically staffed and equipped to provide intense treatment to newborns with serious medical problems or to those suffering from complications of premature birth. The unit must be separate from the newborn nursery and provide specialized care to all ill infants, including those with the very lowest birth weights (less than 1500 grams). Beds and equipment must be set up and staffed in a unit specifically designated for newborn patients. A full-time neonatologist serves as director of an NICU.

intensive care, pediatric A separate medical and nursing care unit providing advanced and highly specialized care solely to pediatric patients. The unit is staffed with highly trained health-care providers and nurses who operate and monitor specialized equipment used to monitor and treat patients who have suffered injury, shock, trauma, or serious illness requiring comprehensive care and monitoring. Beds and equipment must be set up and staffed in a unit specifically designated for pediatric patients.

intensive care, surgical A special medical and nursing care unit providing advanced and highly specialized care to high-risk patients just out of surgery who require advanced postoperative monitoring and treatment.

intensive care unit (ICU) A specialized nursing unit that concentrates in one area within a hospital, specifically, those seriously ill patients needing constant nursing care, monitoring, and observation on a concentrated, continuous basis. Some intensive care units limit their services to certain types of patients such as coronary care, surgical intensive care, and newborn intensive care units. *See also progressive patient care.*

intent 1. To commit an act with a purpose or reason. 2. The aim or purpose of using certain means to reach a particular goal. 3. In criminal law, for a crime to exist, an intent must be demonstrated by the prosecuting attorney.

intention 1. To do something with intent; the doing of an act on purpose. 2. That which is intended or planned.

intentional infliction of emotional distress Also referred to as "outrage," this is when an individual purposely does outrageous behaviors or extreme acts to another person to the extent that it causes extreme emotional upset and mental suffering; an intentional tort.

intentional tort In health law, this is whenever damage, injury, or harm is done to another person willfully, intentionally, and without just cause or excuse yet is not explicitly covered by statutory law. Some intentional torts can be treated as crimes rather than civil wrongs or can be treated as both.

intent of standard According to JCAHO, this is a brief explanation of the meaning and significance of standards used to assess and determine quality of health care in health-care facilities.

inter- Prefix meaning "together"; among; between.

inter To bury; place in the earth.

inter alia (Lat.) Among other things.

interceptor sewers In environmental health, these are large sewer lines that control the flow of the sewage to a treatment plant in a combined system. In a storm, they allow some of the sewage to flow directly into a receiving stream, thus preventing an overload of the plant by a sudden surge of water into the sewers. They are also used in separate systems to collect the flows from main and trunk sewers and carry them to treatment points.

intercompany comparison In health-care administration, this is a management method used to evaluate the effectiveness and efficiency of a health-care facility or organization by comparing one's own facility or operation to industry standards and/or other similar facilities or organizations in the area using standard measures such as revenue, expenses, length of stay, occupation rates, and staffing ratios.

interdiction Prohibition.

interdisciplinary In health-care delivery, this is when various health-care providers and allied health personnel come together to function as a team with a common goal, function, program, or service, each within the limits of their own professional domains; interactive programming or functioning across disciplines.

interdisciplinary patient care plan In long-term care, this is when the nursing care plan sets forth measures of therapy and care to enhance the medical, physical, emotional, and social needs of the resident. The plan must include measurable goals, the methods and approaches used to provide health-care and social services, the department or program responsible for the various aspects of care, and the role that each of the various health-care providers, allied health professionals, and social and nursing personnel will play in completing the patient care.

interest 1. A person's personal or financial involvement in an action. 2. Any right in property. 3. Extra money or profit received for lending money. 4. Money paid for the use of another person's money. 5. The money paid for the use of someone else's money; the cost incurred for borrowing funds expressed as a percentage of the total loan.

interest-adjusted method In insurance, this is a method of presenting the costs of life insurance by giving consideration to the time value of money used for premiums.

interest charge In health-care finance, this is an additional charge made on unpaid bills after a certain period of time. Some health facilities believe that finance charges provide additional revenue to the health facility and allow for competition for the patient's dollar with other businesses. Many administrators of health facilities believe that finance charges are inappropriate in health care.

interested person Any person who has testified or presented arguments at a public hearing or board meeting or who volunteers to assist in carrying out a service for a health-care organization or to serve on committees.

interest expense In health-care finance, these are the funds paid out in interest on capital indebtedness and current debt and considered by third-party payers to be an allowable cost.

interest groups Small or large numbers of people who have a common cause of concern; numbers of people who organize for political action, to support a cause, or to put pressure on members of a legislature to vote in favor of their cause. In health care, those groups with common causes or interest are physicians, nurses, hospitals, nursing homes, HMOs, etc.

interest, insurable *See insurable interest.*

interest rate 1. In health-care finance, this is the amount or level at which invested money grows. 2. The percentage of cost or charge that is assessed on borrowed money by the owner of the money against the borrower. *See interest.*

interest test In managed care or health administration, this is a means or method used to ascertain a commitment or a concern that is strong enough to cause persons to participate in a program, service, or cause.

interface In health-care information management and computerized medical records and business office activities, this is a hardware device that links two computer components and allows them to receive and transmit data and information between the two.

interfaces In occupational health, these are the relationships between two or more system components or between the work environment and one or more system components. Human performance is a function of the physical interfaces between people and equipment, the environment within which people or equipment work, the type and amount or training people receive, the accuracy and ease of use of the procedures people are given for guidance, and the effectiveness of the organizations in which they work.

interference When two different parties make a claim on what may be the same discovery, invention, or production such as two researchers inventing a medical device in two different institutions removed from each other at the same time and applying for a patent at the same time.

interim 1. In the middle or between. 2. A temporary or intermediate period; meanwhile. 3. Intervening period.

interim facilities Health-care institutions designed to provide patient examining rooms, administrative space, or teaching or research space on a short-term (less than 10-year) basis while more permanent facilities are being planned and constructed.

interim patient record A temporary document, sometimes a computer printout, that is created by the computer until the patient is discharged or the treatment ends.

interlocking directorates When a person serves as a director of two or more corporations.

interlocutory 1. Intermediate; provisional. 2. Discussion or dialogue going on while a lawsuit is in progress. 3. Presented or announced during the course of a lawsuit. 4. Not final or definitive.

intermediary 1. A public or private agency or organization selected by health-care providers who enter into an agreement with the Secretary of Health and Human Services under the Hospital Insurance Program (Part A) of Medicare to pay claims and perform other functions for the secretary with respect to such providers. Usually, but not necessarily, this is a Blue Cross plan or other private insurance company. In managed care, this is an agent of a health-care insurance company or health plan who handles the payment of care received at health-care facilities or from health-care providers. 2. A knowledgeable benefits professional such as a benefits consultant who assists plan sponsors in designing, purchasing, and administering health insurance programs. *See also carrier; fiscal agent; fiscal intermediary.*

intermediary letter A letter from the Bureau of Health Insurance to the intermediaries in the Medicare program that provides them with administrative direction or policy. These letters form a numbered series from which the Social Security Administration has made policy for the Medicare program over the last decade.

intermediate care A form of long-term care, this is advanced personal care given to an individual, most often elderly, who is a resident or a patient in a long-term-care health-care facility or receiving home health care by social service personnel, nursing assistants, and LPNs who offer supervised administration of medications, self-medication activities, special or modified diets, dressing changes, injections, etc. under the supervision of a registered nurse and orders of the attending physician. The level of care is greater than personal care, which requires no nursing supervision, and is less than skilled care, which requires registered nurse care and is directed by a physician.

intermediate care bed classification In long-term care, this is when beds are designated for patients requiring skilled nursing and supportive care on less than a continuous basis.

intermediate care facility (ICF) An institution recognized under the Medicaid program that is licensed under state law to provide health-related care and services on a regular basis to individuals who do not require the degree of care or treatment that a hospital or skilled nursing facility is designed to provide but who, because of their mental or physical condition, require care and services (above the level of room and board) that can be made available to them only through institutional facilities. Public institutions for care of the mentally retarded or people with related conditions are also included. The distinction between "health-related care and services" and "room and board" has often proven difficult to make but is important because ICFs are subject to quite different regulations and coverage than are institutions that do not provide health-related care and services such as board and care homes. The National Institute of Medicine Report recommended to Medicare and Medicaid and the Health Care Financing Administration that only one level of care be designated and that the two levels of nursing care be done away with.

intermediate care facility for the developmentally disabled (ICF-DD) A long-term-care facility with the capacity of 4 to 15 beds and providing 24-hour, 7-day-a-week personal care, habilitation, developmental, and supportive social and health-care services to developmentally disabled persons whose primary need is for developmental services and who have a recurring but intermittent need for skilled nursing services. Each individual is required to receive a comprehensive medical, dental, social, and psychological evaluation including vision and hearing screening and laboratory examinations determined necessary by the physician prior to admission under Medicaid laws and with periodic medical reviews. *See intermediate care facility for the developmentally disabled—habilitative.*

intermediate care facility for the developmentally disabled—habilitative A long-term-care facility with the capacity of 4 to 15 beds and providing 24-hour, 7-day-a-week personal care, habilitation, developmental, and supportive social and health-care services to developmentally disabled persons who have intermittent, recurring need for nursing and therapy services but have not been certified by a physician as requiring the availability of continuous skilled nursing care. *See intermediate care facility for the developmentally disabled.*

intermediate care facility for the mentally retarded (ICF/MR) A health-care facility designated solely for the care of the mentally retarded at an intermediate level of care.

intermediate care unit In long-term care, this is a part of a skilled nursing facility or a special unit in the facility or other health-care facility that is set aside, organized, and staffed for midlevels of long-term care that provide care that is more than supervisory/custodial care and less than skilled nursing care. *See intermediate care.*

intermediate emergency medical technician (IEMT) *See IEMT; EMT-I; emergency medical technician.*

intermediate life support As used in emergency medical services, this is the prevention and treatment of shock, stoppage of bleeding, assurance of breathing, and basic first aid in a traumatized or injured victim.

intermediate product protocol In health-care delivery, this is when a common expectation or procedure is established and accepted as the standard method or the usual and customary approach to be used.

intermediate products In health-care delivery, using a systems approach, this is concerned with outputs of certain aspects of processes used in the delivery of health care such as the admissions process, patient bed days, inpatient food services, laboratory tests, and X rays, which are viewed as inputs or processes that affect outcomes or the final product of health-care delivery such as quality diagnosis, treatment, and patient care.

intermediate sanctions Under Medicare and Medicaid, these are the penalties imposed on health-care facilities by Medicare or Medicaid that fall short of termination of the facility's contract imposed by states against health-care facilities that are determined to be out of compliance with state and federal regulations.

intermediate service *See services; levels of service; intermediate care.*

intermediate variable In biomedical research or epidemiology, this is any variable or factor that occurs between the action of the independent and dependent variables. This midlevel variation between the dependent and independent variables can be observed and affects the outcomes of a research design. *See independent variable; dependent variable.*

intermittent 1. Off and on; periodic; once in a while; occasionally; now and then. 2. A disease that entirely subsides or ceases at certain intervals, as in chills, fever, and shivering. 3. In health-care finance, this is any accounting reviews done or payments made periodically or at intervals.

intermittent care In home health care, this is care provided to patients in their residence for a week or two on a regular basis and then on an on-again, off-again basis as needed.

intermittent irrigation In medical care, this is a patient care activity, usually done in a long-term-care setting; the same as plain irrigation but done through a closed catheter system at designated intervals.

intermittent pollution control system In environmental health, this is a dispersion technique that varies the rate at which pollutants are emitted into the atmosphere according to meteorological conditions and/or ambient concentrations of the pollutant to prevent ground-level concentrations in excess of applicable ambient air quality standards.

intern A graduate of a medical, osteopathic, or dental school serving a first-year period of graduate clinical training called a "medical internship." *See internship.*

intern, health administration An undergraduate or graduate student serving in an educationally supervised field experience in a health-care facility or in health service administration. Undergraduates are more often referred to as "interns," and graduate health administration students are administrative residents or fellows and work with top management of health-care organizations. *See administrative residency.*

intern, nurse A graduate nurse who receives advanced formal training in a specialty or clinical area and works under the direction and supervision of a head nurse or nurse specialist.

internal assessment In strategic health planning, this is the process of reviewing a health-care organizations, policies, corporate culture, resources, and personnel and their skills and characteristics, attitudes, support from administration, technology abilities, etc. to determine if the organization can or will support the strategic plan of the organization.

internal audit In health-care financial management and accounting, this is the preparation of financial statements, the analysis of financial records, and the assessment of the financial status of a health-care organization done in-house by the organization's own accountants and bookkeepers.

internal consistency In health administration research, this is one form of reliability found in research questionnaires that is based on how well the findings of the questionnaire are correlated with the concepts, constructs, and theoretical principles behind each of the questions used to make up the research instrument (questionnaire); how well the questions correlate with one another.

internal control In health administration, this involves procedures, processes, and managerial action to coordinate the methods, measures, and accountability used to safeguard the health-care organization's assets, check on accuracy and reliability of bookkeeping and accounting data, assess administrative units of service and data, assess operational efficiencies, and encourage change in policies that are not working well.

internal disaster plan See *disaster plan*.

internal feedback In health-care administration, this is inside, or intrinsic, responses one gives back either in writing or verbally.

internal medicine A medical specialty involving advanced training for physicians in the principles and procedures involved in diagnosing and treating diseases on the internal structures of the body without the use of surgical procedures. Some internal medicine physicians are primary care physicians, others specialize in areas such as arthritis, and others treat mostly geriatric patients. Also referred to as an "internist." See *geriatrician*.

internal quality audit In health-care administration and as a part of quality management activities, this is a procedure carried out by staff or internal committees through which health-care institutions can determine if their services meet preestablished standards.

internal rate of return (IRR) In health-care financial management, this is a complex method of assessing capital expenditure proposals; the amount of income that comes to the health-care organization on an investment. If a health-care service or program can generate more money than the cost of capital, the service is acceptable. It is calculated by finding the discount rate that equates the present value of future cash flows to the cost of the investment.

Internal Revenue Code The U.S. government's tax laws.

Internal Revenue Code—IPA regulations In managed care, IPAs are treated as a single employer for the purposes of determining retirement plans for employees/participants as long as the plan complies with applicable antidiscrimination, eligibility, vesting, contribution, and benefit limit requirements under the Internal Revenue Code, even if the health plan has no employees of its own.

internal storage In health-care information management and computers, this is the memory inside the microchip of a computer as opposed to external storage such as a diskette, hard disk, or magnetic tape. Also referred to as "RAM" (random access memory).

internal validity 1. In health services research, this is a construct used to determine if the findings of an evaluation or questionnaire are directly related to the outcome of the service or program being evaluated; the strength of the findings or facts and how believable they are. 2. In epidemiology or biomedical research, this construct is used to determine if a test, instrument, or questionnaire measures within itself what it was designed to measure; to assess the assumptions, constructs, and theory on which the measure was developed to determine or prove the soundness of the measure. See *validity*.

International Classification of Clinical Services (ICCS) A classification system for hospital services or clinical services provided in other medical facilities. This classification and coding system was developed by the Commission on Professional and Hospital Activities to standardize patient data and to aid in the computerization of patient care data. The categories include laboratory services, pharmaceuticals, diagnostic imaging, anesthesia cardiology, physical medicine, respiratory therapy, nursing, and several other categories.

International Classification of Disease, Adapted for Use in the United States (ICDA) A U.S. Public Health Service official adaptation of a system for classifying diseases and operations for the purpose of indexing hospital records; developed by the World Health Organization. Diseases are grouped according to the problems they present. For example, the major infective and parasitic diseases are listed in one section and all malignant neoplasms in another. A three-digit numerical code is used to number the major disease categories. Subdivisions within categories are numbered with a four-digit code. The ICDA is revised every 10 years.

International Classification of Disease, 9th Revision, Clinical Modification (ICD-9-CM) Based on the official version of the World Health Organization's ninth revision of the International Classification of Diseases (ICD-9), it has been modified for use in all clinical settings in the United States and is designed for the classification of morbidity and mortality information for statistical purposes. It is used for the indexing of hospital records by diseases, procedures, and operations and for data storage and retrieval. For coding purposes, it uses a numerical three-digit number plus a one- or two-decimal digit system. The ICD-9-CM is compatible with the WHO ICD-9 classification system and is required for reporting diagnoses and diseases to the U.S. Public Health Service and the U.S. Health Care Financing Administration programs. The continuous maintenance of this system is the responsibility of the U.S. government, and it became effective January 1, 1979. The codes derived from ICD-9-CM are also used to determine DRG assignments.

International Classification of Health Problems in Primary Care–2 (ICHPPC–2) The various reasons for an individual's visit to a primary care health-care provider are classified into injuries, conditions, and diseases that would warrant a physician visit. Based on the International Classification of Diseases, this classification is adapted for physician use, accounting for the vagueness of some diagnoses.

International Classification of Impairments, Disabilities and Handicaps Using the ICDA, this presents the formal classification of the various types and extent of disabilities in three levels: impairment, disability, and handicap. *See impairments; disability; handicapped.*

International Epidemiological Association (IEA) Founded in 1950, this is a multinational professional society for individuals interested in epidemiology. The IEA is interested in epidemiological studies, methods, and applications of disease control, epidemiological principles to clinical medicine, and health services. The IEA conducts seminars and workshops and encourages epidemiological workshops.

international law Law that applies to the relationships and transactions between countries; the set of principles that determines the country in which a complaint or dispute should be heard.

International Union for Health Education An international professional organization with five aims: 1) to assert the role of health education in the economic and social development of human communities and to keep its theoretical basis up to date; 2) to provide international exchanges among those responsible for the health aspects of economic and social development through the organization of conferences, seminars, and working parties; 3) to contribute to the growth of knowledge on the role of health education and the promotion, protection, and restoration of health; 4) to ensure the international dissemination of publications and research relating to health education; and 5) to develop working relations with international institutions, governments, and nongovernmental organizations. It was formed in 1951 and publishes a journal, *Hygie.*

internist A specially trained physician who is able to diagnose and treat diseases and disorders of the internal organs without the use of surgery; a physician who practices internal medicine. *See internal medicine.*

internship Any period of on-the-job training that is part of a larger educational program. In medicine, dentistry, podiatry, and some other health professions, this has been a 1-year program of graduate medical education in a clinical setting and usually follows graduation from medical school. Practically all physicians take internships, although they are required for licensure in only 39 of the 55 licensing jurisdictions. An internship usually is required for granting of staff privileges. Internships are less common, with 1- to 5-year residencies being more common, and are started in the first year after graduation with one's medical degree, gradually eliminating the 1-year internships.

Inter-Plan Bank A service provided by the Blue Cross system under which a subscriber receiving care outside the subscriber's Blue Cross Plan's area will have bills paid by the local plan.

interpleader 1. In health law, this a procedure to cause a third person to enter into a lawsuit or risk losing his or her claim. 2. In insurance, when there are conflicting claimants to an insurance policy, this allows an insurance company to pay the proceeds of an insurance policy to the court and lets the court determine the proper recipient.

interposition Where a state may reject an order from the federal government if it believes the federal government has overstepped its authority. The Tenth Amendment of the U.S. Constitution provides to the states those powers not delegated to the federal government.

interpretation 1. The reading into or deciding of the meaning of a written document. 2. A psychological or psychiatric technique used in some psychological testing and in psychoanalysis (both individual and group). The significance and meaning of behavior, perception, and emotions are constructed into a meaningful form.

interrogatories In health law and the litigation process, these are a part of the discovery process in which written questions are given to the opposing parties in a lawsuit to get written facts and answers given under oath to questions put forth; written questions addressed to a witness with answers given under oath.

in terrorum (Lat.) In threat.

inter se (Lat.) Among themselves.

interstate agencies In environmental health, any agencies of two or more municipalities in different states, or agencies established by two or more states, with authority to provide for the management of air pollution, solid wastes, or other environmental matters serving two or more municipalities located in different states.

interstate air pollution agencies In environmental health, these are air pollution control agencies established by two or more states or two more municipalities located in different states.

interstate carrier water supplies Sources of water for drinking and sanitary use on airplanes, buses, trains, and ships operating in more than one state. These sources of water are federally regulated.

interval scale In epidemiology and descriptive statistics, this is when data or information are divided into categories with equal distance between categories or units of measure. The interval scale has no zero point, the number structure in the interval data has a value assigned to it, and the distance between the number differences provides measurement. The differences between numbers are equal. An example is found in IQ scales. In most major IQ tests, 100 is considered an average, or normal, score.

intervening cause 1. An indirect cause of an accident or other injury that removes the blame from the person who was the original cause. 2. In health law, this is a cause that comes between the event and the original, or proximate, cause.

intervening variable In epidemiology or biomedical research, this is when a factor or value is altered so that it blocks or alters the effects of other variables in the study. *See intermediate variable; independent variable.*

intervenor In health law, this is a person who becomes a party to a lawsuit between two other parties without being legally required to do so.

intervention 1. In health law, this is a third party entering in an existing lawsuit between two other parties. 2. Any strategy, procedure, therapy, approach, method, or technique that changes, stops, deters, or interacts with a problem, disorder, disease, or disability of a patient, group, or community. 3. The criteria used and applied by the peer review process in assessing the medical care and treatment given an individual patient that are meant to influence the direction and activity of the attending physician in providing care to the patient. 4. In health administration, this is a strategy, incorporating techniques or methods, that actually reaches a group, community, or population.

intervention levels In environmental health, these are the levels usually specified in advance by the competent authority for use in abnormal situations; if the value of the quantity of interest exceeds or is predicted to exceed a particular level, appropriate remedial action may have to be taken. Also referred to as "protective actions guides" or "emergency reference levels."

intervention study In epidemiology or biomedical research, this is a research design used to test cause-effect relationships by modifying the possible or probable causes to determine if they affected cause-effect relationships.

interventionist approach In health-care delivery, this is when health-care providers take the initiative in the health-care delivery process rather than leaving the initiative to the patient.

interventionist forecasting In strategic health planning, this is the process of identifying and incorporating different ways that the forecaster can influence future health-care utilization through the forecast.

interview A structured communication process for the purpose of obtaining information or to evaluate progress.

interview schedule In epidemiology or biomedical research, this is a survey instrument or survey questionnaire that is constructed in a logical manner, often considering how the data are entered into computer software programs, and that uses well-constructed, set questions based on sound theoretical constructs and concepts that standardize the process. The questionnaire is filled out in an interview. *See internal validity; reliability.*

inter vivos (Lat.) Between the living.

intestate To die without making a will; dying and leaving property that is not disposed of in a will.

intolerable cruelty Meanness or cruelty but of a more serious nature.

in toto (Lat.) In whole; complete.

intra- Prefix meaning "within."

intracompany comparison In health administration, this is a method of assessment that assists management in determining the efficiency and effectiveness of the organization's operations by comparing it with other like organizations in the region or state.

intrapreneur In health administration and strategic planning, this is the mindset of employees within a health-care organization that encourages the creation of new services, systems, or approaches. An entrepreneur spirit in the organization is allowed and encouraged.

intravenous (IV) Within a vein. Refers to how a needle is inserted into a vein of a patient. The needle has a receptacle on top to receive IV lines, syringes, or other forms of injection into the needle once the needle is in the patient's vein.

intravenous lines In medical care, this is the process of delivering care to a patient by placing a needle in veins of the body to easily inject fluids and drugs. The system of tubes connects the IV needles to a bottle or bag(s) of fluids and/or injection ports to efficiently inject drugs into the solutions, tubes, and the body.

intravenous team A group of specially trained nurses who administer intravenous therapy under the direction of a physician.

intra vires (Lat.) Within powers.

intrinsic evidence In health law, these are facts from within a case or evidence gained from a document itself.

introduction of evidence In health law, this is evidence presented for use or acceptance as facts in a trial.

introjection In mental health, this is a mental mechanism whereby loved or hated objects are used symbolically in oneself.

intropunitive In mental health and psychiatry/psychology, this is turning hatred and anger inward toward oneself; commonly a characteristic of depressed persons.

introversion In mental health and psychiatry/psychology, this is the fear of interacting with others or entering into unfamiliar situations; turning in on oneself, with no interest in others or the world.

intrust 1. To allow another to hold property, money, or items of value. 2. To deliver something to another with trust, with an understanding as to what it will be used for and with the understanding that it will be honored. *See also entrust.*

intubation In medical care, this is the process of inserting a tube into the body.

inure To take effect; to result; to come into use.

inurement Use; to a person's benefit; to illegally divert funds of a nonprofit corporation to wrongfully benefit an individual, especially a member of a governing body or administration.

invalid 1. Of no force. 2. Useless. 3. Not binding; lacking legal force; having no authority or value.

invariable form In formal health-care meetings and hearings using parliamentary procedure, this is a motion that is not flexible, can be stated in only one way, and is not subject to change or amendment,

invasion In law, this is the unwarranted or undesired interference in the rights of others; encroachment on one's rights.

invasion of privacy In health law, this is the unwarranted encroachment on the personal and private rights of another through the wrongful viewing of private records or information and/or subjecting the person to undesired publicity.

invasive procedure In medical care and the process of delivering patient care services, this is any treatment or procedure involving a puncture or incision of the skin or insertion of an instrument or foreign material into the body including but not limited to percutaneous aspirations and biopsies, cardiac and vascular catheterizations, endoscopies, angioplasties, and implantations but excluding venipuncture and intravenous therapy (JCAHO for acute-care facilities).

inventory 1. Counting all items or goods in stock. 2. A detailed accounting of all items or property. 3. The supply of goods in a hospital's possession, including surgical supplies, drugs, medicine, medical supplies, office supplies, and medical record supplies and all items kept on hand and in reserve in central supply and in the department of materials management.

4. The value of supplies of a hospital, clinic, or nursing home.

in ventre sa mere (French) In this mother's womb. Referring to an unborn child.

inversion In environmental health, this is an atmospheric condition caused by a layer of warm air preventing the rise of cooling air trapped beneath it. This prevents the rise of pollutants that might otherwise be dispersed and can cause an air pollution episode. Also referred to as "thermal inversion."

investigational new drug (IND) A drug available solely for experimental purposes because its safety and effectiveness are not yet approved by the FDA for marketing to the general public. Prescription of the drug is limited to those experts qualified by training and experience to investigate its safety and effectiveness. Use of the drug in humans requires approval by the FDA of an IND application, which provides reports of animal toxicity tests, a description of proposed clinical trials, and a list of the names and qualifications of the investigators. *See also new drug application; new drug.*

investigations In environmental health, these are the detailed systematic searches to uncover the who, what, when, where, why, and how of occurrences and to determine what corrective actions are needed to prevent a recurrence.

investigative consumer report In managed care and insurance, this is a special report that is prepared about an enrollee of a health plan or insurance policyholder containing information about the insured's occupation, personal habits, hobbies, and finances. *See inspection report.*

investigator In epidemiology and biomedical research, this is the key person responsible for organizing and conducting research studies. Also referred to as "principal investigator" (PI). *See principal investigator.*

investment In health-care finance, this is the buying or the adding on of capital stock during a given time period. *See capital stock.*

investment department In managed care and insurance, this is an administrative unit that examines the financial marketplace, recommends investment strategies to the company's finance committee, and manages the company's investments according to the policies established by the governing board. Depending on the organization's financial structure, this administrative unit may also take an active role in investments and serve as advisors to the president and board of directors in mergers and acquisitions.

investment sensitive insurance products In managed care and insurance, these are plans or policies that vary according to future interest rates or investments. Benefit amounts for plans or policies cannot be predicted in advance beyond any guaranteed minimums.

investor-owned hospital *See proprietary hospital.*

investor-owned for-profit hospitals Acute-care medical care facilities controlled by a corporation that is managed on a for-profit basis as set forth by its corporate standing and Internal Revenue Code.

invidious Offensive.

invitation Inviting someone to come into your building or facility or onto your property. Under the law of negligence, a hospital must be careful for the safety of the public invited in to avoid liability.

invitee Under law, this is person who by either implied or express invitation goes onto the property of another. A caller, such as a drug salesman, may be not an invitee but a licensee.

invoice In materials management in a health-care facility, this is a list of goods, usually giving prices and numbers item by item; a bill presented to a customer listing items sold to that customer that now need to be paid for.

involuntary commitment In health law, this is the admission of an individual to a mental health facility against his or her will. A commitment proceeding is required that must demonstrate a danger to oneself, a danger to others, or an inability to take care of one's own health and welfare. The last issue may not be required in all states.

involuntary manslaughter To unintentionally cause the death of another human being. This is against the law even though unintentional.

involuntary nonsuit In the litigation and trial process, this is where the plaintiff fails to appear or fails to produce evidence on which a jury could find a verdict.

involuntary smoke Also called "secondhand smoke," "passive smoke," or "slip-stream smoke," this is the breathing in of air filled with tobacco smoke, exposing the nonsmoker to health risks similar to those of smokers.

involutional melancholia In mental health and psychiatry/psychology, this is depression that occurs at middle age or the menopausal period, characterized by insomnia, anxiety, and paranoia. There is usually no history of a previous mental illness.

involutional psychotic reaction See *involutional melancholia.*

IOC Inspection of care.

IOM Institute of Medicine.

ionizing radiation 1. In laser technology as used in health care, this is electromagnetic radiation that produces ions or disrupts molecular structure. 2. Radiation (e.g., alpha, beta, or gamma) that can remove electrons from atoms. 3. Any electromagnetic or particulate radiation capable of producing ions, directly or indirectly, in their passage through matter; biological material.

IPA See *independent practice association; individual practice association; independent physicians association.*

IPA model HMO In managed care, this is an independent practice association of one of the four different managed-care models. The IPA model contracts with groups of physicians in private practice. The association manages the contract with the HMO and provides administrative services to the IPA. See *independent physician association; individual practice association.*

IPCP See *interdisciplinary patient care plan.*

IPO See *independent practitioner organization.*

ippissimis verbis (Lat.) In the very same words. In the exact words.

IPR See *independent professional review.*

ipse dixit (Lat.) He himself said it.

ipso facto (Lat.) By the fact itself.

IQ Intelligence quotient. A measure of intelligence based on a psychological test.

IRB See *institutional review board.*

IRP See *Individual Responsibility Program.*

irradiated food In public health, this is food that has been subjected to brief radioactivity, usually by gamma rays, to kill insects, bacteria, and mold and to preserve it without refrigeration or freezing.

irradiation 1. In occupational health and safety, this is the exposure to rays that can penetrate the body such as X rays, gamma rays, infrared rays, or ultraviolet rays. 2. Exposure to radiation of wavelengths shorter than those of visible light (X rays, gamma rays, infrared rays, or ultraviolet rays) for medical purposes, destroying bacteria in milk or other foodstuffs, or inducing polymerization of monomers or vulcanization of rubber.

irrational In health-care administration and/or emotional health, this is the making of decisions that appear correct but are not; a state of emotional confusion.

irregularity 1. In health administration, this is the failure to use proper procedures. 2. In health law, this is the failure to take the usual or proper formal steps. This may invalidate a lawsuit or cause a default judgment.

irrelevant Not important or unrelated to the issue.

irreparable injury 1. In health law and recovery from liability, this is harm that cannot be overcome, repaired, or properly reinstated by money alone. 2. Harm that is serious enough to justify an injunction.

irresistible impulse Loss of control caused by temporary insanity; an impulse or urge that is so beyond control that a person cannot refrain from committing a crime; a questionable test used to decide if a person will be treated as a criminal or as a mental patient

irrevocable 1. Not capable of being undone or revoked. 2. Incapable of being recalled, stopped, or changed. 3. Not able to be repealed or annulled.

irrigation, plain In medical care, this is the process of introducing a solution into the bladder through a catheter and then emptying the solution out.

irritant In occupational health and environmental health, this is an agent or substance that causes unpleasant responses such as itching, swelling, allergic reactions, or other tissue reactions.

irritating materials Any liquid or solid substances that, on contact with fire or when exposed to air, give off dangerous or intensely irritating fumes but do not include any material classed as a Poison Class A. Examples are tear gas, brombenzylcyanide, gas identification kits, and diphenylchlorasine.

IRS Internal Revenue Service.

ISD See *intensity, severity, and discharge screening criteria.*

ISD review system See *intensity, severity, and discharge screening criteria.*

ISO See *insurance service officer.*

isolation This is the placing of a patient in a private room, removed from other patients, visitors, and all but a few staff, and is done when the patient has a highly infectious or communicable disease or special disorder; the segregation of patients with infectious and communicable disease or other diseases for a specified time. Three types are common: 1) strict: limiting the movement and social contacts of a patient suffering from or a carrier of a communicable disease to prevent the spread of the disease to others; 2) modified: making an effort to control specified aspects of care to prevent cross-infection; and 3) reverse: the seclusion of a patient in a near germ-free environment to protect the patient from cross-infection. Also referred to as "quarantine." *See quarantine.*

isolation bed In health services, a bed maintained in a private room in a health-care facility to accommodate any patient who may need to be quarantined or isolated from other persons because of a highly infectious disease or other related condition.

isolation incubator In hospitals, this is a bassinet incubator maintained for use by premature newborns or other newborns needing isolation.

isotope One or more chemical elements in which all atoms have the same atomic number, with each separate one having varying atomic weights.

issue 1. Something in contention. 2. An event, action, or occurrence entered into. 3. Conflict. 4. To promulgate or give out officially. 5. The fact or law being discussed. 6. A single point of dispute. 7. Descendants, children, grandchildren. 8. Joint submission of a claim for a decision at law.

-ist A suffix meaning "specialist."

itemize To list each piece or object item by item; breaking a list down into individual separated parts.

IV *See intravenous.*

IVP Intravenous pyelogram. In medical care and testing, this is the injection of iodine dye into a vein to serve as a contrast media that is then easily exposed to and shows up on an X ray so that a picture can be taken of the renal pelvis of the kidney to look for kidney stones or other disorders of the kidney.

IV piggyback The attachment of a second intravenous (IV) solution onto the initial IV line, making one solution piggybacked onto the original one.

J

j. Abbreviation for judge, justice, or journal.

jactitation A false, boastful statement resulting in harm to another.

jail fever In public health, this is slang for "typhus fever."

JAMA *Journal of the American Medical Association*.

jargon The technical or characteristic terminology of a particular group, profession, or culture.

JCAH Joint Commission on Accreditation of Hospitals, the former name for the Joint Commission on Accreditation of Healthcare Organizations.

JCAHO *See Joint Commission on Accreditation of Healthcare Organizations*.

JCAHO five-star rating system The Joint Commission on Accreditation of Healthcare Organizations has devised a five-star rating system for disclosure to the public as to the level of accreditation and quality of a hospital, nursing home, or other health-care organization. Five stars means excellent, or that most standards are met. Four stars means above average, or that many standards have been met. Three stars means good, or that a majority of standards have been met. Two stars means marginal, or that some standards have been met. One star means poor, or that few or no standards have been met.

JCAHO rating system *See JCAHO five-star rating system*.

JCAHPO *See Joint Commission on Allied Health Personnel in Ophthalmology*.

JD Juris doctor; doctor of jurisprudence. The basic law degree that replaced the LLB. Other law degrees offered include the LLM, LLD, BL, JCD, and DCL.

Jehovah's Witnesses A church and religious group with certain beliefs regarding health care. They do not believe in blood transfusions yet believe in surgery. These beliefs present legally complex problems in emergency care and surgery because it is almost impossible to perform some surgical procedures or provide emergency care for extensive and serious injuries and wounds without a transfusion of blood.

Jenner, Edward An English doctor who contributed to the fields of epidemiology and public health by observing that dairymaids who had cowpox did not get smallpox. Dr. Jenner inoculated persons with cowpox, then with smallpox, and they did not get the disease. The process of immunizing populations against smallpox has led to the virtual elimination the disease.

jeopardy 1. Risk; danger; hazard; peril. 2. The defendant's risk of being convicted in a criminal trial.

JIT *See just in time*.

JNOV *See judgment non obstante veredicto*.

job absence *See absenteeism*.

job analysis In health administration and human resource management, this is an assessment and evaluation process used to collect, evaluate, and organize job information about each position.

job analysis schedule In health administration and human resource management, this is a standardized questionnaire or checklist that uses a uniform manner to collect information about various jobs or positions.

jobber 1. A purchaser; one who purchases and sells goods or services for others. 2. A wholesaler or middleman. 3. One who does work by the job. 4. One who carries on official business for profit.

job code In health administration and human resource management, this is a set of numbers or letters or a combination of both used to provide quick identification of job roles and job summaries.

job description A statement of key features, qualifications, experiences, work conditions, requirements, and duties of work to be performed. The statement is based on a job analysis and may also include lines of authority. It may also designate the supervisor or level of placement as well as objectives of the job. This also refers to the requirements of a specific job category.

job dissatisfaction In health administration, this is a result of the lack of acceptance of job circumstances, ineffective policy, pettiness of management, unhappiness, or disfavor that workers have for their positions and/or the health-care organization. *See job satisfaction*.

job enlargement In health administration, this is the adding of additional or different tasks or assignments to an already existing job description. It can be used to increase productivity and provide more responsibility and authority; mistakenly used as a motivation tool. *See job enrichment.*

job enrichment In health administration and human resource management, this is where employees perform job-related activities that require a higher level of skill, ability, and training. Task modification, added responsibility, work autonomy, elevated position, motivation, and some redistribution of power among workers are some characteristics of job enrichment. *See job enlargement.*

job evaluations In health administration and human resource management, this is a systematic procedure used to assess the relative worth of various positions or jobs in the organization.

job families In health administration and human resource management, this is the grouping of various jobs or positions that are similar in that they require similar skills.

job-flo In health administration and human resource management, this is a monthly report describing positions filled, jobs vacated, turnover, and frequently listed jobs or position openings.

job grading In health administration and human resource management, this is one type of job assessment where various jobs are assigned to predetermined classifications according to the position's determined relative worth to the health-care organization. Also referred to as "job classification."

job holder reports In health administration and human resource management, this is a summary and status report provided to the workers of a health-care organization that sets forth its status and economic condition and performance for a specified time period.

job instruction training In health administration and human resource management, this is actual training provided directly to employees while performing their jobs. Also referred to as "on-the-job training," or "OJT."

job performance standards In health administration and human resource management, this is a part of the performance appraisal process where levels of job performance and work requirements become the expected standard for an employee for a specific position; the level of quality and standards of performance expected from a worker in a particular position.

job posting In health administration and human resource management, this is where all positions available and unfilled in the organization and the job qualifications and requirements of each are placed on company bulletin boards, put in a newsletter, and made public.

job progression ladder In health administration and human resource management, this is the development of career paths in an organization that allows workers to advance. Where some jobs have prerequisites, workers are allowed to acquire the needed training and skills.

job ranking In health administration and human resource management, this is one approach to job assessment that uses a subjective placement or categorization of each job according to the value each position has to the organization.

job rotation In health administration and human resource management, this is a training and professional development approach that allows the worker to spend several months observing and working in each department of the health-care organization to learn how each area operates, resulting in administrative training on the organization's overall operations; moving from one job to another to acquire more skills and a variety of jobs.

job safety analysis In occupational health and safety, this is a systematic approach to reviewing the safeness of a job and is used as a technique to uncover inherent or potential hazards. Five steps are used in the analysis: 1) select the job, 2) break the job down into steps, 3) identify the hazards, 4) determine the necessary controls, and 5) evaluate the controls.

job satisfaction In health administration, this is the acceptance, contentment, happiness, or favorableness workers have for their positions and the health-care organization. *See job dissatisfaction.*

job sharing In health administration, this is a scheduling approach that allows two or more employees the opportunity to have the same job by working different shifts or days on a part-time basis to fill a full-time position.

job specification In health administration and human resource management, this outlines what a job requires of workers and the training, skills, and education needed to successfully fill the position. *See job description.*

Job Training Partnership Act of 1983 In human resource management, this is a federal law that provided funding for training people in new, employable skills.

John Doe 1. In law, this is a fictitious name used in lawsuits where no real defendant is yet known; also placed in legal documents when the actual person is not known at the time the document was written. 2. The name assigned to a body of an unknown dead person kept in a hospital or county morgue until it is identified.

joinder 1. The bringing together of causes. 2. Uniting together. 3. Accepting an issue as offered.

joinder of claims In health law, this is when a party who has filed a lawsuit or is asserting a claim joins that claim with other claims that are already filed against the opposing party.

joinder of issues In health law, this is a situation when a lawsuit is in an advanced state in which one side claims facts to be true and the opposing side denies them; the point in the litigation process where all facts and evidence come together to point the case toward a trial in a court of law.

joinder of parties 1. In health law, this when several parties to a lawsuit are united as parties to an action. 2. In law, this is all persons against whom rights are claimed as either coplaintiffs or codefendants; a new person joining a lawsuit on either side of the complaint or suit.

joint 1. Combined, shared, united, undivided. 2. A joint effort owned by two or more parties. 3. Slang for marijuana cigarette.

joint adventure *See joint venture.*

joint and several 1. Where the creditor has the option to sue the debtors either as a group or individually. 2. United together in an obligation either individually or collectively.

Joint Commission on the Accreditation of Healthcare Organizations (JCAHO) A private, nonprofit organization whose purpose is to encourage the attainment of uniformly high standards and quality of institutional medical care. Comprised of representatives of the American Hospital Association, the American Medical Association, the American College of Physicians, and the American College of Surgeons, the organization establishes guidelines for the operation of hospitals and other health facilities and conducts survey and accreditation programs. A staff of medical inspectors will visit hospitals by invitation and examine the operation of the hospital, the organization of its medical staff, and its patient records. Hospitals with 25 or more beds are eligible for review. On the basis of inspection reports, the hospital may be granted "full accreditation" (for 3 years), "provisional accreditation" (for 1 year), or none. Accreditation has been used by, or adopted as a requirement of, specific public programs and funding agencies. For example, hospitals participating in the Medicare program are deemed to have met most conditions of participation if they are accredited by the JCAHO or are deemed to have met the requirements for licensure as a hospital as required by state licensing agencies. The JCAHO operates accreditation programs for hospitals, nursing homes, hospices, home care programs, psychiatric and substance abuse treatment programs, HMOs, and ambulatory care facilities. Accreditation is voluntary, although many third-party payers and state governments require accreditation for payment and licensure.

Joint Commission on Accreditation of Hospitals (JCAH) *See Joint Commission on the Accreditation of Healthcare Organizations (JCAHO).*

Joint Commission on Allied Health Personnel in Ophthalmology A national professional organization that establishes standards and guidelines of training and procedures for allied and ancillary personnel in the delivery of ophthalmological services.

Joint Commission, performance evaluation procedure for auditing and improving patient care (PEP) A patient and health-care audit system developed by the Joint Commission on the Accreditation of Healthcare Organizations (JCAHO) that involves setting of criteria, determining acceptable exceptions, and then examining representative data and information to see if the health care provided has met the criteria. If it has not, recommendations are provided.

joint conference committee In hospital administration, these are the officers from the hospital's administrative team, the medical staff, and members of the governing board who help maintain communications between board and medical staff. This committee, though common, is not always found in hospitals and health-care facilities.

joint health planning The collaborative effort of two or more health-care organizations to develop a strategic plan aimed at serving the health-care needs of a city, county, region, or target area in which both are located and serve. The organizations share data, support services, clinical services, purchasing, and administrative functions yet do not share income or assets.

joint planning *See joint health planning.*

joint powers authority product In managed care, this is the organizing of a number of entities such as school districts into a single, large medical care insurance purchasing group. The group is formed into one large group for the purpose of soliciting and purchasing medical care coverage on a more cost-effective basis than if purchased by each separate district or if traditional medical care programs are purchased.

joint purchasing agreement A formal agreement between two or more health facilities or organizations to purchase professional services, equipment, or supplies. The agreements simplify purchasing or result in economies of scale intended to lower costs to the programs. The purchased services or supplies may be shared or simply distributed among the programs.

joint studies committees In health administration and labor relations, when representatives from both management and a union arrange to hold meetings, other than at the bargaining table, over topics of mutual concern to arrive at mutually satisfactory solutions.

joint underwriting association (JUA) An association consisting of all insurers authorized by a state to write a certain kind of insurance, usually some form of liability insurance such as malpractice insurance. Such associations may be required or voluntarily agree to write malpractice insurance on a self-supporting basis. They may write such insurance on an exclusive basis, which means individual carriers cannot write such insurance, or on a nonexclusive basis. The JUA approach has been used in state legislation to ensure the availability of malpractice insurance.

joint venture 1. A business deal or administrative effort between two persons, companies, or organizations (e.g., between two hospitals). Two or more parties or corporations become involved in or enter into a business as co-owners of specific services or programs to share profits, managerial control, risk, and losses. 2. A one-time group business deal. 3. Partnerships can be one legal form of joint venture. *See joint venture strategies.*

joint venture strategies In strategic planning for health services, this is an approach for undertaking a business opportunity or the development of new services with another organization that a single health-care facility or organization cannot do well alone. Using a consortium-type arrangement, the process of banding together is a means of making a workable whole out of several parts; several small health facilities joining resources together to build strength, expertise, and power by size. The complementary size and expertise of two or more organizations can overcome political, financial, training, management, and purchasing barriers and can get reduced prices and group purchasing advantages. Other strategies and advantages include the ability to access technology too costly to approach alone such as a mobile MRI scanner or to develop and implement a health-care service that would not succeed without the resources and expertise of two or more parties.

joule In laser technology, this is a unit of energy (1 joule = 1 watt second).

journal 1. A written book or record that is updated regularly. 2. A periodical professional magazine. 3. In accounting, this is the chronological listing of all the organization's financial transactions.

jousting Complaining, belittling, blaming, or criticizing others to defend what one has written in the medical chart or to others in person or in court when defending the medical record.

JP *See justice of the peace.*

JPA Product *See joint powers authority product.*

JUA *See joint underwriting association.*

judge 1. The person placed in judgment and who presides over and runs a courtroom. 2. One who decides all legal questions and cases. 3. To decide or evaluate. 4. A person appointed to make decisions.

judge advocate A military legal officer who acts as a judge or a lawyer.

judge-made law 1. Law created by judicial precedent rather than by a statute. 2. Where a judge changes the law to reflect an intent that was never contemplated by the legislature. *See also common law; judicial opinion.*

judgment (judgement) 1. In law, this is the official determination of a judge or court on legal matters heard; a final decision based on the evidence and facts of a case. 2. Comparing or evaluating one's choices within one's own set of values for the purpose of choosing a course of action. Judgment is intact if one's behavior is consistent with reality and impaired if the chosen course of action is not consistent with reality.

judgment creditor In health-care finance, this is a creditor who has proven that a debt is due and has obtained a judgment from the court to collect it.

judgment debtor In health-care finance, this is one against whom a judgment has been made and who must make payments to the judgment creditor.

judgment, estopped by In law, this is an estoppel imposed by a valid decision previously handed down by a competent court. *See estoppel.*

judgment in personam In law, this is a judgment against a specific person over whom the court has jurisdiction.

judgment, interlocutory In law, this is a judgment made during the litigation process to settle a point that must be determined before continuing (not a final determination of a case).

judgment non obstante veredicto (JNOV) (Lat.) Judgment notwithstanding a verdict; when a judge overrules the decision of a jury; an act that is contrary to law.

judgment note In health-care finance, this is the document a debtor gives to a creditor to allow a confession of judgment.

judicial 1. Judges, courts, statutes, law, and their functions. 2. Related to a court or judge. 3. Dealing with jurisprudence. 4. The branch of government that interprets law and decides legal issues (as opposed to the legislative branch).

judicial action Any legal or court action.

judicial comity In law, this is a court in one jurisdiction that utilizes the decisions of equal and superior courts in other jurisdictions to make decisions as a matter of practice rather than as matter of law.

judicial confession In law, this is a confession made before a judge or court.

judicial errors In law, these are errors of the court that require a reversal or a revision of opinion.

judicial notice A court's recognition of certain facts that are susceptible to readily available proof or that are of common knowledge without the necessity of proof (e.g., the result of a sharp knife drawn over skin).

judicial officers In public and environmental health, this is an employee appointed by a federal agency such as the Environmental Protection Agency (EPA). Under the EPA, this person must be an attorney who is not employed in the Office of Enforcement or the Office of Water and Waste Management and cannot participate in the consideration or decision of a case in which he or she performed investigative or prosecutorial functions or that is factually related to such a case.

judicial opinion 1. Judge-made laws. 2. Final decisions made by judges on the appellate level that are referred to at a later date and are used to make new decisions on new cases. 3. In law, this is when a precedent is set by a court's decision on previous cases and thus are used to determine future disputes.

judicial question In law, this is a dispute heard and decided by a court.

judicial review In health law and regulatory activity, this is the power of a court to review laws, to declare a statute unconstitutional, and/or to interpret laws; political controls over administration. It is used to ensure that an administrative agency is acting in accord with the will of the political branches according to the legislation that created it. This process provides an independent check on the validity of regulations. Courts may be used to determine the correctness of an administrative regulatory agency's interpretation of a rule and may change it. *See Administrative Procedure Act.*

judiciary The branch of government that judges, reviews, studies, and interprets the law. *See also judicial.*

Julian date In managed care, this is the process of identifying a date using a code for the numerical days of the year. For example, in the Julian date of 4323, 4 is the last digit of the year 1994, and 323 is the 323rd day of the year.

juniority In health administration and human resource management, this is the opposite of seniority and has the provision attached to it that, should layoffs occur, the persons who have first choice to be laid off are the senior workers, who may accept or refuse. If those with the most seniority do not accept, management can choose to lay off the most junior workers first.

jura eodem modo destituuntur quo constituunter (Lat.) Laws are challenged, changed, and removed by the same process and means by which they are constituted.

jura fiscalia (Lat.) Fiscal rights.

jural Basic law of rights and obligations; legal rights and obligations as opposed to moral rights.

jurat A statement on an affidavit swearing to where, when, and before whom it was sworn.

jure uxoris (Lat.) The right of a wife.

juridical 1. Related to the court system or a judge. 2. Conforming to law and the court. 3. Regular legal procedures.

jurisdiction 1. The region or geographical area within which a court has the authority, right, and power to carry out its prescribed activities. 2. The subject matters that a court has the authority to hear and decide on and that are legally binding. 3. The right to decide a question properly presented in court. 4. The limitation on the courts, judges, police, etc.

jurisdictional dispute In health administration and labor management, this is a dispute between unions; dealing with union members and what the members are or are not allowed to do.

juris doctorate (JD) Doctor of laws. The basic law degree. *See JD.*

jurisprudence 1. The study and philosophy of law. 2. System of laws; study of the form and structure of the legal system. 3. The science of law; a general term describing the course of judicial decision. Also used interchangeably as a popular synonym for "law."

jurist 1. Judge. 2. An expert in the field of law.

juristic act An act having a legal ramification.

juristic person 1. Legal aspects of the individual person. 2. For legal purposes, natural persons, individuals, and corporations.

juror A person who serves on a jury.

jury Several persons randomly selected and put under oath to weigh and review facts of a case, determine fairness and truth, and decide guilt or innocence. A grand jury is used to review complaints and accusations about crimes and hear preliminary evidence. Formal accusations or indictments are then made. A trial jury hears evidence and decides guilt or innocence on criminal cases or liability in civil actions.

jury commission A special selected group of private citizens with authority to select names of jurors.

jury list In the litigation process and voir dire, this is a list of prospective jurors from which a jury is selected. *See voir dire.*

jus (Lat.) Right; justice; law; a body of law.

jus disponendi (Lat.) The right of disposing.

jus mariti (Lat.) The right of the husband.

just 1. True, correct, proper, rightful, equitable. 2. Legal, lawful. 3. Impartial, right, fair, upright, honest.

just cause In health administration and human resource management, this is a legal reason deemed morally right and fair for imposing discipline on an employee as long as the employer has allowed for due process. *See Skelly procedure.*

jus tertii (Lat.) 1. The right to property by a person not involved in a lawsuit. 2. The right of a third party.

justice 1. The use of legal authority and power to uphold that which is right, fair, and lawful. 2. Impartiality, fairness, and equality in treatment under the law. 3. Dealing uprightly with others. 4. Legal administration. 5. A judge of higher courts.

justice of the peace (JP) A judge or court at the local level.

justiciable In law and the litigation process, these are issues or decisions that can properly be determined in a judicial proceeding.

justification 1. In health law, this is the act of showing that something is right or just; a good enough reason; ability of a fact to stand up in court; that which justifies. 2. In health-care administration, this is a written statement of purpose, reason, need, proof, and fact that a piece of equipment be purchased, a renovation completed, a staff member hired, or an administrative decision made.

just in time In health-care administration, this is a form of purchasing and inventory control where little material or product is kept on hand and the needed goods are delivered just in the amount and at the time they are needed.

juvenile 1. Pertaining to youth, adolescence, or childhood. 2. Immature; immature behavior.

juvenile court The court used to hear cases of either delinquent or neglected children and arrested adolescents.

juxtaposition Side by side; close together.

J visa A special visa category authorized by the U.S. Information and Educational Exchange (Smith-Mundt) Act of 1948. It is a product of the concept of the educational exchange initiated by the Fulbright program. Individuals with J visas may be admitted to the United States for the purpose of pursuing a full-time program of study (such as residency) but must be absent from the United States for 2 years after their studies have ended before they can reenter as an immigrant. In 1970, legislation was passed that eliminated this requirement for foreign medical graduates coming to the United States on private funds as long as they were not from a country where their special skills were in short supply. However, waivers may be obtained by physicians who are from countries where their skills are in short supply if the home country has not objected to their immigration to the United States. Waivers are rarely, if ever, denied, primarily for lack of objection from home countries. *See also labor certification, schedule A.*

K

Kahn test In medical care, this is a blood test that can diagnose cancer and syphilis.

kangaroo court 1. A mock court 2. An unofficial court with no authority or legal powers.

KCF *See key clinical findings.*

Kefauver-Harris Amendment A 1962 amendment to the federal Food, Drug, and Cosmetic Act that requires that effectiveness of new drugs be demonstrated before being allowed to be used on patients and prescribed by physicians. The law was extended in 1976 to include the safety and effectiveness of medical devices. Devices must be demonstrated and proven effective before they are allowed in the treatment of patients.

Kelly forceps In medical care, this is a type of small surgical clamp used to stop the flow of blood from blood vessels by clamping off the vessel; a hemostat.

kelvin scale A measure of temperature that uses absolute zero as its minimum reading. Scale units correspond in magnitude to those of Celsius.

Kentucky January A program designed to teach students about the problems of delivering health care in a rural community. The project was supported by the Division of Associated Health Professions and the Area Health Education System of the Kentucky State Council on Public Higher Education. The project provided allied health students an overview of the totality of health care in a variety of practical situations and was supported by an Allied Health Special Project Grant to the University of Kentucky.

Keogh Act plan A plan, available since 1963, under the Self-Employed Individual's Tax Retirement Act (Keogh Act), that permits a self-employed individual (such as a private physician) to establish a formal retirement plan and to obtain tax advantages similar to those available for qualified corporate pension plans. Self-employed individuals can annually set aside up to 15% of earned income or a set amount and take a tax deduction for it.

Kerr-Mills Act The popular name for the Social Security Act's amendments of 1960 that expanded and modified the federal government's existing responsibility for assisting the states in paying for medical care for the aged poor. The act liberalized federal sharing in vendor payments for medical care under the federal/state old-age cash assistance program. It also created a new public assistance category, Medical Assistance for the Aged (MAA). The medically indigent individuals or families eligible for assistance under this program were persons age 65 or over whose incomes were high enough that they were not eligible for old-age assistance but who needed help in meeting the costs of their medical care. The federal share of medical payments ranged between 50% and 80% depending on the per capita income of the states, with no limitation on the maximum amount of payment. The Social Security amendments of 1965 established the Medicaid program, which substituted a single program of federal assistance for medical vendor payments under the categorical cash assistance and MAA programs. The concept of medical indigency was extended to needy, disabled, blind, and dependent children and their families. In July 1970, federal sharing in vendor payments became available only under Medicaid.

key clinical findings (KCF) A measure of the severity of an illness or injury. Used in standardized medical terminology, the findings are based on objective clinical findings such as X rays, lab test results, and CT scans. The most serious clinical level of severity is the likelihood of organ failure.

key employee life insurance A special life insurance for top administrators or chief executive officers of health-care facilities to indemnify the facility or organization for the loss of a key person in the organization.

key function In the accreditation of hospitals, these are important organizational activities that increase the probability of desired patient outcomes (JCAHO for acute-care facilities).

key indicators In health-care delivery in long-term care, these are measures of quality of care and quality of life of nursing home residents based on care given, outcomes, and the process and manner through which the care is provided. *See health status indicators; activities of daily living.*

Key Indicators, Probes and Scoring method *See KIPS.*

key issues or constraints affecting plan implementation The factors and limitations deemed to be influential or deleterious to the implementation of a health plan.

key jobs In health administration and human resource management, these are positions in a health-care facility or organization that are essential for effective and efficient functioning of the organization; common positions found in the health-care industry based on the importance they have to the operation of the organization and/or based on supply and demand and manpower shortage areas.

key-man health insurance An individual or group insurance policy designed to protect an essential employee or employees of a firm against the loss of income resulting from disability. If desired, it may be written for the benefit of the employer, who usually continues to pay the salary during periods of disability. *See key-person insurance.*

key numbers A legal referencing system that classifies legal subjects by topics and subtopics with a key number and sign of a key given to each topic. It is used to find cases listed by subject in the *American Digest System* and the *National Reporter System.*

key performance area *See performance area.*

key-person insurance A specialized disability or life insurance designed to provide money to beneficiaries (the health-care organization) in the event that the key individual(s) (top administrator) dies and his or her absence causes a major monetary loss to the organization. The organization is the owner of the key-person policy and is the legal beneficiary. *See key-man health insurance.*

key primary professional In health-care delivery and patient visits to managed-care clinics, this the first entry-level health-care provider seen for general medical care (e.g., general practitioner, family physician, or physician assistant).

key process A process believed, on the basis of evidence or expert consensus, to increase the probability of desired patient outcome (JCAHO for acute-care facilities). *See process.*

Kg Kilogram.

Kg-m. Kilogram-meter.

kHz Kilohertz.

kickback Money for favors given to a public or corporate official for personal use, for a favor done, or for sending a deal to the person paying the kickback.

kidney dialysis *See renal dialysis.*

kidney dialysis unit *See hemodialysis unit.*

killing by misadventure The accidental killing of a person while engaged in a lawful activity.

kilogauss One thousand gauss. A measurement used in magnetic resonance imaging (MRI) technology, it measures the power or strength of an MRI machine (somewhat like horsepower of an automobile engine). *See gauss.*

kin *See kindred.*

kind 1. A group, class, or division. 2. Humane treatment.

kindred 1. Blood relationships, family, kinfolk. 2. In epidemiological investigations, family tree retrospective studies are used to identify diseases in blood relatives or disease patterns handed down from generation to generation. *See genealogy; kinship.*

kinematograph A device used to show pictures of objects in motion.

kinesiology The study of the motion and biomechanics of the human body.

kinesthesia The awareness one has of the position and movement of parts of one's body.

kineticist A specialist in kinetics.

kinetics The study of the rate of change of certain factors in the body.

kinetocardiogram In medical care and diagnosis of the heart, this is a device that records slow vibration of the chest in the area of the heart.

kinetocardiography In medical care and diagnosis of the heart, this is a the recording of vibration (usually slow) of the chest in the area of the heart.

kinetograph A device used to record movements in the muscles or organs.

kinship Persons who are descendants of a common ancestor. Kinship relationships are often the subject of chronic or genetic diseases and conditions in epidemiological investigations. *See kin; genealogy.*

KIPS Key Indicators, Probes and Scoring method. An accreditation scoring method, used by the Joint Commission on the Accreditation of Healthcare Organizations (JCAHO), for assessing compliance with certain phases of the accreditation process.

KIPS survey guide A publication of the Joint Commission on the Accreditation of Healthcare Organizations (JCAHO) that provides direction on using the *Key Indicators, Probes and Scoring* method for assessing accreditation compliance with certain phases and standards of the survey process.

Kirklin system In medical care and diagnosis of cancer, this is a tumor assessment approach used to determine the extent of the spread of tumors, their seriousness, and the potential survivability of the patient.

kite In health-care finance, this is a negotiable instrument having no value that is written to temporarily maintain credit or to raise money.

kiting 1. Writing checks on a checking account before putting enough money in to cover them. 2. Increasing the quantity of a drug ordered by a prescription. Either the pharmacist or the patient may kite the quantity of the original prescription. When done by a pharmacist, he or she then provides the patient with the quantity originally prescribed but bills a third party, such as Medicaid, for the larger quantity. When done by a patient, it is usually because the patient is dependent on the drug in question. *See also shorting; fraud.*

kleptomania In mental health services and psychiatry, this is a personality disorder characterized by an irresistible compulsion to steal.

Kline test In medical care, this is a test for syphilis.

km Kilometer.

kneeling bus A special feature included on some public buses to accommodate the elderly and disabled. The mechanism consists of a deflatable air bag, permitting the front end of the bus to be lowered to pick up passengers at stops. This feature is usually included in addition to ramps or lifts that accommodate wheelchairs and a stationary floor height of not more than 22 inches.

Knights-move thought A thought process disorder seen in some schizophrenic patients characterized by bizarre and tortuous ideas.

knowingly With full knowledge, design, and intention.

known human effects In environmental health, this is a commonly recognized health effect caused by a particular substance or mixture as described in scientific publications or stated on a company's product label or material safety data sheets. However, an effect is not a known human effect if it was a significantly more severe toxic effect than previously described, was a manifestation of a toxic effect after a significantly short exposure period or lower exposure level than described, and was by an exposure route different than described.

known precedents In environmental health, occupational health, and safety, this is the use of technical information from past experience and existing data to assist in hazard or accident analysis. The information comes from sources such as regulations, manuals, experts, studies, and reports directed toward solutions to known problems.

Knox-Keene Act *See health maintenance organization.*

Knox-Keene Health Care Service Plan Act of 1975 A leading landmark law passed in California in 1975, setting rules and regulations for health maintenance organizations (managed care) and establishing the licensing of health plans. The act is administered by the Department of Corporations and manages licensure, complaints, concerns, and registration of new health plans and managed-care organizations that fall under this law. *See health maintenance organization.*

Koch, Robert A famous German (Prussian) scientist and epidemiologist and one of the first true microbiologists (1843–1910). He was the first to develop the technique of staining bacteria so that they show up under a microscope and to develop fixed microscope slides. He discovered and identified many strains of bacteria by photographing them.

Koch's postulates Concepts and principles of epidemiology set forth by Dr. Robert Koch that helped determine cause-effect relationships between pathogens and a disease. Four of Koch's postulates are 1) the agent must be shown to be present in every case of the disease by isolation in pure culture; 2) the agent must not be found in cases of other disease; 3) once isolated, the agent must be capable of reproducing the disease in experimental animals; and 4) the agent must be recovered from the experimental disease produced. *See Evans' Postulates (Epidemiological).*

Korsakoff's psychosis A mental disorder of alcoholism with symptoms of memory loss, lying, and concocting stories to cover up the problem.

kosher That which is sanctioned by Jewish law.

krypton-81m The most short-lived radioactive isotope gas used in medical treatment, having a half-life of 13 seconds.

kv Kilovolt.

kvp Kilovolt peak.

K-Y jelly In medical care, this is a salve used to lubricate fingers, hands, or devices used in the physical examination of a patient.

kymograph A device used to record physiological reactions on a graph placed on a revolving drum.

PLATE 1

THE SKELETAL SYSTEM
(front view)

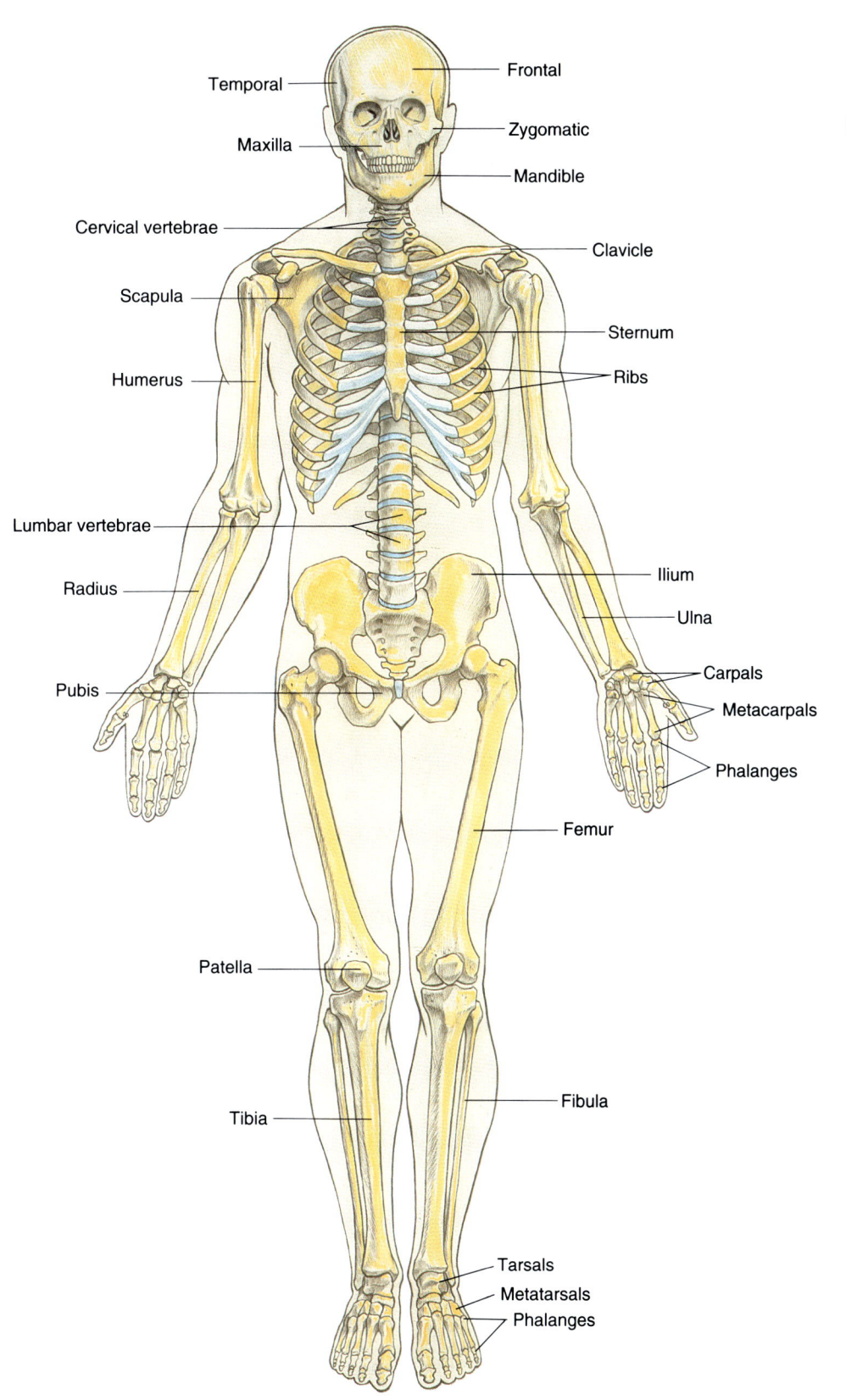

Copyright © 1991 Jones and Bartlett Publishers, Inc. Artist: Vincent Perez

PLATE 2

THE SKELETAL SYSTEM
(side and back views)

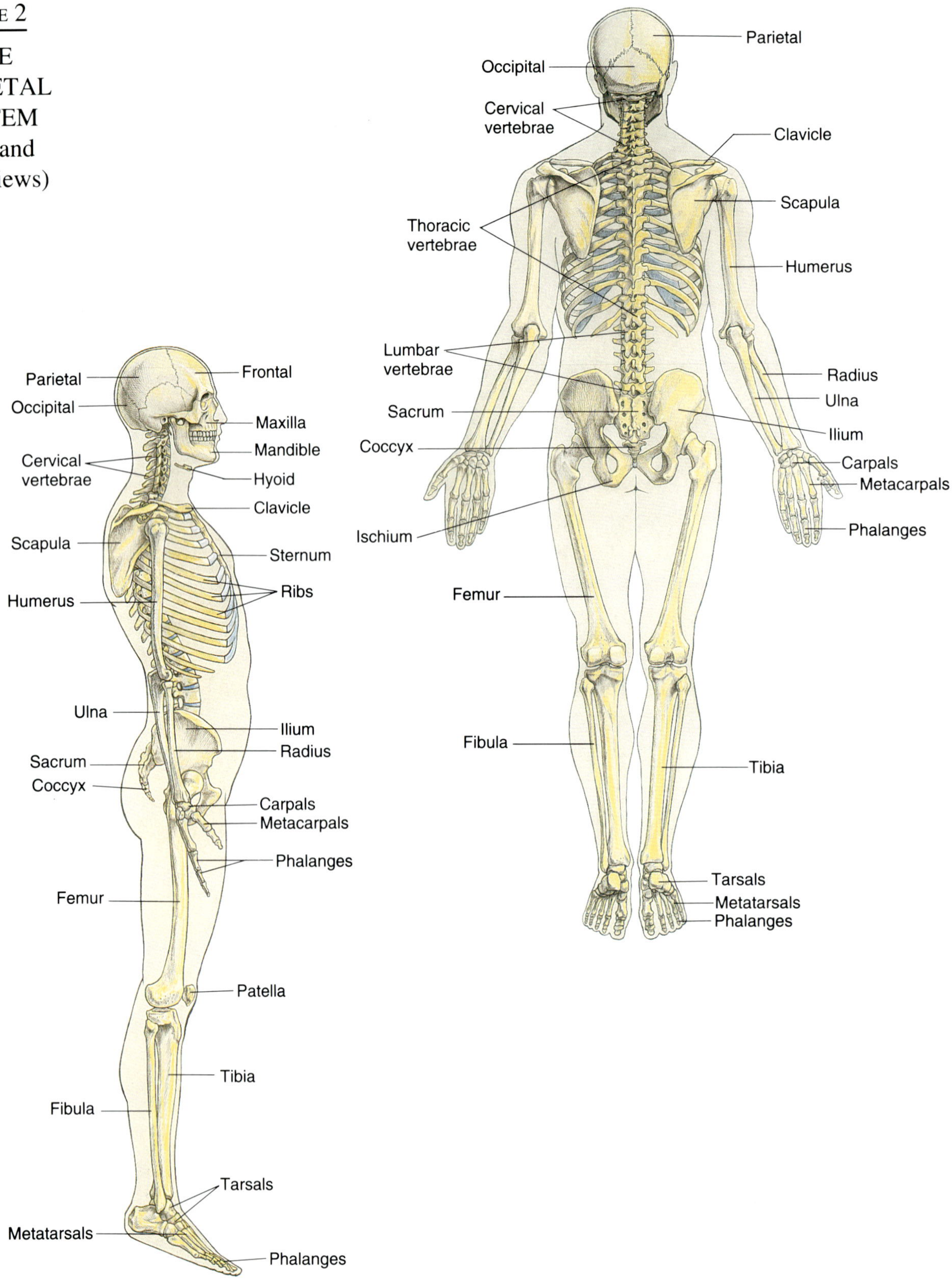

Copyright © 1991 Jones and Bartlett Publishers, Inc. Artist: Vincent Perez

PLATE 3

THE MUSCULAR SYSTEM
(front view)

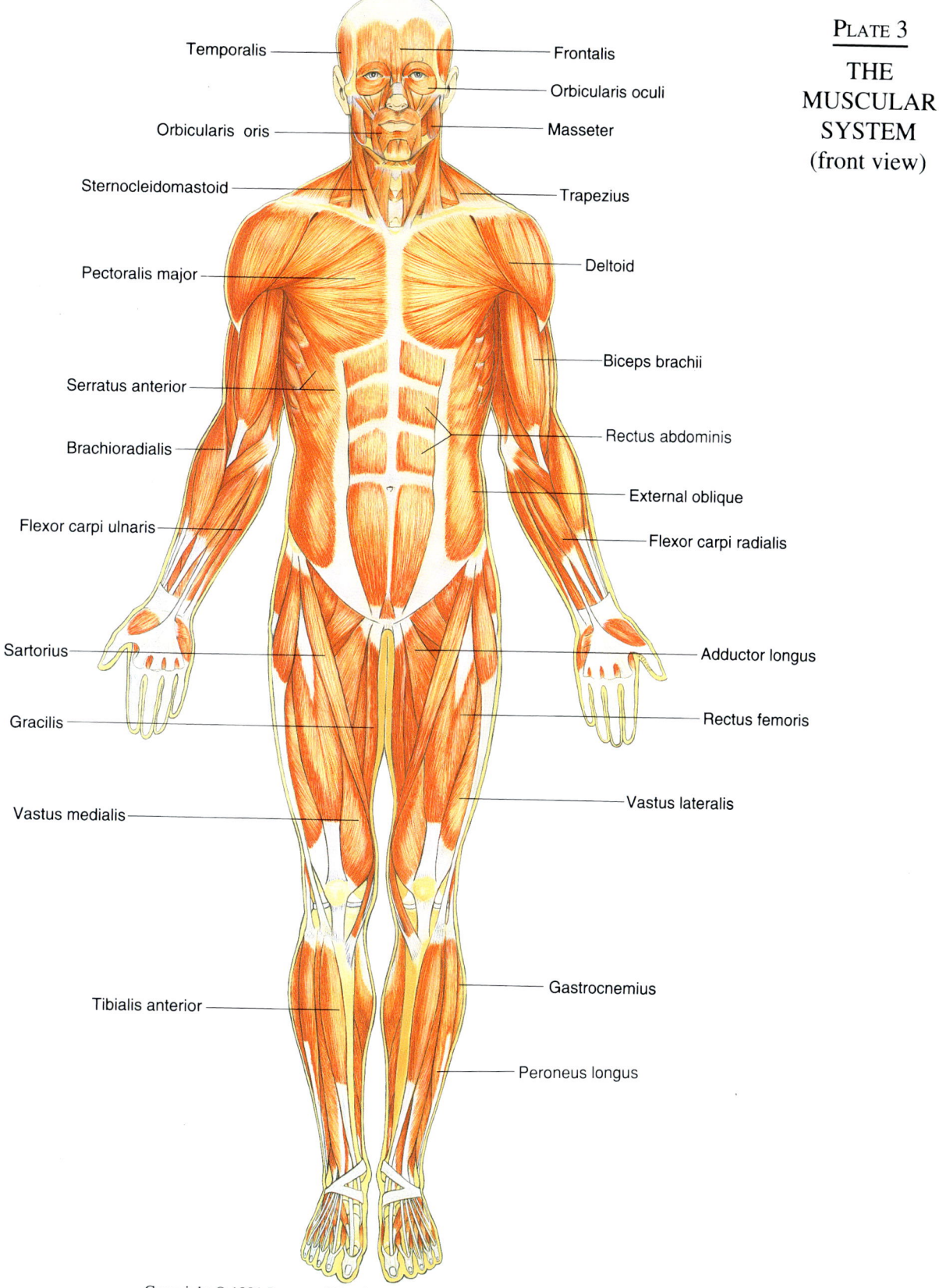

- Temporalis
- Frontalis
- Orbicularis oculi
- Orbicularis oris
- Masseter
- Sternocleidomastoid
- Trapezius
- Pectoralis major
- Deltoid
- Biceps brachii
- Serratus anterior
- Rectus abdominis
- Brachioradialis
- External oblique
- Flexor carpi ulnaris
- Flexor carpi radialis
- Sartorius
- Adductor longus
- Gracilis
- Rectus femoris
- Vastus medialis
- Vastus lateralis
- Tibialis anterior
- Gastrocnemius
- Peroneus longus

Copyright © 1991 Jones and Bartlett Publishers, Inc. Artist: Vincent Perez

PLATE 4

THE MUSCULAR SYSTEM
(side and back views)

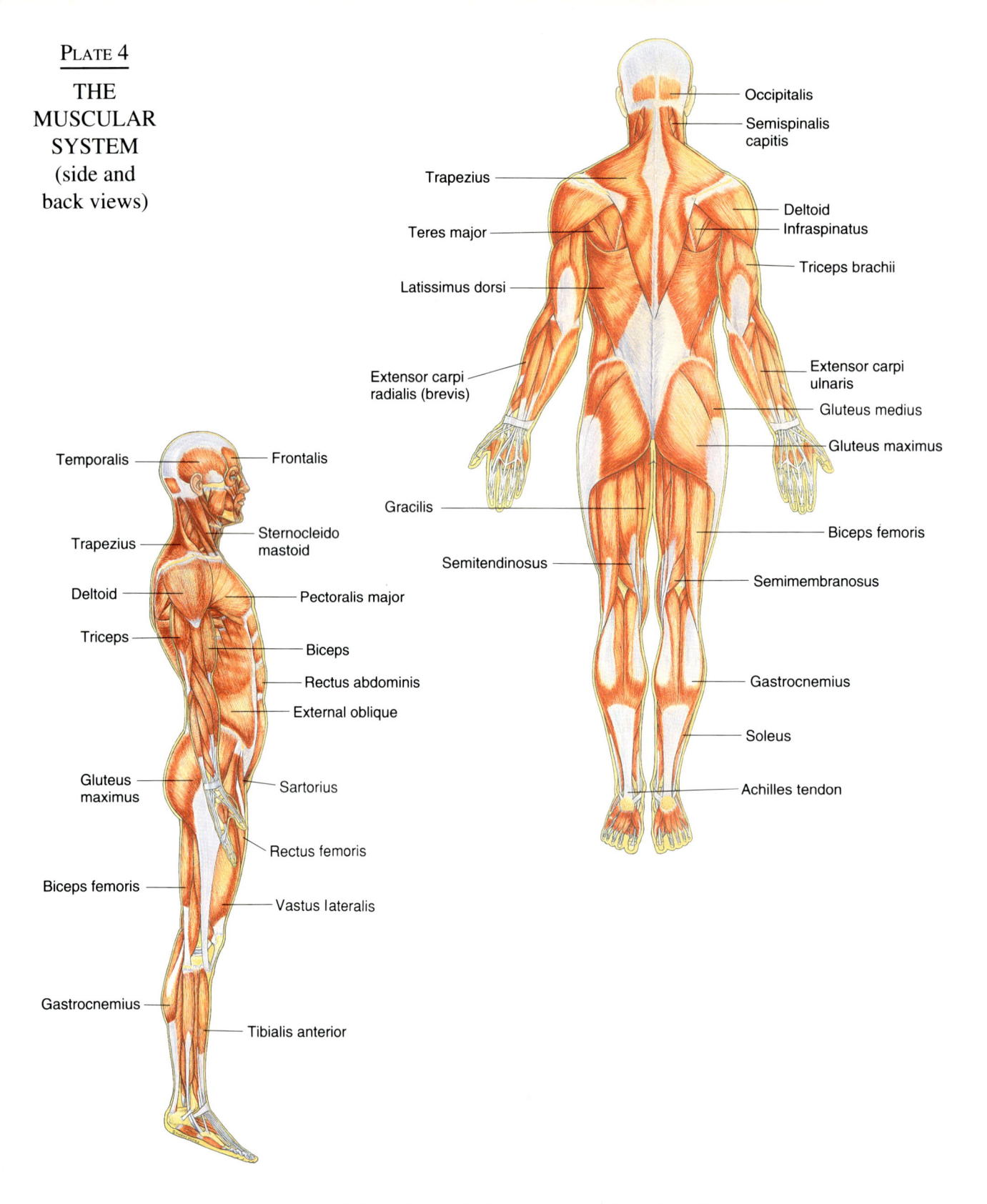

Copyright © 1991 Jones and Bartlett Publishers, Inc. Artist: Vincent Perez

PLATE 5

THE SKULL
and
MUSCLES OF
THE HEAD

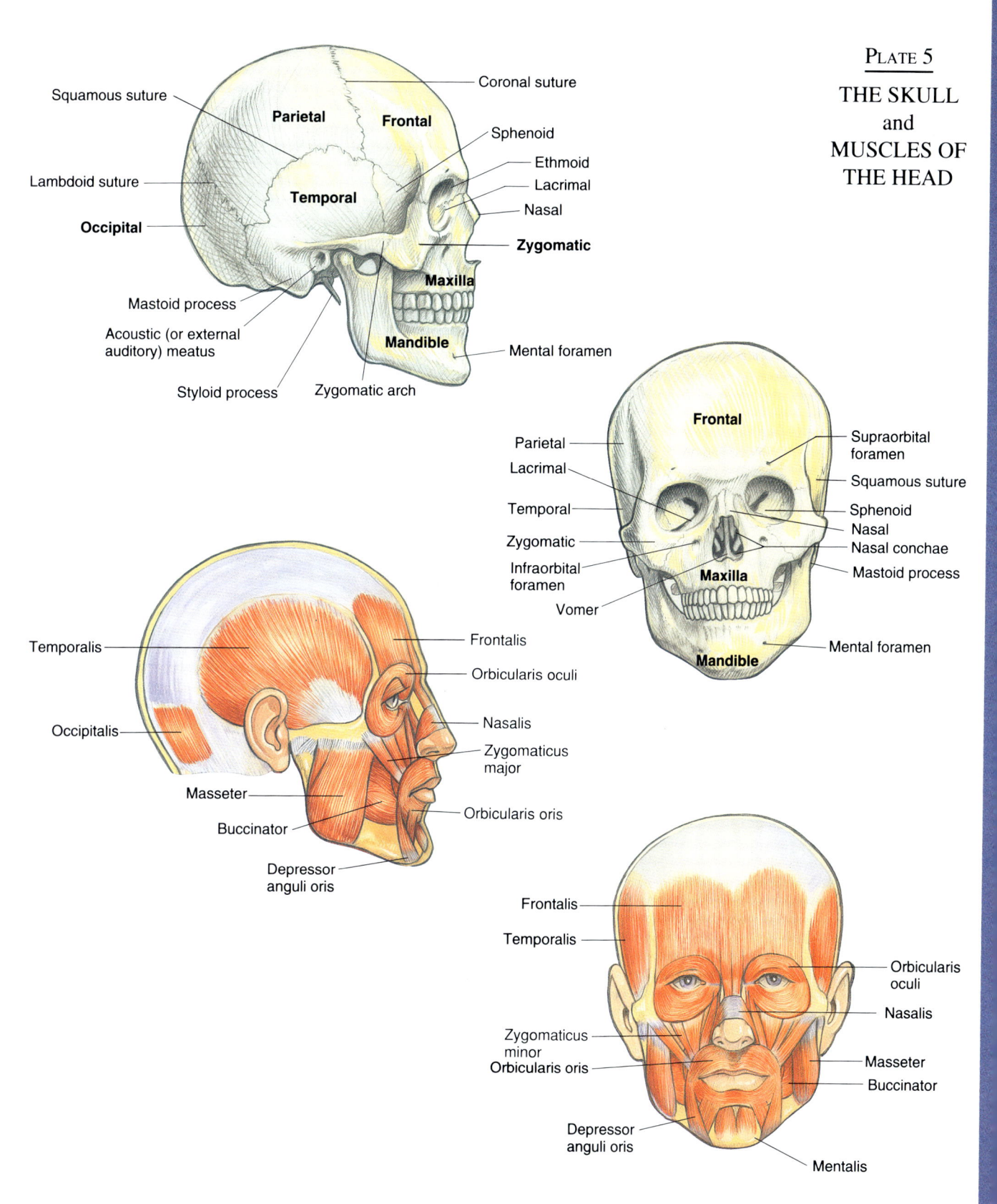

Copyright © 1991 Jones and Bartlett Publishers, Inc. Artist: Vincent Perez

PLATE 6

THE ARTERIAL SYSTEM and THE VENOUS SYSTEM

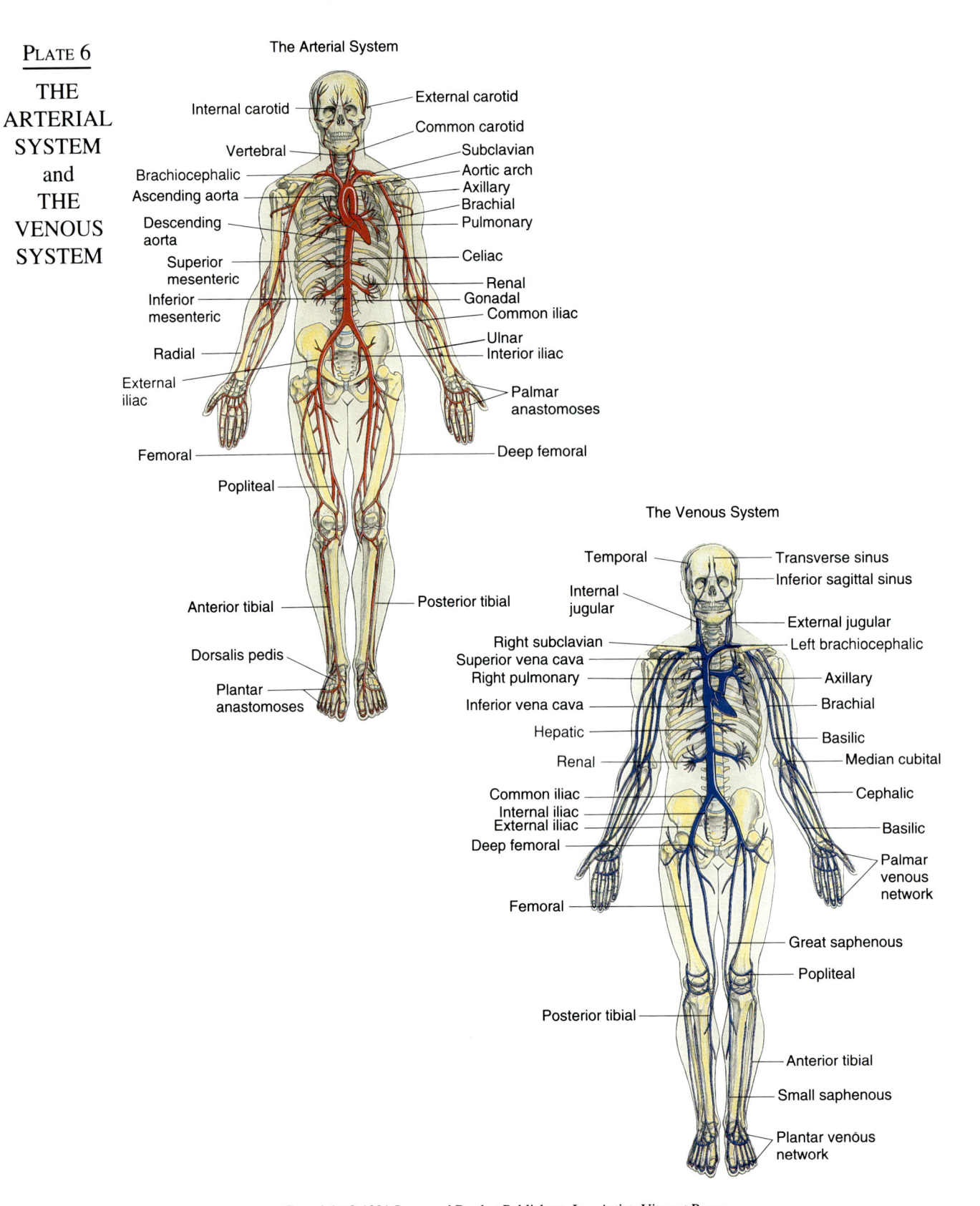

Copyright © 1991 Jones and Bartlett Publishers, Inc. Artist: Vincent Perez

PLATE 7

THE ARTERIAL-VENOUS SYSTEM

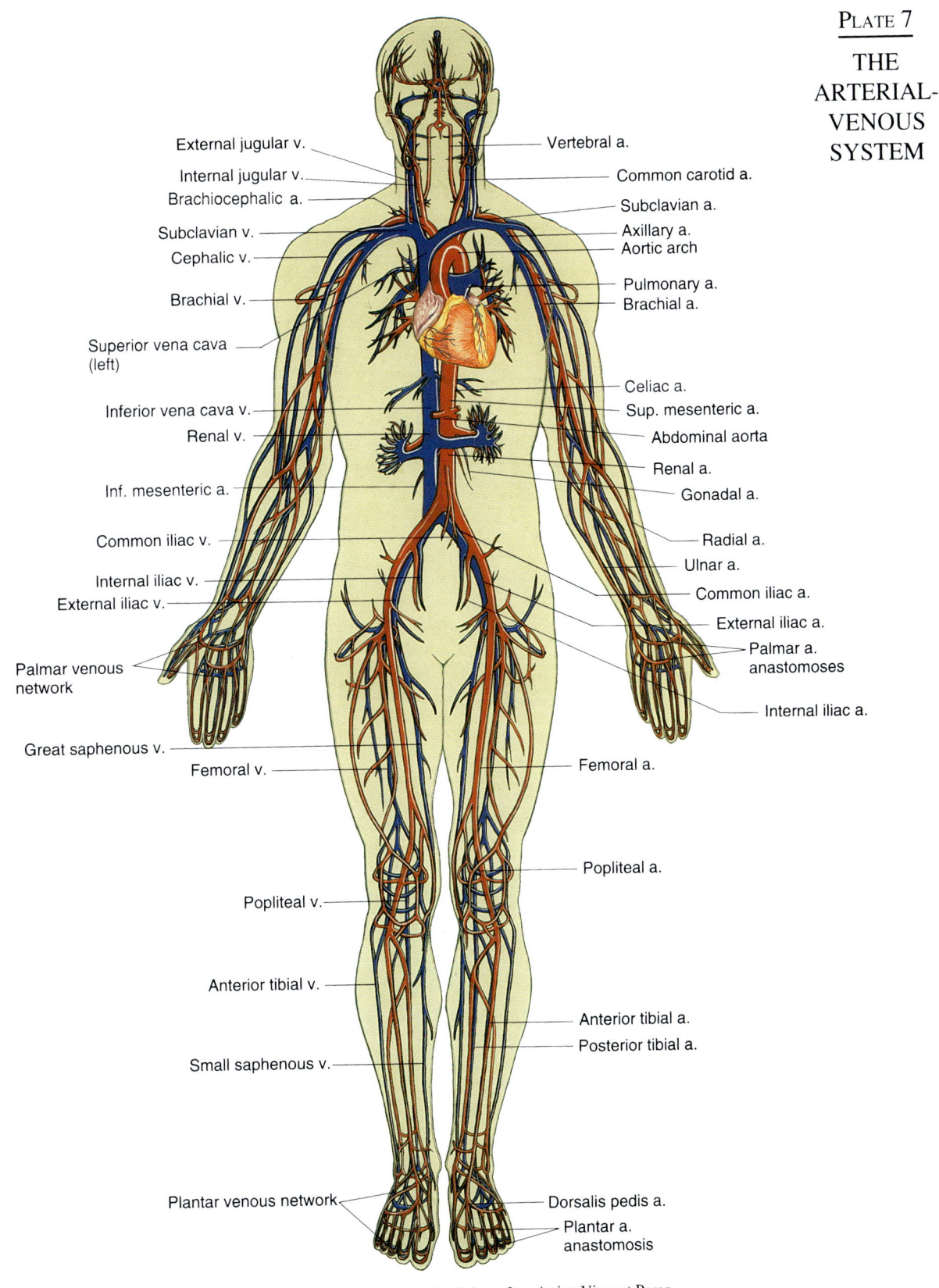

Copyright © 1991 Jones and Bartlett Publishers, Inc. Artist: Vincent Perez

Plate 8

THE HEART and BLOOD CIRCUITS

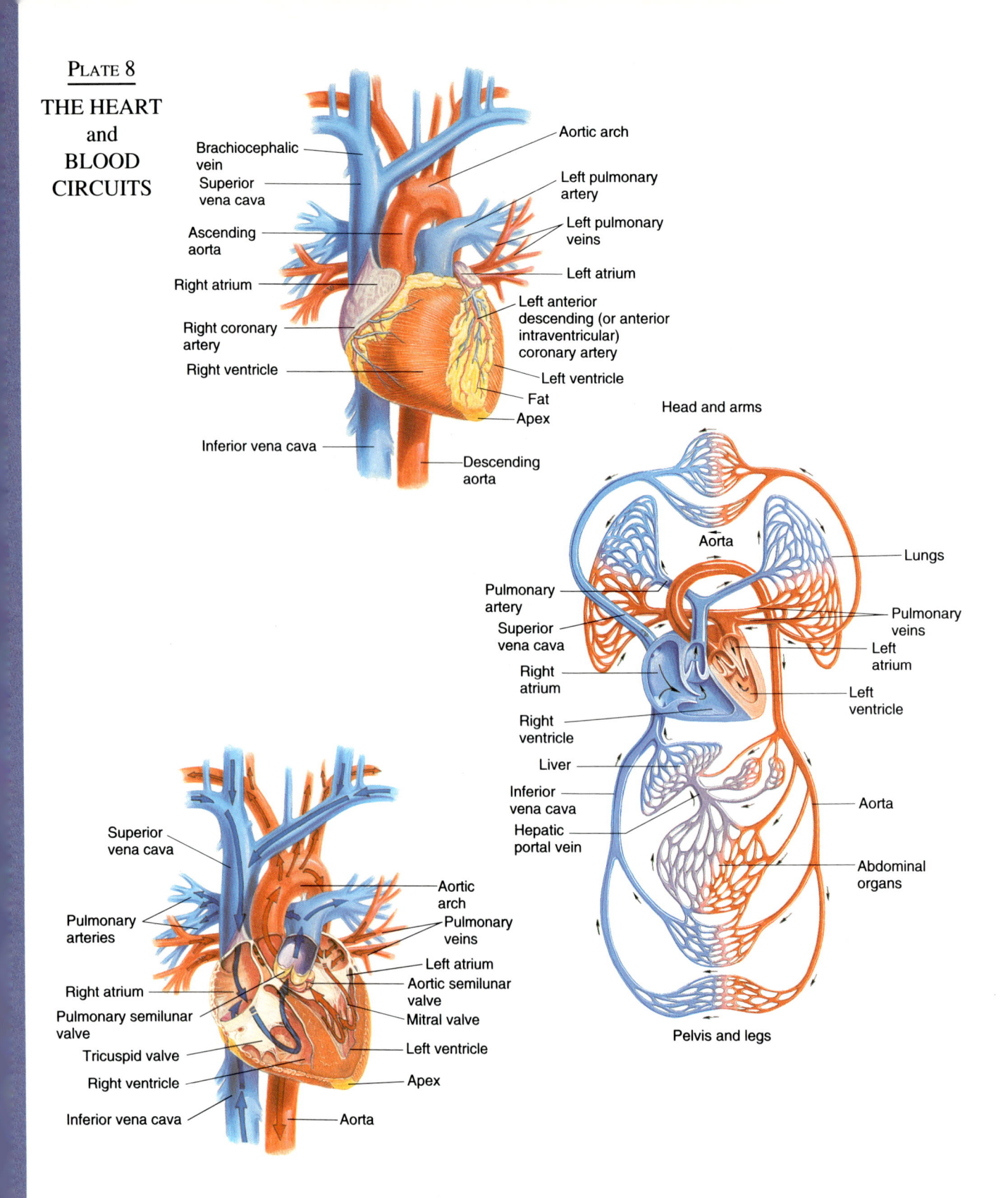

Copyright © 1991 Jones and Bartlett Publishers, Inc. Artist: Vincent Perez

PLATE 9

THE ENDOCRINE SYSTEM

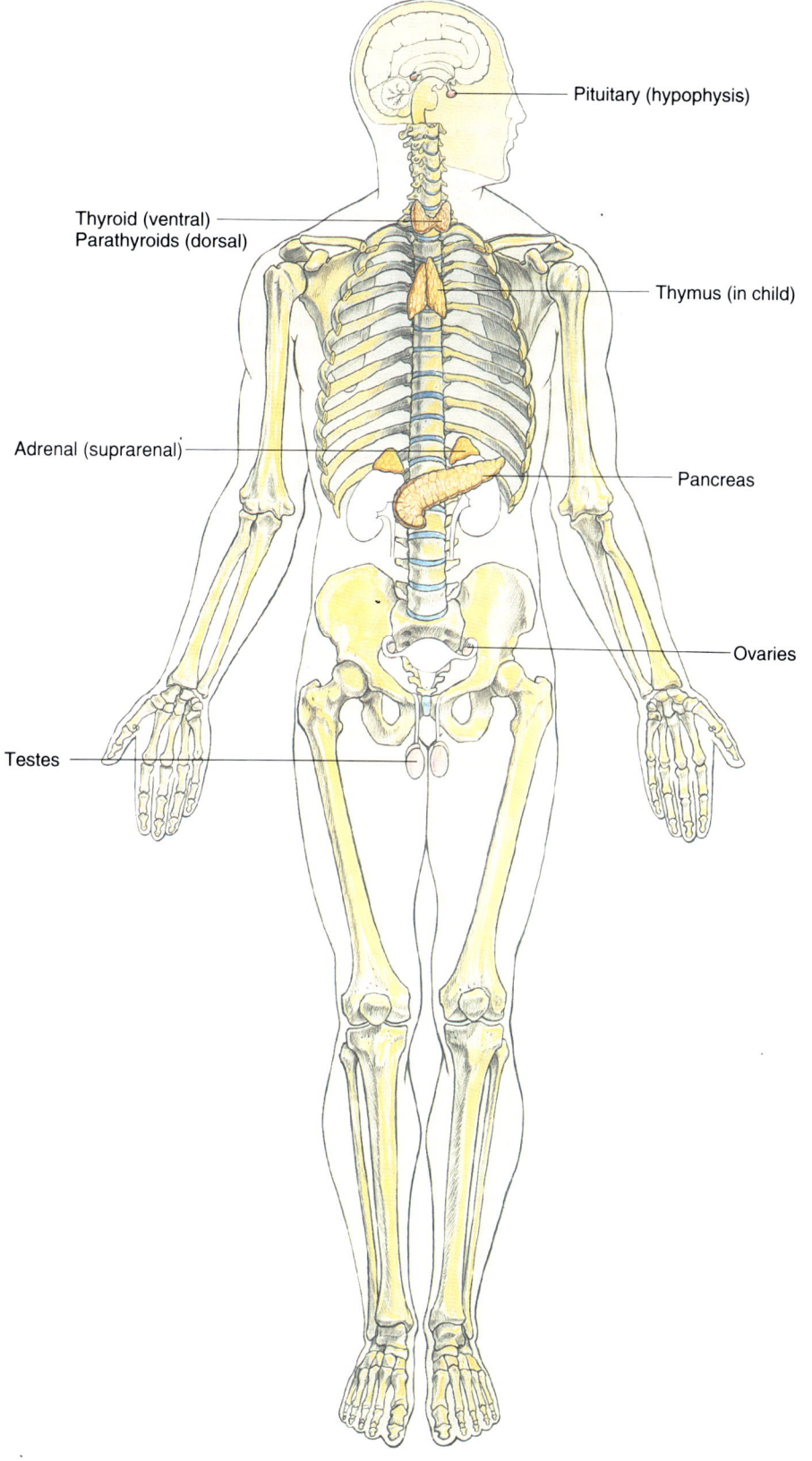

- Pituitary (hypophysis)
- Thyroid (ventral)
- Parathyroids (dorsal)
- Thymus (in child)
- Adrenal (suprarenal)
- Pancreas
- Ovaries
- Testes

Copyright © 1991 Jones and Bartlett Publishers, Inc. Artist: Vincent Perez

PLATE 10

THE LYMPHATIC SYSTEM

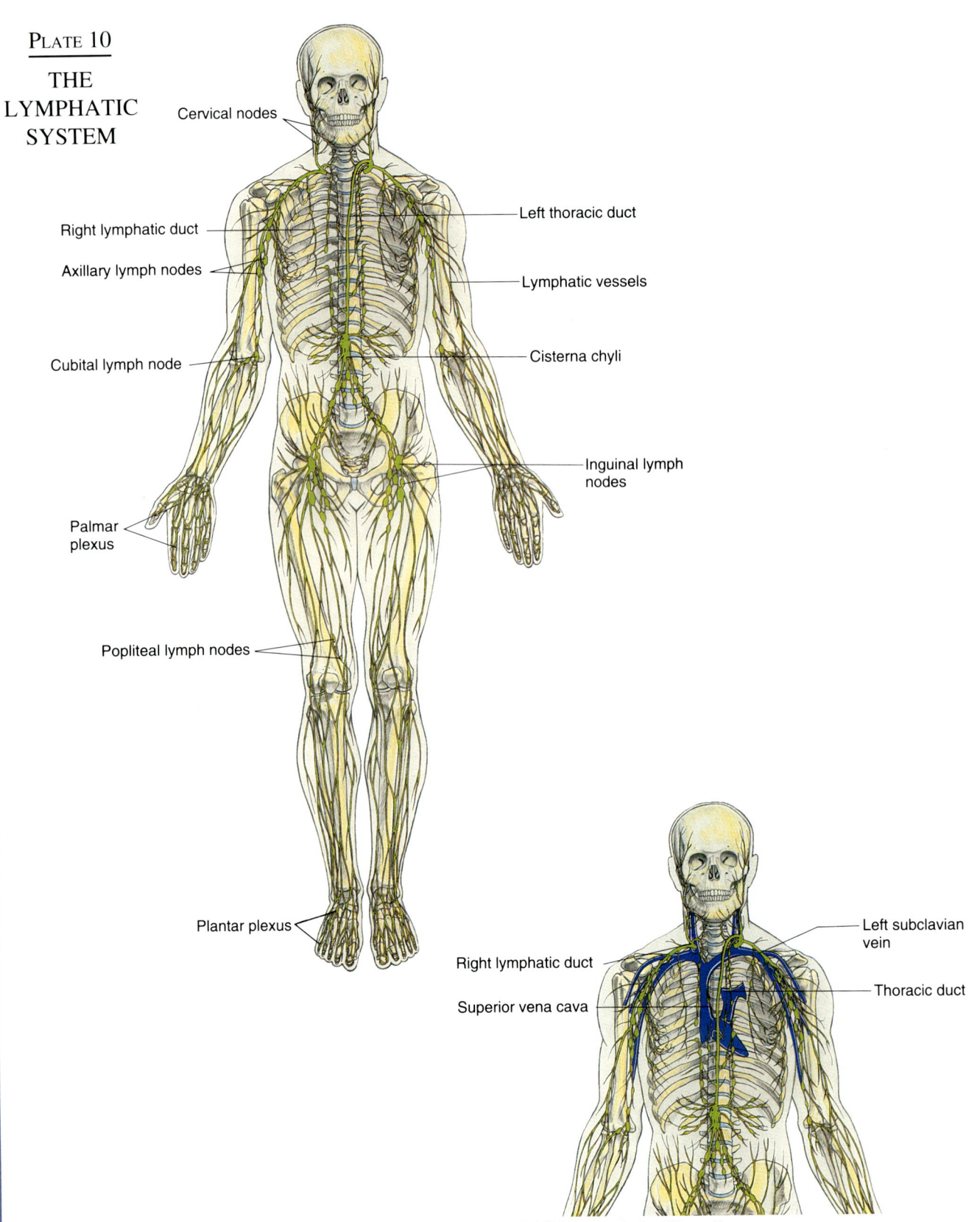

- Cervical nodes
- Right lymphatic duct
- Axillary lymph nodes
- Cubital lymph node
- Palmar plexus
- Popliteal lymph nodes
- Plantar plexus
- Left thoracic duct
- Lymphatic vessels
- Cisterna chyli
- Inguinal lymph nodes
- Right lymphatic duct
- Superior vena cava
- Left subclavian vein
- Thoracic duct

Copyright © 1991 Jones and Bartlett Publishers, Inc. Artist: Vincent Perez

PLATE 11

THE NERVOUS SYSTEM and THE BRAIN (surface and midsagittal views)

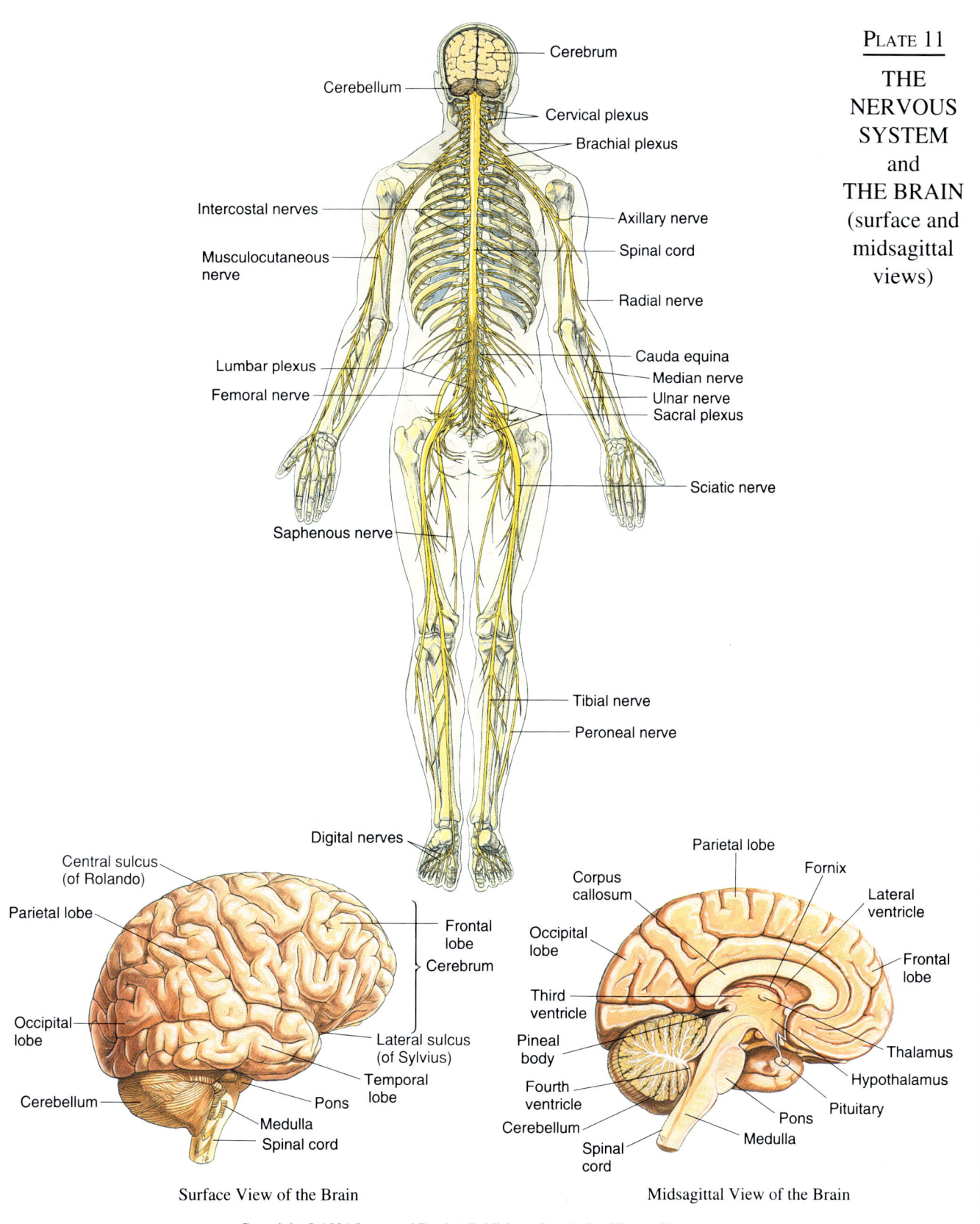

- Cerebrum
- Cerebellum
- Cervical plexus
- Brachial plexus
- Intercostal nerves
- Axillary nerve
- Musculocutaneous nerve
- Spinal cord
- Radial nerve
- Cauda equina
- Lumbar plexus
- Median nerve
- Femoral nerve
- Ulnar nerve
- Sacral plexus
- Sciatic nerve
- Saphenous nerve
- Tibial nerve
- Peroneal nerve
- Digital nerves

Surface View of the Brain
- Central sulcus (of Rolando)
- Parietal lobe
- Frontal lobe
- Cerebrum
- Occipital lobe
- Lateral sulcus (of Sylvius)
- Temporal lobe
- Cerebellum
- Pons
- Medulla
- Spinal cord

Midsagittal View of the Brain
- Parietal lobe
- Corpus callosum
- Fornix
- Lateral ventricle
- Occipital lobe
- Frontal lobe
- Third ventricle
- Pineal body
- Thalamus
- Hypothalamus
- Fourth ventricle
- Pituitary
- Cerebellum
- Pons
- Spinal cord
- Medulla

Copyright © 1991 Jones and Bartlett Publishers, Inc. Artist: Vincent Perez

Plate 12
The Viscera

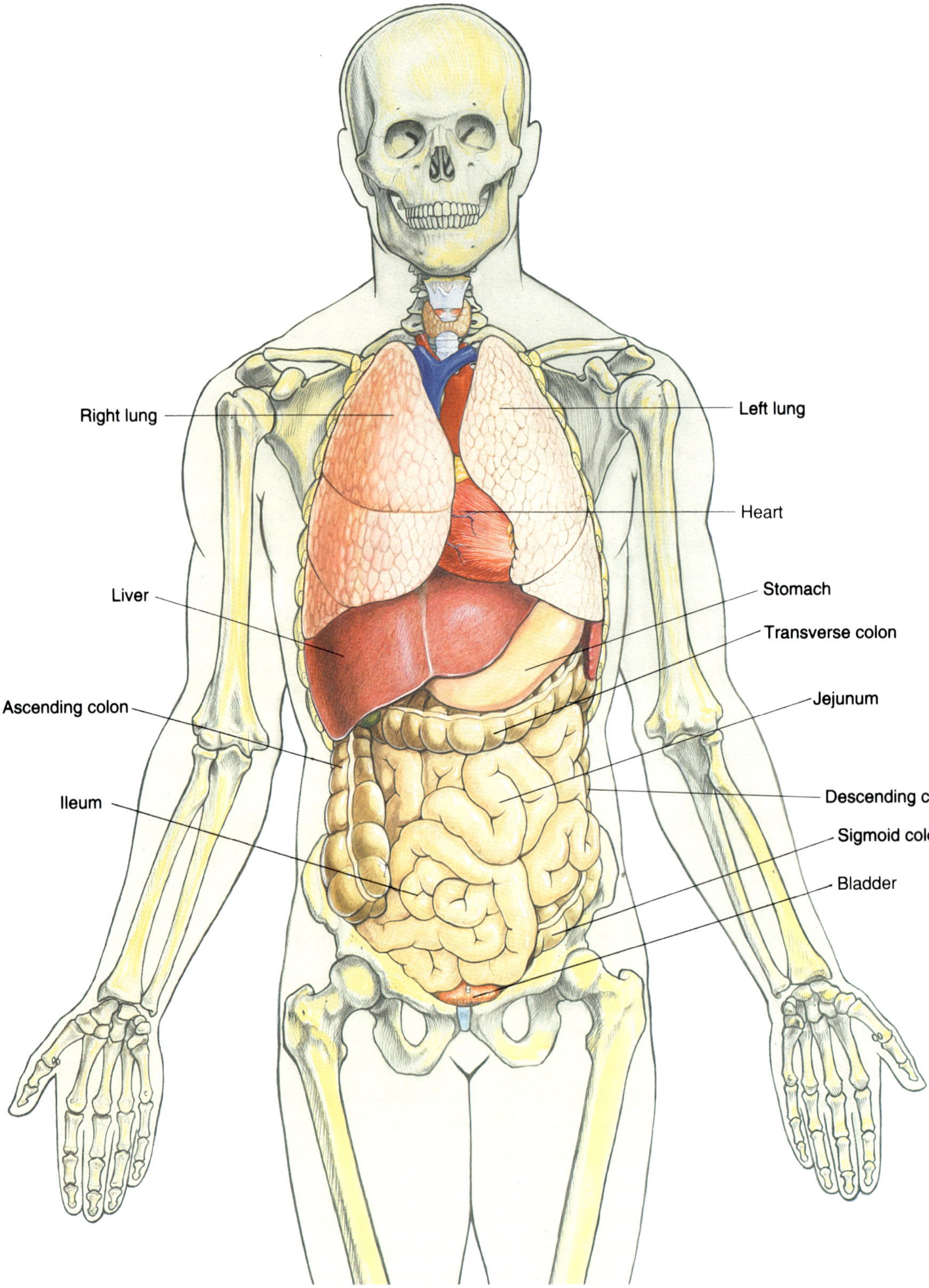

PLATE 13

THE RESPIRATORY SYSTEM

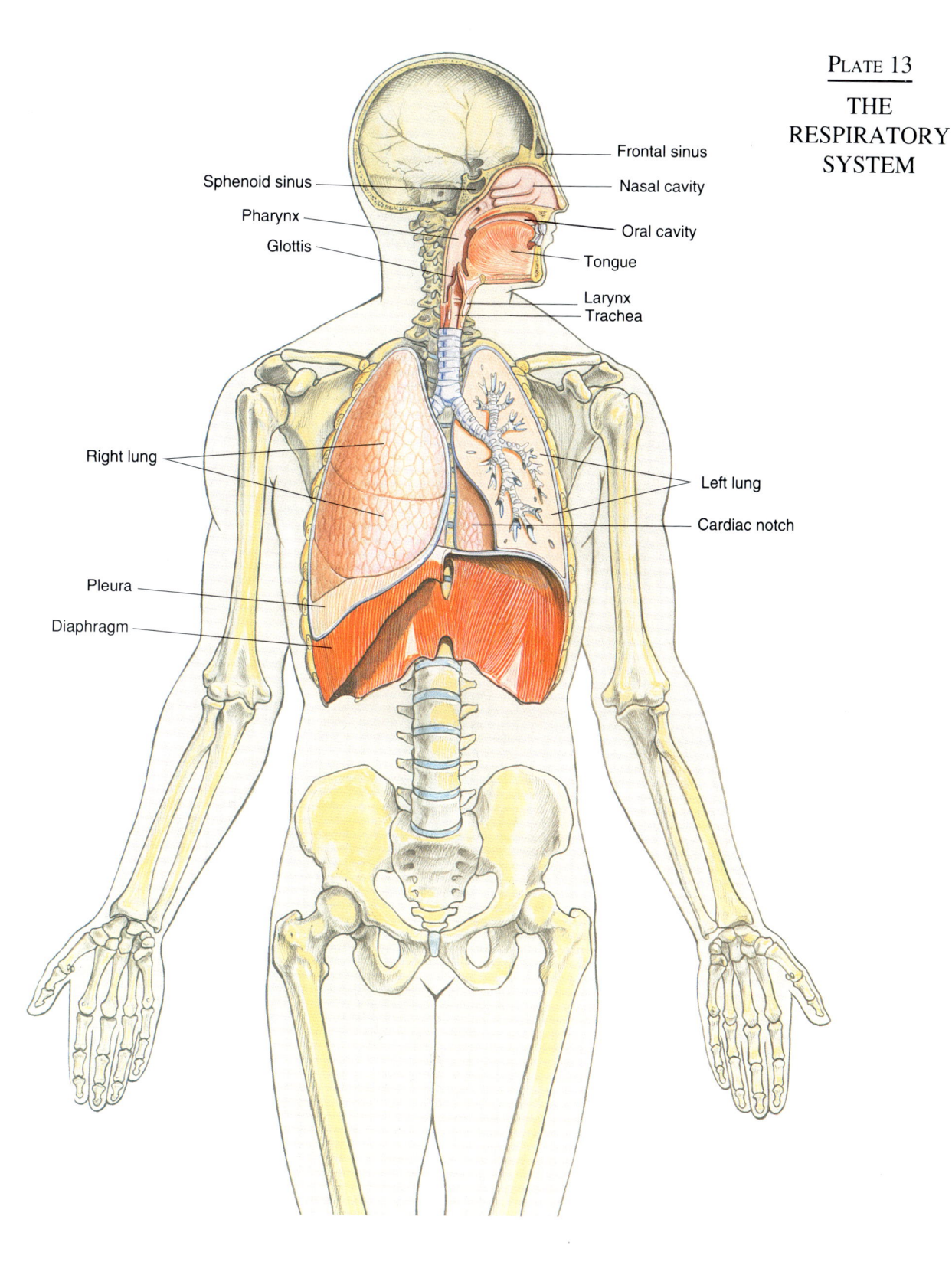

- Frontal sinus
- Sphenoid sinus
- Nasal cavity
- Pharynx
- Oral cavity
- Glottis
- Tongue
- Larynx
- Trachea
- Right lung
- Left lung
- Cardiac notch
- Pleura
- Diaphragm

Copyright © 1991 Jones and Bartlett Publishers, Inc. Artist: Vincent Perez

Plate 14
THE DIGESTIVE SYSTEM

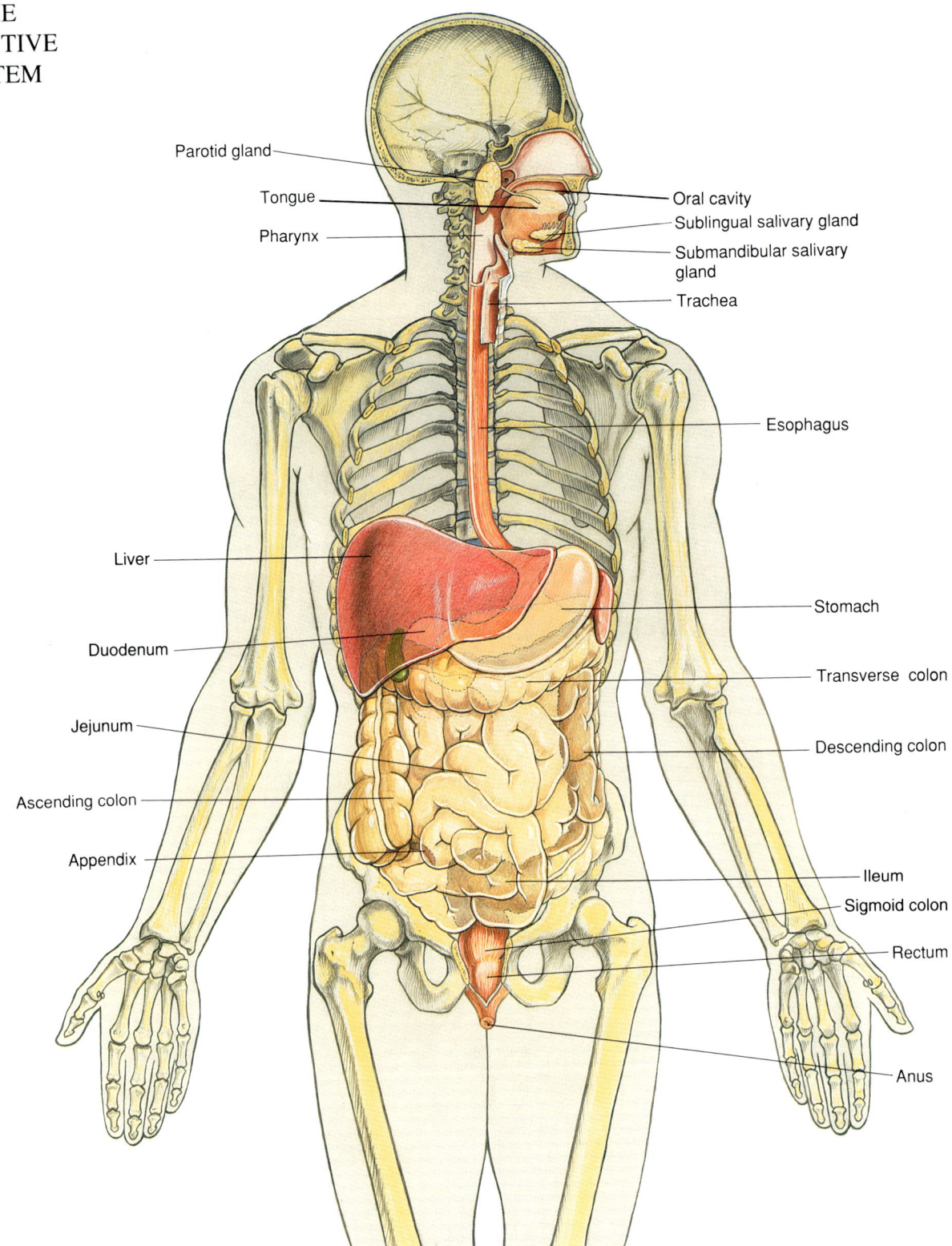

Copyright © 1991 Jones and Bartlett Publishers, Inc. Artist: Vincent Perez

PLATE 15

THE URINARY SYSTEM
and
THE FEMALE AND MALE REPRODUCTIVE SYSTEMS

- Inferior vena cava
- Abdominal aorta
- Renal vein
- Renal artery
- Right kidney
- Left kidney
- Right ureter
- Left ureter
- External iliac vein
- External iliac artery
- Urinary bladder
- Urethra

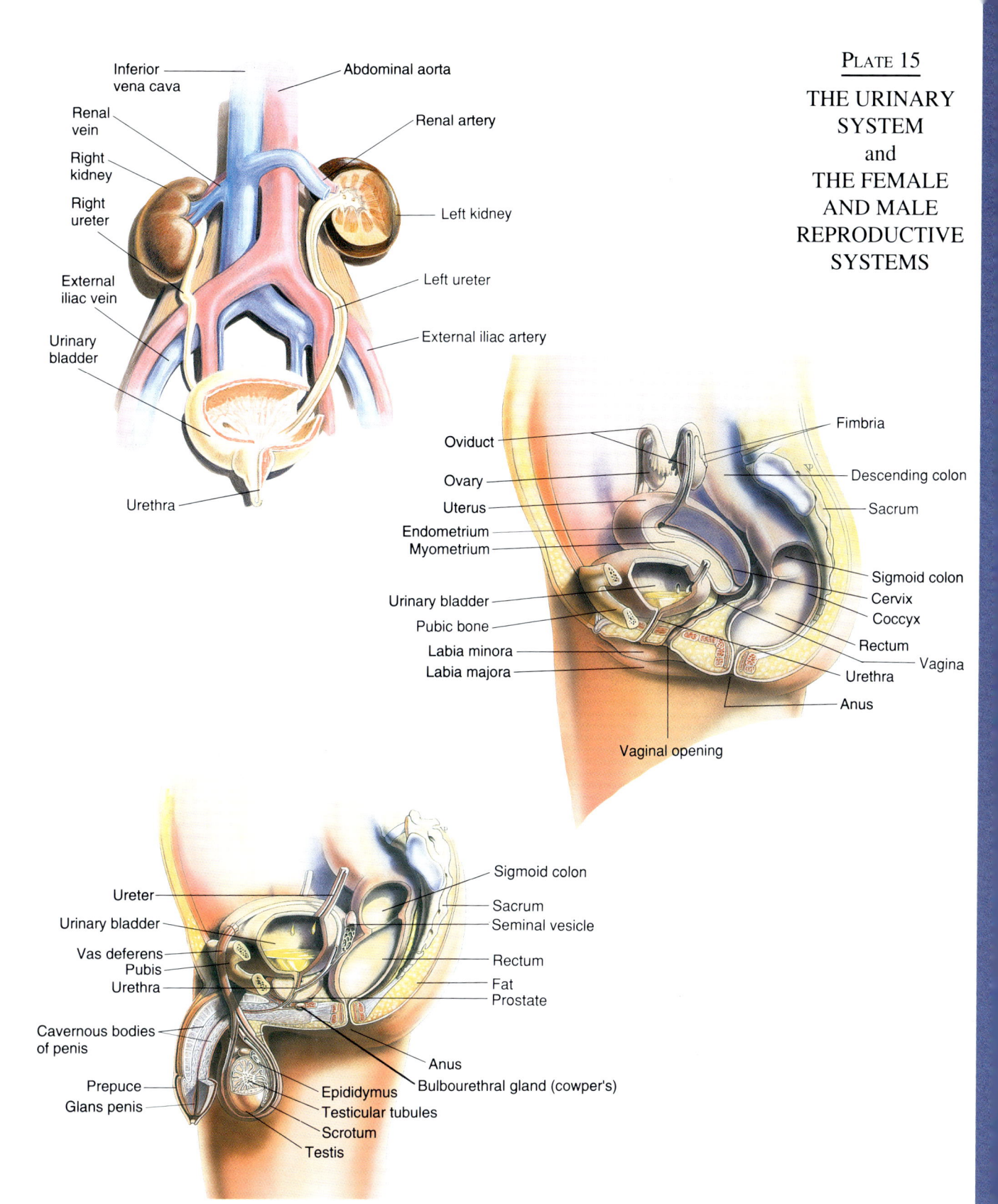

- Oviduct
- Fimbria
- Ovary
- Descending colon
- Uterus
- Sacrum
- Endometrium
- Myometrium
- Sigmoid colon
- Urinary bladder
- Cervix
- Pubic bone
- Coccyx
- Labia minora
- Rectum
- Labia majora
- Vagina
- Urethra
- Anus
- Vaginal opening

- Ureter
- Sigmoid colon
- Urinary bladder
- Sacrum
- Vas deferens
- Seminal vesicle
- Pubis
- Rectum
- Urethra
- Fat
- Prostate
- Cavernous bodies of penis
- Anus
- Prepuce
- Bulbourethral gland (cowper's)
- Glans penis
- Epididymus
- Testicular tubules
- Scrotum
- Testis

Copyright © 1991 Jones and Bartlett Publishers, Inc. Artist: Vincent Perez

Plate 16

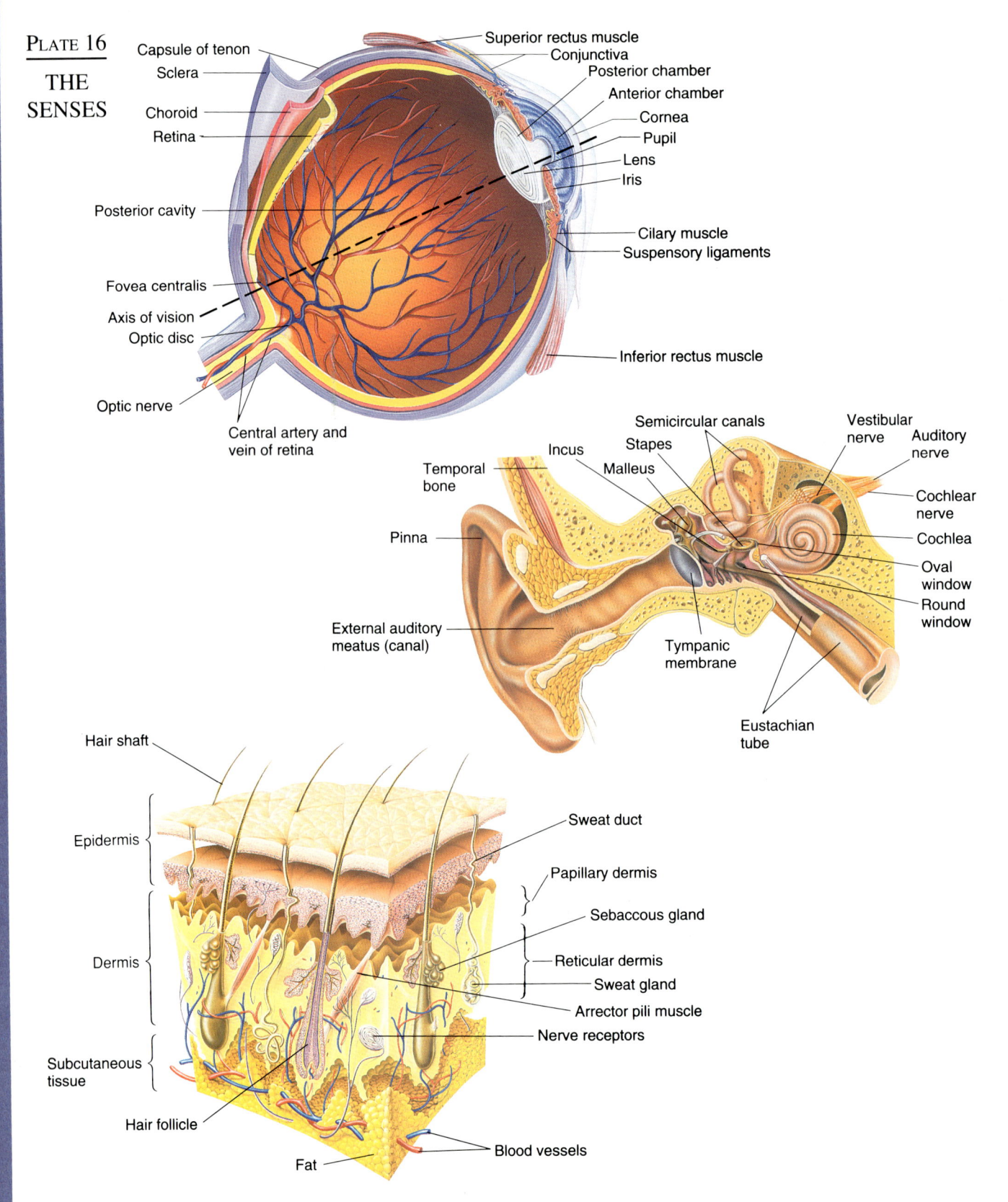

THE SENSES

L

labeling 1. All labels and other written, printed, or graphic matter on or accompanying a food, drug, device, or cosmetic or any of their containers or wrappers (Section 201[m] of the Federal Food, Drug and Cosmetic Act). Labeling for all these products is regulated by the Food and Drug Administration (FDA), whereas advertising for these products (with the exception of prescription drugs) is regulated by the Federal Trade Commission. Labeling cannot contain any false or misleading statements and must include adequate directions for use, unless exempt by regulation. Courts have taken a broad view of the term "labeling" in FDA cases: it includes all written material associated with a product (including leaflets, books, and reprints of journal articles or materials that explain or are designed to be used with the product) and point-of purchase display material (such as placards and signs). Written material need not have been provided to the purchaser at the same time as the product to be considered labeling. 2. In environmental health, this is all written, printed, or graphic matter accompanying pesticides or devices at any time or to which reference is made to the accompanying written literature. *See also package insert; Physician's Desk Reference; compendium.*

labels In environmental health, this is the written, printed, or graphic material accompanying chemicals, pesticides, or devices or their containers.

labile Unstable, rapidly changing emotions.

labor 1. In health-care delivery, this is the physiological and mechanical process of a mother going through contractions of the uterus to expel the fetus, thus giving birth. 2. In health administration, this refers to employees organizing and forming a union to represent the workers to the management of a health-care organization.

labor agreement In health administration and labor relations, this is a contract or other legal document negotiated between health-care workers and the management of the health-care organization that contains the various provisions governing their working relationship as well as terms and conditions of employment.

laboratory A facility where clinical specimens are tested and results obtained and recorded; a testing and research facility that is specially equipped and staffed with technologists, research professionals, and technicians in a medical research institution, freestanding laboratory, public health department, or health-care facility where clinical specimens are grown, tested, and evaluated and the results recorded. In clinical health care, results are provided to physicians to assist in diagnosis, evaluation, patient care, and treatment. *See clinical laboratory; pathology and clinical laboratory services.*

laboratory animal technician One who possesses knowledge and skills in the care and protection of experimental research animals and whose training has been oriented to laboratory animals. *See also animal technician.*

laboratory assistant A person who works under the direct supervision of a medical technologist, pathologist, physician, or qualified scientist in performing routine laboratory procedures requiring basic technical skills and minimal independent judgment in the areas of chemistry, hematology, and microbiology.

laboratory audits In medical laboratories, this is an evaluation done to ensure that all necessary quality control activities and mechanisms are being applied by a laboratory to deliver a quality product. Personnel qualifications are assessed to see if they are qualified to perform assigned tasks. Evaluation is also done to determine if adequate facilities and equipment are available, complete documentation (including chain-of-custody of sample) is being implemented, proper analytical methodology is being used, adequate analytical quality control (including reference samples, control charts, and documented corrective action measures) are being provided, and acceptable data handling and documentation techniques are being used.

laboratory technician *See laboratory assistant; medical laboratory technician; medical laboratory scientist.*

laboratory testing, decentralized 1. In hospitals, this the process of having analytical testing performed at sites in the hospital but physically located outside the hospital's central laboratory. Testing sites are under the jurisdiction of the organized pathology and clinical laboratory or another department/service. Examples of such testing include bedside testing and on-unit testing such as occult-blood testing, serological screens (e.g., mononucleosis or streptococcus), urinalysis, gram stains, and glucose meter testing. 2. For the purposes of JCAHO standards, decentralized laboratory testing does not include testing in satellite laboratories under the jurisdiction of the organized pathology and clinical laboratories that perform tests such as "stat" laboratory tests or off-site hemoglobins, meatocrits, or electrolytes. Decentralized laboratory testing does not include "special function laboratories" such as blood gas laboratories, most sites where intraoperative testing is performed, and cytogenetic laboratories. Also not included are endocrinology laboratories that are not under the jurisdiction of the organized pathology and clinical laboratory but that are sufficiently sophisticated to warrant evaluation using all the standards (JCAHO for acute-care facilities).

laboratory training In administrative training in management, this is a practical, experiential learning process that uses the group process in training to enhance interpersonal skills or case studies to enhance assessment and decision-making skills.

labor certification This is certification by the U.S. Department of Labor that must be obtained by certain aliens such as foreign medical graduates seeking to emigrate to the United States to work before they may obtain a visa. People in occupations that the Department of Labor feels are in short supply throughout the country are given such certification after review of the applicant's qualifications (such as ECFMG certification). *See also schedule A; J visa.*

labor-delivery-recovery-postpartum suites (LDRPSs) In health-care delivery and hospitals, these are specialty rooms in which a mother who is in the labor and delivery process can remain in the same room through her entire stay in the hospital, including recovery. The room is a homelike bedroom that the patient remains in during postpartum recovery until her discharge. Surgical procedures such as caesarean sections cannot be performed in these specialty bedrooms, in which case the mother must be moved to a surgery suite. In the past, patients were moved from the labor and delivery suites to a surgery suite to deliver the baby and to a different room with different staffing for recovery and postpartum. The location of the nursery by the postpartum rooms in older hospitals helped determine the location of postpartum placement. The current arrangement is to have a single suite for all activities but surgical procedures, which have to occur in the operating room. Also called "birthing rooms."

labor dispute In health administration and labor relations, this is a disagreement between employees of a health-care organization who are members of a union and an employer over job content, work environment, benefits, wages, etc. A labor strike is possible as a result of a labor dispute.

Labor Management Relations Act of 1947 (LMRA) Also know as the Taft-Hartley Act, this act amended the National Labor Relations Act of 1935, which set specific union actions considered to be unfair labor practices. This act also created the Federal Mediation and Conciliation Service, which enables the president of the United States to exercise his power over labor matters and can issue injunctions over labor strikes in a national emergency.

Labor Management Reporting and Disclosure Act of 1959 (LMRDA) *See Landrum-Griffin Act.*

labor market 1. In health administration and human resource management, this is the general region or general geographical area in which the health-care organization does its recruitment. 2. The types and amounts of health-care professional manpower available at any one time for employment.

labor market analysis In health administration and human resource management, this is the assessment of the health-care organization's labor market that evaluates the current level and future availability of health manpower.

labor room A specially maintained room in a maternity ward of a hospital for women who are in labor. Both the mother and the unborn child can be monitored to ensure that normal labor is in progress or to ascertain fetal distress or other complications that may require emergency intervention.

labor turnover The rate at which health-care employees are hired to fill work positions and then vacate them, all occurring in a health-care facility's work force. *See turnover.*

labor union An organization formally established to represent employees to management with the goal of improving benefits, wages, and working conditions.

laches 1. In law and the litigation process, this is an unjustified or inexcusable delay in filing or asserting a legal claim that results in the claim being dismissed. Neglecting or omitting the assertion of a legal claim on time.

laetrile A drug derived from apricot pits. Some claim that it has therapeutic value in treating various forms of cancer, whereas other authorities claim it has no value and could possibly be harmful because it contains a cyanide compound.

lagoon In environmental health and water pollution management, this is any shallow pond where sunlight, bacterial action, and oxygen work to purify wastewater or to store wastewater or spent nuclear fuel rods.

lag study In managed care, this is an assessment of a health plan and its management with a report to inform health plan administration how old the claims are that are being processed and how much is paid out each month. The study accounts for both the current month and earlier months on a month-by-month basis. The report compares the monthly payout to the amount of money accrued for expenses each month. This is a useful health plan management tool because it determines if the health plan's reserves are adequate to meet expenses.

laissez faire 1. The attitude that business should have little governmental interference so that individuals can pursue their own self-interests; unfettered competition will maintain prices and wages at normal levels. 2. In health administration, this is a management approach that includes leaving the employees alone to work with a degree of autonomy, having trust and confidence in their abilities, empowering the worker, and thus delegating to them much responsibility. 3. Generally, this is letting people alone; noninterference; letting people fix their own working conditions.

LaMaze A popular orientation toward natural childbirth based on reconditioning the expectant mother from realization of pain to concentration on breathing and relaxation techniques. Expectant mothers are taught different breathing regimens for each stage of labor and are taught to focus on something in the first stage.

land disposal In environmental health, this is the placement of solid, liquid, or hazardous waste in or on the land and includes but is not limited to placement in a landfill, surface impoundment, waste pile, injection well, land treatment facility, salt dome formation, salt bed formation, underground mine or cave, or concrete vault or bunker intended for disposal purposes.

land disposal facilities In environmental health, these are the facilities at which hazardous wastes are applied onto or into the soil surface. Such facilities are disposal facilities only if the waste remains after closure.

land disposal unit In environmental health, this is the placement of solid, liquid, hazardous, or radioactive waste in a landfill, surface impoundment, waste pile, injection well, land treatment facility, salt dome formation, salt bed formation, underground mine or cave, or concrete vault or bunker intended for disposal purposes.

land farming of waste In environmental health, this is a waste disposal process in which hazardous waste is deposited on or in soil and is naturally degraded by microbes.

landfill cells 1. In environmental health, these are the sites for disposal of solid waste in which compacted layers are covered with soil. 2. Discrete deposits in a hazardous waste landfill that uses a liner to provide isolation of hazardous wastes from other wastes or cells such as trenches or pits.

landfills In environmental health and solid waste management, these are referred to as "sanitary landfills," which are land-based disposal sites for nonhazardous solid wastes at which the waste is spread in layers, compacted to the smallest practical volume, and covered with soil or other material at the end of each operating day and with a deep layer of dirt when finally closed.

landfills, specially designated In environmental health and solid waste management, these are solid waste disposal sites, complete with long-term protection, provided to maintain the quality of surface and subsurface waters from pesticides, pesticide containers, and pesticide-related wastes deposited therein and against hazards to public health and the environment. Such sites are to be located in such places and engineered in such a manner as to avoid direct hydraulic continuity with surface and subsurface waters and any leachate or subsurface flow into the disposal area, all of which should be contained within the site unless treatment is provided. Monitoring wells should be established and sampling and analysis programs conducted. The location of the disposal site should be permanently recorded in the local department of public health or environmental health services.

Landrum-Griffin Act A federal act (known as the Labor Management Reporting and Disclosure Act of 1959 [LMRDA]) that allows rights to members of a union. This act amended the National Labor Relations Act. It changed the Taft-Hartley Act and regulates the internal affairs of unions. This was enacted because of fiscal abuse and poor administration by some unions.

Lanham Act A federal statute enacted in 1964 that controls the laws of trademarks and trade names.

laparascopic surgery In medical care, this is abdominal surgery through the use of an endoscope that is inserted into the abdomen for seeing inside the abdominal cavity. The surgery is done with small incisions using physical cutting, lasers, and special techniques under local anesthesia.

lapse 1. In law, this is the termination of a right because of its lack of use within a set time period. 2. Forfeiture of a privilege by failing to meet on obligation. 3. In insurance, the termination of an insurance policy on the policyholder's failure to pay the premium within the time required.

lapsed funds Federal budget funds that are no longer available for obligation because of the expiration of the period for which they were available.

lapse rate In managed care and insurance, this is the probability that a health plan policy that was in effect at the beginning of the policy year will run out by the end of the policy year. Also referred to as "withdrawal rate" or "voluntary termination rate."

lapsus calmi (Lat.) A slip of the pen.

lapsus linguae (Lat.) A slip of the tongue.

laptop computer A portable personal computer that runs on its own power and systems and is as capable and powerful as most desktop computers.

larceny In criminal law, this is stealing or felonious thievery. *See felony.*

large quantities In environmental health, this pertains to hazardous or radioactive materials transportation. When the amounts are massive, they are subject to requirements for being carried on highways designated as preferred routes.

large sample research In epidemiology and health services research, this is a research sampling concept that uses the premise that research findings become more accurate as sample size approaches the size of the population being studied.

laryngoscope In medical care, this is a visual examining instrument with a light used to view the larynx.

laryngoscopy In medical care, this is the process of visually examining the larynx with a laryngoscope.

LAS *See local adaptation syndrome.*

lascivious To excite lustful desires; immoral.

laser An acronym that stands for "light amplification by stimulated emission of radiation." This is an instrument or device that produces a thin, highly controllable, intense-energy beam of light that can be directed or aimed at will. Three basic types exist: argon, CO_2 and Nd: YAG. Each has distinct uses.

laser medium In laser technology, this is any source or substance capable of giving rise to a laser light source.

laser safety officer A health-care professional who is knowledgeable in the evaluation and control of laser hazards and has authority to supervise the control of laser-related health hazards. *See occupational health and safety.*

laser surgery case sources Patients for laser surgery come from several sources, including shifting conventional outpatient or inpatient surgery to laser surgery, shifting traditional procedures to laser procedures, increases in outpatient market using laser surgery, and patient demand for the safer, simpler, less invasive, and quick-healing laser surgery.

laser system In laser terminology, this is a device that is an assembly of electrical, mechanical, and optical components that includes the laser and the needed mechanisms and processes to allow it to function correctly.

last clear chance In health law, this is the concept that a person is legally liable if he or she has the last clear chance to avoid injury or damage and fails to do so.

last dollar coverage Insurance coverage without upper limits or maximums regardless of how great are the benefits payable. *See also first-dollar coverage.*

last in, first out (LIFO) In health administration and materials management, this is a method of inventory and valuation where materials or costs are processed or expended in reverse chronological order of being placed into the inventory.

last resort In law and the litigation process, this is

a court of last appeal from which there is no further or higher appeal in the appeals process; final court of appeals.

late fetal death rate In epidemiology and public health, this is the number of fetal deaths with stated or presumed gestation of 28 weeks or more per 1000 live births plus late fetal deaths.

late majority In public health education and public health, this is the segment of the population most difficult to reach through mass communication channels or those most difficult to convince of the need to accept new health practices and health information; also, those who cannot get to the source or those who suffer culture and language barriers or financial restraints.

latency In health information management, computerized medical records, and business office activities, this is the time delay from the initiation of inputting information or data into a computer to experiencing the computer's response.

latent Remaining hidden or undeveloped; not apparent.

latent defect A defect that is hidden and not readily or easily discoverable on inspection; opposite of "apparent defect."

latent immunizations In epidemiology and public health, this is the development of immunity in an individual caused by an induced inapparent case of the disease resulting from a vaccine. *See immunity; immunity acquired.*

latent infection In public health and epidemiology, this is when an individual is infected with a pathogen and the infection persists without symptoms or only mild symptoms and is not detected by blood tests or other tests.

latent period In epidemiology, public health, and the transmission of disease, this is the observed delay between exposure to an agent or disease-causing pathogen and the manifestation of the signs and symptoms of the disease; the time from infection of the host to detection of the presence of a disease.

lateral Side; on the side, away from the midline.

lateral sewers In environmental health, these are smaller, side sewer pipes that run under city streets, feed the main sewer line, and receive sewage from homes and businesses.

late-remittance offer In managed care and insurance, this is a marketing and customer relations approach used to encourage a reinstatement of lapsed policies. This policy or approach specifies that the health plan will accept an overdue premium after the grace period and expiration date and will reinstate the policy without requiring the completion of a new application or proof of insurability.

later maturity In gerontology, this is a phase of the life cycle in the later years of life from age 60 to 74.

laundry and linen services In hospitals and health-care facility administration, these are services that are a part of central supply or the materials management department that collect, sort, wash, dry, press, and mend sheets, gowns, uniforms, and other cloth items used in a health-care setting.

Laveran, Alphonse A French physician and a prominent historical figure (1845–1922) in public health and epidemiology who is credited with identifying the malaria parasite in Algeria in 1880.

law 1. Any set of rules established to control acts or behavior. 2. A complete set of rules and limitations of a culture or society and government; statutes, codes, ordinances, standards, rules, regulations, and judicial decision/case law are all forms of law. 3. An act or a bill passed by a legislature. 4. The regulations, principles, standards, and rules of a government imposed on and used to protect citizens and society. 5. The system of justice and courts that uses rules to defend rights, property, fairness, business, society, and human activity. *See common law; statutes; lex scripte; non lex scripte; case law; tort law; negligence; malpractice; contract law; criminal law; law of agency.*

law department In managed-care plans and insurance companies, these are full-time lawyers who make sure that the organization complies with state and federal laws and insurance department regulations. They study current and proposed legislation to determine possible effects on the health plan's operations, advise the claim administration department if and when claims are disputed, assist in tax law, and represent the organization as counsel in any outside litigation. Other legal activities can include title searches, policy assessment, investment agreements evaluation, contracts, and litigation reviews and assessment.

lawful Allowed by law; legal; authorized by law; legitimate.

law of agency In health law, this is the area of law establishing the legal relationship between principal and agent (employer and employee) where the agent is to act on behalf, and instead, of the principal in negotiating and transacting business and has authority delegated to him or her from the principal; often used in the context of employee and employer, with the employer as the principal and the employee as the agent. The agent, or employee, is the one whose physical conduct is under the control of and subject to the legal source or authority, or the employer. Under tort law, this is also referred to as a "master-servant relationship." In health care, the physician is seen as the master, and nurses or other allied health professionals are legally seen as servants. The master, or principal, is vicariously liable for the acts of the servant or agent under tort law. *See agent; agency; principal; master; servant; captain of the ship; borrowed servant; vicarious liability.*

law of effect In health education and health promotion, the law suggests that people learn to repeat behaviors having favorable consequences and learn to avoid behaviors having unfavorable consequences (based on the book the *Law of Effect* by psychologist E. L. Thorndike, 1874–1949).

law of large numbers In insurance liability determination and risk research activities, this is a statistical method used to show that as the number of exposures to risk increases, the more probable it becomes that actual loss, damage, or harm will occur and will equal probable loss experience.

law of the case 1. Refusal to reopen a settled case. 2. Acknowledging a previous decision on a specific subject matter.

law reports A published series of legal reports containing case decisions as decided by a court.

lawsuit A case brought before a civil court to have a judge or jury settle a dispute.

lawyer One who is trained, schooled, and licensed to practice law and who professionally advises, counsels, and represents others on legal matters. Synonymous with "attorney."

lay A nonprofessional person; the general public or an average individual.

lay advocate A legal paraprofessional who helps in legal matters or who helps represent persons in hearings of public agencies.

layoffs In health administration and human resources management, this is the separation of workers from the health-care organization because of financial downturns, changes in the economic climate, or business reorganizations.

LCC *See Local Coordinating Committee.*

LCGME *See Liaison Committee on Graduate Medical Education.*

LCME *See Liaison Committee on Medical Education.*

LDRS Labor-delivery-recovery suites. *See labor-delivery-recovery-postpartum suites.*

LEAA Law Enforcement Assistance Administration. A federal agency that provides money and expertise to states and local governments to deter crime.

leachates In environmental health, these are liquids that result when flowing water collects contaminants as it trickles through solid wastes, mostly in landfills, but also occurs from agricultural waste, pesticides, or fertilizers. Leaching may occur in farming areas, feedlots, and landfills and may result in hazardous substances entering surface water, groundwater, or soil; water and other liquids that have percolated through solid waste and have extracted dissolved or suspended materials from the wastes (EPA).

leaching 1. The removal of mineral substances from the soil by the action of erosion. 2. In public and environmental health, this is the passing of surface water over garbage or solid wastes that have been placed in the ground that allows the flowing water to pick up substances and chemicals and take them with it. The water washes harmful agents, chemicals, hazardous waste, and substances such as pathogens or radioactive material out of the waste into the groundwater. These harmful substances work their way underground to pollute water supplies such as wells, rivers, and lakes. In the past, outdoor toilets and cesspools were serious health hazards because the leaching process contaminated well water. 3. The process by which soluble constituents are dissolved and carried down through the soil by a percolating fluid, usually water. Leaching may occur in industrial sites, farming areas, feedlots, various areas of cities, and landfills and may result in hazardous substances entering surface water, groundwater, or soil (EPA).

lead In environmental health, this is a heavy metal that is hazardous to human health if breathed, absorbed, or swallowed and can result in lead poisoning. It was used in gasoline, paints, and plumbing compounds, all of which have been sharply restricted or eliminated by state and federal laws.

leader A person who is focused on change, activity, and process; one with high potential in the field; a visionary who possesses a charismatic personality who, as an enthusiastic communicator, shares excitement for his or her vision with others, empowering and motivating disciples to carry forth the vision; one who has a clear vision of where the organization is going and what it is to become; one who has the ability to communicate direction to others and show enthusiasm for the vision while motivating others to work toward the vision and to work the system to get things done.

leadership Having traits and characteristics that motivate, inspire, and empower others to carry forth the vision of the leader. Traits of leadership include being a visionary; empowering others; building trust; showing integrity and understanding; being exemplary, charismatic, and action oriented; and being a communicator and motivator. Leadership involves identifying future problems and setting needed problem-solving mechanisms in motion, making critical decisions regarding the development and maintenance of an organization, and the ability to inspire higher levels of motivation through highly complex, changing, uncertain, turbulent environments. This is also the behavior expected of a manager, causing motivation to exist within subordinates and other individuals and achieving organizational goals and objectives through their own innate drive. Motivation in subordinates inspired by the leadership traits and skills of a manager is observable even if some of the drive results from other sources.

leadership interview In the JCAHO accreditation process, this is a meeting with the senior leadership of the hospital for the purpose of making an assessment of how the hospital's leaders work together in quality improvement activities, the roles that each of the major components of the hospital play in its management, and the extent to which the standards and requirements for communication and cooperation are being met by the hospital (JCAHO for acute-care facilities).

leaders, organization In the JCAHO accreditation process, this is the group of individuals who set expectations, develop plans, and implement procedures to assess and improve the quality of the organization's governance, management, clinical, and support functions and processes. Leaders include at least the leaders of the governing body, the chief executive officer and other senior managers, the elected and/or appointed leaders of the medical staff and clinical departments and other medical staff members in the organization's administrative positions, the nursing executive and other senior nursing leaders, and other key leaders (JCAHO for acute-care facilities).

leading case A landmark decision or a case decided in a court of appeals that sets a precedent or establishes a principle of law.

leading causes of death *See causes of death in the United States.*

leading question In the litigation process and legal proceedings or in an investigation, this is a question asked in such a way as to suggest the answer that is sought be stated by the person being questioned.

lead time 1. In health administration, this is the time between when a decision is actually made and when the decision is made operational. 2. As used in medicine and public health, this describes the time gained from early detection, diagnosis, and treatment of certain diseases such as cancer, thus reducing the extent, and increasing the treatability, of the disease.

learning In health education and health promotion, this is the acquisition of knowledge, attitudes, skills, and experience that results in behavioral change and enabling individuals to function (an ongoing process).

learning curve The rate at which one learns a skill, process, technique, or educational material through time. A line graph can be plotted and drawn to represent the rate and extent of learning that occurs.

learning principles In health education and health promotion, these are concepts, elements, guidelines, and approaches to assist individuals in learning about their own health and health behavior in the most effective manner.

lease 1. A contract used in the rental of land or buildings. 2. The legal document or agreement allowing one to use something such as land, a building, or equipment for a set payment at fixed intervals.

leasehold In health administration real estate management, this is an estate or property held under a lease; an estate for a fixed term of years.

leave 1. To go away from. 2. A permission granted. 3. A formal farewell.

leave of absence (LOA) 1. In health administration and human resource management, this is allowing an employee to leave for an extended period of time for professional development, education, training, or other personal reasons and promising a job when they return. 2. Allowing a patient to be away from the hospital or nursing home for a certain period of time such as a few hours, days, or weeks with the agreement that the patient return at a certain time to complete treatment. The leave or return is not counted as a discharge or an admission. This rarely occurs.

LeBoyer A method of delivering a baby that advocates that the delivery room have soft music, low lights, a warm temperature, and calm voices. The newborn is given a bath immediately following birth to enhance transition into the new environment. Named after a French physician who believes that traditional obstetrics causes trauma to a baby at birth. Some LeBoyer approaches have the baby born underwater to reduce trauma to mother and baby.

L.Ed. Lawyer's edition of the *U.S. Supreme Court Reports.*

Ledermann model (formula) In public health and health services research, this is a statistical approach used to determine the extent of and/or the distribution of alcoholism in a given population.

ledger 1. In accounting, this is an account book used in bookkeeping to record monetary transactions. 2. In health-care finance, this is the collection of all a health-care organization's business and financial accounts. Also referred to as a "general ledger."

Leeuwenhoek, Antoni Van The individual credited with the development and first use of the microscope. Leeuwenhoek (1632–1723) was the first to view organisms under a microscope that he termed "animalcules," contributing to the germ theory of disease.

legacy 1. A gift given by a will. 2. The disposition of personal property by a will.

legal Required or allowed by law; authorized by or permitted by law; not stopped or forbidden by law; concerning the law.

legal age The age of majority, anywhere from age 18 to 21, depending on the state.

legal aid *See legal assistance.*

legal assistance A free or partially subsidized legal aid program to help low-income individuals, especially the elderly, with wills, legal guardianships, and other legal matters.

legal cap Legal stationery or paper; a long tablet of paper with wide left-hand margins and a narrow right-hand margin, often numbered.

legal consideration In contract law, this is something of value or worth that is legally binding as recognized by the courts as part of consideration in a contract.

legal detriment 1. Taking on liabilities enforceable by law. 2. Changing one's financial position. 3. Subjecting oneself to duties that are enforceable in court.

legal ethics The professional behavior, honesty, and duties owed by all professionals to their clients, to other professionals, and to the public. *See ethics.*

legal fiction To use something that is false or nonexistent as if it were true. Legal fictions are created and used to help do justice. In health law, this is an assumption made by a court that is used to decide a dispute even though it is not supported by facts.

legal insurance A group insurance plan offered to employees by employers that reimburses insured persons when they need certain legal expenses, much like medical insurance.

legal malpractice The failure of an attorney to use such skill, prudence, and diligence as an attorney of ordinary skill and capacity commonly possesses and exercises in the performance of tasks that he or she undertakes. When such failure proximately causes damage, it gives rise to a tort, and a lawsuit may be filed with the court.

legal proceedings 1. Any legal actions in a court. 2. In the litigation process, this is the correct process of presenting a legal action and having it heard in court according to established rules and procedures in law.

legal realism A part of jurisprudence utilizing psychology, anthropology, business, sociology, economics, and the practicalities of life to explain or make legal decisions or judgments.

legal representative One who legally represents or handles another's involvement in the law, a court suit, a trial, or a hearing. *See also lawyer.*

legal residence The place in which a person actually lives; a domicile.

legal right A right that is guaranteed by law or that would hold up in court.

legal services corporation The federal program of legal aid.

legal tender Official medium of exchange such as money.

legend The legal term for a prescription drug; the statement, "Caution: federal law prohibits dispensing without prescription," required by Section 503(b)(4) of the federal Food, Drug, and Cosmetic Act as part of the labeling of all prescription drugs (and only such drugs); any dangerous drug listed under any state professional legal code.

legend drug A drug required by law to be prescribed by a physician. *See legend.*

legislate To renew, create, enact, and pass laws such as statutes; ordinances passed by a legislative body.

legislation 1. The process or system through which laws are created, enacted, passed, or removed. 2. Bills in the process of being considered to be made into law.

legislative 1. The lawmaking part of government. 2. Lawmaking activities requiring the action of a legislature to pass and expedite the implementation of the regulations through administrative health agencies.

legislative authority The act or statute giving an executive agency the authority to write regulations that will implement that act or statute.

legislative courts Higher-level courts established by a legislature such as Congress, state legislatures, or the U.S. Constitution.

legislative facts Evidence and information that aid administrative agencies in deciding legal questions on statutes to write regulations or rules.

legislative history The written record of the development of an act of Congress or a state legislature. It may be used in writing rules or by courts in interpreting the law to ascertain or detail the intent of Congress if the act is ambiguous or lacking in detail. The legislative history is listed in the slip law and consists of the House, Senate, and conference committee reports (if any) and the House and Senate floor debates. The history, particularly the committee reports, often contains the only available complete explanation of the meaning and intent of the law.

legislative intent 1. The process by which a judge or agency decides what the lawmakers meant when they passed a law. This process utilizes legislative records and hearing reports; a way of interpreting statutes. 2. The intent or purpose of enacting a statute that a court analyzes to assist in interpreting a vague statute or regulation or one in conflict with another law.

legislative purpose rule *See legislative intent.*

legislator Any public official who is responsible for lawmaking.

length of hospital stay The duration of days, exclusive of the day of discharge, that a patient spends in a short-stay acute-care inpatient facility. *See average length of stay.*

length of stay (LOS) 1. The length of an inpatient's stay in a hospital or other health facility. Length of stay is one measure of utilization of health facilities and is reported as an average number of days spent in a facility per admission or discharge. It is calculated as follows: total number of days a patient stays in a facility for all discharges and deaths during the same period. 2. In utilization review under the Prospective Payment System (PPS)/DRGs, an appropriate LOS may be assigned each patient on admission. Average LOSs vary and are measured for people with various ages, specific diagnoses, or sources of payment. 3. In PRO and PPS/DRG review, LOS is a criterion used on the basis of past data that defines the expected average point at which patients of similar age and diagnoses have been found to be discharged. *See average length of stay; prospective payment system; diagnosis-related groups; PRO.*

length of stay, average *See average length of stay.*

length-of-stay certification A written order by the attending physician that ensures that the continued stay in a health-care facility is within the criteria of being medically necessary. The order includes diagnosis, complications, plan for care, and anticipated length of stay. This order is to justify any length of stay beyond the predetermined expected length of stay for the illness or DRG. Also called "rectification."

length of stay for discharges This is the time between the date of admission and the date of discharge. *See length of stay.*

length of stay for residents In long-term-care facilities, this is the time from the point of admission until a reporting time, as used in public health surveys (National Nursing Home Survey). *See length of stay.*

leniency bias In health administration and human resource management, this is the slanted, subjective, and high level of perception given an employee that influences the rating of him or her higher on their performance appraisal than their performance justifies; similar to the halo effect.

LEPC *See local emergency planning commission.*

lesion In medical care, this is damage; injury; a change or deterioration in a part of one's body caused by injury or illness; an area of tissue that does not function because of damage from trauma or disease. Ulcers, abscesses, and tumors are considered lesions.

less allowance for uncollectables In health-care finance, this is subtracting from the gross operating revenue the reduction in revenue from serving medically indigent patients and courtesy allowances. It can also include all bad-debt service.

lesser offense In criminal law, this is a less serious crime or a lesser part of a more serious crime.

lethal Causing death; an event or agent capable of causing death.

lethal concentration, low In environmental and occupational health, this is the lowest concentration of a chemical at which only some test animals die following inhalation exposure.

lethal dose In environmental and occupational health, this is the dose of a toxicant that will kill 50% of the test organisms within a designated period of time. The lower the lethal dose, the more toxic the compound.

lethal dose, low In environmental and occupational health, this is the lowest dose of a chemical at which some test animals die following exposure.

lethal dose of radiation In environmental and occupational health, this is the amount of ionizing radiation exposure required to cause death. A brief (within 4 days) whole-body gamma exposure of 600 roentgens would be a lethal dose for most people.

letter 1. The exact, specific, precise, and literal meaning of a law or document, as used in "the letter of the law." 2. The precise language of a subject or policy rather than its philosophical intent. 3. A formal document (as a letter of attorney) as drawn up by someone with legal authority.

letter distribution classification In medical records administration, a list used in classifying documents. The system was prepared by the U.S. Department of the Navy and the Social Security Administration and demonstrates how certain letters of the alphabet, used in alphabetical order, expand in a filing system. The expansion of the files containing the letters is expressed in percentages.

letter of credit In health-care financial management, a formal statement provided by a money-lending institution indicating that it will support a financial agreement.

letters of administration In law and health law, this is a court-drawn document specifically identifying and instructing a person to take charge of the distribution of the property of a dead person.

letters rogatory In law and the litigation process, this is a request from a court of one jurisdiction to a court of another jurisdiction. It is usually a request that a witness be examined by interrogatories.

letters testamentary *See letters of administration.*

level of care 1. In health-care delivery, this is the degree of treatment, services, and procedures needed. The extent of care depends on the type, severity, and seriousness of the illness, disability, or injury of the patient admitted for health-care services. 2. In long-term-care facilities, these are the types and numbers of chronic diseases and disabilities, which, with the residents' ability to care for themselves, determines the level of care needed; the amount of medical care and assistance with activities of daily living needed by individuals. Three levels of care are generally recognized in long-term care: personal care, intermediate care, and skilled nursing care. *See levels of medical care; primary care; secondary care; tertiary care; level-of-care criteria; levels of prevention.*

level-of-care criteria In health-care delivery, these are standards utilized to determine the acceptable and appropriate level of care for a patient. These criteria are based on the illness and disability that the patient has, the services available in the health-care facility, and whether it is an acute-care or long-term-care facility. *See also levels of care.*

level of commitment In strategic health planning, this is the extent to which a health-care organization and its administrators demonstrate they believe in a project and support it. Support and commitment are observed by the allocation of time, resources, and money allotted to plan and implement the proposed program or service.

level of concern In environmental health, especially air pollution control in a hazardous waste emergency, this is the concentration of an extremely hazardous substance in the air from which there may be serious irreversible health effects or death as a result of a single exposure for a relatively short time period.

level premium In managed care and insurance, this is where an insurance premium remains the same each year of the payment period.

levels of care *See levels of medical care; levels of prevention; level of care.*

levels of medical care In health-care delivery, this is the type, amount, and severity of the disease process or condition being diagnosed and treated; the type of physician who has the proper skill, training, and experience to treat the disease; and the type and level of medical care facilities and services necessary to support the health-care provider in his or her diagnosis and treatment of the various levels and severity of diseases and injuries. 2. Three levels of acute medical care or services are identified: primary care, secondary care, and tertiary care. *See primary care; secondary care; tertiary care; level-of-care criteria; level of care.*

levels of potential hazards In environmental and occupational health and hazardous waste management, three levels of potential hazard have been identified. Level 1 potential hazards have the potential for causing a severe injury or fatality, potentially fatal occupational illness, or loss of the facility. Level 2 potential hazards have the potential for causing minor injury, minor occupational illness, or major property damage or the potential for resulting in or contributing to unnecessary exposure to radiation or toxic substances. Level 3 potential hazards have little potential for threatening safety, health, or property.

levels of prevention Three levels of disease and injury prevention services are used: primary prevention, secondary prevention, and tertiary prevention. *See primary prevention; secondary prevention; tertiary prevention; levels of medical care.*

levels of service 1. In health-care delivery and in the provision of medical services in hospitals, clinics, or HMOs, these include the different types and intensity of the various medical care procedures such as how minimal or how extensive examinations, evaluations, treatment, counseling, and conferences with or concerning patients are needed and how much and how intense preventive pediatric and adult health supervision necessitate a wide variation in skill, effort, and time required for prevention, diagnosis, and treatment of illness and the promotion of optimal health. 2. There are seven levels of recognized services: minimal, brief, limited, intermediate, extended, comprehensive, and unusually complex. 3. Three levels of medical care or services are used: primary care, secondary care, and tertiary care. 4. Three levels of disease and injury prevention services are used: primary prevention, secondary prevention, and tertiary prevention. *See primary care; secondary care; tertiary care; primary prevention; secondary prevention; tertiary prevention; service.*

leverage In health-care financial management, this is the ability of a health-care organization to meet long-term debts, needs, and obligations as measured by such financial ratios as capitalization ratio, cash flow/total debt ratio, debt assets ratio, debt/equity ratio, debt service coverage ratio, equity financing ratio, and fixed assets financing ratio.

leveraging In health-care financial management, this is the use of equity, financial worth, or investments to enter into larger financing or investment situations.

leveraging, operating In health administration, this is the ratio of variable to fixed costs. Small amounts of resources, labor, and materials put into new units of service can increase productivity and make the cost of operations low and the operating leverage high.

lewd Unacceptable in a sexual way; immoral. *See lascivious.*

lex (Lat.) Law; a collection of laws.

lex domicilii (Lat.) The law of the domicile.

lex fori (Lat.) Law of the court. The law of a state or county where a dispute was decided.

lex loci (Lat.) The law of the place; law of the local. The legal jurisdiction of the state or country where the acts of a civil suit occurred or a contract was made.

lex loci contractus (Lat.) The law of the place of a contract.

lex non scripta (Lat.) Unwritten law.

lex rei sitae (Lat.) The law of the place of a dispute.

lex scripta (Lat.) Written law.

LHD Local health department.

liabilities *See liability.*

liability 1. A loss; an incident; an occurrence, obligation, or involvement that is a disadvantage. 2. Something one is bound to do or an obligation one is bound to fulfill by law and justice. A liability may be enforced by the court and is usually financial; the cost of meeting a court-determined obligation; an obligation one is bound to fulfill by law. Liabilities are usually financial or can be expressed in financial terms. 3. An act one is legally answerable for. 4. In health-care finance, this is the counterpart of assets such as current debt, short-term debt, and long-term debt; an amount owed. 5. To be liable; being obligated to pay. 6. In managed care, this is the amount the health plan owes its creditors and the actual and expected claims of its policy owners and their beneficiaries. 7. As used in environmental health, these are any probable future sacrifices of economic benefits arising from present obligations to transfer assets or provide services to other entities in the future as a result of past transactions or events.

liability, corporate In health-care law, this is the legal accountability and responsibility of the incorporated health-care organization rather than that of an individual or administrator. The liability of employees, physicians, and patients is covered by the hospital or other incorporated institution. *See liability; vicarious liability.*

liability insurance 1. Insurance taken out with an insurance company against loss, damage, injury, or harm done to person or property. 2. A contract in which an insurance company pays for any loss in return for the payment of insurance premiums.

liability, joint and several In health-care law, this is when the defendant is made up of several parties and shares in any legal liability to the plaintiff.

liability, product *See product liability.*

liability, professional *See professional liability; malpractice.*

liability, strict In health law, in a liability or malpractice case, the plaintiff does not need to show negligence on the defendant's part. The responsibility for injury is imposed by law without regard to any determination of fault. In tort law, the injury or damages are required to be shown. *See fault; liability; malpractice.*

liable 1. Legally bound. 2. Legally required to make good any loss, damage, or harm done. 3. Being responsible for one's acts such as harm done to another.

Liaison Committee on Graduate Medical Education (LCGME) A subgroup of the Coordinating Council on Medical Education intended to serve as the accrediting agency for graduate medical education. Application to be officially designated in this role is expected to be submitted to the U.S. Office of Education. The committee includes representatives of the American Board of Medical Specialists, the American Hospital Association, the American Medical Association, the Association of American Medical Colleges, and the Council on Medical Specialty Societies.

Liaison Committee on Medical Education (LCME) A joint committee of the American Medical Association (AMA) and the Association of American Medical Colleges (AAMC) responsible for accrediting medical schools. Established in 1942, the LCME is recognized for this purpose by the U.S. Commissioner of Education and the National Commission on Accrediting. The committee is made up of six representatives of the AMA Council on Medical Education, six representatives of the AAMC Executive Council, two representatives of the public, and one representative of the federal government. Although all medical schools are now accredited, there are different types and grades of accreditation that are not consistent among schools. In addition to accreditation, the LCME and the two councils it represents have also been performing advisory functions for the medical schools with respect to their programs.

libel A written defamation of character; a common-law wrong; false and malicious written statements that cause harm or injury to a person's profession, position, or reputation. Statements in writing or on film that include defamatory remarks. Libel is actionable without proof of actual damage. *See defamation of character; slander.*

libelant The plaintiff.

libelous 1. To be defamatory in nature. 2. To cause harm or injury to a person's position, profession, or reputation. *See slander; defamation of character.*

liberty 1. Freedom; to be free from any unlawful, forceful, or illegal personal false imprisonment or restraint. 2. The personal right to be free within established limits.

librarian, health science or medical A person who has graduated from an accredited medical or health science library program who provides library services to health-care professionals and works in a medical school, school of allied health, medical society, hospital, or health-care facility library. *See also medical librarian.*

librarian, medical records *See medical record administrator; registered records administrator; accredited records technician.*

library 1. A department or organization that retains a collection of books and periodicals and offers the services of acquisition and retrieval of books, articles, and information. 2. A special unit in a health-care organization that is staffed and equipped to offer acquisition services as well as a collection of current medical and health periodicals and books and the ability to retrieve professional books, periodicals, and other related information needed by health-care providers. Multimedia services may or may not be housed in this type of library. 3. In health-care information management, computers, or computerized medical records, this is an electronic storage system containing one or more definitions or program modules that can be relocated and then incorporated into other computer programs; a group of computerized documents or parts of a software program.

library, health sciences Also referred to as a "medical library," this is a special department in a health-care organization that provides for the acquisition, collection, and retrieval of medical and health-care information, including interhospital library services and computerized literature searches.

library, medical *See library, health sciences.*

Library of Congress system A system of storing or shelving books by subject area and a number assigned at the time of publication and copyrighted by the Library of Congress.

library, patient A collection of popular books and periodicals for use by patients, usually maintained on a less formal basis than a regular library.

license 1. A form of permission granted to an individual or organization by competent authority, usually public (government), to engage in a practice, occupation, or activity that would otherwise be unlawful. Because a license is needed to begin lawful practice, it is usually granted on the basis of examination and/or proof of education rather than measures of performance. Practicing or operating a hospital or health-care facility without a license is unlawful. When a license is given, it is usually permanent but may be conditioned on annual payment of a fee, proof of continuing education, or proof of competence. Common grounds for revocation of a license include incompetence, commission of a crime (whether or not related to the licensed practice), or moral turpitude. Possession of a professional license from one state may not ensure the ability to obtain a license from another state. There is no national licensure system for medical and allied health professions even though requirements are often nearly standardized as to constitute a national system (national certification or registration is not licensure). 2. Acting without legal restraint; disregarding the law. 3. Formal permission authorized by law as indicated by a certificate or document to perform or do some professional act. 4. Permission to practice or deviate from a strict rule of conduct. *See national boards; Federation Licensing Examination; accreditation; registration; certification.*

licensed This means to be in compliance with state codes governing the practice of a profession or the operation of a health-care organization that requires licensure; possessing the legal right and proper certificate and documentation to practice a profession or operate a health-care facility or organization.

licensed beds The number of beds in a hospital or nursing home that the state health facilities licensing agency has authorized the institution to maintain, fill, and manage.

licensed hospital *See hospital, licensed.*

licensed independent practitioner Any individual who is permitted by law and by the hospital to provide patient care services without direction or supervision but within the scope of the individual's license and in accordance with individually granted clinical privileges (JCAHO for acute-care facilities).

licensed nurse A registered (which usually means licensed) nurse or licensed vocational nurse who has met the requirements and has been licensed by the state in which he or she practices. *See licensed nursing personnel; licensed practical nurse; licensed vocational nurse; registered nurse.*

licensed nursing personnel Under Medicare, registered nurses or practical (vocational) nurses licensed by the state in which practicing.

licensed practical nurse (LPN) 1. A nurse who has practical experience in the provision of nursing care and/or has completed a 9-month to 1-year education program but is not a graduate of a formal bachelors degree, associate degree, or diploma school program of nursing education. The education, required experience, licensure, and job responsibilities of LPNs are fairly variable. Less well trained than a registered nurse (RN), the LPN can conduct many functions that overlap with those of the RN. 2. According to JCAHO accreditation of long-term-care facilities, a nurse who is a graduate of an approved school of practical (vocational) nursing and/or is licensed to practice as a practical (vocational) nurse. Synonymous with "LVN." *See licensed vocational nurse.*

licensed psychiatric technician This is an entry-level allied health mental health worker recognized and licensed in some states who usually requires training as a psychiatric technician often taken at a community college. Some community colleges offer an AS degree in the area. These individuals, once licensed, usually work in state hospitals or county mental health services.

licensed vocational nurse (LVN) The same as a licensed practical nurse but referred to by the

LVN title in some states. Less well trained than a registered nurse (RN), the LVN has many functions that overlap with those of the RN. Synonymous with "LPN." *See licensed practical nurse.*

licensee 1. One who holds a license; the person, persons, firm, partnership, association, organization, company, corporation, business trust, political subdivision of the state, or other governmental agency to whom a license has been issued. 2. A person allowed on property with permission but without invitation or enticement. 3. Used in tort law to identify an invited person or guest as a licensee, not an invitee.

licensure 1. The process by which an agency of the government grants permission to persons meeting predetermined qualifications to engage in a given occupation and/or to use a particular title; the process of the government granting permission to an individual or organization to engage in activities otherwise prohibited by law. 2. The government granting permission to institutions such as hospitals to perform certain specified functions once the organization or facility meets certain standards of performance. 3. A legal right granted by a government agency in compliance with a statute governing occupations such as medicine or nursing or the operation of an activity such as a hospital (JCAHO for acute-care facilities).

licensure and certification The granting of permission to provide home health-care services and other facilities including shelter care, long-term care, and acute care.

licensure, limited Physician licensure restricting practice to a specific institution (such as a mental hospital) designated by the state. Holders of these licenses are often foreign medical graduates.

licentiousness 1. Acting with disregard for ethics, law, or rights of others. 2. Lewdness or unacceptable behavior.

lien In health administration and the management of a health-care organization's real estate, this is a legal claim or encumbrance against property rather than a claim against a contract.

lienee In health administration and the management of a health-care organization's real estate, this is a person who has a lien against him or her; a person whose property is subject to a lien.

lienor One who holds a lien.

lieu (French) Place.

life care centers Retirement communities that provide residents with apartment housing, meals, housekeeping, security, recreation, and comprehensive health care for a monthly fee. Most centers also have a nursing home on their premises. On top of the monthly fee, residents pay an entry fee that may range from $40,000 to $200,000, depending on the apartment chosen. Some centers retain up to 25% and may refund up to 75% of this entrance fee if the resident moves or dies. The life care system guarantees prepaid health care, assistance in any aspect of daily living, and on-site nursing home care for all residents. This gives residents the security of stable financial and living arrangements regardless of how their medical conditions change.

life care/continuing care communities In long-term care and housing for the elderly, this is a community that provides a whole range of services and programs for elderly residents, including homes, apartments for independent living, home care services, clinics and visits by physicians and nurses, and a nursing home facility. Payment is usually by an initial membership fee, and monthly fees are based on the type and amount of services an individual or couple may need, including housekeeping and health and social services for the remainder of his or her life.

life change events/experiences In behavioral health, these are stress-caused experiences or events that people have as they go through life. Any change, disruption, or event in life can result in stress, which can produce a change in one's health, affect the immune system's effectiveness, or diminish the body's response to disease. Thomas Holmes, MD, and Richard Rahe, MD, developed the Social Readjustment Scale, also referred to as the Schedule of Recent Experiences, which lists 43 life change events, both positive and negative, that produce stress. The theoretical foundation of the scale is that if one had a certain level of stress in the last year, there is an equivalent possibility of being ill in the next year. *See stressor; dystressor; benestressor; eustress; stress.*

life costs Mortality, morbidity, and suffering associated with a given medical procedure or disease. Life costs of diagnosis and therapy may be contrasted with their financial costs. The use of life costs in assessing the costs of medical procedures avoids the need for assigning dollar values to mortality and morbidity.

life cycle In gerontology, these are the stages of development that an individual experiences in the life span.

life events *See life change events/experiences.*

life expectancy In epidemiology and public health, this is the average span of time an individual born at a certain point in time can reasonably expect to live or the number of years remaining that a person is expected to live on reaching a certain age. The average number of years of life remaining for a person at a particular age is based on a given set of age-specific death rates, generally the mortality conditions existing in the period mentioned. Life expectancy is determined by race, sex, or other characteristics using age-specific death rates for the population with that characteristic. *See longevity; age-specific death rates.*

life in being The time remaining in which a person has to live.

life insurance Insurance that pays a specific amount to the beneficiary when the insured dies. Various types of life insurance include whole life, term, and straight (or ordinary) life. Various approaches include the following: 1) commercial term life (group): a group insurance paid to the survivor(s) on the death of the insured and provided by an employer for each of his employees; 2) commercial term life (individual): an individual insurance paid to survivor(s) on the death of the insured; coverage for a single person is usually purchased by or for that person; 3) commercial whole life (group): a group insurance in which payment is made to survivor(s) on the death of the insured to a certain age or, if still alive, on reaching that age, to the insured; provided by an employer for each employee; 4) commercial whole life (individual): an individual insurance policy in which payment is made to survivor(s) on the death of the insured to a certain age or, if still alive on reaching that age, to the insured; coverage is for a single person, usually purchased by or for that person.

life review In gerontology and some mental health programs, a reappraisal of worth and redefinition of one's purpose in life.

lifes In managed care, this refers to an enrollee or numbers of enrollees who are covered by a managed-care plan; a measure of the size and capacity of managed-care programs (e.g., a health plan may have 25,000 enrolled lifes).

Life Safety Code A fire safety code prepared by the National Fire Protection Association. The provisions of this code relating to hospitals and nursing facilities must, except in cases where a waiver is granted, be met by facilities certified for participation under Medicare and Medicaid. The Secretary of Health and Human Services may accept a state's fire and safety code in lieu of the currently accepted edition of the Life Safety Code if the state code will provide adequate protection for inpatients of nursing facilities. Actual fire inspections are carried out at the local level by the fire marshall to determine whether a physical plant is structurally safe and adequately prepared against fire and escape from it. The code is based on the Southern Standard Building Code, which contains optimum, not minimum, standards. Accreditation by JCAHO requires that health facilities meet this code.

life safety management program A component of a hospital's plant, technology, risk management, and safety program designed to protect patients, personnel, visitors, and property from fire and the products of combustion and to provide for the safe use of buildings and grounds (JCAHO for acute-care facilities).

lifestyle The values, beliefs, behaviors, habits, and activities utilized in one's daily living as influenced and affected by physiological, emotional, behavioral, psychosocial, cultural, environmental, economic, and spiritual factors; patterns of habituated behavior over time that are health related but not necessarily health directed. Behaviors that are negative or risk taking include tobacco use, alcohol consumption, overeating, being overweight, lack of fitness, and drug abuse. Behaviors that are positive or health enhancing are a proper diet, not smoking, exercise and fitness, maintaining proper weight, no drug use and abuse or alcohol consumption, safety consciousness, and successful stress-coping ability.

life support system In hospitals and medical care, this is the technology, equipment, and services needed to provide life-sustaining functions of the heart, lungs, kidneys, and nutrition for a patient who has failure of one or more of these organs.

life table In public health and epidemiology, this is a table based on age-specific mortality rates that predicts the probability of dying at a given age; a method of describing the survival possibilities in populations and patterns of mortality.

Survival data are time specific and use cumulative probabilities of survival of a cohort or population throughout the life span. Life tables use summary-of-death observations in populations over a period of time. In epidemiology, life tables are used to analyze mortality patterns as well as any disease or condition affecting life expectancy having an endpoint such as occupational related diseases or certain chronic diseases. A life table provides data and information on every age known across the life span. Tables showing age-groups by 5-year intervals are referred to as "modified life tables." John Graunt developed life tables and studies to show the different patterns of mortality in London in the 1600s. Graunt found that higher levels of death occurred consistently in some parts of London than in others. *See life table, current/period; life table, cohort/generation; survivorship studies.*

life table, clinical Life tables based on the outcome results of a cohort or population based on their exposure or clinical history. *See life table.*

life table, cohort/generation Life tables that present actual survival data of a population or cohort of the same birth year. *See life table.*

life table, current/period Life tables that present death data over a brief time period based on data on the middle of that period, whether it be 1, 2, or 3 years. This presents combined mortality data by age of the population group in a specified short time period. *See life table.*

life table, expectation of life function In epidemiology, this is the average number of years remaining for those who survive to a certain age (age x). For example, if you live to be 45 years of age in Mexico, you have a life expectancy of 40 years of age, or you will live until age 85. Also referred to as "average future life time." *See life table.*

life table, modified Tables that show age-groups by 5-year intervals instead of showing each and every year of the known life span up to and including the oldest age known to be reached (in 1994, age 116 was the oldest proven age). *See life table.*

life table, survivorship function Persons from a certain population who will survive or remain free of an endpoint disease or condition to a certain age (age x) under age-specific death rates for a stated year; the cumulative function of specific mortality rates for ages below a certain age (such as age 45). *See life table.*

lifetime disability benefit A payment to a disabled person to help replace lost income as long as he or she is totally disabled, even for a lifetime.

lifetime maximum In managed care and medical insurance or other insurance, this is a limit that some plans set on the total benefits the plan will pay to the enrollee or beneficiary.

lifetime prevalence In public health and epidemiology, this is the proportion of the population who have had a certain disease at any time in their lives.

lifetime reserve Under Part A of Medicare, this is a reserve of 60 days of inpatient hospital care available over an individual's lifetime that the individual may use after he or she has used the maximum 90 days allowed in a single benefit period. *See also spell of illness.*

L.I.F.O. Last in, first out. In health administration, this is a material management method used to determine the value and method of usage of an inventory. *See first in, last out.*

lifting station In environmental health, this is a mechanical device installed in a sewer or water system or other liquid-carrying pipeline that moves the liquid to a higher level.

lifts In environmental health, as used in sanitary landfills, this is a compacted layer of solid waste and the top layer of cover material such as soil.

light pen In health-care information management systems, this is a device resembling a pencil or stylus that is used as an input medium into a computer and works by touching it to an electronic pad or the screen of a CRT.

limestone scrubbing In environmental health and air pollution control, this is a process in which sulfur gases moving through smoke pipes toward a smokestack are passed through a limestone-and-water solution to remove sulfur before they reach the atmosphere.

limitation 1. A time restriction. 2. To be restricted or limited. 3. A time period fixed by law during which a legal action can be brought, must occur, or can be settled. 4. In managed care, this is any provision other than an exclusion that restricts coverage under a group subscriber contract. *See statute of limitations.*

limitation of activity Persons having a chronic condition are classified according to the extent to which activities are limited because of the condition: 1) persons unable to carry on major activity, 2) persons limited in the amount or kind of major activity performed, 3) persons not limited in major activity but otherwise limited, and 4) persons not limited in activity. Individuals are also classified by age-group: 1) ordinary play for children under 5 years of age, 2) attending school for persons 5 to 17 years of age, 3) working or keeping house for persons 18 to 69 years of age, and 4) capacity for independent living (bathe, dress, eat and prepare food, shop, clean house, etc.). *See activities of daily living.*

limited 1. Narrowed; restricted. 2. Restricting the liability of shareholders of a corporation so they cannot be sued for corporate actions. 3. The English equivalent of corporation, abbreviated "Ltd."

limited insurance In managed care and medical insurance, this is a contract that covers only specified diseases or accidents and restricts indemnity payments. The insuring clause of contracts can be either limited or comprehensive.

limited partnership In health administration and legal ownership structures, this is one type of a business owner arrangement where two or three physicians, psychologists, or other healthcare practitioners act as general partners and are responsible for all acts of the partnership. Other individuals involved or a part of the group may be limited partners and may purchase an interest in the group but have no voice in the management. The limited partnership minimizes liability exposure of partners to the amount of their investment. By law, a partnership requires at least one general partner who is subject to the claims of the creditors, whereas the limited partners may be exposed only to the extent of the investment. The disadvantage of a limited partnership is finding and identifying an entity willing to take on the responsibility of a general partner.

limited quantity In environmental health, this is a maximum amount of hazardous material for which there is a specific labeling and packing exception, when specified as such in a section applicable to a particular material, with the exception of Poison B materials.

limited-service rural hospitals (LSRHs) A low-volume rural hospital that has downsized its acute-care capacity and has shifted its focus toward meeting the community's needs for emergency and primary care services and possibly long-term-care needs. There is no single approach to this type of hospital but rather a continuum of possibilities that depend on the needs of the community. Usually 24-hour emergency care is offered with a limited number of inpatient beds and a limited length of stay such as 72 or 96 hours. Outpatient services become important to such hospitals. *See eaches/peaches.*

limited services *See services; levels of service.*

limiting factors In environmental health, this is any condition whose absence or excessive concentration is incompatible with the needs or tolerance of a species or population and that may have a negative influence on the ability to grow or even survive.

limits In environmental health, these are the values of a quantity that must not be exceeded. For example, limits in radiation protection are primary, secondary, derived, authorized, and operational.

limits of liability In insurance, especially liability insurance, these are the limits on dollar coverage contained in an insurance policy. Malpractice insurance generally contains such limits on the amounts payable for an individual claim or in the policy year. Excess coverage describes insurance with limits higher than these conventional amounts. It may also be used to refer to limits on professional liability imposed by law. Several states have enacted legislation that would, for example, place a limit of $500,000 on any malpractice award. Such laws are being challenged as to their legality and, in some instances, have been ruled unconstitutional; this is referred to as "tort reform."

limnology In environmental health, this is the study of the physical, chemical, meteorological, and biological aspects of fresh water.

Lindbergh Act The federal statute that makes it illegal to transport a kidnapped person across the border of a state.

line In health administration and organizational structuring, this is a method of determining the hierarchical organizational structure and lines of authority in a health-care organization. Line positions are within the chain of command, and staff positions are supportive of administration or line personnel.

lineal Made up of lines; in line.

lineal relationships As used in epidemiological investigations, this is a direct line to one's ancestors. *See kinship; genealogy.*

line and staff In health administration, this refers to organizational structure and roles of personnel in large health-care organizations. Line sets forth the chain of command and is a part of authority. Line authority refers to superior and subordinate relationships. Staff refers to the supportive and auxiliary nature of the personnel in these positions, which are there to support line executives and line personnel. Staff can only make recommendations to line personnel. Line authority is based on superior-subordinate relationships and occupying positions of authority in the organizational chart.

linear In health planning, health-care management, and health services research, this is a relationship in which each unit of change in one variable is associated with a proportionate amount of change in a second variable and in which the direction of the relationship does not change.

linear regression *See regression.*

line authority In health administration, this is direct authority over subordinates; authority managers have to direct others and make decisions about the health-care organization's operations. *See line and staff.*

line chart A health-care management tool in the form of a graph that depicts movement, progress, and shortcomings and aids administrators in comprehending the flow of activity and the organization's success or failure.

line management In health administration, these are management positions on which responsibility falls for the accomplishment of the organization's primary mission(s), as distinguished from staff organization, which supports the organization's primary mission(s).

line of balance In safety and public health analysis, when assessing accidents, a 45-degree line indicating the norm in accident frequency/severity plotting on log paper or a computer statistics program. Deviations from the line of balance provide important clues to future risk.

line of credit In health-care finance, this is the highest allowable amount of credit given to a customer.

line organizations 1. In health administration in public or environmental health agencies, these are any departments or organizations in the parent company or project responsible for accomplishing the primary goals. 2. In governmental public health and environmental health agencies, this is the unbroken chain of command that extends from the Secretary of Health and Human Services, through the Undersecretary, to the program senior officials, who set program policy and plan and develop assigned programs, to field organization managers, who are responsible to the program senior officials for execution of the programs, to contractors, who conduct the programs. Public health, environment, safety, and health are integral parts of each.

line printer In health-care information management, this is a type of computer printer that prints a full line at a time and can reach speeds of up to 3000 lines per minute.

liners 1. In environmental health and solid waste management, these are relatively impermeable barriers designed to prevent leachate from leaking from a landfill. Liner materials include plastic and dense clay; any continuous layer of natural or man-made materials beneath or on the sides of a surface impoundment, landfill, or landfill cell that restricts the downward or lateral escape of hazardous waste, hazardous waste constituents, and leachate. 2. In environmental health and clean water management, these are inserts or sleeves for sewer pipes to prevent leakage or infiltration.

line units Measures of accountability hierarchy directly concerned with the principal product or outcomes of the health-care organization; those segments of organizational activity directly involved in the production of the health-care organization's services. Also referred to as "units of service" or "clinical units." *See units of service.*

liniment An oily salve, lotion, or liquid used on the skin.

linkages program In health-care delivery and long-term care, this is a service that provides case management and referral services to a variety of community support services for elderly persons at risk of institutionalization.

liquid The ability to sell assets rapidly and without a loss.

liquidate 1. To clear up, pay off, or settle an account or debt. 2. To make into cash. 3. To settle the affairs of a company, organization, or business and distribute its money or goods.

liquidated Paid up or settled up.

liquidated claim 1. A claim or debt bound by an agreement or by a court order. 2. Ascertained; established; fixed; settled. 3. In law, this is a claim having a specific fixed amount put on it by the court or by a mutual agreement.

liquidated damages In contract law, these are money amounts established by the parties to a contract that must be paid off. The party breaching the contract would pay damages to the other party. *See damages, liquidated.*

liquidation 1. To liquidate. 2. The ending or closing of a business or company by selling off all goods and assets.

liquidation strategy In strategic health planning, this is one strategy (though the least desired one) where the liquidation process means terminating a program or service, laying off personnel, halting employee benefits, and selling off all goods, equipment, and assets.

liquidity In health-care financial management, this is the relative strength or weakness of the health-care organization's financial position as assessed by ratios such as the acid test ratio, current ratio, quick ratio, and working capital ratio; the ability to pay accounts payable when they are due on the basis of the level of cash and securities owned by the health-care organization.

liquidity ratio In health-care financial management, this is one measure of a health-care organization's ability to pay its bills. A ratio is used to assess the viability of the health-care organization. If the ratio is too high, the organization may have invested too much in working capital, especially accounts receivable. If the ratio is too low, the hospital is at risk of not being able to pay its short-term financial obligations. A good ratio is between 1.50 and 2.00, as this is the health-care and hospital industry's norm and is taken into consideration by credit rating firms. The liquidity ratio formula follows:

$$\frac{\text{Current assets}}{\text{Current liabilities}} = \text{Current ratio}$$

lis pendens (Lat.) 1. A notice that a lawsuit is pending; a suit awaiting filing. 2. The public announcement of a pending suit against certain property that gives notice to anyone, especially prospective buyers, that property is subject to a claim.

list A company, health facility, or other organization placed on a roster for being found in violation of government regulations. Facilities or firms on such rosters are often debarred from obtaining government contracts because they violated certain regulations. In the environmental health areas, these could include sections of the Clean Air Act or the Clean Water Act.

listed According to JCAHO for psychiatric, alcoholism, and drug abuse facilities accreditation purposes, equipment or materials included in a list published by a nationally recognized testing laboratory, inspection agency, or other organization concerned with product evaluation. The organization periodically inspects the production of listed equipment or materials, and the organization's list states that the equipment or material either meets nationally recognized standards or has been tested and found suitable for use in a specified manner.

lithium therapy In psychiatry and mental health services, this is one of the first successful chemotherapy treatments used for treating mental illness. Lithium is a naturally occurring salt and is a treatment for manic emotional states; a form of chemotherapy with lithium salts.

lithotripsy The common term for "extracorporeal shock wave lithotripsy." Shock waves are generated underwater by a "spark plug" electrode. Ignition of the electrode generates a spark that vaporizes a small amount of water. A shock wave produced by this action can be transmitted through water and biological tissue. When the energy is concentrated, it can cause kidney and urinary stones to crumble or fragment in the kidney or ureter while causing little or no damage to the tissue. The procedure is 89% to 99% successful. The shock waves created by this device are not the same as ultrasound because they are more powerful than mere sound waves. If urinary stones are very large, two or more treatments may be used to pulverize them.

lithotripter The medical device used to conduct lithotripsy treatments for kidney stones and gallstones in patients. *See lithotripsy.*

litigant A party to litigation.

litigate The act of carrying on a lawsuit; to hold a trial; to go through the litigation process.

litigation The process of carrying on a lawsuit; the act of resolving a dispute through the court system.

litigious 1. One who likes to create and bring lawsuits; starting many lawsuits. 2. Subject to disagreement, debate, or dispute.

live birth The complete expulsion or extraction of a product of conception from a mother, irrespective of the duration of the pregnancy, that, after such separation, breathes or shows any other evidence of life such as beating of the heart, pulsation of the umbilical cord, or definite movement of voluntary muscles, whether or not the umbilical cord has been cut or the placenta is attached; each product of such a birth is considered live born (WHO and National Center for Health Statistics). It should be noted that this definition includes no requirement that the product of conception be viable or capable of independent life and thus includes very early and patently nonviable fetuses. It has been suggested by some health professionals that a viability criterion be included in the definition.

live-birth order In public health and epidemiology, this is an item from the birth certificate that indicates the number of live births a woman has had and the order in which they occurred, including the birth being recorded.

live-in unit In hospital administration, this is a room kept and maintained in a hospital for use by parents or persons who wish to stay with their hospitalized children or other relatives.

living trust A trust in effect while the person creating it is still living.

living will A document executed prior to an illness stating that, should circumstances arise where there is no chance of recovery from an illness or injury, the person creating or signing the document would prefer being allowed to die without being placed on machines or technology that prolong life by artificial means. Living wills are recognized by some, but not all, states' legal systems.

LLB Bachelor of laws. The basic law degree, later replaced by the JD.

LLD Doctor of laws.

LLM Master of laws.

LMRDA Labor Management Reporting and Disclosure Act of 1959. *See Landrum-Griffin Act.*

LOA *See leave of absence.*

load To enter data or other information into a computer for use.

loading In managed care and medical insurance, this is the amount added to the premium or actuarial value of the coverage (expected or average amounts payable to the insured) used to cover the operating expenses of the insurer and for maintaining the business (i.e., the amount added to the pure premium needed to meet anticipated liabilities for expenses, contingencies, profits, or special situations). Loading costs for group health insurance range from 5% to 25% of premiums; for individual health insurance, they go as high as 40% to 60%.

loan consent In health-care finance, these are interest rates, expressed in percentage form of indebtedness, that do not change during the term of the loan.

loan constant In health-care financial management, this is interest rates in percentage form (representing indebtedness) that remain unchanged during the term of the loan.

loan package In health-care financial management, this is a financial proposal containing all items and estimates necessary for a money-lending agency to decide whether to give a loan. These items would include information on the borrower, a loan application, a credit report, a financial statement, employment letters, and information and estimates on the property or equipment.

loan ratio In health-care financial management, this is a ratio of the amount of a loan to the value of property. Usually, the higher the percentage, the greater the interest charged. Maximum percentages for banks, savings and loans, or government-insured loans are set by statute.

loath Unwilling; reluctant; indisposed; averse; disinclined.

LOB Line of business. Also referred to in managed care as "product line."

lobbying Efforts to influence a governmental official in the performance of his or her duty. Federal legislation governing lobbying activities (Title III of the Legislative Reorganization Act of 1946) does not define the terms "lobbying" or "lobbyist." The act requires registration by any person "who, by himself or through any agent or employee or other persons in any manner whatsoever, directly or indirectly, solicits, collects, or receives money or any other thing of value to be used principally to aid or the principal purpose of which person is to aid the passage or defeat of any legislation by the Congress." Paid lobbyists are required to register with the Clerk of the House and the Secretary of the Senate and to file quarterly financial reports with the House Clerk. The term derives from the frequent presence of lobbyists in the lobbies of congressional and other governmental chambers.

lobbyists These are advocates representing health or other interests for certain segments of society or special interest groups and are paid to persuade government officials to represent the special interests of a group or industry.

lobotomy In medical care, this is a neurosurgical procedure in which one or more nerve areas in a lobe of the cerebrum of the brain are severed. Prefrontal lobotomy is the disconnecting through surgery of one or more nerve tracts in the prefrontal area of the brain. This treatment has been used in certain severe mental disorders that do not respond to other treatments.

local action 1. A lawsuit brought in one place or one locale. 2. Actions that of necessity or because of jurisdiction must be brought in a specific place. 3. Actions against a locality.

local adaptation syndrome (LAS) In behavioral health, this is the reaction of one's body or body parts to stress.

local area network In health-care information management, this is the connecting of two or more computer systems of several health-care organizations in a restricted region or area to share common services or participate in a shared service agreement.

local bank The bank or branch bank that is nearest to the health-care facility; a home-owned and locally operated bank in the local community. It usually is supported by the community hospital, which is also owned and operated by the community as compared to a national banking chain with headquarters in another city.

local coordinating committee In managed care, this is when representatives of a health plan and the Voluntary Hospitals of America establish goals for the maintenance of an effective local provider network.

local education agencies As defined by Section 198 of the Elementary and Secondary Education Act of 1965, this is the owner of any private, nonprofit elementary or secondary school building and the governing authority of any school operated under the defense dependents' education system provided for under the Defense Dependents Education Act of 1978.

local emergency planning commission A subunit of emergency response planning districts composed of elected, law enforcement, and civil defense officials; firefighting organizations; first aid, health, hospital, environmental, and transportation workers; community groups; news media; and companies that produce, use, or store chemicals. The Emergency Planning and Community Right-to-Know Act (EPCRA) requires each state to have a state emergency response commission.

local health-care executive association (group) In health administration, this is the establishment of a local group of health-care executives into a formal (or informal) society for the purpose of networking and professional development.

local health departments (LHDs) Public health services, clinics, and programs operated by municipal or county governments that provide basic public health, epidemiological, preventive care, health promotion and health education, disease assessment, prevention and control programs, and environmental health services. The mission of LHDs is the prevention and control of disease and injury in their communities. Also referred to as the "public health department" or the "health department."

local governments Any county, city, village, town, district, or political subdivisions of a state, Indian tribe or authorized tribal organization, or Alaskan native village or organization, including any rural community or unincorporated town or village or any other local public entity.

local initiative 1. In public health, health-care delivery, or health planning, as set by federal and state governmental administrative bodies, these are suggested, funding-supported, or mandated activities to city and county government agencies. State or federal agencies encourage the development of health programs or services that are believed to be needed at the local level and that must be investigated, assessed, planned, and implemented at the city or county level. The activity must occur at, be administered by, and be beneficial to the local community. 2. A comprehensive managed-care system developed by city or county government. The health plan responsible for arranging for all covered health-care services for the majority of Medicaid (Medi-Cal) beneficiaries on a capitated, full-risk basis.

local issues In public health, health-care delivery, or health planning, these are concerns identified by local groups and residents that are considered important to them.

locality In Medicare, the geographic area from which an insurance carrier derives prevailing charges for the purpose of making reasonable charge determinations. Usually, a locality is a political or economic subdivision of a state and should include a cross-section of the population with respect to economic and other characteristics. *See also catchment area; health service area; standard metropolitan statistical area.*

locality rule In health law and medical malpractice, this is a rule that bases the standard of care that a physician owes a patient on the standard of care that is generally attained in a specific locality or community. The most restrictive form of the rule is that the measure of a physician's duty of care to a patient is that degree of care, skill, and diligence used by physicians generally in the same locality or community. A less restrictive form holds that a physician owes that degree of care to a patient that is exercised by physicians generally in the same or similar localities or communities. The rationale for the more expansive rule, being applied more widely by courts today, is that the earlier emphasis on locality is no longer appropriate in light of better communications and the standardization of hospital procedures, medical practice, and physician licensure brought about by state statutes and regulations. Also referred to as the "community standard of care." Some states have a statewide standard of care. *See malpractice; cause of action; negligence.*

local option The choices of city or county government to exercise or choose how to implement certain regulations such as the regulation of the sale of alcoholic beverages that is used in prohibition or restriction of alcohol sales in certain cities or counties.

local unions In health administration and labor relations, these are the smallest organizational units of a union and are responsible for representing the union members in the local hospital or health-care organization.

location In health-care information management and computers, this is an address in a computer software program or in a computer's memory chip indicating where a piece of information and/or data is stored.

lock-box banking In managed care, this is a method of collecting premiums in which premium payments are received at a post office box and the bank has authorization to collect the mail. All premium payments are deposited directly by the bank.

locked files In health-care information management and computers, this is the insertion of written locks into premanufactured software to serve as a security measure. Because these locks prevent the copying of the disk or diskette, marketing and sales of the product are also protected.

locked ward This is a medical and nursing unit found in some hospitals and long-term-care facilities, usually mental health-care facilities and state hospitals. The unit has limited access to the outside and is kept locked because the patients are a danger either to themselves or to others; also, a unit kept for the criminally insane or for prisoners with medical problems.

lock hospital An acute-care medical facility used to treat sexually transmitted diseases.

lock-in 1. In health-care financial management, this is a loan that does not allow prepayment so that the borrower is "locked in" to the loan for a specified period. 2. In managed care, this is when the organization has authority and responsibility to control health and requires that all health care for beneficiaries be provided and authorized by the HMO. Except for emergency care, this applies only under the risk-type Medicare contract.

lock-in provision *See lock-in.*

lockout Locking the employees out so that they cannot work, a tactic used by unions or employers when a dispute is unsettled.

loco parentis *See in loco parentis.*

locum tenens (Lat.) To live in the place of. In health care, a physician who is hired to work temporarily in place of another.

locus (Lat.) 1. Place. 2. Anatomical place of origin.

locus poenitentiae (Lat.) 1. Place of repentance. 2. A point, place, or opportunity to withdraw from a contemplated agreement; a point at which one may withdraw from committing a crime; renouncing the intention to commit a criminal act.

locus sigilli (L.S.) (Lat.) The place of the seal. The place on a document where a seal is affixed.

lodger One who stays in a building owned and operated by another (e.g., a patient admitted to and staying in a hospital). The person staying has little control over the room lived in. This is a controversial issue with nursing home residents in terms of the degree of control they have over a room being paid for on a long-stay basis; more like an apartment than a hotel.

log A journal or record frequently used to record daily or periodic events or advancements in one's activities or projects.

logging in 1. Creating a log; recording or creating an original record. 2. In medical records, the process of documenting in the logbook, file, or journal used for controlling the removal and return of medical records and the returned status of a medical record to the medical record department.

logic function In health-care information management and computers, this is a computer function that compares numbers and tests data for certain conditions.

logic trees As used in epidemiology and decision

making, these are diagrams in the shape of a tree that use different geometric symbols to aid a user in systematically portraying information in a logical sequence and showing relationships between elements of the tree with decision points at various branches of the tree. Trees may be positive or negative. Also called "fault trees."

-logy Suffix meaning "the study of."

long-arm statute A statute in some states that allows a court to have jurisdiction over items or persons involved in a claim or dispute who are in another state at that time.

longevity Long life; aged; span of life; life expectancy; the average age a certain segment of the population or race lives; the age one reaches in life; one's length of life; how long a species lives; how long humans live. *See life expectancy.*

longitudinal health record In medical care and medical record administration, this is a patient record that includes medical and treatment information collected from a patient's birth to the current date, including present medical care and treatment activity.

longitudinal study In epidemiology and health and biomedical research, this is a research design that collects data over long time periods where research events and variables are connected and data collected in intervals at set points in time over a span of years from the same individuals and for the same research factors each time. Longitudinal studies are usually prospective in approach. Cohorts are often used in these long-term studies. *See cohort; cohort studies; cross-sectional studies.*

long-range plan An organizational plan developed to ensure the future viability of a health-care organization. The elements of the plan are determined by the services offered and the amount of business in which the health-care organization expects to participate in the future. The plan may require need assessments, the anticipated cost of replacing existing facilities, manpower needed, the amount of profit that must be produced, how depreciation funds will be used, how new programs and services will be financed, and other resources that are needed.

long-range recommended actions In health-care administration and planning, these are actions proposed to satisfy and ensure the attainment of the stated goals and objectives. *See strategic planning; health planning; objectives; goals.*

long-stayers In long-term care, this refers to nursing home residents who are no longer able to live outside institutions and who generally reside in the facility for a long time, usually years, and who often die there.

long-stay inpatient setting *See long-stay setting.*

long-stay setting A setting that provides health-care services to patients who stay overnight or longer in the institution and where 50% or more of the patients remain in the institution 30 days or longer. A long-stay setting may be the usual place of residence for some of or all its patients. *See also long-term care; long-term-care facilities.*

long-term capital gain In health-care financial management, this is income or financial gain on the sale of a capital asset that has been owned for a specified time (usually 1 year or longer) and that is taxed at a special rate.

long-term care (LTC) These are medical care and personal care services required by persons who are chronically ill, aged, disabled, or retarded and provided in an institution or at home on a long-term basis; care provided for nonacute conditions, including skilled nursing care for a person with an extended or permanent disability. This level of care requires supervision and frequent services of a skilled nurse and intermediate care such as the routine provision of lower-level related-care nursing care, personal care, and support services; residential care. The term is often used more narrowly to refer only to long-term institutional care such as that provided in nursing homes, homes for the retarded, and mental hospitals. Ambulatory health services such as home health care, provided on a long-term basis, are seen as alternatives to long-term institutional care and are also considered long-term care.

long-term-care administrator This is a person trained in a specialized area of health administration and focuses on the operation of long-term-care facilities. He or she directs, plans, controls, and coordinates operations and activities of extended care facilities. Often referred to as "nursing home administrators." *See also administrator, skilled nursing facility; nursing home administrator.*

long-term-care alternatives *See Area Agency on Aging; independent living.*

long-term-care case management For persons challenged with chronic illness or physical disability, this is a system of individuals such as social workers who arrange for all support and social services, personal needs, health care, and therapy in the following care areas: acute, chronic, long-term institutional, home health, home and community based, managed, rehabilitation, and subacute. *See Area Agency on Aging; independent living; case management.*

long-term-care facilities 1. Nursing homes that provide continuity of care for the aged or chronically ill patient. These institutions may provide skilled nursing care, intermediate care, or rehabilitative care or programs for the convalescing patient. Recreational therapy, physical and occupational therapies, social services, and nutritional and other special services are provided for ambulatory and bedridden patients. Long-term-care facilities generally offer a comprehensive care program and are usually participants in Medicare and Medicaid programs. 2. Facilities designed, staffed, and equipped to render comprehensive, long-range health services to those in need of such services. *See nursing home; convalescent hospital; state hospitals.*

long-term-care indicators Measures of healthcare delivery for older adults and/or the chronically ill or disabled, these are factors that indicate what services are needed or the level of care the individual receives in the formal and informal health-care systems such as how well they do with the activities of daily living or limitations of activities. The needed level of care is based on the numbers of chronic diseases and the severity of each. Also of concern is information on projected use and patterns of utilization. *See also social disability; alternatives to institutional care; health status indicators; markers for caregivers; limitations of activities.*

long-term-care institution A health-care facility for residents/patients, with nursing care and limited medical care provided over a prolonged time period, usually more than 30 days. The care provided usually includes medical, nursing, social, recreational, and supportive care services. *See nursing home; long-term-care facilities.*

long-term care—skilled nursing Physicians' services and continuous professional nursing supervision to patients who are not in an acute phase of illness and who currently require primarily convalescent rehabilitative and/or restorative services. May include home health care and/or extended care units. Can include, but is not restricted to, Medicare-/Medicaid-certified skilled nursing care. Beds must be set up and staffed specifically designated for long-term-care service. *See subacute care.*

long-term-care unit A medical and nursing unit located in a hospital to accommodate chronic cases prior to discharge to a nursing home, a group home, a board and care facility, or home health care. Beds must be set up, staffed, and specifically designated for this service. Also referred to as an "extended care unit," a "subacute care unit," or, if located in a hospital, a "transitional care unit." *See also extended care unit; skilled nursing unit.*

long-term contract As used in environmental health, this is an agreement used in relation to solid waste supply; contracts of sufficient duration to ensure the viability of a resource recovery facility to the extent that such viability depends on the supply of solid waste.

long-term debt In health-care financial management, this is the value of installment notes, bonds, or collateral trust bonds minus the portion of debt principal due in the next year or longer.

long-term disability income insurance Benefits paid to a covered an insured disabled person as long as he or she remains disabled. *See long-term disability insurance.*

long-term disability insurance A form of insurance that provides a proportion of a disabled employee's wage. Such policies often have long waiting periods and seldom allow the employee to attain the same level of income that existed before the disability.

long-term financing In health-care finance, these are loans financed for a term of 10 years or more.

long-term home health care The provision of providing care in the home by bringing health-care professions into the homes of the sick or disabled homebound elderly. Home health services provide care and supervision by physicians, nurses, social workers, and therapists who, through their combined efforts, restore health to, and provide and maintain the health, safety, and stability of, the patient. The social worker team member arranges for support and homemaker services. The goal is to assist patients over a long period of time to help them remain in their own homes and avoid institutionalization. *See visiting nurses association; home health agency.*

long-term hospital *See hospital, long-term; long-*

term care; long-term-care facilities; long-stay setting; convalescent hospitals.

loop In health-care information management and computers, this is a repetition of a group of instructions in a computer program routine until certain conditions are reached.

looping In diagnosis-related groups (DRGs), a grouper process used for searching all listed diagnoses to determine any comorbidity or complications related to the principal diagnosis; searching all procedures for specific ones such as operating room procedures or other specified ones as indicated by a decision tree.

looseleaf service Books published in looseleaf binders that have current reports on various areas of law. As laws are passed or changes made, new pages are issued to be added to or to replace the old ones.

LOS *See length of stay.*

LOS/ELOS/ALOS Length of stay/estimated length of stay/average length of stay. *See length of stay; average length of stay.*

loser A department or service in a hospital or health-care facility that does not generate enough money to support itself, thus a service or department that loses money; a department or service that causes a continued deficit in the budget. Also referred to as a "cost center."

loss 1. Destroyed; wasted away; failure to win. 2. In insurance, for the insurance carrier, this is the basis for a claim under the terms of an insurance policy. 3. In liability and property insurance, this is any diminution of quantity, quality, or value of property resulting from the occurrence of some peril or hazard. 4. In health-care financial management, this is when a health-care organization has a decrease in income, assets, and resources to the point that expense exceeds income. This financial state is viewed as a serious threat to the organization if it occurs over a period of time.

loss control management In health administration, this is the application of professional management techniques and skills to program activities specifically intended to minimize losses involved with undesired events resulting from the pure risks of business such as risk avoidance, loss prevention, and loss reduction.

loss-of-income benefits Payments made to an insured person to help replace income lost through the inability to work caused by a disability covered by insurance.

loss ratio In managed care and medical insurance, this is the proportion of losses incurred to the amount of premiums collected. This ratio is calculated by determining the results of paid claims and incurred claims plus expenses divided by the paid premiums. As used in general insurance, this is a ratio calculated by dividing the amount of losses by the amount of the premium(s); normally expressed as a percentage of the premiums.

lost-time accidents In occupational health and safety, these are severe job-related accidents that cause employees to lose time from and productivity on their jobs.

lost workdays In occupational health and safety, these are those days on which, because of occupational injury or illness, the employee was away from work or limited to restricted work activity; days on which the worker would have worked but could not because of the work-related injury or illness. *See restricted work activity.*

lot 1. A piece of land of predetermined size. 2. Items that are a separate sale, delivery, or purchase. 3. A portion or a parcel. 4. A number of items in a group.

loth Unwilling. *See loath.*

lotions Liquids or salves that have limited medicinal value and often contain an insoluble powder.

low birth weight In medical care, this is a live birth or a fetal death weight less than 2500 grams (5 pounds, 8 ounces). Very low birth weight is considered to be 1500 grams (3 pounds, 4.5 ounces) or less.

lower court In law, this is a court that has only limited authority or that handles special areas (e.g., traffic or small-claims court).

lowest achievable emission rate In environmental health, under the Clean Air Act, this is the rate of emissions that 1) is the most stringent emission limitation contained in the implementation plan of any state for polluting sources unless the owner or operator of the proposed source demonstrates that such limitations are not achievable and 2) is the most stringent emissions limitation achieved in practice, whichever is more stringent.

low-volume DRGs Those diagnosis-related groups having five or fewer patients during a hospital base year.

LPN *See licensed practical nurse.*

L.S. *See locus sigilli.*

LSD *See lysergic acid diethylamide.*
LSRHs *See limited-service rural hospitals.*
LTC *See long-term care.*
Ltd. *See limited.*
lucre Profit or gain. Often used with a negative connotation in referring to profit gotten in a somewhat illegal, unethical, or immoral way.
lumbar puncture In medical care, this is the insertion of a needle into the lumbar region of the spinal canal. Also known as a "spinal tap."
lump sum settlement 1. In health-care finance, this is a payment of a debt in one large payment at one time rather than in smaller amounts over time. 2. Payment of a large sum of money to settle a debt. 3. Payment of benefits of medical insurance in one check to the injured party or beneficiary.
lunacy Insanity; craziness; mental illness.
Lung Association *See American Lung Association.*
lung classes In occupational health, this is a classification scheme used to designate the clearance of inhaled radioactive materials from the lung. Materials are classified on the basis of their period of retention in the pulmonary region of the lungs. *D* (Day) indicates a biological half-life of less than 10 days, *W* (Week) a half-life of 10–100 days, and *Y* (Year) a half-life greater than 100 days.
LVN *See licensed vocational nurse.*
lysergic acid diethylamide (LSD) A potent psychogenic drug first derived in 1942, LSD produces psychotic-like symptoms, behavior changes, hallucinations, delusions, and time-space disorientation.
lysis of a fever In medical care, this is the gradual reduction of a high body temperature back to its normal level.

M

MA *See medical assistant; medical audit.*
MAAC *See maximum allowable actual charge.*
MAC *See maximum allowable charge; Maximum Allowable Cost Program.*
M and E *See monitoring and evaluation.*
machine language In computers, this is the actual language recognized and used by the computer when running business or medical records software programs or doing other operations.
macro- Prefix meaning "large."
MAF *See medical assistance facilities.*
MAGIC In health information management and computerized health services, a commercial program developed for health care using a combination of software programs, operating systems, and programming language developed by Meditech, founder of the S computer system. *See also Meditech; MUMPS; CAPER.*
magistrate 1. A judge, usually in local and regional courts, who is limited in function and power. 2. A public officer. 3. A justice of the peace.
magna culpa (Lat.) Great fault or blame. Gross negligence.
magnetic resonance imaging (MRI) A high-quality form of anatomical imaging through advanced technological equipment that can develop visual images of the inside of the body that are more clear than X rays or CT scans and safer than X rays because it does not have the risk of radiation exposure. A diagnostic technology and procedure utilizing a giant magnet that allows the physician to observe and quantify the magnetic characteristics of atomic nuclei in varying states of energy such as in the human body. To take the scan, a patient is positioned in the center of the large circular magnet and in its magnetic field. As the magnetic field is rotated and a radio frequency signal beamed through the body, some of the nuclei absorb the radio waves, and the structure of the tissue and organs changes the radio waves' direction, thus causing them to "resonate." The radio signals with its changes are picked up by an antenna and then processed by a computer into an image of the body or organ being examined. Formerly known as "nuclear magnetic resonance."
magnetic resonance therapy (MRT) A spin-off of magnetic resonance imaging (MRI) that gives physical detailed cross-sectional images of the body's organs. Whereas in the MRI the patient is inserted into the hole of a large donut-shaped magnet, in MRT two large donut-shaped magnets are separated by about 2 feet, allowing a physician or two (one on each side) to stand between the two magnets. The part of the patient to be operated on is placed in the middle, between the two magnets, allowing the surgeons to do surgery while using the MRI imaging capabilities. The work being done is seen on the MRI/CRT monitor screens. The physician can direct the images as needed by using surgical tools equipped to emit infrared light as needed by stepping on a foot pedal. The electronic eyes of the MRI sense the infrared light and shoot a picture each time it is stimulated by the light. Less invasive surgery can be done because the body does not need to be opened up to see what is being done.
magnetic tape 1. Audio recording tape. 2. In computers, a storage, input, and output medium in which data are recorded on the surface of a strip of tape in the form of magnetized spots.
Maharishi Ayur-Veda prevention of disease This is the traditional medical system of India and one of the oldest and most comprehensive systems of natural health care and healing. It restores Ayurvedic procedures in accordance within this healing system's classical approaches to promoting a balance between the mind, body, behavior, and environment.
mailbox rule In health law and contracts, this is when an acceptance to an offer is effective on the basis of when it is posted in the mailbox. At that moment, a contract is formed, and the offer cannot thereafter be revoked.
mail kit In managed care and medical insurance, this is a packet of direct-mail literature that includes all forms, materials, and literature that an enrollee needs to select a health plan and apply for a policy.
mail-order insurance This is health and other disability insurance secured in response to public or personal solicitation by mail and advertising. It usually requires no physical examination but rather a statement of health completed by the subscriber. It becomes effective on return of the application by mail and approval by the mail-order insurer. The scant health information required, the complexities of medical histo-

ries, and the relative difficulty of excluding preexisting conditions have contributed to relatively high premiums and loadings and low rates of claims recovery.

maim To harm or cripple; to injure a person.

main earner in family In government programs, eligibility assessment for public health, medical care programs, and/or social services, a family must define one person as the major source of income. In a single-person family, the one person is to be the main earner. In a married couple's family with no children or a married couple with a large family, or, in the case of cohabitation, the adult in the labor force earning the most income, or, if unemployed, the one with greatest potential earning power, or the one with the most retirement or disability income or if equal, the male is designated the main earner.

mainframe In the computer aspects of health information management, this is a large, centrally located computer capable of storing massive amounts of data and information. This computer has the capacity for multiple use, multiple terminals, and hard disk or tape storage.

main motion In formal health-care meetings or hearings under parliamentary procedure, this is the presentation of a principal concept or principle to the assembly for its discussion and a vote.

main program In the computer aspects of health information management, this is a basic software program that contains instructions to start the computer and its programs to function and run. This is the portion of the program that has primary control over the operations to be performed by the rest of the programs, including the instructions for subprograms that perform specific functions.

mainstream In a specialized Medicaid managed care under MediCal in California, this is where contracts in the various regions of the state are made with a non–government-operated HMO selected through a competitive bid process to provide medical care to certain MediCal beneficiaries for a capitated fee. *See local initiative; two-plan model.*

mainstreaming In handicapped services, this is the process of arranging for individuals with some physical or mental limitations to move into opportunities to work or participate in the average or normal walks of life or work.

maintainor 1. In health law, this is when a third party interferes in a lawsuit in which he or she has no interest and is done so to assist one of the parties against the other. 2. One who supports a lawsuit.

maintenance 1. The offense committed by a maintainor. 2. Unethical or illegal support of a lawsuit 3. Unethical financial support of a client by an attorney while a lawsuit is pending.

maintenance department *See physical plant and maintenance department.*

maintenance drug therapy In medical care, this is the reduction of a drug dose in a patient to the minimal therapeutic level to prevent a relapse of a disease or condition.

maintenance expenses In managed care or insurance, this is the cost of keeping a health plan or medical insurance policy active and in force; the time the agent and office personnel who service a policy spend working on each policy, including the cost of processing the annual premium and the policy dividend payments.

maintenance factors In motivation theory developed by Frederick Herzberg, PhD, these are elements of work such as attempting to motivate a person with something like company policy or job security that instead lead to employee job dissatisfaction when used or when resources are not adequately provided or available. Also referred to as "hygiene factors" or "dissatisfiers." *See hygiene factors.*

maintenance of facilities In health-care facility management, this is the amount of money or work needed for maintenance, including physical plant improvements or additions to present facilities, to be in compliance with regulations and to meet accreditation and quality standards.

maintenance services 1. In health-care delivery, these are services provided to individuals with chronic physical and mental conditions to prevent their deterioration as well as services provided to individuals in need of assistance in activities of daily living. The purpose of such services is to enable an individual to participate in the community to the fullest degree to which that individual is capable. Maintenance services do not include habilitative or rehabilitative services because the primary purpose of these services is to restore and increase functional ability rather than maintain an existing level of function. 2. In health administration, these are services provided for a hospital or health-care facility by its department of engineering and/or maintenance, with some assistance from housekeeping, that support the upkeep and repair of the facility's physical plant, both inside and out. *See also engineering and maintenance department; levels of prevention.*

major activity In public health and health promotion research, this is the principal activity of a person or of his or her age-sex group. For those 1 to 5 years of age, it refers to ordinary play with other children; for those 5 to 17 years of age, it refers to school attendance; and for those 18 years of age and over, it usually refers to a job, housework, or school attendance.

major complicating and comorbid (in DRGs) *See complicating and comorbid.*

major diagnostic categories (MDCs) In medical records, coding of diseases, and DRGs, this is a broad classification of diagnoses. There were 83 original coding systems oriented to DRGs, and in the revised DRGs 23 subdivisions were created on the basis of body and organ systems and are associated with the ICD-9-CM coding system. *See also DRGs; ICD-9-CM.*

major emitting facilities In environmental health, any stationary facilities or sources of air pollutants that directly emit or have the potential to emit 100 tons or more per year of any air pollutant, including any major emitting facility or source of fugitive emissions of any such pollutant.

majority 1. In formal health-care meetings, this is when more than half the board or committee cast their votes in one direction or the other. 2. The age at which one can legally manage his or her own affairs, enter into contracts, and be held accountable by law. Referred to as "age of majority." 3. More than half; greatest percentage; the most or greatest amount. *See age of majority.*

majority vote In formal health-care meetings or hearings under parliamentary procedure, when more than half the total number of the assembly presents an authorized voice vote or when the authorized ballot votes represent more than half the legal voters; 51% or more of the vote.

major medical 1. In medical insurance, this is designed to offset heavy uncovered medical expenses resulting from catastrophic or prolonged illness or injuries. Generally, such policies do not provide first-dollar coverage but do provide benefit payments of 75% to 80% of all types of medical expenses above a certain base amount paid by the insured. Most major medical policies contain maximums on the total amount that will be paid (e.g., $50,000); thus they do not provide last-dollar coverage or complete protection against catastrophic costs. However, there is a trend toward $250,000 limits or even unlimited plans. In addition, benefit payments are often 100% of expenses after the individual has incurred some large amount ($500 to $2,000) of out-of-pocket expenses. Some of the various financing mechanisms for major medical include 1) Medicare Part A, 2) Medicare Part B, 3) Medicaid, 4) CHAMPUS (Civilian Health and Medical Program of the Uniformed Services), 5) veterans benefits, and 6) private commercial insurance through one's employment or paid by oneself. Major medical insurance policies can be carried alone or in combination with other medical care insurance or health plans as supplemental insurance policies. 2. Medical insurance that covers only serious illnesses requiring extensive surgery, treatments, and long lengths of stay in the hospital, all of which are very costly. Regular medical insurance often has cost limits; thus major medical insurance goes into effect to cover costly treatments and medical bills not covered by other medical insurance. Also referred to as "catastrophic medical insurance."

major medical expense insurance Health insurance to finance the expense of major illnesses and injuries. Major medical policies usually include a deductible clause, which means that the individual or another insurer contributes to the cost of the medical expenses; a policy especially designed to help offset heavy medical expenses resulting from catastrophic or prolonged illness or injury. *See also major medical.*

major modification In environmental health and under the Clean Air Act, this is any modification to major stationary sources of air pollution emissions. It provides significant pollutant increase levels below which a modification is not considered major.

major release In environmental health, this is the emission or dumping of any quantity of hazardous substances, pollutants, or contaminants that pose a substantial threat to public health or welfare or the environment or that result in significant public concern.

Major Risk Medical Insurance Board A government-created board that oversees the Health Insurance Plan of California (HIPC), a cooperative group insurance purchasing alliance created to serve small business from 5 to 50 employees. Created by the California state legislature, the board defines the coverage, negotiates the premium rates, and oversees all health plans. The board, developed to implement the HIPC, negotiates with insurance carriers in six different cost-of-living areas established across the state of California. A report care is issued for each health plan for the consumer by the board. *See Health Insurance Plan of California; community health purchasing alliances.*

major secondary diagnosis Under medical expenses billing under a prospective/DRG system or a capitation plan, this is a complication or a new disease, disorder, or related condition associated with the principal diagnosis that requires treatment during the patient's hospital stay and is not the diagnosis for which the patient was admitted to the hospital.

major stationary source In environmental health, this is any permanently located, nonmoveable air pollutant source that has the potential to emit more the 100 tons of air pollution matter per year.

major surgery In medical care, this is surgery in which the operative procedure is hazardous. Major surgery is sometimes distinguished from minor surgery according to whether it requires a general anesthetic, involves an amputation above the ankle or wrist, or includes entering one of the body cavities (abdomen, chest, or head).

major third-party payers In medical insurance and managed care, these are any large regional or nationally founded organized insurance carriers, managed-care plans, or state or federal governmental medical insurance programs that pay hospitals or health-care providers directly for the services rendered to enrollees or policy beneficiaries.

major tranquilizer Drugs that have antipsychotic properties. The phenothiazines, thioxanthenes, butyrophenones, and reserpine derivatives are typical major tranquilizers, which are also known as "neuroleptics" or "antipsychotics."

maker 1. In health law, this is the one who makes or prepares a legal document. 2. One who signs a negotiable instrument that binds the signer or maker to pay on it (e.g., a check).

make-whole remedies In health administration and human resource management, this is when a worker is mistreated on the job and the health-care organization or its agents are in violation of employment laws. After due process and appropriate hearings and being proven in legal proceedings and activities, the organization is required to make up the losses that were suffered by the employee because of the wrongdoing.

mal- Prefix meaning "bad."

mala fides (Lat.) Bad faith.

mala in se (Lat.) 1. Wrong in itself. Natural wrongs (e.g., murder). 2. An act that is morally wrong, independent of any statute that may declare it wrong. *See malum in se.*

malaise A general feeling of being unwell, restless, or indisposed.

mala prohibita (Lat.) That which men agree is bad and must not be allowed. Man-made laws, as opposed to wrongs, which are obvious and naturally bad in themselves. *See malum prohibitum; mala in se.*

malefactor One who has committed a crime.

malfeasance Committing an illegal or evil act.

malfunction In environmental health, this is any sudden failure of air pollution control or process equipment or the failure of a process to operate in a normal or usual manner so that emissions of pollutants are increased.

malice Intentionally causing harm or injury without just cause or excuse.

malice aforethought In tort law and criminal law, this when an act is done with an evil intention but not necessarily with an intent to produce a negative result. *See intentional tort.*

malicious 1. With malice or negative intent. 2. In health, tort, and criminal law, this is an intent to harm someone or to commit a serious crime. 3. Done intentionally without excuse. *See intentional tort.*

malicious prosecution In health law, this is the process of arresting someone for filing a lawsuit against a party without just reason or probable cause, lacking merit, with malice intent, and for harassment reasons. This may be legal grounds for a countersuit. A case against a plaintiff must have been decided in favor of the defendant, and the defendant must prove there was no probable cause to show that the defendant was liable and that the plaintiff acted with malice intent when suing the defendant.

malingering The willful, deliberate, and fraudulent feigning or exaggeration of the symptoms of illness or injury for the purpose of achieving a consciously desired end such as collecting insurance or some other benefits.

malnutrition Any nutritional disorder; imbalance in the intake of the various nutrients.

mal ojo (Spanish) Evil eye. A disorder that occurs in the Hispanic culture, it is characterized by a female child experiencing an adult looking at her with lust, thus causing a curse-type disorder to fall on the child.

malpractice 1. Professional misconduct or lack of ordinary skill, improper discharge of duties, or failure to take necessary precautions and to meet the standards of care, resulting in jury to another; failure in the performance of a professional act that causes injury to another. 2. A subprinciple of tort law and negligence. A professional is liable for misconduct, unreasonable lack of skill or fidelity in professional or fiduciary duties, evil practice, illegal or immoral conduct, or any unreasonable incompetence that results in damages or injuries to another individual. For some professions such as medicine, malpractice insurance can cover the costs of lawsuits instituted against the professional and/or any damages assessed by the court, usually up to a maximum limit. In medical malpractice, it is required that the patient demonstrate some injury, harm, or damage and that the injury be caused by negligence in the delivery of care or treatment. This term is applied to negligent misconduct of most all professionals such as physicians, nurses, dentists, lawyers, engineers, accountants, and other applicable professions. *See locality rule; cause of action; foreseeability; reasonableness; scope of practice; standard of care; negligence; tort law.*

malpractice insurance A specialized liability insurance used to protect professionals against the risk of suffering financial damage from a lawsuit that may be filed against a professional who is at risk in his or her practice, a health-care provider as a result of injury, or damage to a patient caused by alleged negligence in providing medical care and treatment. Also know as "professional liability insurance." *See malpractice.*

mal puesto (Spanish) Bad or evil place. A disorder related to sorcery that occurs in the Hispanic culture. It is believed that an illness or disorder is caused by passing, going in, or having an association with a place or spot that is evil.

maltreatment Improper or unskillful treatment of a patient by a health-care provider through neglect or lack of knowledge or skill. This principal does not imply that such conduct by the health-care provider is either willful or grossly careless in the treatment of the patient.

malum in se Naturally evil; evil in itself. An act that, by its very nature, goes against the principles of natural, moral, or public law. *See mala in se.*

malum prohibitum (Lat.) 1. Any wrong that is prohibited. 2. An act made wrong because it is prohibited by a statute. 3. Conventional wrongs; things thought to be harmful or wrong. 4. Breaking man-made rules (e.g., breaking a speed limit). *See mal prohibita.*

managed care 1. Any health-care delivery system that controls both the delivery and the cost of care in such a way that expenses, quality, utilization, operations, and costs are controlled; originally referred to as "prepaid health care." Historically, health-care delivery has been controlled by those who delivered the care and received the payments rather than by those who funded the care. Managed care reverses this and takes the choice of physician and hospital away from the consumer/member and somewhat controls the activities of the health-care provider, especially the physician and the hospital. This approach influences utilization of services, cost-effectiveness of delivery, and quality and uses a prepaid and/or capitated payment structure as an incentive to reduce utilization, expense, and cost. Utilization review, hospital precertification and quality assurance programs, preventive care, and health promotion are integral parts of the HMO, PPO, IPA, or other health plan. Different financial incentives and management controls have been put in place to direct patients to efficient providers who provide appropriate care in a cost-effective manner. Decision making by health-care providers are altered by a complex system of financial incentives, penalties, and administrative procedures that enter into the doctor-patient relationship. A balance between appropriate and quality care and how to achieve both the most economically are the driving forces in this approach to health-care delivery. The various types and approaches of managed care include staff-model HMO, open-ended HMO, group-model HMO, independent practice HMO, open-panel IPA–model HMO, preferred provider organizations, exclusive provider organizations, multiple options plans, and OSA (other strange arrangements). Also referred to as "health plans." 2. From a public care or public health prospective, this is a planned, comprehensive approach to the provision of health care that combines clinical services and administrative procedures in an integrated, coordinated system that is carefully constructed to provide timely access to primary care and other necessary services in a cost-effective manner. It is intended to increase utilization of clinical preventive services and thus reduce the unnecessary use of emergency rooms for ambulatory care and eliminate preventable hospitalizations. 3. From a federal perspective, this is a health-care system that integrates the financing and delivery of appropriate health-care services to covered individuals by arrangements with selected providers to furnish a comprehensive set of services, explicit standards for the selection of health-care providers, formal programs for ongoing quality assurance and utilization review, and significant financial incentives for members to use providers and procedures with the plan. Health maintenance organizations, IPAs, and PPOs fall under the managed-care umbrella. *See prepaid health care; prepaid health plan; health plan; capitation; cost controls.*

managed-care firm A general term for insurance companies that contract prepaid health care to health-care providers and beneficiaries to contain costs to all three entities of a health plan: the beneficiary, the health-care providers, and the insurance company. This organization negotiates contracts for managed care, decides which services are to be offered and which health-care providers will offer the care, and reimbursement levels and approaches, including capitation, cost of service, quality-of-care monitoring, and packaging of the plan and its terms while containing costs and conserving resources.

managed-care MediCal Medicaid beneficiaries are transitioned to managed-care programs so that comprehensive coverage can be provided and costs of health care reduced. The managed-care programs are to improve beneficiary access to quality primary and preventive health-care services; improve beneficiary health status and outcomes by emphasizing health maintenance, health education, preventive care, and early detection and treatment; generate fundamental long-term cost containment by improving the health status of medically underserved populations; educate beneficiaries about the benefits of and rights under managed care; improve quality assurance; promote the delivery of quality care through a system that ensures fiscal and programmatic accountability; support culturally appropriate services; ensure the timely provision of services in appropriate settings and effectively manage the use of technology; reduce duplication of services and enable resources to be shifted from acute and specialty care to primary and preventive care; use managed-care expertise from the public and private sectors; purchase care from organized managed-care plans under capitated at-risk arrangements that use administrative efficiencies; and improve patterns of practice, volume purchasing, and economies of scale.

managed-care organizations *See managed care; managed-care firms.*

managed-care plan, emergency care The provision in managed-care plans to ensure that beneficiaries of a health plan will be able to obtain emergency care when needed. Education regarding the use of and approaches to obtaining emergency care are provided to members, including patient transfer requirements and the reimbursement structure.

managed-care plans A health-care financing, medical insurance, and health-care delivery approach that places controls on the use of medical services including preapproval for elective hospital admissions, second opinions for surgery, and case management. *See managed care.*

managed choice In managed care, this is a health plan approach that combines elements of several managed-care programs and includes benefits similar to those for prepaid health care/HMOs for authorized services with an option to self-refer at a significantly lower benefit level. Each member selects a primary care physician who serves as the member's medical care manager. Also referred to as a "swing-out plan," "point-of-purchase plan," or "point-of-service plan."

managed collaboration In managed care and managed competition, this is the integration and interactivity of third-party payers, health plans, hospitals, medical groups, surgi-centers, outpatient clinics, and long-term care under one organizational structure to fit into a health alliance structure.

managed competition 1. A financing strategy used in managed-care programs where the health plans that do a better job of improving quality and cutting costs are rewarded with more members/subscribers and revenue; those health plans that have poor quality and higher costs realize low revenue. Such approaches seek to minimize the incentive for health plans to select risks for individual plans that allow a free ride. This is not the management of competition but rather the restriction of competition through the creation of large health plans and eliminating smaller plans that cannot compete because of financial structure, restraints, and incentives. Beneficiaries and physicians have limited choice. The system is to be oriented to preventive care and health promotion. Large groups of employees use their combined bargaining clout and purchasing power to acquire lower priced health-care services from health plans and health-care networks of providers and insurance companies that will be forced into competition so that each can be more efficient and cost-effective. It is the restructuring of the health-care system so that competitive forces can lower costs and improve quality of care. Cost caps, which are fairer to the consumer who is able to pay for costs, are implemented. 2. Managed competition establishes health-care "sponsors," or Health Insurance Purchasing Cooperatives (HIPCs), which function as buyers for their members, offering a variety of competing health plans. Employers would pay for coverage for their employees, whereas the self-employed and those not covered by public programs would buy their own coverage with public subsidies as needed. The health-care system is restructured so that the health-care marketplace and its competitive forces can lower costs and improve quality of care. It also encourages individuals to choose cost-effective health-care services. Medicare and Medicaid remain the same. Employers pay a set amount for health plans regardless of the one chosen by the employee; if the plan costs more than the employer's contribution, the employee pays the difference. Tax incentives are applied, encouraging selection of the lowest-cost plan. Incentives also would encourage health plans to keep costs down, making them competitive. The provision to set premiums on the basis of risk is removed.

managed health care *See managed care.*

managed health-care plan In health-care delivery, these are prepaid medical care services that integrate the delivery, utilization, management, and financing of health-care delivery with enrolled members. Organized health-care providers, health systems, or networks are contracted with to share financial risk and include built-in incentives to ensure quality of care and cost-effectiveness in the delivery of care and services and to minimize utilization. Databases, data gathering, and information management systems are employed to assess and monitor utilization patterns and the cost of medical care and health services by the members.

management 1. Getting things done through people. 2. The process of planning, organizing, controlling, coordinating, communicating, commanding, and directing work that utilizes people, ideas, and resources to achieve organizational goals and objectives and to be responsible for the results. 3. Using a systems approach, the process of allocating an organization's inputs (human and economic resources) by planning, organizing, directing, and controlling for the purpose of producing outputs (goods and services) desired by its customers so that organizational objectives are accomplished. In the process, work is performed with and through an organization's personnel in an ever-changing environment. 4. Some governmental agencies consider this to be all personnel above the level of job and task supervisors serving in a command role in the organizational structure. *See functions of a manager; health-care administration.*

management and administrative services The activities performed to direct and conduct the affairs of an entire hospital, or components thereof, as established by policies of the hospital. Standards are applied to evaluate the quality of a hospital's management and administrative services (JCAHO for acute-care facilities).

management and organization assessment As used in governmental health agencies or other organizations, this is an evaluation of the effectiveness and the strengths and weaknesses of programs or contract services. A bottom-up analysis is often integrated with the findings identified by concurrent environmental, safety, and health assessments. Information and documents are gathered to support the assessment, including but not limited to organizational charts and functions, facility or site layout, a description of operations, an environmental survey, contract provisions, budgets, incident reports, internal self-assessments, and corrective actions.

management audit In health administration, this is the assessment of financial statements, status, and management by a certified public accountant or other knowledgeable professional who reviews adherence to governing policy, profit capability, controls, operating procedures, and relations with employees, customers, patients, clients, and the general public.

management by objectives (MBO) A process whereby top, middle, and lower levels of management jointly identify the organization's mission and goals. Once goals are defined, measurable objectives are developed for each area of responsibility and for each worker in terms of the expected results. Using objectives as measures and guides for the operation of a department or business unit, this allows for the assessment of conditions and performance of each member and work unit. *See also goal; objective; management.*

management data 1. Information, statistics, and other inputs used by all levels of administration for decision making and better operation of the health-care facility. 2. In medical records, the information retrieved from patient medical records and used by health-care providers and facility administrators to make decisions and develop policies. 3. The information tools of management such as policy and procedure manuals, bylaws, budgets, statistics, planning documents, worksheets, contracts, and any other source of information available to assist administrators in providing effective and efficient management.

management engineering A process of providing quantitative figures, facts, and costs for use in making management decisions; another term for "management science."

management functions *See functions of a manager; management.*

management information In health administration, this is the data and knowledge needed by administrators to formulate goals and objectives, to determine if they are being met, and to support decision making.

management information system (MIS) A system (frequently automated or computer based) that processes data, makes information available, and produces the necessary information in proper form and at appropriate intervals for the management of a health-care organization or facility. The system should measure program progress toward objectives and report costs and problems needing attention.

management inventories In health administration and human resource management, this is an assessment, review, and summary of the education, skills, and abilities of management personnel.

management letter In health-care finance, this is a formal written statement and summary from the audit firm of the findings of an external audit to the governing board that accompanies the audited financial report.

management of migrations In environmental health, these are actions taken to minimize and mitigate the migration of hazardous substances or pollutants or contaminants and the effects of such migration. Action is taken when the hazardous substances are no longer at or near the area where they were originally located or in situations where a source cannot be adequately identified or characterized. Measures include provisions of alternative water supplies, management of plume of contamination, or treatment of groundwater aquifers.

management oversight and risk tree (MORT) In health services administration, this is a disciplined logic or decision tree used to systematically relate and integrate a wide variety of management or safety concepts. It focuses on three main concerns: specific oversights or emissions, assumed risks, and general management system weakness. MORT analysis asks the question, Are all the factors of the management system necessary, sufficient, and organized in such a manner as to ensure that the overall program or service will be as held out to the customer, to the public, to the organization itself, and to other groups as appropriate?

management rights In health administration and labor relations, these are the discretions and freedoms that an employer needs to manage a health-care organization in an effective manner. They are reserved by management in the labor agreement.

management service organization A legal health-care corporation created to merge medical groups, physician groups, and hospitals under one corporate structure, forming a corporate superstructure for its management. Also formed to provide practice management services to physicians or to medical groups or related entities combined together under one managerial structure. An administrative and corporate structure used in medical care to combine various entities of health-care delivery together to form a comprehensive full-service health-care delivery organization, thus creating special advantages for managed-care contracting, group purchasing, and developing a competitive advantage.

management systems In health administration, these are organizational and administrative approaches and operating philosophies and theories such as PERT or MBO.

management team In health administration, these are top personnel who hold managerial positions in a health services organization who cooperatively work as a group to plan, coordinate, evaluate, direct, and apply the principles and practices of communication, strategic planning, efficiency, effectiveness, quality, policy, and other important organizational and managerial concepts and practices to the organization's operation through an integrated effort. *See functions of a manager; management.*

manager 1. A person who is in charge of and administers the business aspects of a health-care organization, department, service, or company. 2. A member of the House of Representatives who conducts an impeachment hearing in the Senate. 3. One who conducts the affairs of a business or department in a health-care facility or organization. Any person in a health-care organization who is formally designated to be accountable for the work of others. *See functions of a manager; health services administrator; management; midmanager; supervisor.*

managerial control In health administration, this is the process by which an administrator establishes accountability in workers and ensures that resources are obtained and used in an effective and efficient manner to achieve the goals and objectives of the health-care organization.

managerial functions *See functions of a manager; management.*

managing patient resources In managed care, from the health plan's perspective, this puts the primary care physician in control of the efficiency and effectiveness with which patients are cared for and treated. The health plan and the contracting medical groups and hospitals must know what services they are responsible for and create a health-care delivery system that best serves the patient while not wasting resources and containing costs.

mandamus (Lat.) 1. We command. 2. An order issued by a court to a public official, commanding him or her to perform an act that is his or her duty. 3. A writ that tells a governmental department to do something.

mandate 1. A directive or an order from a high official or higher court. 2. A command; an order. 3. Authorization or power to do certain acts.

mandated benefits In managed care, these are the services and products required by state or federal law provided to policyholders, enrollees, or members or their eligible dependents by health plans.

mandated providers In managed care, these are nonphysician health-care practitioners (e.g., podiatrists, psychologists, optometrists, and chiropractors) who provide care and whose licensed service must be included in the benefits and coverage of a health plan as set forth by state or federal law.

mandate, employer (large) In the National Health Security program and health-care reform and under universal coverage plans, this is required medical care insurance coverage where all employers with more than 100 employees are required to offer employees and their dependents a set of choices of health plans that provide a standard medical care benefits package. This is to be offered to employees and their dependents who work more than 30 hours per week or over 1000 hours per year. The employer must make a set contribution of a minimum amount of the lowest health plan to help pay the premiums of the worker.

mandate, individual and small employers In the National Health Security program and health-care reform and under universal coverage plans, this is required medical care insurance coverage where part-time employees who are not covered by any medical insurance or health plan and who work less than 1000 hours per year obtain coverage. An employer with more than 100 employees who work less than 1000 hours per year and persons not employed or covered or firms with less than 100 employees will be required to purchase coverage and offer a menu of plans. Small employers may be required to make monthly payroll deductions and pay the proper plan or system for the coverage. Individuals are required to purchase coverage.

mandates See *mandate, employer (large); mandate, individual and small employers.*

mandatory 1. Obligatory; required; commanded by formal power or authority; must be followed or obeyed. 2. Imperative; that which must be completed as requested.

mandatory licensure State laws that require that all persons who practice in a particular profession (e.g., nursing or medicine) be licensed.

manic-depressive illness In psychiatry/psychology and mental health services, this is a mental disorder characterized by severe changes of mood that have a tendency to recur. In the manic state, the patient is elated and hyperactive. In the depressed state, the patient suffers from a depressed mood, anxiety, clinical depression, and possible physical slowing down, which has physical symptoms. In the cyclic form of the disorder, the affected person has at least one of each kind of episode. The official psychiatric terminology is "bipolar disorder."

manifests In environmental health, these are the forms used for identifying the quantity, composition, and origin, routing, and destination of hazardous waste during transportation from the point of generation to the point of disposal treatment or storage.

manipulative therapy A treatment used by osteopathic physicians and chiropractors that involves using the hands to adjust the body, particularly the spine, and other bones and muscles.

man-made air pollution In environmental health, this is any air pollution that results directly or indirectly from human activities.

manpower The type, level, number, and distribution of personnel needed to accomplish the goals and objectives of an institution, organization, program, or region.

manpower schedule In health administration and human resource management, this is part of a health-care organization's plan of operations in which a health-care manager estimates the number of personnel needed to produce the clinical and nonclinical aspects of health services forecasted. The plan includes the expense of salaries, training, recruitment, hiring of new workers, and benefits.

manslaughter 1. The unpremeditated killing of another person; one form of homicide. 2. Illegally killing a person without malice, either expressed or implied. 3. The taking of another person's life in a sudden heat of anger. This is unlawful and may be voluntary or involuntary. Also referred to as "criminal negligence."

Mantel-Hanzel estimate In epidemiology, this is an adjusted odds ratio used to estimate relative risk using matched and grouped sets of data; a weighted average of individual odds ratios.

manual accounts payable check In health-care financial management, this is revenue such as a check that is processed manually by accounts payable. Occasionally, the customer services department of a health plan will request a manual accounts payable check in lieu of the claims department being able to process an appropriate or timely check. Referred to as a "manual A/P check."

manual arts therapist One who utilizes industrial arts such as woodworking and graphic arts to rehabilitate disabled patients. Under the direction of a physician, he or she plans and administers rehabilitation programs. A 4-year bachelors degree in manual arts therapy, industrial arts, or industrial education, supplemented by a minimum 2-month clinical training program, is usually required. Clinical training is offered by both hospitals and rehabilitation centers.

manual rate(s) 1. In health-care financial management, this is the premium rate developed for group insurance coverage from a health plan's standard rate tables, normally referred to as its "rate manual" or "underwriting manual." A manual rate is also called a "book rate." 2. In managed care, these are standard mortality rates that are developed independently of the mortality experience of any particular group, are based on averages, and are used for determining the premium rate for a small group of potential enrollees; demographic and epidemiological rates based on a health plan's data and average claims information and adjusted for group-specific demographic, regional, and industry factors or benefit or coverage variations.

manual rate making In medical and liability insurance, a process used to quote uniform rates for special types of risks to liability and certain categories of risk exposure and determined by referring to preestablished rates as found in a rate manual.

manual therapies Treatments and therapies that are used on conditions related to jammed nerves or arteries in the spinal cord or other spinal column–related misalignments. Therapeutic modalities are mechanical and based on diagnostic information about the movement pattern of the patient. Diseases are interpreted as the result of a complex of nerve-related factors that drive the internal bodily systems out of balance. *See chiropractic.*

manufacture formulations In environmental health, this is a list of substances or component parts as described by the maker of a coating or pesticide.

MAP *See medical audit program.*

maps In epidemiology or occupational health and safety, these are drawings used to illustrate the physical relationships of elements of people, equipment, materials, buildings, and environmental structures associated with a disease outbreak, an accident, or another incident.

March of Dimes This is a national volunteer health agency that originally had the mission of fund-raising to provide research, education, and assistance to victims of polio. When polio became controlled, the March of Dimes chose another important cause to support: birth defects. To help deter and remove birth defects from society, the March of Dimes' mission includes fund-raising to support research and public health education and to provide assistance to families with a member suffering from a major birth defect.

marginal benefit In health-care delivery, this is the amount of a value or benefit realized from an additional unit of care, treatment, or period of stay.

marginal cost In health economics and financing, the change in the total cost of producing services that results from a small or unit change in the quantity of services being produced. Marginal cost is the appropriate cost concept to consider when contemplating program expansion or contraction. Economies of scale win results from the expansion of a program when marginal cost is less than the average or unit cost.

marginal tax rate The tax rate, or percentage, that is applied on the last increment of income for the purpose of computing federal or other income taxes.

marijuana Dried leaves and flowers of the cannabis sativa (Indian hemp) plant, which can cause physical, mental, or emotional changes when smoked or ingested in sufficient quantity. The physical changes include increased heart rate and blood pressure, dryness of the mouth, increased appetite, and occasional nausea, vomiting, and diarrhea. The mental or emotional changes include dreamy level of consciousness, disruptive chain of thoughts, disturbances of time and space, and alterations of mood. In strong doses, marijuana can produce hallucinations and, at times, paranoid ideas and suspiciousness.

marital Pertaining to marriage.

marital counseling Marriage counseling. A trained counselor assists married couples in resolving problems that arise and trouble them in their relationship.

marital status In public health and health services research, these are categories of married or unmarried. "Married" includes all married people, including those separated from their spouses. "Unmarried" includes those who are single (never married), divorced, or widowed.

MARK In environmental health, this is the descriptive name, instructions, cautions, or other information applied to PCBs and PCB items.

marked-sensed punching method In health information management, a technique for detecting special pencil marks entered in certain locations on a card that the computer reads and then automatically translates into punched holes.

market In health administration, this is the actual or potential purchasers of a health-care service or product.

marketable security In health-care finance, this is a short-term financial instrument that is bought or sold without a loss in principal; often used as a short-term investment for temporary surplus cash balances.

market administration In health administration, this is the management of the various markets and products of a health-care organization such as birthing centers, women's services, heart catheter labs, and outpatient surgery centers. *See marketing; marketing, health-care.*

market area In health administration or managed care, this is the target geographic area or areas of greatest market potential. The market area is not necessarily the same as the defined service area or geographic area and may overlap. *See target population; catchment area.*

market-driven health-care organization Any health-care organization shaped by and responsive to the needs of the customer, marketplace, and consumers who make up the marketplace.

market-driven system Any health-care organization that must be responsive to the conditions of the health-care market and the needs, wants, expectations, and demands of its customers, including third-party payers (those who pay for the services), physicians (those who admit patients, order the services, and play the role of the gatekeeper), and patients (the consumer).

marketing 1. An applied discipline that focuses on the successful management of relationships and transactions between and among significant groups both inside and outside the health-care organization. Offering something of value to the customer (patient, physician, or third-party payer) in exchange for something of value. The functions and activities include but are not limited to market research, product and service development (e.g., product and service design and testing), promotion (pricing, advertising, and selling), distribution, and communications. In health-care marketing, three customers are identified: the patient/family, third-party payers, and physicians. 2. Finding out what people want and doing more of it; finding out what customers do not want and doing less of that. *See marketing, 4 P's of.*

marketing audit A systematic, critical, impartial review, appraisal, and thorough evaluation and examination of a health-care organization's marketing plans, operations, activities, and market position. Included in the assessment is a review of goals, objectives, policies, and assumptions that underlie them. The personnel, methods, organizational structure, budget, methods, approaches, and procedures used to achieve the marketing goals and objectives of the health-care organization are assessed and critically evaluated. Marketing audits are done to ensure that up-to-date information is used; to keep up with the changing, dynamic nature of the health-care industry; and to periodically monitor the health-care organization's position and activities so that it can be effective and responsive to market changes, needs, and preferences.

marketing committee 1. In managed care, this is a multidisciplinary, multidepartmental committee that provides input, insights, and recommendations into the approach and structure of insurance contracts, including interdepartmental input into the specific coverages to be included in the contracts as well as premium rates, co-payment rates, and guarantees. 2. In health administration, this is a multidisciplinary group that reviews and assesses the health-care organization's marketing needs and may conduct marketing audits to make recommendations on marketing. *See marketing audit.*

marketing department In managed care, this is the administrative unit responsible for promoting and ensuring that health plan services and products are accessible and available to the beneficiaries/members. This administrative unit conducts market research; communicates the benefits; develops ad campaigns; advertises, promotes, and assists in developing new services; and assesses and assists in revising existing services to meet the member and health plan needs and organizational goals.

marketing, 4 P's of In health-care marketing, these are four words beginning with the letter "P" used to ensure that a good marketing program exists if all four are covered: product (service), price, place, and promotion. *See marketing.*

marketing, health-care The assessment of consumer health-care needs and the subsequent planning of activities to increase the health-care organization's clientele and income. The application and use of basic marketing concepts and principles for use in the communication, selling, promoting, and advertising of health services as appropriate and effective. Marketing principles as used in the modern industries and manufacturing for the selling of goods are often found ineffective in the marketing of health-care services. Specialized approaches, techniques, methods, and processes are used and needed in marketing health services that are unique to the health-care industry because it functions much differently than the other industries in the United States. Marketing of health services requires a through understanding of the health-care delivery and services and the special differences and approaches for it to be effective. Ill-conceived marketing campaigns aimed at the wrong audiences and run at the wrong times can be costly to health services and organizations. *See also health planning; strategic health planning; advertising, health care.*

marketing mix In health-care marketing, this is the process of employing all marketing approaches, methods, and tools in an integrated way to cover all facets of the market being targeted.

marketing plan In health administration and health services delivery, this is a final document that results from the planning process that specifies the health-care organization's marketing goals, objectives, approaches, direction, and strategies to be used to achieve the plan and the specific goals and objectives for each critical service or product line.

marketing, strategic health-care The process of utilizing business marketing ideas, concepts, and processes to increase a hospital's or other health-care facility's market share of the health-care business available to a health-care organization.

market mix In health-care marketing, this is to ensure that the services being sold, offered, or communicated to the customer are of the right type, amount, and level to meet customer needs and ensure that the proper population strata, age, race, education, occupation, income, catchment area, and other related factors are of the right type, balance, and numbers to produce the best possible utilization and profitability.

market oriented In health administration and strategic planning, this is a managerial approach and administrative mind-set that identifies the needs and interests of the target population and catchment area while exploring avenues through which to meet the needs of the health-care organization's customers.

market research Information- and data-gathering approaches and methods used to discover the attitudes, expectations, preferences, needs, and wants of customers or potential customers of a health-care organization and to learn how to satisfy those desires. The aim is to provide the health-care organization with data and information that will help in decision making, resulting in being able to offer and deliver greater satisfaction to target markets, customers, and the community. *See market segment; target population.*

market segment In health-care marketing and health delivery assessment, this is any specific group or subset of a population with similar needs that differ from other populations. It is identified by a set of characteristics used to forecast or influence their use of health services (e.g., age, race, sex, geographic location, residence, education level, marital status, and family composition). *See target population; catchment area.*

market share In health-care delivery assessment, this is the proportion of all health services utilization that a health-care provider is able to capture over a certain time period. The share of individual services or product lines can be calculated for retention and flow and by specific service categories.

market share position In health-care delivery assessment, this is the assessment and determination of what proportion of health-care customers an organization has been able to attract in terms of competing health services. Market growth strategies that fortify or improve the market share are considered and then implemented by the health-care organization to better the position.

market testing To make available a service or product to consumers to determine its acceptability, attractiveness, desirability, need, or demand and to see how it influences consumer behavior; a pilot test used to see if a product or service is wanted or needed. *See pilot study.*

market value In health-care finance, this is the financial worth of an asset based on current prices or the purchasing price; one method for appraising the value of property or equipment by comparing the price of similar properties or equipment (comparables) recently sold and the circumstances of the sales.

market value approach In health-care finance, this is one method for appraising the value of property or equipment by comparing the price of similar properties or equipment (comparables) recently sold and the circumstances of the sales.

markup A meeting of a congressional committee at which the committee itself writes laws to recommend to the full Congress, makes decisions on appropriations, or otherwise makes policy; usually takes place after a public hearing on the subject matter. *See also executive session.*

married In public health and health services research, this a category of health status that includes all married people, including those separated from their spouses. *See marital status; unmarried.*

marshaling 1. The act of ordering, arranging, or ranking. 2. The arranging and ranking of capital assets when planning to pay off debts.

Martindale-Hubbell A set of reference books listing lawyers by location and area of practice.

MAS *See medical audit system.*

Massachusetts General Hospital's Multi-Programming System (MUMPS) A medical computer language developed with the support of grants from the National Center for Health Services Research. This was supposedly the first computer language developed for the health-care field. MUMPS was developed to handle medical data, and it has a system that is easily updated. It is easy to use, flexible, and inexpensive and can improve the efficiency and effectiveness of health-care delivery because it uses time and database sharing and a hierarchical file structure. *See also CAPER.*

mass basis *See service on mass basis.*

mass communication in health The transfer of health information to a large and usually heterogeneous population, usually by means of such media as direct mail, newspapers, magazines, radio, television, or motion pictures (Joint Committee on Health Education Terminology).

mass merchandising A possible insurance benefit offered to personnel working in a health-care facility that involves the sale of group property insurance through a payroll deduction. Most of these types of insurance offerings are aimed at automobile and homeowners coverage.

mass storage In the computer aspects of health information management, this is a storage medium such as a hard disk or tape that allows for the storing of large amounts of health-care data and/or patient information.

MAST *See military assistance to safety and traffic.*

mastectomy The surgical removal of the breast.

master 1. In health law, this is the responsible person; the source of authority. 2. An employer or principal person who is responsible for the acts of employees; in the physician/nurse relationship, the physician is the master and the nurse is legally the servant. 3. The person who is responsible for acts of those working under him or her. *See principle; agent; agency; law of agency.*

master budget In health-care financial management, this is the main overall budget of a hospital or health-care facility or organization that is composed of all the departmental and division budgets in the organization.

master contract In managed care, this is a legal contract between a health plan or insurance company and a group policyholder. This contract provides the details on the medical coverage or insurance benefits of a large number of employees or members under a single contract; a managed-care contract for a large employment group or other group that sets forth the conditions, terms, services, products, and persons covered by a health plan contract.

master group contract *See master contract.*

master lease In health-care finance and contracts, this is the major, or main, lease that controls subsequent leases or subleases.

master patient index In health information management and health-care delivery, this is a brief list of information and data that assists in the identification and location of health records and patient charts.

master policy In managed care, this is a legal contract between a health plan or insurance company and a group of employees or insurance policyholders.

MAST suit Military Anti-Shock Trousers. Used in emergency care to treat hypovolemic or cardiogenic shock, this suit consists of pants that are pulled on the legs, up to and over the abdomen, and then inflated. The pressure compresses the veins, thus increasing venous return to the heart.

matched controls In epidemiology and health services research, this is the process of ensuring that a study is sound in comparing subjects and controls. Every effort should be made by the investigator to ensure that controls or control groups and subjects in all comparison groups are as much alike as possible so that confounding variables and discrepancies in the study are reduced.

matching In epidemiology and health services research, this is an important aspect of research design because it deals with the control of confounding variables. Matching is the process of selecting controls so that the controls have similar effects or characteristics in a study to the subjects or cases. It attempts to make the subjects comparable with controls. Several approaches to matching have be used: caliper matching, which matches ages closely together; pair matching, which pairs individual cases with controls on a case-for-case basis; frequency matching, which matches case and control characteristics with frequency distributions so that both are the same or similar in cases and controls; and category matching, which groups broad categories such as age, education, occupation, and race.

matching funds Money, equipment, vehicles, buildings, office space, and sometimes personnel provided by local health and human service agencies to be used as a contribution to a project for which the federal government is providing a grant, demonstration contract, or other contract. The federal government usually provides three-fourths of the money the first year of funding, with one-fourth being "matched," or provided, by the state or local agency. Some grants are provided on a diminishing federal contribution basis (e.g., three-fourths by the federal government and one-fourth by the agency the first year, half by each the second year, and one-fourth by the federal government and three-fourths by the agency the third year), all done with the idea that once the federal government initiates a program, it will be so good that the local government will pick up the funding and continue it. This approach has not been effective for the most part because state and local governments usually cannot generate the extra money to compensate for the withdrawn federal funds nor afford to fund every new program the federal agencies can come up with.

matching grants In grant acquisition and fundraising, money given to an agency or organization on the condition that the agency contribute a similar amount of funds for the activity.

material 1. Essential; necessary; pertinent; getting to the basic issue. 2. Facts or evidence important enough to sway the final decision of a case. 3. Tools, resources, and equipment needed to get work done or to deliver health services.

material allegation An allegation that is a part of a claim or a defense.

material evidence In health law, these are the facts and evidence that prove or disprove substantial matters of a dispute.

material fact 1. In health law, this is a fact that is central and basic to the final decision of a case. 2. A fact that could influence the type and nature of an insurance policy.

material issue In law and the litigation process, this is a disputed issue subject to the trial process.

material safety data sheets In environmental health, this is a compilation of information required under the OSHA Communication Standard (Superfund Amendments and Reauthorization Act) on the identity of hazardous chemicals, health, physical hazards, exposure limits, and precautions.

materials management department In hospitals or other health-care facilities, this is a department that is also known as "purchasing and stores." It is responsible for ordering supplies, materials, furniture, and equipment, both medical and administrative. It purchases, receives, maintains, and stores an inventory and delivers these items to the appropriate areas in the health-care facility.

materials management department head A mid-management-level position, usually found in a hospital or other health-care facility, having the responsibility for the day-to-day operations of the materials management department. Administrative responsibilities involve inventory control, purchasing, procurement, storage, control, and distribution of business, office, and medical supplies.

material witness A person who knows specific facts and who can provide relevant evidence and testimony at trial.

maternal Related to being a mother; belonging to or coming from a mother.

maternal and child health In public health and health services, this is the provision of health for women of childbearing age and for children.

maternal and child health services (MCH) Organized health and social services for mothers (especially for family planning and pregnancy-related services), their children, and sometimes fathers. Mothers and children are often considered particularly vulnerable populations with special health needs and their health being a matter of high public priority. Therefore, such services are sometimes separately organized and funded from other health services. One example is the Maternal and Child Health Program operated by the federal government under the authority of Title V of the Social Security Act.

maternal death Any death resulting from complications of pregnancy or childbirth. *See maternal mortality.*

maternal mortality In epidemiology and public health, this is the death of mothers caused by complications of pregnancy, childbirth, and puerperium (the period of 42 days following the termination of a pregnancy). Common causes include uterine hemorrhage, toxemia, complications of pregnancy, or underlying medical conditions such as infections or diabetes.

maternal mortality rate In epidemiology and public health, this is the number of deaths of mothers caused by complications of pregnancy, childbirth, and puerperium (the period of 42 days following the termination of a pregnancy) attributed to pregnancy and the birth process compared to the number of live births per 1000,

10,000, or 100,000 live births within a specific time period, usually 1 year. The maternal mortality rate formula follows:

$$\frac{\text{Number of deaths from puerperal causes in a given geographical area during a given time period}}{\text{Number of live births that occurred among the population of the same geographic area and during the same time period}} \times 1000$$

maternity Related to all aspects of being, or the process of becoming, a mother.

maternity benefits Medical insurance coverage for the costs of pregnancy, labor, delivery, and in some cases family planning, postpartum care, and complications of pregnancy. Various medical insurance policies or plans take different approaches and apply different conditions to maternity benefits. *See also exclusions; flat maternity; swap maternity; switch maternity.*

maternity patient Females to which health and medical care that is related to the process of becoming a mother is provided; a pregnant female under the care of a licensed health-care provider.

maternity ward The medical and nursing unit in a health-care facility staffed and equipped to assist pregnant women in the labor, delivery, and birth process and to provide medical care for any complications of birth. Also called a "maternity center." *See also birthing room.*

matriarchal order The culturally accepted family structure when the mother is head of the house or family.

matrilineal Descending through the female side of the family.

matrix organization In health administration and organizational structuring, this is a vertically coordinated hierarchical structure approach using the traditional chain of command and departmentalization while implementing a horizontally coordinated, or lateral, structure across departments using patient care teams. A grid approach to work scheduling is used for these teams to work in the most needed areas. A project manager temporarily borrows personnel with certain skills, training, licenses, or talent that he or she needs on a project or service from a functional department. The project manager, not the functional department head, supervises the people borrowed during the loan period. This approach has been used in some public health departments to ensure the ability to conduct clinics in various locations on a rotating basis with a full staffing pattern of health-care providers, nurses, and allied health support personnel.

matrix scheduling In health administration, this is a grid approach used in scheduling work to set work for patient care teams to have them work in the most needed areas or locations. This approach has been used in some public health departments to ensure the ability to conduct clinics in various locations on a rotating basis and have a complete patient care team available. Matrix scheduling is a very efficient use of health-care manpower, but high levels of stress and burnout, as well as low morale and loss of job satisfaction, have been observed in some patient care teams.

matter 1. A subject or issue worthy of dispute or discussion; an important fact. 2. An event, deal, or transaction. 3. An issue of a lawsuit.

matter in pais Facts that are not a matter of record.

matter of fact An issue or concern solved by obvious facts and evidence or the testimony of the witnesses.

matter of law Any question solved through the process of testing the issues through applying the law to the matters and facts of the case.

matter of record 1. In law, this is the official recording of an issue or statement of the court as it is stated. 2. Any matter or issue that is recorded and can be proven by the record of the court; an issue that can be proven by checking official records of the court.

maturation 1. The process of growth in all areas of life (including physical, emotional, and social dimensions) to full development in each and all aspects. 2. When a life insurance policy has reached the maximum amount. 3. In health-care financial management, this is when the principal will be repaid to a bondholder.

maturity 1. When a debt, an obligation, or insurance becomes due. 2. The date or time when a document is in full force or fully developed.

maturity date 1. In health-care financial management, this is the date on which the principal will be repaid to a bondholder. 2. When a life insurance policy has reached the maximum amount.

maxim 1. Specific and concise statement about

the law. 2. A principle or rule of conduct that works when applied to most cases. 3. A general statement of truth; a law or rule.

maximization The manipulation of census data and information to optimize hospital reimbursement.

maximum allowable actual charge (MAAC) In health-care financial management, this is the highest amount or limit a physician may charge a Medicare beneficiary for any treatment, therapy, or service. The MAAC applies only to those nonparticipating physicians who do not take Medicare patients, whereas under an assigned care agreement the physician must accept the Medicare-approved charge for the visit as set forth by the Medicare Public Law passed in 1986.

maximum allowable charge (MAC) In health-care financial management, this is the greatest amount. Often this is a list of generic prescription medications that a health plan will cover or a list of items and the cost that a vendor may charge for something but not necessarily the minimum charge; often used in pharmacy contracting. Also referred to as "maximum allowable charge list" or "fee maximum," which is often used in conjunction with "professional fees." *See maximum allowable cost program.*

Maximum Allowable Cost Program (MACP) A federal program that limits reimbursement for prescription drugs under the Medicare and Medicaid programs and public health service projects to the lowest cost at which the drug is generally available. Specifically, the program limits reimbursement for drugs under programs administered by the Department of Health and Human Services to the lowest of the maximum allowable cost (MAC) of the drug, if any, plus a reasonable dispensing fee, the acquisition cost of the drug plus a dispensing fee, or the providers' usual and customary charge to the general public for the drug. The MAC is the lowest unit price at which a drug available from several sources or manufacturers can be purchased on a national basis. Also referred to as "maximum allowable charge."

maximum contaminant level 1. In environmental health, this is the greatest level of a contaminant in drinking water at which no known or anticipated adverse effect on the health of persons could occur and that allows an adequate margin of safety. These are nonenforceable health goals. 2. In environmental health, this is the greatest permissible level of a contaminant in water that is delivered to the free-flowing outlet of the ultimate user of a public water system, except in the case of turbidity, where the maximum permissible level is measured at the point of entry to the distribution system. Excluded are contaminants added to water under circumstances controlled by use, except those from corrosion of piping and plumbing caused by water quality.

maximum foreseeable loss In health-care financial management, this is the largest loss that could possibly happen under the worst circumstances.

maximum out-of-pocket costs In managed care, this is the limit placed on the total co-payments, deductibles, and co-insurance under a benefit contract that a health plan member must pay.

maximum permissible dose In environmental health, this is the greatest amount of radiation that will produce no detectable damage over the normal life span when received by persons working with ionizing radiation.

maximum permissible exposure (MPE) In laser technology, this is the level of radiation levels to which a person may be exposed without hazardous effects or adverse biological changes in the skin or eyes.

maximum possible loss In health-care financial management, this is the largest loss that could possibly happen under the worst circumstances.

maximum security unit In mental health services, this is the part of a mental institution used for persons who have committed crimes or who are considered dangerous to others or themselves.

may As used in JCAHO accreditation, a qualifying verb that reflects an acceptable and recognized method but one that is not necessarily preferred. *See also shall; should.*

mayhem 1. To maim another person. 2. To intentionally maim, mutilate, or injure a person's body. 3. Violently causing a serious wound. 4. To limit or deprive a person's bodily function that he or she would need for self-defense.

MBO *See management by objectives.*

MCAT *See Medical College Admission Test.*

McCarran-Ferguson Act A federal law passed on March 9, 1945 (15 U.S.C. 101, 115), that declares a general policy that federal laws that regulate or affect business and commerce are not to be interpreted as affecting the insurance business unless specifically provided for. Prior to a Supreme Court decision in 1944, insurance was not considered a matter of commerce and thus was not subject to federal law. When the Supreme Court found insurance to be a matter of commerce, it became necessary to clarify the effect of existing federal law on it. The act has the effect of leaving regulation of insurance to the states unless specifically undertaken in federal law.

MCE Medical care evaluation. One aspect of a quality assurance program in hospitals and other medical care settings that assesses and reviews the process and delivery of medical care treatment and services. *See medical care evaluation.*

MCES Medical Care Evaluation Study. *See patient care audit.*

MCEPEN Midwest Continuing Education Professional Education Nurses.

MCH *See maternal and child health.*

MCHR Medical Committee for Human Rights.

MCPI *See Medical Consumer Price Index.*

MD Doctor of medicine; doctorate of medicine; medical doctorate degree; medical doctor. Anyone possessing a medical degree from a recognized and accredited school of medicine. Having a medical doctorate degree is contingent on graduating from an accredited medical school with a medical degree, not on licensure as a physician.

MDC *See major diagnostic category.*

MDS *See minimum data set.*

meals on wheels One of several long-term-care support services provided to the elderly or handicapped who are unable to cook for themselves. Inexpensive, nutritious meals are delivered to individuals in their homes. The meals are priced on the recipient's ability to pay and serve additional functions such as allowing for some socialization and enabling the delivery person to look in on isolated persons should they fall or become ill.

mean Average, a statistical measurement; the adding of a set of scores and then dividing by the total number of scores; the arithmetic average; used as a measure of central tendency with median and mode for a more complete picture of the data.

mean annual loss The average loss per year over a period of years; sum of losses during a period divided by years in the period.

mean deviation Average variation, a statistical measure of variation, derived by dividing the sum of deviations in a set of variables by the number of cases involved. *See also average deviation; standard deviation.*

means testing In the assessment of eligibility for health or social services programs, income and assets are examined to determine if the required low income and limited assets are within the guidelines and the law. The amount of income and assets are tested to ensure eligibility for those on poverty-level incomes. *See eligibility; poverty; acute poverty; chronic poverty; medically indigent.*

measure The assignment of numbers to objects or variables under observation; to evaluate, assess, or compare.

measurement 1. In epidemiology and biomedical research, these are the methods and procedures used for systematic observation, evaluation, and assessment; the assignment of numbers to variables or research data. 2. Psychological testing.

measures of a health-care system *See measures of health services.*

measures of central tendency In epidemiology and health services research, this is the mean, median, and mode of a set of data. This also describes how data are distributed in a normal distribution curve.

measures of health services In health-care delivery, the commonly used indicators or characteristics of a health-care service or system are accessibility, acceptability, satisfaction, availability, capacity, cost, quality, and continuity of care. Also referred to as "characteristics of a health-care system."

measures of management In health administration, the commonly used indicators or characteristics of management activities are quality, quantity, efficiency, effectiveness, costs, use of resources, and survivability.

measures of severity in diagnosis-related groups *See complicating and comorbid.*

mechanical aeration In environmental health, this is the use of mechanical means and energy to inject air into water to cause a waste stream of water to absorb oxygen.

mechanically altered diet A special diet altered in texture for patients with certain medical conditions, physical limitations, or mastication problems. Also called a "soft diet."

mechanical transmission In public health and epidemiology, this describes how communicable diseases are transmitted from one person to another, usually by fomites or vectors. *See fomite; vector.*

med. Short for "medication."

medex Physician assistant (PA) programs developed specifically for former military medical corpsmen with medical duty experience. Most medex practitioners have been trained to work as primary care generalist physician assistants, with some specifically trained to work with specialist physicians. The first such program was begun in 1969 by Richard A. Smith at the University of Washington in cooperation with the Washington State Medical Association. The first programs generally consisted of 3 months of university training and 12 months of preceptorship. Most medex programs converted into regular PA programs, which now consist of 2 years of intense training, resulting in a general medical care practitioner who is as well trained (if not better) than most of the former GPs (general practitioners) who had medical degrees.

media nox (Lat.) Midnight.

median The midpoint in a set of numbers as used in a measure of central tendency. *See mean and mode.*

median lethal concentration In biomedical research and environmental health research, this is the concentration level at which 50% of test animals die when exposed by inhalation for a specified time.

median lethal dose In biomedical research and environmental health research, this is the dose at which 50% of test animals die following exposure. A dose is usually given in milligrams per kilogram of body weight of the test animal.

mediate data Information and statistics from which facts can, with a reasonable amount of certainty, be inferred.

mediate testimony Secondary evidence.

mediating variable In epidemiology, this is any factor responsible for enabling or altering the relationship between a cause and an effect. For example, women who nurse a child in their late teens or early twenties have a reduced incidence of breast cancer in the ages before menopause. Nursing and age are mediating variables.

mediation 1. Friendly intercession. 2. An invited intervention in a dispute. 3. Calling in an intermediary. 4. A third party who is used to decide issues and provide solutions to disputes. The decision has no legal backing and differs from arbitration, which can have the backing of a court.

medic 1. A physician, doctor, or surgeon. 2. A medical student, intern, or resident. 3. A military medical corpsman who gives first aid and medical care in the field or in combat.

medicable That which can be cured, healed, or medically treated.

Medicaid The federally aided, state-operated, and state-administered program that provides medical benefits for certain low-income persons. The program, authorized by Title XIX of the Social Security Act, is basically for the poor. It does not cover all the poor, however, but only persons who are members of one of the categories of people who can be covered under the welfare cash payment programs: the aged, the blind, the disabled, and members of families with dependent children where one parent is absent, incapacitated, or unemployed. Under certain circumstances, states may provide Medicaid coverage for children under age 21 who are not categorically related. Subject to broad federal guidelines, states determine the benefits covered, program eligibility, rates of payment for providers, and methods of administering the program. Arizona was the only state not to adopt a standard Medicaid program and did not have one for years, but in 1983 it implemented a different version, referred to as AHCCCS. *See eligibility, Medicaid; medically indigent; AHCCCS.*

Medicaid agency The state-level administrative department that administers the medical care insurance program for the poor and that also processes the claims and makes payment for Medicaid to local health facilities and services.

Medicaid gap Persons with monthly income above or below certain amounts so that they are not eligible for Medicaid.

Medicaid mill A health program that solely or primarily serves Medicaid beneficiaries, typically on an ambulatory basis. The mills originated in the ghettos of New York City and are still found primarily in urban slums with few other medical services. They are usually organized on a for-profit basis, are characterized by their great productivity, and are frequently accused of a variety of abuses. *See also family ganging, ping-ponging.*

Medicaid Retrospective Reimbursement System The state-administered reimbursement structure for health care for the poor in which a facility's costs are reimbursed after expenditure. Each state has different allowable costs and limits and may vary costs by such factors as size of facility, local, or region.

MediCal California's version of Medicaid. *See Medicaid.*

medical 1. Pertaining to the science, study, or practice of medicine; the art of healing diseases or providing treatment and cures for illness and disease. 2. In JCAHO accreditation, this pertains to or deals with the healing arts and the science of medicine. 3. Nonsurgical treatment. 4. Medical treatment (adjective).

medical application In some types of insurance, this is when an applicant for insurance is required to undergo some form of medical exam.

Medical Alert Foundation International A worldwide association that assists individuals with medical conditions by providing bracelets and tags stamped with the medical alert symbol to attract the attention of health-care providers and emergency medical personnel. It also serves as a clearinghouse for foundation members. The foundation serves as a backup system of information on the medical conditions of its members by having a toll-free number stamped on the back of the medical alert tag that can be called in an emergency.

medical alert tags Metal bracelets, dog tags, necklaces, or other items with the words "Medical Alert" printed in red on one side. In case of an emergency, the tag provides first aid personnel or health-care providers with critical information about a victim's medical condition. If no information is printed on the tag, a collect phone number usually is. Wallet cards are also carried with medical and personal information on them. The medical alert symbol is recognized throughout the world as a warning that the one who wears it has a medical condition or may be wearing a medical device.

medical assistance 1. Medical care and treatment provided by a health-care provider. 2. Assistance to help pay for the cost of medical care. *See Medicaid.*

medical assistance facilities In health-care delivery, especially in rural areas, this is a health-care facility that is an alternative to the traditional rural hospital. Some rural hospitals in selected states (e.g., Montana) have been granted a waiver from Medicare to provide care under this new delivery system approach. The hospitals have no bed limit, but the length of stay is limited to 96 hours. The rural short-stay facilities are encouraged (but not required) to transfer the more seriously ill or injured patients to larger medical centers within the 96-hour time period or after stabilization of the patient. Some rural hospitals are attached to nursing homes that are not considered part of the acute-care medical assistance facility because they provide long-term care. *See caches/peaches; alternative rural hospitals project; combined facility; limited-service rural hospitals; rural primary care hospitals.*

Medical Assistance Program The health-care program for the poor authorized by Title XIX of the Social Security Act (Medicaid).

medical assistant An individual who works in a doctor's office or under the direction of a physician to perform functions related to office administration and minor clinical activities. Office duties include insurance billing, accounting, report keeping, medical records, medical transcription, ICD-9-CM coding, and public relations. Clinical duties include minor aspects of patient examination, assessing vital signs, assisting with physical exams and treatment, routine laboratory procedures, and use of biomedical electronic office and evaluation equipment.

medical associations 1. Legal, formal associations such as cooperatives, corporations, and chartered institutions; some partnerships of three or more practitioners that fit the broader definition of a legal association. The grouping of many single practitioners under one legal organizational structure can also be referred to as a "medical association." 2. Professional national organizations that have some aspect of health care or medical treatment as the premise or focus of the organization (e.g., the American Medical Association, the American College of Surgeons, or the American Academy of Pediatrics). 3. Local medical societies.

medical audit A detailed retrospective review and evaluation of selected medical records by qualified professional staff. Medical audits are used in some hospitals, group practices, and occasionally in private, independent practices for evaluating professional performance by comparing that performance with accepted criteria, standards, and current professional judgment. A medical audit is usually concerned with the care of a given illness and is undertaken to identify deficiencies in that care in anticipation of educational programs to improve it. *See also concurrent review; medical care evaluation.*

medical audit committee In a hospital or clinical setting, this is a group of health-care personnel responsible for the evaluation of patient care and treatment given to patients by the medical profession and other health-care providers who provide direct patient care.

medical audit follow-up In a hospital or clinical setting, these are recommendations of the medical audit committee and the steps taken or action initiated. Follow-up must be immediate if the problems are life or health threatening. Appropriate documentation must be completed to show the status and improvement a patient has made toward recovery and discharge.

medical audit program (MAP) An extension of the Professional Activity Study (PAS) in which data are displayed in comprehensive quarterly reports by hospital departments. In the evaluation of clinical patient care, this is the process of collecting and analyzing the data and information on patient status, patient care activities, diagnostic procedures, diagnosis, treatments, and therapy. The reports are used by hospital clinical departments in conducting a comprehensive medical audit and in retrospective utilization review. *See also commission on professional and hospital activities.*

medical audit study (MAS) In a hospital or clinical setting and in a medical audit, this is the application and practical aspects of the audit.

medical care 1. The process of providing patient education, prevention, protection, safety, maintenance, diagnosis, evaluation, assessment, therapy, surgery, medications, and treatment primarily tied to injury, illness, disability, and disorders experienced by humans. 2. Treatment and therapy of individuals under the supervision and control of physicians. 3. All personal health-care and institutional care activities, including nonphysician care (e.g., home health care), dental care, nursing homes, eye care, physical therapy, and nursing care. The term "health care" has been used widely to mean "medical care." The term "medical care" is more correct because "health care" reflects an individual's effort to enhance health status, health behaviors, lifestyle, habits, preventive care, health promotion, and overall well-being and to avoid the use of medical care providers, services, and facilities. 4. Care and treatment provided under the direction of a physician. 5. Care and treatment provided directly by a physician.

medical care appraisal programs Subunits of a broader program that include the review of admitting diagnoses, utilization review of health-care services, assessment of therapy and treatment, and review of the results of treatment and discharge.

medical care distribution *See geographic maldistribution.*

medical care evaluation (MCE) 1. In medical care and clinical settings, these are studies that review the quality of health care and treatment rendered; a retrospective medical care review in which an in-depth assessment of the quality and/or nature of the use of selected health services or programs is made. Restudy of an MCE assesses the effectiveness of corrective actions taken to correct deficiencies identified in the original study but does not necessarily repeat or replicate the original study. Utilization review requirements under Medicare and Medicaid require utilization review committees in hospitals and skilled nursing facilities to have at least one such study in progress at all times. Such studies are also required by the PRO program. 2. In-depth assessment of the delivery and organization of health-care services designed to ensure that said services are appropriate, of optimum quality, and provided in a timely way. *See also medical audit.*

medical care outcome In medical care, this comprises the final results of treatment and therapy and the effect of the treatment on the patient's illness, disability, disorder, or condition, whether acute or chronic.

medical care unit A unit in a health-care facility staffed and equipped to provide general therapy and treatment by medical personnel to persons who are admitted to the unit. *See also inpatient care unit.*

medical center 1. Any health-care facility offering a range of medical care services on inpatient and outpatient bases. Sometimes used interchangeably with "hospital." 2. A health sciences center serving a regional area and affiliated with a university; a teaching hospital that offers a range of health-care services and treatments, some of which are highly specialized because the facility is attached to or affiliated with a medical school, school of nursing, and possibly other teaching programs such as pharmacy, medical radiography, or physical therapy.

medical center, academic A medical school and its affiliated teaching hospital, research facilities, support units, laboratories, library, outpatient care facilities, and allied health professions training programs.

Medical College Admission Test (MCAT) A nationally standardized test generally required or strongly recommended by nearly all medical schools in the United States as part of the admissions process. The results of the test are evaluated by admissions committees along with other information about the student's education, background, and evidence of the student's ability to handle medical school coursework. The test is designed to provide objective measures of academic ability and achievement through tests of verbal ability, quantitative ability, scientific knowledge, and general information. It cannot and does not claim to measure motivation, the nature or sincerity of interest in the study of medicine, or the personal characteristics that are of basic importance to the practitioner or teacher of medicine.

medical communications specialist An individual who knows the properties and capabilities of communications media and applies this knowledge to the design and improvement of communication processes in the health field.

medical computer language See MUMPS; CAPER.

medical computer specialist An individual who combines a knowledge of computer science and health science to provide systems and programming support in the medical field.

medical consultation The request by the attending physician for another physician or a member of the medical staff to review the patient's medical history, examine the patient, administer additional tests, and then present the attending physician with findings, opinions, and recommendations about the patient's case and possible treatment and therapy.

Medical Consumer Price Index (MCPI) The medical component of the Consumer Price Index. It gives the trends in medical care charges on the basis of specific indicators of hospital, dental, medical, and drug prices.

medical deduction The federal income tax deduction for expenditures on health insurance and other medical expenses in excess of 5% of income.

medical/dental secretary An individual with clerical/secretarial skills who knows medical terminology and some medical insurance billing and office practice procedures to assist physicians or dentists in their medical practices using medical shorthand, typing, computers, filing, accounting, and appointment scheduling and performing receptionist and general office management duties.

medical device See device; Kefauver-Harris Amendment.

medical director 1. A physician who is in charge of medical matters in a health facility or organization and who is usually appointed by the governing body to function in a leadership capacity, which is the chief of staff in a hospital or vice president for medical affairs. The scope of responsibilities varies with each position, facility, or organization but generally includes patient/doctor relations and doctor/doctor or doctor/administration relations. It may or may not include business or nonmedical administrative duties. 2. In a long-term-care facility, this is the physician responsible for the health status of all patients, coordination of medical care by other physicians, and adequacy and appropriateness of patient care and medical services; the physician on staff who is responsible for resident care policies, the development of relations with other physicians, and the coordination of medical care for all residents. 3. A physician in a hospital, medical group, nursing home, or other clinical setting who is responsible for the implementation of patient care policies and who works with administration and other physicians to ensure quality patient care.

medical education 1. The training given medical students in an accredited medical school. 2. Continuing medical education is provided to practicing physicians to keep them up to date on new developments in their fields and to keep their certifications and licenses current. 3. Graduate medical education is provided to practicing physicians to keep them current on new developments in their fields and to keep their certifications and licenses current.

medical education director The physician on the medical staff of a hospital who coordinates continuing medical education activities for the medical staff of the hospital. Many hospitals rotate this responsibility among the medical staff.

medical eligibility Those eligible for Medicare, Part A, hospital insurance benefits. Eligibility applies to individuals age 65 or over who are entitled to monthly Social Security benefits, qualified railroad retirement beneficiaries age 65 or over, and uninsured persons age 65 or over who meet the requirements of a special transitional provision. Permanently disabled persons were given eligibility in 1972 by Public Law 92603 (H.R. 1). Supplementary medical insurance, Part B, is also available effective July 1973. A person eligible for hospital insurance is enrolled automatically.

medical emergency The sudden, unexpected onset of an illness or condition, manifesting symptoms such as severe chest pains, convulsive seizure, hemorrhage, or unconsciousness; not to be confused with accidental injury. *See accident; first aid.*

medical ethics A set of guidelines and principles established to direct and govern physicians and the medical community in the practice of medicine and any related activities. The guiding principles address issues such as doctor-patient relationships, dealing with the patient's family, interaction with the community, fellow physicians, and expected professional conduct.

medical evaluation study (MCES) *See patient care audit; medical care evaluation.*

medical examination A physical and medical assessment and evaluation conducted by a physician or physician extender. A medical history is taken, physical and clinical information from various tests is gathered, laboratory assessments of bodily fluids are made, and a physical assessment, including such information as weight, height, blood pressure, pulse, and heart and lung sounds, is made.

medical examiner 1. A coroner or related public health officer. 2. A physician who examines applicants for insurance purposes.

medical expense insurance In health insurance, this provides benefits and pays the cost for medical care on an inpatient or outpatient basis. *See medical insurance.*

Medical Explorer Post A program of the Boy Scouts of America set up for males and females between the ages of 15 and 17 years that allows participation in, and presents programs to familiarize its members with, career opportunities in the health-care field.

medical exposure In medical care, this is the exposure of an individual to radiation resulting from the medical examination or treatment involving radiation-producing substances or X rays.

medical foundation An organization of physicians, generally sponsored by a state or local medical association. It is a separate, autonomous corporation with its own board of directors. Every physician member of the medical society may apply for membership in the foundation and, on acceptance, participate in all its activities. A foundation is concerned with the delivery of medical services at a reasonable cost. The foundation believes in the free choice of a physician and hospital by the patient, fee-for-service reimbursement, and local peer review. Many foundations operate as prepaid group practices or as individual practice associations for an HMO. Although these are prepaid on a capitation basis for services to some or all their patients, they still pay their individual members on a fee-for-service basis for the services they give. Some foundations are organized only for peer review purposes or other specific functions. Sometime referred to as a "foundation for medical care."

medical graduate, foreign (FMG) *See foreign medical graduate.*

medical graduate, United States (USMG) Any graduate of a U.S., Puerto Rican, or Canadian medical school.

medical graduate, United States foreign (USFMG) A graduate of a medical school outside the United States, Puerto Rico, or Canada who was a U.S. citizen at the time of graduation.

medical group A partnership, association, or group of physicians, dentists, psychologists, podiatrists, or other licensed health-care providers collaborating in the practice of their specialty. Usually, the majority of the members are licensed professionals who engage in coordinating the practice of their professions and the delivery of health care. Some group practices pool their income and use a portion of it to employ an administrator and staff and then distribute the remainder among themselves according to prearranged agreements. The pooling of income and administrative activities allows for acquiring and sharing support services and equipment (lab services, X-ray facilities, pharmacy, medical records department, and appropriate personnel) and locating them conveniently in-house. Some IPAs and HMOs are arranged in a modified group practice configuration. *See medical group management; group practice; individual practice association; health maintenance organization; prepaid group practice; multispecialty group.*

medical group management 1. In health administration, these are the planning, organizing, directing, coordinating, and controlling activities needed to administer a group of physicians who have joined together to form a physician group operation to benefit from shared overhead and expenses; to centralize administration, financial management, and medical records administration; and to have in-house lab and X-ray services, reduced costs of operation, and the ability to contract with managed-care programs and treat patients in a centralized clinic. 2. One of several career paths that a health-care administrator can take, as compared to hospital or long-term-care administration.

Medical Group Management Association (MGMA) The official national professional organization for administrators and managers of medical groups, clinics, group practices, and related physician group practice organizations. *See also Medical Group Management Information Service.*

Medical Group Management Information Service (MGMIS) Activity of the Medical Group Management Association located in Denver, Colorado, formerly known as the Library Reference Service. The purpose of the MGMIS is to assist persons involved in or desiring to learn more about the management of medical group practices, health maintenance organizations, and evolving forms of medical care in which group practice is an essential organizational component. The service provides opportunities for continuing education for MGMA members and others in medical group business management by collecting, classifying, storing, and disseminating information on medical group business management and by stimulating the creation of new information. The service was the first to cover medical group practice management on a national scale.

medical group practice *See medical group; medical group management; group practice.*

medical habilitation and rehabilitation services The medical evaluation of the needs of the ill or disabled individual and the design, management, and evaluation of a habilitation or rehabilitation program to meet those needs.

medical history A component of the medical record consisting of an account of a patient's history. It is obtained whenever possible from the patient and includes at least the following information: chief complaint, details of the present illness, relevant past personal and family disease and medical history, and a relevant inventory of body systems (JCAHO for acute-care facilities).

medical hotel Also referred to as a "hospital/hotel," this is a facility used to fill the gap in service between an inpatient hospital admission and home. Patients are released from the hospital but stay in a hospital-owned hotel, which is very near the hospital so that the patient can access treatment in the hospital. The patient may come to the hospital as an outpatient for specialized treatment such as cancer therapy. Most are equipped with 24-hour call buttons for emergencies, and some use home care visits if the patient is bedfast. All amenities of a hotel are found in the rooms. In some facilities, food services are provided from a restaurant-type menu through the hospital's food service. Family members or guests of the patient are allowed to stay in the hospital/hotel while a family member is in the hospital. Also called a "hotel/hospital."

medical illness severity grouping system (Medisgroups) A classification system that rates patients by severity of illness using clinical information and objective data abstracted from the medical record of the patient for analysis and severity determination. *See severity of illness.*

medical illustrator An artist who demonstrates medical facts by the creation of illustrations, models, or teaching films; serves as a consultant, advisor, and administrator in the field of medical illustration.

Medical Impairment Bureau (MIB) A clearinghouse of information on people who have applied for life insurance in the past. Any adverse medical findings on previous medical examinations are recorded in code and sent to companies subscribing to the service. This service raises interesting legal and confidentiality questions, especially with respect to information produced by medical examinations.

Medical Indemnity of America, Inc. (MIA) A stock insurance company organized in Ohio in 1950 by the Blue Shield plans to serve as a national enrollment agency, to assist individual plans in negotiating contracts, and to serve large national accounts in which two or more plans are involved.

medical indigency Not having sufficient income to pay for adequate medical care without depriving oneself or one's family or dependents of food, clothing, shelter, and other essentials of living. Medical indigency may occur when a self-supporting individual under ordinary conditions is able to provide basic maintenance for himself and his family and, in the case of catastrophic illness, is unable to finance the total cost of medical care. *See also medically indigent; spend-down; medically needy; working poor.*

medical indigent *See medical indigency; near poor; medically indigent; working poor.*

Medical Information Bureau (MIB) A national organization that serves as a clearinghouse for medical information for the life insurance industry. Insurance companies must join and become members to access MIB-coded information, which is limited to authorized medical, underwriting, and claim personnel in the member companies. Health status indicators, as well as health impairments and test findings of potential policyholders, are forwarded to MIB from member companies with which the consumers have applied for life insurance policies.

medical insurance Also more commonly and incorrectly referred to as "health insurance," this type of insurance coverage provides benefits for medical care on an inpatient or outpatient basis; a financing mechanism that takes the risk of paying for the extensive cost and high charges incurred in medical care away from the average person and places it on the insurance company even though the insured person and his or her employer pay the monthly premiums. The health plan or insurance company may limit the amount it will pay per visit or may pay the total amount for all visits, hospital room and board, surgery, surgeon's fees, drugs, treatments, therapies, nursing care, and all other related costs. It may also exclude the first few visits to the physician at the beginning of an illness and have a deductible or co-payment.

medicalization To make a medical condition or medical issue out of something that previously was not considered medical; to redefine certain disorders or conditions previously considered legal, moral, or social problems into medical problems in their origin and therefore medically treatable.

medical jurisprudence Philosophical aspects of law that deal with medical care and health-care delivery. *See forensic medicine; malpractice; jurisprudence.*

medical laboratory An educational program that trains individuals in the basic principles and practices of clinical laboratory procedures utilized by lab assistants. *See laboratory; medical technologist; medical laboratory technician.*

medical laboratory assistant *See medical laboratory; medical laboratory technician.*

medical laboratory scientist Performs clinical analysis procedures and research in medical/clinical laboratories utilizing disciplines such as chemistry, biochemistry, bacteriology, and microbiology. Training at the graduate level is required. *See also laboratory; laboratory technician; medical technologist.*

medical laboratory technician Individuals who perform routine clinical laboratory tests that require minimal exercise of independent judgment. Under the supervision of a medical technologist or pathologist, they perform laboratory tests in chemistry (qualitative and quantitative analyses of body constituents), hematology (blood counts and blood cell identification), urinalysis, blood banking (routine typing and cross-matching and immunological tests for the detection of antibodies), microbiology (antibiotic susceptibility testing), and parasitology (organism identification). Certification is awarded by the Board of Registry following successful completion of an examination. The requirements for taking the certifying examination include a high school diploma or equivalent, either graduation from an AMA-approved school or completion of a basic military laboratory course, and 1 year of experience.

medical laboratory technology An educational program that prepares individuals to perform bacteriological, biological, microbiological, and chemical tests to provide data to physicians for the diagnosis and treatment of disease. All activities are done under the supervision of a microbiologist or pathologist.

medical librarian An individual with a degree in library science who has specialized knowledge of medical librarianship and bibliography and uses that background to acquire, organize, catalog, retrieve, and disseminate medical information. *See librarian, health science or medical.*

Medical Literature Analysis and Retrieval System (MEDLARS) A computer-based information database access system of the U.S. National Library of Medicine.

medical loss ratio In managed care, this is the ratio between the cost of delivering medical care and the expense experienced by the health plan. Insurance companies often have a loss ratio of 96% or more. Well-managed health plans may have a medical loss ratio of 75% to 85% even though cost, expense, and overhead are higher. Medical loss ratios are dependent on the amount of revenue brought in as well as the cost of delivering health care. If the member rates are too low, the ratio may be high even though the actual cost of delivering care is within reason.

medically A medical concern; according to the rules of medicine; for the purpose of curing and healing.

medically indigent A person who is capable of sustaining him- or herself financially and is able to pay for the basics in life but is too poor to meet medical expenses or buy health insurance. Refers either to persons whose income is low enough so that they can pay for their basic living costs but not their routine medical care or to persons with generally adequate income who suddenly face catastrophically large medical bills. *See also medical indigency; medically needy; acute poverty; working poor; spend-down.*

medically necessary In health-care delivery, this is any care, treatment, therapy, or service provided by a health-care provider that is usual, appropriate, and consistent with standard treatments or procedures and that fits the diagnosis. The services and care that fall within the standard of practice of the health professionals in the community that, if not provided, would adversely affect the health status and condition of the patient and fall below the quality of care expected. *See medical necessity; medical necessity determination.*

medically needy In the Medicaid program, persons who have enough income and resources to pay for their basic living expenses (and so do not need welfare) but not enough to pay for their medical care. Medicaid law requires that the standard for income used by a state to determine if someone is medically needy cannot exceed 133% of the maximum amount paid to a family of similar size under the welfare program for families with dependent children (AFDC). To be eligible as medically needy, people must fall into one of the categories of people who are covered under the welfare cash assistance programs: aged, blind, disabled, or members of families with dependent children where one parent is absent, incapacitated, or unemployed. They receive benefits if their income, after deducting medical expenses, is low enough to meet the eligibility standard. *See also spend-down.*

medically underserved area (MUA) 1. A geographic location that has insufficient health resources in manpower or facilities to meet the medical needs of the resident population or to have inadequate access to health care as determined by an agency of the federal government. Such areas are also sometimes defined by measuring the health status of the resident population rather than the supply of resources; an area with an unhealthy population is considered underserved. 2. A comprehensive federal designation of a geographic area that is designed to measure the extent of personal health-care services and needs in that area. It is based on a set of four weighted tables, each of which measures an important aspect of the health resources or needs of the area: 1) the percentage of the population below the poverty level, 2) the percentage of the population over 65 years of age, 3) the infant mortality rate, and 4) primary care physicians per 1000 population.

medically underserved population (MUP) The population of an urban or rural area with a shortage of personal health services or another population group having a shortage of such services. A medically underserved population may not reside in a particular medically underserved area or be defined by its place of residence. Thus migrants, Native Americans, or the inmates of a prison or mental hospital may constitute such a population. Under the Public Health Services Act, this designation allows such populations to have priority for federal assistance, especially in HMOs and the National Health Service Corporation. Populations not meeting the criteria of a medically underserved area may be designated as underserved on the basis of unusual local conditions that may affect the health-care delivery or access at the local area or in a certain population.

Medical mall Ambulatory health services, clinics

plus doctor offices, and medically related retail stores aligned with banks, credit unions, or other appropriate businesses, of which all located in the same retail building and grouped together for customer convenience. Health education centers, health stores, mammogram screening facilities, birthing centers, and diagnostic imaging and Alzheimer's diagnosis centers have been used in addition to traditional medical services.

medical malpractice In health law, this is a subprinciple of negligence and tort law. For the injured patient, recovery from the injury, harm, or damage comes through filing a lawsuit. The plaintiff must show 1) the existence of the patient-physician relationship and his or her duty to the patient; 2) a lack of adherence to the standard of care; 3) harm, damage, or injury that can be remedied by a court of law though recovery; and 4) a causal relationship between the harm, injury, or damage stated in the lawsuit and the failure of the physician to stay within the standard of care or to have misconduct. *See malpractice; recovery; standard of care; negligence; tort law; cause of action.*

Medical Management Analysis (MMA) This is a system for conducting screenings of disease occurrence to detect problem cases in which quality-of-care problems arise.

medical model One of the philosophical approaches used to explain how health-care professionals deal with illness. This approach evolved from the end of the 18th century, when diseases were determined to be separate entities. This model assumes that illness is involuntary and biologically and organically based and that when the state of illness falls below a level of acceptability to the individual or community, it must be cured by treating the symptoms and the supposed cause (i.e., disease). Through diagnosis, interpretation, and treatment of illness (tasks that are the sole responsibility of the physician), the person can be rid of the cause of disease and, if so, will overcome the illness and become healthy again. People are to be viewed as patients, and it is their role to unquestionably cooperate and obey the physician's orders. If a disease is identifiable, it is presupposed that the cause will be able to be found through biomedical research. With the acceptance of psychogenic and psychosomatic illnesses by many sectors of the medical and health-care community, this model, as a philosophical way of thinking, has been challenged and is being expanded to no longer discount the brain or the mind's ability to affect the health of the body.

medical necessity In determining eligibility for home health care under Medicare, necessity indicates that it is medically contraindicated for the patient to leave home. Patients requiring the aid of supportive devices are included (e.g., a wheelchair-confined patient who requires special transportation to obtain medical services such as a wheelchair van). What is thought to be medically needed often is determined by individual physicians and governmental guidelines on the basis of the prevailing medical consensus of the time or area. *See medically necessary; eligibility; home health care.*

medical necessity determination In managed care and medical insurance, this is a formal judgment about a treatment that attempts to determine whether it was important to the overall health status of the individual. It usually is done for the purpose of making payments or reimbursement to a health plan. Plastic surgery, nose repair, or other cosmetic surgery often is determined not to be medically necessary.

medical need *See medical necessity.*

medical neglect The lack of providing medical care when warranted; failing to give medical treatment to those in need, especially to children, which could be a form of negligence.

medical office assistant An employee who helps a physician examine and treat patients and performs the administrative tasks required to maintain an efficient medical practice. For example, he or she may prepare patients for examination or treatment, take patient temperatures, measure height and weight, sterilize instruments, and assist in certain examinations or treatments. This assistant may also act as secretary, receptionist, and bookkeeper for the physician. *See also medical assistant.*

medical oncology The physician board subspecialty under the internal medicine specialty that deals with tumors, cancer, and their treatment, especially with chemotherapy and radiation.

medical outcome studies An assessment of the final result of medical care experience of patients as investigated on a national basis using a comprehensive survey instrument that is self-administered, telephone administered, or used in a personal interview. Items assessed include physical functioning, role limitations from physical and mental problems, pain, social functioning, general mental health, vitality, and general health perception. The survey is developed and conducted by the International Resource Center for Health Care Assessment, Boston, Massachusetts.

medical personnel A broad term meaning any worker or professional involved directly in the treatment and care of patients in the provision of medical care (e.g., physicians, nurses, allied health professionals, biomedical engineers, and risk managers), excluding personnel who work in a health-care setting, but have no direct contact with the patient (e.g., administrators, physical plant workers, food service workers, and maintenance workers).

medical photographer An individual specially trained to utilize photography to capture medical phenomena on film for later use in teaching, research, writing and publication, or other educational uses in the medical and biological sciences.

medical practice act The statute passed by each state legislature legally setting forth the principles and regulations of the practice of medicine within each state.

medical practice plan As used in clinical training of physicians in medical schools, these are the policies and procedures under which faculty and medical students render patient care and health services in a medical education setting while delivering full quality care to the patients. Also called a "clinical practice plan" or "faculty practice plan."

medical radiation dosimetrist An individual involved in treatment planning and radiation dosage calculation, usually under a physician's or radiologist's supervision; calculates radiation dosage in the treatment of malignant disease and plans the direction of radiation to its target in the safest way. The minimum required education is a bachelors degree, but graduate training is preferable.

medical radiation physicist, qualified According to JCAHO for accreditation purposes, an individual who is certified by the American Board of Radiology in the appropriate disciplines of radiological physics, including diagnostic, therapeutic, and/or medical nuclear physics, or an individual who demonstrates equivalent competency in these disciplines. *See diagnostic radiology services.*

medical radiographer An X-ray technician or radiologic technologist; one who is trained in X-ray diagnostic radiology, therapeutic radiology, and/or nuclear medicine. *See also radiographer.*

medical radiography Term for "radiologic" or "X-ray technology."

medical record 1. The patient record, which contains sufficient information to clearly identify the patient, to justify his or her diagnosis and treatment, and to document the results accurately. The record 1) serves as the basis for planning and continuity of patient care; 2) provides a means of communication among physicians and any professional contributing to the patient's care; 3) furnishes documentary evidence of the patient's course of illness and treatment; 4) serves as a basis for review, study, and evaluation; 5) serves in protecting the legal interests of the patient, hospital, and responsible practitioner; and 6) provides data for use in research and education. Medical records are not usually readily available to the patient because they are difficult for the patient to read, and the contents are kept confidential. However, the patient does have the legal right to all information in the medical record and to a copy. Each healthcare provider in rendering care to a patient usually keeps an independent record of that care. 2. In JCAHO long-term-care facility accreditation, clinical documentation of an individual's health care, including but not limited to the medical, nursing, social, and rehabilitative care provided to a patient/resident. 3. The account of patient encounters, care, and treatment compiled by physicians and other health-care professionals, including a medical history; present illness; primary and secondary diagnoses; an abstract of the records; findings on examinations and from tests; details of treatment, procedures, and therapies; and notes on progress. The medical record is a legal record of care (JCAHO for acute-care facilities). *See also problem-oriented medical record.*

medical record abstract The essential material of a medical record that has been selected, separated, and summarized onto a form or into a predetermined format for the purpose of compiling data for quality care management, financial management, health-care delivery management, and research purposes, including epidemiological retrospective research.

medical record abstracter An individual trained in medical records administration who is responsible for lifting specific information from the medical record onto a form, into a predetermined format, or for computer entry.

medical record abstracting process The selection and separation of essential material of a medical record or other source document (JCAHO for acute-care facilities).

medical record coding process The process of substituting a symbol (such as a numerical code) for a medical term (such as a diagnosis or procedure) (JCAHO for acute-care facilities).

medical record committee A committee of hospital personnel who assist in upgrading medical records to make them more efficient to use. The handling and storage of medical records may also be a task for this committee.

medical record, complete A medical record is complete when its contents reflect the primary and secondary diagnoses and contain the results of diagnostic tests, therapy rendered, conditions, and all aspects of the in-hospital progress of the patient as well as notes on the condition of the patient at time of discharge. The contents also include any required clinical resume or final progress notes, which are assembled and authenticated, and all final diagnoses. Complications are recorded without the use of symbols or abbreviations (JCAHO for acute-care facilities).

medical record, computerized In health information management and patient record management, this is a computer-based medical record system that is instantaneously accessed and readily available to health-care providers for inputting treatment and its progress or for making available output of all medical care activities in the record. Some systems are networked with the financial office, inventory control, and other areas needing access to patient care data.

medical record designee In long-term care, this is an individual who has the responsibility for medical records administration and the maintenance of the medical records for residents in the facility, often under the supervision of a registered records administrator (RRA) or an accredited records technician (ART) consultant.

medical record entry Writing or placing information in the medical record. An individual who is involved with the care of the patient makes a note or record in the patient's medical record regarding treatment, occurrence, progress, or therapy, using standardized approaches and protocol, including the entering of time and date for each writing. Only those directly involved with patient care are allowed to write in the medical record.

medical record index A record storing system that quickly retrieves the medical record number and basic information of a previously admitted patient.

medical record legibility The degree to which handwritten entries in a medical record can be read or deciphered (JCAHO for acute-care facilities).

medical record librarian An antiquated term used to identify a registered records administrator or accredited records technician. *See registered records administrator; accredited records technician.*

medical record practitioner (MRP) For Medicare purposes, a person who 1) is eligible for certification as a registered records administrator (RRA) or an accredited records technician (ART) by the American Medical Record Association (AMRA) or 2) is a graduate of a school of medical record science that is accredited jointly by the Council on Medical Education of the American Medical Association and the AMRA. *See also medical records technician; registered records administrator; accredited records technician.*

medical record, problem-oriented *See problem-oriented medical record.*

medical record progress notes A component of the medical record consisting of pertinent chronological handwritten reports entered into the medical record by physicians and nurses or other appropriate health-care providers of the patient's course of treatment, therapy, surveillance, assessment, and progress (JCAHO for acute-care facilities).

medical records administrator (MRA) Referred to as a "registered records administrator" (RRA), this is an individual who plans, designs, and manages systems of patient administrative and clinical data and patient medical records in all types of health-care institutions. The minimum educational requirement for professional registration as a medical records administrator is a bachelors degree in medical records science or medical records administration in a program accredited by the American Medical Association in collaboration with the American Medical Record Association (AMRA). The AMRA maintains a list of persons who have successfully completed the national registration examination. Recent graduates must meet a continuing education requirement 5 years after initial registration. The administrator is the most highly trained of several types of medical records personnel, including the medical records technician. *See medical record administrator, qualified; registered records administrator; accredited records technicians.*

medical records administrator, qualified 1. According to JCAHO for accreditation, a registered records administrator who has successfully passed an appropriate examination conducted by the American Medical Record Association (AMRA) or who has the documented equivalent in education and training. 2. For JCAHO accreditation of long-term-care facilities, an individual who is eligible for certification as a registered records administrator (RRA) or an accredited records technician (ART) by the AMRA, who is a graduate of a school of medical record science accredited by the AMRA, or who has documented equivalent training and/or experience.

medical records analyst An individual who works in a medical records department and is assigned the duties of abstracting and compiling data from medical records on patients' inpatient stays. A person trained in medical records administration who is responsible for lifting specific data from the medical record to determine the importance of those data for hospital, health-care delivery, and financial management; also responsible for constructing computerized summaries in spreadsheets or databases for statistical assessment. Analysis includes interpretation and projects from the data that will aid in health administration activities.

medical record science An allied health profession that deals with making, compiling, understanding, controlling, administering, abstracting, analyzing, computerizing, storing, retrieving, and classifying data on patients and their medical care and with all the legal aspects of medical records.

medical records department An administrative unit in a health-care facility, under the direction of a registered records administrator (RRA) that manages, maintains, stores, and retrieves both old and new patient records and that codes diagnoses and procedures using the ICD-9-CM system. Additional activities include transcribing physicians' dictation; assisting in quality assurance; participating in utilization review processes; processing the legal and authorized release of medical records information; indexing health records; maintaining a tumor registry system; abstracting, retaining, and gathering data for research and quantitative analysis; and reporting and administering the medical record aspects of the PPS/DRG reimbursement system.

medical record services In health administration, these are the activities designed to ensure the accuracy, completeness, timeliness, and accessibility of the medical record to the health-care provider and the safe, secure, and confidential storage of patients' medical records. Standards are applied to evaluate a hospital's performance in providing medical record services (JCAHO for acute-care facilities).

medical records review function A responsibility of the medical staff carried out in cooperation with other relevant departments/services to monitor, evaluate, and improve the quality of medical record documentation (i.e., the degree to which medical record documentation is accurate and complete and is performed in a timely manner) (JCAHO for acute-care facilities).

medical records technician An allied health worker who provides records administration and maintenance assistance to medical records administrators by performing many essential technical activities in the medical records department of a health-care institution or agency. Duties are varied and depend on the size of the facility in which they work. In a small facility, they are likely to work independently with only occasional consultation with a medical records administrator. In some cases, they may be employed as directors of medical records departments. In general, medical records technicians compile and maintain medical records and review them for completeness and accuracy. They code symptoms, diseases, operations, procedures, and other therapies according to standard classification systems and post codes on medical records to facilitate information retrieval. Technicians maintain and use a variety of health record indexes and compile medical care and census data for public health and other statistical reports. They assist the medical staff by tabulating data from records for research purposes and for use in evaluating and planning health-care services programs. Other responsibilities include transcription, directing the day-to-day operations of a medical records department, and either filing or directing the filing by medical records clerks. Also referred to as an "accredited records technician." *See accredited records technician; medical records technician, qualified.*

medical records technician, qualified According to JCAHO for the accreditation of health-care facilities, this is an accredited records technician who has successfully passed the appropriate accreditation examination conducted by the American Medical Record Association or who has the documented equivalent in education and training.

medical records technology An educational program that prepares individuals in medical records administration to develop statistical reports, code diseases and medical procedures, maintain indexes according to accepted procedures, and deal with the legal aspects of medical records and other administrative tasks in managing a medical records department. Graduates are usually eligible for ART or RRA certification. *See registered records administrator; accredited records technician; medical records administrator.*

medical review An assessment of medical care required by Medicaid made by a team composed of physicians and other appropriate health and social service personnel of the continuing need for care of each inpatient in a long-term-care facility. By law, the team must review the care being provided, the adequacy of the services available, the necessity and desirability of the continued placement of such patients in the facility, and the feasibility of meeting patients' health-care needs through alternate institutional or noninstitutional services. Medical review differs from utilization review in that it requires evaluation of each individual patient and an analysis of the appropriateness of specific treatment in a given institution, whereas utilization review is often done on a sample basis with special attention to certain procedures, conditions, or lengths of stay. *See also continued stay review.*

medical review agency The professional review organization of Medicare's Prospective Payment System that was established to administer the review and surveillance of quality and utilization in hospitals and health-care provider practices, including fraud deterrence.

medical savings accounts (MSA) A proposed form of medical expenses payment that embraces the concept of universal coverage. The MSA is an attempt to put the control of medical care payments and cost savings into the consumer's hands by having all workers open a savings account at work to be used for tax exempt health-care expenses. Usually the plan includes a large deductible to encourage individuals to spend less on health care. The MSA uses a special personal savings account instead of putting money into insurance premiums or paying into a third-party payer insurance company for coverage. Under the MSA it is believed that consumers will shop around, refuse unneeded treatment, and get the best buys because it is their own money and not an anonymous insurance company. Any money left over after certain time periods and/or when the savings account is large enough goes back to the owner (the worker who put it in). Several different approaches to this same concept have been proposed.

medical secretary An individual with secretarial skills and a background in medical terminology and possibly with insurance knowledge who performs secretarial duties in a physician's office, in an office in a health-care facility, or on a medical unit of a hospital or clinic. Sometimes referred to as a "unit clerk" or "ward clerk." *See also unit clerk; medical assistant.*

medical self-help The basics of first aid, home self-care, emergency care, and medical care, all expanded to cover medical care situations where no doctors are available and thus is provided to oneself or one's family members.

medical service plan An organization for the billing, collection, distribution, and/or use of specifically identified portions of professional fees covered by participating physicians.

medical services 1. The range of programs of treatment, therapy, and rehabilitation provided by medical personnel and facilities as requested by an individual and rendered by physicians, dentists, and their professional assistants such as nurses or dental hygienists. 2. In health insurance, services provided by the primary physician who refers the patient to another physician. 3. All medical care and treatment offered to patients at their request and provided by physicians, physician extenders (PAs or NPs), dentists, nurses, and allied health professionals and administered by formally organized health-care organizations.

Medical Services Administration (MSA) A bureau of the federal government that administers the Medicaid program. It is part of the Social and Rehabilitation Service, which administers most of the welfare programs in the Department of Health and Human Services. Direct administration of Medicaid programs is carried out at the state level by state Medicaid programs. California's program is referred to as Medi-Cal and Arizona's as AHCCCS. *See AHCCCS.*

medical social worker An individual who acts as a liaison between organized social services and those who need those services to solve medical problems. This person is prepared to identify and understand the social and emotional factors underlying a patient's illness and to communicate those factors to the health team. He or she assists patients and their families in understanding and accepting the treatment necessary to maximize medical benefits and in adjusting to permanent and temporary effects of illness. These professionals also work with discharge planning and help arrange for support and social services in the community.

medical society A local association for physicians made up of the practicing physicians in the geographical area or of a specialty area. Also referred to as a "medical association."

medical specialties Many medical specialties are now available for advanced training for physicians and to enhance the level and quality of medical care to the public. The following medical specialties practice in the United States: pediatrics, pediatric allergy, pediatric cardiology, family practice, psychiatry, internal medicine, geriatrics, cardiology, ear/nose/throat, pulmonary diseases, neurology, nephrology, allergy, and dermatology. Surgical specialties include neurological, orthopedic, otolaryngological, colorectal, urologic, head and neck, traumatic, plastic, and pediatric. Other specialties include pathology, child psychiatry, radiology, radiation oncology, emergency medicine, sports medicine, aerospace medicine, occupational medicine, preventive medicine, and public health. A separate area of medical practice, but not considered a specialty, is osteopathic medicine. Chiropractic is not a medical specialty but a separate profession. *See chiropractic; osteopathic medicine.*

medical staff 1. Collectively, the physicians, dentists, and other professionals responsible for medical care in a hospital or other health facility or agency. Such staff may be full or part time, employed by the hospital or not, and include all professionals who wish to be included (open staff) or just those who meet various standards of competence or specialization (closed staff). Staff privileges may or may not be permanent or may be conditional on continued evidence of competence. 2. A hospital administrative unit and medical practice body that has the overall responsibility for the quality of the professional services provided by practitioners with clinical privileges and also the responsibility of accounting to the hospital administrator and governing body. The medical staff includes fully licensed physicians and may include other licensed individuals permitted by law and by the hospital to provide patient care services independently in the hospital such as podiatrists, oral surgeons (who are dentists), and psychologists. Members have delineated clinical privileges that allow them to provide patient care services independently within the scope of their clinical privileges. Members and all others with individual clinical privileges are subject to medical staff and departmental bylaws and are subject to review as part of the hospital's quality assessment and improvement activities. Standards are applied to evaluate the quality of a hospital's medical staff performance (JCAHO for acute-care facilities). The categories of medical staff for JCAHO accreditation of hospitals are active and associate, or those regular and full-time participants on the medical staff at the hospital, and courtesy, consulting, honorary, provisional, and others who are nonregular attenders. Board-certified status is also used in selecting medical staff members and physicians who have passed an examination given by a medical specialty board and who have been certified by that board as specialists. In accreditation, only the primary certification board is used for physicians certified by more than one board. Medical staff members are listed by medical specialty (JCAHO for acute-care facilities). *See medical specialties.*

medical staff, active Members of the hospital medical staff who currently admit patients and who have full hospital privileges and responsibilities, including some administration and committee work as granted by the board of governors and the hospital's administration.

medical staff, associate A special status on the medical staff of a health-care facility offered to some psychologists, podiatrists, chiropractors, dentists, and other nonphysician qualified health-care practitioners allowing them special or limited hospital privileges; an interim appointment of a physician, dentist, or podiatrist to the medical staff with privileges accorded a regular or active medical staff physician. Some hospital medical staff bylaws do not allow full participation of associates in medical staff political and administrative activities.

medical staff bylaws 1. The policies, procedures, rules, right, obligations, and regulations that define the duties, qualifications, and methods of selection of health-care providers for a hospital medical staff and positions plus the method of selection of medical staff officers. Bylaws are drafted and created by the medical staff and approved by administration and the governing body. Policies are created on credentials, operation and function expectations, and any limitations. 2. An official document that describes the organization, roles, and responsibilities of the medical staff. The bylaws are developed, adopted, and periodically reviewed by the medical staff and approved by the governing body (JCAHO for acute-care facilities).

medical staff, categories of privileges Six categories of medical staff granted medical care privileges in a hospital may include active, courtesy, consulting, provisional, honorary (including retired), and administrative. These vary from hospital to hospital and by region of the country. *See medical staff privilege levels.*

medical staff corporation In hospital administration, this is when the medical staff organization takes out articles of incorporation, establishes itself as a separate legal corporation from the hospital, and then contracts back its services to the hospital. This process establishes the medical staff as an incorporated body much like the hospital has been incorporated and makes both legally separate.

medical staff, courtesy In hospital administration, these are health-care providers who are qualified for an appointment to the medical staff of a hospital but who are allowed only temporary staff privileges to admit patients; a physician who is not a regular active or associate member of the medical staff and does not participate in regular medical staff activities.

medical staff equivalent In JCAHO long-term-care facility accreditation, an organized medical staff that provides services to one or more facilities or that serves a group of facilities.

medical staff executive committee An administrative group of medical staff members (a majority of whom are licensed physician members of the medical staff practicing in the hospital, selected by the medical staff, or appointed in accordance with governing body bylaws) who are responsible for making specific recommendations to the administration and the governing body for its approval and for receiving and acting on reports and recommendations from medical staff committees, clinical departments/services, and assigned activity groups (JCAHO for acute-care facilities).

medical staff, honorary Retired physicians or those no longer practicing medicine who are allowed to participate in certain medical staff activities, medical staff management, and hospital administration as a gesture of respect and courtesy, realizing they have much to contribute to the administration of the hospital but no longer having admitting privileges.

medical staff organization In hospital administration, this is the administrative unit and structure that governs and represents physicians on the medical staff and affiliated staff members of a hospital to the hospital's administration and board of directors. The organization of the medical staff provides a management structure to represent all physicians on the medical staff and a communication structure to hospital administration and the board of directors allowing input into hospital operations. *See medical staff.*

medical staff privilege levels In hospital administration, these vary from hospital to hospital and by region of the country but usually consist of active, associate, and courtesy, honorary, consulting, provisional, special, and nonphysician. *See medical staff; medical staff, categories of privileges.*

medical staff privileges In hospital administration, this is when the administration and board of directors legally accept a physician or other special nonphysicians (podiatrists, dentists, psychologists) to admit, treat, do surgery, provide consultation, test, and discharge patients from a hospital as determined and approved by the medical staff and the board of directors. *See medical staff; medical staff, categories of privileges.*

medical staff, provisional Also referred to as "associate medical staff." *See medical staff, associate.*

medical staff recruitment plan In hospital administration, this is one aspect of the hospital's strategic plan or long-range operational plan used to establish the size, medical specialties needed, areas of physician shortages, future medical areas and services to be developed, the types of services the hospital will provide, and the impact that medical staff functioning will have on the hospital's future.

medical statistics *See vital statistics; biostatistics; descriptive statistics.*

medical subject headings (MeSH) A literature listing from the National Library of Medicine (NLM) on current biomedical literature produced annually and published by the NLM through the National Technical Information Services of the U.S. Department of Commerce.

medical supplies In the delivery of medical care, these are products essential to providing medical care. Certain products or items are required to function in a specific manner or to provide specific therapeutic or diagnostic outcomes or effect as required by the health-care provider to provide the proper and appropriate treatment or care. Such items include syringes, needles, surgical dressings, catheters, sanitizing solutions, irrigating solutions, and disposable tubes.

medical/surgical 1. A nursing unit in a hospital that utilizes nursing techniques and procedures in providing care to patients in surgical operative and postoperative settings; one of the most common medical and nursing care units found in a hospital. 2. A specialty area of nursing training and practice that cares for patients in surgical operative and postoperative levels of recovery.

medical/surgical intensive care In hospital organizational structure, this is a patient care unit in a hospital that provides a level of patient care more intensive than the usual medical and surgical care unit found in hospitals. The care is provided under physician orders and approved nursing care plans. These intensive care units are supervised by physician specialists and staffed with specially trained nursing personnel. The units are equipped with specialized monitoring and life support equipment to assist in treatment, therapy, observation, nursing, and recovery of patients who require intensified, comprehensive observation and care because of serious levels of sickness or injury such as trauma, surgical recovery, and life-threatening conditions.

medical technician This is an individual who is trained to carry out some functions of MDs or DOs, especially in emergency situations outside hospitals and during transport to hospitals, when limited but intense life support services are needed. Some medical personnel such as paramedics, surgical technicians, and emergency room technicians are highly trained and specialized.

medical technologist A specially trained individual who performs a wide range of complex and specialized procedures in all general areas of the clinical laboratory. The minimum educational requirement for one of several certification programs in medical technology is a bachelors degree with appropriate science course requirements plus a 12-month structured AMA-approved medical technology internship program and an examination. The medical technologist is the most highly trained of several types of clinical laboratory personnel, including the medical laboratory technician and medical laboratory assistant. As highly skilled laboratory scientists with a strong generalist orientation, medical technologists have the ability to perform or supervise tests and procedures in hematology, bacteriology, serology, immunology, clinical chemistry, blood banking, urinalysis, mycology, and parasitology. They perform complex analyses requiring the exercise of independent judgment, correlate test results, and must be able to interpret their findings with respect to disease or normality. They must have knowledge of physiological conditions affecting test results and must produce reliable and valid results that can be confirmed by statistical measurements of precision and accuracy. Also referred to as a "biochemistry technologist," "blood technologist," or "microbiology technologist." *See medical laboratory technician; medical technologist, qualified; pathology and clinical laboratory.*

medical technologist, qualified According to JCAHO for accreditation, an individual who is a graduate of a medical technology program approved by a nationally recognized body or who has the documented equivalent in education, training, and/or experience who meets current legal requirements of licensure or registration and who is currently competent in the field.

medical technology 1. A set of techniques, drugs, equipment, and procedures used by health-care professionals in delivering medical care to individuals and the system within which such care is delivered (Office of Technology Assessment). 2. An educational program that prepares individuals as highly skilled microbiological and medical laboratory scientists with an in-depth ability to perform complex and specialized medical laboratory procedures and to work in all phases of a medical lab, including advanced bioelectronic and computer equipment. This person is trained to be responsible for the complex analysis of pathological specimens and for judgment concerning the presence or absence of disease-producing microorganisms. Many programs require a 5-year bachelor of science degree and 1 year of clinical education experience in a hospital.

medical trade area An area from which one or more specified providers draw their patients; similar to a catchment area except that a catchment area is defined by the type of patient rather than the provider.

medical transcriptionist An individual skilled in typing, medical spelling, medical terminology, and the proper format of medical records and reports and who can transcribe medical dictation using mechanical dictating equipment.

medical treatment Medical care, surgery, or therapy administered by a physician or registered professional personnel under the standing orders of a physician. Medical treatment does not include first aid treatment (e.g., one-time care of minor scratches, cuts, burns, or splinters that do not require professional care), even though such care is provided by a physician or registered professional personnel. *See definitive care; emergency care; first aid.*

medical waste In environmental health and hazardous waste, these are discarded materials from treatment and surgery in hospitals, clinics, and medical practice that have the potential to cause infections if not handled and discarded properly. The solid or liquid by-products generated in the diagnosis, treatment, or immunization of human beings or animals in research or in the production or testing of biologicals; does not include household waste or most industrial waste.

medicament A drug or herb used for healing, treating, curing, or relieving pain; a medicine.

Medicare Health insurance for the aged. A nationwide health insurance program for people age 65 and over, for persons eligible for Social Security disability payments for over 2 years, and for certain workers and their dependents who need kidney transplantation or dialysis. Health insurance protection is available to insured persons without regard to income. Monies from payroll taxes and premiums from beneficiaries are deposited in special trust funds for use in meeting the expenses incurred by the insured. The program was enacted July 30, 1965, as Title XVIII of the Social Security Act and became effective July 1, 1966. It consists of two separate but coordinated programs: hospital insurance (Part A) and supplementary medical (physician) insurance (Part B).

Medicare beneficiary Any U.S. citizen over age 65 or who meets other eligibility requirements and who has been designated by the federal Social Security Administration as eligible or entitled to participate in Medicare and to receive benefits. *See Medicare.*

Medicare benefits As outlined in the *Social Security Handbook*, a person with hospital insurance protection (Part A) may have benefits paid on his or her behalf or, in certain cases, paid to him or her for covered health-care services. The medical insurance plan (Part B) adds to the protection provided by the basic hospital insurance plan and covers a substantial part of physicians' services, surgery, and a number of other health items and services. The benefit period includes 90 days of hospital care plus a lifetime reserve of 60 days. A benefit period begins when a person is admitted to a participating hospital and terminates after a person has not been a patient for 60 consecutive days in the hospital or in a skilled nursing home. The hospital insurance plan covers the cost of general hospital care, room and board, operations, drugs, medical supplies, diagnostic tests, laboratory fees, and physical therapy. Some services not allowed are telephone, television, private room (except as a medical necessity), and personal items. The cost to the patient includes the initial hospital deductible, which is revised every year.

Medicare case mix index In health-care delivery, this is an indication of the severity of illness in treated Medicare patients. The severity index is "1" for a national average. Numbers higher than "1" indicate a high level of severity. The higher the numbers, the higher the severity of an illness. *See case mix; case mix index; case severity.*

Medicare co-insurance *See Medicare supplementary insurance.*

Medicare conditions of participation A uniform payment system used by Medicare under the Health Care Financing Administration that sets forth requirements that hospitals and other institutional providers must meet to be allowed to receive payment for health care provided to Medicare patients. An example of a condition is that a hospital must have a utilization review system in place.

Medicare cost-based reimbursement A uniform payment system used by Medicare under the Health Care Financing Administration that is based on a health-care provider's or health-care facility's costs for providing services, treatments, or therapy.

Medicare insured group (MIG) 1. One approach to Medicare contracting with health plans established by the Health Care Financing Administration. Risk-based contracts with HMOs and competitive medical plans offer better control over retiree health costs for employers, unions, and Medicare. Elements of this approach include risk assumption by the health plan other than the federal government for total health benefits, prospective payment based on an enrolled group's medical treatment experience instead of average costs, and monitoring to ensure high-quality care. 2. A specialized health insurance or health plan or program that provides medical care and services to Medicare beneficiaries in which a managed-care plan, union, or corporation assumes responsibilities for all aspects of medical care provided to a group of older adults (age 65 and older) in return for a set payment from Medicare. Often referred to as "senior plans" or other similar titles.

Medicare intermediary In health-care finance, this is a private company that becomes a fiscal agent and handles Medicare medical care claims and payments for the Health Care Financing Administration. Often the organization is already in the medical insurance business (e.g., Blue Cross and Blue Shield, Aetna, and Mutual of Omaha plans). The tasks of an intermediary include determining reasonable costs for services or products covered, making payment, containing costs, assessing utilization, and protecting against unnecessary use of covered services of Part A. Hospitals, home health agencies, nursing homes, and HMO contracts are examples of health-care providers that use Medicare intermediaries. Also referred to as "Medicare carriers." *See intermediary.*

Medicare/Medicaid (MediCal) This covers persons enrolled for medical benefits under Medicare and Medicaid (MediCal in California). Also referred to as "Medi-Medi."

Medicare/Medicaid Automated Certification System (MMACS) In health-care information management systems, this is a database system operated by the Health Care Financing Administration to collect data from all state survey agencies who conduct Medicare and Medicaid certification activities for health-care facilities and services.

Medicare/Medicaid beneficiary One who is eligible to receive medical care coverage for health services under both Medicare and Medicaid.

Medicare operating margin Payments received by a health-care provider from Medicare less the operation costs of the physician or health-care facility covered by Medicare payments divided by Medicare revenues and multiplied by 100. Medicare revenues and costs not covered under the Prospective Payment System (e.g., capital expenditures and medical education) are excluded.

Medicare participating physician Any physician who has taken assignment on all claims from all Medicare beneficiaries in return for a set fee payment and certain incentives.

Medicare risk competitive medical plans *See Medicare risk health maintenance organizations.*

Medicare risk health maintenance organizations In managed care, these are health plan options established to cover all medical care needs and expenses for Medicare patients for a set fee. Medicare patients under such HMO plans are required to use only those hospitals and physicians under contract with and identified by the health plan. Also called "competitive medical plans" (CMPs).

Medicare supplementary insurance This is any medical insurance policy that covers those areas that Medicare falls short of covering and is exclusively for those persons over age 65 with end-stage renal disease or who are disabled and enrolled in Medicare. Also referred to as "co-insurance." *See Medigap; Medigap policy.*

Medicare supplement policy An insurance policy that covers the cost of the portion of services and care not covered by Medicare. Some managed-care plans guarantee a policyholder's deductibles, co-payments, and co-insurance costs. *See co-insurance.*

medicaster A medical charlatan or quack.

medicate In medical care, this means "to treat with medicine or drugs."

medication 1. Drugs and pharmaceutical substances and preparations used in the treatment of patients. 2. In JCAHO accreditation, any substance, whether prescribed or over the counter, taken orally or injected, inserted, topically applied, or otherwise administered to a patient. 3. Any chemical compound, remedy, or noninfectious biological substance, the action of which is not solely mechanical, that may be administered to patients by any route to aid in the diagnosis, treatment, or prevention of disease or other abnormal condition; to relieve pain or suffering; or to control or improve any psychological or pathological condition. Products that contain medications but are primarily used for cosmetic or other purposes do not fit the true definition of a medication.

medication administration The route or process by which drugs are taken or administered. The five R's of medication administration are right medication, right dosage, right patient, right time, and through the right route such as intravenous, intramuscular, or oral. Four methods are usually used: 1) oral administration, by which the drug is taken by mouth for absorption into the gastrointestinal tract; 2) inhalation administration, by which drugs in gas or vapor form are breathed in through the nose and absorbed by the respiratory tract; 3) topical administration, by which drugs such as lotions, ointments, lozenges, or suppositories are absorbed through the skin or mucous membranes; and 4) parenteral administration, by which drugs in a solution or in suspension are administered by injection or intravenously. Some methods of parenteral administration include intradermal: injecting a small amount of a solution just below the surface of the skin, forming a wheal (this method is used for a local rather than a systemic effect, e.g., local anesthetic or tuberculosis skin test); intravenous: injecting varying amounts of soluble solutions directly into a vein for immediate absorption; subcutaneous or hypodermic: injecting a small amount of highly soluble medication into the tissue directly under the skin; and intramuscular: injecting a large amount of a solution into the muscle.

medication aide In JCAHO long-term-care facility accreditation, any unlicensed personnel who have successfully completed a state-approved training program in medication administration.

medication error In the process of health-care delivery, especially the administration of drugs and other substances to patients, this is a mistake or a failure in medication processing and administration. The multiple levels of personnel, the transcription process from prescriptions, and the prescription-filling process in the pharmacy and mix-ups by physician or nurses just prior to administration all have the potential to contribute to an error in drug administration. Adherence to the five R's of medication administration (right medication, right dosage, right patient, right time, and through the right route such as intravenous, intramuscular, or oral) helps eliminate errors in the process of administering medications. *See medication administration.*

medication order An order for drugs or pharmaceuticals, issued by a physician, dentist, podiatrist, or other legally qualified professional, to be procured from a pharmacy and administered to a patient in a health-care facility or long-term-care institution by a qualified individual under physician supervision.

medicinal Having the ability to heal or relieve disease.

medicine 1. The art, science, and practice of promoting, maintaining, and restoring individual health and of diagnosing and treating disease. 2. Drugs or other substances used other than surgery in the treatment of diseases or conditions. *See allopathy; homeopathy; osteopathy; chiropractic.*

medicine, general An educational program that describes the principles and procedures used in the observation, diagnosis, care, and treatment of illness, disease, injury, disorders, deformity, disability, or other anomalies in humans that are studied by medical and nursing students and certain other allied health professionals.

medico (Spanish) Physician (or an equivalent health-care practitioner).

medico, ca (Spanish) Medical, medicinal personal construct. *See construct.*

medicolegal Pertaining to medicine and law.

medicredit One of several proposed national health insurance plans designed to encourage the voluntary purchase of qualified private health insurance policies by granting tax credits against personal income taxes to finance, in part or in whole, the premium cost of such plans. In addition, the proposal would provide for the federal payment of premiums for qualified policies for poor individuals or families with no tax liability.

Medigap Areas of medical care coverage not covered by Medicare medical insurance.

Medigap insurance Supplemental insurance designed to fill in some of the gaps in Medicare coverage or the gaps between private insurance and Medicare coverage.

Medigap policy A medical care insurance policy sold as a supplemental insurance policy to Medicare participants, usually to cover co-payments and deductibles not covered by Medicare.

MEDIHC (Military Experience Directed Into Health Careers) A program that recruits qualified veterans with military health-care experience and attempts to place them in health-care jobs in areas of health personnel shortages.

medi medi The term used to describe individuals who are enrolled in both Medicare and Medicaid for medical insurance benefits. *See Medicare/Medicaid.*

MEDIPHOR (Monitoring and Evaluation of Drug Interactions in Pharmacy-Oriented Reporting) Developed by the National Center for Health Services Research, this is a computerized drug interaction screening and reporting system that can be a component of a pharmacy billing and inventory system to alert physicians to possible adverse drug interactions. When a pharmacist enters a new drug into the computer, the computer checks with the patient's drug profile for negative drug interactions and generates a report as to any expected adverse reaction.

MedisGroups *See Medical Illness Severity Grouping System.*

MEDIS GRPS A shortened form of "medical groupings." Used in quality assurance and utilization review, this is a commercially sold program that uses clinically accepted information to assess the severity of a patient's illness for admitting diagnosis. This may include laboratory findings, radiological tests, and physical exam results indicating abnormal health conditions. Patients are assigned to one of five levels of illness severity ranging from 0 to 4. This system validates whether the utilization review correctly targets the in-depth review process and organizes the utilization management approach into three levels of admission: low admission severity, medium admission severity requiring close monitoring, and high admission severity requiring intensive planning. This program is marketed to help quality assurance and utilization review activities while helping to avert DRG cost overruns.

Meditech A private company founded by Neil Papalardo, who, as a graduate student at MIT, worked under a federal grant at Massachusetts General Hospital to develop a computerized hospital information system. The result was the MUMPS system and programming language. As the system was developed with federal funds, the software was public domain. Papalardo then formed this corporation to market the system. *See also Massachusetts General Hospital's Multi-Programming System.*

MEDLARS (Medical Literature Analysis and Retrieval System) A computerized database literature search system that is tied into *Index Medicus,* the *Index to Dental Literature,* the *International Nursing Index* and other literature databases.

MEDLINE A medical library computerized bibliographic search and acquisition system (MEDLARS' on-line system).

MEDPAR A Health Care Financing Administration data file of bills for a 20% sample of Medicare beneficiaries discharged from short-stay hospitals; contains billed charge data and clinical characteristics such as principal diagnosis and principal procedures.

MEDRECS A medical records abstracting system developed by McAuto of the McDonnell Douglas Health Information System based in St. Louis, Missouri. It is designed to collect, edit, analyze, and report information using a personal computer. Used by some hospitals, the system replaced the old MR II system. It provides DRG groupers, a master patient index, and a medical record deficiency system. The system maintains and provides statistics, indexes, and special reports to medical records and a health-care facility's administration.

meeting A formal gathering of a task force, committee, work group, board, or society in an assembly of its members who stay together for a set time period or until certain goals are reached (except for breaks or a recess).

meeting of minds A clear understanding and mutual agreement of the terms of a contract by both parties, having no secret purpose or intent. Both sides of a contract are in total agreement of the terms of the contract. Also referred to as "mutual assent" as used in contract law. *See mutual assent; contract.*

megavoltage radiation therapy A specialized form of radiation therapy for cancer using cobalt units and linear accelerators with or without electron beam therapy capability, betatrons, and Van De Graaff machines. This equipment generates supervoltage and megavolts for deep therapy cancer treatment.

melancholia A geriatric related term, this is also an old term for depression, often seen in older adults but not limited to older age-groups. Involutional melancholia refers to a debilitating state of depression.

melancholia agitata A geriatric related term, this is an agitated depression, common to senile psychosis.

member 1. Belonging to an organized group or effort. 2. A part of the body, usually a limb. 3. In managed care, this is any person who has entered into a contractual agreement with a prepaid health-care program or health plan under which the health-care organization agrees to assume the responsibility of providing basic medical care and services and any supplementary health care needed by the persons enrolled, even if it includes contracting out for some services. Any person enrolled and eligible to receive or receiving benefits from a health plan, HMO or medical care policy; a participant in a health plan, also called an "enrollee," "subscriber," "policyholder," "beneficiary," or "eligible dependent." Usually this includes all people who enroll or subscribe for benefits and their eligible dependents; any individual enrolled as a subscriber or an eligible dependent of a subscriber and for whom the health plan has accepted the responsibility of providing medical care and health services and such supplemental health services as may be contracted for. 4. In insurance, any person who is a policyholder; an eligible subscriber or eligible dependent who is enrolled under a group subscriber agreement. 5. In health administration, persons who participate in a health-care organization's internal system or activities; one of the hospitals or health-care facilities in a system of hospitals and health services. 6. In a hospital, this includes all employees, administrators, staff, physicians, trustees, volunteers, other nonemployed providers (podiatrists, dentists, psychologist, etc.), or other persons internally affiliated with the hospital. *See also subscriber; insured; beneficiary.*

member category In managed care or medical insurance, this is a level of care, patient type, or treatment classification of a health-care provider that is used to determine reimbursement levels for health-care providers.

member certificate In managed care or medical insurance, this is documentation that a person is a member of the health plan and is eligible for medical benefits coverage.

member co-payment A type of cost sharing in which the insured pays a specified amount per unit of service (e.g., $1.00 per visit or half the cost of prescription drugs) and the insurer the remainder of the cost. Unlike co-insurance, the amount of the co-payment does not vary with the cost of services.

member month(s) 1. In managed care, this is used to assess premium income, which is equivalent to one member for whom the health plan has realized 1 month's premium of income; one member enrolled for 1 month in a health plan. One member enrolled for 3 months is 3 member months as is three members enrolled for 1 month; the total of all months that each health plan member was covered. A health plan with 20,000 members in January and 25,000 members in February equals 45,000 total member months for the year as of the end of February.

membership corporation A corporation, created for social, charitable, or political purposes, that is a nonprofit or nonstock organization.

members per year In managed care or medical insurance, this is the number of enrollees in a health plan in a 1-year period. The formula for members per year follows:

$$\frac{\text{Member months}}{\text{12 months}}$$

memorandum 1. A written record of events; a semiformal written communication. 2. A written summary of a meeting. 3. A written proposed agreement. 4. A message from one member of an organization to another. 5. A document establishing that a contract exists. 6. In law, this is a brief submitted to a judge. 7. A brief written summary of the terms of a contract, promise, or legal transaction.

memorandum decision An appellate court's decision that determines which party prevails but gives no reason for the decision.

memorandum of understanding 1. A letter of agreement of certain administrative or contractual issues between two administrative units, two agencies, two different hospitals, etc. 2. An agreement, usually between a PRO and a hospital, fiscal intermediary, or state agency, identifying the respective responsibilities of each party for various activities and costs.

memory 1. In mental health, this is the ability to retrieve past impressions, knowledge, learnings, experiences, and ideas. 2. Storage in a computer; the part of a computer that stores or holds data.

mens rea (Lat.) Guilty mind; wrongful intent; with a harmful purpose.

mental adaptive mechanisms See *mental mechanisms*.

mental age A measure of mental ability as determined by standard psychological testing. *See also IQ; Stanford-Binet intelligence test; Wechsler intelligence scales.*

mental anguish Strong mental or emotional feelings that occur during or after an injury. One may be able to recover damages for mental anguish in a lawsuit. Also referred to as "mental suffering" or "pain and suffering."

mental cruelty Meanness, harassment, demeaning encounters, controlling behavior, and verbal attack, on the part of one spouse done to the other, that lacks physical harm but causes mental distress or anguish to such a degree that the marriage is intolerable. This has been grounds for divorce in some states.

mental disorder A general term for abnormal functioning or capacity of the mind, emotions and related behavior; the absence of mental health; any of several disorders listed in the *International Classification of Disease, 9th Revision, Clinical Modification* (ICD-9-CM) or the *Diagnostic and Statistical Manual of Mental Disorders, Third Edition—Revised* (DSM-III-R). Also referred to as "mental disease" or "mental illness."

mental distress See *stress; mental illness*.

mental health 1. The capacity of an individual to maintain self-esteem and self-confidence, have a good self-concept, believe in oneself, do acceptable behaviors, and form and maintain harmonious relations with others at school or work or in marriage and families; understanding and knowing how to contribute constructively to work and society and to changes in the social and physical environment while achieving a harmonious, balanced satisfaction of potentially conflicting instinctive drives. Such a definition should be compared with that of "health." Mental health is a concept influenced by mental capacity, emotional stability, socially accepted behavior, biological makeup, social and cultural experiences, and other factors. 2. Operationally defined as the absence of any identifiable or significant mental disorder or mental pathology and sometimes used as a synonym for "mental illness" (e.g., mental health services or mental health benefits). *See psychiatric; psychopathology; mental illness; health; mental health promotion.*

mental health/human services An educational program that prepares individuals to assist in the care and treatment of the mentally ill, emotionally disturbed, frail aged, those suffering from substance abuse, and the handicapped. Individual, marital, and family counseling and psychotherapy is used to counsel and instruct persons suffering from emotional, mental, or social dysfunction to help the suffering individual develop new patterns of living. Tasks may or may not include assisting in drug therapy as appropriate under the supervision of a physician.

mental health organization 1. More correctly, these are mental illness organizations, which are any administratively distinct public or private agencies or institutions whose primary concern is the provision of direct mental care services to the mentally ill or emotionally disturbed; all state, county, and private psychiatric hospitals, psychiatric services of general hospitals, residential treatment centers for emotionally disturbed children, federally funded community health centers (prior to 1983), freestanding outpatient psychiatric clinics, partial care organizations, and multiservice mental health organizations. 2. Mental health associations that do mental health education and promote good mental and emotional health and behavior are considered mental health organizations.

mental health plan The plan of a city, county, or state that addresses the provision of services designed to prevent emotional, social, and behavioral dysfunctions in its residents.

mental health promotion A specialized phase of health promotion that aims to develop good coping skills, stress management, communication, self-esteem, self-concept, self-confidence, and acceptable behavior to form and maintain harmonious relationships with others in school, at work, and in marriage and families. Individuals are taught to contribute constructively to work and society, to deal with changes in the social and physical environment, and to achieve a harmonious, balanced satisfaction of potentially conflicting instinctive drives. Mental health promotion takes into account emotional, behavioral, mental, and biological states as well as social and cultural and other influencing factors. Some of the approaches and methods used to promote mental well-being include education, group experiences, personal growth exercises and experiences, teaching of coping skills, training in communication skills, stress management, and group and personal counseling. *See mental health promotion; mental health; health promotion.*

mental health promotion services Programs or activities that encourage or promote optimum mental, behavioral, and emotional well-being among individuals in the community, often including coordination, support, and consultation with mental health associations, public schools, police, health-care organizations, colleges and universities, churches, and other concerned entities. *See mental health promotion; mental health; health promotion.*

mental health provider This is a licensed psychiatrist, psychologist, social worker, or psychotherapist or any hospital, health-care facility, psychiatric care center, or other mental health facility that is licensed, certified, or accredited to provide mental health services.

mental health services The diagnosis and treatment of emotional and mental diseases, behavioral problems, marital or family problems, and conditions or their symptoms through counseling, psychotherapy, or the administration of medication and specialized therapy. Professional and technical staff provide programs or activities to clients or residents aimed at improving mental, behavioral, emotional, psychological, or psychiatric well-being. Treatment plans are developed through the diagnosis and evaluation of mental, behavioral, and emotional status; through concern for the prevention of deviations from mental and emotional well being; and/or to provide treatment and therapy through a planned regimen. All these help the client or resident regain, maintain, and/or increase mental and emotional function and ability. Counseling, psychotherapy, group therapy, psychotropic medications, biofeedback, hypnosis, and behavior therapy are some of the modalities used in general inpatient and outpatient psychiatric services, alcohol and substance abuse treatment centers, outpatient community health centers, hospital-based psychiatric treatment facilities, private practice, private mental health centers, or other inpatient or outpatient facilities to develop a functional and effective level of mental well-being.

mental health supplies and services In a psychiatric setting, these are any items or products used in the diagnosis and treatment of psychiatric disorders, mental illness, behavioral disorders, alcoholism, or substance abuse.

mental health technologist *See human services/mental health technologist.*

mental hygiene A somewhat antiquated term meaning "mental health" or "mental well-being"; the maintenance of the state of one's emotional, behavioral, and mental well-being; having a high level of self-acceptance, acceptance of others, self-esteem, and self-confidence as well as a positive self-concept, adequate love, purpose in life, good coping skills, social responsibility, self-control, and self-discipline. The term has also been occasionally used to mean "psychiatry" or "psychology" or to refer to some aspect of the activities and processes of psychiatry, psychology, psychiatric nursing, or social work. *See mental health; mental well-being.*

mental illness All forms of illness in which psychological, intellectual, emotional, or behavioral disturbances are the dominating feature. The term is relative and variable and includes a wide range of types (such as psychic and physical, neurotic and psychotic) and severity. It is useful to distinguish mental diseases (those with an identifiable physical cause) from mental illness (those with no known cause and those with emotional, familial, social, or other roots), but this is not done routinely. *See also mental health.*

mentally ill In law and psychiatry, this is when a person is considered a danger to himself or herself or to others or cannot take care of his or her own health and welfare. *See mental illness; mental health.*

mentally incompetent Mental competency is a legally defined mental state determined by the courts and court-appointed mental health professionals such as psychiatrists and psychologists who use the basic definition of mental incompetency as set by state law. Most states use the "danger to self, danger to others" concept to determine mental illness. In mentally impaired or elderly persons who suffer mental impairment, the courts may impose a conservatorship or guardianship on the basis of the court's determination that the individual in question cannot take care of his or her finances, health, and welfare (including medical care and informed consent) and thus is placed under a court-appointed conservator or guardian. *See mentally ill; mental illness; incompetent.*

mental mechanisms In psychology/psychiatry and mental health, these are coping and mental defense behavior adjustments that occur consciously or unconsciously. Mental mechanisms help one compensate for emotional, social, or environmental stress, pain, struggles, or voids used to cope with and to overcome insecurity, defend one's pride, blame, shift the blame, provide an alibi, deny a problem while saving face, or justify actions in some other way.

mental retardation The absence of normal mental development, usually measured by the intelligence quotient and considered to be present in individuals scoring less than 70 on the Stanford-Binet scale, according to which various types (intellectual or emotional) and degrees (borderline, 68–85; mild, 57–67; moderate, 36–51; severe, 20–35; and profound, under 20) are described. Mental retardation is one type of developmental disability and mental disorder.

mental retardation aide One who works under the supervision of a professional staff in attending to the physical needs and well-being of mentally retarded patients.

mental retardation services In mental health care and long-term care, these are programs, activities, or facilities that provide health-related care and services on a regular basis to patients with developmental or mental impairment who do not require the degree of treatment or care that a skilled nursing unit is designed to provide. In nursing homes, long-term-care beds must be set up and staffed in a unit specifically designed for this service.

mental status 1. The level of emotional, behavioral, or mental well-being possessed by an individual at any one time. 2. The results of a psychiatric examination in which a patient's general mental health, speech patterns, perception, general mood, and other characteristics are assessed or renewed.

mental status exam This is an evaluation of a person's awareness and mental capabilities used in psychiatry to be somewhat equivalent to the physical exam in medicine. When conducting this evaluation, the psychiatrist looks at several areas: general appearance, behavior, flow of thought and speech, affect, mental content, sensory-motor activity, intellectual resources, insight, and judgment. The exam is often given to elderly persons who are presenile or in more advanced stages of senility or victims of a stroke. Often this exam is administered by psychiatrists, psychologists, counselors, social workers, physicians, psychiatric nurses, or other mental health professionals to determine the mental capacity and the level of understanding a person has of the current world. Part of the exam includes asking the patient questions that are simple for normal, alert persons but difficult for individuals with diminished mental alertness (e.g., the date, current place, who is the president of the United States, other key or prominent individuals, current events, and family member names).

mental suffering *See mental anguish.*

mental well-being A feeling of contentment, high self-esteem, strong self-confidence, high self-perception, emotional stability, peace of mind, and satisfaction with life. *See mental health; mental hygiene.*

mentor In health administration, this is when an experienced and well-educated person, usually an administrator, offers a young, new, and inexperienced person, training, advice, counseling, and special attention and assistance in career development as well as experience and exposure to actual job-related tasks and activities plus the needed coaching, teaching, and support to direct the person down a successful career path; a friend; a wise and faithful counselor or teacher.

menu A listing of programs or choices in a program that allows certain actions or interactions. In human resource management, this is a method of presenting medical care employee benefits by offering a wide selection and listing of various health plans or medical insurance options available for employees to select from.

Merck Manual A widely used medical book on medical diagnosis and therapy that presents each disease and disorder in a standardized way. Some areas it discusses are etiology, epidemiology, pathology, symptoms and signs, diagnosis and prognosis, prophylaxis, treatment, and complications. It is published by the Merck pharmaceutical company.

Merck Manual of Geriatrics This is a widely used medical book similar to the *Merck Manual*, but it is focused on medical diagnosis and therapy for older adults and addresses the unique aspects of medicine affecting geriatric patients.

mercury A heavy metal that can accumulate in the environment and is highly toxic if breathed or swallowed; includes all particulates, vapors, aerosols, and compounds of this element.

merge Under corporate law, legally and officially bringing together two or more separate health-care organizations or facilities under one organizational, administrative, and financial structure. *See also multi-institution organization.*

merger The legal process, under corporate law, of combining two health-care organizations into one functioning entity. The joining of two or more independent health-care facilities or organizations under a solely owned organization by acquisition of a major portion of stocks and/or assets. *See also merge; multi-institution organization.*

merger and acquisition strategies In strategic planning in health-care organizations, this is a health-care market positioning strategy that involves the combining of two or more health-care organizations into one or when one health-care organization purchases or takes over another health-care organization and absorbs it into its own operations or operates it as a subsidiary or division. *See strategic planning.*

merit-based promotions In health administration and human resources management, this is when an employee is promoted to a more responsible position by being an outstanding worker with superior performance that is recognized by management.

merit raises In health administration and human resources management, this is when an employee is provided with a monetary reward because of outstanding performance or a level of performance above the usual. These are given to the worker in addition to any cost-of-living or promotion raises.

MeSh Medical subject headings.

MeShs Medical staff hospital joint venture companies. *See joint venture.*

mesmerism Another term for "hypnotism" or a trance-type mental state; the first name given to hypnosis. The term was named after a French medical quack, Anton Mesmer, who in the late 1700s claimed cures through magnetism and is credited with discovering hypnosis.

messenger and transport service In health-care facilities, this is a service that provides for the delivery of mail and supplies and for the transportation of patients within the hospital.

meta-analysis In health services and biomedical research, this is a research methodology involving extensively searching the professional literature on a topic and then conducting an analysis on the findings of the search. The frequency, topic, and related concepts are assessed, as are constructs, association, and causation. The process includes an extensive review of related or relevant literature and ruling out methodological shortcomings of the studies such as sampling and designs problems, reliable and valid instruments issues, and proper use of controls. An accurate, objective aggregation and the findings of the studies are put into a quantitative description. Variables are weighted and descriptive statistics developed. The combining and compiling of findings, variables, risk factors, and other data based on hypotheses or some research premise is completed. *See meta-evaluation.*

metabolic disease screening Preventive procedures for detecting disease in respiration, circulation, peristalsis, muscle tone, body temperature, glandular activity, and other functions of the body.

metabolites In environmental health, these are substances produced in or by biological processes and derived from a pesticide.

meta-evaluation In health services and biomedical research, this is a research methodology that assesses the rigor and internal validity of research studies by looking at several standards or criteria such as appropriateness of research design, sampling process, sample size, characteristics of the study population, quality of the instruments, questionnaires, or modes of measurement and intervention. *See meta-analysis.*

-meter Suffix meaning "measure."

methadone A drug used mostly in the detoxification and maintenance of heroin addicts. Methadone hydrochloride is a long-acting, synthetic narcotic drug developed in Germany as a substitute for morphine.

method 18 In environmental health, this is an Environmental Protection Agency technique of testing concentrations of volatile organic compounds that uses gas chromatographic techniques to measure the concentration of individual volatile organic compounds in a gas stream.

method 24 In environmental health, this is an Environmental Protection Agency technique of determining density, water content, and total volatile content (water and volatile organic compounds) of coatings.

method 25 In environmental health, this is an Environmental Protection Agency reference technique of determining the volatile organic compound concentration in a gas stream.

method effectiveness In the delivery of health care, this is the extent or level to which a therapy, medicine, or treatment meets its intended outcome or falls short of achieving its intended result. A shortcoming may be caused by a lack of patient compliance or improper administration by the health-care provider.

method failure In the delivery of health care, this is when a therapy, medicine, or treatment fails in its use or purpose.

method of voting In formal health-care meetings using parliamentary procedure, this is an approach to voting that is used on a formal motion before the body. Examples are voice vote, vote by rising (standing), roll call (reading the name of each board member and ascertaining his or her position on the vote), or secret ballot.

methodology The approaches, sequence of activities, strategies, and techniques employed in a scientific study. The literal meaning is "to study methods; the study of methods." Also referred to as "method."

methods In health education, this refers to any of a multitude of education and communication techniques used to accommodate the learning or behavior change process in individual or community health. Tools and learning approaches used to assist learning include but are not limited to instruction in or presenting of health information to individuals or groups, printed material, electronic media, movies, videotape, role playing, computerized instruction, group discussion, group exercises, health counseling, gaming, storytelling, and individualized programmed learning.

"me too" drug A drug that is identical, similar, or closely related to a drug product for which a new drug application (NDA) has been approved. Many "me too" drugs on the market are essentially copies of approved new drugs but were introduced by the manufacturers without Food and Drug Administration approval on the theory that the NDA holder, or pioneer drug, had become generally recognized as safe and effective. Other "me too" products are being marketed with abbreviated new drug applications (ANDAs) that require the submission of manufacturing, bioavailability, and labeling information but not data relating to safety and effectiveness, which are assumed to be established. *See also generally recognized as effective; generally recognized as safe; generic drug.*

metrazol shock treatment In psychiatric treatment, this is a rarely used form of shock treatment in which convulsive seizure is induced by the injection of the drug Metrazol.

metropolitan statistical area (MSA) A designation of an urban area by the federal Office of Management and Budget of the federal Committee on Metropolitan Statistical Areas. An MSA is either an area that contains a city or an urbanized area with a population of at least 50,000 with a total metropolitan population of 100,000. All MSAs are defined by entire counties. An MSA may not only include the central county but also additional, adjacent counties that have close economic and social connections in that county. There is no limit to the number of adjacent counties included in an MSA as long as the counties are integrated with the central city. An MSA is not limited to a single state, as boundaries may cross state lines. Any county not in an MSA is deemed a rural area. The Medicare Prospective Payment System uses the MSA designations to adjust a hospital's prospective payment rate on the basis of its urban or rural location. Facilities in urban areas are paid at a higher rate because they generally incur higher costs, especially for wages.

METs Multiple Employer Trusts.

MGMA *See Medical Group Management Association.*

MGMIS *See Medical Group Management Information Service.*

MHC *See migrant health center.*

MHREF Montana Hospital Research and Educational Foundation.

MHS Multihospital system.

MIA *See Medical Indemnity of America, Inc.*
miasma Vapors in the air; poor quality of air.
miasmata *See miasma; miasma theory of disease.*
miasma theory of disease In epidemiology, this is an ancient set of beliefs that was considered the state of the art in medicine in determining the cause of disease. The theory attributed epidemics to a bad quality of air, vapors, mists, smells, or things floating in the air, all that created poisonous atmospheric or environmental conditions that caused disease. One example is malaria, which literally means "bad air."
miasmic theory of disease *See miasma; miasma theory of disease.*
MIB *See Medical Impairment Bureau.*
MIC *See mobile intensive care.*
MICR Magnetic ink character recognition. A medium used for inputting information and data into a computer.
microbes In epidemiology and public health, these are microscopic organisms such as algae, animals, viruses, bacteria, fungi, and protozoa, some of which cause disease.
microbial pesticides In environmental health, these are microorganisms that are used to control a pest and are of low toxicity to humans.
microbiologist A professional biological scientist involved in the study and analysis of bacteria, viruses, fungi, molds, parasites, and other microorganisms. This scientist may work in public health, medical laboratories, private labs, research, medical schools, and colleges and universities and in the training of technologists and technicians.
microbiologist, medical A biological scientist who works exclusively in a medical setting studying and analyzing microorganism samples taken from patients.
microbiology The study, preparation, staining, examination, classification, and analysis of life processes of bacteria, viruses, fungi, molds, parasites, and other microorganisms using microscopes and advanced technologies such as the electron microscope to see and analyze organisms not visible to the naked eye. The study of microorganisms, microbes, and molecules of life.
microbiology laboratory *See medical laboratory.*
microbiology technologist A technically trained laboratory worker who works with minimum supervision from a pathologist, physician, or laboratory director in performing bacteriological, viral, parasitological, immunologic, and serologic procedures in a clinical laboratory setting; generally not a medical technologist by degree or training, but education in microbiology is required. *See also medical technologist.*
microbiology technology An educational program that prepares individuals to work with minimum supervision from a pathologist physician or laboratory director in performing bacteriological, viral, parasitological, immunologic, and serologic procedures in a clinical laboratory setting.
microcomputer Any computer small enough to fit on a desk or in a briefcase used for personal needs or business activities. Also referred to as a "personal computer."
microfiche A small, rectangular sheet of microfilm containing a multitude of microimages in a grid pattern that must be read with magnification. Titles are large enough to be read with the naked eye, but printing on the film must be read with a special reader.
microfilm An information storage method where positive films are used to store information that is reduced in size without altering or changing the information content or the original document. This process allows reduced storage requirements, mailing costs, and use of paper products. Microfilm is processed on rolls, cartridges, and film cards (called "microfiche").
microfilming The process of reducing, through photographic means, records, documents, and reports to miniature form on film; commonly used with medical records.
microorganism 1. Bacteria, fungi, and viruses. 2. Organisms too small to be seen with the naked eye. Also called "microbes."
middle age In gerontology, this is the phase of the life cycle between the younger and growth years and older age periods; ages 40 to 59 according to some sources, but others move the ages down to 35 to 55 years.
middle majority As used in public health education and health services delivery, this is the segment of the population who accepts new concepts or ideas after early adopters do and prior to the latecomers or those possessing reluctance to new ideas. This group is influenced by the mass media, endorsements by noted personalities or prominent organizations, and personal recommendations of friends and associates or the organizations they are affiliated with; not necessarily the same as the "silent majority."

middle management In health administration, these are individuals in hospitals, medical groups, health plans, or other health-care organizations who are in midlevel administration positions such as supervisor, director, coordinator, or department head; administrative positions above and over employees and below upper management. *See midmanagement; midmanager.*

midlevel practitioner The roles of the physician assistant, nurse practitioner, and nurse midwife are at the midlevel practitioner level; nonphysicians who deliver medical care under the supervision of a physician. Also called "physician extenders." *See physician assistant; nurse practitioner; nurse midwife.*

midmanagement A level of administration in a hospital or health-care organization that is below and under top management and above charge persons (e.g., charge nurse) and employees that requires much upward and downward communication to support both employees and supervisors while also supporting upper-level management. Midmanagers and supervisors are considered midmanagement personnel and are the entry level to the uppermost echelon of the organization. In some organizations, midmanagement may or may not include supervisors, charge persons, or directors. *See midmanager.*

midmanager An individual who has responsibility and authority over certain designated areas and supervisory personnel, charge persons, and employees in health-care organizations. The person filling this position is to plan, initiate, and execute programs; direct and communicate organizational goals; ensure that tasks are completed, objectives achieved, services performed, and performance assessed; interpret and apply policies; work standards; motivate; and control and assist employees while interacting and communicating with and supporting and assisting top-level administrators. May also be called "directors."

midnight census A hospital patient count taken at midnight each night of the year. *See average daily census.*

midwife *See nurse midwife.*

miedo (Spanish) Fear, dread, or apprehension. An early form of mal puesto, where the victim is usually so frightened that he or she imagines seeing frightful things that do not exist. *See also mal puesto; demencia.*

MIG Medicare insured group. A new approach to Medicare contracting. *See Medicare insured group.*

migraine A severe headache affecting one or both sides of the brain; may also manifest as nausea and disturbed vision.

migrant health center (MHC) A health-care facility (usually a clinic) located in or, if a mobile unit, transported to the agricultural areas where migrant workers work or near their housing. These special medical care systems of rendering care to a highly needy population receive federal funding and state or local support to provide primary health care to migrant and seasonal farm workers and their families.

migration *See migration of pollutants; management of migration.*

migration of pollutants The movement or transporting of hazardous substances from the disposal site by means of air, surface water, or groundwater. *See management of migration; leaching; leachates.*

migration (migrant) studies In epidemiology, this is to assess and analyze the movement of individuals or groups of people from one locale to another by studying the different disease transmission and distribution patterns of both locales based on physical, social, cultural, and biological factors; genetic characteristics; genealogy and family history disease patterns; death rates; and disease patterns in both old and new population groups. The current and past places of residence or origin are compared for similarity and differences in their mortality and morbidity history. Patterns of diseases of large numbers of migrants from the same country or culture are studied and compared as the migrants enter into new living places.

milieu therapy A method of therapy that emphasizes a positive socioenvironmental situation for the benefit of the patient.

Military Assistance to Safety and Traffic (MAST) Begun in 1972, this service uses military helicopters and medical corpsmen to provide emergency medical assistance to civilian victims of traffic accidents and other medical emergencies, especially in rural areas. It is used in Texas, Arizona, Idaho, Utah, Colorado, and Washington.

military hospital Acute-care medical facilities owned and operated by the federal government on military bases, administered by military personnel, and funded by the Department of Defense for treating active-duty military personnel and their dependents. Some civilian personnel work in such facilities, but the hospitals are staffed mainly by military health-care providers, nurses, allied health workers, and health administration personnel.

milliequivalent The numbers of grams of a solute in 1 milliliter of a normal solution; abbreviated "mEq."

milliliter A metric unit of measures of volume equal to 1 cubic centimeter; abbreviated "ml."

minicomputer A computer that is smaller than a mainframe computer and larger than a personal (micro) computer yet can perform the same functions of a mainframe.

minim A unit of liquid measure equal to 0.0616 ml.

minimal brain dysfunction In mental health services, this is a behavior pattern of childhood characterized by learning problems, hyperactivity, irritability, and short attention span.

minimal care unit A nursing unit in some health-care facilities, but mostly long-term-care institutions, that provides treatment to ambulatory patients who are able to care for most of their own needs yet who need nutritional support, help with medications, and some nursing care. *See also personal care.*

minimal differential risk In biomedical research, this is the process of evaluating the difference in risks of treatments. The risk between two or more treatments, therapies, medicines, procedures, or surgical approaches is studied and evaluated to determine how great the risk of one approach is over another or if the risk or an unwanted outcome between the two approaches exists.

minimal services *See services; levels of service; level of care.*

minimum and maximum enrollment In public managed-care initiatives through local public health departments, this is the level of enrollments set by the state department of health services that each local initiative has set to provide a stable volume of business needed to support the participating traditional and safety net providers and to allow the mainstream plan sufficient volume of members to maintain its economic viability while allowing Medicaid beneficiaries a choice. Federal law has established a minimum enrollment level for both the local initiative and the mainstream plan at 22,500. Maximum enrollment limits for either plan are computed by region. *See local initiative; mainstream.*

minimum data set (MDS) 1. In health services research, this is basic research information and the core of data needed and acquired from medical records to conduct retrospective or other research studies. 2. In long-term care and under OBRA, this is a set of screening and assessment elements, common definitions, and coding categories needed for a comprehensive assessment of nursing home residents. The information in the MDS standardizes data and communication about a resident's problems and conditions in the long-term-care facility, between facilities, and with outside agencies. The general categories used to assess each resident using the MDS are as follows: identification and background information, cognitive patterns, communication/hearing patterns, vision patterns, physical functioning and structural problems, continence in the last 14 days, psychosocial well-being, mood and behavior patterns, activity pursuit patterns, disease diagnoses, health conditions, oral/nutritional status, oral health/dental status, medication use, and special treatment and procedures.

minimum deposit business In insurance, this is where the value of the insurance policy is used as a loan to pay the premiums. The policy owners have the insurance company pay their premiums out of the cash value of the policy and bill them for a premium only if there is insufficient cash value to pay the premium.

minimum fragment distance In occupational health and safety, this is the least distance required for the protection of personnel in the open, in an inhabited building, and on public traffic routes from hazardous flying fragments as would be found in an explosion; also used in the military to study explosive devices.

minimum premium In managed care or medical insurance, this is where an employer pays only a portion of the cost of a health plan or insurance policy to the insurance company to cover the cost of administration and services and for a specific stop-loss policy. The employer places payments into a special fund account that the insurance company draws on to pay for claims.

Minnesota Multiphasic Personality Inventory (MMPI) In mental health services, this is a questionnaire-type psychological test for individuals age 16 and over. It consists of 550 true-or-false statements coded in 14 scales ranging from a social scale to a schizophrenia scale. It is the leading measure of mental status used in clinical settings and in a court of law to verify mental illness or absence thereof.

minority elderly In gerontology, this is the subgroup of older adults who experience difficulty in accessing health and social services by being among the underrepresented groups in society.

minority opinion In law, this is a stated deposition that goes against the majority of opinions. The opinion is of such importance that any disagreement is also presented in the form of a formal written statement. It is often used by Supreme Court judges or in formal hearings or meetings where the decisions have an important effect on others.

minority vote In formal health-care meetings or hearings using parliamentary procedure, any votes that represent less than half the assembly.

minor releases In environmental health, these are releases of hazardous substances, pollutants, or contaminants that pose minimal threat to public health or welfare or the environment.

minor surgery In medical care, this is surgery in which the operative procedure is not hazardous and is often done on an outpatient basis (e.g., repair of lacerations, treatment of some simple fractures, and biopsies). *See also major surgery.*

minor tranquilizer A drug used to diminish stress, restlessness, and pathological anxiety without producing any antipsychotic effect. Meprobamate and diazapoxides are commonly used minor tranquilizers.

minutes In JCAHO accreditation, a record of business introduced, transactions and reports made, conclusions reached, and recommendations made. Reports of officers and committees may be summarized briefly or mentioned as having been presented. In either case, a copy of the report is filed in the committee report book and the page number included in the minutes.

MIO *See multi-institutional organization.*

MIS *See management information system.*

miscellaneous expenses Hospital costs, other than for room and board, such as X-ray, drug, laboratory, or other ancillary charges that are not separately itemized.

miscellaneous units In environmental health and hazardous waste management, these are measures of hazardous waste management units where hazardous wastes are treated, stored, or disposed of. These do not include containers, tanks, surface impoundments, piles, land treatment units, landfills, incinerators, boilers, industrial furnaces, or underground injection wells with appropriate technical standards or units eligible for research, development, and demonstration permits.

misclassification In epidemiology and health services research, this is the incorrect placement of data, cases, subjects, characteristics, or values into an inappropriate or incorrect category in the process of tabulation and analysis.

misdemeanor In criminal law, this is an unlawful act or crime of a less serious nature than a felony and punishable by a fine and/or short-term jail sentence.

misfeasance In tort law, this is the performance of a legal act but in an improper or negligent manner; doing an illegal or improper act; doing something wrong or illicit but not necessarily against the law but harmful.

mishap Synonym for "accident."

misjoinder In health law, this is the improper joinder of claims or parties involved in a lawsuit.

mislaid property Equipment, personal items, or property put in place by a rightful owner and then forgotten. Such property is not considered lost.

misnomer 1. A mistake. 2. An error in an explanation. 3. A name wrongly used for an individual or a corporation. When the correct party can be identified. In contract law, a misnomer will not void a contract.

misprision 1. Misconduct in or failure in a public duty. 2. Negligence in one's duty. 3. Negligence, malpractice, failing to carry out the responsibility of a high public office. 4. Failing to report a crime.

misprision of felony Concealing a felony one is not an accessory to.

misprision of office Incompetence or contempt in the administration of one's official office; misconduct in public office.

misrepresentation In health law, this is a false or misleading presentation of oneself. A statement that is not known to the individual to be false as made is an innocent misrepresentation. Knowingly making a false or untrue statement is a fraudulent misrepresentation. The use of misleading statements to induce a prospective purchase is prohibited in any insurance sales practice.

misrepresentation of fact In health law, this is a

false or misleading statement; when a physician, nurse, or other health-care provider deliberately misleads a patient; when a nurse or physician makes an untrue statement about a treatment of procedure to obtain a patient's consent to proceed with treatment when it is felt that the patient might refuse if he or she knew all about the procedure and its potential.

mission In health administration and strategic planning, these are the aspirations and benefits a health-care organization intends to contribute to its catchment area, target population, customers, and community.

mission statement 1. A goal-type statement for health-care organizations and facilities that contains detailed information providing the direction and purpose of the organization; an enduring statement used in strategic planning for health-care organizations that shows direction and serves as a guide for future planning and decision making. A mission statement should contain the philosophy, values, and beliefs of the organization; the organization's desired public image; identification of service area or population; and in some cases the use of technologies, unique offerings or services, commitment to survival and growth, the level and type of services provided, major functions of the organization, special programs or services to be provided, and special formal and informal relationships to be established with other organizations. 2. A written expression that sets forth the purpose of a hospital or a component thereof. It usually precedes the formation of the hospital's goals and objectives or a component thereof (JCAHO for acute-care facilities).

misstatement-of-age clause In managed care or insurance, this is a statement in an insurance policy requiring an adjustment of the amount of insurance payable in the event the owner of the policy misrepresented his or her age.

mistrial 1. In law and the litigation process, this is a trial that has been stopped and invalidated because some fundamental procedure was not followed. 2. A trial that has not been carried through to completion. 3. A trial that the judge dismisses because of a major defect in procedure.

mists In environmental health, these are liquid droplets suspended in the air that are generated by condensation from a gaseous to a liquid state or by breaking up and dispersing a liquid by atomizing; fine liquid droplets of any liquid suspended in the air. Usually, mists range in size from 500 to 40 microns, whereas fog particles are smaller than 40 microns.

mitered corner A manner of folding sheets and blankets into a triangular shape and tucking in the sheets on a hospital bed so that the corners overlap and are well anchored. *See hospital corner.*

mitigate 1. To alleviate; to diminish or reduce. 2. To lower the extent of a decision.

mitigating circumstances Facts that justify a reduction in the charge against a person; providing a more lenient sentence or reducing the damages in a civil suit.

mitigation 1. In law, this is reduction; lowering the severity of a penalty or punishment. 2. In environmental health, these are measures taken to reduce adverse effects on the environment.

mitigation of damages In health law, these are facts or evidence that demonstrate that the amount of a claim for damages is too high, unjustified, or unrealistic.

mittimus The court order used to send a convicted person to prison; a writ that transfers records from one court to another.

mixed liquor In environmental health and liquid waste management, this is a mixture of activated sludge and water containing organic matter undergoing activated sludge treatment in an aeration tank.

mixed model In managed care, this is a health plan that combines two or more types of health-care delivery systems such as when a health plan or HMO uses both a closed-panel and an open-panel delivery system together.

mixed wastes In environmental health, these are wastes that contain both radioactive and hazardous materials; any wastes that meet the definition of a hazardous waste and contain radioactive waste.

mixing zone In environmental health and water pollution control, this is the place where wastes and water mix, not a place where effluents are treated. Limited volumes of water serve as zones of initial dilution in the immediate vicinity of the plant discharge point where receiving (rivers, streams, or lakes). Water quality here does not meet standards.

MLA Major life activity.

MLP *See midlevel practitioner.*

MMACS Medicare Medicaid Automated Certification System.

MME *See major medical expense.*

MMPI *See Minnesota Multiphasic Personality Inventory.*

M'Naughten's Rule In law, this is a test of criminal responsibility that states that a person is not aware of the nature and extent of his or her acts because of mental incompetence and so cannot be held responsible for those acts.

mnemonic 1. Mental devices intended to help one remember something. 2. In computers, this is an alphabetic representation of a function or a machine instruction.

m.o. (Lat.) Modus operandi. Mode or method of operation. *See modus operandi.*

mobile intensive care (MIC) Personnel trained at various levels to provide efficient emergency care to the ill or injured at the scene of an accident and during transportation of the victim to the emergency care center or emergency room. The care provided in a MIC system is provided by advanced life-support teams.

mobile setting A movable structure or specially equipped vehicle used to provide continuing or periodic health-care services in a location selected to ensure geographic accessibility to an identified target population; also, a vehicle used to provide health-care services during transportation of patients (e.g., ambulances, mobile screening units, and mobile birthing center vehicles). *See mobile intensive care.*

MODCO *See modified co-insurance plan.*

mode The number or value that occurs most frequently in a series of numbers or observations that are ordered from least to most; used as a measure of central tendency. *See mean; median.*

mode of transmission In epidemiology, several methods are recognized by which diseases can be spread in a population of susceptible individuals. The following are the most common modes of disease transmission: airborne, contact, enteric, fomites, vectorborne, and waterborne. Airborne transmission results from the inhalation by susceptibles of pathogen-contaminated droplets (e.g., tuberculosis) and dust particles (e.g., Hantavirus) suspended in the air. Contact transmission results from either direct or indirect contact such as touching (indirect transmission via saliva from a rabid dog), a bite (rabies), oral or sexual contact (AIDS), or with an individual (or animal) who is ill with the disease when the disease is in a communicable stage. Enteric transmission results from the ingestion of pathogens, commonly found in feces, by susceptible persons, usually through contaminated hands, food, drink, or water (e.g., typhoid fever or cholera). Fomite transmission results from direct or indirect contact by susceptible victims with contaminated inanimate objects such as a commonly shared drinking glass (e.g., diphtheria) or surgical instruments (e.g., staphylococcal nosocomial infection). Vectorborne transmission results when nonhuman intermediate host and carrier such as a fly (e.g., trachoma or onchocerciasis), flea (e.g., bubonic plague), mosquito (e.g., malaria), or rat (e.g., bubonic plague) transfers disease from one organism to another (e.g., from rat to flea to human). Waterborne transmission results from the ingestion of untreated water that has been contaminated with pathogens (e.g., cholera or shigellosis) by a susceptible individual.

model As used in epidemiology or health education and health promotion, this is when relevant facts, information, and constructs that delineate, organize, and make up a composite of theories are synthesized into a sequence of activities.

model A An automated, computerized system of the national Blue Cross Association for processing Medicare admissions and paying claims.

modeling 1. In health education and health promotion, this is an individual who is looked up to as a standard of excellence to be imitated. The concept is also valuable in the development of health administrators. 2. In environmental health, this is an investigative technique using a mathematical or physical representation of a system or theory that accounts for all or some of its own properties; used to test the effect of changes in system components on the overall performance of the system. *See mentor.*

modem In health information management and computers, this is a device that changes electronic signals that are otherwise incompatible and makes them compatible, thus enabling a computer to receive or transmit information over telephone lines.

modernization In health-care facility physical plant management, this is the remodeling, renovation, or sometimes replacement of health facilities and equipment to bring them up to current construction standards and into compliance with fire and safety codes or to meet contemporary health delivery needs and capabilities. It usually implies no increase in facility capacity (e.g., the total number of available beds would not be increased unless that was the intent).

modification A reduction, change, or alteration; a slight change or revision; a limitation or qualification.

modified co-insurance plan (MODCO) In managed care and insurance, this is when a reinsurer receives its share of premium revenues less the proportionate amount for expenses, overhead, commissions, and taxes. Money reserves are held for the entire policy for the insurance company.

modified community rating In managed care or medical insurance, this is an assessment of the delivery and utilization of a health plan or health services in a certain community or area and is based on demographic data such as age and sex.

modified diet Therapeutic or special preparation of foods for patients who require nutritional modification of food for rehabilitation and recovery or health maintenance (e.g., a salt-free diet).

modified fee-for-service In health-care finance or managed care, this is where the health-care provider is paid on a standard fee-for-services basis but with upper limits placed on the payment by the health plan or insurance company.

modifiers In health insurance and medical records coding, these are adjustments to the description of service that is allowed. They are provided in a procedure coding manual. The use of modifiers permits the physician to indicate those circumstances under which the usual procedure is altered (increased or decreased) and/or the service itself is changed from that described by its five-digit code. The modifier code system is used by the majority of physicians in only a small portion of services because relatively few of the modifiers will be applicable to their practices. Properly used, the modifiers obviate the necessity for more extensive reporting of the modifying circumstances. Specific modifiers are listed at the beginning of each section in the procedure coding manual.

modus (Lat.) Method, manner, or way. The means or system used.

modus operandi (m.o.) (Lat.) Method of operation. A specific technique, a set of circumstances, specific characteristics, or methods of a person's actions; the usual methods employed by a specific criminal.

moiety Half; one of two equal parts.

money market In health-care finance, this is the short-term financial system through which funds are borrowed or loaned for short periods by health-care organizations for special projects or to meet financial needs.

monitor 1. In environmental health, occupational health, and safety, this is closely checking out and observing contaminated areas to determine whether they are safe for workers. 2. In medical care, this is to keep watch on the condition of a patient through close visual observation and to view displays of equipment attached to various organs of the patient's body. 3. A CRT/TV type of screen that presents a display of data, information, or graphic presentation and that is used with computers, EKG machines, fetal heart monitors, etc.

monitoring 1. In health administration and services delivery, this is the constant and ongoing process of surveillance and measurement of utilization, checking schedules, tracking activities, observing outcomes, and assessing and determining compliance and performance. 2. In medical care, this is the close watching and surveillance of patients by personal contact and video camera/TV screen to assess their condition through close visual observation. This also includes tracking and closely following the patterns of physiological response through electronic and technological means using CRT displays, paper graphs, and other displays of the activity picked up by equipment attached to various parts of the patient's body. All this is done to keep track of and closely observe any changes in the patient's status. 3. In environmental and public health, this is periodic or continuous surveillance or testing to determine the level of compliance with regulations and pollutant levels in various media or in humans, animals, or other living things; a set of observation and data collection methods used to detect and measure deviations of current operations; actions intended to detect and evaluate radiological conditions.

monitoring and evaluation According to JCAHO for the accreditation of hospitals, this is an evaluation process designed to help hospitals effectively use their quality assessment and improvement resources by focusing on high-priority quality-of-care issues. The process includes identifying the most important aspects of the care that the hospital (or department/service) provides; using indicators to systematically monitor these aspects of care; evaluating the care, at least when thresholds are approached or reached, to identify opportunities for improvement or problems; taking actions to improve care and solve problems; evaluating the effectiveness of those actions; and communicating findings through established channels (JCAHO for acute-care facilities).

monitoring systems In environmental and public health, these are mechanical, chemical, or electronic sensing devices used to sample, analyze, and provide a record of emissions or process parameters of pollution.

monitoring wells In environmental and public health, these are wells drilled at a hazardous waste management facility or Superfund site to collect groundwater samples for the purpose of physical, chemical, or biological analysis to determine the amounts, types, and distribution of contaminants in the groundwater beneath a site.

monitrend In hospital administration and health-care delivery, this is a program system developed by the American Hospital Association to compare internal data of specific hospitals with other similar institutions within the region, state, or nation.

monogamous A single relationship; a single sexual and love relationship between husband and wife; having a single partner; physicians practicing in a single hospital.

monopoly One organization that controls the manufacture, sale, or distribution of a single kind of good or service.

Montgomery straps In medical care and in patient care, these are special ties used to hold dressings in place over a wound on the body.

moot 1. A hypothetical subject for argument; not genuine, undecided, unsettled. 2. Abstract; not a real dispute. 3. For the sake of argument; a practice situation.

morale hazard Any danger or hazard resulting from a subconscious desire in a person to create loss, harm, or injury; a concern for insurance companies, especially those dealing in liability.

moral turpitude 1. Lewd or immoral behavior. 2. In criminal law, this is a crime that is more than just breaking the law and includes the commission of bizarre acts; acts of baseness or vileness.

moratorium An authorized and enforced delay.

morbidity 1. Disease; sickness; illness; infirmity. 2. The extent of acute or chronic disease, illness, injury, or disability existing in a defined population within a prescribed time. Disease is usually expressed in general or specific rates of incidence or prevalence; used to refer to an episode of disease. 3. The Expert Committee on Health Statistics of the World Health Organization measures morbidity three ways: by the number of persons ill, by the disease experienced, and by the duration of the illness. 4. In epidemiology, these are sickness rates of both acute and chronic disease. The morbidity rate is the number of persons ill in a certain population compared to the total population at risk multiplied by 1000, 10,000, or 100,000, all covering a specific time period. Common morbidity rates are incidence rates, prevalence rates, and attack rates. *See incidence; incidence rate; prevalence; prevalence rate; attack rate; comorbidity; mortality; spell of illness.*

morbidity, compression of In epidemiology, public health, and gerontology, this is the process of diseases occurring more at one time or in a phase of life than others. Children have more communicable disease early in life. Older adults have the good fortune of being healthy in the younger years of life with multiple illnesses occurring in the later years.

morbidity, expansion of In epidemiology, public health, and gerontology, this is the process of disease occurrences being spread throughout life into the very late years of life, especially as people live longer and are healthier.

morbidity incidence rate The number of reported cases of a specific or any given disease during a period of a year per 1000, 10,000, or 100,000 population. An estimate is usually made in the middle of the year. More commonly and correctly referred to as the "incidence rate." *See incidence; incidence rate.*

morbidity prevalence rate The number of cases of a given disease at a particular time per 100,000 population. *See also prevalence.*

morbidity rates *See incidence rate; prevalence rate; morbidity; comorbidity.*

morbidity survey In epidemiology and public health, this is a research approach used to estimate the incidence or prevalence of a disease in a group, population, community, or region. *See prevalence.*

Morgan clamp In medical care, this is a specialized clamp used in circumcision that substitutes for cutting the foreskin.

morgue A special unit found in large hospitals, some public health departments, and county medical examiner departments that provides for the postmortem examination and storage of dead bodies. Cadavers may also be processed and embalmed in this unit if located in a medical school or related setting. *See also autopsy.*

moron An obsolete term to distinguish a level or degree of mental retardation in any slightly retarded individual; a former classification of mental deficiency used to describe a person with an IQ ranging from 50 to 75; a person mentally equal or inferior to a child between ages 8 and 12; the highest classification of mental retardation above imbecile and idiot. *See idiot; imbecile; mental retardation.*

morphology The branch of science that studies the structure and form of things or living organisms.

MORT *See management oversight and risk tree.*

mortality Death; used to describe the relation of deaths to the population in which they occur. The mortality rate (death rate) expresses the number of deaths in a unit of population within a prescribed time and may be expressed as crude death rates (e.g., total deaths in relation to total population during a year) or as rates specific for diseases and, sometimes, for age, sex, or other attributes (e.g., number of deaths from cancer in white males in relation to the white male population during a year). *See mortality rate; perinatal mortality.*

mortality curve In epidemiology and public health, this is a line graph that represents the mortality rate as it changes from age to age. *See population pyramid; mortality table; life tables.*

mortality list In managed care, this is a listing of deceased members enrolled in a health plan, especially those health plans for the elderly.

mortality rate 1. The death rate; the frequency with which death occurs in a defined group of people in a specified time period. 2. Life insurance costs and premiums for individuals are based in part on the mortality rate for a person's age-group. 3. The mortality rate as used in public health and epidemiology is the number of deaths in a unit of population within a prescribed time (usually 1 year) multiplied by 1000, 10,000, or 100,000. The mortality rate formula follows:

$$\frac{\text{Number of deaths in a specific time period}}{\text{Total population in the same time period}} \times 1000$$

mortality statistical tables In epidemiology, public health, vital statistics, and insurance underwriting, these are tables of information on death occurrences compiled from death certificates. Published by public health departments at the state and local levels, these tables show death rates by age, sex, cause, race, income, education, and other characteristics.

mortality table In epidemiology, public health, vital statistics, and insurance underwriting, this is a graphic presentation of the number of deaths per thousand and life expectancy for various ages; tables that show the probabilities of living and dying at various ages in a large population. The table of greatest use in the United States is that of the Commissioner's Standard Ordinary Table of 1958 (CSO).

mortgage In health administration and real estate and property management, this is the legal document by which real estate is offered as security for the repayment of a loan and through which the lender can claim the property if the borrower does not make the loan payments when due; property offered as security for payment of a debt with the borrower retaining the possession and full use of the property.

mortgage bond In health-care financial management, this is a bondholder's claim against a corporation's assets that are sought through a mortgage against the company's property.

morto- Prefix meaning "death."

MOS *See medical outcomes studies.*

motion 1. In the litigation process, this is requesting a court to rule on an issue or provide an order directing some act to be done. 2. In formal health-care meetings, this is a procedure used in a meeting to propose an action. 3. In law, this is a request that the court dismiss the case.

motivation In health administration or health promotion, this is internal drive, innate response, or personal reasons to take action because of the interest or value a person places on the action, behavior, or process.

motivational factors Psychological or personal values that cause a person to take action, do a behavior, participate in a process, complete work, and function and perform a high level of excellence. Factors identified as motivational are recognition, achievement, advancement, responsibility, satisfaction from completing work, self-interest, power, control, guilt, and fear.

MOTNAC *Manual of Tumor Nomenclature.*

motor vehicle In public health and safety, this is any mechanically or electrically powered device not operated on rails on which or by which any person or property may be transported on a long highway. The load on a motor vehicle or trailer attached to it is considered part of the vehicle. Tractors and motorized machinery are included while self-propelled in transit or used for transportation. Also included are motor scooters, motorcycles, motorized bicycles, and snowmobiles (but not airplanes).

motor vehicle accident In public health and safety, this is any accident involving a motor vehicle in transport (in motion, in readiness for motion, or on a roadway but not parked in a designated parking area) that results in death, injury, or property damage.

motor vehicle nontraffic accident In public health and safety, this is any motor vehicle accident that occurs entirely in any place other than a trafficway.

motor vehicle traffic accident For public health and safety, this is any accident involving a motor vehicle, that occurs on a trafficway that is a way or place, any part of which is open to the use of the public for the purpose of vehicular traffic.

MOU *See memorandum of understanding.*

mouth care In long-term care, helping the disabled elderly, handicapped, or bedridden person with oral health activities such as brushing, flossing, and rinsing the oral cavity; usually done by nursing assistants or aides.

movant 1. One who makes a motion. 2. In formal health-care meetings, this is the person who makes a formal motion. 3. One who initiates a motion before a court.

move The act of putting a motion into discussion.

moving averages In health services research, this is a forecasting technique that calculates average health services utilization across two or more past time periods. These averages are then used as a basis for projecting future utilization patterns.

moving motor vehicle accident This is when any motor vehicle accident occurs where at least one of the motor vehicles involved in the accident was moving at the time of the accident. Such accidents are categorized as "traffic" and "nontraffic" accidents. *See motor vehicle; motor vehicle nontraffic accident; motor vehicle traffic accident.*

MPCA Michigan Primary Care Association.

Mr. Gallagher In hospital administration, this is a code word used in some hospitals to indicate a fire. It is announced through the hospital's public address systems to alert the personnel and staff of a fire. The code word is used to not alarm the patients, guests, families, or other persons in the hospital. Most hospitals now have the ability to contain flame conditions and handle fire emergencies when they occur so that all patients in the facility may not need to be alerted unnecessarily. Another term used is "code red."

MRI *See magnetic resonance imaging.*

MR II/IP A hospital medical record information system developed by McAuto, a division of the McDonnell Douglas Corporation, which uses the computer to collect, edit, analyze, and report information from inpatient medical records.

MRP *See medical record practitioner.*

MRT *See magnetic resonance therapy.*

MSA *See metropolitan statistical area; medical savings account.*

MSO *See management service organization.*

MSIS *See multistate information system.*

MUA *See medically underserved area.*

MUA/P Medically underserved area/population.

MUG MUMPS users group. An organization of medical computer specialists who use and work with the MUMPS program. *See MUMPS.*

multidisciplinary In long-term care, geriatrics, gerontology, and health-care delivery, this is one health-care delivery approach that assumes that all disciplines of the various health professions and allied health areas are concerned with and have special application to the older adult. Each of the various health and medical care domains contribute appropriate care for their background and expertise to elderly patients using a total person model to meet all aspects of an older person's needs, including medical and personal care and psychosocial needs. *See interdisciplinary; multidisciplinary team.*

multidisciplinary team According to JCAHO for psychiatric, alcoholism, and drug abuse facilities accreditation purposes, a group of clinical staff members composed of representatives from different professions, disciplines, or service areas.

multifactorial etiology In epidemiology, this is disease causation from many factors, agents, or causes. *See multiple causation.*

multihospital See multihospital system.

multihospital system When two or more hospitals are owned, managed, sponsored, or leased by a single common health-care corporation. *See also multis; multiinstitutional organization.*

multiinstitutional organization (MIO) In health-care organization structuring, this is two or more acute-care facilities under a single management and ownership. Most MIOs are investor owned, and they are quite common in health care because of the need to contain costs. There are significant cost advantages through shared purchasing and laboratory services. They also have an advantage in strategic planning because they gain the ability to compete for a larger market share of health-care and support services.

multilateral Many sided; on many sides.

multiphasic screening In school health, health promotion, and preventive care activities, this is the combined use of a group or battery of screening tests as a preventive measure to attempt to identify any of the several diseases being screened for in an apparently healthy population; used in schools, universities, health fairs, and work sites.

multiple causation In epidemiology and public health, this refers to certain diseases or conditions that may have more than one source, agent, or cause, especially chronic, occupational, and lifestyle and behaviorally caused diseases and conditions. Certain combination of agents or circumstances can create the factors needed for a cause, which leads to an effect. *See web of causation.*

multiple line insurer In managed care, this is an insurance broker who can underwrite all types of insurance including medical insurance with the exception of life insurance.

multiple option plan In managed care and human resource management of benefits, this is one health plan structure or menu offering that allows employees the choice of enrolling under one of several different types of health plans (e.g., HMO, IPA, PPO, or a major medical indemnity plan).

multiple personality In psychiatry or abnormal psychology, this is a term for a dissociative reaction in which a person has two or more distinctive personalities, each often not knowing the others.

multiple risk In epidemiology and public health, this is when more than one risk factor, agent, condition, or circumstance is present to cause a disease, injury, condition, illness, or malady to occur. A combined effect of several risk factors together ensures a greater cause-effect relationship than each risk factor would by itself. An example is that of the combined effects of living in a high-smog area, smoking, and having a family history of lung cancer. As effects of risk are added to each other, the risk of getting the disease increases and may result in a synergistic effect from the cause.

multiplicity of actions In health law, this is act of improperly filing several lawsuits on the same issue.

multiprocessing In health-care information management, this is the simultaneous execution of two or more computer programs by a computer that contains more than one internal central processing unit.

multiprogramming In health-care information management, this is when a program is written to allow more than one activity or task to be executed at one time, even with one central processing unit.

multipurpose senior citizen center In aging services, this is a community center that provides food services (congregate dining), social programs, recreational programs, socialization, support services, and organized activities for older adults.

multipurpose senior services programs In aging services, this is a comprehensive social and health case management to help frail elderly persons remain living in their own homes independently. *See Area Agency on Aging.*

multis Multi–health-care services corporations. Health-care organizations that have many phases, levels, services, or facilities within a single common organizational structure. Such organizations use vertical integration, horizontal diversification, or both. A multi has numerous health-care services and facilities of different sizes, serving different organizational needs, different patient needs or specialty areas, and different catchment areas and target populations. A multi may have a hospital, nursing home, or home health agency in its horizontal diversification and an in-house laboratory and laundry in its vertical integration. *See multihospital system.*

multiservice mental health organization Any psychiatric or psychological institution that directly provides two or more psychologically related services and is not a hospital, psychiatric hospital, or residential treatment center.

multisource drug A drug available from more than one manufacturer or distributor, often under different brand names. Limits on reimbursement are more likely to be feasible for multisource drugs than for drugs available from only a single source. A drug may not be available from more than one source because it is

multispecialty group

protected by a patent, only one company has obtained FDA marketing approval, or the demand for it is such that only one supplier has entered the market. *See also Maximum Allowable Cost Program.*

multispecialty group A medical group composed of three or more physicians representing two or more fields of medicine.

multistate information system In medical records, an automated information system used to interchange mental patients' records.

multithreading In health information management and computers, this is the concurrent processing of more than one command at a time by a computer program.

MUMPS Massachusetts General Hospital's Multi-Programming System. In health-care information management, this is a medical computer language that was developed and demonstrated through grants from the National Center for Health Services Research (NCHSR) and put into practical use between 1970 and 1980. Prior to the development of MUMPS, no such computer language existed for health care. FORTRAN and COBOL did not adapt well to medical use because they required a lengthy process. MUMPS handles a broad range of medical data and is easily updated. The language is flexible and easy to learn, inexpensive to use, and improves the quality and efficiency of health care. Some of its features include time and database sharing and a hierarchical file structure. *See CAPER.*

municipal Local governments; city, town, or village government.

municipal bonds In health-care finance, this is a form of funding or financing issued by a state, city, county, or village. Any interest is exempt from federal income taxes. This is a common source of funding for hospital construction loans.

municipal corporation A city government; a municipality.

municipal hospital *See hospital, city; hospital, city-county.*

municipal law City laws, usually called "ordinances."

municipal local governments Usually city government and its laws.

municipalities From a public health or health services perspective, these are cities, towns, boroughs, villages, counties, parishes, districts, or other public governmental bodies created by or pursuant to state law with the responsibility for the planning or administration of public health, environmental health, solid waste management, or health services; Indian tribes or authorized tribal organizations or Alaskan Native villages or organizations; any rural community or unincorporated towns or villages or any other public entities for which an application for assistance is made by a state or political subdivision thereof.

municipal solid wastes In environmental health, this is the garbage, refuse, sludge, waste, and other discarded materials resulting from residential and nonindustrial operations and activities such as household activities, office functions, and commercial housekeeping wastes.

MUP *See medically underserved population.*

murder In criminal law, this is the lay term for "homicide," which is the general unlawful killing of another human being with malice aforethought. Manslaughter is an unplanned murder with no premeditation or malice aforethought. Second-degree murder lacks the premeditation aspect but is still an unlawful act. First-degree murder is premeditated. *See homicide.*

music therapist A health-care professional who engages physically and mentally ill patients in individual and group musical activities to accomplish therapeutic aims, to create an environment conducive to therapy, and to influence behavior. This professional usually has a bachelors degree in music therapy and is registered with the National Association for Music Therapy.

mutagens Substances that can cause a change in genetic material.

mutate To bring about a change in a genetic constitution of a cell by altering its DNA.

mutatis mutandis (Lat.) With necessary detailed changes. A part of a document may remain the same, but names can be changed.

mutilate 1. To mangle or maim. 2. To damage or injure; to cut off a limb.

mutilation 1. The act of cutting, shredding, tearing, or otherwise destroying a document. 2. To destroy its legal effect. 3. The act of injuring or mutilating.

mutual aid groups Voluntary groups of people who join with peers who all suffer from the same problem. Individual aid is offered to provide support, understanding, and assistance in coping with a chronic disease or disability. Alcoholics Anonymous is one example.

mutual assent In health-care contracting and contract law, this is the amount of agreement between parties to a contract based on the evidence of an offer and acceptance of the contract; an equal understanding of the terms of a contract as understood by both parties of the contract; agreement of both sides of a contract based on whatever a reasonable person making a contract would think the terms of the contract meant. *See meeting of the minds.*

mutual benefit associations Fraternal or social organizations or corporations for the relief of members of the organization from specified perils or costs such as the costs of illness. Such associations pay losses, with assessments on their members intended to liquidate specific losses, rather than by fixed premiums payable in advance.

mutual company A company or business in which the consumers are the owners and also receive profits from the company.

mutual fund 1. A business or company established as an investors' pool. 2. A group that jointly invests money and buys stock in other companies.

mutual insurance company Insurance companies that have no capital stock and that are owned by the policyholders. Earnings over and above payment of losses, operating expenses, and reserves are the property of the policyholders and are returned to them through dividends or reduced premiums. *See also stock insurance company.*

mutuality of contract 1. In health law and contracts, this is the reciprocity of obligation that makes a contract binding. 2. A binding obligation of performance. Each side of a formal agreement must keep a promise to do an act to make a contract binding.

mutual mistake A misunderstanding on the same important issue by both parties to a contract sufficient to negate or void the contract.

MVSR Monthly vital statistics report.

myelogram In medical care, this is an X ray of the spinal cord.

myocardial infarction Heart attack; cardiac arrest; obstruction of the blood flow to an area of cardiac tissue.

mysophobia Fear of germs or dirt.

N

NACHRI National Association of Children's Hospitals and Related Institutions.

NADSP See National Association of Dental Service Plans.

NAEMT National Association of Emergency Medical Technicians.

NAHMOR National Association of HMO Regulators.

NAIC See National Association of Insurance Commissioners.

naive forecasting In health-care delivery and health services utilization, this is a utilization projecting process that has little concern with the causes of utilization, barriers to them, or any related factors that might alter utilization patterns.

naked 1. Incomplete. 2. Lacking authority. 3. Without force.

named insured 1. The person whose name appears on an insurance policy for health, life, or property; the policyholder. 2. The policyholder of an insurance policy.

named peril contract An insurance policy that lists disasters that will be covered by the insurance policy.

NAP-NAP See National Association of Pediatric Nurse Associates/Practitioners.

NAPNES See National Association for Practical Nurse Education and Service.

NAQAP National Association of Quality Assurance Professionals.

narcosis Drug-induced stupor.

narcosynthesis In mental health services, this is to conduct psychoanalysis while the patient is sedated.

narcotic A drug that causes insensibility and stupor while relieving pain.

narcotic blockade In medical care and treatment of substance abuse, this is the use of specific drugs to inhibit the effects of other drugs such as heroin; a technique used in the treatment of opiate addicts.

narcotic drug As set forth in the Comprehensive Drug Abuse Prevention and Control Act of 1970, this is any of the following drugs, whether produced directly or indirectly by extraction from substances of vegetable origin, independently by means of chemical synthesis, or by a combination of extraction and chemical synthesis: opium, coca leaves, and opiates; a compound, manufacture, salt, derivative or preparation of opium, coca leaves, or opiates; and a substance (and any compound, manufacture, salt, derivative, or preparation thereof) that is chemically identical with any of the substances referred to above. The term is used very irregularly, sometimes referring to any drug that dulls the senses and reduces pain and sometimes describing any drug whose use is subject to special governmental control. Narcotics include heroin, morphine, Demerol, and methadone. They do not, by the first definition, include marijuana, hallucinogens, amphetamines, or barbiturates. The narcotics are among the most common causes of drug dependence. See also schedule of controlled substances.

NARL No adverse response level.

narrative notes In medical records, this is a written record that relates, reports, or reviews facts about a patient and that includes but is not limited to observations, patients' reactions to care, and response to treatment.

narrow construction In constitutional law, this is the part of jurisprudence that holds the courts, especially the U.S. and State Supreme courts, to being bound by the literal and exact wording of the Constitution, by the original intent of the framers of the U.S. Constitution, or both. Also referred to as "judicial restraint."

nasal-gastric feeding In medical care, this is the process of passing a tube through a patient's nose into the stomach to provide liquid nutrition for those who are unable to take nourishment by mouth.

nasogastric tube In medical care, this is a tube inserted through the nose and nasal passage through the throat into the stomach to deliver medications, nutrition, or food or to drain secretions.

nati- Prefix meaning "birth."

national accounts In medical insurance, a national group with employees in two or more insurance plan areas that designates one location as the control plan for all enrollment and coverage history for members of that group. Claims received in a local plan are wired to the control plan for payment approval.

national ambient air quality standards In environmental health, these are air quality standards established by the Environmental Protection Association that apply to outside air.

National Association for Practical Nurse Education and Service (NAPNES) An organization concerned with practical nurse education and services. The NAPNES provides accrediting and consulting services for schools involved in practical nurse training as well as educational services.

National Association for Public Health Policy (NAPHP) A nationwide nonprofit professional organization founded in 1979 to improve the health of the people of the United States by helping to develop health policy and to formulate and initiate legislation to implement health policies and supporting measures, all strengthening public health services. The NAPHP helps establish a national health program in three areas: disease prevention, medical care, and standard of living. Policy efforts are directed at supporting local, state, and federal health departments in implementing comprehensive prevention programs; controlling exposure to environmental, workplace, and marketplace hazards; removing barriers to medical care; and promoting healthful standards of employment, income, housing, education, and recreation. National headquarters is located in South Burlington, Vermont.

National Association for Search and Rescue A nationwide professional organization concerned with upgrading and maintaining search and rescue knowledge, abilities, techniques, and skills while supporting and promoting search and rescue professionals. Headquarters is located in La Jolla, California.

National Association of Area Agencies on Aging A nonprofit organization that represents the interests of Area Agencies on Aging. Its mission is to promote national policies that would allow elderly Americans to remain independent in their communities and homes for as long as possible. The primary objective is to provide leadership to area agencies and to enhance their central role in the national network on aging.

National Association of Community Health Centers (NACHC) Administrators, personnel, or professionals who work in or are associated with the operation of community health centers. The activities of the NACHC include education and training, information dissemination, problem solving, shared services, technical assistance, advocacy, research, collaboration, policy analysis and monitoring, and serving as a clearinghouse. National headquarters is located in Washington, D.C.

National Association of Dental Service Plans (NADSP) A national professional organization of professionals in dental prepayment plans developed with the cooperation of the American Dental Association (ADA). It was underwritten by ADA but now is an autonomous agency supported by state dental service plans and dental societies. *See Delta Dental Plan.*

National Association of Emergency Medical Technicians The nationwide professional organization concerned with upgrading and maintaining the knowledge, abilities, and skills of emergency medical technicians (EMTs) and supporting and promoting the EMT profession. Headquarters is located in Newton Highlands, Massachusetts.

National Association of Insurance Commissioners (NAIC) The nationwide professional organization of state insurance commissioners organized and designed to promote consistent and fair regulations that affect the insurance industry. A private organization with no governmental powers, it participates in governmental hearings; sets standards; makes recommendations about rules, policies, and regulations; and applies political pressure to individual state insurance commissioners, legislatures, and the insurance industry to influence decisions regarding various types of insurance such as medical, major medical, managed-care programs, home health care, long-term care, and life.

National Association of Pediatric Nurse Associates/Practitioners (NAP-NAP) The nationwide nonprofit professional organization for pediatric nurse practitioners that provides advancement and continuing education for nurses who are prepared by training, clinical experience, education, licensure, or certification to provide primary care to pediatric patients under the supervision of a physician. This organization cooperates and works in conjunction with the American Academy of Pediatrics.

National Association of Quality Assurance Professionals The nationwide professional organization for persons involved with quality assurance management or related quality services activities. It includes many employees of health-care facilities.

National Association of Urban Critical Access Hospitals The nationwide professional organization that represents hospitals serving a disproportionate share of poverty level and elderly patients, often overutilizing emergency rooms. Such hospitals rely heavily on the Medicare and Medicaid programs for financing. Some 250 hospitals located in urban areas across the United States are of the critical access type.

national board examinations National standardized tests used to assess competence in medical and allied health professionals developed and administered by the National Board of Medical Examiners. They are given in three parts, which are generally taken during the second and final years of medical school and the internship year. Successful completion of the national boards is a requirement for licensure as a physician in some states and an acceptable alternative to the state's own medical examinations in other states. *See also Federation Licensing Examination.*

National Board of Medical Examiners (NBME) An organization founded in 1915 that includes among its members representatives from the Federation of State Medical Boards of the United States, the Council on Medical Education of the American Medical Association, the Association of American Medical Colleges, the American Hospital Association, the armed services, the U.S. Public Health Service, and the Veterans Administration. Members at large are elected from among leaders in medicine throughout the United States. The purposes of the board are to prepare and administer qualifying examinations of such high quality that legal agencies governing the practice of medicine within each state may, at their discretion, grant successful candidates a license without further examination; to consult and cooperate with the examining boards of the states; to consult and cooperate with medical schools and other organizations or institutions concerned with maintaining the advancing quality of medical education; to assist medical specialty boards and societies in establishing measurement of clinical knowledge and competence for purposes of certification and assessment; and to study and develop methods of testing and evaluating medical knowledge and competence.

National Bureau of Standards (NBS) A division of the Department of Commerce, the NBS establishes measurement standards for industry and science that are considered the best and most accurate. Some agencies or entities must follow the standards set by NBS as set by law. This organization conducts research and reviews technology to improve standards. It also provides the approved standards to commerce, federal agencies, and state and local governments.

national capacity variances In environmental health, these are nationwide variances based on inadequate waste management or treatment capacity. The Environmental Protection Agency included provisions in regulations for specific wastes that allow a variance from the land disposal restrictions.

National Center for Health Care Technology (NCHCT) A federal organization established by an act of Congress (P.L. 95623) to provide for the assessment of health-care and medical technologies. The center supports the undertaking of research and synthesizes the results for health-care providers, consumers, industry, government agencies, and any organization in need of such findings and information.

National Center for Health Services Research (NCHSR) A federal organization established to research and analyze how Americans utilize health-care services. Patterns of use, character of health expenditures, cost of health care, the influence of Medicare and Medicaid programs, and related health-care concerns are some of their study activities.

National Cholesterol Education Program A program of the National Institutes of Health, National Heart, Lung, and Blood Institute, that develops and updates recommendations for cholesterol management, educational content, and health areas of concern such as low density lipoproteins (LDLs), coronary heart disease (CHD), high-density lipoprotein (HDL), high fat foods in the diet, physical fitness, dietary therapy, and weight loss.

National Coalition of Hispanic Health and Human Services Organizations A private nonprofit organization dedicated to improving the health and psychosocial well-being of the nation's Hispanic population. The organization provides national leadership in identifying and responding to health and human services needs of Mexican American, Puerto Rican, Cuban American, Central American, and Latin American populations and works with community-based organizations to conduct research, education, and training in areas such as mental health chronic disease health promotion and disease prevention, substance abuse, and maternal and child health. Headquarters is located in Washington, D.C.

National Commission for Health Education Credentialing (NCHEC) A nationwide professional organization, organized in 1988 for the health education profession, that evolved from the work of the National Task Force on the Preparation and Practice of Health Educators, which started its works in 1978, and was charged with developing a credentialing system. The NCHEC has three purposes: 1) to certify health education specialists, 2) to promote professional development, and 3) to strengthen professional preparation. It is organized into three administration divisions representing each of the three areas. The certification offered is that of certified health education specialist (CHES). National headquarters is located in New York City. *See certified health education specialist (CHES).*

National Committee for Quality Assurance (NCQA) A national accrediting body for medical groups, including those affiliated with HMOs, that review quality improvement, utilization management, credentialing, member rights and responsibilities, preventive care services, medical records, administration, and other factors. The NCQA uses a rating of standards approach on completion of the accreditation survey.

National Council for International Health (NCIH) A worldwide professional organization, established in 1971 as a nonprofit organization, that works with health professionals, policymakers, the media, and the public to advance and strengthen the response of the United States to international health issues, especially in developing countries. Headquarters is located in Washington, D.C.

National Council of State EMS Training Coordinators An organization that coordinates communication between the various state EMS training coordinators across the nation. Other activities include working out reciprocity between states, certification and recertification standards, and standardizing and upgrading the system.

national drug code (DC) A nationwide drug and substance classification system used for identification of drugs. The DC is similar to the Uniform Product Code (UPC) classification system.

National Eldercare Developed as a national program to ensure the self-sufficiency of older adults in the community who are at risk by the federal Administration on Aging to fill critical gaps in the system of services and support for older adults and to raise public awareness to prepare for changes in the demographics of the population in the older age-groups.

National Eldercare Institute on Health Promotion Developed by the U.S. Administration on Aging to work cooperatively with the National Eldercare campaign. The institute is to encourage healthful behaviors, reduce the risk of chronic and preventable conditions, and maintain and improve functioning in physically or mentally impaired older adults. The objectives of the institute include serving as a knowledge base and program resource on health promotion, disease, and disability prevention for vulnerable older persons and their caregivers; promoting the effective transfer, dissemination, and utilization of relevant information on health promotion across the continuum of care; providing training and technical assistance on health promotion and aging; focusing on agencies and organizations comprising the national, state, and community of Eldercare coalitions.

National Electronic Information Corporation A private corporation and claims clearinghouse owned by about 30 commercial insurance companies that also provides consultation, direction on medical insurance forms such as the UB-82 (a paper billing form) and UB-92 (a computerized billing form), both developed by the National Uniform Billing Committee and ANSI 837, another computerized billing form developed by the American National Standards Institute. *See National Uniform Billing Committee; American National Standards Institute.*

national emissions standards for hazardous air pollutants (NESHAPS) In environmental health, these are standards set by the Environmental Protection Agency for air pollutants not covered by the National Ambient Air Quality Standards that may cause an increase in deaths or in serious irreversible or incapacitating illness. Primary standards are designed to protect human health; secondary standards are to protect public welfare.

National Environmental Health Association (NEHA) An official national organization for professionals and academicians in the field of environmental health that provides a forum for education, annual conventions, advancement of the profession, training, consultations, input into government standards and regulations, and technical assistance. Members of NEHA work to provide a healthful environment for all and to keep abreast of developments in the fields of public and environmental health and protection. The NEHA publishes the *Journal of Environmental Health*. National headquarters is located in Denver, Colorado.

National Environmental Policy Act A public law established to declare a national policy that encourages productive and enjoyable harmony between man and his environment, to promote efforts that will prevent or eliminate damage to the environment and the biosphere and stimulate the health and welfare of humans, to enrich the understanding of the ecological systems and natural resources important to the nation, and to establish a Council on Environmental Quality.

National Environmental Policy Act Documents In environmental health management activities, these are forms or formal written required papers used to meet this act and supportive regulations. Documents include environmental assessments, findings of no significant impact, notices of intent to prepare an environmental impact statement, record of decision, and categorical exclusion determination.

National Eye Institute (NEI) A division of the National Institutes of Health. This organization conducts and supports research on diseases and normal functioning of the visual system, the eyes, and rehabilitation of the visually handicapped.

National Federation of Licensed Practical Nurses (NFLPN) The official national organization for licensed practical or vocational nurses. Founded in 1949, the federation establishes policy, is the official voice for LPNs, conducts workshops, and holds an annual convention. The NFLPN also represents LPNs in all affairs of the profession relating to its welfare and its role in nursing. Its official publication is the journal *Nursing Care*.

National Fire Protection Association (NFPA) The nationwide professional society concerned with fire safety in homes and in institutions, especially health-care facilities. The NFPA is the organization that developed and maintains the *Life Safety Code*, which sets standards for fire safety in nursing homes and hospitals. The Joint Commission on the Accreditation of Healthcare Organizations relies on The *Life Safety Code* for health-care facility accreditation.

National Formulary (NF) A compendium of standards for certain drugs and preparations that are not included in the *U.S. Pharmacopeia*. It is revised every 5 years and is recognized as a book of official standards by the Pure Food and Drug Act of 1906. *See also formulary; compendium.*

national guidelines for health planning Under the former Health Systems Agency regulations, these were documents on policies and procedures issued by the Department of Health and Human Services as required by Section 1501 of P.L. 93-641. The guidelines concerned national health policy and standards regarding the appropriate supply, distribution, and organization of health resources, and national health planning goals, all which still have some use and applicability.

national health board Under President Clinton's 1994 Health Security Program proposal, this would have been a national advisory and policy board over a federal universal coverage health plan. It would collect data on utilization, outcomes, pricing, and quality information for national use; determine and establish risk adjustments; and set the federally standardized benefit package.

National Health Care Expenditures Study (NHCES) A research project and series of reports on the critical national health policy issues for legislative bodies, government agencies, health planning agencies, health professionals, health administration training programs, and any organization interested in the formulation of health-care policies.

national health expenditures A measure that estimates the amount of health-care dollars spent for all health services and supplies, health-related research, and construction activities used in the United States during a specified time period. Detailed estimates are made available by source of expenditure such as direct payment, private medical insurance, and government medical insurance programs as well as by type of expenditure such as hospitals, physicians, and drugs. Data are compiled from a variety of sources, including providers of care.

national health insurance (NHI) Proposed prepaid comprehensive insurance programs that would be mandatory for all citizens. Coverage would be universal and funded by payroll deductions and government funds. The federal government would be primarily responsible for ensuring medical coverage for all. *See also national health service; social insurance; socialized medicine; managed competition; health security program.*

National Health Planning and Resource Development Act (NHRD) A law passed by Congress in 1974 that created a national health planning system and set forth the governmental mechanism to create the now-defunct health systems agencies, state health planning and development agencies, and statewide health coordinating councils. It also created certificates of need, which were responsible for health planning and resource development across the United States from 1974 through October 1986, when the law was removed. *See also health planning; health systems agency; state health planning and development agency; statewide health coordinating council.*

national health priorities *See Healthy People 2000.*

national health service (NHS) Often used synonymously with "national health insurance." It is referred to as the national health service because it is a health program that the federal government directly operates as a health system to serve some or all of its citizens as a national health insurance program. The government insures or otherwise arranges financing for health care without arranging for, owning, or operating the health service (although NHI proposals usually include some measures of regulation of financed service aspects of the plan). *See also social insurance; socialized medicine.*

National Health Interview Survey (NHIS) Formerly referred to as the National Health Survey (NHS). A continuing health survey by the National Center for Health Statistics of the Department of Health and Human Services that includes studies to determine the extent of illness and disability in the population of the United States. The study describes the use of health services by Americans and gathers related access and utilization information. It conducts a continuing household interview survey of a sample of the population, surveys certain medical records and a sample of the population through health examinations, and conducts related developmental and evaluative studies.

National Health Service Corps (NHSC) A program that places the U.S. Public Health Service personnel in areas of the country with a critical shortage of health manpower for the purpose of improving the delivery of health care and medical services to persons residing in such areas. The corps was established by the Emergency Health Personnel Act of 1970 (P.L. 91-623), as amended by the Emergency Health Personnel Act Amendments of 1972 (P.L. 92-585, Section 329 of the PHS Act). The first corps members were assigned in January 1972. *See also medically underserved population.*

National Health Service Corps programs Services and projects operated by the federal government pursuant to Section 329(b) of the Public Health Service Act, the Manpower Training Act of 1971 (P.L. 92-157), and Section 74(F) of the Public Health Service Act as amended.

National Hospital Panel Survey A study conducted by the American Hospital Association (AHA) each month to gather data from randomly selected member hospitals across the country. An average of 30 hospitals are asked to participate by furnishing information on finances, staffing levels, utilization of services, length of stay, occupancy rates, etc. Findings are distributed to all AHA members on a regular basis.

National Institute of Child Health and Human Development (NICHHD) A division of the National Institutes of Health that is concerned with research and education related to the development and health status of children.

National Institute of Occupational Safety and Health (NIOSH) Under the Centers for Disease Control and Prevention, NIOSH conducts research and studies, makes recommendations for the prevention of work-related illnesses and injuries, and develops standards related to work environment, occupational health, and safety. Established by the Occupational Safety and Health Act of 1970, NIOSH's responsibilities include investigating potentially hazardous working conditions as requested by employers and employees; evaluating hazards in the workplace, ranging from chemicals to machinery; creating and disseminating methods for preventing disease, injury, and disability; conducting research and providing scientifically valid recommendations for protecting workers; and providing education and training to individuals preparing for or actively working in the field of occupational safety and health. NIOSH identifies causes of work-related diseases and injuries and the potential hazards of new work technologies and practices.

National Institute of Standards and Testing A federal research and development organization that sets standards for commerce, industry, and government and tests new technologies to verify quality and set standards.

National Institutes of Health (NIH) This is one of the major institutes under the Department of Health and Human Services that has several subunits, including the National Library of Medicine, the Fogarty International Center for the Advanced Study of Health Sciences, and eleven research institutes that carry out and support programs of basic and clinical research. The eleven institutes are the National Institute on Aging; the National Cancer Institute; the National Heart, Lung, and Blood Institute; the National Institute of Dental Research; the National Institute of Neurological and Communicative Disorders and Stroke; the National Institute of Arthritis, Diabetes, and Digestive and Kidney Diseases; the National Institute of Allergy and Infectious Diseases; the National Institute of Child Health and Human Development; the National Institute of General Medical Sciences; the National Eye Institute; and the National Institute of Environmental Health Sciences.

National Interns and Residents Matching Program (NIRMP) The official cooperative plan for first-year appointments in graduate medical education of the American Hospital Association, the American Protestant Hospital Association, the Association of American Medical Colleges, the Catholic Hospital Association, the American Medical Association, the American Student Medical Association, and the American Board of Medical Specialties. The program operates as a clearinghouse to match preferences of medical students for internships and residencies with available positions in accord with hospital lists of preferences among graduating students. To participate in the program, hospital program directors sign the program's hospital agreement, which commits the institution to participate in the NIRMP as a corporate entity and to list with the NIRMP all programs and positions being made available to students.

National Labor Relations Board (NLRB) An independent federal regulatory commission appointed by the president of the United States with approval by the Senate. Its purposes include the administration of the Wagner and Taft-Hartley Acts when unfair labor relations/union practices arise. The NLRB holds elections for bargaining representatives; supervises union interest elections; holds hearings of complaints of unfair labor and union practices that affect interstate commerce; conducts labor investigations; seeks court orders, injunctions, and cease and desist orders; and files complaints in the courts.

National League for Nursing (NLN) A national official nursing organization with responsibility for improving nursing education and services. Individual membership in the NLN is open to anyone providing nursing care, from registered nurses to nursing assistants, as well as institutional membership for nursing programs to be accredited. Among the many roles of the NLN, it is the official accrediting body for schools of nursing. Its official journal is *Nursing Outlook*.

National Library of Medicine (NLM) A library administered by the U.S. government that collects and maintains a comprehensive library collection on medicine located in Washington, D.C.

National Male Nurses' Association (NMNA) A nationwide organization that promotes education, development, interests, practice, and professional status of males in the nursing profession.

national pollutant discharge elimination system In environmental healh and under Section 402 of the Clean Water Act, this establishes a permit for discharges into water and provides standards by which such permits may be granted.

National Practitioner Data Bank (NPDB) A computerized data bank created by the Health Care Quality Improvement Act of 1986 (HCQIA). The law went into effect in 1990 and created a clearinghouse for malpractice claims against physicians. Three actions are required by the law: 1) any insurance company or private party that makes a payment on a malpractice claim must report it to the NPDB, 2) any board of medical examiners that disciplines or imposes sanctions against a licensed physician must report it to the NPDB, and 3) any medical staff member of a hospital who takes any action affecting a physician's hospital privileges for a period longer than 1 month must report it to the NPDB. Information from the NPDB is available to select entities such as hospital administration, boards of trustees of hospitals, medical staff credential committees, and home health agencies.

national priorities list (hazardous waste sites) (NPL) In environmental health, this is a formal listing of the nation's worst hazardous waste sites as established by the Comprehensive Environmental Response, Compensation, and Liability Act. It includes the EPA's list of the most serious uncontrolled or abandoned hazardous waste sites identified by possible long-term remedial action under the Superfund. A site must be on the NPL to receive money from the trust fund for remedial action. The list is based primarily on the score a site receives from the Hazard Ranking System. The EPA is required to update the NPL at least once a year.

National Registry of Emergency Medical Technicians (NREMT) The organization that provides educational programs for EMTs leading to national certification, establishes qualifications for eligibility to certify, and maintains a national directory of registered EMTs. The NREMT conducts written and practical examinations for the certification of the EMT-A, EMT-I, and EMT-P.

National Reporter System In health law and case law, these are court cases in book form that cover decisions of appellate courts. They are reported by region and include all federal cases and state court cases decided by the court of last resort. For example, the North Eastern Reporter, which covers Illinois, Indiana, Massachusetts, New York, and Ohio, is abbreviated N.E. or, if in the second edition, N.E. 2d.

National Response Center In environmental health, this is the federal operations center that receives notifications of all releases of oil and hazardous substances into the environment. The center, open 24 hours a day, is operated by the U.S. Coast Guard, which evaluates all reports and notifies the appropriate agency.

national response teams In environmental health, these consist of representatives of 13 federal agencies that, as teams, coordinate federal responses to nationally significant incidents of pollution and provide advice and technical assistance to the responding agencies before and during a response.

National Rural Health Association (NRHA) A nationwide professional nonprofit organization, established in 1978, with the primary mission to improve the health care of rural Americans. Membership is composed of individuals and institutions with rural interests who provide leadership on rural health issues through advocacy, communication, education, and research. The NRHA's goals are to create a better understanding of health and health-care problems unique to rural areas; represent and articulate the health-care views of rural America; provide a forum for the exchange and distribution of ideas, information, research, and methods relative to the improvement of rural health; and develop positive solutions applicable at the local, regional, and national levels. National headquarters is located in Kansas City, Missouri.

National Safety Council A national nonprofit organization whose mission is to educate and influence society to adopt safety and health policies, practices, and procedures that prevent and mitigate human and economic losses arising from accidental causes and adverse occupational and environmental health exposures. National headquarters is located in Washington, D.C.

National Society of Patient Representatives An affiliate of the American Hospital Association, this is the nationwide professional organization for patient representatives who work in hospitals as patient advocates and/or with insurance billing procedures. *See patient representative.*

national structured evaluation A systematic assessment of alcohol and other drug abuse prevention approaches implemented nationwide. The Anti-Drug Abuse Act of 1988 authorized several federal agencies to establish substance abuse prevention projects and required formal project evaluations. The key agencies involved in this evaluation process include the U.S. Public Health Service and the Center for Substance Abuse Prevention.

National Student Nurses Association (NSNA) A nationwide professional nonprofit organization established for students in training to become nurses. The organization promotes the cause of student nurse education and their professional development. *Imprint* is its official monthly publication.

National Uniform Billing Committee (NUBC) This is a consortium of health-care providers and third-party payers that created the UB-82, a standardized paper billing form, and the UB-92, an electronic/computerized standard billing form. The NUBC is working toward national uniformity of billing in these and other forms.

national unions In health administration and labor relations, these are the nationwide parent organizations that are administratively over and affiliated with many of the local unions found in some health-care organizations.

Native American One whose family ancestry originates on the American continents; American Indians; the more correct term identifying those people erroneously called "Indians," who are truly from India, not the Americas.

natural barrier In environmental health and solid waste management, these are the physical, chemical, and hydrological characteristics of the geological environment at a solid waste disposal site that individually and collectively act to retard or preclude waste migration.

natural childbirth A very general orientation where the mother is awake and aware at the birth of her child. Although she has gone through some preparation to decrease and minimize the use of pain-reduction drugs, the birth is not painless.

natural death act The law that allows the removal of life-sustaining equipment and procedures from patients with a terminal illness by their request. The patient requests that a written document titled "living will" or "Health Care Durable Power of Attorney" be written and witnessed prior to any illness and entering the hospital. The same effect can be accomplished by a durable power of attorney. *See living will; durable power of attorney.*

natural experiment In epidemiology, this refers to any outbreak of disease that occurs in a population where subjects with different characteristics have common exposures to the disease. Because of natural circumstances, individuals in the population are exposed to the diseases in a manner that resembles a planned research design such as observed by Dr. John Snow in London in his study of cholera. Cholera occurred in one area of the city where people received water from two different water companies. One company supplied upstream water from the Thames River that was more pure, whereas the other got its water out of the Thames in the middle of London, where it was contaminated. Those receiving contaminated water got cholera, and those receiving the cleaner upstream water did not get cholera. Recipients of water subscribed for water at random, as did the manner in which the water company connected water lines to the houses. This random connection process offered random sampling by natural circumstance instead of through planned research design, resulting in the same research effect by accident or through natural events.

natural history of disease In epidemiology and public health, these are the stages that a disease goes through in its course of growth, infection and illness, death, or recovery. Communicable diseases have different stages than chronic or occupational diseases. Communicable diseases are caused by pathogenic microorganisms that cause disease. In upper respiratory diseases, the natural course of the disease has several stages: a period of exposure; an incubation period, where the pathogen grows in the body; a prodromal period, where symptoms begin to appear; a clinical stage called the fastigium period; a defervescence period, which is the beginning of recovery; a convalescence period, where the individual is feeling better but not totally recovered and could relapse; and a final recovery, or defection, period. In the fastigium period, if the person continues to get worse instead of recovering, death can result, completing that part of the natural course of events. Chronic diseases such a heart disease, cancer, or diabetes have their own natural course of development and events, many of which are multifactorial in cause including individual lifestyles and behavior.

natural history study In epidemiology, this is a study of risk factors or variables associated with influencing the course of a disease or condition and developing self-defeating or health-risk behaviors or social and behavioral patterns as they have occurred in the past or as they occur over time without intervention or interference.

natural law 1. Wrongs that are considered immoral, dangerous, or harmful by most societies. 2. Rules of conduct that are the same everywhere. 3. The rules that are basic to society and human behavior. 4. Moral law. *See also mala in se; common law.*

natural person In law, these are the rights of a citizen; a human being; distinguished from an artificial legal creation such as a corporation, which also has many of the rights of a natural person.

natural rate of increase In epidemiology, this is the growth rate of a population that occurs naturally from babies being born while subtracting the deaths. *See growth rate of population.*

naturopath A nonmedical health practitioner who practices therapy using light, heat, water, nutrition, etc. but no drugs in treatment.

naturopathy A drugless system of therapy, making use of physical forces such as air, light, water, diet, heat, and massage, dedicated to restoring or stimulating in the body the person's ability to heal him- or herself. The naturopathic physician will attempt to clear the body of homotoxine (imbalance of vitalizing and disruptive forces) by fasting, provoking vomiting, and applying lavements (internal cleansing). Hydrotherapy, massage, herbal medicines, diet, and nutritional therapy may also be used in treatment. In modern times, this is sometimes associated with chiropractic. *See lavement; clyster; chiropractic.*

nausea The sensation that one has to vomit.

N.B. *See nota bene.*

NBME *See National Board of Medical Examiners.*

NCA National Council on Aging.

NCC Noncomplicating and comorbid (in DRGs). *See complicating and comorbid.*

NCCNHR National Citizen's Coalition for Nursing Home Reform.

NCHCT *See National Center for Health Care Technology.*

NCHS National Center for Health Statistics.

NCHSR *See National Center for Health Services Research.*

NCQA *See National Committee for Quality Assurance.*

NDA *See new drug application.*

NDC National drug codes.

Nd: Yag In laser technology, this is yyitrium aluminum garnet doped with neodymium, which is a man-made crystal capable of producing laser beams.

ne exeat (Lat.) A writ forbidding a person from leaving a local city or area.

near poor Those people who make enough money to meet daily needs but who cannot meet poverty guidelines to qualify for any type of county, state, or federal assistance when an emergency arises. This group of people makes too much money to receive aid and too little money to pay for medical bills, automobile bills, major house repairs, or other emergencies. They usually also have no insurance to help pay for these emergencies.

near surface disposal facilities In environmental health and hazardous waste management, these are landfills or similar land disposal facilities in which radioactive waste is disposed of within the upper 30 meters of the earth's surface.

nebulize Change a liquid, medication, or other substance into a mist or spray.

nebulizer An atomizer or sprayer; a mist maker.

necessary and sufficient cause In epidemiology, this is a concept of causality and association. In disease, illness, disability, or death, certain casual factors are always required to be present for the effect to occur. When the cause is always followed by the effect (i.e., disease, injury, or death), then, for the casualty and association to be ensured, the cause must precede (be necessary), be of enough strength or amount (sufficient), and result in the effect (i.e., disease, injury, or death). *See association, causation, causality, cause.*

necessary cause A condition or factor that must be present or that is necessary for a specific disease to occur.

necessitates immediate medical or surgical intervention In medical care, this is an injury or illness that can cause permanent damage to the body if timely medical or surgical intervention is not done to prevent permanent impairment using the appropriate medical devices.

necro- Prefix meaning "death."

necromania Unhealthy preoccupation with dead bodies. Also called "necrophilia."

necropsy Another term for "autopsy"; occasionally used to refer to the autopsy of animals in medical research institutions.

necrosis The dying of bodily tissue; dead tissue.

NEDEL No epidemiological detectable exposure level.

need 1. An action or item that is essential, indispensable, required, or cannot be lived without. A condition marked by lack or want. The presence or absence of a need can and should be measured by an objective criterion or standard. Needs may or may not be perceived or expressed by the person in need and must be distinguished from demands and expressed desires. Like appropriateness, need is frequently and irregularly used in health care with respect to health facilities, services, and people. In health-care delivery, it is important to specify what thing's or action's need is being considered, by what criteria the need is to be established, by whom (provider, consumer, or third party), and with what effect (as payment for services by insurance or a third-party payer may be a condition on which a provision of service is based). 2. That which is wanted or necessary for health, comfort, or well-being. 3. In medical care, this is an estimation of the interventions or treatment required based on the diagnosis of a problem. In populations, this is the number of people eligible to benefit from the intervention(s), treatments, or procedures. *See also certificate of need; medically needy; medical necessity.*

need assessment 1. In health planning and program development, this is the portion of the plan and program development process that involves assessment of health status, identification of gaps in services, health organization, and goal setting done prior to setting objectives and priorities. 2. An evaluation of a group, population, community, or separate individuals to identify deficiencies both perceived and unperceived. 3. In health administration and human resource management, this is the identification of an employee's shortcomings, lacks, deficits, problems, and challenges that can be met through education, training, and development.

need evaluation A research study used to determine future health-care needs of a given geographical or catchment area in which a health-care organization or system determines which services or programs it should offer to meet the needs of the health-care consumers in the study area. Some studies can be interinstitutional and involve a multi-institutional system.

need for a specific allied health occupation An adequate minimum quantity and quality of persons in an allied health occupation that the consensus of a wide variety of persons believe ought to be available to the citizens of the United States for the purpose of remaining or becoming reasonably healthy.

need for care In health-care delivery and health planning, this is a determination by the health plan or health planning organization of the amount and level of medical care a person or population requires.

nefas (Lat.) Wrong, unjust.

negative averment 1. A negative declaration. 2. A positive declaration in which some negative is used. 3. A statement in the negative.

negative covenant In law, this is when a party agrees and is obliged to refrain from committing an act, usually having to do with the use of real property.

negative operating margin In health-care finance, this is a loss that occurs when costs of operation exceed revenues.

negative pregnant In a testimony, a denial that implies an affirmation of the truth or a fact.

neglect 1. Carelessness. 2. Failure to do that which normally is expected to be done. 3. Lack of due care. 4. Failure to properly care for a child. 5. Habitual lack of attention.

negligence 1. In health law and tort law, this is the failure to exercise reasonable, usual, ordinary, or expected care, resulting in harm or injury. 2. Doing something carelessly or failing to do something that should have been done. 3. The omission of doing what a reasonable person would do, using ordinary considerations that commonly regulate human behavior. 4. The doing of some act, behavior, or activity that a reasonable and prudent man would not do. Characterized by inattention, recklessness, thoughtlessness, wantonness, and inadvertence. The law of negligence is based on reasonable care under all circumstances. Negligence is often referred to in degrees of care or degrees of failure to exercise the proper degree of care. These degrees are "gross," "ordinary," and "slight." These degrees indicate only that certain levels of care or caution are required, but failure to exercise care at a demanded or expected level is negligence. *See tort; malpractice; comparative negligence; contributory negligence; gross negligence; ordinary negligence; passive negligence; slight negligence; subsequent negligence; wanton negligence; willful negligence; reasonable man; standard of care; foreseeability, doctrine of.*

negligence per se In health law and tort law, this is a harmful act or the omission of an act that is viewed as negligent because it is against the law or against the common practice or prudence that any careful person would not have done or made an omission of. Negligence per se is determined by a jury as it examines the law that was violated or how the lack of diligent care, prudence, and proximate cause was exercised to cause damage.

negligence, professional In health law and tort law, this is any harm, injury, or damage caused to another party because of the failure of any professional to exercise that degree of prudence, care, and skill practiced by other professionals in the same profession with similar skill and training and under similar conditions.

negligent 1. Not exercising due care. 2. Careless. 3. The commission of an act or the failure to perform an act that a "reasonable man (person)" would not do under the same circumstance.

negotiable instrument In business law, this is a document that has been signed and that contains a promise to pay a specific sum on demand or at a specific time. Negotiable instruments include checks, notes, drafts, and bills of exchange and must state that they are payable to a specific individual or to the bearer. These documents are covered by the Uniform Commercial Code.

negotiate 1. To bring about a compromise by negotiation. 2. To discuss, arrange, or bargain. 3. Do business. 4. To place into circulation. 5. To tender a negotiable instrument for payment.

negotiated underwriting In health-care finance, this is the bargaining for and sale of bonds by an insurance company on a private basis as opposed to announcing and advertising publicly for bids. In hospital bond underwriting, the deals are discussed and bargained for privately because of special market considerations.

negotiating The process of understanding the agendas, wants, needs, motivations, and positions of the other party to a bargaining session while establishing a baseline and framework for discussion, setting a balance for the interaction that allows a win-win situation for both parties; a fundamental process of contract law and managed-care agreement formation.

negotiation 1. Conferring, bargaining, or discussing a matter by two sides of an issue; a fundamental function of management. 2. Carrying on a win-win discussion and give/take communication by two parties to reach an agreement, compromise, or mutually acceptable outcome in a situation where preferences for outcomes are negatively related, the two parties are interdependent, and the two parties are divided by a conflict of interest and tend to disagree in a relationship that is voluntarily entered into. 3. The process by which a negotiable instrument is presented for payment. 4. In managed-care contracting, this is the bargaining, discussion, and agreements regarding the terms of services provided by health-care providers and payment structures and levels by health plans for contracted HMOs, PPOs, and other managed-care services.

NEIC National Electronic Insurance Codes.

neighborhood health center (NHC) Developed in the 1960s with funds from the Office of Economic Opportunity and the old Department of Health, Education and Welfare, these centers provided comprehensive ambulatory services for special populations consisting mostly of the poor and elderly. The neighborhood health centers were developed to overcome the demeaning, impersonal, and crowded conditions at county hospitals or state medical school teaching hospitals' outpatient services. A broad range of primary and secondary ambulatory care services are provided by salaried physicians and other health-care providers, and emphasis is placed on preventive health care with some nonmedical support services also provided. Consumers were to have a major role in the governing of the facility. These centers are mostly no longer in operation.

NEJM *See New England Journal of Medicine.*

nematocides In public health and environmental health, this is a chemical agent that is destructive to roundworms or threadworms in the nematode family.

nematodes In public health, this is a parasite to humans (e.g., hookworm). These are invertebrate animals of the phylum nemathelminthes and the class nematoda; unsegmented round worms with elongated, fusiform, or saclike bodies covered with cuticle and inhabiting soil, water, plants, or plant parts; may also be called "nemas" or "eelworms."

nemine contradicente (Lat.) No one dissenting or contradicting.

nemine dissentiente (Lat.) Unanimous.

nemo (Lat.) No one.

nemo dat quod non habet (Lat.) No one can give what he does not have.

nemo est supra leges (Lat.) No one is above the law.

nemo potest plus juris ad alium trans ferre quam ipse habet (Lat.) No one can transfer a greater right to another than he himself has.

neo- Prefix meaning "new."

neonatal Newborn; infants from the moment of birth through 28 days. *See neonatal period.*

neonatal death Any death that occurs during the first 27 days of life.

neonatal intensive care In hospital medical care delivery, these are highly specialized levels of care for newborn babies, especially those of low birth weight (less than 1500 grams), the most ill newborns, or those with serious developmental or medical problems. Such newborns must be separated from the regular newborn nursery so that advanced and highly skilled medical and nursing care can be provided under the direction of a neonatologist.

neonatal intensive care unit In hospital medical care, this is a special, highly trained and staffed medical and nursing care unit equipped with high technology and special bassinets or incubator-type cribs with equipment and devices for monitoring premature babies, newborns with medical problems, or infants recovering from surgery. Mechanical ventilation, feeding tubes, oxygen therapy, heart and lung monitors, and intravenous therapy are examples of the advanced care and technology provided.

neonatal intermediate care In hospital medical care, this is a specially equipped and staffed medical and nursing care unit that specifically provides intermediate or recovery care to newborn infants. This unit has special capabilities such as immediate resuscitation, intravenous therapy, prolonged oxygen therapy, and monitoring but is not equipped at the level of an intensive care unit.

neonatal mortality 1. In epidemiology and public health, this is the death (mortality) of live-born children who have not reached 4 weeks or 1 month of age, usually measured as a rate: the number of neonatal deaths per 1000 live births in a given area or program and certain time period. Early neonatal deaths (those occurring in the first week of life) are sometimes also reported. 2. As used in medical care delivery in perinatal care, this is the cumulative death rate of live-born infants within 28 days of birth; 28 days old. *See also mortality; infant mortality; perinatal mortality.*

neonatal mortality rate The numbers of deaths under 28 days of age per 1000 live births. The neonatal mortality rate formula follows:

$$\frac{\text{Number of newborn deaths under 28 days in 1 year}}{\text{Number of live births in the same time period}} \times 1000$$

neonatal-perinatal medicine A subspecialty of pediatrics that focuses on the assessment, treatment, and medical care of newborn infants at and surrounding the period of birth.

neonatal period The interval from the time of birth to the time the infant becomes 28 days of age; the first 28 days of life.

neonatal unit A medical and nursing care unit for healthy newborn infants.

neonatologist A licensed physician who has completed a medical residency in neonatology and who specializes in the area of newborn infants, especially during the first month of life.

neonatology The medical specialty that provides treatment and care for newborn infants in the first month of life, especially those that have low birth weights (less than 1500 grams), the most ill newborns, those just out of surgery, or those with serious developmental or medical problems.

neo-no-fault compensation In health law, this is a no-fault approach to compensation for harmed or injured patients resulting from a bad outcome of medical care.

neoplasm A new growth; a tumor.

nephrology A licensed physician practicing in the subspecialty of internal medicine that focuses on the assessment, treatment, and medical care of diseases, conditions, and disorders of the kidney and urinary system.

nepotism Hiring one's relative.

nested design In health services and biomedical research, this is a study design that combines two study designs to get the best out of both designs. The advantages of a nested design are lower costs and more data acquired in a shorter time period.

net 1. Actual items remaining. 2. Free from charges, expenses, commissions, and fees. 3. In health-care finance, this is what remains after all expenses or debts have been paid. 4. Actual weight, excluding the weight of the container. 5. What remains after everything is deducted.

net amount at risk In insurance and managed care, this the face amount of a policy minus the reserves of the policy at the end of the policy year.

net autopsy rate The comparison of all inpatient autopsies to all inpatient deaths minus all unautopsied cases for the medical examiner or coroner during a certain time period.

net benefit In insurance and managed care, this when there is a surplus of benefits after all costs are included.

net income The difference between a health facility's adjusted gross income and its operating expenses. This may or may not include depreciation figures.

net lease A lease requiring payment of not only rent but also taxes, insurance, utilities, and maintenance.

net loss ratio In managed care, this is used to determine the total claims liability and all expenses divided by the total premiums income, which shows the health plan's or insurance company's loss ratio after accounting for all expenses incurred. The net loss ratio formula follows:

$$\frac{\text{Total claims liabilities and all expenses}}{\text{All premium income}}$$

net migration In public health, health services delivery, and epidemiology, this is the statistical difference between emigration and immigration.

net migration rate In public health, health services delivery, and epidemiology, this is the statistical effect on a city, county, state, nation, or other population of emigration and immigration. The difference is stated as a rate of increase or decrease in a specific population in a specific time period per 1000, 10,000, or 100,000 population.

net national saving In health economics, it is theorized that the more a nation saves in savings accounts or other saving-type investments, the more prosperous and productive a country is. Savings include all budget surpluses at the federal, state, and local government levels as well as undistributed corporate profits. Social Security funds add to these savings reserves.

net patient revenue In health-care finance, this is the gross patient revenue minus deductions for contractual adjustments (patient expenses not paid by insurers), bad debt, charity care, uncollected accounts, and related costs.

net premiums In managed care and insurance, these are the premiums derived from combining mortality rates and interest rates; the profit from premiums, not taking into account operational expenses, agent's commissions, and administrative costs that must be added onto the premium rate to charge enough to make a profit and continue operations.

net present value In health-care finance, this is the evaluation of capital expenditures proposals. It is determined by subtracting the net investment required by a project from the projected cash inflows the project or equipment will generate. If the project's net present value is greater than zero, it is to be accepted. If the value is less than zero, then plans, resources, or services should be adjusted or rejected.

net profit from operations In health-care finance, this is the total income after expenses from operations plus unrestricted contributions and investment income.

net profit margin ratio In health-care finance, this is a measure of how much gross revenue is retained by the health-care organization in the form of a net profit from operations and nonoperating revenue. This is determined by dividing net profit from net operating revenue. The net profit margin ratio formula follows:

$$\frac{\text{Net profit}}{\text{Net revenue}}$$

See operating margins.

net reproduction rate (NRR) In public health and epidemiology, this rate is used to determine population growth as it occurs from one major time period to another or from one generation to the next. The rate is determined by taking the average number of female live births that occur in a population of female newborns during their lifetime based on current fertility and mortality rates, assuming they will remain constant. This rate accounts for the fact that some females will die before completing childbearing years. A rate of 1.0 indicates that enough daughters are being born to allow the population to replace itself over the next given time period.

net revenue In health-care finance, this is the actual income received by the health-care organization as opposed to what is initially posted in accounting procedures. This is equal to gross revenue minus adjustments for bad debts, uncollected debts, charity, and discounts to health plans.

net single premium In managed care and insurance, this is the value of the policy or health plan benefits that are expected to be paid; the amount of money that must be collected at the time a policy is issued to ensure that there will be enough money to pay the benefit of the policy, assuming that interest rates remain the same, interest is earned at the expected rate, and member claims occur at the projected rate.

net total revenue In health-care finance, this is the net patient revenue plus all revenue of the health-care organization, including donations, grants, contributions, endowment revenue, and other revenue not derived from patient care.

networking To make acquaintances in one's professional field; a process used by health professionals to develop acquaintances, friends, and colleagues in their fields to collaborate on projects, serve on boards, and get to know key individuals who are strategically placed in the industry and who may assist one another in accomplishing goals and solving problems or that one can turn to for support, assistance in job searches, or advancing one's career.

network interfacing unit (NIU) In health-care information management, this is a computer-linking device that streamlines hospital information systems. Developed jointly by researchers at the University of California at San Francisco and the Applied Physics Laboratory at Johns Hopkins University. The device enables dissimilar computer systems to plug into a network to allow two different computers to "talk" to each other.

network model In managed care, this is a health maintenance organization or preferred physician provider program that contracts with two or more independent medical groups to provide physician services under a managed-care contract.

network model HMO In managed care, this is when a health maintenance organization contracts with two or more single or multispecialty physician medical groups for patient care services. Physicians use their own offices, clinics, and facilities and may see non–managed-care patients.

net worth In health-care finance, this is the difference between total assets and liabilities of an individual, hospital, nursing home, corporation, etc.

neuroleptic A major tranquilizer. *See antipsychotic drug.*

neurologic Pertaining to the nervous system.

neurological surgery *See neurosurgery.*

neurologist A physician who has a board certification and the required graduate medical residency specializing in disorders and diseases of the brain, spinal cord, and all parts of the nervous system.

neurology The medical specialty dealing with disorders and diseases of the brain, the spinal cord, and the human nervous system.

neuromagnetometer In medical care, this is a new device for imaging brain function by detecting magnetic fields created by the brain's electrical activity. This technology is noninvasive and is less expensive than other imaging devices yet has equal or better resolution.

neuropathology A subspecialty of the medical field of pathology that focuses on the diagnosis and treatment of all diseases, conditions, and disorders of the brain and spinal cord and disease states in all other parts of the nervous system.

neuropsychiatry A medical specialty that incorporates psychiatry and neurology.

neurosis A form of mental illness characterized by anxiety. Although neuroses do not overtly distort reality, they can be severe enough to impair one's effectiveness and functioning. Types of neurosis include anxiety, hysterical, phobic, obsessive-compulsive, depressive, neurasthenic, depersonalization, and hypochondriacal. This term is of limited use in psychiatric diagnosis because of its vagueness and has mostly been eliminated from use.

neurosurgeon A physician specialist who has completed a residency and is board certified and specializes in surgical diagnosis and surgical treatment of diseases, conditions, and disorders of the brain, spinal cord, and all parts of the nervous system.

neurosurgery A medical specialty that is involved in the process of diagnosis and surgical treatment of diseases and disorders of the brain, spinal cord, and all other parts of the nervous system.

newborn Those infants that are alive from the moment of birth through 28 days. *See neonatal; neonatal period.*

newborn boarder baby In health-care delivery and hospital medical care, this is a newborn who has to stay in the hospital much longer than the average length of stay common to the normal healthy baby because of illness, prematurity, or underdevelopment. The mother is discharged from the hospital, and the newborn baby remains in the nursery under the care of nurses. Such circumstances are very costly, especially under capitated or managed-care contracts. The long stay deprives the mother of nurturing the infant and interferes with bonding.

new drug A drug for which premarketing approval is required by the Federal Food, Drug, and Cosmetic Act. A new drug is any drug that is not generally recognized, among experts qualified by scientific training and experience to evaluate the safety and effectiveness of drugs, as safe and effective for use under its prescribed conditions of use. Since 1962, most new prescription drugs have been subject to the new drug application and premarket approval process. The vast majority of drugs marketed over-the-counter, however, have not been through the new drug approval process. *See also GRAS; GRAE; not new; "me too" drug.*

new drug application (NDA) An application that must be approved by the FDA before any new drug is marketed to the general public. Once the application is approved, the drug may be prescribed by any physician or other health professional authorized to prescribe under state law. The NDA must include reports of animal and clinical investigations; a list of ingredients including the active drug and any vehicle, excipient, binder, filler, flavoring, and coloring; a description of manufacturing methods and quality control procedures; samples of the drug; and the proposed labeling. Approval of an NDA must be based on valid scientific evidence that the drug is safe, usually through adequate and well-controlled clinical studies (such as random sample controlled trials or blind studies) demonstrating that it is effective for its intended uses. An NDA commonly refers to the FDA's approval of an application (i.e., the manufacturer's license to market the drug). *See also investigational new drug.*

New England Journal of Medicine A leading current periodical covering medicine, epidemiological studies, and public health, published weekly by the Massachusetts Medical Society.

new illness In medical care insurance for the purpose of determining financial reimbursement, this is an illness that begins with a series of office visits separated by 120 days from the date of the last visit.

New Jersey rule A form of tort reform, this is a ruling by the Supreme Court of New Jersey that held that contingency fees must be scheduled according to the size of the award with the percentage of the award going to the claimant's lawyer declining as the size of the award increases. For example, in New Jersey, lawyers may receive 50% of a $1000 settlement but only 10% of any amount recovered over $100,000. A number of states have adopted variations of the New Jersey rule.

new matter New issues or facts that have not previously been alleged in a pleading.

new patient One new to the physician, office, or facility. The initial comprehensive history and examination need not be done at the time of the first visit.

newspaper policy Life or health insurance sold in newspapers.

next cause In health-care law and tort law, this is the closest or most related cause of harm or injury; the proximate cause. *See also proximate cause.*

next friend A person not formally appointed who acts on behalf of or represents one who is legally incapable or is disabled such as an infant or someone who is retarded.

next of kin Family or those closely related to a dead person, usually the spouse, children, or brothers and sisters.

nexus (Lat.) A connection; a link in a series; a joining.

NF *See National Formulary.*

NFLPN *See National Federation of Licensed Practical Nurses.*

NFPA National Fire Protection Association.

NGA National Governors Association.

NHC *See neighborhood health center.*

NHI *See national health insurance.*

NHL National Health Lawyer Association.

NHRD *See National Health Planning and Resource Development Act.*

NHS *See National Health Survey; national health service.*

NHSC *See National Health Services Corps.*

NIA National Institute on Aging.

NICU Neonatal intensive care unit.

night In vehicular safety, this is the time interval between sunset and sunrise.

night care In hospital medical care, this is a special unit or administrative arrangement offered to patients allowing them to spend nighttime hours in a nursing care unit of a health-care facility to receive treatment and therapy.

night hospital 1. A halfway house facility. 2. A part-time hospital in which psychiatric patients are allowed to work and function in the outside community during the day and work hours and then return to the hospital at night.

Nightingale, Florence The founder of the profession of nursing, Nightingale (1820–1910) established nursing as an integral part of health care during the Crimean War. She established the first school of nursing at St. Thomas's Hospital in London, setting high education and nursing standards. Her contribution to medical records and health-care administration was done by showing the importance of the statistical analysis of hospital medical records, as she was also a hospital administrator (superintendent). She was noted for her two publications: *Notes on Hospitals* and *Notes on Nursing*. Her contribution to public health was through her cause of promoting sanitation measures in India.

Nightingale ward In hospital administration, nursing services, and health-care delivery, this is a special hospital unit design suggested by Florence Nightingale. Ward size was limited to promote air circulation, sanitation, cleanliness, and patient comfort. Though wards are not used much in modern hospitals, the notion of limiting patient interaction, windows, proper lighting, and patient comfort are now central to hospital construction and administration.

night terror In psychiatry, this is a sleep disturbance characterized by sweating, talking incoherently, crying, sleepwalking, and often showing fear or talking about fearful situations. This is not a nightmare because the person does not remember any part of the night terror, whereas nightmares cause no physical reaction and are remembered.

NIH *See National Institutes of Health.*

nihil (Lat.) Nothing.

nil (Lat.) Nothing.

NIMBY Not in my back yard. A saying used to describe the reaction of citizens who do not want a mental health clinic, halfway house, group home, etc. in their neighborhoods or who oppose the construction of a nuclear reactor, sanitary landfill, hazardous waste site, or other public health facility, etc. near their homes, areas, or towns.

NIMH National Institute of Mental Health.

NIOSH *See National Institute of Occupational Safety and Health.*

NIRMP *See National Interns and Residents Matching Program.*

nisi (Lat.) Unless. In law, this is a court order that will be enforced unless the person named appears in court to show cause why it should not be enforced.

nisi prius court (Lat.) A court that conducts a trial with a judge and a jury. This court is distinguished from an appellate court.

nitrates In environmental health, these are compounds containing nitrogen that can exist in the atmosphere or as a dissolved gas in water and that can have harmful effects on humans and animals. Nitrates in water can cause severe illness in infants and cows.

nitrification In environmental health, this is the process whereby ammonia in wastewater is oxidized to nitrite and then to nitrate by bacterial and chemical reactions.

nitrites In environmental health, this is an intermediate in the process of nitrification; nitrous oxide salts used in food preservation.

nitrogen dioxide (NO_2) In environmental health, this is the result of nitric oxide combining with oxygen in the atmosphere, resulting in the brown cloud seen in air pollution; a major component of photochemical smog.

nitrogenous wastes In environmental health, these are any animal or vegetable residues that contain significant amounts of nitrogen.

nitrogen oxides (NO) In environmental health, this is a product of combustion from transportation (mostly automobiles) and stationary sources (industrial plants) and is a major contributor to the formation of ozone in the troposphere and acid deposition.

NIU *See network interfacing unit.*

NLADA National Legal Aid and Defender Association.

NLM National Library of Medicine.

NLN *See National League for Nursing.*

NLRA National Labor Relations Act.

NLRB *See National Labor Relations Board.*

NM Nuclear medicine.

NMA National Medical Association.

NMCUES *See National Medical Care Utilization and Expenditures Survey.*

NMR *See nuclear magnetic resonance.*

NMRI Nuclear magnetic resonance imaging.

NNHS National Nursing Home Survey.

no adverse response level (NARL) In environmental health, this is a measure of the level of soil contamination. Through animal studies it is determined if hazardous waste embedded in the soil is below the level hazardous to humans or if it will have any adverse effects on humans.

no code order In medical care, this is a "do not resuscitate" order given for certain patients at their own or their family's request. A clear notice attached to the outside of the medical record is often done as a means of notifying the nursing and medical staff. *See Natural Death Act; living will.*

no contest Not challenged. *See nolo contendere.*

nocti- Prefix meaning "night."

nocturnal enuresis The lack of control of the bladder at night while sleeping; bedwetting.

no epidemiological detectable exposure level In environmental health, this is a phrase that describes toxic levels of hazardous material in polluted soil. Developed by the Montana Department of Health and Environmental Sciences in conjunction with the Centers for Disease Control and Prevention, this measures human environmental exposure to toxic substances in polluted soil and is used to determine if the exposure is at high enough levels to have toxicity and to produce symptoms in the exposed cases.

no-fault insurance 1. Automobile insurance that provides coverage against injury or other loss without the need to determine responsibility for an accident. Coverage and benefits vary widely and exist in only a few states. 2. One suggested proposed solution to tort reform, especially in medical malpractice suits and litigation where courts are not used to determine fault but a certain amount of money is awarded to the individual patient without a formal trial.

noise Any unwanted sound.

nolle prosequi (Lat.) In law, this is a plaintiff or a prosecutor deciding and announcing that he or she will not further prosecute a pending case. When a case ends, it is nolled or nolled prossed.

nolo contendere (Lat.) I will not contest it; no contest. In criminal law, this is admitting only part of the guilt or being guilty indirectly without admitting guilt.

nomenclature A system of terms or labels used to classify or describe an object or device; system of names used in a branch of science.

nominal 1. Slight, small, token amount. 2. Not real or substantial; in name only.

nominal damages In health law, this is compensation given to the plaintiff when the case is proven but the actual injury or loss was not proven.

nominal group process In health care marketing or community health services development, this is an interactive group technique used to increase creative thinking and decision making; to combine individual effort such as in assessing community needs. The method involves bringing consumers or patients together in groups to present their opinions without any critique from the group such as in a brainstorming session. The results are then rated by the group through a confidential written response, which reduces interference and minimizes bias on the ratings from interpersonal dynamics and social status.

nominal scale In descriptive statistics as used in epidemiology and public health, this is a means of classifying observations into separate categories such as sex, age, race, types of disorders, diagnoses, and procedures.

nomination In formal health-care meetings or organizations using parliamentary procedure, this is the presentation of an official proposal indicating a person as a candidate for an office or position of an organization or assembly.

nomogram In health services research or epidemiology, this is an uncommon statistical technique consisting of a line graph presenting scales for the variables involved. The line is drawn in such a way that corresponding values for each variable lie in a straight line intersecting all the scales.

non (Lat.) Not.

non- Prefix meaning "not"; giving a negative direction or force to a root word.

nonage Not yet of legal age; still a minor. *See age of majority.*

nonassertion As used in communication in health services and assertiveness training, this is to violate one's own rights by not expressing honest feelings, thoughts, and beliefs and permitting others to take unfair advantage. Expression of one's thoughts and feelings in an apologetic, indifferent, self-effacing manner so others can easily disregard them; to appease others to avoid conflict.

nonassigned Health-care providers who will not accept patients or programs under certain health-care programs administered by the federal government such as Medicare or Medicaid.

nonattainment areas In environmental health and air pollution, this is any geographical or political area that is shown by monitored data or that is calculated by air quality modeling (or other methods determined by the administrator to be reliable) to exceed any national ambient air quality standard for such pollutant; any geographic areas that do not meet one or more of the National Ambient Air Quality Standards for the pollutants set forth in the Clean Air Act.

noncancelable and guaranteed renewable policy An insurance policy that the insured has the right to continue in force to a specified age by the timely payment of premiums. During the specified period that the policy is in force, the insured has no right to make any unilateral change in any provision of the policy.

noncan insurance A special type of health and medical insurance that is not cancelable and is guaranteed to be renewable at a specified premium.

noncommunity hospitals Acute-care health-care facilities including federal government hospitals, long-term-care hospitals, hospital units of institutions, psychiatric hospitals, tuberculosis hospitals, respiratory hospitals, rehabilitation hospitals, chronic disease hospitals, facilities for substance abuse and alcoholism, and institutions for the mentally retarded. The four major categories of hospitals included in this category are federal government, nonfederal government, not-for-profit nongovernment, and for-profit/investor owned.

noncommunity water systems In environmental health, these are public water systems that do not serve city or community housing but are systems for water supplies to camp sites, national parks, etc.

noncomplicating and comorbid (in DRGs) *See complicating and comorbid.*

non compos mentis (Lat.) 1. Not of sound mind. 2. Insane; suffering a mental illness. *See also insanity.*

nonconcurrent study In epidemiology, this is used synonymously with "historical cohort study." *See historical cohort study.*

nonconfining sickness In managed care and medical insurance, this is an illness that prevents the insured person from working but does not result in confinement to a hospital or to one's home.

nonconforming beds In hospitals, nursing homes, or other licensed or accredited health-care facilities, these are beds that are deficient according to regulations, certification, or accreditation standards because of unsuitable structural frames, missing fire and safety devices, being housed in unsuitable rooms or environment, or lacking appropriate ancillary services.

noncontact cooling water In environmental health, this is water used for reducing the temperature of a manufacturing process where the water used in the cooling process does not come in direct contact with any raw material, intermediate product, waste product, or finished product yet may come out of the plant in a heated state.

noncontact cooling water pollutants In environmental health, this is when water used for reducing the temperature of a manufacturing process does not come in direct contact with any raw material, intermediate product, waste product, or finished product yet is polluted and/or heated, alerting one to other possible sources of pollution in the water.

noncontributory *See noncontributory benefit plans.*

noncontributory benefit plans 1. In managed care and human resource management, these are fringe benefit plans paid for by the employer such as a medical care plan being totally paid for by the employer with no worker contribution required. 2. In managed care, this is a group insurance plan financed entirely by the group policyholder. Under such a plan, the enrollment of group members is automatic, and all eligible group members are covered.

noncontributory insurance Group medical insurance for which the employer pays the entire premium.

noncontributory plans *See noncontributory benefit plans.*

nonconventional pollutants In environmental health, these are any pollutants that are not listed or that are poorly understood by the scientific community.

nondelegated hospital A hospital for which all Professional Review Organization (PRO) program health-care review activities are performed by a PRO. *See Professional review organization.*

nondetects In environmental health, these are chemicals that are not detected in a particular sample above a certain limit.

nondirective counseling In mental health care and psychotherapy, this is process of skillfully listening to a disturbed client/employee, encouraging him or her to share problems or concerns, listening for understanding with empathy, and guiding yet allowing the individual to arrive at his or her own appropriate solutions.

nondirectory (structured) In health information management and computers, this is a storage volume set up sequentially with no directory for it as a volume. File information such as file name, type, length, and date are in each file on the volume. Volumes can include diskette, disk, magtape, or cassette.

nondisabling injury An injury or illness that may require medical care but does not produce loss of working time or income.

nondisclosure 1. Failure to disclose. 2. Not telling all the facts.

non-dissent No one dissenting.

nonduplication of benefits In managed care, this is when a patient is covered under more than one health plan or one group of medical or dental insurance programs where the carrier with a nonduplication provision, as distinguished from a coordination of benefits provision, assumes no liability, frequently leaving the patient with out-of-pocket expenses.

nonexclusive territory In insurance, this is the use of a general agency system in which an insurance company having several general agents may represent the same insurance company.

nonexempt distinct part unit In a hospital, this is usually an extended care unit, often a separate wing of the facility certified by Medicare or Medicaid that has a different pay rate structure than regular Medicare patients in the main inpatient beds of the hospital. This unit is viewed by the payment sources as a separate facility; thus patients are discharged and readmitted to the distinct part as a transfer-in as if it were a different facility. *See distinct part.*

nonfatal cases without lost workdays In occupational safety and health (OSHA), these are cases that do not involve fatalities or lost workdays but result in medical treatment other than first aid, loss of consciousness, transfer to another job, or diagnosis of occupational illness.

nonfatal injury accident In safety and public health, this is an accident in which at least one person is injured and no injury results in death.

nonfeasance 1. In health and tort law, this the failure to perform a duty or act that one is required to perform; failure to perform a required duty. 2. When a professional is required to perform a duty and fails to do so.

nonfederal Agencies, programs, health facilities, institutions, or organizations not operated by the U.S. government.

nonfederal government hospital Acute-care health-care facilities that are operated by state or local governments but are not operated by the U.S. government. *See community hospital; nonprofit hospital; hospital.*

nonfile-structured device A device such as line printer or terminal on which data can be organized as if in multiple files.

nonforfeiture options In insurance, these are the different approaches or ways used to get policy owners the cash value of an insurance policy due to them.

nongovernment not-for-profit hospitals Acute-care, short-stay health-care facilities that have 501(b) nonprofit organization tax status. Such hospitals usually include community hospitals, religious affiliated hospitals, cooperative hospitals, and health-care institutions owned and managed by fraternal societies.

nonhospital ambulatory care organization In health-care delivery, this is any walk-in, outpatient 1-day treatment center, clinic, or facility that operates as and is accredited under the designation of an ambulatory care center and is accredited as a separate organization by JCAHO.

noninvasive Not entering the body. In medical care, this is any diagnostic or treatment procedure or technique that does not enter or penetrate the tissues of the body, including having no needle pricks, punctures, or surgical cuts in the process.

noninvasive cardiac assessment In the delivery of medical care, these are the studies, evaluations, and testing activities concerning the healthy functioning of the heart that do not cut into or enter the internal parts of the body or heart. Such assessment activities include stress testing, stress EKG, exercise stress evaluation, echocardiography, CT scans, and MRI imaging.

nonledger accounts In health-care finance, these are used to record assets and liabilities not affected by cash transactions.

nonmaternal death The death of a woman that is indirectly related to the childbirth process but is not directly related to the actual childbirth and that occurs in a hospital or birthing center. *See also death rate.*

nonmedical application In medical insurance and managed care, this is an application completed by a potential member in which he or she is not required to go through a medical exam.

nonmetropolitan area A standard statistical area for a small community or county that contains a population of less than 50,000 as determined by the federal Office of Management and Budget. *See metropolitan statistical area.*

nonmetropolitan statistical area Any rural area that is not included under the metropolitan statistical area designation. *See nonmetropolitan area.*

nonmoving motor vehicle accident In the assessment of motor vehicle accidents, this is any motor vehicle accident where, at the time of the accident, the vehicle was stationary and not moving.

nonobservable adverse effect In environmental health, this is when, in a dose response experiment, the experimental exposure level represented the highest level tested at which no adverse effects were demonstrated.

non obstante verdict (NOV) (Lat.) Notwithstanding the verdict. In the legal procedures of a court, this is when a judge overrules a jury by rendering the judgment in a lawsuit to one side when the jury gave the verdict to the other side.

nonoccupational policy A contract that insures a person against off-the-job accident or sickness. It does not cover disability resulting from injury or sickness covered by workers' compensation. Group accident and sickness policies are frequently nonoccupational.

nonoperating revenue In health-care finance and hospital administration, the monies from patient care, patient medical and nursing services, or sale of goods used in the provision of health care that are not directly related to the actual day-to-day operation of the hospital. These may include endowed funds, gifts, interest, or profit from for-profit holding companies.

nonoperating revenue ratio In health-care finance and hospital administration, this a ratio formula used to help monitor the financial stability of a hospital. The ratio indicates how dependent a hospital is on nonoperating revenue such as unrestricted donations, grants, gifts, or investment income. The calculation of this ratio and the implications of its results indicate if hospital operations are the source of revenue loss. If multiplied by 100, making the findings a percentage, and if the percentage is large and is an increase from past percentages, this suggests that the hospital may be having financial problems caused by patient-generated revenue being down or that gifts, donations, and grants are up. If the percentage is high, the hospital is relying more on nonoperating revenue for its survival than is wise to do from a financial management point of view. Nonoperating revenue formulas follow:

$$\frac{\text{Nonoperating revenue}}{\text{Net profit}} = \text{Ratio}$$

$$\frac{\text{Nonoperating revenue}}{\text{Net profit}} \times 100 = \text{Percentage}$$

nonoperational storage tanks In environmental health, this is any underground storage tank in which regulated substances will not be deposited or from which regulated substances will not be dispensed.

nonownership liability When a liability occurs, even when the hospital or health-care facility does not own the property whose use has caused damage, harm, injury, or loss to another's property or person.

nonparametric data In epidemiology, this a form of descriptive statistics that uses nominal and ordinal scale data to make inferences about values or information of a group or population. Data that are not useful or appropriate for parametric data defaults to and is analyzed as nonparametric data.

nonparticipating hospital A hospital that has not contracted with a reciprocating health plan.

nonparticipating insurance company See stock insurance company.

nonparticipating policy In insurance, this is the typical insurance policy (e.g., term insurance) in which the policyholder does not share in the surplus revenue.

nonparticipating provider (NON-PAR) In managed care, this is a health-care provider who has not entered into a contract with a managed-care health plan to render services under a group subscriber agreement.

nonparticipating provider indemnity benefits In managed care, this is a type of medical care coverage that pays for services provided by health-care providers not under contract with the health plan. Member benefits are covered on an indemnity basis, usually with high co-payments and deductibles.

nonpathogen A microorganism that is not disease producing.

nonphysician health-care providers Any healthcare professional who does not hold a doctor of medicine, doctor of osteopathy, or equivalent degree yet is qualified or licensed to provide direct patient care. Included are nurses, psychologists, physical therapists, respiratory therapists, social workers, etc.

nonphysician practitioners This includes dentists, podiatrists, clinical psychologists, nurse midwives, and chiropractors who are allowed some medical staff privileges in a hospital. According to JCAHO, only podiatrists and dentists/oral surgeons usually have full admission authority and privileges; others have limitations on their medical staff privileges.

nonpoint sources In environmental health, these are diffuse water pollution sources and do not have a single point of origin or are not introduced into a receiving stream from a specific outlet. The pollutants are generally carried off the land by storm water runoff. The commonly used categories for nonpoint sources are agriculture, forestry, urban, mining, construction, dams and channels, land disposal, and saltwater intrusion.

nonprobability samples A nontraditional sampling technique that allows an arbitrary choice approach to sampling. This diminishes the objectivity of the sample.

nonprofit 1. Any nongovernment school, institution, agency, organization, corporation, religious organization, or association in which no part of the net earnings goes to an individual or benefits any private shareholder or individual. 2. An Internal Revenue Service tax status (501)b designation of an organization that requires the overattained funds to be reverted back into the organization so that no shareholder or individual can gain profits from it. Church-related and community hospitals are usually nonprofit organizations.

nonprofit hospital Any hospital corporation that turns its profits back into the hospital and has a nontaxable status. It is usually community owned or owned by a church or society or other service-oriented organization; hospitals with a nonprofit status (501)b as determined by the Internal Revenue Service. *See also proprietary hospital; nonprofit voluntary hospital; community hospital.*

nonprofit voluntary hospital Any short-stay acute-care inpatient health-care facility that has oversight from the community through a board of directors who represent the community and is a not a governmental, religious, or for-profit hospital; a community hospital. *See community hospital.*

nonproportional reinsurance In group medical insurance and life insurance, this is where the proportion of the risk carried by the main insurance company and the proportion of the risk carried by the reinsurer are not known to either party at the time the reinsurance treaty is completed.

nonproprietary (nonprofit) nursing home A long-term-care facility that has an Internal Revenue tax status as nonprofit. It turns all overattained funds back into the institution instead of going to owners or stockholders. Often this type of facility is operated by a religious or fraternal organization. *See also nursing home.*

non prosequitur (Lat.) 1. He does not follow up. 2. In law and the litigation process, this is a judgment given to a defendant because the plaintiff has failed to follow up on a lawsuit or claim that has been filed. 3. A default judgment.

nonredundant data In health-care information management, this is information, numbers, or statistical information that appears a minimum number of times in a database, is easily accessible in case more information is needed, and has more information than the master file contains.

non repet (Lat.) Do not repeat.

nonrevenue producing cost centers In health care financial management, these are those departments, programs, units, or support services that have a high overhead, that provide necessary services to the overall function of a full-service hospital, and that are essential but do not produce income (such as social services).

non–service-connected disability In the Veterans Administration health-care program, a disability that was not incurred or aggravated in the line of duty during active military service. Care is available from the program for such disabilities on a bed-available basis after service-connected disabilities are cared for.

nonsmoker risk class In medical insurance and other insurance, these are individuals who are considered to be less of a risk to insurance companies as they have not smoked tobacco for a specified period of time prior to applying for insurance, usually 12 months, and thus pay lower than standard insurance premiums.

nonstochastic effects In environmental health, these are the effects for which the severity of the effect varies with the dose and for which a threshold may exist.

nonstochastic radiation effects In environmental health, these are the effects of radiation for which a threshold exists and above which the severity of the effect varies with the dose.

nonsudden accidental occurrences In safety and health, these are the events that take place over time and involve continuous or repeated exposure.

nonsuit In the litigation process, this is a judgment against a plaintiff when the plaintiff fails to prove his or her case or fails to appear in court; a judgment made not fully on the merits of the case but on the failure to present a prima facie case. *See also directed verdict.*

nontarget organisms In environmental health and public health, these are the flora, fauna, and humans not intended to be controlled, injured, made ill, killed, or detrimentally affected in any way by a pesticide (or other chemical) or microorganism.

nontraffic moving motor vehicle accident In safety and health assessment or traffic safety research, this is any crash or collision between two or more vehicles or a vehicle and a stationary object that occurred entirely in any place other than a public street or highway, usually on private property.

nontransient noncommunity water systems In environmental health, these are public water systems that do not serve city or community housing but that regularly serve at least 25 of the same persons over 6 months per year.

nonurgent Any minor or nonacute emergency not requiring the resources of an emergency service.

nonverbal communication Body language; communication through facial expression, gestures, and posture. Such expressions or gestures can exclude spoken words or be used to give emphasis to the spoken word.

nonviable 1. Not capable of living. 2. Not capable of succeeding.

no observable effect level 1. In environmental health and dose response evaluation or experiments, this is the experimental exposure level representing the highest level tested at which no effects at all were demonstrated. 2. In environmental health, this is a measure of contamination levels in polluted soil where research animals are exposed to soil polluted with a hazardous substance to determine effects on humans to show that the level of contamination is below the level hazardous to humans.

Nork case Refers to the legal case of *Gonzales v. Nork and Mercy Hospital of Sacramento, California* (Cal. Super. Ct. No. 228-566, Sacramento County, Nov. 1973), which legally helped to define a hospital's responsibility for the actions of its medical staff members.

norm(s) 1. Numerical or statistical measure(s) of usual observed performance. For example, a norm for care of appendicitis would be the usual percentage of appendices removed in cases diagnosed as appendicitis that are shown by pathology to be diseased. A norm can be used as a standard but does not necessarily serve as one. Both norm and standard imply single, proper values rather than a range. 2. The average, normal, usual, or expected behavior, action, ability, or level of achievement.

normal distribution A bell-shaped curve that graphically depicts the mathematical setup of all observations of an average population and how observations usually fall, with 68% of all observations in the middle and the remainder at each end. Sixty-eight percent of the observations fall within 1 standard deviation to the left and right of the mathematical mean, 95% within 2 standard deviations of the mean, and 99% within 3 standard deviations of the mean.

normal limits In public health, health promotion, and medicine, health and health status are viewed as falling within a range or continuum having upper and lower limits indicating at what level illness is present. When a medical test is given to a patient, one's health status or level of illness is based on whether the results fall within a previously set of standards or limits. When the test results fall within the high or low cutoff points, that means they have fallen within normal limits.

normal saline An isotonic concentration of salt (NaCl) in water.

normative Fitting within standards or norms; normal; usual within accepted values.

normative effect In health education, health promotion, or community health services, this is an observed expected response or influence on social patterns. It is anticipated that expected certain behaviors will occur in or be taken by individuals and groups under certain conditions or circumstances.

normo- Prefix meaning "rule," "order," "average," or "normal."

Norris-Laguardia Act A federal act established in 1932 to prevent certain injunctions against strikers or unions and prohibits "yellow dog" contracts.

nos- Prefix meaning "relating to disease"; of disease.

nosocomial Pertaining to or originating from a hospital.

nosocomial infection Any infection acquired by a patient during the process of receiving health-care services or from staying in a hospital, nursing home, or other health-care facility; hospital-acquired infections or infectious diseases. See *iatrogenic*.

nosocomial infection rate In epidemiology and infection control in hospitals or other inpatient facilities, this is the number of patients with nosocomial infection divided by the number of patients at risk of developing a nosocomial infection. Rates may be stratified by age or payment source or by taking into account certain patient factors that may predispose a specified group of patients to an increased risk of acquiring a nosocomial infection. Also called "rate stratification by infection risk" (JCAHO for acute-care facilities). The nosocomial infection rate formula follows:

$$\frac{\text{Number of cases of nosocomial infection in a certain time period}}{\text{Number of patients at risk of developing a nosocomial infection in the same time period}} \times 1000 \text{ (or } \times 100\text{)}$$

See *incidence; incidence rate*.

nosography Making a record of or the documentation of the classification of diseases; development of a disease nomenclature; the science of the description of disease.

nosology The science of the classification of diseases; classification of sick persons into categories; a nomenclature of disease; study of the classification of disease.

nosopoetic Producing diseases.

no-strike clause In health administration and labor relations, this is a statement placed in a labor contract by management whereby a union relinquishes its right to strike.

nostrum A quack medicine; patent medicine; a medicine that has the ingredients kept secret to protect sales by the inventor; any quack device, scheme, or plan.

nota bene (N.B.) (Lat.) 1. Mark well. 2. Note well. 3. Observe (used for emphasis in writing).

notarized affidavit In health law, this is a statement or document signed in the presence of a notary public, who also signs to witness that the signature is that of the person signing the statement. Under these conditions, the person signing the document attests that the statement or document is true, under penalty of perjury. This can be a less formal form of written testimony.

notary public A minor public official who witnesses signatures on documents, administers oaths, certifies the validity of signatures and legal documents, and performs witnessing duties for the business and legal community.

notary subpoena A part of the pretrial discovery process whereby a special procedure is used to expedite the litigation process. A subpoena is issued by a notary public and then the appropriate medical record taken to an attorney's office instead of the pretrial hearing or court.

notation voting Boards or legislatures casting votes without any meeting, a practice that is usually not ethical or legal.

not-certified facilities Hospitals, nursing homes, substance abuse treatment facilities, or psychiatric institutions that are not approved as Medicare or Medicaid providers.

notch In managed care or medical care insurance, this is a sudden and sharp discontinuity in medical or financial benefits for individuals with slightly different income. In certain public and medical assistance programs, one additional dollar of income can mean a total loss of benefits. For example, in Medicaid, families just below the income eligibility standard receive fully subsidized coverage while families with only slightly more income and just above eligibility standards receive no benefits. This may provide families with substantial incentives to restrict their incomes to remain eligible.

Spend-down provisions are used to compensate for notches. A notch may also occur when, without change in eligibility, cost-sharing requirements increase suddenly with a small change in income.

note 1. A legal document that may be exchanged for money. Whoever signs a monetary note promises to pay a specific amount of money by a certain time. 2. A record of a legal proceeding or ruling in a court.

notes payable A document indicating obligations incurred and due by a health-care facility, including a promise to obtain a short-term loan to pay off the debt; a document used to postpone payment to a creditor or vendor.

not-for-profit carriers In managed-care or insurance programs, service corporation or prepayment health plans organized under state not-for-profit statutes (e.g., Delta Dental Plan and Blue Cross and Blue Shield Plans).

not-for-profit hospital See *proprietary hospital, nonprofit*.

notice 1. To become aware of. 2. To pay attention to. 3. To give a formal warning to. 4. A formal action that can be part of a legal agreement. 5. The act of delivering legal documents.

notice of availability (environmental impact statement) A formal notice, published in the *Federal Register*, that announces the issuance and public availability of a draft or final environmental impact statement. Agency Notice of Availability is the official public notification of an environmental impact statement.

notice of intent (Environmental Impact Statement) A notice given that an environmental impact statement will be prepared. The notice describes the proposed action and possible alternative, describes the agency's proposed scooping process, including whether a scooping meeting will be held and where and when, and states the name and address of a person in the agency who can answer questions.

notice of lis pendens See *lispendens*.

notice of loss In liability insurance, this is a provision in a policy that requires an insured health-care provider to notify the insurer of any damage or loss within a specified period of time.

notice to produce In health law, this is a lawful notice requiring a party or witness to bring certain documents for inspection by a party or to trial.

notifiable In public health, epidemiology, and medical care, these are any diseases that health-care providers are required (usually by law) to report to federal, state, or local public health officials when diagnosed (such as AIDS, tuberculosis, diphtheria, and syphilis). Notifiable diseases are those of public interest by reason of their infectiousness, severity, or frequency. *See also registration; quarantine.*

notifiable diseases In public health, epidemiology, and medical care, these are any communicable diseases that are of public concern by reason of their contagiousness, severity, or frequency that health-care providers (physicians, hospitals, and physician extenders) are required by law to report to local or state public health officials or to the federal Centers for Disease Control and Prevention. The following is the 1994 list of notifiable diseases in the United States:

AIDS (acquired immunodeficiency syndrome)
Amebiasis
Aseptic meningitis
Botulism
Brucellosis
Chancroid
Cholera
Diphtheria
Encephalitis, primary
Encephalitis, post-infectious
Gonorrhea
Granuloma inguinale
Hantavirus
Hepatitis A
Hepatitis B
Hepatitis, non-A, non-B
Hepatitis, unspecified
Legionellosis
Leprosy
Leptospirosis
Lymphogranuloma venereum
Malaria
Measles (rubeola)
Meningoccocal infections
Mumps
Pertussis (whooping cough)
Plague
Poliomyelitis, paralytic
Psittacosis
Rabies, human
Rheumatic fever
Rubella (German measles)
Rubella, congenital syndrome
Salmonellosis
Syphilis, total all stages
Tetanus
Toxic-shock syndrome
Trichinosis
Tularemia
Typhoid fever
Typhus fever, flea-borne (endemic, murine) and tick-borne (Rocky Mountain spotted fever)
Varicella (chicken pox)

notification of changes in patient status For Medicare purposes, a facility must have appropriate written policies and procedures relating to notification of the patient's attending physician and other responsible persons in the event of an accident involving the patient; other significant changes in the patient's physical, mental, or emotional status; patient charges, billings, and related administrative matters. Except in a medical emergency, a patient is not transferred or discharged, nor is treatment altered radically, without consultation with the patient or, if he or she is incompetent, without prior notification of next of kin or guardian.

not new A drug for which premarketing approval by the Food and Drug Administration is not or is no longer required. A drug may become "not new" on a ruling by the FDA that the safeguards applicable to approved new drugs (e.g., maintenance of records and submission of reports) are no longer required. *See also "me too" drug.*

notorious Common knowledge; known to all.

NOV *See non obstante verdict.*

novation 1. In managed care, this is the substitution of a new health plan contract for an earlier one, thus ending old agreements or promises. 2. A new formal contract that ends all related previous agreements. 3. Placing a new professional in a responsible position held previously by a person under a contractual agreement.

NP *See nurse practitioner.*

NPDB National Provider Data Base.

NPHPRS *See National Public Health Program Reporting System.*

NPL *See national priorities list (hazardous waste sites).*

NPRM Notice of proposed rule making.

NREMT *See National Registry of Emergency Medical Technicians.*

NRHA *See National Rural Health Association.*

NSA National Security Agency.

NSF 1. National Science Foundation. 2. Not sufficient funds.

nuclear facilities In environmental health, these are facilities whose operations involve radioactive materials in such form and quantity that a significant nuclear hazard potentially exists to the employees or the general public. Included are facilities that 1) produce, process, or store radioactive liquid or solid waste, fissionable materials, or tritium; 2) conduct separations operations; 3) conduct irradiated materials inspections, fuel fabrication, decontamination, or recovery operations; or 4) conduct fuel enrichment operations. Incidental use of radioactive materials in a facility operation (e.g., check sources, radioactive sources, and X-ray machines) does not necessarily require the facility to be in this definition. Accelerators and reactors and their operations are also not included.

nuclear family 1. Immediate members of a family, including the parents and the children. 2. As used in JCAHO accreditation, the conjugal family, composed of parents and children living under one roof. This is assumed to be the dominant form of family life today, as compared to the extended family in the past in which the conjugal family plus blood relatives from two or more generations lived under one roof. Modified extended families are still very much in evidence where two or more generations live in close proximity and maintain close contact but are not living under one roof. The mobility of society has contributed to the breakup of the extended and nuclear families. *See family health.*

nuclear incidents In environmental health, these are any occurrences, including an extraordinary nuclear occurrence, with the United States causing, within or outside the United States, bodily injury, sickness, disease, or death, loss of or damage to property, or loss of use of property arising out of or resulting from the radioactive, toxic, explosive, or other hazardous properties of source, special nuclear, or by-product material.

nuclear magnetic resonance (NMR) The former term for magnetic resonance imaging. The term was changed to more clearly represent the true activities of the technology and procedure. The change eliminated the term "nuclear" because it has a negative connotation and is misleading in that the procedure uses no radiation or nuclear energy. *See magnetic resonance imaging.*

nuclear medical technology An educational training program that prepares individuals to prepare and administer radioactive isotopes and to measure glandular and other bodily activity in therapeutic, diagnostic, and tracer studies using a variety of equipment specially designed and constructed to handle radioactive materials and be traced in the body.

nuclear medicine 1. For JCAHO accreditation purposes, the scientific and clinical discipline concerned with diagnostic, therapeutic, and investigative use of radionuclides. 2. The medical specialty that is concerned with the use of radioactivity, radiation therapy, radioactive chemicals, and technology used in therapy, diagnosis, and treatment of diseases and conditions.

nuclear medicine physician A medical doctor who has completed advanced training and a residency in the diagnosis and treatment of diseases and disorders necessitating the use of radioactive isotopes.

nuclear medicine services 1. A medical service unit in a hospital that provides for the diagnosis and treatment of diseases and disorders through the use of radioactive isotopes. 2. The delivery of scientific and clinical care involving the diagnostic, therapeutic (exclusive of sealed radium sources), and investigative use of radionuclides. Standards are applied to evaluate a hospital's performance in providing nuclear medicine services (JCAHO for acute-care facilities).

nuclear medicine technologist 1. Nuclear medicine technologists are involved in both diagnostic and therapeutic procedures, preparing and using radioactive nuclides in laboratory procedures, scanning or imaging, and function studies. Under the guidance of a nuclear medicine physician, the technologist receives, positions, and attends to patients, makes dose calculations for in vivo studies, performs a wide variety of diagnostic tests on human beings or on body fluids, and applies radioactive materials in treatment procedures. Nuclear medicine technologists are responsible for the safe disposal or storage of radioactive materials and for the inventory and control of radiopharmaceuticals. Nearly all nuclear medicine technologists are employed in hospitals or clinics. 2. An allied health profession in which specially trained individuals who have completed a 1-year (or longer) training program in nuclear medicine technology and who administer and measure radioactive nucleotides in diagnostic and therapeutic applications, all under the supervision of a nuclear medicine physician.

nuclear radiation A process that accompanies the transformation of atoms from unstable to stable states by the release of excess energy in the form of electromagnetic waves or atomic particles.

Nuclear Regulatory Commission The federal agency responsible for regulating commercial nuclear power plants and other commercial nuclear operations pursuant to the Atomic Energy Act of 1954, as amended.

nuclear threat incidents In environmental health, these are situations involving the threatened, attempted, or actual theft, loss, or unauthorized possession of source or special nuclear material, radioactive by-products, nuclear explosive devices, improvised devices (either separately or in combination with explosives), or radioactive dispersal devices or the threatened use of these items.

nuclear winter The prediction by some scientists that smoke and debris rising from massive fires resulting from a nuclear war could enter the atmosphere and block out sunlight for weeks or months. The scientists making this prediction project a cooling of the earth's surface and changes in the climate that could, for example, negatively affect agricultural weather patterns.

nude pact See *nudum pactum*.

nudum pactum (Lat.) A bare agreement; a promise not supported by consideration and therefore not enforceable. It is completed only by honesty and goodwill.

nugatory A wasted effort; ineffectual; futile.

nuisance 1. Anything that unnecessarily or unreasonably annoys or disturbs. 2. Violating the public's health, safety, or decency.

null Nothing; having no legal effect or validity; void.

null hypothesis In health services and biomedical research, this is when the expected hypothesis and outcome is stated in a way that says nothing will happen or rejecting this position once results have been found.

nullify 1. To void. 2. To render invalid.

nullity 1. Nothing. 2. Having no legal force. 3. Ineffectual.

number index In medical records, this is a chronological listing of all medical record numbers with cross-references to names of patients.

numbering system A method of identifying patients restricted to numbers assigned by the administration. It is used for grouping sets of medical records. Each medical record is labeled using the assigned numbers for filing in a systematic manner for ease of storage and retrieval.

numerator In epidemiology and descriptive statistics, this is the top number of a rate formula presented in the form of a fraction; the top portion of a fraction.

numerical continuum scale Relative to clinical aspects of health care, this is a line on which clinical measurements fall (e.g., height, weight, blood pressure).

numerical rating system In managed care and insurance, this is a technique used since the 1900s for classifying risk in which both medical and nonmedical factors are evaluated according to a numerical value–driven system where each risk factor is assigned a numerical value on the basis of its impact on mortality.

nunc dimittis (Lat.) 1. Now let you depart. 2. A departure or farewell, usually from life. 3. A dismissal.

nunc pro tunc (Lat.) 1. Now for then. 2. Acts performed with a retroactive effect. 3. Legal authority that clears the health-care provider for giving treatment that has already been done.

nuncupative will An oral declaration, intended to serve as a will, that is made shortly before death and later put in writing by one of the witnesses.

nurse A professional health-care provider who works under the direction of a physician and who is qualified by education and authorized by state law to provide for patients, nurturing, care, education, support, administration of medications, therapy, and other activities that fall within the scope and practice of nursing. There are many different types, specialties, and levels of nursing whose titles are generally descriptive of their special responsibilities (such as charge or head, hospital, private or private duty, public health, pediatric, or school). Also referred to as "RN" (registered nurse). *See registered nurse; nurse anesthetist; nurse practitioner; nursing.*

nurse aide Any individual providing nursing-related services to residents or patients under the supervision of a registered nurse. They perform tasks delegated or assigned by the professional nursing staff and assist in activities of daily living and in direct patient care of a routine nature, making beds, escorting patients to other health facility departments, setting up and moving equipment, delivering messages, counting linens, etc. Tasks may also include, where policy permits, the taking of vital signs and, in the case of orderlies, performing heavier work in the nursing unit, maintaining equipment, setting up traction, and performing male catheterization. Also referred to as "hospital attendants," "nursing assistants," "nurse attendants," "orderlies," or some other variation. *See also nursing assistant; orderly.*

nurse anesthetist A registered nurse with special training in anesthesia who works under the supervision of an anesthesiologist or physician in administering anesthetic agents to patients before and during surgical and obstetrical procedures and operations. *See also certified registered nurse anesthetist.*

nurse anesthetist, certified See *certified registered nurse anesthetist*.

nurse anesthetist, qualified According to JCAHO for accreditation, a registered nurse who has graduated from a school of nurse anesthesia, accredited by the Council on Accreditation of Educational Programs of Nurse Anesthesia or its predecessor and who has been certified or is eligible for certification as a nurse anesthetist by the Council on Certification of Nurse Anesthetists or who has the documented equivalent in training and/or experience, meets any current legal requirements of licensure or registration, and is currently competent in the field.

nurse, associate 1. A community college graduate who majored in and graduated from an accredited associate degree program in nursing. 2. A nurse team member who carries out primary care nursing plans for the patient.

nurse-bed ratio In health-care administration, this is a method used to determine the number of full-time equivalent nursing personnel to the number of beds. This ratio can be used in health-care facilities by its administration to determine staffing ratio and needs. It can also be used in health planning to determine health manpower needs at the community, county, state, and national levels. The formula for nurse-bed ratio follows:

$$\frac{\text{Number of full-time equivalent nursing personnel}}{\text{Total number of beds}}$$

nurse, cardiac care A registered nurse who, through advanced training and experience, works in a cardiac care medical and nursing hospital unit providing specialized care to patients recovering from heart and cardiovascular system diseases or surgery.

nurse, certified A registered nurse who has met all credentialing requirements and has been certified for specialization in 1 of about 20 different specialty areas in clinical and administrative nursing. Certification is conducted by the American Nurses Association and many other professional and nursing organizations.

nurse, certified critical care (CCRN) A registered nurse who has met the credentialing criteria of the American Association of Critical-Care Nurses (AACN), shown competence in critical care nursing, passed an exam administered by the Center for Occupational and Professional Assessment of the Educational Testing Service in the field, and received official and valid certification as a critical care nurse. See *nurse critical care*.

nurse, charge The nurse on shift who is responsible for the supervision and management of other registered nurses, licensed practical nurses, and nursing assistants and/or all activities of a medical and nursing unit in the health-care facility.

nurse, circulating An operating room nurse who, by virtue of advanced training and experience, assists in surgery. This registered nurse secures needed equipment and materials, assists with surgery as needed, and maintains a safe environment during surgical procedures.

nurse, clinical instructor The registered nurse on the faculty of a school of nursing who is a regular member of the health-care facility staff and who is qualified to supervise student nurses in a clinical health-care setting.

nurse clinician A patient care specialist in the nursing profession who works with nursing problems in areas of direct patient care and may focus on special diseases, conditions, or groups such as cancer/oncology patients, geriatrics, pediatrics, and pregnant women in labor and delivery.

nurse, community health A registered nurse who works in the community and not in a health-care facility. Nurses who work in home care, school nursing, public health, occupational health, and health agencies are considered community health nurses. Public health nursing is a specialty area with specific parameters and is not necessarily synonymous with community health nursing.

nurse, critical care A registered nurse who, through advanced training and experience, provides specialized and advanced health care to patients in an intensive care unit who require 24-hour monitoring and care. See *nurse, certified critical care*.

nurse, diploma A registered nurse who graduated from a hospital-based nursing school that granted a 3-year diploma instead of an associate or bachelors degree.

nurse, float A registered nurse who is a regular staff member of a health-care facility but who is not assigned to a regular medical or nursing unit. Instead, the float nurse works wherever needed in the facility.

nurse, floor A registered nurse who works in nursing practice, having only direct patient care responsibilities in a nursing/patient care unit of a hospital such a medical/surgical unit.

nurse, general duty A registered nurse without specialization who works in nursing practice, providing direct patient care in any of a variety of nursing/patient care units of a hospital.

nurse, graduate 1. A registered nurse with a masters degree or other graduate degree in nursing. 2. A nurse who graduated from an associate or bachelors degree program at a college or university. 3. A nurse who has a degree in nursing but is not licensed.

nurse, head The nurse responsible for an entire medical or nursing unit and who directs, supervises, and manages other registered nurses, licensed practical nurses, and nursing assistants on the care unit.

nurse, intensive care A registered nurse who specializes in working in intensive care, cardiac care, neonatal intensive care, or other critical care units. *See nurse, critical care.*

nurse, licensed practical (LPN) The lowest level of licensure in the practice of nursing care. Any individual who has completed the educational and clinical training (usually 1 year) required for licensure at this level as determined by the state board of nursing for that state and who has passed the appropriate examination. Once licensed, this individual may practice under the direction of a supervisory nurse to carry out a variety of nursing activities. In some states, they are referred to as "licensed vocational nurses" (LVNs).

nurse, licensed vocational The equivalent of a licensed practical nurse. *See also licensed practical nurses.*

nurse midwife A registered nurse who, by virtue of added knowledge and skill gained through an organized program of study and clinical experience recognized by the American College of Nurse-Midwives, has extended the limits of practice into the management and care of mothers and babies from the prenatal to the postpartum period.

nurse midwifery practice The independent management of care of normal newborns and mothers antepartally, intrapartally, postpartally, and/or gynecologically. Such practice is in accord with the *Functions, Standards and Qualifications for Nurse-Midwifery Practice* as defined by the American College of Nurse-Midwives.

nurse, occupational health A registered nurse with specialization in industrial and occupational nursing who works in private companies dealing with the unique medical and injury problems of the workplace or heavy industry.

nurse, operating room A registered nurse with advanced training and experience who assists in surgery. The operating room nurse hands the physician tools and materials, assists in the surgical techniques and procedures, and may also aid the surgery by securing needed equipment and materials in the absence of the circulating nurse and provide assistance to the nurse anesthetist, anesthesiologist, and assistant surgeon as needed. *See also circulating nurse.*

nurse, pool A registered nurse who works for a private nurse staffing agency and reports to work at the hospital, nursing home, or clinic that has contracted with the staffing agency for a temporary nurse. The nurse is employed by the staffing agency and under the supervision of the contracting institution as a temporary employee.

nurse, practical *See nurse, licensed practical.*

Nurse Practice Act The law (statute) passed at the state level establishing and governing the education, licensure, and practice of nursing in each particular state.

nurse practitioner (NP) A registered nurse qualified through the completion of a formal program of study, usually at the masters degree level, designed to prepare and specially train registered nurses to provide primary care, diagnosis and treatment, and clinical intervention, including procedures common to primary health care in physician offices, clinics, homes, and ambulatory care facilities, long-term-care facilities, and other health-care institutions. Nurse practitioners generally function under the supervision of a physician but not necessarily in his or her presence. They are usually salaried rather than reimbursed on a fee-for-service basis, although the supervising physician may receive fee-for-service reimbursement. Referred to as a "physician extender." *See also physician assistant; medex; physician extender.*

nurse, primary care A registered nurse who provides basic nursing care as a regular staff member of a health-care facility or who works for a family practice or pediatric physician in private practice or in public health, outpatient clinics, or any other primary health-care setting. This nurse functions as a generalist in various areas of nursing practice, including some levels of emergency care. In some hospitals, a primary care nurse may provide all nursing care to the same patients throughout their entire stay in the hospital.

nurse, private duty A registered nurse who works in a private home providing nursing care to homebound persons and who is paid directly by the employer. Such a nurse is an independent employee and is not associated with a visiting nursing service or health-care agency or facility. The supervising physician is the patient's private doctor.

nurse, PRN Nurse as needed. In a hospital, this is to have a nurse(s) on standby or available to be pulled out of their current work unit to report to any unit in the health-care facility as needed. *See nurse, pool; nurse, float.*

nurse, professional A movement initiated in 1985 to distinguish diploma and associate degree nurse graduates from bachelor degree graduates, spearheaded at the annual American Nursing Association conference held in Hawaii. This conference set forth the notion of two levels of nurses; technical nurses (those with diplomas and associate degrees) and professional nurses (those with bachelors degrees and above). Over two thirds of registered nurses are of the technical level type, and the movement toward having two levels has met with minimal acceptance.

nurse, psychiatric In mental health services, this is a registered nurse who is a member of the mental health-care team who works with patients in a psychiatric hospital and conducts individual, family, and group psychotherapy.

nurse, public health A registered nurse who has education, clinical training, and specialization in public health. When hiring public health nurses, most government-administered public health departments require a minimum of a bachelors degree with a specialty in public health. Public health nurses often work in the provision of medical care for local or state health departments or private agencies.

nurse, registered *See registered nurse.*

nursery Any unit, facility, or center where newborns or infants are observed, nurtured, and cared for; facilities and services for newborns. *See nursery, newborn; nursery, premature.*

nursery, newborn A medical and nursing care unit in a health-care facility specially equipped and staffed to care for newly delivered infants who may need treatment and nursing care up to 28 days or longer.

nursery, premature A medical and nursing care unit in a health-care facility specially equipped and staffed to care for newly delivered infants who were born prior to the normal gestation period and who are in need of advanced and special treatment and nursing care because of their low birth weight and immature growth and development (usually under 2500 grams).

nurse, school A registered nurse who has met the requirements of being a registered nurse and completed all education and training required by school districts and county and state departments of education to work as a school nurse and who has received the proper credential to serve as a nurse in the school setting.

nurse, scrub An operating room nurse or technician who assists in surgery. *See also nurse, operating room.*

nurse's fees In medical insurance and some managed-care programs, this is a provision sometimes found in a medical expense reimbursement policy that allows for payment of nursing services provided to a patient. In most cases, the services are provided by a visiting nurse or a home care agency nurse in the home.

nurse, staff A registered nurse or licensed practical nurse who fills a regular nursing position in a health-care facility and who is responsible for direct patient care in one of several different types of medical and nursing units of the health-care institution.

nurse, student An individual enrolled in a nursing school or academic department of nursing. Part of the educational requirement includes clinical training under the supervision of a clinical instructor and faculty member in charge of clinical instruction.

nurse supervisor The nurse who is responsible for an entire nursing service area or two or more nursing care units and who supervises and manages other nurses and all management activities of the assigned nursing service in the health-care facility, including administration of all phases of nursing care and personnel. This is a midmanagement nursing position.

nurse, technical It has been suggested that these are registered nurses who hold a diploma or associate degree in nursing. *See nurse, professional.*

nursing 1. To assist sick or well individuals in the performance of activities contributing to health or recovery from injury or illness (or to a peaceful death) that they would perform themselves unaided if they had the necessary strength, will, or knowledge to do so (International Council of Nurses). Assisting patients in carrying out therapeutic plans initiated by physicians and other health professionals and assisting other members of the medical team in performing the nursing function and understanding health needs of patients. The specific content of nursing care varies in different countries and situations, and it is important to note that, as defined, it is not given solely by nurses but also by many other laypersons, paraprofessionals, and advanced specialty trained nurses such as nurse practitioners. 2. The provision of physical, emotional care, and educational services to a patient to support recovery from an illness or injury, to improve the ability to function in his or her environment, and to help the patient regain independence as rapidly as possible. *See nursing care.*

nursing administration 1. The largest management unit found within a health-care facility, usually headed by one of the top management team (an assistant or associate administrator of nursing services or vice president of clinical services or patient care services) who usually has a masters of nursing or masters of health administration or related graduate degree. This management unit is responsible for the coordination, supervision, planning, budgeting, controlling, and directing of all nursing activities in a health-care facility. 2. An educational program that describes the techniques and procedures for managing nursing personnel and services in health-care facilities, agencies, and institutions.

nursing assistant A term that is currently replacing "nurse aide," "attendant," and "orderly" as it provides more prestige to the position and has no gender-related connotation. This person usually performs an increasing number of duties such as bed making, feeding, bathing, temperature taking, elevation, and assisting the patient and the nursing staff in some nursing duties. *See also nurse aide; orderly.*

nursing audit Review of a patient's charts by other nursing peers to determine the competency of nursing care.

nursing care Nursing care is provided on four different levels: 1) promotion of health, 2) prevention of further disease or injury, 3) illness recovery and the restoration to normal activities and health, and 4) consoling the dying. Professional nursing care activities can include the following: application of dressings and bandages; assisting patients with basic needs; administering drugs, medications, and treatments; bowel and bladder retraining; catheterization; enemas; full bed bath; injections; irrigation; nasal feeding; oxygen therapy; temperature; pulse and respiration; blood pressure measurement; patient observation with regard to response and adaptation and response to treatment; teaching self-care; patient education; counseling on health matters; directing rehabilitation activities; patient aftercare; and planning and providing mental, social, and emotional support for the patient. *See also nursing; nursing process.*

nursing care home A facility that provides long-term care; another term for "nursing home" or "convalescent hospital" with the primary function of providing nursing care or subacute care but excluding acute medical care. The facility is staffed with one or more registered nurses or licensed practical nurses. *See nursing home; skilled nursing facility; intermediate care facility.*

nursing care objectives In medical and nursing care services, this is a part of the nursing care plan. These are the action-oriented, outcome driven, measurable activities that need to be completed for each patient to provide quality care, reduce the stress of treatment and recovery, and expedite patient recovery. *See nursing care plan.*

nursing care plan In medical and nursing care services, this is a document of planned patient care activities and nursing care objectives that is used to assess and determine needs and manage and coordinate patient care activities for each individual patient in a nursing care unit. *See care plan.*

nursing care unit In medical and nursing care services, this is a unit within the nursing service of a hospital, nursing home, or other health-care institution that provides continuous nursing care; any ward, floor, or health-care unit specifically organized as a nursing service in a health-care facility to offer regular and continuous nursing care services to patients. *See nursing services.*

nursing department One of the key administrative unit of a hospital, nursing home, or medical clinic responsible for all nursing service activities in the organization. In a hospital, this unit is under the direction of an assistant administrator or vice president of nursing services. *See nursing services.*

nursing differential Because elderly patients were presumed to need more nursing services than the general population, Medicare formerly reimbursed hospitals and skilled nursing facilities (SNFs) for nursing services at a rate higher than that paid by insurance companies that serve the general population. Prior to 1981, this added amount equaled 8.5% of total inpatient routine nursing salary costs. The passage of the Omnibus Budget Reconciliation Act of 1981 reduced that added percentage to 5% for hospitals but retained the 8.5% rate for SNFs. The Tax Equity and Fiscal Responsibility Act of 1982 eliminated the differential for both hospitals and SNFs and was effective for cost-reporting periods ending after September 1982.

nursing, director of A top administrative position and the top nursing administrative position in a hospital or other health-care facility filled by a registered nurse, usually with a masters degree in administration, who is responsible for all nursing services in the hospital. In the hospital, the term "director of nursing" has been elevated to a more appropriate level, more correctly identifying the position and title at the assistant administrator, chief nursing officer, or vice president level to better reflect the level of responsibility and importance that goes with the position and its contribution to the management team of a hospital or health-care facility. Directors of nursing serve as key administrative personnel who are responsible for all nursing care in nursing homes, home health agencies, medical clinics, medical groups, public health clinics, and other health-care facilities. They hold various titles such as chief nurse officer.

nursing, general An educational program that describes the techniques and procedures for providing care for the sick and disabled, including the administration of medical care and treatment and assisting physicians in providing examinations, treatment, and therapies and planning patient education and follow-up care.

nursing HMO *See HMO; nursing.*

nursing home 1. Generally, a wide range of institutions, other than hospitals, that provide various levels of maintenance, personal, or nursing care to people who are unable to care for themselves on a long-term basis. These include freestanding institutions or identifiable components of other health facilities that provide nursing care and related services. Nursing homes include skilled nursing facilities, intermediate care facilities, convalescent hospitals, and extended care facilities but not boarding homes. 2. Any institution caring for the elderly and/or patients in need of skilled nursing care on a long-term basis. Usually, it is expected that a certain level of nursing care be given. Nursing homes offer custodial and personal care, nursing care, as well as social and rehabilitative services. The facility should be well-equipped, clean, and pleasant with a caring, courteous, cheerful, well-trained staff. 3. A long-term-care facility that has three or more beds, provides residential living and inpatient personal nursing care on a 24-hour basis, has 50% or more of its residents receiving one or more nursing services, and has at least one or more registered nurse or licensed practical nurse for 35 or more hours (full time) of employment per week (as per the terms of accreditation, certification, or licensure as per state laws which vary). *See also long-term-care facilities; skilled nursing facility; intermediate care facility.*

nursing home administration In health administration, this is the performance of any managerial act or the making of any administrative decisions involved in planning, organizing, directing, and controlling the operation of a long-term-care facility.

nursing home administrator The chief administrative officer responsible and licensed to conduct the overall day-to-day management of a long-term-care facility that is licensed as a nursing home by the state in which it operates.

nursing home operator Refers to the individual responsible for the administration of a nursing home. This may be the administrator or the owner. *See also administrator, skilled nursing facility; long-term-care administrator; administrator, qualified.*

nursing home owner The individual, company, or corporation that is the legal owner of the facility and under whose name the licensing of the facility is registered by the state. The owner may be a licensed nursing home administrator who manages the facility or a corporation that hires a licensed administrator.

nursing process The methods, procedures, practices, and steps that a nurse uses when planning and implementing patient care. It is based on the scientific method of problem solving and includes four basic components: assessment, planning, implementation, and evaluation.

nursing, psychiatric/mental health 1. A branch of nursing education that trains students in the techniques and procedures for providing care to patients exhibiting psychological or psychiatric pathology. 2. A specialized nursing unit in a health-care facility that provides care on an inpatient and outpatient basis for patients who suffer from emotional, behavioral, and mental disorders. *See also nurse, psychiatric.*

nursing, public health A branch of nursing education that focuses on the preventive and curative aspects of nursing and allows nurses to work with normal and special high-risk groups in a community to provide preventive health-care services.

nursing service 1. In JCAHO hospital accreditation, these are patient care services pertaining to the curative, restorative, and preventive aspects of nursing that are performed and/or supervised by a registered nurse pursuant to the medical care plan of the practitioner and the nursing care plan. 2. In JCAHO long-term-care facility accreditation, these are patient/resident care services that pertain to the curative, restorative, and preventive aspects of nursing and that are under the supervision of a registered nurse pursuant to the multidisciplinary patient/resident plan of care. 3. The coordination, implementation, monitoring, and management of resident care plans, including provision of personal care services, monitoring resident responsiveness to environment, range-of-motion exercises, application of sterile dressings, skin care, nasogastric tubes, intravenous fluids, catheterization, and administration of medications (Title 22, California). *See nursing; nursing care unit.*

nursing service administrator A registered nurse generally trained at the masters degree level (MSN, MHA, or other related degree) who is responsible for the overall management of a hospital or health-care facility nursing service and is an assistant or associate administrator on the facility's management team. *See also nursing administration; nursing, director of.*

nursing staff Registered nurses, licensed practical/vocational nurses, nursing assistants, and other nursing personnel who perform nursing care in a health-care organization (JCAHO for acute-care facilities).

nursing, team An organized approach to providing patient care and implementing nursing care plans in medical and nursing units in a health-care facility. Usually, this involves assigning one nurse to provide the same care, assessment, or nursing activity to each patient in the unit. A leader usually meets with the team, and assignments are determined and designated to the nurses on the team.

nursing team leader In a team nursing approach, the nurse who is in charge of managing patient care activities and designating nursing care responsibilities to each nurse on the nursing team.

nursing unit 1. In a hospital or other health-care facility, this is a physical division of the institution determined by medical specialty or service provided (e.g., medical, surgical, recovery, coronary care, intensive care, obstetrical, pediatric and psychiatric units). A supervisor or charge nurse of a unit who manages several professional staff and other support personnel such as aides, orderlies, ward clerks, and unit managers. 2. In JCAHO accreditation, an organized jurisdiction in which nursing services are provided on a continuous basis. 3. A designated patient care area of a facility that is planned, organized, operated, and maintained to function as a unit. It includes patients' rooms and adequate support accommodations, services, and personnel providing nursing care and necessary management of patients (Title 22, California).

nurture To feed; to nourish; to promote the development of; to educate; to rear or bring up.

nutrient Substances found in food that are digested and absorbed by the body and used as food and energy needed to sustain life.

nutrition The science of food (the nutrients and other substances therein), their action, interaction, and balance in relation to health and disease and the processes by which the organism ingests, digests, absorbs, transports, utilizes, and excretes food substances. In addition, nutrition must be concerned with social, economic, cultural, and psychological implications of food and eating (Council on Foods and Nutrition, American Medical Association).

nutritional care The application of the science and art of human nutrition in helping people select and obtain food for the primary purpose of nourishing their bodies in health or disease throughout the life cycle. This participation may be in food service systems management, nutritional education programs, or dietary counseling.

nutritional deficiency disease A disease which is caused by an insufficient quantity of necessary vitamins and minerals in the body resulting from the lack of a proper diet.

nutritionist A trained member of the health-care team who adapts and applies food and nutrient information to the solution of food problems, the control of disease, and the promotion of health. Performs nutrition research, instructs groups and individuals about nutritional requirements, and helps people develop meal patterns to meet their nutritional needs.

nutritionist, clinical *See dietitian; dietitian, clinical; dietitian, registered; dietitian, qualified.*

nutritional services 1. Services in a health-care facility that are designed to provide inexpensive, nutritionally sound meals to patients. 2. In long-term care, a nutrition program that provides nutritional meals to elderly people in group dining arrangements at senior centers or other meal sites.

O

OAA Older Americans Act.
OASDHI See Old-Age, Survivors, Disability and Health Insurance Program.
oath 1. The giving of a solemn declaration of truth in a court of law. 2. Swearing to tell the truth. There are two basic types of oaths: assertory oath, or asserting that something is true, and promissory oath, or making a promise to do something.
OB *See organizational behavior.*
obese Having a high amount of fatty tissue over normal body weight; being more than 20% over one's normal body weight based on one's weight at age 20.
OB/GYN Obstetrician/gynecologist.
obiter In passing; incidentally.
obiter dictum (Lat.) Something said in passing. Words in a judicial opinion, not a part of a legal decision; a general comment of a judge.
object 1. In law, this to oppose an action or statement of the opposing party in court as being incorrect, biased, improper, unfair, or failing to follow procedure. 2. To assert that a decision or action made by a judge is incorrect or wrong. 3. To express opposition; to formally oppose.
objection 1. Having grounds to object. 2. Presenting an adverse argument. 3. Disapproval. 4. Disagreement. 5. An expression of disapproval.
objection to the consideration of a motion In formal health-care organization meetings using parliamentary procedure, this is an incidental motion used to avoid the consideration of an undesirable or impractical motion. This is applied to a main motion as soon as it is opened up to discussion and before any amendments are made. It does not require a second, an amendment, or a discussion. The vote must be two thirds to dismiss the main motion and sustain the objection.
objective 1. Something that is determinable, known, and external to one's mind; actual or real; reality. 2. Features and characteristics of an object. 3. Being without judgment, prejudice, bias, or a demeaning position. 4. A sign, symptom, or condition easily observed by persons other than patients such as their physicians. 5. A lens in a microscope. 6. In health planning or health administration, this is any short-term, measurable, specific statement of an activity having a specific time limit or time line for completion and measurable outcomes. It is usually a quantified statement of a desired outcome in the near future. Objectives are used to reach goals and specify who, to what extent, under what conditions, and by what standards certain activities are to be performed and completed. They also specify expected outcomes and the period of time in which these activities are performed and completed. 7. According to JCAHO for psychiatric, alcoholism, and drug abuse facilities accreditation purposes, an expected result or condition that takes less time to achieve than a goal, is stated in measurable terms, has a specified time for achievement, and is related to the attainment of a goal. 8. A defined result of specific activity to be achieved in a finite period of time by a specified person or number of people that states who will do what, how much, and by when. *See outcome measures.*
objective probability distributions In probability and inferential statistics used in biomedical research and epidemiology, this is the following of standardized statistical procedures to determine probability distributions.
objective risk In health, medical, and liability insurance, this is used to determine the relative variation of actual loss from the potential for loss.
obligation 1. A legal duty. 2. An expectation created by a contract. 3. An official written promise; a duty to perform a written promise. 4. A duty to perform or act. 5. An agreement or promise bound by a legal penalty.
obligations 1. In the federal budget, these are the dollar amounts of orders placed, contracts awarded, services rendered, or other commitments of federal budget authority made by federal agencies during a given period that will require outlays of federal funds. 2. Debts owed or agreements yet to be completed or fulfilled.
obligatory Legally or morally bound.
obligee 1. One to whom a duty is owed. 2. A person to whom another party is bound by a contract. 3. One on whose behalf an obligation exists.
obligor 1. One who owes another a duty. 2. One who binds him- or herself to another party by a contract.

obliterate 1. To destroy. 2. To erase. 3. To cross out written words or phrases. 4. To remove all traces of something.

obloquy 1. To cause shame or disgrace. 2. To blame. 3. To censure. 4. To reproach. 5. Verbal abuse or reproach.

OBRA *See Omnibus Budget Reconciliation Act.*

OBRA/SOBRA *See Sixth Omnibus Reconciliation Act of 1985; Omnibus Budget Reconciliation Act.*

OBS *See organic brain syndrome.*

obscene Immoral; lewd; filthy; foul; indecent.

obscenity 1. An obscene act or presentation. 2. The state of being morally and socially unacceptable.

observation In epidemiology, this is to take notice of any change in a subject of a study; the change in a health status indicator or in a research cohort.

observational studies In epidemiology, this is the study of the natural course of events that have occurred in the past (retrospective studies) and the study of events when and as they occur (cross-sectional studies). This method is based on the concept that any change in one trait or variable that is observed can cause changes in other variables. Changes are caused not by the researcher but occur naturally. Also referred to as "observational method."

observer error In epidemiology and biomedical research, this is a research error caused by observer shortcomings or mistakes in making observations during research or analyzing results. *See observer variation.*

observer variation In epidemiology and biomedical research, this is when researchers make different observations of the same research phenomena but arrive at different results or conclusions. The extent to which the findings of a set of researchers vary from one another.

obsessive-compulsive personality A personality disorder in which a person is overattentive to detail, does repetitive behaviors, and is excessively conscientious, demanding, and usually overinhibited.

obsolescence In health administration, this is when an employee or piece of equipment no longer possesses the knowledge or ability to perform at the level required; outmoded or outdated.

obstetric(s) 1. The care and treatment of pregnant women up to and including the labor and delivery process. 2. The medical specialty concerned with any activity involved in providing care to pregnant mothers relating to the care, preventive care, diagnosis, treatment, and surgery associated with pregnancy and the birthing process. 3. In a health-care facility, a medical care unit equipped and staffed specifically to provide care to mothers going through labor and childbirth, including labor rooms, delivery rooms, and birthing centers. *See also obstetric services.*

obstetric care Medical care received from a health-care provider, usually an obstetrician or nurse midwife, during pregnancy, labor, and delivery and the period immediately following birth.

obstetric care unit A medical and nursing care unit of a hospital, birthing center, or women's health-care center. One or all three levels of service are used: 1) those for uncomplicated maternity and newborns and for uncomplicated cases, 2) those having a majority of complicated outcomes and in need of special neonatal services, and 3) those having a high level of need for care and services for serious outcomes, illnesses, complications, and abnormalities and providing full-time nursing supervision by specially trained nurses and staff. Beds must be set up and staffed in a unit specifically designated for this service.

obstetrical technician Under the supervision of the nursing and medical staff, the obstetrical technician assists in the care of women in labor and in delivery rooms before, during, and after delivery. Such an individual may perform various hygienic and routine laboratory procedures, sterilize and maintain equipment, and maintain supplies in the delivery rooms.

obstetrical technology A nursing-related instructional program that prepares individuals to assist in the care of a mother's labor and delivery room needs before, during, and after the delivery process. All the activities of obstetrical technology are done under the supervision of a qualified physician, midwife, nurse practitioner, or nurse and include performing hygienic procedures, routine laboratory and sterilization activities, and other support activities related to assisting in the birth process.

obstetrician A physician specialist who has completed board certification and an approved residency to provide care, diagnosis, and treatment to mothers in pregnancy and labor and during the childbirth process.

obstetrics The branch of surgery dealing with the management of pregnancy, labor, delivery, and all aspects of the childbirth process.

obstetrics and gynecology A medical specialty that focuses on the study, diagnosis, treatment, and procedures of diseases, disorders, conditions, and medical problems of a woman's reproductive system as well as the childbirth process.

obstetric services The diagnosis and treatment of any abnormalities during pregnancy and services for the promotion and maintenance of optimum mental and physical well-being of the individual woman and her child from the onset of labor until the end of the perinatal period, including diagnosis and treatment of prenatal conditions and complications, labor assistance and care, delivery, and postpartum and newborn care.

obstructing justice 1. Stopping or interfering with the functioning of the courts, the litigation process, or court officials. 2. Keeping a witness from appearing in court. 3. Withholding evidence.

occasion of service In health-care delivery, this is the process of providing health-care services, whether in a health-care facility, an outpatient service, or a practitioner's office; the care provided to a patient by a health-care provider. Such services might include diagnosis, lab visits, therapy, treatment, immunization, physical exam, or surgery; a specific provision of care or service rendered to a patient.

occult 1. Concealed; hidden; secret. 2. Acts or occurrences that are mysterious, supernatural, and beyond human understanding. 3. Mystic arts and studies related to magic, witchcraft, astrology, satanism, or folk beliefs.

occupancy 1. The ratio of the inpatient census to the number of available beds, usually calculated and presented as a percentage of beds in use. The ratio of the average daily census to the average number of beds (i.e., statistical beds) maintained during the reporting period. The number of statistical beds may differ from the actual bed count at the close of the reporting period. 2. In hospitals, this is the ratio of the average number of inpatients (excluding newborns) receiving care to the average number of beds in a hospital set up and staffed for use (i.e., statistical beds) during a particular reporting period (American Hospital Association). *See also occupancy rate.*

occupancy, percentage of The proportion of actual inpatient days to the possible or maximum inpatient days. Bed capacity is used to determine maximum inpatient days. The percentage of occupancy is determined by dividing the actual inpatient days of service by the number of possible inpatient days if each designated bed would have been occupied every day in the period of time being used for the determination. The percentage of occupancy formula follows:

$$\frac{\text{Actual inpatient days}}{\text{Number of beds in service} \times 365 \text{ days}} \times 100$$

See also day, occupied bed.

occupancy rate A measure of inpatient hospital use determined by dividing available bed days by patient days; occupied beds divided by available beds times a multiple of hundreds in a specific time period. It measures the average percentage of a hospital's beds occupied and may be institution-wide or specific for one department or service. The occupancy rate formula follows:

$$\frac{\text{Average daily census (occupied beds)}}{\substack{\text{Number of hospitals beds available} \\ \text{during the same time period}}} \times 100$$

occupancy rate for health-care facilities (nonhospitals) The occupancy rate for facilities other than hospitals is calculated as the number of residents reported divided by the number of beds reported in the same time period. The health-care facilities occupancy rate formula follows:

$$\frac{\text{Number of residents}}{\substack{\text{Number of beds in} \\ \text{the same time period}}} \times 100$$

occupation 1. The principal vocation or economic producing skill in one's life. The skill, training, or ability to produce economic gain that engages one's time. The business or vocational trade that one follows to produce a livelihood. One's training, skills, interest, education, and abilities related to procuring a living. 2. In government studies of work, this is each person over 14 years of age who is considered when assessing a population for occupation. Occupations involving any type of farm work are classified by the U.S. Bureau of Labor Statistics in the farm category. Blue-collar occupations cover heavy physical work, the operation of service vehicles, work in manufacturing or processing, and skilled trades or crafts. White-collar occupations include office or clerical work, sales, management or administrative work, and professionals and technical specialties. Examples of service occupations include waiters, nurses, teachers, social workers, police officers, and nurses aides.

occupational doses In occupational health and radiation safety, this is the exposure of individuals to radiation in a restrictive area or in the course of employment in which the individual's duties involve exposure to radiation, provided that occupational doses are not deemed to include any exposure of an individual to radiation for the purpose of medical diagnosis or therapy of an exposed individual.

occupational exposure In occupational health and safety, this is any exposure of a worker to any unhealthy or disease-causing agent during a period of work.

occupational health A program and its related services located in the workplace designed to maintain a high health status of the workforce through safety and the prevention of occupational diseases, disability, and accidents or deaths with the ultimate goal of reducing lost productivity and work time. An effective occupational program includes the following services and components: maintenance of a healthful work environment, comprehensive safety system, emergency care and first aid, immunizations, health exams, health screening, fit-for-duty assessments, surveillance of personnel in high-risk positions, drug testing per regulations or policy, diagnosis and treatment, health promotion and health education, health intervention and health counseling programs, medical records system, and primary care nursing and medical services.

occupational health and safety Actions taken to ensure the recognition, prevention, and control of occupational health hazards and illnesses and to promote the physical and mental well-being of employed persons. *See occupational health; Occupational Safety and Health Act; Occupational Safety and Health Administration.*

Occupational Health and Safety Act *See Occupational Safety and Health Act.*

Occupational Health and Safety Administration *See Occupational Safety and Health Administration.*

occupational health and safety incidence rate *See incident rate; occupational health and safety; average lost workdays.*

occupational health nursing A specialty in the field of nursing where registered nurses work in industrial settings to provide support to primary medical care and health screening and provide first aid, education, and related nursing activities at the workplace.

occupational health services Health services concerned with the physical, mental, and social well-being of humans in relation to their working environment. The concern is thus larger than the safety of the workplace and includes health status and job satisfaction. In the United States, the principal federal statute concerned with occupational health is the Occupational Safety and Health Act administered by the Occupational Safety and Health Administration (OSHA) and the National Institute of Occupational Safety and Health (NIOSH).

occupational illness 1. Any disease, condition, malady, or disorder (acute or chronic) resulting from a work-related exposure or incident or caused by environmental factors such as inhalation, absorption, ingestion, or direct contact with harmful, hazardous, infectious or disease-causing substances or agents found in the workplace. 2. Abnormal physical conditions or disorders of an employee, other than those resulting from an occupational injury, caused by exposure to environmental factors associated with employment. It includes but is not limited to, acute or chronic illness or diseases that may be caused by inhalation, absorption, ingestion, direct contact, or radiation.

occupational injury Any traumatic harm to a body part, organ, or system such as a laceration, fracture, sprain, strain, amputation, abrasion, poisoning, scrape, impaled object, or puncture wound as a result of a work accident or any unplanned harmful exposure to an agent in a work environment, including any single instantaneous exposure or incidents.

occupational medical program A program developed in the workplace to ensure the health and safety of employees in their work environments through the application of occupational medicine principles: 1) determine the physical and mental fitness of employees to perform job assignments with undue hazards to themselves, fellow employees, or the public; 2) ensure the early detection and treatment of employee illness or injuries by means of scheduled periodic health screening, evaluations, and unscheduled employee visits; and 4) contribute to the maintenance of good employee health through the application of preventive medicine measures such as immunizations, alcohol and drug abuse programs, and health counseling.

occupational medicine A specialty branch of medicine that deals with the health protection and health maintenance of employees with special reference to job hazards, job stresses, and work environment hazards; the medical specialty that provides primary care and preventive medicine in industrial settings; care, treatment, and prevention of occupational related injuries and illnesses arising out of the course of employment.

Occupational Outlook Handbook A book published on a regular basis by the U.S. Departement of Labor showing different types of occupations and the future need for certain jobs and occupations including health services and public health areas.

Occupational Safety and Health Act of 1970 (OSHA) A federal law enacted to ensure that every working man and woman in the United States has a safe and healthful working environment. The act, which took effect on April 28, 1971, was created by Senator Harrison A. Williams of New Jersey and Congressman William Steiger of Wisconsin (the Williams-Steiger Act). It authorizes the Secretary of Labor to set mandatory standards for safety and health, provides for research and development in industrial health, encourages the institution of new industrial health programs, and provides for enforcement of established standards. In each state, a state-level agency, created by law, is to be established that sets standards, creates regulations, enforces the regulations, educates, plans, and implements the state-level OSHA programs. The standards at the state level must be at least as stringent as the federal standards in providing a safe and healthful workplace. The state OSHA agency reports directly to the U.S. Department of Labor. The following work areas are to be covered by federal and state OSHA programs: environmental control; fire protection; hand and portable power tools; hazardous materials; machinery and machine guarding; materials handling and storage; medical and first aid; occupational health; powered platforms; man lifts; vehicle-mounted work platforms; protective equipment; walking and work surfaces; and welding, cutting, and brazing of metal.

Occupational Safety and Health Administration (OSHA) An agency under the Department of Labor that was created by Section 6(a) of the Williams-Steiger Occupational Safety and Health Act of 1970 (84 Stat. 1593 and P.L. 91-596) and implemented on April 28, 1971. The act provides for the revocation, modification, and promulgation of occupational safety or health standards, any national consensus standard, or any federal standard established by regulations, unless determined that the promulgation of such a standard would not result in improved safety or health for specifically designated employees. OSHA does the following activities: conducts inspections and investigations and issues citations and penalties; requires employers to keep records of safety and health data; petitions the courts to restrain imminent dangerous situations; and approves or rejects state plans for state-level plans under the act. The legislative purpose of this provision is to establish standards with which industries are generally familiar. On adoption, those interested and affected persons will have already had an opportunity to express their views. The act also sets forth the following activities: education and training of employers and employees; consultation with employers (companies or organizations) and employees regarding the prevention of illnesses and injuries; grant funds to states for research, investigations, research, and demonstration projects; technical assistance and support; and the creation of a data and statistical system for occupational health and safety.

Occupational Safety and Health Review Commission A federal agency charged with the review of appeals and fines for safety and health violations given to companies, organizations, or employers by the Occupational Safety and Health Administration.

occupational therapist (OT) A graduate of an occupational therapy curriculum accredited jointly by the Council on Medical Education of the American Medical Association and the American Occupational Therapy Association and who is registered or who is eligible for registration by the American Occupational Therapy Association. A specially trained individual who evaluates the self-care, work, leisure, and task performance skills of well and disabled patients of all ages. The OT plans and implements activities of daily living, work, homemaking, and social and interpersonal activities designed to restore, develop, and/or maintain the client's ability to satisfactorily accomplish daily living tasks. Formal educational preparation of an occupational therapist requires at least 4 academic years of college or university work leading to a bachelors degree plus a minimum of 6 months of fieldwork experience. Persons already having a bachelors degree in a field other than occupational therapy may enroll in a postbaccalaureate program leading to a masters degree in occupational therapy or a certificate of proficiency in occupational therapy. *See also occupational therapist, qualified.*

occupational therapist, qualified According to JCAHO for psychiatric, alcoholism, and drug abuse facilities accreditation purposes, an individual who is a graduate of an occupational therapy program approved by a nationally recognized accrediting body or who currently holds certification by the American Occupational Therapy Association as a registered occupational therapist or who has the documented equivalent in education, training, and/or experience. This individual must meet any current legal requirements of licensure or registration and must be currently competent in the field. *See physical rehabilitation services.*

occupational therapy (OT) The evaluation, diagnosis, and treatment of problems interfering with functional performance in persons impaired by physical illness or injury, emotional disorder, congenital or developmental disability, or the aging process. Specific occupational therapy services include but are not limited to activities of daily living; the design, fabrication, and application of splints; sensorimotor activities; the use of specifically designed crafts; guidance in the selection and use of adaptive equipment; therapeutic activities to enhance functional performance; prevocational evaluation and training; and consultation concerning the adaptation of physical environments for the handicapped. These services are provided to individuals or groups through medical, health, educational, and social systems for the maintenance of health.

occupational therapy aide An entry-level allied health worker who works in a hospital, clinic, or rehabilitation center assisting occupational therapists in applying occupational therapy services, care, and rehabilitation under the direction of a registered occupational therapist as prescribed by a physician. In some states, this position or the individual filling this role must spend less than 50% of their time as an activities therapist.

occupational therapy assistant For Medicare purposes, a person who is eligible for certification as a certified occupational therapy assistant by the American Occupational Therapy Association or has 2 years of appropriate experience as an occupational therapy assistant and has achieved a satisfactory grade on a proficiency examination approved by the Secretary of the Department of Health and Human Services, except that such determination of proficiency shall not apply with respect to persons initially licensed by a state or seeking initial qualification as an assistant after December 21, 1977; an individual certified or eligible for certification by the American Occupational Therapy Association or by state law to serve as an occupational therapy assistant in a hospital, clinic, or rehabilitation center directly assisting occupational therapists in planning and applying occupational therapy services, care, and rehabilitation as prescribed by a physician and done under the direction of a registered occupational therapist. In some states, this position or the individual filling this role must spend less than 50% of their time as an activities therapist.

occupational therapy department *See occupational therapy; occupational therapy services.*

occupational therapy services A service unit usually found within larger health-care facilities staffed and equipped to provide exercises and tasks to assist persons in redeveloping or regaining some of the normal skills of daily life that were lost through disability, disease, injury, or disorder. These services are conducted as prescribed by physicians and are administered by or under the supervision of qualified occupational therapists.

occupiable area In health administration and environmental health and safety, this is the portion of the gross area available for use by an occupant's personnel or furnishings, including space available jointly to various occupants of the buildings such as auditoriums, health units, and snack bars. Excluded is space devoted to operations and maintenance, including shops, gear rooms, and storage. Occupiable area is computed by measuring from the occupant's side of ceiling-high corridor partitions or partitions enclosing mechanical, toilet, or custodial space to the inside finish of permanent exterior building walls or the face of the convector if the convector occupies a least 50% of the length of exterior wall. When separated by partitions, measurements are taken from the center line of partitions.

occupied bed day *See occupancy, percentage of; day, occupied bed.*

occurrence 1. In epidemiology this is the frequency of disease in a population. 2. In environmental health, this is any deviation from a planned or expected behavior or course of events if they have environmental protection, safety, or health protection significance. *See off normal occurrences; incidence; prevalence.*

occurrence-based coverage In insurance, this is when a policy covers an event that happens during the time period of coverage regardless of when the claim is filed.

occurrence basis In liability insurance policies, a clause that states that certain specific or minor acts must have occurred under certain conditions and the results must be caused by an accident and be totally unintended while the overall effect or major occurrence itself is allowed to be a deliberate act of the person holding the insurance policy.

occurrence policy An insurance policy covering any employee of a health-care facility or hospital during which an incident (such as malpractice) occurred even if the person who did it or who caused the liability is no longer employed or if the hospital is no longer covered by that policy.

occurrence reporting In quality management activities in hospitals or clinical settings, this is notifying proper officials of cases of diseases or conditions detected in a screening process as part of a medical management analysis program used in some hospitals and clinics. *See occurrence screening.*

occurrence reports Written evaluations of an event or condition that are prepared in sufficient detail to enable the reader to assess the significance, consequences, or implications and to evaluate the actions being proposed or employed to correct the condition or to avoid recurrence.

occurrence screening In quality management activities in hospitals or clinical settings, this is an evaluation process done by examining medical records and related medical care treatment and therapy. Assessment is done to obtain treatment information and identify cases that have had adverse events or adverse patient occurrences according to predefined criteria, which is all part of a quality medical management analysis program used in some hospitals and clinics. *See occurrence reporting.*

OD *See optometrist.*

odds *See odds ratio.*

odds ratio In epidemiology, this is the ratio of the chance that something is true to the chance that it is false; the ratio of the chances that a disease exists among the exposed to the chance that the disease will not exist in the unexposed; the ratio of two odds.

odium Hatred; general ill-feeling against someone.

O/E *See order/entry system.*

O&E Operating expenses. Operations and equipment.

OEO Office of Economic Opportunity.

of counsel 1. Employed as a lawyer. 2. One who assists a lawyer.

off 1. Postponed. 2. Ended. 3. Terminated.

offense Commission of a crime; breaking of laws.

offer 1. To present a proposal. 2. To make a proposition. 3. To attempt to have evidence admitted into a trial. 4. In contract law, a proposal to make a deal.

office In public health and health services research, this is the practice or workplace of any physician in private practice, including physicians connected with prepaid group practices. Any location for a physician's ambulatory practice other than hospitals, nursing homes, other extended care facilities, patients' homes, industrial clinics, college clinics, and family practicing clinics, including private offices in hospitals.

office audit system In quality management of physicians, this is used to determining the quality of care rendered to patients in private practice or medical clinics.

office automation In health-care information management, this is the use of computers and other electronic devices and equipment to improve information management, communication, availability of data and statistics, and overall productivity by increasing efficiency, effectiveness, speed, communication, and accuracy for the transfer of information among members of a work group or management team.

office-based physicians In health services research, these are medical doctors who spend the majority of their time working in practices based in private offices; hospital-based physicians spend the plurality of their time as salaried physicians in hospitals.

office-based practice In managed care, this is any health-care provider who provides the provisions of primary or basic medical care in their independent private practice located in physical space removed from a hospital or other health-care institution.

office call *See visit; office visit.*

Office of Civilian Radioactive Waste Management Established by the Nuclear Waste Policy Act of 1982, this office has the responsibility for the Nuclear Waste Fund and for the management of federal programs for recommending, constructing, and operating repositories for disposal of high-level radioactive waste and spent nuclear fuel; interim storage of spent nuclear fuel; monitored retrievable storage and research, development, and demonstration regarding disposal of high-level radioactive waste and spent nuclear fuel.

Office of Environmental Restoration and Waste Management This agency provides program policy guidance and manages the assessment and cleanup of inactive waste sites and facilities, continues safe and effective waste management operations, and develops and implements an aggressively applied waste research and development program to provide innovative environmental technologies that yield permanent disposal solutions at reduced costs.

Office of Health Maintenance Organizations (OHMO) A former division of the Public Health Service of the Department of Health and Human Services, this office administered federal activities affecting health maintenance organizations. The title was changed to Office of Prepaid Health Care. Referred to as the Central Office. *See Office of Prepaid Health Care.*

Office of Management and Budget (OMB) An agency of the federal executive branch of government that is responsible for researching, assessing, preparing, and controlling the budget submitted by the president to Congress each year. It also evaluates, formulates, and coordinates management procedures and program objectives within and among federal departments and agencies; supervises the assumptions of planning and the allocation, distribution, and spending of federal monies by government agencies during the year; and provides the president with recommendations on budget proposals and legislative enactments on a routine basis.

Office of Personnel Management (OPM) The federal agency that administers the Federal Employees Health Benefits plans. Managed-care plans contract with this office to provide medical care coverage for federal employees.

Office of Prepaid Health Care (OPHC) A division of the Health Care Financing Administration that oversees federal qualification and compliance and directs the affairs of federal HMO activities. It also administers and is responsible for regulations, standards, and federal activities affecting prepaid health plans, including health maintenance organizations. Formerly a part of the Public Health Service and called the Office of Health Maintenance Organizations. Referred to as the Central Office.

Office of Professional Standards Review (OPSR) A federal agency that reports to the Assistant Secretary of the Department of Health and Human Services, the official who is responsible for the activities of Professional Standards Review organizations. *See also professional review organization.*

Office of Technology Assessment (OTA) A federal agency that reports to Congress and that assesses new technology and determines its use and merits, including medical technology.

Office of the Assistant Secretary for Environment, Safety and Health This agency ensures that departmental programs are in compliance with environmental safety and health regulations and that environmental and safety impacts of department programs receive management review.

officer In health administration and health law, this is any individual in a position of authority in a health-care organization who is either elected or appointed to that position; persons in leadership and management positions of a corporation who are appointed by a board of directors and are given legal authority and responsibility to manage the day-to-day operations and activities of a health-care corporation.

officers of the court All personnel who work in or assist the court.

office visit(s) Services performed by a physician in his or her own office or in an office in an outpatient, ambulatory clinic of a health maintenance organization; physician diagnosis, exams, care, treatments, or services provided in an office setting. *See also visit.*

official 1. One holding a position of authority. 2. Directives from one in authority. 3. In pharmacy, pharmaceuticals authorized for medical use. 4. Authoritative.

official health agency Any governmental or public supported organization mandated by law or regulation for the control of diseases, the reduction of death and disability, the improvement of health status, and the protection of the health of the public.

official notice Information or mandates coming from a source of authority, usually an administrative agency.

off-line In computerized health-care services and medical records, the equipment and devices not currently being used in the computer system or, if still attached, not under the direct control of the computer.

off normal occurrences In environmental health and occupational health and safety, these are abnormal or unplanned events or conditions that adversely affect, potentially affect, or are indicative of degradation in the safety, security, environmental, or health protection performance or operation of a facility.

offset A counterclaim; a setoff.

offshore captive company A liability insurance company established by health-care providers or a group of providers outside the United States, often in the Caribbean Islands, created for the provision of issuing malpractice insurance coverage to its members.

off-site facilities In environmental health, this is any hazardous waste treatment, storage, or disposal area located at a place away from the site where the waste was generated.

off-the-job safety programs In occupational health and safety, this is a part of a company's safety program directed to workers when not in the work environment. As an extension of an occupational safety program, the aim of these programs is to get employees to follow the same safe practices used on the job when participating in nonwork activities away from the job. An effective safety program away from work can result in injury and illness prevention and can reduce costly employee absences caused by accidents, injuries, and disabilities and can show a commitment to worker well-being.

of record Officially recorded.

OHMO Office of Health Maintenance Organizations/Office of Prepaid Health Care. *See health maintenance organization.*

oil In environmental health and according to the Clean Water Act, this is any oil product in any form, including but not limited to petroleum, fuel oils, sludges, oil refuses, and oils mixed with wastes other than dredged spoil.

oil spills In environmental health, any accidental or intentional discharge of oil that reaches bodies of water. These can be controlled by chemical dispersion, combustion, mechanical containment, or adsorption (EPA).

ointment A semisolid salve or lotion that is rubbed on parts of the body.

old age In gerontology, this refers to phases of life at the end of life, often considered to be the period past the age of 75 years.

Old-Age, Survivors, Disability and Health Insurance Program (OASDHI) A program administered by the Social Security Administration that provides monthly cash benefits to retired and disabled workers and their dependents and to survivors of insured workers; it also provides health insurance benefits for persons aged 65 and over and for the disabled under age 65. The health insurance component of OASDHI was initiated in 1965 and is generally known as Medicare. The legislative authority for the program is found in the Social Security Act, originally enacted in 1935.

oldest-old In gerontology, this refers to the final phase of life at the very end of life, often considered past the age of 85 years.

old guard Any group of persons who have long tenure in an organization, are conservative, defend the old way of doing things, and are resistant to organizational change.

oligarchy Power and control is in the hands of a few.

oligo- A combining form that means small, few, or scant.

oligopoly In health economics, this is the control of a service in a limited market by a limited number of companies or suppliers. When health services or health-care providers are so few and competition is so limited, the actions of any one of them will affect pricing and thus have measurable affect on competitors.

olograph *See holograph.*

-ology Suffix meaning "the study of."

-oma Suffix meaning "morbid growth"; "tumor."

OMB *See Office of Management and Budget.*

ombudsman (Swedish) 1. A special advocate or public official who acts as an advocate for a specified group (such as the residents of a nursing home) with power to investigate illicit acts or misconduct and provide legal help in any wrongdoing. An advocate who investigates and resolves complaints on behalf of residents in long-term-care facilities, often relating to administrative action that affects the residents' rights, health, safety, and welfare; provides information and findings as to appropriate and proper public agencies regarding the problems with an expected intervention or remedy; provides training of volunteers and promotes the development of citizens organizations to participate in the ombudsman program. 2. One who monitors the development and implementation of state or local laws and policies that may affect the operations and function of long-term-care facilities and the rights of residents who reside there.

omission Being omitted, not included, or neglected. An act of omission is failing to do what is expected or what is a part of one's duty. *See also act of omission; negligence.*

omit 1. To purposefully leave out; to fail to include; to not give or provide; to not mention. 2. To neglect; to fail to do or to use.

omnibus (Lat.) 1. Containing two or more separate items. 2. Concerning two or more different and independent subjects.

Omnibus Budget Reconciliation Act of 1987 (OBRA) This federal act sets forth reform in Medicare and Medicaid nursing care facility benefits, nursing home operations, and administration to better serve and benefit the nursing home resident with rehabilitation as a foundation of the reforms. Patients rights are set forth, and admission agreement/contracts are required. Residents shall be free of chemical and physical restraints, and if used there will be a specific and clear documentation by the medical director or the patient's physician and nursing staff justifying the restraint use. A comprehensive assessment of any newly admitted resident is to be completed by nursing facility staff within 14 days of admission and annually thereafter. All residents are to be supported in maintaining their highest practical level of functioning. Residents have the right to refuse medical treatment. The facility is to provide adequate staffing to meet the OBRA guidelines, including an adequate number of licensed nurses and rehabilitation personnel. Other requirements imposed on nursing homes include rules on recruiting and training all nursing assistants (aides) such as providing 75 hours of training within 90 days of hire (53 topics to be covered) and quality assurance programs to be effectively implemented and functioning. Providers are allowed to represent Medicare beneficiaries during the appeals process. *See Sixth Omnibus Reconciliation Act of 1985.*

OMR *See on-line medical record.*

once-over To take a quick and comprehensive check for the last time; a swift examination; an appraisal in a rapid yet complete fashion.

oncogenic Any substance that causes tumors, whether benign or malignant.

oncologist A physician who has completed a special residency in the diagnosis and treatment of tumors and cancer utilizing radioisotopes and other specialized technology.

oncology A medical specialty for the diagnosis and treatment of tumors and cancer.

oncology department In hospitals, this is a specially equipped and staffed medical care unit found in a major health-care facility providing for the diagnosis and treatment of tumors and cancer.

oncometer An instrument of medicine used to measure variation in size of the internal organs of the abdominal cavity.

on cost In health-care finance, this is overhead or overhead expenses.

on demand 1. Immediately payable. 2. Something must be presented or given up on the presentation of an official document or note.

onerous Burdensome. In contract law, this is when one party's obligations exceed his or her advantages. The agreement is thus onerous.

one-party coverage In medical insurance; one person or family coverage; coverage for the subscriber only.

one-to-one nursing care An approach to organizing care for patients in a health-care facility where one nurse is assigned to provide total care for one patient during that nurse's shift. *See also primary care nursing.*

on-ground tanks In environmental health, these are stationary devices designed to contain an accumulation of regulated substances and constructed of nonearthen materials such as concrete, steel, or plastic. These provide structural support and are situated so that the bottoms of the tanks are on the same level as the adjacent surrounding surfaces and the external tank bottoms cannot be visually inspected.

ONHA Office of Nursing Home Affairs.

on-line In health-care information management, computers, and data processing, this is when all equipment that provides direct interface with the computer's central processing unit is installed and functioning.

on-line data processing In health-care information management, this is a method of processing medical records or business data in which input and output are under the control of a central processing unit. Current information is introduced into the processing system as soon as it occurs. Direct storage is needed for transactions to be processed in a timely manner.

on-line medical records (OMRs) In health-care information management, this is total computerization of the actual medical record to allow easy data and information entry and instant access. The medical record is created in the computer throughout the patient's stay, just as a paper medical record is created. Another, more acceptable approach (for legal and signature reasons) is the placing of the total medical record in the computer once the patient is discharged. More common is the abstracting of pertinent information from the discharged patient's medical record and entering this limited but important information into the computer for management statistics and research purposes. Immediate access to the medical record is readily available through access terminals once it has been entered. The most effective OMRs are those that are fully integrated and that have terminals at the patient's bedside and are connected to all aspects and phases of operations and business activities of the hospital, interacting with all pertinent operations and capturing information in medical records, business accounts, and materials management inventory control.

on-line processing *See on-line data processing.*

on-scene coordinators In environmental health, these are predesignated EPA, U.S. Coast Guard, or Department of Defense officials who coordinate and direct Superfund removal actions or Clean Water Act oil or hazardous spill corrective actions and directly coordinate and direct the removal actions of releases of hazardous substances, pollutants, or contaminants from Department of Defense vessels and facilities.

onset of condition In medical care or epidemiology, this is the time at the beginning of a condition and can vary because of circumstance and/or age. This can be the time when an agent or pathogen is introduced into the host, when the malady was first discovered, when the individual first felt ill or showed signs of illness, when a person became injured, the time the family of a child was made aware of the illness or injury, or the time the health-care provider is sought regarding the illness or injury.

on-site discharges In environmental health, these are airborne and liquid wastes discharged to on-site treatment or disposal systems such as sewage lagoons, retention, ponds, and cribs for settling, decay, or storage on-site.

on-site facilities In environmental health and hazardous waste management, these are hazardous waste treatment, storage, or disposal areas that are located on the site on which they are generated.

on-the-floor In formal health-care meetings using parliamentary procedure, this is a motion being considered by the group or board.

on-the-job training In health administration, this is any informal education or learning experiences or task development that occurs in the workplace; doing the actual tasks the worker will be expected to perform as a regular employee on the job.

ONTR Orders not to resuscitate. The order is also stated as "DNR" (do not resuscitate).

onus Burden; encumbrance.

onus probandi (Lat.) Burden of proof.

opacity In environmental health, this is the amount of light obscured by particulate pollution in the air. Clear window glass has zero opacity, a brick wall 100% opacity. Opacity is used as an indicator of changes in performance of particulate matter pollution control systems and of the degree to which emissions reduce the transmission of light (EPA).

OP code *See operation code.*

OPD *See outpatient department.*

open 1. To begin. 2. To make available. 3. To be visible. 4. To have no time limitation. 5. To be frank and honest with nothing hidden.

open access In managed care, this is when the

health plan allows a member to self-refer for specialty care or allows a member to visit any participating health-care provider without a referral from a gatekeeper physician. Also referred to as "open panel." *See open panel.*

open account In health-care finance and materials management, this is a credit arrangement between a health-care organization and a supplier where orders are taken by the supplier without payment and supplies charged to an account. The hospital or health-care facility is billed at a future date. The health-care facility accountants record this as accounts payable.

open and shut In law, this is an issue or case that is easily, clearly, and obviously determined and ended.

open burning In environmental health and air pollution control, these are uncontrolled fires in an open dump or in backyards or fields in the community.

open communication In health-care delivery, the patient-physician relationship, or health administration, this is when employees or patients feel unrestrained to freely express relevant messages.

open contract In managed care, this is a special contract under which an organization's bylaws and constitution are a part of an insurance contract. Any amendments to the bylaws or constitution also amend the contract but do not diminish benefits that the organization is contractually obligated to pay.

open-door policy An unrestricted or unlimited admission or allowance of lower-level employees to a manager or executive; a policy that allows employees to go to their boss or a higher level of management with any problem or concerns without fear of reprisal by their boss; the acceptance by all levels of administration of an employee's right to go over a boss's head.

open-end credit In health-care finance, revolving charge plans (e.g., credit cards) that can be paid off in small payments.

open ended In managed care, this is any health plan that offers a variety of benefit approaches to enrollees, giving them freedom to choose services and approaches to the various arrangements with flexibility in benefits and financial incentives; multiple options and restrictions with varying health-care providers and payor risk arrangements and the increase in administrative accountability.

open-ended HMO In managed care, this is one approach to a prepaid health plan, also referred to a point-of-service plan where members are allowed to choose providers and receive medical care outside the health plan, but usually at a higher cost. *See open ended.*

open-ended lines In environmental health and air pollution control in industrial sites, this is any line, except pressure release lines, having one end in contact with process fluid and one open to the atmosphere, either directly or through an open valve.

open-ended programs In the federal budget, entitlement programs for which eligibility requirements are determined by law (e.g., Medicaid). Actual obligations and resultant outlays are limited only by the number of eligible persons who apply for benefits and the actual benefits received. *See also entitlement authority.*

open-ended valve In environmental health and air pollution control in industrial sites, this is any valve, except pressure release valves, having one side of the valve in contact with process fluid and one side open to the atmosphere, either directly or through open piping.

open enrollment In managed care or medical insurance benefit offerings to employer groups, this is a period each year when new or continuing subscribers and eligible dependents who failed to enroll when first eligible may elect to enroll in a medical insurance plan or a managed-care plan from a list of two or more plans being offered or to select a new or alternate health plan. This is usually done preceding the employer's group plan anniversary or during a set period each year. Evidence of insurability or waiting periods are usually waived in open enrollment. Open enrollment periods may be used in the sale of either group or individual insurance and may be the only period of the year when insurance is available. Individuals perceived as high risk (perhaps because of preexisting conditions) may be subjected to higher premiums or exclusions during open enrollment periods. In the Health Maintenance Organization Act of 1973 (P.L. 93-222), the term refers to periodic opportunities for the general public, on a first-come, first-served basis, to join a health maintenance organization (HMO). The law requires that HMOs have at least one annual open enrollment period during which an HMO accepts, "up to its capacity, individuals in the order that they apply" unless the HMO can demonstrate to the Department of

Health and Human Services (DHHS) that open enrollment would threaten its economic viability. In such cases, the DHHS can waive the open enrollment requirement for a period of up to 3 years.

open enrollment period In human resource management employee benefits and managed care, this is a time period each year during which subscribers to a health benefit program have an opportunity to select an alternate health plan from the list being offered, usually without evidence of insurability or waiting periods. The annually offered period when an employee may change health plans. The requirement that, for a period of 1 month per year, an HMO accepts into the health plan any individual eligible for coverage, regardless of health status, and charges the regular standard fee rate.

open-heart surgery In medical care, this is a tertiary level of surgical care using a specially equipped and environmentally controlled surgical operating theater staffed with highly trained medical specialists and specially trained surgical teams who open a patient's chest while being supported by advanced technological equipment through which blood is recirculated and oxygenated. Highly advanced technological equipment is used for the surgical repair of heart conditions, replacement of heart valves, or restoration of circulation to the heart.

open-heart surgery unit An advanced specialized surgical theater in a hospital that is specially designed, equipped, and staffed to provide advanced surgery by specialized physicians for patients suffering from heart disease. *See open-heart surgery.*

opening statement In law, this is the first remark by the plaintiff to a jury at the start of a trial.

open medical staff In hospital administration, this is when the board of trustees, administration, and the organized medical staff extend hospital privileges to any licensed physician applying. A medical staffing approach that is not under the closed model, this approach has limited use in large medical centers, whereas in small rural hospitals it is more common.

open minded 1. Being open to progress or new ideas without prejudgments, preevaluations, or bias. 2. Free from prejudice.

openness Being frank and forthright and not hiding or withholding information or secrets; having trust in one's communication with another; a willingness to disclose.

open panel In managed care, this is a health plan that contracts with private practice physicians and medical groups to provide medical care in their own offices to enrollees of a health plan. Health maintenance organizations, PPOs, and IPAs are operated under such a health-care delivery arrangement.

open-panel group practice A managed-care plan in which the beneficiary chooses among the health-care providers participating or in which physicians accept or refuse clients.

open shop 1. A hospital or other health-care organization where both union and nonunion persons may work. 2. When both union and nonunion workers can be employed in the same institution.

open staff In hospital administration, this is where any licensed physician may admit and care for his or her own private patient in the hospital without going through a medical staff admission or review. The hospital has no set medical staff size nor sets forth the type of physician or specialty needed on its medical staff. This was a widespread practice but is now very rare.

open systems activities In health-care strategic planning, these are outward-looking strategies through which an organization selects its options and shares services, negotiations, and bargaining agreements.

open wound In medical care, first aid, or emergency care, this is any injury or wound where the skin or mucous membrane has been cut open to expose underlying tissue.

operand Something that is operated on. In computerized health-care services, this is identified by an address that is part of an instruction in a health-care software program.

operant conditioning In mental health services, this is a term created by the psychologist B. F. Skinner to describe behavioral responses that occur as a result of reinforcers. A behavior therapy theory and process by which environmental or social events called reinforcers are done to an individual following a behavior that needs to be changed or strengthened, depending on whether it is negative or positive, so that the behavior is likely to occur more or less in the future.

operating budget In health administration, this is the plan developed by a health-care organization for the expenditure of funds for the coming year. The plan forecasts the level of new and return business that the organization is expected to produce (as well as operating expenses, capital expenditures, and new staffing needs) and provides standards of performance against which the manager can measure productivity and business activity.

operating cost-effectiveness In health-care finance, this is the financial ratio of the operating costs of a health service or program compared to a specific effect of the service.

operating costs In health-care finance, these are the financial requirements necessary to operate a health services facility. This includes any costs incurred after the date the activities commenced and normally includes the costs of personnel, material, supplies, overhead, contracts, leases, purchased services, fees, depreciation, expenses, and interest paid; the direct, indirect and variable expenses incurred in the operations of a health-care facility.

operating expenses The costs of running a business, including salaries, utilities, day-to-day expenses, taxes, insurance and employee-related expenses, plus a reserve of money for replacement items; a common component of a profit-and-loss statement.

operating income In health-care finance, this is the proportion of the revenue left after expenses. The operating income formula follows:

$$\text{Total operating income} - \text{expenses}$$

operating margin In health-care finance, this is the proportion out of each dollar the hospital generates. The only money the hospital is allowed to keep can come only from an operation's income. The operating margin is compared with past performance and with the budget and the operating margins of hospitals in the region. The operating margin percentage formula follows:

$$\frac{\text{Operating income}}{\text{Total operating revenues}} \times 100$$

operating margin ratio In health-care finance, this ratio is used to determine profitability of the health-care organization. The profit or loss from operations is compared to the net operating revenue, that is, how much revenue generated from operations is sustained as a net profit or loss. The operating margin ratio formula follows:

$$\frac{\text{Profit or loss from operations}}{\text{Net operating revenues (net sales)}}$$

See net profit margins.

operating revenue In health-care finance, the gross amount of money earned by a hospital or health-care facility based on accrual accounting procedures utilizing established rates. *See also other operating revenue.*

operating revenue, other *See other operating revenue.*

operating room (OR) A medical unit in a hospital or surgicenter that is specially designed, equipped, and staffed to provide for general surgery for a variety of disorders or conditions in ill or injured patients.

operating room nurse *See nurse, operating room.*

operating room procedure hierarchy In hospital administration, under DRGs, this includes all procedures conducted in an operating room that are rated as to their degree of risk and resource consumption. A patient with two or more procedures is classified into the top of a three-tier hierarchy of most important or applicable procedure category. Also referred to as "surgical hierarchy."

operating room procedures In hospital administration, under PPS/DRGs, these are procedures designated in the ICD-9-CM procedure manual (volume 3) that are performed in a fully equipped operating room or those physician-determined procedures that are significant in terms of degree of risk or in resource consumption. Physicians were asked to review all procedures in the procedure manual and classify them as either an "operating room procedure" or as a "non–operating room procedure."

operating room technician This individual works as a general technical assistant on the surgical team under the direct supervision of the operating room nurse and the medical staff. He or she prepares patients for surgery, maintains antiseptic conditions, arranges supplies and instruments, and assists the surgeon during operations.

operating room technician, certified An operating room technician who has met established requirements of experience and training and has passed an examination as stipulated by the Association of Operating Room Technicians.

operating system In information management and computerized health-care services, a software program that organizes the computer's internal memory, allowing it to function and execute application software programs.

operation 1. Any medical procedure or act performed on the body with instruments or by the hands of a physician or surgeon; surgical procedures; surgical treatment done in a hospital or surgical suite of a clinic where the patient undergoes special preparation; sanitation measures are taken; sterile fields are established; special tools and equipment are arranged for; monitoring equipment provided; special staffing by assistants, nurses, and technicians are scheduled; anesthesia is arranged for; and postoperative care is scheduled and provided. 2. In computerized health-care services and medical records, a software program step undertaken and executed by the computer; any single computer instruction that is entered into the computer, then run and completed.

operational accidents In health and safety, these are events stemming from technological and man-made hazards that present a potential risk to life, health, property, or the environment.

operational information In health administration, this is training and communication needed by the various types and levels of employees of a health-care organization to successfully perform work in various functions or services.

operational mode A way of classifying medical group practices. Most medical group practices have been freestanding and operated on a fee-for-service basis and have not been linked contractually or organizationally to another organization or entity such as a hospital or medical school. The classification is possible under an operational mode: freestanding, hospital affiliated, university affiliated, industry affiliated, or university hospital affiliated.

operational performance in health-care organizations Indicators of operational performance are the comparison with actual desired levels of inventory, occupancy rates in hospitals, and waiting times in physicians' offices, etc.

operational planning In health planning, this is an objective-oriented planning approach utilizing operating management activities and including scheduling and resource allocation to achieve a health-care facility's goals and overall mission. This approach is integrated with other methods of planning. *See also planning; health planning; strategic planning; objective; goal.*

operational readiness In occupational health and safety and environmental health, this is a state attained by verification of every significant detail of preparation for operations to ensure safe startup and operation and the correction of hazardous omissions in design and plans and the initiation of retrofit prior to accidents.

operational readiness review In occupational health and safety and environmental health, this is a structured method for determining that a project, process, or facility is ready to operate and occupy and that includes, as a minimum, a review of the readiness of the plant, hardware, personnel, and procedures. It also includes a determination of compliance with environmental, safety, and health standards.

operational research In health services research, this is the study of the organization and function of the health services, health-care facilities, or health administration conducted to enhance utilization, efficiency, and effectiveness.

operation code (OP code) A part of computer machine language instruction that tells the central processing unit which actions to perform.

operation of law In law, this is the process by which rights or liabilities are given to or are owned by a person automatically without his or her act or cooperation.

operations and maintenance 1. In environmental health, the activities conducted at a site after a Superfund site action is completed to ensure that the action is effective and operating properly. 2. Actions taken after construction to ensure that facilities constructed to treat waste water will be properly operated, maintained, and managed to achieve efficiency levels and prescribed effluent limitations in an optimum manner.

OPHC *See Office of Prepaid Health Care.*

ophthalmic dispenser An individual who adapts and fits corrective eyewear as prescribed by the ophthalmologist or optometrist.

ophthalmic laboratory technician A technician who grinds lenses and fabricates eyewear to prescription.

ophthalmic medical assistant Under the direction and supervision of the ophthalmologist, this person performs a variety of tasks, including technical laboratory duties and office assistance. Ophthalmic assistants take medical histories, administer diagnostic tests using precision instruments, make anatomical and functional ocular measurements, and test eye functions including visual acuity, visual fields, and sensorimotor functions. They often carry out very technical measuring and testing procedures and in some cases provide technical assistance to the ophthalmologist in ophthalmic surgery. They change eye dressings, administer eyedrops or oral medications, and instruct patients in inserting, removing, and caring for contact lenses. Other duties include caring for and maintaining optical and surgical instruments.

ophthalmic medical technologist (technician) (OMT) An allied health profession that assists in the practice of ophthalmology. *See ophthalmic medical assistant.*

ophthalmic photographer *See ophthalmic photography.*

ophthalmic photographic technologist *See ophthalmic photography technician.*

ophthalmic photography A specialized field dealing solely with the eyes and related problems. There are two major divisions of ophthalmic photography. The first, slit lamp photography, deals with photography of the anterior segment of the eye. The camera has an independent variable-width beam of illuminating light (thus, slit lamp) that can be rotated through a 180-degree arc in front of the eye. This method gives illumination of etiologies that may otherwise be obscured in normal floodlamp–type photography. Corneal endothelial cells may be illuminated and counted by this method, as may iris and crystalline lens disease entities. The second division, posterior (or fundus) photography, involves two areas of study in the posterior segment of the eye. In the first area, fundus photography is a static color documentation of the interior of the eye using a specially prepared optical system allowing the photographer to view and photograph the retina and vitreous through a dilated pupil with 35mm film. A technique known as stereophotography reveals elevation differences in the retina and abnormalities in the vitreous. The other aspect of fundus photography is called fluorescein angiography, which involves a photographic technique (formulated by Novotney and Alvis in 1961) of injecting an intravenous bolus of sodium fluorescein, then taking rapid sequential photographs of the vasculature of the retinal areas as the dye enters the vascular system.

ophthalmic photography technician An allied health profession that utilizes the photographing of the inner parts of the eye for diagnostic or research purposes. Formalized training mostly occurs in clinical practice and through certification.

ophthalmic services 1. A department found in health maintenance organizations, freestanding centers, and some hospitals that provides diagnosis and treatment of vision defects, diseases, and disorders. The service also includes vision testing, administering treatment including surgery, preparing and fitting eyeglasses and contact lenses, and prescribing corrective eye exercises. 2. An educational program that prepares persons to assist ophthalmologists or optometrists in identifying vision defects, performing tests, assisting in examinations, assisting in preparation for surgery, fitting eyeglasses or contact lenses, educating patients, and providing directions for corrective eye exercises.

ophthalmologist (DO or MD) A physician specializing in the diagnosis, medical care, treatment, and surgery of all eye diseases and abnormal conditions, including refractive errors. This individual may prescribe drugs and lenses and performs surgery or other treatment. *See also optician.*

ophthalmology The medical specialty that focuses on the diagnosis and treatment of diseases, conditions, and disorders of the eye and its supportive tissue and structures as well as the anatomy and physiology of the eye.

ophthalmoscope A handheld instrument used to examine the interior of the eye that utilizes a high-powered focused light.

opinion 1. In health law, this is a decision or statement given by a judge about the outcome or final decision of a case. 2. A statement by a lawyer for a client, giving a belief about how the law applies to the case under consideration.

opinion evidence What a witness believes about facts rather than what the witness saw or heard. Opinion evidence is usually admissible only when it comes from an expert witness such as a physician.

opinion of the court In law, this is the decision given by an appellate court; one judge writing the opinion for the court. Judges who agree, but for different reasons, may write their opinions explaining their reasons. Judges who disagree with the majority may write dissenting opinions.

OPM *See Office of Personnel Management.*

opportunistic infection In medical care and epidemiology, this is an infection caused by normally nonpathogenic organisms in a host whose resistance has been decreased. Victims of AIDS and diabetes mellitus often experience this type of infection.

opportunistic organism In medical care and epidemiology, this is an unusual infection caused by an organism that usually does not cause an infection under normal circumstances.

opportunity cost In health economics, the value that resources would have if used in the best possible way or in another specified alternative way. When opportunity costs exceed the value that the resources have in the way they are being used, they represent lost opportunities to receive value from the resources. An opportunity cost of devoting physician time to tertiary care is the lost value of devoting the same time to primary care. Opportunity cost is the appropriate cost concept to consider when making resource allocation decisions. Actual costs often, but not always, can be assumed to represent or be proportional to opportunity costs. *See also marginal cost.*

opprobrious Infamous; not worthy of respect; disgraceful; abusive.

opprobrium Disgrace or reproach as a result of a wrongdoing; shame.

OPSR *See Office of Professional Standards Review.*

-opsy Suffix meaning "view."

optemetrics The art and trade of making, fitting, adjusting, or repairing eyeglasses, contact lenses, and other vision-wear and ophthalmic devices.

optical axis In laser technology, this is the optical centerline passing through a laser tube, optical fiber, or some type of lens structure.

optical fiber In laser technology, this is a filament of optical glass or quartz material that can carry light long distances with no significant loss of laser strength.

optically pumped laser In laser technology, this is a laser in which electrons are excited into an upper energy state by the absorption of light from an auxiliary light source.

optical scanner A computer-driven device that photoelectrically speed-reads data from a page and puts it directly into a computer.

optical scanning A method utilizing an optical scanner for reading symbols and converting them to data into a computer through the use of magnetic ink or optical marks.

optician A health-care worker who fits, supplies, and adjusts eyeglasses according to prescriptions written by ophthalmologists or optometrists to correct a patient's optical or muscular vision defect. In some states, opticians also fit contact lenses but do not examine the eyes or prescribe treatment. Qualification for initial licensure usually includes successful completion of written, oral, and practical examinations. Apprenticeships are required in most licensing states, an alternative being the completion of a 1- or 2-year training program.

opticianry The place and practice of optemetrics whereby an optician makes, selects, fits, adjusts, and repairs glasses, contact lenses, and other vision-wear and ophthalmic devices.

optimization In health administration, this is the allocation of scarce health-care resources that are maximized to the benefit of the health-care organization.

option As used in law, when a person is allowed to pay money for the right to buy or sell something at a certain place and within a certain time.

optional services In managed care, these are services that may be provided or covered by a health plan or provider and, if provided, will be paid for in addition to any required services that must be offered. In addition to the required services under Medicaid, if states elect to include any of the optional services in their programs, matching funds under Title XIX are available. The optional services states may offer prescribed drugs; clinic services; dental services; eyeglasses; private-duty nursing; skilled nursing facility services for individuals under 21; care for patients under 21 in psychiatric hospitals; intermediate care facility services; prosthetic devices; physical therapy and related services; other diagnostic, screening, preventive, and rehabilitation services; optometrist, podiatrist, and chiropractor services; care for persons 65 or older in institutions for mental diseases; and care for patients 65 and older in tuberculosis institutions. States may also offer any medical care, or any other type of remedial care recognized under state law, furnished by licensed practitioners within the scope of their practice as defined by state law, that is not specifically excluded from coverage by Title XIX (exclusions are care or services for inmates of public nonmedical institutions; inpatient services in a mental institution for individuals over 21 and under 65, and services for persons under 65 in a tuberculosis institution). *See also basic health services; supplemental health services.*

option contract In contract law, this is a contract supported by consideration that allows the right to buy on the terms stated and for a specific period of time. The offeror may not withdraw or revise the terms of the offer.

optometric assistant One who performs a variety of tasks that are generally less complex than those of the optometric technician: keeping records, acting as receptionist, assisting patients with frame selection, and ordering prescribed lenses. This person may do visual-acuity testing, color vision screening, and visual field testing. In addition, an assistant may also provide patients with instructions on the use and care of different types of lenses. The specific duties are determined by the employing optometrist. In large practices, the assistant may specialize in any of the following functions: laboratory, contact lens, visual training, chair-side assistance, or office administration. Assistants in smaller practices may assume all these duties. Most optometric assistants work for optometrists engaged in private practices of varying sizes. Others are employed by clinics, government agencies, optical instrument manufacturers, health maintenance organizations, and various branches of the armed forces.

optometric technician An individual who assists the optometrist with vision care services by measuring the curvature of the cornea, testing the ability of the patient to see numbers or letters of a specific size at a specified distance, and recording eye pressures or tensions. The technician also determines the power of lenses in old and new prescriptions, assists the patient in frame selection, and takes facial and frame measurements. He or she may also perform ophthalmic laboratory work, modify conventional glasses or contact lenses, keep an inventory of optometric materials, and clean and care for instruments. Other duties may include bookkeeping, secretarial, and office management responsibilities. In all cases, duties are performed under the supervision and guidance of an optometrist.

optometric technology An educational program that prepares persons to perform a variety of vision care procedures such as fitting contact lenses or visual training under the supervision of an ophthalmologist or optometrist.

optometrist (OD) A practitioner concerned with problems of vision who specializes in prescribing corrective lenses and diagnosing but not treating conditions of the eye. Optometrists examine the eyes and related structures to determine the presence of any abnormality and prescribe and adapt lenses or other optical aids. They do not prescribe drugs, make definitive diagnosis of or treat eye diseases, or perform surgery. An accredited doctor of optometry degree requires a minimum of 2 years of preoptometry college education and 4 years of professional training in a school of optometry. The degree and an optometry board examination are required by all states for licensure for the practice of optometry. Effective October 30, 1972, a state that previously covered optometric services under Medicaid and that in its Medicaid formal plan specifically provides coverage for eye care under physicians' services that an optometrist is licensed to perform must reimburse such care whether provided by a physician or an optometrist. Optometrists thus may not be excluded as potential providers in these states. *See also ophthalmologist; optician.*

optometry A profession concerned with the problems of human vision. Practitioners of optometry are called optometrists (OD) and examine the eyes and related structures to determine the presence of any visual, muscular, or neurological abnormality. Optometrists prescribe and adapt lenses or other optical aids and may use visual training aids (orthoptics) when indicated to preserve or restore maximum efficiency of vision. Most optometrists fit and supply the eyeglasses they prescribe. Some states have passed legislation that allows optometrists to prescribe drugs in the treatment of patients.

-or Suffix meaning "one who."

OR *See operating room.*

oral Referring to the mouth.

oral hygiene The cleaning and freshening of a one's own teeth, gums, and mouth on a constant and regular basis.

oral and maxillofacial surgeon, qualified An individual who has successfully completed a postgraduate program in oral and maxillofacial surgery accredited by a nationally recognized accrediting body approved by the U.S. Department of Education (JCAHO for acute-care facilities).

oral contract 1. A contract that is spoken and is not in writing. 2. A verbally expressed contract 3. In contract law, this is an express agreement as opposed to an implied agreement.

oral/maxial/facial surgery A surgical subspecialty that utilizes the principles and techniques of restorative surgery to the area of the jaw and face to treat diseases, injuries, or deformities.

oral pathology A specialty area of dentistry or medicine that focuses on the functional and structural changes and diseases affecting the mouth, teeth, bones, and gums.

oral surgeon A physician or dentist who has completed a specialty in surgical treatment of maxillofacial area under general anesthesia.

oral surgery A specialty of dentistry or medicine in which a dentist performs surgery on a patient's maxillofacial area under general anesthesia in a specially equipped operating room or surgical suite.

ORD Office of Research and Development.

order 1. A written directive from a judge. 2. A directive of a court to appear at a trial or hearing. 3. A command given by a public official. 4. A direction to pay something. 5. A command to perform a task or complete a job or participate in a work activity given to a subordinate by superior administrative personnel. 6. The directive of a physician to a physician assistant, nurse practitioner, physical therapist, nurse, technician, etc. regarding patient care, treatments, therapies, examinations, or other care activities.

order/entry system (O/E) In health-care information management, this is a series of software programs written in the MAGIC programming language that facilitates on-line, real-time ordering of services of patients by transmitting orders to the appropriate areas of the health-care facility while updating patients' financial charges and records. The program accepts daily nursing care plans, unfilled orders, central supply lists, etc.

orderly A hospital attendant with no professional training or schooling, most often a male, who does nonnursing general chores, especially attending to the needs of male patients and transporting patients. *See also nurse aide; nursing assistant.*

order not to resuscitate A directive in a patient's medical record stating that lifesaving procedures such as cardiopulmonary resuscitation (CPR) should not be used.

order of business In formal health-care meetings and hearings using parliamentary procedures, the formal sequencing of items to be covered in a meeting or assembly. Business is arranged in the order in which items are to be presented to the assembly for discussion and formal action.

orders of the day In formal health-care meetings, this is the agenda, or the scheduled program of business activities used in meetings that are of long duration such as conventions. Also referred to as "agenda of the day" or "agenda of business."

order to show cause A court order made ex parte requiring a party to appear in court to show cause as to why a claim or decision should not be made final. *See also rule nisi.*

ordinal scale In descriptive statistics, this is a method of giving order to various categories of subjects or numbers to allow for the comparison between categories such that one category signifies more or less of a variable than another category. Different numbers signify different amounts of the quality being measured. An example is a three-point Likert scale ranging from very dissatisfied to moderately satisfied to very satisfied. *See also nominal scale.*

ordinance A law, statute, or regulation passed by a municipal legislative body; laws created by a city council for a city.

ordinary agency system In managed care and insurance, this is a distribution system using commissioned agents to solicit applications, sell insurance policies, collect initial premiums, and provide customer services.

ordinary negligence In health law, the lack or omission of care that an ordinary, prudent, and reasonable person would usually take for his or her own care; the failure to exercise care of an ordinarily reasonable and prudent person in the same situation. Under nominal circumstances, a person is expected to know and understand the results of his or her acts. *See also negligence.*

ordinary person In health law, this is any person of average diligence, reasonableness, prudence, and care.

ordinate axis In descriptive statistics used in health-care management or public health, the vertical side of a chart or graph; the side on which the frequency of responses or other frequency-based data are presented.

Oregon health-care rationing plan A specialized health-care rationing plan developed in Oregon for the state's Medicaid plan that provides for medical insurance for all citizens of the state but does not cover some expensive procedures. A list of 709 medical procedures or treatments was developed and ranked according to costs and benefits. Procedures falling below item number 587 are not to be covered by Medicaid. An example of those excluded may be advanced cases of AIDS with less than 6 months to live.

organ bank A service provided in some major

hospitals that is a repository for a supply of human tissue, organs, and bone acquired and maintained for use or replacement in needy patients or for research.

organic 1. Referring to or derived from living organisms. 2. In chemistry, any compound containing carbon.

organic brain syndrome (OBS) A psychotic or nonpsychotic disorder caused by impaired organic functioning of the brain.

organic disease Any illness caused by damage or a change in an organ or tissue.

organic law 1. Basic. 2. The most fundamental of governmental law.

organic matter Compounds containing the natural element carbon.

organism As used in epidemiology and public health, this is any living thing such as a human being, animal, insect, or microorganism (germ), especially ones that can harbor disease, serve as a reservoir of disease, or be a pathogen of disease.

organization 1. An executive system for structuring and ordering interpersonal and work relationships of individuals in a workplace, a company, an agency, an institution, or a cause. Positions in the structure are differentiated in authority, status, responsibility, accountability, role, and objectives to reach a common goal or accomplish a mission. 2. The hierarchical arrangement and orderly structuring of individuals in companies, agencies, or institutions by position, level of authority, and responsibility and the delineation of the flow of communication and authority upward and downward in the institution; a system using policy and rules to guide behavior and business while providing each member with the values that bond them together for long-term strategic purposes. 3. To bring order to chaos to meet objectives, expectations, and performances successfully and to accomplish tasks efficiently and effectively; being organized; marshaling and coordinating resources to meet program goals or to implement a program. *See organizing.*

organizational behavior (OB) 1. An area of management focusing on the application of learning, research findings, and behavioral science concepts and theory and how they affect people and their behavior in organizational settings. Additionally, this field utilizes empirical methods of research, inquiry, and interpretation derived from counseling psychology, social psychology, behavioral psychology, clinical psychology, sociology, anthropology, and political science to observe and understand behavioral phenomena in organizations. 2. The merging of individual, group, and organizational actions and their study on the basis of industrial/organizational psychology and management and organizational theory based in the foundations of social psychology, psychometrics, sociology, anthropology, and management. The topics of OB can include motivation, leadership, and job attitudes; job design, absenteeism, turnover, and individual worker differences; and job performance, job satisfaction, corporate culture, power, and politics.

organizational chart In health administration, this is a graphic representation showing the line of authority, reporting channels, and place of position and responsibility of the officers and staff of a health-care facility, agency, or organization.

organizational climate In hospitals or other health-care organizations, this is the positive/favorableness or negative/unfavorableness of the work environment, treatment of personnel, and attitudes of management and workers in the organization.

organizational development (OD) A specialty area of management that uses behavioral science, organizational behavior, and management principles to assess problems in an organization by using a planned change approach. The program attempts to change a total organization through the use of behavioral science theory such as establishing an organizational culture and values. Assessment and evaluation procedures, systems management for the whole organization, behavioral science methodologies, and group processes are used to determine the organizational climate or dysfunction. Information presentation and a group of other change techniques are then implemented to increase an organization's effectiveness and efficiency with the ultimate aim of increasing employee morale, job satisfaction, corporate culture, productivity, and the quality of work while reducing employee turnover to bring about planned change.

organizational performance The ability of a health-care organization to properly articulate and coordinate its various components necessary for the delivery of efficient and effective quality hospital care to patients.

organizational performance processes There are two main performance assessment processes:

1) vertical differentiation, which establishes the hierarchy in a health-care organization, and 2) horizontal differentiation, which helps separate activities through the foundation of departments and sections.

organizational structure *See structure, organizational.*

organization for quality In health administration and quality improvement, this is the process of structuring organizational activities to effectively serve the accomplishment of the goals of the health-care facility, physicians, patients, and the organization's objectives.

organization leaders *See leaders, organization.*

organized Administratively and functionally structured to bring about order, efficiency, effectiveness, and productivity.

organized medical staff In JCAHO accreditation, a formal organization of practitioners with the delegated responsibility and authority to maintain proper standards of patient/resident care and to plan for continued betterment of that care.

organized outpatient services In health-care delivery, these are ambulatory health services offered by appointment with a health-care provider and may include diagnosis, testing, exams, treatment, therapy, outpatient surgery, and other nonemergency conditions as ordered by a staff physician or a referral physician.

organized social work services Part of the social services department in a hospital or health facility directed and staffed by properly educated, trained, certified, and otherwise qualified persons who provide assistance and counsel to patients and their families. Assistance is provided to patients and families in coping with social, emotional, relationship, economic, and financial matters associated with illness or disability, including discharge planning to arrange for nursing home care, home health, or community support services.

organizing In health-care administration, this is a function of the manager or administrator where administrative and personnel activities and processes are given structure, order, logical courses of action, sequencing of events, staffing, work flow structure, scheduling, time management, neatness of effort, etc. on the basis of efficiency and effectiveness of work to produce quality managerial outcomes. *See organization; functions of a manager.*

organizing committee In health administration and labor relations, this is a group of employees in a health-care organization that organizes (or attempts to) fellow workers into a labor organization.

organ procurement agency (OPA) A private service or organization that has established a system to identify and track patients in need and to obtain human body parts and organs for transplantation in persons needing them. A donor system is established and used to make organs available in a timely manner to those who need them or to store those organs that can be stored until needed.

ORH Office of Rural Health.

ORHP Office of Rural Health Policy.

orientation 1. Awareness of time, place, and person. 2. A guided adjustment of a worker to a new work environment, situation, or organization; a training program conducted by health-care facilities for new employees, usually a half or whole day in length. In this program, the new employee is acquainted with the history of the facility, introduced to key administrative people, informed of security and safety issues, presented with major policies and procedures, informed of employee benefits, and presented with public relations issues and other information deemed pertinent for new employees. *See also reality orientation.*

orientation and training In hospitals or other health-care organizations, this is the training and education of new employees to an organization and its rules, culture, policies, and expectations. This activity reinforces the employee's ability to be successful at work, communicates conditions of employment, introduces key administrators, informs workers of rules and policies of the organization, instills pride, establishes organizational climate and values, and aids in understanding and becoming committed to the mission statement and overall commitment and loyalty to the organization and its success.

orientation program In hospitals or other health care organizations, this is an educational experience for new employees to acquaint them with their roles, expectation, policies, and fellow workers. *See orientation and training.*

original jurisdiction The initial authority of a court to try a case or to hear an appeal.

orphans In insurance, these are policy owners whose agents are no longer available to provide customer service.

ortho- Prefix meaning "straight," "correct," or "normal." Correction of deformities or maladjustments.

orthodontics A dental specialty that describes the principles and techniques involved in the prevention and correction of dental and oral anomalies and misalignment of teeth and nominal biting processes.

orthodontic surgery A specialty in surgery focusing on the principles and techniques involved in correcting dental and oral anomalies by surgical procedures.

orthogenics The study and treatment of defects.

orthognathic A dental or orthopedic specialty area that pertains to the bones of the face and teeth; having a straight jaw and profile.

orthognathic surgery Dental or orthopedic surgical procedures that treat deformities or problems in the bones of the face, jaw, and teeth.

orthopedic assistant An individual trained to assist a physician in applying, adjusting, and removing casts; assembling traction devices and/or exercise frames; fitting strappings and splints; and adjusting crutches and walkers to fit patients.

orthopedics A specialty in medicine that focuses on the diagnosis, treatment, preservation, and restoration of the skeletal system and related structures.

orthopedics department A medical unit in a health-care facility staffed and equipped to provide services for the diagnosis, treatment, preservation, and restoration of the musculoskeletal system under the supervision of an orthopedic surgeon or other physician.

orthopedic sports medicine A subspecialty of orthopedic medicine that treats injuries, skeletal system and related structural problems, or conditions that result from sports activities or accidents.

orthopedic surgeon A physician who has completed a postgraduate approved surgical residency who is board certified and specializes in the branch of medicine and orthopedics that is surgically oriented, focusing on the repair of bones and the restoration of the functions of the skeletal system and its related structure and function.

orthopedic surgery 1. In medical care, this is the provision of surgical repair or treatment of the skeletal system and its articulations and associated structures by a licensed and board-certified orthopedic surgeon. 2. A specialty of medicine involved in correcting diseases, fractures, and deformities of bones, joints, and the skeletal system through the use of surgical procedures.

orthopod Slang for "orthopedic surgeon."

orthopsychiatry A therapy method used in the study and treatment of human behavior as used by psychiatry, psychology, and other sciences to promote healthy emotional and behavioral growth and development.

orthoptics A technique of eye exercises designed to correct the visual axes of eyes not properly coordinated for binocular vision. *See also orthoptist.*

orthoptist A specially trained individual who works under the supervision of an ophthalmologist in testing for certain eye muscle imbalances and teaching the patient exercises to correct eye coordination defects. Most work in the private offices of ophthalmologists, whereas others are employed in hospitals and clinics. The American Orthoptic Council, the regulating board for orthoptists, administers the national board examination. A trained orthoptist needs a minimum of 2 years of college and 15 months of training in a training center or 24 months of preceptorship training.

orthostatism Erect posture of the body in standing position.

orthotic The process of protecting; to restore or improve function.

orthotic/prosthetic assistant One who assists the orthotist/prosthetist in caring for patients by making casts, measurements, and model specifications and fitting supportive appliances and/or artificial limbs.

orthotics assistant *See orthopedic assistant.*

orthotic technician A specially trained individual who assists a physician in applying, adjusting, and removing casts; assembling traction devices and/or exercise frames; fitting splints; and adjusting crutches and walkers to fit patients. This person may also provide patient education on how to walk with crutches and walkers and how to care for casts and braces.

orthotist *See prosthetist.*

orthotist/prosthetist One who writes specifications for and makes, fits, and repairs braces and appliances and/or artificial limbs following the prescription of physicians.

OSHA Occupational Safety and Health Administration or Occupational Safety and Health Act. *See Occupational Safety and Health Administration.*

-osis Suffix meaning "abnormal condition."

ostensible 1. That which is intended to be obvious. 2. That which is apparent or visible. 3. The power a principal gives to an agent. 4. The authority a physician gives to a nurse or medical technologist.

osteopath (DO) Doctor of osteopathic medicine. A physician who has graduated from an accredited school of osteopathic medicine and generally practices family medicine and may also specialize. Osteopathic therapy and treatment includes the manipulation of body parts. The theoretical basis for this branch of medicine is based on the loss of the structural integrity of the body as a source of somatic abnormalities and disease and may use manipulative techniques on the skeletal system and neuromuscular structure in treatment as well as traditional allopathic medical treatments, therapies, and practices. *See also osteopathy; allopathic physician*.

osteopathic medicine An educational program that teaches a system of therapy utilizing accepted medical, surgical, and physical manipulation methods in diagnosis and treatment with emphasis on normal body mechanics and manipulation techniques for detecting and correcting faulty body structure. *See also osteopathy*.

osteopathic medicine, doctor of (DO) *See osteopath*.

osteopathic physician *See osteopath*.

osteopathy A school of healing based on the theory originally set forth in 1874 by Dr. Andrew Taylor Still that the normal body, when in balance, is a vital mechanical organism naturally capable of making its own responses to and defense against disease, infections, and other toxic conditions. The body is seen as structurally and functionally coordinated and interdependent. The osteopath seeks to correct any peculiar position of the joints or tissues or peculiarity of diet or environment that may be a factor in destroying natural resistance. Measures taken may be physical, hygienic, medicinal, and surgical. Osteopaths are licensed to perform medicine and surgery in all states, are eligible for graduate medical education in either osteopathic or allopathic programs, are reimbursed by Medicare and Medicaid for their services, are supported under health manpower legislation, and are generally treated equally with allopathic physicians. *See also homeopathy; naturopathy*.

osteoporosis A disorder most common among elderly persons in long-term care. Osteoporosis results from a reduction in the quality of bone tissue, especially in women, because of the aging process and is complicated by a decrease in protein and certain minerals in the diet.

-ostomy Suffix meaning "to make a new opening."

OT *See occupational therapy; occupational therapist*.

OTA *See Office of Technology Assessment*.

OTC (drug) *See over-the-counter drug*.

other accident In health and safety and public health research, this includes all injuries that occur in public places such as falling or tripping on a sidewalk and includes all nonaccidental injuries such as homicide attempt injuries and suicide attempts.

other diagnosis In diagnosis-related groups, any existing condition other than the principal diagnosis at the time of admission to health-care facility or one that develops subsequent to the admission and that affects the length of stay or the treatment needed. Conditions or diagnoses related to an earlier illness or those that have no bearing on the current hospital stay are excluded.

other operating revenue In health-care financing, revenue acquired from nonpatient care services and from sales of goods or services to nonpatients such as the health-care facility's staff or family of patients. Examples include revenue from cafeteria sales to visitors and staff and over-the-counter pharmacy sales. *See also operating revenue*.

other physician In long-term care, this is a salaried physician, other than the medial director, who supervises the care of residents when the attending physician is not available; a physician available to provide emergency services on a 24-hour-a-day basis.

other weird arrangements Describes the unique, creative, or unusual approach or manner in which managed-care plans are organized, structured, or arranged beyond the usual health maintenance organization, preferred provider organization, or independent practice association.

otolaryngologist A physician with a specialty in the diagnosis, treatment, and therapy of injuries, conditions, or diseases of the ear, nose, and throat. Also referred to as an "ENT" or "ear, nose, and throat specialist."

otolaryngology A medical specialty that does diagnosis and treatment of the ear and upper respiratory system, including the larynx.

otologist A physician who specializes in surgery and diseases of the ear.

-otomy Suffix meaning "incision."

otorhinolaryngology (ENT—ear, nose, and throat) A medical specialty that performs diagnosis and treatment of the ear, nose, and nasopharynx. A specialty in medicine that focuses on the anatomy, physiology, disorders, and care and treatment of the ear, nose, and throat. Also called "otolaryngology." *See also otolaryngologist.*

outage insurance A special form of loss insurance applicable to losses experienced when an essential piece of equipment is not functioning because of a peril or accident.

outcome(s) 1. Under OBRA, this is any end result or final consequence of medical practice, patient care, delivery of services, support, or assistance. 2. The end and final result of any process, function, performance, or service delivery; the ultimate product. 3. The final result of attempting to complete goals and objectives; the end results of objectives. 4. In public health and epidemiology, this is the ultimate product of a service or treatment measured in the context of a population's mortality, morbidity, and vital statistics. 5. In medical care, this is the final result of medical treatment, therapy, rehabilitation, and course of stay as an inpatient in a hospital.

outcome evaluation 1. In health promotion or health-care delivery, this is the assessment of the final effects of a program or service on the lives of the participants in terms of health status improvement. 2. In health education, this is a measurement process used to determine the effectiveness and results of health education methods, modalities, or processes on the basis of knowledge gained, attitudinal adjustments, or behavioral change and ultimately seeing an increase in health status. Operationally, health education final results take time to occur, so longitudinal assessment is required for objective observation of the ultimate results. 3. The determination of the effectiveness of a health education program or service based on the ultimate results of the objectives, including long-term changes in health status, social benefits, and quality of life.

outcome management In health administration, this is an assessment of the final results of health-care services; administrative activities used to evaluate the quality of service, health-care delivery, and administrative activities.

outcomes management standards board In managed care, this is a health-care reform proposal to ensure patient/consumer education and information and to report the results of the effectiveness of new health-care approaches.

outcome measures A measure of the quality of medical care in which the standard is the attainment of a specified end result or outcome. The outcome of medical care is measured with such parameters as improved health, lowered mortality and morbidity, improvement in abnormal states (such as elevated blood pressure), and increased health status. The process of tracking clinical treatment and its final result, including the assessment of function and morbidity measures. Disease has a "natural history" or course in which medical care seeks to intervene. To measure the effectiveness of a particular medical action in altering a disease's natural history is to carry out an outcome measure. Such measures are a way to determine the quality, effectiveness, and efficiency of medical care. A cost-benefit analysis of medical care is also one measure. It is possible to carry out a random controlled trials using outcome measures to compare the therapeutic effect of any drug or medical procedure on a disease as compared to its "natural history" without treatment or with a treatment already in use. Some commonly used outcome measures are length of stay, length of treatment required, readmissions, hours of therapy required daily, final results of treatment, payer expense for treatment, patient satisfaction, and discharge destination. *See also input measure; process measure; output measure; health status; health status indicator.*

outcomes, value-scaled In public health or health services delivery, this is a measure of the results of programs or services based on values assigned to scales used to depict a range of importance or level of benefit or lack of benefit to participants or patients (e.g., a low to high five-point value scale of a health behavior affecting health status of a population).

outfall In environmental health and water pollution control, this is the place where an effluent is discharged into receiving waters.

outflow In public health or health services delivery, this is a measure of the proportion of individuals in a service area, catchment area, or target population who leave the locale for the same service elsewhere. *See outmigration.*

outlay for personal health services In health-care delivery and managed care, these are the revenues used to deliver medical care to individuals and are calculated by taking total charges for health services received during the year plus prepaid and insurance premiums for insurance to cover personal health services. Costs include family co-payment and regular charges but not employer contributions or co-insurance or other payments.

outlays In the federal budget, these are actual expenditures of federal funds, including checks issued, interest accrued on the public debt, or other payments (minus refunds and reimbursements). Total budget outlays consist of the sum of the outlays from appropriations and other funds included in the budget universe less off-setting receipts. Off-budget federal agencies are not included in the budget universe, and their outlays are excluded from total budget outlays. Although budget authority is usually obligated in the fiscal year for which it is appropriated, it may be used as an outlay, once obligated, over several years.

outlier In the Medicare Prospective Payment System/Diagnosis Related Groups (PPS/DRG) system, a patient case displaying atypical characteristics relative to other patients in a DRG; cases falling outside the norms of the PPS/DRG system. Under Medicare, this is a patient with an unusually long length of stay or overly expensive hospital cost who is billed by charges rather than DRG rates. It refers to extremes experienced in receiving care in a health-care facility as compared to the typical or average patient such as low and high lengths of stay, death, leaving against medical advice, admitted and discharged the same day, low-volume DRGs, or clinical outliers. Such special cases receiving additional payments from Medicare must be approved by the peer review organization.

outmigration In epidemiology or health-care delivery, this is the residents moving out of one community or area to live elsewhere; the movement by rural residents from their communities to urban areas to procure health care and other services; to leave an area with high infestation of a disease to a low-disease area.

out of area In managed care, this is any care or treatment rendered or obtained to a health plan member outside the geographical or service area limits of the health plan in which he or she is enrolled. Coverage of care is limited to emergency care.

out-of-area benefits In managed care, this is the emergency care coverage a health plan enrollee has when he or she is outside the defined service area and away from contracted health-care providers. Some health plans offer unlimited out-of-area emergency coverage, whereas others have a limit on the dollar amount and rules about reimbursement procedures and may require immediate transfer to contract health facilities in the service area.

out-of-area care In managed care, this is medical care rendered to a health plan member when the member is beyond the service area of the health plan. Health plans such as health maintenance organizations are required by federal law to define their service area. *See out of area; out-of-area service.*

out-of-area insurance *See insurance, out-of-area.*

out-of-area service In managed care, these are medical services provided to a health plan enrollee by health-care providers not under a health plan contract and outside the health plan's service area. Health plans usually do not pay for services outside the contract or service area unless a delay in treatment would have adversely affected the health status or medical condition of the patient.

out of plan In managed care, this is any service or medical care obtained by a plan member without the authorization of the health plan.

out-of-pocket costs In managed care, this is money paid by enrollees for medical care outside and exclusive of any health plan coverage such as any required co-payments, co-insurance, or deductibles. *See out-of-pocket expenditures.*

out-of-pocket expenditures In managed care, this is money paid by an individual or family member (enrollee) for medical care outside and exclusive of any health plan or medical care insurance benefits and includes any required co-payments, co-insurance, or deductibles. The amount paid for medical care directly by individuals out of their own budgets and not paid by any third-party payer. Out-of-pocket expenditures are calculated by dividing total annual out-of-pocket expenditures by total person-year equivalents.

out-of-pocket expenses In managed care and insurance, these are costs borne directly by a patient without benefit of insurance. Unless insured, these include patient payments under cost-sharing provisions; the amount of money paid directly by an individual or dependent exclusive of any part paid by a health plan, medical insurance, or other persons or agencies; the amount of money a health plan member must pay before the health plan will pay any amount.

out-of-pocket limit In managed care and insurance, this is the total amount, after all costs are covered, that a member is required to pay for him- or herself and dependents and will be required to pay no more than a predetermined amount as set forth in the contract. Some exclusions may be stated and require some out-of-pocket costs for areas such as mental health or some medical devices.

outpatient A patient who receives ambulatory care at a hospital's outpatient clinic, surgicenter, ambulatory care center, or other health facility without being admitted to the facility as an inpatient. This usually does not mean people receiving services from a physician's office or other health service not designated as giving inpatient care; an individual not admitted nor confined to a bed as a bedpatient in a hospital but treated at a health-care facility. Also referred to as "same-day patients," "clinic patients," "walk-in patients," or "ambulatory patients."

outpatient care 1. Medical care provided at a hospital or other health-care facility to an ambulatory patient in an ambulatory care center in the facility but not admitted and not staying overnight. 2. In mental health services, these are ambulatory mental health services provided in a duration of less than 3 hours at a single visit on an individual, group, or family basis, usually in a clinic or similar ambulatory health-care facility. Emergency care on a walk-in basis as well as mental health care provided by mobile teams who visit patients outside the formal facility setting. 3. In managed care, this is any medical treatment provided to the member of a health plan who is not admitted to, or serving as an inpatient in, a health-care facility. Any medical care provided on an ambulatory care basis at a hospital or clinic without being admitted for an overnight stay.

outpatient department (OPD) The department that provides nonemergency ambulatory care as contrasted with formal admission to the hospital and inpatient care. The department may have several specialty clinics and may be staffed by full-time doctors, nurses, clerks, and technicians.

outpatient department, organized According to JCAHO, this is a service or clinic of a hospital established to provide nonemergency medical care for ambulatory patients.

outpatient medical facility A facility designed to provide a limited or full spectrum of health and medical services (including health education and maintenance, preventive services, diagnosis, treatment, and rehabilitation) to individuals who do not require hospitalization or institutionalization.

outpatient prescription drugs In medical care, these are medicines, pharmaceutical preparations, or other substances written by and under the orders of a physician that can be given to or taken by patients outside the inpatient areas of a hospital.

outpatient programs According to JCAHO for psychiatric, alcoholism, and drug abuse facilities accreditation purposes, programs that provide services to persons who generally do not need the level of care associated with the more restrictive environments of inpatient or residential programs. Such programs are usually located in facilities classified as business occupancies in chapter 13 of the 1973 edition of the *Life Safety Code* (NFPA 101). *See also partial day program.*

outpatient services Health-care services provided to patients on an ambulatory basis rather than by admission to a hospital or other healthcare facility. These services may be a part of a hospital and may augment its inpatient services or be provided at a freestanding facility; therapies, programs, treatments, and diagnostic studies that can be safely and effectively provided to ambulatory patients who are treated and leave the same day and that can be performed in a department that is part of a hospital, clinic, or health center. *See ambulatory surgery center.*

outpatient social work In hospitals or other health-care facilities, this is social support services or social work activities provided in the outpatient department or areas of a health-care facility.

outpatient surgery Medical care surgical treatment or diagnostic procedures in an ambulatory care center of a hospital that do not require admission as an inpatient to the hospital even though the surgery is performed in the hospital. *See ambulatory surgery.*

outpatient surgery services In hospital administration and health-care delivery, these are scheduled surgical treatments or diagnostic activities rendered to patients in a hospital who are not admitted as inpatients or do not have an overnight stay in the hospital. Surgery and recovery activities are provided in operating suites designed to accommodate 1-day ambulatory surgery situations in units specially designated as surgical units, operating rooms, and recovery rooms in an ambulatory care area or center.

outpatient treatment Medical care, therapies, and treatment procedures in an ambulatory care center of a hospital or other setting outside a hospital that do not require admission as an inpatient. *See ambulatory surgery.*

outpatient visit 1. Health and medical services provided to a patient on an ambulatory basis while spending less than 2 hours in a facility. Services provided may include any test, examination, patient education and prevention, treatment, or other service or procedure provided by qualified physicians, nurses, and allied health-care providers. Outpatient care is usually either emergency, outpatient surgery, or other clinical services not requiring an overnight inpatient hospital stay; walk-in visits by patients for medical, dental, or diagnostic services but who are not lodged in the hospital, are not admitted as inpatients, and leave the same day after recovery from treatment or surgery. 2. Each appearance by an ambulatory patient to each unit of a hospital in the capacity of an outpatient counts as one outpatient visit. A visit consists of one or more occasions of service (each test, examination, treatment, or procedure rendered to an outpatient counts as one occasion of service). Outpatient visit assessment is the best measure of outpatient services utilization and is done in several areas: emergency, professional contact visits, outpatient therapy and treatment visits, and ancillary service visits. Occasions of service are useful as a visit verification measure.

outplacement In human resource management, this is when a health-care organization provides some assistance to former employees in preparing for, searching for, and finding jobs as a result of layoffs caused by budget cuts or downsizing.

output 1. In health information management, this is the data that come out of a computer after its input information has been processed. 2. The process of transferring data from an internal to an external storage area of a computer. 3. The end product of any activity. It is often associated with communication processes, information systems, production tasks, and management activities. 4. In health-care delivery, this is the final result of a patient receiving medical treatment, therapy, or services; the end product of a course of treatment or a stay in a health-care facility.

output contract A contract in which a buyer agrees to purchase the entire production or output of a particular item. *See also requirements contract.*

output coupler In laser technology, this is a reflective mirror that allows only a portion of the beam to escape from the laser cavity.

output descriptions A detailed explanation of what descriptors will be produced by a computer from using a software application (e.g., patient number, name, DRG principal diagnosis, and length of stay).

output measure Measures of the productivity of health programs and manpower, process measures, or outcome measures. *See outcome measures.*

output media In health-care information management, these are the forms, tapes, printouts, or devices on which processed information appears.

output objectives In health planning and health administration, these are the measurable end results of planned activities used to accomplish the aims of a program, service, or unit.

outputs In health administration and health-care delivery, these are the number of units of service produced by various units, programs, or services in the provision of patient care or to other centers in the health-care facility.

Outrageous Conduct, Doctrine of Any act or behavior that is beyond all decency and is regarded as unacceptable and intolerable.

outreach According to JCAHO for psychiatric, alcoholism, and drug abuse facilities accreditation purposes, the process of systematically interacting with the community to identify those in need of services, alerting persons and their families to the availability of services, locating needed services, and enabling persons to enter the service delivery system.

outreach worker A social service professional or paraprofessional worker who goes into the community to visit individuals in need of social or health care. The worker attempts to establish a level of need and types of services required.

outside containers In environmental health and hazardous waste management, these are strong containers (other than a freight container), serving as the outermost enclosure, used in transporting hazardous material.

outside counsel In health administration or managed care, these are attorneys hired from a law firm to represent the health-care organization in legal matters.

outside directors Members of a board of trustees who are community leaders or business personnel not employed by the health-care organization.

overbed cradle A specialized frame set over a patient while lying in bed used to protect the body from contact with the bed covers.

overbedded In health-care delivery, this is the number of hospital beds or nursing home beds that are in excess of what is needed and/or used on an average in a hospital or other health-care facility or in a region or geographic area; a measure of a health-care system or facility and its capacity or overcapacity, implying increased costs and wasted resources resulting from a lack of use.

overcome 1. To prevail over. 2. To master.

overcompensation In mental health, this is an exaggerated effort to overcome real or imagined physical or psychological deficit or insufficiencies.

overdraft In health-care finance, this is to withdraw more money from an account than is in the account.

overfill releases In environmental health, these are liquid or polluted water releases into the environment that occur when a tank is filled beyond its capacity, resulting in a discharge of the regulated substance into the environment.

overfire air In environmental health, this is the air that is forced up to the top of an incinerator or boiler to fan the flames.

overhead In health-care financial management, this is the general operating costs that are distributed to all the revenue-producing operations of the entity but that are not directly attributable to a single activity; costs that are not payroll but that include fringe benefits and all expenses related to patient care operations.

overland flow In environmental health, this is a wastewater cleansing method where polluted water is allowed to flow over a sloped surface. As the water flows over the materials on the surface, the contaminants are removed and the water becomes clean as it is collected at the bottom of the slope.

overlapping territory In managed care and insurance, this is the catchment area or geographical area open to other health plans or agents for sales of medical benefit packages; when a part of a sales region is covered by both an individual agent and a general agent of an insurance company.

overmatching In biomedical and epidemiology research design activities, this is a subject selection process that can distort or block true causal associations between independent and dependent variables; the matching of variables when it is not necessary such as when no effect on the dependent variable will occur. The creation of an overelaborate design and its result have no outcome effect.

overnutrition The oversupply of calories, vitamins, minerals, or other nutrients; excess consumption of calories and lack of a balanced diet.

overpack In environmental health and hazardous waste management, this is an enclosure that is used by a single consignor to provide protection or convenience in handling of a package or to consolidate two or more packages. Overpack excludes the freight container.

overreach In contract law, when a party in a superior position makes unfair demands or requires concessions from the party in an inferior bargaining position.

overrule 1. To have authority over. 2. In law, this is to supersede; a higher court rejecting the legal principles on which the case was based; a superior court voiding a lower court's opinion.

oversight and omissions 1. In health administration, these are things that are overlooked or left out of an organization's plans because of inadvertence, which causes delays, problems, or failures in achieving stated goals. 2. In risk management, all contributing factors in an accident sequence are seen as specific oversights and omissions until such time as they are transferred to assumed risk.

overstocked In health administration material management and health-care finance, this is when supplies on hand and inventory exceed demand, which may cause a drain on cash flow.

overt 1. An act outwardly done. 2. Any action done with no attempt to conceal it. 3. Open; clear. 4. Extremely obvious.

over-the-counter drug (OTC drug) A drug that is advertised and sold directly to the public without prescription (e.g., aspirin).

overtime In health administration and human resource management, this any amount of time worked beyond the expected, set, or standard workday or workweek. Some personnel may require payment of overtime wages as set forth by federal or state wage and hour laws. For exempt employees (professional staff), payment for extra hours worked is built into the basic salary, income distribution, or bonus plans. Certain statutes require that certain nonphysician and nonprofessional personnel be paid overtime for extra hours of work. Provisions should be made in personnel handbooks to clearly indicate which employees must be paid overtime according to law.

overwintering In epidemiology, this is when a vector has reduced activity over the winter season but the pathogen persists through the cooler winter months. How much of an epidemic will occur in the summer depends on how well vector-borne pathogens survive in the host over the winter.

OWA *See other weird arrangements.*

owner's equity In health-care finance, this is the difference between the assets and liabilities of a health-care organization. Also referred to as the organization's "net worth."

ownership disclosure Making public information by a health program of all ownership interests in the program. By law, each skilled nursing facility participating in Medicare and Medicaid must supply ownership information to the state survey agency, and each intermediate care facility must supply such information to the state licensing agency. Full and complete information must be supplied 1) on the identity of each person having (directly or indirectly) an ownership interest of 10% or more in such facility; 2) in the case of a facility organized as a corporation, each officer and director of the corporation; and 3) in the case of the facility organized as a partnership, each partner. Any changes that affect the accuracy of this information must be promptly reported.

oxidants In environmental health and air pollution, these are substances containing oxygen that react chemically in air to produce a new substance; the primary ingredient of photochemical smog.

oxidation ponds In environmental health, these are man-made lakes in which waste is consumed by bacteria. These are used mostly with other wastewater treatment processes. An oxidation pond is basically the same as a sewage lagoon.

oxo- Prefix meaning "oxygen."

oyer and terminer (French) Hear and decide. Some higher criminal courts carry this title.

ozone Found in two layers of the atmosphere: the stratosphere and the troposphere. In the stratosphere (the atmospheric layer beginning 7 to 10 miles above the earth's surface), ozone is formed of naturally occurring oxygen, which provides a protective layer shielding the earth from ultraviolet radiation's harmful health effects on humans and the environment. In the troposphere, ozone is a chemical oxidant and a major component of photochemical smog. Ozone can seriously affect the human respiratory system and is one of the most prevalent and widespread of all the criteria pollutants for which the Clean Air Act required the EPA to set standards. Ozone is produced through complex chemical reactions of nitrogen oxides, which are among the primary pollutants emitted by combustion sources, by decay of organic matter, by hydrocarbons released into the atmosphere through combustion, by vapors from decay of organic materials, and by handling and processing of petroleum products and sunlight.

P

P Probability. As used in the analysis of biomedical and health services empirical research using inferential statistics, results and findings are stated in terms of the probability that results do or do not occur by chance and that they do so at a certain level of confidence (e.g., a 95% level of confidence that the finding is not caused by chance alone). A 5% probability that the research findings could only occur by chance is a .05 probability level. Also referred to as "P value."

P&T Pharmacy and therapeutics.

PA Professional association; physician advisor; public accountant. *See also physician assistant.*

PAC Preadmission certification; products of ambulatory care.

pacemaker In medical care, this is an electronic medical device that sends an electrical signal to the heart's nervous tissue to stimulate each heartbeat when the natural heartbeat response is defective, erratic, or nonexistent. The pacemaker device is implanted under the skin in the chest area, and electrodes are attached to or in the heart.

package insert A labeling process approved by the Food and Drug Administration for prescription drug products that accompanies the product when shipped by the manufacturer to the physician or pharmacist but that usually does not accompany a dispensed prescription. The package insert is directed at the prescribing professional, principally the physician, and states the appropriate uses of a drug, the mode of administration, dosage information, contraindications, and warnings. The legal effect of prescribing the drug in ways not described in the package is unclear. *See also compendium; Physician's Desk Reference.*

packed red blood cells In blood bank operations, these are red blood cells that have been separated from the plasma and are administered to patients separately.

packed towers In environmental health, these are pollution control devices that force dirty air through a tower packed with crushed rock or wood chips while liquid is sprayed over the packing material. The pollutants in the airstream either dissolve or chemically react with the liquid and help clean the air.

packing 1. In health law, this is attempting to sway a legal decision through improperly placing persons on a jury, a court, or an agency hearing. 2. In medical care, this is the process of filling an open wound with an absorbent material such as gauze.

pact An agreement.

pactum (Lat.) 1. A pact. 2. A bargain.

PAHO *See Pan American Health Organization.*

paid claims In managed care, this is the amount of money paid to health-care providers to satisfy the contractual liability of the health plan sponsor or insurance carrier. Excluded is any member liability for ineligible charges or for deductibles or co-payments. If capitation contracts or other fee schedules are contracted for by the managed-care plan with the insurance carrier, lower paid claims liability usually results.

paid claims loss ratio In managed care, this is the ratio from paid claims divided by total premiums.

paid FTE Full-time equivalent employees who are fully paid. In health administration and human resources management, this is all full-time equivalents (FTEs) calculated using all hours paid, including such items as personal time off, sick pay, holidays, vacation, or leave.

pain Any unpleasant feeling or sensation of physical suffering experienced by the stimulation of certain nerve endings; may be caused by threat or disease, blows to body, injury, or mental perception.

pain and suffering In health law and the recovery process in tort law, negligence, or malpractice, this is the nonvisible or noneconomic injury that accompanies an adverse event experience by a plaintiff in the delivery of health care or from other harm or loss as a result of negligence. Under some circumstances, court and juries are allowed under law to compensate victims of negligence beyond basic recovery for pain and suffering that resulted from the experiences associated with the actual injury, loss, or damage. *See recovery; tort law; negligence; malpractice.*

pain management program In medical care delivery, this a therapy program that assists patients in pain who have little or no relief in the control of chronic pain and when the disease cannot be treated or removed and symptom control is one of the few remaining alternatives. Some patients who suffer from cancer or other painful chronic diseases are often the participants in such a program, which involves a multidisciplinary health-care team providing symptom relief through pain control.

pain-pleasure principle A psychological concept stating that people tend to seek pleasure and avoid pain. Also referred to as "hedonism."

pain threshold The amount of stimulation required for pain to be felt.

paired comparison In health administration and human resource management, this is a performance appraisal method where each employee is compared to all others in a work area, section, or department. Each is compared one at a time to determine which of the employees are the most outstanding in their job performance according to the job characteristics being compared. When all workers have been rated against each job characteristic and one another, the employee who comes out most favorably most often is ranked first, and so on, two being compared each time until all are ranked.

paired sampling In health services and biomedical research, this is a research sampling process used to place subjects equally into research and control groups. Subjects are identified and paired by common characteristics such as age or education, and then one of the pair is assigned to the research group and the other to the control group.

pairing 1. Two or more persons not voting on a certain bill in a legislature. 2. Agreeing to refrain from. 3. A biomedical research sampling process where research subjects are grouped in twos by certain common characteristics, then one of the two is put into the research pool and the other into the control group pool.

pais (French) Outside the court.

palliative Providing relief but not a cure.

palpable 1. That which is tangible, plain, easily seen, obviously evident, or clear to the mind. 2. Notorious, usually in reference to an error or an abuse of authority.

palpation Feeling something with the hands and the fingers.

pan- Prefix meaning "all," "common to all," "across," or "every."

Pan American Health Organization An international public health organization for health of the Inter-American System. It also serves as the Regional Office for the World Health Organization and is part of the United Nations system. The PAHO collaborates throughout the Americas with Ministries of Health and Social Services, other governmental and nongovernmental institutions, organizations, universities, community groups, and others to strengthen national and local health systems to improve the health of the people of the Americas. The PAHO employs scientific and technical experts to promote primary care and public health activities through targeting vulnerable groups, communities, and areas to improve their health status. Activities include eradication of communicable diseases such as smallpox, polio, cholera, and diarrheal disease plus public health and environmental health measures such as clean drinking water, liquid waste control, vector control, elimination of occupational health hazards, and the degradation of the environment. The association was founded in 1902 with headquarters located in Washington, D.C.

pandemic In epidemiology, this is an outbreak of a disease that is widespread or worldwide; epidemics across large populations and widespread geographical areas.

pander 1. To procure. 2. To solicit prostitution. 3. To provide a means to help one satisfy vices or ambitions.

panel 1. A jury list. 2. The group of jurors as a whole. 3. A group of judges or arbitrators used to decide an issue. 4. In managed-care and health-care finance, this is a payment mechanism that groups patients under one health-care provider (physician) who agrees to be responsible for their health care and who is then paid on a capitation basis for a set period of time (e.g., 1 month or 1 year). The health-care provider usually agrees to see this group of patients for whatever care is needed within a range of services previously agreed on. The income to the health-care provider is usually based on the number of patients in the group (panel) rather than on the number and type of patients seen and services rendered. Thus there is an incentive to see the least number of patients possible while retaining a high quality of care and reducing the number and type of services rendered to individual patients. This method is used in institutional approaches to health-care delivery, especially in managed care and managed competition. *See open panel.*

panel group practice *See closed-panel group practice; open-panel group practice.*

paper of a lawsuit All documents; short for "commercial paper"; a negotiable instrument.

PAR *See preadmission review.*

par 1. At face value. 2. Equal to a preestablished value.

parachute, golden In health administration and human resource management, this is an employment agreement for top administrators for protection against wrongful termination that was created to offer some financial protection to the administrator in the event of the loss of one's position/employment. Severance pay, regular pay, and benefits to continue for a specified time period are usual conditions of a golden parachute employment contract.

paradigm A model; a system, schematic, or framework; a construct or framework of a set of interactions in and between activities.

paradigm change When the principles and concepts of a system or model and related interactions and activities are different than the ones used to start the model. *See paradigm shift.*

paradigm lock When a health administrator is stuck in or continues in a line of thinking about systems and models while the industry and society are moving in a different direction and into new models and approaches.

paradigm shift As used in health administration and health systems, this is when the foundational constructs, principles, and rules of health-care delivery or health systems management no longer are useful or effective and thus change to a new set of rules, approaches, methods, and principles; a change in the way the health administrator thinks and views managerial systems or models and how the administrator of a health facility or health-care organization approaches management and leadership on the basis of new models and frameworks using new lines of thinking; a change in strategic philosophical thought, approaches, and methods of health-care delivery or health administration; a new way of seeing an old problem or model.

paralegal A nonlawyer who works to assist a lawyer.

parallel citation A court's decision that is published in more than one publication.

parallel interface In health information management, this is computer hardware that allows all information or data in a computer to be transferred to another computer or unit simultaneously.

paralogia *See evasion.*

paralysis The loss of all or part of one's motor function in a part of the body.

paralysis agitans *See Parkinsonism.*

paramedic An individual with an advanced level of training, beyond that of the emergency medical technician, who responds to medical emergencies, evaluates the nature of the emergency, and carries out specified diagnostic and treatment procedures under standing orders or who carries out treatment while in direct communication with a physician. Paramedics may provide advanced life support services such as intravenous drug administration and cardiac arrhythmia control. *See also emergency medical technician.*

paramedical Having indirect or peripheral association with the practice of medicine; loosely or distantly connected to medical care.

paramedical personnel All nonphysician health personnel including health aides, record keepers, family health workers, nutritionists, dental hygienists, medical technicians, physician assistants, and health associates. This is a general term, and no list of occupations that meets this category are agreed on. *See also allied health personnel; emergency medical technician.*

parameters 1. Factors, variables, or issues that vary according to application on the basis of different situations. In health-care delivery, the factors that contribute to the status of a patient are parameters such as a drug given, procedure completed, or test conducted, which all have a bearing on the outcome of the patient or, in research, the final results of the research activity. 2. In computer software programming, a variable given as a constant value for a specific purpose or to initiate a certain process. *See variable.*

parameters, practice Strategies for patient management developed to assist practitioners in clinical decision making, including standards, guidelines, and other patient management strategies (JCAHO for acute-care facilities).

parametric data In epidemiology and statistics, this uses interval and ratio scale data that are quantitative, can have mathematical and statistical methods applied to them, and consider the distribution of the data.

paramnesia A memory disorder in which reality and fantasy are confused. It is observed in certain types of schizophrenia and organic brain syndromes.

paramour An illicit lover; a person who substitutes for or replaces a husband or wife with another lover but without any legal right or marital obligation.

paranoid In psychiatry, this is a mental state marked by symptoms of systematized delusions and disorganization, fear, and excessive distrust.

paranormal medicine Therapies that go beyond the mainstream of usual medical practice but have been found useful in augmenting medical treatment such as biofeedback, biorelease, humor as an intervention, rebirthing, unitive psychology, alpha training, autogenic training, Gestalt therapy, deep relaxation, visualization therapy, or any technique that provides self-renewal and self-transcendence.

paraplegia Paralysis from the waist down; paralysis of both legs, usually caused by damage to the spinal cord or adjacent nerves as a result of injury or disease. Sensation may or may not be lost, and motor and muscle function may be absent depending on the level and extent of destruction.

parapraxis In psychiatry, this describes blunt statements blurted out or slips of the tongue caused by unconscious thoughts.

paraprofessional A person who assists a professional or who performs some of the basic duties of a professional. In health care, these are usually identified as allied health professionals. *See also allied health professional.*

paraprofessional services In community health and aging services, these are services, therapies, or support activities provided to patients in their own homes such as home attendants, homemakers, home health aides, housekeepers, and home repair personnel. Such personnel provide basic support, on-site training, personal support, and guidance and assist the disabled or elderly to function at the highest level possible in their own homes.

parasite Any organism that cannot live independently without its host; any plant or animal organism that lives off or on another plant or animal to obtain its subsistence and nourishment.

parasitic disease In public health, epidemiology, and medical care, this is a disease that is caused by a plant or animal living within or on another living organism, obtaining subsistence at the host's expense.

parasympathetic nervous system The segment of the autonomic nervous system that controls the life-sustaining organs of the body.

parens (Lat.) Equals.

parens patriae (Lat.) The power and right of government to take over the treatment or care for minors or others who cannot legally care for themselves.

parental rejection Withholding of love, affection, and attention from a child by one or both parents. The child develops great emotional needs and/or hostility, which can be directed outward in the form of tantrums or inward against himself or herself in the form of psychosomatic disorders, self-hate, self-pity, or self-destructive behavior; similar to love deprivation or emotional abuse.

parent corporation A legally established corporation that directly owns at least 50% of the voting stock of a corporation that is facility owned or operated.

parenteral Piercing mucous membranes or the skin barrier through such events as needle sticks, human bites, cuts, and abrasions.

parenteral IV feeding *See parenteral nutrition.*

parenteral nutrition The process of giving a patient nutrients in a manner and by a route other than is considered normal ingestion by mouth. Nutrients are put into the body by intravenous tubes or other routes such as subcutaneously, intramuscularly, or intradermally. *See total parenteral nutrition.*

parenteral product According to JCAHO for psychiatric, alcoholism, and drug abuse facilities accreditation purposes, a sterile, pharmaceutical preparation ingested by the body through a route other than the alimentary canal.

pares (Lat.) Equals.

paresthesia Strange feelings or sensations felt on the skin, including burning, tickling, and tingling.

Pareto analysis This is a method of collecting statistics, information, and data and arranging it in descending order of frequency as it relates to the type or causes of administrative or productivity problems.

Pareto principle The 20/80 rule: 20% of patients use up 80% of the resources, 20% of volunteers do 80% of the work, etc.

pari delicto (Lat.) Equal fault.

pari materia (Lat.) On the same subject; interdependent.

pari passu (Lat.) Equally; without preference or discrimination.

parity 1. Equality. 2. In epidemiology, the classification of women by the number of live-born children (e.g., a woman of parity 4 has had four live-born children). 3. In medical usage, the classification of women by the total number of births they have had, including both live births and stillbirths; the total number of times a woman has been pregnant minus the number of abortions and/or miscarriages occurring up to 28 weeks of gestation.

Parkinsonism A chronic disease as manifested by rhythmic muscular tremors known as pill rolling and accompanied by spasticity and rigidity of movement, propulsive gait, droopy posture, and masklike facial expression. It is usually seen in later life as a result of arteriosclerotic changes in the basal ganglia.

Parkinsonism-like effect A common side effect of antipsychotic drugs. Typical symptoms include motor retardation, physical rigidity, changes in posture, tremor, and autonomic nervous system disturbances.

parliamentary authority In formal health-care meetings or hearings, a procedure manual that follows Robert's Rules of Order or other parliamentary procedure guidelines. The manual is adopted by the health-care organization as its official guide to parliamentary procedure and is used to govern the business of official and formal assemblies not otherwise stated in the constitution and bylaws of the assembly or health-care organization.

parliamentary law Rules, policy, and procedures used by legislatures to conduct business.

parol evidence In health law, these are facts or proof given verbally rather than in writing.

parol evidence rule In substantive law, a rule declaring that when an agreement between two parties has been reached and when the terms of the contract have been written, oral evidence will not supersede the written contract.

parol promise A simple contract; a verbal promise.

Part A intermediaries In health-care financing through Medicare, these are business organizations, often medical insurance companies, that become contractors who accept billing from and make payments to hospitals, nursing homes, and home health agencies on behalf of the Health Care Financing Administration (HCFA). *See Medicare.*

Part B carriers In health-care financing through Medicare, these are business organizations, often medical insurance companies, that become contractors who accept billing from and make payments to physicians, laboratories, and suppliers for noninstitutional services to Medicare patients on behalf of the Health Care Financing Administration (HCFA). *See Medicare.*

partial care treatment In mental health services, this is a planned program of mental health treatment services generally provided in visits of 3 or more hours to groups of patients. Included in the psychiatric services are therapy programs that emphasize intensive short-term therapy and rehabilitation; programs that focus on recreation and/or occupational program activities, including sheltered workshops; and education and training programs, including special education classes, therapeutic nursery schools, and vocational training.

partial closure In environmental health and hazardous waste, this is allowing some units to operate while ending the use of a hazardous waste management unit in accordance with regulatory requirements; the closure of a tank, landfill, cell, surface impoundment, waste pile, or other hazardous waste management unit while other units continue to operate.

partial day programs According to JCAHO for psychiatric, alcoholism, and drug abuse facilities accreditation purposes, programs that provide services to persons who generally do not require the level of care provided in the more restrictive environments of residential or inpatient programs. Partial day programs are designed for patients who spend only part of a 24-hour period in the facility. They provide sleeping accommodations and are usually located in facilities classified as residential occupancies in chapter 11 of the 1973 edition of the *Life Safety Code* (NFPA 101). Partial day programs that provide treatment and care services only during the day are usually located in facilities classified as business occupancies in chapter 13 of the 1973 edition of the *Life Safety Code.*

partial disability In insurance, any illness or injury that prevents a person from performing some of the functions of his or her regular job.

partial hospitalization 1. Formal programs of care in a hospital or other institution for periods of less than 24 hours a day, typically involving services usually provided to inpatients. There are two principal types: 1) night hospitalization, which is for patients who need hospitalization but who can work or attend school outside the hospital during the day, and 2) day hospitalization, which is for people who require inpatient diagnostic or treatment services but who can safely spend nights and weekends at home. 2. Substance abuse and alcohol or mental health programs conducted in the day without inpatient admissions that provide clinical services at a hospital as an alternative or follow-up to the prior inpatient hospitalization. 3. In mental health services, this is a planned transitional program of outpatient psychiatric care and/or halfway houses provided after discharge from inpatient psychiatric hospitalization or residential treatment programs when a patient no longer requires 24-hour psychiatric care.

partialization In mental health care, this is breaking down a client's problems into manageable segments or areas.

partially delegated hospital A hospital to which the PRO has assigned either concurrent review or MCE study functions; may also indicate that in the concurrent review process the hospital assumes the responsibility for either the physician advisor or the review coordinator function. The PRO retains final responsibility for the effective performance of all reviews conducted by the hospital review committee. *See also medical care evaluation; professional review organization.*

partial psychiatric hospitalization A method of therapy and treatment of mental illness in which the patient goes to a hospital on a part-time basis. *See also day hospital; night hospital; weekend hospital.*

participating hospital A hospital that has an agreement or contract with a medical insurance company or managed-care plan to provide hospital services to its enrolled members.

participating insurance company *See mutual insurance company.*

participating physician In managed care, this is a physician who has contracted with a health plan insurance group or enrolled with an insurance company and agreed to accept its patients. Also called a "member physician."

participating physician agreement A contract that a physician signs with the Health Care Financing Administration (HCFA) to accept Medicare patients and assignment on all Medicare claims and to follow the HCFA's procedures and policies. Agreements are renewed annually. This is a contract that a physician makes with a health plan or an insurance agency to accept the health plan's patients, follow the agency's procedures and policies, and submit the health plan's paperwork for reimbursement.

participating provider In managed care, this is a medical care professional or health-care provider who is licensed to provide health care and has a written agreement (contract) with a health plan to provide medical services to health plan subscribers. Providers may be physicians, pharmacies, hospitals, nursing homes, medical groups, or other practitioners, services, or facilities.

participating special facility A nonhospital health-care facility that has a written agreement with an insurance company or health plan and provides a specialized type of care.

participation 1. In managed care, this is an agreement whereby a physician participates in a health plan or medical insurance plan and agrees to accept the plan's preestablished fee or reasonable charge as the maximum amount that can be collected for services rendered. A nonparticipating physician may charge more than the insurance program's maximum allowable amount for a particular service. The patient is then liable for and must pay out-of-pocket the costs above the allowed amount. This system was developed in the private sector as a method of providing the insured with specific health-care services with no out-of-pocket costs. 2. In Medicare and Medicaid, this is any physician who accepts reimbursement from either program. Approximately half of Medicare claims are paid to physicians who participate by accepting assignment. Any physician accepting Medicaid payments must accept them as payment in full. A hospital or other health program is called a "participating provider" when it meets the various requirements of, and accepts reimbursement from, a public or private health insurance program. 3. In managed care, these are the groups of employees enrolled in managed-care services or health plans for medical coverage as determined by the percentage of the total number of eligible employees. A 70% participation requirement level means that 70% of eligible employees must enroll for coverage for the plan to be offered and include dependents. 4. In health-care finance, this is when a bank or other financial lender is willing to be actively involved in a building project or the institution of a new service that a health-care organization is undertaking. The lending institution's involvement requires a percentage of the gross sales, profit, or interest gained. This approach to financing projects is done when it is difficult to obtain financing through other means.

participation rates In public health and health services delivery, these are the percentages of working-age men and women in the work force.

participative counseling In mental health services, this is one approach to psychotherapy that seeks to utilize the better parts of directive and nondirective psychotherapy. The counselor and the client both actively participate in the counseling process in an interactive manner.

particulars 1. The specific details of a complaint. 2. Items listed on a bill or ledger.

particulars, bill of 1. An itemized written account of the issues of a claim. 2. An informal statement by a plaintiff as to a cause of action, or a defendant's setoff.

particulate loading In environmental health and air pollution, this is the mass of particulate per unit volume of air or water.

particulate matter In environmental health and air pollution, these are the microscopic particles of solid matter suspended in the air, including both nontoxic materials (e.g., soot, dust, and dirt) and toxic materials (e.g., lead, asbestos, suspended sulfates, and nitrates); finely divided solid or liquid airborne material with an aerodynamic diameter smaller than 100 micrometers.

particulate matter emissions In environmental health and air pollution, these are all finely divided solid or liquid material, other than uncombined water, emitted to the ambient air as measured by applicable reference methods or by a test specified by an environmental regulatory agency.

particulates In environmental health and air pollution, these are fine solid microscopic particles such as dust, smoke, fumes, or smog found in air or in emissions into the air.

parties Several persons or groups of persons involved in a lawsuit; all persons or organizations involved in a legal proceeding.

partner An individual in a partnership. A "silent" partner is one not publicly known as a partner. A "special" or "limited" partner puts in a fixed amount of money, gets a fixed amount of profit, and is usually not liable for anything beyond the initial investment.

partnership A business agreement between two or more persons who agree to share profits and losses in an unincorporated business arrangement. Each partner is a legal agent of the other and can be legally held responsible for the acts of the other, including malpractice, torts, or negligence, and each is legally bound by the acts of the other. In a partnership, each partner has a vested interest and incentive in the business, decisions, policymaking, and profit. The disadvantages of a partnership are that the partners share responsibility for the professional and business mistakes of one another and that all legal liability and tax benefits are limited. A partnership can be dissolved on the withdrawal of a single partner. *See also limited partnership.*

Partnership for Health A synonym for the former federally imposed comprehensive health planning program. The first set of amendments to the program were made in 1967 by P.L. 90-174, which was given the short title Partnership for Health Amendments of 1967.

part-time layoffs In health administration and human resources management, this is when a health-care organization has workers stay home without pay for a part of each week. Also called "furlough days" or "call-off days."

-partum Suffix meaning "birth."

parturition The process of delivery a baby; giving birth.

party 1. A person taking part in a transaction, lawsuit, or any legal claim. 2. Persons taking part in a transaction or proceeding.

party of the first part A phrase used instead of the name of a party in a document.

par value In health-care finance, the face value of trust deeds, mortgages, and stocks based on the balance owed without considering any discount.

PAS *See professional activity study/survey.*

PAS norms Professional Activity Study norms. These are the results of the Commission on Professional and Hospital Activities, which examines issues such as average lengths of stay in various regions of the United States, which is used to set standard estimates (norms) of lengths of stay (LOSs). Many different types of measures and indicators of health care are studied and developed. *See health status indicators; measures of health services.*

pass 1. To pronounce. 2. To pass judgment. 3. Enacted successfully.

passenger variable In health services and biomedical research, this is a third-level influencing variable that affects the outcome of research and is either tied to, carried by, or separate from the independent or intervening variable; a third level of explanation as to the reasons for what might appear as a cause-effect relationship or other results of a research outcome that accounts for the association of any change in the dependent variable that goes beyond the influence of the independent variable.

passim (Lat.) 1. Here and there. 2. In various places. 3. Throughout. 4. General reference to a work.

passive 1. Inactive. 2. Not involved. 3. Apathetic.

passive exercise In medical care rehabilitation, these are therapeutic exercise in which the movement is provided not by the patient but by a machine or therapist.

passive forecasting In strategic health planning, this is a planning or forecasting process that assumes that the planner has no way of influencing future utilization of services from either an objective or a subjective perspective.

passive negligence In health law, the defects, obstacles, or problems on the premises of a healthcare facility that if ignored cause danger from the mere physical condition of the property itself and that pose a liability risk. In legal liability, the defects, obstacles, or problems that are allowed to exist, are not fixed or maintained, and are dangerous simply because of the physical condition of the property or physical plant.

passive smoke Secondhand smoke or slipstream smoke imposed on nonsmokers by other persons smoking tobacco; a form of indoor air pollution that is harmful to one's health and has been known to contribute to cancers of the respiratory system. *See secondhand smoke; slipstream smoke.*

passivity Lethargic; lacking energy or will.

Pasteur, Louis An important historical figure in epidemiology and a pioneer in bacteriology, Pasteur (1822–1829) was the first chemist to be admitted to the French Academy of Medicine because of his work on discovering the pathogens of many diseases such as rabies and anthrax and for developing immunizations against them. He also found that pathogenic bacteria could live only within certain temperature ranges and that if certain foodstuffs such as milk are heated to a high temperature, bacteria are killed, thus the term "pasteurization." He is also known for his famous quote "Chance discoveries occur only in the well-prepared mind."

pastoral counseling *See chaplain; chaplaincy service; psychotherapy.*

PAT *See preadmission testing.*

PATCH *See Planned Approach to Community Health.*

patency Open; not shut or clogged.

patent 1. Apparent; evident; plainly visible. 2. Open; obvious. 3. A right to control the manufacture and sale of a discovery or invention. 4. A grant of privilege or property by the government.

paternal Belonging to or coming from the father.

paternalism In health administration, as used in management, this is when a supervisor or manager assumes that he or she alone is the best judge of employee needs and fails to respond to employee needs or suggestions.

paternity suit A lawsuit used to prove that a person is the real father of an illegitimate child. This is usually done to enforce his obligations to provide child support.

-path Suffix meaning "One suffering from a disease"; one who treats illness/patients by a system.

path analysis In epidemiological causality and association analysis, this deals with the linkage of the sequence of events and how variables are configured and related to one another. Probable and less probable linkages, paths, and connections between variables and paths are analyzed to eliminate the improbable linkages.

path-based patient care In managed care, these are overall goals and objectives of focused care plans and treatment processes that are identified that include the use of critical paths as a resource management tool. Selected paths are explored with universal paths modified as needed to be most effective.

path-goal strategy In health administration, this is a human resource strategy used to improve the path toward the goal by trying to improve outcomes at the end of the path by changing policy, procedure, and personnel efficiency.

patho- Prefix meaning "disease."

pathogen 1. In epidemiology and medical care, this is any organism such as a bacteria, virus, worm, or other parasite that can produce disease; a disease-causing organism. 2. In environmental health, these are microorganisms that can cause disease in other organisms or in humans, animals, and plants. They may be bacteria, viruses, or parasites and are found in sewage, in runoff from animal farms, or rural areas populated with domestic and/or wild animals, and in water used for swimming. Fish and shellfish contaminated by pathogens, or the contaminated water itself, can cause serious illness.

pathogenesis In epidemiology and medical care, this is the process by which certain disease-causing organisms produce disease. *See etiology.*

pathogenicity In epidemiology and medical care, this is the ability of an agent or organism to produce or cause disease; capability of an organism to produce illness.

pathogenicity of infectious agents In epidemiology, this is the ratio of the number of individuals with a pathogen-caused illness compared to the number of those exposed to the infectious agent.

pathological Abnormal or diseased.

pathologist A medical doctor who specializes in the study of the etiology of disease and diseased tissue. This physician practices in laboratories and morgues and carries out wet lab and epidemiological research, including autopsies.

pathologist, anatomical A physician who analyzes the gross aspects of tissue samples from patients and microscopically studies cells, tissues, and body organs presented to the pathology lab. This specialist studies tissue cells taken from biopsy, autopsy, amputation, childbirth, and body fluids to make a determination of disease states.

pathologist, clinical A physician who specializes in the assessment and study of disease states of cells and tissue in a clinical laboratory setting.

pathology The study of disease processes.

pathology, anatomic Services relating to surgical pathology, autopsy, and cytology (JCAHO for acute-care services).

pathology and clinical laboratory services The programs or services providing information on diagnosis, prevention, or treatment of disease through the examination of the structural and functional changes in tissues and organs of the body that cause or are caused by disease. Standards are applied to evaluate a hospital's performance in providing pathology and clinical laboratory services (JCAHO for acute-care facilities).

pathology, clinical In hospital and health facilities administration and in the delivery of medical care, these are services relating to the solution of clinical problems, especially the use of laboratory methods in clinical diagnosis; includes clinical chemistry, bacteriology and mycology, parasitology, virology, clinical microscopy, hematology, serology, and radiobioassay (JCAHO for acute-care facilities).

pathology department A clinical department and service in most major health-care facilities that examines and analyzes tests on human tissue, bone, and excretions and that assists in the diagnosis and treatment of patients. This department is under the supervision of a physician and, in a large health-care facility or hospital, may include many subdepartments and allied health personnel such as medical technologists who do special analysis and related research.

pathology, forensic A medical specialty dealing with laboratory analysis and assessment of human tissue and bodily fluids that has legal implications, especially as they may be related to the commission of a crime.

pathology lab *See pathology department.*

pathology service *See pathology department.*

pathology, surgical A medical specialty dealing with laboratory analysis and assessment of human tissue removed during surgical procedures, especially as used in diagnosis.

-pathy Suffix meaning "disease process."

patient 1. One who receives health services. Also referred to as a "consumer." 2. An individual being diagnosed or treated or receiving medical care under the auspices of a physician, health-care provider, health-care facility, or other medical personnel working in the health-care organization. 3. Any person admitted to a skilled nursing facility for observation, diagnosis, or treatment. *See also inpatient; outpatient; private patient; service patient.*

patient accounts In health-care finance, this is the financial record keeping of payment, credit, third-party payers, and collection activities of patients after discharge from a health-care facility.

patient accounts manager In health-care finance, this is an individual who works in the business office of a health-care facility and is in charge of financial records and payments related to patients discharged from the facility. *See also patient accounts.*

patient activities coordinator, qualified For JCAHO accreditation of long-term-care facilities, an individual who is licensed or registered, if applicable, in the state in which he or she is practicing and is eligible for registration as a therapeutic recreation specialist by the National Therapeutic Recreation Society; or an individual who has had at least 2 years of experience in a social or recreational program within the last 5 years, 1 year of which was full time in a patient/resident activities program in a health-care setting; or an individual who is a qualified occupational therapist or occupational therapy assistant; or an individual who has the equivalent training and/or experience.

patient advocacy In health-care delivery, especially in health-care facilities, this is the process whereby patients are assisted with complaints or problems regarding the delivery of medical care. A patient representative or ombudsman is often the professional who is involved in such matters. *See patient representative.*

patient advocate A person or professional who acts on the patient's behalf. *See patient representative.*

patient, ambulatory 1. Any individual who can walk into or from a health-care facility or treatment center unassisted, is not wheelchair bound or dependent on crutches, and walks freely when healthy. 2. In long-term care, this is an individual who is able to leave a building unassisted under emergency conditions.

patient assessment computerized system (PAC) In long-term care, this is a standard resident assessment system developed by a private nursing home corporation, the National Health Corporation of Murfreesboro, Tennessee.

patient assistance services In health-care delivery in health facilities, these are activities done or problems solved for the patient such as helping with toileting, mail, showers, and reading.

patient bed days *See patient days.*

patient care and services (PaCS) A patient care survey protocol developed for Medicare by the Health Care Financing Administration.

patient care audit The objective and systematic review of medical records by qualified personnel to assess the quality and quantity of medical care as compared to predetermined standards.

patient care committee An assembly of medical, nursing, and allied health-care providers who meet on a regular basis to review patient care standards and practices as compared to preset standards.

patient care coordinator In health administration and nursing care, this is the nurse with responsibility for the administration of patient care activities in a medical and nursing care unit(s) in a health-care facility. *See also nurse, charge; nurse supervisor.*

patient care manager (PCM) In hospital administration, this is the individual, often a primary care physician, responsible for ascertaining which services are needed by a patient to improve quality of care, ensure that all necessary care is rendered, and contain costs.

patient care plan A special plan developed under the direction of a physician by the nursing staff for the care and rehabilitation of each patient in the care unit. *See also nursing care plan.*

patient care policies In long-term-care administration, these are required written rules that guide the type, level, and amount of nursing care and medical services provided in nursing homes.

patient care profile In long-term care, this is a standard resident assessment system developed by William Thomas, a nursing home administrator in New Hampshire, and used by the Hillhaven Corporation.

patient care unit A medical and nursing care unit specially staffed with appropriate nursing and support personnel and equipped to care for persons admitted to the health-care facility. This patient care service is operated under the supervision of physicians who attend to the specialized needs of patients and the attending physician, who directs the care of his or her own patients.

patient-carried personal health record Medical and treatment records such as immunization records and disease histories about one's own medical history or family medical experiences that are kept and stored by private individuals.

patient census In health administration, this is the number of patients occupying beds as inpatients in a health-care facility for a specific period of time. Usually the patient count is conducted at midnight or a standard preset time and is done every 24 hours. Also called the "midnight census."

patient compliance When a patient follows physician's orders and treatment prescriptions; when a patient adheres to, follows through, and completes a treatment plan by taking the prescribed drugs, presenting himself or herself for therapy, and following prescribed orders when away from the health-care provider and/or facilities.

patient condition A statement provided to the public about the status of the type and severity of the illness of a patient, especially a public figure. The levels used are usually critical, serious, poor, fair, and good. Other levels are stable, guarded, and improving.

patient consent *See informed consent.*

patient data Any or all information gathered on a person receiving care or treatment from a health-care provider.

patient day expenses *See expenses per inpatient day.*

patient days In health administration, a measure of health-care institutional use, usually measured as the number of inpatients at a specified time (e.g., midnight). These are also the total number of inpatient days of care provided in a specified or set time period. For example, if there were 60 inpatients in a health facility for each of 10 days, this would be 600 patient days for this set time period. Also, these are the services rendered to one patient over a 24-hour period. *See also occupancy rate.*

patient days of care In health administration, any or all health care provided to a patient as it relates to the daily totals of the patient census for a certain time period.

patient discharge In health administration, the time when a patient is formally released from the care of a physician and from the health-care facility.

patient-driven management In hospital administration, this describes a managerial and philosophical position taken by hospital administration whereby all operations and activities directly translate into being for the benefit of the patient. *See patient-focused care.*

patient education 1. Health-teaching and self-care information instruction and counseling experiences designed to influence patient learning during the period in which a person receives preventive, diagnostic, therapeutic, and/or rehabilitative services, including experiences that arise from coping with symptoms; referral to sources of information; prevention, diagnosis, and care; and contacts with health institutions, health personnel, family, and other patients (Joint Committee on Health Education Terminology). 2. A specially designed or planned combination of learning and motivation activities used to assist people who have an illness, disease, injury, or disorder to change their behavior and beliefs toward a lifestyle conducive to good health.

patient education department A service and administrative unit in a health-care facility that provides health information and instruction to patients and their families about their conditions prior to discharge from the institution.

patient education plan Education and health counseling goals and objectives related to treatment and therapeutic regimens, medical procedures, and self-care for a patient or his or her family to carry out.

patient educator An individual with advanced education and specialized training in communication, interpersonal skills, and educational methods who also has medical expertise to teach and motivate patients. This individual has additional knowledge and skills in new medical technologies, belief structures, motivation, patient counseling, educational media, and behavior modification so that, when being assisted in a combination of learning, belief modification, behavior change, and value clarification activities, the patient can activate and adopt behaviors conducive to wellness and a healthful lifestyle.

patient-focused care In hospital administration, this is a philosophical and managerial approach to hospital operations that departs from the physician-focused and administration-driven hospital organization to one that reorganizes the resources of the hospital, staff, administration, physicians, technology, and supplies around the patient's needs. The needs of physicians take a less prominent position in the delivery of patient care than the needs of the patient. Attention is focused not on a professional classification system of patient care, staff retention and financial management, physician satisfaction, and reduced operational expenses but on increased patient satisfaction with administrative factors and concerns falling in line as appropriate. *See patient-driven management.*

patient ledger In health-care finance, this is the account of the charges rendered to individual patients in hospitals, health-care facilities, or other health services.

patient lives *See covered lives; lives.*

patient management categories (PCMs) In medical care delivery, these are the different levels of the severity of illness that can be quantified on the basis of the perceived needs of the patient for diagnostic, treatment, or therapeutic purposes.

patient management guideline In health administration and medical care, this is the setting of the acceptable pattern of diagnosis, treatment, and expected outcomes for a specific set of procedures, treatments, diseases, or conditions that is formalized by knowledgeable health-care providers and specialists familiar with the diseases or procedures.

patient margin In health-care finance, this is a measure of the profitability of health services or medical care rendered to patients. It is calculated as patient care revenues minus total costs divided by patient care revenues. The patient margin formula follows:

$$\frac{\text{Patient care revenues} - \text{Total costs}}{\text{Patient care revenues}}$$

patient mix In hospital or long-term-care facility administration, this is the numbers and types of patients served by a hospital or other health program. Patients may be classified according to their place of residence, socioeconomic characteristics, diagnoses, severity of illness, or source of payment. Knowledge of a program's patient mix is important for planning and comparative purposes. *See also patient origin study; scope of services.*

patient no-fault compensation As an alternative to medical malpractice, this is a no-fault system of compensating patients harmed by medical treatment.

patient, nonambulatory In long-term care, this is an individual who is unable to leave a building unassisted under emergency conditions or who is dependent on mechanical aids such as crutches, walkers, and wheelchairs and includes profoundly or severely mentally retarded persons.

patient origin study A study, usually undertaken by an individual health-care facility, hospital, health service or program, or health planning agency, to determine the geographic distribution of the places of residence of the patients served by one or more health services. Such studies help define catchment and medical trade areas and are useful in locating and planning the development of new services.

patient representative An allied health professional who has the responsibility of meeting the personal, social, and comfort needs of the patient; helps with problems; and responds to patient's inquiries and concerns about his or her care. As an advocate, the patient representative serves as a part of the health-care institution's complaint mechanism and supports the institution's risk management program while solving patient problems. *See patient service representative.*

patient representative department A service and administrative unit in a health-care facility that is staffed by qualified personnel to inquire into problems or concerns expressed by patients. The service provides a mediation mechanism for the patient and the administration of the facility to solve complaints and issues while ensuring respect for patients' rights.

patient representative services An organized hospital service that has specialized personnel to assist and support patients and hospital staff with solutions to any organizational or facility problems that negatively affect the patient's stay, the delivery of quality care, and efficient services.

patient's bill of rights Documents made available to patients describing their rights under treatment by or through a health-care provider or facility (for an example of a patient's bill of rights, see Appendix IV).

patient's data set In health-care information management, this a computer record of facts and informational items that relates to the episode of care. Included in the data set are the patient's identity number, patient identity demographics, attending physician, dates of treatment, primary and secondary diagnoses, procedures and therapeutics, etc.

Patient Self-Determination Act (PSDA) Passed by U.S. Congress in 1990 as part of the Omnibus Reconciliation Act (OBRA 90), the PSDA requires health-care providers to inform patients of their rights to make health-care decisions and to execute advanced directives. The PSDA requires health-care providers to educate staff and the community regarding PSDA rights. A health plan is to be developed for each individual on admission or enrollment, setting forth the exercise of the individual's right to accept or refuse medical or surgical treatment. Most important is the statement of the individual on life support use and on advanced directives. An advanced directive consists of written instructions regarding the provision of health care when an individual is incapacitated such as a durable-power-of-attorney for health care, which is a declaration pursuant to a living will. A statement is made to the effect that the organization respects a patient's right to self-determination in medical care decision making. Discrimination based on whether the patient has executed an advanced directive for health care is not allowed. Two types of advanced directives are used: First, a legal agent, who is to make the decisions, can be appointed and, second, the individual can state choices and decisions about life-sustaining treatment if incapacitated, namely, whether to continue with treatment and life support machines and technology when incapacitated or to have life-sustaining equipment turned off if no hope of recovery is seen. *See durable-power-of-attorney for health care; advanced directives.*

patient service representative A person who works in a hospital assisting with Medicare, Medicaid, and private insurance company forms and with the money collection process. This role can be contrasted with that of the patient representative, who is a social service worker, counselor, and advocate of the patient. *See also patient representative.*

patient's representative An individual who is authorized to make decisions pertaining to medical treatment for patients who lack the capacity to understand their rights and the nature and consequences of proposed treatment. Within the constraints of statutory and case law, individuals who may act as a patient's representative include a conservator or a guardian or a person designated as a durable-power-of-attorney for health care or the parents or guardians of minor patients.

patient's right to privacy The guaranteed protection of a patient's medical record. No unauthorized persons are allowed to view the patient's medical record or one's own body with consent. The right applies to any communications made to the physician and entered in the medical record and on all matters relating to medical treatment. Some states have passed statutes that allow personal information to be released to governmental agencies or pharmaceutical companies as long as the patient's privacy and anonymity are preserved. *See privacy; privileged communications; fiduciary relationship.*

patients' rights Rights to which an individual is entitled while receiving medical attention. These include right to privacy, right to refuse treatment, right to treatment in the case of long-term care or mental health care, and all civil rights granted and guaranteed by the Constitution of the United States.

patriarchal A family system in which the father is the head of the family.

patrilineal Descending through the male line.

pattern analysis In health-care delivery, this is a program used to evaluate the effectiveness of patient care by comparing medical care data, trends in patient care, or occasions of service and utilizing certain variables or characteristics.

pattern bargaining In labor relations, this when the same basic labor relations agreement is used for several other hospitals, health-care facilities, or organizations in the same areas.

pattern in data *See data.*

patterns and practice In human resource management and affirmative action, this is to discourage and halt discrimination that may be found to exist against a large number of individuals who are in a protected class.

paucital In health law, this is legal relationships in personam.

Paul v. Virginia An 1868 U.S. Supreme Court decision that decided that insurance is not commerce and that established the right of individual states to regulate insurance.

payable 1. Owing. 2. To be paid now or in the future; that which is due.

payback period In health-care finance, this is a finance and budgeting method that determines the length of time needed to recover the initial investment of money in a project. Often discounted cash flow analysis is not used in determining the payback period and therefore is not as effective in making long-term decisions as is the adjusted rate of return or net present value.

payee 1. To whom a negotiable instrument is made out. 2. To whom something has been paid or is about to be paid.

payer An insurance company, governmental entity, or health plan that pays the money to health-care providers for the rendering of medical care, therapies, treatments, procedures, and services. Also referred to as "third-party payers."

pay-for-knowledge compensation system In human relations management, this is when bonuses or incentives are offered to workers as incentives for them to develop new skills or knowledge that benefit the organization, in some cases resulting in higher pay. In some hospitals and health maintenance organizations, college courses that apply to work are paid for, or a set amount of money for such activities is provided each year for each employee.

payment In health-care finance, this is the amount of money that is paid out or transferred on behalf of the recipient from one or more paying source or agents to the providers of the health services.

payment, cost-based In health-care finance, this is one method of payment of medical care programs by third parties, typically medical insurance plans or government agencies, for services delivered to patients. In cost-related systems, the amount of payment is based on the cost of delivering the service by the provider based on his or her charges. The actual payment may be based on any one of several different formulas, such as full cost, full cost plus an additional percentage, allowable costs, or a fraction of costs.

payment, fee-for-service In health-care finance, this is payment of a fee by the patient to a physician for the performance of a specific service, procedure, or care rendered.

payment, lump sum In health-care finance, this is payment for professional patient care services based on a negotiated agreement between the payer and individual physicians, physician groups, or institutions. The agreement establishes the services to be provided, the amount of payment, and who will provide the services and describes the client group without necessarily specifying the population of the group or the services to be provided its members. This payment method is used by the Maternal and Child Health Program (Title V) and by many state and local governments to provide physician services to specified client groups.

payment, unified In hospital administration and financial management, this is payment for services of teaching physicians and house officers in cases where the latter are employees of a physician organization rather than of the hospital.

payout standards In human resource management, these are the levels of performance, quality of efficiency or effectiveness achieved, or other benchmarks that are used to determine whether an incentive or award has been earned and should be paid to the employee.

payroll In health-care finance, this is payment of wages to employees entitled to monetary compensation for work or personal services rendered. Payments are also made for payroll-associated costs such as insurance, income tax, retirement, and Social Security withholdings.

payroll costs Wages, salaries, and benefit expenses.

payroll deduction In health-care finance and health administration, this is a specified amount taken out of one's paycheck to finance a benefit. Payroll deductions may be either a set payroll tax (e.g., the Social Security tax) or a required payment for a benefit (e.g., a group health insurance premium). A payroll deduction generally refers to any amount withheld from the earnings of an employee.

payroll tax In health-care finance and health administration, this is a tax liability imposed on an employer or employee to finance a specific benefit in the health field. Payroll tax is often used synonymously with "Social Security tax." Such a tax is not applied on total payroll but rather on the wages of each employee up to a set maximum. The ceiling on wages to which tax is applied means that the tax rate varies with income in a regressive manner. A government requirement that an employer pay a set portion of the premium on group health insurance benefits for employees is in reality a payroll tax on the employer, although it is not often recognized as such. Because the amount paid by the employer would be a set amount per employee not related to the amount of an individual's earnings, its impact as a tax would be regressive. The IRS collects half from employees (7.51%), and the employer pays half, whereas self-employed persons pay both halves less a 2% tax credit. Of this, 2.9% goes into the Hospital Insurance Trust Fund to pay for Medicare.

PC Personal computer. *See also professional corporation.*

PCA *See patient care audit.*

PCBs *See polychlorinated biphenyls.*

PCB articles, containers, equipment, and items In environmental health, these are any manufactured packaging, products, or goods that contain, or whose surface has been in direct contact with, polychlorinated biphenyls (PCBs). Common items containing the toxic, persistent, hazardous chemical PCB are electronic capacitors, transformers, electric motors, pumps, pipes, microwave ovens, fluorescent light ballasts, and other electronic equipment.

PCB waste In environmental health, this is any

manufactured packaging, product, or good that contains polychlorinated biphenyls (PCBs) at such a level (500 ppm or greater) as to be required by law to be incinerated.

PCC *See primary care center.*

PCDDs *See polychlorinated dibenzo-p-dioxins.*

PCDFs *See polychlorinated dibenzofurans.*

PCM *See patient care manager.*

PCP 1. Primary care physician. In managed care, PCPs (primary care physicians) are designated as gatekeepers. 2. Abbreviation for phencyclidine hydrochloride, an illicit drug of abuse used as a hallucinogen. *See primary care physician; gatekeeper.*

PC/PM *See per contract per month.*

PCU *See patient care unit.*

PDR *See Physician's Desk Reference.*

PEC *See potentially compensable event.*

peculation Embezzlement.

pecuniary Pertaining to or related to money; having monetary concern.

pedestrian In health and safety and public health, this is any person involved in a motor vehicle accident who is not a passenger in or on a motor vehicle or trailer or other item pulled by a vehicle. In some reporting activities, this may include persons injured on children's coaster wagons, sleds, tricycles, rollerskates, skateboards, rollerblades, etc. Included are persons boarding, off-loading, jumping, or falling from motor vehicles.

pediatrician A board-certified physician who provides medical care for children from the moment of birth to the age of 14 (or 16), with some pediatricians practicing adolescent medicine; a primary care physician who may practice some minor surgery. Some pediatricians become subspecialists (e.g., cardiac care or gastroenterology).

pediatric(s) Child medical care. Refers to the health and medical care of children and adolescents; medical care rendered to child patients from birth to age 14; medical care provided to child patients by or under the orders of a pediatrician who also approves nursing care plans. Family physicians also provide pediatric care. This also refers to the type and level of care for children in a hospital or other definitive care setting.

pediatric aide An allied health technician who assists in providing health care to children or young adults. These persons work under the supervision of nursing personnel, physicians, or other qualified professionals such as child psychologists.

pediatric beds In a hospital, these are hospital beds in a children's unit assigned for regular patient use by child patients and maintained for children under age 14, excluding newborns.

pediatric cardiology The recognized medical subspecialty of pediatrics dealing with heart and related cardiovascular problems of children.

pediatric endocrinology The recognized medical subspecialty of pediatrics dealing with disease and functioning of the major ductless glands and organs of the body as found to occur in children.

pediatric gastroenterology The recognized medical subspecialty of pediatrics dealing with disease and functioning of the major organs of the digestive system, including the stomach, intestines, gallbladder, and bile duct, as found to occur in children.

pediatric hemato-oncology The recognized medical subspecialty of pediatrics dealing with diseases of the blood and blood-forming organs and with cancer and tumors and their treatment as found to occur in children.

pediatric intensive care In a hospital, this is a specialized children's unit that provides advanced levels of care to child patients who have been injured or traumatized or have life-threatening diseases or disorders that require comprehensive intensified care, monitoring, and observation. The level of care and monitoring is more intense than that usually provided in regular pediatric units. It is staffed with specially trained nurses and personnel and contains monitoring and specialized support equipment for treatment, all done under the supervision of physician pediatric specialists.

pediatric medical/surgical care In a hospital, this is a specialized children's unit that provides care to individuals who have not yet reached age 14, are admitted to this unit by a pediatrician, and are in the hospital on a short-term basis for diagnosis and treatment of injury, illness, conditions, or disorders.

pediatric nephrology The recognized medical subspecialty of pediatrics dealing with disease and functioning of the urinary system and kidneys as found to occur in children.

pediatric nurse practitioner A physician extender who is a nurse with advanced medical practitioner training and the minimum of a masters degree with a specialization in primary care of children.

pediatric orthopedics The recognized medical subspecialty of pediatrics dealing with disease and functioning of the bones and surgical repair of bones as found to occur in children.

pediatric service A medical and nursing unit found in a health-care facility specially staffed to provide for the diagnosis and treatment of newborns, infants, and children.

pediatric surgery The recognized medical subspecialty of pediatrics and/or surgery with practice limited to surgical treatment and repair of conditions in infants and children.

pediculosis In medical care and public and school health, this is the infestation of children or a general population with lice, usually head lice; also a prison health concern.

pedodontics The branch of dentistry concerned with the diagnosis and treatment of dental conditions in children.

peer review 1. The evaluation of one another by practicing physicians or other health-care providers, by colleagues, or by the medical staff to see how well services are performed by all medical personnel and health-care providers and how appropriate the services are in meeting patient needs to assess the effectiveness and efficiency of services provided by all health-care professionals (peers) in practice. Peer review has been advocated as the only possible form of quality control for medical services because it is said that only a physician's professional peers can judge his or her work. Peer review has been criticized as having inherent conflicts of interest because some believe that physicians will not properly judge one another and that reviews do not adequately reflect patient objectives and points of view. 2. Peer review is also done by professional review organizations (PROs), which receive federal guidance and funding from the Department of Health and Human Services and are staffed by physicians, osteopaths, and nonphysicians such as nurses or physician assistants. Duties include the establishment of criteria, norms, and standards for diagnosis and treatment of disease encountered, all based on input, process, and outcome measures determined in local PROs. Professional review organizations develop utilization review programs in hospitals to assess findings that are inconsistent with established norms such as hospital length of stays that are too long. *See professional review organization; professional review committee.*

peer review committee An assembly of physicians created for the purpose of evaluating the quality and effectiveness of patient care provided by physicians. *See professional review organization.*

peer review organization (PRO) The organizations that replaced the PSRO programs, which were repealed by the Tax Equity and Fiscal Responsibility Act of 1982. Under the new PRO program, the Department of Health and Human Services contracts with peer review organizations composed of a representative number of licensed physicians practicing in a PRO area to review medical care services to Medicare participants for the Health Care Financing Administration. Each state has a PRO that exists to ensure that quality care is provided to Medicare patients, that care meets medically recognized standards of quality, and that care is provided in the appropriate medical care settings. Physicians, nurses, physical therapists, and other health-care providers make up the staff of the PRO and are hired to assist in evaluating the medical necessity of care and to investigate the quality of care of health care providers assigned under Medicare. *See professional review organization.*

peers Equals; those of the same rank or status.

pejoration A worsening.

pelf, pelfe Ill-gotten gains; booty.

penal Punishment or punishable; concerning a penalty; pertaining to criminal law.

penalty 1. In health law, this is a punishment imposed by law for violating a contract or a regulation. 2. In managed care, this is the price paid for the breach of a managed-care contract. 3. In health-care finance, this is a fee imposed for missing a payment deadline.

pendency After the beginning and prior to terminating.

pendente lite (Lat.) In health law, this is a pending lawsuit; during the period a lawsuit is being heard.

pendent jurisdiction The authority given to federal courts to hear and decide all issues against a defendant, even if the issues are not involved with federal law.

pending Not yet decided; not finished or completed; awaiting completion or approval.

pending motion In formal health-care meetings,

this is the item of business on the floor that is being discussed but not yet concluded or passed.

pending question In formal health-care meetings and hearings using parliamentary procedure, a motion in front of the assembly that has not yet been voted on.

penetration In managed care or insurance marketing, the percentage of possible subscribers who have in fact contracted for benefits (subscribed); the amount of business a health plan has been able to capture in certain subscriber groups; similar to market penetration. Sometimes used synonymously with "participation."

penetration ratio The actual admissions in a health-care facility or persons enrolled in managed-care plans per 1000 population as compared to national averages.

Penrose drain A flexible, rubber tube used to drain secretions from a wound or incision.

Pension Reform Act of 1974 The Employee Retirement Income Security Act of 1974 (P.L. 93-406). This act established mandatory rules for retirement plan participation. The vesting of participants' rights by means of a three-way option plan with minimum funding standards and more stringent fiduciary laws is also required. Financial statements are to be audited. A pension benefit guaranty corporation is to be established to insure plans against failure. The law does not require an employer to establish plans, nor does it apply to all retirement plans.

people All persons in a nation or state; all persons as a whole; a population.

peoples medical society A large health-care consumer organization; a nonprofit patient advocacy organization.

PEP Performance evaluation procedure. *See Joint Commission, performance evaluation procedure for auditing and improving patient care.*

per (Lat.) By; through; by means of; during.

per 100 adjusted census The ratio of personnel to adjusted average daily census, each on a 100 census basis.

per autre vie (Lat.) 1. For another life. 2. For as long as another, specified person is alive.

per capita (Lat.) 1. By the head. 2. Individual person sharing equally.

perceived health status In health promotion and public health, this is an average person's judgment of his or her own health status relative to others of the same age based on a four-point continuum such as poor, good, fair, and excellent.

perceived need In health-care delivery, this is the level of desire possessed by the consumer about the type, kind, or availability of health services and may not be congruent with that of the health-care provider, health plan, or payer.

perceived risks In environmental health and safety, these are risks as a person or worker believes or understands them to be, whether actual or not.

percentage lease A specialized lease sometimes used with business property as it is based on a percentage of income generated by the lessee to determine the rent. A minimum fee is established in case of a low volume of activity.

percentage participation In managed care or medical insurance, this is one stipulation in an insurance contract that states that the insurer will share losses with the insured person in an agreed-on proportion. An 80-20 participation is common: the insured person pays 20% of his or her losses (similar to paying a deductible) and the insurance company the remaining 80%.

percentile A statistical value based on a scale of 100. A percentile is used to place people in groups on the scale of 100 to compare how they rank with the rest of the members in the group. It is used extensively to report the results of psychological testing and in health care to analyze case mix, hospital patient care loads, and utilization (differs from "percentage"). Also referred to as "percentile ranking."

percent of occupancy In health administration and relevant to health-care facility census figures and case management statistics, the ratio of total inpatient days of service for a specified time period to the total inpatient bed days for the same period; the ratio of the total inpatient service days for a specific time period times 100 over the total inpatient bed count days for the same time period. The percent of occupancy formula follows:

$$\frac{\text{Total inpatient service days for a certain time period}}{\text{Total inpatient bed count days for the same period}} \times 100$$

perception The meaningful organization of a person's intellectual, sensory, and emotional capacities; the understanding of an experience or knowledge; an awareness of a person, thing, or situation.

percipient Perceiving; one who perceives or sees something.

percolation In environmental health, this is the movement of water from the earth's surface downward and radially through the subsurface soil layers, usually continuing downward to the groundwater; water flowing and passing through rock, soil, sand, and other matter that helps to clean it.

per contract per month (PC/PM) In managed care, this is the amount of money associated with each active and effective contract holder (e.g., an employment group) or by each subscriber or each member for each month.

per curiam (Lat.) 1. By the court. 2. By the entire court, as opposed to by a single judge.

per diem (Lat.) By the day. Through the course of the day; used in reference to compensation for meals, lodging, expenses, etc. incurred in a day of work or services. Travel allowances are provided on a "per diem" basis. In managed care, this is a daily amount, often used in conjunction with a hospital and medical group contract, whereby a daily charge is established for a health plan member in the hospital medical group regardless of the actual services provided.

per diem charge In health-care finance and health administration, this is the amount of money charged for services, care, or treatment over the course of 1 day. *See also hospital service charge; per diem cost.*

per diem cost Cost per day. Hospital or other inpatient institutional costs per day or for a day of care. Hospitals occasionally charge for their services on the basis of a per diem rate derived by dividing their total costs by the number of inpatient days of care given. Per diem costs are averages and do not reflect true costs for each patient. With this approach, patients who use few hospital services (typically those at the end of a short stay) subsidize those who need much more care (those just admitted) or those who have long lengths of stay. Thus the per diem approach is said to give hospitals an incentive to prolong hospital stays. *See also cost per patient day.*

per diem cost per patient day In health administration and health-care financial management, this is the cost of running a health-care facility divided by the number of inpatient days in the same time period. *See cost per patient day.*

per diem rate *See per diem cost per patient day.*

per diem reimbursement In managed care and health-care finance, this is when a hospital or other health-care organization receives payment from a health plan or insurance company for care rendered to an enrollee on the basis of a set rate per day rather than on charges. This form of payment can be varied by service such as medical/surgical charges or intensive care charges, or it can be a standard charge regardless of type, level, or intensity of services.

peremptory 1. Barring further action. 2. Absolute; conclusive; final. 3. Not requiring an explanation. 4. Cause not need to be shown. 5. Arbitrary; decisive. 6. That which cannot be denied, opposed, or changed.

peremptory challenge In law, this a challenge to a prospective juror used to disqualify him from being impaneled for no given reason. Peremptory challenges vary and are established by statute.

peremptory ruling A judge's decision that overrules the final decision of a jury.

PERF Perfusion or perfusionist.

perfect 1. To leave nothing wanting. 2. Complete; enforceable; exact. 3. Without defect; totally correct; without flaw.

perfidy 1. The deliberate violation of an agreement. 2. The violation or breach of trust and faith.

performance 1. Carrying out a deal, promise, or contract. 2. Completing an obligation according to present terms. 3. The ability of an individual, group, or organization to carry out processes that increase the probability of desired outcomes (JCAHO for acute-care facilities).

performance appraisal A work measurement process and administrative activity used in the work setting to evaluate work performance, task abilities, effectiveness on the job, and skill level and ability. It can also be used to determine the need for training and education for individuals or groups in organizations. Job and work assessments are used as an information source for reviewing worker's achievement of objectives and work activity and can be used for merit recognition, promotion, personnel change, personal and staff development, organizational modification, and job description refinement. Information gained from evaluation and appraisal of job performance is useful in planning, organizing, controlling, and directing work performance. *See graphic rating scale.*

performance area An element of an accreditation decision grid used by JCAHO that consists of a performance score process resulting from aggregation of a number of related standards compliance scores. For example, infection control and emergency services are two performance areas for which a performance score is calculated for use in the accreditation decision process (JCAHO for acute-care facilities).

performance area, key An element of the accreditation process used by JCAHO that consists of identifying performance areas that are important in the delivery of quality medical care. For example, infection control and emergency services are key performance areas for most hospitals (JCAHO for acute-care facilities).

performance assessments In environmental health, this is the systematic analysis of the potential risks posed by waste management systems to the public and environment and a comparison of those risks to establish levels of performance and related objectives.

performance-based training Any systematic approach to training that is based on tasks and the related knowledge and skills required for competent job performance.

performance budget In health administration and health-care financial management, this is a budgeting method that shows at the end of the accounting period what income was realized and what costs should have been in the actual operations of the facility.

performance evaluation See *performance appraisal*.

performance evaluation samples In laboratory management, this refers to samples provided to a laboratory for the purpose of demonstrating that the laboratory can successfully analyze the samples within limits of performance specified. The true value of the concentration of the reference materials is unknown to the laboratory at the time of the analysis.

performance measures In health administration and human resource management, these are ratings used to evaluate employee performance. See *performance appraisal; graphic rating scale*.

performance rating scales In health administration and human resource management, these are personnel evaluation forms used in the performance appraisal process to assess an employee and his or her on-the-job performance. Often the form consists of traits and characteristics used to describe work and is usually followed by a five-point rating scale ranging from poor to excellent. See *graphic rating scale*.

performance, specific 1. Carrying out a contract according to specific terms. 2. In health law, this is to seek a remedy. One may sue for specific performance rather than for damages for nonperformance.

performance standards In health administration and human resource management, these are the measures, criteria, or benchmarks against which performance is measured.

performance testing In health information management, this is a pilot run of a computer application program to determine if a program works and if the results are functional.

perfusion In medical care, this is advanced health-care technology that allows the circulating of blood or other liquid through the heart, lungs, or other organs or tissue, often assisted by heart-lung machines and pumping devices.

perfusionist An allied health professional who has specialized training in assisting physicians, especially in surgery, in the circulating of blood and other liquids through the heart, lungs, or other organs or tissue and who is specialized in the operation of heart-lung machines and related technology.

perfusion technologist See *cardiovascular perfusionist*.

peril In insurance, this is cause of a possible loss such as an accident, death, sickness, fire, flood, or burglary. See also *insurance; hazard*.

perinatal In epidemiology and medical care, this pertains to the time just before and shortly after birth.

perinatal care Medical care that pertains to or occurs in the period shortly before and after birth, beginning with the completion of the 20th to the 28th week of gestation and ending 7 to 28 days after birth.

perinatal deaths In epidemiology and medical care, these are all fetal deaths of 20 or more weeks gestation plus neonatal deaths. See *perinatal mortality; perinatal mortality rate*.

perinatal mortality In epidemiology and medical care, these are deaths during the late prenatal period (after the 28th week of gestation or with a fetus weighing over 1000 grams, including stillbirths; fetal and neonatal deaths combined), during the birth process, surrounding the birth process, or in the early neonatal period (first week after birth). It is usually measured as a rate: number of perinatal deaths per 1000 live births in a given area or program and within a given time period. *See also health status; infant mortality; neonatal mortality.*

perinatal mortality rate In epidemiology and medical care, this is the number of perinatal deaths (fetal and neonatal deaths combined) per 1000 live births in a given area or program and time period; the number of late fetal deaths plus infant deaths with 7 days of birth per 1000 live births; fetal deaths (28 weeks + of gestation) plus postnatal deaths (first week) (which is the number of perinatal deaths) divided by fetal deaths (28 weeks + of gestation) plus live births times 1000. In some World Health Organization (WHO) reporting countries, the baby has to be over 1000 grams to be included. The perinatal mortality rate WHO formula follows:

$$\frac{\text{Number of perinatal deaths}}{\text{Number of live births in the same period}} \times 1000$$

The perinatal mortality rate used in most industrialized countries is fetal deaths (28 weeks + of gestation) plus postnatal deaths (first week) (which is the number of perinatal deaths) divided by fetal deaths (28 weeks + of gestation) plus live births times 1000 within a specified time period. The formula for perinatal mortality rate for industrialized nations follows:

$$\frac{\text{Fetal deaths + Postnatal deaths}}{\text{Fetal deaths + Live births}} \times 1000$$

perinatal mortality ratio The annual number of perinatal deaths as a proportion of the annual number of live births. *See perinatal mortality rate.*

perinatal period In epidemiology and medical care, this is the period shortly before and just after the birth of a child, including the time period of the completion of the 28th week of gestation and ending 4 weeks after childbirth.

periodic interim payment (PIP) In health-care finance under Medicare, this is when the intermediary pays hospitals, home health agencies, nursing homes, or other health-care providers on a spaced but regular basis (e.g., monthly or semimonthly) on the basis of estimated usual revenue and services generated and adjusted periodically when actual accounting and submissions are completed.

periodic payments In health-care finance under Medicare, this is when the intermediary pays hospitals, home health agencies, nursing homes, or other health-care providers in installments instead of lump sums; installment payments paid over time and received or paid on a regular basis as per financial arrangements and agreements.

periodic table The systemic classification of elements according to atomic numbers.

periodontics The branch of dentistry concerned with diseases and problems affecting the mucous membranes, gums, and support structure of the teeth.

period prevalence 1. In epidemiology, this is a measure of prevalence for a certain disease as determined for a specific point in time. Added to this are all new cases and recurrences of the disease during a succeeding period of time. Another perspective is that this is the number of cases of a condition known to have existed during a specified period of time regardless of whether they began during that period or an earlier period. 2. The total number of individuals known to have had the disease at any time during a specified time span or period of time. The period prevalence rate formula follows:

$$\frac{\begin{array}{c}\text{Number of cases of the disease}\\ \text{that existed within a time period}\end{array}}{\text{Average study population}} \times 1000$$

peripheral device Any device separate from the computer that can provide input to or accept output from the computer.

perjury 1. Lying under oath. 2. Giving false testimony or swearing falsely to a document; evidence or facts in a legal proceeding.

perm. Permanent.

permanent As used in health care, this is nonreversible impairment or damage.

permanent disability An illness or injury that prevents an insured person from performing all the functions of his or her regular job; any degree of nonpermanent nonfatal injury; any injury resulting in the loss of use of any part of the body or any permanent impairment of function of the body or body part. *See permanent partial disabilities; permanent total disabilities.*

permanent fund In health-care finance, this is a grant or gift of money to a health-care organization from which only the interest can be used; an endowment account that can be used to provide the institution financial viability but cannot be spent.

permanently and totally disabled As used in the Social Security Act and its administration, this describes those individuals who apply for and meet the definition of disability to qualify for Social Security and Medicare benefits.

permanent partial disabilities Injuries other than death or permanent total disability that result in the loss or complete loss of use of any member or part of a member of the body or any permanent impairment of functions of the body or body part. Loss disregards any preexisting disability of the injured member or impaired body function.

permanent total disabilities Injuries other than death that deny gainful occupation and permanently and that totally incapacitate an employee or result in the partial or complete loss of use (in one accident) of both eyes; one eye and one hand, arm, leg, or foot; or any two of the following not on the same limb: hand, arm, foot, or leg.

permanent vegetative state Used to describe the condition of patients who have suffered a stroke or other form of brain damage where the higher brain functions are permanently and obviously absent in a patient.

per member per month (PM/PM) In managed care, this describes one type of capitation payment plan. This is what health plans and health-care providers use as an indicator of revenue, expenses, or utilization of services per member per month (e.g., health-care providers may receive a capitation amount of $44 per month per patient); a unit of measure of enrollee activity, identifying each active member of a health plan for each month the member was active. The formula for PM/PM follows:

$$\frac{\text{Number of subscriber units}}{\text{Number of member months}}$$

per member per year (PM/PY) In managed care, this is what health plans and health-care providers use as an indicator of revenue, expenses, or utilization of services per member per year. For example, patients may visit the physician an average of 4.1 times per member per year.

permissible exposure limit In occupational health and safety, these are standards or measures developed to safeguard employee's health and sets forth the acceptable type and level of exposure to radiation, dangerous agents, chemicals, or other forms of contamination found in the workplace.

permissive 1. Allowed. 2. Tolerated.

permissive licensure A legal rule that allows practitioners who are not licensed to practice but does not offer them protection from the licensing agency or organization.

permit Any authorization, license, or equivalent control document issued by the proper authority, agency, or governmental body to participate in or carry out specific activities or functions authorized by the permit.

perpetrator 1. One who commits a crime. 2. By whose agency or direction an illicit act occurs.

perpetual consent In health law, this is continual consent for medical treatment. Some insurance companies and other third-party payers request this type of consent because it has no time limit set on its validity. This could violate what is considered current or ongoing consent, informed consent, and confidentiality.

perpetual inventory In health administration, this is a stock control system where the number of units of goods at any time may be obtained directly from the records and without an actual physical count of the goods. A record is kept in units and/or values for stocked items or goods. This is also a running record of items or goods ordered, received, and used and of the balance left on hand.

perpetuating testimony In health law, this is a method of gathering and preserving testimony; a deposition taken from a person who is ill or a person who is about to leave the state.

perpetuation of evidence In health law, this is ensuring that evidence is available for a trial that may occur at a later date.

perquisites In health administration and human resources management, these are benefits incidental to a job or position other than salary.

per quod (Lat.) Whereby.

per se (Lat.) In and of itself. By itself, himself, or herself; alone; taken along; inherent.

persistence In epidemiology and health services research, this is the extent to which previous patterns of disease, illness, or conditions continue to characterize observations in the future.

persistency In insurance, the rate at which policies written in a given line of insurance or for members of a given group are maintained in force until the completion of the terms of the policies.

persistent pesticides In environmental health, these are pesticides that break down very slowly or do not break down chemically and that remain in the environment after the growing season or for extended periods of time.

person 1. A human being or an individual or incorporated group having certain legal rights or responsibilities; a natural person, as opposed to a corporation, which is called an artificial person. 2. In epidemiology, this refers to all factors relating to the people aspects of public health and a population contributing to the cause and spread of disease, disability, or death; one of three epidemiological factors that are considered in a disease investigation: time, place, or person; the traits, characteristics, and dimensions of individuals that make up the health and social profile of a group or population; factors or traits that affect a group's health status such as age, race, gender, education, occupation, marital status, family integrity, religion, income, socioeconomic status, health services utilization, and fertility rate. *See place; time; epidemiology.*

personal 1. Private; individual; not public. 2. Having to do with movable property as opposed to affixed property. 3. Belonging to a person.

personal care In nursing home care, this is assistance in walking, buttoning clothes, getting in and out of bed, bathing, dressing, eating, taking drugs, and preparing special diets prescribed by a physician. *See activities of daily living; intermediate care.*

personal care facility A long-term-care facility that provides 24-hour general assistance plus limited nursing care, assistance with nutrition, bathing, dressing, and medication. *See personal care; intermediate care facility; skilled nursing facility.*

personal care home A long-term-care facility that provides 24-hour general assistance with its primary function to provide supervised assistance to the elderly or others who have problems with activities of daily living. A nurse may or may not be employed.

personal care home with nursing A long-term-care facility that has fewer than half the residents receiving nursing care. In addition, such homes must employ one or more registered nurses or licensed practical (vocational) nurses or must provide administration of medications and treatments in accordance with physicians' orders; have supervision of therapies or medications; assist with bathing, dressing, eating, ambulation, and other activities of daily living; or provide three or more personal services.

personal care home without nursing A long-term-care facility in which no resident receives formal nursing care. These homes provide administration of medications and treatments in accordance with physicians' orders; have supervision of self-administered medications; assist with bathing, dressing, eating, ambulation, and other activities of daily living; or provide three or more personal services.

personal care services In long-term care, these are activities required of elderly persons in custodial or supervisory care, including activities of daily living.

personal employee time (PET) In health administration and human resource management, in some major health-care facilities, employees are allowed to accumulate a certain number hours of personal time off based on the number of days worked, called PET hours/days. Sick days or other forms of days off may or may not be used if PET time is used, depending on the policies of the organization.

personal health 1. The basic dimensions of total well-being and wholistic health, including social, biological/physiological, emotional, spiritual/values, mental dimensions, the absence of pathological conditions, and a perceived sense of well-being. Also considered is the ability to be economically viable in ones' culture and society. 2. In health education, this is a course of study that addresses personal hygiene, all aspects of preventive care, and health promotion and that presents the skills, knowledge, and ability to be a healthy individual and to use health services to maintain and increase ones' personal health status.

personal health care In health-care delivery, this is a major subsystem of the overall health-care system that includes services delivered to individuals to improve or maintain health status. Major service categories in personal health care include prevention and detection, diagnosis and treatment, habilitation and rehabilitation, maintenance, and personal health-care support.

personal health-care expenditures In health-care finance, these are outlays for goods and services relating directly to patient care. The expenditures in this category are total national health expenditures minus expenditures for research and construction, expenses for administering health insurance programs, and expenditures for government public health activities.

personal health-care services Under MediCal (Medicaid) in California, these are managed-care plans operating under a two-plan model: a local initiative under government control and a mainstream approach that is a contracted private health plan. These plans are contractually responsible for providing almost all MediCal covered personal health-care services to enrolled children and adults. Included are all necessary clinical assessments, preventive care, and treatment services. Some children's care services remain intact, and prepaid dental care is included.

personal health-care support services Patient care activities that do not involve direct medical care but that assist in the prevention, diagnosis, and treatment of diseases or conditions or in the habilitation, rehabilitation, or maintenance of ill or disabled individuals.

personal health services These are all health services provided to individuals and are contrasted with services such as environmental, community health, and public health services, which are usually directed at populations, not individuals, and are undertaken to protect activities and to promote healthful environments, behavior, or lifestyles; medical care services provided on an outpatient basis such as medical care received in primary care physician offices, dentist offices, well-child clinics, adult day health-care centers, student health centers, and home health care.

personal health status The level of health of the individuals in a population.

personal injury Harm done to a person's body; the harm or injury a person suffers.

personality 1. Personal property. 2. The constant configuration and behavior of a person, showing his or her physical, emotional, and mental status as well as attitudes, beliefs, and interests, which are the sum total of adjustment to life. 3. In mental health and socialization, this is the ability to elicit positive responses from others.

personality test In mental health services, psychology, and psychiatry, this is a psychological test used to identify an individual's perceptions, motivations, emotionality, interpersonal interaction abilities, and attitudinal traits.

personal leave days In health administration and human resource management, these are sick days or other days of leave that an employee is entitled to take as a part of the benefits of working for the health-care organization. Often called "PTO (personal time off) days" or "personal employee time (PET) days."

personal physician A physician who assumes responsibility for the comprehensive medical care of an individual on a continuing basis. The physician obtains professional assistance or consultations when needed for services he or she is not qualified to provide and coordinates the care provided by other professional personnel in light of his or her knowledge and understanding of the patient as a whole. Although personal physicians will have an interest in the patient's family as it affects the patient, they may not serve the entire family directly (e.g., a pediatrician may serve as a personal physician for children and an internist or other specialist adults). Personal physician is sometimes more simply defined for any given patient as the one the patient designates as his or her personal or principal physician. *See also family physician; private patient.*

personal producing general agent (PPGA) In insurance and managed care, this is a general agent who works as a broker under contract with several insurance companies and spends the majority of his or her time selling insurance rather than building and managing an agency.

personal property 1. Items that can be moved or removed and that are not permanently affixed to or a part of real estate; items that can be removed without seriously damaging or diminishing the functional value of either the property or real estate. 2. In health-care settings, these are the personal effects of a patient that need to be inventoried and accounted for and returned to the patient on discharge or request.

personal protective equipment In occupational health and safety and the protection of medical care workers, this is any specialized clothing or equipment worn by an employee for protection against a hazard. General work clothes (e.g., uniforms, pants, shirts, or blouses) not intended to function as protection against a hazard are not considered to be personal protective equipment.

personal services In health-care delivery, these are the extra activities and services provided to patients, more for patient comfort and to increase patient satisfaction, than are necessary for medical care and treatment.

personal time-off days (PTO) In health administration and human resource management, this type of leave is used instead of sick days to allow time off for personal matters the employee is entitled to take as a part of the benefits of working for the health-care organization.

persona non grata (Lat.) An unwelcome person. A person who is unacceptable.

personnel Individuals included on a health-care facility's payroll. Personnel are recorded as full-time equivalents (FTEs), which are calculated by adding the number of full-time persons to half of the number of part-time personnel, not including interns, residents, administrative residents, and other trainees. *See also full-time equivalents; personnel, full-time equivalent employee.*

personnel audit In health administration and human resources management, this is when the personnel department or administration evaluates personnel activities used in the health-care organization such as staffing patterns, organizational chart/position assessment, types of manpower needed, downsizing possibilities, and combining of positions.

personnel barriers In health administration and human resources management, these are cultural, physical, racial, or prejudicial obstacles against workers or those seeking work. For already employed individuals, these could also be obstacles to advancement, promotion, or development.

personnel department In health administration and human resources management, this is an administrative department that recruits, interviews, and screens applicants for health-care facility positions; provides benefits; and maintains salary scales. The department keeps records of present and past employees and provides orientation for new employees. The director of personnel maintains a control system over positions of employment so that jobs cannot be increased without approval of the administration. Personnel departments are also involved with labor relations and risk appraisal.

personnel, full-time equivalent employee (FTE) In health administration and human resources management, this is an estimate of full-time equivalent employees where administration counts two part-time employees. A full-time employee works 35 hours or more a week; 35 hours of a part-time employee's work per week is sometimes counted as one full-time employee.

personnel management 1. The process of administering human resources in health-care organizations and includes activities such as recruitment, maintaining personnel files, meeting affirmative action requirements, developing job descriptions, managing personnel benefits, and screening applicants. 2. The study of how to employ, screen, train, develop, utilize, evaluate, promote, advance, maintain, and retain the proper number and types of workers while meeting worker needs and providing benefits.

personnel monitoring equipment In environmental health, this is any device designed to be worn or carried by an individual worker for the purpose of estimating the dose of a chemical or hazardous substance received by that individual. Examples are film badges, pocket dosimeters, and thermoluminescent dosimeters.

personnel per adjusted census In hospital administration and human resources management, this is the ratio of personnel to the adjusted average daily census, each on a 100-census basis. *See personnel.*

personnel record According to JCAHO for psychiatric, alcoholism, and drug abuse facilities accreditation purposes, the complete employment record of a staff member, including job application, education and employment history, performance evaluation, and, when applicable, evidence of current licensure, certification, or registration.

persons 1. In epidemiology, this is used to describe the people characteristics of populations. 2. In epidemiology, this is used to imply person-year equivalents; per person, number of persons, or percentage of persons; "in person-years" refers to persons weighted by the proportion of the year that they fall into a population or demographic category. *See person-years; person.*

person-time In epidemiology, this is often used as a denominator of rates (e.g., incidence rates) where a unit of time is combined with person characteristics; the sum of units of time that research subjects in a study have, plus person factors; a unit of measure combining elements of time and the traits of the person. *See person years.*

person-time incidence rates The number of new

cases of a disease that occur per a unit of time and unit of population at a point in time.

person-to-person (mode of) transmission In epidemiology, this is a direct method of the spread of disease from one individual to another such as touching, breathing, or sneezing on another or kissing or sexual contact; one of the several methods through which infectious diseases can be spread. *See fomite; airborne transmission; foodborne transmission; carrier.*

person-years 1. In epidemiology or longitudinal studies, attrition of subjects causes different subjects to be used in the study or research. Thus, people are studied or are observed for varying lengths of time and do not contribute equally to the population at risk. To weigh the contribution a person makes to a study, a time-and-person unit is used for the denominator of any rates used. Person-years are computed by summing the total months by sample members in the population during the research study year and dividing this sum by 12, which allows an adjustment for sample members who were not in the population the entire study year and accounts for those who died, moved, were institutionalized, or entered the study later on. 2. In longitudinal studies, this is where subjects are followed over time and each person contributes a person-year for each year of participation (e.g., 50 subjects in a study for 5 years is 250 person-years). *See also prevalence; incidence.*

per stirpes (Lat.) 1. By roots. 2. A method of dividing by estates, by representation, or by groups whereby the children share equally in their deceased parents' share.

persuasive authority All law that a judge might use in making a decision. A persuasive decision often is given by a famous judge or comes from a powerful court.

per subscriber per month Used in managed care to describe enrollments and related revenues generated and expected levels of utilization of medical care services at the individual enrollee level.

perverse incentive In managed care, this is a motivation inherent in a health delivery or financing system that is to the system's disadvantage. In a fee-for-service delivery system, the incentive is to use up resources rather than conserve them by overtreatment or overtesting, whereas in prepaid or capitated programs there is an incentive to undertreat, undertest, discharge patients early, and conserve resources.

PERT *See program evaluation and review technique.*

per thousand members per year (PTMPY) In health-care delivery and managed-care utilization, one manner in which health services utilization is reported. Hospital utilization is expressed as days per thousand members per year.

pesticide-related wastes In environmental health, these are all pesticide-containing wastes or by-products that are produced in the manufacturing or processing of a pesticide and that are to be discarded but that, pursuant to acceptable pesticide manufacturing or processing operations, are not ordinarily a part of or contained in an industrial waste stream discharged into a sewer or the waters of a state.

pesticides In environmental health, this is a group of chemicals used to control or kill pests such as rats, insects, fungi, and bacteria that affect humans or agricultural products, including insecticides, herbicides, fungicides, rodenticides, miticides, fumigants, and repellents; substances or mixtures of chemicals intended for preventing, destroying, repelling, or mitigating any pest or as a plant regulator, defoliant, or desiccant. Pesticides can accumulate in the food chain and/or contaminate the environment if misused. *See suspension; suspension, emergency.*

pesticide tolerance In environmental health, this is the amount of pesticide residue allowed by law to remain in or on a harvested crop. By using various safety factors, the EPA sets levels well below the point where the chemicals might be harmful to consumers. *See suspension; suspension, emergency.*

pests In environmental health, these are insects, rodents, nematodes, fungi, weeds, or other forms of terrestrial or aquatic plant or animal life or viral, bacterial, or microorganisms that are injurious to health or the environment.

PET *See positron emission tomography; personal employee time.*

PET scan *See positron emission tomography.*

Peter Principle A concept in administration suggesting that, in business or large organizations, individuals, especially managers, rise administratively to their level of incompetence (developed by Laurence J. Peter).

petition 1. In law and the litigation process, this is a written prayer or request for certain things or what a court takes a particular action on; an official plea on an issue or compliant. Sometimes used synonymously with "complaint." 2. A written application for redress. 3. A request made to a public official. *See prayer.*

petitioner 1. In law and the litigation process, this is the plaintiff; one who initiates a petition; one who petitions the court. 2. One initiating an appeal to a higher court; an appellant.

petit jury In law and the litigation process, this is a lower-level jury; a trial jury.

petit larceny A misdemeanor; stealing property of little value, usually less than $50.

petty theft In criminal law, this is petty larceny; theft of something of little value.

pH The acidity or alkalinity of a solution, with neutral being designated 7, acidity 0–7, and alkalinity 7–14.

PH Pharmaceutical services.

PHA Public Housing Administration.

phantom limb In medical care and an amputation situation, this is a sensation felt by a patient that a body part is still attached even though it has been amputated. This occurs because the severed nerves provide continual nervous activity and sensation to the brain.

phantom pain A pain that continues to exist in a limb after the limb has been removed such as pain perceived to be in a foot after it has been amputated.

phantoms In medical radiography activities and training, these are models of body parts made from dense plastic to simulate radiation interaction characteristics of a human or animal body, thus not requiring the use of humans, to reduce exposure risk.

pharmaceuticals Drugs, chemical substances, and other related preparations used by private individuals at home and by patients under the care of a health-care provider, including prescribed medicinals and antibiotics as well as over-the-counter drugs such as aspirin, vitamins, and amino acids for both human and animal use. *See also drug.*

pharmaceutical services Activities pertaining to the appropriate, safe, and effective storage, preparation, dispensing, and administration of drugs. Standards are applied to evaluate a hospital's performance in providing pharmaceutical services (JCAHO for acute-care facilities).

pharmaceutical services, decentralized Storage, preparation, and dispensing of drugs performed at hospital sites physically located outside the hospital's central pharmacy. Also called "satellite pharmacies" (JCAHO for acute-care facilities).

pharmacist 1. A professional qualified by education and authorized by law (usually by license) to practice pharmacy. 2. In long-term care, this is an individual licensed to practice pharmacy who a health-care facility is required to use for various purposes, including providing consultation on pharmacy services, establishing a system of records of controlled drugs, overseeing records and reconciling controlled drugs, and/or performing a monthly drug regimen review for each resident. 3. Under Medicare, an individual who is licensed as a pharmacist by the state in which he or she practices and has training or experience in the specialized functions of institutional pharmacy such as residencies in hospital pharmacy, seminars on institutional pharmacy, and related training programs. 4. According to JCAHO for accreditation purposes, an individual who has a degree in pharmacy and is licensed and registered to prepare, preserve, compound, and dispense drugs and chemicals in the state in which he or she practices.

pharmacist, licensed Individuals who have met the requirement for licensure in the state, allowing them to prepare, compound, sell, and distribute medicinal products.

pharmaco- Prefix meaning "drug" or "chemical."

pharmacologist A health-care professional who has graduated from a recognized school of pharmacy with a degree in pharmacology. Included in the training are required clinical experiences and research involving drugs.

pharmacology The science of drugs, including their composition, uses, actions, and interactions.

pharmacopoeia A list of products, substances, or drugs used in medicine, including their description and formulas.

pharmacy 1. The science, art, and practice of preparing, preserving, compounding, dispensing, and giving appropriate instruction in the use of drugs; a place where drugs are compounded, prepared, stored, or dispensed. 2. A place where pharmacology is practiced. In a health-care facility, this department or service purchases drugs and medications, maintains a supply, and fills requisitions for medical care services and nursing units. It also may fill prescriptions for individual patients. The department is run by the chief pharmacist, and a special drug and therapeutics committee provides communication and interaction with the medical staff. The pharmacy maintains the formulary, which is a list of drugs that the medical staff finds acceptable for use in the hospital. Generic names are listed, and the pharmacist may substitute drugs that are clinically the same. This reduces drug inventories and helps contain the cost of drugs as it allows bulk purchasing and the use of low-cost generic name drugs. *See also formulary.*

pharmacy and therapeutics committee (P&T) In managed care, this is a group of physicians from an array of medical specialties organized as an advisory committee to health plans to provide input into the types, effectiveness, and safe use of prescription drugs and to develop and administer the health plan's drug formulary. The committee also serves as a official link between administration, medical staff, and pharmacy activities of the health plan.

pharmacy and therapeutics function The medical staff responsibility carried out in cooperation with the pharmaceutical department/service. The nursing department/service, management and administrative services, and other services and individuals monitor, evaluate, and improve the policies and procedures relating to drug and diagnostic testing material and investigational or experimental drug usage; develop and maintain a drug formulary; and review all significant untoward drug reactions. Standards are applied to evaluate a hospital's performance of the pharmacy and therapeutics function (JCAHO for acute-care facilities).

pharmacy assistant One who works under the supervision of a pharmacist assisting him or her in selected activities including medication profile reviews for drug incompatibilities, prescription packaging, handling of purchase records, and inventory control. Where state law permits, the pharmacy assistant may administer drugs to patients under the supervision of a registered pharmacist.

pharmacy committee An assembly of physicians and/or pharmacists that has the responsibility for developing policies, procedures, and practices concerning the selection and distribution procedures of drugs and the pharmacopoeia for a health-care facility.

pharmacy department An administrative department and service unit in a health-care facility that is responsible for dispensing, storage, control, security, and preparation of pharmaceuticals and drugs as well as public prescription filling.

pharmacy, part-time A small simplified pharmacy controlled and supervised by a part-time registered pharmacist who is employed by the health-care facility or is under contract, as in a nursing home or psychiatric or other health-care facility.

pharmacy profile record system A form of medical record that may be computerized, allowing for the immediate retrieval of drug information on a patient, especially previously dispensed medications. When a prescription is present, a profile card is pulled or a computerized CRT picture is presented that gives previous drug prescriptions/usage for all members of a family living at the same address.

pharmacy services In hospitals or clinics, these are used to assist the pharmacist in selected activities in pharmacy departments to provide pharmaceutical services to patients, nurses, and physicians.

pharmacy technician An individual who assists a pharmacist with a variety of tasks and activities such as conducting medication profile reviews for drug incompatibilities, typing labels, inventory control, prescription packaging, dealing with purchase records, and product ordering, all done under the supervision of the licensed pharmacist. *See pharmacy assistant.*

phased disposal In environmental health, this is a method of solid waste and tailings management and disposal using lined impoundment landfills (meeting regulations of no greater than 40 acres in an area) that are immediately filled on becoming dried and covered to meet federal standards.

phenols In environmental health, these are organic compounds that are by-products of petroleum refining, tanning, and textile, dye, and resin manufacturing. Low concentrations cause taste and odor problems in water, and high concentrations can kill aquatic life and humans.

phenothiazine In psychiatry and medical care, this is a drug known for its antipsychotic properties. As a class, the phenothiazine derivatives are among the most widely used drugs in treatment of mental and emotional disorder in psychiatric practice.

philanthropy director A high-level administrator in a health-care organization or hospital with the task of fund-raising and acquiring gifts for the facility. Usually referred to as the "director or vice president of development" or the "foundation director."

philo- Prefix meaning "attracted to" or "to like" or "to love."

phlebotomist A nurse, medical technologist, medical laboratory technologist, or other allied health technologist who draws blood from patients for laboratory analysis or in blood banks from blood donors.

PHN Public health nurse.

PHO *See physician-hospital organization.*

phobia A pathological, restraining fear associated with an object, a place, or an event.

-phobia Suffix meaning "fear of a situation."

phobo- Prefix meaning "fear."

-phoria Suffix meaning "emotions," "feeling," or "mental state."

phosphates In environmental health, these are certain chemicals compounds containing phosphorus; fertilizers.

phosphorus In environmental health, this is an essential chemical food element that contributes to the eutrophication of lakes, streams, and other bodies of water. Increased levels of phosphorus result from the discharge of phosphorus-containing materials into surface waters.

photochemical smog In environmental health, this is any air pollution caused by a variety of chemical reactions and pollutants such as ozone and/or nitrous dioxides.

photon In laser beam technology, this refers to the smallest division of a light beam that retains properties of the beam as measured by frequency, wavelength, and energy.

photo scan A medical imaging approach using a two-dimensional picture of the gamma rays emitted by a radioisotope and showing a varying concentration of bones and tissues in the body with a printout from the light source of the exposure on the film.

phototherapy In medical care, this is a treatment usually used on babies suffering from hyperbilirubinemia and jaundice. Bilirubin levels usually drop to normal after specific time exposure under these special lights.

PHP *See prepaid health plan.*

PHS *See Public Health Service.*

PHS Act *See Public Health Service Act.*

-phylaxis Suffix meaning "protection."

physiatrics Rehabilitation, physical therapy, and physical medicine. *See also physical medicine.*

physiatrist A licensed physician who specializes in providing and prescribing physical therapy for patients needing physical rehabilitation.

physiatrist, qualified For JCAHO accreditation of long-term-care facilities, a licensed physician who is certified or eligible for examination either by the American Board of Physical Medicine and Rehabilitation or by a specialty related to rehabilitation or who has the documented equivalent in training and/or experience.

physical and chemical treatments In environmental health, these are processes generally used in large-scale wastewater treatment facilities. Physical processes may involve air stripping or filtration. Chemical treatment includes coagulation, chlorination, or ozone addition. In liquid waste management, this refers to treatment processes used to treat toxic materials in surface waters and groundwaters, oil spills, and some methods of dealing with hazardous materials on or in the ground.

physical evaluation In health administration and facilities planning activities, this is a study of the potential of continuing, expanding, or contracting a hospital's facilities in a manner that permits the physical plant to meet recognized standards or local regulations for health facilities as well as the continuous operational requirements of the institution.

physical examination In medical care, this is the inspection, examination, and assessment of a patient's body by a health-care provider qualified to do so by utilizing tests, special tools and instruments to determine health status, levels of wellness, or signs and symptoms of illness and disease.

physical examination (long-term care) A complete medical physical exam and history must be completed for all residents of long-term-care facilities within 5 days prior to admission or within 72 hours following admission (Title 22 California, OBRA).

physical fact 1. A fact that is obvious and indisputable. 2. An unquestionable fact; law of nature.

physical harm In occupational health and safety, this is injury and/or illness as well as adverse mental neurological or systemic effects resulting from a harmful or injurious exposure at work or from circumstances encountered in the course of employment.

physical medicine A department that may include specialty areas such as physiatry and physical and rehabilitative medicine and performing diagnosis, therapy, and treatment of the disabled, convalescent, and physically handicapped patient using heat, cold, exercise, water, etc. Physical therapists assist the physiatrist and provide much of the therapy. Occupational therapy and speech therapy may also be included in this department.

physical medicine and rehabilitation *See physical medicine.*

physical medicine services According to JCAHO accreditation, these services include physical therapy, occupational therapy, or other physical restorative and maintenance services that are provided in the specialty of physical medicine.

physical plant and maintenance department The department of a health-care facility responsible for repair and maintenance of the facility. It also maintains the steam and heating plant, electricity, air conditioning, emergency power, equipment, buildings, fire alarm systems, elevators, grounds, and parking lots.

physical prompt In mental health care, this is a signal or gesture that is used to alert an individual to do task responses by doing a behavior or doing an activity in training or that encourages a certain behavior.

physical rehabilitation services The professional and technical care that assists physically disabled persons to increase, attain, and/or maintain functional capacity. Standards are applied to evaluate a hospital's performance in providing rehabilitation services (JCAHO).

physical restraint Any physical or mechanical device or material attached or adjacent to a patient's body that the patient cannot remove easily and that has the effect of restricting the patient's freedom of movement. This does not include the use of the least restrictive immobilization reasonably necessary to administer treatment of a therapeutic, noncontinuous nature (such as immobilization of a patient's arm for an injection), as long as the restraint is removed on the administration of such treatment. This does not apply for continuously administered treatments such as intravenous therapy.

physical therapist (PT) 1. A specially trained and licensed individual who uses physical agents, biomechanical and neurophysiological principles, and assertive devices to relieve pain, restore maximum function, and prevent disability following disease, injury, or loss of a bodily part. Physical therapists are employed by rehabilitation centers, schools, societies for crippled children, and public health agencies. A license is required to practice physical therapy in the 50 states, the District of Columbia, Puerto Rico, and the Virgin Islands. To obtain a license, an applicant must have the appropriate bachelors or a masters degree or a certificate from an approved school of physical therapy and pass a state board examination. The minimum education required in some states is at the masters degree level. 2. According to JCAHO, this is an individual who is a graduate of a physical therapy, approved by a nationally recognized accreditation body, or who has the documented equivalent in training, education, and/or experience who meets any current legal requirements of licensure or registration and who is currently competent in the field.

physical therapist, qualified consultant For Medicare purposes, a person who is licensed as a physical therapist by the state in which he or she practices and 1) has graduated from a physical therapy curriculum approved by the American Physical Therapy Association, by the Council on Medical Education and Hospitals of the American Medical Association, or jointly by both; 2) prior to January 1, 1966, was admitted to membership by the American Physical Therapy Association, was admitted to registration by the American Registry of Physical Therapists, or has graduated from a physical therapy curriculum in a 4-year college or university approved by a state department of education; 3) has 2 years of appropriate experience as a physical therapist and has achieved a satisfactory grade on a proficiency examination approved by the secretary, except that such determinations of proficiency shall not apply with respect to persons initially licensed by a state or seeking qualification as a physical therapist after December 21, 1977; 4) was licensed or registered prior to January 1, 1966, and prior to January 1, 1970, and had 15 years of full-time experience in the treatment of illness or injury through the practice of physical therapy in which services were rendered under the order and direction of attending and referring physicians; or 5) if trained outside the United States, was graduated since 1928 from a physical therapy curriculum approved in the country in which the curriculum was located and in which there is a member organization of the World Confederation of Physical Therapy, has 1 year of experience under the supervision of an active member of the American Physical Therapy Association, and has successfully completed a qualifying examination as prescribed by the American Physical Therapy Association.

physical therapy (PT) An allied health specialty that employs the use of physical agents, electrotherapy, gymnastics, massage, ultrasound, light, hydrotherapy, exercise, heat, cold, and neurophysiological principles and devices to relieve pain, regain body strength, adjust to physical defects, restore maximum function, and prevent disability following disease, injury, or loss of a body part.

physical therapy aide An individual who assists a physical therapist by cleaning and setting up equipment, assisting in lifting and moving patients, keeping records, escorting patients to and from patient care units, doing clerical chores, and performing other patient-related activities. *See physical therapy assistant.*

physical therapy assistant An individual working under the direction and supervision of a physical therapist who assists patients in therapy and rehabilitation. Under the supervision of a physical therapist, this person also helps in some clerical duties, maintenance work, housekeeping, supportive chores, equipment assembly and maintenance, and specified treatment programs. This individual also assists physical therapists in patient therapy and safety precautions.

physical therapy department A specially staffed and equipped administrative and service unit in a health-care facility that provides rehabilitative and restorative services for patients referred for physical therapy and care. *See also physical therapy; physical therapist.*

physical therapy services Therapies, treatments, and services provided to patients in facilities developed for the purpose of rendering physical therapy activities as prescribed by physicians and administered under the direction of a qualified physical therapist. *See physical therapy department.*

physician 1. A professional person qualified by medical education in an approved and accredited school (MD and DO) who has met licensure requirements, has the clinical experience, and is authorized by law (usually by having obtained a license) to practice medicine. 2. According to JCAHO, this is an individual who has received a doctor of medicine or doctor of osteopathy degree and is currently fully licensed to practice medicine. *See also teaching physician.*

physician, active Medical doctors who are currently licensed and practicing medicine on a regular basis, regardless of the number of hours worked per week.

physician, admitting In medical care delivery, this is the medical doctor who, by having medical staff privileges, authorizes the admission of a patient to a health-care facility.

physician advisors In quality care issues related to medical care, these are practicing physicians who work for professional review organizations as consultants to review medical records and assess appropriateness of care and patterns of delivery for quality of care.

physician, alternate In long-term care, this is the medical doctor, often the medical director of a nursing home, who takes over responsibility for patient care when the attending or family physician is absent.

physician assistant (PA) A specially trained, licensed, or credentialed individual who performs basic primary medical care and treatment under the direction of a supervising licensed physician. Such tasks might otherwise be performed by the physician such as taking medical histories, performing examinations, ordering and interpreting tests, making diagnoses, and determining and providing treatments, including minor surgery and writing prescriptions. Many PAs were corpsman or paramedics initially trained by the military and later trained further in medical schools to assist physicians in civilian health services. These programs were referred to as "medex programs" and were started at Duke University in 1967. Physician assistants are usually salaried rather than reimbursed on a fee-for-service basis, although the supervising physicians may receive fee-for-service payment for their services. The PA usually must have at least 2 years of college, though many people with masters degree and even doctorates have become PAs, have some medical care experience, and undergo 2 years of intense medical training, much like the academic and clinical training of a physician but greatly compressed in time and intensity. A PA is any individual certified as a PA by the proper licensing body of the state. Also known as a "physician extender." *See also medex; physician extender; nurse practitioner.*

physician assistant (PA), certification Physician assistants are certified by the National Commission on the Certification of Physician Assistants by passing an exam developed by the National Board of Medical Examiners. They must earn 100 hours of continuing medical education every 2 years and complete a recertification exam every 6 years.

physician assistant (PA), primary care These individuals, who represent the majority of physician assistants, perform physician-delegated functions in the areas of family practice, general internal medicine, general practice, pediatrics, emergency medicine, and obstetrics. They take medical histories, perform detailed physical examinations, conduct visual and auditory tests, conduct minor treatments and surgery, and otherwise assist the physician in patient care responsibilities.

physician assistant (PA), role of Physician assistants and physicians work together with other health-care providers in a unique partnership. Even though PAs work under the supervision of a physician, the physician need not be present when the PA is seeing patients. The relationship between the PA and the physician is based on mutual trust and reliance. The physician can delegate tasks to the PA on the basis of experience, education, and practice setting, complementing each other while providing medical care to patients. The PA provides both diagnostic and therapeutic health care so that physicians can spend more time on complex patient problems. Studies have show that PAs can perform 80% of the duties that would otherwise require a physician. They allow physicians to see more patients, freeing up more time to spend with patients while reducing patient waiting times. They participate in a wide range of primary care activities and/or can specialize in a particular area of medicine such as family practice, surgery, and internal and emergency medicine.

physician assistant (PA), specialty Physician assistants who have developed a specialty area and perform physician-delegated functions in such areas as orthopedics, surgery, urology, pathology, allergy, and dermatology. These individuals take case histories, perform physical examinations, conduct routine tests appropriate to the medical specialty, perform routine laboratory tests, perform basic primary medical care and treatment, and otherwise assist physicians in specialty-oriented patient care responsibilities.

physician assistant training program Affiliated with an accredited medical school, this is an educational program that prepares individuals to effectively provide primary health care under the supervision of a physician with current graduates being as well trained as the general practitioner physician of the past. These are highly intense training experiences where the curriculum compresses 4 years of medical school into 2 years, with the graduates having highly developed medical skills in the primary care levels of care. The PA usually must have at least 2 years of college, though many have a masters degree, and even some with doctoral degrees have become PAs, have some medical care experience, and undergo 2 years of intense medical training. *See also physician assistant.*

physician associate Also referred to as "physician assistant." *See physician assistant.*

physician, attending The primary physician legally responsible for the care of a patient. In cases where a patient's care is paid for by public funds such as in a teaching or county hospital, the physician chosen from among members of its medical staff is typically assigned patients on their admission to the hospital or is one of the teaching physicians or his or her charges; the physician chosen by a patient or a patient's representative to be responsible for the medical treatment of the patient in a health facility; the physician assigned to and responsible for the care of a patient in a teaching hospital who may also have the role of teaching and supervising residents and interns.

physician, board certified A medical doctor who has completed his or her medical education, received the medical doctorate degree, who has also completed an approved residency program and successfully passed all testing and examination processes (board exams) allowing the physician to be certified in a recognized and approved specialty area. *See specialty.*

physician, board eligible A medical doctor who has completed his or her medical education, received a medical degree, has completed an approved residency program, and is eligible for testing and certification examination processes in a recognized and approved specialty area but has not yet completed the exam portion or full certification. *See specialty.*

physician care, expenditures for *See expenditures for physician care.*

physician, contact Any consultation with a physician, in person or by telephone, for examination, diagnosis, treatment, or advice, excluding hospital inpatients or patients seen on a mass basis. Any contact associated with the individual patient about whom medical advice is sought, even if that person does not actually see or consult with the physician, such as a mother taking her child to see the doctor, with the contact ascribed to the child. Each patient treated in a setting (such as a home) makes each separate treatment a contact. Any test or X ray in the physician's office or outpatient center is a physician contact, as is advice on the phone or in a physician's home visit or any direct professional exchange between an ambulatory patient and a physician or a member of his or her staff dealing with medical care and the rendering of medical care services; services directly provided by a physician, nurse, PA, NP, or other individual acting under the supervision of a physician; family practitioners, general internists, pediatricians, geriatricians, obstetricians, and other primary care doctors who make up the majority of physicians of first contact in the medical care system; physicians engaging in primary care and seeing patients.

physician contingency reserve (PCR) In managed care, this is when a health plan holds back in reserve a portion of claim payments due health-care providers/physicians as an assurance and incentive for appropriate utilization and quality of care. The amount is retained by the health plan and is credited to the physician's account. The health plan may use the funds if additional funds are needed to pay claims. The funds are returned to the physician at various times as agreed on by the contract and at varying levels, which are determined by the performance or productivity of the physicians compared to their peers. Also referred to as a "withhold."

physician, critical care A physician who specializes in the care of patients suffering from serious illness or injuries. These physicians work in cardiac care units, intensive care units, emergency rooms, or trauma rooms to provide continual high levels of care.

physician, emergency care A licensed physician with advanced training in emergency medicine who provides immediate advanced medical care for patients suffering from trauma and injury caused by accidents or seriously acute illnesses. Such a physician usually practices in an emergency room and works on a contract, salary, or stipend basis.

physician executive A medical doctor who has assumed an administrative or top executive position in a health-care organization.

physician extenders A physician assistant (PA), nurse practitioner (NP), clinical nurse specialist, certified midwife, or one who performs physician-delegated tasks, treatments, care, and services. Minimally trained health-care providers educated to do certain medical tasks and treatments formerly reserved for physicians. Both PAs and NPs are used heavily in health maintenance organizations, but the original intent was to use physician extenders to better distribute medical care services, especially to rural areas. *See physician assistant; medex; nurse practitioner.*

physician, geographic A full-time salaried staff physician who is paid for clinical and administrative services to the hospital.

physician, graduate A medical doctor who has completed his or her medical education and who has received a medical degree (MD or DO) and who is taking post-MD training.

physician, hospital-based Several medical specialties often work in or out of hospitals rather than in private practice: anesthesiologists, pathologists, radiologists, emergency room physicians, and in some cases psychiatrists and primary care physicians in outpatient centers in a hospital. In some states (e.g., California) physicians are not allowed to be employed by a hospital unless they are in a teaching hospital situation of one of the specialties that practices in a hospital such as anesthesiologists, pathologists, radiologists, or emergency room physicians. *See hospital-based physician.*

physician hospital organization (PHO) Under managed care and managed competition, this is a corporate entity created jointly by a hospital and a physician group to pursue contracts with third-party payers, health plans, and employee groups through employers. Some PHOs have organizational structures similar to those of health maintenance organizations or other similar managed-care approaches, providing their own risk-bearing arrangements, sharing in the surpluses, and being accountable for the disbursement of funds.

physician licensure The process by which a state grants permission to an individual who has graduated from an accredited medical school to practice medicine on finding that the individual has met acceptable qualifications and standards. Physician licensure also involves ongoing state regulation of physicians, including the state's authority to revoke or otherwise restrict a physician's license to practice (JCAHO).

physician member of the medical staff A doctor of medicine or doctor of osteopathy who, by virtue of education, training, and demonstrated competence, is granted medical staff membership and clinical privileges by the hospital to perform specified diagnostic or therapeutic procedures (JCAHO for acute-care facilities).

physician, nonparticipating Under Medicare, this is a health-care provider who has not accepted a contract with Medicare, restricting him or her from receiving payment from Medicare or charging a Medicare patient the difference between the usual fee and the Medicare payment amount.

physician, office-based Medical doctors who spend most of their time working in practices based in private offices.

physician, participating Under Medicare, this is a health-care provider who has accepted a contract with Medicare, allowing him or her to receive payment from Medicare and who must accept the payment from Medicare without adding any charges to make up any differences between usual charges and contract charges.

Physician Payment Review Commission A special policy body established by the federal government under the Comprehensive Omnibus Budget Reconciliation Act of 1985 (P.L. 99-272) that makes recommendations to Congress and the Secretary of Health and Human Services on various issues relating to changes in physician payment under Medicare. In 1992, a change was made in Medicare's payment method to physicians to a relative value scale of the resources that go into physician care.

physician, primary care *See primary care physician.*

physician recruitment In health administration, this is the managerial process of locating, recruiting, soliciting, and convincing physicians to join a medical group, move to a rural community, join the medical staff of a hospital, etc. Perks, benefits, and incentives are offered to some physicians to entice them to join a health-care organization such as a medical group.

physician, referring A primary health-care provider who requests another physician, usually a specialist, to give a consultation or assume care of the patient.

physician, resident A medical doctor who has graduated from an accredited and recognized medical school, is on the staff of a hospital, and is undertaking advanced training in a specialty area. *See also resident; residency.*

physician, salaried A physician in full-time clinical practice providing service to patients in a hospital and on the payroll of that facility.

physicians' and surgeons' professional liability insurance *See malpractice insurance.*

physician's current procedural terminology (CPT) 1. An American Medical Association publication that has disease and injury classified by procedures with treatments primarily carried out by a physician using a numerical code for identification and insurance reimbursement submission. 2. In managed care, this is a listing of medical treatments, therapies, and care activities and procedures performed by practitioners and physicians. Each treatment or procedure is given a five-digit code to provide a standard for reporting physician medical care activity and an industrywide standard and method of reliable communication.

Physician's Desk Reference (PDR) An annually published compendium of information on prescription drugs and diagnostic products published primarily for physicians and widely used as a reference document in the medical field. The information included in the book is mostly identical with a drug's labeling or package insert and covers indications, effects, dosages, administration, and any relevant warnings, hazards, contraindications, side effects, and precautions. The PDR is distributed free or at reduced cost to many physicians and other providers through the patronage of drug manufacturers who have paid for having information on their products included. It is the one of the most widely used and readily available source of identifying drugs by picture. The drugs are listed by brand name for each manufacturer and are indexed by manufacturer, brand name, drug classification, and generic and chemical names.

physician services (general requirements) In long-term care, these are services provided by physicians responsible for the care of individual patients in the facility. All persons admitted or accepted for care by the skilled nursing facility shall be under the care of a physician selected by the patient or a patient's authorized representative. In long-term care, physician services must include a patient evaluation, including a written report of a physical examination within 5 days prior to admission or within 72 hours following admission.

Physicians for Human Rights A professional nonprofit organization that concerns itself with the rights of humans in prison camps, prison, jail, or confinement situations, opposing torture, vicarious trauma, and mistreatment.

physician shortage area An area with an inadequate supply of physicians, usually defined as an area having a physician-to-population ratio less than a specified standard such as 1 physician per 1000 persons. *See also medically underserved area.*

physician specialty Any specific branch of medicine in which a physician may concentrate. The specialty classification used by the Bureau of Health Professions and National Ambulatory Medical Care Survey and the American Medical Association include primary care specialties such as family practice, internal medicine, and pediatrics; medical specialties such as internal medicine, pediatrics, allergy, cardiovascular disease, dermatology, gastroenterology, pediatric allergy, cardiology, and pulmonary diseases; and surgical specialties such as general surgery, neurological surgery, obstetrics and gynecology, ophthalmology, orthopedic surgery, otolaryngology, plastic surgery, colon and rectal surgery, thoracic surgery, and urology. Other specialties are aerospace medicine, anesthesiology, child psychiatry, geriatrics, neurology, occupational medicine, pathology, physical medicine and rehabilitation, preventive medicine, psychiatry, public health, and radiology.

physician's profile A compilation of each doctor's charges and the payments made to him or her through the years for each specific professional service rendered to a patient as kept by a medical insurance carrier, hospital, or other institution or agency. As charges are increased, so are payments, and the profile is then updated through the use of computer data.

physician's services 1. Any professional treatment, therapy, or care rendered by licensed medical doctors, including surgery, consultation, and home, office, and institutional calls or visits. 2. Any service performed by a licensed medical doctor at a long-term-care facility except services performed by a resident's personal physician.

physician, teaching Any fully trained physician (e.g., MD, DO, or DDS) not enrolled in a graduate training program who is responsible for or directly engaged in any patient care activities performed by a physician and for the instruction, supervision, or both of interns, residents, or fellows who are participating in a medical educational program. *See teaching physician.*

physician visit insurance In managed care and medical care insurance, this is insurance that pays for all or part of the cost of an encounter with a medical doctor or his or her treatment staff such as physician assistance in his or her office for nonsurgical treatments or procedures; an insurance plan that pays for office visits for a specified visit or when a deductible has been met.

physician visits, mean number In health services research, these are the average totals of all visits related to hospitalized illness, other major non-hospitalized illnesses, pregnancy, other minor illnesses and routine checkups, immunizations, physician ordered tests, X rays, and ophthalmologist visits in the physician's office. This also includes seeing either a physician or an osteopath or his or her nurse or a technician in the patient's home, doctor's office, private clinic, outpatient department or emergency room, industrial clinic, school camps, dispensary, college health service, or any other clinic, including public health clinics; the average number of doctor visits for persons seeing a doctor.

physician visits, place of Five different places of treatment encounters by medical doctors have been identified: 1) home: house calls; 2) Office: fee-for-service patient encounters with a medical doctor in his or her private office, clinic, prepaid medical group, outpatient facility, or health center (excluding hospitals); 3) outpatient department: a patient encounter with a medical doctor in an organized ambulatory or walk-in treatment center, freestanding industrial care facility, freestanding medical care center and seen by a private physician, salaried house staff physician, or physician extender under the direction of a physician; 4) emergency room: a patient encounter with a medical doctor in an emergency room of a hospital but distinct from an outpatient clinic with an appointment; and 5) other: a patient encounter with a medical doctor in a student health center, employee/industrial clinic, public health clinic, HMO clinic, labor union clinic, or other clinic that is not in one of the other categories above.

physician visits, prenatal In health services research, this is the number of times a patient comes to a medical doctor in connection with a live birth occurring during the time period of study, usually 1 year. Visits usually include per delivery and postpartum visits to the physician's office and exclude hospital-based visits.

physio- Prefix meaning "nature."

physiology The study of the biochemical and physical functioning of living organisms and their parts; the process and function of human organs and tissue, including biochemical and physical actions.

physiotherapist A member of the health-care team who assists patients with problems related to the musculoskeletal system. *See also physical therapy.*

physiotherapy Therapy and rehabilitation techniques utilizing physical agents such as hydrotherapy, heat, and light rays.

physPRC *See Physician's Payment Review Commission.*

pica A hunger for something not fit to eat; eating dirt or other inorganic matter not meant for human consumption (e.g., lead paint chips).

Pick's disease A presenile degenerative brain disease. *See also Alzheimer's disease.*

pie charts A circle graph that shows percentage distributions in pie-shaped wedges.

piercing the corporate veil A court's refusal to recognize a corporation as a legal entity, making those individuals who run the corporation personally responsible for its activity.

pig A container made out of lead used to ship or store radioactive materials.

piggyback loan In health-care finance, this is a loan made jointly by two or more banks or other loan institutions under a trust deed or mortgage. The lenders are classified as "subordinate," or the one with a lesser percentage and thus high risk, and "portion," or the one with the greatest percentage of loan and thus at the greatest risk of loss.

pilot investigation *See pilot study.*

pilot project In health planning or program development, this is the implementation of the skeleton of a program or service or a trial run of a service or program to see if it is useful, if it will work, or if it is economically feasible to implement and operate; a dry run of a program in which little experience exists and that is done to see how things will go or how the program or service will work. It can also be a modified or simplified run of a project prior to implementing a full blown project. This consists of shortened versions of the main project fully implemented but not the full project; the first project implemented in a series of similar projects with the first serving as the test project. Also called a "test case."

pilot study In epidemiology or biomedical research, this is the implementation of a trial run of a research project to see if it is useful or if it is economically feasible to implement, often done to identify problems and set baseline data; the first run of a research project done on a small scale to test it out prior to conducting it on a large-scale basis.

PIN Provider identification number.

ping-ponging The practice of passing a patient from one physician to another in a health program for unnecessary cursory examinations so that the program can charge the patient's third party for a physician visit to each physician. The practice and term originated in Medicaid mills.

pink lady A volunteer member of a health-care facility's volunteer auxiliary, so called because of the pink uniform worn. *See also auxilian; auxiliary, hospital.*

PIP *See periodic interim payment.*

PIRO People, ideas, resources, objectives. A management concept identifying what a manager works with. *See also management.*

P.L. *See public law.*

P.L. 93-641 *See National Health Planning and Resource Development Act of 1974; Health System Agency.*

place In epidemiology, these are geographical, regional, or area factors or political boundaries that influence or contribute to the cause, prevalence, or occurrence of disease in a population. The natural, physical, or topographical features or boundaries that affect, restrict, limit, or allow for the presence of disease or its restriction. The location, physical features, lay of the land, and layout of cities or buildings and the role they play in the containment or spread of disease. *See time; person; epidemiology.*

placebo An inactive or inert substance, preparation, or procedure (such as a sugar pill or an injection of sugar water) used in random-controlled trials to determine the efficacy of the substance, treatment, or preparation being tried. A placebo may also be given to deceive, please, or gratify a patient or physician or subject of a research study.

placebo effect In biomedical research, this is when a change or reaction in the research subject is a result of the subject believing so strongly in the curative effect of the drug or treatment, even if a fake one is administered, that he or she responds to or is healed from his or her belief in the treatment rather than the actual treatment or therapeutic intervention.

place of occurrence In health law, this is where the event occurred.

place of residence 1. In health law, this is where an individual legally lives or maintains as the legal place of living; legal residency. 2. In public health, this is where a person lives. It is stated as the legal residency, especially as used in reporting live births or fetal deaths, where the residence of the mother is used. 3. In health services, this is the place where a subject or patient lives inside a metropolitan statistical area (MSA) or outside an MSA. Place of residence inside an MSA is classified as either a central city area or not central city.

place of service In managed care and health services delivery, this is the physical address or location where medical care is agreed on to be provided such as at a clinic, hospital, or physician's office.

plaga (Lat.) Blow or strike. The root of plague.

plagiarism Illegally using art, protected writings, or literary compositions of another and passing it off as one's own work.

plague 1. Derived from the Latin "plaga," meaning "blow" or "strike." 2. Broad disease devastation on large populations. 3. An acute infectious disease with a high mortality rate; primarily diseases of rats and rodents transmitted to man by a vector, usually a flea, with the most common form being bubonic plague.

plain error rule In law and the litigation process, this is a rule that allows an appeals court to reverse a decision because of an error in the proceedings, even if no objection was given during the proceeding.

plaintiff 1. In law and the litigation process, this is the person initiating a lawsuit against another person or party; the person or persons who bring a civil action against the defendant; the person initiating a petition; the one filing a claim. 2. The party who has been harmed or injured and has brought a lawsuit to seek damages.

plaintiff in error In law and the litigation process, this is the appellant who seeks a review of a decision; an appellant.

plan 1. A set of decisions describing what short- or long-range actions should be taken to produce future changes to attain explicitly stated and desired results. 2. Used to refer to a managed-care health plan; an insurance company or the medical coverage provided by not-for-profit medical insurance organizations. 3. Using the problem-oriented medical record approach, a method of organizing activities into three parts: collecting further data, initial treatment, and patient data. This creates a plan of action indicating what the patient must do and shows the results of the patient's own activities in the management of the problem. Exam and test results and review of the prognosis are also provided. A plan can be used in educating patients with regard to changes they must make in their lifestyles to recover fully or live comfortably with their illness or condition. *See also problem-oriented medical record.*

plan development process In health planning, this is a cyclical process used for expressing community values and long-range aspirations for health status and health system performance, projecting and evaluating the capabilities of current health services to address health status needs, and designing and choosing among which actions will close the gaps between projected and desired levels of community health and health service performance.

plan hospital *See plan provider.*

plan, implementation *See Annual Implementation Plan.*

Planned Approach to Community Health (PATCH) In health promotion, this is a cooperative program of technical assistance aimed at federally established priority health problems that is supported by the Centers for Disease Control and Prevention (CDC) to strengthen state and local health departments' abilities to plan, implement, and evaluate community-based health promotion activities.

planner A health services administration professional whose professional activities are involved with the process of conducting planning activities, need assessments, program development, implementation, and evaluation activities. The most desirable levels of education and training for this professional usually include an advanced degree in health planning, health services administration, or public health.

planning 1. The most primary of all the functions of a manager; a key activity of administrators and managers that is used to determine a preferred course of future action for an organization, service, or institution. 2. The conscious design of desired future states (described in a plan by its goals and objectives and its description and selection among alternative means of achieving the goals and objectives), the activities necessary to designing (such as data gathering and analysis), and the assurance that the plan is achieved. There are many different definitions of planning and descriptions of different types, including long-range, or perspective (covering 15 or more years); midrange, or strategic (5–15 years); short-term, or tactical (1–3 years); health facilities; manpower; community or program; categorical or comprehensive health; nominative (based on norms or standards with legal basis); and inductive or deductive (used when the planning is done locally, then consolidated and used at state and federal levels). 3. The process of identifying needs, setting priorities, setting goals, writing outcome objectives, identifying causes of problems, setting implementation activities, developing time lines, assessing internal and external resources, identifying barriers, and allocating resources and personnel to implement and achieve program goals and objectives. *See also health planning; operational planning; strategic planning; priority levels; planning; functions of a manager.*

planning and program development *See program development.*

planning cycle In health planning, this is the scheduled sequence of a set of formal steps and procedures to be performed over a predetermined period of time to complete planning activities. The planning cycle is repeated for each successive planning period and ends with the implementation of the plan and the evaluation process.

planning grant Funds allocated to support the planning process that are used to develop methods and refine approaches for carrying out research, program development and implementation, demonstration projects, or initiating pilot projects.

planning, levels of In health or institutional planning, several levels are used, and each level must have goals supported with objectives and long-range recommended actions and resource requirements to meet these goals and objectives. At the macrogovernmental level, planning is done for the nationwide health system (regional, state, county, and city) on both the medical care delivery side and the public health side. Levels of planning also occur in privately owned national or international hospital and health-care systems as well as regional and local health-care systems. In the micro sense, various approaches to planning occur in a health-care system or institution such as a hospital or managed-care organization. Some of the various levels at which planning can occur are health-care system delivery and utilization planning (such as in a large HMO with its own hospitals and clinics), strategic planning, long-range planning, short-term planning, tactical planning, operational planning, budgetary planning, and program development. *See planning; program development.*

planning, long-range Envisioning where a health-care organization would like to be operationally and in terms of physical plant, programs, facilities and service; what the organization should look like in 5 years and 10 years and what changes and resources are needed to ensure that the plan will occur. Also referred to as "long-term planning." *See strategic planning.*

planning, short-term A tactical plan that positions where a health-care organization must be operationally in terms of physical plant, programs, facilities, and service in the next year as well as the second and third years and what changes and resources are needed to ensure that the plan will occur while sensing and responding to the changing social and economic environment. Short-term plans are flexible and are adjusted to respond to current events while supporting the long-range plan and ensuring that both plans will occur. *See strategic planning.*

planning, strategic *See strategic planning.*

planning system A formal set of rational procedures to guide the process of decision making during the development of a plan. This includes steps in data collection and analysis for projections of the future, establishment of goals and objectives, and generation of alternative actions and selection among them.

plan of care *See patient care plan.*

plan of correction In health facility accreditation, certification, and licensure, these are actions to be taken and the forms used to document the procedures and time frame for correcting violations of certification or regulations as cited by the survey team.

plan of correction, conditional accreditation In JCAHO accreditation, this is a written plan approved by the JCAHO staff that outlines the activities the health-care organization will take to address compliance issues that caused the decision of conditional accreditation; the plan is the basis for the follow-up survey 6 months following approval of the plan.

plan of correction, plant technology and safety management In JCAHO accreditation, this is a written statement approved by the JCAHO staff that details the procedures to be taken to correct existing life safety deficiencies and lists the extraordinary life safety measures to be implemented to temporarily reduce the hazards associated with the deficiencies.

plan provider In managed care, these are physicians, hospitals, or other health-care providers who have contracted with a health plan to render services to members in accordance with provisions of the group subscriber agreement.

plan selection In past government planning for the health-care system, this was the fourth phase of plan development, which involved an analysis of the costs, benefits, and cost-effectiveness of implementing alternative plans. The alternatives are compared with respect to their overall effect on all priority objectives, their respective feasibility, public acceptability, and comparative cost. Plan selection ends with a selection of the preferred alternative plan.

plant age and depreciation In health administration and health-care financial management, this is to assess the age of the hospital or nursing home's physical plant. Many health-care facilities have been added on, and thus the age may vary from one physical location to another within the same facility. Age is also a function of keeping up with technology and refurbishing older physical plant structures. Thus an approximation of a health-care facility's age may be averaged by referring to the fixed assets section of the balance sheet for accumulated depreciation and to the operating expense section of the statement of operations for annual depreciation expense. A rule of thumb is that if the health-care facility exceeds the age of that of the competing facilities, it becomes expensive to replace fixed assets, thus the administrator should account for this by setting aside monies and supplementing all depreciation charged as an operating expense, thus ensuring that money will be available to maintain capital assets in a current condition and that the physical plant and equipment are kept up. This is referred to as "fund depreciation" (setting aside funds equal to the depreciation, ensuring that money is available, and not spending these funds for operation while periodically adding to the fund to ensure that the facility can be kept comparatively and competitively young). The age of a health-care facility can be estimated by dividing accumulated depreciation by annual depreciation expense:

$$\frac{\text{Accumulated depreciation}}{\text{Annual depreciation}} = \frac{\text{Overall age of facility}}{\text{(in years)}}$$

plant condition In health administration, this is to assess the buildings, structures, and physical plant and to determine its structural integrity, upkeep, maintenance, newness, overall condition, and appearance.

plant engineer The person administratively responsible for the physical plant of a hospital or other health-care institution.

plant fund In health-care finance, this is an account used to record the financial activities and transactions of a health-care organization's purchases, expenses, and investments in land, structures, buildings, and equipment.

plant operations In health-care administration, these are the heating, cooling, operation, and maintenance activities of the physical facilities, equipment, buildings, grounds, and structures.

plant, technology, and safety management In hospital administration, this is the organizational management program designed to provide a physical environment free of hazards and to manage staff activities to reduce the risk of human injury. Standards are applied to evaluate a hospital's performance in providing plant technology and safety management (JCAHO for acute-care facilities). *See risk management; safety committee.*

plant, technology, and safety management standards In hospital accreditation, these are the criteria used to establish life safety, safety management, and equipment and utilities management activities and functions to establish quality management of the physical environment (JCAHO for acute-care facilities).

plasma The fluid portion of the blood.

plastic surgery A medical specialty that focuses on the techniques involved in repairing, replacing, or correcting malformed, injured, or deformed parts of the body. This surgeon performs cosmetic and reconstructive surgery.

plea 1. In health law, this is a defendant's official answer to a complaint. 2. A motion or pleading to a court. 3. In equity, an answer as to why a suit should not be heard or entered.

plea bargaining In criminal law, this is the process of making a deal between a prosecutor and the defendant's lawyer and is used to reduce sentencing or the charges against the defendant.

plead 1. In law and the litigation process, this is to make a pleading; to present a motion to a court. 2. To argue a case in a hearing or trial.

pleading In law, this is filing an official written statement to a court; the first document filed as a complaint in a lawsuit. The response to the complaint is the answer. Motions and all documents given to a court are usually called "pleadings."

plea in abatement In health law, this is a plea that does not challenge the complaint but challenges the manner, place, or time a dispute is brought.

plea in bar In law, this is a plea that defeats a plaintiff's entire action.

pledge Allowing possession of personal property to be given to another person until the completion of a promise or the payment of a debt; a promise to pay.

pledging of accounts receivable In health-care financial management, this is using the accounts receivable of a health-care organization to secure a loan, usually based on short-term borrowing from financial institutions. The lender may legally and physically acquire or take over accounts due the health-care organization if the loan defaults but usually does so with recourse to the borrower.

plenary 1. Full; whole; complete. 2. Concerning every person or every thing.

PLI Practicing Law Institute. A nonprofit publishing and legal continuing education organization.

PLM *See product line management.*

plumes In environmental health, these are 1) visible or measurable discharges of a contaminant from a given point of origin that can be visible or thermal in water or visible in the air (e.g., plumes of smoke), 2) areas of measurable and potentially harmful radiation leaking from a damaged reactor, and 3) the distances from a toxic release considered dangerous for those exposed to the leaking fumes.

pluralism 1. In health-care delivery, the overall health-care system is multifaceted. It has many subsystems and a variety of methods and approaches that are put together according to the needs of the consumer, not the system. 2. In psychiatry, the idea that a multitude of factors may affect one's behavior.

plurality 1. In formal health-care meetings and hearings using parliamentary procedures, when more votes are cast for one measure or candidate but are less than a majority. 2. The greatest number; more than half.

PM Postmortem.

PM/DRGs Pediatric modified diagnosis-related groups.

PMIS *See PRO Management Information System.*

PM/PM Per member per month. As used in managed care, this describes one type of capitation payment plan. *See per member per month.*

PM/PY Per member per year.

PM$_{10}$ emissions In environmental health, these are the fine solid or liquid materials with an aerodynamic diameter less than or equal to a nominal 10 micrometers as measured by proper test equipment emitted to the ambient air.

pneumoencephalogram An X ray of the cerebrospinal spaces after they are filled with air.

pneumoventriculogram An X ray of the ventricles of the brain after oxygen is put into them.

PNP Pediatric nurse practitioner.

pocket part A booklet that supplements a law book and is kept in a special pocket that is part of the back inside cover of the book.

podiatric assistant One who assists the podiatrist by preparing patients for treatment, sterilizing instruments, performing general office duties, and assisting in preparation of dressings, administration of treatments, and development of X rays.

podiatric services The services relevant to the diagnosis, care, and treatment of conditions, disorders, diseases, and injuries of the foot and toe to inpatients and/or outpatients.

podiatrist 1. A health professional responsible for the examination, diagnosis, preventive care, treatment, and care of diseases and disorders of the human foot. A podiatrist performs surgical and other operative procedures, prescribes corrective devices, and administers drugs and physical therapy. 2. Under Medicare, a doctor of podiatry is considered a "physician" but only with respect to functions he or she is legally authorized to perform by the state in which he or she performs them. However, certain types of foot treatment or care are excluded, whether performed by a doctor of medicine or a doctor of podiatry. 3. According to JCAHO, an individual who has received a doctor of podiatric medicine degree and is currently fully licensed to practice podiatry. *See also podiatry.*

podiatry A branch of medicine that provides for the diagnosis, treatment, and preventive care of conditions, disorders, diseases, and dysfunctions of the foot and, in some states, the hand. Surgical and operative procedures are performed and corrective devices prescribed, as are drugs and physical therapy if needed.

point 1. An important issue that is the focus of concern or attention. 2. A legal issue or argument 3. Money charged for lending money. 3. In laser technology and environmental health, this a source of radiation whose dimensions are small enough, compared to distance and source and receptor, to be neglected in calculations.

point of disinfectant application In environmental health, this is the point where the disinfectant is applied to water and the water downstream of the point is not subject to recontamination by surface water runoff.

point-of-entry treatment In environmental health and water pollution control and treatment, this is any device applied to the drinking water entering a house or building for the purpose of reducing contaminants in the drinking water distributed in the building.

point of order In formal health-care meetings and hearings using parliamentary procedure, an assertion presented to the presiding officer that a procedure should be corrected or rules adhered to.

point-of-purchase plan *See managed choice.*

point of sale In health-care information management systems, used in pharmacies, business offices, food services, and other places where goods are sold, this is a computer-driven checkout system where transactions are picked up electronically from a bar code, setting charges and notifying the computerized inventory control systems.

point-of-service HMO *See point of service; point-of-service plan.*

point of service (POS) In managed care, this is an open-ended health plan that not only provides or arranges for the provision of health services but also allows the subscriber/plan member the option to seek a health-care provider outside the designed list or panel of contracted health-care providers. This type of health plan provides health-care sources that are differentiated by the financial responsibility and benefits and often for the convenience of health plan members. Health plan members may receive health services at the direction and discretion of the primary care health plan physicians. Members can seek care from a panel of contracted providers or from a nonparticipating provider of the member's choice. The members have a greater financial incentive to obtain care through the health plan or from a contracted health-care provider because co-payments, deductibles, and the filing of insurance forms are often imposed on the member who seeks a private health-care provider.

point-of-service option *See point-of-service plan.*

point-of-service plan In managed care, this is one health plan option where the member who anticipates using a private physician or hospital in addition to an HMO has an option to choose the different health-care providers, outside the health plan, but with different benefit levels. Several approaches are used: the health plan may allow enrollees to obtain some limited medical care from nonparticipating health-care providers; the health plan may provide coverage for nonparticipating providers through a supplemental medical insurance policy, including major medical coverage; a health plan such as a PPO may provide both participating and nonparticipating coverage; and any combination that may be desired by the subscriber group can be used. *See point of service, managed choice.*

point prevalence In epidemiology, this is a measure of the number of people in a population who have a disease at a given point in time or on a certain date; the frequency of a disease or condition at a designated point in time; the number of persons with a disease, condition, or disorder or attribute in a group or population at a single specified point in time; the number of existing cases of a disease at a point in time;

a cross-sectional study of a disease at a point in time. The point prevalence rate formula follows:

$$\frac{\text{Number of existing cases of the disease at a point in time}}{\text{Total study population}}$$

point prevalence average annual estimate In epidemiology, this is when the prevalence of a condition is measured regularly in an ongoing manner over an extended time period such as once a week for a year. The resulting estimate of prevalence is an average of the 52 weekly prevalence estimates.

points In health finance, this is the same as percentages. Any charge rate of three points is the same as 3% of the gross amount used as a fee or charge.

points and authorities In law, this is a memorandum used to support a legal position.

point source epidemic In epidemiology, this is when a disease outbreak is investigated until it is traced back to its point of origin, which is a specific place or location and/or person; when a single person in a specific location is identified as the cause and source of a disease outbreak.

point sources In environmental health, these are stationary locations or fixed facilities from which pollutants are discharged or emitted. Any single identifiable sources of pollution such as a pipe, ditch, smokestack, factory discharge pipe, feedlot, or a floating vessel.

point system In health administration and human resource management, this is a job assessment system that evaluates the importance of the key tasks and activities of a job and the position itself using a point system to determine the relative worth of each position in the organization.

poisons Substances that in relatively small doses have an action that either destroys life or seriously impairs the functions of the body's organs or tissue.

poisons, class A Extremely dangerous poisons that include poisonous gases or liquids of such a nature that a very small amount of the gas, vapor, or liquid, mixed with air, would be dangerous to life. Some class A poisons include liquid bromoacetone, cyanogen gas, liquid nitrogen peroxide, and phosphine.

poisons, class B Poisons that are not as dangerous as class A poisons. This class includes substances, liquid or solid (including pastes and semisolids) other than class A or irritating materials, that are known to be so toxic to humans as to provide a hazard to health during transportation and that, in the absence of adequate data on human toxicity, are presumed to be toxic to humans on the basis of results with test animals (e.g., oral toxicity testing). Arsenic acid (solid), liquid chloropicrin, and solid cocculus are examples of class B poisons.

poisson probability distribution A statistical presentation of a probability in which more than one occurrence can happen in a given time and where the mean is equal to its variance; a statistical distribution curve used to present the occurrence of a distribution of sporadic, isolated, or rare data points that occur in a continuum over time or space.

POL Physician-owned laboratory; physician-operated laboratory; physician office laboratory.

police power A government's power to create, carry out, and enforce laws or restrict rights for the health, safety, and welfare of the public; the power to license.

policies 1. Guidelines, rules, and directives established in companies and health-care organizations within which employees must perform their work. 2. In public health or environmental health, these are written statements that express the wisdom, philosophy, experiences, and beliefs of an organization's senior managers for future guidance toward attainment of goals and objectives. 3. The standard method of communicating, performing work, and following procedures; step-by-step methods of performing work-related tasks; rules of work and the workplace.

policies and procedures The act, method, and manner of proceeding in some process or course of action; a particular course of action or way of doing something such as policies and procedures governing the medical staff credentialing process (JCAHO for acute-care facilities).

policy 1. A course of action adopted and pursued by a government, individual, or organization; any course of action adopted as proper, advantageous, or expedient. The U.S. Congress makes policy on health-related matters by writing legislation and conducting oversight activities. 2. In managed care or insurance, this is a written contract of insurance between an insurer and the insured. 3. In the executive branch of the federal government, these are documents that interpret or enlarge on rules and are sometimes referred to as "guidelines."

Policies bear the same relationship to rules (regulations) as rules do to law, except that, unlike regulations, they do not have the force of law. 4. In health administration, these are the general rules and guidelines of a health-care organization used to provide direction and order to work and the workplace, reduce confusion, and enhance productivity and efficiency; objectives and rules guiding the activities of a health-care organization providing authority for allocation of resources.

policy adjustment An adjustment in bookkeeping used to account for all monies. *See also administrative adjustment.*

policy analysis In health administration and health services delivery, this is the evaluation and measurement process by which broad questions of need, scope, allocation, utilization, capacity, resources, and goals are critically assessed.

policy dividends In insurance and managed care, this is the policy owner's share of the surplus that is equally divided and payable to the policy owner at the end of the policy year; a return of part of the premiums paid by policy owners used to keep the policy in force for the year.

policy formation 1. In health administration, this is the determination of a general course of action to include informing key managers, coordinating activities, and implementing an administrative decision. 2. Development of specific rules, regulations, expectations, and procedures that support the organization's mission, goals, and objectives as well as facility- and department-level procedures and activities of the health-care organization.

policyholder In managed care or insurance, this is any individual, company, or organization that has purchased an insurance policy or that holds a group medical insurance or managed-care contract. Group policy owners do not have the same rights as individuals.

policyholder's surplus In managed care and insurance, this is the excess revenue as seen on an insurer's balance sheet, showing the net worth of an insurer (assets minus liabilities).

policy owner *See policyholder.*

policy owner service department In health plans, this is the administrative unit that provides assistance to a company's policy owners, agents, and beneficiaries. This department is responsible for handling requests for information, interpreting policy language, answering questions about coverage, making changes as needed in the policy such as beneficiary designation, sending premium notices out, collecting payments, calculating and processing policy loans, processing commission payments for company agents, and dealing with nonforfeiture options, dividends, and surrenders and mode of premium payment.

policy, public General rules and expectations used in controlling a society; health and social services of or representatives of that society. *See public policy.*

policy reserve In insurance and managed care, this is a liability account used to identify the amount of assets that are expected to be sufficient to pay future claims, including future premiums to be received from already existing policies. Also referred to as "legal reserve."

policy term In managed care or medical insurance, this is the period for which an insurance policy provides coverage or is in force.

polio *See poliomyelitis.*

poliomyelitis In medical care, this is an acute viral disease marked clinically by fever, sore throat, headache, vomiting, and often stiffness of the neck and back. Severe forms often result in paralysis of various limbs or parts of the body. Commonly called "polio."

political question An issue that courts cannot and will not hear because it is a decision to be made by the executive branch of government.

pollen A natural or background air pollutant; a fine dust produced by plants from the fertilizing element of flowering plants.

polling the jury In the litigation and trial process, this is asking each individual jury member for his or her decision; to question jurors one at a time in court; requiring a jury to voice its verdict.

pollutant or contaminant In environmental health, this is any element, substance, compound, or mixture, including disease-causing agents, that after release into the environment and on exposure, ingestion, inhalation, or assimilation into any organism, either directly from the environment or indirectly by ingestion through food chains, will or may reasonably be anticipated to cause death, disease, behavioral abnormalities, cancer, genetic mutation, physiological malfunctions (including malfunctions in reproduction), or physical deformations in such organisms or their offspring.

pollutants Any substance introduced into the environment that renders the atmosphere or water foul or noxious to health or that adversely affects the usefulness of a resource.

pollution 1. In environmental health, this is the contamination of water, air, food, or soil beyond that what is natural or nominal, toxic, or harmful to health. The presence of matter or energy whose nature, location, or quantity produces undesired environmental effects. 2. According to the Clean Water Act, these are man-made or man-induced alterations of the physical, biological, and radiological integrity of water.

pollution liability In environmental health, this is legal liability for injuries arising from the release of hazardous substances or pollutants or contaminants.

pollution standard index In environmental health and air pollution, this is a measure of adverse health effects of air pollution levels in major cities.

poly- Prefix meaning "many."

polychlorinated biphenyls (PCBs) Chemical substances limited to the biphenyl molecule that have been chlorinated to varying degrees or any combination of substances that contains such chemicals. According to the EPA, this is a group of toxic, persistent chemicals used in transformers and capacitors for insulating purposes and in gas pipeline systems as a lubricant. Their sale and use was banned by law in 1979.

polychlorinated dibenzofurans. One of a group of toxic and hazardous compound in the environment that accumulate because they are resistant to microbial and chemical breakdown. They accumulate in both plant and animal tissues, soil, fly ash, and other biological material.

polychlorinated dibenzo-p-dioxins One of a group of toxic and hazardous compounds in the environment that accumulate because they are resistant to microbial and chemical breakdown. They accumulate in both plant and animal tissues, soil, fly ash, and other biological material.

polydrug A medicinal substance, usually narcotic, that contains many different drugs.

polyelectrolytes In environmental health, these are synthetic chemicals that help solids clump together during sewage treatment.

POMR *See problem-oriented medical record.*

ponderal index An alternative approach to measuring human body mass instead of using just straight weight. It is calculated by height divided by the cube root of body weight.

pool *See insurance pool.*

pooled income fund In health-care finance, this is a fund to which several donors transfer property yet retain an interest income from, and give the remainder to, a single foundation or charity.

pooling In managed care, this is the process of combining insurance risk for all health plan accounts and employee groups of enrollees or numbers of subscriber groups into one risk pool.

pool nursing In hospital administration, this is a management strategy used to lessen the effects of variation in occupancy rates of nursing units and nurse staffing needs. An administratively centralized grouping of staff nurses is allocated to work units where needed such as being sent to work in nursing units where the occupancy rate and census are high and being pulled back from low census units. One staffing approach would be the matrix scheduling/grid.

pool, nursing A private agency that contracts with health-care facilities to provide nursing personnel and other allied health professionals on a temporary basis in times of manpower shortages or to avoid employing excessive personnel when occupancy rates are up temporarily. Also called "temporary nursing agencies" or "temporary health-care employment agencies."

pool, risk In managed care, this is an employment group or health plan account as identified by size of group, location, number of enrollees, and claim dollars that exceed a certain level per enrollee, in which revenue and expenses are combined. Attempts are made to identify the expected claim use (liability to the health plan) and the required funding to support the medical care claims.

poor *See poverty.*

popular name tables Legal reference charts used to find laws and statutes by their popular names.

population 1. The inhabitants of an area or region; groupings of individual cultures, ethnicity, and races; groups of people living together. 2. The study of the characteristics of people living together in a region such as patterns of birth, death, or migration changes. 3. The group from which a research sample is drawn. *See demography; person.*

population and family planning services Health services provided to individuals to control population and family size through the use of contraceptives.

population and family planning specialist One who serves in an administrative and planning role specifically oriented toward the use of demography, demographic techniques, and reproductive physiology to plan, conduct, and evaluate family planning programs. *See also family planning.*

population attributable risk The amount of disease associated with an agent or disease exposure in a group, community, or population. If expressed as a percentage, it is referred to as "population attributable risk percent." *See attributable fraction.*

population based In public health, this is a community defined by political and geographical boundaries from which studies are taken; also used as a denominator for an epidemiological rate.

population-based public health services In medical care services delivery under Medicaid and public health services, this provides for linkages between public health department services and Medicaid managed-care programs and is a plan that builds on existing managed-care program requirements, including requirements for plans to provide clinical preventive services, compliance with schedules, and understanding the roles of and coordinating with local public health departments.

population density The number or concentration of people living in a defined area.

population excess rate In epidemiology, this is the rate of disease in a population compared to the nonexposed individuals in the same population or the amount of disease associated with exposure levels and numbers of nonexposed in a population; the relationship of the amount of disease that exists in a population compared to the level of exposure.

population medicine The study of disease rates, exposures, epidemics, and other communicable and chronic disease phenomena that occur in groups or populations and the resultant impact these have on public health, medical care delivery, and health status of the population. *See public health; community medicine; preventive medicine.*

population momentum In public health, epidemiology, or health services, this is when a fertility rate (number of women ages 15–44) decline is seen in a community, state, or country yet the number of births continues to increase, causing a growth situation among the population even while death rates remain static. One reason for this occurrence is an increase in the number of children born per female.

population pyramid In epidemiology and public health, this is a graphic and pictorial representation of the numbers of females compared to males in a population for each age-group across the life span in a population group. This is usually constructed as a bar graph with the youngest age-group for both male and female bars at the bottom and the oldest at the top and with males on the left and females on the right. Age groupings are usually every 5 years. Industrialized nations that have high life expectancy in all age-groups cause the pyramid to lose much of its shape. When pyramids are re-created over time, changes in population trends can be observed in different age-groups and large or small age cohorts observed as they move though the generations and up the pyramid.

population segment In health-care delivery, this is the quantifiable number of persons who share similar health-care service needs that can be translated into a relatively predictable pattern of health services utilization.

portability In national health security plans and national health insurance, this is the ability of individuals to take their medical insurance or health plan coverage with them on losing their job or changing their residence or life's circumstance, guaranteeing that continuous medical care coverage goes with them.

portability clause In managed care and insurance, this is a statement in the policy that allows workers to transfer accumulated benefits to their subsequent employer when they change jobs. This has also applied to pensions.

portability of benefits In national health security plans and in universal health-care coverage, this refers to individuals being able to take their medical care coverage with them no matter what happens in life's circumstances so that coverage will be available if a job is lost, if one moves, or if one is no longer under his or her former health plan.

portent of embarrassment The fear of being demeaned or belittled for inferior or inadequate performance in one's duty in one's profession.

portfolio In health-care finance, this is a group of investments managed by a financial management firm for the health-care organization.

POS *See point of sale.*

positional authority In health administration, this is the formal managerial authority given by the administration of the organization through being appointed to an administrative position. The amount of authority held by the position depends on the level of the position, the delegation process, and empowerment activities of upper administration.

position analysis questionnaire (PAQ) In health administration and human resources management, this is a standardized form that collects specific information about various positions in the health-care organization.

position control In health administration and human resources management, this is the process of the management team of the health-care organization reviewing the number of position created and the numbers of persons hired to fill them.

position description In health administration and human resources management, this usually details the job title; tasks, activities, responsibilities of the position; salary and benefits; job requirements; and minimum qualifications that a candidate for the job must have to be considered for the position.

positioning In strategic health planning and marketing, this is the process of assessing the competitive environment and determining how to place the health-care organization in a strong competitive and progressive position in the local or regional health-care marketplace so that it will have a strong and successful future.

positive evidence In health law, this is the direct and final proof of an issue.

positive exposure In environmental health, this is any recorded exposure, corrected for background, greater than the established minimum detection limit of the monitoring device or the measuring technique employed.

positive law Statutes enacted by a legislature.

positive motion In formal health-care meetings and hearings using parliamentary procedures, when a motion has more "yes" votes than "no" votes.

positive operating margin In health-care financial management, this is a surplus of revenue that occurs when income exceeds costs of operation.

Positron Emission Tomography (PET) Invented in 1973, the PET scanner can electronically peer into the skull to learn how brain cells react to a radioactive substance that is almost painlessly injected into the body. It allows one to look at the brain not only to localize brain disturbances but also to measure how severe they are.

posse commitatus (Lat.) 1. The power of the state. 2. Citizens used by law officers to help enforce the law, usually only in an emergency.

possession 1. To have ownership and control. 2. Rightful occupancy of land or buildings. 3. Holding and keeping something.

possessory action A legal action used to gain and control property but with no attempt to get legal ownership.

post- Prefix meaning "after" or "past."

postacute convalescence In health-care delivery, this is the recovery period of a patient following an acute spell of illness or a stay in an acute-care hospital where the patient recovers in a convalescent hospital, transitional care unit, or at home under the care of a home health agency or family.

postclosure In environmental health, this is the time period following the shutdown of a waste management or manufacturing facility. For environmental pollution monitoring purposes, this is usually 30 years.

postconsumer wastes (PCW) In environmental health, these are materials or products that have served their intended use and have been discarded for disposal or recovery after passing through the hands of the final user. Postconsumer wastes are a part of the broader category called "recycled materials."

postdate To date a document later than the date it is signed.

posterior frame A frame on which the patient lies when he or she is in a supine position.

postero- Prefix meaning "back" or "behind."

postmortem (Lat.) After death. Autopsy of a dead body to investigate the medical cause of death.

postmortem care In hospitals or nursing homes, this is the preparation of the deceased by health-care providers for transportation to a mortuary, funeral home, or morgue.

postmortem examination An autopsy; the examination of a dead body to ascertain cause of death. The body and its organs are dissected by a physician, usually a pathologist, to determine the actual physiological cause of death. *See autopsy.*

postnatal Following the birth of a child.

postneonatal death In epidemiology and public health, this is any death occurring between the 28th day of life and the end of the first year of life (365th day).

postneonatal mortality In epidemiology and public health, these are deaths that occur from 28 days through the 365th day after birth. *See neonatal mortality.*

postneonatal mortality rate In epidemiology and public health, this is the annual number of postneonatal deaths as a proportion of the annual number of live births (per 1000 live births). The rate is the number of deaths that occur from 28 days to 365 days after birth per 1000 live births. The postneonatal mortality rate formula follows:

$$\frac{\text{Number of deaths from 28 days through 365 days}}{\text{Number of live births}} \times 1000$$

See neonatal mortality rate; perinatal mortality rate.

postoperative care In hospitals or surgical centers, this is a series of activities beginning at the time a patient is removed from surgery where nursing and technical staff care for the patient by meeting the patient's psychological, medical, and physical needs directly after surgery.

postoperative recovery room A medical and nursing unit used exclusively to monitor patients recovering from the effects of surgery, including observation of patients who are recovering and going through withdrawal from anesthesia and psychological support and observation to ensure that the patient returns to a state of physiological and mental stability.

postpartum Following childbirth; following delivery.

postpartum care Medical care following childbirth; hospital visits and care by a health-care provider associated with and following the birth of a baby.

postprandial After a meal.

postsecondary health education program In school health education, this is a planned set of health education policies, procedures, activities, and services directed to students, faculty, and/or staff of colleges, universities, and other higher education institutions. This includes but is not limited to 1) general health courses for students, 2) employee and student health promotion activities, 3) health services, 4) professional preparation of health educators and other professionals, 5) self-help groups, and 6) student life (Joint Committee on Health Education Terminology).

potable water Water that is safe for drinking and cooking; water safe for human consumption.

potency In health services delivery, this is the ability to bring about health planning and health service delivery in the health-care system at an acceptable level of quality.

potentially compensable event (PCE) In managed care and insurance, this is an issue or occurrence related to risk; any risk that occurs when there is a possibility that a medical diagnosis or treatment failed to meet a required standard of care, causing an injury to a patient. A patient can make an allegation of negligence, or an internal quality/risk inquiry may discover the chance that poor care caused the injury.

potentially infectious materials In environmental health, public health, and medical care activities, these are body fluids and tissues that have the ability to cause or spread disease. The following body fluids are those listed as being of concern: semen, vaginal secretions, cerebrospinal fluid, synovial fluid, pleural fluid, pericardial fluid, peritoneal fluid, amniotic fluid, saliva in dental procedures, any body fluid visibly contaminated with blood, and all body fluids in situations where it is difficult or impossible to differentiate between body fluids. Also included are any unfixed tissues or organs other than intact skin from humans and HIV-containing cell or tissue cultures, organ cultures, and HIV- or HBV-containing culture media and other solutions: blood, organs, and other tissues from experimental animals infected with HIV or HBV.

potentially responsible parties In environmental health, these are any individuals or companies, owners, operators, transporters, or generators who potentially are responsible for or contribute to contamination problems at Superfund or polluted sites. The EPA requires legal actions to be taken against entities that pollute to clean up hazardous waste sites they have contaminated.

potential to emit In environmental health, this is the maximum capacity of a stationary source to emit a pollutant under its physical and operational design. Any physical or operational limitation on the capacity or the source to emit a pollutant, including air pollution control equipment and restrictions on hours of operation or on the type or amount of material combusted, stored, or processed, shall be treated as part of its design if limitation or the effect it would have on emissions is federally enforceable. Secondary emissions do not count in determining the potential to emit from a stationary source.

potential years of life lost (PYLL) In epidemiology and public health, this is a measure of early unwarranted deaths in a population and their economic and social impact. Disease, injury, and occupational hazards that cause early or youthful unnecessary deaths have a negative impact on productivity and economic stability of a society and are thus a concern for public health and the development of public policy to reduce PYLL, which is calculated by the sum of premature lives lost divided by all persons dying from the same cause in the same time period that the same individuals would have lived to normal life expectancy.

poverty 1. The condition of having an inadequate supply of money, resources, goods, or means of subsistence. The poor live under conditions that weaken their condition economically, socially, physically, and mentally and that are compounded by poor health, malnutrition, inadequate housing, poor heating, and lack of sanitary facilities. To compound these health hazards, several social factors adversely influence the way that those in poverty perceive and use the health-care system. There may be cultural differences in perceptions of illness and its appropriate medical treatment. The main cause of poverty seems to lie mostly in the lack of motivation to gain skills, education, and vocational training and the lack of purchasing power. Some of the working poor may not be able to take time from work to see a doctor. The poor may not have access to the knowledge of how, when, and where to obtain medical care. Finally, there is inadequate information among the poor on how to maintain a healthful living environment. The federal government has no national standard for poverty, but each federal agency that offers assistance to the poor has set its own standards and guidelines. Under the Aid for Families with Dependent Children (AFDC) program, the poverty levels vary significantly by state. Under the Supplemental Security Income (SSI) program, a nationwide standard has been established. Medicaid income levels are based on, but are not necessarily equivalent to, the levels established under AFDC and SSI. All these vary and are raised with inflation; to be eligible in 1994 the elderly person cannot have more the $2,000 in savings. 2. The smallest amount of income required to afford basic necessities at the lowest level of living of an average family purchased at the lowest realistic cost. Any economic status below this is to live in poverty. It is estimated that the average citizen spends a third of his or her income on food, thus setting the poverty level at three times the amount of the lowest realistic food budget. This somewhat dated formula, developed in the 1960s, was associated with the consumer price index and is believed to be skewed (Social Security Administration).

poverty, acute The segment of the population who are suddenly impoverished after living most of their lives with an adequate income. This group includes the unemployed or those who are retired and are required to live with a reduced income. The acutely poor must find ways to adapt to their new status. Some are able to find work and reestablish themselves, whereas others become depressed and suffer from poor mental and physical health caused by the loss of a standard of living and lack of income.

poverty area An urban or rural geographic area with a high proportion of low-income families. Average income is used to define a poverty area, but other indicators such as housing conditions, illegitimate birth rates, and incidence of juvenile delinquency are sometimes added to define geographic areas with poverty conditions.

poverty, chronic The segment of the population who have spent their entire lives below standard poverty levels. They usually have no realistic hope of changing their life situation because of a lack of knowledge of how to live above the poverty level.

poverty level The socioeconomic status of an individual or family and the amount of money available to families or individuals above which it is possible to achieve an adequate standard of living and inadequate below that level. Poverty levels are artificially established by government agencies and vary with the general area in which people live; the location in a community and inflation can be manipulated for political ends.

poverty line *See poverty level; poverty.*

power 1. The right, ability, or authority to control something, to carry out tasks, or to ensure that rules or laws are upheld; determining who gets ahead, gets rewarded, and makes what decisions; the capacity to modify the conduct of others while avoiding modification of one's own position or behavior; the ability to get others to act in a manner contrary to immediate interests or personal long-range goals while not being forced into submissiveness against one's will. 2. In health administration, this is the authority of a manager's position; recognizing the ability to control and have authority over others, especially subordinates, such as determining status, work schedules and time, income, promotion, work assignments, location of work, and self-determination in tasks and assignments.

power density In laser technology, this is the measurement of power concentration within the laser spot measured in watts per square centimeter.

power meter In laser technology, this is an instrument used to measure the power in a laser beam, which is important when used in medical treatment.

power of appointment A document that gives someone the power to decide who receives money or property from an estate and how it will be used.

power of a statistical test In health services research, this is the probability that the outcome of the research is strong enough and the sample size large enough to accept the research hypothesis.

power of attorney A legal document giving an individual the power to act as a legal representative, attorney, or agent of another in certain situations. What is allowed, including limitations, is clearly spelled out in the document. *See durable-power-of-attorney; conservatorship; guardianship.*

power of attorney, durable *See durable-power-of-attorney.*

PPA *See preferred provider arrangement.*

PPC *See progressive patient care.*

PPGP *See prepaid group practice.*

PPO *See preferred provider organization.*

PPS *See prospective payment system.*

practical nurse *See licensed practical nurse.*

practical nursing An educational program that prepares persons to assist in nursing care functions and activities under the direction and supervision of a registered nurse, physician, dentist, or other qualified health-care provider. *See licensed practical nurse.*

practice 1. The use of one's knowledge in a particular profession. The practice of medicine is the exercise of one's knowledge in the promotion of health and the treatment of disease. 2. A usual or customary way of doing things. 3. Procedures used in pleading and in court. 4. To repeat a behavior over and over until it is easily done.

practice parameters In medical care delivery, these are the approaches, techniques, methods, assessments, evaluations, treatments, procedures, and strategies used in individual patient management. *See practice; parameters.*

practice plan *See medical service plan.*

practice privileges In JCAHO long-term-care facility accreditation, permission to render care within well-defined limits on the basis of the individual's professional license and his or her training, experience, competence, ability, and judgment.

practitioner 1. One who practices a profession; a physician or other health-care professional who provides health-care services. 2. According to JCAHO long-term-care accreditation, any appropriately licensed individual who may be granted clinical privileges in the hospital, specifically physicians (MD or DO), dentists, and podiatrists.

praecipe In health law, this is an official motion or request of a court that does not need a judge's approval but the approval of a clerk of the court.

prayer 1. A request hoped for or desired as a part of a legal pleading. 2. In health law, this is asking for relief, help, action, damages, and recovery from harm, injury, or damage caused by the other party to a lawsuit.

preadmission certification In hospital administration, this is the review of the need for proposed inpatient services prior to the time of admission to an institution. Preestablished criteria are used to review and determine the need for and appropriateness of inpatient care. *See also concurrent review; prior authorization.*

preadmission process In hospital administration, this is the process of completing and signing appropriate forms, participating in tests and exams ordered by the physician, and completing all medical, business, and policy activities of the formal admission process by the patient for the physician. *See also admission; admission, preadmission process for; admission, inpatient.*

preadmission screening (PAS) In long-term care, this is an evaluation of patients prior to entering a nursing home as expected by Medicare so that therapy and care can be started immediately on admission to contain costs and keep lengths of stay as short as possible. *See case management.*

preadmission testing (PAT) In hospital administration, these are tests and examinations performed in the hospital on an outpatient basis prior to admission for care as an inpatient.

preamble The introduction to a document (e.g., a summary of why it was written).

preauthorized payment system In insurance and some managed-care plans, this is a method of payment in which the policy owner or member signs an authorization for the health plan or insurance company to withdraw funds from the policy owner's bank account in the amount of the premium each month and at the same time; authorizes the bank to honor the withdrawals without the member's signature.

precatory 1. A recommendation that is advisory only. 2. Counseling that is not legally binding. 3. Expression of a desire of something wanted.

precaution 1. Any measure, caution, or care taken beforehand to avoid danger, failure, or harm. 2. To warn or advise in advance to prevent harm or misdeeds; preventive warning. 3. Actions taken in advance to secure certain advantages.

precautionary Taking preventive measures; advisory warnings.

PRECEDE An acronym for Predisposing, Reinforcing, and Enabling Causes in Educational Diagnosis and Evaluation. In health promotion and health education, this is a seven-phase health education planning model that directs a health educator's efforts to results rather than inputs. The seven phases are included under the general areas of epidemiological and social diagnosis, behavioral diagnosis, educational diagnosis, and administrative diagnosis.

precedent 1. In law and the litigation process, this is a judicial interpretation of a legal issue that will be followed in the future. 2. A court decision and understanding giving authority and direction on how to decide a future similar issue of law. Landmark cases are formed by the process of using the findings of the landmark case to decide future cases, thus establishing a precedent. 3. Something that must occur before something else may be accomplished or take place; a new standard that arises from past practices.

preceptorship In health administration or clinical training for health-care practitioners or allied health workers, this is where a student is placed under a professional in the field who serves as a preceptor. The student has the experiential or field-based part of his or her education under the supervision of an active practitioner at the worksite.

precept A directive given by a person having authority to give such a command.

precipe *See praecipe.*

precipitating factors In epidemiology, these are those occurrences or elements associated with the onset of disease, injury, conditions, disorders, or death such as a set of events, agents, lifestyle, behaviors, risk-taking behaviors, or exposures.

precipitation In environmental health, this is the removal of solids from liquid waste so that the hazardous solid portion can be disposed of safely; removal of particles from airborne emissions.

precipitators In environmental health, these are air pollution control devices that collect particles from an emission.

precision In health administration, health services delivery, and health planning, this is a forecasting technique used to identify how close, accurate, or narrow the range of a forecast is to reality or how broad the range of uncertainty is that accompanies a forecast.

precognition 1. In health law, this is interviewing and questioning a witness before a hearing or a trial begins. 2. In psychology, thoughts or emotional states that are at a lower conscious level and have not yet reached the thinking, or conscious, level.

predentistry Educational preparation leading to a bachelors degree that allows a predentistry student to apply to an accredited school of dentistry. This usually includes all premedical admission educational requirements such as study at the college level with 1 year of chemistry, 1 year of biological sciences, and 1 year of physics.

prediction In health administration, health services delivery, and health planning, this is a forecasting technique used to identify relationships between past utilization and capacity patterns and related influencing factors and then is extrapolated to future utilization needs, patterns, and capacity.

predictive maintenance In occupational health and safety, these are actions necessary to monitor, find trends, and analyze the parameters, performance characteristics, properties, and signatures associated with equipment, systems, or facilities that are indicative of decreasing performance or impending failure.

predictive value In epidemiology, testing, and screening, this is the process of demonstrating through statistical analysis that a medical test of a disease has the ability to accurately predict results at a safe and high statistical level; the ability to show that a person with a positive test result does in fact have the disease as the test showed and at the same level of severity. Sensitivity and specificity of a test are used to determine the predictive value of the test. *See sensitivity; specificity.*

predisposing factor 1. In health promotion, preventive care, and health education, this is any characteristic, condition, or circumstance that affects a patient or community to be motivated toward a certain health behavior. 2. In public health and epidemiology, these are factors or elements that cause an individual or host to react in a particular manner to a particular environmental condition or disease agent such as the presence or absence of levels of immunity, susceptibility, or other factors that sensitize, condition, or allow the reaction to occur, including age, gender, race, genetic makeup, martial status, family structure, educational level, existence of a concurrent condition, past illnesses, past exposures, and attitudes toward a healthy lifestyle. From an epidemiological perspective, using the necessary-and-sufficient test, these factors are usually necessary to be present for a disease or condition to occur but may not require any sufficient level.

preemption 1. The first right or chance to be in line to purchase or receive something. 2. The act of doing or the right to do something before somebody else does it.

preemptive A right to the exclusion of others.

preexisting condition 1. An injury that has occurred, a disease contracted, or physical condition that existed prior to or that first manifested itself prior to the issuance of a medical insurance policy. Such a condition may cause an exclusion from medical care coverage under the policy for costs resulting from the condition. Some policies will cover the condition only after a specified waiting period. Such criterion is not to be allowed under universal coverage plans. 2. A disease, injury, or condition for which treatment was rendered prior to a health plan or medical care insurance policy being in force and that was not disclosed on the application.

preexisting condition limitation In medical insurance and managed care, the limit placed on benefits allowed for a medical condition that the enrollee had prior to becoming insured. *See preexisting condition.*

preexisting conditions provision In health plans and medical insurance contracts, this has been a statement used in the policy that states that until the member or policy owner has been under the policy for a certain time, usually 2 years, that no benefit is payable if the condition that produced the claim existed prior to the issue date and was not disclosed on the application.

preference 1. The paying of a debt by an insolvent debtor. 2. Right to be paid first before other creditors.

preferential debts In health-care financial management, these are debts in bankruptcy having priority; debts that can be satisfied before others.

preferred beneficiary In life insurance, this is the spouse, children, parents, and grandchildren of the insured. Policy owners can make beneficiary changes, designating the preferred beneficiary without consent from the currently named beneficiary, but consent must be obtained to name a nonpreferred beneficiary.

preferred provider arrangement This is the same as a preferred provider organization. *See preferred provider organization.*

preferred provider option In managed care, this is one approach to a health plan where certain health-care providers are designated by third-party payers as the providers who are selected or preferred because they are cost-effective and are contracted for care for health plan enrollees. When an enrollee receives care from the preferred provider, physician charges are paid by the health plan, but if a patient seeks care from another physician, fees will not be fully covered.

preferred provider organization (PPO) In managed care, these are specialized health-care delivery organizations formed by hospitals, physicians, medical groups, or health plans that negotiate fee schedules with insurance companies, thus becoming preferred. Preferred provider organizations offer lower prices to insurers in return for a larger patient care population and faster reimbursement of submitted claims.

The health plan or insurance company requires its policyholders to meet their health-care needs from health-care providers on a list because they use an advanced reduced fee schedule that saves money for all involved, especially the employer. Preferred provider organizations agree to provide as good of medical care and as extensive of coverage as would be covered by private health-care providers. This gives the employee a financial incentive to use the preferred provider, but unlike an HMO, the patient is not locked into staying with the PPO. Claims screening and utilization review analysis must be conducted by the PPO. Hospital-based PPOs have been used to increase average daily census and to compete with HMOs.

preferred provider panels As used in some legal literature and other documents, this is another term for "preferred provider arrangement" or "preferred provider organization." *See preferred provider organization.*

preferred providers In managed care, these are health-care providers such as physicians, hospitals, medical groups, dentists, or other health-care providers and practitioners who are under contract to provide medical care services to subscribers enrolled in a specific health plan.

preferred risk class In health services delivery and epidemiology, these are individuals who have a longer-than-normal life expectancy, usually identified as being nonsmokers, not drinking alcohol, having a regular exercise routine, having a good diet, being an acceptable weight range, and having a good family medical history.

preferred stock In health-care finance, these are stock investments of the health-care organization carrying a fixed specified dividend payment stated when it is issued. Preferred stockholders do not have voting rights as under common stocks.

prefix with the year In hospital administration and patient information management, this is a system of assigning numbers to patients. Within that number, the year of current treatment is included.

Pregnancy Discrimination Act of 1978 An amendment to the Civil Rights Act of 1964 that prevents discrimination in employment against women who are pregnant and able to perform their jobs.

prejudice 1. Bias; a strong belief in something or against someone. 2. Favoring one side in a dispute. 3. Harmful to one's rights such as in prejudicial error, which is a serious enough error to be appealed. 4. Negative evaluations, beliefs, judgments, or opinions formed without factual knowledge. 5. Irrational suspicion or hatred.

prejudice, with In health law, the final judgment adverse to the plaintiff, just as if the action had been tried to the end.

prejudice, without In health law, these are negotiations, decisions, agreements, offers, admissions, and judgments that are carried out at no risk to the parties involved.

preliminary title report In health-care financial and real estate management, this is a document showing the specific conditions of a title prior to a sale or loan transaction. This document is necessary to show that the title is clear and free so that the title insurance policy can be issued once a transaction is closed.

premanufacture notification In environmental health, this is a requirement by the Environmental Protection Agency (EPA) that a chemical manufacturer has to show that a chemical has been thoroughly tested and must give 90 days notification to the EPA of its plans to manufacture the chemical.

premature In medical care and childbirth, this is a live birth or fetal death occurring before the 37th week of gestation.

premature birth In medical care and childbirth, these are infants born between the 20th and 36th weeks of gestation. Also referred to as "preterm births."

premature nursery A separate medical and nursing care unit in a hospital that is specifically staffed and equipped to care for newborns whose weight is 2500 grams (5.512 lb.) or less. Because these infants are born before the complete maturation of body systems has been achieved, complications often occur. The premature nursery handles difficulties present in the premature baby.

premedicine The course of study, usually leading to a bachelors degree, that prepares a student to apply to an accredited school of medicine and includes study at the college level with 1 year of chemistry, 1 year of physics, and 1 year of biological sciences.

premeditation 1. A predetermined act. 2. Planning in advance about how to do something. 3. Deliberation. 4. Prior consideration.

premium 1. Money paid to an insurance company for insurance coverage. 2. Payment made periodically to keep an insurance policy in force; payment to an insurance company required to keep a group subscriber agreement in force, which is prepaid. 3. In managed care, this is the amount of money or consideration that is paid by an insured person or policyholder (or on his or her behalf) to an insurer or third party for insurance coverage under an insurance policy. The premium is generally paid in periodic amounts. It is related to the actuarial value of the benefits provided by the policy plus fees to cover administrative costs, profit, etc. Premium amounts for employment-related insurance are often split between employers and employees. Premiums paid by the employer are nontaxable income for the employee. Premiums are paid for coverage whether benefits are actually used or not; they should not be confused with cost-sharing devices such as copayments and deductibles, which are paid only if benefits are actually used.

premium receipt book In insurance, this is a booklet given to the policy owner that contains renumbered receipts that are signed by the insurance agent when the premium is collected.

premium/surplus ratio In health-care finance and insurance, the comparison of money received by the insurance company through clientele premiums compared to the policyholder's surplus. Some companies desire the ratio to fall between 2:1 and 3:1.

prenatal In medical care and childbirth, this is before birth; the period of time in pregnancy just prior to birth.

prenatal care In public health and medical care services, this is the provision of providing preventive care to pregnant women such as proper nutrition and weight gain; freedom from drug, tobacco, and alcohol use; and regular exercise and check-ups from the time of conception until labor and delivery occurs, all done to ensure a healthy pregnancy, optimum health of the mother and child, and an uneventful birth of a healthy infant. Prenatal care has been classified in three different levels: inadequate: no prenatal visits, prenatal care started after 28 weeks of gestation, and the week that care was started is unknown with less than 10 visits; intermediate: care started with 14 weeks of conception, but the number of visits is less than five, or care was started at 1 to 28 weeks of gestation and the number of visits is less than 10, or the week of care started is unknown but the number of visits is 10 to 19; adequate: care is started within 14 weeks of conception with the number of visits being five or more, the care started at 15 to 28 weeks of gestation, and the number of visits is 10 or more, or the week of care is unknown, but the number of visits is 20 or more.

prenatal physician visits *See physician visits, prenatal.*

preoperative In medical care, this is before surgery; prior to or preceding a surgical procedure or operation.

preoperative care In the provision of medical care, this is the period prior to undergoing surgery when psychological and physical preparations are made according to the special needs of the individual patient. Preparation for surgery may start at home by diet and liquid restrictions, but in the hospital it starts from the time the patient is admitted to the hospital to the actual time of the surgical operation, with the ordering of tests, room assignments, operating room schedules, ordering of drugs and diet, etc.

prepaid care In managed care, this is any healthcare plan offering potential patients an opportunity to pay for their health-care needs on an installment basis prior to getting sick, similar to an insurance policy. If services are required, they are provided for free or for a small fee. If services are not needed, then others benefit from the collective contributions of all the subscribers.

prepaid expenses In health-care finance, this is an accrual accounting method that pays for goods or services in advance, thus providing a savings to the organization in the next operating and budget cycle; expenses that a health-care facility has paid before actually receiving the product or service; products or services paid for but not yet used or consumed in health-care facility operations. Examples are leases, rentals, insurance premiums, and interest.

prepaid group practice (PPGP) A formal association of three or more physicians that provides a defined set of services to persons over a specified time period in return for a fixed periodic prepayment made in advance of the use of service. *See also group practice; medical foundation; health maintenance organization.*

prepaid group practice plan In managed care and medical insurance plans, these are organizations under which specified health services are provided by participating physicians to a pre-enrolled group of persons who pay fixed periodic payments in advance. If a health insurance carrier is involved, it contracts to pay in advance for the full range of health and medical services to which the insured is entitled under the terms of the health insurance contract. One approach to such a plan is a health maintenance organization. *See also health maintenance organization.*

prepaid health plan (PHP) In managed care, this is a contract between an insurer and a subscriber or group of subscribers whereby the PHP provides a specified set of health benefits in return for a periodic premium. This is the foundation of managed care, especially health maintenance organizations. Prepaid health plans have four attributes: 1) an organized system of health care in a geographic area, 2) a specified set of comprehensive health maintenance and treatment services, 3) a voluntarily enrolled group of persons, and 4) a predetermined and fixed period prepayment made by or on behalf of each person or family enrolled without regard to the amount of service provided to a particular person or family unit.

prepared childbirth A course of study that prepares expectant parents for childbirth. These courses include general information, hospital tours, educational experiences, and classes on any of several methods of managing labor.

preparedness The training of personnel, acquisition of resources and facilities, and testing of emergency plans and procedures to ensure an effective response to an emergency.

prepayment The payment for health-care services in advance. To pay insurance companies, PPOs, HMOs, or related health-care organizations a set fee for health-care services to be provided at a future date if needed.

prepayment penalty In health-care financial management, this is money charged for the privilege of paying off a debt in advance.

prepayment plan *See managed care; health plan; prepaid health plan.*

prepayment premiums Medical insurance benefits paid for in advance, generally through monthly premiums. In managed care, this is any medical care insurance payment paid ahead of time to a provider for anticipated services (e.g., an expectant mother paying in advance for maternity care), sometimes distinguished from medical insurance as referring to payment to organizations (e.g., HMOs, prepaid group practices, and medical foundations) that, unlike an insurance company, take responsibility for arranging and providing needed services as well as paying for them.

prepayment provision In health-care finance, this is the option in any financial arrangement such as a loan that specifies at what time or on what terms repayment of the principal amount may be made prior to maturity without penalty; often used in bonds or mortgages.

prepharmacy A course of study that prepares an individual to enter a professional school of pharmacy, often a major in chemistry at the bachelors degree level.

preponderance of evidence In health law, evidence of greater weight that is adequate to overcome doubt and to dispel speculation. As used in tort law, negligence, and malpractice, this is enough proof to tip the scales of justice and the decision of a jury or judge in favor of one party or the other of a lawsuit. Fifty-one percent of proof is what is needed in civil lawsuits to win a decision and tip the scales of justice.

prerogative An exclusive privilege, advantage, or power; a special choice of a person; having official power or receiving special allowances or privileges.

prerogatives of the physician Several exclusive privileges are reserved for licensed physicians with clinical privileges at a hospital; admission of patients, treatment, prescribing of drugs, surgery, and the discharge of patients from a hospital.

prerogative writs In law and the litigation process, this is a special action of a court taken only under certain circumstances (e.g., a mandamus or habeas corpus).

presbyopia A vision disorder that occurs in old age because the lens of the eye tends to solidify in a certain shape, muscles atrophy, and the person loses the ability to focus.

prescription 1. A document allowing open possession and limited to a specific time period set by law. 2. The acquisition of rights to property by long-term uninterrupted use. 3. A written order or direction for the preparation and administration of a drug, therapy, or other remedy by a physician, dentist, or other practitioner licensed by law to administer such a drug or therapy. Prescriptions may be written as orders in hospitals and other institutions for drugs to be given to inpatients or given to outpatients to be filled by a pharmacist. The prescription properly specifies the drug to be given, the amount of the drug to be dispensed, and the directions necessary for patient use of the drug or therapy to be rendered.

prescription drug *See prescription medication.*

prescription medication A drug available to the public only by prescription and approved by the Food and Drug Administration. The availability of such drugs is thus limited because the drug is considered dangerous if used without a physician's supervision. The prescription process is pursuant to law, and prescriptions are dispensed only by legally licensed physicians and pharmacists. *See also ethical drug; over-the-counter drug.*

present 1. In the here and now. 2. Immediate. 3. The one at hand. *See also presentment.*

presentation An instructional program used in training or educational activities and given one time on one topic in a limited time period. *See also in-service education; presentment.*

presentence investigation 1. An investigation carried out by court-appointed physicians, psychologists, social workers, or psychiatrists to learn of a person's background. This is done to ascertain his or her potential for rehabilitation or integration back into society.

presentment 1. Presenting a negotiable instrument and expecting payment on it. 2. A statement from a grand jury to a court stating that it believes that a crime has been committed and that the named person is responsible.

presents 1. This document. 2. An educated estimate with facts to back it up; an inference based on usual occurrences.

present value In health-care financial management, this is the current value of cash flows that will be received or paid later. The value of money is adjusted for inflation for the time value of money and is discounted at the same interest rate. The amount that must be invested at the beginning of a transaction to have it increase to a specified amount at a set future date. Also referred to as "present value of money."

president *See chief executive officer; administrator.*

president of medical staff In hospital administration, this is a physician on a hospital's medical staff who is chosen or elected by the entire medical staff to serve for a set time period as the leader and as a liaison between the medical staff and the hospital's administrative staff and to handle the administrative needs of the medical staff.

president's budget The federal budget for a particular fiscal year specifying proposed budget authority, obligations, and outlays transmitted to Congress by the president in accordance with the Budget and Accounting Act of 1921, as amended. Some elements of the budget such as the estimates for the legislative branch and the judiciary are included without review by the Office of Management and Budget or approval by the president. The budget is presently submitted in January for the fiscal year beginning during the calendar year.

President's Health Security Plan *See Health Care Reform Taskforce.*

President's Taskforce on Health-Care Reform *See Health Care Reform Taskforce.*

pressor Any stimulation causing physiological and psychological stress. *See stressor; dystressor.*

pressor test Specialized tests that assess the types and amounts of reaction to artificially generated or externally imposed stimulation that produces stress, causing physiological and/or psychological reactions. *See stressor.*

pressure sewers In environmental health liquid waste management, this is a system of pipes in which water, wastewater, or other liquid is transported to a higher elevation by use of pumping force.

pressure sore Decubitus ulcer or bedsore. A skin disorder commonly occurring in persons confined to lengthy lying or sitting positions, such as bedfast elderly patients in long-term-care facilities or wheelchair-bound persons. It is caused by continuous pressure in a localized area, interfering with circulation, resulting in an open sore. Recent studies show that urine from incontinence furthers the potential for a decubitus ulcer.

presumption 1. To assume that a fact is true by reviewing the factual occurrence of other events. 2. A conclusion. 3. A presumption of fact is an assumption that because one thing is true, another thing is also true.

presumption of innocence Assuming that a person is innocent of any wrongdoing until guilt is established by evidence and proven by due process of law.

preterlegal Beyond the law; illegal; illicit; not legal.

preterm birth Infants born between the 20th and 36th weeks of gestation.

pretermit To neglect.

pretreatment In environmental health, this is the process used to reduce, eliminate, or alter the nature of wastewater pollutants from nondomestic sources before they are discharged into publicly owned treatment works.

pretreatment facilities In environmental health, these are water treatment facilities that reduce, eliminate, or alter the nature of wastewater pollutants from nondomestic sources before they are discharged into publicly owned treatment works.

pretrial screening panel In health law, this is a panel of physicians, attorneys, judges, and insurance representatives who assess and review medical malpractice cases in terms of the strength and validity of the case. Amounts of dollar settlements are considered and recommended. If the offer or decision is not acceptable, a lawsuit can be filed. Also called "arbitration panels" and, in health law, "malpractice screening panels."

prevailing charge(s) In the absence of unusual medical treatments and services, prevailing charges are generally used; a charge that falls within the range of charges most frequently used in a locality for a particular medical service or procedure. The top of this range establishes an overall limitation on the charges that a carrier will accept as reasonable for a given service without adequate special justification. Current Medicare rules state that the limit of an area's prevailing charge is to be the 75th percentile of the customary charges for a given service by the physicians in a given area. For example, if customary charges for an appendectomy in a locality were distributed so that 10% of the services were rendered by physicians whose customary charge was $150, 40% by physicians who charged $200, 40% who charged $250, and 10% who charged $300 or more, then the prevailing charge would be $250 because this is the level that would cover at least 75% of the cases. *See customary, prevailing and reasonable charges; actual charge; fractionation.*

prevailing charge locality Under Medicare in certain geographic localities, Medicare sets the customary and reasonable charges and sets payment structures under Part B for medical services provided by physicians and other assigned health-care providers. Medicare established about 240 separate prevailing charge localities across the United States.

prevailing fee The usual, customary, regular, and reasonable charge for medical care services in the local area, region, or state.

prevailing wage rates In health administration and human resource management, these are the most common levels of pay for a given job in a specific category in a geographical area and are determined by wage and salary surveys.

prevalence In epidemiology, this is the number of cases of a given disease in a given population over a given time period or at a point in time; the number of cases of disease, conditions, infected persons, or persons with some other attribute present at a particular time in relation to the size of the population from which it is drawn; a measure of the extent of the existence of a disease, condition or medical problem in a population based on the number of cases (old and new) existing in the population at a given time. When a time qualification is not stated, it usually means at a specific point in time such as midyear. It is a measurement of morbidity at a point in time (e.g., the number of cases of measles in the county as of the first of July). The prevalence of arthritis is high relative to its incidence. Prevalence equals incidence times average case duration. *See also point prevalence; period prevalence; lifetime prevalence; incidence; incidence rates.*

prevalence, annual In epidemiology and public health, this is an index used to determine the total number of persons with a disease or condition at any time during a single year. Included are cases of the disease occurring before but extending through the designated time period (1 year) as well as those having new onset of the disease during the year.

prevalence, average annual estimate point *See point prevalence average annual estimate.*

prevalence, lifetime In epidemiology, this is the total number of persons known to have had a disease, condition, or disorder for most of their life or at least part of it.

prevalence of conditions In public health and epidemiology, this is the number of persons who have the condition at a given point in time. Prevalence of acute conditions is seldom used, as incidence is used to determine acute conditions.

prevalence, period *See period prevalence.*

prevalence, point *See point prevalence.*

prevalence rate The total number of all cases of a disease, condition, disorder, or infected persons during a particular interval of time or at a specific point in time divided by the population at risk of having the attribute or disease in the same time frame or midway through the time period per 1000 population. One difficulty in determining prevalence rates is in defining and choosing the most appropriate denominator (i.e., setting the population at risk). The prevalence rate formula follows:

$$\frac{\text{Total number of cases of the disease at a given time}}{\text{Total population at risk at a given time}} \times 1000$$

See also point prevalence; period prevalence.

prevalence study In epidemiology, this assesses the extent of the existence of a disease, condition, or medical problem in a population, accounting for the number of cases (old and new) existing in the population at a single given point in time (cross-sectional view). Also referred to as a "cross-sectional study."

preventable fraction In epidemiology, as an explanation of how herd immunity works, it is observed that if a fraction of the susceptible people in a population is protected against a communicable disease by either having been exposed to it and having developed a natural immunity or having been immunized against it, and should an outbreak occur, only a fraction (percentage) would ever get ill. It is recommended that if an 85% level of immunization exists in a population, this protects against the possibility of an epidemic (herd immunity). This establishes that a proportion of the population would be prevented from getting the disease if the whole population were exposed to the disease; the comparison of the proportion of exposed to unexposed susceptibles in a population during an epidemic. *See herd immunity.*

preventative A vaccine, drug, or substance taken by an individual or given to a patient as a preventive measure against disease. *See preventive.*

prevented fraction In epidemiology, this is the percentage of a total population exposed to a disease who have avoided the disease by immunization or prior exposure; the comparison of the proportion of exposed to unexposed susceptibles in a population during an epidemic.

prevention 1. Stopping something harmful or damaging before it has a chance to occur; anticipating harm or damage. 2. In public health and health services, this is to preserve and restore health; to avoid or stop illness, injury, sickness, disorders, conditions, maladies, or medical problems before they occur while minimizing suffering, pain, and stress; the elimination or avoidance of accidents, injury, or risk factors to health, disease-causing agents, pathogens, or other sources of disease or disability. *See preventive care; health promotion; health education; prevention, levels of.*

prevention and detection services Programs and activities delivered to individuals to promote optimum physical and mental well-being, including protection from the development of disease and ill health, or to identify disease or ill health at the presymptomatic or unrecognized symptomatic stage to permit early intervention.

prevention, levels of In preventive medicine, public health, and epidemiology, three levels of prevention are recognized that correspond with the three levels of medical care: primary, secondary, and tertiary. All three levels of prevention are affected by economic, social, educational, medical, behavioral, lifestyle, and environmental factors at both the individual and community levels. *See primary prevention; secondary prevention; tertiary prevention.*

prevention of disease *See preventive care; prevention, primary; health promotion.*

prevention of disease, Maharishi Ayur-Veda The traditional medical system of India, this is the oldest system of natural health care. It is comprehensive in that it restores Ayurvedic procedures in accordance with classical approaches and promotes a balance in the mind, body, behavior, and environment.

prevention of significant deterioration In environmental health and air pollution control, this is an Environmental Protection Agency program in which state and/or federal permits are required that are intended to restrict emissions for new or modified sources in places where air quality is already better than required to meet primary and secondary ambient air quality standards.

prevention, primary Halting any occurrence of a disease or disorder in the first instance before it happens. Health promotion, health education, and health protection are three main facets of primary prevention. Lifestyle changes, community health education, health screening, school health education, health activation, good prenatal care, good behavioral choices, proper nutrition, and safety and healthy conditions at home, at school, or in the workplace are all primary prevention activities. Fundamental public health measures and activities such as sanitation; infection control; immunizations; protection of food, milk, and water supplies; environmental protection; and protection against occupational hazards and accidents are all basic to primary prevention. Basic personal hygiene and public health measures have had a major impact on halting communicable disease epidemics. Immunizations, infection control (e.g., hand washing), refrigeration of foods, garbage collection, solid and liquid waste management, water supply protection and treatment, and general sanitation have reduced infectious disease threats to populations. Treatment and health care by physicians needs to be replaced with primary prevention, including adequate economic support for health promotion and disease and injury prevention programs and activities.

prevention, secondary Aimed at health screening and detection activities used to discover pathogenic states in individuals in a population. If pathogenic states are discovered early, diagnosis and early treatment can prevent conditions from progressing and spreading in the population, and the progress of disease, disability, disorders, or death can be retarded or halted. Secondary prevention has the aim of blocking the progression of disease or keeping an injury from developing into an impairment or disability. One aspect of health promotion that has been effective in secondary prevention is health screening programs. Early detection, referral, and prompt treatment can either cure the disease or halt it at the earliest stages of development. At the very least, early detection can slow the progress of a disease, prevent complications, limit disability, and halt or reverse the communicability of an infectious disease. Early intervention and treatment of a disease in single cases can prevent groups or major populations from acquiring communicable diseases. Such interventions provide primary prevention for persons not exposed and secondary prevention for those already infected. Additionally, secondary prevention can maintain already healthy behaviors and reverse unhealthy lifestyles through health education and behavior change programs such as smoking cessation, weight loss, stress reduction, health counseling, or early admission into a drug treatment program.

prevention, tertiary Aims to retard or block the progression of a disability, condition, or disorder to keep it from becoming advanced and in need of excessive and unnecessary care. Tertiary prevention consists of limiting any disability by providing rehabilitation where a disease, injury, or disorder has already occurred and has left damage. At this level, the goal is to help diseased, disabled, or injured individuals avoid unnecessary use of health-care services and avoid becoming dependent on health-care practitioners and institutions. Prompt diagnosis and treatment, followed by proper rehabilitation and posttreatment recovery along with proper patient education, behavior change, and lifestyle changes, are all necessary so that diseases or disorders will not recur. At the very minimum, the progression of the disease or disorder or injury needs to be slowed and checked.

preventive Action or intervention taken preceding an event or occurrence to stop it from taking place or manifesting itself. Medical care provided or health services provided to populations that prevent an occurrence of diseases, disability, or death. *See preventative; preventive care; preventive medicine; health promotion; health education.*

preventive care Comprehensive care emphasizing halting diseases, disorders, conditions, injuries, or deaths before they occur and the early detection and early treatment of conditions. The restriction of the occurrence of a disease, conditions, or disorders, this involves care, therapy, or treatment designed to prevent disease, conditions, injuries, and their consequences. Health promotion, health education, lifestyle changes, health screening, medical exams, good prenatal care, good behavioral choices, proper nutrition, wellness, self-care, safety, and healthy conditions at home, school, or the workplace are all preventive care activities. Basic public health activities such as sanitation, infection control, immunizations, protection of food, milk and water supplies, environmental protection, and protection against occupational hazards and accidents are also considered basic to preventive care. Three levels of prevention have been identified: primary, secondary, and tertiary. *See preventive medicine; prevention, levels of; public health; health promotion; health education.*

preventive detention The unconstitutional act of holding a person against his or her will, assuming that he or she may commit an illegal act or crime.

preventive discipline In health administration and human resource management, this is any action taken in the workplace toward employees to encourage them to follow policies, rules, or standards to avoid infractions.

preventive law Helping a person to avoid legal problems.

preventive medicine Medical care aimed at preventing disease or its consequences and carried out by medical practitioners, usually on a patient care level. It includes health-care programs aimed at warding off illnesses (e.g., immunizations), early detection of disease (e.g., pap smears), and inhibiting further deterioration of the body (e.g., exercise or prophylactic surgery). Preventive medicine was developed subsequent to bacteriology and was concerned in its early history with specific medical control measures taken against the agents of infectious diseases. With increasing knowledge of nutritional, malignant, and other chronic diseases, the scope of preventive medicine has been extended. It is now assumed that most if not all problems are preventable at some stage of their development. Preventive medicine now includes health education, with the general aim of improving the healthfulness of the environment and one's relationship with it through such things as avoidance of hazardous substances, modified diet, and family planning. In particular, the promotion of health through altering behavior, especially by health education, is gaining prominence as a component of preventive care. In preventive medicine, three levels of prevention are identified: primary, secondary, and tertiary. *See also public health; consultation and education services; community medicine; health education; prevention, levels of.*

preventive psychiatry *See community psychology.*

preveterinary medicine A course of study that prepares students at the baccalaureate level to enter an accredited school of veterinary medicine, usually including standard premed requirements (i.e., 1 year each of biology, chemistry, and physics).

previous question In formal health-care meetings using parliamentary procedure, this is a submotion that is used to close the discussion. If the motion is passed, it stops discussion, puts the pending motion up for a vote, and requires a two-thirds vote.

PRI *See program-related investment.*

price blending In health-care finance, this is the process of comparing the national average reimbursement under the Medicare Prospective Payment System for a certain DRG with the actual costs of providing care and then having the cost of the DRG adjusted.

price fixing In health-care finance, this is when two or more health-care providers agree that all should charge the same high price for certain services, treatments, or procedures, a practice that is illegal in most states under antitrust laws.

price-in elastic demand In managed care and health-care financial management, this is when government and insurance companies create a condition in which managed-care plans are given rewards for raising, not lowering, prices.

price variance In health-care finance, this is the assessment of how actual prices agree with budgeted prices. The difference between the actual prices and the budgeted prices are multiplied by the actual quantity of goods or services purchased. Also called "rate variance."

prima facie (Lat.) 1. At first sight; on the face of it; on the first appearance. 2. Presumably; a fact considered to be true unless proven otherwise.

prima facie case In health law, this is a case based on evidence that appears to be sufficient enough to determine a negative outcome for the defendant.

primary authority In law, this is the first and basic binding source of power, right, and legal authorization.

primary care Basic or general medical care provided at the point where the patient first seeks assistance from the medical care system. Usually this care is for the simpler, more common illnesses. The primary care provider usually assumes ongoing responsibility for the patient in health maintenance, therapy, and treatment of illness. Being at the first entry point to the health-care system, it does not require highly advanced and sophisticated equipment or specialized resources. Care is comprehensive, as this level of care takes responsibility for the overall coordination of the care for the patient's health problems, whether medical/biological, mental, emotional, or behavioral. This level of practitioner has the responsibility for preserving resources by serving in the role of a gatekeeper in an ambulatory care setting. The appropriate use of referrals, consultants, and community resources is an important part of effective primary care. Such care is generally provided by physicians but is increasingly provided by other personnel such as physician assistants and family nurse practitioners. *See also family physician; personal physician; secondary care; tertiary care.*

primary care center *See primary care; primary care facilities.*

primary care facilities Health-care institutions and services, regardless of location or structure, that offer first-level on-demand services to the public and serve as the first entry to the health-care system; entities designed, equipped, staffed, organized, and operated as an integral part of a comprehensive health-care system and offering basic entry-level health and medical services that are available, personalized, and offered in continuous fashion on an outpatient basis.

primary care nurse *See nurse, primary care.*

primary care network (PCN) In managed care, this is a group of primary care practitioners who together share a health plan risk of providing care to patients who are enrollees of a particular health plan.

primary care nursing One approach to nursing practice in a health-care facility where one registered nurse assumes responsibility for several patients in a nursing care unit and provides the whole range of basic nursing care for these patients while they are inpatients in the facility. *See nurse, primary care; nursing, team.*

primary care physician A physician engaged in the basic entry level of medical care and who practices general medicine and is usually the first professional medical care practitioner seen in an ambulatory care setting when a patient enters the health-care system. Doctors who are considered primary care physicians most often have been licensed in and are board certified in one of the following: family practice, basic internal medicine, pediatrics, geriatrics, obstetrics/gynecology, and in some cases psychiatry or emergency medicine. Some government programs limit the designation to family and general practitioners, pediatricians, obstetricians and gynecologists, and general internists. Under managed care, this physician is designated by a health plan to be the "case manager" or "gatekeeper" of a health plan member's health care in an ambulatory or inpatient setting and is expected to control resources and limit and make only appropriate referrals to specialists.

primary care provider The health-care practitioner, physician, or physician extender who is responsible for supervising, coordinating, and providing the first instance of treatment, initial entry medical services, the most basic care, primary treatment, and definitive care and making referrals and ensuring continuity of care to patients. *See primary care; primary care specialties.*

primary care specialties Physicians who are licensed, engage in the practice of medicine, and are the health-care providers of first contact when the patient enters the health-care system; usually includes general practice, family practice, internal medicine, geriatrics, pediatrics, obstetrics and gynecology, and possibly psychiatry.

primary care system Entry levels or family practice levels of medical care rendered to patients on the first instance of medical care delivery whether the care is provided in a physician's office, clinic, medical group, health maintenance organization, or industrial clinic. The system has seven parts: 1) assessment of total patient needs before these are categorized by specialty; 2) elaboration of a plan for meeting those needs in order of their importance; 3) determination of who shall meet the defined needs, be they physicians, nonphysician members of the health team, or social agencies; 4) follow-up to see that needs are met; 5) continuous, coordinated, and comprehensive care; 6) attention at each step to personal, social, and family dimensions of the patient's problem; and 7) continual health maintenance and disease prevention, which is viewed as important as cure and rehabilitation (Committee on Medical Schools and the Association of American Medical Colleges, The Pellegrino Committee).

primary case In epidemiology, this is the first case of disease in an epidemic and not always the first diagnosed; the first case of disease introduced into a group or population. *See index case.*

primary coverage In managed care, these are the basic benefits of a health plan under the benefit rules of insurance for which the health plan is obligated to pay the enrollee's eligible expenses without consideration of other benefits or coverage.

primary diagnosis 1. In medical care, this is the most serious and principal reason the patient has entered the health-care system for treatment and is the main disease or condition diagnosed by a health-care provider entered into the patients medical record. 2. Under the Medicare and PPS/DRG reimbursement system, this is the diagnosis that will be paid for and is listed in the medical record as the key purpose for treatment or hospitalization.

primary drinking water regulations In environmental health, this applies to public water systems and specifies a contaminant level that will have no adverse effect on human health, as established by regulation and public health law, as set forth in the Clean Water Act.

primary emission control In environmental health, actions taken and devices installed at the very source of a potential for pollution such as the hoods, ducts, and control devices used to capture, convey, and collect process emissions in labs or processing areas of plants.

primary environmental monitors In environmental health, these are specialized machines and devices legally required to monitor ongoing discharges; devices placed closest to the point of discharge that are used to determine if discharges are within specified limits; equipment that actuates automatically in response to set level signals from such a monitor. These do not include equipment in a general area, remediation, or compliance monitoring programs.

primary evidence In health law, this is the first, best, and surest proof.

primary gain The reduction of tension, anxiety symptoms, or conflict in neurotic or stress disorders.

primary health care scope and setting The range of basic and primary care ambulatory services formed for the provision of evaluating, diagnosing, and treating illnesses, injuries, diseases, conditions, or disorders to promote physical, dental, and mental health. Services are offered in physicians' offices, ambulatory clinics, outpatient centers, public health centers, HMOs, public health clinics, neighborhood health centers, or other primary care centers and are offered by family practice, internal medicine, emergency care, or other primary care physicians, psychologists, social workers, physician assistants, nurse practitioners, and other physician extenders. The services offered embrace preventive, patient education, and other health maintenance activities and are distinguished from secondary and tertiary care, which are offered in inpatient care settings.

primary limits In environmental health especially related to radiation, these are the values of dose equivalents and/or effective dose equivalents applying to an individual. In the case of a member of the public, the limit is taken to apply to the average dose in the critical group.

primary loss In health-care finance, this is the amount of money that is used as a deductible in a credit insurance policy to hedge against bad debt and that reflects the normal credit losses a health-care facility experiences in bad debt; the actual amount lost from uncollectables and bad debt.

primary nursing *See primary care nursing.*

primary payer An insurer obligated to pay losses prior to any liability of other secondary insurers. Under current law, Medicare is a primary payer with respect to Medicaid; for a person eligible under both programs, Medicaid pays only for benefits not covered under Medicare or after Medicare benefits are exhausted. *See also duplication of benefits; coordination of benefits.*

primary prevention One of three recognized levels of prevention. *See prevention, primary; prevention, secondary; prevention, tertiary.*

primary psychological prevention Measures needed to prevent an emotional or mental disorder, which could be as basic as proper nutrition, nurturing in infancy, safe environment, or solid family structure.

primary reserve In managed care or insurance, this is the part of an insurance company's reserves set aside for losses incurred but not reported (IBNR).

primary standards, air pollution In environmental health, these are the national primary ambient air quality standards promulgated pursuant to Section 109 of the Clean Air Act.

primary storage unit In health information management and computers, this is a part of the central processing unit that holds data and programs. Also called the "main memory."

primary waste treatment In environmental health and liquid waste management, these are the first steps employed in wastewater treatment. Screens and sedimentation tanks are used to remove most material that floats or will settle. Primary treatment results in the removal of about 30% of the carbonaceous biochemical oxygen demand from domestic sewage.

primary work group In health-care organizations such as hospitals, this is the smallest social aggregate of organizational activity that produces work or outcomes; persons whom an individual interacts with, relies on, and works with on a daily basis.

prime First; high quality; major; original; most important; the best.

prime carrier In managed care, this is the initial insurance carrier with first payment responsibilities.

prime lending rate In health-care financial management, this is the interest rate charged by major commercial banks on short-term commercial loans to its most favored health-care organization customers. Mortgages are not included in these loans.

prime rate In health-care finance, this is the rate of interest on loans that banks charge to large, strong health-care organizations.

primogeniture First child born.

principal 1. Head; director; main; major; chief; most important; primary. 2. The most legally responsible person in a relationship. 3. A basic sum of money; the amount of money originally borrowed or invested. 4. A person acting on his or her own behalf. 5. One in a position of authority. 6. An employer, a physician, or anyone who gives another person (an agent) authority to do things or work for him or her. 7. The main person committing a crime.

principal diagnosis The diagnosis of a condition, disease, disorder, disability, or injury established after examination, testing, and patient assessment as the chief reason for an occasion of service in a health-care facility or from a health-care provider; the most life- and health-threatening condition that is responsible for a patient's admission to a hospital; the major health-care disorder or disease used in determining a DRG classification and referenced with the ICD-9-CM.

principal investigator In research grants for health-care demonstration projects or services or in health services and medical research grants, the key administrative person responsible for overseeing and managing all activities of the project and ensuring quality and completion. Also called the "project director."

principal procedure A procedure performed for a definitive treatment and not for diagnostic, exploratory, assessment, or testing purposes; also a procedure needed to treat a complication of the principal diagnosis; the procedure that is most directly related to the principal diagnosis and is identifiable in the third volume of the ICD-9-CM.

principle 1. A doctrine. 2. A rule or belief used to determine an issue. 3. A legal truth. 4. A basic legal expectation or doctrine.

principle of indemnity In health-care finance and insurance, a limit on the actual amount of money a health-care organization may collect against the cash value of property that has been insured.

principle of insurable interest In health-care finance, this is a situation where the health-care organization must show a financial interest in the item being insured as a precondition to recovery in event of loss. This legal principle prevents insurance from becoming a gambling contract. *See also recovery.*

print media advertising In health promotion and health-care marketing, these are all advertisements placed in newspapers, magazines, and journals.

printout 1. In health information management, this is a typed document produced by a computer interfaced with a printer to produce a "hard copy," or printed document, of data or information from the memory of a computer. 2. In medical records, a computer-generated patient and DRG admission sheet.

prion A recently identified form of infectious agent that causes some diseases previously thought to be caused by viruses (from "proteinaceous infectious particle").

prior authorization 1. In medical insurance, this is an administrative procedure where a doctor or dentist submits a treatment plan to the insurance carrier before treatment is initiated. This procedure is common in dental contracts, eye care, some managed-care plans, and the Medicaid program. Also referred to as "preauthorization," "precertification," "predetermination," "preestimate of cost," or "pretreatment estimate." 2. In health care, a requirement imposed by a third party under some systems of utilization review that a provider must justify before a peer review committee, insurance company representative, or state agent the need for delivering a particular service to a patient before actually providing the service to receive reimbursement. Generally, prior authorization is required for nonemergency services that are expensive or particularly likely to be overused or abused. 3. In managed care, this is an approval obtained by a plan provider from the health plan and/or the medical director of a specific medical group through which the member receives services prior to rendering specific services covered under the group subscriber agreement.

prior claim In health-care finance, this is when a business fails and its assets are sold to raise money to pay its debts. If a health-care organization such as a hospital has any claims against the business, they will be paid to the hospital before other claims are processed and paid.

prior determination In medical insurance and managed care, this is similar to prior authorization but less restrictive in that payment will be made if prior authorization is not sought, provided that it would have approved the service as needed.

prior hearing In health law, this is a previously held hearing of an administrative agency that is required to occur before any action can be taken.

priorities In health administration or health planning, this is the relative importance and emphasis attached to various goals and objectives and the actions designed to achieve them; ranking activities by importance or by sequence of occurrence needed.

priority Lists, problems, concerns, ramifications, and alternatives ranked according to desirability, preference, importance, value, and effectiveness. Alternatives or choices ranked according to feasibility, value, and/or importance.

priority groups In health services delivery and health manpower shortage areas, work groups are ranked into four groups according to population-to-practitioner ratios and indications of high need and insufficient capacity. A designation of 1 signifies the highest need.

priority levels (in planning) In health or institutional planning, there are several levels used, and each level must have goals supported with objectives and long-range recommended actions and resource requirements to meet the goals and objectives. At the macrogovernmental level, planning is done for the nationwide health system (regional, state, county, and city), on both the medical care delivery side and the public health side. Levels of planning also occur in privately owned national or international hospital and health-care systems as well as regional and local health-care systems. In a micro sense, various approaches to planning occur in a health-care system or institution such as a hospital or managed-care organization. Health-care system delivery and utilization planning (such as in a large HMO with its own hospitals and clinics), strategic planning, long-range planning, short-term planning, tactical planning, operational planning, budgetary planning, and program development are some of the various levels at which planning can occur.

priority objective In health administration and health planning, this is an aim or activity that is compared to and evaluated against all other aims or activities and is determined to be of greatest relative importance and thus is ranked first in order for implementation or execution.

priority problem list In health services administration, this is a management system wherein problems and deficiencies in an organization are categorized as to need for attention and importance (based on input from the organization's line and staff managers). After categorization, the most money and time is spent on these high-priority items.

prison hospital A small health-care facility staffed and equipped on the dispensary level to treat minor acute problems for those within the confines of a prison. In many states, prisoners with serious health and medical problems are taken to county or state teaching hospitals under tight guard. *See also security hospital.*

privacy 1. The right to have one's personal life and activities kept to oneself, to be left alone, and to not be presented to the public. 2. Respect for confidential information of a person.

Privacy Act of 1974 A federal law that protects the privacy of individuals about whom the federal government has information. Government agencies must provide safeguards against misuse (not use it without permission) and individuals must be able to find out what data are kept on them and how those data are used. Individuals must be given a means through which to correct inaccurate information.

privacy of employees, right to Employees of health-care organizations have the right to not be unnecessarily subjected to lie-detector tests, drug tests, electronic monitoring of work and the workplace, or other practices done as a matter of routine procedure that might violate an employee's right to privacy, unless in an investigation where wrongdoing is highly suspected and probable cause exits. Then tests such as a polygraph test may be used when investigating losses of resources in a hospital, stealing of trade secrets such as in research, or drug testing when drug use on the job is suspected.

privacy, right to In health law and the process of delivering health services, the individual has the right to not have his or her name or picture or other likeness used for commercial purposes without permission, not have any intrusion on his or her affairs of seclusion (briefcase searched), not have publication of information that places that individual in false light, or have any public disclosure of private fact about an individual that an ordinary person would find objectionable.

private Individual and personal; not for use by the general public or government.

private-duty nurse A registered nurse who provides skilled nursing services in a person's home to care for a single sick, injured, or disabled individual who pays the nurse directly for services rendered; may be a LVN/LPN or an RN.

private expenditures In health-care delivery, these are outlays of money, paid-for services rendered and paid by nongovernmental sources such as consumers' self-payment, insurance companies, private industry, church social services, philanthropic organizations, and other nonpatient care sources.

private health agency A nongovernmental agency concerned with the improvement of health or related medical issues that is organized as 1) nonprofit incorporated (voluntary), 2) nonprofit unincorporated (voluntary), or 3) proprietary (commercial). A nonprofit or for-profit organization devoted to providing primary, secondary, and/or tertiary health services that may include health education or health promotion activities (Joint Committee on Health Education Terminology). Examples of such agencies are the American Heart Association, the American Cancer Society, the American Lung Association, and the American Red Cross. Also called a "voluntary health agency."

private health insurance Medical insurance used for any disease, medical, or related conditions needing treatment where expenditures of money and use of resources are required, with the insurance being used as a benefit to pay for physician or hospital care.

private hospital Hospitals owned by individuals, groups, or corporations who operate the institution as a for-profit entity and are not owned by a religious organization, community nonprofit corporation, or any government entity. *See hospital, investor owned; hospital, proprietary (for profit); hospital, private.*

private law 1. Law dealing with private individuals or groups. 2. The law controlling relationships among and between persons and groups. 3. Laws that deal with the private sector and/or its relationship to society and between private parties.

private patient 1. A patient whose care is the responsibility of an individual health professional (usually a physician) who is paid directly by the patient or a third party for his or her services. The physician is called a personal physician and the patient is his or her private patient. Private patients usually have a hospital or nursing home room to themselves and are contrasted with public, service, or ward patients, whose care is the responsibility of a medical care program, government programs, managed-care plans, or an institution. Public patients are often cared for by an individual practitioner paid by the program (such as a member of the house staff of a hospital), but the program, rather than the individual, is paid for the care. The distinction is important to third-party payers (including Medicare) because situations arise in which payment is made to both a program and an individual practitioner for the same services. 2. A patient occupying a private room. *See also private practice.*

private placement In health-care financial management, this is the process of investing money in the private money market such as banks, insurance companies, pension funds, and real estate.

private practice Medical practice in which the practitioner and his or her practice are independent of any external policy control. The practitioner is usually self-employed, except when he or she is salaried by a partnership in which he or she is a partner. Sometimes wrongly used synonymously with either "fee-for-service practice" (the practitioner may sell services by another method, e.g., capitation) or "solo practice" (group practice may also be private). The opposite of private practice is not necessarily public in the sense of employment by government. Practitioners salaried by private hospitals are not usually thought to be in private practice. Private practice also involves the small business management aspects of a physician practicing medicine in solo or small group practice; not being salaried by an institution or government institution.

private placement agencies In health administration, these are private businesses that assist health-care professionals seeking work to find employment. Also referred to as "headhunters."

private placements In health-care finance, these are investments offered to specific institutions that are not required to be registered with governmental agencies.

private room In health-care facilities, this is when a patient has his or her own room. A private room is more costly because it is occupied by only one person, as opposed to a semiprivate room; accommodations for one patient and one bed and total privacy.

privilege 1. Permission to do something not usually allowed. 2. A special right to be preferred. 3. Exempt from regular duty; getting preferential treatment.

privileged communication Any statement, paper, or document made in confidence or trust to a counselor, psychologist, physician, lawyer, or spouse. The law protects a fiduciary relationship from being required to reveal confidential information, even in a trial. See *fiduciary relationship*.

privileged staff (medical) In hospital administration, this is a medical staff to which any licensed physician or other qualified medical care practitioner may apply, but the hospital limits selection to those who meet the standards and guidelines of experience, certification, education, etc. See *open medical staff; closed medical staff*.

privileged motions In formal health-care meetings and hearings using parliamentary procedures, this is a motion affecting the comfort or needs of the assembly or one of its participating members and thus has the highest level of precedence.

privileged relations A special or confidential relationship between two persons that would exempt them from being forced to testify against each other on the basis of any communication they might have had such as physician and patient or psychologist and client. See also *fiduciary*.

privileges 1. The right of a physician to practice medicine at a specific hospital. 2. In medical care and hospital administration, these are rights granted to physicians and other medical staff members to participate in various forms of medical treatment, procedures, and surgery as well as the admission of patients and prescribing therapy and medications. The types, amount, and extent of rights and treatments allowed are determined by the medical staff and administration on the basis of education, board certifications, completed internships, and residencies and past experience. See *privileges, hospital; privileges, admitting*.

privileges, admitting In hospital administration, this is the right granted by the board of trustees and hospital administration to a licensed medical doctor allowing him or her to admit patients to the hospital and perform treatments, surgery and other therapies, and medical care activities. See *privileges, hospital; privileges, clinical*.

privileges and immunities 1. A principle provided by the U.S. Constitution that no state may treat a person from another state unfairly. 2. No state shall make or enforce any law that shall abridge the privileges or immunities of citizens of the United States.

privileges, clinical A licensed physician granted full medical staff hospital privileges by the board of directors and the medical staff and allowed to practice in the facility according to his or her training and ability.

privileges, emergency In hospital medical staff administration, this is a courtesy medical staff privilege given on a temporary basis to an attending physician whose patient is admitted on an emergency basis to a hospital to which the physician has no medical staff privileges.

privileges, hospital The opportunity to practice medicine in a hospital given to a licensed and board-certified physician who is granted full medical staff privileges by the hospital's board of directors, administration, and medical staff and who is allowed to exercise physician's prerogatives in the hospital according to his or her training and ability as shown by board certifications and experience.

privileges, temporary See *privileges, emergency*.

privity 1. Private information. 2. Having inside information. 3. Having a direct financial relationship. 4. Rights and duties of a contract. 5. Mutual relationships to the same right or property.

privy One who is privity of a contract or with another person; one who is allowed access to confidential information about a contract or a private matter.

PRN As needed; medication, treatment, or care to be given only when needed or as desired.

PRO *See peer review organization; professional review organization.*

pro- (Lat.) Prefix meaning "for."

proactive In health administration and strategic management, this is the process of using foresight and projecting managerial activity into the future as compared to activities of the present; actively taking charge of circumstances to control managerial direction and outcomes, as opposed to crisis management or being reactive.

proactive management In health administration, this is when the management team and the chief executive officer anticipate problems and take positive action to minimize problems rather than waiting until problems occur and then reacting to them.

probability 1. The chance of some event or action occurring; the number of times that an event is likely to occur as compared to the number of possible occurrences. 2. In health law, this refers to a person having reason to believe that a procedure, treatment, medical event or use of a device caused or contributed to an adverse medical event or outcome. 3. In statistics, this is the degree of belief or the relative frequency that an event in a sequence of random trials is likely to occur. 4. A ratio of the number of times an event occurs divided by the number of times it is possible to occur. A probability of 1 means the event is certain. A probability of 0 means the event is impossible. A flipped coin has a probability of 0.5 of being heads (or tails).

probability distribution In statistics and biostatistics, a mutually exclusive and exhaustive list of all possible events that may occur by chance in the selection or sampling process.

probable cause for arrest In criminal law, this is an arrest for strong circumstances that are more than a suspicion but less than proven facts that a crime has been committed.

probable causes In safety, these are causes attributed to an accident or incident as most likely in the absence of positive proof.

probate The court that handles the distribution of an estate or will. It may also handle such matters as mental illness commitments.

probation 1. In criminal law and the penal system, this is allowing a convicted person to stay out of jail on the basis of expected good behavior and the condition that he or she will commit no further illegal acts. 2. A trial period sometimes given to new employees to see if they are capable of doing the work or if they will fit into the job. In governmental jobs, it is usually a period of 6 months, and in some hospitals it is 90 days.

probationary period In managed care, this is a specified number of days after the date of the issuance of the policy during which coverage is not afforded for sickness; the first 90 or 180 days of employment or other time period. *See also waiting period.*

probative Tending to prove fact; providing actual proof.

probity Honesty.

problem Any behavior of patients that disrupts, disturbs, or endangers their health and well-being, thus requiring attention by the attending physician for additional diagnosis, observation, therapy, or treatment.

Problem-Oriented Medical Information System (PROMIS) A computerized medical record system. Medical database and source tapes, along with functional specification and documentation of PROMIS, were developed by the Medical Center Hospital of Vermont with the support of the National Center for Health Services Research (NCHSR). PROMIS categorizes patient data according to relevant medical problems, recording the reasons for each medical service provided and how it relates to the total regimen of care. PROMIS also provides a guide to basic medical practices for each phase of care and warns of inadvisable therapy and drugs.

problem-oriented medical record (POMR) A medical record in which information and conclusions contained in the record are organized to describe each of the patient's problems. The description properly includes subjective, objective, and significant negative information, discussion, and conclusions and diagnostic and treatment plans with respect to each problem. The record, which was developed by Lawrence Weed, MD, has gained increasing acceptance and can be contrasted with the traditional medical record, which is less formally organized and usually records all information from each source together (history, physical exam, and laboratory) without regard to the problems that the information describes.

problem-solving interviews In human resources management, this is a type of interview that relies on asking problem-oriented questions that are hypothetical in nature. The person being interviewed is evaluated on how well he or she solves the problems.

pro bono (Lat.) Free or charitable legal services for a community or public organization.

pro bono publico (Lat.) For the good of the public.

procatarctic cause A historical epidemiological term that identified the causes of certain diseases to be associated with lifestyle and behavior.

procedural law 1. The process of carrying out the procedures necessary for a lawsuit. 2. Law governing procedure or practice.

procedural motion In formal health-care meetings and hearings using parliamentary procedure, a motion that presents a question related to procedure, as distinguished from a regular motion.

procedural services In health-care delivery, these are medical care activities that rely on the use of medical devices or clinical skills as compared to administrative services.

procedure 1. A method or technique used in therapy or treatment; the manipulation, surgery, or treatment of a patient by a health-care practitioner; any service a doctor renders to a patient as coded from a procedure coding manual; a surgical or nonsurgical operation, diagnostic activity, or special treatment assigned by the physician to the record of the patient discharged from inpatient service of a short-stay hospital. Operative activities, surgical operations, and/or special treatments are all categorized as procedures. Any medical technology using drugs, devices, and practitioner skills and knowledge. 2. The step-by-step method used in carrying out legal actions. 3. A step-by-step outline of the mode used by a hospital or other institution to accomplish a specific objective or task. 4. Written or established methods by which a company or organization operates to accomplish its objectives; a sequence of actions that collectively accomplish some desired task.

procedure capture In medical care delivery, this is the process by which a health-care provider is chosen to provide medical care or services over others; the persuading of referral sources to make the referrals to a select or specific health-care provider.

procedure coding manual A booklet produced by medical and health insurance companies to help the health-care provider file an insurance claim. A code and narrative description is provided for services, treatments, and procedures in the areas of medicine, surgery, radiology, nuclear medicine, pathology, and special services. *See also ICD-9-CM.*

procedure expectation In medical practice, this is the anticipation of various tasks and activities of clinical care such as injections and physical examinations.

procedure manual A collection of written rules and procedures used as a guide for persons working for an organization.

PROCEED Policy, Regulatory and Organizational Constructs in Educational and Environmental Development. In health promotion and health education, this is an outgrowth of and the activities following the diagnostic planning phases of the PRECEDE model developed by Lawrence W. Green and Marshall W. Krueter while at the Johns Hopkins University. PROCEED is a set of relationships and procedures used as a comprehensive strategy to address the implementation of advocacy, policy, regulation, and organization in large-scale community health promotion efforts. *See PRECEDE; PATCH.*

proceeding 1. Process and procedure of a hearing. 2. The orderly process of a lawsuit or hearing. 3. A record of a hearing or court.

process 1. In the litigation process, this is an order for a defendant to appear in court or risk losing the lawsuit. 2. A summons. 3. A court order that takes jurisdiction over person or property. 4. In health planning and program development, this is carrying out the method of doing things; step-by-step activities done to accomplish goals and objectives. 5. In health-care delivery, these are regular procedures moving forth step by step. 6. In JCAHO accreditation, this is a goal-directed, interrelated series of actions, events, mechanisms, or steps.

process control charts In health administration and health planning, these graphs show activities, outcomes, and administrative performance over time, showing appropriate data and statistics.

process emissions In environmental health and air pollution control, these are inorganic emissions captured directly at the source of generation.

process evaluation 1. In health education and health promotion, these are assessments obtained during the implementation of health promotion program activities used to control, ensure, provide feedback, or improve the quality of performance or delivery of the program; used to assess how well a program is being implemented by reviewing the external features of the program such as instructor training, quality of the learning resources, appropriateness and thoroughness of the instructional materials, and objectives and quality of instructional plans. Assessments are also done on the actual health promotion courses or activities and the final outcomes of the experience as determined by the participants. The assessment results should show limitations and precise and valid outcomes, identifying the strengths and weaknesses of the program, its implementation, and the processes it went through. 2. In health administration, this is the assessment of inputs such as policies, resource utilization, personnel, budgets, quality of services, medical and nursing practice activities, and any managerial concerns observed during implementation.

processing In health information management, these are the activities of performing specified computer operations on the input side to produce meaningful results on the output side.

processing cycle In health information management, computerized health services, and medical records, a batch-run method of computer interactive processing using real time.

process measure An indicator of the quality of medical care; documenting and assessing the methods and procedures used in providing a health service or the medical care utilized with various populations to evaluate the quality of the services or care provided (e.g., the fraction of people with hypertension who receive an intravenous pyelogram or the percentage of cases of strep throat that are cultured before treatment). Process measures do not necessarily measure the results of care, although they measure the use of diagnostic and treatment methods that have been proven to be effective. Generally, such measures indicate the degree of conformity with standards established by peer groups or with expectations formulated by leaders in the profession. *See also input measure; outcome measure; output measure.*

processor In health information management and computerized health services, this is a hardware device that receives data and information and breaks it down using software programs into language parts that the computer recognizes. In computer software, a program that compiles, assembles, translates, and relates computer functions according to a specific computer programming language.

process units In environmental health, this is equipment assembled to produce a volatile hazardous air pollutant (VHAP) or its derivatives as intermediates or final products; equipment assembled to use in VHAP in the production of a product. Process units can operate independently if supplied with sufficient feed or raw materials and sufficient product storage facilities.

process wastewater 1. In environmental health, this is any water that, during manufacturing or processing, comes into contact with or results from the production or use of any raw material, intermediate product, finished product, by-product or waste product. 2. In environmental health, this is when pollutants are present in processed wastewater.

process weight In environmental health, this is the total weight of all materials, including fuel, used in a manufacturing process. It is used to calculate the allowable particulate emission rate from the process.

prochain ami (French) Next friend.

pro confesso (Lat.) As confessed.

proctor Someone given authority to oversee or to manage another person's activity; supervision of a testing or evaluation process.

proctoscope A lighted optical instrument used to visually examine the interior of the rectum.

proctoscopy The act of viewing the interior of the rectum with a lighted optical instrument.

procure 1. To acquire or gain something for someone. 2. Obtain or solicit.

producing cause *See proximate cause.*

product In health-care marketing, this is a set of activities or experiences offered and consumed by patients in a manner that is different from other industries. Examples are a single visit to a physician, spending a day in the hospital, an entire length of stay, and the completion of a procedure such as a surgical operation or session of therapy.

product accumulator vessels In environmental health, these are any distillate receivers, bottoms receivers, surge control vessels, or product separators in volatile hazardous air pollutant (VHAP) service that are vented to the atmosphere either directly or through a vacuum-producing system. Product accumulator vessels are in VHAP service if the liquids or the vapors in the vessel are at least 10% by weight VHAP.

product design objectives In health administration and health-care marketing, these are the aims, activities, and measurable outcomes of the programs and services to be provided to the customer (patient, physician, third-party payer) and the benefits that should result to the health-care organizations.

product-driven organization In health administration and health-care marketing, this is where the marketing of the health-care organization is aimed at selling the services and program of the organization. Image, community role, and related issues are ignored. Administration focuses all activities on the customer (patient), the physician, and third-party payers.

product evaluation committee An assembly of health-care providers, administrators, and materials management or purchasing personnel who have the responsibility of assessing new products for use in the health-care facility and who advise for or against the purchase and use of the goods.

production The process, act, or behavior used to produce goods or services.

production bonuses In health administration, this is a monetary incentive system where an employee is rewarded for achieving certain preset productivity or performance goals. Additional compensation or rewards or a salary raise is provided to employees when they surpass the goals. *See motivation.*

productive FTE In health administration, this is the calculation of full-time-equivalent staffing based only on time worked and excludes holidays, vacation, sick leave, and personal time off.

productivity 1. The amount of output that can be obtained from a unit of input by utilizing production measures. Physician productivity generally is measured by the number of physician hours spent, the number of patient visits, the number of procedures performed (i.e., for surgeons), and the expenditure of supplies. A unit of output is measured by the number of patients seen, the number of office visits, and the dollar amount of income generated. 2. The ratio of the health-care organization's output (services and programs) divided by its input (resources, personnel, capital, materials). *See units of service.*

product liability Holding liable those manufacturers and sellers of goods to consumers, users, and bystanders for any physical harm or property damage caused by the good or product; liability arising out of manufactured goods after they leave the premises (applies to the manufacturer and those who handle or distribute the goods). *See torts; negligence.*

product life cycle In health-care marketing, this is the pattern of use, demand, and consumer behavior found to affect a specific product or service, with different patterns of interest emerging such as how new it is and how and when competition causes a change in demand.

product line In health-care marketing, this is any set of services or goods that can be used by or that is experienced by the patient that can be viewed and used as a product measure.

product line analysis In diagnosis-related groups (DRGs) review and assessment, some DRGs are found to make money and others to lose money. Thus, it must be determined which DRGs are most cost-effective for the facility. These DRGs become the facility's product line.

product line management In health-care marketing and health-care administration, this is the identification of services offered by the health-care organization that are revenue generators and the assessment and management of all service resource requirements, operational demands, marketability of the service, accessibility, information management system needs, competition, and image in the community and how all facets of services offered by a health-care organization are delivered.

professio juris (Lat.) In contract law, where one state or country decides all legal issues of a contractual agreement.

profession A group of persons with a common interest united together for advancement of that interest.

professional An individual who has completed the formal education and examination required for membership in a profession. Certification or licensure by regional or national professional associations is required for membership, reflecting community sanction or approval. Usually for a person to be a professional there is a body of systematic scientific knowledge and technical skill required. The members function with a degree of autonomy and authority under the assumption that they alone have the expertise to make decisions in their area of competence. Medicine is an occupation that most closely approaches the prototype of a profession.

Professional Activity Study (PAS) A shared-computer medical record information system purchased by hospitals from the Commission on Professional and Hospital Activities (CPHA) in Ann Arbor, Michigan, a nonprofit computer center. Information flows into the system through a discharge abstract completed by the hospital medical record department on every discharged patient. The patient information is displayed back to the hospital in a series of monthly, semiannual, and annual reports that compare average lengths of stay, number and types of tests used, and autopsy rates for given diagnostic conditions with those of other hospitals of similar size and scope of services (good examples of process measures). *See PAS norms.*

professional association(s) 1. In health services, these are groups of health-care professionals who, because of their training, career area, or profession, voluntarily join together in a formal society to further their profession, professional development, education, and affiliation (can also refer to labor organizations). 2. In corporate law, this is a form of legal incorporation of professional practices and organizations allowed in some states. Another term for "professional corporation." *See professional corporation.*

professional component In medical insurance, under certain circumstances, the physician may wish to submit a charge for the professional component of a procedure rather than for a technical component. Under these circumstances, the professional component charge is identified by adding a modifier number to the usual procedure number found in the procedure coding manual when filing insurance forms. *See also procedure coding manual.*

professional corporation (PC) A legal entity established to function in the business world distinct from its several members. A PC is created and operates under authority from a state through the articles of incorporation. This legal entity may be for-profit, not-for-profit, a personal holding company, or for tax shelter purposes under Subchapter S of the Internal Revenue Code. Also referred to as a "professional association," a PC requires shareholders to be licensed in the same profession (e.g., medicine, dentistry, or architecture), with sole incorporates acting as members of the board of directors. The advantages of a PC are freedom from personally being sued (instead the PC is sued), limited liability for the professional stockholder(s), centralized administration, continuity of corporate life, free transferability of stock, and tax shelters. The disadvantages are the loss of a degree of stockholder autonomy in decision policy making, scrutiny from state and federal governments, substantial legal service requirements, and the possibility of double taxation.

professional development In health administration and human resource management, this is the process of strengthening abilities, skills, and knowledge in an area of expertise, communication, and human relations or to advance technical knowledge and skills in specialized areas.

professional liability In health law, these are obligations of health-care providers or their professional liability insurers to pay for damages resulting from acts of negligence or of omission or commission that a medical care practitioner may commit in the process of treating patients. The term is sometimes preferred by physicians to the term "medical malpractice" because it does not necessarily imply negligence. This term also describes the professional performance and skill obligations of all types of professionals (e.g., lawyers, architects, engineers, and other health practitioners, as well as physicians).

professional liability insurance *See malpractice insurance.*

professional library and health information services In JCAHO accreditation of hospitals, these are activities designed to meet the information, education, and, when appropriate, research-related needs of a hospital. Standards are applied to evaluate a hospital's performance in providing professional library and health information services.

professional nurse A licensed nurse who has graduated from a nursing school accredited by the National League of Nursing with a bachelors, masters, or doctorate in nursing.

professional personnel In medical care services, these are physicians, physician assistants, chiropractors, dentists, dental hygienists and licensed practical nurses, pharmacists, physical therapists, podiatrists, registered nurses, and other allied health occupations at the professional level. Those health-care providers or their supportive technicians and technologists are licensed in the state where they practice, and licensure usually requires the completion of an appropriate degree or certificate program for that profession; may be classified according to specialty, place of practice, or other criteria.

professional review organization (PRO) A specialized medical care auditing organization staffed by physicians, nurses, and other allied health-care professionals removed from the health-care facility. They evaluate quality and sequencing and coding procedures used by the facility to ensure the intermediary that the health-care facility is not coding diagnoses and procedures incorrectly in an effort to increase reimbursement. Hospitals and other health-care facilities are required to contract with this organization, which is selected by the intermediary. *See peer review organization.*

professional service corporation (PSC) *See professional association; professional corporation.*

professional services Relevant to health-care finance, these are revenue-producing services, usually ancillary services such as pharmacy, X ray, and laboratory as well as major cost-producing areas such as operating rooms and recovery rooms. In hospital administration, this is a revenue category that identifies revenues from the professional or ancillary services such as X ray, laboratory, pharmacy, or specialty areas such as rooms or central supply.

Professional Standards Review Organization (PSRO) 1. A former medical review organization that was physician controlled and charged with reviewing the services provided to patients who are covered by Medicare, Medicaid, and maternal and child health programs. These were changed to PROs (peer review organizations) in 1983–85, when Medicare's Prospective Payment System was implemented. The aim of the organization was to review services rendered and determine if they were medically necessary. Services are provided in accordance with professional criteria, norms, and standards and are provided in an appropriate setting. The creation of the Professional Standards Review Organization was mandated in 1972 by Congress in the 1972 amendments to the Social Security Act (P.L. 92-603) to ensure that health-care services and items utilized in health care for which payments are made under Titles V, XVIII, and XIX of the Social Security Act conform to the appropriate and expected high professional standards of health care and are delivered in the most effective, efficient, and economical manner possible while ensuring quality of care. Two fundamental review concepts are used in health care settings: 1) physicians are the most appropriate individuals to assess the quality of medical care and 2) local peer review is the most effective means for ensuring that health-care resources and facilities are appropriately utilized. Four major goals of the PSRO program were 1) to ensure that health-care services are of acceptable professional quality; 2) to ensure appropriate utilization of health-care facilities at the most economical level while being consistent with professional standards; 3) to identify lack of quality and overutilization problems in health-care practices while working toward improvement; and 4) to attempt to obtain voluntary correction of inappropriate or unnecessary practitioner and facility practices and, where unable to do so, recommending sanctions against such practitioners and facilities. *See also advisory group; peer review organization.*

proffer 1. To offer. 2. To present for acceptance. 3. Avowal. 4. To offer services.

proficiency testing Assessing technical knowledge and skills related to the performance requirements of a specific job, whether such knowledge and skills were acquired through formal or informal means. Section 241 of the Social Security Amendments of 1972 (P.L. 92-603) requires the Secretary of Health and Human Services (HHS), in carrying out functions relating to qualifications for health manpower, to develop and conduct a program to determine the proficiency of individuals in performing the duties and functions of practical nurses, therapists, medical technologists and cytotechnologists, radiologic technologists, psychiatric technicians, or other health-care technicians and technologists. The program is to use formal testing of the proficiency of individuals and is not to deny any individual who otherwise meets the proficiency requirements for any health-care specialty a satisfactory proficiency rating solely because of his or her failure to meet formal educational or professional membership requirements. Proficiency examinations are to determine the necessary work qualifications of health personnel (therapists, technologists, technicians, and others) who do not otherwise meet the formal education, professional membership, or other specified criteria established under Medicare regulations so that services provided by these individuals will be eligible for payment. *See also equivalency testing.*

profile In health-care delivery and health planning, this is a longitudinal or cross-sectional aggregation of medical care data. Patient profiles list all the services provided to a particular patient during a specified period of time. Physician, hospital, or population profiles are statistical summaries of the pattern of practice of an individual physician, a specific hospital, or the medical experience of a specific population. Diagnostic profiles are a subcategory of physician, hospital, or population profiles with regard to a specific condition or diagnosis.

profile analysis In medical records and PRO review processes, a method used to determine the effectiveness of the PRO review process or the health-care facility's utilization review program by comparing like information and finding differences over time.

profit In health administration and health-care financial management, this is money left over from patient care and operation revenues after all expenses are paid. The gain made by the sale of goods or services after deducting the value of the labor, materials, rents, interest on capital, and other expenses involved in the production of the good or service. Economists define "profit" as return on capital investment and distinguish normal (competitive) and excessive (more than competitive) profit. Profit in the sense of a profit-making or proprietary institution is present when any of the net earnings of the institution inure to the benefit of any individual. The concept of profit is very hard to define operationally, and unreasonable or excessive profit is even more difficult, as some believe there is no such thing as excessive profit. It is important to recognize that reasonable profit on investment must vary with the risks involved in the investment. Profit bears a close relationship to the balance of supply and demand, being a measure of unmet demand. In nonprofit organizations, this is referred to as "excess of revenues over expenses" or "overattainment of funds."

profit-and-loss statement In health-care finance, this is one kind of a financial statement that sets forth revenues, allowances, adjustments, income, and expenses with a statement at the bottom indicating a gain or loss for the period. According to acceptable accounting procedures, losses are enclosed in parentheses.

profit center Any service, area, program, or department in a health-care facility that produces more money than it expends in its operation; any service or group of services in a health-care facility that generates a profit.

profit driven In health administration, this is when a hospital or other health-care organization puts excessive emphasis and managerial focus on producing a profit and meeting budgetary constraints than is put on other equally important activities such as patient care, proper staffing, and maintenance and is often done at the expense of quality care, lack of upkeep, and overworked staff.

profit-sharing plan In some health-care organizations, this is a special financial structure that enables eligible employees to receive a proportion of the health-care organization's profits if a profit is made and if certain conditions or agreements are met. Two type of plans are used: current and deferred.

pro forma (Lat.) As a matter of form; a formality.

prognosis In medical care, this is the prediction or opinion of the outcome of a disease, condition, or disorder; medical prediction of the course and probable outcome of a treatment, injury, illness, or condition.

program 1. In computerized medical records, medical insurance, business records, or medical research, a group of related routines that solves a given problem or commands the computer. A plan or routine for solving a problem on a computer. 2. Another term for service, project, agency, or department. 3. A set of planned activities designed to achieve specified objectives over a given period of time. 4. A group of projects providing related services that together address a common purpose (e.g., a maternal and child health program). 5. According to JCAHO for psychiatric, alcoholism, and drug abuse facilities accreditation purposes, a general term for an organized system of services designed to address the treatment needs of patients (JCAHO for acute-care facilities). 6. An outline of work to be done or a prearranged plan or procedure. *See service; department.*

program area 1. In health administration, this is a unit, program, or department where the same or similar health service activities occur; all related services and care units' responsibilities falling under the organizational head of one department. 2. In health administration and strategic health planning, this is where the total group of services and program activities in a health-care organization are directed toward the same goals, outcomes, and end results.

program coordinator Director or head of a service or project; the individual appointed to be administratively responsible for controlling, planning, directing, supervising, scheduling, and operating a service or project. Synonymous with "midmanager," "department head," and "supervisor."

program development 1. A part of planning or grant-writing activities that involves the determination of a need and then the evaluation of gaps in service delivery. Once needs and gaps are identified, specific activities, time lines, procedures, staff, budgets, materials, equipment, and office resources needed to implement the new program can be determined. 2. The process of completing the activities of long-range or strategic planning. 3. The process of writing and debugging software programs.

program directives In health administration and planning, these are the aims or desired results that are set forth for each department, program, or service and that define operational direction and provide a basic framework for operational planning, budget planning, and decisions.

program effectiveness The extent or level of quality and quantity that a program has attained in meeting objectives as a result of planned activity required to meet program goals.

program efficiency The resourceful use of time, materials, and personnel in the attainment of a program's objectives as compared to total resources expended.

program evaluation 1. According to JCAHO for psychiatric, alcoholism, and drug abuse facilities accreditation purposes, an assessment component of a facility that determines the degree to which a program is meeting its stated goals and objectives. 2. In health promotion and health education, this is the process of ascertaining and ensuring outcomes and determining the effectiveness of health promotion programs.

program evaluation and review technique (PERT) A management technique that assists personnel in the accomplishment of an objective; a system that helps identify activities essential to completing a project while assisting in establishing the best schedule for its completion. Many approaches to this management method exist. The critical path method (CPM) is one adaptation of PERT that is often used and is more specific in its time frames.

programmatic proposals *See proposal, program.*

programmed instruction In health education or human resource training, this is where all curriculum or instructional materials fall under a self-guided format that does not require the presence of an instructor and that uses instructional aides and media education devices such as textbooks, videotapes, computers, programmed texts, workbooks, interactive computer programs, or television or other formats to provide individuals with information about the subject and a chance to respond to the information immediately. Participants receive instant feedback and insights into their progress.

programming 1. The process of steps and procedures to be taken to produce a report or document. 2. To command a computer to perform certain functions.

program objective A statement of activity directed toward a desired outcome specifying who is to do what, how much, and at what point in time, according to the implementation of a plan. *See objective.*

program proposals *See proposal, program.*

program-related investment (PRI) In health-care finance and health planning and program development, when a health-care organization such as a hospital turns to foundations and philanthropic organizations for financial assistance, the philanthropic organization offers a low-interest loan instead of the traditional grant.

program synergy The process of cooperation, collaboration, teamwork, and communication across and within health services, programs,

departments of health facilities, and health-care organizations.

progress in debate In formal health-care meetings, this is when a change occurs in the meeting process or where the assembly takes a different position on a motion or question before the floor. When an assembly adopts a motion or approves business matters, this affects the assembly and results in a change in parliamentary situation.

progressive discipline In health administration and human resource management, this is the process of taking a step-by-step approach to coach, guide, discuss, and warn employees for repeated offenses, documenting each occurrence along the way. Such progression usually starts with oral requests, discussions, and warnings, progressing to employee conferences, counseling sessions, and written warnings, allowing the employee to take corrective action, all done prior to considering the termination of the employee.

progressive patient care (PPC) A system under which patients are grouped together in units depending on their type, level, and need for care as determined by the severity of their illness rather than by consideration of medical specialty. There are three conventional levels or stages of progressive patient care: intensive care, intermediate care, and minimal care down to self-care. With the development of intensive care units and transitional care units in hospitals, the concept of progressive patient care has been recognized as a needed service by hospitals and other health facilities, whether planned or in response to need or market forces.

progressive rates In managed care, this is an approach used by some health plans to set new rates, which is done usually monthly, quarterly, or semiannually. New or renewal members with anniversaries that fall with the time period automatically are subject to the new rates or the prevailing rates in effect during that time period. Some health plans will guarantee the rates for one benefit year. Such an approach helps contain rate changes on a group-to-group basis for each benefit year and offers a better rate parity than a fixed rate structure for the fiscal year.

progressive tax In human resource management, this is a tax taken from an employee's paycheck that takes an increasing proportion of income as income rises such as the federal personal income tax. Incremental increases in taxable income are subject to an increased marginal tax rate. *See also regressive tax; proportional tax.*

progress notes In medical care and medical records, this is the hour-by-hour or day-by-day notation in the medical record by the physician of his or her assessment of treatment, services, and the prescribed care of the patient and the patient's progress toward recovery. The patient's medical record contains information concerning the patient's condition, needs, drug reactions or responses, recovery, improvements, general well-being, and results of tests and examinations. As the patient's conditions change, so does the treatment plan, and these factors are progressively noted by the physician in the medical record and are supported by nursing notes.

pro hac vice (Lat.) For one particular occasion only; for this occasion.

prohibition A legal order to stop or not engage in certain acts.

prohibition, writ of 1. A court order. 2. In health law, this is a writ directing a person not to do something that the court has been made aware of. 3. A writ from a higher court to a lower court directing it to cease certain activities.

project In health-care delivery, program planning and implementation, or health administration, these are a set of activities to be carried out by a provider organization or in a health facility by a health administrator. Projects include development and demonstration of manpower, budgets, feasibility studies, assessment and evaluation of services, outcome studies, operations, and operating policies (e.g., administrative action and tasks necessary to establish and operate an outpatient surgery center). *See health planning; program development.*

project grant A grant of federal funds to a public or private agency or organization for a specified purpose authorized by law such as the development of an emergency medical services system or the planning, development, and operation of a health education program.

Project Hope An international nonprofit health services organization that started in 1958 to share American medical techniques, training, and technology with the world, especially underdeveloped countries. In its early days, a large hospital ship was used. More recently, training of local indigenous inhabitants in medical care and public health has been done. Also, educational programs aimed at local peoples are used to help improve the health status of people across the globe, all through the use of volunteer physicians, nurses, health educators, and other support personnel. The journal *Health Affairs* is one key publication.

projection 1. In mental health, this is a mental defense mechanism that is indicative of poor communication skills, a distorted sense of responsibility, and not owning up to self-responsibility and is used to blame or place responsibility on another for one's own failures, actions, inadequacies, shortcomings, or mistakes. 2. In health administration and strategic health planning, this is a forecasting method using past health services utilization patterns and data to predict utilization patterns into the future.

projection method In insurance, this is a technique used to keep annuity tables up to date where it is assumed that death rates at any given age decrease or improve at a constant percentage each year.

projection of need (hospital bed capacity) A model for projecting the number of acute-care short-stay inpatient facilities using a modified Hill-Burton model as developed for use by former health system agencies. Current population, current patient days, projected population, and occupancy rates are used to determine bed need in this model. All population figures are in thousands, and occupancy of 85% is used.

Step 1: $\text{Current use rate} = \dfrac{\text{Patient days}}{\text{Population}}$

Step 2: $\text{Projected average daily census} = \dfrac{\text{Projected population} \times \text{current use rate}}{365 \text{ days}}$

Step 3: $\text{Bed need} = \dfrac{\text{Projected average daily census}}{\text{Occupancy rate}}$

projective test A psychological test that helps a subject reveal his or her own feelings, intelligence level, personality, or psychopathology. Examples include the Rorschach Inkblot Test and the Thematic Apperception Test.

prolix Verbose, drawn out; wordy, tedious, tiresome, prolonged.

prolonged use of a device Medical devices used over a long period of time that lead to dependence on the device and the inability to regain use of a normal bodily function such as indwelling catheters, gastrostomy tubes, and nasal/gastric tubes.

PRO Management Information System (PMIS) A management information system designed to transmit, process, and analyze information about the PRO program and project operations so that sound decisions about program operation and policy can be made. At present, PMIS is composed of three interrelated components: the Deliverable Monitoring System, the Federal Reports Manual, and the Contract Management Manual.

PROMIS *See Problem-Oriented Medical Information System.*

promise 1. An ethical obligation to keep an agreement that commits the person who made it to keep the agreement or do an act; ethically bound to keep one's word. 2. An orally expressed or written statement by one person to another to do something or to perform the conditions of the agreement. 3. An agreement usually involving something of value to be given in return for services performed.

promisee In health law and contracts, this is the party to whom a promise or an agreement is made.

promisor In health law and contracts, this is the party who makes a promise or agreement.

promissory estoppel In contract law, this is a binding promise that expects some action to be taken by a promisee. Such a promise is legally binding and has the effect of a contract. If it is unfair or causes an injustice, it is not binding. This is a promise given by one party to influence a second party to rely on a promise/contract and does so to a detriment. When the promise is relied on and injustice results, the promising party can be held legally liable.

promissory note In law, this is a written promise to pay, as agreed, a sum of money at a certain time or place.

promotion In health administration and human resource management, this is the process of advancing or moving an employee up to a better position at higher pay, responsibility, or organizational level.

promulgate 1. To publish. 2. To formally announce. 3. To make public. 4. To officially and formally present to the public.

prone Lying face down.

proof Sufficient and convincing evidence to show that there is no doubt that the facts are true.

proof of loss In health law and insurance, this is a

contractual right of an insurance carrier or service corporation to request verification of services rendered through the submission of claim forms, radiographs, dental study models, or other diagnostic material.

proof-of-loss clause In liability insurance, a statement in the policy that requires the insured organization to prove the amount and type of loss suffered by the organization as a condition of recovering the claim.

ProPAC *See Prospective Payment Assessment Commission.*

proper 1. Acceptable actions. 2. Having a substantial interest 3. Suitable or appropriate.

property 1. A solid, tangible item that may be owned. 2. Any item or object belonging to someone.

property, buildings, and equipment An asset category identifying the health-care organization's investment in buildings, land, equipment, or other capital items.

property damage accident Any event that causes damage to property but in which no person is injured. *See tort law.*

property loss The dollar cost of restoring damaged facilities or equipment to their original condition, whether or not such restoration actually occurs. In determining loss, the estimated damage to the building and contents shall include replacement cost, less salvage value, plus the cost of decontamination and cleanup. Effects on program continuity, auxiliary costs of fire extinguishment, and consequent effects on related areas should be included so that the effects and cost estimates can be determined. *See tort; recovery.*

prophylaxis Preventive treatment; prevention of disease. *See preventative.*

proponent 1. One who makes an offer or proposal. 2. A person who puts forward an item, object, or suggestion.

proportion In epidemiology and descriptive statistics, this is a ratio where the numerator is included in the denominator. Dividing a numerator by a denominator results in a decimal number, which, if multiplied by 100, results in a percentage.

proportional reinsurance In insurance, this is an arrangement under this special type of insurance used with individual insurance, where the proportion of the risk to be carried is known to both the ceding company and the reinsurer at the time the reinsurance treaty is made.

proportional tax In human resource management, this is a tax that takes a constant proportion of income as income changes. The Social Security payroll tax is proportional up to the $14,000 limit on income to which it applies. *See also progressive tax; regressive tax.*

proportionate mortality rate In epidemiology, this is the number of deaths from a certain cause in a specific period of time per 1000 total deaths for the same period. If the mortality of groups with different causes, characteristics, and distributions in the causes of death are used for cross-comparison, misleading results may occur. The proportionate mortality rate formula follows:

$$\frac{\text{Deaths from a specific cause in a time period}}{\text{Total deaths in same time period}} \times 1000$$

proposal 1. A proposition; a written plan for a project that is to be considered for implementation. 2. In grant writing, a document prepared for program development that is then submitted to foundations, corporations, or government agencies to request funding. Such support serves to initiate, implement, or operate a program or project or to apply for monies for capital improvements or equipment purchases. This document includes a description of the organization, the need for the project, objectives and goals, a budget, plans and procedures, and a means for project evaluation.

proposal, program In health planning or program development, this is the process of requesting the use of organizational resources to develop a new service or project for a department or unit of a health-care organization that will affect or enhance only that particular department, program, or service. The proposal must state how it will help fulfill the overall goals and mission of the health-care organization. Also referred to as a "programmatic proposal."

proposition In formal health-care meetings and hearings using parliamentary procedure, this is the presentation of a motion, resolution, report, or proposal to the assembly for consideration and action.

propositus In genetics and genealogical epidemiological studies, this is the first identified member of a family tree to manifest a genetic trait, especially a genetically transmitted disease in a family. Referred to as the "genetic index case."

propound 1. To offer. 2. To make a proposal. 3. To put forward; to make a proposition.

proprietary 1. Holding property. 2. Profit making. 3. Operated for the purpose of gaining a profit. 4. Having to do with ownership. 5. Legal right to ownership.

proprietary drug Any medicine or pharmaceutical preparation manufactured for and sold to the general public without a prescription.

proprietary function 1. In health-care organizations, this is the performance of a function by the board of directors that generally does not fall under general governmental duties of the board but deals more with the day-to-day operation of the health-care organization, usually delegated to the administrator; the right to private daily operations. 2. Dealing with rights of private ownership and the day-to-day operations of a business.

proprietary hospital A privately owned hospital operated for the purpose of making a profit for its owners. Proprietary hospitals are often owned by physicians for the care of their own and others' patients. There is also a growing number of investor-owned hospitals, usually operated by a parent corporation that operates a chain of hospitals. Proprietary hospitals are usually owned by individuals, partnerships, or corporations.

pro rata Proportionately; by a percentage, fixed rate, or share.

pro rata liability clause A statement in a liability insurance policy requiring that insurance companies proportionally share in any losses that the particular coverage bears compared to the total coverage of the risk or peril.

pro rata treaty In liability insurance, when premiums and losses are proportionally shared as stated in the policy; often found in reinsurance policies.

prorate 1. Break down or divide in sections. 2. Lots, pieces, or items portioned in downward increments.

prorating In health-care financial management, this is the allocation of an expenditure to two or more different accounts. The allocation is made in proportion to the gain that the expenditure provides in relation to the programs for which the accounts were established.

proration In insurance, this is an adjustment of insurance benefits paid because of a mistake in the premiums paid or the existence of other insurance covering the same accident or disability.

prorogation 1. A delay; putting off. 2. A continuance.

pro se (Lat.) For himself on his own behalf.

prosector A pathologist's assistant who assists in autopsies and related postmortem exam activities, including the dissection and preparation of pathological specimens for examination by the pathologist or lab.

prosectorial science A branch of anatomy utilizing principles of dissection and identification to make displays for anatomical demonstrations.

prosecute To begin and carry out a civil lawsuit; to bring to trial a person charged with a crime.

prosecutor A lawyer who works for a county, city, or state as a representative of that government who presents the cases against an accused person and asks the court to convict that person of the crime that he or she committed.

prospecting In managed care and insurance, this is searching for or seeking out potential subscribers or members for health plans or insurance.

prospection In health administration and planning, this is a forecasting method focusing on future issues that can be understood and projected with regard to health services utilization while disregarding past experience and past patterns of utilization.

prospective 1. Forward in time; events or occurrences of the future. 2. Laws that are preventive. 3. In health services research, this is the process of analyzing data at a point in time and in the future after subjects are exposed to some intervening variable, forward-looking research.

prospective budget In health-care financial management, this is a detailed plan of the projected services, revenues, costs, and volume for the next fiscal year.

prospective consent In medical care and health law, this is a form of consent often requested by third-party payers for the release of information prior to a patient being admitted to a health-care facility or receiving any treatment. This approach to consent is questioned by some legal authorities as it requires the patient to relinquish the right to privacy before knowing whether the information is confidential or what therapy or treatment will be required.

prospective payment In health-care finance, this is payment made before a service is rendered and is based on a fee schedule set in advance and accepted as payment in full by the health-care provider; the opposite of a fee-for-service or cost reimbursement payment system.

Prospective Payment Assessment Commission (ProPAC) A committee (group) of health policy and health finance experts who monitor the Prospective Payment System for the Health Care Financing Administration by evaluating data and recommending policy. The commission was established by the same law (P.L. 98-21) that created the Prospective Payment System/Diagnosis-Related Groups. The commission also advises the Secretary of Health and Human Services on health-care finance and health-care delivery issues.

Prospective Payment System (PPS) In health-care finance, the Health Care Financing Administration (HCFA) developed and implemented this third-party payment approach to paying health-care facilities for their Medicare patients in 1983. This system replaced the retrospective cost-based method of reimbursement effected in 1968. In this system, HCFA determined how much it will pay for each diagnosis-related group, and that is what the health-care facility receives, regardless of costs incurred in treating the Medicare patient or the patient's length of stay. There is no end-of-year adjustment offered and no reimbursement related to cost, forcing the health-care facility to either manage costs within the limits of these available revenues, lose money, or discharge the patient prior to full recovery. Quality assurance mechanisms are used to prevent premature discharge of patients and to preserve quality of care. *See also diagnosis-related groups; retrospective reimbursement; prospective reimbursement.*

prospective reimbursement In health-care finance, this is any method of paying hospitals or other health programs certain amounts or rates of payment established in advance for the coming year on the basis of a contract or an agreement between third-party payers and health-care providers. Medical care and health services are paid predetermined amounts regardless of the costs actually incurred. This system of reimbursement is designed to introduce a degree of constraint on charges or cost increases by setting limits on amounts paid during a future period. In some cases, such systems provide incentives for improved efficiency by sharing savings with institutions that perform at lower-than-anticipated costs. A prospective reimbursement system based on diagnosis-related groups (DRGs) was instituted by the Health Care Financing Administration (HCFA) in 1983 for Medicare inpatient hospital services. Predetermined and predicted classes and volumes of patients are used to determine the amount to be paid for each DRG prior to any patient receiving services. Payment is limited to the predetermined amount with no concern for cost or length of stay, and one rate per DRG is paid regardless of what happens to the patient as reimbursement is based on average costs for areas or regions. *See also diagnosis-related groups; Prospective Payment System (PPS); Section 222.*

prospective review In health-care delivery and medical care, this is a procedure used to review the patient's care prior to receiving care to plan for appropriate admission procedures, placement, and level of care and mainly to determine the medical necessity of the patient's admission.

prospective study In biomedical and health services research, this is an inquiry or research project planned to observe events that have not yet occurred or that will occur in the future. This is in contrast to a retrospective study, which examines events that have already occurred; research projects used to study groups of cohorts, variables, or events as they occur in the future.

prospects In managed care and insurance, these are potential subscribers or members for health plans or insurance.

prospectus 1. A document of future events. 2. A document of a planned future financial deal. 3. A statement about a corporation's or company's stocks and about securities issued as an invitation for investment.

prosthesis Any device, instrument, or object that is an artificial body part used to replace a part that has been amputated.

prosthetic/orthotic assistant or technician Individuals who assist the prosthetist/orthotist in caring for patients by making casts, taking measurements or model specifications, and fitting supportive appliances or artificial limbs.

prosthetist An allied health professional who writes specifications for, and makes, fits, and repairs, braces, appliances, and artificial limbs. Also referred to as an "orthotist."

prosthetist, certified A specialist in physical medicine who has successfully passed the American Orthotic and Prosthetic Association certifying examination and thus is certified to fit and repair braces, prostheses, appliances, and artificial limbs for handicapped patients.

prosthodontics A program of study that instructs individuals in the principles and techniques of constructing artificial devices and the restoration and maintenance of oral function by the replacement of missing teeth and other oral structures with artificial devices.

pro tanto (Lat.) For so much; to that extent.

protected class See protected groups.

protected groups In human resources management and affirmative action administration, these are individuals or classes of people who fall into a category that legally allows them to be protected from discrimination under one or more laws (e.g., under Title VII of the 1964 Civil Rights Act).

protective barriers In occupational health and safety, these are barriers of radiation-absorbing material such as lead, concrete, plaster, and plastic used to reduce radiation exposure. Two levels of protective barriers are identified: primary, which are sufficient to attenuate a useful radiation beam to the required degree, and secondary, which are sufficient to attenuate stray or scattered radiation to the required degree.

protective housing In laser technology, this is a shield or guard designed to prevent access to radiant power or energy at levels higher than the intended classification limits.

protective order A temporary court order allowing one side of a legal proceeding to not show documents or evidence that were officially requested by the opposing party.

Proteinaceous infectious particle See prion.

pro tem Short for "pro tempore."

pro tempore (Lat.) For the time being. Commonly shortened to "pro tem."

proto- Prefix meaning "first."

protocol 1. A formal set of ideas, principles, or expectations governing the actions of health-care providers or other personnel in a health-care facility. 2. In computers, the rules or conventions governing the formats and timing of information exchange between two communicating devices or processes. 3. In medical care, this is a written plan for the treatment and care of a condition injury or disease that is adopted by the medical staff as the method, approach, or manner in which future cases will be handled or will serve as a plan of action to be used by practitioners in health maintenance organizations, hospitals, medical groups, etc.

provider 1. A licensed physician or other medical care practitioner or health-care facility or institution that renders medical care; individuals or organizations in the provision of medical care services. 2. In Medicare, an institutional provider is a hospital, skilled nursing facility, home health agency, hospice, or certain providers of outpatient physical therapy services. These providers receive prospective or retrospective cost-related reimbursement. Other Medicare providers, paid on a charge basis, are called "suppliers." Individual providers include individuals who practice independently of institutional providers such as physicians. The former health planning law (P.L. 93-641) defined an individual provider as one (Section 1531[3] of the PHS Act) who is a direct provider of health care (including a physician, dentist, nurse, podiatrist, or physician assistant) in that the individual's primary current activity is the provision of medical care to individuals or the administration of facilities or institutions (including hospitals, long-term-care facilities, outpatient facilities, and health maintenance organizations) in which such care is provided and, when required by state law, the individual has received professional training in the provision of such care or in such administration and is licensed or certified for such provision or administration. 3. Physicians, physician assistants, nurse practitioners, hospitals, clinics, medical groups, health centers, or medical care institutions that render medical care. 4. In managed care, this is a medical care practitioner or a hospital, medical clinic, or institution that is under contract with a health plan to render services to plan members.

provider-driven system In health-care economics and finance, this is the delivery and provisions of medical care being controlled, influenced, and stimulated by health-care providers. Needs of patients, delivery of care, referrals, consultations, testing, evaluation, and rendering of medical care services are all within total control of the physicians and other health-care providers. See managed care; managed competition.

provider, institutional In Medicare, this is a hospital, skilled nursing facility, home health agency, hospice, or certain providers of outpatient physical therapy services.

provider of health care *See provider.*

provider participation In health-care finance, this is a health-care provider that has accepted assignment to treat Medicare or Medicaid patients covered by either or both plans.

provider reimbursement review board (PRRB) In health-care finance, this is a subunit of the Health Care Financing Administration (HCFA) that conducts hearings and renders decisions on appeals from health-care providers accepting Medicare reimbursements. The decisions of the PRRB are subject to further review by the administrator of HCFA and by federal district courts.

provider-sponsored networks (PSNs) Under Medicare, this is a group or alliance of health-care providers who may contract directly with Medicare under federal certification guidelines with a point-of-service option allowed. The PSN would be required to provide a substantial proportion of the benefits found in past Medicare benefits packages. Each network/plan would have to apply to the state for a license. If the state denies the request, an application could then be made to the Department of Health and Human Services.

providers of service An individual or institution rendering medical care to patients. In Medicare, an institutional provider is a hospital, skilled nursing facility, home health agency, hospice, or certain providers of outpatient physical therapy services.

province 1. An area of responsibility. 2. An expected duty.

provisional 1. Temporarily applied. 2. Applicable. 3. To temporarily enforce a law. 4. In some states, a provisional nursing home administrator's license is often used and issued on a temporary basis and is in effect only until testing or other licensing procedures are passed and completed.

provisional remedy In health law, this is a legal but temporary remedy for an immediate condition or circumstance; an injunction; a temporary enforcement of the law.

provisional staff In hospital administration, these are physicians or other professional health-care providers who have only recently been accepted for medical staff privileges on a probationary basis. In many health-care facilities, initial appointments to the medical staff are provisional until the health-care provider achieves regular status. Honorary and consulting status are not considered provisional.

proviso (Lat.) 1. A condition that is set. 2. A qualification made or a limitation placed in a legal paper. 3. A provision. 4. Being provided.

provocation 1. Inciting hostility or anger. 2. An act by another that entices rage, upset, resentment, or irritation.

proximate In immediate relation to or with something else.

proximate cause 1. In health law, this is the direct or actual cause that led to an accident, damage, harm, or injury; the single most important cause of the damages; the key act prior to injury without which such injury would not have resulted. 2. In health law, this is an act of omission for which a legal claim is filed with the courts that is actually or directly related to the cause of harm, damage, or injury. The cause does not have to be the closest cause in terms of time, location, or space in relation to the injury. The cause is not always the event that set the incident in motion. 3. The causal factors that directly produced the effect without intervention of any other cause; the causes nearest to the effect in time and space.

proximo (Lat.) Next.

proxy 1. A person who stands in for another person. 2. One appointed to represent another. 3. In formal health-care meetings using parliamentary procedure, this is a signed statement that transfers a person's right to vote to another or allows another to participate in place of the person signing the statement.

PRRB *See provider reimbursement review board.*

prudent buyer principle The principle that Medicare should not reimburse a provider for a cost that is not reasonable because it is in excess of the amount that a prudent and cost-conscious buyer would be expected to pay. For example, an organization that does not seek the customary discount on bulk purchases could, through this principle, be reimbursed for less than the full purchase price.

PSC Professional service corporation.

pseudo- Prefix meaning "fake" or "false."

PSNs *See provider-sponsored networks.*

PS/PM Per subscriber/per month. Used in managed care to describe enrollments and related revenues generated and expected levels of utilization of medical care services.

PSRO *See Professional Standards Review Organization.*

PSRO Management Information System (PMIS) *See PRO Management Information System.*

psyche The mind.

psychiatric 1. Pertaining to the study of the mind and mental processes, especially abnormal states or mental illness. 2. Refers to those health-care services, therapies, or treatments related to emotional disturbances as well as mental illness and behavioral and developmental problems.

psychiatric aide A technical level assistant with minimal training and experience in mental health care who assists psychiatrists, psychologists, social workers, counselors, psychiatric nurses, or other qualified professional mental health-care providers. This person works under supervision to help provide care and to assist in therapeutic programs for patients who are inpatients in a psychiatric unit of a health-care facility or a mental hospital. *See also psychiatric technician.*

psychiatric care Acute or long-term care provided to emotionally, behaviorally, or mentally disturbed patients on an outpatient or inpatient basis, with therapy and treatment provided under the direction of a psychiatrist, psychologist, or other qualified mental health-care provider, including psychiatric nurses or social workers. Patients are accepted for diagnosis and treatment or may be admitted to a freestanding psychiatric hospital or a health-care facility's psychiatric unit on the basis of a physician's orders. In health-care facilities, inpatient beds are established, and the unit is properly staffed in a medical care unit specifically designed for psychiatric care. This type of care may also include medical, nursing, and psychotherapeutic care. Long-term psychiatric care can include intensive supervision for chronically mentally incompetent and chronically mentally ill patients. This also includes mental illness care provided to patients as set forth in definitions from the National Institutes of Mental Health and includes any of several psychiatric disorders listed in the ICD-9-CM or the DSM-IV.

psychiatric child/adolescent services In mental health care, this is a service that provides care to emotionally disturbed children and adolescents, including those admitted for diagnosis and treatment.

psychiatric consultation and education services The provision of interpretive mental health services to community agencies such as schools, police, courts, and welfare agencies. Such outreach expands mental health information, knowledge, and skills to individuals who need it and educates those not in the field about mental health.

psychiatric consultation and liaison services In mental health care, this is a service that provides organized psychiatric consultation and liaison services to nonpsychiatric staff and/or departments on psychological aspects of medical care that may be generic or specific to individual patients.

psychiatric day treatment (day care) In mental health services, this is the provision of mental illness diagnosis, treatment, and a planned therapeutic program during most or all of the day for people needing broader programs than are possible through outpatient visits but less intense treatment than would require hospitalization as an inpatient.

psychiatric educational services In mental health services, this is a service that provides psychiatric educational programs to community agencies and workers (e.g., schools, police, courts, public health nurses, welfare agencies, clergy). The purpose is to expand the mental health knowledge and competence of personnel not working in the mental health field and to promote good mental health through improved understanding, attitudes, and behavioral patterns.

psychiatric emergency services Programs or facilities, usually hospital based, available on a 24-hour basis to provide unscheduled outpatient care to ambulatory patients needing immediate care, diagnosis, evaluation, crisis intervention, and assistance to those persons experiencing acute emotional or mental distress.

psychiatric foster care Any planned post-inpatient mental health-care observation and therapy provided in an approved foster home by competent and trained foster parents.

psychiatric geriatric services The provision of care to emotionally disturbed elderly patients, including those admitted for diagnosis and treatment.

psychiatric home care Any planned, home-based mental health care, including therapy in the patient's home augmented by outpatient care or individual psychotherapy in a community mental health center.

psychiatric hospital Acute-care short-stay facilities primarily concerned with providing diagnosis, inpatient care, and treatment for the mentally ill or persons with psychiatric-related illnesses, generally operated by a state or county and by private corporations. *See hospital, psychiatric.*

psychiatric inpatient care The provision of mental illness diagnosis and treatment to persons requiring 24-hour medical or psychiatric supervision admitted as inpatients to a psychiatric inpatient facility or unit.

psychiatric inpatient care unit A special unit in a health-care facility offering inpatient care for patients suffering emotional, behavioral, and mental problems.

psychiatric nurse *See nurse, psychiatric.*

psychiatric outpatient care The provision of mental illness diagnosis and treatment to persons on an ambulatory outpatient basis that does not involve any admission process or overnight stay in an inpatient facility.

psychiatric outpatient clinics, freestanding Administratively distinct facilities that have the primary purpose of providing nonresidential mental health services and where psychiatrists assume medical responsibility for all patients and/or direct the mental health program.

psychiatric outpatient services Ambulatory health-care services, diagnosis, and treatment offered in a variety of settings such as private practice, private mental health centers, and nonprofit community mental health centers and in hospital ambulatory mental health treatment services for outpatients suffering from emotional, developmental, behavioral, or mental disorders.

psychiatric partial hospitalization *See partial psychiatric hospitalization.*

psychiatric partial hospitalization program Organized hospital facilities and services for day care and/or night care for psychiatric patients who do not require inpatient care 24 hours a day.

psychiatric services Mental health and psychiatric services provided in hospitals that are either separate psychiatric inpatient, outpatient, or partial hospitalization services with assigned staff and space, all done under the care and supervision of a licensed psychiatrist. *See psychiatric care.*

psychiatric technician One who works under the supervision of professional or technical personnel in caring for mentally ill patients in a psychiatric medical care facility. This person assists in carrying out the prescribed treatment plan for the patient, maintains consistent attitudes in communicating with the patient in keeping with the treatment plan, and carries out assigned individual and group activities with patients. *See also psychiatric aide.*

psychiatrist A physician who has completed a residency, is board certified, and specializes in the study, diagnosis, and treatment of mental, emotional, and behavioral disorders. After receiving the doctor of medicine degree, the psychiatrist-in-training spends 3 years as a resident in psychiatry in a psychiatric hospital setting.

psychiatrist, qualified According to JCAHO for psychiatric, alcoholism, and drug abuse facilities accreditation purposes, a doctor of medicine who specializes in the assessment and treatment of individuals having psychiatric disorders and who is fully licensed to practice medicine in the state in which he or she practices.

psychiatry The branch of medicine that deals with behavioral, emotional, or mental disorders and related physiological or neurological involvement.

psychic In reference to the mind.

psychic costs In health law and mental health, these are the stresses, upsets, strains, and anxieties that affect an individual's mental health status in periods of change, stress, and social disruption.

psycho- Prefix meaning "mind."

psychoactive drug A drug that alters one's mental or emotional state. Such a drug may help a person to overcome depression, anxiety, or rigidity of thought and behavior. This drug may be used in conjunction with psychotherapy.

psychoanalysis Sigmund Freud's system of mental investigation and psychotherapy; a technique for determining and understanding the mental processes. Psychoanalysis includes the use of free association, catharsis, effects of the father and mother on emotional stability, and the analysis and interpretation of dreams, resistance, and transference.

psychographic data Statistics that describe what the consumers and customers think, respond to, or believe about issues relevant to the health services being offered. Market mix, place, product, services, promotion, and price all contribute to psychographic data.

psychographic profiles Using data about what customers (patients, physicians, third-party payers) think to develop a profile that shows what they expect from the health-care organization. Such findings can reveal what motivations lie behind choosing a hospital or facility, ascertaining the characteristics and practice style of health-care providers and enabling the development of more effective marketing approaches and strategies for the health-care organization.

psychographics In health-care marketing and planning, this is subjective data and information gathered from individuals and customers with regard to what they feel and believe about health services, health facilities, medical care practitioners, hospital or clinic administration, and their satisfaction with their experience and its potential effect on their health status. Such data can be used by health organizations and their administration in developing strategies, marketing, and forecasts and projecting need.

psychological aging In gerontology, these are life's changes and the accompanying adaptive and coping mechanisms that affect one's psychosocial status associated with the aging process.

psychological autopsy An approach to investigating death that goes beyond the four classes of death listed in the *International Classification of Diseases* and *Causes of Death*. The nonmedical investigator searches for the reason for the death by using a retrospective epidemiological approach, asking questions such as the following: (1) What motivated them? Why did the individual do it? (2) How did the individual really die, and why at that particular time? Many deaths are not explainable in medical terms, so behavioral scientists search beyond the medical explanation for other reasons such as self-fulfilling prophecy, subconscious death wishes, risk taking, doing something on a dare, brinkmanship games, suicide in deaths not considered suicide, or other psychological death-related phenomena.

psychologist A specially trained professional, usually with an advanced degree (MA or a PhD from a program approved by the American Psychological Association) and clinical training who specializes in the study of mental processes and the treatment of mental disorders through testing and psychotherapy and who in most states is licensed to practice as a psychologist. *See also psychologist, qualified; Council for the National Register of Health Service Providers in Psychology.*

psychologist, clinical 1. An individual who has completed a doctoral degree with a major in clinical psychology and who has completed a 1-year internship in a clinical setting approved by the American Psychological Association. History and philosophy of psychology, abnormal psychology, personality, psychopathology, behavior modification, psychotherapy, statistics, research, and testing are subjects basic to this professional. The clinical aspects of the training include assessment, testing, interpretation, and evaluation of patients presenting emotional, behavioral, and mental disorders. This person is also trained in providing such therapeutic interventions as behavioral therapy, psychotherapy, crisis intervention, and other appropriate forms of therapy. 2. A psychologist licensed by the state licensing board who usually is required to possess a doctoral degree in psychology from an educational institution meeting the criteria of the state board and in some states is required to have 2 years of clinical experience in a multidisciplinary facility licensed and operated by the state to provide health care or is listed in the National Register of Health Services Providers in Psychology as adopted by the Council for the National Register of Health Service Providers in Psychology.

psychologist, qualified According to JCAHO for psychiatric, alcoholism, and drug abuse facilities accreditation purposes, an individual who meets current legal requirements of licensure, registration, or certification in the state in which the services are rendered, who is currently competent in the field, and who either possesses a doctoral degree in psychology and at least 2 years of clinical experience in a recognized health-care setting or has the documented equivalent in education, training, and/or experience and is currently competent in the field.

psychology The study of the mind and mental and emotional processes.

psychometric Relating to the process of assessing, evaluating, and measuring an individual's mental health status, behavior, emotionality, and intelligence.

psychometry The science of measuring psychological functioning and capacity through the use of psychological tests.

psychomotor Body activity or skills related to cerebral or psychic activity.

psychomotor performance Behavior, actions, and activities that rely on mental processes as they interact with and relate to muscular responses.

psychopathic personality One who behaves in unacceptable ways; doing bizarre behaviors without remorse or any sense of morality. *See also antisocial personality.*

psychopathology 1. The branch of psychology or psychiatry that deals with mental illness. 2. The existence of emotional or mental illness.

psychopharmacology The study of drugs and their effects on mental and behavioral processes.

psychophysiological disorder Any emotional or mental disorder characterized by physical symptoms related to mental processes. *See also psychosomatic illness.*

psychoprophylaxis Psychological preparation to prevent pain.

psychosis Mental illness where a person's mental awareness, emotional response, recognition of reality, communication, and ability to relate to others are impaired enough to interfere with the capacity to deal with the ordinary demands of life. Psychoses are subdivided into two major types: functional psychoses and those associated with organic brain syndromes.

psychosomatic "Psycho" refers to mind, and "somatic" refers to body; how the mind affects the well-being of the body or causes it to respond.

psychosomatic illness Disease in which psychological and other nonphysical factors play a causative role. For example, asthma, vasomotor rhinitis, peptic ulcer, colonic disorders, arterial hypertension, chronic urticaria, coronary disease, and hyperthyroidism are considered to have mental and emotional causation. Psychosomatic disorders should be distinguished from mental disorders and from the psychic effects of diseases that are not psychically caused. *See also psychophysiological disorder.*

psychosurgery A surgical treatment procedure in which some region of the brain is destroyed to alleviate a severe and otherwise intractable mental or personality disorder. The early and crude surgical approaches to lobotomy have been replaced by the advanced techniques of psychosurgery. Psychosurgery is differentiated from brain surgery in that brain surgery is directed at repairing damaged brain tissue or alleviating symptoms resulting from tumors, accidents, infections, or any other disorder where the cause of brain impairment is clear. Psychosurgery includes the destruction of what appears to be normal and healthy brain tissue to eliminate or "cure" serious behavioral and emotional symptoms that other treatment modalities such as drug therapy and psychotherapy have been ineffectual in treating.

psychotherapist A professional mental healthcare provider trained in the techniques and skills of therapeutic interventions such as psychotherapy used to minimize emotional, behavioral, antisocial, or other mental problems without the use of drug or medical intervention.

psychotherapy A planned and organized treatment for mental illness and behavioral disturbances by a trained person through therapeutic intervention, both verbal and nonverbal, with attempts to remove emotional disturbance, change patterns of behavior, and encourage personality growth and development. Psychotherapy is distinguished from other forms of psychiatric treatment such as drugs, psychosurgery, electric shock treatment, and insulin coma treatment.

psychotropic Dealing with the psychopharmacological, physiological, and biochemical aspects of the central nervous system of the human body.

psychotropic drug Any drug that affects psychopharmacological, physiological aspects in the body and the psychic functioning of the brain and central nervous system and that in turn affects behavior and/or emotionality. This includes but is not limited to any drug that is mind or mood altering or that produces drug dependence.

PT *See physical therapy; physical therapist.*

PTMPY *See per thousand members per year.*

PTSM *See plant, technology, and safety management.*

public 1. All persons of a society, community, state, or nation. 2. A state, nation, or community as a whole. 3. Affecting all persons.

public accidents In public health and safety, this is any accident other than motor vehicle accidents that occur in the use of public premises, including deaths from recreation, swimming, auto races, boxing, football, hang gliding, hunting, non–motorvehicle transportation, accidents involving public buildings, and deaths from natural disasters such as earthquakes, hurricanes, and tornadoes, even if they occurred in a private home or its premises. Excluded are work-related accidents or those that occur while in the process of exercising activities of gainful employment.

public accountability See *accountable, accountability*.

public deaths Deaths that occur accidentally on property other than that owned by the victim.

public defender A lawyer provided by the government to represent persons accused of a crime who cannot afford a lawyer. *See also prosecutor*.

public domain 1. Owned by the government. 2. Free for anyone's use. 3. Items that are not protected by a patent or a copyright; government-produced publications that are open for use by anyone.

public doses In environmental health and radiation safety, the doses of radiation received by members of the general public from exposure to radioactive material released by a facility under the control or direction of the Department of Energy.

public expenditures In health-care finance, these are outlays for services provided or paid for by federal, state, or local government agencies or expenditures required by governmental action (e.g., workers' compensation insurance payments).

public health The science that deals with the improvement of the health status of the public or a community by organized governmental effort through detection, prevention, and control activities to reduce disease, disorders, conditions, disability, and death. Public health activities are generally those that are less effective when undertaken on an individual basis and do not typically include direct personal health or medical care services. Recognized public health activities include epidemiology, preventive care, health promotion, immunizations, communicable disease control, chronic disease control, sanitation, maternal and child health, preventive medicine, quarantine, environmental health, occupational health and safety programs, dental health, laboratory services, air and water quality, water and food protection, health education, and family planning. *See public health model standards; health promotion; preventive medicine; preventive care; health education; prevention, levels of; epidemiology*.

public health administration A specialized area of health services administration that focuses on the public administration and management aspects of local public health departments and related government health agencies. In addition to responsibility for the organization, administration, and function of public health services and programmatic areas and activities, the following areas are also a part of the role and function of public health administration: laws, regulations, planning, political responsibilities, financial management, organizational behavior, motivation and change, human resources and personnel management, community organization and planning, epidemiology, clinical management, laboratory management, public health education and health promotion, boards, advisory groups, management, organization and scheduling, span of control, collective bargaining, civil service, equal opportunity employment, financial management, accounting, budgeting, fiscal public policy, audits, policy development, public relations, media affairs, and public administration. *See health services administration; management; public health model standards*.

public health agency A governmental tax-supported organization mandated by law or regulation for the protection and improvement of the health of the public (Joint Committee on Health Education Terminology).

Public Health Councils The new name for the Board of Public Health as recommended by the National Institute of Health, which sets forth the role, political representation, effort, and direction for change to be taken by these councils.

public health education 1. Often used synonymously with "community health education" to refer to five basic phases or types of activities, including community analysis, sensitization, publicity, education, and motivation aimed at attitude and health behavior change. 2. A process designed to help improve and maintain the health status of the general population. Also referred to as "community health education." *See community health education*.

public health educator A person with professional preparation in health education and health sciences (usually a bachelors, masters, or doctorate in health education, health promotion, or preventive care), including training in the application of selected content from relevant medical, social, and behavioral sciences used to educate and influence individuals and group behavior change; learning; mobilization of community health action; and the planning, implementation, and evaluation of health education programs. The specific educational methods in which the public health educator is trained include community organization, program planning and evaluation, health content, communications, group work, and consultation. Also included in the preparation are epidemiology, biostatistics, environmental health, microbiology, and health administration (adapted from the Joint Committee on Health Education Terminology). *See community health educator.*

public health model standards The American Public Health Association, the National Organization for State Health Officers, county health officials, local health officers, and the U.S. Public Health Service developed what became known as the *Model Standards: A Guide for Community Preventive Health Services,* which has served as a guide and set of standards for organizing public health activities at the local level. The *Model Standards* lists 34 categories of public health services that should be available at the local level.

public health plan A plan of the public health department at the state and local levels that addresses the provision of health-care services and public and environmental health to the residents of the state or area.

public health practice The science and art of preventing disease, prolonging life, changing behavior and lifestyles, promoting health and well-being in populations through government-organized community efforts for the sanitation of the environment, the control of communicable disease and infections, the control of chronic disease, the organization of early diagnosis and prevention of disease, and the education of individuals and groups of people on health and wellness, lifestyle, and behavior factors that influence the health status of populations.

Public Health Service (PHS) An agency of the federal Department of Health and Human Services. Its administrative head is the U.S. Surgeon General. The PHS regulates diverse areas of public health concerns such as the medical

---

Model Standards: A Guide for Community Preventive Health Services

Administration and supporting services
Aging and dependent populations
Air quality
Alcohol and drug abuse and addiction
Chronic disease control
Communicable disease control
    Immunizations
    Sexually transmitted diseases
    Tuberculosis
Dental health
Emergency medical services
Epidemiology and surveillance
Family planning
Food protection
Genetic disease control
Health education
Home health services
Housing services
Injury control
Institutional services
Laboratory services

Maternal and child health
Mental health
Noise control
Nutrition services
Occupational safety and health
Primary care
Radiological health
Sanitation in facilities
    Child care facilities
    All public buildings
    Mobile home parks
    Recreational areas
School health
Schools
Solid waste management
Tobacco use and addiction
Toxic and hazardous substances
Vector and animal control
Violent and abusive behavior
Water (safe drinking)

(Source: American Public Health Association, the National Organizations for State Health Officers, County Health Officials, Local Health Officers, and the U.S. Public Health Service)

examination of aliens; Native American health programs; and quarantine, inspection, and licensing procedures. It administers grants to many kinds of health-care facilities and programs and provides fellowships and internships to those training in the health professions. Health promotion, preventive care, and disease prevention are major activities. It is also involved in national health planning and resource development, including the certification of health maintenance organizations.

Public Health Service Act An act of Congress providing legislative authority for federal health activities (42 U.S.C. 201–300) originally enacted July 1, 1944. Generally, the act contains authority for public health programs, biomedical research, health manpower training, family planning, emergency medical services systems, HMOs, regulation of drinking water supplies, and health planning and resources development. Many amendments to the PHS Act have been completed to revise, extend, or add new authority to it such as the HMO Act of 1973.

public health surveillance A health data collecting process that includes not only the systematic collection of information but also the analysis, interpretation, dissemination, and use of health information. In the health objectives for the United States as set forth in *Healthy People 2000*, surveillance and data systems was one of the five major areas of focus. Public health surveillance and data systems provide information on morbidity, mortality, and disability from acute and chronic conditions; injuries; and personal, behavioral, occupational, and environmental risk factors. Such factors are associated with illness, premature death, morbidity and mortality prevention, control, and treatment services and costs. Results of the surveillance and data collection and analysis are used to better understand the health status of the population to plan, implement, describe, and evaluate public health programs that control and prevent adverse health events.

public hearings Informal or formal public meetings used to provide the public with the opportunity to give comments and to permit an exchange of information and opinion on a proposed rule or regulation.

public information interviews In JCAHO accreditation activities, this is the opportunity for the presentation of information by the public or interested parties during an on-site accreditation survey as well as by personnel and staff of the hospital undergoing accreditation surveys.

public insurance A special type of managed-care or medical insurance coverage offered and controlled by a government agency and administered by a private agency. *See local initiative.*

public interest Anything that can have an effect on the general public.

public law (P.L.) 1. A federal act passed by Congress. 2. The area or class of law that deals with the government or the relationship between the government and individuals or organizations; laws that deal with the government and the public domain. 3. Law that handles disputes, or controls relationships, between private parties and government; law of the government as opposed to private law. Also referred to as "administrative law."

public offerings In health-care finance, these are stocks and bonds offered for sale to the general public and are required to be registered with appropriate governmental agencies.

public patient Any patient in a health-care facility that has his or her care paid for by government or public funds and who is referred to as public, service, or ward patients whose care is the responsibility of a medical care program, a government reimbursement program, a specialized contracted managed-care plan, or an institution. Public patients are often cared for by an individual practitioner paid by the program (e.g., a member of a governmental hospital housestaff), but the program, rather than the individual, is paid for rendering the care. *See service patient; private patient.*

public policy Laws and general rules to determine standards of public behavior for the good of the people. Laws are passed, on the basis of what is for the general public's good, to create services, regulations, or activities that affect the public as a whole.

public relations Any form of communications intended to promote goodwill or to create a favorable public image for a business or organization.

public relations department In health administration, this is an administrative unit in a health-care organization, usually a hospital, responsible for meeting the public and the press in an official capacity to release information, announce special events, or represent the facility and its patients. This unit is responsible for producing brochures, pamphlets, reports, and promotional materials to enhance or strengthen the image of the facility.

public relations director The administrator responsible for coordinating, planning, and organizing formal public communication activities of a health-care facility to enhance the facility's image.

public responsibility In health-care quality improvement, these are concerns, practices, and policies established by health-care facilities and health-care organizations that address social responsiveness, ethics, public health, environmental and occupational health, safety, and all appropriate facets of social responsibility.

public water systems In environmental health, these are systems that provide piped water for human consumption to at least 15 service connections or that regularly serve 25 individuals. Public water systems are either community water systems or noncommunity water systems for a total of a least 60 days per year.

publication of service A method of serving a summons by printing it in a newspaper.

publici juris (Lat.) 1. Of public right. 2. Rights that are universal.

published exposure levels Exposure limits as published in the *National Institutes of Safety and Health (NIOSH) Recommendations for Occupational Health Standards* and *Threshold Limit Values and Biological Exposure Indices* by the American Conference of Governmental Industrial Hygienists.

puerperal Pertaining to the birth process, this refers to a mother who has just given birth or the period immediately following childbirth.

puerperal fever Childbed fever, a systemic bacterial infection, often started in the open wound left in the uterus caused by the expulsion of the placenta following childbirth; septicemia following childbirth when unsanitary conditions exist, often because of unsterile obstetric equipment and techniques or unsanitary treatment procedures.

puerperium That period of time, up to 6 weeks, following childbirth in which physiological and anatomical changes occur in the mother because of being pregnant, including the change and adjustment to motherhood and recovery from pregnancy.

puffing 1. Creating a belief in a patient or consumer that something is better than it actually is. 2. Intentionally giving misleading information.

puisne A lower-level person; an associate or subordinate, not a chief or superior.

pulmonary diseases 1. Infections, conditions, and disorders that deal with the lungs and the respiratory tract. 2. A specialty of internal medicine that evaluates, diagnoses, and treats conditions, diseases, and disorders of the lungs and respiratory system.

pulmonary function laboratory A specially equipped and staffed therapy unit in a health-care facility used for diagnosis, assessment, therapy, and treatment of patients suffering from respiratory disorders.

pulmonary specialist *See pulmonologist.*

pulmonologist A physician certified and licensed to practice medicine in the medical specialty area concerned with diseases of the lungs.

pulsed duration In laser technology, this is how long the laser pulse lasts, usually measured as the time interval between the half-power points or the leading and trailing edges of the pulse.

pulsed laser In laser technology, this is a laser that delivers its energy in the form of single pulse or a train of pulses. Often the standard used is the duration of a pulse of 0.25 seconds.

pumping, laser In laser technology, this is the process of raising the atoms of an active medium to higher energy levels.

punitive damages 1. In health law, this is a monetary charge made by a court to a person who has been harmed extending beyond the amount of recovery from harm, injury, or damage and is above and over the amount of actual loss, serving to punish the defendant for his or her behavior. The tacking of additional amounts of money to the amount of recovery is to send a message to others in the health professions that such actions are unacceptable to society and the courts. A large monetary award given to serve as a punishment. The award often is not related to the actual cost of the injury or harm suffered, but its purpose is to prevent a similar act from happening again in the future. The money is given to the injured party as a warning to the party who caused the harm and future parties who may do a similar act. May also be referred to as "exemplary damage." *See also damages, exemplary; recovery.*

purchase 1. To legally buy or acquire. 2. A transaction creating an agreement to acquire property.

purchase order In health administration materials management, this is the authorization for a person to buy or deliver goods or perform services or the promise to pay for goods or services in written form.

purchasing agent In health administration materials management, this is the administrative person responsible for the selection and procurement of goods, supplies, equipment, and other items necessary for the efficient and effective functioning of a health-care facility. *See also materials management department.*

purchasing alliances 1. In health administration and health finance, this is the process of two or more hospitals, medical groups, or any combination of health-care organizations, services, or facilities that band together in a formal agreement for the purchasing of goods in bulk to reduce cost. 2. The joining together of health-care facilities, practitioners, and services to form a large full-service health-care organization to be selected by federal health-care programs as a health-care provider for an area or region. *See group purchasing; health alliances.*

purchasing and stores *See materials management department.*

purchasing department *See materials management department.*

purchasing group 1. In environmental health management, this is any group of persons who have as one of its purposes the purchase of pollution liability insurance on a group basis. 2. In health administration, this is when two or more health-care facilities or systems band together for the purpose of buying goods, supplies, and equipment to get a reduced purchase price from buying the products in bulk or in mass quantities.

pure premium In insurance or managed care, this is the portion of money paid by the insured organization to retain its insurance policy. This reflects the basic costs of loss but does not include profit or overhead.

pure risk In liability insurance, the potential of any peril or disaster certain to produce loss.

purge 1. To clean. 2. To clear from a charge. 3. To remove guilt. 4. To clear from a contract. 5. To eliminate; to clear a name. 6. In medical records, the removal of all unnecessary paper from each medical record prior to placing it in permanent storage.

purport 1. To act as if real. 2. To imply. 3. To profess. 4. To give an impression. 5. To present a false impression.

pursuant 1. According to; in accordance with. 2. Carrying out an act with authority to do so; within the scope of responsibility or authority.

purview 1. The meaning, design, or reason for a statute or other law. 2. Range, scope, or extent.

putative 1. To be alleged. 2. To be commonly known as. 3. A supposed occurrence or status.

putrescible In public health, this is a substance able to rot quickly enough to cause odors and attract flies.

putting the motion In formal health-care meetings using parliamentary procedure, this is to vote on the motion on the floor.

pyelogram In medical care, this is a roentgenogram of the kidney and ureter that shows the pelvis of the kidney.

pygmalion effect In health administration and personnel management, the notion that personnel will do what is expected of them. People live up to the highest expectations of what others hold of them.

pyrolysis Decomposition of chemicals by extreme heat.

pyrophoric materials Any substances that under normal conditions are liable to cause fires through friction, would combust if hit with an impact, or, if heat is produced from manufacturing or processing, is persistently retrained as to create a serious transportation or disposal hazard.

Q

QA *See quality assurance.*
QALY *See quality-adjusted life year.*
QAP *See quality assurance program.*
QAM *See quality assurance monitor.*
QI *See quality improvement.*
QM *See quality management.*
QRO *See quality review organization.*
Q-spoiled *See Q-switched laser.*
Q-switched laser A pulsating laser capable of extremely high peak powers for very short durations.
Q-switching In laser technology, this is when one of the resonator mirrors made from nonreflective material is used during an interval of pumping the laser. It is switched to a highly reflective mirror, and, as a result of the switch, all the stored energy in the medium during the pumping interval is emitted in a powerful pulse of light but lasts only for about 10 billionths of a second.
qua (Lat.) 1. As. 2. In the capacity of. 3. Considered as. 4. In and of itself.
quack One who deceives the public, consumers, or patients about his or her ability to treat or cure disease by pretending to have knowledge and training in medicine.
quackery Fraudulent medical claims; falsely claiming the ability to cure disease; fraudulently implying to consumers or patients that machines, devices, procedures, nostrums, or contrived substances that are basically ineffective, useless, or possibly harmful will treat or cure diseases or medical conditions.
quadrangular therapy Marital therapy that involves four people: the married couple and two therapists. Sometimes this may be one therapist for each spouse.
quadriplegia Paralysis that eliminates the use of all four limbs of the body; being paralyzed in both arms and both legs.
quaere (Lat.) 1. To query, doubt, or question. 2. That which follows is open to question or doubt.
qualifiable worker In human resource management, this is any individual who currently falls short of the requirements, knowledge, skills, and abilities to perform a job but who can become qualified with additional training and experience.
qualification 1. To be eligible. 2. Meeting certain requirements. 3. A restriction. 4. Putting limitations on something. 5. In health services, meeting standards for program eligibility, licensure, reimbursement, or other benefits. Thus, a qualified educational program meets accreditation standards, a qualified HMO (for the benefit of mandated dual choice under Section 1310 of the PHS Act) meets the standards imposed by the HMO Act, and a qualified provider for reimbursement by an insurance program meets its conditions of participation.
qualified 1. To be officially recognized; formal demonstration or acceptance. 2. To be officially or formally accepted or recognized by an organization, profession, or agency as an indication that the person or organization has met certain criteria or standards. 3. To be eligible to participate in a profession or licensing program or be accepted by governmental programs.
qualified acceptance The acceptance of an agreement or a deal that is limited or conditional.
qualified administrator In JCAHO accreditation, this is an individual who is currently licensed by the state in which practicing, if applicable, and is qualified by training and experience for the proper discharge of his or her delegated responsibilities. *See health administration; health services administrator; administration of skilled nursing facility; long-term-care administrator; administrator, qualified.*
qualified audiologist *See audiologist, qualified.*
qualified dietetic service supervisor *See dietetic service supervisor, qualified.*
qualified dietitian *See dietitian, qualified.*
qualified handicapped Individuals who are mentally or physically handicapped and who, with reasonable accommodations, perform life's daily functions and work activities successfully.
qualified impairment insurance A limiting form of a special class of insurance restricting benefits to a particular condition or injury; a form of preexisting-condition restrictions that is not acceptable under universal coverage.
qualified medical beneficiary (QMB) *See qualified Medicare beneficiary.*
qualified medical radiation physicist *See medical radiation physicist, qualified.*
qualified medical record administrator *See medical records administrator, qualified.*

qualified medical records technician *See medical records technician, qualified.*

qualified medical technologist *See medical technologist, qualified.*

qualified Medicare beneficiary (QMB) In medical care, this is an individual whose income falls below 100% of the federal poverty guidelines so that the state must pay all the Medicare Part B fees, including premiums, deductibles, and copayments.

qualified nurse anesthetist *See nurse anesthetist, qualified.*

qualified occupational therapist *See occupational therapist, qualified.*

qualified patient activities coordinator *See patient activities coordinator, qualified.*

qualified pharmacist *See pharmacist.*

qualified physiatrist *See physiatrist, qualified.*

qualified physical therapist *See physical therapist.*

qualified psychologist *See psychologist, qualified.*

qualified radiologic technologist *See radiologic technologist.*

qualified right The right to do certain things for certain purposes and under certain circumstances (e.g., the prerogatives of the physician). *See prerogatives of a physician.*

qualified social worker *See social worker, qualified.*

qualified speech-language pathologist *See speech pathologist.*

qualify To become eligible.

qualitative analysis Used to determine the quality or nature of the elements of a problem, compound, or substance.

qualitative data In epidemiology and descriptive statistics, these are the nominal scale and ordinal scale data that describe sex, race, religion, occupation, or descriptive factors of concern or interest.

quality 1. A measure of the degree to which health services delivered to a patient, regardless of by whom or in what setting provided, resemble satisfactory delivery of services as determined by health professionals. Quality is frequently described as having three dimensions: quality of input resources (e.g., certification of the facility and the training of individual providers), quality of the process of service delivery (e.g., use of appropriate procedures for a given condition), and quality of outcome of service use (e.g., actual improvement in conditions or the reduction of harmful effects); doing the best possible job that can be done; doing work or tasks or performing at the highest achievable level, striving for excellence in all phases of work and life. 2. The nature, kind, or character of someone or something, hence the degree or grade of excellence possessed by the person or thing; the appropriateness of a set of professional activities or services based on the objectives they are intended to serve or the extent to which achievable value is achieved or as determined by meeting customer expectations and satisfaction; a characteristic of effectiveness and efficiency measured with respect to individual medical services, the various services received by individuals or groups of patients, individuals or groups of providers, or health programs or facilities. This can also be measured in terms of technical competence, acceptability of the service or outcome, humanity, need, acceptability, appropriateness, inputs structure, process, or outcomes. 3. Under total quality management activities, this is doing the right thing right consistently to ensure the best possible outcomes, customer satisfaction, retention of good employees, and sound financial performance; understanding expectations and needs of customers with never-ending quality improvement, as everything in an organization can be improved, and all employees are to be involved; meeting or exceeding the requirements of customers and making it a continuous improvement effort. 4. The degree to which health services for individuals and populations increase the likelihood of desired health outcomes and are consistent with current professional knowledge (Institute of Medicine). *See also quality of care; efficacy; effectiveness, Quality Assurance Program; medical review; peer review; utilization review.*

quality-adjusted life year (QALY) In epidemiology and health promotion, this is a measure of well-being that measures mental, physical, and social functioning. By multiplying the measure of well-being by the number years of life remaining at each age interval, an estimate of the years of healthy life for a population can be determined. The calculation of years of healthy life uses life tables and the average number of years of life remaining at the beginning of each age interval. Also needed are age-specific estimates of the well-being of a population compared to the population of the life table.

quality and performance plans In health-care marketing, this is the process of planning and operationalizing marketing strategies by identifying those requirements needed to achieve leadership in market segments identified as ones chosen to dominate, meeting and using key health service requirements and performance indicators, and identifying the resources needed to meet marketing management requirements.

quality and resource management *See quality management.*

quality assessment 1. Measuring or comparing the method or practice used with an accepted standard commonly used to determine the expected level or degree of excellence; measurement of professional and/or technical skill and outcomes as compared with accepted standards used to determine degree of excellence. 2. In JCAHO accreditation, this is the measurement of the technical and interpersonal aspects of health care and services and the outcomes of that care and service. It provides information that may be used in quality improvement activities.

quality assessment and improvement Ongoing activities designed to objectively and systematically evaluate the quality of patient care and medical services, pursue opportunities to improve care and services, and resolve identified problems. Standards are applied to evaluate the quality of a hospital's performance in conducting quality assessment and improvement activities (JCAHO accreditation).

quality assurance 1. Activities and programs intended to ensure the quality of care in a defined medical setting or program. Such programs must include educational or other components intended to remedy identified deficiencies in quality as well as the components necessary to identify such deficiencies (e.g., peer or utilization review components) and assess the program's own effectiveness. A program that identifies quality deficiencies and responds only with negative sanctions (e.g., denial of reimbursement) is not usually considered a quality assurance program, although the latter may include the use of such sanctions. Such programs are required of HMOs and other health programs assisted under authority of the PHS Act. 2. Under the Medicare Prospective Payment System, this is any quality assurance program administered under a utilization review program using DRG data in medical reviews or evaluations of medical care plans. Intrahospital comparisons are made on the basis of length of stay, most common DRGs treated in the hospital, costs, charges, and services used by persons in certain illness groups. Regional and PRO comparisons can be made, as can comparisons of suspected problems in DRG groups. Analyses of age-groups, cohorts, types of specialties utilized, physician usage, case mix, etc. can be conducted. Hospital statistics and public health data can be cross-analyzed and hospital performance determined. Early and late discharges are screened to ensure quality of care because early discharges can save money for the health-care facility. 3. In managed care, this is a formal set of quality improvement and quality management activities implemented and managed to ensure that quality of medical care and services are rendered. Activities include quality assessments and corrective actions taken to discover and remedy deficiencies. Comprehensive continuous quality improvement programs are required to ensure quality in patient care services, administration, and support services. 4. Long-term and continuous accountability for professional activities whereby customers know they receive appropriate and quality services and care; formal review of services and medical care rendered through assessment and corrective actions taken to remedy deficiencies identified in patient care, support services, and administration.

quality assurance coordinator *See quality assurance manager.*

quality assurance manager In hospital administration and quality management, this is the administrative person responsible for quality assurance and quality improvement programs and activities whose duties include the gathering of information, data, and statistics on quality issues; setting up and assisting quality assurance and improvement committees; record keeping; assisting with accreditation preparation; planning quality improvement activities; and reporting to the management team.

quality assurance mechanism A review conducted by the medical staff using retrospective review methods. Quality of care is compared to local health-care facility standards to ensure that standards are met, plans developed, and deficiencies corrected and that any problem is reassessed and a plan developed to overcome the problem.

quality assurance monitor In health administration and quality management, this is the part of a quality assurance program that addresses issues concerning physicians, the medical staff, nursing care, and other patient care areas. The Commission on Professional and Hospital Activities conducts a Professional Activity Study (PAS), which addresses issues related to patient care. The findings of the PAS are computerized as case abstracts and are compared with established patient care and clinical standards with the findings reported through the hospital's quality management.

quality assurance professional A health-care provider or practitioner who is trained and has experience in the development and management of quality assurance programs, serves in a quality assurance management position, and usually is a member of the National Association of Quality Assurance Professionals and may be certified as a certified professional in quality assurance (CPQA).

Quality Assurance Program (QAP) A program developed by the American Hospital Association for use by hospital administrators and medical staff in the development of a hospital program to ensure the quality of the care provided in the hospital.

quality circles (QCs) In health administration and quality management, this is an ongoing management tool continuously used for eliciting more productivity, receiving input from all levels of workers, assisting in declining morale, solving work-related problems, and helping to move an organization to new levels of participative management while creating and preserving quality in the health-care facility. These activities are done through a voluntary group of health-care organization employees chosen from throughout all facets of the organization and are led by a person trained as a facilitator to identify quality problems and arrive at quality solutions.

quality circles, elements of In health administration and quality management, this is a management tool that consists of a task force of 3 to 12 employees from all levels of jobs and positions who work in the same health-care organization and who meet on a regular basis, about 1 hour per week on company time. The group meets to assess statistical and performance data and to review information, procedures, and processes used on the job that affect work quality, morale, the work area, and the delivery of health-care services. Much of the activity of the task force is to assess problems and areas of concern; brainstorm solutions that improve quality, effectiveness, and efficiency; present to administration recommendations for authorization to change policy; and implement new approaches or solutions.

quality control 1. In health administration and quality management, this is the monitoring, assessing, and surveillance mechanisms of procedures for producing evidence of quality. 2. In environmental health, this is a system of procedures, checks, audits, and corrective actions taken to ensure that all research design and performance, environmental monitoring and sampling, and other technical and reporting activities are of the highest achievable quality.

quality food Food that has been selected, prepared, and served in such a manner as to retain or enhance natural flavor and identity, to conserve nutrients, and to be acceptable, attractive, and microbiologically and chemically safe.

quality function deployment 1. In quality management and quality improvement, this is a technique, method, or process that identifies customer and technical requirements, prevents potential problems, increases customer satisfaction, and improves development cycles and better internal transfer of knowledge to help health-care organizations focus on the aspects, services, programs, and health-care delivery features that are most important to the customer. Activities include analyzing customer needs, prioritizing organizational quality improvement process activities, and getting to know what satisfies the customer, including patients, physicians, third-party payers, and employees. 2. In health-care marketing, this is when the health-care organization focuses on customer wants and integrates these into the marketing and service delivery process.

quality health care In health services and medical care delivery, this is the extent to which the type, amount and level, and appropriateness of care achieve the highest level of medical care possible and expected. *See quality; quality of care.*

quality improvement 1. In health administration and quality management, this is the process of striving for and achieving superior and, many times, unprecedented levels of performance. The process of identifying health-care delivery problems, testing solutions to the problems, and constantly monitoring the solutions for continuous improvement. 2. In JCAHO accreditation, this is an approach to the ongoing study and improvement of the process of providing health-care services to meet the needs of patients and others.

quality improvement, continuous See *continuous quality improvement.*

quality improvement process In health administration and quality management, this is a five-step process employed to continually improve quality in health-care organizations: 1) define the problem; 2) organize a team in the organization that understands the organization and its functions, processes, and activities; 3) diagnose problems from a quality improvement perspective; 4) design and test improvements; and 5) apply improvements while continually improving the process.

quality improvement standards and leadership requirements The health-care facility's leaders are to set expectations, develop plans, and implement procedures to assess and improve the quality of the organization's governance, management, clinical, and support processes: 1) Leaders are to undertake education concerning the approaches and methods of continuous quality improvement. 2) Leaders are to set priorities for organization-wide quality improvement activities designed to improve patient outcomes. 3) Leaders allocate adequate resources for assessment and improvement of the organization's governance, managerial, clinical, and support processes through assigning personnel to participate in quality improvement activities; provide adequate time for personnel to participate in quality improvement activities; and develop and provide information systems and appropriate data management processes to facilitate the collection, management, and analysis of data needed for quality improvement. 4) Leaders ensure that the organization's staff is trained in assessing and improving the process that contributes to improved patient outcomes. 5) Leaders individually and jointly develop and participate in mechanisms to foster communication among individuals and among components of the organization and to coordinate internal activities. 6) Leaders analyze and evaluate the effectiveness of their contributions to improving quality (JCAHO).

quality management An ongoing and continuous effort to evaluate and improve quality of health services with the goal of continuous improvement of the entire health organization and its services and systems; a management activity aimed at improving effectiveness and efficiency in the delivery of health services. Effectiveness from a quality view is the extent to which realistic goals are achieved. Efficiency from a quality view is the extent to which health service resources are effectively used to reach quality goals.

quality management of health care In health administration and quality management, this is a continuous management process used to assess and improve medical care and treatment. See *quality of care.*

quality management, total See *total quality management.*

quality of care As a measure or indication of the health-care system, the degree of excellence or conformity to standards that the various components of the health-care system adhere to; the degree to which medical care is rendered by competent and qualified health-care providers to individuals or groups of people, with the likelihood of desired and beneficial health outcomes that are consistent with current medical knowledge, technical competence, need, appropriateness, acceptability, and humanity. Quality of care is determined by the level of performance or abilities in efficiency, efficacy, access, and satisfaction of care. Availability, acceptability, and continuity of care may also be used as measures of quality of care. See *quality.*

quality of life The perception, belief, or expectancy of individuals or groups that their health and personal needs are being satisfied without being denied opportunities to achieve personal growth, well-being, happiness, and fulfillment.

quality of patient care The degree to which patient care services increase the probability of desired patient outcomes and reduce the probability of undesired outcomes, given the current state of knowledge. Potential components of quality include accessibility of care, appropriateness of care, continuity of care, effectiveness of care, efficacy of care, efficiency of care, patient perspective issues, safety of the care environment, and timeliness of care (JCAHO accreditation of hospitals).

quality of services The nature and grade of services being provided to the residents of a particular community at a given point in time.

quality of work life In health administration and human resource management, these are efforts made by a health-care organization to give employees an opportunity to affect the way their jobs are done and to show that their overall contributions to the organization are well-received; to provide good working conditions, have good supervision and good pay and benefits, and have an interesting, challenging, and personally rewarding position.

Quality Review Bulletin **(QRB)** A monthly publication on quality-of-care issues in hospitals and other health-care facilities and institutions published by the Joint Commission on the Accreditation of Healthcare Organizations (JCAHO).

Quality Review Organization Under Medicare's Health Care Financing Administration, this is a medical care review organization under contract to the Health Care Financing Administration (HCFA) that reviews the quality of care provided by managed-care health plans, hospitals, HMOs, posthospital care settings, and ambulatory care facilities. *See Medicare; quality review organization.*

quality staircase In health administration and quality management, this is a technique and method of visualizing quality improvement efforts developed by Joseph M. Juran. In health-care services, quality improvement must be constantly monitored and improved, thus moving up and improving as if going up a staircase in steps of improvement.

quantify To measure or express in numbers.

quantiles In health services research or data analysis, this is the process of distributing data or information into groups of equal and ordered subgroups such as tenths, quarters, or hundredths. The terms for these various distributions are centiles (hundredths), deciles (tenths), quintiles (fifths), quartiles (quarters), and terciles (thirds).

quantitation limit In environmental health, this is the lowest level at which a chemical may be accurately and reproducibly quantitated; usually equal to the detection limit multiplied by a factors of 3 to 5 but varying between chemicals and between samples.

quantitative analysis Used to determine the quantity and nature of elements in a problem, substance, or compound.

quantitative data In inferential statistics, these are the interval and ratio scale data with numerical quantities that can be analyzed by all levels of mathematical methods, including probability statistics.

quantitative risk assessment (QRA) In environmental health, this is a health risk exposures assessment approach that is conducted by scientists for a broad range of applications. Such an assessment is used mainly to evaluate the relationship between environmental exposures and potential occurrences of disease, conditions, injury, and death and is used in environmental epidemiology.

quantity A goal and/or measure of a health-care organization, health service, health-care system, health-care entity, management, or operations; the aspects of outputs, productivity, and capacity and how much there is available and provided; how much is offered to the consumer or customer of a health service, organization, or system as compared to other similar organizations or systems.

quantity of services A measure of a health-care system used to assess the amount and numbers and levels of health services, health facilities, and health-care providers in a community, region, or area; ensuring that an adequate number and types of services are available to meet the medical needs of a population. *See quantity.*

quantity variance A method of determining how well the quantity of a resource was used or controlled; the difference between the actual quantities used and the budgeted quantities for production multiplied by a standard price. Also called "usage variance."

quantum meruit (Lat.) 1. As much as one merits or deserves. 2. In law and the litigation process, this is bringing suit on the basis of an implied promise or an assumed contract.

quantum valebat (Lat.) 1. As much as they were worth. 2. In law and the litigation process, this is a claim started to recover the cost of goods delivered and based on an implied promise to pay.

quarantine In public health and epidemiology, this is the limitation of freedom of movement of susceptible persons or animals that have, or have been exposed to, a communicable disease to prevent the spread of the disease; restricting of individuals or families ill with a communicable disease to their own homes until the disease is over or no longer communicable or infective; the place of detention of such persons or animals or the act of detaining vessels or travelers suspected of having communicable diseases at ports or places for inspection or disinfection. *See isolation; public health; infection control; epidemiology.*

quarantine by personal surveillance In public health, epidemiology, and medical care, this is the close supervision, tracking, and/or an imposed partial restriction of certain freedoms of certain persons or animals infected with selected communicable diseases to keep track of their state of infectivity or their contact with others to control or eliminate the ability to spread a disease. For example, persons with typhoid fever are required by law to register with a public health department, are not allowed to work in food services, and are to report their whereabouts at all times.

quarantine by segregation In public health and epidemiology, this is the limitation of freedom of movement or the separation of parts of a population or group of persons or animals infected with a communicable disease for a period no longer the longest part of the incubation period, keeping them apart from others to observe, study, or restrict contact with others to control and eliminate the ability to spread the disease. In some hospitals or nursing homes, specially designated isolation rooms are used to segregate infected patients from all other patients so that special sanitary, infection control, and quarantine precautions and measures can be taken by the nursing and medical staff.

quarantine, complete In public health, this is the total limitation of freedom of movement of persons or animals infected with a communicable disease for a period no longer than the longest part of the incubation period to restrict contact with others to control and eliminate the ability to spread the disease.

quarantine, modified In public health and epidemiology, this is the partial limitation of freedom of movement of persons or animals infected with a communicable disease for a period no longer than the longest part of the incubation period to restrict contact with others to control and eliminate the ability to spread the disease. An example is keeping children who are infected with chickenpox home and out of school until they are no longer communicable.

quare (Lat.) Wherefore.

quare clausum fregit (Lat.) A legal action against a trespass used to recover damages by an unlawful entry.

quarter of coverage In Social Security and Medicare, this is when an eligible person earns enough income at work during one fourth of a calendar year to cover Social Security and to have it counted toward entitlement for Social Security and Medicare.

quash 1. To make void. 2. To overthrow. 3. To annul. 4. To suppress. 5. To completely do away with.

quasi (Lat.) 1. To a certain degree. 2. Analogous to. 3. Almost. 4. As if. 5. Similar. 6. Kind of; like unto it.

quasi contract 1. An implied contract. 2. A promise with no express agreement. 3. A legal obligation imposed by law with the force and legal consequences of a contract; used to prevent unfair personal gain at the unfair advantage or expense of others.

quasi-experimental design In health services research, this is a research design that has much of the traditional experimental research design in place but lacks certain design elements such as the action of the independent variable, the sampling process, and the balance between control and research groups.

quasi judicial 1. A semijudicial case. 2. Deciding function of an administrative agency.

quench tanks In environmental health, these are water-filled tanks used to cool incinerator residues or hot materials during industrial processes.

query Question; to question or ask; to inquire.

question In formal health administration meetings using parliamentary procedure, a proposal, idea, business item, or proposition presented to the assembly for a decision or vote. Stating "Question" means "I am ready to vote on the motion."

questions of privilege In health administration meetings using parliamentary procedure, this motion, called a point of privilege, is entered with concern for the welfare of the assembly in mind, such as might be used to introduce guests or provide a professional environment by asking a person to withdraw statements or comments. The chair must make a decision about the motion.

queue To form into a line while waiting to be treated or served; a line or file of people or things to be served or brought into service.

qui (Lat.) 1. He or she. 2. He or she who. 3. One who commits an act.

quick assets Anything that can be directly and immediately turned into cash.

quick ratio In health-care finance, this is a measure of a health-care organization's financial liquidity. It is calculated by dividing the sum of cash, marketable securities, and net accounts receivable by current liabilities. The quick ratio formula follows:

$$\frac{\text{Cash + Marketable securities + Net accounts receivable}}{\text{Current liabilities}}$$

quid pro quo (Lat.) 1. Something for something. 2. One thing of value given for another. 3. Consideration. 4. An exchange of items of similar value. 5. Something required in return for another thing of like value; used in the consideration of health manpower legislation to refer to requirements of health professional schools set as conditions of their receiving federal capitation payments.

quiescent Silent; dormant; inactive, as in a letter or document being silent or inactive.

quiet 1. Inactive. 2. Having no interference. 3. Undisturbed.

Quinlan case In health law, this is the somewhat landmark case (decided at the state level, not by the U.S. Supreme Court) of Karen Quinlan, a 22-year-old brain-damaged patient who became comatose after taking excessive amounts of drugs and alcohol and who was kept in a vegetative state for years on a mechanical respirator. Quinlan's parents requested that she be removed from the life-sustaining equipment, but the health-care providers refused. The father was appointed by the court as her legal guardian and had the life support system removed, a decision that was supported by the New Jersey Supreme Court. On removal of the breathing equipment, Ms Quinlan continued to breathe and was maintained on antibiotics and nutritional feeding tubes for a lengthy period of time and eventually died in 1985. The legal issues were the right to determine (to refuse) medical treatment on the basis of the right to privacy (In re Quinlan, 70 N.J. 10, 355 A.2d 647, *cert. denied*, 429 U.S. 922 [1976]).

quit 1. To leave a position of employment. 2. To give up possession of a place or position. 3. To end a relationship. 4. To discontinue or stop something; to leave.

qui timet (Lat.) 1. Because of fears. 2. A court order similar to an injunction. 3. To protect a person who fears he or she is in jeopardy.

quo ad hoc (Lat.) 1. To this extent. 2. With respect to the following.

quo animo (Lat.) With what intention or motive.

quod (Lat.) 1. That. 2. That which.

quod vide (Lat.) Used in legal references to mean "See that word"; refers the reader to a notation, abbreviated "q.v." and in law books "Q.V."

quorum In formal and official health-care meetings, this is the required number of persons who must be present at a meeting to take action, officially conduct business, or legally function as a group as set by the organization's by-laws. The number is often a majority, such as more than half the board of directors.

quota sampling In epidemiology, health services, and biomedical research, this is one form of research sample selection where subjects are selected as they are available or show up until the quota is met according to certain traits (e.g., a certain amount of females or males are needed in the study or a certain number of individuals in each age-group are selected until the number needed in each age-group for the study is reached).

quota share treaty A reinsurance program where the insurance company accepts a percentage of premiums and also the loss of certain designated types of insurance.

quo warranto (Lat.) 1. To show by what right one has the authority to perform an act. 2. With what authority. 3. Legally questioning the right of a person to undertake an act or hold an office.

q.v. *See quod vide.*

R

rabbi The spiritual head of a congregation and synagogue of Jews for religious practice and worship; clergyman who is ordained to conduct professional religious activities, is a teacher of the law and ritual, decides religious law, and serves as the leader of Jewish synagogues and religious ceremonies; may serve as a chaplain in a Jewish hospital or for those of the Jewish faith in any other health-care facility.

race In public health and health services, this is a classification process whereby individuals are placed in categories as determined by racial background. In 1976 the Federal Governments Data Systems, including the Census Bureau, created racial categories through a series of interviews. Persons age 17 years or older in national interviews were asked of their racial background and if they could best be described as American Indian or Alaskan Native, Asian or Pacific Islander, black, white, or other. They were also asked if their main national origin or ancestry was among one of the following: Puerto Rican, Cuban, Mexican, Mexicano, Mexican-American, Chicano, Latin American, or Spanish, all of which were classified as Hispanic. Depending on the source of data classification, race may be based on self-classification or on observation by an interviewer or others filling out survey questionnaires. If parents are of different races and one is white, the child is assigned the other parent's race. If either parent is Hawaiian, the child is classified as Hawaiian. In other cases where parents are of two different races, the child is assigned the father's race. In epidemiology, this is one aspect of the "person" and is part of vital statistics.

race/ethnicity In public health and health services, this is the classification of individuals by background, culture, racial ancestry, and heritage. Often individuals are assigned racial/ethnic groups such as white, black, Hispanic, and all other (American Indian, Pacific Islander, Asian, and other). There exists a need by the federal government, other government entities, and research organizations to develop a more diverse and clearly delineated set of racial and ethnic classification system because of the misjustice afforded American Indians, Asians, Pacific Islanders, and Hispanics who have a great deal of cultural and ethnic diversity within their groups yet are classified as "other." Even though this is a complex process, research should be more diligent in reflecting more closely the actual race/ethnicity of the respondents.

race statute In legal aspects of managing a healthcare organization's property, this is the party who first files a claim on or interest in real property and has prior legal right to that claim.

rad The standard measure of radioactive dose, superseding the Roentgen. The Atomic Energy Commission has established conservative limits of exposure for the protection of workers around radiation.

radiant energy (Q) In laser technology, this is the energy emitted, transferred, or received in the form of radiation and is referred to by the measurement unit of a joule (j).

radiation 1. The emission of very fast atomic particles or rays. Some elements are naturally radioactive, whereas others become radioactive after bombardment with a radioactive material; emission of rays from the nucleus of an atom; any form of energy propagated as rays, waves, or streams of energetic particles. 2. In environmental health, this is the emission and propagation of energy through space or through a material medium in the form of waves such as electromagnetic, sound, or elastic waves. Classification of radiation is Hertzian, infrared, visible (light), ultraviolet, X ray, alpha, beta, gamma, mixed, cosmic, or unknown.

radiation absorbed dose In environmental health, this is a unit of radiation. One rad of absorbed dose is equal to .01 joules per kilogram.

radiation areas In environmental health, this is any place accessible to humans in which there exists radiation at such levels that a major portion of the body could receive, in any 1 hour, a dose in excess of 5 millirems or, in any 5 consecutive days, a dose in excess of 100 millirems.

radiation-induced genetic effects In medical science, these are any changes induced in both somatic and germinal cells by radiation; radiation-induced hereditary diseases.

radiation oncology services In hospital cancer treatment services, this is the delivery of care pertaining to the use of radiation therapy for patients with tumors. In the accreditation process and quality assessment, standards are applied to evaluate a hospital's performance in providing radiation oncology services.

radiation protection officers In occupational health and safety, these are individuals who by training are technically competent persons designated by the management of the health-care organization to supervise the application of radiation protection regulations and to provide advice on all relevant aspects of radiation protection.

radiation safety Actions taken to protect the community from unnecessary exposure to ionizing and nonionizing radiation from controllable industrial and nuclear sources and to minimize exposure of patients and medical personnel to clinical radiation. Major areas of radiation safety concerns are industrial radiation, medical radiation, and radioactive wastes. Safety is concerned with the recognition, evaluation, and control of risks from radiation exposure or risk of exposure.

radiation shields In occupational health and safety, these are materials interposed between a source of radiation and persons or equipment or other objects to attenuate the radiation.

radiation standards In occupational health and safety, these are the levels and regulations that set maximum exposure limits for protection of the public from radioactive materials (EPA).

radiation therapist An allied health-care professional who assists the physician in treating a patient through the therapeutic use of radiation. *See also radiation therapy technologist; health physicist.*

radiation therapy A treatment modality used to reverse the spread of cancer and to cure diseases through the use of radioisotopes and various forms of radiation. Treatments are provided in specialized facilities located in hospitals or other health-care facilities. Ionizing radiation is used in the treatment of cancer patients by a radiation therapist or a physician qualified in therapeutic radiology.

radiation therapy technologist Allied health personnel who use equipment to generate X rays and electron beams in the therapeutic treatment of disease under the direction of a physician with a specialization as a radiologist. This technologist exposes specific areas of the body to prescribed doses of ionizing radiation, observes and reports patient reactions, and assists in tumor localization and dosimetric procedures. They assist in maintaining the proper operation of controlling devices and equipment, observe safety measures for patients and clinical personnel, help maintain patient records, and assist in the preparation and handling of radioactive materials used in treatment procedures. Nearly all radiation therapy technologists are employed in hospitals or clinics and are supervised by a physician in the operation of a variety of laboratory equipment such a high-energy linear accelerators, radioactive isotopes, and particle generators and are usually graduates of a 12-month program or an associate degree program in the field.

radio- Prefix meaning "rays," "X rays," or "radius."

radioactive articles In occupational health and safety, these are any manufactured instruments and articles such as an instrument, clock, electronic tube or apparatus, or similar instruments and articles having radioactive materials as a component part.

radioactive contamination In occupational health and safety, this is the deposition of radioactive material in any place it is not desired and particularly in any place where its presence may be harmful. The harm may contaminate, or it may invalidate an experiment or procedure or be a source of excessive exposure to personnel.

radioactive contents In occupational health and safety and environmental health and hazardous waste management, these are any radioactive materials together with any contaminated liquids or gases in a package.

radioactive decay In occupational health and safety and medical care, this is the disintegration of the nucleus of an unstable nuclide by the spontaneous emission of charged particles and/or photons.

radioactive effluent In environmental health, these are any airborne or liquid radioactive materials discharged into the environment.

radioactive half-life The time required for a radioactive substance to lose 50% of its activity by decay. Each radio nuclide has a different half-life.

radioactive implants In medical care, these are the insertion of radioactive material such as radium, cobalt-60, cesium-137, or iridium-19 into the body for the treatment of malignancies.

radioactive materials Any materials or combination of materials that spontaneously emit ionizing radiation; any material having a specific activity greater than 0.002 microcuries per gram.

radioactive mixed wastes Any radioactive materials that also contain hazardous waste constituents.

radioactive substances *See radioactive materials.*

radioactive waste In occupational health and safety and environmental health, these are all solid or fluid materials of no value containing radioactivity; discarded items such as clothing, containers, equipment rubble, residues, or soils contaminated with radioactivity; soils, equipment, or other items containing induced radioactivity such that the levels exceed safe limits for unconditional release; any waste materials containing radioactive materials that exceed concentrations that may render them dangerous.

radioactive waste management In occupational health and safety, this is the planning, organizing, and controlling of activities that provide for the collection, storage, transportation, transfer, processing, treatment, and disposal of radioactive wastes.

radioactivity In medical care, occupational health and safety, and environmental health, emission of energy in the form of alpha, beta, or gamma radiation. A few elements such as radium are naturally radioactive, whereas others are induced; the property or characteristics of radioactive materials that spontaneously disintegrate with the emission of energy in the form of radiation. The unit of measure for radioactivity is the curie.

radiobiology The study of radiation's effect on living things.

radiochemical Any compound, substance, or mixture containing a sufficient amount of radioactivity to be detected by a Geiger counter.

radiodiagnosis A diagnostic procedure that involves X-ray examination.

radio frequency radiation 1. A form of radiation that does not change the structure of atoms but does heat tissue and may cause harmful biological effects. 2. Microwaves, radio waves, and low-frequency electromagnetic fields from high-voltage transmission lines.

radiographer Under the general direction of a physician, usually a radiologist, radiographers are primarily responsible for the operation of X-ray equipment and the preparation of patients for various types of diagnostic procedures. Radiographers prepare radio opaque mixtures administered to patients so that internal organs may be observed and identified on film, position patients, adjust X-ray equipment to correct settings, and determine proper voltage, current, and exposure time for the production of radiographs. These technologists use anatomical knowledge, positioning of the body, and radiographic techniques to create anatomical radiographically generated structures on radiographic film using X rays. They assist the radiologist in fluoroscopic procedures and are responsible for maintaining equipment in proper working order, processing film, and keeping patient records. Although examinations are normally conducted in the hospital or a physician's office, radiographers are also capable of operating mobile X-ray equipment at the patient's bedside or in the hospital operating room. The extent of the services provided by the radiographer varies with employment settings and other circumstances. In some states, the range of duties of the radiographer is limited by law (e.g., they are prohibited from injecting contrast media into patients). In most locations, however, the range of duties is determined by the hospital, clinic, or other place of employment. In other situations, the range of duties is determined by the physician responsible for radiographic diagnosis. These technologists usually have a 2-year associate degree in radiography or a bachelors degree in the area. *See also radiologic technologists.*

radiographic medical technology An educational training program that prepares individuals to apply Roentgen rays and radioactive substances to patients for diagnostic and therapeutic purposes under the supervision of a radiologist. Training includes instruction in anatomy, physiology, physics, radiographic positioning techniques, radiation protection, equipment maintenance, film processing, and darkroom techniques.

radioimmunoassay Antibody reaction based on the use of a substance labeled radioactive that reacts with the substance being tested (e.g., hepatitis antigen).

radioisotope A radioactive chemical element, some of which are used in medicine for diagnostic and therapeutic purposes in nuclear medicine and oncology.

radioisotope facility A specialized nuclear medicine service of a radiation therapy department in a hospital.

radiological accidents The loss of control of radioactive materials that presents a potential hazard to personnel, public health, property, or the environment or that exceeds the established limit for exposure to ionizing radiation.

radiological area monitoring In occupational health and safety, this is the routine checking of the level of radiation or of radioactive contamination of any particular area, building, room, or equipment.

radiological monitoring In occupational health and safety, this is periodic or continuous determination of the amounts of ionizing radiation or radioactive contamination present in an occupied region as a safety measure for purposes of health protection.

radiological surveys In occupational health and safety, these are processes used in the evaluation of the radiation hazards incident to the production, use, and existence of radioactive materials or other sources of radiation under a specific set of conditions. Assessment activities customarily include a physical survey of the disposition of materials and equipment, measurements or estimates of the levels of radiation that may be involved, and a sufficient knowledge of processes using or affecting these materials to predict hazards resulting from expected or possible changes in materials or equipment.

radiological warfare The purposeful use of radioactive contaminated materials as a weapon of offense in a nuclear war.

radiologic personnel In hospitals and clinics, these are technicians or technologists such as medical radiographers, ultrasound technologists, health physics technicians, radiation monitors, radiation protectors, radiologic assistants, X-ray assistants, personnel radiation monitors, radiation therapy technicians, and nuclear medicine technicians who participate in diagnostic or oncology treatment activities. Technologists usually have more training and advanced experience than technicians.

radiologic technologist An individual who maintains and safely uses X-ray, CT, and MRI equipment and supplies to demonstrate portions of the human body on X-ray film or fluoroscopic or computer screen for diagnostic purposes and may supervise and/or teach other radiologic personnel. Approximately one third work for hospitals, the remainder work for independent X-ray laboratories or multispecialty clinics and in physician's offices and government agencies. The American Medical Association Council on Medical Education formerly approved radiologic technology programs conducted by hospitals and medical schools and by colleges with hospital affiliation. Programs are open to high school graduates, although a few require 1 or 2 years of college. The length of training varies from a minimum of 2 years in a hospital radiology department or a junior college in affiliation with one or more hospitals offering an associate degree to a 4-year university degree.

radiologic technologist, registered A medical radiographer who has met the necessary educational, internship, and externship requirements and has graduated from a program in radiologic technology approved by the Council on Medical Education of the American Medical Association or who has equivalent training and education, has successfully passed an examination, and is registered by the American College of Radiology and the American Society of Radiologic Technologists.

radiologic technologist, qualified See *radiologic technologist; radiologic technologist, registered; diagnostic radiology services.*

radiologist A licensed physician who has advanced training, has completed a residency, and specializes in radiology, including the diagnosis and evaluation of X-ray, CT, and MRI scans as well as the use of radiation in the treatment of disease, especially cancer, mainly through the use of radioisotopes.

radiologists, anesthesiologists, and pathologists (RAPs) The small group of physicians who commonly do most of their medical practice in hospitals. Emergency medicine physicians who work in the hospital emergency room are also often considered among the four physicians who do their work at the hospital and who are allowed to be hired or salaried by a hospital even in states that restrict hospitals from hiring physicians. Under the Prospective Payment System (PPS) and Diagnosis-Related Groups (DRGs), RAP physicians work is paid through the hospital rather than directly to the physicians.

radiology A medical specialty and branch of medicine that uses ionizing radiation for diagnosis and therapy. X-ray and nuclear medicine, as well as CT and MRI scans, are used and are often now referred to as "imaging medicine."

Diagnostic nuclear radiology, diagnostic radiology, and therapeutic radiology are branches of radiology that use radiation or radioactive substances for diagnosis and treatment.

radiology department (service) A clinical department in a health-care facility where patients go for X rays, CT scans, PET scans, or MRI imaging and that is staffed by radiologic technologists who work under the direct supervision of a radiologist. Some departments are called medical imaging departments because of advances in technology and the addition of CT scanners and MRI imaging.

radio-opaque Being visible to X ray. Substances that make body structures visible or opaque are iodine and barium salts.

radiotherapy In medical care, this is the treatment of tumors and cancer and related diseases with the application of relatively high dosages of radiation and the use of electromagnetic radiation of several varieties.

radiotoxicity In medical care, this is the potential of an isotope to cause damage to living tissue by absorption of energy from the disintegration of the radioactive material introduced into the body.

radium (Ra) A metallic radioactive element with a half-life of 1602 to 1622 years, radium exists in a continuous state of disintegration and so is useful in treating disease because it kills cells, especially young, immature, actively growing, abnormal cells such as cancer cells.

radium therapy The treatment of cancer and other diseases through the use of radioisotopes.

radon (Rn) A radioactive element with a half-life of 3.8 days, radon is a gas that is a by-product of radium disintegration.

RADTT Radiation therapy technologist.

RAG Regional Advisory Group.

Rahe, Richard, MD One of the pioneers in stress research, he and Thomas Holmes, MD, both psychiatrists at the University of Washington at the time, developed the first measure of stress caused by life change events. A 43-question scale/research instrument (referred to as the Social Readjustment Rating Scale, the Schedule of Recent Events, and the Schedule of Life Change Experiences) was developed to identify stressful life change experiences.

raise an issue To present a concern or an issue; the presentation of a claim in a pleading, in the trial proceeding, or in litigation process.

raison d'etre (French) Reason for being.

RAM Random access memory. In computers, the place where the program being used is stored in the computer's memory.

R and C Reasonable and customary. In managed care, this term clarifies patient care charges that have been billed to the health plan on the basis of a fee-for-services reimbursement structure.

RAND Corporation A nonprofit health and social services research organization that was established in 1948 to further and promote scientific, educational, and charitable purposes, all for the public's welfare and security of the United States of America. Rigorous analyses of significant national problems are undertaken to provide policymakers and the public with facts, insights, and scientific findings on the concerns surrounding policy issues. Through the RAND Graduate School of Policy Studies, graduate education is provided, leading to a doctoral degree in policy analysis. Research, dissemination, and educational activities are financially supported by federal, state, and local governments through grants and contracts and through grants from foundations, philanthropic organizations, and corporate funds. An endowment fund, as well as fees that are charged for services, is also established to generate funding.

random 1. A statistical and research design term that refers to the process of research subjects or case selection where a subject is selected by chance or without any bias or planning; to be purposefully controlled or governed by chance while avoiding a deterministic approach of subject selection. 2. In epidemiology or health services research, these are any of a number of approaches used as objective and unbiased means of selecting subjects, thus allowing all subjects of a research study an equal and fair chance of being selected for either the research group or the control group.

random access The ability to obtain information and data from where it is located in the computer without being dependent on the location of previously obtained data. *See random*.

random assignment In epidemiology and health services research, this is the process by which each subject of a study has an equal opportunity to be included in either the experimental group or the control group, ensuring equal composition of both groups and unbiased placement of subjects in the research process. *See random; randomization.*

random controlled trial (RCT) In health services and biomedical research, this is an experimental prospective study for assessing the effects of a particular drug or medical procedure in which subjects are assigned on a random basis to either of two groups: experimental or control. The experimental group receives the drug or procedure, whereas the control group does not. A series of laboratory tests and clinical examinations are performed on both groups in an attempt to detect any difference, usually using the double-blind technique. The goals of these drug studies are to determine how the drug is absorbed, metabolized, and eliminated; levels of the drug that are tolerated; any obvious toxic effects; long-term toxic and carcinogenic effects; the effectiveness of the drug in prevention or control of a disease or symptom; and the safe and appropriate dosage of the drug for the various patients in whom it will be used. *See random; randomization.*

random error In epidemiology, health services, and biomedical research, this is an unbiased and unpredictable error that occurs in the process of research and where the mean tends toward zero in repeated experiments or measures.

randomization 1. In epidemiology, statistics, and research design, this is the probability or chance of selection; a planned scientific unbiased purposeful choosing process or methodology by which cases or subjects are selected, all having a fixed, equal chance and determinate probability of being selected or not being selected as determined by a predetermined planned selection process as opposed to a haphazard approach. 2. In epidemiology, health services, and biomedical research, this is the process by which cases, subjects, or individuals are chosen for either the study or the control group. *See random.*

random sample In epidemiology, statistics, and research design, this is a case or subject that has been selected not by a haphazard chance but by a planned selection process based on chance where all subjects have a chance of being selected without bias, with all samples being taken from a set of potential subjects, and with all cases having a chance for selection. *See random; randomization; random sampling.*

random sampling In epidemiology, health services, and biomedical research, this is the process by which each subject of research or each unit of observation has an equal chance of being included in the study, ensuring an unbiased representation of the total population to which findings are generalized. Subjects are chosen solely by chance or by a system that guarantees a random chance selection. *See random; randomization; random sample.*

range In statistics, a measure of variation determined by the end values; the distance between the highest and lowest number or values in a series of numbers or observations. The highest number from a series of numbers minus the lowest number equals the range score.

range of distribution In statistics, this is the difference between the highest score and the lowest score in a set of numbers. *See range.*

range of motion (ROM) The extent of movement in a given joint. Each joint has a normal range. A range of motion of particular importance in rehabilitation is the functional range, which is less than normal but enables the limited joint or combination of joints to be functional for performing activities of daily living.

ranking scale In descriptive statistics using an ordinal scale, as used in epidemiology, this is the process of establishing a high to low arrangement of selections from lowest to highest with numbers assigned to each level of ranking. In a research questionnaire, it is common to use a Likert scale arrangement such as a five-point scale ranging from most desirable to least desirable, with a set of scales presented for each question and only one choice being selected.

RAP *See resident assessment protocol; RAP MDs.*

RAP area trigger In long-term care, this is when a risk factor common to long-term-care patients is experienced by a resident of a nursing home (e.g., a pressure sore or fall), initiating intervention activities by the nursing or social services staff. *See resident assessment protocol.*

rape 1. To take by force. 2. Forced sexual intercourse with an unwilling victim; a felony.

RAP MDs Radiologist, Anesthesiologist, Pathologist. Physicians who are usually employed by a hospital and who practice their profession in the confines of the hospital. *See radiologists, anesthesiologists, and pathologists.*

rapport In health administration and human resources management, this is a harmonious accord between two persons. In a group, it is the mutual responsiveness, as shown by spontaneous and sympathetic understanding of one another's needs.

RAPs *See RAP MDs; radiologists, anesthesiologists, and pathologists.*

rap sessions In human resources management in health-care organizations, these are communication meetings between managers and groups of employees to discuss complaints and concerns, take suggestions, elicit opinions, and answer questions. This term is somewhat dated.

raspatory In medical care, this is a file-like surgical instrument used to scrape bone surface; a surgical steel rasp.

rate 1. A fixed amount, usually based on a formula or adjustable fee based on a set standard. 2. A regular or usual fee charged to all persons for the same service or care. 3. In managed care, this is the premium that is charged to employer groups for their specific benefit package and is usually prepaid; the amount of money per enrollment classification paid to a health plan for medical coverage and charged on a monthly basis. 4. In epidemiology and descriptive statistics, this is any figure expressed as a rate that indicates the number of occurrences, cases, or incidents of any given occurrence as they relate to the general population of an area in the same time period (e.g., 20 deaths per 1000 live births). Rates are composed of the exposed group, subgroup, cases of illness, etc. and are included in the numerator for a specific time period. The numerator is a part of the population of the denominator. The numerator is divided by the denominator for the same time period, which consists of the total population, general population, the population at risk, etc. and must be multiplied by 1000 or 10,000 or 100,000. "Rate" is often confused with "ratio" and "proportion." *See ratio; mortality rate; incidence rate; proportion.*

rate, blended In health-care finance and under the Prospective Payment System of the Health Care Financing Administration, this is used to designate a rate formed by combining the hospital-specific rate and the preestablished Medicare rate.

rate cell verification *See HCFA rate cell verification.*

rate, death *See mortality rate.*

rate difference In epidemiology and descriptive statistics, this is the difference seen when two rates are compared (e.g., comparing the rate of a population exposed to a disease to the rate of a similar population not exposed to the same cause of disease). The difference of rates helps determine causation relationships.

rate fixing In health-care finance, this is the power to control fees, set charges, or control the rate of exchange that a hospital, health-care facility, or company may get for its services.

rate, hospital-specific In health-care finance and under the Prospective Payment System of the Health Care Financing Administration, this is one approach to calculating a hospital's reimbursement that focuses on the past financial activity of a single hospital to help determine rates of reimbursements.

rate, inclusive In health-care finance, this is a prospective payment method where a single charge is assessed for a day of inpatient care for all services provided, with no regard for the number of procedures, treatments, tests, or services provided or the level of care needed.

rate, interim In health-care finance, this is a retrospective reimbursement method where the amount paid to a provider by a third-party payer occurs on a periodic basis.

rate making In managed care and insurance, this is a method of assessing and determining pricing structures for various types of insurance; establishing premium rates for a health plan and its various types of coverage. Actuaries, as well as health plans, consider many factors when setting life insurance rates such as mortality rates, age of clientele, morbidity levels, and utilization rates. Financial considerations include interest rates, expenses, lapse rates, and taxes.

rate, morbidity *See incidence rate; prevalence rate.*

rate, mortality *See mortality rate.*

rate, occupancy In hospital administration, this the comparison between occupied hospital beds and total available beds, expressed as a rate. The rate is determined by dividing the numerator, which consists of the average number of beds occupied for a specific time period, by the denominator, which includes average number of beds available in the same time period multiplied by 100. The occupancy rate formula follows:

$$\frac{\text{Average number of beds occupied for a specific time period}}{\text{Average number of beds available in the same time period}} \times 1000$$

rate odds ratio *See odds ratio.*

rate of return In health-care finance, this is the earnings received on an investment given as a percentage of the cost or of the purchase price.

rate, per diem In hospital administration, this is determined by placing total cost in the numerator and the total number of inpatient days for the same time period in the denominator. This is a crude rate that does not take into account specific rates such as cause, disease, severity, diagnosis, and procedure. The per diem rate formula follows:

$$\frac{\text{Total costs for patient care for a specific time period}}{\text{Total number of inpatient days for the same time period}} \times 1000$$

rate process In managed care, this is the assessment of an employer group or a member of a health plan to set a premium rate on the basis of the type of risk. Key factors considered in the risk rating are age, sex, location, type of industry, base capitation, plan design, family size, demographics, and overhead and administrative costs.

rate ranges In human resource management, these are entry-level salaries up to the highest amounts of pay available that have been set for each job classification in the health services organization.

rate ratio The ratio of two rates. In epidemiology, this formula is used to compare the unexposed population to the exposed population by calculating a ratio for both groups and then calculating a rate using the rates for both groups. *See relative risk; rate; ratio.*

rate review In health-care finance, this is a prospective assessment of a health-care facility's financial information, budget data, and related charges and costs to determine reasonableness of rates and rate increases. This is usually conducted by third-party payers or government agencies.

rate, room In hospital administration, this is the cost the hospital charges for 1 day of care, services, hotel charges, board, and basic nursing care. This rate differs from the inclusive rate. Also referred to as "daily service charge."

rate, rural In health-care finance under the Prospective Payment System of the Health Care Financing Administration, this is a special and different Medicare rate for hospitals that must be classified as rural, including being over 25 miles from the next nearest hospital in the SMSA.

rates, adjusted or standardized Used in epidemiology and vital statistics, these rates are used to compare two population groups in which the age distribution differs.

rate setting In health-care finance, this the process of attempting to contain costs and control the cost of health care delivery by regulating charges for health care (done by government agencies). In managed care, rates are set by contract negotiations rather than government regulations. *See also rate fixing; rate review.*

rate stratification by infection risk *See nosocomial infection rate.*

rate, urban In health-care finance under the Prospective Payment System of the Health Care Financing Administration, this is a special and different Medicare rate for hospitals that must be classified as urban.

ratification 1. The formal approval of a document. 2. Confirmation of an act. 3. Adoption by proper authority of a proposed action.

rating The process of determining rates or the cost of insurance for individuals, groups, or classes of risks.

rating process In managed care and insurance, this is the process of assessing an eligible employee group or individuals to determine premium rates on the basis of the type of risk the group presents. Risk factors used in the rating formula are age/sex factors, location, type of industry, base capitation factor, average family size, benefit plan design, demographics, potential utilization, and administration costs.

rating scale In human resource management, this is a questionnaire established for use in the performance appraisal process that requires the supervisor (the rater) to provide an evaluation of a worker's performance. Job performance is assessed along a range of possible levels of performance as set forth in a scale that usually ranges from inadequate to very satisfactory on a 1-to-5 scale. The most common is the graphic rating scale, which uses objective job descriptors and traits arranged on a 1-to-5 rating scale.

rating system, five-star *See JCAHO five-star rating system.*

ratio The results of comparing one quantity to another; a numerical expression used to compare how a population relates to the total population or a segment thereof; a fixed relation between two items, things, or populations as expressed in degrees; the quotient of a quantity divided by another like or similar to the first (shown as a fraction). If the numerator is divided by the denominator, the result is a proportion that is expressed as a decimal and if multiplied by 100 becomes a percentage; used in epidemiology, health-care finance, descriptive statistics, quantitative analysis, etc.

ratio analysis 1. In descriptive statistics, this is the assessment of the proportionate relationship between two different amounts or between sets of ratios. 2. In health-care finance and health-care administration, this is the assessment by a health administrator of the various financial ratios used in health-care financial management to determine financial viability. Examples are the following: current ratio, quick ratio, acid test ratio, working capital ratio, liquidity ratio, leverage ratio, and efficiency ratio.

ratio decidendi (Lat.) 1. In health law, this is the basic and essential issue used in deciding a case. 2. The major reason for, or the determining factor in, a decision.

rational behavior therapy (RBT) In mental health services, this is a highly directive form of psychotherapy embracing the cognitive and behavioral areas of psychology. It is used to teach people rational thinking and reasoning skills instead of perceiving the world from a subjective opinion viewpoint, encouraging less emotional upset and being better able to cope with life's problems. This therapy is derived from cognitive theory, learning theory, and behavior therapy and goes beyond behavioral conditioning and reinforcers. *See also rational self-counseling.*

rational emotive therapy (RET) In mental health services, this form of cognitive psychotherapy, developed by Albert Ellis, PhD, is contrasted with psychoanalysis, behavior modification, traditional behavior therapy, and other related theories as it utilizes an A-B-C theory of personality disturbance (A is the activating event, B is the belief system, and C is disturbed emotional consequences), which helps a person with emotional problems overcome inappropriate feelings and behaviors in a relatively brief time period. It employs several cognitive, emotional, and behavioral therapy methods while creating a philosophical view of life. Also referred to as "cognitive-behavioral therapy."

rationalization In mental health, this is a mental or defense mechanism in which a person justifies feelings, behavior, and motives that would otherwise be intolerable.

rational self-analysis (RSA) In mental health services, this is the homework behavioral therapy aspect of rational behavioral therapy and rational self-counseling that actively involves the patient in his or her own therapy. Such self-analysis helps the patient engage in calm, objective self-analysis as opposed to emotionally charged, distorted decisions. It helps separate feelings from thoughts, thus allowing one to have an objective view of events. It relies on an A-B-C-D approach to events or upsetting situations where self-talk, emotions, and facts are separated. "A" represents facts and is compared to "B," which is the self-talk about the event, "C" represents feelings and emotions and the subjective aspects, and "D" is irrational self-talk and is compared to "B." Emotions are compared to the facts.

rational self-counseling (RSC) In mental health services, this is a personal approach to rational behavioral therapy that is a constant and continual process that the patient or client does in everyday living to overcome mental, emotional, and behavioral problems. A rational self-analysis is done to help the patient or client learn be a more rational person, thus having less emotional upset and fewer self-defeating behaviors.

rational service areas In health services delivery, this the designation of the area to be served by a health-care organization; the logical catchment area of a health service based on criteria such as size, natural boundaries, transportation routes, and language barriers.

rational validity In human resource management in health services, these are the tests that assess skills needed to perform well on the job or to ascertain skills needed for good job performance where an obvious relationship between performance and certain skills and traits is needed for success on the job.

ratio of cost to charges In health-care finance, this is the comparison of total charges to total costs for a procedure, service, treatment, therapy, good, or equipment; used as an accounting technique to ensure that the cost is less than the charges to ensure that a loss does not occur and that a profit is realized.

ratio of program costs to charges In health-care finance, this is a method of dividing and partitioning departmental costs among third-party-payer services on the basis of the comparison of total costs to total charges.

ratio scale In descriptive statistics, this scale of measurement has much of the same characteristics as the interval scale plus a zero point. Examples of ratio scales include a tire gauge, thermometer, weight measuring scale, speedometer, and number of participants attending an immunization clinic or participating in a survey. The ratio scale relies on an equal distance between all numbers and a consistent value of all numbers and the distance between them in the scale. The distance between 7 and 8 is the same as the distance between 77 and 78, 50 is half the amount of 100, 30 is twice the amount of 15, etc. Ratio scales are used in time assessments, elapsed time, scores of exams, etc. Ratio scales are basic to most descriptive and inferential statistical analyses and are, at the least, a starting point for most analyses; also used in epidemiology.

raw data 1. In health information management, these are the facts processed by a computer to produce new data or information. In health services research, this is any unprocessed information and data that have not yet been analyzed. 2. In occupational health and safety, these are any laboratory worksheets, records, notes, memoranda, or exact copies that are the result of original observations and activities of a study.

raw sewage In environmental health and liquid waste management, this is untreated wastewater.

RBRVS Resource-based relative value scale (used under Medicare). *See relative value scale.*

RBT *See rational behavior therapy.*

RCC *See ratio of costs to charges; ratio of program costs to charges.*

RCRA *See Resource Conservation and Recovery Act.*

RCRA and HSWA Resource Conservation and Recovery Act (RCRA) and the Hazardous and Solid Waste Amendments (HSWA). *See Resource Conservation and Recovery Act.*

RCT *See random controlled trial.*

R.D. *See registered dietician.*

re (Lat.) Concerning; in the matter of; in the case of. *See also in re.*

reach In health services delivery, this is the ability of a program to contact, influence, or impact those attending or those exposed to an intervention or service.

reaction formation In mental health, this is a mental or defense mechanism wherein attitudes and behavior are adopted that are the opposite of beliefs or impulses the individual has.

reactive effects In health promotion, epidemiology, and health services evaluation, this is when subjects of evaluation processes or research respond or react to the experimental or surrounding conditions as well as to the evaluation or research in which they are participants, thus challenging the external validity of the evaluation of the research, service, or program.

reactive management In health administration, this is when administrative action and decision making is a reaction instead of a planned move; decisions are made in response to changes, challenges, or problems rather than planning for and developing strategies and anticipating and developing interventions ahead of time before events occur.

readiness In mental health care or health education processes, this is the state of being ready and accepting, having an open mind, and being open to intellectual, emotional, or behavioral growth; maturation, growth and development needed to be able to perform certain activities such as learning. Referred to as "readiness to learn."

readmission In hospital administration, this is returning a discharged patient to the hospital shortly after discharge with the second admission related to the cause of the original admission; a second admission related to the same diagnosis or illness as the original admission, often because of complications, recurrence of the problem, or failure of treatment in the original course of stay and treatment. A condition, illness, injury, or diagnosis different from the first admission would be considered a new admission.

readmission, rate *See readmission rate.*

readmission rate In hospital administration, this the comparison of a hospital's patients who re-enter the health-care facility within a given time period after being discharged. The readmission rate formula follows:

$$\frac{\text{Total number of patients readmitted for a given time period}}{\text{Total number of patient discharges for the same time period}} \times 1000$$

readmit *See readmission.*

read-only memory (ROM) In health information management and computers, this a computer's memory that can be read but not altered by computer instructions.

real estate investment trusts (REIT) In health-care finance, this is one form of investment used in the health-care industry and is considered a relatively safe investment, especially if a certificate of need is required for construction of long-term-care facilities.

real evidence In health law, these are actual objects used to prove facts or used for evidence and shown to a judge or jury (e.g., X rays, medical records, items or objects used in a crime, wounds, and fingerprints).

realistic job preview In health administration and human resource management, this is a recruitment and orientation approach where the job applicant is permitted to see and participate in the type of work, equipment, and working conditions involved in the actual job prior to accepting the job or the hiring decision being made.

reality Having an objective view of things and factual events.

reality orientation A form of therapy used on withdrawn persons or those who have given up. James C. Folsom first organized a "reality-orientation program" in Winter Veterans Administration Hospital in Topeka, Kansas, in 1958. Folsom believed patients are not ready for remotivation until they have gone through the reality orientation classes. The program is ideally suited for patients who have been institutionalized for long periods of time or have moderate to severe organic brain impairment. The treatment involves having patients presented repeatedly with basic personal and current information, beginning with the patient's name, where he or she is, and the date. Only when these basic facts have been relearned is the patient presented with other facts such as age, hometown, former occupation, family, weather, and events of the day.

reality principle In psychoanalytic theory, the construct that pleasure represents the instinctual wishes of a person and is normally modified by the demands, expectations, and requirements of society.

reality testing In mental health, this is to constantly evaluate the world around you so as to differentiate adequately between reality and the appearance of reality in one's internal world; to seek and receive feedback on facts and realities of life.

reality therapist In mental health services, this a psychotherapist with specialized training who assists the chronically mentally ill to become reoriented to time, place, and person.

reality therapy In mental health services, this is a form of psychotherapy developed by William Glasser, MD and based somewhat on psychiatric theory. It leads patients toward reality and toward grappling successfully with the tangible and intangible aspects of the real world; a therapy that takes the patient toward reality and responsibility in the here and now.

realize 1. To make real. 2. To convert into monetary form. 3. To cash in.

realized In health law or health administration, this is to have something come to you; to have an understanding; to receive money or property.

realized profit In health-care finance, this is the actual possession of money gained or profits earned and available.

real property law The area of law dealing with the purchase, ownership, transfer, and rights related to real estate.

real time In health information management and computers, this is the actual time used by a computer; the actual time taken to perform a computation on a computer.

real time processing In health-care information management and computers, this is an on-line functioning system that allows for interactive processing of data or information to keep all activities current.

reasonable 1. Denoting a decision based on the facts of a situation or case rather than on an abstract legal principle. 2. Possessing the ability to think clearly. 3. Being able to reach sound and competent conclusions. 4. Acting in a sound or sensible manner.

reasonable act In health law, this is any act that may fairly, justly, and reasonably be expected or required of a party or person.

reasonable and customary charges In health-care finance and managed care, these are the amounts of money most commonly or most frequently charged and the prevailing fees for certain health services or medical procedures in a certain locale or geographic area. Managed care or medical insurance reimbursements are often based on this concept. *See reasonable charge.*

reasonable assistance Aid and care given in emergencies by one capable of providing basic emergency care.

reasonable care In health law, this is the amount of knowledge and skill ordinarily used by a competent health-care provider with equal experience and education in treating the sick and injured. *See also reasonable man; standard of care.*

reasonable charge In health-care finance, for any specific service covered under Medicare, the lower of the customary charge by a particular physician for that service and the prevailing charge by physicians in the geographic area for that service. Reimbursement is based on the lower of the reasonable and actual charges; the amount of coverage allowed for a given health service or medical procedure or supply as set by Medicare for a certain locale. The term is used for any charge payable by an insurance program, which is determined in a similar but not necessarily identical fashion. *See also comparability provision; Section 224.*

reasonable charges In health-care finance, this is done on an individual physician basis by the Medicare Part B carrier. In the absence of unusual treatment or procedures, this is the lowest of a health-care provider's customary charges, the prevailing charge, the actual charge, or the carrier's charge for a comparable service.

reasonable cost 1. In health-care finance, this is generally the amount that a third-party payer using cost-related reimbursement will actually reimburse. Under Medicare, reasonable costs are costs actually incurred in delivering health services, excluding any part of such incurred costs found to be unnecessary for the efficient delivery of needed health services (see Section 1861 of the Social Security Act). The items or elements of cost, both direct and indirect, that the regulations specify as reimbursable are known as "allowable costs." Such costs are reimbursable on the basis of a facility's actual costs to the extent that they are reasonable and related to patient care. Under certain conditions, the following items may be included as reasonable allowable costs: capital depreciation; interest expenses; educational activities; research costs related to patient care; unrestricted grants, gifts, and income from endowments; value of services of nonpaid workers; compensation of owners; payments to related organizations; return on equity capital of proprietary providers; and the inpatient routine nursing differential. Bad debts may only be included to the extent that institutions fail in good-faith efforts to collect the debts. 2. In environmental health and hazardous waste cleanup, these are amounts that may be recovered for the cost of performing a damage assessment; when the injury determination quantification and damage determination phases have a well-defined relationship to one another and are coordinated. *See also Section 223; reasonable and customary charges.*

reasonable doubt In health law, this is knowledge of facts that induces doubt in the mind of an ordinary and prudent person.

reasonable man (person) 1. In health law, this is a theoretical, ordinary person who possesses the same physical characteristics of the defendant, who possesses foreseeability, and who is of good judgment; an ideal person possessing the same characteristics, background, knowledge, skills, and physical makeup of any average person; an expected standard of behavior. *See also ordinary person; foreseeability, doctrine of; standard of care.*

reasonableness In health law, this is having average, basic, yet good judgment; being fair, observant, and sensible and having a degree of common sense. *See reasonable man (person).*

reasonableness doctrine *See reasonable man (person).*

reasonable reimbursement In managed care, this is negotiated between the health plan and health-care provider, as managed care desires the rates to be as low as possible and the amounts predictable. The health-care provider cannot lose money and be able to maintain an effective, profitable, and growing organization if the rates are too low or just meet expenses because equipment wears out, technology advances, personnel need raises, and growth must be planned for. Risk should be shared fairly by both sides.

reasonably prudent man doctrine A person who uses ordinary care and skill. *See reasonable man (person).*

reason for examination In heath services delivery and utilization evaluation, this addresses the purpose that a client/patient presents him- or herself for medical examination such as not feeling well; to meet a requirement such as in employment, school, athletics, and licensure.

rebating In managed care and insurance, this is the process of offering a prospective client or employer group a special inducement to purchase the policy or accept the plan on the basis of a return of some funds or a part of the commissions. This practice is prohibited in most states in the insurance industry.

rebut 1. To dispute. 2. To defeat the effect 3. To oppose. 4. To answer to. 5. To take away the effect of the evidence of an argument.

rebuttal In health law, this is the act of refuting through argumentation, evidence, or proof.

rebutting evidence In health law, this is evidence

used to disprove evidence introduced by the opposing party.

recall The process of recollecting thoughts, words, and actions of a past event in an attempt to remember what actually happened.

recall judgment To revoke or reverse a judgment.

recaption 1. To recover that which was removed. 2. To take back that which was given away or taken.

receipt 1. A printed or written acknowledgment of payment for an object, item, or good that has been received. 2. The act of receiving.

receivables In health-care finance, this is the money owed to the health-care organization but not yet received or collected. These funds are considered current assets even though not yet collected or received and thus are a part of the financial picture and the organization's financial viability. Most hospitals run an average of 60 days on most accounts of gross revenues prior to receiving the money. *See accounts receivable.*

receivables ratio In health-care finance, this represents the monies owed but not yet received or collected. The total or gross amount of money tied up in receivables is divided by the average amount of all revenues generated per day (total revenue per year divided by 365 days.) The receivables ratio formula follows:

$$\frac{\text{Gross accounts receivable}}{\text{Average revenue per day}} = \text{Days of revenue outstanding}$$

receive a report In formal health-care organization meetings using parliamentary procedure, this is to have an oral presentation of the report. It does not necessarily mean it is to be approved by the committee or board or that official action is to be taken on it. Often a statement is made by the chair for the minutes of the meeting to "receive the report as read." A motion is not needed.

receiver 1. One who takes or holds property or items of value. 2. A person appointed by a court to hold and manage money or property. 3. One who accepts stolen goods.

receiver pendiente lite In health law, this is a noninvolved or impartial person appointed by the court during litigation to manage, oversee, or hold money and accounts or manage bankruptcy or foreclosures.

receivership 1. Being in the hands of a receiver. 2. In law, this is to have business affairs taken over by a receiver appointed by a court; a court placing money or property into the hands of a receiver to preserve it for those entitled to it.

receiving stream In environmental health, these are creeks or rivers that receive outfall discharge of wastewater effluents.

receiving waters In environmental health, these are creeks, rivers, lakes, oceans, or other watercourses or bodies of water into which wastewater or treated effluents are discharged.

recency effect In health administration and human resource management, this is when a supervisor allows recent employee performance to sway the overall long-term evaluation. The rater rates the employee in the performance appraisal only on the basis of recent work behavior, which could have positive or negative effects, depending on how positive or negative the results of the recent work events were.

recertification *See length-of-stay certification.*

recess In health law, this is a break in a court proceeding or formal meeting for a short period of time.

recession of contract In law, this is the rescinding or annulment of a contract. *See also rescind.*

recidivism 1. Relative to health-care services, the percentage of discharged patients who are subsequently rehospitalized; readmission rates; a relapse requiring readmission to a facility or program. 2. To continually back or support criminal or antisocial behavior, habits, or activities.

recidivist 1. A repeating offender. 2. A habitual or continued lawbreaker.

recipient 1. In health-care delivery, this is any individual who receives health services. In health care, these are patients, residents (in long-term care), or clients (in mental health services). 2. Under Medicaid this is a person who is designated by the Medicaid agency as eligible to receive Medicaid benefits. 3. In managed care, this is the individual enrolled in a health plan who is the beneficiary of services and is the actual person receiving the care, treatment, or therapy.

reciprocal An offer made by each side or by each other; a mutual action.

reciprocate To give and take in exchange; to interchange or give something in return.

reciprocity 1. In licensure of health professionals, the recognition by one state of the licenses of a second state when the latter state extends the same recognition to licenses of the former state. Licensing requirements in the two states must usually be equivalent before formal or informal reciprocal agreements are made. "Reciprocity" is often used interchangeably with the term "endorsement." 2. The act, process, or principles of law where a state allows the same or similar privileges to citizens from another state; an agreement where states exchange privileges or penalties. 3. A mutual and reciprocal agreement. 4. In managed care, this is an agreement between two more health plans whereby a member may receive treatment that cannot be postponed from another prepaid plan for illness or injuries until they can return to their service area.

recission 1. In the federal budget, this is enacted legislation canceling previous budget authority provided by Congress. Recissions proposed by the president must be transmitted in a special message to Congress. Under Section 1012 of the Congressional Budget and Impoundment Control Act of 1974, unless Congress approves a recission bill within 45 days of continuous session, the budget authority in question must be made available for obligation. 2. In insurance, cancellation with repayment of premiums of a policy.

recital In law, this is an official written statement explaining the purpose and meaning of a document or the reason for the transaction that the document covers.

reckless In health law, this is negligent; careless; not heeding the consequences of one's actions.

recoding 1. In medical records, this is changing an original diagnosis from the primary diagnosis to a secondary or tertiary level diagnosis and reassigning a new, more accurate primary diagnosis that better reflects the severity of the condition, injury, or illness. 2. The process of taking data from one classification and placing it into a new or different classification. 3. The process of evaluating the original code assigned to data, a procedure, a disease classification, or a diagnosis and reassigning it to another, more specific and proper category or code.

recognition 1. The identification of facts, evidence, or an object previously known or seen. 2. Formal approval. 3. Items or acts that come under the scrutiny of the law. 4. In health law, this is an item or incident that is recognized by law. 5. In formal health-care meetings using parliamentary procedure, this is when members of the board or committee are recognized by the chair by stating their names or stating that the chair recognizes them and that they have the floor.

recognizance 1. A legal agreement to do a particular act. 2. A type of bail bond used so that a person will be obligated to appear in court at a later date. 3. An obligation that is a part of a court record.

recommended actions and implementation strategies In health services and health planning, these are methods and/or techniques to be utilized by health planning in the accomplishment of organizational or system goals.

recommended medical audit and action In medical records, the steps or tasks that must be accomplished as a result of a completed audit by the medical audit committee. The tasks must be clearly set forth, problems identified, and the change effectively accomplished.

reconcile 1. To restore a relationship. 2. To adjust or settle differences. 3. To make consistent.

reconciliation The restoration of a broken or disrupted relationship. A settlement or adjustment of differences or disagreements.

reconsideration In health-care finance, under Medicare, this is a review of an unfavorable claims adjudication for institutional care under Part A upon the request of the beneficiary, his representatives, or the provider. Request for reconsideration is made to the intermediary.

record 1. An official written, printed, or published report of public acts, such as a court record or legislative record. 2. A body of facts that is known and preserved. 3. A formal written account of a case including a written history of actions taken, evidence shown, documents filed, decisions made, and opinions written.

record 1. To officially write out in permanent form. 2. To register; to mark or make an indication in written form.

record, certificate of need In the review of certificate of need (CON) applications used by some states, this includes all modifications, amendments, or supplements as well as memos, analysis, and data used to evaluate the application; also includes all correspondence or memoranda submitted by the applicant or other affected persons as well as transcripts, recordings, and testimony from public hearings. All statements of matters officially noticed and all findings, recommendations, opinions, or reports issued by any concerned party as well as transcripts of all oral proceedings before hearing bodies make up the CON application record.

record, computer A collection of related items of data or information treated as a unit.

record control In medical records and health-care information management, these are policies and procedures used to ensure a permanent location of records and the related abstracted data to define limits of access to records and data by specified personnel or parties and to retain the current location of a record or its abstracted information.

record destruction program In medical records and health-care information management, this is a plan to routinely purge or eliminate specified records from the files as determined by a predetermined time schedule within legal and regulatory limits.

recording method In insurance, this is a method of changing the beneficiary of a life insurance policy by the policy owner and notifying the insurance company in writing of the change of beneficiary.

record linkage In health information management, this is the method or technique of gathering information about health-care services and other related health events for one patient from many different sources such as hospital stays, immunizations, and visits to physicians. This scattered information is brought together in a common file or record through the use of a computer. A second approach is to pull together by computer a set of common data from many records such as a certain diagnosis from all hospital medical records in 1 year or, in vital statistics, to pull from birth or death certificates significant health events that are removed from one another in time and place but that contribute to a picture of health status for a community; commonly used for epidemiological research.

recorded instruments In health law, certain certified copies of officially written documents such as deeds, conveyances, bonds, mortgages, or other written reports completed in the process of doing regular business activities can be accepted as evidence in a court of law. Certain documents such as deeds, conveyances, bonds, mortgages, or licenses are considered official, verified, legal, or certified if they have undergone some recording process and are accepted as evidence in a court of law. In health care, this includes medical records, incident reports (not part of a patient's record), X rays, and any other formal documents created in the process of providing patient care. Administrative reports, bylaws, policies, incidence reports, and medical records are often considered recorded instruments.

record of decision In public or environmental health, this is a concise public record of an administrative agency's decision on a proposed action for which an environmental impact statement was prepared and that includes the alternatives considered, the environmentally preferable alternative, factors balanced in the decision, and mitigation measures and monitoring to minimize harm.

records administrator, registered See *registered records administrator*.

recoup 1. To recover or regain. 2. To make a note or agreement good. 3. To repay or reimburse.

recoupment In health law, this is the deduction from a sum owed to a plaintiff that grows out of the same transaction between the parties and is based on the plaintiff's failure to fully perform on a contract.

recourse 1. The right to receive payment on a negotiable instrument from anyone who has endorsed it if the person who created it fails to make payment. 2. An appeal for aid or protection. 3. Legal avenues that can be used to recover damages.

recourse arrangement In health-care finance, this is used in accounts receivable financing where the health-care organization sells its accounts receivable to a financial institution under an agreement as part of a financial deal or for collateral or direct payment. Accounts receivable cannot be collected by the health-care organization. When the deal is settled and accounts are paid off, the health-care organization must repurchase the accounts from the financial institution.

recover 1. To receive compensation for damages through the judgment of a court 2. To win a lawsuit. 3. To get back or make up for losses or damage through legal means. 4. Money being paid for damages.

recoverable In environmental health and solid waste management, this is the capability and likelihood of being recovered from solid waste for a commercial or industrial use.

recoverable materials In environmental health and solid waste management, these are waste materials and by-products recovered or diverted from solid waste. This term does not include materials or by-products generated from and commonly reused in the original manufacturing process.

recovery 1. In health law, this is the act of restitution; regaining loss or damage; the money awarded to the plaintiff in a judgment of a civil lawsuit equal to the loss, injury, or damage; the plaintiff of a lawsuit to be assisted by the courts to be returned to the level of functioning that existed prior to injury, damage, or loss. The money is not given to the plaintiff as a punishment against the defendant but is given to bring the injured party back to the state he or she was in prior to experiencing the damage, injury, or loss caused by the defendant. This also means to be recovered from harm, damage, or injury caused by the negligence or malpractice of others; the money realized by the plaintiff from the defendant on winning a lawsuit to bring the injured party back to the same level of functioning prior to the injury or harm. 2. In medical care, this is the regaining of strength, physical and physiological functions, health, and wellness after a spell of illness, injury, or surgery; postoperative care in the time period immediately following surgery until strength returns and the effects of the drugs and anesthesia have worn off to where the patient is alert and stable.

recovery room In medical care, this is a specially staffed and equipped area, usually in a hospital or surgery center adjacent to surgery suites, where a patient is taken directly after surgery. Nurses monitor vital signs and closely observe the patient while recovering from the effects of the anesthesia, trauma, and shock of an operation prior to being transferred to a unit in the hospital or before allowing the patient to leave the health-care facility.

recreational director A person who is usually trained and certified as a recreational therapist responsible for planning and implementing recreational therapy activities, usually in long-term-care facilities or psychiatric or related institutions.

recreational therapist A person with training and specialization in therapeutic recreation who is registered or eligible for registration as such by the National Therapeutic Recreation Society and who directs recreational activities in long-term-care facilities or recreation centers for special populations such as the elderly, retarded, or mentally ill. The therapist plans, organizes, and directs medically approved activities to provide a means of therapy and socialization, including sports, trips, dramatics, exercise, and arts and crafts. These activities assist patients in recovering from physical or mental illness and in coping with temporary or permanent disability. In some pediatric settings, these are referred to as "child-life workers."

recreational therapy A therapeutic modality that activates social interactions, leisure, crafts, arts, and enjoyment in a therapeutic manner. The recreational therapist is concerned with all dimensions of the total person with the aim of providing rehabilitation. The recreational therapist helps patients in nursing homes, state hospitals, or other long-term-care facilities.

recreational therapy technician This technician assists the recreational therapist in conducting medically approved recreational programs such as exercise programs, dramatics, and arts and crafts.

recreational therapy technology A course of study that prepares technicians to assist the recreational therapist in conducting medically approved recreation programs. *See also recreational therapy technician.*

recredentialing The assessment of the continued quality, skills, competency, and ability of health-care providers on a regular interval, often through continuing education or in some cases clinical, written, or oral exams.

recrimination In health law, this is the act of answering an accusation or a charge brought by another person; a counterclaim.

recrudescence In epidemiology, medical care, or infection control, this is the reactivation or recurrence of an infection; the return of symptoms after the remission of a disease or infection; to get worse.

recurdescent In epidemiology, medical care, or infection control, this is the renewal or recurrence of an infection or of disease activity after a period of inactivity.

recruitment In health administration and human resource management, this is the process of determining job requirements and attracting, advertising for, screening, interviewing, and selecting the most qualified personnel to fill vacant positions while staying within equal opportunity employment guidelines. Finding, attracting, and hiring highly qualified and capable applicants for employment in health-care organizations.

recruitment, external In health administration and human resource management, this is meeting all aspects and processes of recruitment and staying within equal opportunity employment guidelines while seeking, attracting, and soliciting qualified personnel from outside the health-care organization whether on a local, regional, or national basis.

recruitment, internal In health administration and human resource management, this is meeting all aspects and processes of recruitment and staying within equal opportunity employment guidelines while seeking, attracting, and soliciting qualified personnel from inside the health-care organization, opening opportunities for advancement, promotions, retraining, and transfers. If no suitable candidates are found in the organization, external recruitment can be initiated.

recruitment, internal/external In health administration and human resource management, this is used in some cases to recruit personnel both inside and outside the health care organization and done simultaneously with internal staff having the right of first selection. This is done especially if management has the belief that the chances of finding an internal candidate are limited. All managerial and legal ramifications of the recruitment process are employed as in any other recruitment.

rectal digital examination In medical care, this is an examination of the rectum using a gloved finger.

rectal tube In medical and nursing care, this is a tube inserted into a patient's rectum or colon to help in the expulsion of gas.

recuperate 1. To regain. 2. To recover.

recurring clause A provision in some managed-care and medical insurance policies that specifies a period of time during which the recurrence of a condition is considered a continuation of a prior period of disability or hospital confinement rather than a separate spell of illness.

recusation In health law, this is the procedure of disqualifying a judge from a lawsuit or an official hearing because of personal vested interest or bias.

recycled materials In environmental health, these are materials that may be utilized in place of raw or virgin materials in manufacturing a product and consist of materials derived from postconsumer waste, industrial scrap, agricultural wastes, and other sources, all of which can be used in the manufacture of new products. *See postconsumer waste.*

recycled oil In environmental health, these are any used oils that are reprocessed or reused following original use for any purpose (including the purpose for which the oil was originally used). Also referred to as "re-refined," "reclaimed," "burned" or "reprocessed" oil.

recycled PCBs In environmental health, this is any intentionally manufactured polychlorinated biphenyls (PCBs) that appear in the processing of paper products or asphalt roofing materials as PCB-contaminated raw materials. The PCB-concentration amounts are monitored and controlled at the following levels. In paper manufactured in or imported into the United States, there must be an annual average of less than 25 ppm with a 50 ppm maximum, no detectable concentrations in asphalt roofing materials, added to water discharged from a processing site less than 3 micrograms per liter, at the point of emissions being vented to ambient air less than 10 ppm, and disposal of any other process wastes above concentrations of 50 ppm PCB.

recycling In environmental health, this is the process of minimizing the generation of waste by recovering usable products that might otherwise become waste such as recycling aluminum cans, newspaper and wastepaper, plastics, glass, metals, wood, steel, green wastes, and other products. *See postconsumer waste.*

red-circle rates In health administration and human resources management, these are wages or salaries that are inappropriate for a given job or level or position.

redeem 1. To repurchase. 2. To reclaim property. 3. To make good. 4. To turn in for cash. 5. To rescue.

redemption 1. Returning an item for cash. 2. A seller's right to buy back from the buyer, at an agreed-on price, an item sold.

redress 1. To receive reparation or indemnity. 2. In health law, this is to receive satisfaction or compensation from injury or harm done. 3. Payment provided for harm done.

reduced paid-up insurance option In life insurance and some other forms of insurance, this is when under a nonforfeiture option the cash value of an insurance policy is used as a single premium payment on the purchase of another insurance policy on the basis of the face amount of fully paid insurance of the same kind and for the same time period as the policy that is surrendered.

reductio ad absurdum (Lat.) 1. Reduce to the absurd. 2. Showing an issue or argument that leads to an unfounded and absurd conclusion.

reductionist In medical care, this is an approach to diagnosis that seeks to identify the cause of the illness or condition on the basis of testing, laboratory findings, and medical assessments that indicate the internal condition of the patient and that consider the factors that could contribute to the illness or condition in the immediate environment from which the patient emerged.

reductionist diagnosis In medical care, this is the use of testing, X ray, and assessment to determine the cause of disease or conditions. *See expansionist diagnosis.*

redundant 1. Excessive; more than enough. 2. Overabundant; repetitious.

Reed, Walter, MD A pathologist/bacteriologist physician serving the U.S. Army in the tropics who established the epidemiological connection between yellow fever and the mosquito as the vector and mode of transmission. Until 1900, yellow fever killed thousands of people in yearly epidemics. As head of the U.S. Army Yellow Fever Commission, Reed's experiments showed how the disease is transmitted. Reed was born on September 13, 1851, in Belroi, Virginia, and received a doctor of medicine degree before age 18 from the University of Virginia. In 1869 he received a second doctor of medicine degree from the Bellevue Hospital Medical College in New York City, then worked for the New York City and Brooklyn boards of health. In 1875 he entered the Army Medical Corps as a medical officer. In 1890 he studied at Johns Hopkins Hospital and was appointed professor of bacteriology and clinical microscopy at the Army Medical School in Washington, D.C. Reed headed a committee to investigate epidemics of typhoid fever raging through army camps. It was found that flies and dust were helping to spread the disease. Dr. Reed recommended sanitation measures that reduced the disease rate. He was then appointed in 1900 as head of the Yellow Fever Commission, which was organized to combat the disease among troops stationed in Havana, Cuba. In a series of controlled experiments, they proved the theory. As strict mosquito-control measures were enforced, yellow fever epidemics ceased. A neglected chronic appendicitis caused his death on November 22, 1902. A major Army hospital in Washington, D.C., is named for him.

reengineering In strategic health planning and health-care administration, this is the process of changing the organizational structure of a hospital, other health-care organization, or in some cases certain divisions, departments, or administrative entities of the organization to increase organizational efficiency and effectiveness while enhancing quality. To accomplish needed changes, administrative approaches, organizational chart structuring, financial management strategies, managerial paradigms, corporate culture approaches, and philosophical positions to overall administration are greatly modified or entirely redone to accommodate broader changes in the medical care field and delivery system, especially in the areas of medical care financing and basic delivery of health care.

reentry intervals In occupational health and safety, these are periods of time immediately following the application of a pesticide during which unprotected workers should not enter a field.

refer 1. To direct attention to. 2. To turn a case over to another lawyer. 3. To direct a patient to a professional who has specialized qualifications or has been appointed to, or has more knowledge of, the problem or disorder.

referee 1. In health law, this is an official appointed to hear arguments or arbitrate disputes. 2. An arbitrator.

reference 1. The act of submitting a matter for settlement. 2. Any promise written into a contract where a party will agree to submit certain disputes to arbitration; sending a case to a referee for a decision. 3. To provide information about one's character, credit, or qualifications.

reference dose (RFD) In occupational health and safety, these are the toxicity values used in evaluating noncarcinogenic effects and are listed as chronic RFDs, subchronic RFDs, and developmental RFDs.

reference levels In environmental health, and health and safety, these are the values of quantities that govern a particular course of action. Such levels may be established for any of the quantities determined in the practice of radiation protection. These indicate when they are reached or exceeded and are not to be confused with or considered limits of exposure.

reference man In environmental health and health and safety, this is a hypothetical aggregation of a human's (male or female) physical and physiological characteristics arrived at by international consensus. Such characteristics are used by researchers and public health workers to standardize results of experiments and related biological insults from ionizing radiation to a common base. For example, this fictitious organism is assumed to inhale 8400 cubic meters of air in a year and ingest 730 liters of water; also used in dosimetery for radiation protection purposes.

reference methods In environmental health and health and safety, these are approaches used for sampling and analyzing the ambient air for an air pollutant by standardized measurements.

reference projection In health planning for health services delivery, these are forecasts of expected future levels on various types of health planning data if no actions are taken to alter current activities and commitments. Reference projections include such data as indicators, related demographic and environmental factors, resources, financial factors, and health service utilization. The health status, health services, and resources presented by the reference projection is sometimes termed the "base case" for a particular population.

reference standards In environmental health and health and safety, these are tested and preestablished levels that must be maintained by manufactures, organizations, or other entities to protect the environment, humans, and the ecology of the earth.

reference substance In environmental health and health and safety, these are any chemical agents, mixtures, or materials that are administered to or are used in analyzing a test in the course of a study for the purposes of establishing a basis for comparison with the test substance for known chemical or biological measurements.

referendum Placing a proposed law or repeal of a law to the vote of the people rather than enacting it through the legislative process.

referent That which is referred to.

referral 1. In medical care delivery, this is the practice of sending a patient to another practitioner or to another program or services for consultation when the referring source is not prepared or qualified to provide such service. In contrast to referral for consultation, referral for services involves a delegation of responsibility for patient care to another practitioner or program, and the referring source may or may not follow up to ensure that services are received. As a physician sends a patient to another physician or health-care provider who is a specialist, the referring physician turns over primary responsibility for health care of the patient from one physician to another; in insurance, this is not considered a consultation. 2. In managed care, this is the recommendation by a health-care provider or health plan for a member to receive care or services from a different health-care provider, clinic, or facility and to have it covered.

referral center A rural short-stay health-care facility that stabilizes patients who are then transferred to larger medical centers. In urban areas, this can be a freestanding emergency center or neighborhood or industrial treatment center that, as a part of its role, stabilizes patients until they can be transported to a tertiary care medical center. *See eaches/peaches.*

referral for services In medical care, this is the delegation of responsibility for patient care to another practitioner or program. The referring source may or may not follow up to ensure that services are received. *See referral.*

referral protocols In medical care delivery, these are procedures that are followed when referring patients from one service or health-care professional to another.

referral provider 1. In medical care delivery, this is a health-care provider who renders a service, treatment, or procedure to a patient of another physician on the basis of a referral process or agreement. 2. In managed care, this is the physician or health-care provider who has sent a patient to another health plan physician or health-care provider in the same health-care system or health plan.

referred pain Pain that is felt in one area but the source of pain is from another area (e.g., a kidney pain may be referred to the back muscles).

referring physician 1. In medical care delivery, this is a medical doctor who sends a patient to another physician or health-care provider for consultation, examination, testing, treatment, or procedures, often because the referring physician is not qualified or capable of providing the needed services. 2. In managed care, this is a physician who has a patient sent to him or her by another health-care provider, usually in the health-care system, for testing, examination, or surgery or to have specific or special procedures performed on the patient, often because the referring health-care provider is not prepared or qualified to provide the necessary services or procedures.

refinement In epidemiology, health promotion, or health services research, this is the process of establishing subcategories of research variables to have a closer description or clear details of cause-effect relationships such as the development of different subcategories of cholesterol testing (e.g., total cholesterol being specified into LDL and HDL).

reflection In laser technology and radiation, this is the deviation of radiation following the beams striking a surface.

reflex An involuntary activity as a response to a stimulus.

reformation The change of a written agreement by a court, usually done for the legal betterment of all involved.

refreezing In health administration, this is the integration of what has been experienced or learned about a process and function of some entity into practice. This concept also has an application to health education and health promotion.

refreshing memory In health law, this is the use of documents or items to help remind a witness of details.

refund To give back; to repay.

refunding 1. To refinance a debt. 2. The act of returning money for an unacceptable or damaged item or goods.

refuse In environmental health, this is synonymous with "solid waste" and includes sludge, trash, garbage, and discarded material, including solid, liquid, and semiliquid wastes or contained gaseous materials resulting from industrial, commercial, mining, and agricultural operations and from community activities or from a waste treatment plant, water supply treatment plant, or air pollution control facility. This does not include solid or dissolved materials in irrigation return flows or industrial discharges that are point sources subject to permits under the Federal Water Pollution Control Act (EPA).

refuse reclamation In environmental health, this is the conversion of solid waste into useful products such as composting organic wastes to make soil conditioners or separating aluminum and other metals for melting and recycling.

refutation The act of proving statements, propositions, proposals, evidence, documents, or arguments as false or erroneous.

refute To use argument, discussion, or evidence to disprove statements or facts.

regeneration Renewal of damaged or lost cells or tissues.

regimen In medical care, this is a pattern of activity; a planned course of treatment or a therapy program for patient care.

regional issues Concerns identified and considered as being important to regional groups; local health services and health systems matters and concerns.

regionalization 1. In the late 1960s and early 1970s, the federal government asked each state to develop regions within their states to receive grants, contracts, and other funding and to plan social and health service programs. Regional governmental associations were established to receive the funding, manage grants, and develop programs and do planning. These were called Councils of Governments (COGs). 2. In a managed-care system or large HMOs, a system of cooperative arrangements of services among health-care providers of various health services components to deliver services on a regional basis. The regionalization may encompass varying levels of specialization with respect to the specific type of service and requires specialized manpower and facilities such as obstetrics. The shared services approach allows certain needs like obstetrics to be effectively met in a single facility or clinic in an area by the coordinated efforts of several institutions or services.

Regional Medical Program (RMP) A former regional medical services, demonstration, and research entity that created programs for the care of heart disease, cancer, stroke, and related diseases and oriented toward initiating and improving continuing education, nursing services, and intensive care units at the regional level. As a program under federal support for regional health and medical care organizations, this was developed as a cooperative agreement among medical schools, research centers, and health-care institutions to improve care for heart disease, cancer, strokes, and related diseases; created by P.L. 89-239, which was found in Title IX of the PHS Act. Some features of the RMP program were discontinued and combined into the health planning program authorized by P.L. 93-641 and were called health systems agencies (which in turn were discontinued in 1986). *See health systems agency.*

regional response teams In environmental health, this is a representative of federal, local, and state agencies who may assist in the coordination of activities at the request of the on-scene coordinator before and during a Superfund response action (EPA).

register 1. In epidemiology, this is a set of records of vital statistics and public facts such as births, deaths, and marriages that was created because of the legal requirement that such events be recorded as public record. 2. The official document or log where legal data or vital statistics are officially recorded and maintained. 3. The public official who keeps vital records. 4. To record information. 5. A log or journal used to record a request for information or a medical record. 6. In public health and epidemiology, this is a record or file of information or data on all cases of a disease that is retained by a public health department on the population of a community, allowing prevalence, incidence, recrudescence, survivability, and death rates to be established.

registered 1. Facts or information recorded in an official record. 2. To have one's name recorded in a public record or with a legally created office that shows one's legal approval to practice a profession such as registered nurse. *See also licensing; certification; registration.*

registered bonds In health-care finance, these are financial bonds that are registered with a bond trustee who determines ownership. Sale or transfer of ownership of bonds must be registered with the bond trustee for new owners to receive principal and interest.

registered care technologist (RCT) A nurse-type technologist position created by the American Medical Association to meet the nursing needs of hospitals and clinics during nurse shortages. This is a new class of bedside patient care worker. The RCT would report to the nurse supervisor on the floor of a hospital or the professional in charge of a department in which the RCT works (e.g., in the emergency department, the RCT would report to the department director, who is often a physician). All RCTs would be required to meet state licensure. Most nursing associations and groups oppose this new allied health professional.

registered dietitian (RD) An American Dietetic Association (ADA) dietitian who has successfully completed the ADA examination for registration and maintains registration by meeting continuing education requirements. In providing nutritional care, the RD applies the science and art of human nutrition in helping people select and obtain food for the primary purpose of nourishing their bodies in health or disease throughout the life cycle. This participation may be in single or combined functions, in food service systems management, in extending knowledge of food and nutrition principles, in teaching these principles for application according to particular situations, or in dietary counseling. *See also clinical dietitian.*

registered environmental health specialist *See sanitarian, registered.*

registered hospital Any health-care facility recognized and accepted by the American Hospital Association as having the facilities, staff, equipment, and necessary attributes of a hospital and having paid the required fees for registration. About 98% of hospitals are registered.

registered nurse (RN) 1. A professional health-care worker who has graduated from a formal approved program of nursing education (associate degree, diploma, and bachelors degree graduates) and licensed by the appropriate state authority. Registered nurses are the most highly educated nurses and have the widest scope of responsibility in all aspects of nursing care. 2. A nurse who has graduated from a formal program of nursing education and been licensed by the appropriate state licensing board and authority to practice nursing. They are responsible for the direct patient care and the quality of care of all types of nursing that patients receive. Some nurses specialize in the type of care setting they work in such as neonatal intensive care nurse, operating room nurse, emergency room nurse, pediatric nurse, and home health nurse. This includes clinical nurse specialists and some nurse practitioners who primarily perform nursing, not physician-delegated tasks. Educational training of nurses ranges from 2-year associate degrees to hospital-based diploma schools to 4-year college graduates as well as masters and doctoral trained persons. Even with advanced degrees in nursing, the basic licensure and registration requirements of a nurse must be met. 3. According to JCAHO for accreditation purposes, a nurse who is a graduate of an approved school of nursing and who is licensed to practice as a registered nurse; an individual who is qualified by an approved postsecondary program or baccalaureate or higher degree in nursing and licensed by the state, commonwealth, or territory to practice professional nursing. *See also nurse; licensed practical nurse; nurse practitioner; nurse anesthetist.*

registered physical therapist (RPT) A person licensed in physical therapy and trained to provide therapy for and to treat disability, injury, and disease by external physical means such as massage, exercise, heat, and light. *See also physical therapist.*

registered records administrator (RRA) An individual who is registered through the American Medical Records Association who plans, develops, and administers medical records systems for public, private, and military health-care facilities This individual collects and analyzes patient and institutional data and creates and implements policies and procedures for the collection, storage, retrieval, and release of data for medical, administrative, legal, and research purposes. In smaller facilities, a medical records administrator might be hired as a consultant to oversee the facility's own staff. In some agencies or institutions, tasks described as those of the administrator might be performed by technicians. In large hospitals, chief medical records administrators direct and coordinate all medical records staff activities, including supervision, training, systems planning, administration, and data analyses. In larger settings, the medical records administrator functions in a more complex professional and administrative role and is responsible for planning and developing records systems that meet the standards of a variety of accrediting and regulatory agencies. The administrator designs health records abstracting systems used by staff and researchers and directs the preparation of indexes as well as the collection and analysis of data. Employment settings beyond the hospital include outpatient clinics, ambulatory care centers, health maintenance organizations, nursing homes, professional standards review organizations, government and insurance agencies, universities and colleges, and research centers. *See also medical records administrator, qualified.*

registered respiratory therapist According to JCAHO for accreditation purposes, an individual who has been registered by the National Board for Respiratory Therapy, Inc., after successfully completing all requirements for education, experience, and examination.

registered sanitarian *See sanitarian, registered.*

registrar An official with authority to keep official records; a government official who has the responsibility to keep and maintain records in vital statistics and public health. These usually include birth, death, marriage and divorce records, and other legal documents of public interest such as property deeds.

registration 1. The process of recording. 2. The act of creating a special list of names. 3. The process by which qualified individuals are listed on an official roster maintained by a governmental or nongovernmental agency called a "register." Standards for registration may include the successful completion of a written examination given by a registry, membership in a professional association maintaining the registry, and education and experience such as graduation from an approved program or equivalent experience. This is where the term "registered nurse" was derived. Nurses are now licensed. Registration is a form of credentialing and is similar to certification. 4. In public health and epidemiology, this is recording and tracking persons with certain threatening, notifiable diseases. 5. In public health and vital statistics, this is recording vital events of interest to public health such as births, deaths, marital status, and divorces. 6. The act of establishing an official and permanent record of births, deaths, marital status, divorces, etc. 7. The formal listing with the Environmental Protection Agency of a new pesticide before it can be sold or distributed in intra- or interstate commerce. The product must be registered under the Federal Insecticide, Fungicide and Rodenticide Act. The EPA is responsible for registration (premarket licensing) of pesticides on the basis of data demonstrating that they will not cause unreasonable adverse effects on human health or the environment when used according to approved label directions.

registration area Each state and territory is a registration area for the federal government through which data are collected on the occurrence of births and deaths. Established reporting standards are used based on exactness, completeness, and promptness in reporting. States are encouraged to adopt the reporting processes and standards. Mortality registration was first established in 1880, and the reporting process started in 1890 in 10 states, the District of Columbia, and several cities. The District of Columbia was established as the first registration area in 1915. In 1933 all states in the Union were developed into registration areas for both birth and death registration. Currently all 50 states, Puerto Rico, the U.S. Virgin Islands, and Guam, are included as part of the U.S. total. The United States has separate registration areas for birth, death, marriage, and divorce statistics. Data are collected annually from the states whose registration data are at least 90% complete.

registration standards In environmental health, these are the published reviews of all the data available on active ingredients in pesticides.

registry 1. In public health, epidemiology, and vital statistics, this is a system of recording and compiling diseases, conditions, or vital events that relate to or affect the health status of the public. 2. In managed-care and health-care delivery, this is a list of individuals who have given explicit indication that they use or rely on a given health professional or program for the services that the professional or program is able to provide. A panel is sometimes used in preference to a registry with respect to individual practitioners. The nature of the actual financial and other relationships between a program and the people on its registry is quite variable. 3. An organization that conducts a registration program for health manpower and compiles lists of individual health professionals who it has registered (done by professional societies or associations). 4. A temporary manpower employment pool where health-care professionals sign up with and work for a temporary employment agency and placement organization and do the work at a health-care facility or for a health-care organization as needed and are paid on a per diem basis. See also catchment area; enrollment period; roster; register.

registry, birth defect A system of recording and tracking all congenital anomalies to create a study population for research using comparisons of environmental factors as a cause and the genetic basis of birth defects and related disorders.

registry, cancer See registry; tumor.

registry pool Health-care professionals who work for a temporary employment agency. See registry.

registry staff In health administration and human resource management and staffing, these are clinical personnel provided to a health-care facility by a placement service on a temporary or day-by-day basis.

registry, tumor A system of recording cancerous tumors, creating a database of each and every tumor or cancer diagnosed and treated in a health-care facility, usually through a computer network; often the responsibility of a medical records department of a hospital. Some states have computerized record linkages with hospitals, public health departments, and cancer research institutes to obtain complete and accurate data on cancer and tumors.

registry, twin A nationwide system of recording and tracking all twins to create a study population for research using comparisons of environmental factors and the genetic basis of diseases and disorders.

regression 1. In mental health, this is a defense mechanism in which a person mentally returns to earlier thoughts or behaviors. 2. In biostatistics, this is the process of doing linear statistical estimates of the value of Y at any given X on a contingency table or regression graph. 3. A statistical forecasting method used in predicting utilization of health services by predicting the value of usage correlated with facts and knowledge about related influencing factors and influences on utilization.

regression analysis In biostatistics, this is a procedure for predicting the value of one variable on the basis of facts known about other variables that influence and affect the original variable; the effect of the independent variable(s) on the dependent variable. Mathematically finding how Y as a function of X can make linear predictions of their relationships, how Y can be predicted from X, and how the relationship of Y correlates with X.

regression to the mean In biostatistics, this is how the results of test scores or research findings come closer to the averages on the basis of a comparison of pretests to posttests, regardless of the independent variable; the results of research findings or test results that gravitate toward the average of the test population.

regressive tax A tax that takes a decreasing proportion of income as income rises such as sales taxes and the Social Security payroll tax on earnings above the maximum to which the tax applies This tax is a constant percentage of income up to the maximum level (wage base) or a proportional tax up to that level. *See also progressive tax; marginal tax rate; proportional tax.*

regular 1. By established rule or order. 2. A usual custom. 3. Steady; uniform; with no unusual deviation or variations. 4. Lawfully conforming to usual practice.

regular medical expense insurance In medical insurance, this is coverage that provides benefits through payment toward the cost of health services such as doctor fees for nonsurgical care provided at a hospital, at home, or in a physician's office. This also includes X rays or laboratory tests performed outside the hospital or other health-care facility.

regularly maintained beds In hospitals or other inpatient health-care facilities, these are beds set up, maintained, set aside, and staffed for daily operation and use. A hospital may be licensed for a certain number of beds, but that does not mean that all beds are kept available for immediate use, so a count of those beds kept ready for use on a regular basis better describes the immediate operation capacity of the hospital.

regular medical insurance In some medical insurance, this is a type of coverage that covers only a physician's services and procedures other than surgical procedures.

regular source of care The usual medical care provider, clinic, or place where the patient goes for medical care, treatment, or medical advice.

regulate 1. To control. 2. To adjust to a standard. 3. To govern according to predetermined rules to keep in proper order.

regulated substances In environmental health, these are chemicals, compounds, or materials whose manufacture, generation, transportation, alteration, or disposition is regulated under any federal or state statutes.

regulated waste In environmental health and hazardous waste management, these are any potentially infectious materials, liquid or semiliquid blood, or other potentially infectious materials; contaminated items that would release blood or other potentially infectious materials in a liquid or semiliquid state if compressed; items that are caked with dried blood or other potentially infectious materials and are capable of releasing these materials during handling; contaminated sharps; and pathological and microbiological wastes containing blood or other potentially infectious materials are all considered hazardous and are regulated.

regulation 1. The intervention by government or accreditation associations in the health system by means of rules and policies that typically influence, control, or set standards for services provided in the health system. Regulation involves the setting, resources, services provided, and the manner in which providers of service are reimbursed. 2. The imposition of government into private industry, health-care institutions, health services, health-care systems, or health insurance industry to control entry into or change the behavior of participants in that marketplace through specification of rules or standards for the participants. Regulatory programs include some certification, some registration, licensure, environmental control, public health control, certificate of need, and Professional Review Organizations (PRO) programs. 3. The act of enforcing policies, standards, rules, or laws.

regulations Legally enforceable written rules backed by statutory law developed by official governmental administrative agencies as mandated by the proper official lawmaking body for which compliance is sought by proper administrative agencies such as the Occupational Safety and Health Administration, the Environmental Protection Agency, Medicaid, the fire marshal's office, public health departments, environmental health services, and air quality management districts that also administer, enforce, change, and interpret the regulations; specific and detailed aspects of some statutes created by administrative agencies. Regulations are often concerned with issues related to health care or public health, and, if created in the proper manner and do not conflict with constitutional rights, they have the full force of the law. *See Administrative Procedure Act.*

regulatory agency Any agency or subagency of the government that, under statutory mandate, creates regulations, administers and enforces rules and regulations for the purpose of health protection, and controls any health or related activity in a particular area (e.g., the federal Food and Drug Administration, the Occupational Safety and Health Administration, the Environmental Protection Association, and local public or environmental health departments). *See Administrative Procedure Act.*

regulatory organizations In public or environmental health, these are governmental agencies responsible for decision making and the implementation and enforcement of regulatory action. *See regulatory agency; regulations.*

rehabilitate 1. To restore to a former state, rank, or privilege. 2. To restore health, function, and physical strength skills and abilities to an injured, disabled, or ill patient.

rehabilitation 1. Restoration of form and function following an illness or injury; any array of restorative and therapy services. 2. The combined and coordinated use of medical, social, educational, and vocational measures for training or retraining individuals disabled by disease or injury to the highest possible level of functional ability. Social and medical care planned and designed to restore patients to their former level of functioning, capacity, or health status, including independent living activities. Several different types of rehabilitation are distinguished: vocational, social, medical, and educational. Habilitation is used for similar activities undertaken for individuals born with limited functional ability as compared with people who have lost abilities because of disease or injury. 3. Coordinated multidisciplinary procedures, treatment, therapies, and techniques used to restore and achieve maximal function and optimal adjustment for a patient to prevent relapses or recurrences of the condition or disability under the direction of a physician knowledgeable and experienced in physical or rehabilitative medicine; therapy and social support geared to activate the patient's abilities, self-belief, and recoverable functions, including individual and group psychotherapy, directed socialization, vocational retraining, education, physical therapy, occupational therapy, and recreational therapy. 4. In occupational health, this is the return of employees to work after medical attention with as little work time lost as possible; to attempt to minimize disrupted lives, economic loss, loss in productivity, and the restoration of health, activities of daily living, and functioning of workers. *See habilitation maintenance service; activities of daily living.*

Rehabilitation Act (1973) A federal law prohibiting discrimination against the handicapped, especially qualified handicapped individuals who could hold employment or a position. The law originally applied to employers who received federal monies and most federal agencies.

rehabilitation counselor An individual who helps disabled persons to become aware of and secure rehabilitation services designed to prepare them for gainful employment and to follow up on job satisfaction after placement. Types and levels of training are varied, but a masters or doctoral degree in rehabilitative counseling or counseling psychology is often preferred.

rehabilitation counselor aide Under the supervision of the rehabilitation counselor, this individual assists in developing and implementing a rehabilitation plan for clients. Specifically, the aide may conduct interviews, locate employment opportunities, match clients with available jobs, and locate individuals in need of counseling or rehabilitation services.

rehabilitation facility A health-care facility specially designed, equipped, and staffed to provide multidisciplinary medical, psychological, social, occupational therapy services, and physical restorative care to disabled or handicapped individuals with the aim of assisting them in recovering to their maximum level of functioning, activities of daily living, and health status and in many cases acquiring vocational skills and training to allow them to acquire employment on discharge or return to their prior position; an institution or center that provides medical, social, vocational, and educational programs and services with the aim of improving disabilities or impairments caused by injury or illness.

rehabilitation hospital *See hospital, rehabilitation; rehabilitation facility.*

rehabilitation, medical In occupational health, this is the required medical therapy and treatment a disabled worker receives in a definitive medical care setting under the supervision and care of a licensed physician and supportive rehabilitation personnel to treat an injury, impairment, or condition and to restore normal function and health status. In many states, vocational rehabilitation includes medical diagnosis and evaluation, surgery, psychological support, fittings for prostheses, and health restoration. Minor injuries are taken care of in the company clinic, and serious injuries or impairments are treated at the hospital or rehabilitation hospital. If injuries are serious, workers' compensation laws require employers and third-party payers to pay the cost of rehabilitation. For chronic disabilities, the third-party payer attempts to manage the care, including the selection of rehabilitation services that utilize medical rehabilitative personnel such as physical and occupational therapists.

rehabilitation outpatient services An organized and coordinated multidisciplinary approach providing rehabilitative, physical restorative, occupational therapy, vocational training, and mental health counseling services under physicians to ambulatory patients.

rehabilitation potential In medical care, these are the goals physicians and therapists have for an injured or ill patient with regard to what level of recovery is possible; the ability to return a patient's normal functioning and restoration to their usual daily activity. Issues considered are activities of daily living, ability for self-care, emotional and social well-being, independent living, and management of the specific medical problem.

rehabilitation program An organized rehabilitative program offered in an inpatient, outpatient, or home health setting.

rehabilitation unit The administrative unit of a health-care facility specially equipped and staffed to provide rehabilitative programs for handicapped, injured, or disabled persons.

rehabilitation, vocational In occupational health, this is the process of preparing injured workers to return to work, to assist in finding a new occupation, or to provide training to continue on their old job or seek a new position. Counselors and trainers are the personnel most often found working in this area of rehabilitation and may or may not be under the supervision of a physician. Retraining, vocational development, and skill acquisition is the focus of this type of rehabilitation. This form of therapy or approach to rehabilitation is used when medical rehabilitation falls short in its effort to restore the worker to the position held before being injured. Training is needed to overcome limitations or learn to compensate for injuries or disabilities. New occupations or skills may be part of the rehabilitation process. In many states, vocational rehabilitation includes medical diagnosis and evaluation, surgery, psychological support, fittings for prostheses, and health and social related services as well as the traditional vocational rehabilitative approaches such as education, vocational training, on-the-job training, and job placement. In some states, workers' compensation programs support vocational rehabilitation.

rehabilitative care *See rehabilitative services.*

rehabilitative nursing care In long-term care, this is a care plan directed at assisting each resident in achieving and maintaining the highest level of self-care, personal care, and independence possible in the context of the living circumstances, chronic disease, and disability present by using any combination of psychosocial rehabilitation, physical therapy, recreational therapy, speech therapy, and occupational therapy as needed and appropriate.

rehabilitative services Medical care and psychological and therapeutic services provided to restore and/or improve lost bodily and/or mental function following illness, injury, or disease. *See habilitative maintenance service.*

rehearing In health law, this is to hold a second hearing on a matter previously decided to allow evidence previously omitted to be presented or to correct errors.

reimbursement In health-care finance, this is paying back monies expended to provide health-care services; the process by which health-care providers receive payment for services rendered from a third-party payer. Payment is done by third parties who represent the patient/member or member's dependents.

reimbursement account In human resource benefits, this is a salary deduction system allowing employees to pay for medical expense coverage not covered by the regular medical benefits or health plans. Prior to the beginning of the benefit year, the employee predicts the medical care expenses for the coming year, and one twelfth of that amount is deducted each month for the entire benefit year and put into an account in the company. The employee pays the medical bills, which are then reimbursed from the special account by the company after submitting the receipts to the company. These accounts are often accompanied by premium conversion accounts.

reimbursement, cost-based *See cost-based reimbursement.*

reimbursement, cost control In health-care finance, DRG reimbursement systems provide several approaches through which health-care facilities can receive reimbursement (e.g., by price per case or by indexation). Under price per case, the patient population is distributed among the groups, and rates are then set for each DRG. Rates are prospectively set and paid regardless of costs incurred or length of stay. Thus, the administration of the health-care facility must avoid unnecessary costs because the excesses in payment are retained by the facility. Under the indexation approach, per diem reimbursement methods are retained with reasonable costs being adjusted to reflect case mix.

reimbursement period In environmental health, this is the time period when the data from the last nonduplicative test to be completed under a test rule are submitted to the Environmental Protection Agency (EPA) and ends after an amount of time equal to that which had been required to develop data or after 5 years.

reimbursement, prospective See *prospective reimbursement*.

reimbursement, retroactive In health-care finance, this is a payment system where third-party payers pay additional money to a health-care facility for services not included in the original request for reimbursement.

reimbursement, retrospective See *retrospective reimbursement*.

reimbursement specialist In health-care financial management, this is a professional who specializes in preparing statements and documents for submission to third-party payers for reimbursement and who negotiates payment systems and reimbursement methods with the third-party payers.

reinforcement In behavioral psychology and behavioral health, this is the presentation or removal of an event or reinforcer after a response; the increase in the frequency of a response that is immediately followed by a consequence.

reinforcement schedule In behavioral psychology and behavioral health, these are the different means, approaches, or factors that ensure that a behavior will continue to be repeated or persist; rules for providing reinforcement stimulus specifying the conditions that must be met for a reinforcer to be delivered.

reinforcer In behavioral psychology and behavioral health, this is any event, factor, or consequence that increases the frequency of a behavior.

reinforcing factors 1. In behavioral psychology and behavioral health, these are any punishments or rewards used as a consequence of a behavior to strengthen the motivation of a behavior directly after it occurs. 2. In epidemiology and health promotion, these are issues, concepts, or variables that support the continuation, perpetuation, or aggravation of a problem, condition, disorder, disease, or pattern of self-defeating behavior on the negative side or factors that enhance, encourage, and promote the continuation of positive and self-enhancing behavior. The factors that characterize reinforcement are repetitiveness, recurrence, or persistence of the behavior.

reinstate In health law, this is to return to a place, state, or condition that had been lost or revoked.

reinstated benefits In managed care, this is when the health plan will allow a member to return to maximum benefits on the basis of the policy and the insurance schedule after a certain time period has elapsed while not receiving benefits.

reinstatement In medical insurance and managed care, this is the resumption of coverage under a lapsed or revoked insurance policy; to allow insurance or managed-care coverage to be reestablished once revoked or discontinued; to restore a lapsed policy to a premium paying status according to the terms of the policy contract.

reinsurance In managed care and insurance, this is the practice of one insurance company buying insurance from a second company for the purpose of protecting itself against part or all of the losses it might incur in the process of honoring the claims of its policyholders. The original company is called the "ceding company" and the second the "assuming company" or "reinsurer." Reinsurance may be sought by the ceding company for several reasons: 1) to protect itself against losses in individual cases beyond a certain amount where competition requires it to offer policies providing coverage in excess of these amounts, 2) to offer protection against catastrophic losses in a certain line of insurance such as aviation accident insurance, or 3) to protect against mistakes in rating and underwriting in entering a new line of insurance. A managed-care plan's approach to limiting liability through the practice of purchasing insurance from another company to protect itself against part or all losses incurred from processing and honoring all classes of members. The risk comes when certain dollar limits are exceeded from the fluctuation or extremes in variation of utilization and cost, especially in start-up periods. Self-insurance is preferred because reinsurance is expensive. Thus, as the managed care company grows in financial security, reinsurance is discontinued. Some states may provide reinsurance for certain types of managed-care plans. Also referred to as "stop-loss" or "risk-control" insurance.

reinsurance treaty In managed care, this is an insurance contract between a reinsurer and a ceding company. Three type of reinsurance treaties are used: automatic, facultative, and facultative-obligatory. *See reinsurance.*

reinsurer An insurance company that agrees to accept the transfer of risk from one managed-care company (the ceding company) to another insurance company called the "reinsurer." Also referred to as the "assuming company."

REIT *See real estate investment trusts.*

relapsing fever In managed care, this is when a high temperature returns to normal for 1 or more days and then returns to a fever state.

related factor In health services delivery or public health, this is any factor that has an impact on the quality of a population's health or that affects the ability of the health system to perform as desired. Trends in population density, ethnicity, occupation, and poverty are presumed to affect mortality, morbidity, and conditions. Polluting effects of industry and man-made systems also affect health status.

related system Any system that exists for a primary purpose other than improving and maintaining health but that may also affect the state of health of residents and the performance of the health system (e.g., education, welfare, and economic development).

relational data system In health information management systems, this is a flexible information and data retrieval system that allows for the retrospective creation of a data category or a definition after the fact.

relation by objectives In labor relations, this is a program established by the Federal Mediation and Conciliation Service with the aim of improving labor-management relationships and cooperation between the two parties.

relative biological effectiveness In occupational health and radiation safety, for a particular living organism or part of an organism, the ratio of the absorbed dose of a reference radiation that produces a specified biological effect to the absorbed dose of the radiation of interest that produces the same biological effect.

relative odds *See odds ratio.*

relative risk (RR) In epidemiology, this is a ratio of the risk of mortality or the incidence of a disease in a population exposed to a given risk factor (numerator) to the mortality or incidence in those not exposed in the same population (denominator). Relative risk with a ratio of 1.0 indicates that there is no greater risk in the exposed than in the not exposed. Often used for rare occurrence or diseases, "relative risk" is synonymous with "risk ratio" and "odds ratio" and has been used as a ratio for the forces of morbidity. *See odds ratio.*

relative survival rate In public health and chronic disease epidemiology, this is a comparison of the observed survival rate for the patient group to the expected survival rate for persons in the general population similar to the patient group with respect to age, sex, race, and calendar year of observation. The 5-year relative survival rate is used to estimate the proportion of cancer patients potentially curable. Because over half of all cancers occur in person 65 years of age and older, many of these individuals die of other causes with no evidence or recurrence of their cancer. Thus, because this rate is obtained by adjusting observed survival for the normal life expectancy of the general population of the same age, the relative survival rate is an estimate of the chance of surviving the effects of cancer.

relative value services In managed care, this is a system used to assign values to various medical procedures on the basis of a standardized unit of measure, allowing a comparison of medical services across health-care providers, clinics, and facilities in terms of setting a pricing structure that is reflective of true costs. A system based on these premises was developed in California and was ruled by the Federal Trade Commission as a form of price fixing.

relative value scale (RVS) In health services or medical care delivery and under Prospective Payment System (PPS) and Diagnosis-Related Groups (DRGs) of Medicare, this is a coded listing of physicians or other professional services using a unit system or cardinal ranking to indicate the relative value of the various services rendered or to provide a value to each in a manner such that the difference between the numerical ranking for any two services or procedures is a measure of the difference in value between them. The system takes into account the time, skill, and overhead cost required for each service but does not usually consider the relative cost-effectiveness of the services, the relative need or demand for each service, or the importance of a service to people's health. The units in this scale are based on median charges by physicians. Appropriate conversion factors are used to translate the abstract units in the scale to dollar fees for each service. Given individual and local variations in practice, the RVS can be used voluntarily as a guide to physicians in establishing fees for services and as a guide for insurance carriers and government agencies in determining appropriate reimbursement (e.g., use of relative value scales under Medicare where there is no customary or prevailing charge for a covered service). One example is the scale prepared and revised periodically by the California Medical Association, which includes independent scales for medicine, anesthesia, surgery, radiology, and pathology. Relative value scales can contain biases favoring certain specialties (such as surgery) or types of services (highly technical or specialized) over others. *See also fractionation.*

relative value unit (RVU) In health administration, this is one approach to a unit of service system with a level of importance value assigned to each medical procedure, treatment, or health-care service so that comparisons of resources can be done. *See relative value scale.*

relator 1. In health law, this is the name of one against whom a legal action is brought; the name placed on a legal action or claim filed.

release 1. To set free; to sign a document relieving responsibility of a second party, as in signing a release form. 2. In contract law, this is to be free from an obligation or from a penalty, as in a contract; to be released from a contract. 3. In medical insurance, this is to give up a claim to the person who owes the claim; a written document surrendering a claim or interest to another or to a third party (e.g., a medical record may be released to a court or an attorney). *See also release of information; informed consent.*

release detection In environmental health, this is the process of determining whether a release of a regulated substance has occurred from the underground storage tank system into the environment or into the interstitial space between the tank and its secondary barrier or the secondary containment area around it.

release form In health law, this is a statement signed by a patient that releases a health-care facility or provider from responsibility or liability caused by the patient refusing treatment, refusing to cooperate, or refusing to follow a doctor's orders. A release of side rails is also a common release form that protects the health-care facility from liability if the patient falls out of bed. Another release form is a temporary absence release, which gives a patient temporary leave from the hospital.

release of information In health law, this is a consent form that must be signed by the patient before any information may be given to an insurance company, attorney, or other third party.

releases In environmental health, this is any spilling, leaking, pumping, pouring, emitting, emptying, discharging, injecting, escaping, leaching, dumping, or otherwise disposing of substances into the environment. This includes abandoning/discarding any type of receptacle containing substances or the stockpiling of a reportable quantity of a hazardous substance in an enclosed containment structure. Any spill, leak, emission, discharge, escape, leaching, or disposing from an underground storage tank into groundwater, surface water, or subsurface soils.

relevant 1. Pertinent. 2. Having to do with the case at hand. 3. Having importance or impact on an issue in a lawsuit.

reliability 1. In health services or biomedical research, this is the reproducibility or replication of an experimental result. 2. As used in testing, this is when a test is repeatable and if it measures accurately and consistently the same things from one time to the next; a test that yields consistent results each time a subject takes it; how well it is replicated; a test that shows predictability over time; consistency of test scores obtained by the same persons when retested under identical conditions and with an identical or equivalent form of the test; a degree of stability observed in measurement device or test when it is repeated under identical conditions. *See also validity; validity, test.*

reliable data In health services or biomedical research, this is information or facts acquired by objective means; obtaining information by using concrete verifiable means or accepted sampling techniques.

reliance interest In health law, this is one who has depended on the acts or words of another and has incurred loss as a result.

relief 1. Aid or help provided by a court to a person initiating a claim or a lawsuit; that money or restoration of damages or harm sought after by a plaintiff through a lawsuit. 2. Charitable help given to the poor.

relocation program 1. In human resources management, this is when a large health-care organization or health-care system offers certain classes of employees assistance with moving to a new locale when it is required as part of their job or as a promotion. 2. In some governmental programs, there have been special social and economic assistance programs established to help purchase a home and pay for expenses related to forced moves of certain segments of special population groups. Under some unusual circumstances, some Native American families have been required to move and establish new living arrangements and locations such as being forced to move from living in certain places in reservations (e.g., the joint-use area between the Navajo and Hopi tribes in Arizona).

rem Radiation-equivalent-man or roentgen-equivalent-man. A unit of radiation dose equivalence.

rem (Lat.) 1. Thing or item. 2. Showing that actions are brought against an item rather than a person. *See in rem.*

REM (sleep) The deep-sleep period during which the sleeper exhibits rapid eye movements (REMs). This period occupies 20% to 25% of total sleep time and is needed for deep and complete sleep.

remand 1. In law and the litigation process, this is to return or send back, as in a higher court remanding a case to a lower court. 2. To commit to custody again. 3. To ask for more information on a particular point.

remedial 1. Used as a cure. 2. Able to correct a deficiency.

remedial actions In environmental health, these are actions consistent with a permanent remedy taken instead of, or in addition to, removal action in the event of a release or threatened release of a hazardous substance into the environment to prevent or minimize the release of hazardous substances so that they do not migrate to cause substantial danger to present or future public health or the environment.

remedial investigations In environmental health, this is an in-depth study designed to gather data necessary to determine the nature of and extent of contamination at a hazardous waste or Superfund site; establish criteria for cleaning up the site. These identify preliminary alternatives for remedial actions and support the technical and cost analysis of the alternatives. This is done with a feasibility study and is complementary to it. *See feasibility study.*

remedial profession Health-care personnel who assist handicapped persons achieve living and work abilities at a level that is as near normal as possible. These health-care professionals usually include recreational therapists, occupational therapists, speech therapists, physical therapists, and rehabilitation psychologists.

remedial statute 1. A new law created to correct or overcome an inadequacy found in a previously passed law. 2. A law providing a remedy or solution. 3. An intervening law.

remedies In environmental health, these are actions consistent with removal actions taken in the event of a release or threatened release of a hazardous substance into the environment; to prevent or minimize the release of hazardous substances so that they do not migrate to cause substantial danger to present or future public health or welfare or the environment.

remedy 1. In law, this is a part of the legal process used to prevent, redress, or compensate damaged parties. 2. The result of an action removing or correcting a wrong or misdeeds. 3. To make right or provide relief.

reminiscence Thinking about, reflecting on, and remembering the events, experiences, and significant activities of the earlier years of life.

reminiscent therapy In long-term care and gerontological services, this is a therapeutic interactive process whereby a therapist or counselor assists older adults with reality orientation by attempting to put meaning into life when the patient is removed from former, familiar living circumstances. The older adult is assisted in recalling the meaningful events and experiences of the past.

remise 1. A release of a claim; to give up; to surrender. 2. To forgive.

remission 1. Forgiving a penalty or forfeiture. 2. The period at the end of the course of a disease when symptoms diminish and disappear but the disease has not gone away.

remit 1. To submit or return. 2. To make less severe. 3. To give up. 4. To pay. 5. To forgive or pardon. 6. To refrain from demanding or insisting on.

remittance In health-care finance, this is money sent in or sent forward to another person or to a business such as a hospital or physician's office.

remittent fever A fever in which there is a wide

range of elevated temperatures over a 24-hour period.

remittitur 1. In health law, this is the authority of a judge to decrease an award given by a jury. 2. In health law, this is the authority of an appeals court to turn down a new trial if the two parties agree to a smaller award than would be given in court.

remittitur of record A case from an appeals court sent to a lower trial court to have the judgment of the higher court carried out.

remoteness 1. Far off in time. 2. Lacking cause and effect. 3. Not likely to be related. 4. In health law, this is lacking proximate cause; where the relationship between the supposed cause of harm or injury and the actual cause is lacking; so distantly removed from cause that damages cannot be fairly awarded.

remotivation 1. A therapy modality used as a means of reaching and motivating long-term, chronic patients residing in nursing homes and mental hospitals who do not seem interested in improvement and discharge. Remotivation must be followed by therapeutic activities leading toward rehabilitation through programs such as occupational and recreational therapy and vocational and social rehabilitation. Remotivation has been used extensively in nursing homes to stimulate and encourage therapeutic social participation. Arts and crafts and group activities such as movies, games, or singing are important remotivation factors because they offer social interaction. 2. A group therapy technique administered by nursing service personnel in a long-term-care facility or mental hospital. Withdrawn patients are put into social situations to stimulate their communication skills and interest in self, others, and their environment.

removable claim A legally filed claim that may be removed or transferred to another court.

removal 1. In environmental health, this is the cleanup of released hazardous substances from the environment. Such actions are required in the event of the release of hazardous substances into the environment. 2. Taking away from; the state of being removed; movement from one place to another.

removal actions In environmental health, this is any short-term, expedient response to cleaning up and taking away hazardous substances.

removal of a case Transferring a case from one court to another.

removal of cause 1. A change of venue. 2. To transfer a lawsuit from one jurisdiction to another.

renal dialysis In medical care, this is the use of an artificial kidney machine to treat patients with chronic kidney problems or kidney failure. The process involves cleaning the blood of waste materials normally removed by the kidneys by having the blood flow from an artery through an artificial membrane where impurities are removed and then returning the cleansed blood through a vein.

renal dialysis center A medical care facility, either freestanding or part of a hospital, equipped and staffed for the specific purpose of providing renal dialysis to kidney patients. The center usually offers the full spectrum of diagnostic, therapeutic, and rehabilitative services for renal dialysis and related kidney treatment and care, all under a licensed physician with a specialty in renal diseases. Kidney transplantation is usually done in a hospital surgical unit or a surgery center and is not a part of the center.

renal dialysis unit A medical care department in a hospital that is equipped and staffed to provide renal dialysis to kidney patients. *See renal dialysis; renal dialysis center; hemodialysis unit.*

renal failure In medical care, this is the total cessation of the kidney function caused by disease, injury, or drugs. It may be permanent or temporary and may require renal dialysis or hemodialysis.

render 1. To declare. 2. To give up. 3. To pay. 4. To perform. 5. To pronounce or state as a final decision.

rendering judgment The act of giving a decision on a case in court.

renewal 1. In contract law, this is the retention of a contract; to keep an agreement open; to restart a previously held contract. 2. In insurance, the continuance of coverage under a policy beyond its original period by the acceptance of a premium for a new policy period.

renew a motion In formal health-care meetings and hearings using parliamentary procedure, the presentation of a motion to the assembly for a second or third time.

renewal at company option In managed care, this is the right a company has to stop insuring employees as individuals, but the company cannot stop paying benefits provided by the health plan or under medical insurance in the middle of an illness or treatment.

renewal commission In managed care or insurance, these are the financial commissions paid to agents for a specified number of years after the first policy year. The rate of pay is usually lower than the first-year commission rate and is paid only on the policies that are still active.

renounce 1. To disown. 2. To fail to accept. 3. To cast off, reject. 4. To give up in an open manner. 5. To abandon. 6. To surrender.

renovation In health facilities, this is altering and renewing the structure of a building in any way and must include any one or more facility components. Operations in which load-supporting structural members are wrecked or taken out are excluded.

rental value insurance A type of insurance covering the loss of property rented by a health-care facility in the event the insured rented property becomes damaged or is destroyed.

renunciation 1. The act of disowning. 2. The giving up of a right; rejecting a right without giving it to another. 3. The act of casting off.

renvoi (French) In law, this is a rule by which a court may use the laws of the accused person's own state to decide a case.

reparable injury Any harm or wrong that can be fixed, repaired, overcome, or compensated for with money.

reparation 1. In health law, this is providing redress for a wrong; remedying or overcoming a mistake with the payment of money.

repeal 1. In law, this is the act of removing a statute by passing a new one to override it, take the place of the original one, or remove the law entirely. 2. In formal meetings in health-care organizations using parliamentary procedure, this is when the board or directors or committee desires to change a former motion, decision, or action. A formal motion to repeal is presented to the board and is acted on using usual parliamentary procedures and requires a two-thirds vote. On passage of the repeal motion, the secretary is directed to "strike the former motion from the records."

repeatability In health services or biomedical research, this is when a study is conducted many times and the same results occur again and again; identical or close results occur each time an experiment or test is conducted, making the process predictable and reliable. *See replication; reliability.*

repeated measurement studies *See repeated measures.*

repeated measures In epidemiology cohort longitudinal studies, this is the process of ensuring that the same traits, factors, and variables of the cohort are measured over and over at each re-evaluation.

repetition In health education, the review and repeating of certain health information or facts helps in learning and retention of the knowledge.

repetitively pulsed laser In laser technology, this is a specialized laser with multiple pulses of radiant energy that occur in a repeated sequence.

replacement In managed care and insurance, this is the act of surrendering an insurance policy or changing coverage under a health plan or medical insurance policy to clear the way to purchase a new policy or enroll in a different health plan.

replacement charts In health administration and human resource management, these are visual representations, in the form of charts, of the future organizational structure of the health-care organization that lay out who will be promoted and who will replace whom when job openings occur; based on a "promote from within" philosophy.

replacement cost In health-care finance, this is the inflated current market price of goods or a product used to replace a capital purchase of a similar kind.

replacement cost insurance Insurance that pays the current cost to replace health-care property damaged or destroyed, without any deduction for depreciation.

replevin A court action or a lawsuit used to recover personal property held by another.

replevy The act of having personal property returned to the party who owns it because a lawsuit was filed for the replevin of property.

replication In health services or biomedical research, this is the completion of a study, experiment, or survey several times to confirm results, increase the reliability and validity, and obtain better control of sampling error. *See reliability.*

reply 1. In law, this is a response provided in the pleading state. 2. The plaintiff's returned answer; a response to a counterclaim.

report 1. In health law, this is any formal, written document on proceedings or legal actions. 2. Any written summary or overview.

reportable diseases In epidemiology and public health, diseases that pose a danger to groups and populations that have the potential to cause death or disability and that, according to state and federal laws, regulations, or municipal ordinances, attending physicians must report to the health officer. The Centers for Disease Control and Prevention refers to these as "notifiable diseases." *See notifiable diseases.*

report card In health-care reform, managed competition, and managed-care activities, this is a standardized medical care delivery quality report of managed-care and health maintenance organizations made available to the public so that members, dependents, and potential members can compare various health plans and choose the best plan on the basis of quality of care and cost. Published performance results based on the health plan's own quality measures have been used. Some measures include yearly mammogram rates for women over 50, caesarean-section rates, and chemical dependency readmission rates. Most managed-care programs use administrative guidelines established by the National Committee for Quality Assurance, a national accreditation agency for health maintenance organizations located in Washington, D.C.

reported significant observations In occupational health and safety, this is a means of obtaining feedback from the work level on factors that contribute to an accident situation. A specialized questionnaire is used to obtain the reports and observations.

reporter 1. The published decisions of judges. 2. One who compiles or writes reports. 3. Looseleaf binders of current reports and developments in law.

reporting area In the National Vital Statistics System, these are areas designated by boundaries from which each are required to report on birth certificates. What is reported may vary according to state. Different states report standardized as well as various other characteristics such as the month during which prenatal care began or the educational level of the mother.

reporting form Special fire insurance that requires the health-care organization to periodically report the number, type, and location of insured property.

reports In law, these are the decisions of cases that are published and distributed, usually of appellant courts, all of which contribute to the building of case law.

represent 1. To speak or act under one's authority. 2. To do business for. 3. To stand in for or to act for another person.

representation 1. The act of representing. 2. A statement of fact. 3. An argument made on behalf of another person. 4. In managed care and insurance, this is an application statement made by the health-care organization to the insurance company prior to a contract being approved by the insurer, thus affecting the willingness of the insurance company to accept the risk.

representative 1. A person authorized to act and speak for others. 2. One who represents another person. 3. A public official elected to the House of Representatives.

representative action The bringing of a lawsuit by a stockholder of a corporation to overcome wrongdoings of other stockholders or to claim a right for a company or hospital.

representative sample In health services and biomedical research, this is a sampling process whereby the researcher ensures that the sample taken from the research population was not just randomly selected but was selected through some objective methodology and that it truly reflects the traits and characteristics of the study population; allowing all members of a population an equal chance of being selected for the study and ensuring that the subjects represent the study population. 2. In environmental health, this a sample of a whole area such as a lagoon, landfill, slough, or water supply that can be expected to exhibit the average properties of the whole area. *See randomization; random sampling.*

repression In mental health, this is a mental or defense mechanism that suppresses or removes unacceptable thoughts, experiences, ideas, and emotional impulses from consciousness.

reproducibility In health services and biomedical research, this is redoing or replicating a research study in the same manner and form as the original research and obtaining the same or similar results; repeatability of research.

reproduction rate *See gross reproduction rate; net reproduction rate.*

reproduction rate, gross *See gross reproduction rate.*

reproduction rate, net *See net reproduction rate.*

reproductive-age women According to government definitions, these are all women between and including the ages of 15 and 44 years. In reality, the reproductive-age range is more like 11 to 50 years, and women as old as 65 have had babies in recent times. Also referred to as "fertility."

reproductive health services A clinic, center, or unit in a health-care facility that offers family planning information and services, child-spacing assistance, and fertility testing.

reprocessing In environmental health, this is the dissolution of a used product or material and the separation and reuse of the precious parts and the reusable items; the recycling or reusing of materials after their original intended use to recover valuable materials and remove waste.

reprography 1. Copying. 2. Photographic copy machine or other copying process. *See also Xerox.*

repudiate 1. To refuse to recognize or accept something as due. 2. To disown. 3. To reject. 4. To renounce a responsibility. 5. To refuse an obligation.

repudiation of a contract Refusal to complete a contract.

repugnancy 1. To have high dislike for something. 2. To be contradictory. 3. Inconsistency, as when one part of a document is correct, thus making another part of it false.

repugnant 1. To be at variance with or to offer resistance to. 2. Highly distasteful. 3. Opposed to. 4. Contrary and inconsistent.

request for proposal (RFP) 1. In grant writing, this is a solicitation from a foundation or governmental agency notifying interested parties in the professional community that monies are available for selected or specified demonstration or research projects. 2. In hospital or health-care facilities, these are requests for proposals of bids from vendors when shopping for large-scale equipment such as computer systems and MRI and PET scanners.

required request law *See routine inquiry law.*

required services 1. Services that must be offered by a health program to meet some external standard or regulation. Under Title XIX of the Social Security Act, each state must offer certain basic health services before it can qualify as having a Medicaid program and qualify for federal matching funds. The required services are hospital services; laboratory and X-ray services; skilled nursing facility services for individuals 21 years and over; early and periodic screening, diagnosis, and treatment services for individuals under 21; family planning services; physicians' services; and home health-care services for all persons eligible for skilled nursing care. It is important to note that within these requirements states may determine the scope and extent of benefits. States may offer additional, optional services in their Medicaid programs. 2. In some states, long-term-care facilities are required to provide but not be limited to providing the following required services: physicians, skilled nursing, dietary, pharmaceutical, activity program, in-service training, special treatment for mentally disordered individuals, rehabilitation and physical therapy, dental and oral hygiene, emergency care, podiatrists, psychologists, and transportation. These services ensure that all orders, written by a person lawfully authorized to prescribe, shall be carried out unless contraindicated.

requirements contract 1. A contract where a manufacturer agrees to furnish the contractor with as many items as may be required or where a service agrees to furnish the contractor with as many visits or services as required. 2. When a health-care facility agrees to purchase a certain product and abide by the requirements of that product (e.g., to buy a certain type of syringe and to agree to use only that company's inserts in it).

requisition 1. A written request made for an item, good, or property to which one is rightfully entitled. 2. A claim made by authority. 3. A written demand for items needed.

reregistration In environmental health, this is the reevaluation and relicensing of existing pesticides originally registered prior to current scientific and regulatory standards. The EPA reregisters pesticides through its Registration Standards Program.

res (Lat.) 1. A thing; object or items. 2. The issues or actions that are in rem.

rescind 1. To cancel or terminate. 2. To annul or end a contract. 3. To release a party from obligation.

research Conscious action to investigate or acquire deeper knowledge or new facts about scientific or technical subjects; the process of using data, findings, facts and information to verify and ascertain facts about that which is assumed to exist or that which is based on subjective observations; proving that which is speculated about; planned investigations, surveys, inquiries, or experimental trials used to prove or disprove facts or hypotheses. Research can explore or investigate information retrospectively (backward in time), cross-sectionally (at a point in time), or prospectively (forward in time). In health services, scientific investigation or inquiry is classified into several categories: biomedical, behavioral, technological or organizational, and services delivery.

research and development The extension of investigative findings and theories of a scientific or technical nature into practical application for experimental or demonstration purposes, including the production and testing of models, devices, equipment, and processes.

research committee In managed care and insurance organizations, this is a multidepartmental group that assesses and studies issues and concerns related to membership, health-care delivery patterns, utilization, medical outcomes, cost-effectiveness, demographics, and related information that impacts the health plan. The insurance committee for an insurance company also assesses products and their development and implementation, underwriting practices, operations, procedures, and actuarial issues.

research design The process of planning, setting up, conducting subject selection and controls, using sampling methodologies, and choosing design methodology and scientifically accepted approaches of inquiry that produce unbiased, objective, and credible findings. Research designs can explore or investigate information retrospectively (backward in time), cross-sectionally (at a point in time), or prospectively (forward in time). Experimental design that is a prospective type of study involves having at least two research groups (one treatment group and one control group) from which certain factors or variables are assessed and evaluated statistically. How treatment groups and the control groups are established is determined by the approach to be chosen. Sometimes researchers and subjects are not allowed to know who is getting the treatment and who is not. These are called blind studies, and many arrangements are available (e.g., double-blind studies). Survey research often uses many of these same design approaches, including control groups. Survey research is key to collecting information from populations for epidemiological and public health purposes.

research, epidemiological *See epidemiological research.*

research grants Money awarded to scientists for the purpose of testing new ideas or developing new areas of knowledge.

Research Grants Index A federal publication produced by the Department of Health and Human Services that indexes current health research supported by the federal government.

research laboratory In hazardous waste and potentially infectious materials management, federal regulations define this as any laboratory producing or using research laboratory–scale amounts of HIV or HBV. Research laboratories may produce high concentrations of HIV or HBV but not in the volume found in production facilities.

research sampling techniques Methods of selecting representative samples of a population; research sampling methods that increase effectiveness and objectivity in predicting findings and the ability to predict future findings or project the results to general populations.

resectoscope In medical care, this is a surgical instrument used in resection of the prostate or tumors from the bladder; one type of an endoscope.

reserpine A drug made from the root of the *Rauwolfia serpentina* plant. This alkaloid extract is used primarily as an antihypertensive agent. It was once used as an antipsychotic agent because of its sedative effect.

reserve 1. An amount of money set aside by an insurance company to guarantee its ability to fulfill its commitments to future claims. 2. To hold back for later use. 3. To keep control of. 4. To keep as one's own. 5. Restraint in speech or actions.

reserve accounts In health-care finance, these are profits or funds set aside for a specific reason, fund, or commitment.

reserves 1. In managed care and insurance, this is a financial management method establishing a fund for retaining monies already committed to certain services or financial liabilities (e.g., services yet to be delivered, money yet to be spent, and obligations yet to be met). Thus the money is retained in the reserve fund for these purpose. A percentage of health plan premiums or insurance premiums are used to support the reserve fund. 2. A balance sheet account set up to report liabilities still to be faced by an insurance company under active insurance policies. The purpose is to secure an accurate picture of the financial condition of the organization (by permitting conversion of disbursements from a paid to an accrual basis). The company sets the amount of reserves in accord with its own estimates, state laws, and recommendations of supervisory officials and national organizations. Regulatory agencies can accept the reserves or refuse them as inadequate or excessive. For example, in Blue Cross plans, reserves are set aside to cover average monthly claims and operating expenses for a certain time period. 3. Reserves, while estimated, are all obligated amounts and have four principal components: reserves for known liabilities not yet paid, reserves for losses incurred but unreported, reserves for future benefits, and other reserves for various special purposes, including contingency reserves for unforeseen circumstances.

reservoir 1. In epidemiology, this is an organism or medium that harbors a disease such as an animal, human, or nutritional substance that promotes the propagation of a pathogen; one of four factors identified to contribute to the cause of a disease outbreak as identified in the epidemiology triangle. The other three factors are agent, host, and time. 2. In environmental health, this is any natural or artificial holding area used to store, regulate, or control water or liquids. *See epidemiology triangle.*

reservoir of infection In epidemiology, this refers to any soil, plant, insect, animal, human, or any combination thereof in which a pathogen or infectious agent lives and thrives, depends on the organism for its survival, and can be transmitted to a host. *See agent; host and time.*

res gestae (Lat.) 1. Things done or the thing done. 2. The acts and words of an event that provide a clearer understanding of it. 3. A transaction. 4. Everything said and done as part of a single incident.

residence In census gathering activities and public health research, this is how the type and size of places where individuals live are classified: large urban (The ten largest Standard Metropolitan Statistical Areas), other urban (all other urban residences), rural nonfarm, and rural farm. Other classifications are Standard Metropolitan Statistical Area (central city); Standard Metropolitan Statistical Area (other); urban (non-Standard Metropolitan Statistical Area); rural, nonfarm; and rural, farm.

residency A prolonged (usually 1 or more complete years) period of on-the-job training that may be a part of a formal educational program or may be undertaken separately after completion of a formal program, sometimes to fulfill a requirement for credentialing. In medicine, dentistry, podiatry, and some other medical professions, residencies are the principal part of graduate medical education, beginning after either graduation or internship and lasting 2 to 7 years and providing specialty training. Most physicians take residencies in 1 of the 23 specialty areas, although they are not required for licensure as a physician. Residencies are needed for board eligibility. In health-care administration, most masters degrees in health-care administration require an extensive on-the-job administrative field experience or internship called an "administrative residency." *See administrative residency; resident, administrative.*

residency, administrative *See administrative residency; resident, administrative.*

residency, medical *See residency.*

resident 1. The status of and title given to a graduate of a medical, osteopathic, or dental school who has gone on for further training and is completing an advanced period of postgraduate training in a specialization area, usually in a hospital or clinic. This represents the first and subsequent years of clinical graduate training by treating patients under the supervision of other physicians. Certification or board eligibility is often the final outcome. 2. In health administration, this is the title of a student participating in an administrative residency/internship program in hospital administration, medical group management, health maintenance organization administration, or health services administration through on-the-job management training in a health-care organization. The administrative student works under the supervision of a top-level administrator who serves as a mentor and supervisor for administrative training. 2. Any individual residing within the boundaries of a state regardless of the length of stay. 3. The label often given a patient in a nursing home, indicating that the individual lives in the nursing home and is not a patient in a short-stay hospital but is residing there for the long term and thus needs to be viewed differently than an individual in the facility for a short-term stay because the nursing home is more like their new home than a hospital. A person who has been formally admitted to but not discharged from a long-term-care facility.

resident, administrative A graduate student, usually in a masters in health administration program, who, through an educationally controlled program, works in an administrative capacity under the direction of a top-level healthcare administrator/preceptor in a health-care organization to gain advanced practical experience in the tasks and responsibilities of high-level health-care management, which is required as part of the graduation requirements.

resident assessment protocol (RAP) In long-term-care administration and patient care, this is the identification of problems, complications, and risk factors common to long-term-care patients. A list of 18 problems, complications, and risk factors that may need intervention or referral has been identified. These factors are seen as trigger areas because they start action toward intervention of treatment: delirium, cognitive loss/dementia, visual function, communication, activities of daily living functional/have rehabilitation potential, urinary incontinence and indwelling catheter, psychosocial well-being, mood state, behavioral problem, activities, falls, nutritional status, feeding tubes, dehydration/fluid maintenance, dental care, pressure ulcers, psychotropic drug use, and physical restraints needed.

residential areas In community or public health, these are areas where people live or reside; housing and the property on which homes or buildings are located, including neighborhood playgrounds, parks, and other public areas in the community.

residential care A house or other domicile that provides room and board in a protective environment with a program planned to meet the residents' nutritional, social, and spiritual needs. Also called "board and care homes."

residential care and elderly housing A specialized housing approach for older adults who are healthy, mobile, and independent and require little or no medical care or nursing services but may require some assistance in the activities of daily living. Sheltered care living for developmentally disabled persons, long-term psychiatric care, and board and care for the elderly are all included in this type of housing arrangement.

residential care facility A long-term-care facility where a protective care environment is provided, including room, board, and personal care on a 24-hour basis, to elderly persons not needing skilled institutional care but where social and daily living needs rather than medical needs are stressed. These individuals find it difficult to remain in their own homes because of health and medical problems and need minor care and personal living assistance. Trained staff often includes an LVN who provides personal care, assistance, personal hygiene, assistance with medications, and social and recreational activities. Examples of these institutions include centers for the developmentally disabled, halfway houses, personal care facilities, and therapeutic communities for the elderly and mentally ill.

residential health-care facility (RHCF) See *residential treatment facility*.

residential home care See *home health care; foster care*.

residential programs According to JCAHO for psychiatric, alcoholism, and drug abuse facilities accreditation purposes, programs that provide services to persons who require a less restrictive environment than individuals in an inpatient program and who are capable of self-preservation during an internal disaster. Such programs are usually located in facilities classified as residential occupancies in Chapter 11 of the 1973 edition of the Life Safety Code (NFPA 101).

residential solid wastes In environmental health, this is garbage, rubbish, trash, and other solid waste resulting from the normal activities of households.

residential treatment care In mental health services, this is the provision of overnight mental health care in conjunction with an intensive treatment program in a setting other than a hospital. Included are centers for emotionally disturbed children and residential treatment centers for mentally ill adults.

residential treatment facility A live-in center where a patient receives treatment appropriate for his or her particular needs. A children's residential treatment facility often will furnish educational training and therapy for the emotionally disturbed child.

residential treatment centers for emotionally disturbed children 1. A residential care center for children with emotional and behavior problems that must meet all the following criteria: 1) not licensed as a psychiatric hospital and has the primary purpose of providing individually planned mental health treatment services in conjunction with residential care; 2) has a clinical program directed by a psychiatrist, psychologist, social worker, or graduate trained psychiatric nurse; 3) serves children and youth primarily under the age of 18; and 4) the primary reason for the majority of admissions is mental illness as classified by DSM-IIIR/ICD-9-CM codes, other than mental retardation, developmental disability, and substance abuse–related disorders. 2. A live-in residential institution serving children with emotional and behavioral problems that provides therapy, treatment and rehabilitative services under the supervision of a psychiatrist and other clinical staff such as psychologists and social workers.

residential treatment facility for emotionally disturbed children See *residential treatment centers for emotionally disturbed children.*

resident, long-term-care An individual who is an inpatient in a convalescent center or nursing home who needs basic nursing care but does not need the level of care provided in a hospital setting.

resident, medical See *resident.*

resident population In public health and epidemiology, these are persons living in the United States, including members of the armed forces stationed in the United States and their families as well as foreigners working or studying in the United States. Excluded are foreign military, naval, and diplomatic personnel and their families located in the United States and residing in embassies or similar quarters of other countries as well as Americans living abroad. The resident population is often the denominator when calculating birth and death rates and incidence rates of disease.

residual In environmental health, this is the amount of a pollutant remaining in the environment after a natural or technological process has taken place (e.g., the sludge remaining after initial wastewater treatment or particulates remaining in the air after the air passes through a scrubbing or other air cleaning process).

residual disinfectant concentration In environmental health, this is the concentration of disinfectant measured in milligrams per liter in a representative sample of water.

residual risks In public health, these are any risks that remain after the application of resources for prevention or mitigation.

residuary 1. That which is left over. 2. Pertaining to those parts remaining after other parts have been disposed of or removed.

residues In environmental health, these are hazardous materials remaining after shipping as may be found in a tank car or boat tanker after its contents have been unloaded to the maximum extent practicable and before it is either refilled or cleaned of hazardous materials and purged to remove any hazardous vapors.

residuum (Lat.) A balance; a residue.

resile 1. To withdraw. 2. To recede from an issue, cause, or purpose.

res integra (Lat.) 1. Whole thing. 2. As yet undecided and without precedent.

res ipsa loquitur (Lat.) 1. The thing speaks for itself. 2. The shift of the burden of proof from the plaintiff to the defendant; when the obvious becomes evident in and of itself such as a surgical instrument found inside a patient following an operation. 3. In malpractice, a legal doctrine or presumption that, when an injury occurs to a plaintiff through a situation under the sole and exclusive control of the defendant and where such injury would not normally occur if the one in control had used due care, was diligent in work effort, and was reasonably careful, the defendant is negligent (e.g., when a surgeon leaves a clamp or another item in the abdomen of a patient). Influencing factors or elements are 1) the event would not normally have occurred in the absence of negligence, 2) the defendant must have had exclusive control over the instrumentality that caused the injury, and 3) the plaintiff must not have contributed to the injury (Ybarra v. Spangard, 25 Cal. 2d 486, 154 P. 2d 687 [1944]).

resistance to change 1. In health administration and organizational behavior, this is when employees would prefer that things remain as they are and prefer the status quo or show outright opposition to new or different ideas, technology, human resource realignment, management approaches, or organizational rearrangement. 2. In health promotion and behavioral health, this is when individuals or groups resist adapting a healthier lifestyle or fail to give up self-destructive habits or behaviors.

resistive behaviors In mental health, these are behaviors that inhibit change, compliance, involvement, and cooperation.

res judicata (Lat.) 1. A thing decided. 2. A matter once decided by judgment or a competent court cannot thereafter be reconsidered by the same or another court.

resolution 1. A decision of the court. 2. An official opinion of a governmental body or legislature. 3. A principle that is created by a vote but does not become law. 4. In health services and biomedical research, this is the level of effectiveness of a test and its ability to produce highly credible results; the power of the test.

resonant cavity In laser technology, this is the structure or area located between the high reflective mirror and the output coupler that sustains any whole number of half wavelengths.

resort 1. To apply to something for help. 2. The gaining of an end. 3. In law, this is the final end, as in the last resort (e.g., a court of last resort is the final court of appeal).

resource Any person, thing, or action needed for living or to improve the quality of life.

resource-based relative values scale (RBRVS) In managed care, this is a system of classification used to determine health-care provider reimbursement by health plans. The classification system measures skill and training needed to deliver a certain health service, procedure, or treatment. The system has the intent of reevaluating Medicare's tendency to overcompensate procedures and services such as surgery and testing while underpaying primary care services that take time such as spending time with patients doing patient education and conducting physical and diagnostic exams. This system, started in 1992, has a major new approach to compensating physicians for Medicare services. *See relative value scale.*

resource capacity The amount and distribution of services that can be provided by the usable, available resources in a given geographic area.

resource conservation In environmental health, this is the reduction of the amounts of solid waste that are generated, reduction of overall resource consumption, and utilization of recovered resources.

Resource Conservation and Recovery Act (RCRA) In environmental health, these are the federal laws passed in 1976 to provide federal and state hazardous waste management regulations and guidelines that promote the protection of health and the environment and conserve valuable material and energy resources. In 1984 the Hazardous and Solid Waste Amendments (HSWA) were passed. The original law requires industry to identify and list all hazardous wastes and to note the toxicity, persistence, degradability in nature, potential for accumulation in tissue, and other characteristics of the waste materials. The RCRA sets forth rules and standards for hazardous waste generators to protect human health and the environment. The HSWA added to the RCRA by requiring corrective action to be taken at sites with continuing hazardous waste releases. The RCRA sets forth performance standards for treatment, storage, and disposal facilities and also includes the requirements for record keeping, container labeling, component disclosure, and use of a manifest system to track hazardous waste movement for reporting to the Environmental Protection Agency. The original law deals with old chemicals, not new ones. The regulations are designed to deal with the chemicals as they are thrown away. When the chemical is already classified as a hazardous waste, it requires cradle-to-grave tracking through a manifest. The law regulates treatment, storage, and disposal facilities. *See treatment, storage, and disposal facilities.*

resource development In health-care delivery and development, these are activities that focus on the education, training, and skill development of allied health and health-care professionals and their recruitment. This also deals with the construction, renovation, and modernization of health-care facilities.

resource recovery In environmental health, this is the process of recovering material or energy from solid waste.

resource recovery facilities In environmental health, these are the facilities at which solid waste is processed for the purpose of extracting, converting to energy, or otherwise separating and preparing solid waste for reuse and recycling.

resource recovery systems In environmental health, these are the solid waste management systems that provide collection, separation, recycling, and recovery of solid wastes, including disposal of nonrecoverable waste residues.

resource requirements The identification of the material, money, and manpower necessary to reach a goal.

resources 1. Sources of support available to an individual in addition to one's regular earned or unearned income. Generally, resources refer to an individual's wealth or property (including cash savings, stocks and bonds, a home, other real estate, the cash value of life insurance, an automobile, or jewelry) that could be converted to cash if necessary. Existing programs for the poor generally set a limit on the total amount of resources an individual or family may have and still be eligible. Most existing resource tests exempt a home of reasonable value on the basis that it would not be reasonable to require selling a home to qualify for benefits. 2. The providers, institutions, health manpower, and facilities used for the provision of health services in the national health-care system or local health system. 3. In health administration, these are items or materials necessary for a health-care organization to operate effectively and efficiently such as skilled personnel, professional personnel, equipment, money, and supplies.

resources development Activities that focus especially on the recruitment and education of health-care professionals or the construction and modernization of health-care facilities.

resource utilization groups (RUGs) A prospective, case mix reimbursement system for long-term-care facilities first developed in New York State; a standard method of grouping nursing home patients by the services they require. Nursing home patients are classified into nine groups that reflect an increasingly greater level of care needed to assist the patient in activities of daily living (ADLs). Each RUG is then weighted, and the care of a patient with minimal needs is reimbursed at a lower rate than a patient requiring total care. Such a system encourages the use of noninstitutional care for patients with minimal needs because there is no financial incentive to keep them in an institutional setting. Likewise, there would be less of a financial burden to care for patients requiring higher levels of resource use because rates are weighted to compensate for those additional resources. The RUGs system would require careful monitoring to ensure that patients are not allowed to deteriorate just so that the facility may qualify for higher reimbursement.

respirator In medical care, this is a device used to assist with or take over the breathing functions of patients who have difficulty breathing on their own and who have temporary or permanent diseases, conditions, or disorders of the lungs or pulmonary or cardiopulmonary system.

respiratory arrest In medical care, this is a medical emergency that occurs when a patient ceases to breathe. Artificial respiration is used to restore breathing, or, in a definitive care setting, oxygen is used. If heart failure accompanies respiratory arrest, CPR (cardiopulmonary resuscitation) is used.

respiratory care department According to JCAHO for hospital accreditation purposes, an organizational unit of the hospital designed for the provision of ventilator support and associated services to patients.

respiratory care services According to JCAHO for hospital accreditation purposes, this is an organizational unit in a hospital that provides for the delivery of care to provide ventilator support and associated services for patients. Standards are applied to evaluate a hospital's performance in providing respiratory care services.

respiratory care technician According to JCAHO for accreditation purposes, this individual has been certified by the National Board for Respiratory Care after successfully completing all education, experience, and examination requirements.

respiratory disease unit A specially equipped and staffed unit in a health-care facility for the provision of assessment and treatment activities for patients with respiratory disorders, conditions, and diseases.

respiratory distress syndrome (RDS) A medical care concern for infants, this is an acute respiratory condition in premature infants caused by a deficiency of pulmonary development and pulmonary surface area to absorb adequate oxygen. In severe cases, mechanical devices and equipment are employed to assist the infant in breathing.

respiratory therapist 1. An individual who works under a physician's supervision and administers prescribed respiratory drugs, therapy, care, and life support to patients with deficiencies and abnormalities of the lungs and cardiopulmonary system. The respiratory therapist has a variety of duties: setting up, operating, and monitoring devices such as respirators, mechanical ventilators, therapeutic gas administration apparatus, environmental control systems, and aerosol generators; performing bronchopulmonary drainage; assisting patients with breathing exercises; and monitoring patients' physiological responses to therapy. In many work settings, respiratory therapists are required to exercise a considerable degree of independent clinical judgment in the respiratory care of patients under the direct or indirect supervision of a physician. Further, the respiratory therapist is expected to be capable of serving as a technical resource to the physician regarding current practices in respiratory care and to the hospital staff regarding safe and effective therapies. In addition, therapists may supervise trainees and technicians. Respiratory therapists are almost always employed by hospitals. They cover intensive care units, newborn nurseries, surgical and medical areas, and emergency rooms. This training and knowledge in respiratory therapy comes from a formal academic and clinical training experience of at least 2 years. 2. According to JCAHO for accreditation purposes, a respiratory therapist has successfully completed a training program accredited by the Joint Review Committee for Respiratory Therapy Education and is eligible to take the registry examination administered by the National Board for Respiratory Therapy, Inc., or has the documented equivalent in training and/or experience. *See also registered respiratory therapist.*

respiratory therapist, registered *See registered respiratory therapist.*

respiratory therapy 1. A course of study that includes instruction in ventilator therapy, cardiorespiratory rehabilitation, microenvironmental control, and diagnostic testing of the patient's respiratory system. 2. The clinical diagnosis, assessment, exercises, testing, therapy, and treatment of breathing and respiratory diseases, disorders, and conditions through the administration of oxygen, potent drugs, and other gases through inhalation or positive pressure.

respiratory therapy assistant An individual who assists the respiratory therapist in carrying out prescribed diagnostic testing, therapy, and treatment and transporting patients as well as assisting with the specialized equipment used in the unit.

respiratory therapy services Health-care services that are staffed and equipped to treat, manage, and control the care of patients with deficiencies and abnormalities in the cardiopulmonary system through the administration of oxygen and appropriate drugs by inhalation or positive air pressure.

respiratory therapy technician 1. A technician who works under the supervision of a respiratory therapist or a physician and performs clinical duties essentially identical to those of the therapist. This person practices the specialized technical aspects, skills, and knowledge of general respiratory therapeutics, which is gained by completing at least a 1 year of formal education and clinical experience. Generally, however, this individual does not engage in teaching, administration, supervision, or evaluation of new equipment and therapeutic modalities. Although duties vary with the employing institution, technicians usually exercise a lesser degree of independent judgment and responsibility than that of a respiratory therapist, usually because their formal training in anatomy, physiology, pharmacology, and clinical practice is less extensive than that of the therapist. Primarily working in hospital settings, technicians provide treatment and maintain patient records. 2. According to JCAHO for accreditation purposes, this is an individual who has successfully completed a training program accredited by the American Medical Association Committee on Allied Health and Education and Accreditation in collaboration with the Joint Review Committee for Respiratory Therapy Education and is eligible to take the certification examination administered by the National Board for Respiratory Therapy, Inc., or has the documented equivalent in training and/or experience.

respiratory therapy technician, certified *See respiratory therapy technician.*

respiratory therapy technology A course of study that prepares persons to operate and maintain equipment used in therapy and supportive treatment functions of the body's respiratory system. Under the direction of a physician, oxygen, therapeutic gases, and mist inhalants are administered to patients. This program also trains individuals to respond to emergency situations and provide therapy to patients with severe respiratory disorders requiring intensive care. Minor repair of equipment is also taught.

respite To rest from; a temporarily relief; an interval of rest; temporary period of relief or rest.

respite care Short-term care provided by nonfamily members to ill or disabled dependent family members, such as a mentally retarded child, an ill elderly person, or a disabled family member, in a special center or agency or in the home to relieve the family or caregivers from their 24-hour, 7-day-a-week care and supervision; services or facilities that provide short-term placement of dependent persons to provide caregivers or family members time away to handle emergencies, have rest, be relieved of care for a period of time, take vacations, meet planned absences, shop, or handle personal affairs.

respite care center A facility that can accept and accommodate handicapped, elderly, or disabled persons for short-term placement to provide short-term rest and relief from caregiving.

respite care registry program A service provided to caregivers or family members where a temporary employment agency of qualified personnel are available to provide respite services.

respondeat superior (Lat.) 1. Let the superior answer; let the master respond. 2. A legal principle, founded in principles of vicarious liability, under the law of agency where an employer such as a health service organization is the master and is responsible for the actions of those under its employ (agents) who carry out their duties of employment. Liability can exist for the superior/principal in situations where wrongful acts are committed by an agent. This principle often applies to the relationship between physicians and allied health-care providers. 3. In malpractice, a form of vicarious liability whereby an employer is held liable for the wrongful acts of an employee even though the employer's conduct is without fault. Before liability predicated on respondeat superior may be imposed on an employer, it is necessary that a master/servant (i.e., controlling) relationship exist between the employer and employee and that the wrongful act of the employee occur within the scope of his or her employment. The doctrine of respondeat superior does not absolve the original wrongdoer, the employee, of liability for a wrongful act. Not only may the injured party sue the employee directly, but the employer may seek indemnification from him or her.

respondent 1. In law, this is the one who answers or responds; the party against whom an appeal is made or a motion is filed. 2. An appellee.

response actions In environmental health, these are actions on either a short-term or a long-term removal response that may include but are not limited to removing hazardous materials from a site to an approved hazardous waste facility for treatment, containment, or destruction; containing the wastes safely on-site; and identifying and removing the source of groundwater contamination and halting further migration of contaminants. Also included are methods that protect human health and the environment from asbestos-containing materials.

response rate 1. In emergency health services delivery, this is the generally acceptable maximum allowable time for a victim to wait to receive medical aid without suffering long-term effects from an injury or illness. 2. In health services and biomedical research or epidemiology, this is how well a research project is participated in or how many completed and returned research surveys are received. It is often stated in research that a 50% return rate on questionnaire research, especially when using a mail-in questionnaire approach, is a good response rate. If made into a true mathematical rate, it is calculated by dividing the total number of returned questionnaires in the numerator by the total study population in the denominator and multiplying them by 100.

response time 1. In computers, the time a computer system takes to give a response to the user. 2. In emergency care, this is the amount of time taken to respond to a medical, fire, or police emergency; total elapsed time from the receipt of the call by the ambulance, paramedics, air ambulance/helicopter, or fire department until they arrive at the location of the accident or emergency.

responsibility 1. In health administration and management, this is one of three elements of the delegation process. For an administrator is to be effective and successful, he or she must delegate an equal amount of authority and responsibility with a follow-up (return and report) accountability system. When all three delegation elements are present, an employee is empowered to be successful at the delegated task. 2. The obligation of a worker to perform work or tasks as required by a superior. Responsibility is work-related activities given to an employee to follow through with, accomplish, and complete; an employee's obligation to perform certain assigned duties.

responsibility accounting 1. In health administration and financial management, this is the process of accounting for and reporting all operational activity in a health-care organization by a responsibility center. Also referred to as "responsibility reporting." 2. In health-care financial management, this is an accounting system that uses historical, current, and projected statistical and monetary data as they relate to revenues and expenses to keep track of and account for financial activities in each designated organizational unit that produces revenues or incurs expenses. *See responsibility center.*

responsibility center In health administration and management, this is the most basic unit of organizational activity found at the lowest supervisory level. In health-care organizations, centers of responsibility are determined by administration and may be reflected in the organizational chart. Some examples of responsibility centers in a hospital are nursing services, outpatient/ambulatory surgery, operations, and ancillary services. Each responsibility center has an administrator who is in charge of and responsible for all activities of this administrative unit.

responsibility center manager In health administration and management, this is the supervisor or administrator who does all the planning, coordination, communication, and controlling and has overall charge of and accountability for activities in the responsibility center. Sometimes called a "first-line supervisor," "charge nurse," or "primary monitor."

responsibility reporting *See responsibility accounting.*

responsibility to duty In health law, this is an obligation to perform an act or carry out a duty. When a health-care provider is expected to render reasonable assistance to an injured or sick party, a responsibility to duty exists.

responsible party 1. In health law, liability, or medical malpractice, this is the person or persons who are at fault; the ones who have a role in the proximate cause of the injury, harm, or damage. 2. The health-care provider who is legally responsible for placement of a patient in a health-care facility. 3. The legal guardian or conservator of a patient who holds the legal rights of the patient with regard to treatment decisions, informed consent, and payment and care on discharge.

REST Respiratory therapist.

restart In computers, to resume a program; to execute a software program again.

rest homes In long-term care, these are facilities that provide only custodial care, usually to elderly persons with some chronic diseases. Some homes offer limited nursing care but do not have a licensed, well-trained staff such as that found in an intermediate care facility or skilled nursing home; a lay term for a nursing home, convalescent hospital, board and care home, or custodial care home.

restitution 1. The act of restoring or giving back. 2. To make good on or to keep a promise. 3. The restoration of a right or property to one unjustly deprived of it.

restoration In environmental health, these are the actions taken to return an injured person, property, or other resource to its original condition as measured in terms of the physical, chemical, or biological properties or the services it previously provided when such actions are in addition to response actions completed or anticipated and when such actions exceed the level of response determined appropriate (EPA).

restrain 1. To deprive one from liberty. 2. To stop an issue or action. 3. To restrict or limit. 4. To hinder or obstruct. 5. To hold back or interpose on a proceeding.

restraining order A temporary court order given without a trial or hearing that provides for the status quo to remain until a formal action or hearing can be held to determine the necessary action. Also referred to as a "TRO" (temporary restraining order).

restraint 1. An action occasionally used in nursing homes or mental institutions to hold patients down so that they will not harm themselves or others. Drugs are now more widely used to calm patients, and physical restraints are necessary less often. The wrongful use of restraints can be legally viewed as a deprivation of liberty or false imprisonment with legal consequences if used without doctor's orders or just reason such as protecting a patient from harming him- or herself, and then only short-term, temporary use is allowed. 2. According to JCAHO for psychiatric, alcoholism, and drug abuse facilities accreditation purposes, a physical or mechanical device used to restrict the movement of the whole body or a portion of a patient's body. This does not include mechanisms used to assist a patient in obtaining and maintaining normative body functioning (e.g., braces and wheelchairs). 3. According to JCAHO hospital accreditation standards, this is the use of physical or mechanical devices to restrain the involuntary movements of a patient or a portion of the patient's body as a means of controlling his or her physical activities to protect the patient or others from injury. This form of restraint differs from mechanisms usually and customarily employed during medical, diagnostic, or surgical procedures that are considered a regular part of such procedures. Such mechanisms include but are not limited to body restraint during surgery, arm restraint during intravenous administration, and temporary physical restraint prior to administration of electroconvulsive therapy. Some devices are not considered restraint interventions, including those used to protect the patient such as bed rails, tabletop chairs, protective nets, helmets, or the temporary use of halter-type or soft-chest restraints and mechanisms (e.g., orthopedic appliances, braces, wheelchairs, or other appliances) and those used to posturally support the patient or assist him or her in obtaining and maintaining normative bodily functioning. *See chemical restraints; physical restraints.*

restricted activity day In assessing disability or the need for rehabilitation, it must be determined whether or when an individual must cut down on his or her usual activities for a whole day because of an illness or injury. "Usual activities" means that, for any one day, these are the activities, appointments, encounters, or daily living things that an individual would ordinarily do on that day. For school-aged children, usual activities are the usual activities that are a part of the child's daily regular pattern and that are influenced and controlled by the child's age, school attendance and schedules, weather, extracurricular activities, etc. For older adults, this usually consists of the ability to complete their usual routine. Any interference or cutting down on usual activity is restricted activity, which does not imply complete inactivity but does account for being able to do only minimal activities for one whole day. Persons with chronic diseases often do not report restricted activity days because they see the daily care of the disease as a part of their regular routine yet could have restricted daily activity. A day spent confined to bed or a day at home from work or school because of injury or illness is a restricted activity day. In public health surveys, unduplicated counts of bed-disability, work-loss, and school-loss days as well as other days during which a person cut down on his or her usual activities are considered restricted activity days; the number of days a person experiences at least one of the following: cut-down days, school-loss days for children, work-loss days for adults over 18 years of age, and bed days. For example, being the most inclusive and least descriptive measure, 3 days of restricted activity also can mean 3 bed days because of a serious illness or 3 days where an individual merely cut down on his or her activities because of a minor injury or illness. *See disability day; bed disability; restriction of activity.*

restricted area In environmental health, this is any area to which access is controlled by the licensee for purposes of protection of individuals from exposure to radioactive materials, radiation, or hazardous materials.

restricted assets In health-care financial management, especially nonprofit health-care organizations and hospitals, these are funds such as grants, endowments, earmarked funds, or pension monies that are established and set aside for a designated purpose and cannot be used for any other purpose. Also referred to as "restricted funds."

restricted debate In formal health-care meetings and hearings using parliamentary procedure, a formal discussion restricted to a proposed motion, a submotion, or a minor motion or how a minor motion relates to the main motion yet does not open up discussion of the main motion.

restricted funds In health-care financial management, especially nonprofit health-care organizations and hospitals, these are monies such as endowments, grants, earmarked funds, or pension monies that have a designated purpose and must be used for that purpose as specified by the grantors, donors, or granting agencies; funds with limited or designated use; monies given to a health-care facility that can be spent for specific projects or purposes. Similar to restricted assets. *See restricted assets.*

restricted use In environmental health, this is when a pesticide is registered, and some or all its uses are classified under the Federal Insecticide Fungicide Rodenticide Act (FIFRA) regulations for restricted use if the pesticide requires special handling because of its toxicity. Restricted-use pesticides may be applied only by trained, certified applicators or those under their direct supervision. *See restricted-use pesticide.*

restricted-use pesticide In environmental health, this is when a pesticide is classified for restricted use under the provisions of the Federal Insecticide Fungicide Rodenticide Act (FIFRA), which states that if the administrator determines that the pesticide, when applied in accordance with its directions for use, warnings, and cautions and for the uses for which it is registered, or for one or more of such uses, or in accordance with widespread and commonly recognized practice, may generally cause, without additional regulatory restrictions, unreasonable adverse effects on the environment, including injury to the applicator, he shall classify the pesticide, or the particular use or uses to which the determination applies, for restricted use.

restricted work activity In occupational health and safety, these are days a worker was assigned to a temporary job due to injury or illness, or the employee worked at a permanent job less than full-time or worked at a permanently assigned job but could not perform all activities or duties associated with it or expected in that job. If the worker becomes ill on the job, lost workday calculations usually do not include the day of the onset of illness or day of injury. *See lost work days.*

restriction of activity For public health research purposes, four types of restricted activity are used: bed days, work-loss days, school-loss days, and cut-down days. Work-loss days include only those in the work life span, ages 18 through 65. School-loss days include children ages 5 through 17. Both acute and chronic conditions account for restricted activities and may or not be the sole cause of restricted activity. Also, this is any behavior associated with having a limitation placed on, or cutting back of, activity because of long-term or short-term illness, injury, or conditions or when what an individual is normally capable of doing is restricted, which can be a short-term reduction in activities that an individual is accustomed to doing or when a person's activities fall below his or her normal capacity.

restrictive indorsement In health-care finance, this is signing a check or negotiable instrument so that it ends its negotiability (e.g., "For deposit only to the account of Riverview Hospital").

restructuring In health-care administration, this is the process of reorganizing a hospital or other health-care organization, usually for the purpose of improving quality, efficiency, and effectiveness of the organization or to accommodate new services, demographic shifts in the catchment area, new approaches to the delivery of care, or changes in the economic, social, and political climate.

RESTT Respiratory therapy technician.

result 1. The final outcome and conclusions of a research study; representing the findings of a study or the outcome of a test or intervention. 2. A value or quantity derived at by calculation.

résumé A summarized account or listing of an individual's education, training, professional experience, career activities, personal data, honors, and other qualifications relevant to a position for which he or she is applying or to the activities of a research proposal requesting funds. Also called a "curriculum vitae" (CV), or "vitae," the difference being that a curriculum vitae outlines relevant course work or training, whereas a résumé may not.

resuscitation In medical care or emergency care, this is the revival of a person who is not breathing or whose heart is not beating by applying cardiopulmonary resuscitation (CPR) and/or artificial respiration. In a definitive care setting, specialized equipment that aids with the flow of oxygen and provides external electrical stimulation to the heart may be used to revive a patient.

RET *See rational emotive therapy.*

retail outlet distribution system In managed care or insurance, this is a system of storefronts where future members or customers can purchase insurance or health plan coverage by contacting an agent or insurance company representative directly by going into the office or storefront in a shopping center, shopping mall, or other retail outlet so that potential health plan members or insurance consumers can shop for insurance while shopping for other personal items.

retainer An advance fee paid to a professional to enlist his or her services.

retaliatory law In insurance law, when one state passes a statute imposing a burden through taxation on certain insurance companies operating within its boundaries and other states follow by imposing a similar burden on insurance companies chartered in the first state.

retardation The lack of or slowness in the development or progress of a person. Mental retardation is a slowness of intellectual maturation. Psychomotor retardation is slow psychic activity, motor activity, or both. This form can be observed in pathological depression. *See IQ.*

retention 1. In managed care, this is when a portion of the premiums for a health plan benefit or medical care coverage is kept by the insurance company or health plan to cover internal costs or for profitability of the company. Also referred to as "administrative costs." 2. In liability insurance, this is the portion of a risk retained by the insurance company for its own account while carrying the balance to a reinsurer; the portion of risk retained by a company or health-care organization, the balance being transferred to a commercial insurance company. 3. In health-care marketing, community development, and health services utilization, this is the number of persons available in the catchment area, services area, or market of the health-care organization who remain in, seek, and use services in the catchment area. 4. In medical science as related to occupational and environmental health, this is the fraction of a chemical or substance remaining in the body or an organ at any given time after exposure and the normal elimination of the majority of the substance by regular bodily processes.

retention limit In managed care and insurance, this is the total or maximum amount of insurance that the health plan or insurance company may carry on any one person or risk situation at its own risk. Any higher amounts above this limit must be covered by a reinsurance company.

retention/retrieval In health information management and computers, this is the storage of data for future use in a manner that makes it available for call-up as needed.

retention/retrieval manual In medical records administration, this is the policy-and-procedures document describing what is to be completed, how it is to be accomplished, the methods and techniques to be used, and productivity levels expected for various phases in handling medical records. Guidelines for retaining, checking out, returning, and storing medical records are also outlined, as are physician use and how to legally protect the health-care provider, facility, and patient.

retirement centers A complex of homes, apartments, stores, cafeterias, clubs, etc. A retirement center may provide a broad range of apartment-like living arrangements, condominiums, recreational programs, and intermediate care facilities. Some short-term skilled nursing care may be provided. See also *life care centers*.

retirement income credit Setting aside income each year for retirement and not paying taxes on it until retirement, when taxes come due but are then lower.

retract 1. To take back. 2. To withdraw or disavow a statement, offer, or promise.

retractor In medical care and surgery, this is a surgical instrument used to retract or pull open the cut edges of skin, muscle, and tissue. This tool assists in opening up a cavity for the operation site.

retrenchment strategies In health strategic planning, this is a short-term strategy used during periods of uncertainty about the economic state of affairs and organizational financial strain where the organization tightens financial activities and assumes a no-growth position, improves efficiency, possibly downsizes the organization, eliminates cost areas, and reduces expenses. Some activities common to retrenchment are reduction in hiring new personnel, allowing normal attrition of staff, making retirement offers, trimming administrative staff, postponing capital expenditure projects, extending the use of equipment, delaying replacement of equipment, retiring obsolete equipment, dropping services that cost money to operate and do not produce revenue, hiring lower cost personnel, restructuring work schedules including reduced workdays or workweeks, reorganizing work flow, reducing inventory on hand, reusing items that can be recycled, and reducing use of disposable items.

retro 1. Before or back; backward. 2. Behind, previous, or past.

retro- Prefix meaning "behind."

retroactive date In managed care and insurance, this is when, in a claims-made insurance policy, a date is stated for the earliest time that any past covered incident or event could occur.

retroactive denial In health-care finance, this is disapproval of reimbursement based on retrospective reviews of a patient's case. Many third-party payers allow an appeals process in which the health-care provider or a health-care facility's representative can present further documentation from the patient's medical record.

retroactive law 1. Law that changes the legal status of laws already passed or actions previously done. 2. Applying laws to past actions. 3. Laws having the power to affect past acts.

retroactive premium adjustment In managed care, this is when a change in health plan coverage or enrollment status causes a change in the member's premium and notice was received after the effective date of the change by the health plan or insurance company.

retroactive reimbursement In health-care finance, this is the payment to a health-care provider for procedures and treatment rendered that were not submitted or accounted for at the time of the original reimbursement submission.

retrocession In managed care or liability insurance, this is a process through which a reinsurer can buy insurance from another insurance company under an insurance treaty and each participating member of the reinsuring pool participates equally in the risk.

retrocessionaire In managed care or liability insurance, this is a reinsurance company that is willing to accept the excess risk of another reinsurer.

retrospective Refers to events, activities, facts, data, or occurrences of the past.

retrospective cost-based reimbursement In health-care finance, this is one approach to paying for health-care services, usually in hospitals, where treatments, procedures, and medical care are paid by third-party payers once care has been rendered. Historically in the United States, physicians and clinics were paid on the basis of charges rather than expenses incurred and costs of care, whereas hospitals have been paid by cost incurred, especially under self-pay, Medicare, and Medicaid. Many capitation and prospective payment approaches have replaced this payment method.

retrospective denial In health-care finance, these are cost-containment incentive programs placed on health-care providers to encourage scrutiny of treatment and to cause providers to consider the cost of care and overutilization. The health plan or intermediary decides on submission of the claim and, after the care has been delivered, to not pay for questionable services or treatments provided or those that appear to be inappropriate.

retrospective payment In health-care finance, this is when payment is made to a health-care provider after care is given. This is the fee-for-service approach to payment.

retrospective-prospective study In epidemiology and health services research, this is a cohort study that first collects and analyzes historical data on a cohort study population and then, on the same cohort subjects, conducts prospective studies and data-gathering activities.

retrospective rate derivation In managed care, this is when a health plan policy or insurance policy has an addendum providing for risk sharing by an employer, making the employer responsible for all or part of the risk beyond basic coverage for the contract year. The employer may be at risk for all or part of the percentage of the health-care costs on the basis of a negotiated arrangement. The health plan/carrier may also be required to return to the employer any excess of premium dollars if medical care costs are less than the total premium dollars used during the contract period.

retrospective rating In malpractice or liability insurance, this is a pricing method in which a premium depends on the actual loss experience of the insured and the premium is adjusted to reflect past experience with loss or having a good record with no lawsuits filed against the party seeking insurance.

retrospective reimbursement system In health-care finance, this a third-party payment system in which reimbursement amounts are based on the charges or costs of care already rendered. Amounts reimbursed are limited by preset caps, ceilings, or an agreed-on percentage of actual costs incurred.

retrospective review 1. In managed care using epidemiological research or outcome studies, this is a research method used to determine medical necessity of treatments or procedures, utilization assessments, or appropriate billing practices for services rendered. 2. A study approach that occurs after health services have been delivered and reimbursement issued and is used to monitor expenditures in areas that are selected for review.

retrospective study In epidemiology and health services research, this is a research design approach that looks backward in time to observe events that have already occurred; evaluation and data gathering and assessment using historical documents and data. Epidemiological studies often use backward-looking research activities utilizing cohort study groupings or case-control study methods, which often rely on records and documents, especially medical, public health, or vital event records, compared with prospective studies, which are planned to observe future events that have not yet occurred. A study methodology in which the medical history of individuals or groups of people are examined for exposure to pathogens, certain treatment procedures, or potentially causative agents. *See research; prospective study; cross-sectional study.*

return 1. In law and the litigation process, this is a report from a court official or peace officer stating that he or she has carried out an order from the court or why it was not carried out. 2. Income, yield, or profit. 3. To begin or to appear again. 4. To go back to a place. 5. To say in reply; to answer.

return date In law and the litigation process, this is the date by which a party must answer a complaint or pleading after receiving a summons to appear before a judge or in court.

return on assets In health-care finance, this is an important indicator of profitability based on the capacity of the health-care organization to produce a profit from its assets; the extent to which retained profits are adequate to finance capital assets. The formula for return on assets is excess income (profit) divided by total assets times 100 (Standard & Poors):

$$\frac{\text{Net profit}}{\text{Total assets}} = \text{Return on assets}$$

return on equity In health-care finance, this is an important indicator and test of profitability of a health-care organization and represents the amount of profit a health-care organization makes as a percentage of its fund balance. The formula for return on equity is excess income (profit) divided by fund balances (equity) times 100:

$$\frac{\text{Net profit}}{\text{Fund balance (equity)}} = \text{Return on equity}$$

return on investment (ROI) The monetary gain received for money or resources invested; a measure of a service or production operation's performance.

reuse In environmental health, this is the process of minimizing the generation of waste by recovering usable products that might otherwise become waste. Examples are the recycling of aluminum, wastepaper, and glass (EPA).

rev. 1. Revised; revision. 2. Reviewed.

revenue 1. Income; money. 2. Increase in money from services or operations of a service or program; money gained. 3. Money returned on investment. 4. Money gained through taxation. 5. The gross amount of earnings received by an entity for the operation of a service, program, or other activity. 6. In managed care, these are the premium dollars received by a health plan from the benefit or employer group for medical care coverage and administrative services. *See also premium.*

revenue bond In health-care finance, these are monies payable solely from the revenue generated from the operation of the project being financed. In hospital revenue bonds, the financing is payable from the gross receipts of the hospital. Government bonds are backed by the income the bond issuer expects to receive from the project for which the bonds were issued. Government-funded bond issues for government-run health-care organizations such as public health initiatives or public hospitals often rely on taxes for repayment.

revenue budget In health-care finance and budget planning, this is a financial plan for the use of finances established on a yearly basis, indicating the amount of revenue the health-care organization plans to receive or take in over the next year. This financial plan sets forth the limitations of all budgets in the organization and must be prepared before expense budgets can be developed. *See budgeting.*

revenue codes In managed care, these are the various code descriptors of cost centers in a hospital or institution for standardized services such as surgery or physical therapy. Managed-care plans use a standardized list of revenue codes.

revenue, gross patient In health-care finance, these are all inpatient and outpatient monies generated by payments received from or on behalf of the patient; revenues from services rendered to patients, including payments received from or on behalf of individual patients.

revenue, net In health-care finance, these are the total monies generated from patients, or the gross patient revenue less deductions for contractual adjustments, bad debts, uncollected debt, charity care, stipends for physicians, and other costs.

revenue, net total Net patient revenue plus all other revenue, including contributions, endowment revenue, government grants, and all other payments not made on behalf of individual patients.

revenue, other operating *See other operating revenue.*

revenue-producing cost centers Departments in a health-care facility providing direct services for which patients are required to pay, thereby generating revenue. Examples include pharmacy, X-ray, and laboratory services. *See non-revenue–producing cost centers.*

revenue sharing Federal governmental grants provided to cities, counties, or states to redistribute tax monies to local governments for the purpose of developing and enhancing public safety, transportation, recreation, social services, and environmental health and public health services.

reversal In health law, this is the changing of a decision or judgment; the changing or annulment of a decision of a lower court or hearing.

reverse 1. In law, this is to set aside a decision of a lower court or to change the judgment. 2. To annul, vacate, or change; to turn a decision backward.

reverse discrimination In human resource management, this is the process of fairly or unfairly seeking to hire or promote a member of a protected class over an equally (or better) qualified applicant who is not a member of a protected class.

reverse osmosis In environmental health, this is a water treatment process used in small water systems by adding pressure to force water through a semipermeable membrane. This process also removes most drinking water contaminants and is used in wastewater treatment.

reverse protocol In medical care, this is the act of prescribing a treatment or drug on the basis of complaints or opinions of the patient rather than following the premise that a diagnosis of certain disease exists, testing confirms the diagnosis, and the findings require an acceptable drug(s) or therapies.

reversible error In health law, this is an error made by a lower court or trial court that has an effect on an appellant's basic rights, thus warranting a reversal of the decision by the appellate court.

revert To go back to; to return property or rights back to the original or former owner. When a guardianship or conservatorship ends, all civil rights revert back to the individual.

review 1. In health law, this is when a pretrial hearing, arbitration panel, malpractice screening panel, or court examines a case. 2. In states with certificate-of-need laws, this is when the state health planning and review agencies have the right to assess, evaluate, and make recommendations on certificate of need.

review, admissions *See admissions review.*

review, capital expenditure *See capital expenditure review.*

review, claims *See review of claims.*

review, concurrent *See concurrent review.*

review, continued stay *See continued stay review.*

review coordinator The administrator responsible for the direction and management of the utilization review program. This individual functions as the key person in dealing with the various personnel and phases of the review process to include patients, attending and consulting physicians, health-care facility administration, and outside agencies such as professional review organizations (PROs). *See professional review organizations.*

review, medical services In medical care, this is a retrospective assessment record of the appropriateness of treatments, procedures, therapy, and services.

review of claims In health-care finance, a retrospective assessment of insurance companies, government Health Care Financing Administration agencies, or other third-party payers of requests for reimbursement. It is conducted for the purpose of determining if the third-party payer is liable for meeting the reimbursement request as well as for determining the eligibility of beneficiaries, the necessity and appropriateness of the services provided, and the reasonableness of the charges and costs.

review, peer *See peer review.*

review, rate *See rate review.*

review, retrospective *See retrospective review.*

review, utilization *See utilization review.*

revised statutes In law, this is a code or record of statutes in book form that does not include temporary and repealed statutes. The official written law of a state, county, or city is also referred to as the "code." Statutes are usually placed in the book in the order that they were passed.

revive 1. To bring back. 2. To restore to the original state or its legal force. 3. To bring back from a state of neglect; to restore life to something.

revocation 1. To take back. 2. To end; to make void. 3. The act of annulling a repeal or a reversal.

revoke 1. To cancel or rescind. 2. To take back or cancel. 3. To reduce or eliminate the legal effect of something.

rex (Lat.) King.

RFP *See request for proposal.*

RFVC Reason For Visit Classification.

RHC Rural health clinic.

RHCF Residential health-care facility. *See residential treatment facility.*

rheumatologist A licensed physician who has completed a residency, is board certified, and specializes in the treatment of infections, diseases, and pain in the joints, especially rheumatism. This is often a subspecialty of the internal medicine specialty.

rheumatology A medical subspecialty of internal medicine dealing with the treatment of infections, diseases, and pain in the joints, especially rheumatism and other rheumatic disorders and conditions; a medical specialty in which a physician can complete a residency and board certification.

RICS Residents In Community Services. A specialized program developed for the coordination of community services used by nursing home residents.

rider 1. In insurance, a legal document that modifies the protection provided by an insurance policy. It may expand or decrease the payable benefits by adding or excluding certain conditions from a policy's coverage. In managed care and medical insurance, this is any additional coverage that exceeds the basic coverage that is offered to employer groups. Additional coverage may be subject to additional charges to the member or dependents; an attachment to any standardized insurance policy added at the request of the policyholder used to obtain additional coverage for a fee. The attachment becomes a part of the insurance contract. 2. In the process of creating laws, an addition to a legislative bill that is added after the bill has been through the proper committee. 3. An attachment to a larger document.

right 1. An ethical expectation. 2. Something that is moral, fair, just, and honorable. 3. Right of action; an enforceable claim. 4. To restore to a proper condition; to correct. 5. Legal authority to control certain actions of others. Every right has a corresponding duty. Rights as used in law refer to legal rights; those things that are legally just.

rightful Having a just claim according to law.

right of action 1. Any legal issue that is enforceable by a court. 2. Any legal claim or fact great enough to demand judicial attention.

right of recovery In health insurance, in the event payment is made for any condition for which a third party may be responsible, the insurance company will be entitled to the proceeds of any settlement up to the amount paid. The same applies to payments made in excess of charges.

right to die In health law, this is the right an individual has to refuse heroic, life-sustaining, and lifesaving treatments or measures; the right to refuse treatment and to accept the process of disease as it leads to death.

right to privacy See *patient's right to privacy; patient's bill of rights; Appendix IV*.

right to treatment A phrase developed in the 1960s that applies mainly to patients in mental hospitals who were warehoused and sometimes abused and denied treatment. Persons with mental problems who are brought into custody or admitted to a health-care facility are not to be held for a period of time longer than the state law allows without treatment (usually 48 or 72 hours). If not treated, the person must be released. The term has been expanded to include any person in a long-term-care facility who should have the right to receive adequate therapy and treatment. Long-term-care and psychiatric patients are to be provided with the same quality and quantity of care they would receive as a private patient in an acute-care hospital.

right-to-work law State laws prohibiting unions from requiring a person to join a union to work at that place of employment or from denying employment because of membership or lack of membership in a labor organization. These laws outlaw closed shops and union shops.

rigidity A psychiatric term referring to a person's resistance to change.

rigor mortis The stiffening of the body after death caused by physiological and biochemical changes in the tissues of the body.

Ringlemann chart In environmental health and air pollution control, this is a series of shaded illustrations used to measure the opacity of air pollution emissions. The chart ranges from light gray through black and is used to set and enforce emission standards (EPA).

riparian habitats In environmental health, these are areas adjacent to rivers and streams having a high density, diversity, and productivity of plant and animal species relative to nearby uplands (EPA).

riparian rights In environmental health, this is the entitlement of a landowner to the water on or bordering his or her property, including the right to prevent diversion or misuse of upstream waters. This is generally a matter of state law (EPA).

risk 1. In insurance, the designation of specific individual or property insured by an insurance policy against loss from some peril or hazard.

2. The probability that the loss will occur. 3. In health services research, this is the relationship between exposures, experiences, and outcomes observed in the research group compared to the control group; experiencing no negative outcomes. 4. In health promotion and public health, this is the chance that an event or exposure will lead to some disease, condition, disability, or even death. Risk has also been used to describe the probability of some unfavorable outcome of a health- or medically related event or experience. Association and risk can be measured statistically and statistical probabilities generated regarding the chance of risk. *See also insurable risk; at risk; risk factors.*

risk adjustment In managed care, insurance, and health care delivery, this is using a level of risk measurement process such as severity of illness to establish risk to the patient and to the insurance plan and to adjust reimbursement, acceptable lengths of stay, and types and amount of treatment allowed; the process of trying to compensate companies that have an unusually high number of high-cost enrollees.

risk analysis In managed care and health services delivery, this is the process of assessing the anticipated medical care costs for a prospective employer group to determine what product, coverage, benefit level, or pricing structure to offer to best meet the needs of the future beneficiaries and retain profitability for the health plan or insurance company.

risk assessment 1. In environmental health and occupational health and safety, this is the qualitative and quantitative evaluation performed in an effort to define the risk posed to human health and/or the environment by the presence or potential presence or use of specific pollutants. 2. In managed care, this is the process where insurers estimate anticipated claims costs of enrollees. The insurer assesses past claims or use of health-care services or facilities, demographics, and geography and assesses the level of risk involved and the likelihood that an enrollee will require health-care services.

risk charge The fraction of a premium that goes to generate or replenish surpluses that a carrier must develop to protect against the possibility of excessive losses under its policies. Profits, if any, on the sale of insurance are also taken from the surpluses developed using risk charges. The risk charge is sometimes referred to as "retention" or "retention rate."

risk class In managed care and insurance, this is a group of beneficiaries or an employer group that has substantially the same types and amounts of risk to the insurance company. The more common classes of risk used by most insurance companies are standard, preferred, nonsmoker, nondrinker, substandard, and uninsurable.

risk communication In environmental health, this is the exchange of information about health or environmental risks between risk assessors, risk managers, the general public, news media, interest groups, etc. (EPA).

risk contract In managed care, this is an agreement between Medicare/Health Care Financing Administration (HCFA) and a health plan that requires the managed-care plan to furnish, at the minimum, all Medicare-covered services to Medicare-eligible members on an annual basis for certain predetermined, fixed monthly payment rates from HCFA and a monthly premium that is paid by the member. The managed-care plan is liable for services and treatment regardless of the type, severity, extent, or degree of illness and associated expenses.

risk control The elimination and management of factors or circumstances encountered by patients and employees that pose a threat to their safety and comfort while being a potential lawsuit liability. This is a part of risk management and quality assurance because it helps to identify negligence, deficiencies, and mistakes and helps determine the difference between levels in quality of care.

risk control insurance *See reinsurance.*

risk difference In health services research and epidemiology, this is the difference in risk of two different risk experiences or factors.

risk factors 1. In health promotion, epidemiology, and public health, these are experiences, events, behaviors, acts, or aspects of lifestyle or behavior that increase the chances of acquiring or developing a disease, condition, injury, illness, disorder, or disability or of dying; behaviors or exposures associated with increased risk of a disease, injury, condition, or disability that can develop later in life. If a certain risk is associated with an elevated frequency of occurrence of a disease, disorder, injury, disability, or early death and an association can be explained on the basis of a cause-effect relationship, it would be considered a risk factor. Risk factors are not only important to identify but are used in the measurement of health status. Frequency, magnitude, level of exposure to a population, and prevention activities all rely on research data that demonstrate the effect of the risk factor on a group or population. Thus, any factors associated with disease, disability, injury, or death by virtue of an elevated relative risk are risk factors. Risk factors can be caused by a predisposing factor, attribute, or risk exposure, and because of an exposure there is an increased probability of a bad outcome such as illness, injury or disability, or death with an epidemiological causality or association being present. Risk factors can be determined by reducing or modifying the exposure to the risk and then observing the outcome. 2. In epidemiology, these are the characteristics of individuals such as familial history, socialization, culture, health traditions and beliefs, behaviors, genetic makeup, and environmental exposures that increase the chance of disease, injury, disability, or death as determined and measured by relative risk for that population.

risk HMOs *See Medicare risk health maintenance organizations*

risk identification systems In a health-care organization's quality assurance programs, these are the processes used to determine potential legal claims. The systems serve as a centralized data collection and use system that helps to identify trends in employee illness and injury. The systems are also used to do trend analysis for ancillary staff, analyze financial matters related to risk management and equipment failures, and identify interdepartmental, system, medical staff, and incidence problems and other risk-related issues and concerns.

risk, impaired or substandard An insurance applicant whose physical condition does not meet the standards of required health.

risk management 1. The assessment and control of the obvious and identifiable risks to which a health-care facility has or might be subject to. The management of risk involves analyzing all possibilities for loss and determining how to reduce risk exposures by reducing, eliminating, or transferring the risk and by obtaining insurance to cover risks that cannot be eliminated or that are unforeseen. Having a financial and liability awareness focus, this is the science of identifying, monitoring, tracking, trending, evaluating, correcting, intervening, and ensuring against risks that could cause liability lawsuits or financial loss. Risk management must identify immediate or future problems to minimize threat of losses and prevent future losses. Major concerns are process and procedures for eliminating the cause of losses previously experienced or anticipated by health-care organizations and their visitors, patients, and employees while improving quality. 2. In environmental health, this is the process of evaluating alternative regulatory and nonregulatory responses to risk and selecting among them. The selection process requires the consideration of legal, economic, and social factors. *See plant technology and safety management.*

risk management activities According to JCAHO for accreditation purposes, these are clinical and administrative activities that hospitals undertake to identify, evaluate, and reduce the risk of injury and loss to patients, personnel, visitors, and the institution itself while reducing lawsuits, liability, and related expenses such as insurance premiums. Standards are applied to evaluate a hospital's performance in conducting risk management designed to identify, evaluate, and reduce the risk of patient injury associated with care and services.

risk manager The administrator who is responsible for the management, assessment, and elimination of environmental risk factors that could affect patients, visitors, or personnel while in the health-care facility.

risk marker In health promotion and public health, this is a key, obvious, or well-proven behavior, activity, or attribute that has been associated with increased chances of acquiring a disease; a risk factor that can be used as an indicator of an increased risk and should be observed and modified in susceptibles or in an entire population group. A risk factor is similar to a health status indicator but is more specific to one disease or condition and can be changed or reduced. *See risk factor; health status indicator.*

risk pool In managed care, this is a risk-sharing approach whereby an agreement between a health plan and a provider group is made where a portion of the capitation fees are put into special fund accounts on a periodic basis and treatment and procedures paid for through a claim system and evaluated against a predetermined standard. The funds of the pool are divided between the health plan and the provider on the basis of the degree of health services utilization. As utilization rates increase, the amount of funds that will be paid to the providers decreases. Methods of calculation, charges, and payment structures are determined by health plan/provider contract agreements. *See risk sharing.*

risk pooling In managed care, medical insurance, and all insurance, this is the process of having large numbers of individuals with a low probability of illness, injury, disability, or death or other loss share cost by placing monthly payments of funds (premiums) into a central account and then all sharing the costs of high-expense events when they occur, hopefully to a small number of the persons contributing. The idea is to have a large number of contributors and a small number of persons withdrawing funds to pay for the expenses of medical care, damage, or loss. This approach reduces individual risk to the amount of the insurance premium rather than requiring a single person to pay for the full cost of the medical care loss or damage. These are the fundamental principles behind all insurance.

risk ratio This is the process of assessing the observed divided by the expected; the strength of association that exits between exposure and endpoint. A value of 1.0 equals no risk. The risk ratio formula follows:

$$\frac{\text{Observed factors or events}}{\text{Expected outcomes}} = \text{Risk}$$

See relative risk.

risk retention In liability insurance, a method of dealing with risk by bearing the results of the risk within the organization rather than transferring it.

risk retention group Any corporation or other limited liability association or insurance company whose primary activity consists of assuming and spreading all or any portion of liability of its group members. It is organized for the primary purpose of serving as an insurance company, is authorized to engage in the business of insurance under the laws of any state, and does not exclude any person from membership in the group solely to provide for a member of such a group a competitive advantage over such a person.

risks Quantitative or qualitative expressions of possible loss that consider both the probability that a hazard will cause harm and the consequences of that event.

risk selection In managed care and insurance, this is the process by which insurers try to enroll healthy members who will not use the services or who will use few programs or services. An attempt is also made to identify and deny coverage to individuals who show characteristics that indicate they will be high consumers of health care and have high utilization.

risk sharing In managed care and insurance, this is the process whereby a health plan and a contracted health-care provider each accept partial responsibility for the financial risk and benefit from profits resulting from delivering medical care and treatment for enrolled members. If health care is provided in an inefficient manner, loss could occur, and if done in a cost-effective manner, rewards could result. Also referred to as an "incentive pool."

rites of passage Ceremonial rites marking transition from one social status to another. As used in gerontology and retirement studies, it refers to both explicit and implicit role status that is denoted by some occurrence that allows role change.

ritual 1. Automatic activity. 2. Behavior with a cultural origin.

ritualistic behavior In psychiatry and mental health care, these are repetitive acts performed in a compulsive manner to relieve anxiety.

RMP *See Regional Medical Program.*

RN *See registered nurse.*

RNA Ribonucleic acid, which is produced by DNA. It is important to memory function. *See also DNA.*

RO $>$ 1 The symbol for when a virus has the capability of causing disease and emerges to cause illness or an epidemic.

RO Receive only. In computers, these are printers or CRT displays used for output only, having no input capabilities.

robbery 1. Forcible stealing. 2. In criminal law, this is illegally taking personal property by force or fear.

Robinson-Patman Act of 1936 In health law and antitrust law, this act prohibits price discrimination and does not allow the lowering of prices below those charged by competitors.

robust design In quality health services delivery, this is building into services, treatment, and the delivery system the highest level of competence, equipment, delivery, and quality.

rodenticides In environmental health, this is any chemical or agent used to destroy rats or other rodent pests or to prevent them from damaging food, crops, etc. (EPA).

roentgen The unit of measurement of X-ray or gamma radiation.

roentgen equivalent, man A unit of ionizing radiation equal to the amount that produces the same damage to humans as 1 roentgen or high-voltage X rays (EPA).

roentgeno- Prefix meaning "X rays."

roentgenogram A film produced by photography with roentgen rays.

Roe v. Wade A decision of the U.S. Supreme Court in 1973 that liberalized existing abortion laws. One of the landmark decisions that gave unusual credence to the vague, ominous, and undefined concept of "state's interest" against that of the individual. The Court ruled that once the fetus is viable, it was in the state's interest to protect the potential life and that it became compelling to do so. Restrictive state abortion laws were stated as being unconstitutional and violating the individual's (the pregnant woman's) right to privacy to make decisions concerning her own body.

rogatory letters In health law, this is a formal request by a court of one jurisdiction or state to another court asking that a witness be examined by interrogatories and that the records of that examination be returned to the original court.

ROI *See return on investment.*

role 1. Any pattern of behavior that a person takes on as a part of his or her own behavior and personality. When a behavior pattern conforms with the expectations of society, it is a complementary role. If it does not conform with the expectation of others, it is a noncomplementary role. 2. A defined organizational position in a health-care organization and in a work group that is associated with specific functions to be performed as well as expected behaviors that are a part of the job, position, or profession. *See also identification; injunction.*

roleless role The ambiguity of role caused by retirement wherein there are few explicit expectations or rules regarding behavior or performance.

role reversal In gerontology, this is when a child no longer obtains care and support from their parents. Instead, the children become the caregivers, and the parents become the dependents because of the aging process and the development of chronic diseases late in life.

rolfing In mental health, this is a specialized therapeutic massage used to release emotional stress from the muscles. *See structural integration.*

roll 1. Any official record of a proceeding. 2. A list of names for official purposes.

ROM *See read-only memory; range of motion.*

room accommodations Description of the types of patient care rooms provided in a facility (e.g., private, semi-private, or ward).

room and board 1. Routine or daily patient services, including all food services, housekeeping, bed and bedding, etc., that contribute to the basic housing and support needs of patients. 2. In health-care financial management, this is a revenue category that identifies routine services or daily patient services and includes revenue generated from room, food services, and general nursing services.

rooming in A service offered to mothers that allows them to share room and accommodations with their newborn infants. Some hospitals extend this service to pediatric patients who are required to have a lengthy stay in the hospital.

room rate Basic inpatient per diem charges for a stay in a health-care facility. In hospitals these are the basic hotel charges for a patient's stay. *See cost per patient day.*

Rorschach test In psychiatry and mental health care, this is a special type of projective test in which the patient reveals perceptions, attitudes, and emotions by responding to a set of inkblot pictures.

roster A list of patients served by a given health-care provider or program. The roster may be derived from a registry or list of visits, but the listing of an individual on a roster does not necessarily imply any ongoing relationship between the program and the individual. *See also catchment area.*

rough fish In environmental health, these are fish that are not prized for eating (e.g., gar, carp, and suckers) and that are more tolerant of changing environmental conditions than game species (EPA).

rounds Physicians or medical students in training (or possibly nurses, dietitians, clinic pharmacists, physician assistants, or other health care providers) visiting the bedsides of hospitalized patients to assess treatment and note progress of the patient. *See also ward rounds; grand rounds.*

rounds, ground In medical education, this is a

tradition in most medical schools where weekly presentations are held in a large auditorium where unusual medical cases are presented to medical school faculty and medical students. Also included are special presentations on topics of concern to medical education such as gerontology, medical malpractice, and ethics. Some grand rounds presentations can be used as CME (continuing medical education) credits. A part of the tradition is for the participants to challenge the speaker on his or her background, research, and literature knowledge.

rounds, teaching *See rounds, ward.*

rounds, ward In medical education, this is the process of supervising and teaching clinical skills and knowledge to physicians-in-training by seeing patients in the hospital at bedside to review the patient's conditions, diseases, treatments, and recovery and to assess the knowledge, decisions, and prescribed treatments set forth by the students. Similar processes and activities are used in nursing and allied health professionals in clinical training. Also called "teaching rounds."

routine care Regular and usual medical care extended to any patient who requires institutionalization as a result of a medical disorder and/or surgery but whose malady is not severe enough to require specialized or tertiary care.

routine inquiry law In health law, this is a law passed in some states that requires health-care providers to develop a regular system of asking families of deceased patients to donate organs and body parts for medical use and/or for use in transplants. Also referred to as a "required request law."

routine services *See services, routine.*

routine wastes In environmental health, these are various kinds of trash, rubbish, garbage, or, in the case of a hospital or clinic, biohazards that are generated in the normal course of operations and doing business.

RPCH *See rural primary care hospitals; eaches/peaches.*

RPT *See registered physical therapist.*

RRA *See registered records administrator.*

RRC Rural referral center.

RSA *See rational self-analysis.*

RSC *See rational self-counseling.*

RT Respiratory therapist; radiological technologist. Also referred to as a "rad tech."

rubber stamp signature A physician's signature made into a rubber stamp and used on medical records or prescriptions in health facilities that the physician may not frequent very often (e.g., a nursing home). The physician may later confirm the rubber stamp signature with his or her own official signature. *See also authentication.*

rubbish In environmental health, this is the solid waste, excluding food waste and ashes, from homes, institutions, and workplaces (EPA).

rubella German measles. A type of mild viral infection marked by a pink rash, fever, and lymph node enlargement.

rubric 1. A title or heading for a law. 2. In epidemiology, this is used to describe the system used for the classification of diseases; a label for a category in a classification system.

RUGs Regulated unit of groups. In VA hospitals, this is the process where a special coding system was developed using the same diagnoses grouped together for use only in VA hospitals.

rule 1. A standard. 2. A principle of conduct. 3. An established usage of law. 4. A usual course of action. 5. To govern. 6. In law and the court process, this is to establish by a legal decision, as a judge does in court to settle a legal issue or decide a motion. 7. To settle an objection raised by one side in a legal dispute. 8. In the executive branch of the federal government, an agency statement of general or particular applicability and future effect designed to implement, interpret, or prescribe law or policy or to describe the organization, procedure, or practice requirements of an agency. Rules are published in the *Federal Register*. A rule, once adopted in accordance with the procedures specified in the Administrative Procedure Act (Title V, U.S.C.), has the force of law and is a regulation. Commonly called a "regulation."

rule-making procedures In health law and regulations making, these are the activities that are part of and are required under, the Administrative Procedures Act (APA). Three approaches to rule making are allowed under the APA: formal, informal, and exempted. Formal rule making is when regulations are required by statute to be made by a governmental administrative agency that holds a hearing as set forth by the APA's formal adjudication process. When a rule-making authority statute requires it, a formal trial-type hearing must be conducted, and interested persons must be provided with an opportunity to testify and cross-examine adverse witnesses. Input is allowed from the interested public before making the rule formal and making it a regulation. Informal rule making (also referred to as "notice and comment"), as set forth in Section 533 of the APA, is used when a governmental agency issues substantive rules. When a statute merely authorizes an administrative agency to create and implement regulations and the regulations affect the rights of private parties, the agency is required to exercise the informal rule-making requirements of notice and comment. Three procedural requirements must be met: 1) Prior notice of a hearing must be published, for federal laws the *Federal Register* is used, and for local communities the local newspapers are used. 2) The administrative agency must give interested persons an opportunity to participate, which means that they may submit written comments, present data, and offer views, opinions, and arguments. Oral hearings are not required under this section of the APA. 3) The administrative agency must consider all public comments and then issue as part of its final regulations a concise general statement about the basis and purpose of the rule that has been made. Exempted rule making is a bit vague and unclear, but it exempts input from the public on military, foreign affairs functions, or administrative agency management that may require national secrecy. These activities are subject to judicial review if adequate justification is lacking for excluding public participation.

rule nisi 1. Order to show cause. 2. An order that is to take effect unless the person shows cause why it should not.

rule of discovery In health law and tort law, this is when a statute of limitations is not active and in effect until the injured party becomes aware of or should have known that an injury or harm had occurred. In some states, statutes of limitations begin to toll on discovery by the victim of the harm or injury. *See discovery.*

rule of law A general guide to conduct in law, government, or health agencies that is applied by government officials and supported by governmental authority. The highest authority of a government is its laws.

rules and regulations The specific and detailed aspects of a statute that have the full force of the law and are part of the originating statute; clear and concise written statements of policy or a statute, setting forth certain activities, levels of performance, standards, or the level of quality expected or not allowed in a health-care facility, businesses, plants, or services under the jurisdiction of environmental or public health.

rules of exclusion A legal standard that allows evidence offered to be excluded from the record of proceedings or from being received in evidence if it is not properly qualified or identified. The administrator of a medical records department or qualified staff can take medical records to court and testify as to their validity.

rules of reason In health law and antitrust, this is an element of law that sets forth the principle that only unreasonable restraints of trade are prohibited that have a detrimental effect on hospitals and physicians and their ability to contract.

ruling A decision or judgment made on a legal issue.

run 1. Having legal effect. 2. To be in effect during a specific time period. 3. To be written or related. 4. To go through successfully. 5. To expose oneself to. 6. To allow or permit. 7. To accrue or mount up. 8. A period of operation. 9. To pursue and catch, as to run down a debt. 10. In computers, a single but continuous execution of a program. 11. In environmental health and air pollution control, this is the net period of time during which an emission sample is collected and may be either intermittent or continuous within the limits of good engineering practice.

runoff In environmental health, this is precipitation, snow melt, or irrigation water that runs off land into streams or other surface water and can carry pollutants from the air, crops, and residential and industrial areas into the receiving waters (EPA).

run-on In environmental health, this is any rainwater, leachate, or other liquid that drains over land onto any part of a facility (EPA).

rural 1. A vague and ambiguous term. Some federal agencies state that a rural area is any city or town with a population under 35,000 to 50,000. Other organizations and agencies set the population numbers much lower. The distance to populated areas or health and economic centers are also factors that are considered. Frontier is also a classification used to denote places that have a population density of less than 6 persons per square mile. 2. For a hospital to be classified as rural, it must be 25 miles or more from the next closest hospital in the SMSA. 3. In public health and safety (for motor vehicle reporting), this includes communities of less than 5,000 inhabitants, except those classified as urban by the U.S. Census Bureau.

rural health care Because of a lack of facilities and specialists, the health care available in remote areas of the United States is usually emergency care or primary care delivered by a general practice/family practice, osteopathic, internal medicine physician or by physician assistants, nurse practitioners, midwives, EMTs, paramedics, or other physician extenders. Patients are usually stabilized until being transported to advanced secondary or tertiary care facilities located in larger population centers. Many rural areas have no physician because of the lack of incentive for physicians to practice in these areas.

rural health centers Rural health clinics, offering basic primary care and emergency services, established and staffed by allied health personnel.

rural health clinic Under Medicare, to be reimbursed for care provided by physician extenders in a rural clinic, the clinic must be located in a rural area where the supply of physicians, medical facilities, and services is limited and not sufficient to meet the needs of the population. The definition can also include areas designated by the Public Health Service Act as being medically served. The lack of physician services and only those clinics that are not directed or staffed by a full-time physician would meet the eligibility requirements. *See certified rural health clinic.*

rural health initiative projects Health underserved rural area projects under the U.S. Public Health Service developed to provide health care to some 1.2 million rural Americans, including migrant and seasonal workers. These clinics may be staffed and managed by the National Health Service Corps (NHSC) of the U.S. Public Health Service and are somewhat like neighborhood health centers except that they are located in remotely populated areas.

rural primary care hospital (RPCH) 1. The Department of Health and Human Services has allowed several states (California, Colorado, Kansas, New York, North Carolina, South Dakota, and West Virginia) to develop essential access community hospitals (eaches) and rural primary care hospitals (peaches), allowing some rural hospitals to convert the hospital from a general acute-care facility into a primary care facility. The RPCHs are linked with larger eaches, which provide backup emergency and medical care and agree to accept all patient transfers. This approach is used to revive financially ailing and underutilized rural hospitals. Criteria for a RPCH include being located in rural areas; having no more than six inpatient beds; being allowed to provide care for 72 hours or less; midlevel practitioners such as physicians assistants or nurse practitioners providing inpatient care; and providing the services of a dietitian, pharmacist, laboratory technician, medical technologist, and radiologic technologist on a part-time basis; created by P.L. 101-239. 2. A special designation for hospitals in rural areas that must restructure their organization and facility to survive, stay in operation, and meet the needs of its community. Such hospitals must be located in a rural area or in an urban county whose geographic area is substantially larger than the average area for urban counties and whose hospital service area is similar to the service area of hospitals located in rural areas. No more than 6 acute-care beds or 12 acute-care beds that are swing beds are allowed. Long-term-care beds can be allowed up to licensed levels. Average length of stay (ALOS) may not exceed 72 hours over a 12-month period, but exceptions are allowed for inclement weather and emergency situations. Mandatory services include inpatient medical care subject to length-of-stay limits, emergency care on a 24-hour basis, and laboratory and radiology. Restricted services are inpatient surgery and services requiring general anesthesia. *See medical assistance facilities; essential access community hospital.*

rural referral centers (RRCs) A large regional medical center or tertiary care hospital located in a rural area that services a wide geographic area. These hospitals, as certified under Medicare, must meet certain bed size (usually 75 beds or larger), meet certain referral characteristics, and are eligible for special considerations under the Medicare PPS/DRG system of reimbursement. *See essential access community hospital.*

RVS *See relative value scale; relative value of services.*
RVU *See relative value unit.*
Rx Prescription, therapy, or treatment.

S

SA 1. Societe Anonyme (French), abbreviation for "corporation." 2. Sociedad Anonima (Spanish), abbreviation for "corporation." 3. Surgical and anesthesia services.

SAC *See Subarea Advisory Council.*

sacrosanct (Lat.) Not to be violated; sacred.

sadism 1. In mental health, this is a psychological disorder, often a sexual deviation, in which sexual gratification is achieved by inflicting pain and humiliation on the sex partner. It generally refers to inflicting of pain or causing physical harm to others with no emotional remorse. In some cases, pleasure is derived with no sexual implications involved. 2. Deliberate cruelty. 3. Destructive-aggressive attitudes in an individual.

sadist One who derives pleasure from inflicting physical or psychological pain on others in both social or sexual encounters.

sadomasochistic relationship Any relationship where enjoyment is achieved from the suffering by one person and the enjoyment of inflicting pain by the other person. Both can be attractions in the relationship.

SADR Severity adjusted death rate. *See case severity.*

safe In health and safety, this is a condition wherein risks are as low as can be achieved and present no significant residual risk.

Safe Drinking Water Act In environmental health, this is a federal law that created a national comprehensive framework through which the public can be assured of quality and safe drinking water supplies. It assumes quality water at the time it reaches the consumer in the community rather than pretreatment quality of the source of supply. Regulations specify contaminants that the EPA determines to have an adverse effect on human health. The EPA's primary standards require maximum contaminant levels. Secondary standards cover aesthetics of the drinking water. *See sanitary surveys; secondary drinking water regulations; secondary maximum contaminant levels; secure maximum contaminant levels.*

safeguard 1. A person or thing that protects. 2. To provide security. 3. To protect or defend.

safeguards In environmental health and radiation protection and safety, these are physical protection, material accounting, and material control measures designed to date, prevent, detect, and respond to unauthorized possession, use, or sabotage of special nuclear materials.

safe harbor guidelines Controls and restraints that were proposed to be placed on physicians and their ownership of health-care facilities to limit ownership to 40%.

safe harbor regulations Proposed regulations from the U.S. Department of Health and Human Services for health-care providers and hospitals specifying which practices would not be unethical under the Medicare and Medicaid anti-kickback provision to avoid fraud and abuse.

safe place statutes In occupational health and safety, these are laws in some states requiring an employer to eliminate all unguarded dangers from the workplace.

safety 1. In daily living or in occupational health and safety, this is any device, act, or behavior that is protective or keeps an individual from danger, harm, or injury; the diligent avoidance of circumstances or the potential for harm, injury, or loss of property; the control of accidental loss or injury. 2. In medical care, this is the probability that use of a particular drug, device, method, or medical procedure will not cause unintended or unanticipated harm, disease, pain, or injury. Safety is, in this context, a relative concept that must be balanced against the effectiveness of the drug or procedure in question. Drugs or procedures known to cause harm, disease, or injury when used are not usually thought of as unsafe if the benefits they give exceed the damage. The federal Food, Drug and Cosmetic Act requires a demonstration of safety for drugs marketed for human use. No similar requirement exists for most other medical procedures paid for or regulated under federal or state law. 3. Free from hazard or danger; the control of accidental loss or injury.

safety analysis process In health and safety, this is the identification of hazards, the analysis of hazard control, and the analysis of residual risk.

safety and health assessments In health and safety, these are processes and activities that involve a comprehensive periodic review of all aspects of an organization's operations and functioning that affect health and safety, including organization and administration, operations, maintenance, training and certification, auxiliary systems, emergency preparedness, technical support, security and safety interfaces, experimental activities, site and facility safety review, nuclear criticality safety, radiological protection, fire protection, packaging and transportation, quality verification, personnel protection, aviation safety, and medical services.

safety and health committee In health and safety, this is a group of individuals who represent the organization to advise and aid management and employees on matters of safety and health for the health-care organization. Some committees may get involved in essential monitoring, education, investigative, and evaluative tasks. The responsibilities of the committee are safety and health instruction, inspection of the facility, planning improvements that affect procedures and regulations, updating work practices and hazard controls, assessing the impact of work task changes, field testing of protective equipment, monitoring and evaluating effectiveness of recommendations and improvements, communications, and studying and analyzing accident and injury data, all to assist compliance with OSHA regulations.

safety and health directors In any organization, this is an administrative person who is the primary manager responsible for the overview and coordination of the occupational safety and health program.

safety appraisal, functional *See safety appraisals.*

safety appraisal, management *See safety appraisals.*

safety appraisals In safety management, this is a review of a safety/loss control program's effectiveness. Reviews can be conducted as a management appraisal, a functional appraisal, or a comprehensive appraisal, which combines the previous two. A management safety appraisal is a review and evaluation of management performance covering all safety disciplines and management responsibilities to ensure a proper safety loss/control program. A functional safety appraisal is a review of a safety specialty discipline (e.g., industrial safety, industrial hygiene, and fire protection) to verify that applicable elements of the safety/loss control program have been developed, documented, and effectively implemented in accordance with specific safety/loss control requirements and needs.

safety barriers In health and safety, these are structures such as guardrails or protective shields that restrict access to prevent, control, or minimize the unnecessary risk of an accident or injury.

safety committee In hospital administration, this is an in-house hospital committee composed of representatives from various departments and medical staff who plan, implement, and monitor a facility-wide safety program under the guidance of a safety manager or director. *See plant technology and safety management.*

safety device/system In safety management, this consists of permanently installed safety-related equipment related to processes, major equipment, and major personnel hazards. Not included are boundary ropes, chains, goggles, and other minor items.

safety limits In safety management, these are the restraints and restrictions placed on risk situations necessary to provide reasonable protection to the integrity of certain physical barriers that guard against the uncontrolled release of radioactivity or a potential accident situation.

safety management A component of a hospital's physical plant, technology, and safety management program that combines five elements: 1) general safety, 2) safety education, 3) emergency preparedness, 4) hazardous materials and wastes, and 5) safety devices and operational practices. Standards are applied to evaluate a hospital's performance in conducting safety management programs (JCAHO).

safety manager In hospital or health facility administration, this is an administrative person responsible for the day-to-day safety, fire, and disaster protection and the prevention activities of a health-care facility, its personnel, and its patients. Also called a "safety director."

Safety Medical Devices Act In 1990, the FDA developed regulations on the safety of medical devices and is authorized to enforce related regulations. The law places a regulatory burden on companies that develop, produce, and distribute medical equipment, machines, technology, and devices. Reports must be filed when a health-care provider becomes aware of the probability that a device has caused harm or injury or has contributed to the death of a patient. Both the FDA and the manufacturer must be notified. The FDA must submit reports to Congress on the safety benefits of user reporting. The General Accounting Office must assess compliance by health-care facilities, and the FDA has regulatory authority over hospitals with regard to the medical devices and reporting. Hospital records can be accessed and investigations conducted. Monetary amounts allowed by the law are to not exceed $15,000 for single infractions, and multiple violations are not to exceed $1,000,000 for failure to report injuries or deaths.

safety net providers Under Medicaid (MediCal in California), this is an administrative process used to transition public health and Medicaid clients into managed-care programs under local initiatives and the mainstream program to preserve existing clinical relationships among providers and patients and to retain providers who are familiar with and interested in caring for MediCal beneficiaries. The local health departments serve to ensure that care will continue through local initiatives, which is when local health departments offer internal managed-care programs to the public health clientele and Medicaid patients. Care can also be obtained through contracts with private-sector managed-care programs, referred to as "mainstream."

safety of care In hospital administration, this is the degree to which the hospital environment is free from hazard or danger (JCAHO).

safety program review In health and safety, this is the assessment of safety programs to ensure that a planned and measured program exists having low-cost and high-volume services, that it allows for professional growth, and that it uses up-to-date methods. Also included are the definition of ideals and policy; description and schematics; monitoring, audit, and comparison techniques; professional staff; management peer committees; organization for improvement; block function and work schematics; and scope and integration of the review and safety program services.

safety reviews In health and safety, these are deliberate and critical examinations of the safety impact of proposed activities or an ongoing activity related to the development, site selection, design, construction, operation, maintenance, and modification of a facility using radioactive materials or hazardous waste.

safe work permit In health and safety and hazardous waste management, this is a document allowing employees to perform potentially hazardous work and outlining necessary safeguards and procedures. Several approval procedures are required before work can begin.

said As used in health law documents, a somewhat vague and overused legal term meaning "already referred to" or "the one mentioned before."

salaried sales distribution systems In managed care and insurance, this is a sales and marketing approach that uses in-house employees to sell and service insurance and health plan policies. The sales personnel can work independently or through private insurance agents and can also serve in customer relations by distributing group insurance products.

sale and lease back method *See sale-leaseback.*

sale-leaseback In health administration and health care finance, this is the process of selling a piece of equipment or a machine to an organization or business and then, as part of the same transaction, arranging to lease the equipment back, all of which is agreed on at the onset of the transaction.

sales expense budget In health-care financial management and managed-care marketing, this is one approach to a budgetary plan for expenses based primarily on the costs incurred in marketing and sales with the largest budget item being commissions.

salts In environmental health, these are minerals that water picks up as it passes through the air; over, under, and through the ground; and as it is used by households and industry; the reaction product when a metal displaces the hydrogen with an acid.

saltwater intrusion In environmental health, this is the invasion of fresh surface water or groundwater by saltwater. If the saltwater comes from the ocean, it may be called "seawater intrusion" (EPA).

salvage value In health-care financial management, this is the worth given a capital asset at the end of a specified period. It is the current market worth of the item or equipment being considered for replacement in a capital budget.

Samaritanism In medical and nursing care, this is a caring attitude and patient care approach that considers how the patient feels, not just treating the disease; reassurance and support to an individual having pain or troubled by a disease, illness, or disability.

same-day surgery *See outpatient surgery; surgicenter; ambulatory care; ambulatory care center; ambulatory care services; ambulatory health-care ser-*

vices; ambulatory services settings; surgery, ambulatory.

sample In epidemiology or health services research, these are individuals, subjects, or cases selected from a study group or a population to represent a representative cross-section of the total population. Samples are usually drawn at random, but samples of convenience are often used as well.

sample bias In epidemiology, this is when the sampling process falls short of being objective and free from prejudice, confounding variables, or vested or personal interest. In conducting epidemiological studies of populations, several types of bias are encountered. Visibility bias includes only those who are identifiable or are at hand and excludes those not easily identifiable or easy to access. Order bias occurs when people are chosen by alphabetical or numerical order, street address, or other sequential ordering. The tendency is to use people at the beginning of the alphabet or top of a list too often and to include the end people (names) rarely. Accessibility bias occurs when field interviewers are allowed to pick the sample. They tend to pick those persons who are most easily reached. Cluster bias happens when the subject clusters are set too closely together such as when those subjects who live close to one another may interact and share information. Affinity bias occurs when people interview those whom they tend to be drawn to. *See bias.*

sample, blanket survey In epidemiology, this sampling process tries to interview all possible recipients of a population, community, or target population for a service or program. A blanket survey is almost impossible to accomplish. This approach supports the notion that the larger the sample size, the smaller the error in predicting need. This is very costly and thus is not used as often.

sample, cluster In epidemiology, this sampling process is used if the study population is dispersed, gathered, or arranged in unusual patterns geographically or in separated places or spread over a large geographic area. This sampling approach lends itself to mail surveys or person-to-person interviews or telephone approaches. If travel time and costs are high for interviews, cluster sampling is more economical. Again, basic random sampling is to be used. A large sample size needs to be maintained if cluster sampling is to produce accurate results. Groups of people that cluster together are sampled, for example, university students, church members, club members, public schools, race, cultural bound groups, and housing tracks. Sampling involves the initial sampling of groups of clusters and the sampling of each element of the clusters. Cluster approaches are used when it is impractical to compile a complete list of characteristics or influencing variables of a study population. In a city, a set of city blocks could be selected for sampling. From the selected city blocks, sampling is done for all of those living there. Sampling of subgroups within the city blocks based on race, for example, could also be done. This is also referred to as "multistage sampling."

sample, density In epidemiology, this sampling process is used in case control and longitudinal studies as a method of selecting controls. This approach conducts sampling from incident cases over a specific period of time. Sampling and assessment of controls is done through the entire study period. The aim of this sampling approach is to reduce bias by constant sampling of both subject and controls instead of using a cross-sectional approach of doing the assessment at a single point in time. As time passes, patterns of exposure to disease and health factors occur in both subjects and controls in longitudinal studies. Changes occur over long periods of time, and sampling needs to account for such changes.

sample, EPSEM In epidemiology or health services research, this means "equal probability of selection method sample." Basic random sampling is one example of this approach in which all subjects have the same chance of being selected.

sample, grab In health-care marketing and health services research, this is somewhat like a sample of convenience and is often done by doing surveys in a shopping mall, on the telephone, or with whomever is handy and will participate. It differs from a sample of convenience in that it uses not large groups but rather the place where high numbers of persons pass or frequent.

sample of convenience In epidemiological studies, this sampling approach is when and where the research accepts persons as subjects who are easily accessible in large groups and who are willing (or compelled) participants in a study. This approach often includes recipients of a service, those who attend a clinic, are available at a worksite, or are enrolled in classes in a college or public or private schools. This approach is adequate as long as the sample size is large and includes a high percentage of the study population. Generalizations are drawn from the findings and often applied to the larger population. Even though this is one of the most commonly used approaches, it is one sampling approach that lends itself to much bias and is often criticized by behavioral science researchers, especially if results are generalized to the general population.

sample, probability *See sample, random.*

sample, quota In epidemiology, this sampling process is used when an interview approach is used. Random sampling should be used. Interviews are assigned a quota of a given number of interviews from each segment or cluster. Problems arise in quota sampling if hourly wages are used. Assigned quotas and payment per number are more cost-effective and productive, but efforts should be made to ensure that the forms are filled out honestly and ethically by or with research subjects.

sample, random In epidemiology, this sampling process takes overt steps to ensure that all persons in a study population have an equal chance of being selected without bias in a fair and objective manner. This is used when the sample is quite large and uses a true random approach in selecting subjects, for example, cutting up a list of names and selecting them out of a hat and ensuring that a set percentage is chosen, selecting every seventh person from a computer printout of all persons in a study group, using a random numbers table, using a computer program that generates random numbers, or selecting every eleventh person in a phone book. "Random" has two dimensions: 1) the assigning of people to groups so that each person has an equal chance of being selected to participate in the study and 2) the selection of individuals to participate as subjects from the research population. Random selection is used in need assessment studies more often than random assignment. Random assignment is used more in epidemiological surveys and is the more accepted form of research sampling. Also referred to as a "probability sample."

sample, self-selection/volunteer participation In epidemiology, this sampling approach uses a survey that is given to individuals such as patients at a public health clinic who are willing to fill out the form, making it somewhat of a sample of convenience. As a general rule, this sampling approach has more bias in it than other forms. Research has shown that certain types of persons will participate more than others in filling out research forms. The type of people who are willing to fill out a survey form usually are more educated, have a higher occupational status, have a high need for approval, have a high IQ, and are low in authoritarianism.

sample size In epidemiology, this is the process of selecting the best size of the study population for the type of research to be done. One rule is to use the largest sample size as possible or realistic, given the constraints of time, logistics, and money. Statistical curves show that the smaller the sample size, the larger the error in predictability. The larger the sample, the smaller the error in predictability.

sample, stratified random In epidemiology and health services research, subjects or cases are drawn from a population or research study group to ensure that each and every level of the population is represented as determined by age, race, income, and socioeconomic placement and that all have an equal chance of being drawn. This sampling process is done by dividing the study population into several segments, levels, or strata and sampling a different proportion of each. This selection or stratification process is often based on economic or demographic characteristics, age, or other variables that sensibly lend themselves to dividing the population into segments. Random sampling approaches are used in each level, group, or strata. *See stratified sample.*

sampling 1. In epidemiology and health services research, this is the process of selecting subjects from a study group or population; the process of choosing a case or a research group to be in a study. 2. In environmental health, this is the process of taking a representative small portion or quantity of something for testing or analysis. *See sample; sampling and sample selection.*

sampling and sample selection In epidemiology, health services research, and survey research, sampling should consider the kind of study and approach to be used and the kinds of findings anticipated. Empirical research sampling approaches should be used. With regard to sampling, the size of the sample must be large enough to be representative of the study population. The reason for sampling is to get responses that show a true picture of conditions, disease, injuries, or disabilities and to have reliable data that can be analyzed without asking each and every person in the entire population. The main reason to use sampling is to cut cost and effort yet predict need or determine problems as opposed to surveying an entire population.

sampling frame In epidemiological studies, this is a list of individuals that identifies all persons or households or living units in a population at a single point in time.

sampling plans In environmental health, these are documents outlining goals and objectives for continuous data collection activities on areas such as air, water, pesticides, and hazardous waste. The plan should describe the organization and responsibilities, project description, objectives, scope, schedule of tasks, time line and milestones, data usage, monitoring network/sampling analysis, and design rationale. Also included should be data quality objectives, sampling procedures, calibration, analytical methods, documentation/data reduction/reporting, data assessment, audits, corrective action, reports, and safety.

sampling variation In epidemiology or health services research, this is the possibility that the results of the study will vary because the subjects are chosen at random. All subjects will differ, as will the study group to which they belong, and the study results will differ because of the sampling process.

sanatorium An institution where patients were treated for chronic physical diseases (such as tuberculosis) or mental illnesses or where a patient is nursed and treated during a period of recuperation; a facility with a focus on preservation and advancement of health as much as rehabilitation or recuperation.

sanction 1. Formal consent or approval by an official in authority to give it. 2. To condone or approve of another person's actions or behavior. 3. A punishment provided by law to ensure that the law is obeyed. 4. Power to enforce a law. 5. In managed care, this is a reprimand by a health plan of a participating provider for a variety of reasons.

sand filters In environmental health, these are structures that remove some suspended solids from sewage. Air and bacteria decompose additional wastes filtering through the sand so that cleaner water drains from the bed (EPA).

sandwich model of discipline In health administration and human resource management, this is the process of counseling or critiquing employees where a positive comment is made. The corrective direction or criticism is then made and is followed by an positive final comment.

sane 1. Mentally sound. 2. Of healthy mind. 3. A legal rather than a psychiatric term indicating that an individual is in possession of a competent and stable mental state.

sanitarian A public health or environmental health worker who is involved with health protection activities, conducts sanitation inspections, and enforces public health and environmental health regulations. *See sanitarian, registered.*

sanitarian, registered (RS) In public health and environmental health, this is an individual who has successfully passed a registration/licensure exam in sanitation measures and environmental health for the state and usually is required to have completed a bachelors degree in public health, community health, or environmental health or a closely related degree major that includes 30 semester units of selected science courses. This public health/environmental health professional usually works in health protection activities for a local, regional, or state public health department of a department of environmental health services with the purpose of enforcing regulations and ensuring that sanitary conditions exist in food services and public eating establishments, milk products, swimming pools, water supplies, liquid waste control and management, solid waste control and management, air pollution control, food protection, and safety and occupational health. In some states this professional is now referred to as a "registered environmental specialist."

sanitarium A health-care facility established for the treatment or recuperation of physical or mental disorders focusing more on prophylactic care than therapeutic care.

sanitary 1. To be clean, sterile, or free of disease, dirt, or contamination; conducive to health. 2. To take measures to ensure that no pathogens, infections, contaminants, dirt, or disease-producing or unclean materials are present.

sanitary engineering structures In environmental health, these are tanks, reservoirs, and other structures commonly used in water and waste treatment works where dense, impermeable concrete with high resistance to chemical attack is required.

sanitary landfills In environmental health, this is a disposal facility employing an engineered method of disposing of solid wastes in land in a manner that minimizes environmental hazards by spreading the solid wastes in thin layers, compacting the solid wastes to the smallest practical volume, and applying cover material, usually dirt, at the end of each working day. The structure and management must comply with EPA guidelines for land disposal of solid wastes as prescribed by 40 CER 241. *See landfill.*

sanitary sewers In environmental health, these are underground pipes that carry only domestic or industrial waste and not gutter runoff or storm water (EPA).

sanitary surveys In environmental health and safe water management, these are on-site reviews of the water sources, facilities, equipment, operation, and maintenance of a public water system to evaluate the adequacy of those elements for producing and distributing safe drinking water (EPA).

sanitation 1. In public health, these are established procedures that help reduce the growth and spread of communicable disease and infectious organisms and in turn reduce health hazards in the community or health-care facilities. The application of measures for the protection of health to create environmental conditions that are conducive to health. Cleanliness, garbage removal and control, sewage control, insect control, rodent and rat control, clean water supplies, hand washing, and clean food handling and cooking utensils are all basic to good sanitation. Sanitation is foundational to public health. In health-care facilities and medical care, sterilization, sanitizing equipment and materials, and advanced infection control procedures are also sanitation measures. 2. In environmental health, this is the control of physical factors in the human environment that could harm development, health, and survival (EPA).

sanitize To kill all, and reduce the presence of, microbiological organisms in or on articles to levels judged safe by public health authorities.

sanitizer In public health, this is any chemical or agent such as chlorine, iodine, or high heat that can reduce or eliminate the presence of microorganisms, especially pathogens and infection-causing agents or any contaminants.

sanity 1. Soundness of mind. 2. Having a stable emotional and mental state.

SAP *See service assessment program.*

satellite clinic A primary care and ambulatory care facility located near the workplace or where people live to provide better accessibility and availability to emergency or primary care services. If advanced health care is needed, then the patient is referred or transferred to a parent organization such as a hospital, major clinic, or medical center.

satellite hospital *See hospital, satellite.*

satellite record system The storage of those medical records needed on a current basis at the site of care removed from the hospital or main treatment site (e.g., an ambulatory neighborhood clinic). Records may be retained at the remote site for a period of time and then returned to the central medical record department for permanent filing once the course of treatment is completed or the patient is transferred to the central facility.

satisfaction 1. Payment of a debt 2. Reparation for injury or insult. 3. Completion of an obligation. 4. In health-care delivery, this refers to the feelings and perceptions concerning the course of treatment or stay that a patient experienced. It also can be used as a measure of health-care delivery.

satisfaction, patient In health-care delivery, hospital administration, or clinic management, this is the degree or level of happiness or unhappiness; the extent of positive or negative experiences that a patient experiences or perceives in the process of being seen, treated, examined, and attended to in a medical care setting based on how the staff responded to and treated the patient and how he or she was attended to by staff, nursing personnel, allied health workers, and physicians. Timeliness in treatment, listening to concerns, response to needs, effectiveness in medical treatment and therapy, a caring attitude, personal respect and nice treatment, waiting times, time lapse before appointments and return appointments, and related issues all contribute to patient satisfaction.

satisfaction piece In health law, this is a memo from both the plaintiff and the defendant that is filed with the court to acknowledge the satisfactory settlement of a lawsuit.

satisfaction survey, patient In health-care administration, this is a process, tool, or mechanism used to measure and evaluate the course of treatment and how well a patient was attended to, respected, and responded to. A questionnaire is usually developed that is presented to the patient at an a appropriate time or sent to the patient's home after the course of treatment ends. Included in the survey are issues or concerns common to a patient satisfaction such as timeliness in treatment, listening to concerns, answering questions, responding to needs, effectiveness in medical treatment and therapy, a caring attitude, personal respect, being treated nicely, short waiting times, time lapse before appointments and return appointments, and related issues.

saturated zones In environmental health and safe water management, these are subsurface areas in which all pores and cracks are filled with water under pressure equal to or greater than that of the atmosphere.

saturation In health-care marketing and managed care, this is the point at which further market penetration is improbable, the competition is great, or costs will be excessive; when a health plan or HMO achieves maximum market penetration either in a subscriber group or in the market itself. The health plan's goal is to retain enrollees and its saturation level and not lose subscribers to competition. Marketing and expansion efforts are assessed to increase market share and learn how to expand the service area or market. *See also penetration.*

satyriasis An unhealthy preoccupation with sexual needs or desires in men. This condition may be caused by an organic brain disease or psychiatric dysfunction and is similar to nymphomania in women.

save 1. To spare. 2. To avoid; to prevent. 3. To hold until later. 4. To reserve something. 5. To preserve a document.

save-harmless statutes In health law, these are written laws or codes in some states that permit or require an agency to repay employees for damages lost in civil suits because of an act of negligence or tort on the employees' part. This is done while carrying on the business of the agency.

savings bank life insurance In insurance, this is any insurance policy sold by savings banks to people who live or work in the state in which the insurance is sold. Connecticut, Massachusetts, and New York are three states that allow such insurance.

SBU Strategic business unit.

SC Service corporation. *See professional association; professional corporation.*

scab In labor relations management, this is a nonunion worker; a worker who is not a member of the union who replaces a striking union worker.

scanlon plan In health administration and human resource management, this refers to an incentive program that attempts to motivate employees by some form of compensation to reduce labor costs and conserve resources to levels above those previously experienced by the health-care organization.

scarcity area In health-care delivery or community health, this is an area lacking an adequate supply of one particular health service or all health services. Synonymous with "medically underserved area."

scatter diagram *See scattergram.*

scattergram In epidemiology or health services research, this is the representation of data by a chart of dots. The dots represent the distribution of two different variables and their relationship to each other. The values of the X variable is placed on one axis and the values of Y are placed on the other axis. Dots are plotted according to their numerical value. A line is often drawn through the mean of the dots, and slope is calculated to make it into a correlation. This can be done, calculated, and drawn by desktop or mainframe computer statistical programs.

SCBA *See self-contained breathing apparatus.*

SCH *See sole community hospital.*

schedule 1. List. 2. A written list of things to be accomplished in a certain order or at a certain time.

schedule A 1. The list of occupations that the Department of Labor considers to be in short supply throughout the United States for purposes of labor certification. 2. In health-care financial management and income tax, this is the main tax form that is filled out and filed with the Internal Revenue Service.

schedule bond In insurance and personnel bonding activities, this is a fidelity bond listing employees by name and the amounts for which they are bonded.

schedule C In health-care financial management and income tax, this is the business operations tax form that is filled out and filed with the Internal Revenue Service and is connected to schedule A.

scheduled benefit provision *See allocated benefit provision.*

schedule of compliance In environmental health and pollution control, this is a schedule of required measures, including an enforceable sequence of actions or operations leading to compliance with an emission limitation, other limitation, prohibition, or standard (EPA).

schedule of controlled substances Under the Federal Comprehensive Drug Abuse Prevention and Control Act of 1970, drugs were classified by schedule for the purpose of legal control. Possession of any controlled substance without a prescription is illegal, and no distinction in the penalty language is made between drugs or different schedules. In violations concerning the manufacture and sale of controlled substances, a distinction between schedules is made. Schedules I, II, III, IV, and V are updated and reviewed each year. Schedule I: A drug or substance that has a high potential for abuse, has no current accepted medical use, and lacks accepted safe usage under medical supervision, including drugs such as heroin, LSD, mescaline, psilocybin, DMT, marijuana, and hashish. Schedule II: A drug or substance that has a high potential for abuse, has currently accepted medical use (even with restrictions), and may lead to severe psychological or physical dependence to include drugs such as (but not limited to) opium, methadone, Demerol, codeine, and cocaine. Schedule III: A drug or substance that has a potential for abuse but less potential than those in schedules I and II, has a currently accepted medical use, and may lead to moderate or low physical dependence or high psychological dependence, including such drugs as paregoric, barbiturates, Doriden, and amphetamines. Schedule IV: A drug or substance that has a low potential for abuse, has currently accepted medical use, and may lead to limited physical or psychological dependence, including drugs such as equinol and Miltown. Schedule V: A drug or substance that has low abuse potential, has a currently accepted medical use, and has limited physical and psychological dependence.

schedule of drugs See *schedule of controlled substances*.

schedules In managed care or medical insurance, this is the basis for determining certain health insurance benefits. These lists set forth specific amounts of money that the health plan or insurance company will lay out for specific procedures (e.g., the policy will pay up to $1,200 for hip replacement surgery).

schema In mental health, this is a psychological process of organization of intellectual or cognitive acts into a larger organization. Intellectual acts are not discrete or chaotic but are organized. A cognitive plan that determines the sequence of behaviors that often leads to the solution of a problem (Jean Piaget).

schematics Functional diagrams showing the secession of functions or processes required to attain a desired output.

schizocaria An acute form of schizophrenia, often referred to as "catastrophic schizophrenia." It is a disorder in which the patient's personality deteriorates at a very rapid rate.

schizoid personality A personality disorder characterized by shyness, oversensitivity, and sometimes eccentricity. These people are usually detached and appear unemotional in the face of stressful events and experiences.

schizophrenia A psychotic mental disorder characterized by disturbances in thought processes, mood, language, and behavior. Thought disturbance is shown through a distortion of reality manifested by delusions, incomplete thoughts or expressions, and hallucinations accompanied by a fragmentation of mental and perceptual associations resulting in incoherent speech. Mood disturbance is shown by inappropriate emotional responses. Behavior problems are seen as ambivalence, apathetic withdrawal, and bizarre activity. Also known as "dementia praecox," the different forms of schizophrenia include simple, hebephrenic, catatonic, paranoid, schizoaffective, childhood, residual, latent, chronic undifferentiated, and acute schizophrenic episode.

school health The total aspects of the health of the school-age child in the school setting, including the school environment, control of diseases, health screening programs, first aid and emergency care, and the child's overall physical, social, and psychological well-being. See *school health program; school health services; school health education*.

school health education 1. The health education process associated with health activities planned and conducted under the supervision of school personnel with the involvement of appropriate community health personnel and utilization of appropriate community resources; one component of the comprehensive school health program that includes the development, delivery, and evaluation of a planned instructional program and other activities for students preschool through grade 12 and for parents and for school staff and is designed to positively influence the health knowledge, attitudes, and skills of individuals (Joint Committee on Health Education Terminology). 2. A portion of a comprehensive school health program that includes curriculum and programs planned by people from the community and by health education teachers and administrators from within the school. It is taught only by teachers specially trained and prepared to teach health education; curriculum and programming covering the scope of health issues and teaching responsibility for one's personal health.

school health education curriculum All the health opportunities affecting learning and behavior of children and youth in the total school curriculum. These health experiences occur in both school and community settings as the individual interacts with the environment, including other students, school personnel, parents, and community members (Joint Committee on Health Education Terminology).

school health education curriculum guides The plans or framework for the curriculum that are developed and implemented cooperatively by health personnel, teachers, administrators, students, parents, and community representatives, preferably under the leadership of a qualified health educator (Joint Committee on Health Education Terminology).

school health educator 1. An individual with professional preparation in health education or health science who is qualified for certification as a health teacher and for participation in the development, improvement, and coordination of school and community health education programs. 2. An education practitioner who is professionally prepared in the field of school health education, meets state teaching requirements, and demonstrates competence in the development, delivery, and evaluation of curricula for students and adults in the school setting that enhance health knowledge, attitudes, lifestyle, and problem-solving skills (Joint Committee on Health Education Terminology).

school health program The composite of procedures and activities designed to protect and promote the well-being of students and school personnel. These procedures and activities include those organized in school health services, providing a healthful environment and health education (Joint Committee on Health Education Terminology).

school health services 1. The part of the school health program provided by physicians, nurses, dentists, health educators, other allied health personnel, social workers, teachers, and others to evaluate and promote the health of students and school personnel. These services are designed to ensure access to and the appropriate use of primary health-care services, appraise the health status of pupils and school personnel, help prevent and control communicable disease, provide emergency care for injury or sudden illness, promote and provide optimum sanitary conditions and safe facilities and environment, and provide concurrent learning opportunities that are conducive to the maintenance and promotion of individual and community health (Joint Committee on Health Education Terminology). 2. A part of a comprehensive school health program that includes school readiness programs, health appraisals, health counseling, interacting with teachers and parents concerning student health problems, emergency care and first aid activities, immunization and communicable disease control, public health concerns, community health education activities, and medical records maintenance.

school-loss day In public health, this is when a student 5 to 17 years of age missed more than half a normal day from school in which he or she has been currently enrolled because of a disease, condition, injury, or illness. *See disability.*

school medical adviser A physician who serves as a consultant for a school district to assist the school in medical matters and procedures to enhance the health and well-being of the students and school personnel.

school nurse Health-care practitioners who make up the largest group of health-care providers in school health services. School nurse responsibilities include activities to promote dental, mental, emotional, and physical health; to teach about health; to serve as a health counselor to students, parents, and teachers; and to be medical professional liaisons for students, parents, teachers, and physicians. School nurses advise schools of unsanitary and environmental conditions, monitor disease control and the spread of communicable disease, and provide emergency care for students and school personnel. School nurses also participate in a number of preventive programs such as vision and hearing screenings and immunization programs.

school nurse practitioner (SNP) A registered nurse who has a school nurse credential (as required in some states) and has advanced training as a nurse practitioner with a specialization in school nursing.

school of nursing *See collegiate school of nursing.*

school rule In health law and medical malpractice, this is similar to the community standard of care but instead of being based on the standard of care expected in a community, the standard is based on the medical specialty and is not recognized or used in all states. The standard of care is measured by the degree of care exercised by or expected of physicians with the same board specialty or medical specialization, which is the referred to as the "school" to which they belong. One is judged by peers with the same medical specialty, and only medical expert witnesses can be drawn from other physicians with the same medical specialty.

science information management In epidemiology, biomedical research, and outcome studies, this is the process of identifying priorities of information needed; retrieving valid, current, accurate, and relevant data; proper analysis, tabulation, assessment, interpretation, and use of the results and findings to improve outcomes.

scienter (Lat.) 1. Knowingly; knowledge with guilt 2. In fraud, knowingly having an intent to deceive.

scientific congruence in association and causation In epidemiology, this is when association and causation of any disease, condition, disability, or injury must be congruent and compatible with and be based on and supported by current epidemiological, biomedical, and scientific knowledge and information. Proof of association and causation can include responses of control groups, evidence of reactions from those not getting the illness and those excluded from the exposure or event, and proof from those who are exposed and who become cases with the disease or malady.

scientific emphasis In medical education in the United States, premedical students are usually required to complete 1 year of biological sciences, 1 year of chemistry, and 1 year of physics for admission to medical school. Much of this science is repeated in depth in the first 2 years of medical school. The physician then graduates as more of a scientist than a physician, with much emphasis on scientific testing and treatment with pharmaceuticals while having minimum training in preventive medicine, public health, patient relations, nutrition, and psychobehavioral causes of diseases or treatment through the whole-person philosophy.

Scientology A religious movement begun in 1952 that teaches immortality and reincarnation and claims a sure psychotherapeutic method for freeing the individual from personal problems, for increasing human abilities, and for speeding recovery from sickness, injury, and mental disorder.

scintigraphy In medical care testing and radiographic imaging, this is an X-ray imaging type of procedure in which an agent or substance that emits radioactive waves is injected into the body. A camera with special film sensitive to the radioactive emissions then photographs that part of the body under study (e.g., the retina of the eye). *See ophthalmic photography.*

scintilla (Lat.) 1. A spark or trace. The slightest bit of evidence.

scire facias (Lat.) 1. Cause it to be known. 2. A judge's order to a defendant to appear in court and to show cause as to why a record should not be used against him or her.

SCM Society of Computer Medicine.

scope The extent of activities or range of operations that will be undertaken and/or accomplished.

-scope Suffix meaning "instrument for visual examination."

scope and setting, primary health-care The range of basic and primary care ambulatory services formed for the provision of evaluating, diagnosing, and treating illnesses, injuries, diseases, conditions, or disorders to promote physical, dental, and mental health. Services are offered in physicians' offices, ambulatory clinics, outpatient centers, public health centers, HMOs, public health clinics, neighborhood health centers, or other primary care centers and are offered by family practice, internal medicine, emergency care, or other primary care physicians, health educators, psychologists, and social workers as well as physician assistants, nurse practitioners, and other physician extenders. The services offered embrace preventive, patient education, and other health maintenance and health promotion activities and are distinguished from secondary and tertiary care, which are advanced-care levels in inpatient settings.

scope of care and services In hospital administration, this is an inventory of processes that make up a specified medical care or administrative function such as activities performed by governance, management, clinical staff, and/or support personnel (JCAHO).

scope of employment Professional activities that a person is specifically employed to do or that may be implied from specific duties.

scope of practice In medical care delivery, these are the treatments, therapies, and patient care activities, techniques, or methods that an allied health care professional or nurse is legally allowed to do. These may or may not be a part of the physician's prerogatives.

scope of practice act The state law that sets forth the treatments, therapies, and patient care activities, techniques, or methods that allied health-care professionals or nurses are legally allowed to do in the practice of their professions, and in the process of caring for or treating patients.

scope of services In health-care delivery, this is the number, intensity, or complexity of services provided by a hospital or health program. Scope of services is measured in a number of different ways so that the capacity and nature of different programs may be compared. A program's scope of services should reflect, and be adequate to meet, the needs of its patient mix.

scopo- Prefix meaning "visual examination."

scoring guidelines *See guideline, scoring.*

scotoma In psychology and psychiatry, this describes a person's psychological blind spot; one's unawareness.

screening 1. In health promotion and epidemiology, this is the use of quick and simple tests or procedures to identify and separate persons who are apparently well but who have or may be at risk of a disease from those who probably do not have the disease; a series of tests to identify individuals with a disease or risk of disease; to identify well persons from sick persons and to identify suspects for more definitive diagnostic studies; to give diagnostic tests to large groups of individuals to detect disease. 2. One use of screening is multiple screening (or multiphasic screening), which is the combination of a battery of screening tests for various diseases performed by technicians under medical direction and applied to large groups of apparently well persons. 3. An initial, cursory claims review by insurance companies intended to identify claims that are obviously not covered or are deficient in some way. 4. In psychology and psychiatry, an initial evaluation of a patient that includes medical and psychiatric history, psychological testing, and mental status evaluation to formulate a diagnosis to determine a patient's suitability for a particular treatment modality. 5. In environmental health, this is the use of screen materials or structures to remove coarse floating and suspended solids from sewage (EPA). *See also sensitivity; specificity; preventive medicine; early and periodic screening, diagnosis, and treatment; screening, multiphasic.*

screening clinic A clinic that provides the initial assessment of patients seeking care to determine what services they need, with what priority, and sometimes where treatment of minor problems will be done. *See also triage.*

screening, generic 1. In health promotion, this is to test and evaluate as many individuals in a population as possible without regard to existing diagnoses or conditions. 2. In hospital administration and medical practice, this is to test and evaluate as many patients in a hospital study population as possible without regard to existing diagnoses or conditions to discover adverse outcome, patient care incidents, oversights, lack of quality care, lack of diligence in patient care, nosocomial infections, iatrogenic occurrences, etc.

screening interview In health administration and human resource management, this is a special interview used to eliminate various applicants who clearly do not have the education, skills, ability, or experience for a specific job or position.

screening level In testing and screening measurements, this is the usual point of concern or the cutoff level at which the results of the test indicate a health concern such as blood pressure in adults exceeding 140/90 or total cholesterol exceeding 220 points.

screening, mass In health promotion, this is to test and evaluate as many individuals in a population or community as possible to detect a disease or condition or increase the health status of the population.

screening, multiphasic In health promotion and school health, this is to test and evaluate high numbers of individuals in a population or public setting with batteries of tests to identify well persons from sick persons. These are set up in shopping malls, schools, universities, senior citizen centers, etc., and normal individuals usually visit several stations for a different test at each station so that persons suspected of having a disease can be identified and sent for more definitive medical diagnostic studies or reassured by good results and reinforced for good health practices; to give batteries of diagnostic tests in public settings to large groups of individuals in order to detect disease. *See screening.*

screening, occurrence In hospital administration and medical practice and quality assurance processes, this is to assess as many patient's medical records in a hospital study population as possible to identify cases in which an adverse occurrence occurred on the basis of certain areas of treatment, medical care, diagnoses, or conditions. The findings can be used as outcome studies to reduce occurrences or can be used in risk management to reduce chance of liability. More commonly called "outcome studies," "medical care evaluation," or "medical audit." *See medical audit; medical care evaluation.*

screening panels In health law, these are fact-finding bodies used during the early stages of a malpractice dispute. There are two basic types of screening panels in use: physicians' defense panels, which seek to develop the best possible defense for the physician who faces a real or potential malpractice claim, and joint physician and lawyer panels, whose purpose is to look at the facts of the case for both the physician and the plaintiff and decide on its merits.

screening tests, characteristics of In health promotion, this is the development or use of a test designed to evaluate populations of people for certain disease, disorders, or conditions that can be referred to a physician or that can be prevented if detected soon enough. Such tests must be effective and efficient and produce high-quality results, including high levels of accuracy, high yields, reliability, validity, good sensitivity, good specificity, and reproducibility and must be precise and easily administered.

screen memory In mental health, this is a psychological process that causes one to forget or is used to cover up or repress a painful memory.

scrub In medical care in preparation for surgery, this term has come to have the broader meaning of thoroughly preparing for surgery by putting on sterile surgical garments, washing and scrubbing one's hands and arms with disinfectant soap prior to putting on latex or rubber gloves, and masking, all as a part of infection control. The term is derived from the narrower, more historical meaning of thoroughly scrubbing hands and arms prior to surgery when rubber gloves were not yet used.

scrubbers In environmental health, these are air pollution cleaning devices that use a spray of water or reactant or a dry process to trap pollutants in emissions.

scrubs *See surgical scrubs.*

scurrilous 1. Using abusive language. 2. Vulgar; indecent. 3. Verbal abuse.

scut work In hospital administration, this is a slang term used by house staff or others who work in health care facilities to describe undesirable work, usually dirty, tedious, or trivial work such as paperwork, cleaning up after patients, or work that could always be done by most anyone.

SDMIX South Dakota Medical Information Exchange.

SDTs *See self-directed teams.*

S.E. In law, the South Eastern Reporter of the National Reporter System.

seal An authenticating mark on a document (e.g., a notary or corporate seal).

sealed sources In environmental health and hazardous material management, these are radiation sources whose structures are such as to prevent any dispersion of the radioactive material into the environment under normal conditions of use.

sealed verdict In law, this is a verdict decided while a court is not in session. Thus the verdict is placed in an envelope and sealed, and the jury separates. The verdict is pronounced later in court.

seamless system In national universal healthcare coverage, this is a health-care delivery and medical insurance coverage system that does not limit a person's ability to see a physician or get health care because of state or county political boundaries. That is, a patient in a rural area who lives next to a state line or across the street from a different county can easily access health care in the next state or county without worrying about crossing state lines or political boundaries.

seamless web of care In health-care delivery and health systems, this is a health-care delivery system that has no cracks in the system that a patient might fall through, is vertically integrated, and has alternative systems available, including home health care, case management, and an integrated information management system. Thus the system must be comprehensive, and all types and levels of care must be available with total universal coverage.

search firms In human resources management, this is a private business established to help health-care organizations locate hard-to-find personnel or manpower specialties or locate and place top-level executives. Also referred to as "headhunters."

search warrant In law, this is a court order issued by a magistrate to a police officer who has shown probable cause for a search of a property. This warrant allows the police officer to search real or personal property for evidence, stolen goods, or illicit materials.

seasonable Within a reasonable period of time.

seasonal variation In epidemiology, this is a causation factor related to the time element of epidemiological investigations. Seasonal change can influence the presence or the diminishing of certain diseases because the mode of transmission or source of the disease can be affected by weather and temperature. For example, malaria, yellow fever, and encephalitis are more common in the summer months because the mosquito is the vector, and meningitis, influenza, or common colds are more common in the winter months, being transmitted by airborne or fomite methods.

SEC Securities and Exchange Commission.

seclusion 1. According to JCAHO for psychiatric, alcoholism, and drug abuse facilities accreditation purposes, a procedure that isolates the patient to a specific environmental area removed from the patient community. 2. According to JCAHO in acute-care or long-term-care facilities, this means the involuntary confinement of a patient alone in a single room from which the patient is physically prevented from leaving for a period of time. Seclusion does not mean nonclinical involuntary confinement based on legally mandated reasons such as a person confined to a room who is facing serious criminal charges or who is serving a sentence in a prison or jail. *See isolation; quarantine.*

second aid The performance of assistance after the time of any immediate or temporary need; continuous health care. *See also secondary care.*

secondary attack rate In epidemiology, this is where a susceptible individual acquires an infection from a primary source. Secondary transmissions are found only in certain types of communicable diseases and can occur only through certain routes of transmission, the most common being person-to-person contact. This is the frequency with which infection occurs among susceptible individuals on the basis of the incubation period of the disease following exposure to an infectious person. This is a specific attack rate with the numerator consisting of persons who have gotten the disease from a primary source and the denominator consisting of the population at risk. The type of disease, levels of immunity, and ability of the disease to recur all have to be considered when determining the denominator. The formula for secondary attack rate follows:

$$\frac{\text{Total number of persons who got the disease from a previous infected person (primary source)}}{\text{Population at risk}} \times 1000$$

See attack rates.

secondary authority In law, this is any indirect authority, opinions, or sources other than actual decisions by an appellate court in the governing jurisdiction.

secondary boycott Indirect pressure or indirectly withholding of services.

secondary care In health-care delivery, the services provided by medical specialists who generally do not have first contact with patients; medical care services provided by hospitals or medical specialists to patients who are referred for care by the primary care health-care provider and in some cases through self-referral; medical care that is advanced and supplemental to primary care. Some specialists such as internal medicine physicians, urologists, cardiologists, psychiatrists, obstetricians, gynecologists, and ophthalmologists are considered secondary care health-care providers but do not include subspecialties or highly specialized physicians. General inpatient hospital care, ambulatory surgery, and some outpatient care are usually considered secondary care. There has been a trend toward self-referral for secondary care services rather than by referral from primary care providers. In managed care, the patient is to first seek care from primary care providers and is then referred to secondary and/or tertiary care providers as needed. *See also primary care; tertiary care.*

secondary care facilities In health-care delivery, these are facilities such as general acute hospitals or ambulatory surgical centers that render care that requires a degree of sophistication and skills and that is usually associated with the confinement of the patient for a definite period of time; usual hospital care, procedures, and treatment.

secondary carrier In managed care and insurance, this is the insurance carrier responsible for payment to the health plan after the primary health plan or carrier has paid for the enrollee's treatment or encounter with a health-care provider.

secondary data In epidemiology, health services research, or health-care marketing, this is the use of facts, statistics, and information gathered as primary data by some other agency or entity such as governmental agencies, insurance companies, research institutions, or published reports and accessed later by the epidemiologist for a retrospective study.

secondary diagnosis In medical care, these are conditions that coexist with a primary diagnosis at the time of admission or that subsequently develop after admission and affect the treatment and care received and the length of stay in the health-care facility; a disease or condition identified by a health-care provider in addition to the chief reason for seeking medical care.

secondary drinking water regulations In environmental health and safe drinking water management, these are regulations that apply to public water systems and that specify the maximum contaminant levels that, in the judgment of the state or the EPA, are requisite to protect the public welfare. Such regulations may apply to any contaminant in drinking water that may adversely affect the odor or appearance of such water and consequently may cause a substantial number of the persons served by the public water system providing such water to discontinue its use or that may otherwise adversely affect the public welfare. Such regulations vary according to geographic or other circumstances. *See Safe Drinking Water Act.*

secondary emissions In environmental health and air pollution control, these are pollutants that are spewed into the atmosphere as a result of the construction or operations of an existing stationary facility but do not come from the existing stationary facility; emissions from vehicles, ships, or trains coming to or leaving existing stationary facilities; emissions that escape capture by a primary emission control system.

secondary evidence In health law, this is evidence that is not from primary or forthright sources (e.g., oral testimony of the contents of a lost document).

secondary gain The recognition, attention, and advantage that a person gains from being ill (e.g., gifts, pampering, and the release from responsibility).

secondary hood system In health and safety and environmental health, this is equipment such as hoods, ducts, fans, and dampers that is used to capture and transport secondary inorganic pollutants and emissions.

secondary limits In health and safety and radiation safety, these are the values of the dose equivalent indices (deep or shallow) in the case of external exposure or of annual limits on intake in the case of internal exposure which can be used to obtain an indirect assessment of compliance with primary limits.

secondary maximum contaminant levels (SMCLs) In environmental health and safe water management, these apply to public water systems and are requisite to protect the public welfare. They are the maximum permissible levels of a contaminant in water delivered to the free-flowing outlet of the ultimate user of public water system; contaminants added to the water under circumstances controlled by the user, except those resulting from corrosion of piping and plumbing caused by water quality. *See Safe Drinking Water Act; sanitary surveys; secondary drinking water regulations.*

secondary prevention In public health, epidemiology, health promotion, and preventive medicine, these are health screening and detection activities used to discover pathogenic states in individuals in a population. If pathogenic states are discovered early, diagnosis and early treatment can prevent conditions from progressing and from spreading in a population and can stop or slow the progress of disease, disability, disorders, or death; blocking the progression of disease or an injury from developing into an impairment or disability; early detection, referral, and prompt treatment to either cure a disease or halt it at the earliest stages of development as possible. Early detection can slow the progress of a disease, prevent complications, limit disability, and halt or reverse the communicability of an infectious disease. Early intervention and treatment of a disease in single cases can prevent groups or major populations from acquiring communicable diseases. Primary prevention best helps persons not exposed, and secondary prevention is for those already infected. Secondary prevention can maintain already healthy behaviors and reverse unhealthy lifestyles through health education and behavior change programs such as smoking cessation, weight loss, stress reduction, health counseling, or early admission into a drug treatment program. *See primary prevention; tertiary prevention.*

secondary procedures Therapeutic and diagnostic procedures beyond the principal diagnosis and performed during a patient stay.

secondary psychological prevention Measures needed to prevent an emotional or mental disease process through prevention based on early findings, therapy, and treatment.

secondary smoke *See secondhand smoke.*

secondary standards In environmental health, this is a national secondary ambient air quality standard promulgated pursuant to the National Ambient Air Quality Standards.

secondary treatment In environmental health and liquid waste management, this is the second step in most waste treatment systems in which bacteria consume the organic parts of the waste. It is accomplished by bringing together waste, bacteria, and oxygen in trickling filters or in the activated sludge process. This treatment removes floating and settleable solids and about 90% of the oxygen-demanding substances and suspended solids. Disinfection is the final stage of secondary treatment. *See primary treatment; tertiary treatment.*

secondhand smoke In environmental health, this is a form of indoor air pollution that results from raw tobacco burning into the open air that nonsmokers often end up breathing, causing the nonsmoker to breath air polluted with harsh tobacco smoke, the particulate matter, and the related unhealthy chemicals and carcinogenic substances. The Environmental Protection Agency refers to this as environmental tobacco smoke (ETS) because it is considered a form of indoor air pollution. Tobacco smoke has long been recognized as a major cause of mortality and morbidity. Secondhand smoke is dilute compared to mainstream smoke, but if inhaled it is chemically similar to mainstream smoke and has many of the same carcinogenic and toxic agents. On the basis of a multitude of epidemiology studies and analysis and following the EPA guidelines for carcinogen risk assessment, the EPA concluded that environmental tobacco smoke is a Group A (known human) carcinogen. Also referred to as "secondary smoke," "slipstream smoke," and "indoor pollution." *See involuntary smoking.*

second opinion In medical care, this is the medical examination and assessment of a patient with accompanying new diagnoses and recommendations provided by a second physician to confirm previous diagnoses and recommendations of the first physician.

second opinion program In medical care, this is a mechanism established by a health-care organization, medical service, or insurance organization to provide and encourage second opinions of recommended medical procedures and diagnoses.

second surgical opinion Under managed care, this is a verification and information-seeking process for the enrollee in a health plan who is encouraged to obtain additional opinions from other health-care providers/surgeons before making a final decision about a serious surgical procedure. In health plans, it is common for a list of surgical procedures to be developed jointly by the enrollee and the secondary care provider or specialist.

section In professional association or areas of specialization, these are organized members of a medical subspecialty.

section 89 A statute under the Internal Revenue Service Code that requires certain employee benefit plans to meet five qualifications for them to be nontaxable to covered employees. Welfare benefit plans are subject to this section of the IRS code.

section 125 In human relations and personnel management, this refers to a flexible benefit plan as set forth in this section of the federal Internal Revenue Service Code, which defines such plans and allows employee contributions to benefit plans be made with pretax dollars.

section 222 A section of the Social Security Amendments of 1972 (P.L. 92-603) that authorized the former secretary of HEW (now HHS) to undertake, with respect to Medicare, studies, experiments, or demonstration projects on prospective reimbursement of facilities; ambulatory surgical centers (surgicenters); intermediate care and homemaker services (with respect to the extended-care benefit under Medicare); elimination or reduction of the 3-day prior hospitalization requirement for admission to a skilled nursing facility; determination of the most appropriate methods of reimbursing the services of physicians' assistants and nurse practitioners; provision for day-care services to older persons who are eligible under Medicare and Medicaid; and possible means of making the services of clinical psychologists more generally available under Medicare and Medicaid.

section 223 A section of the Social Security Amendments of 1972 (P.L. 92-603) that requires the secretary of HEW to establish limits on the overall direct or indirect costs that will be recognized as reasonable under Medicare for comparable services in comparable facilities in an area. The secretary is also permitted to establish maximum acceptable costs in such facilities with respect to items or services (e.g., food or standby costs). The beneficiary is liable (except in the case of emergency care) for any amounts determined as excessive (except there are no charges for excessive amounts in a facility in which one's admitting physician has a direct or indirect ownership interest).

section 224 A section of the Social Security Amendments of 1972 (P.L. 92-603) that places a limit on Medicare and Medicaid reimbursement of charges recognized as reasonable. The law recognizes as reasonable those charges that fall within the 75th percentile of all charges for a similar service in a locality. Increases in physicians' fees allowable for Medicare purposes are indexed to a factor that takes into account increased costs of practice and the increase in general earnings levels in an area. Section 224 further provides that, with respect to reasonable charges for medical supplies and equipment, only the lowest charges at which supplies and equipment of similar quality are widely and consistently available in a locality may be recognized.

section 314(d) A section of the PHS Act that authorized formula grants by the federal government to the states for their unrestricted use in funding state and local health programs and activities.

section 504 A section of the Rehabilitation Act of 1973 (P.L. 93-112) as amended. This section provides access to hospitals with reasonable accommodations for handicapped people and prohibits discrimination against handicapped people for employment.

section 1122 A former section of the Social Security Act added by P.L. 92-603 that stated that payments would not be made to health-care facilities under Medicare or Medicaid for certain disapproved capital expenditures determined to be inconsistent with former state or local governmental health systems agency plans. Public Law 93-641, the National Health Planning and Resources Development Act of 1974 (which ended in 1986), required states to participate in the section 1122 program for cost containment purposes to have the state health planning and development agency serve as the section 1122 agency for purposes of required reviews. *See also capital expenditure review; certificate of need.*

sector In computers, a part or area of a disk, diskette, or other storage medium.

secular trends In epidemiology and demographics, this is the tracking of diseases, conditions, injury occurrences, disability, or death over long-term periods to show trends in their occurrence, usually no less than 10 years; tracking disease and demographic statistics and changes over long durations of time. Also referred to as ''temporal trends.''

secure 1. Free from fear, care, or worry. 2. Confident. 3. To provide confidence in the payment of an obligation. 4. To guarantee repayment. 5. To gain possession of.

secured bonds In health-care financial management where corporate bonds are used for projects like hospital construction, the corporate bond is backed up by the organization's assets to meet a bondholder's claims. If payment is not made when the bonds come due, and if cash is not available, the bond-issuing company has the right to all assets and properties to meet the amount of the bond. If there is a payment default, the bondholders have the first claim on the specified assets and may sell them to turn the assets into cash to meet the bond obligation.

secured creditor One to whom money is owed and is protected by a mortgage or security interest in the property of the debtor.

secure maximum contaminant levels In environmental health and safe water management, these are the maximum permissible levels of a contaminant in water delivered to the free-flowing outlet of the ultimate user of a water supply, the consumer, or contamination resulting from corrosion of piping and plumbing caused by water quality. *See Safe Drinking Water Act.*

securities In health finance, these are stocks, bonds, or other financial legal documents or notes that verify that shares of stock in a company exist.

securities law In law, these are elements of law that interpret and apply statutory and regulatory requirements governing and controlling the sale and purchase of investment systems, such as stocks and bonds.

security 1. The quality or state of being safe; certain; protection. 2. Something given as a guarantee of performance, protection, or payment. 3. A quasi-police service or officer in a health-care facility; private guards who watch over and protect the staff, patients, and property of hospitals or other health-care facilities.

security department In health-care administration, this is the administrative unit responsible for crime prevention, safety, control, and security of a health-care facility and its property, patients, and personnel while in the facility or on its premises.

security director The administrator responsible for the day-to-day operation of the security department and security activities in a health-care facility.

security guard An employee of the security department with responsibility for protecting the health-care facility against crime, fire, and any illegal activity while ensuring the safety of the patients and personnel in the facility or on the premises.

security hospital A health-care facility serving an inmate population in a prison, jail, or mental institution where patients must be guarded. *See also prison hospital.*

sedative 1. Tending to calm or soothe. 2. Any drug that produces a calming or relaxing effect through central nervous system depression. Some sedative drugs are barbiturates, chloral hydrate, paraldehyde, and bromide.

sedimentation In environmental health and liquid waste management, this is letting solids settle out of wastewater by gravity during wastewater treatment (EPA). *See secondary treatment.*

sedimentation tanks In environmental health and liquid waste management, these are the holding structures or areas for wastewater where floating wastes are skimmed off and settled solids are removed for disposal (EPA). *See secondary treatment; primary treatment; tertiary treatment.*

sediments In environmental health and ecology, these are soil, sand, and minerals washed from land into water, usually after rain. These substances pile up in reservoirs, rivers, and harbors; destroy fish and nesting areas and holes of water animals; and cloud the water so that needed sunlight might not reach aquatic plants. Careless farming, mining, and building activities will expose sediment materials, allowing them to be washed off the land after rainfalls.

sedition The promotion of public disorder against the government.

seduce 1. To lead astray. 2. To entice from duty. 3. To tempt to do wrong.

seed money Funds provided or set aside to start a project or program; money used to match monies given as a gift or through a grant to start a project.

segmentation 1. In managed care and insurance, this is a process by which the insurance company divides general accounts into different and distinct parts that identify each of the company's major lines of business such as life insurance, accident insurance, health plans, senior plans, and CHAMPUS plans. 2. In health-care marketing, this is targeting advertising, services, or public relations activities toward a certain population group or geographic area.

Segment, Target, Research, Assess, Provide Products (STRAP) In health strategic planning and health-care marketing, STRAP stands for segment (identify market segments, e.g., by demographic traits), target (which segment to target for the marketing activity), research (identify the needs of the target population), assess (evaluate; compare outputs to inputs and processes), and products or services that meet the needs or desires of the target population.

segregated account *See separate account.*

seize To take property legally; to legally possess; to put into possession.

seizure 1. A public official taking property into custody as a direct result of a person violating the law. 2. A neurological disorder characterized by loss of awareness and control.

select and ultimate mortality tables In epidemiology, vital statistics, and insurance, these are death tables that show the mortality rates for the policyholders for a certain age cohort and compared to the projected greatest length of time the person is expected to live. These types of tables are used for calculating dividends, dividend scales, and premium rates.

select group In insurance, these are potential insurance applicants who are accepted for insurance policies at standard rates. Mortality rates are better for select groups than for the general population. *See select mortality; select and ultimate mortality tables.*

selection 1. In epidemiology and health services research, this is the sampling of subjects for the study group and control/comparison group so that they are representative of the total study population. Failing to take into account differences in characteristics might be attributed to selection and could account for any differences in outcomes. 2. In population genetics, these are cultural, traditional, behavioral, and familial traits and characteristics that set physiological status, general well-being, or disease states and related genetic results that are determined and result from mate selection and their offspring, who then grow and develop in various subgroups of a general population.

selection bias *See sampling bias.*

selection interviews In health administration and human relations management, this is a process through which an applicant for a position and the potential employer participate in communication processes in person or by a telephone conference that may include answering a set of questions and/or a discussion of the applicant's skills, abilities, and potential to fill the position. If the interview is done in person, observations of behaviors, interpersonal interactions, and communication skills are also observed. Phone interviews are often done to screen out applicants and save interview costs and time but have many limitations and fall short of being effective as a selection interview.

selection process In health administration and human relations management, this is a process consisting of several steps used to advertise, recruit, screen, interview, and hire candidates for a position.

selection ratio In health administration and human relations management, this is the number of job applicants hired compared to the total number of applicants.

selective contracting In managed care, this is one approach to modifying the way health-care providers practice and deliver health care, thus switching responsibility of control processes from the health plan or third-party payer to health-care providers (both hospitals and physicians). Gatekeepers are made of primary care physicians, reducing the role of the specialist and increasing the role of the primary care practitioner, thus redistributing resources and reducing costs. Education and feedback are also used to show practitioners how they compare to other similar health-care providers in costs, use of resources, testing, etc.

selective pesticides In environmental health, these are chemicals designed to affect only certain types of pests or insects, leaving other plants and animals unharmed (EPA).

selectman A person chosen to sit on a board of officials. Mostly used in New England, this person serves in the capacity of a mayor.

select mortality tables 1. In epidemiology, vital statistics, and insurance, these are mortality tables derived from the use of only death experiences of a select group. 2. In life insurance, mortality tables are based on both age of the person insured at the time the policy was issued and the time period since the writing of the insurance policy. *See select and ultimate mortality tables.*

select period In epidemiology, vital statistics, and insurance, this is the calculation of mortality rates using the length of time during which the effects of selection are assumed to be observable and significant (e.g., 5 to 10 years or 10 to 20 years). *See secular trend.*

select risk fact finder In managed care, this is a document that lists and presents all medical data and information about a prospective employer group that is a potential new account.

self-actualization The term used by Abraham Maslow to describe the highest level of mental well-being, self-confidence, inner peace, mental and emotional development, and personality adjustment.

self-administered group insurance plan In managed care and insurance, the policyholder is required to take care of most paperwork and administrative work for the health plan. The policyholder maintains detailed records of group membership; processes forms; responds to routine requests, changes in beneficiaries and in name and address changes; and in some cases prepares certificates for new group members. Each month or quarter, the policyholder prepares a premium statement that shows the services used and the computation of the premium due and then sends it to the carrier along with premium payments.

self-care 1. In hospital or nursing home care, this is when an inpatient can dress him- or herself, walk about, eat without assistance, take his or her own medications, and cope with activities of daily living. 2. Individuals who have learned minor medical care and procedures such as the observation and reporting of symptoms and vital signs, health record keeping, treating minor illness, and injuries such as cuts. Such individuals can self-treat 70% of illnesses and not require a physician. 3. Medical treatment and cures given to oneself for common or simple medical problems or chronic disease. Self-diagnosis, over-the-counter drugs, home remedies, nutrition, herbs, and folk remedies may be employed or may be used to augment definitive and allopathic care.

self-care dialysis unit A medical care facility where long-term dialysis maintenance is performed by a trained patient, with appropriate professional supervision by trained personnel, all under the supervision of a physician.

self-care dialysis training unit A medical care facility where patients on dialysis or their helpers or family are trained to perform all procedures in dialysis self-management so it can be done at home, under appropriate professional supervision by trained personnel, all under the supervision of a physician.

self-care unit A hospital unit that offers medical supervision without nursing care. Individuals in a self-care unit are capable of caring for themselves and need supervision only with diet, medications, bathing, etc; most often seen in long-term-care facilities and VA and rehabilitation hospitals. *See also personal care; custodial care.*

self-contained breathing apparatus (SCBA) In environmental health and hazardous waste, this is a special type of respiratory protection equipment used in hazardous waste operations and cleanup. Two types are used: open circuit and closed circuit. Open-circuit SCBA equipment consists of a gas cylinder, a pressure demand/reducer valve, inhalation/exhalation valves, and a face piece. The gas cylinder contains compressed air that is inhaled through the pressure valve and exhaled into the ambient air. Both are positive pressure and approved by the National Institute of Occupational Health and Safety (NIOSH) and the Mine Safety and Health Administration (MSHA) for use in atmospheres that are immediately dangerous to life and health. Closed-circuit SCBA equipment consists of a gas cylinder, an inflatable bag or chamber with a moving diaphragm, and a face mask piece. The worker inhales from the bag/reservoir and exhales back into the system through an absorbent material that removes carbon dioxide. Amount of usable time in the equipment is one of the main considerations when selecting which type to use.

self-dealing One who acts for oneself rather than helping an agent or the person for whom one works.

self-defense The right to employ aggression or physical force against a person who is threatening one's own person, property, or name. Force is acceptable only when the threat was not provoked, when there is no reasonable escape, and when the force is not disproportionate to the threat.

self-determination In mental health services, this is the process of the therapist permitting clients to decide and direct their own lives and affairs while under the direction of a therapist.

self-directed team In health administration, this is a group of employees who are responsible for planning and scheduling their own work, making work-related decisions, solving problems, and managing themselves and their own tasks, work areas, and areas of responsibilities with minimum supervision while serving the customers of the health-care organization. Because employees are empowered and motivation factors incorporated, the results are increased quality, productivity, and morale and reduced turnover, absenteeism, and labor costs.

self-efficacy In mental health and psychology, this is a construct from social learning theory; a belief held by a person that one is capable of doing certain acts or behaviors and fulfilling certain expectations or accomplishments.

self-evaluation A critical assessment of a facility or training program measured against accreditation objects, criteria, and standards. Also called a "self-study." *See self-study.*

self-executing 1. A law or court action that requires no further official action for it to be enforced or put into effect. 2. A will executed by the testator and witnesses and verified by a notary public and thus needing no other proof to be admitted into probate.

self-funding In health-care finance and insurance, this is when a health-care organization decides to develop a special account or investment fund to meet the risk and insurance obligations out of its own resources.

self-funding groups In managed care, this is when private business or commercial organizations absorb the costs of covering employee's medical care. The health plan can serve as its own provider of the medical care, drugs, and related bills of the group for all actual medical costs incurred plus an administrative fee for operations and overhead; a self-insurance approach for large companies.

self-governance 1. Self-rule; being totally responsible for administration and functions of an organization or a department of an organization even though it is a part of a larger organization; allowed responsibility, authority, accountability, and decision making for certain delegated tasks, functions, or activities or the total operation of a division or department. 2. In hospital administration and medical staff management, this is when a hospital's board of directors delegates specific responsibilities and duties to the director of the medical staff and the medical staff organization of the hospital; evaluation and selection of physicians for the medical staff, monitoring and control of patient care quality practice patterns and activities of the medical staff physicians, and assessing the need for new facilities and equipment.

self-help 1. Taking a legal action without authority and planning to suffer the consequences. 2. Giving first aid or primary health care to oneself or family. Also called "medical self-help" or "self-care." *See also self-care; medical self-help.*

self-help group In mental health and social services, this is to bring together a group of individuals who have a common concern or problem. Through group therapy sessions, 10 to 15 persons engage in discussions, sharing emotional support and assistance designed to bring help to one another in dealing with a problem, struggle, concern, or interest.

self-insurance The practice of an individual, group of individuals, employer, or organization assuming complete responsibility for losses that might be insured against such as malpractice losses, medical expenses, and/or other losses caused by illness. A certain level of funds must be verified to cover liability or loss, as an insurance policy would do. In such cases, medical expenses would most likely be financed out of current income, personal savings, a fund developed for the purpose, and/or some other combination of personal assets. Self-insurance is contrasted with the practice of purchasing insurance by the payment of a premium to some third party (an insurance company or government agency). Actually, self-insurance is not a formal form of insurance.

self-insured In managed care, this is a health plan where the risk for medical cost is assumed by the company rather than an insurance company or managed-care company. Under ERISA, self-insured insurance or health plans are exempt from certain regulatory mandates such as premium taxes and mandatory benefits. Self-insured organizations often contract with health plans or insurance companies to manage the benefits and the administrative aspects of the plan (called third-party administrators or administrative services only). Self-funded organizations can limit liability through stop-loss insurance. *See third-party administrators.*

self-pay Patients who pay their own hospital bills out of their own pockets without insurance benefits; patients who do not have or use medical care or hospital insurance.

self-pity A mental or defense mechanism that involves self-blaming, a negative mind-set, giving up, feeling rejected, feeling that there is no hope or that no one cares, or shifting the responsibility of life's disappointments from oneself to others or to the environment. The conscious mind shares the feeling of thwarted desire of the unconscious mind, thus creating inner harmony. As one feels sorry for oneself, self-pity becomes a form of projection. Self-pity is destructive to the personality because it is a negative cognitive set promoting a defeatist attitude while avoiding self-responsibility and can lead to a maladaptive personality, self-destructive behavior, and even clinical depression.

self-responsible patient In hospital administration, medical care delivery, and health-care finance, this is when a patient has to pay out of his or her funds for either all or part of a hospital bill or physician's fees because they lack third-party medical insurance or membership in a managed-care health plan. *See self-pay.*

self-study The process of conducting the equivalent of an accreditation survey, licensure review, or eligibility assessment for participation in a reimbursement program such as Medicare but done internally by the organization's own staff to determine readiness for the full survey and the ability to pass the survey and to discover shortcomings and lack of compliance with standards and criteria.

semantic barriers In human relations, these are the problems and limitations that arise from the choice of words with which we communicate.

semi- Prefix meaning "half."

semiannual Twice a year; a 6-month time period. The first semiannual period concludes on the last day of the last month during the 180 days from the start date.

semiconfined aquifers In environmental health and safe water management of groundwater, this is an aquifer that is partially confined by soil layers of low permeability through which recharge and discharge of water can occur.

semiprivate Splitting privacy in half. "Semi" means "half," thus it should be viewed as two beds or two patients in one room.

semiprivate patient In a hospital, nursing home, patient care hotel, or other health-care facility, this is when a patient is required to share the room with one or more patients.

semiprivate room A patient's room in a hospital or nursing home room with two or more beds; two patients per room; two to four beds per room. In some definitions, a ward is four beds or more, and in other definitions three or more. "Semi" means "half," thus it should be viewed as two beds per room but has taken on the meaning of partially private because some semiprivate rooms in some hospitals and nursing homes have as many as four beds.

semivariable costs In health-care financial management, these are revenues that are fixed over a certain range of volume and change to different levels beyond that volume.

Semmelwis, Ignaz Philipp One of the early epidemiologist and infection control leaders and researchers at the beginning of the scientific knowledge explosion of the 1800s. Semmelwis (1818–1865) discovered that infection was spread from person to person contact and by airborne transmission. He was first to discover that chlorinated lime (chlorine) can kill germs. He was also noted for his attention to scientific inquiry and the understanding of epidemiological methodology that he employed in discovering how childbed fever (puerperal fever) was spread in the lying-in-hospital Allgemeines Krankenhaus in Vienna. He was able to finally observe how putrid matter on the hands of medical students acquired from doing the required autopsy work in the dissecting room of the hospital was spread from one newly delivered female patient to the next because of unclean hands. He laid the groundwork for understanding the importance of sanitation, and, through handwashing techniques and the sanitation of medical tools and equipment, he was able to reduce maternal mortality in maternity hospital wards to almost zero. Unfortunately, his work was not widely published, nor was the new knowledge well-accepted because of the blind adherence to the misleading Hippocratic theory of disease by the medical community at the time.

senescence A part of the aging process, usually the second half of life, that could increase vulnerability to any life occurrence.

senile dementia Memory loss and loss of certain bodily functions occurring usually after the age of 65 in which any cerebral pathology other than that for senile atrophic change can be reasonably excluded. It includes the following: 1) delirium, or senile dementia with superimposed reversible episodes of an acute confused state; 2) delusional type, or senile dementia characterized by development in advanced old age (progressive) and delusions, varying from simple, poorly formed paranoid delusions to highly fanned paranoid delusional states with hallucinations (also referred to as "paranoid type"); and 3) depressed type, or senile dementia characterized by development in advanced old age (progressive) and depressive features, ranging from mild to severe forms of manic-depressive affective psychosis. Disturbance of the sleep-waking cycle and preoccupation with dead people are often particularly prominent (ICD-9-CM, vol. 1).

senile psychosis One form of mental illness found mainly in the aged. It may be marked by the physiological involution of the brain itself. *See also organic brain syndrome.*

senility A vague term used to describe any emotional and mental degeneration that occurs in old age.

senior center recreation services A therapeutic recreation program that has the goal of increasing the vigor and social interactions of elderly people by providing formal social activities and a central meeting place. In addition, senior centers can serve as a referral service to link the senior citizen with needed supportive services.

senior citizen policies Contracts insuring persons 65 years or over with policies that are supplemental to the coverage afforded by the Medicare program.

senior citizens' residences Apartment complexes usually limited to elderly persons who can manage fairly well for themselves but need daily supervision. A clinic is provided, and a nurse may be available to visit residents in need of assistance. Some facilities have "resident clubs" or an association that plans activities for residents. Most of these residences have a manager and provide special services. Grounds usually are well-maintained, safe, and comfortable.

senior community service employment program Under Title V of the Older Americans Act, this is a service that provides part-time employment training opportunities to low-income persons 55 years old and older to assist in the transition of enrollees of a health plan or medical insurance policy to an unsubsidized employment situation.

senior health plan medical risk contract In managed care, this is a contractual agreement between the Health Care Financing Administration (HCFA) and a managed-care health plan that is paid a rate based on the contractual agreement per member per month to provide health-care services to the enrollees of a senior citizen health plan. Under the agreement, the health plan assumes the risk in the event the health-care costs exceed HCFA's payment to the health plan.

senior home and health care Long-term-care and aging services offered by some county-level agencies such as the county Office on Aging, which is primarily a case management service, designed to provide a compliment of services to keep frail elderly seniors in their homes instead of being placed in institutions. Case management activities include home interviews to determine needs and problems of the elderly person, identification of services and resources in the community to meet the found needs, and arranging for services, resources, periodic evaluation, and advocacy on behalf of the senior client.

seniority Longevity on the job; the length of time of a worker's employment in relation to all other employees; length of time with the organization.

seniority-based promotions In health administration and human resource management, this is when a worker who has been with the organization for a long time is promoted into a new position solely on the basis of longevity with the organization.

senior management The high-ranking administrative officials of an organization; the top administrative layer of administration in a large health-care organization. Also referred to as the "management team."

senior membership program A service for older adults offering benefits such as information, claims assistance, education and senior wellness programs, and discounts for other hospital services; may charge an application fee.

senior plan In managed care, this is a medical care insurance benefit package available through a health plan to nonworking individuals over age 65 and often associated with Medicare through a contract with the Health Care Financing Administration (HCFA) and Medicare.

senior plan network (SNP) In managed care, this is an alliance of health plans that offers membership to the over-65 age-group in the senior plan part of an HMO. Medicare contracts with the HMO, which prepays most or all of the medical care costs as it does for most regular enrollees.

sensitivity 1. In epidemiology and testing, this is a measure of the ability of a diagnostic or screening test to correctly identify those with the disease and to have their tests be positive on the screening test; the proportion of true positive cases correctly identified as positive; the ability to avoid missing cases of persons with the disease in a population. This shows the proportion of truly diseased persons in a population who underwent screening and who are correctly identified as being diseased by the screening test. A test may be very sensitive without being very specific and show few false negatives. Sensitivity is also a measure of the ability to identify the true positives in a screening test or the ability of medical tests to detect a disease or that something is wrong. For a test to be highly reliable, it must have a high level of sensitivity. 2. Capable of responding to a stimulus, such as bacteria responding to an antibiotic. 3. In mental health services, counseling and psychology, and human relations, this is to have understanding and awareness of a person's emotional, mental, and social needs. *See specificity; screening.*

sensitivity and specificity of a test *See sensitivity; specificity.*

sensoristasis The need for sensory stimulation.

sensors In environmental health and some medical care equipment or health-care facility areas, these are devices that measure a physical quantity or the change in a physical quantity such as temperature, pressure, flow rate, pH, or liquid level.

sensory deficit Partial or complete impairment of any stimulus to one's sensory organs.

sensory deprivation A lack of sensory stimulation or the impulses that are conveyed from the sensory organs to the brain.

sensory overload Excessive amounts of sound or visual sensory stimulation.

sentinel health events In health-care delivery, these are medical conditions that, by virtue of their presence or prevalence in a population, indicate a lack of access to acceptable, quality, primary health-care services. Examples include dehydration in infants; measles, mumps, or polio in children; and advanced breast cancer or invasive cervical cancer in adult women.

separate account In insurance, this is a special money account maintained separately from the insurance company's general accounts to better manage the funds used for nonguaranteed insurance products. With accounts held differently from the general accounts, the insurance company is able to modify investment strategies while maintaining the insurance company's regular insurance accounts. May also be referred to as a "segregated account."

separate billing In health-care finance and patient billing, this is when a patient or the insurance carrier receives one bill for physician services, a different bill for hospital services, and other bills for additional physician's services such as the anesthesiologist, the radiologist, and the pathologist.

separate maintenance In law, this is support money paid by one married person to the other while separated and not living together as husband and wife.

separation 1. A husband and wife no longer living together by mutual agreement; a legal marital separation. 2. A legal document designed to distinguish who gets what and who pays what until the divorce is complete. This is temporary but could be permanent if no divorce is filed. 3. Synonymous with "patient discharge"; formal release from a health-care facility.

separation of duties In health-care financial management, this is a security method for handling money whereby the receipt-writing process, the acceptance of money, and receivables and deposits are all managed so that the individual who receives money is different from the one who posts money and is different from the one who deposits it. All this is done to maintain honesty in the workers and to avoid embezzlement.

separation of powers The balancing of power of each branch of the government by assigning different roles and responsibilities to each so that any one branch does not become too powerful.

sepso- Prefix meaning "infection."

septic Putrefaction; decomposition.

septic tanks In environmental health, these are underground liquid waste storage tanks for human and other liquid wastes generated by homes that lack connection to a regular sewer systems that feeds into a treatment plant. The waste goes directly from the house to the tank, where the organic waste decomposes by bacteria and the sludge settles to the bottom. The lighter liquid effluent, which is mostly free of solids, flows out of the tanks into the ground through drainpipes into a drainage field. The heavier, more solid sludge is pumped out periodically and disposed of. *See cesspool.*

sequential access In health information management and computers, this is a process used by a computer to find information or data by searching for its location sequentially on the basis of the previous location rather than by random searching. The computer reads all the records in order or sequence.

sequential access storage medium *See sequential access.*

sequential analysis In epidemiology and health services research, this is the research design process of placing cases and controls in pairs and thus being able to examine and compare each pair and their results as they occur. The data are accumulated longitudinally with results added to previous findings as they come available.

sequester 1. To isolate. 2. To hold aside. 3. To deposit. 4. To set apart. 5. To seclude, as to sequester witnesses or the jury during a trial.

serial bonds In health-care financial management, these are different issues of bonds with different maturities that are retired either in equal annual amounts or on a level debt service basis.

serial communications In computers, this is when information is sent in sequence. The least important bit is transmitted first and the most significant bit last, all preceded by a start bit and ending with a stop bit.

serial numbering A medical record numbering system that assigns a patient a new number at each admission to the health-care facility.

serial unit numbering A medical record numbering system that assigns a patient a new number for each occasion of service. All old medical records are retrieved and reassigned the new number.

seriatim (Lat.) One by one; in order of occurrence or priority.

series In health-care financial management, these are bonds purchased at one time and with the same monies but issued at intervals with different dates. They may or may not mature at the same time.

serious illness or injury In medical care, this is any life-threatening event that can result in permanent impairment of a body function or permanent damage to a bodily tissue, organ, or structure, necessitating immediate medical or surgical intervention into any possible permanent disability, impairment, or damage to the body or its organs, tissues, or structures.

seriousness In health and safety and health law, this applies to any situation for which a clear and present danger exists to patients, workers, or members of the public.

serious violation In occupational health and safety, a violation of safety and health regulations is determined by asking two questions that must be answered yes: 1) Is there a substantial probability that death or serious physical harm could result? 2) Did the employer know, or with the exercise of reasonable diligence should have known, of the hazard? (OSHA).

seroepidemiology The combining of epidemiology and medical care as a unique form of epidemiological study approach by using blood and body fluid testing to assess changes in the characteristics of serum levels of specific antibodies, thus detecting and tracking infectious diseases in specific populations by identifying carriers and subclinical and latent infections in patients through serum testing.

serologist A subspecialty of microbiology or medical technology. This professional scientist prepares serums for the evaluation and diagnosis of diseases or prepares blood and serum preparations for use in immunizations and vaccinations against diseases.

serology A subspecialty area of microbiology and hematology that focuses on the study of blood and serums and their analysis and development; the study of serums, which are the fluids of the body and blood; the preparation and development of serums for use against disease.

serology technologist A medical technologist who works with blood and serums as used in the diagnosis of diseases and their treatment or works in the development of immunizations and vaccines.

serum The clear substance of a fluid left after separation by a centrifuge; the liquid portion of blood as opposed to the solid particles.

serum hepatitis Hepatitis B.

servant 1. In health law, tort law, and the law of agency, this person is employed by and under the control of and subject to another person who is in a position of authority's commands and orders; an individual under the control of the master. 2. In agency law, this is the agent. A person serving as a servant or agent is responsible to carry out the orders given by the master or principal, who is also responsible for the acts of the servant. Legally speaking, a physician is a master, and the nurse or other allied health-care provider is the servant in the working relationship of medical care delivery. *See also master; agent; respondeat superior; vicarious liability.*

service(s) A functional division of a hospital or of its medical staff; also the delivery of care (JCAHO).

service 1. The act of delivering or issuing a legal document such as a summons, a court order, an injunction, or a writ to the person named in it and done so in the prescribed legal manner as to comply with due process of law. 2. Professional functions and duties. 3. To receive a special benefit or advantage. 4. Continual and regular payments on a debt. 5. To provide help or aid to those in need of such help. 6. A unit of health care. There is no standard term for a single unit of health care, whatever that unit may be. Both "service" and "procedure" are often used to refer to units of health care (e.g., a health service or a medical procedure). A hospital can offer pediatric services or substance abuse services. "Service" is sometimes used synonymously with "encounter" but should be differentiated because an encounter may include several services. It is also used synonymously with "department," "program," "department," "division," or "unit"; a treatment, act of patient care, or act done for a patient in a health-care system.

service area 1. In community health or health-care delivery, this is the geographic area or portion of a region in which all or a majority of an institution's patients reside or are drawn from. This may be a special planning area defined by law and not related to market or natural catchment areas. The population base of services that is served by a health-care facility may be only a part of the total community if other health-care facilities are in the area. 2. The geographical area that a managed-care plan, home health agency, hospital, or medial group decides it will provide services to or from which it will draw the majority of its patients. 3. In Medicare and Medicaid contracts, this is the identification of locations of health plan member areas, which are determined by areas designated by the U.S. Postal Service ZIP codes after an assessment to ensure adequate access to health-care services by health plan members. 4. In managed care, this is the catchment area, or the territory within certain boundaries, that a health plan designates for offering benefit plans and providing medical care to its members on the basis of the ability of the health plan to maintain easy access to medical care services. Some health plans consider radius of miles from the clinics or health service sites, whereas others use ZIP codes or city or county boundaries. These are geographical areas served by a health plan as approved by state regulatory agencies or detailed in the certificate of authority. *See also catchment area; target group.*

service assessment program In managed-care and health-care financial management, this is conducting internal audits to assess accuracy and the timeliness of claims payment, enrollment data entry, and provider data entry.

service benefits In managed care or insurance, these are benefits received as a result of prepayment or insurance whereby payment is made directly to the provider of services or the hospital or other medical care programs for covered services provided by them to eligible persons. Service benefits may be full-service benefits, meaning that the health plan fully reimburses the hospital. Full-service benefits may also be available when the program itself provides the service as in a prepaid group practice. Partial service benefits cover only part of the expenses, the remainder being paid by the beneficiary through some form of cost sharing. *See also indemnity benefits; vendor payment.*

service-connected disability In the Veterans Administration health-care program, a disability or disease incurred or aggravated in the line of duty in active military service. These disabilities are the primary concern of the program. *See also non–service-connected disability; adjunct disability.*

service connectors In environmental health and safe water management, these are pipes that carry tap water from the public water main to a building or house.

service contract In managed care or medical insurance, this is when the benefits of a contract with a health plan or insurance carrier are the medical care services and treatment received as opposed to life insurance, where the benefits come in the form of money called an "indemnity benefit."

service fees In managed care or insurance, these are the monies paid to an insurance agent that are a small percentage of premiums payable after the renewal commissions have ceased.

service, hospital-based In hospital administration, this is the range of services that are common to a general hospital and include many of the following programs or units: general medical and surgical, diagnostic and therapeutic, imaging and radiology, laboratory, psychiatric, respiratory and tuberculosis, obstetrics and gynecology, eye-ear-nose-throat, outpatient, pharmacy, orthopedic, surgery, pediatrics, rehabilitation, rehabilitation, chronic disease, alcoholism and chemical dependency, and home health care.

service intensity In health-care delivery, this is the quantity, quality, and complexity of health-care services provided per admission that culminates over time such as having 15 X rays, 25 lab tests, 11 physical therapy appointments, 8 pharmacy prescriptions, and 2 surgical procedures per hospital stay.

service location In managed care and health services delivery, this is any place or area where an HMO patient or health plan member obtains medical care by the medical care groups and other health-care providers as set forth in the terms of the managed-care contract.

service mode In mental health services, these are the various kinds of mental health and psychiatric services such as inpatient care, outpatient care, day treatment, residential treatment care, and partial care.

service of process In law, this is the official notification that in some way a person is involved in a legal action or court proceeding. Notification may be done in person or, under certain situations, by mail or by publication of the notice in a newspaper.

service-of-process statute 1. The law creating the legal procedure of "service of process." 2. In insurance, the state law that allows a person to bring a suit against any insurance company doing business in the state in which the insurance company is legally operating and is incorporated. *See also service of process.*

service patient A patient whose care is the responsibility of a health program or institution (usually a hospital). Service patients are often cared for by an individual practitioner paid by the program (typically a member of a hospital's house staff), but the program, not the individual, is paid for the care. Sometimes called a "public patient" or "ward patient." *See also private patient.*

service received on a mass basis In public health, this is when a treatment, procedure, or screening test is administered identically to all persons who have arrived at the site for the purpose of receiving the service. Such services have included chest X rays, immunizations, diabetes testing, cholesterol screening, and mammograms.

services 1. Groupings of patients, departments, treatments, personnel, and physicians (e.g., pediatric, surgical, medical, obstetrical, or outpatient services). Most groupings of services and personnel are called "departments" (e.g., X ray and nursing). 2. Care or services as provided by health-care providers at different levels are defined below. For health insurance purposes, each of these levels is given a code number from the procedure coding manual for each type of care provided: 1) minimal services include injections, dressings, and minimal care, not necessarily requiring the presence of the physician; 2) brief services require a brief period of time and minimal effort by the physician; 3) limited services require limited effort or judgment such as abbreviated or interval history, limited examination, or discussion of findings and/or treatment; 4) intermediate services may include a complete history and examination of one or more organ systems or an in-depth counseling or discussion of the findings but does not require a comprehensive examination of the patient as a whole; 5) extended services require an unusual amount of time, effort, or judgment but not a complete examination of the patient as a whole; 6) comprehensive services provide an in-depth evaluation of the patient; and 7) unusually complex services arise when a complex medical problem necessitates a comprehensive history and complete examination, extensive review of prior medical records, compilation, and assessment of data. 3. According to JCAHO for accreditation purposes, a functional division of the hospital or of the medical staff; also used to indicate the delivery of care. *See also levels of service.*

services, critical care *See critical care services.*

service site In Medicare and Medicaid, this is the place designated by the contracting health plan where members receive primary care physician services.

services, routine In health administration and health-care financial management, these are the usual and customary services provided to persons who are inpatients in a health-care facility. Routine services usually include room, board, nursing care, heat and lights, maintenance, and housekeeping, whereas medical care or extras such as rehabilitation, testing, or special equipment are considered charges beyond routine services.

services type In mental health services, these are the various approaches used in providing mental health and psychiatric services such as inpatient care, outpatient care, residential treatment care, and partial care.

service unit or care unit A health-care area or ward in a health-care facility that offers medical and nursing care to persons on an inpatient basis. Patients are grouped together by related diagnoses, types of treatment needed, or specialty of the medical staff.

servient 1. Serving. 2. Being a slave to something.

servitude 1. Slavery; bondage. 2. To place restrictions and burdens on something or someone.

session 1. An assembly of people such as in a court, hearing, or legislature. 2. A day or a period of time in which a court or legislature meets. 3. Continuous periodic gatherings or meetings; a series of single meetings such as in conventions. 4. In health-care administration, this is a regular meeting of the board of directors.

session laws The publication of laws and statutes in the order, or by session, in which they were ruled on and passed.

SET Surrogate embryo transfer; Strategy Evaluation Technique.

set aside 1. To cancel. 2. To void or annul. 3. To revoke a judgment or a court ruling. 4. To declare a verdict void.

setback In environmental health and building codes, this is a building offset from the front of the property line, sidewalk, street, or right-of-way.

set down In health law, this is to schedule a case or lawsuit for trial or hearing.

setoff 1. A counterclaim that is unrelated to the lawsuit at hand. 2. The extinguishing or mitigation of a claim brought against the defendant by payment of money.

settle 1. In health law, this is to reach an agreement out of court about an issue, disagreement, damage, debt, or disposition of a lawsuit. 2. To finish or end completely. 3. To put into a fixed state or position. 4. To agree on or adjust to. 5. To make final, firm, and solid. 6. To dispose of. 7. To become fixed and assume a lasting form. 8. To determine. 9. To create a trust. 10. In liability or medical malpractice lawsuits, this is when both sides of a lawsuit meet and agree on what it would take to satisfy the needs, repair the damages, or solve the harm done to the injured party before trial and outside of court, the litigation process, and the legal system.

settleable solids In environmental health and liquid waste management, these are materials suspended in wastewater that are heavy enough to sink to the bottom of the wastewater treatment system or treatment tank (EPA).

settlement 1. The payment of a debt or obligation. 2. The adjustment made on a dispute. 3. In insurance, payment to the policyholder of claims made against the insurance. 4. The amount of money used to settle a liability or malpractice lawsuit or obligation. 5. In liability or medical malpractice lawsuits, this is the process of both sides of a lawsuit agreeing on what it would take to satisfy the needs, damages, or harm done to the injured party who brought the lawsuit and done outside of court, the litigation process, and the legal system.

settlement, structured See structured settlement.

settling chamber In environmental health and air pollution control, this is a series of screens placed in the way of flue gases to slow the stream of air, thus helping gravity pull particles out of the emission into a collection area and clean the air of particulate matter (EPA).

settling tanks In environmental health and liquid waste management, this is a holding container or area for wastewater where heavier particles sink to the bottom for removal and disposal (EPA).

sever 1. To end or cut off. 2. To pull apart 3. To be torn apart. 4. In health law, this is to hear a person's case in a separate place and at a different time removed from a current trial.

severable 1. Divided; disunited. 2. Separable. 3. Capable of a separate existence.

several 1. Having many or more than one. 2. To be distinct and separate. 3. Individual. 4. Independent.

severally Each its own way; separate; distinct.

severalty ownership 1. Having single or sole ownership. 2. A health facility or nursing home with ownership by one person.

severance pay In health administration and human resource management, this is a sum of money paid to workers when they are released from employment in a health-care organization, especially if it occurs under favorable circumstances such as program cuts. Workers terminated under unfavorable conditions usually are not eligible for severance pay.

severity 1. The seriousness of a situation, event, occurrence, illness, injury, or disability; how bad something is or has become. 2. How complex, extensive, extreme, or serious a disease or injury has become; the degree to which an injury or illness compromises the health and safety of a patient or resident; the opposite extreme of health or well-being.

severity of illness 1. In prospective payment system/diagnosis-related groups, this is a continuum of the extent of illness, care, treatment, and resources needed to care for a disease at various extents or levels of seriousness of an illness or injury. A mild case of an illness may require minimal treatment and use minimal resources with costs being minimal, but a serious case of the same disease can use up an extensive amount of resources and cost a great deal to treat to bring the patient to an acceptable level of recovery and wellness. 2. In managed care and medical care, this when a panel of physicians rates the extent or level of illness on the basis of need for medical care and physician intervention. Four levels can be used: 1) preventive or reassurance only; 2) symptomatic relief; 3) a condition that is severe enough that it must be seen by a physician; and 4) hospitalization and advanced specialized treatment. If the illness or injury falls in the last two categories as needing an examination or treatment. The extensiveness, magnitude, complexity, and seriousness of a disease, injury, or condition. *See AS-SCORE; case severity.*

severity of illness score In medical care and health-care delivery, this is when a quantitative number is assigned to a disease or condition on the basis of a qualitative assessment of severity for each disease. A number is assigned according to how extensive or serious the illness is for each patient, arriving at a final number that indicates the severity of the illness. Several models have been developed and are used in reimbursement and in quality-of-care measurements.

sewage In environmental health and liquid waste management, this is the liquid wastewater that passes through sewers; the waste and wastewater produced by residential and commercial establishments and discharged into sewers (EPA).

sewage lagoons In environmental health and liquid waste management, these are man-made lakes or bodies of water in which liquid waste is consumed by bacteria. These are used most frequently with other liquid waste treatment processes.

sewage sludge In environmental health and liquid waste management, this is the semisolid liquid waste produced at sewage treatment plants or in septic tanks of which disposal is regulated under the Clean Water Act (EPA).

sewer In public health and environmental health, this is a underground pipe system that accepts, contains, controls, and keeps liquid waste from the public or population to protect people from disease and foul odors while the liquid waste flows to a treatment facility. The man-made underground conduit for carrying off liquid waste, wastewater, and refuse (EPA); a channel or conduit that carries wastewater, storm water, and runoff to a sewage treatment plant. Sanitary sewers carry household, industrial, and commercial waste. Storm sewers carry water runoff from rain, snow, lawn watering, and street gutters.

sewerage In environmental health and liquid waste management, this is the system of sewers; the entire system of sewage collection, treatment, and disposal (EPA).

sewers, lateral *See lateral sewers.*

sex In epidemiology, public health, and vital statistics, this is used to designate gender; one variable of the "person" aspects of epidemiology. In community-based research, if gender is not provided, it may be assigned on the basis of first name or, in interview situations, through observation; the gender of the subject, interviewee, or enrollee recorded by the observations of the staff or researcher.

sex ratio In epidemiology, public health, and vital statistics, this is the number of females per 100 males; the ratio of one gender to the other. When the ratio is more than 100, there are more of one sex than the other. In the United States, there are more females than males. More males are born than females, but because of infant deaths the ratio declines with age so that by old age more females than males exist. The formula for sex ratio follows:

$$\frac{\text{Males}}{\text{Females}} \times 100 = \text{Men per 100 women}$$

sexual child abuse Contacts or interactions between a child and an adult when the child is being used for sexual stimulation by another person (National Center on Child Abuse and Neglect); any act that uses a child for sexual arousal or sexual gratification.

sexual dimorphism The physical, emotional, and psychological difference between males and females.

sexual harassment In human resource management, a vague and difficult concept to deal with, define, and determine. This is any uncalled-for, unnecessary focusing on the sexuality of the opposite sex (both female and male) in the workplace, including the use of implications of sexual favors being required for advancement, rewards, or pay raises with fear of reprisals for refusing, which is called "quid pro quo" (Latin for "something-for-something"), where the worker must submit to sexual favors to advance or get rewards or suffer consequences for not submitting. Another form is when, in the workplace, behaviors, comments, and innuendo with sexual undertones are done to the point of being demeaning, causing a person much stress, discomfort, and feelings of harassment. This is called a "hostile environment," where sexual overtones and implications make the workplace a stressful and unhealthy environment to work in. Sincere romantic advances have not qualified as sexual harassment. Sexual harassment is a form of workplace discrimination as set forth by the Civil Rights Act of 1964.

sexually transmitted diseases (STDs) A major concern for public health, epidemiology, and the health status of populations, these are any diseases that may be transmitted by person-to-person transmission through sexual contact. Examples are syphilis, gonorrhea, chlamydia, herpes II (genital herpes), and AIDS. Also called "venereal diseases."

shall According to JCAHO for psychiatric, alcoholism, and drug abuse facilities accreditation purposes, this indicates a mandatory standard.

shall or must According to JCAHO, this indicates a mandatory statement or the only acceptable method under the current standards. *See also should; may.*

sham 1. False; fake. 2. Deceiving. 3. A pretense or fraud.

sham pleading In health law, this is a pleading that appears fair on the surface but is founded on an error or mistakes in the facts or has a fraudulent pretense.

share 1. A stock in a corporation. 2. An equitable part given. 3. To have a common possession.

shared care services *See custodial care; personal care.*

shared computer systems 1. In health information management systems, this is a centralized computer system that offers computer services to medical records, the business office, or any other service or administrative unit in the health-care facility, all from the same computer system. 2. A commercial service outside the health-care facility that offers computer services and programs to the facility to collect, process, and report information, data, and statistics on patient services and need assessments, all on the basis of abstracts of patient's stay. 3. Computer services that provide analysis and reports of the client hospital as compared with hospital performance of similar facilities.

shared services In health administration, this is the coordinated, or otherwise explicitly agreed-on, sharing of responsibility for the provision of medical or nonmedical services on the part of two or more otherwise independent hospitals or other health programs to eliminate duplication. The sharing of medical services might include, for example, an agreement that one hospital provide all pediatric care needed in a community and no obstetrical services while another undertook the reverse. One example is imaging equipment placed in a semitrailer and moved from one hospital to the next throughout the week as a shared service. Examples of shared nonmedical services include joint laundry or dietary services for two or more nursing homes. Common laundry services purchased by two or more health programs from one independent retailer of laundry services are not usually thought of as shared services unless the health programs own or otherwise control the retailer.

shared services organization In health administration, this is an organization created to provide joint use of a single service, thus reducing costs and duplication of services and effort. The organization is a separate legal entity and offers fair and equal use to the sponsoring institutions.

shared support services Programs or services shared by health-care institutions such as laundry, purchasing, and data processing. *See also shared services.*

shareholder Synonymous with "stockholder," this is someone who holds financial stock in a corporation.

share of cost Under Medicaid, this is when a family's (or person's) net income beyond the needs of maintenance and daily living must be paid or obligated toward paying for health-care services prior to being certified and receiving Medicaid cards.

sharps In medical care delivery, these are any pointed objects or blades such as needles, syringes, scalpels, or other disposable instruments that could possibly injure the health-care provider in the process of providing patient care. Special precautions are used in handling sharp or pointed instruments, including not trying to recap needles or putting covers on scalpels to avoid accidental punctures or cuts in health-care providers after treating patients.

sharps safe In medical care delivery, this is a specialized container used to dispose of needles, scalpels, or other sharp or pointed patient treatment instruments. Safes are usually made of several layers of cardboard with durable plastic bag liners. Safes are used to provide easy and quick disposal of used needles and cutting instruments so that the health-care provider does not attempt to replace the cap on the instrument, thus avoiding a possible accidental puncture or cut and any resulting life-threatening infection or diseases. The safe is also used as a biohazard and infection control device by holding and keeping infected needles and blades from being used again, from accidentally being used on another patient, and by protecting the health-care provider from injury from instruments infected by patient treatment activities. Safes and their contents are disposed of by biohazard personnel and approved methods.

Shattuck, Lemuel One of the first key public health figures in the United States of America. Shattuck (1793–1859) was a politician and physician who developed several pubic health reports, including a landmark document titled *The Report of the Sanitary Commission of Massachusetts, 1848*. Often called the Shattuck Report, it was used as the basis for the development of the first State Board of Health for the Commonwealth of Massachusetts.

SHCC *See statewide health coordinating council.*

sheepskin A natural skin of a sheep or a synthetic one used by long-term-care patients or handicapped persons to protect bony areas such as hips, elbows, or ankles and to prevent pressure sores.

shelf sitters In health administration and human resource management, this is a slang term used to describe managers who are immobile in their growth and professional promotion who block job advancement opportunities or promotions for others.

sheltered care In long-term care, this is limited care to individuals with special needs provided by aides and nurses as well as by staff who provide assistance with daily living, housekeeping, food and nutrition, bathing, and personal hygiene in a safe and secure live-in facility.

sheltered care institution A special health-care facility that provides personal care and permanent accommodations for retarded, mentally ill, or other handicapped persons.

sheltered workshop A health and social service providing assistance and protection, vocational training, work experience, or vocational rehabilitation in a protected and controlled environment and/or work setting that is offered to physically or mentally disabled persons on an ambulatory basis or in a residential setting in an institution.

Shepard's Citations A legal publication for use in reference to cases and statutes that reflects all subsequent cases that cite or refer to a principal case.

Sherman Act A federal antitrust law used to stop any combination of organizational arrangements or agreements that cause a restraint of trade or create monopolies; concerned with agreements between competitors that have the ability to restrain trade and lead to monopoly power. Associated with the Clayton Act, the Sherman Act is aimed at anticompetitive agreements between rival firms, as can exist in health-care environments, who have the ability to do price fixing, divide markets, and control the dynamics of a free market.

shielding In environmental health, this is high-density protective material placed over or between a radioactive source and its surroundings to reduce radiation exposure.

shielding materials In environmental health and occupational health and safety, this is any material used to absorb and effectively reduce the intensity of radiation and in some cases eliminate it. Lead, concrete, aluminum, water, and plastic are examples of commonly used shielding material.

shifting 1. Changing. 2. Transferring or changing position. 3. In health law, this is to change testimony or an account of what happened.

SHMO *See social health maintenance organization.*

shock In medical care and emergency medicine, this is the rapid fall in the body's circulation of blood and the lowering of blood pressure following some injury, surgical operation, physical trauma, emotionally traumatic event, or the administration of anesthesia.

shoe-leather epidemiology In epidemiological investigation of a disease outbreak, this consists of investigation activities in the field such as doing door-to-door interviews. It is used extensively in person-to-person communicable disease investigations, especially with sexually transmitted diseases.

shop book rule In health law, if books or records are kept in the usual course of business, they may be entered into court as evidence as long as they are proper and held in proper custody.

shop steward A worker in a large organization who is elected by the workers or the labor union to represent the workers in dealings with the employer and to help enforce union policy and rules. *See steward.*

short cause In law, this is the part of a lawsuit or a case that must be heard by a judge but that will not take up much time, so the waiting period is shortened. Also called a "short calendar."

shortened workweeks In hospital administration and human resource management, this is a flexible scheduling approach that allows full-time workers to put in 40 hours of work per week in less than the traditional 5 days (e.g., four 10-hour days).

shorting In the ethical and legal aspects of medical care and health-care administration, this is purposefully dispensing a quantity of a drug that is less than the quantity prescribed for the purpose of increasing profit by charging for the prescribed amount. *See also kiting; fraud.*

short-range actions In health administration and strategic planning, these are well-defined changes that must be made in the next year if long-range actions are to be implemented and objectives achieved by the time specified. Short-range actions are more explicit than long-range actions in that they usually specify individuals or agencies who should take primary responsibility for the implementation of a short-range action.

short sale In health-care finance, this is a contract made for the quick sale of stock by a seller who does not own it; used to profit from an expected fall in price of the stock under consideration.

short stayers In long-term care, these are nursing home residents with acute or subacute illnesses who generally come from hospitals to convalesce and who are then discharged back to the hospital or home or who have a high possibility of dying in a very short time.

short-stay hospitals These are acute-care facilities that have an average length of overnight inpatient stay of less than 30 days; any acute-care facility in which the type of services provided is general: maternity, eye-ear-nose-throat, children's, or osteopathic. *See hospital; acute-care hospital.*

short-stay inpatient setting *See short-stay setting; short-stay hospitals.*

short-stay setting In health-care delivery, this is providing health-care services to patients who stay overnight as inpatients in the institution, 50% or more of whom return to their normal place of residence within 30 days of entering the institution. *See also short-term hospital.*

short-term capital gain In tax law, the amount of profit gained from the sale of a capital asset held less than 1 year.

short-term disability income insurance A provision in insurance to pay benefits to a disabled person as long as he or she remains disabled. Coverage is usually up to a specified period of time but not to exceed 2 years.

short-term financing In health-care finance, the obligations or debts having a maturity of less than 1 year.

short-term hospital These institutions are determined by the average length of stay of the inpatients. According to the American Hospital Association, a short-term hospital has over 50% of all inpatients admitted to units with an average length of stay of less than 30 days. Also referred to as an "acute-care facility." *See hospital; short-stay setting; acute-care hospital.*

short title In Congress, the shorter, less formal, common title given an act of Congress by its authors. Short titles include the Health Maintenance Organization Act of 1973 (P.L. 93-222) and the National Health Planning and Resources Development Act of 1975 (P.L. 93-641).

should According to JCAHO, the interpretation of a standard to reflect the commonly accepted method yet allowing for the use of effective alternates. *See also shall or must; may.*

show cause In health law, this is a court order issued to require someone to appear in court so that he or she can explain why the court should not carry out a decision or a proposed act. If he or she fails to appear or to give good enough reasons why the court should not act on the issue, the court will go ahead with the decision on the action.

SHP *See State Health Plan.*

SHPDA *See state health planning and development agency.*

shyster A dishonest or unscrupulous person.

si (Lat.) If.

sibship All brothers and sisters born to the same mother.

sic (Lat.) 1. Same in context. Thus; so; in such a way. 2. An error that was made in the original document and copied correctly by the last writer; not an error in the current publication or reproduction.

sickness Used synonymously with disease and illness, generally not a clearly defined illness; not well, unhealthy, being ill or diseased; having a condition or disorder.

sick role To assume a role of wanting to be pampered and freed from life's responsibilities because of illness; desiring sympathy and remorse for an illness or injury from others, especially caregivers, family, or health-care providers.

sick role behavior Being dependent and subservient to health-care providers and caregivers, wanting to be cared for, and seeking much sympathy for one's illness or disability; patient compliance and responding to the caregiving processes; behaviors of those who consider themselves ill or disabled to recover and return to wellness and reclaim one's health; giving in to one's illness or injury to expedite healing and restoration of health.

side effect Unwanted or unintended physical, emotional, or mental complications as a result of using a drug.

SIDS *See sudden infant death syndrome.*

sievert In environmental health and occupational health and safety, this is a unit of ionizing radiation equal to the amount that produces the same damage to humans as 1 roentgen of high-voltage X rays.

sight 1. Payable when presented or requested. Also referred to as a "sight bill," "sight draft," or "at sight." 2. Being able to see; within view.

sigmoidoscope In medical care, this is a specialized instrument used to visually examine the sigmoid colon.

sigmoidoscopy In medical care, this is to examine the interior of the sigmoid colon by the use of an endoscope or sigmoidoscope.

sign 1. In medical care, this is one of the factors used in diagnosis and in determining the causes of illness. A communicable disease is usually caused by a single pathogen, whereas syndromes rely on a set of signs that usually run together. Physicians rely on symptoms, signs, and findings of tests (e.g., blood tests, tissues samples, and X rays) to determine diagnosis and the presence of illnesses, disorders, or conditions. 2. The means through which deaf people can learn to communicate as in signing the alphabet; the use of sign language. *See symptom.*

signal words In environmental health, these are the words used on pesticide labels such as "Danger," "Warning," or "Caution," to indicate the level of toxicity of the chemicals in the container.

signatory One who signs.

signature One's name signed by hand.

significance In research and statistics, this refers to statistical chance of occurrence of events or the level of probability. *See statistical significance.*

significant adverse reaction In occupational health and safety, these are the physiological responses that may indicate a substantial impairment of normal activities or long-lasting or irreversible damage to health or the environment.

significant deterioration In environmental health and pollution control, this is any increased level of or new pollution resulting from a new source in a previously clean area (EPA).

significant environmental compliance issues In environmental health law, these are circumstances or events that have the potential of being precedent setting or controversial and that involve several levels of governmental regulatory health agencies.

significant impairment In environmental health and air pollution control, this is visibility impairment that interferes with the management, protection, preservation, or enjoyment of the visitor's visual experience to mandatory Class I federal areas, which are national parks, preserves, and wilderness areas. Determination is made on a case-by-case basis, accounting for geographic extent, intensity, duration, frequency, and time of the visibility impairment and how these factors correlate with times of visitor use, frequency, and times of natural conditions that reduce visibility.

significant municipal facilities In environmental health, water pollution, and liquid waste management, these are publicly owned sewage treatment plants that discharge a million gallons or more of water per day and are considered to have the potential for polluting or having a substantial effect on the quality of receiving waters (EPA).

significant procedure Treatment and surgical procedures included in the ICD-9-CM (Volume 3). *See also principal procedure.*

significant source of groundwater In environmental health and safe water management, this is any aquifer that is saturated with water having less than 10,000 milligrams per liter of total dissolved solids; is within 2500 feet of the land surface; has a transmissivity greater than 200 gallons per day per foot, provided that any formation or part of a formation included in the source of groundwater has a hydraulic conductivity greater than 2 gallons per day per square foot; and is capable of continuously yielding a least 10,000 gallons per day to a pumped or flowing well for a period of at least 1 year. This is any aquifer that provides the primary source of water for a community water system.

significant violations In environmental health law and regulations, these are any violations by point source dischargers of sufficient magnitude and/or duration to be a regulatory priority (EPA).

silt In environmental health, these are fine particles of sand or rock picked up by the air or water and deposited as sediment (EPA).

silviculture In environmental health, this refers to the management of forest land and overcutting of trees for timber, which sometimes contributes to water pollution, especially when done by the clear-cutting method (EPA).

simple 1. Plain; uncomplicated; not involved; not elaborate. 2. Not aggravated or complicated, as in a simple fracture.

simple contract In contract law, this is an orally expressed contract; a contract that is not sealed.

simple interest In health-care financial management, this is to pay interest only on the original amount of money that was borrowed or invested.

simple treatment Radiation therapy and oncology treatment of benign or malignant diseases requiring simple field localization or simple beam-shaping devices, single field treatment, or surface or intracavitary therapy applied without general anesthesia.

Sims position A semiprone examination position in which a patient lies on the left side with the right knee and thigh drawn up above the left leg. The left arm is placed in back of the patient and hangs over the edge of the examining table. The patient's chest is forward so that the patient rests on it.

simulate 1. To make a pretense. 2. To take on the appearance. 3. To imitate. 4. To pretend. 5. To use mockups or models to demonstrate a scientific fact such as causation of disease.

simulator A computer or other piece of equipment that imitates or mimics the actions and reactions of a system or condition, showing the effects of various applied changes.

sine (Lat.) Without.

sine die (Lat.) 1. Without day. 2. An adjournment at which the participants do not set a date for another appearance or meeting.

sine prole (Lat.) 1. Without issue. 2. Without child.

sine qua non (Lat.) 1. Without. 2. A condition or situation that cannot be done away with. 3. An indispensable element.

single-carrier replacement In managed care, this is the process whereby the employer group or a purchaser of group medical care coverage obtains insurance coverage for all eligible members and their dependents through only one carrier and drops all other insurance carriers from the account.

single-name paper In law, this is a negotiable instrument with only one original signer or originator.

single-need selling In insurance, this is where a specialized need or a particular financial need that can be met by insurance is singled out. For example, life insurance may be taken out to include enough coverage to ensure the payoff of a mortgage on a house should the sole breadwinner (the insured) die.

single-payer initiative 1. In health-care reform using a socialized medicine system with universal coverage for all, one entity (the federal government) would be responsible and pay for all health care for all U.S. citizens. 2. At the state level, in a managed-care approach to delivering health care to public sector patients, an advisory panel of medical care and health experts working with an elected commissioner would set medical benefits and coverage for all under the plan. Regional differences would be accounted for, including rural areas being able to compete feewise for physicians. An independent consumer council would watch over the process. Existing public health funding would go to the program, businesses would pay a payroll tax based on number of employees, and individuals would also pay a percentage of taxable income based on income level. Physicians and consumers would have to opt in or out of the program, and insurers could continue to offer supplemental policies for such benefits as private hospital rooms and cosmetic surgery. Medicaid and Medicare programs could participate or be billed. *See local initiative.*

single photon emission computerized tomography (SPECT) In medical imaging, this is a nuclear medicine imaging technology that combines existing technology of gamma camera imaging with computed tomographic imaging technology to provide a clear and precise image of the tissue and body parts being viewed.

single proprietorship A business legally owned by one person.

single-specialty group In health-care delivery and medical group organizational structure, a group or clinic that provides medical and health-care services in one area of medical specialization. Common single-specialty groups include anesthesiologists, orthopedic surgeons, family practitioners, pathologists, and radiologists.

single-use (disposable) medical device Any instrument, apparatus, machine, implant, in vitro reagent, or other related article intended for use in the diagnosis or treatment of disease that is labeled by the manufacturer for single use only or in which a caution is included in the accompanying literature or catalog recommending it for one-time use only.

sings Spiritual healing ritual conducted by a Native American medicine man.

sinking In environmental health and water pollution, this is the controlling of oil spills by using an agent to trap the oil and sink it to the bottom of the body of water where the agent and the oil are biodegraded.

sinking agents In environmental health and water pollution, these are the additives or substances applied to oil discharges to sink floating pollutants below the water surface.

sit 1. To officially occupy a seat 2. To meet or hold a session of court 3. To formally carry on official business; to be in session.

sit-down strike In labor relations management, this is a labor strike in which employees stop work and refuse to leave the worksite.

site characterization In environmental health and solid waste and landfill management, this is the program of exploration and research in both the laboratory and the field undertaken to establish the geological conditions and the ranges of parameters of a particular site. The characterization process includes borings, surface excavations, excavation of exploratory shafts, limited subsurface lateral excavations and borings, and in situ testing at depths needed to determine the suitability of the site for a landfill or geologic repository.

site closure and stabilization In environmental health and solid waste and hazardous waste landfill management, these are actions taken on completion of operations of a landfill that prepare the disposal site for custodial care and that ensure that the disposal site will remain stable and will not need ongoing active maintenance.

site development and facility utilization plans In environmental health and solid waste and hazardous waste landfill management, these are formal written documents setting forth goals and objectives and summarizing the various data necessary to plan for the most effective utilization and orderly future development and disposal of facilities at an individual site in accordance with site-related program objectives and requirements.

site inspections In environmental health and hazardous waste management, this is information collected from a Superfund site to determine the extent and severity of hazards posed by the site. It follows, and is more extensive than, the preliminary assessment. The purpose is to gather information necessary to score the site, using the Hazard Ranking System, and to determine if the site presents an immediate threat that requires prompt removal action (EPA).

site-limited intermediates In environmental health and hazardous waste management, this is a substance, chemical, or agent that is manufactured, processed, and used only on-site and not distributed in commerce other than as an impurity or for disposal. Imported intermediates cannot be site limited.

site quality assurance plan In environmental health and landfill and hazardous waste management, this is a written document associated with site sampling activities that presents, in specific terms, the organization, objectives, functional activities, and specific quality assurance (QA) and quality control (QC) activities designed to achieve the data quality goals of a specific project or continuing operations. The QA project plan is prepared for each specific project or operation. The QA project plan is prepared by the responsible program office, regional office, laboratory, contractor, recipient of an assistance agreement, or other responsible organization.

siting In environmental health, this is the process of choosing a location for a landfill, hazardous waste disposal location, sewage treatment plant, water treatment facility, water well, etc.

situs (Lat.) 1. Place. 2. A fixed locale. 3. A location.

six-sigma In statistics and as used in quality assurance, this means that a certain level of defect exists: 99.999997% of the findings are up to standards or are perfect and that a 3.4 defect exists per million parts. Three-sigma means that 99.7% are perfect, and one-sigma means that 68% of the outcomes are perfect or up to standard.

Sixth Omnibus Reconciliation Act (1985) This act created several health-care–related mandates such as the development of quality review organizations (QROs) and empowered QROs and peer review organizations (PROs) to monitor quality of care in Medicare programs and Medicare-contracted programs with HMOs or other managed-care programs. This act also provided for monetary penalties for health plans that fail to provide proper quality care and restricted the types of physicians incentives that a managed-care plan may use when providing care for Medicare enrollees. The act also made disenrollment from managed-care plans far easier for Medicare recipients.

sixty-three–twenty ("63-20") financing In health-care financial management, this is when bonds are issued to a hospital or other nonprofit health-care organization, and, when fully retired, the title is given to a municipality or public agency. Thus a tax-exempt financing approach is needed, requiring a special ruling from the Internal Revenue Service, which uses the 1963 Ruling #20, allowing a tax break for such special financing approaches.

size In hospital administration, this is the number of beds maintained and staffed for use in a health-care facility; the number of beds licensed or approved for use in a health-care facility by state or regional regulatory agencies. Hospitals may be categorized by hospital statistical tables by number of beds (e.g., 6–24, 50–99, 100–199, 200–299, 300–399, 400–499, and 500 plus beds).

size of group 1. In medical group management, this is the number of health-care providers in a group practice determined by the full-time equivalent (FTE) physicians practicing in a group. 2. In managed care, this is the highest number of health plan members enrolled in a group health plan without counting dependents.

Skelly letter In health administration and human resource management, this is a written document used to inform an employee of allegations against him or her with regard to work or job-related problems and the decision to terminate or suspend. *See Skelly procedure.*

Skelly procedure In health administration and human resource management, this is a process of documenting reasons an employee is being brought under disciplinary actions. The procedure includes a written memo or letter used to set forth issues and charges against the employee, access to copies of any or all materials used in arriving at the charges, and the decision to suspend or terminate the employee. The due process part is to allow the employee a time period (e.g., 10 days) to respond to all allegations and the right to appeal the decision to an unbiased party.

skew In descriptive statistics and central tendency, this is the shape or direction of a normal distribution. *See skewness of standard distribution.*

skewed distributions, positive In descriptive statistics and central tendency, this is when a distribution's shape is skewed to the right. This is backward of what seems logical. As the scores pile up left of the mean, this makes the distribution skewed to the right. The skewness is located in the tail. The side of the tail that is the flattest determines the direction of the skewness.

skewed distributions, negative In descriptive statistics and central tendency, this is when a distribution's shape is skewed to the left. The negative skewed distribution shows that the scores piled up above the mean.

skewness of standard distribution In descriptive statistics and central tendency, this is when the shape of the standard distribution bell curve departs from the "normal" distribution. Most sets of numbers do not pile up in a neat, normally distributed pile with most scores in the middle and with half of the scores evenly distributed on the positive and negative side of the mean. Occasionally, though, they pile up toward the positive or negative side, offsetting the distribution and making the distribution skewed. The normal distribution is mostly an ideal that is used as a standard to be compared to. Most often, standard distributions are skewed to either the left or the right or are positively or negatively skewed.

skill A learned psychomotor ability to carry out a function, behavior, action, or activity.

skilled care Long-term nursing care provided by registered nurses to meet the medical, physical, social, and emotional needs of residents or in-patients through the supervision of resident/patient care over long periods.

skilled nursing care In long-term care, this is a comprehensive nonacute nursing service, therapy, or social service provided by or under the supervision of a registered nurse in long-term-care settings on a 24-hour basis, 7 days a week, utilizing planned care practices to incorporate rehabilitation and restorative care as well as regular nursing care methods and procedures in the care of long-term-care residents; the nursing care offered in a skilled nursing facility. *See also skilled nursing facility.*

skilled nursing care bed classification In long-term care, this means that beds are designated for patients requiring skilled nursing care on a continuous and extended basis (Title 22, California).

skilled nursing facility (SNF) 1. This is a long-term-care facility used to provide skilled nursing care 24 hours a day, 7 days a week, to aid in convalescence, recuperation, and maintenance of chronic diseases, conditions, and disorders including medical care, dietary, pharmaceutical services, social services, recreational therapy, and other therapies such as physical, speech, and occupational therapy as needed. 2. Under Medicare and Medicaid, this is an institution that has a transfer agreement with participating hospitals and that is primarily engaged in providing skilled nursing care and related services for patients who require medical or nursing care or rehabilitation services for the rehabilitation of injured, disabled, or sick persons; has formal policies that are developed with the advice of a group of professional personnel, including one or more physicians and one or more registered nurses, to govern the skilled nursing care and related medical or other services it provides; has a physician, a registered professional nurse, or a medical staff responsible for the execution of such policies; has a requirement that the health care of every patient be under the supervision of a physician and has a physician available to furnish necessary medical care in case of an emergency; maintains medical records on all patients; provides 24-hour nursing service and has at least one registered professional nurse employed full time (40 hours per week); provides appropriate methods for the dispensing and administering of drugs and biologicals; has in effect a utilization review plan that meets the requirements of the law; has met the standards established for licensing in the case of an institution in which state or applicable local law provides for the licensing of institutions; has in effect an overall plan and budget, including an annual operating budget and a 3-year capital expenditures plan; provides for a regular program of independent medical review of the patients in the facility to the extent required by the programs in which the facility participates (including medical evaluation of each patient's need for skilled nursing facility care); meets the Life Safety Code; and meets any other conditions relating to the health and safety of individuals who are furnished services in the institution. 3. In rural health, this is a long-term-care facility that may be freestanding but often is a wing or a unit of a small rural hospital and is designated as a "distinct part SNF," which provides skilled nursing care. In a distinct unit in the hospital that provides skilled nursing care, it has beds set and staffed specifically for this service, is owned and operated by the hospital, and meets Medicare certification criteria. 4. A health-care facility or a distinct part of a hospital that provides continuous skilled nursing care and supportive care to patients whose primary need is availability of skilled nursing care on an extended basis. It provides 24-hour inpatient care and as a minimum includes physician, skilled nursing, dietary, pharmaceutical services, and an activity program (Title 22, California). Also referred to as "convalescent hospitals" or "nursing homes."

skilled nursing services Under Medicare for home health care, patient care services pertaining to the curative, restorative, and preventive aspects of nursing performed by or under the supervision of a registered nurse pursuant to the plan of treatment established in consultation with the care team. Skilled nursing services are nursing care activities emphasizing a high level of nursing direction, observation, and skill.

skilled nursing unit A medical and nursing area or ward in an acute-care facility that offers long-term restorative and rehabilitative skilled nursing care as well as usual nursing procedures carried out by registered nurses. Also called "transitional care units" or "subacute care units." *See also skilled nursing care; skilled nursing facility.*

skills inventories In health administration and human resources management, this is an assessment that summarizes and catalogs each worker's or technical workers' skills and abilities, education, training, and experience. This can be used for promoting or assessing quality and productivity for each department, service, or program in the health-care organization.

skimming 1. In managed care and prepaid medical care, where health-care providers are paid on a capitation basis, or in medical insurance, the practice of seeking to enroll only the healthiest people as a way of controlling program costs (because income is constant whether or not services are actually used). 2. In environmental health, this is the use of a machine to remove oil or scum from the surface of surface water (EPA). *See also skimping; creaming; adverse selection.*

skimping In medical care services paid on a prepayment or capitation basis, the practice of denying or delaying the provision of services needed or demanded by enrolled members as a way of controlling costs (because income is constant whether or not services are actually used). The classic example is the denial or delay of cataract surgery. This may be viewed as a form of rationing of care. *See also skimming; adverse selection; rationing of care.*

slander In tort law, this is the oral defamation of character; untrue, false, and defamatory remarks that injure a person's profession, reputation, business, rights, career, etc.; demeaning and harmful spoken defamatory remarks said in front of witnesses.

sleeper effect In health education or mental health services, this is a delayed response to an educational or counseling intervention that is associated with a lag time required for knowledge to be valued and beliefs to be manifest into behaviors.

sliding fee scale In health-care finance, this is a fee schedule structure for some poorer patients, with the amount of fee charged for services rendered varying on the basis of the patient's ability to pay; discounts in charges for services based on the consumer's ability to pay, according to income and family size.

sliding scale deductible In managed care and health-care financial management, this is a deductible that is not set at a fixed amount but that varies according to income. A family is usually required to spend all (a spend-down) or a set percentage of their income over some base amount (e.g., all or 25% of any income over $5000) as deductible before a member can receive medical care benefits. There may be a maximum amount on the deductible. The sliding scale concept can also be applied to co-insurance and co-payments.

slight negligence In tort law, this is the absence of the level of care that persons of extraordinary prudence and foreseeability would expect.

sling In medical care, this is a support used to rest an injured limb, usually an arm, so that pain is reduced, support provided, and the correct position for healing maintained.

slip United States Supreme Court decisions (or other court decisions) that are printed and made readily available soon after the decisions are handed down. Also referred to as a "slip sheet," "slip decision," or "slip opinion."

slip gauges In environmental health and air pollution control, these are instruments that have a probe that moves through the gas or liquid in a storage or transfer container and can detect the level of vinyl chloride in the container by the physical state of the material the gauge discharges.

slip law The final version of an act of Congress and its first official publication. Each public law is printed in the form of a slip law, which also lists but does not include the legislative history of the act, whatever earlier act may be amended by the new law as it is amended, or any explanation or interpretation of the law.

slipper pan A specialized bedpan that has one end flattened to place it easily under the patient.

slipstream smoke *See secondhand smoke.*

slit lamp An instrument with a narrow beam of light, usually used with a special microscope.

slope In epidemiology or health services research, this is a measure of the amount of change observed in long-term trends and changes of health status indicators, health services utilization, and treatment procedures and processes as expressed as units of utilization per a specific time period.

slope factor In environmental health, this is the upper estimate of the probability of a response per unit intake of a chemical over a lifetime. The slope factor is used to estimate an upper-bound probability of an individual developing cancer as a result of a lifetime exposure to a particular level of a potential carcinogen.

slot A position or place in a work or education program where only a limited number of individuals are accepted such as medical school, physician assistant programs, nursing school, and physical therapy.

slow sand filtration In environmental health and safe water management, this is the process of passing raw water over and through a bed of sand at low velocity (less than 0.4 m/h) resulting in substantial particulate removal by physical and biological mechanisms (EPA).

slow virus A pathogen of the virus family, with a long incubation period, sometimes years. Once the disease manifests itself, the symptoms occur slowly, and the course of the disease is usually long and drawn out, with much debilitation and illness. Kuru, the shaking disease of Papua New Guinea, was one of the first discovered. Also referred to as a "retrovirus."

sludge 1. Any muddy or slushy mess. 2. In environmental health and liquid waste management, this is a precipitated solid matter arising from sewage treatment processes; a semisolid residue resulting from any of a number of air or water treatment processes; any solid, semisolid, or liquid waste generated from a municipal commercial or industrial wastewater treatment plant, water supply treatment plant, or air pollution control facility or any other such waste having similar characteristics and effect. Sludge can be a hazardous waste (EPA).

sludge dryer In environmental health and liquid waste management, this is a device used to reduce the moisture content of sludge by heating it to a temperature above 65°C (150°F) directly with combustion gases.

slurries In environmental health and liquid waste management, these are watery mixtures of insoluble matter that result from some pollution control techniques.

slush fund In health-care financial management, this is a special general fund set aside to be used to make payments on or be used for various expenses. This fund usually is accounted for as a one-ledger T account, and the various expense items it is used for are not strictly accounted for in separate accounts. The advantage of a slush fund is the flexibility of its use because it has no budgetary restrictions placed on it as regular budget items do.

small business A company or business having a limited number of employees and relatively low sales volume and limited ability to provide medical care or dental insurance coverage. A small group practice, private practice, clinic, or private nursing home may be considered a small business.

small claims A special court that handles small cases concerning a limited amount of money.

small-group polling In managed care, this refers to small business, either in groups, segments, or an aggregate body, that is combined into a single insurance pool or group of pools. Anticipated claims and premiums rates are set by each pool and not on an aggregate group basis. *See pooling.*

small manufacturers In environmental health and hazardous waste, these are manufacturers of a chemical substance if its total annual sales, when combined with those of its parent company (if any), are less than $40 million. If the annual production volume of a particular chemical substance at any individual site owned or controlled by the manufacturer is greater than 45,400 kg (100,000 lb), the manufacturer shall not qualify as small for purposes of reporting on the production of that chemical at that site, unless the manufacturer qualifies under the definition of a small manufacturer.

small-quantity generators In environmental health and hazardous waste, these are companies that generate less than 1000 kg of hazardous waste in a calendar month.

small subscriber group aggregate In managed care, this is the process of combining small business entities such as small shops, stores, manufacturing plants, professional associations, or groups (e.g., lawyer groups, physician groups, accounting firms, and engineers) into a single large subscriber group for the purpose of purchasing medical care insurance, dental insurance, or managed-care plans. *See small-group pooling.*

smart money Money paid in the form of punitive damages.

SMFP *See State Medical Facilities Plan.*

smog In environmental health, this a type of air pollution made up of dust, fumes, vapors, irritating smoke, or particulate matter in the air that turns to haze when exposed to sunlight; air pollution associated with oxidants (EPA).

smoke Any suspension of burnt or partly burnt organic particles in the air originating from combustion or incomplete combustion. Carbon or soot particles result from the incomplete combustion of carbonaceous materials such as coal or oil. Smoke generally contains water or other droplets as well as dry particles. Tobacco smoke, for example, is a wet smoke composed of minute tarry droplets and suspended particles.

smoke compartment For JCAHO-accredited long-term-care facilities, a subdivision of a floor that is protected by smoke partitions and that provides an area of refuge should another part of the floor become filled with smoke from a fire.

smoke door For JCAHO-accredited long-term-care facilities, a door installed in a smoke partition and constructed to resist the passage of smoke. Wood doors serving this function must have at least a 1¾-inch solid wood or metal core.

smoke partition/wall For JCAHO-accredited long-term-care facilities, a wall or barrier that is constructed to resist the passage of smoke and that has a minimum fire resistance rating of half an hour. Smoke partitions are required to subdivide any floor providing sleeping accommodations for 30 or more patients in existing facilities and to limit the maximum smoke compartment length to 150 feet.

SMP See special multiple-peril policy.

SMSA See standard metropolitan statistical area.

Snellen chart A special chart used in screening programs or in clinical settings to check a person's distance vision. It consists of rows of capital letters placed in random order. The letters are graduated down in size and correlate with the ability to read at certain distances. Only distant vision can be determined.

SNF See skilled nursing facility.

SNODO Standard Nomenclature of Disease and Operations.

SNOMED See Systematized Nomenclature of Medicine.

SNOP Systematized Nomenclature of Pathology.

Snow, John A respected physician and the anesthesiologist to Queen Victoria of England, Dr. Snow (1813–1858) was noted for his medical work with the royal family, including the administering of chloroform at the birth of the Queen's two children. In the 1840s, Snow pioneered equipment used to administer ether safely to patients. His book *On Ether*, published in 1847, remained a standard reference until well into the 20th century. However, Snow is most famous for his pioneering work in epidemiology. Among epidemiologists, Snow is considered one of the most important contributors in the development of the field of epidemiology. Many of the tactics, approaches, concepts, and methodologies he used in his epidemiological work are found useful and of value in epidemiological work today. Snow had an interest in and studied cholera throughout his medical career. From his studies he established sound and useful epidemiologic methodologies. He observed and recorded important factors related to the course of the disease cholera. In the later part of his career, Snow conducted two major investigative studies of cholera. He studied cholera outbreaks in the SoHo and Golden Square districts of London in the Broad Street area. Later in his career as an epidemiologist, Snow studied a cholera epidemic where he compared death rates from cholera with sources of water from two different water companies in London, the Lambeth Water Company, and the Southwark and Vauxhall Water Company. Snow was a founder of the Epidemiological Society. He died on June 16, 1858, in London.

SNU See skilled nursing unit.

So. Southern Reporter of the National Reporter System.

SOAP An approach to the recording of information in a patient's medical record based on the problem-oriented medical method. It stands for "subjective" (what the patient or other information source has told you), "objective" (what you have observed), "assessment" (affirmative statement of the situation), and "plan of action" (future treatment plans). Not all the letters need to be used with each recording of the narrative. There is no necessity to be redundant if the flow sheet in the medical record says what is required.

SOBRA Sixth Omnibus Reconciliation Act of 1985. See OBRA; Omnibus Reconciliation Act.

social actions The behaviors, traditions, and actions of groups or classes of people in society without reference to specific individuals.

social adaptation 1. Adjustment to society. 2. Acceptable interpersonal relationships and transactions. 3. The ability to live in accordance with society's restrictions and demands.

social aging The actions, behaviors, and expectations of members of society as they get into older periods of life and how they relate to society as a group.

social and rehabilitation services (SRS) The administration in the Department of Health and Human Services (HHS) that manages welfare and related programs, including Medicaid, which is the responsibility of SRS's Medical Services Administration. This is not under the direction of HHS's Assistant Secretary for Health, and Medicaid was originally administered separately from the department's other health programs.

social assessment According to JCAHO for psychiatric, alcoholism, and drug abuse facilities accreditation purposes, the process of evaluating each patient's environment, religious background, childhood history, military service history, financial status, reasons for seeking treatment, and other pertinent information that may contribute to the development of the individualized treatment plan.

social breakdown syndrome In mental health services, this is the part of a mental patient's symptomatology that is a direct result of treatment and living conditions in an institution and not a part of the primary illness. Factors related to this condition are labeling, learning the chronic sick role, dysfunctional or lost work and social skills, and role identification with the maladjusted and ill.

social change Modification and evolution of culture, traditions, and the usual way of doing things in society that are influenced by the structure and functions of social interactions that, in turn, are transformed as a result of political mandates, societal expectations, diminished morals and values, loss of family structure, effects of economic forces, influences of business and marketing enterprises, and education and learning, including how groups seek, access, utilize, or avoid the use of health services.

social characteristics The social aspects of the population that affect that population's health and health care.

social class In epidemiology and public health, these are the various strata of society made up of different levels of income, education, and backgrounds that dictates one's status in society.

social desirability In health services or epidemiological research, this is when a subject is reactive to, or is a source of bias in, measurements or tests or tries to satisfy the evaluator or meet the researcher's expectations.

social diagnosis 1. The assessment of the major factors having a negative effect on the quality of life found in a community, group, or population by clarifying concerns in economics, housing, nutrition, work, unemployment, illegitimacy, civic disturbance, etc. 2. In public health and health promotion in a community or population, this is the evaluation of subjective and objective factors of high social interest or priority that are assessed according to their social and economic role and as a measure of the quality of life.

social disability As used in long-term care, social and health services for the elderly, and disabled and handicapped services, a measure of the need for supportive services and for determining persons at risk for institutionalization. It also measures the need for assistance and compares it with unmet social and health services needed where a person is not self-sufficient in performing certain daily living activities. Relates to those persons in jeopardy of losing their independence through medical, health, social, mental, and emotional disability as well as reduced mobility and lack of self-sufficiency, basic personal care, health preservation, and life-sustaining activities. Persons who are not self-sufficient must either find a way to meet life's required needs through support and assistance or try to continue with unmet needs at the risk of being put in health or social jeopardy. Some support may come from formal support services or from informal caregivers such as neighbors or family members. Quality of life can be affected by the level or extent of health and social disability experienced by those in this special population and can lead to becoming frail or vulnerable to institutionalization. Five areas that have been studied as contributors to social disability include housekeeping needs, transportation, social interaction, food preparation and grocery shopping, and obtaining medical care. *See also alternatives to long-term institutional care.*

social drift A sociological term describing the downward mobility of one's social class caused by impaired health, disease, injury, handicap, or disability.

social health maintenance organization (SHMO) An HMO that integrates social services and medical services for delivery solely to an elderly population, usually over age 65. Medicare funding is used to promote competition between health-care services with the aim of reducing the cost of health care and avoiding institutionalization of the elderly. Additional aims of SHMOs are to reduce hospital stays and public expense for Medicare and Medicaid costs to elderly health-care consumers while integrating medical acute and long-term-care systems. Initially designed to integrate acute-care and long-term care for Medicare members.

social HMO *See social health maintenance organization (SHMO).*

social indicator A numerical value given to a social situation that reflects a change in the quality of life.

social insurance A device for the pooling of risks by their transfer to an organization, usually governmental, that is required by law to provide indemnity (cash) or service benefits to or on behalf of covered persons on the occurrence of certain predesignated losses. Characterized by the following conditions: coverage is compulsory by law; except during a transition period following its introduction, eligibility for benefits is derived, in fact or in effect, from contributions having been made to the program by or in respect of the claimant or the person to whom the claimant is a dependent; there is no requirement that the individual demonstrate inadequate financial resources, although a qualified status may need to be established; the methods for determining the benefits are prescribed by law; the benefits for any individual are not usually directly related to contributions made by him or her; the cost is borne primarily by contributions, which are usually made by covered persons, their employers, or both; the plan is administered or at least supervised by the government; and the plan is not established by the government solely for its present or former employees. Examples in the United States include Social Security, railroad retirement, and workers' and unemployment compensation. In other countries, health insurance is often a government-sponsored social insurance program.

socialization 1. The learning of adequate interpersonal skills and proper interaction with other members of a group according to and in general conformity with the roles, behaviors, rules, laws, traditions, culture, and expectations of one's society; development of behavior patterns, acceptance, conformity, and adherence to culture and tradition of the community and lifestyle through modeling or imitating socially acceptable acts and behaviors considered important to society, peers, family, and social groups. 2. The learning of new behaviors and orientations to society or the workplace as one moves into new positions in the social structure of the organization; an ongoing process by which an employee adjusts and adapts to an organization through observation, understanding, and accepting the roles, policies, norms, beliefs, and values held by the health-care organization. 3. Mimicking actions and behaviors portrayed in the media by celebrities and famous personalities.

socialized medicine A medical care system where the organization and provision of medical care services are under direct government control. Administration and the health-care providers are employed by or contract for the provision of services directly with the government.

socially needy Persons who have at least two of the following four barriers and factors: age 75 years or older, handicapped, living alone, or having language or communication limitations.

social medicine A minor branch of medicine related to public health and community medicine where the physician is concerned with disease, injury, disorders, conditions, and death that occur in groups of people, especially people living in groups. The role of the individual in the health and disease of the total group, the family, and the surrounding population is the focus of the practice.

social problem A set of employment, vocational, education, training, adaptive, and societal integration circumstances affecting a significant number of people who are the victim of difficulties; situations and life's circumstances. These are deemed unacceptable by objective evaluations and social interpretation and are viewed as sources of unhappiness and difficulty that affect a significant number of people in a group or population.

social psychiatry A branch of psychiatry that deals with the ecological, sociological, and cultural variables that cause maladaptive behavior.

social reconnaissance In public health, epidemiology, and health promotion, this is the environmental scanning and diagnostic processes used to assess a large geographic area or large population and to seek information and input from individuals with various levels of authority and resources, including community leaders, government officials, and health and social service professionals regarding the needs of the people in the service area or catchment area, their participation in existing services, and their need for new health services or social programs.

Social Security A retirement assistance social insurance provided for most citizens of the United States through the federal government under the Old Age, Survivors, Disability, and Health Insurance Program (OASDHI), created in 1935 to help replace income loss from being retired, elderly, a dependent survivor, or disabled. Medicare, the medical insurance program for the elderly and disabled, is a part of Social Security and was created by the addition of Title 18 to the Social Security Act. *See benefits.*

Social Security Act of 1935 A federal law that established the Social Security Administration, which in turn taxes workers and employers to create a fund for retirement, disability, and death payments and later on established the Medicare medical insurance program for the elderly.

Social Security Administration (SSA) An agency of the Department of Health and Human Services under the Social Security Act of 1935 that manages the Social Security program and the Health Care Financing Administration, the administrative agency that administers and determines eligibility for Medicare.

Social Security number A unique number assigned to each individual in the United States. Originally, the number was needed by workers to be identified as contributors to the federal Social Security system through payroll deductions or direct contributions by small businesses, which in turn was used to enroll for Social Security benefits on retirement at age 65 or if disabled. The number has turned into a national federal governmental identification number and is used by children as listed on the federal level Internal Revenue Services income tax forms and as an identification number in the military, colleges and universities, bank and credit union accounts, etc.

Social Security numbering A method of assigning numbers to medical records whereby patients are identified by their Social Security numbers instead of a sequential numbering system.

Social Security office These are local federal Social Security Administration places of operation and administration through the United States for the public to access the Social Security Administration with problems or concerns. Applications for Social Security and Medicare are accepted and processed, as are Medicare appeals.

Social Security reserves The amount of money in the national Social Security trust fund that remains each year above the amount disbursed in benefits. Intended to help pay for the aging of America (the baby boomers growing into old age), the total is expected to peak at five times the amount of annual outlays by 2018. Between the years 2035 and 2050, the reserves will be used to finance benefits; after 2050, it will leave a degree of burden on the working generation that will depend on the strength of the economy.

Social Security trustees An appointed group of individuals who serve as the board of directors responsible for ensuring Social Security's capacity to serve Americans over the next 75 years. The trustees report to Congress annually and submit the reports and program to the review and scrutiny of an outside advisory panel every 4 years.

Social Security trust funds Several trust funds are developed: old-age survivors' pensions (the largest), retired workers and widows, disability and children's trust funds, and hospital insurance trust funds, which provide Medicare benefits.

social service aide A person who assists social workers by interviewing applicants for services, referring people to available community resources, and doing simple follow-up studies under the supervision of a social worker. There are no specific educational requirements beyond a high school diploma. A 2-year associate degree may be preferred by some employers.

social service department In hospitals, nursing homes, and rehabilitation hospitals, this is the administrative area responsible for social services of the health-care facility that are carried out by medical social workers and possibly psychiatric social workers who focus on the social, economic, mental, support services, and community factors that influence the patient's condition on discharge. Community resources are used to reduce the social, environmental, and emotional barriers to recovery such as financial problems, posthospital care, posthospital placement, discharge planning, and assistance to the patient's family. Social service programs are often closely linked to psychiatry and psychiatric social work services.

social services designee A person identified in an extended care or long-term-care facility to provide social services under the direction of a social work consultant. A designee should have at least 2 years of college education and, preferably, a bachelors degree. Licensure is not required in any state because the function of a social service designee is not itself an occupation but a role specified in Medicare regulations and assigned to an otherwise employed member of the facility's staff.

social support Personal or family relationships that provide emotional, psychological, or material assistance or personal help in time of need.

social support services Community-based services that provide assistance to families in their homes, usually arranged for or coordinated by a social service worker or social worker. These services often include arrangements for the protection or removal of children or family members from violence or abuse, transportation, homemaker services, counseling, rehabilitation, home-delivered meals for the homebound elderly, shopping assistance, assistance with health-care visits, home health care, home repair, conservator or guardianships, nursing home placement, etc.

social unionism In health administration and labor activities, this is taking the activities, power, and social forces of labor beyond the activities of the workplace to a broader level of influence in the social, economic, governmental, and legal policies environment into all levels of government and society.

social work 1. A branch of social science that trains individuals to offer assistance and care, arrange social support systems, and provide social and emotional support to special and needy populations. 2. Services that offer support and social assistance to families and special populations in dealing with personal, social, family, and societal problems. 3. Medical social work offers assistance to patients and their families in dealing with social support needs as well as coping with the results of injury, disease, and disability and to meet social and nutritional support needs on discharge of a health-care facility and/or while at home under the care of a home health agency. *See also medical social worker.*

social work aide A staff person with orientation and on-the-job training who receives supervision from a social worker or social work assistant.

social work assistant 1. According to JCAHO for accreditation purposes, this is an individual with a bachelors degree, preferably with a human services, social welfare, or social work sequence, who is given on-the-job training for specific assignments and responsibilities in the provision of social work services or who has the documented equivalent in education, training, and/or experience. 2. A person with a bachelors degree in the social sciences or related fields and who receives supervision, consultation, and in-service training from a social worker (Title 22, California).

social worker 1. A professionally trained person providing social services, either as an employee of a city or a county social services agency, welfare office, or office on aging or as a member of a health-care team, part of a social service section of a health facility, or as a consultant. Social services are provided to enable a patient, family members, or others to deal with problems of social functioning affecting the health or well-being of the patient. Most trained social workers hold masters degrees in social work (MSW). The bachelors degree in social work (BSW) or human services is an entry-level professional degree. The National Association of Social Workers (NASW) requires that social workers engaging in independent practice have at least an MSW and 2 years of professionally supervised practice in social work methods to be employed in independent practice and be licensed by the state board of licensure or examiners as required.

social worker, health services Individuals who have completed a formal program of study in the identification, assessment, understanding, and treatment of social and emotional factors underlying or contributing to a patient's illness and who communicate the observations and findings to the health-care team and health-care providers. These professionals assist patients and families in case management and the understanding and acceptance of treatment needed to maximize medical benefits and to cope with and adjust to the effects of the illness or injury. Case management assists with understanding and utilizing resources of family and community agencies to enhance recovery and a return to full social and vocational functioning.

social worker, hospital A qualified social worker who works in the hospital setting, offering assistance to patients and their families in dealing with social support needs and in coping with the results of injury, disease, or disability through arranging services and providing counseling on discharge from the hospital. *See also social work; organized social work services.*

social worker, medical An individual who, if required, is licensed by the state, is a graduate of a school or department of social work accredited by the Council of Social Work Education, and has 1 year of social work experience in a medical care setting. *See social work; social worker, health services; medical social worker; social worker, hospital; organized social work services.*

social worker, psychiatric A professional trained in social work who works with psychologists and psychiatrists in a clinic or institutional setting. This professional assesses family, environmental, and social factors that contribute to the patient's illness; works with new patients; and may follow up former patients after discharge. Psychiatric social workers also do individual, family, and group psychotherapy.

social worker, qualified 1. According to JCAHO for psychiatric, alcoholism, and drug abuse facilities accreditation purposes, an individual who has a masters degree from an institution accredited by the Council on Social Work Education, or who has been certified by the Academy of Certified Social Workers, or who has the documented equivalent in education, training, and/or experience. 2. An individual who either has met the requirements of a graduate curriculum leading to a masters degree in a school of social work that is accredited by the council on Social Work Education or has the documented equivalent in education, training, and/or experience (JCAHO for acute-care facilities). 3. For Medicare purposes, a person who is licensed, if applicable, by the state in which practicing, is a graduate of a school of social work accredited or approved by the Council on Social Work Education, and has 1 year of social work experience in a health-care setting. *See organized social work services.*

social work services 1. The delivery of care that assists patients and their families in addressing emotional, social, and economic stresses of illness or injury. Standards are applied to evaluate a hospital's performance in providing social work services. Also called "social services" or "social work." (JCAHO for acute-care facilities). 2. An administrative entity in a health-care facility or community agency that offers social support assistance to patients and their family members by arranging for services, assessing social needs, and providing counseling for any problem arising from injury, illness, or disability or arranging for social and nutritional support services on discharge and/or under the care of a home health agency, all done under the direction of a qualified social worker. *See social support services; organized social work services.*

societal outcomes In health-care delivery, these are less tangible results of medical care and rehabilitation as measured in terms of health-care provider or consumer satisfaction, education, ethical, and legal results.

Society for Healthcare Planning and Marketing A nonprofit professional association for health planners and health-care marketing executives and professionals who work mainly with hospitals. A subaffiliate of the American Hospital Association, the society provides current programs, products, and publications on strategic planning and marketing geared toward hospitals and health-care organizations. The driving principle behind this association is that health planning and marketing in health-care organizations is complementary to and provides direction for the health-care organization and that strategic planning and marketing should be integrated in health-care management.

Society for Human Resource Management A nonprofit national professional association that offers training, education, and resources to professionals and administrators working or interested in personnel management and related human resource functions and activities. They offer accreditation programs for personnel management professionals.

Society of Prospective Medicine An organization that provides an opportunity for individuals to keep up with the rapid changes in the practice of health maintenance and health enhancement. Through identifying the actual and potential health risks for a person, followed by a personalized plan of risk reduction, it is the ultimate in comprehensive and continuing high-level wellness care. Large industrial corporations, life insurance companies, labor unions, community action groups, colleges and universities, religious organizations, and individuals utilize wellness programs on the basis of principles of the Society of Prospective Medicine. The goals include the following: 1) to assist in the development of appropriate risk factors for identified causes of disability and death such as overweight, sedentary lifestyles, smoking, and excessive stress; 2) to seek to identify additional causes of disability and death; 3) to provide for quality evaluation and availability of risk factor data; 4) to advance the teaching of prospective medicine and personal health in medical schools, residency programs, community hospitals, and other educational institutions; 5) to serve as a clearinghouse for professional and lay information about procedures that will enable individuals to adopt healthful lifestyles; and 6) to promote research to evaluate the effectiveness of these changes and mechanisms to motivate individuals to decrease risks and practice positive wellness.

Society of Public Health Education (SOPHE) Formed on October 23, 1949, at the 77th meeting of the American Public Health Association, this is a professional organization for persons with special interest, training, and experience in health education of the public. The society has a particular concern for research in methods of public health education, especially for graduates of schools of public health and those possessing the recognized professional public health degrees (e.g., MPH or DRPH), with the development of professional standards for conducting public health education activities and for promoting the profession. The SOPHE professional journal is *Health Education Quarterly*.

socioeconomic classification In public health and epidemiology, this is the arrangement of individuals into categories on the basis of traits that contribute to prestige in society, attitudes held, values embraced, and factors that affect one's social and economic standing such as level of income, occupation, and education, all of which correlate with health status and use of medical services. Several models and lists have been made, many having limitations often associated with putting people into categories. The lists range from professional occupations to unskilled labor. Some lists account for, and others ignore, the self-employed and business owners.

socioeconomic status In public and community health and health services delivery, this is the position in society held by individuals on the basis of skills, training, and education levels; occupation; levels of income; and financial status.

sociogram Pictorial or diagrammatic presentation of the occurrence of choices, rejections, and indifference in a number of persons involved in a life situation.

sociology The study of groups and social organization.

sociometric distance A method used to measure the degree of perception that one person has for another. It is suggested that the greater the sociometric distance between persons, the more inaccurate is one's evaluation of social relationships.

sociometrist An investigator or researcher who measures interpersonal relations, social structures, and vital statistics of a community.

sociopath In mental health, this is a psychological condition whereby a person does not adhere to societys' moral and ethical standards at the expense of others. Sometimes this personality type commits bizarre crimes with no moral concern or remorse. Sometimes used synonymously with "psychopath."

sociotechnical system In health administration and human resource management, these are changes and developments in the workplace circumstances and the work structure and process of work groups caused by the technology used at work.

soft detergents In environmental health and safe water management, these are cleaning agents that break down in nature.

soft money In health-care organizations, these are temporary funds (not regular budget items) from sources that will not continue the funding and usually are for one-time use (e.g., research project or demonstration project); money that is temporarily available from outside sources and that will end in the near future; not from solid line funding sources such as the regular operating revenue or budget; money that is given to a program or organization on a short-term basis and in limited amounts. When the specific amount is gone, the program or job ends. Sources of soft money usually are grants in specific amounts for specific designated use from federal or state governments, philanthropic organizations, or businesses. *See also hard money.*

software 1. In health information management, this is the collection of computer instructions in programs and routines such as application programs, operating system, programming languages, and translators; also applies to word processors, spreadsheets, databases, graphic programs, art and drawing programs, and statistics programs, including CD interactive audiovisual programs, music programs, and databases. 2. Films, audiotapes, videotapes, slides, etc. used on projectors and audiovisual and media equipment.

soft water In environmental health and safe water management, this is any water that does not contain a significant amount of dissolved minerals such as calcium or magnesium salts.

soil adsorption field In environmental health and liquid waste treatment, this is a subsurface area containing a trench or bed with clean stones and systems of distribution piping through which treated sewage may seep into the surrounding soil for further treatment and disposal (EPA).

soil injection In environmental health, this is the process emplacing pesticides into the soil by applying them in the plowed layers of soil during the process of tilling.

sole community hospital (SCH) A rural hospital that is presumed to be the only source of local inpatient hospital care to local residents because of their isolated location, weather conditions, travel conditions, or absence of other hospitals nearby. The distance from other hospitals and health-care providers, the portion of patients in the service area receiving treatment from the hospital, and being in a rural or non-SMSA are some of the criteria that determine the sole community hospital's status. Sixty-five percent of the SCHs are located in the western United States. Federally designated SCHs receive special considerations under Medicare's Prospective Payment System. This is one class of institutions identified by the Health Care Financing Administration (HCFA) for special treatment under TEFRA (Tax Equity and Fiscal Responsibility Act of 1982) and the Social Security Amendments of 1983, which authorized the PPS/DRG system. The PPS/DRG and TEFRA requirements restricted reimbursement and adversely affected the financial ability of rural hospitals to stay open and serve the rural areas as the available medical care facility. To qualify, an SCH must apply to HCFA and demonstrate its eligibility under the regulations. The designation of an SCH allows a greater weight to hospital-specific cost factors and eligibility for special payments during times of low patient occupancy and volume.

sole proprietorship A single-owner business; a legal one-owner business entity. Most small businesses are of this type, including many medical care practitioners; a one-physician, one-dentist, one-psychologist solo practice approach to ownership of an unincorporated business entity. The physician or psychologist may hire an associate on salary while retaining responsibility for legal matters, management, policy development, and budgetary and financial matters. The advantages of a sole proprietorship are sole ownership, self-determination, simple decision making, and simple financial arrangements. The disadvantages are sole legal and financial responsibility, limited information in decision making, and limited consultations and professional interactions.

solicitation 1. To ask for. 2. Something urgently needed or requested. 3. Something that is enticing. 4. To seek or strongly request.

solicitor general A lawyer or officer for the Department of Justice who represents the U.S. government.

solid waste In environmental health, this is any waste material that requires oxidation or enzyme action to break it down into its basic elements (e.g., paper, tin cans, and yard waste). All trash, garbage, rubbish, or materials that are disposed of in sanitary landfills or that can be recycled such as metals, tires, paper, plastics, glass, and wood.

solid waste–derived fuel In environmental health, this is a fuel produced from the decomposition of solid waste that can be used as a primary or supplementary fuel in conjunction with or in place of fossil fuels. It can be in the form of raw or unprocessed solid waste, shredded or pulped materials that can be burned in an incinerator, gas or oil derived from pyrolyzed solid waste, or gas from the biodegradation and decomposition of solid waste, usually in the form of methane gas.

solid waste disposal In environmental health, this is the final placement or disposition of refuse not salvaged or recycled by burying it in a landfill, dumping it in the ocean, or incinerating it.

Solid Waste Disposal Act In environmental health, this act was passed in 1965 to provide for a national research and development program to improve methods of solid waste disposal and for a program of technical and financial assistance to states and governments for solid waste management. Solid waste experts were assembled into a new office, and grants were made for research, technology demonstration, development of areawide management systems, development of state and interstate plans, and personnel training to eliminate city and town dumps and develop controlled landfill sites.

solid waste management In environmental health, this is the supervised handling of garbage, trash, rubbish, and other solid waste materials from their source through recovery processes to disposal and must include a pro-

solid waste management facilities In environmental health, this is any resource recovery system, organization, building, or components thereof for the collection, separation, storage, transportation, transfer, processing, treatment, or disposal of solid wastes, including hazardous wastes.

solid waste planning In environmental health, this includes assessing needs, setting goals and objectives for the management of resource recovery, and conservation and effective and efficient methods of dealing with solid waste generation problems, including the investigation and consideration of progressive disposal systems such as effective recycling systems, encouragement of free enterprise in the recycling process, and incineration.

solid wastes In environmental health, this includes all nonliquid, nonsoluble materials ranging from municipal garbage to industrial wastes that contain complex and sometimes hazardous substances. Also included are sewage sludge, agricultural refuse, demolition wastes, and mining residues and can include liquids and gases enclosed in containers; all garbage, refuse, rubbish, trash, and other discarded solid materials resulting from industrial and commercial operations and from community activities. It does not include solids or dissolved materials in domestic sewage or other significant pollutants in water resources such as silt, dissolved or suspended solids in industrial wastewater effluents, dissolved materials in irrigation return flows, or other common water pollutants (EPA).

solidification and stabilization In environmental health and liquid waste management, this the removal of wastewater from a waste or changing it chemically to make the waste less permeable and susceptible to transport by water (EPA).

solo practice A physician, psychologist, dentist, podiatrist, or other practitioner who has an office and practices by himself or herself as a self-employed individual. Solo practice is private practice but is not necessarily general practice or fee-for-service practice (solo practitioners may be paid by capitation, although fee-for-service is far more common) and is not a member of a medical group. Solo practice is common among physicians, dentists, psychologists, podiatrists, optometrists, and chiropractors and less common and sometimes illegal in other professions. *See also sole proprietorship.*

solutions In environmental health and hazardous waste, these are any homogeneous liquid mixtures of two or more chemical compounds or elements that will undergo segregation under conditions of normal transportation as hazardous waste.

solvency In health-care finance, this is when a health-care organization has enough money to pay its debts; possessing more assets than liabilities; the ability of a health-care organization to meets its financial obligations when due.

solvent 1. Having the authority to end or dissolve something. 2. Being capable of paying off a debt. 3. A substance or agent that could be water but often is an organic compound that dissolves another substance; substances, usually a liquid capable of dissolving or dispersing one or more other substances (EPA). 4. In environmental health, this is a potential pollutant of water and air if not handled correctly because solvents contain benzene and other harmful substances and contaminants that easily flow into water systems or evaporate into the air.

somatic Referring to the physical body.

somatize In mental health and behavior health areas, this is to unknowingly express emotional concerns as physical symptoms.

somatopsychic A physical illness leading to a mental disorder. *See also psychosomatic illness.*

somnambulism Sleepwalking or motor activity during sleep. It is commonly seen in children. In adults, it is seen in the schizoid personality disorder and certain other types of schizophrenia.

somno- Prefix meaning "sleep."

somo- Prefix meaning "body."

sono- Prefix meaning "sound."

sonoplacentography A technique utilizing ultrasound waves to ascertain the exact position of the placenta during pregnancy.

sonotopography A technique utilizing ultrasound to determine the position of a structure in the body.

soot In environmental health and air pollution control, this is carbon dust formed by incomplete combustion, often the result of inefficient burning of coal, fossil fuels, or tires.

SOP *See standard operating procedure.*

SOPHE *See Society of Public Health Education.*

sorption In environmental health and air pollution control, this is the chemical or physical action of soaking up or attracting substances and is used in many pollution control approaches and systems.

sound 1. Together; whole. 2. Not deteriorating or decaying. 3. In good condition. 4. Healthy. 5. Founded on what is believed to be true. 6. Free from error. 7. Carefully thought out. 8. Dependable. 9. Valid.

soundex system In medical records, a phonetic filing system that utilizes letters and numbers in code to designate names.

sound mind 1. Having a sane, competent, healthy mental state. 2. Legally competent; can make reasonable and thought-out decisions.

source In environmental health, this refers to any place, location, building, facility, plant, factory, structures, equipment, machinery, etc. from which one or more pollutants come.

source control maintenance measures In environmental health, these are measures intended to maintain the effectiveness of source control actions once such actions are operating and functioning properly (e.g., the maintenance of landfill caps and leachate collection systems).

source control remedial action In environmental health, these are measures intended to contain hazardous substances, pollutants, or contaminants where they are located or to eliminate potential contamination by transporting contaminants to a new location. Such actions are appropriate if a substantial concentration or amount remains at or near the point of origin and inadequate barriers exist to retard migration. Such actions may not be appropriate if the contaminants have migrated from the areas where originally located or if the local department of environmental health determines that the contaminants are adequately contained.

source document In medical insurance and medical records administration, this is a paper on which data are originated. Patient charts, doctors' orders, or medical insurance forms can be source documents.

source individual In occupational health and safety and infection control, this is any person, living or dead, whose blood, remains, donated blood or blood components, or other potentially infectious materials may be a source of infectious occupational exposure to employees of a hospital or clinic or patients, clients in institutions for the developmentally disabled, trauma victims, clients of drug and alcohol treatment facilities, and residents of hospices and nursing homes.

source language In health information management, this is the system of symbols and syntax used in computer programs to execute a program.

source-oriented record In medical records, a chart that maintains all reports, information, and data from a given department in one section of the record. Papers are kept in chronological sequence in each area or subsection of the medical record.

sources, stationary In environmental health, these are fixed, nonmoving producers of pollution, mainly power plants, factories, oil refineries, manufacturing companies, chemical plants, etc., using industrial combustion processes; any building, structure, facility, or installations that emit or may emit air pollution for which a national standard exists and is in effect.

sovereign immunity 1. The government's ability to allow or not allow claims to be brought against it. 2. Immunity from laws or claims due to it being the source of power and laws. 3. Designed for a particular purpose.

span of authority In health administration, this is the amount or level of responsibility, power, and decision-making control a manager has over a certain number of employees or departments.

span of control In health administration and human resource management, this the number of workers a manager can effectively and directly supervise for the particular job or work situation. The more workers assigned to a manager's responsibility, the broader the manager's span of control. *See span of authority; span of supervision.*

span of supervision The upper limit to the number of subordinates a manager can effectively supervise.

SPC *See statistical process control.*

special 1. Uncommon. 2. Extraordinary. 3. Differing or distinctive from others. 4. Limited. 5. Unusual.

special appearance In health law or medical malpractice arbitration hearings, this is showing up in court or a hearing for a special reason such as to contest the jurisdiction of a court to hear a case.

special aquatic sites In environmental health, these are geographic areas possessing special ecological characteristics of productivity, habitat, wildlife protection, or other important and easily disrupted ecological values. These areas are generally recognized as significantly influencing or positively contributing to the general overall environmental health or vitality of the entire ecosystem of the region.

special care In medical care, this is care limited to a particular branch of medicine or surgery, delivered by staff who, by virtue of their advanced training, are qualified to deliver such care in a specialized setting.

special care units 1. In health-care facilities, this is an appropriately equipped area of the institution, usually a hospital, that is organized and staffed to take care of a single but serious type of problem such as cardiac care, intensive care, burn units, and neonatal intensive care where there is a concentration of physicians, nurses, and others who have special skills and experience to provide optimal medical care for critically ill patients. 2. According to JCAHO for hospital accreditation purposes, this is a hospital center with a concentration of qualified professional staffing and supportive resources that is established to provide intensive care continuously on a 24-hour basis to critically ill patients. Such units include general intensive care medical/surgical units and other types of units that provide specialized intensive care (e.g., burn and neonatal intensive care). Standards are applied to evaluate a hospital's performance in providing intensive care. *See intensive care units.*

special class insurance In medical insurance, this is coverage for applicants who cannot qualify for a standard policy because of poor health.

special committee *See ad hoc.*

special damages In health law, these are damages that are the actual harm or damage, but not necessarily the result, of the injury.

special diet A modified diet such as low cholesterol, salt free, low sugar, or any other diet that is limited for medical reasons; a diet that limits or adds specified nutrients because of a health condition. Sometimes called a "therapeutic diet." *See also modified diet.*

special health supervision In occupational health, this is a special medical investigation carried out for workers exposed to radiation at working condition A (annual exposures exceeding three-tenths of the dose equivalent limits).

special hospital 1. A health-care institution that has, as its main purpose and function, the provision of diagnostic and treatment services for special types of patients or for specific diseases, medical conditions, or types of care required such as children's hospitals; rehabilitation facilities; tuberculosis sanatoriums; and cancer, osteopathic, orthopedic, and psychiatric hospitals. 2. Unique health-care facilities for mentally ill patients who are a danger to themselves or others and must be kept separate and under security.

special injunction A court order or writ that prohibits acts of a party such as dumping of pollutants indiscriminately.

specialist A physician, dentist, or other health-care provider or practitioner who limits his or her practice to an advanced specific branch of medicine or dentistry other than primary care; a health-care provider with a focused and advanced narrow area of practice. These health-care practitioners usually have advanced concentrated education and training, including clinical internships or residencies in a focused and advanced narrow area of medicine that relates to their medical practice, and are often certified as specialists by a specialty board in areas such as allergy, gastroenterology, cardiology, neurosurgery, and orthopedics. These highly trained practitioners most often practice in large urban medical centers that usually are referral and tertiary care facilities and are rarely found practicing in small rural hospitals. Other practitioners can also be specialists. For example, nurses can concentrate on neonatal intensive care or surgical nursing, and psychologists can specialize in children, family therapy, and testing. Social workers, physical therapists, occupational therapists, speech pathologists, and other practitioners can also have a focused and concentrated area of practice. *See also board eligible; board certified; general practitioner; secondary care; tertiary care.*

specialization 1. In medical care, this is where a health-care practitioner or health-care provider has a focused, limited, concentrated, highly technical, unique set of experiences and training and a highly developed level of expertise, skill, and knowledge in one or two areas and who is exceptionally good at this narrow area of expertise. 2. A health-care institution that offers a focused, limited, narrow, specific set of services that are done exceptionally well.

specialized outpatient program for AIDS In health-care delivery, this is a specialty service providing diagnostic, treatment, continuing care, medical care plans, and counseling and support services for AIDS/ARC patients and their families and acquaintances.

specially designated landfills See *landfills, specially designated*.

special master An official of the court who represents the state to determine the validity of certain facts or the real circumstances surrounding a case.

special meeting See *ad hoc*.

special multiple-peril policy (SMP) In liability insurance, a special policy similar to those offered to home owners but used by businesses because it offers a variety of risk-related coverages related to disasters and acts of nature that cause destruction, damage, or injury.

special pleading In health law, this is the presentation of new facts that offset the matter presented by the opposing party.

special populations 1. In public health, these are individuals who have unique, unusual, or different needs than the mainstream population such as segments of underrepresented minority groups, elderly, mentally retarded, mentally ill, and physically handicapped/disabled persons. 2. In emergency health services and under disaster circumstances or a required evacuation, these are persons who may require special transportation or protective provisions because of institutional confinement, lack of transportation, or being handicapped, disabled, or elderly.

special reviews In environmental health, this is a regulatory process by which existing pesticides suspected of posing unreasonable risks to human health, nontarget organisms, or the environment are referred for review by the EPA. The review requires an intensive risk-benefit analysis with opportunity for public comment. If the risk of any use of a pesticide is found to outweigh social and economic benefits, regulatory actions are developed, ranging from label revisions and use restriction to cancellation or suspension of use (EPA).

special risk insurance Insurance coverage for risks or hazards of a special or unusual nature.

special services In managed care and medical insurance, a service that is generally not a part of basic services but that involves additional services of physicians. Such services or treatments generally are adjunctive to common services. See also *services*.

special source of groundwater See *groundwater, special source of*.

special statute A law that has a special purpose or impact on a particular issue or concern, rather than a general application, common to public health and environmental health.

specialty A focused, advanced, narrow, and concentrated area in a profession; advanced training with supervised practice resulting in a specified set of skills, knowledge, and experience in a specific area of practice or in a subconcentration in a certain discipline; often certified. Practitioners with a concentrated area of practice are called "specialists." Physicians specialists are usually board certified in their specialty area.

specialty board Organizations that certify physicians and dentists as specialists or subspecialists in various fields of medical and dental practice. The standards for certification relate to length and type of training and experience and include written and oral examination of applicants for specialty certification. The boards are not educational institutions, and the certificate from a board is not considered a degree. Specialties and their boards are recognized and approved by the American Board of Medical Specialties in conjunction with the AMA Council on Medical Education. See also *board certified; board eligible*.

specialty care The provision of advanced medical care with a narrow area of focus usually offered by physicians who have specialized and advanced training through a residency or related internship training.

specialty hospital See *hospital, specialty*.

specialty, medical In medical care, this is where a physician has a focused, limited, concentrated, highly technical level of expertise, skill, and knowledge in areas such as the following: cardiology, orthopedics, psychiatry, obstetrics/gynecology, family practice, internal medicine, pediatrics, geriatrics, ophthalmology, dermatology, urology, neurology, neurosurgery, gastroenterology, thoracic surgery, physical medicine, preventive medicine, and ear-nose-throat. Most medical specialty areas require a 2- to 5-year residency and are board certified in their area of specialty. Sixty-five medical specialties and subspecialties are accredited by the Accreditation Council for Graduate Medical Education:

allergy and immunology	emergency medicine
anesthesiology	family practice
critical care	geriatrics
colon/rectal surgery	internal medicine
dermatology	cardiovascular disease

critical care
 endocrinology/metabolism
 hematology
 infectious disease
 medical oncology
 nephrology
 pulmonary disease
 rheumatology
neurological surgery
neurology
 child neurology
nuclear medicine
obstetrics/gynecology
ophthalmology
orthopedic surgery
 hand surgery
 musculoskeletal oncology
 pediatric orthopedics
 sports medicine
otolaryngology
 (ear-nose-throat)
pathology
 blood banking
 chemical pathology
 forensic pathology
 hematology
 immunopathology
 medical microbiology
 neuropathology

pediatrics
 pediatric cardiology
 pediatric endocrinology
 pediatric hemato-oncology
 pediatric nephrology
 neonatal-perinatal rehabilitation
physical medicine/rehabilitation
plastic surgery
preventive medicine, general
 aerospace medicine
 occupational medicine
 public health
psychiatry
 child psychiatry
radiology, diagnostic
radiology, diagnostic-nuclear
radiation oncology
surgery
 critical care
 pediatric surgery
 vascular surgery
 thoracic surgery
urology

specialty society In medicine, this is private association for physicians in certain areas of specialization; a medical association or medical society for specialists.

special verdict In law, this is a decision in which the jury states bare facts as they are determined and on which a verdict is based.

special wastes See *waste, special*.

species In environmental health, this includes any subspecies of fish, wildlife, or plants and any distinct population segment of any species of vertebrate fish or wildlife that interbreeds when mature. Excluded is any species of the class of insect determined to be a pest whose protection under the Endangered Species Act would present an overwhelming and overriding risk to humans.

specification In epidemiology, this is choosing factors or variables to be used in the assessment, analysis, and development of association or causality and the identification of external changes or influences such as confounding variables; to analyze relationships (such as cause-effect relationships) as identified in a study by using a certain approach, model, or technique.

specifications 1. In health facility construction or remodeling, this is a detailed statement of requirements for interior finishes; architectural hardware; and plumbing, electrical, and mechanical systems usual to health-care facilities. 2. In environmental health, this is a clear and accurate description of the technical requirements for materials, products, or services that specifies the minimum requirement for quality and construction of materials and equipment necessary for an acceptable product. In general, these are in the form of written descriptions, drawings, prints, commercial designations, industry standards, and other descriptive references.

specific contagion theory In epidemiology and medical care, this is a theory of infection transmission and control based on the idea that a single and specific cause exists for every communicable disease, usually a single microorganism. This theory is based on the work of Robert Koch of Germany (Prussia) and Louis Pasteur of France conducted in the 1800s on microorganisms and their role in disease. This theory of infection is the founding principle of the germ theory of disease and has influenced how modern medical practice treats infectious disease even today.

specificity In epidemiology and testing, this is a measure of the ability of a diagnostic or screening test to correctly identify the negative results or show the healthy people; the proportion of true negative cases (healthy people) correctly identified as negative on a test; the ability of the test to correctly identify the percentage of those who do not have the disease and are proven to not have the disease as demonstrated by a test; the proportion of nondiseased persons in a population who underwent screening and who are correctly identified as not being diseased by the screening test; ability to identify the true negatives in a screening test and those found to be free from false positives; the ability of a test to rule out cases not possessing a particular disease or condition and to avoid a false positive result. A test may be quite specific without being very sensitive. See *sensitivity; screening*.

specific performance In contract law, this is to be compelled to perform in a contract when money damages for breach of the contract would not be satisfactory.

specific rates In epidemiology, these are focused

and detailed subrates of morbidity, mortality, fertility, and birth rates calculated for select or certain ages, gender, race, demographic characteristics, or other specific events or concerns. *See rates.*

specified disease insurance In medical insurance, this is a unique insurance policy that provides benefits, usually in large amounts or with high maximums, toward the expense of the treatment of a specific disease or diseases named in the policy. Such policies are rarely written but were more common in the past for such diseases as polio and spinal meningitis. Coverage of end-stage renal disease under Medicare can be thought of as an example.

specified professional personnel According to JCAHO for accreditation purposes, individuals who are duly licensed practitioners, members of the house staff, and other personnel qualified to render direct medical care under the supervision of a practitioner who has clinical privileges in the hospital and capable of effectively communicating with patients, medical staff, and hospital personnel.

specimens Any animal or plant or any part thereof; any tissue, blood, serum, product, egg, seed, or root of any human, animal, or plant taken for examination or analysis.

SPECT *See single photon emission computerized tomography.*

specular reflection In laser technology, this is a mirrorlike reflection.

speculative risk In managed care and insurance, this is an insurance risk with an unpredictable outcome thath could produce either profit or loss (e.g., a venture capital investment).

speculum In medical care, this is a specialized medical instrument used to open a body orifice to view an internal cavity; often employed by gynecologists to view the interarea of a female patient's vaginal canal to observe and examine the uterus.

speech disturbance A general term for a variety of verbal or nonverbal communication disorders not caused by an organic problem. *See aphasia; alexia.*

speech-hearing therapy aide An entry-level health-care worker who assists in testing, evaluating, and treating the problems of people with speech and hearing difficulties.

speech-language pathologists Individuals who are licensed as required by state law to practice speech therapy and related services. *See speech pathologist.*

speech-language pathology or audiology An educational program that prepares individuals to evaluate and habilitate hearing, speech, and language disorders such as neurological disturbances, defective articulation, or foreign dialects in children or adults; includes instruction in how to plan, direct, and conduct remedial programs designed to restore or improve the communication efficiency of individuals with hearing or speech impairments.

speech pathologist 1. A health-care provider who is prepared to diagnose and evaluate individual speech and language competencies, abilities, and effectiveness, including assessment of speech and language skills as related to educational, medical, social, and psychological factors. A speech pathologist's responsibilities are as follows: 1) plan, direct, and conduct habilitative and rehabilitative treatment programs to establish and promote communicative efficiency in individuals with communication problems arising from neurological disturbances or defective articulation; 2) provide counseling and guidance to speech- and language-handicapped individuals and their families; 3) provide consultant services to educational, medical, and other professional groups; and 4) teach scientific principles of human communication in educational institutions, direct scientific projects, or conduct research in the areas of voice, speech, and language. 2. For Medicare purposes, a person who is licensed, if applicable, by the state in which practicing and eligible for a certificate of clinical competence in the appropriate area granted by the American Speech and Hearing Association or meets the educational requirements for certification and is in the process of accumulating hours of supervised experience required for certification. 3. A person licensed as such by the state board of Medical Quality Assurance or a person who has a masters degree in the field and is authorized to practice under the supervision of a licensed speech pathologist (Title 22, California).

speech pathology 1. A medically related discipline that evaluates, diagnoses, and provides therapy to patients with speech and language disorders. 2. Clinical therapeutic services for speech and language disorders provided for patients on either an inpatient or an outpatient basis by qualified personnel trained in speech therapy methods and techniques. *See speech screening.*

speech pathology and audiology An educational

program that presents the nature and treatment of hearing and speech disorders, including the principles and techniques of providing therapy to restore functioning to its potential level.

speech pathology services An administrative and therapy unit found in major health-care facilities that provides diagnosis, assessment, evaluation, and therapy for individuals with language and speech disorders.

speech screening According to JCAHO for psychiatric, alcoholism, and drug abuse facilities accreditation purposes, a process of testing articulation in connected speech and formal testing situations; voice in terms of judgments of pitch, intensity, and quality and determinations of appropriate vocal hygiene and fluency, usually measured in terms of frequency and severity of stuttering or dysfluency (based on evaluation of speech flow, sequence, duration, rhythm, rate, and fluency).

speech therapist A person trained to aid persons with speech and language disorders by evaluating, diagnosing, and providing therapy to patients to restore or help retain the ability to speak and use language.

speech therapy The study, evaluation, assessment, examination, treatment, and therapeutic intervention of defects and diseases of the voice, speech, and spoken and written language as well as the use of appropriate substitutional devices and treatment. *See also speech pathologist.*

speech therapy services A program or unit of a health-care organization or agency administered and operated for the purpose of evaluation, assessment, diagnosis, and treatment of inpatients or outpatients with speech and language disorders by licensed professionals who have at least a masters degree in the field of speech pathology and are authorized to practice under the supervision of a licensed speech pathologist.

spell of illness 1. A single disease event. 2. The full course of the disease, including all signs, symptoms, effects, and manifestations of the disease from onset to recovery; running the full course and duration of disease, including any medical care, hospitalization, treatment, or other remediation of the effects of the disease. 3. In Medicare, the benefit period during which Part A hospital insurance benefits are available. A benefit period begins the first time an insured person enters a hospital after his or her hospital insurance begins. It ends after he or she has not been an inpatient in a hospital or skilled nursing facility for 60 days in a row. During each benefit period, the insured individual is entitled to up to 90 days of inpatient hospital care, 100 days in a skilled nursing facility, and an unlimited number of home health visits. An additional lifetime reserve of 60 hospital days may be drawn on when more than 90 days of hospital care are needed in a benefit period. There is no limit to the number of benefit periods an insured person may have. The spell of illness concept means that the program may pay for more than 90 days in a hospital in a given year because, with a new spell of illness, the benefit becomes available again. Additionally, under Medicare the deductible is tied to each spell of illness. Thus, an individual who is hospitalized three times in a year, each in a separate spell of illness, has to pay the deductible of the cost of an inpatient hospital day three times. 4. In managed care and medical insurance under some health plans, this is the time period that begins with the first day of hospitalization or admission to a nursing home and ends when the patient has gone 60 days without being readmitted to either type of health-care facility. This time period that constitutes a benefit period is broken by varying periods of time with indemnity and dread disease coverage. *See benefit period.*

spell of sickness *See spell of illness.*

spendable income Revenue, after taxes and expenses, that can be used or spent.

spend-down Under Medicaid or other governmental social welfare programs, this is a method by which an individual establishes eligibility for the medical care program by reducing gross income through incurring medical expenses until net income (after medical expenses) becomes low enough to make him or her eligible for the program. The individual, in effect, spends income down to a specified eligibility standard by paying for medical care until bills become high enough in relation to income to allow him or her to qualify under the program's standard of being needy, at which point the program benefits begin. The spend-down is the same as a sliding-scale deductible related to the overall income level of the individual. For example, persons are eligible for program benefits if their income is $200 per month or less, a person with an income of $300 per month would be covered after spending $100 out of pocket on medical care, and a person with an income of $350 would not be eligible until medical expenses of $150 are incurred. The term "spend-down" originated in the Medicaid program. An individual whose income makes him or her ineligible for welfare but is still insufficient to pay for medical care can become Medicaid eligible as a medically needy individual by spending some income on medical care. Medicaid covers an individual only if that person is aged, blind, or disabled or a member of a family where one parent is absent, incapacitated, or unemployed, that is, fitting one of the categories of individuals who are covered under the welfare cash payment programs. *See medically indigent; poverty.*

spent material In environmental health or infection control in medical care, this is any material that has been used and, as a result of contamination, can no longer serve the purpose for which it was produced.

sphygmocardiograph In medical care, this is a device used to record a continuous heartbeat via a person's pulse, which is then recorded on a moving graph or oscilloscope.

sphygmograph In medical care, this is a device used to record a continuous pulse of an artery and displaying its strength and rate.

sphygmomanometer In medical care, this is an instrument used to measure blood pressure.

sphygmophone In medical care, this is an instrument used to record activity of the heart using amplified sound waves played through a set of earphones or a speaker.

sphygmoscope In medical care, this is an instrument used for showing the activity of the heart as displayed on an oscilloscope.

spiked samples In environmental health or medical care laboratory activities, this is when a known amount of some unusual substance or substance of planned interest is added to a normal sample of material (gas, liquid, or solid). This is done to check on the performance of a routine analysis or the recovery efficiency of an analytical method.

spill area In environmental health and hazardous material management, this is the area of soil on which visible traces of a spill can be observed, plus 1 foot beyond the visible traces. Any surface or object such as a concrete sidewalk or automobile within the visible trace area or on which visible traces are observed is included in the spill area. This area represents the minimum area assumed to be contaminated by substances such as PCBs in the absence of pre-cleanup sampling data and is thus the minimum area that must be cleaned.

spill boundaries In environmental health and hazardous material management, this is the actual area of contamination as determined by postcleanup sampling to determine actual spill boundaries. The EPA can require additional cleanup when necessary to decontaminate all areas with the spill boundaries to the levels required by regulation.

spills In environmental health and hazardous material management, this includes both intentional and unintentional leaks, spillage, accidents, puncture of tanks or tankers, and uncontrolled discharges where the release results in any quantity of hazardous substances (e.g., PCBs) running off or about to run off the external surface as well as the contamination resulting from any releases.

spin density Synonymous with "nuclear magnetic resonance imaging."

spin-offs In health-care organization and health services delivery, these are administrative units, programs, or services that are separate operating entities that have broken off of the main organization and now operate as self-sufficient and freestanding operations. The originating health-care organization is the primary customer and offers the same services to other organizations or the public.

spiral bandage In first aid, emergency care, or medical care, this is a method of applying a bandage to parts of the body's extremities, usually around joints. The bandage or gauze wrapped around the leg or arm may be twisted a half-turn and overlapped slightly on each wrap to hold a dressing or splint in place.

spiral reverse bandage A bandage applied to extremities of the body to hold dressings in place. Because the limbs are tapered, the bandage is given a half-turn with each wrap to keep it tight.

spirogram In medical care, this is the record, made by a spirograph, of the response to what is being monitored by the machine (e.g., respirations).

spirograph In medical care, this is a device used to record respiration on a graph.

spirometer In medical care and the assessment of lung function, this is device for measuring the volume of air inhaled and exhaled.

spirometry In medical care and the assessment of lung function, this is the measurement of pulmonary capacities.

splint In first aid, emergency care, or medical care, this is a special rigid support attached to a broken or sprained limb to maintain or immobilize a joint, body part, or limb.

split-dollar insurance In managed care, medical insurance, or life insurance, this is an insurance plan in which the employer, as owner of the policy, can name the employees of his or her organization as beneficiaries of the policy with both the employer and the worker paying part of the premium. If an employee dies, the employer receives an amount of the proceeds equal to any cash value of the policy, and the beneficiaries receive any benefits as set forth in the policy.

split-half reliability In epidemiology or health services research, this is a measure of internal consistency of a test, questionnaire, or other research tool based on the strength of the statistical correlation of scores between two halves of the test, questionnaire, or measure when compared in a series of tests and retests.

SPN *See senior plan network.*

spoliation In health law, this is the intentional destruction or mutilation by a third party or an outsider (e.g., the failure of one side of a dispute to come forward with evidence); intentional change or mutilation by an unauthorized party.

sponge 1. Any absorbent pad used in hospitals or surgical operations. 2. A porous, absorbent cloth or other substance such as a pad of gauze or cotton surrounded by gauze used in medical care to absorb fluids such as blood during surgery or to clean wounds caused by injury.

sponge, gelatin absorbable In medical care, this is a sterile, absorbable, water-insoluble, gelatin-based material used in the control of bleeding.

sponsor 1. In managed care, this is a subscriber to a prepaid health-care plan who has dependent beneficiaries. 2. In health administration and human resource management, this is a mentor or administrator who creates or assists in the career development and advancement of another. 3. A large medical supplier or organization that participates in a health-care conference by supplying money and getting market recognition and advertising in return for support; an organization that puts up money to support an effort or a cause.

sponsored malpractice insurance A malpractice insurance plan that involves an agreement by a professional society (e.g., a state medical society) to sponsor a particular insurer's medical malpractice insurance coverage and to cooperate with the insurer in the administration of the coverage. The cooperation may include participation in marketing, claims review, and review of rate making. These have been replaced by professional society–operated plans, joint underwriting associations, state insurance funds, and other arrangements.

sponsors Under proposed universal coverage plans, these are large employers, the government as an employer, and health alliances (Health Plan Stores, or HeLPS) that would all act as sponsors to facilitate personal choice of health plans. They would provide information and incentives for individuals to choose among accountable health plans (AHPs), which are the health-care providers. They would pool risk and achieve economies of scale in purchasing and set rules to ensure equitable coverage of members of the sponsored groups (Jackson Hole Group).

spontaneous combustible materials In environmental health and hazardous material handling, these are any solid waste substances such as a sludges or pastes that may undergo spontaneous heating or self-ignition under conditions normally incident to transportation of such substances or conditions that may undergo an increase in temperature and ignite on contact with the atmosphere.

spontaneous emission In laser technology, this is the natural transition of an atom from a high energy level to a low energy level that emits a photon of light.

spooling In health information management and computers, a technique where slow input and output devices place information on mass storage devices to await processing.

sporadic Irregular occurrences; from time to time; occasionally happening; haphazard appearances; infrequent and unpredictable medical or health events or appearance of a disease.

sporadic disease In epidemiology, this is a disease that occurs in occasional scattered cases.

spore A destruction-resistant body formed by certain microorganisms; resistant cells.

sports medicine A medical specialty in which the physician conducts diagnosis, screening, evaluation, therapy, treatment, and clinic services for the prevention and treatment of injuries in patients resulting from participation in sports, athletic events, or related activities.

sports medicine clinic services Specialized medical care services that provide for the diagnosis, screening, evaluation, therapy, rehabilitation, treatment, and habilitative clinic services for the prevention and treatment of injuries resulting from participation in sports, athletic events, or related activities.

spot map In epidemiology, this is a tool used to identify an element of "place" in an epidemiological investigation. This is used to identify the general physical location of a disease outbreak, exposure, or disease event. A spot map is more generalized than a dot map. The dot map is used to pinpoint the location of each and every case occurrence, whereas a spot map shows a more general area. The use of maps in epidemiology has been common practice since historical times and is an aid in localizing and identifying an epidemic. Geographical and physical barriers can be seen, localization of the outbreak can be observed, and identification where the disease occurrence is and where it is not are seen from plotting spots on a map or locating cases in a dot map. The epidemiologist assumes that risk of exposure is evenly distributed in a population, as are susceptibles. Thus, when high levels of cases occur in selected areas, inferences can be made concerning causation, source of exposure, and high-risk areas.

spot zoning In planning and zoning, this is where zoning regulations are applied to certain areas or property, whereas surrounding land is allowed a different zoning. Sometimes, special changes or spot zoning is allowed for special purposes such as allowing a nursing home or a freestanding emergency medical clinic to be built in a residential area.

spousal abuse The physical, verbal, emotional, or mental attack of a husband or wife by his or her spouse in enough intensity, repetition, and duration to cause physical or emotional harm; to be physically attacked, harmed or injured by one's spouse; to be verbally attacked over and over by one's spouse over a period of time and on a continual basis. The definition of spousal abuse is vague and difficult to define because the totality of the circumstance has to be considered, as does the usual routine of the interactions in a relationship. What is a verbal spat to one person (e.g., verbal encounters) may be more emotionally devastating to another person. Level, intensity, duration, and repeated and continual occurrence all need to be considered. Physical abuse is more obvious and less tolerated, although verbal abuse is also emotionally and mentally crippling.

spouse One's legally married companion; one's partner or companion in marriage; one's legal husband if a female and one's legal wife if a male.

squeal law In health law, this is a statute passed in some states that mandates that any family planning organization or agency must report to parents if a minor is provided with family planning services or counseling. Also called the "squeal rule."

SQUIMP A computer software program code used to analyze Probabilistic Risk Assessment (PRA) information. Developed at the Idaho National Engineering Laboratory near Idaho Falls, Idaho.

SSA *See Social Security Administration.*

SSI *See supplemental security income.*

SSP *See state supplemental payments.*

ST Surgical technician/technologist.

stability reliability In health services or biomedical research, this describes a method of establishing questionnaire or test reliability on the basis of the correlations of scores on exactly the same measurement instrument taken on the same population at two or more different points in time, pairing up each testing situation to the others by subject, to establish the repeatability and thus reliability of the test or questionnaire.

stabilization 1. In medical care, this is to bring a sick, injured, drugged, anesthetized, surgically wounded, or mentally or emotionally distressed patient back to mental and physical homeostasis through allowing the effects of the substances to pass or counting them with additional medications and allowing time to pass, thus returning the body to its normal functioning and state. 2. In environmental health and liquid waste management, this is the conversion of the active organic matter in sludge into inert, harmless material (EPA).

stabilization ponds In environmental health and liquid waste management, these are shallow ponds of water where sunlight, bacterial action, and oxygen work to purify wastewater; also used for the storage of wastewaters or spent nuclear fuel rods.

stable air In environmental health and air pollution, this is a mass of unmoving air caused by a high-pressure weather system so that it holds rather than disperses pollutants. This is often accompanied by a thermal inversion, where a layer of cooler air holds the warmer air in.

stable population In epidemiology, public health, and health-care delivery, this is an assessment of the growth rates of a community and the population distributed across the various age-groups in the population. If each age-group has a low death rate caused by a low disease rate and has a constant and predictable birth rate and if immigration and migration are low and the population remains constant over time, the population is considered stable.

stab wound In emergency and medical care, this is a puncture wound caused by a sharp instrument such as a knife.

stack effect In environmental health and air pollution, this is when smoke, steam, or pollutants rise in an upward plume, as in a chimney, because they are warmer than the surrounding atmosphere.

stack gases In environmental health and air pollution, this is the air coming out of a chimney after being vented from the burner during combustion. The air contains nitrogen, oxides, carbon oxides, water vapor, sulfur oxides, particulate matter, particles, sometimes soot, and many other chemical pollutants.

stacks In environmental health and air pollution, these are large chimneys or smokestacks or other vertical pipes or brick smokestacks that discharge used air and smoke; a source point of air pollution for a plant, factory, or facility that is designed to emit smoke, solids, liquids, and gases into the air and is made up of a pipe or ducts but not including flares (EPA).

staff In hospital administration, this is a position of authority (not function), and staff authority is not inferior to line authority or vice versa. Staff is auxiliary and can only make recommendations to line, line authority being a superior/subordinate relationship in direct line of authority. Staff are usually experts in a specialty and support area and provide advice to line managers and personnel. Line and staff concepts are confusing and have been used in different contexts in different organizations. In some large organizations, "line" refers to the workers doing the labor and "staff" to those in supervisor and management positions.

staff authority In health administration and human resources management, this is the right to advise and direct work but not necessarily direct other employees as a member of staff; having no positional authority; in direct authority over personnel in other departments; the requirement to consult with staff units, who must concur with a decision before action can be taken.

staff development 1. In health administration, this is the ongoing training, skill development, and education of the organization's employees, usually done in-house though the department of staff development, to ensure high levels of quality in the organization's personnel; to help them keep current in the latest knowledge and techniques, and to provide for advanced learning and continuing education, ensuring continued growth and development of the health-care organization's personnel at all levels. 2. Under Medicare, an ongoing educational program that is conducted for the development and improvement of skills of all the facility's personnel, including training related to problems and needs of the aged, ill, and disabled. Employees receive appropriate orientation to the facility and its policies and to their position and duties. In-service training includes, at least, prevention and control of infections, fire prevention and safety, accident prevention, confidentiality of patient information, and preservation of patient dignity, including protection of privacy and personal and property rights. Records of training that indicate the content of, and attendance at, such staff development programs are to be maintained.

staff, hospital In hospital administration, these are the full-time regular employees of a hospital; often excludes physicians on the medical staff. *See medical staff.*

staffing In health administration, this is one of the several functions of a manager where the administrator tries to translate work objectives into the kind of service and care the health-care organization wishes to provide. Responsibility for recruiting and the proper use of the personnel in the organization fall on the manager. Many of the managerial activities of staffing include the efficient and effective supervising and directing of employees in the proper use of time, tasks, resources, and personnel while setting realistic yet high levels of productivity, assigning appropriate work, encouraging quality of output, scheduling work, and maximizing talent and skills of the workers. *See line staff; functions of a manager.*

staffing according to varying patient needs (nursing) In the delivery of medical care and nursing services, one approach of classifying patients into three levels according to their level of severity. Type I patients are self-care, type II intermediate care, and type III critical or intensive care. In hospitals it is assumed that patient types are evenly distributed for staffing reasons, and adjustments are made according to how the patient types deviate from the mean in either severity or minimum care levels. Pool nursing is also used because adjustments can easily and quickly be made to accommodate severity or minimum care levels.

staffing grants Money granted to a health-care institution or agency for the hiring or support of members to staff a project or department.

staffing, nursing In hospitals, nursing homes, and other health-care facilities, this is an attempt by health-care administrators to translate organization, work, and patient care objectives into the quality and type of nursing care the health-care organization wishes to provide in nursing areas. Nursing care staffing has unique factors to consider such as the number of patients on a unit, the level of intensiveness of care or minimal care needed for each patient, and the nursing activities required in each unit or area. Nurse administrators staff each specialty unit separately according to need and intensive levels of care needed and are responsible for keeping work data on each unit on a 24-hour basis, determining time frames needed for each task or activity such as evaluation, nursing assessments, patient care planning, work activity planning, patient teaching and counseling, shift changes, communication with physicians, and paperwork time. Nurse administrators also determine levels of personnel needed for various chores done by nursing assistants, LVNs, and RNs. Patient days per year per patient unit should be kept, as should total nursing hours per year per unit. Continuing education, training, in-service education, committee work, orientation and training, student clinical nurse training, participation in research and outcomes studies, and other activities also need to be accounted and planned for in staffing.

staffing patterns Under Medicare, a facility furnishes to the state survey agency information from payroll records setting forth the average numbers and types of personnel (in full-time equivalents) on each tour of duty during at least 1 week of each quarter. The week to be evaluated is selected by the survey agency.

staffing ratio The total number of employees in a health-care facility or total numbers of employees on a unit who are full-time equivalents divided by the average daily census of the facility or the unit; the total number of hospital employees (FTEs) divided by the average daily census. The staffing ratio formula follows:

$$\frac{\text{Total number of employees (FTEs)}}{\text{Average daily census}}$$

staffing ratio, nursing The total number of nursing staff needed on duty at any given time on a daily basis is determined by comparing the number of hours of care per patient multiplied by the number of clients divided by the hours worked per employee. The formula for nursing staffing ratio follows:

$$\frac{\text{Hours of care/patient} \times \text{Number of patients}}{\text{Hours worked/employee}}$$

staffing table In health administration and human resource management, this is a grid or table listing anticipated employment openings for each position, job, or department in a health-care organization.

staff, medical *See medical staff.*

staff mix accounting In hospital administration and nursing administration, this is the process of budgeting and staffing for the most efficient and effective patient care levels of a nursing unit. One approach includes the following: 1) determining the total number of nursing FTEs; 2) determining gross salaries for each category of nursing employee classification; 3) adding salaries of all positions (ward clerks, nursing assistants, etc.) to the total of the unit's basic labor expenses of the nursing unit; 4) multiplying the unit's basic labor costs by the percentage of employee benefits costs; 5) computing, shift by shift, numbers, mix, salaries, and differentials (accounting for each shift, night differentials, and other related expenses); and 6) summarizing FTEs and adding in differentials.

staff-model HMO In managed care, this is an organizational approach where the health maintenance organization (HMO) employs its own physicians to provide medical care to all its members. It is very much like a medical group model except the doctors work directly for the HMO. All premiums and other revenues accrue to the HMO, which in turn compensates physicians by salary and incentive programs. Generally, all outpatient and ambulatory medical care services are provided in a single clinic setting under the staff model.

staff nurse An LPN or RN who provides usual nursing care services to patients in a health-care facility or agency under the direction of a physician.

staff privileges The privilege of joining the hospital's medical staff granted by a hospital or other inpatient health facility to a physician or other independent medical care practitioner. A practitioner is usually granted staff privileges after meeting certain standards, being accepted by the medical staff and board of trustees of the hospital, and committing him- or herself to carry out certain duties for the hospital such as teaching without pay, serving on committees, or providing emergency or clinic services. It is common for a physician to have staff privileges at more than one hospital. On the other hand, because hospitals accept a limited number of physicians, some practitioners can be excluded and end up with no access to hospital facilities and no staff privileges. The standards used to determine staff privileges sometimes include evaluation by the county medical society, which may give preference to or require membership in that society, which in turn may require membership in the American Medical Association, which formally opposes this practice. Some hospitals limit privileges for certain services to board-eligible or board-certified physicians. Full-time or hospital-based physicians, as well as physicians working in a system such as a prepaid group practice with its own hospital, are not usually thought of as having staff privileges. Many hospitals have several different levels of staff privileges with names like active, associate, courtesy, or limited. Sometimes, staff privileges are called admitting, hospital, practice, or clinical privileges. Open staffing is the process of taking all types of specialties, whereas closed staffing is the process of accepting only specialties that administration believes are needed to enhance the quality and range of care and services offered by the hospital.

staff referral In health administration and human resource management, this is when a current employee is suggested to human resources as a candidate for a new job or a promotion from within the company.

staff units In health administration and human resource management, these are departments, services, or programs in large organizations that provide technical and support activities for the workers involved in direct patient care and treatment. Departments, services, or programs that indirectly contribute to the productivity of the health-care organization through support, tasks, services, materials, and equipment such as accounting, maintenance, supplies, information management systems, and human resources.

stage of disease In epidemiology or medical care, this refers to how far into the course of the disease the case or patient is (e.g., acute stage or chronic stage). Stage identification is used in diagnosis, treatment protocol, prognosis, prevention, and control.

staging In medical care, this is ascertaining how far into the course of a disease a patient is as an estimate and measure of severity of the disease. Different phases of a disease are identified and placed in a stage. Some diseases pass through several stages, and each stage dictates different treatment approaches and protocol. By identifying a patient's level of severity, he or she can be placed in the stage of the disease. This process is called "staging."

stagnation In environmental health and pollution, this is the lack of motion in a mass of water or air, causing it to hold pollutants.

stakeholder 1. In health law, this is a noninvolved party who is selected to hold funds in dispute with the understanding that he or she will turn the goods over once the matter is settled. 2. In health administration, these are all parties that have an interest in, a reliance on, or a concern for or who have a financial interest in or are otherwise tied to the health-care organization; those with a vested interest in the well-being of an organization or community; exchange partners whose power, influence, and views are of enough importance to affect a health-care organization's operation and success; those with a stake in the outcome and thus an interest in the organization's continued success.

stale check In health-care financial management, this is a check or negotiable instrument that has been held beyond its time limit. The time period to cash a check is set by law or is written on the check.

stand-alone computers In health-care information management, these are all desktop, laptop, or personal computers that are not required to be connected to a mainframe computer, even though most personal computers may be connected as needed or on a permanent basis.

standard 1. A professionally developed expression of the range of acceptable variation of performance from a norm or criterion. 2. The value assigned to a particular criterion when measuring health service characteristics. 3. A measure of quantity, quality, weight, extent, or value that is set up as a rule by authority. 4. A statement of expectation that defines the structures and processes that must be substantially in place in an organization to enhance the quality of care (JCAHO).

Standard and Poors In health-care finance, this is a national financial rating organization and system that includes hospitals and managed-care and other health-care organizations in their rating activities. Hospitals and health-care organizations are rated as to their outstanding debt and credit risk, thus affecting the ability of the health-care organization to secure loans and borrow money.

standard benefits In a proposed universal coverage medical care system, this benefit package would provide transportable insurance that would not be tied to employment and would offer coverage for all. Standard benefits would provide a basis for defining universally available services and put governmental and private health plans on the same plane, have side-by-side coverage of health plans, have standardized claim forms and requirements, be insulated from political interference, and be based on scientific documentation, including cost-effectiveness (Jackson Hole Group).

standard class rate (SCR) In managed care and medical care insurance, this is used to determine monthly premium rates by using a base revenue requirement per member or per employee multiplied by certain group demographic information to calculate the monthly rates.

standard deviation In statistics, this is a measure of variation derived by squaring each deviation in a set of scores, taking the average of these squares and taking the square root of the result. The standard deviation, represented by the Greek letter sigma, is one of the most useful measures of variation in statistical computations. In central tendency measures, this is used to show how far certain data points are from the average (mean); the square root of the average of the squares of the deviations from the mean.

standard error In statistics, this is a measure used to determine how much variation exists in test results and how much is caused by chance and error. It also shows how much is caused by experimental influences. The standard error of the mean is arrived at by dividing the standard deviation by the square root of the numbers of measures or, when the number of measures is less than 30, by the square root minus 1.

standard industry code In managed care and medical care insurance, this is a code used to identify the type of industry that an employer group represents such as hospital, banking, insurance, university, manufacturing, and retail.

standardization 1. A common minimum baseline established as an acceptable level of performance or quality; averaging, weighting, and comparing traits, factors, and elements to create a common ground or baseline. 2. In epidemiology, this is comparing specific rates to crude rates to get a feel for what is normal or average; averaging the findings of specific rates of two or more study populations and comparing them to the distribution of a known standard. 3. In testing, this is to use a test or other measure over and over until a very large baseline of data is available so that new testing occurrences can be compared to the baseline data.

standardization of tests In epidemiology and health services research, this shows that a test has been used over a long period of time and has had widespread use, the cutoff levels/values have been well established, and the test has a proven track record over time with normative data. *See sensitivity; specificity; screening.*

standardized mortality ratio (SMR) In epidemiology, this is an age-adjusted ratio and is the process of comparing the total death occurrences in a certain population to that of the total population of expected deaths, often for a certain age-group. Thus, this is the ratio of the number of deaths in a population compared to the number of deaths expected for that age-group. Selected age-groups, occupations, causes, education, religion, race, or other factors can be the focus of the SMR, making it a specific mortality ratio. Some epidemiologists state that the SMR should be expressed as a percentage of the number of observed deaths compared to the deaths that might have been expected to occur in a given population on the basis of past data and experience based on the rate of a standard population. (If results are shown as a percentage, this is no longer a ratio, making it a mortality percentage.) The formula for the standardized mortality ratio follows:

$$\frac{\text{Number of deaths in a population in 1 year}}{\text{Number of deaths expected in an average year}}$$

standardized rate ratio In epidemiology, this is when the numerator and denominator rates are compared to and are reflective of the standard distribution of the same population. This is a ratio of two or more rates and is expressed as a ratio. *See rate ratio.*

standard job performance In health administration and human resource management, this the process and steps for teaching the most systematic way to do a critical job consistently with maximum efficiency.

standard metropolitan statistical area (SMSA) This is used to determine if a community is urban or rural or if a hospital in a certain location is to be determined a rural hospital or an urban hospital. An SMSA is a county or group of contiguous counties containing one or more cities with populations of at least 50,000 or twin cities with a combined population of 50,000 or more. Contiguous counties are included if they are essentially metropolitan in character and are socially and economically integrated with a central city. In New England, towns and cities are used rather than counties in defining SMSAs (U.S. Office of Management and Budget). This is based on the most current census information. The OMB replaced SMSAs with metropolitan statistical areas. *See metropolitan statistical area.*

standard of care 1. In tort law, these are the skills and education commonly possessed by members of a chosen profession that are needed and expected to exist for them to deliver an expected level of care. 2. In health law, this is reasonable and ordinary care, skill, and diligence that ordinary and prudent health-care providers and professionals in good standing should exercise in like or similar cases or situations. This definition is used to include locality or community rules. That is, the health-care provider would be expected to deliver the usual level of care given in that locality or community. The reasonableness (reasonable man) concept and the principle of foreseeability are closely aligned with the standard of care. *See foreseeability; reasonableness; scope of practice; cause of action.*

standard of performance In environmental health and air pollution control, this is a requirement of continuous emission reduction, including any requirement relating to the operation or maintenance of a source to ensure continuous emission control; restrictions on the quantities, rates, and concentrations of chemical, physical, and biological or other constituents that are discharged from new sources into bodies of water.

standard of reasonableness The expected level at which prudent individuals are to act under certain circumstances. *See also reasonableness; reasonable man.*

standard operating procedure (SOP) Formal written procedures officially adopted by a large organization as the usual way of doing things; the routine basis for carrying out work, policy, and procedures.

standard pressure The international standard barometric pressure is 29.92 inches of mercury, or a temperature of 760 mm Hg.

standard rates *See rates, adjusted or standardized.*

standard risk class In managed care or insurance, these are average individuals who have a normal life expectancy and pay usual or standard insurance premiums with most clientele falling into the standard risk class.

standards 1. Generally, a measure set by competent authority as the rule for measuring quantity or quality; a minimum acceptable level of performance, effectiveness, efficiency, quality, or outcomes. 2. In health-care delivery, conformity with standards is usually a condition of licensure, accreditation, or payment for services. Standards may be defined in relation to the actual or predicted effects of care; the performance or credentials of professional personnel, and the physical plant, governance, and administration of facilities and programs. In the PRO program, standards are professionally developed expressions of the range of acceptable variation from a norm or criterion. Thus, the criteria for care of a urinary tract infection might be a urinalysis and urine culture, and the standard might require a urinalysis in 100% of cases and a urine culture only in previously untreated cases. 3. In environmental health, these are physical references used as a basis for comparison or calibration; concepts established by authority, custom, or agreement to serve as a rule to compare against in the measure of quality or the establishment of a practice or procedure.

standards compliance summary report In accreditation activities, under JCAHO, this is a written review of scores, findings, and results of the accreditation survey.

standards-developing groups Committees, subcommittees, boards, or other principal subdivisions of the health services organization that develop, revise, and review standards that are accepted as formal procedures and levels of quality performance for the organization.

standards information management system Computer and software systems that provide access to databases that have preestablished baselines and levels of quality for comparison.

standards manuals Under JCAHO accreditation, five books are used to delineate current standards pertaining to specified types of health care organizations. The books are designed for use in organization self-assessment and are the basis for the survey report forms used by the JCAHO surveyors during on-site surveys. The five manuals are *Accreditation Manual for Hospitals; Accreditation Manual for Ambulatory Health Care; Accreditation Manual for Mental Health, Chemical Dependency, and Mental Retardation/Developmental Disabilities Services; Accreditation Manual for Long Term Care;* and *Accreditation Manual for Home Care.*

standards of participation Under the Medicaid program, this is the criteria of eligibility for participation as set forth in regulation 42 DFR 442.300, in which a state survey agency determines whether an intermediate care facility is eligible to participate in the Medicaid program. Each standard has many subparts, called "elements," that also must be met.

standard survey In long-term care, this a semiannual inspection of nursing homes or convalescent hospitals based on a review of the facility's past performance with concern given to key indicators and interviews using a random sample of residents.

standard temperature The international standard temperature is 69°F or 20°C.

standard wipe test In environmental health and hazardous waste, this is the test for PCBs on solid surfaces using a cleanup to numerical surface standards and sampling by a standard wipe test to verify that the numerical standards are met. The protocol is to use a standard 10 × 10 centimeter template to delineate the area of the test. The wiping medium is a gauze or glass wool pad that has been saturated with hexane, which is stored in sealed glass vials until it is used for the wipe test.

standby commitment In health-care finance, this is a commitment to issue a loan, usually for a period of 1 to 5 years once construction is completed, in the event a regular permanent loan cannot be obtained. This type of loan is usually extended at a higher interest rate than a permanent loan, and a standby fee is charged.

standing In health law, this is the right to bring a lawsuit because the party involved is directly affected by the issues being disputed in the case.

standing committee In health administration, this is a group of individuals brought together to manage certain administrative or business activities under its responsibility for a continuous period, usually lasting the same amount of time as the term of the officers directing the main body or board.

standing orders In medical care, these are written directives that are used or intended to be used in the absence of a health-care provider's physical presence or prescriber's specific order for a specific patient.

standing rules In formal health-care meetings, these are the policies and protocol of the way things are usually done by that committee or board of directors; may also refer to the regular time and place of meetings.

standing to sue In health law, this is where a party has enough cause or enough personal interest in a matter to cause him or her to seek relief through the courts and a lawsuit.

stand mute In law, this is a refusal to plead guilty or not guilty. In the United States, where one is supposed to be innocent until proven guilty, such a stand is often treated as a not-guilty plea; similar to using the Fifth Amendment of the U. S. Constitution to refuse to plead guilty to avoid self-incrimination.

Stanford-Binet intelligence test (scale) A verbal psychological test administered individually to children and adults to test levels of intelligence. *See also IQ; mental age.*

stare decisis (Lat.) 1. Let the decision stand. 2. In law, this is to stand by previous decisions; judge-made law; case law precedents; a doctrine involved with precedent in deciding cases. A court should stick to a sound legal principle created by a previous decision and apply it to all future cases with similar facts unless there is a strong reason not to.

start-up costs In health-care financial management and in planning and program development, these are nonrecurring expenses, including initial planning, marketing, purchase of equipment, construction, remodeling, lease or rent of facilities, supplies, and other capital outlays needed to initiate a new service, program, or project.

stat 1. In health administration and medical care delivery, this is used in a hospital crisis or emergency, meaning "at once"; to respond immediately. 2. In managed-care administration, this is when a certain medical service or intervention requires prompt attention, which may require the patient to bypass the health plan's normal appointment and referral system and review. This usually refers to emergency and treatment outside regular business hours where delays would either be inappropriate or put the patient's life or health in jeopardy.

state 1. To say. 2. To set forth. 3. To declare. 4. A condition or situation. 5. Governmental, legislative, or administrative entities of state government.

state agencies Any governmental administrative entity such as a department, division, board, commission, or center at the state government level that has the legal, statutory, and regulatory responsibility for the oversight and management of official health-related programs for the state.

state approved In nursing, law, and some other professions, the state board of examiners or licensure will approve educational training programs by accepting their graduates for licensure in the state but may not be a nationally accredited program. For example, in some states the state board of nursing examiners will approve a college degree program as eligible to have their graduates sit for the licensing exam and, on passing, be licensed as a registered nurse in the state with the program not accredited by the National League of Nursing and no reciprocity to another state.

state board of medical examiners A state government agency established by the statutes of the state to administer licensure of physicians and oversee the ethical and professional activities of physicians licensed to practice medicine in the state. The board also serves in a peer review role and quality control function and can conduct investigations, restrict practice activities, impose sanctions and punishments, or remove physicians' licenses on violation of the medical practice act or because of unethical behavior or practices. The board reviews the credentials, degrees, and training of physicians who apply for licensure; administers the examinations for licensure; approves or denies licensure; and disciplines or removes licenses as required.

State Comprehensive Health Planning Agency A former health planning agency assisted under Section 314(a) of the PHS Act and added by P.L. 89-749, the Comprehensive Health Planning and Public Health Service Amendments of 1966. The agencies were to develop state comprehensive health planning programs with the assistance of a health planning council broadly representative of the general public and private health organizations in the state with a majority of consumers among its members. Public Law 89-749 was superseded by P.L. 93-641, the National Health Planning and Resources Development Act of 1974, which authorized, at the time, assistance for state health planning and development agencies to replace 314(a) agencies. The new agencies prepared annual state health plans and medical facilities plans. The state agency also served as the designated Section 1122 review agency and administered the certificate-of-need program. Federally driven governmental health planning agencies ceased to exist in October 1986.

state cost commissions In some states, these were state agencies assigned for various health services cost and charge regulation or review responsibilities. The duties of the commission included ensuring that total hospital costs were reasonably related to total services offered, aggregate rates bore a reasonable relationship to aggregate costs, and rates were applied equitably to preclude any possibility of discriminatory pricing among various services and patients of a hospital. These commissions were tied closely to the federally mandated cost containment regulatory health systems agencies of the late 1970s and early 1980s that ceased operation in 1986.

state designated routes In environmental health and hazardous waste management, these are preferred routes selected in accordance with the U.S. Department of Transportation Guidelines for Selecting Preferred Highway Routes for Highway Route Controlled Quantities of Radioactive Materials or an equivalent routing analysis that adequately considers overall risk to the public in case of a mishap or accident.

state director The chief administrative officer of a state health agency.

state emergency response commission A policy- and action-oriented body appointed by the governor to meet the requirement of SARA Title III (Superfund Amendments and Reauthorization Act). Some of the responsibilities include designating emergency planning districts, appointing local emergency planning committees, and supervising and coordinating the statewide emergency response activities.

state employment security agency A state-level merit system employment service that announces jobs that are open in state and county agencies and solicits qualified applicants; also serves as the unemployment office and attempts to match available jobs with job seekers.

state/EPA agreements In environmental health, these are formal agreements between the regional Environmental Protection Agency administrator and the state-level environmental protection department to coordinate EPA and state activities, responsibilities, and programs.

state health agency (SHA) The state-level agency mandated and responsible for oversight and control of all state and local public health and health services activity in the state. The SHA is responsible for setting statewide public health priorities, carrying out national and state mandates, responding to public health hazards, preventing disease and controlling epidemiological activities, ensuring access to health care for underserved medically indigent state residents, and other related and appropriate public health and health services activities. Often the state agency bears a title such as the Department of Health Services, Department of Health and Welfare, or Department of Health and Human Services.

state health manpower plan A plan developed by the state health planning and development agency (SHPDA) that concerns itself with health manpower in the state. *See also state health planning and development agency.*

state health manpower priorities The ranking of the state's health manpower needs and concerns in order of importance.

State Health Plan (SHP) In the cost-containment era of 1974–76, under the control and administration of health systems agencies, these were a combination of the health systems plans for a state as modified by the statewide health coordinating council to represent its decisions as to broad strategic actions and health resource changes recommended over 5 years or more, plus recommendations for their implementation, to alter the future health system to attain explicitly stated goals. Such plans and planning activities ceased when the federally mandated health systems agencies were no longer funded. They folded in October 1986. Some states still produce a state health plan, but planning activities are focused at state and local governmental health agencies rather than all health services and health delivery entities in the state, usually done by the state health planning and development agency (SHPDA) for states that retained such an agency.

state health planning and development agency (SHPDA) Section 1521 of the PHS Act, added by the old P.L. 93-641, which formerly required the establishment of a state health planning and development agency in each state. These were a replacement for existing state CHP agencies. These agencies prepared an annual preliminary state health plan and the state medical facilities plan (Hill-Burton). The agency served as the designated review agency for purposes of Section 1122 of the Social Security Act and administered a certificate-of-need (CON) program. In 1986, when the federally mandated health systems agencies were no longer funded and closed, many SHPDAs also closed down or assumed a planning role for state agencies such as state public health departments or the state department of health services. Certificate of need is also still required in some states with both planning and CON usually administered by the state health planning and development agency (SHPDA) for states that retained such an agency. *See health systems agency; state health agency.*

state health priorities Under the former health systems agencies, the health needs and concerns of the population of the state were ranked according to importance and were subject to intervention by the state health planning and development agency and the health systems agency. Such priority setting, plans, and planning activities ceased when the federally mandated health systems agencies were no longer funded and then folded in October 1986. *See also priorities.*

state hospital A long-term-care psychiatric facility owned and operated by the state government to treat medically indigent mental patients and patients with extensive and extreme cases of mental pathology. Short-stay programs, outpatient treatment, drug and alcohol treatment units, and adolescent treatment units are operated at some state mental hospitals. Also referred to as "state mental hospital."

state implementation plans In environmental health, these are state-level approved plans for the establishment, regulation, and enforcement of air pollution standards based on Section 110 of the Clean Air Act. The act calls for 1) attainment and maintenance of primary ambient air quality standards within 3 years and secondary standards within a reasonable time thereafter, 2) emission standards that limit the quantity of pollutants that can be emitted from facilities or groups of facilities (these limits must at the very least be applicable to the criteria pollutants), and 3) procedures for reviewing the impact that a new source will have on existing and future air quality (EPA).

state long-term-care ombudsman In long-term care and gerontology, this is an appointed or hired professional investigator employed as an unbiased advocate to investigate and resolve complaints made by residents of nursing homes, convalescent hospitals, or other long-term-care facilities.

state medical board *See state board of medical examiners.*

state medical facilities plan (SMFP) Under the former health systems agencies and their regulatory processes, this was a document used to present the decisions reached by the state health planning and development agency. It had to be approved by the statewide health coordinating council, which specified the state requirements for medical facilities. Under Title XVI of the former P.L. 93-641, financial assistance was provided for medical facility construction, modernization, and conversion, depending on the priorities.

state mental hospital *See state hospital.*

statement of affairs In health-care financial management, a financial summary form that is used when filing for bankruptcy.

statement of changes in financial position In health-care financial management, this is a finance report that documents and presents all the health-care organization's sources of revenues and funds and shows how the revenue was used, spent, or applied to operations. Also referred to as a "cash flow statement" or "statement of sources and application of funds."

statement of changes in fund balances In health-care financial management, this is a finance report showing the beginning and ending total net profit or loss. It also reports nonoperating revenue, additions, and deductions that affected the changes in the profits or revenues.

statement of construction A JCAHO document that must be completed by each long-term-care facility prior to a survey. A properly completed statement of construction describes and verifies the basic structural and fire protection characteristics of each building in which patients or residents are housed. In addition, a plan of correction for all physical plant deficiencies identified by authorized inspection agencies or indicated in the JCAHO Statement of Construction and Fire Protection must be submitted.

statement of managers *See conference.*

statement of operations In health-care financial management, this is a finance report showing net profit; revenue and expense records that show a net profit or loss. Also referred to as a "statement of revenues and expenses."

statement of revenues and expenses *See statement of operations.*

statement of sources and application of funds *See statement of changes in financial position.*

state plan Under Medicaid, this a comprehensive written commitment by the state Medicaid agency to administer and supervise the Medicaid program for the state in compliance with federally mandated requirements.

state primary drinking water regulations In environmental health and safe drinking water management, these are drinking water regulations at the state level that are comparable to or more stringent than the national primary drinking water regulations.

state routing agencies In environmental health and hazardous waste management, these are state departments or divisions that are authorized to use the state legal process to impose routing requirements, enforceable by state agencies, on carriers of radioactive materials without regard to intrastate jurisdictional boundaries, including Indian tribes and their lands. A common agency of more than one state as established by interstate compact is also to be established and authorized to regulate hazardous waste traffic that crosses state lines.

state's evidence In law, this is evidence given by an accomplice to a crime as testimony against his or her partners in the crime. For immunity from prosecution a partner in crime testifies against his or her accomplices.

state supplemental payments (SSPs) In 1974, under Social Security, the Supplemental Social Security Income program went into effect, replacing local and state programs for the blind, disabled, and aged. When the state-level programs ended, and if the state program was paying higher monthly payments to its recipients than the new federal program, the state is required to make up the difference and not cause the recipient to experience a cut in payments. The difference is paid by the state and is called "state supplement payment."

state survey agency In health facility licensing and quality control, this is the state-level agency mandated and responsible for surveying and reviewing acute-care hospitals, nursing homes, psychiatric hospitals, home health agencies, and other health-care facilities or agencies to ensure quality and compliance with state-supported services as well as Medicaid and Medicare compliance.

statewide health coordinating council (SHCC) A former state-level council usually affiliated with the state department of health services. The council is made up of providers and consumers. Each SHCC was formed to supervise the state health planning and development agency and to review and coordinate the plans and budgets of the state's health agencies. It may prepare a state health plan. This council was formerly a part of and required by Section 1524 of the PHS Act and was added by P.L. 93-641. Many SHCCs folded when P.L. 93-641 was phased out in 1986, but some states retained them as advisory councils.

statewide issues or needs In health planning, these are concerns identified by entities of state government that are considered of statewide importance.

statim (Lat.) Immediate.

stationary sources *See sources, stationary.*

statistical error 1. In a research study and the analysis of its findings, several sources of errors can occur: computation, analytical approaches, sampling, bias, confounding variables, systemic, type I or type II, and faulty research design. 2. In assessing research and statistical results, two common errors are seen: type I and type II. Type I error is to reject a true hypothesis, and type II error is to accept a false hypothesis.

statistical inference In statistical analysis and presentation of the results and findings, this is the process of accepting or rejecting hypotheses, determining and stating the level of significance and confidence levels for accepting and rejecting hypotheses and findings, and the ability to extrapolate findings to the larger populations and to suggest cause-effect relationships and association.

statistical process control (SPC) In quality control management, this is a computerized system of statistical analysis of quality control centers, activities, charts, and process that are analyzed and used to improve quality of operations in health-care organizations; the use of statistical methods and techniques such as control charts to assess and evaluate outputs; an approach for analyzing factors related to unacceptable outcomes by measuring variation about the mean such as how many cases of readmissions for certain types of treatments occur and how to remedy the situation. Deviations from the norm or expected outcomes are identified so that corrective actions can be taken to maintain statistical control of the process and improve the process and its capability.

statistical quality control (SQC) In quality control management, this is a computerized system of statistical analysis used to measure deviations in outcomes.

statistical significance A statistical measure of reliability that shows that something occurs other than by chance. In statistics, this is a statement of levels of confidence of an occurrence such as a 95% level of confidence that the results of a research study did not occur by chance, or a .05 level of significance.

statistics 1. A body of methodologies, procedures, techniques, and mathematical manipulations dealing with the collection, organization, tabulation, analysis, interpretation, and presentation of findings and results stated in a numerical format. 2. Two major categories of statistics exist: inferential and descriptive. Inferential statistics are used most with empirical health services and biomedical research using interval and ratio scales and quantitative and parametric data. Descriptive statistics are used in epidemiology and consist of rates, ratios, percentages, proportion, central tendency, and related information as well as ordinal, nominal, interval, and ratio scales and qualitative and nonparametric data. 3. A collection of facts and information stated in numerical form, such as vital statistics, which is data on death, births, marriages, and divorces. 4. Calculated sets of data.

status 1. A condition. 2. The position, state, or basic standing of a person or situation or social order of things. 3. The condition of affairs. 4. The legal state of affairs.

status, health The state or level of a person or a population's well-being. *See health status; health status indicators.*

status of the health delivery system An assessment and description of the existing health delivery system and the structures utilized in the provision of health services to the residents of the state.

status value An assessment of a person's position in society as measured by criteria such as income, social prestige, intelligence, professional status, and education.

statute Any law passed by a legislative body; written law; code law; an ordinance or law passed by a lawmaking body such as a state legislature, county board of supervisors, county commission, or city council. In Latin, lex scripte. Synonymous terms are "code," "ordinance," and "municipal law."

statute of frauds *See frauds, statute of.*

statute of limitations A law that establishes and fixes the period of time during which an action may be started or must occur or claims must be filed. Time limitation often depends on the type of legal action or the circumstances of the issue or dispute.

statutes at large In law, these are written laws passed by a legislature that have been collected and printed in the order of their passage.

statutory 1. Established or declared by law, code, or statute. 2. Having to do with a statute. 3. Created by or conforming to statute or code. 4. Defined or required by a statute.

statutory law A law passed by a legislature that is a city, county, state, provincial, or federal lawmaking body.

statutory rape In law, this is an adult over the age of majority having sexual intercourse with a female under the age of majority.

stay 1. To stop or halt. 2. To stop a proceeding. 3. A temporary act by a court order.

STD *See sexually transmitted diseases.*

STEEP analysis In strategic planning, this is a technique for assessing an organization's functioning and role. STEEP stands for Sociological, Technical, Economic, Environmental, and Political, and each factor is assessed strategically as to how it affects, enhances, or inhibits the organization's effectiveness.

steering committee 1. In health administration, this is a formal group of individuals serving as an advisory board to see projects through or give direction to the administrator. 2. In healthcare quality management, this is a part of a quality circle or similar employee involvement effort and includes a top manager and group of individuals who assist in giving quality improvement direction to the manager.

stenographic recording In the litigation process, this is the writing or recording of testimony or court proceedings by a court reporter who uses a paper-punching recording machine, a tape recorder, or a notebook. This differs from a court recorder.

step chart In health administration, this is a management tool that provides a graphic representation of a pattern of gain and loss movement.

step-down In health-care financial management, this is a cost-finding approach involving the single distribution of general service cost center in both general service and final cost centers.

step-down allocation *See step-down; cost finding.*

stepped approach In medical care delivery, this is an intervention method following triage, in which minimal resources or effort are expended on the first group or level, more intensive effort is put into the second level, and the most intensive effort, resources, staffing, and supplies are put into the third, most serious or demanding level.

step-rate plan Medical insurance coverage in which premiums increase with the age of the enrolled member.

stereotaxy In medical care, this is a specialized surgical procedure used in brain surgery. Deep areas of the brain are operated on once a position has been determined utilizing point measurements. The actual surgical procedure is done with electricity, heat or cold, or mechanical means.

stereotype 1. Beliefs and values held in common by the members of a group that conform to a fixed belief system or cultural pattern. 2. Oversimplified evaluation, judgment, or bias about a person or group; preconceived notions about individuals, groups, or cultures, usually not founded in fact or truth; can be a form of prejudice or bias.

stereotypy In psychiatry and mental health care, this is an unusual or excessive continuous repetition of speech or physical activities; a characteristic of catatonic schizophrenia.

sterile Free from germs, pathogens, and microorganisms; aseptic. *See sanitary; sanitation.*

sterile field In medical care and surgery, this is the removal from the patient and the immediate surgical area all items or substances that could infect or contaminate a surgical procedure done by treating (painting) the area of the surgical wound with a strong antiseptic substance such as iodine; having the surgical suite, area, materials, equipment, tools, and personnel free from germs, pathogens, or other infectious agents or contaminants.

sterile technique *See surgical asepsis.*

sterilize The use of physical, heat, steam, or chemical procedures to destroy all microbial life, including highly resistant bacterial endospores.

sterilization 1. The process of making sterile; the destruction of all forms of life, germs, pathogens, or microorganisms by heat and/or chemical means. 2. The surgical procedure that renders an individual incapable of sexual reproduction such as a vasectomy or tubal ligation. 3. In environmental health and pest control, this is the use of radiation and chemicals to damage body cells needed for reproduction. 4. In environmental health, this generally is the destruction of all living organisms in water or on the surfaces of materials or equipment. Sterilization kills all living organisms, whereas disinfection kills most living organisms.

stertor Snoring or sonorous respiration.

stethoscope In medical care and health screening activities, this is an auditory instrument used to hear sounds produced in the body.

steward In labor relations, this is an employee of a company, elected by the workers or appointed by the local union leaders as a representative of all workers, who is a liaison between management and workers and negotiates with management over problems and labor contracts. Also called a "shop steward." *See shop steward.*

stillbirth In medical care, this is the delivery of a fetus that died before or during delivery. Some definitions are limited to fetuses of an age or weight that are potentially or usually viable (e.g., 1000 g or more). If the fetus takes a verified single breath or other sign of life as observed by medical personnel involved with the delivery of the baby, it is not considered a stillborn. *See also perinatal mortality.*

stillborn *See stillbirth.*

stimulant Any drug that produces an exciting or arousing effect and increases physical activity. In psychotropic drugs in addition to these physical responses, an unusually high sense of well-being is experienced. There are different types of stimulants (e.g., central nervous system stimulants, cardiac stimulants, and respiratory stimulants) that produce physiological excitement, arousal, and response.

stimulated emission In laser technology, this is when an incident photon stimulates the transition of another atom from a high energy level to a lower level, emitting an identical photon.

stimulus Anything from the environment, internal or external, that arouses or incites an action or a response.

stimulus-mediation-response In behavioral health and safety, this is the usual way most individuals respond to a stimulus. They receive the stimulus, mediate between the input, recall past experience, and then respond. This is different than the reflex arc response, which is a neurophysiological reaction (e.g., jerking one's hand back quickly from touching a hot object).

stimulus-response A mechanical response to a stimulus when a certain stimulus is given and a certain response expected. Normally, individuals use a thinking and evaluation process instead of responding blindly to a stimulus, unless it is the reflex arc response. *See stimulus-mediation-response.*

stipulation In health law, this is a written agreement between lawyers of two different parties about legal procedures or matters.

stochastic effects Biological effects (the probability rather than the severity) that are a function of the magnitude of the radiation dose without threshold (i.e., stochastic effects are random). Nonstochastic effects are biologically founded, and the severity of the effect in affected individuals varies with the magnitude of the dose above a threshold value.

stock 1. Items or goods for sale by a business. 2. The supply of goods on hand. 3. Shares in a corporation; an investment document showing ownership in a company; a share in the ownership of a business or corporation. 4. In health administration and materials management, this is a quantity of materials, goods, or resources at a particular time necessary to carry on business or operations, such as having a stock of antibiotics in the inventory of the pharmacy.

stock dividend In health-care finance, this is when the health-care organization is paid dividends in additional shares of stock instead of cash. Stock dividends are not recorded as income. The number of additional shares must be recorded and their value included in annual statements.

stockholders In health-care finance, these are the owners of shares of stock in a company. Also called "shareholders," these individuals share in the profits of the company by receiving periodic payments called dividends.

stockholder's derivative suit In law, this is the filing of a lawsuit by a stockholder of a corporation for the corporation while the company itself is not filing the suit.

stockinette In medical care, this is a soft cloth material placed under a cast to protect the skin.

stock insurance company A company owned and controlled by stockholders and operated for the purpose of making a profit, with shares sold to stockholders. The profits go to the owners or those holding shares and is contrasted with a mutual insurance company, where the profits go to the insured.

stock-out In health administration and materials management, this is when a requested inventory item has been used up and is not presently available.

stone center In medical care services, this is a specialized treatment unit that treats kidney and gallstones by advanced technology and equipment; also called a "lithotripsy facility." Lithotripsy pulverizes the stones within the body via sound waves, thus avoiding invasive procedures or surgery to remove the stones. *See lithotripsy.*

stool Waste products from the large intestine; feces. *See also feces.*

stopcock A valve that controls the flow of fluid through a tube.

stop-loss A type of insurance used to purchase coverage from a third-party insurance company to have a risk of some unexpected event or financial loss covered. In the event of a financially catastrophic claim, stop-loss limits the loss for the insurer and purchaser.

stop-loss insurance In managed care, this is a contractual limit such as a health plan accepting risk for any given member up to $50,000 but not to exceed this amount. If the health plan has excessive claims and exceeds the amount for the year's contract, the health plan's loss would stop because it is covered by insurance, which would then be activated. This is when a health plan purchases insurance from another insurance company to reimburse the health plan's cost of providing care if it exceeds a certain level or ceiling. Insurance coverage taken out by a managed-care plan or a self-funded employer to provide protection from losses resulting from claims over a specific dollar amount per member per year (calendar year or illness to illness). Two types are commonly used: 1) specific or individual, where reimbursement is given for claims on any covered individual exceeding a predetermined deductible such as $20,000 or $50,000, and 2) aggregate, which is when reimbursement is paid for claims exceeding a predetermined amount such as 120% of the amount expected in an average year. *See reinsurance.*

stop-loss limit In managed care and insurance, this is a specified amount of money that an insurance policy or health plan will cover in excess of the deductible amount, at which point the level of reimbursement by the health plan increases to full coverage.

stop-loss provision In managed care and insurance, this is a limit in the policy that sets limits on the highest amount of out-of-pocket expenses a member will experience.

stop-loss reinsurance In managed care, this is a type of reinsurance plan where the reinsurer pays the health plan an agreed-on percentage of the net actual claims that exceed an agreed-on contractual percentage of the expected claims for all health plan business during a given period of time.

stop order 1. To give notice to a bank to refuse payment on a check. 2. A standing medical staff order requiring a specific drug or treatment to be discontinued after a specified period of time. The drug or treatment may be resumed if a physician reorders it.

stoppage in transit A merchant's right to stop the delivery of an item or good even after it has been sent.

stop payment and reissue requests In managed care or medical insurance, this is when a health plan or insurance company's claims department gets a request to stop payment of a check or reimbursement and then reissues the check or reimbursement in the event a health-care provider or member does not receive payment.

storage In health information management, this is a device or medium on which data can be entered, retained, and recovered for use; to enter information into a medium such as a chip or diskette for later use.

storage, hazardous waste In environmental health, this is holding hazardous waste for a temporary period at the end of which the waste is treated, disposed of, or stored elsewhere (EPA); temporary holding of waste pending treatment or disposal through such methods as containers, tanks, waste piles, and surface impoundments.

stores *See materials management department.*

storm sewers In environmental health and liquid waste management, these are a system of underground water sewage pipes that are separate from sanitary sewers and that carry only water runoff from building and land surfaces.

storm water In environmental health and liquid waste management, this is surface water that runs off from precipitation or lawn watering and other water that runs in streets gutters and into storm drains.

storm water collection system In environmental health and liquid waste management, piping, pumps, conduits, and any other equipment necessary to collect and transport the flow of surface water runoff resulting from precipitation or domestic, commercial, or industrial wastewater to and from retention areas or any areas where treatment is designed to occur. The collection of storm water and wastewater does not always include treatment.

stowage In environmental health and hazardous waste, this refers to placing hazardous waste on board a vessel.

straight-line depreciation In health-care finance, this is dividing the cost of an item by the number of years of useful service and deducting that amount each year from income tax.

strain 1. Overstretching a muscle, a part of a muscle, or a tendon. 2. Sometimes used synonymously with "stress."

stranger One who is not part of a business transaction; a third party; a person not known to the first party.

STRAP *See Segment, Target, Research, Assess, Provide Products.*

strategic alternatives In strategic health planning, these are various approaches to better organizational structure and positioning of the organization for future success. Eleven different approaches have been identified: 1) status quo, which is maintaining stability and is internally managed; 2) concentration, which is to enhance a single product or service and is internally managed; 3) vertical integration, which is to take on and develop products or services internally that have previously been contracted for through an outside source and has external ramifications; 4) horizontal integration, which is to obtain control of similar services or programs and control the competition and has external ramifications; 5) diversification, which is to go into new services or programs that enhance the overall health-care organization's offerings, making it a more full-service organization, and has both internal management issues and external ramifications; 6) joint ventures, which is a process of spreading risk and sharing costs and services by having a shared service that has complementary benefits to both parties; 7) retrenchment, which is to cut back some services while not expanding others, which is an internal management issue; 8) downsizing, which is to cut back in operations, reduce staff, and remove part of the organization that is not profitable and has both internal and external ramifications (two general downsizing approaches are often used, narrow and deep, which usually cut services and programs and many jobs, and shallow and wide, which relies on turnover, retirements, and work cutbacks such as shortened work weeks or call-off days and tries to retain jobs); 9) divestiture, which is to sell off or close services or programs that do not fit well into the health-care organization or its mission and is an internal management issue; 10) liquidation, which is to close certain operations and sell the goods and equipment and is an internal management issue; and 11) innovation, which is to take initiative and seize excellent opportunities that will enhance the organization that may not always be mainstream and can be both internal and external in their management.

strategic apex In health administration or health policy, this is the top level of a bureaucratic organization responsible for governance, financial management, and planning.

strategic business unit An externally oriented aspect of strategic planning that evaluates departments, services, and programs and their ability to be business profit centers for the parent organization (e.g., an emergency care helicopter service).

strategic health planning A long-term, highly effective and focused planning approach that uses the formulation of mission statements and goals for the health-care organization; the identification of money-generating departments and programs while assessing the health facility's resources. Organizational strengths and weaknesses are evaluated, voids in the system identified, and new programs suggested to help meet the competition currently experienced in the marketplace. Strategic planning must be supported by management to be successful and utilizes a top-down approach. The planning process must be ongoing and have organizational openness; have a free flow of information; have realistic strategies; question underlying assumptions; have competent organizational communication; utilize rational decision making, action, and control; consider the organization's financial situation; and do a major review of the product market with the development of marketing and competitive strategies. The strategic planning process is based on long-term future actions, goals, and objectives and relies on a seven-step process: 1) development or assessment of vision and mission statements; 2) internal and external analysis (SWOT exercises assessments); 3) formulating goals, setting objectives, and assigning responsibility; 4) assessing competition and setting priorities; 5) exploring and evaluating alternatives; 6) decision making; and 7) assessing the long-term actions and consequences. *See SWOT; strategic planning.*

strategic management In health administration and management, this is the managerial process of making quality decisions that set forth the organization's mission, goals, and objectives while determining the most effective and efficient utilization of its resources while ensuring long-range and broad-reaching future effectiveness in a competitive environment and choosing the best strategic alternatives; the whole scope of strategic decision making aimed at positioning and strategy implementation to guide internal activities and external direction and determine and guide long-term performance for a health-care organization as it relates to the industry and business environment; a process that deals with the entrepreneurial activities of the health-care organization aimed at organization renewal, growth and advancement, and selection of strategies that will develop and guide the health-care organization.

strategic opportunities In strategic health planning, these are environmental, business, or community circumstances or situations that provide chances for shifts and advancements in service or program capabilities and increased market share, often based on response to competition, mergers, acquisitions, vertical integration, horizontal integration, and expansion in or moving into a new market niche.

strategic plan The process of assessing internal and external organizational environments and assessing the factors that impede, influence, or enhance organizational operations. Evaluating visions, organizational direction, and mission and developing tactics to accomplish the mission. A critical road map for a health-care organization to follow and closely adhere to in order to cope with future threats, changes in the health-care industry, and competition and to take advantage of future opportunities through goals and objectives that lay out strategies, tactics, and direction for the organization. The plan sets forth a vision, a mission statement, goals, objectives, guidelines, programs, policy revision, environmental surveillance, activities, finances, progressive and aggressive decision making, responsibility, organizational structure, and direction.

strategic planning 1. A long-range planning approach, process, and decision making that uses a variety of creative approaches to assess and evaluate internal effectiveness and external opportunities to the current organization and its operations with long-term implications for management and marketing; forecasting, which predicts future long-term implications of decisions including the market, organizational structure, policy revision, resources, direction, competition, and finance. 2. A rational process by which a health-care organization (e.g., hospital) determines it best course of action. This involves effectively balancing community needs for health services with the organization's strengths and ability to use available resources and producing practical plans to implement financially feasible strategies acceptable to consumer needs (American Hospital Association). *See strategic health planning.*

strategic quality planning In health-care organization quality assurance management, these are plans that incorporate quality as the focus of this long-range plan, which demands action toward quality outcomes. All aspects of the plan embrace quality and usually includes as a minimum quality in customer requirement areas, the effect of industrial projections on quality, effects of competition on quality, identification of opportunities to improve quality to better position the health-care organization with competitors, improving quality in service delivery and meeting consumer needs, and comparing opportunities against risks, resources, and capabilities.

strategic responses In strategic health planning and health-care organization management, these are strategy formulation decisions made about the future of the organization with regard to its mission and long-term future and include making whatever necessary changes it must to position the health-care organization for a sound and competitive future.

strategies 1. In mental health services, these are planned behavior modification and therapy approaches used to complement, supplement, and reinforce the learning and social change process. 2. In strategic health planning, these are tactics used to position oneself in the marketplace and better meet the competition.

strategy A methodological approach or plan of attack (action) that takes into account any problem or barriers and resources necessary to achieve goals and specific objectives. The desired or preferred course of action taken to accomplish mission, goals, and objectives and ensure the future viability and growth of the health-care organization. 2. In strategic health planning and health marketing, this is any means of deploying resources to better position the organization in the competitive market and to achieve the health-care organization's objectives using the organization's strengths, resources, and any potential opportunity for improvement in a competitive environment.

strategy formulation In strategic health planning, this is the administrative and planning process that helps define the health-care organization's visions, philosophy, and mission while establishing goals and objectives and determining and selecting the approaches, tactics, and strategies that it will use and implement in positioning the organization for future success.

strategy, functional In strategic health planning, this is the administrative and planning process where strategies developed and considered are useful and practical, with attainable goals and objectives developed for the main units, entities, services, programs, or departments in the organization such as clinical patient services, financial management, human resources, materials management, and medical staff.

strategy implementation In strategic health planning, this is the administrative and planning process where strategies are determined and decisions made to ensure that strategies are matched with goals and that the organizational structure is effective and receptive to the strategies. This also involves communicating, coordinating, budgeting, and putting the goals and strategies into action while monitoring feedback and the effectiveness of the strategies.

stratification In epidemiology and health services research, this is to separate the subjects of a research study by placing samples in both the study group and the control group according to various logical categories such as age, socioeconomic status, education, income, and occupation.

stratification in health care Access to health care being based on income, age, ethnicity, race, the nature of the disease, and how chronic or disabling a disease is, all causing inequities in the accessibility, availability, and quality of health services.

stratified randomization *See stratified random sample; stratification.*

stratified random sample *See sample, stratified random; sample.*

stratified sample *See stratified random sample; stratified sampling.*

stratified sampling A research sampling approach that divides a population into levels,

strata, or homogeneous groups according to some characteristic or parameter such as race, socioeconomic status, education, type of treatment, or age-group, with samples taken from each of the selected categories. *See sample, stratified; sample.*

stratosphere As an environmental health and air pollution concern, this is the portion of the upper atmosphere that is 10 to 25 miles above the earth.

straw man A person who participates in a business deal from a distance or is involved only on a superficial level; one who takes part in a business transaction in name only.

street or highway In public health and safety, this is the entire width of a public thoroughfare between property lines, any part of which is open for use to the public as a matter of custom and right and thus includes the whole right-of-way such as public and private sidewalks, driveways, lanes, alleys, and medians.

strength In occupational health and safety, this is the usable capacity of a structure or its support members to resist a heavy load within deformation limits.

streptokinase In medical care, this is one of several kinase heart-related drugs. If given as close as possible to a heart attack, the damage and effects of the heart attack are greatly reduced. The drug is produced by bacteria of the beta-hemolytic streptococcal strains. It aborts a heart attack by dissolving clots that block the coronary arteries of the heart.

stress A physical, chemical, psychological, or emotional factor that causes bodily or mental tension, anxiety, or upset and that may also cause disease or fatigue. It can be both negative or positive: distress or eustress, respectively. It stems from a deviation of optimal conditions that an individual cannot easily cope with or adapt or adjust to. *See also stressor; distress; benestressor; eustress; dystressor.*

stress immunity The failure to react to stress. The false notion, often held by executives and professionals who work under high-stress conditions or in stressful environments, that they can adjust to, accommodate, and take on more stress as they get used to it. However, there really is no such thing as immunity to stress, and if allowed to accumulate, it eventually has negative and detrimental effects on one's physical and mental well-being if not minimized, coped with, or reduced and if proper health behaviors such as vigorous daily exercise are not taken to help the body cope with stress.

stress inoculation A concept based on the process of immunization used for the control of communicable disease whereby individuals are exposed to mild levels of a stress that could later be encountered at a more intense level in real life. This prepares them to cope with the more intense stress when it occurs. The concept is based on the belief that if an individual is given the opportunity to deal with a mildly stressful stimulus and is allowed to practice a succession of stress exposures, then, when encountering a somewhat more intense level of stress later on, he or she will be able to handle it and control his or her own behavior. A three-phase process is suggested: educational phase, rehearsal phase, and application phase. The human body has the ability to adapt and adjust to stressful situations, as demonstrated by practices of short-term stressful events as used in sports and war preparation with much success. This theory has not been proven. Some researchers on stress suggest the opposite: that the body cannot build a tolerance to stress only to a certain level and that it then takes its toll on the body, depending on the type and duration of the stressors. *See stress immunity.*

stress interviews In human resource management, these are interviews that rely on a series of harsh, rapid-fire questions intended to upset the applicant to determine how well the applicant deals with tense and stressful situations. Used in certain professions such as job applicants with the police, prison guards, intelligence agencies, and certain military positions. Because health care is a people oriented, caring profession, such interviews have no value in the health-care industry.

stressor Any changes, occurrences, events, or experiences that upset or threaten the physical, mental, spiritual, emotional, social values, belief system, relationship, or economic status of the human organism that cannot be effectively coped with or adapted to. If poor adaptation to stress occurs and if coping skills are lacking, this tends to diminish one's natural resistance to disease and proper functioning at the emotional, social, and physiological levels. When an upset in the normal balance of the body occurs, then stress causes a mental and physiological breakdown of the person. *See also stress; dystressor; benestressor.*

stress performance model A scheme that attempts to show the relationship between stress and job performance.

stress threshold The level of stressors that a person can tolerate before feelings of distress begin; based more on individual perception of life change events or stressful encounters than the actual event itself.

strict 1. Exacting. 2. Severe. 3. Precise. 4. Rigid; governed by rigid or exact rules.

strict foreclosure 1. The right of a creditor to regain property, but only in a special situation. 2. To cancel a debt with the creditor without the debtor being able to sue.

strict liability In health law, this is to be legally responsible for harm done or injury caused even if not at fault; liability without the identification of any fault, negligence, malpractice, knowledge, or acts of omission; liability by being involved in an act that results in harm or injury.

strictness bias In human resource management, this is when employees are rated lower than is justified in their job performance appraisal by their supervisors.

strike 1. In labor management, this is when employees purposely stop work or do not show up for work to force management to concede to workers' demands to gain benefits or win concessions from an employer. 2. To hit or dash against; to deal a blow.

string In computer programming, a connected sequence of characters.

strip In environmental health, this is the removing of friable asbestos materials from any part of a building or facility.

stroke In medical care, this is a cerebral vascular accident (CVA), apoplexy, or any hemorrhage or softening of the brain that results in damage to the cerebral arteries. Paralysis, aphasia, and coma are among the neurological symptoms that accompany this condition. It is caused by a sudden rupture or blockage of a blood vessel in the brain, depriving the brain of its blood supply, resulting in loss of consciousness, paralysis, or other disorders, depending on the site and extent of brain damage. *See also cerebral vascular accident.*

strong potential for harm In long-term care and OBRA, this is when a long-term-care facility practice is observed to be so divergent from accepted principles of good care that a future negative outcome or harm is probable. An example observed in nursing homes is a nurse aide not washing hands between patients, especially after handling feces and soiled linen, creating a high potential for the spread of disease and nosocomial infections.

strontium 90 A beta-minus decay radioisotope; a radionuclide; a nuclide; a hazardous radioactive substance.

struck jury The most qualified or, at least, the most unobjectionable group of persons selected as a jury to try a case; the final members of a jury selected to sit at and hear a trial.

structural integration A deep-massage technique, developed by Ida P. Rolf, PhD, that is designed to help a person realign the body by altering the length and tone of myofascial tissues. It is referred to as "rolfing." Practitioners of "rolfing" believe that misalignment of body structure, resulting from inaccurate learning about posture as well as emotional and physical trauma, may have a detrimental effect on an individual's health, energy, self-image, perceptions, and muscular efficiency.

structural measure An assessment of compliance with standards, expectations, or rules regarding physical facilities. *See input measure.*

structural unemployment This is when people are ready, willing, and able to work as long as they can work in their area of training or expertise but are not working because their skills fail to match jobs that are available. This can be caused by the lack of flexibility in the hiring process by employers or the reluctance of workers to work in an area different than they are used to.

structure In strategic planning or quality assurance management, this is the organizational setup and layout of the organization, which is reviewed to see how resources are used, how effective processes are, and how the setup and layout of the organization affect outcomes and overall quality.

structured group judgment In health administration and health planning, this is a formal decision approach that uses group decision making in planning, eliciting, aggregating, and communicating decision results and is used to reduce the effects of personal or group bias or influences such as personal status, authority, self-serving influences, or self-interests. Also referred to as "group decision making."

structured interviews In health administration and human resource management, this is a job interview that uses a preestablished set of questions that are asked of all potential employees or job applicants.

structured settlement In health law and medical malpractice, this is when the lawsuit is settled prior to going to trial and the payment of damages to the plaintiff is set up on an installment schedule by the defendant, who will also pay the plaintiff for rehabilitation and related medical expenses as they occur. The terms of each settlement are negotiated by both parties and vary from case to case.

structure, organizational The development of logical and consistent relationships among the various components and functions of an organization.

Stryker frame A canvas-covered frame on which a patient lies. It is attached to a metal frame on wheels. The canvas-covered frame is connected at a pivot joint so that the entire frame turns when the patient is turned from his or her back to the abdomen and vice versa. When turning the patient, a second canvas-covered frame is placed on top of the patient, and the two frames are secured with the patient between them like a sandwich. Safety belts are used to hold the frames together. A Foster frame is a similar device.

Stryker saw A handheld electrical saw with a half-blade that oscillates rather than rotates. It is used to remove casts, to perform autopsies, and, in medical education, to dissect cadavers. It has no guards because the manufacturer claims they are not needed.

student nurse *See nurse, student.*

studies 1. Observations and analysis of a phenomenon, concern, development, question, or scientific hypothesis, with the results applied to solving a problem, making a new discovery, making changes, improving services, or implementing a project or service. 2. Any in vivo or in vitro experiments to evaluate or assess substances to predict their fate, toxicity, metabolism, and other characteristics in humans, animals, or plants. Synonymous with "research," "research study," "trial," or "experiment."

study design The structure, methodology, technique, and approach used in health services research or epidemiological research that are developed and implemented according to acceptable scientific designs and methods. *See research design.*

study director In research, this is the individual responsible for conducting an entire research project or an assessment process. In grant-funded or scientific research, this is referred to as the "principal investigator" (PI).

stupor In mental health care, this is a disorder or reaction that causes a disturbance of one's consciousness. The patient is nonreactive and unaware of his or her surroundings. Organically, it is the same as unconsciousness. In psychiatry, it is a form of autism and is found in catatonia disorders and psychotic depression.

sua sponte (Lat.) 1. Voluntarily; of one's own will. 2. On a judge's own motion. 3. Lack of a formal request from the parties of a dispute.

sub (Lat.) Under.

subacute An illness, disease, disorder, or condition that is not quite as serious as a full acute disorder but may become so if not properly cared for; often found in elderly patients in the convalescing period following an illness, surgery, or other treatment; a level of care that requires more than skilled nursing care but is less intense than the medical and nursing care found in an acute-care setting such as a hospital. Patients discharged from hospitals early may enter a nursing home or home care situations under visiting nurses in less than a recovered state and still need some acute care, which makes this subacute care. *See subacute patient care.*

subacute care *See subacute patient care.*

subacute care unit In long-term care, this is a special area or unit, usually in a skilled nursing facility, room, wing, or other location, administratively determined, where advanced nursing care is provided to patients with serious diseases or advanced chronic conditions or who have very recently experienced surgery. Some regulations state that a minimum of one registered nurse and one LPN or LVN is required for each subacute unit to meet nursing hour requirements. It is recommended that a minimum of 5.2 to 6.2 hours of licensed care be provided daily for this level of patient and patient care, depending on patient mix and the number of patients needing respirator care. Special arrangements are needed to establish readily available physician care and emergency care. These units may also be required to contract for lab services, X rays, respiratory therapy, pharmacy, emergency care, etc. *See subacute patient care.*

subacute dietary lethal concentration (LC 50) In environmental health, this is when food substances have a concentration of a chemical or other substance that is harmful, expressed in parts per million, that is lethal to 50% of the test population of animals under test conditions.

subacute patient care High levels of nursing care provided by nursing homes and skilled nursing facilities or home health agencies. Because of the requirements of the prospective payment system under DRGs, elderly patients in need of high-level nursing care are discharged from hospitals early and are transferred to nursing homes. Such care includes postsurgery care, including maintenance of surgical wounds and drains, intravenous drug and nutrient administration, and respirator and ventilator care. *See subacute care.*

subarea In health services delivery, these are community subdivisions of a health service area that are used for localizing input, involvement, and advice for health services systems or managed-care systems.

Subarea Advisory Council (SAC) A former community-based committee or related organization established by the former health systems agencies (HSAs) under past law P.L. 93-641 that was created to advise the HSAs on their functions and to provide an advisory link between the HSA and local communities. Also referred to as Health Advisory Councils (HACs).

subchapter "S" corporation In health-care financial management, this is a business or organization that receives the protection of a corporation but is taxed as a partnership. Some practitioners or group practices may be formed in such a manner.

subchronic reference dose (RFD) In environmental health, this is an estimate of a daily exposure level for the human population, including sensitive subpopulations, that is likely to be without an appreciable risk of deleterious effects if the exposure were to occur for a period of less than 7 years (EPA).

subclinical case In medical care and epidemiology, this is the phase of a disease before it manifests symptoms; pertains to a disease, disorder, or condition that does not present overt clinical symptoms; diseases that may require testing, such as blood and serum tests, to verify a diagnosis and to identify the presence of the disease. Also referred to as "subclinical disease."

subcoma insulin treatment In psychiatric treatment, this is a form of shock treatment in which insulin is used to produce sleepiness and cause a sense of well-being instead of shock or coma.

subconscious In psychiatry, psychology, and mental health, this is the preconscious or unconscious mind.

subcontract In health administration, health services delivery, and managed care, this is when a formal written legal agreement is met by a second formal legal agreement being entered into by a third party, stating that it will have the third party provide services, conduct business, and do certain types of work or activities to meet part of the original agreement. *See contract.*

subcutaneous Beneath the layers of skin; hypodermic.

subjective A mental state or an observation based on emotion, feelings, attitudes, expectations, reactions, and perceptions while lacking facts, observations, documentation, and data that make it objective.

subjective data 1. Signs and symptoms of dysfunction or disease that are perceived as real by the patient. 2. Information based on personal opinion rather than facts.

subjective probability distributions In epidemiology, these are probability distributions arrived at using subjective approaches rather than using standard objective research methods and objective information and data.

subjective risk In liability insurance, this is an insurance risk founded on the mental stability (or lack thereof) in a person who shows uncertainty or doubt as to the results of certain activities.

subjectivity An appraisal, evaluation, and interpretation of something influenced by one's own feelings, perceptions, and thinking as to the quality of the object or experience while not accounting for facts or objectivity.

sub judice (Lat.) In law, this is any concern or issue that could be considered by a court; item before the court; issues for the court's consideration.

sublimation In mental health, this is a mental mechanism or defense mechanism that channels unacceptable behavior into socially acceptable behavior.

subluxation of the spine An incomplete or partial dislocation of two adjacent vertebrae of the spinal column. Normally, the vertebral bodies are squarely situated atop one another. However, when such things as trauma, strain, or certain forms of arthritis intervene, one vertebral body may shift with respect to its neighbor. When the shift does not completely abolish contact between the two normally adjacent surfaces but does alter their position with respect to one another, the abnormally positioned vertebra is said to be subluxed or partially dislocated. Services of chiropractors are covered under Medicare only when such subluxation is demonstrated on an X ray.

submission The act of referring issues to the arbitration process or other legal processes.

submit 1. To refer to the judgment of another. 2. To present for. 3. To refer to. 4. To yield or surrender. 5. To allow to. 6. To introduce evidence.

sub nomine (Lat.) Under the name of; in the name of. In law, this is used to indicate that the name of a case has changed.

suboptimization of objectives In health administration and health planning, this is where one objective can be achieved only at the expense of another objective. Good planning and effective and efficient allocation of resources can help to avoid such management dilemmas.

subordinate 1. Any worker or employee under the supervision and authority of a manager or supervisor; lower in rank. 2. To have less power or authority. 3. Of less value or importance.

subordinated debenture In health-care finance, this is a bond having a claim on the health-care organization's assets only after the major proportion of the debt has been paid off in the event of a liquidation.

subordination Signing an official document in a manner that indicates a weaker or secondary interest or position.

subordination agreement A special agreement whereby an encumbrance is made on the basis of or subject to another encumbrance. A loan for land purchase is made once a subsequent construction loan is finalized.

suborn 1. To induce. 2. To give false testimony. 3. To bribe or entice another to commit perjury.

subornation of perjury In law, this is forcing or enticing a person to lie under oath.

subpoena In law, this is an order of a court commanding a person to appear in court to testify. A penalty may be imposed in the event of failure to appear.

subpoena duces tecum (Lat.) In health law, this is a subpoena that directs a person to bring certain documents to court. For example, a director of medical records may be asked to bring medical records to court.

subrogation 1. To substitute one party for another to claim a right or debt. 2. A provision of an insurance policy that requires an insured individual to turn over any rights he or she may have to the insurer to recover damages from another party to the extent to which he has been reimbursed by the insurer. Some experts have argued that private health insurance should have subrogation rights similar to those in most property insurance policies (e.g., auto or fire); the contractual right of a health plan to recover payments made to a member for care costs after that member has received payment for damages in a lawsuit. Having paid the hospital bill of a policyholder, the health insurance company could assume its right to sue the party whose negligence might have caused the hospitalization and be reimbursed for its outlay to the policyholder. Subrogation rights could help ensure prompt payment of medical expenses without duplication of benefits. Others respond that subrogation is time consuming and expensive and may not offer companies adequate protection against loss. This differs from "coordination of benefits" (COB) in that liability is shared between the parties of a contract under COB, whereas subrogation assigns the right to another party. Few insurers use subrogation voluntarily, and some insurance commissioners forbid its use.

sub rosa (Lat.) Literally means "under the rose." Secretly or privately.

subroutine In health information management and computer programming, this is a set of instructions that can be used to perform a routine on a set of data in a program at various points and can run a routine on the original set of data or on a separate program.

subscribe To write or sign one's name to a document such as a contract. To sign up for something such as an insurance plan or a computer access program or to receive a service, good, or piece of literature on a regular basis for a set time period.

subscriber 1. One who pays into or belongs to a managed-care program, health plan, or group health insurance plan; also called enrollee, certificate holder, insured, policyholder, client, member, patient, or beneficiary. In a strict sense, it means only the individual (family head or employee) who has elected to participate in an insurance or HMO plan for either him- or herself and his or her eligible dependents. 2. In managed care, this is the individual or employee who is responsible for premium payments or whose employment is the basis for eligibility of membership in a health plan or HMO because the employer group makes it possible for the individual to join and the employer pays all or part of the premium; any person who has enrolled in a health plan under a group hospital or medical services agreement or as a member of a special Medicare contract managed-care plan; an employer, union, purchasing pool, association, or group that contracts with a prepaid health plan for medical care.

subscriber certificate *See subscriber contract.*

subscriber contract In managed care, this is a formal written legal agreement setting forth the health plan member's medical care policy. Also referred to as "subscriber certificate" or "member certificate."

subsequent negligence In health law and tort law, this is when a defendant sees or is aware of a possible danger or situation where harm could be done to the plaintiff and fails to exercise due care and precaution to prevent the injury to the plaintiff from occurring.

subsidiary In health-care administration and organizational structure, this is when a smaller supportive health-care organization is owned by a larger parent organization; when one organization is controlled by another and is more than 50% owned by the parent organization.

sub silentio (Lat.) Though silence; with silence; under the veil of silence; without notice; not giving any warning or indication.

subspecialty In medical care, this is where a physician has a focused, limited, concentrated, highly technical level of expertise, skill, and knowledge in a subdivision of a recognized broad specialty area such as pediatric cardiology, child psychiatry, family practice/geriatrics, neurosurgery, or pediatric gastroenterology. Most medical subspecialty areas require a 2- to 5-year residency and are board certified in their area of specialty. *See specialty.*

substance 1. The essence of or the main point of a document. 2. Drugs, alcohol, or other mind-altering chemicals; other chemicals or agents.

substance abuse The excessive use, misuse, or wrongful use of any legal or illegal drugs or alcohol; the use of a substance to the extent that the user is detrimentally affected socially, physically, psychologically, and economically or is caused to be physiologically and/or mentally impaired or dependent; continued use of a drug or drugs, even with knowledge of the harmful effects of the substances on all facets of living; taking of alcohol or drugs at dosages or frequency rates that place the individual and/or family's welfare in a potentially hazardous or endangered position while endangering the public's health, morals, safety, health status, and overall well-being. Also referred to as "drug abuse." *See drug abuse; alcoholism.*

substance abuse plan A state or local government-level health plan of an administrative agency such as a public health department or social services agency that addresses the provision of services to individuals known to be abusers of intoxicants and controlled substances (alcohol or drugs).

substance abuse treatment unit In health-care delivery, this is a specialized service in a hospital or a separate facility where patients are checked in for a specific period of time to withdraw from alcohol or drugs and to undergo treatment, therapy, and rehabilitation for alcoholism or substance abuse and addiction.

substandard health insurance An individual medical insurance policy issued to a person who cannot meet the minimal health requirements of a standard medical insurance policy. Protection is provided, but with an increase in the premium and by a waiver of medical condition or under a special qualified impairment clause.

substandard risk class In insurance, this is a classification of individuals who have health problems, medical impairments, disabilities, or other problems that make their life expectancy shorter than usual or normal for their age. Thus, they have a higher risk of early death and must pay a higher-than-standard insurance premium.

substantial 1. Having a real existence; actual.

2. Valuable. 3. Not imaginary. 4. Worthwhile or of real worth. 5. Complete enough; considerable.

substantial business relationships In health law, this is when two or more different companies, organizations, or businesses have developed a pattern of recent or ongoing business transactions such that a current business relation between the entities exists; the extent of business relationships in existence according to state or contract law to make a guaranteed contract valid and enforceable.

substantial compliance In health-care facilities, when surveyed by the state Medicaid or Medicare agency or licensing agency, this means that the health-care facility is in conformity with the regulations by a licensee to such an extent that patient safety, welfare, and quality of care are ensured (Title 22, California).

substantial interest In public hearings on health regulations or public health care matters such as environmental health regulation passage or certificate-of-need hearings, there may be a conflict of interest held by persons who are serving on a hearing body or a committee. There may be a personal gain or benefit from the decision of the assembly. Any person serving on the committee who will benefit or receive direct or indirect gain or has personal or economic interest in a matter before the hearing body is said to have a substantial interest through ownership, partnership, employment, medical staff privileges, fiduciary relationships, contractual relationships, or financial or creditor involvement or who is serving in a consultive relation with any individual or party involved in the matter being heard by the hearing body. Such persons usually are allowed to remain on a committee and participate in the discussion but may not vote on findings or recommendations.

substantial performance In contract law, performance on the substantial part of the contract but not necessarily on other less important details or parts.

substantiate 1. In health law or hearings, this is to establish the existence of a fact or evidence. 2. To prove true; to verify.

substantive law The legal principles that determine rights and duties, as opposed to procedural or adjective law, which determines procedure and process in legal concerns. *See also procedural law.*

substantive motion In formal health-care meetings and hearings using parliamentary procedure, a presentation of a concrete proposal to the assembly concerning a matter of business to be heard by the assembly; not a matter of procedure or procedural motion.

substate ombudsman In long-term care, this is an agent or representative of the state ombudsman who carries out the duties and responsibilities in an assigned area of the state for the state ombudsman.

substitute consent In health law, this is when informed consent is sought from an individual other than the patient or a legal entity such as a parent or guardian. Legally speaking, only the individual has the right to consent to any medical treatment, surgery, or other treatment that would involve an invasive or chemically induced procedure. Guardianships, conservatorships, and being a parent of a minor allows the legally responsible individual to give consent. Implied consent is more correct than substituted consent, which is technically illegal and unethical. *See informed consent; implied consent.*

substituted judgment doctrine In health law, this is an element of law in some states applied by some courts that requires a conservator or legal guardian to make medical care and treatment decisions for mentally incompetent persons, especially in informed consent situations. The judgment of the guardian is substituted for the mentally incompetent person and is to reflect his or her attitudes and beliefs regarding the treatment.

substituted service A substituted legal procedure for the delivery of subpoenas. The usual method is by in-person delivery. Substituted service would be by mail or publication in a newspaper.

substitution 1. Filling a prescription by a pharmacist with a drug product therapeutically and chemically equivalent to the brand name prescribed. Many states have antisubstitution laws that prohibit the pharmacist from filling a prescription with any product other than the specific product of the manufacturer whose brand name is used on the prescription. 2. In mental health, this is a mental or defense mechanism that replaces one thing with another. Unattainable or unacceptable goals are replaced by ones that are attainable or acceptable. *See also Maximum Allowable Cost Program; generic name.*

succession The act of transferring the deceased's property to his or her heirs.

succession charts In health-care administration and human resource management, this is an organizational chart schematic providing a graphic representation of who the likely candidates are for promotion to key positions in the health-care organization.

succession of care Continuous care maintained from the health-care setting or facility to the following health-care institution or agency or through any transfers or follow-up care. Quantity and quality of care are kept at their highest levels throughout any changes in service settings.

succinylcholine In medical and psychiatric care, this is a drug used as a powerful muscle relaxant. It is used in anesthesia and in electroconvulsive treatment.

suctioning Drawing secretions out of the body by a tube connected to a suction machine.

sudden accidental occurrences In occupational safety, these are events that are not continuous or repeated in nature that cause harm, injury, damage, or property damage.

sudden infant death syndrome (SIDS) The sudden and unexpected death of an infant for reasons that remain unclear even after autopsy. SIDS is the most common cause of death in the postneonatal period.

sudden releases of pressure In occupational health and safety, this is identified as a dangerous condition for workers when there is any sudden, instantaneous release of steam, gas, or heat when subjected to sudden shock or pressure or high temperature.

sue 1. To initiate a civil legal proceeding. 2. To start a lawsuit.

sue and labor clause In liability insurance, a statement in the policy that requires a company or owner to attempt to protect property from extended loss and states that the owner of the insurance policy should attempt to recover the losses from other parties.

suffer 1. To allow or to permit something to happen. 2. To sustain injury, harm, loss, or damage.

sufficient 1. Adequate, solvent, or responsible. 2. Equal to the proposed goal.

suggestibility In mental health care, this is to be open to the power of suggestion or influence, a common observation in persons with hysterical symptoms. This also refers to the ability of patients to participate in hypnosis.

suggestion system In health administration, this is a formal communication method of soliciting, generating, evaluating, and implementing ideas submitted to administration by employees, guests, patients, and their family members for the betterment of the organization and to improve quality, effectiveness, efficiency and productivity. The traditional method is the suggestion box, which works well when diligently used and respected by administration. Mail-in postcards, suggestion forms, survey forms, formal surveys, focus groups, and SWOT analysis are examples.

sui generis (Lat.) 1. Of its own class. 2. One of a kind.

sui juris (Lat.) 1. Of his own right; competent. 2. Having full legal rights.

suit 1. A lawsuit. 2. A civil action taken to court. 3. To seek favor. 4. An action, court procedure, or process at law other than in criminal law.

suitable employment In human resources, this is a job for which the person is best suited because of his or her skills, education, training, abilities, and experience.

sulfur dioxide In environmental health and air pollution, this is a heavy, pungent, colorless, gaseous air pollutant formed primarily by the combustion of fossil fuels.

summary 1. A short, abridged statement. 2. Brief and concise; an abstract or shortened form. 3. Immediate; without a full trial; to prove a case of lack of evidence before going to trial or the conclusion of a trial.

summary judgment In health law, in the pretrial litigation process, when an issue or motion in a lawsuit arises where pleadings, depositions, testimony, interrogatories, admissions, and all other evidence show no material facts, indicating that the lawsuit and the facts and evidence on which it is based are questionable and lack substance, the defendant can ask the claim to be dismissed and the legal proceeding called to a halt. The party who initiated the motion is entitled to a decision or a judgment from the hearing officer or court as a matter of law.

summary plan description In managed care and self-funded health plans, this is the presentation of a health plan in a package form that shows an overview of the entire benefits and is made available to all employees covered by self-funded plans as required by law.

summation conference In JCAHO accreditation, this is an optional conference and is held by the accreditation team after the chief executive officer exit conference and is held for all hospital staff and others to convey general observations about the survey findings and provide preliminary information about the hospital's strengths and weaknesses on the basis of these findings.

summative evaluation In health services research and outcome studies, these are the conclusions and judgments made of a study or of measures about a study population where results and findings are presented about the outcomes and the impact of a program, services, or treatment approach.

summons In law and the litigation process, this is a document that has been certified by the clerk of the court. It is a brief summary of a complaint and states the number of days within which the defendant must answer or appear.

sumptuary law Statutes created to control the sale or use of socially undesirable, harmful, or wasteful products or substances.

Sunshine Act A federal law requiring that meetings of federal agencies be open to the public, with certain specified exceptions. Public announcements must be made (usually in the *Federal Register*) of the time, place, subject, and the agency official to contact for more information. Many state and local governments have similar laws requiring open meetings not only for their own governmental units but also for certain nongovernmental community organizations such as hospitals.

superbill An itemized statement furnished to the patient giving all pertinent information so that the patient may bill the insurance company directly. *See also superticket.*

supercontrollers In health administration organizational structuring using responsibility centers, this is the administrator who supervises responsibility center managers.

superego In Freud's psychoanalytic theory, referring to the unconscious part of the psyche that monitors the id and the ego; concerned primarily with morality, ethics, and social standards.

Superfund In environmental health and hazardous waste, this is a federal program operated under the legislative authority of the Comprehensive Environmental Response Compensation and Liability Act of 1980 (CERCLA) and the Superfund Amendments and Reauthorization Act (SARA) that funds and carries out the EPA solid waste emergency and long-term removal activities. A National Priorities List of sites with serious hazardous waste problems has been established. Other Superfund activities include the investigation of sites for inclusion on the list, determining priority level on the list, determining sites for cleanup, conducting and supervising cleanup, and other remedial activities. *See Comprehensive Environmental Response Compensation and Liability Act.*

Superfund Amendments and Reauthorization Act (SARA) In environmental health and hazardous waste, this is a federal program, enacted in 1986, operated under the legislative authority of the Comprehensive Environmental Response Compensation and Liability Act (CERCLA), which extends and amends this act.

Superfund memorandum of agreement In environmental health and hazardous waste, this is a nonbinding, written document executed by an EPA regional administrator and the head of a state agency that may establish the nature and extent of interaction during the removal, preremedial, remedial and enforcement response process of Superfund site issues. The agreement generally defines the role and responsibilities of both the lead agency and support agencies. This agreement is not site specific, but attachments may address specific sites.

Superfund state contracts In environmental health and hazardous waste, this is a joint, legally binding agreement between the EPA and a state to obtain the necessary assurances before a federally led remedial and cleanup action can begin at a site.

superintendent The head administrator of a health-care facility. The term is used most often in governmental health-care facilities and institutions such as state hospitals or hospitals for the developmentally disabled and is becoming somewhat limited in its use in the health-care field; a title of head administrators in public schools. *See also administrator; chief executive officer.*

superintendent of agencies In insurance, under the home service distribution system, this the administrative person responsible for all insurance agencies and is the link between the home office and district offices.

super IPA An independent practice association where physicians keep their independent businesses but negotiate as a group with payers but as several IPAs merged into one to contract with payers to get even better contracts and rates.

super PHO A physician hospital organization designed to integrate a hospital and its medical staff together so they can contract with health plans or payers as a single lead entity but with several physician hospital organizations merged into one to contract with payers to get even better contracts and rates.

superior 1. High in place, rank, or position. 2. To have power and control over. 3. Preferable or higher in quality. 4. Above.

superior court Court of general and extensive jurisdiction.

supersede 1. To have something set aside. 2. To wipe out. 3. To take the place of. 4. To make old laws or policies unnecessary; to replace a law or document with another one.

supersedeas (Lat.) In practice. A court order that temporarily stops or delays a hearing or court from proceeding.

supersedeas bond A bond used to gain a suspension of judgment, resulting in a delay in the execution of a pending appeal.

superticket A medical bill and related insurance claims combined onto a single sheet to avoid duplication and to keep costs down. Commonly referred to as a "fee ticket," it is utilized in outpatient emergency care or ambulatory services. *See also superbill.*

supervening 1. Newly effective. 2. Interposing. 3. A new policy or procedure.

supervised areas In occupational health and safety, these are areas where radiation levels are such that annual exposure is most unlikely to exceed three-tenths of the occupational dose equivalent limits but may exceed one-tenth of those limits and where special forms of supervision such as area monitoring are applied.

supervising In health administration, this is the facilitation of day-to-day work activities, using good communication, task understanding, mutual respect, clearly delineated tasks, objectives, and expected outcomes while striking a balance between the demands of the job and the assurance of productivity and having good task and work outcomes with employee-centered interactions and expectations.

supervision 1. In health-care organizations, this is the managerial process of influencing, directing, scheduling, assisting, setting forth orders and directives, and other management activities through a midmanager or other level of manager to motivate and direct workers to accomplish day-to-day work activities, objectives, work outcomes, and specified tasks. Administrators at all levels engage in some aspects of supervision activities such as scheduling, influencing, planning, organizing, staffing, directing, and controlling. 2. Under Medicare, authoritative procedural guidance by a qualified person for the accomplishment of a function or activity within his or her sphere of competence, with initial direction and periodic inspection of the actual act of accomplishing the function or activity. Unless otherwise stated in regulations, the supervisor must be on the premises if the person does not meet assistant-level qualifications. 3. One of the several functions of a manager and one of several personnel controls that may include assignment, training, promotion, resource control, segregation, and assignment of duties. 4. In long-term-care settings, this means to instruct employees or subordinates in their duties and to oversee or direct work but does not necessarily require the immediate presence of the supervisor (Title 22, California). *See management; functions of a manager.*

supervision, direct The supervisor shall be present in the same building as the person being supervised and be available for consultation and assistance (Title 22, California).

supervision, immediate The supervisor shall be physically present while a task is being performed by the person being supervised (Title 22, California).

supervisor In health administration, this is a lower level midmanager position serving as a liaison between mid- and top-level management and the working employees. The traits of a supervisor include being a boss, leader, and manager with technical or clinical expertise. Job duties include planning, setting objectives, scheduling and assigning work, coordinating work activities, quality assurance, communicating with the workers and top administration and problem solving, motivating workers, managing and conserving resources, and cooperating and communicating with fellow supervisors and department heads. Supervisors need technical skills of their area, human relations skills, and administrative skills. *See manager; midmanager.*

supervisory care *See personal care; custodial care.*

supervisory care facility A health-care facility that may or may not be licensed by the state and that provides limited nursing and medical care to elderly or handicapped residents. The personnel assist the residents in dressing, nutrition, medications, and some aspects of daily living. An LPN or RN may be required to be in the home on a full-time basis or on a consulting basis, depending on state laws. Also referred to as "custodial care facilities" or "personal care facilities." *See also personal care; custodial care; personal care facility; supervisory care home.*

supervisory care home A health-care facility that provides room, board, and custodial care but less assistance than a nursing home. Such a home provides a residential setting for individuals who need room, board, and assistance in bathing, housekeeping, and taking medications as well as help in case of an emergency. It must be a clean and safe living environment, look after the needs and well-being of the residents on a 24-hour basis, provide three nutritious meals a day along with snacks or access to the kitchen, provide special diets if prescribed, supervise the taking of medication, encourage socialization and participation in planned activities, take action in the event of a crisis, and explain to the newly entering person the rights of residents, including rates and services provided. *See board and care; custodial care; skilled nursing facility.*

supervisory nurse *See nurse, supervisor.*

supervisory programs In health information management, this is any software program that has the primary function of scheduling, allocating, and controlling a computer system and that does not run or process data or information or provide the user with results.

supination Turning the palm upward; lying on the back.

supine The position of lying on one's back facing upward.

supplemental benefit rider In managed care or insurance, this is when a stipulation is added to an insurance policy to provide additional benefits.

supplemental employment benefits In human resource management, this is when the employer provides extra benefits or supplements them. This is also when an employer supplements state unemployment insurance when a worker is laid off.

supplemental health insurance Medical insurance that covers medical expenses not covered by separate health insurance policies already held by the insured. For example, many insurance companies sell insurance to people covered under Medicare to include either the costs of cost sharing required by Medicare, services not covered, or both. Where cost sharing is intended to control utilization, the availability of supplemental health insurance covering cost sharing limits its effectiveness.

supplemental health services In managed care, these are the optional services that HMOs may provide in addition to basic health services and still qualify for federal assistance. They are defined in Section 1302(2) of the PHS Act. These services include facilities for intermediate and long-term care; vision care, which is not included as a basic health-care service; dental services not included as a basic health-care service; mental health care not included as a basic health-care service; long-term physical therapy, physical medicine, and rehabilitative services; the provision of prescription drugs prescribed in the course of care offered by an HMO; and any other services that are not included as basic health-care services that have been approved. These services may be provided by licensed health-care providers in the HMO or IPA or through referral to such services not available in the health-care organization.

supplemental security income (SSI) A program of income support for low-income aged, blind, and disabled persons, established by Title XVI of the Social Security Act. It replaced state welfare programs for the aged, blind, and disabled. This federally administered program pays a monthly basic benefit, and states may supplement this basic benefit amount. Receipt of a federal SSI benefit or a state supplement under the program is often used to establish Medicaid eligibility.

supplemental services In managed care, these are optional services that a health plan may offer coverage for in addition to the basic health plan and its provided services; medical care, health services, and treatment offered by a health plan that exceed those services required by law or that exceed the federal HMO regulations (HMO regulations, Subpart A, 110.101[c], 110.102).

Supplementary Medical Insurance Program (SMI) Also known as Part B, the voluntary portion of Medicare in which all persons entitled to the hospital insurance program (Part A) may enroll. The program is financed on a current basis from monthly premiums paid by persons insured under the program and a matching amount from federal general revenues. During any calendar year, the program will pay (with certain exceptions) 80% of the reasonable charge (as determined by the program) for all covered services after the insured pays a deductible on the costs of such services. Covered services include physician services; home health care; medical and other health services; outpatient hospital services; and laboratory, pathology, and radiologic services. Any individual over 65 may elect to enroll in Part B. However, individuals not eligible for Part A who elect to buy into Part A must also buy into Part B. State welfare agencies may buy Part B coverage for elderly and disabled public assistance recipients and pay the premiums on their behalf. The program contracts with carriers to process claims under the program. The carriers determine amounts to be paid for claims on the basis of reasonable charges. The name, Part B, refers to Part B of Title XVIII of the Social Security Act, the legislative authority for the program. *See also medical eligibility; Medicare.*

supplementary payments In medical malpractice and liability insurance, a requirement placed on insurance companies to pay for defense costs, any interest charged against the judgment, and costs of court bonds. In addition, they must pay the cost of recovery and any dollar judgments handed down by the court. *See also recovery.*

supplementation Partial payment for a portion of the cost of nursing home care by the patient or his or her family. Supplementation was a common requirement in state Medicaid programs in several of the southern states. Prior to 1972, the practice was stopped in response to a directive of the Senate Finance Committee set forth in the report on the 1967 Social Security Amendments. Supplementation should not be confused with the practice of requiring an individual to contribute his or her excess income to assist in payment for nursing home care. Generally, under Medicaid, a nursing home must agree to accept reimbursement from the state as the full amount of its payment for service. Under a system of supplementation, a state pays a certain rate, but the nursing home does not agree to accept that amount as full payment. Instead, it accepts supplementation of the state rate by the individual or his family. The amount the home collects in supplement is not under the control of the state. Supplementation generally was used where the state rate was admittedly not sufficient to pay for the cost of the care.

supplier Generally, any institution, individual, or agency that furnishes a medical item or service. In Medicare, suppliers are distinguished from providers, including hospitals and skilled nursing facilities. Institutions classified as providers are reimbursed by intermediaries on a reasonable cost basis, whereas suppliers, including physicians, nonhospital laboratories, and ambulance companies are paid by carriers on the basis of reasonable charges.

supplies Inexpensive materials, goods, or resources necessary for carrying on operations in a health-care organization such as paper, printer ribbons, pens, and other items that are regularly used in the daily operation of an office or in clinical practice; medical items, usually disposable, such as bandages, tongue depressors, rubbing alcohol, and latex gloves. Supplies are distinguished from permanent and durable capital goods (those whose use lasts over 1 year).

supply In health economics, the quantity of services supplied as the price of the service varies (income and other factors being held constant). For most services, increases in price induce increases in supply. Increases in demand (but not necessarily in need) normally induce an increase in price.

supply and demand In health economics and as a part of classical economic theory, this is when these two economic factors come together to determine the price of a commodity or service. Increased supply and availability increases competition, and prices go down. Short supply and high demand causes prices to rise. These processes are the driving forces behind a free-market and free-enterprise system. Government control, interference and regulations, monopolies, and marketing also affect pricing.

support 1. The financial, moral, and social obligation to provide food, clothing, and shelter for one's immediate family. 2. To bear the weight of; to endure; to bear or put up with. 3. To verify or prove.

support group A formal or informal mental health and social service where a group of persons and possibly family members with the same problem, disease, or condition meet together in a formal group meeting to talk about issues and problems related to the disease or condition to share feelings, concerns, insights, and solutions to problems on how to deal with the pains, frustrations, and stresses encountered. Having an opportunity to talk it out, see commonalties, share feelings, and develop trusted friends among persons with a commonality becomes most therapeutic. In some support groups, names and phone numbers are exchanged so that members can call and get personal support between meetings.

supportive services In long-term care and community health, these are social, nutritional, and related health care services provided to individuals in their homes to avoid institutionalization. Such services include home health care, meals on wheels, transportation services, volunteer visitors, and homemaker services.

support services 1. In health-care facilities and health-care delivery, these are programs or services that ensure efficient management of medical care services and an effective patient care environment and that assist in the delivery of services and ensure continuity of care but are not direct patient care services such as social services, discharge planning, patient representatives, information and referral, and transportation coordination. 2. In managed care and insurance, these are supplemental services provided by an insurance agency or health plan to facilitate the members' ability to use the primary care services of the organization. *See supportive services; ancillary services.*

support staff According to JCAHO for psychiatric, alcoholism, and drug abuse facilities accreditation purposes, employees or volunteers whose primary activities involve clerical, housekeeping, security, laboratory, recordkeeping, and other functions necessary for the overall clinical and administrative operation of the facility.

support system Those individuals who provide support or assist a person in an emergency or crisis.

suppress 1. To subdue. 2. To prevent or disallow. 3. To conceal or keep in. 4. To restrain.

suppress evidence In law, this is to subdue or conceal evidence from being used in a criminal trial by trying to show that it was obtained illegally or that it is irrelevant.

suppression 1. Controlling, hindering, or inhibiting an impulse, emotion, experience, or idea. Suppression is different from repression in that the latter is an unconscious process. 2. Sudden stoppage. 3. A mental or defense mechanism whereby unpleasant feelings and experiences are kept from conscious awareness.

supremacy clause Article VI, Section 2, of the U.S. Constitution: All legal documents or laws made, under the authority of the United States, shall be the supreme law of the land; and the judges in every state shall be bound by them and anything in the Constitution or laws of any state.

supremacy of law In any government, the highest authority is the law, not the citizen's wants. *See also supremacy clause.*

surcharge 1. Additional money added onto something already paid for. 2. An excessive or added charge above the regular price. 3. Any additional word or mark. 4. To overload or overburden.

surety 1. Certainly; that which makes security; assurance that something will happen. 2. A guarantee; security; insurance. 3. One who guarantees or gives assurance.

surety bond In health-care financial management, this is a written financial contract that guarantees the work of a third party. The principal (insurance company or bondholder) is the party required to respond to the second (protected) party for the losses caused by a third party such as a contractor; the party who agrees to make good on any default on the part of a third party in performing duties toward the party protected under the bond.

surface impoundment 1. In environmental health, this is a natural topographic depression, man-made excavation or diked area formed primarily of earthen materials (although it may be lined with man-made materials) that is not an injection well. This is designed to hold an accumulation of liquid wastes or wastes containing fee liquids (EPA). 2. Treatment, storage, or disposal of liquid hazardous wastes in ponds.

surface water In environmental health, these are all waters that are open to the atmosphere and subject to surface runoff (EPA). All waters naturally open and on the earth's surface such as rivers, lakes, reservoirs, streams, impoundments, seas, estuaries, creeks, ponds, runoff, and open stock tanks that are not considered wastewater or liquid waste. *See groundwater.*

surface water resources In environmental health, these are all the waters of the United States, including the sediments suspended in water or lying on the bank, bed, or shoreline and sediments transported through coastal and marine areas. The term does not include groundwater, surface water, or sediments in ponds, lakes, or reservoirs designed for waste treatment.

surgeon A physician who, through advanced training in a residency, specializes in the treatment of diseases, disorders, and conditions through surgery. This physician must be screened and accepted by the medical staff of a hospital prior to being allowed to perform surgery. Provisional status may be granted while the surgeon's application is being approved.

surgeon, general A physician who provides surgical treatment for various body systems, organs, or body parts rather than specializing in one area of surgery with broad but in-depth surgical skills and training.

Surgeon General The chief physician and head administrative officer of the U.S. Public Health Service.

surgeon, operating In medical care and in the process of conducting surgical procedures in an operating room on a patient who has been properly prepared for surgery, this the head surgeon who actually does the cutting and surgical treatment or repair. This physician is responsible for all medical care surrounding the surgical operation, including postsurgery care. Other surgeons, called "assistant surgeons," may assist in the operation. The physician who admits a patient to the hospital or surgical center is the attending physician and may or may not be the operating surgeon.

surgeon, oral A dentist with advanced training in surgical procedures of the mouth and its anatomical dental structures. The oral surgeon provides surgical treatment to patients with diseased, deformed, injured, or dysfunctional mouth tissue, teeth or supportive tissue, or structures of the teeth.

surgery 1. Any operation or manual procedure that requires cutting or destruction of the body's tissues or any invasive procedure undertaken for the diagnosis or treatment of a disease, injury, or other disorder. 2. The branch of medicine concerned with diseases that require, or are responsive to, treatment by cutting into the tissues of the body to repair, restore, or remove injured or disease tissue. 3. Any work done by a surgeon or other physician that includes the cutting of tissues of the body. 4. The title of the room or suite where surgical procedures occur. *See also operation; psychosurgery; major surgery; minor surgery; elective surgery; cosmetic surgery.*

surgery, ambulatory Minor, less complex or less severe surgical procedures done to patients who walk in and leave on the same day who are not admitted to the hospital and return home after the surgery. *See surgicenter; ambulatory care; ambulatory care center; ambulatory care services; ambulatory health-care services; ambulatory services settings.*

surgery, day *See surgicenter; ambulatory care; ambulatory care center; ambulatory care services; ambulatory health-care services; ambulatory services settings.*

surgery department In hospital administration, this is the administrative and service unit of a hospital that provides surgical suites, and recovery rooms and all staff, support personnel, and materials for patients in need of surgical or emergency treatment.

surgery, elective Any medical condition or physical or bodily structure problem that may benefit from surgical repair but can be delayed or is not medically essential is considered elective. Some medical experts suggest that if a surgical treatment can be delayed and scheduled for sometime in the future and is not needed to prevent death or disability, it can be thought of as elective. Others believe that only cosmetic surgery and certain forms of plastic surgery are to be considered elective. Some managed-care and insurance policies will allow surgical treatment to be done only if deemed medically necessary. All other surgery is considered elective.

surgery, major Any surgical procedure that is long in duration, complex in process, extensive in its involvement, has large surgical wounds with much tissue cutting involvement, uses a large surgical team, involves much equipment and high levels of technology, is high in cost, requires hospitalization and inpatient treatment, and has an extensive recovery period.

surgery, minor Any surgical procedure that is short in duration, simple in its process, relatively limited and small in its involvement, has limited surgical wounds with minimal tissue cutting involved, uses a small surgical team, involves little technology, is lower in cost, and probably is done on an outpatient ambulatory basis with a short recovery period at home.

surgery, operating room Surgical procedures and treatment that cannot be done in the emergency room, physicians office, patient's bed, regular treatment room, or minor surgery suite.

surgery, outpatient *See outpatient surgery; surgicenter; ambulatory care; ambulatory care center; ambulatory care services; ambulatory health-care services; ambulatory services settings; surgery, ambulatory.*

surgery requiring hospitalization Any surgical procedure that is long in duration, complex in process, uses a large surgical team, involves much equipment and high levels of technology that should be done in the hospital setting because it requires extensive testing and inpatient treatment, and has an extensive recovery period needing intensive care and continual monitoring.

surgery, same-day *See outpatient surgery; surgicenter; ambulatory care; ambulatory care center; ambulatory care services; ambulatory health-care services; ambulatory services settings; surgery, ambulatory.*

surgery, unjustified These are surgical treatment procedures deemed by a review committee, a panel of peers, or a health plan representative as not being medically necessary. A peer review panel would ask a question such as, "Would the average surgeon with the same background, knowledge, and experience have performed this operation?" Diagnostic, lab tests, X rays, CT scans, MRIs, and other evidence is reviewed and considered to see if surgery is justified or unjustified.

surgery, unnecessary Surgical treatment procedures that were not required and that really did not change the medical condition or the health status of the patient. Disease, illness, or conditions that could have been managed by a physician without surgery. Justified surgery could be unnecessary.

surgical In medical care, these are any methods, operations, techniques, or treatments related to and involving surgery; pertaining to surgery.

surgical and anesthesia services In medical care, this is the delivery of care to any patient in any setting who receives for any purpose by any route 1) general, spinal, or other major regional anesthesia or 2) sedation (with or without analgesia) for which there is a reasonable expectation that, in the manner used, the sedation/analgesia will result in the loss of protective reflexes for a significant percentage of a group of patients (JCAHO for acute-care facilities).

surgical asepsis In medical care and infection control, these are methods or measures taken that render items or objects free from pathogenic and nonpathogenic microorganisms. *See sanitary; sanitation; sterile.*

surgical case review In medical care, this is a medical staff responsibility that entails monitoring, evaluating, and improving the quality of surgical care and the use of other invasive procedures. Standards are applied to evaluate the hospital's performance of the review process (JCAHO for acute-care hospitals).

surgical center An ambulatory, outpatient facility used to provide surgery to patients where an overnight hospital stay is not required and the patient is not admitted as an inpatient. The facilities may be in a hospital or in an outpatient, freestanding medical clinic.

surgical expense insurance In medical insurance this is a type of health insurance policy that provides benefits toward the doctor's operating fees. Benefits usually consist of scheduled amounts for each surgical procedure.

surgical hierarchy *See operating room procedure hierarchy.*

surgical insurance benefits A type of medical insurance used to insure against financial loss caused by surgical expenses.

surgical-medical insurance One type of insurance that is used to pay for all or part of the medical bill for surgical treatment by a surgeon regardless of the setting in which it is done. The medical part of the insurance is to pay for physician visits other than the surgery and any hospitalization that may be required. Part B of Medicare or CHAMPUS is this type of insurance. Also referred to as "major medical."

surgical operations *See surgery.*

surgical procedures, in-hospital In medical care using surgical treatment, this is any cutting process or activity, setting dislocated joints, setting fractures, suturing wounds, circumcisions, and cesarean section deliveries (does not include normal deliveries) done in a hospital to inpatients. The patient usually uses the hospital recovery room and has been admitted as an inpatient using the usual or appropriate hospital-based testing and services.

surgical resident A graduate medical student undergoing advanced training and education, usually for 3 to 5 years, in the methods, approaches, practices, techniques, procedures, protocol, and all relevant physiological, medical, and patient care aspects related and important to the process of conducting surgery.

surgical schedule In managed care or medical insurance, this is a list of cash allowances that are payable for various types of surgery with the maximum amounts based on the severity of the operations.

surgical scrub In medical care and infection control management, this is an infection control measure that includes a thorough cleansing procedure of the hands, wrists, and forearm prior to surgery or entering a sterile situation in which the hands are held higher than the elbows to maintain sterility.

surgical scrubs In medical care surgical procedures and surgical services, this is the sterile clothing worn by the physicians, surgical team, and visitors while doing surgery to maintain infection control and sanitary conditions.

surgical services 1. In health-care delivery and medical care, this is the diagnosis and treatment of physical diseases or conditions or their symptoms by means of operative techniques in conjunction with the administration of local or general anesthesia as appropriate. 2. In insurance, these services mean the work performed by a surgeon in treating diseases, injuries, and deformities by manual or operative means. *See surgical asepsis; sterile; sterile field; sanitary; sanitation.*

surgical specialty In medical care, this is a physician with specialized training in certain aspects of surgery. A physician need not be board certified in the surgical specialty and may be listed as their secondary specialty rather than their primary specialty. General areas considered surgical specialist include general surgery, orthopedic surgery, plastic surgery, neurological surgery (neurosurgery), thoracic surgery, cardiac surgery, colon and rectal surgery, urology, obstetrics, ophthalmology, and otolaryngology.

surgical suite In hospitals or surgical centers, these are specialized rooms that are staffed and equipped as operating rooms with all supportive surgical preparation rooms and services, including scrub rooms, sterile room, recovery rooms, X-ray facilities, and laboratory.

surgical team The combined services of several physicians, often of different specialties, in a surgical operation, plus other highly skilled, specially trained surgical technicians, operating room nurses, other personnel, and various types of complex equipment.

surgical technologist An individual who works as a general technical assistant on the surgical team by arranging supplies and instruments in the operating room, maintaining antiseptic conditions, preparing patients for surgery, and assisting the surgeon during the operation. *See also operating room technician.*

surgical technology *See surgical technologist.*

surgicenter Usually a freestanding ambulatory health-care facility that may be incorporated as a separate business organization and that is usually physically and organizationally separate from a hospital, serving outpatients on a scheduled basis who require surgical treatment exceeding that needed in a physician's office but less serious or severe than those requiring advanced hospital surgical suites and hospitalization. Most minor and some major surgical procedures are done on an ambulatory basis. Also referred to as units for "ambulatory surgery," "day surgery," or "in-and-out surgery." *See ambulatory care; ambulatory care center; ambulatory care services; ambulatory health-care services; ambulatory services settings.*

surplus In managed care and insurance, this is the excess of a company's assets (including any capital) over liabilities; overattainment of funds; profits. Surplus may be used for future dividends or expansion of business or to meet possible unfavorable future developments. Surpluses may be developed and increased intentionally by including an amount in the premium in excess of the pure premium needed to meet anticipated liabilities (known as a "risk charge"). Surpluses are sometimes earmarked in part as contingency reserves and in part as unassigned surplus.

surplus-line market These are insurance companies that provide insurance coverage to areas not covered by domestic insurance companies. Lloyds of London provides much coverage to this market through its special agents or brokers.

surplussage In health administration and materials management, this is an excess of materials or supplies; over and above the required amount; something superfluous or unnecessary.

surprise In law, this is when one party is brought

to trial with no intent or purpose on the part of the opposite party and is presented with an issue that was completely unexpected and unanticipated, resulting in difficulty in presenting his or her side of the case. This situation could cause a new trial or a delay in the present trial.

surrender 1. To give back or give up. 2. To return.

surrogate 1. A person appointed to act for another. 2. A substitute. 3. A judge presiding over matters of probate and intestate succession. 4. A court officer who deals with proving of wills and estates. 5. A substitute person or object.

surrogate mother A female who is impregnated with the sperm of the husband of another woman (or possibly another male's sperm) and who goes through the entire pregnancy, has the child for the couple, and must surrender the child to the couple on birth; a woman who gets pregnant and has a child for another woman.

surrogate parent Any parental or authority figure who acts as a parent for a child and is reactive and sensitive to emotions, feelings, and responses in the child.

surtax Any tax above the normal or expected tax imposed on an item or service.

surveillance (French) To watch over. 1. As used in epidemiology, this is the continual watching over and close observation of the distribution and occurrence of diseases, injuries, illnesses, disorders, or conditions and death through an organized and standardized system of collecting, tabulating, analyzing, reporting, and disseminating data on the death, disease, or injury events. The overall goal of surveillance is to provide prevention and control measures of disease, injury, disability, or death for the public's health and to enhance a population's overall health status. The surveillance process establishes the natural history of a disease, a description of the occurrence of a disease, and epidemic-related insights for determining the time, place, and person aspects of a disease or outbreak. 2. In environmental health, this is the periodic monitoring of performance adequacy; all planned activities performed to ensure compliance with operational specifications established for a project or service. *See epidemiology; environmental assessment.*

surveillance of disease In epidemiology and public health, this is the continual scanning of the environment or population for any occurrence of or the rise and spread of all diseases that can be prevented and controlled or that cause, pain, suffering, disability, or death to institute prevention and control measures.

surveillance systems In environmental health, these are a series of monitoring devices, located strategically throughout the study area, designed to determine environmental quality or pollution activities.

survey 1. A questionnaire, form, interview schedule, or other written instrument used to gather information from large groups of individuals on the basis of individual observations, perceptions, and experiences. 2. The process of conducting a research study or investigation where information is systematically gathered using a survey form or questionnaire to obtain information on individual observations, perceptions, and experiences; questionnaire research that uses retrospective or cross-sectional research designs but does not use experimental designs. Person-to-person interviews, telephone interviews, self-completed forms, mailed-in forms, and group self-completed forms are several approaches used. 3. To scan, preview, observe, or gain information from a population, group, or community. *See survey research.*

survey, accreditation A full organization, facility, and medical care delivery assessment of a health-care organization by a survey team to determine compliance with accreditation standards. The Joint Commission on Accreditation of Healthcare Organizations, the American Health Care Association, the Medical Group Management Association, and the Unified Medical Group Association are examples of associations that conduct accreditation surveys. *See accreditation; accreditation survey.*

survey instrument In survey research, this is the actual questionnaire, interview form, interview schedule, or written checklist used to gather research information from large numbers of people in a population.

survey, focused An accreditation survey that concentrates on and examines only those areas deemed important to the progress of the health-care organization toward compliance with certain accreditation standards.

surveyor An individual who represents a state licensing agency, financing agency, or accredita-

survey research tion organization who physically goes through a health-care facility or organization to ensure it is up to standards. *See accreditation surveyor.*

survey research In epidemiology and health services research, this is a widely used research approach and can use complex research designs be as simple as a one-page questionnaire addressing a single variable or condition in the study population. Survey research requires a good research questionnaire. Developed questionnaires that are valid and reliable are available in published form. Researchers, consulting firms, and government agencies have developed standardized questionnaires that are useful for some studies. Special effort has been put into developing some survey forms so they can be computer scored and analyzed. Questionnaires are often developed by the researcher or in an agency. Questions on the survey form should ask simple, straightforward questions and be asked in a manner that will get the information desired. Wording of the questions should be reviewed, tested, and edited to ensure they are well prepared and ask what you want to know without bias or leading the subject. Avoid writing double negatives into questions. For example, "He has no immunizations, yes or no? There is no clinic nearby, yes or no?" Keep the questions and the questionnaires short and to the point. A major problem is retrieving the questionnaires, so a system to retrieve survey questionnaires needs to be established. Interviews and home visits solve data gathering and questionnaire retrieval problems. Mailed questionnaires are difficult to retrieve. Some seasoned researchers indicate that in mail-out questionnaires, a 50% return rate is considered quite good. Large sample sizes and appropriate sampling methods should be used. Five common approaches to survey research are 1) person-to-person interviews, 2) drop-off and retrieve questionnaire, 3) mailed questionnaires, 4) telephone interviews, and 5) newsletter or magazine surveys. *See epidemiology; sampling.*

surveys 1. In epidemiology and health services research, this is an information-gathering approach using questionnaires, direct observations, interviews, or other means to gather information from groups or populations to estimate norms and identify trends, characteristics, practices, behaviors, attitudes, and interests of individuals sampled from the study population. 2. In environmental health, this is a comprehensive examination of policies, procedures, practices, facilities, and equipment, including field observation of actual conditions.

survey, tailored An accreditation survey that is developed to meet the unique differences of some health-care organizations having unusual arrangements or several types of services and is covered by several different accreditation standards and criteria. *See accreditation, tailored survey.*

survey team A group of professionals who represent a state licensing agency, financing agency, governmental agency, or accreditation organization who physically go through a health-care facility or organization to assess quality and ensure it is up to standards in its operations, functions, activities, care, and treatment of patients. *See accreditation; surveyor.*

survival curve In vital statistics, epidemiology, and public health, this is a line graph that uses 100% as the base to show the percentage of the population still surviving at various intervals of time or various ages. *See population pyramid.*

survival rate The rate at which survivors in a population or group continue to live after exposure to disease, chemicals, or physical agents; individuals of a diseased or exposed group who are alive on a certain date and who are still alive at the end of a certain time interval (e.g., 5 years). The rate is equal to 1 minus the cumulative mortality rate. Current life tables or cohort life tables can be used to study or develop survival rates.

survive 1. To outlive; to live longer than another; to live beyond or through an event. 2. To have the health-care organization make it through difficult economic and financial periods and stay viable and functioning; the goal of any health-care organization.

survivorship, right of The legal right of a person to property of another from outliving or surviving that person.

survivorship studies In vital statistics and epidemiology, this includes the process of analyzing life tables to predict the likelihood of an event occurring. Events such as death are predictable to occur within certain time intervals after the diagnosis of certain diseases. Survivability is also predictable after certain intervals of time in people with certain diseases. Life tables are actually death tables and are based on complex statistical methods for predicting and summarizing death occurrence in a population, and the probability of surviving or dying can be determined statistically for certain ages, diseases, or other occurrences. Insurance companies use life tables to conduct survivorship studies. Various approaches, techniques, and methodologies are used to do survivorship studies and are found in demographic and population study books and resources. John Graunt developed life tables and studies to show the different patterns of mortality in London in the 1600s. Graunt found that higher levels of death occurred consistently in some parts of London than in others. *See life table, current/period; life table, cohort/generation.*

suspect 1. In law, this is to believe in the possibility of someone being guilty of an illegal act without having proof. 2. To conjecture; to consider as questionable. 3. One who is believed to be involved in the committing of a crime.

suspect class Any class of persons identified by a statute for special (discriminatory) treatment; classes identifiable by monetary worth, nationality, race, age, or sex.

suspect or know In epidemiology, this is when a scientific observation suggests the possibility of causation (cause-effect relationships) but has not been demonstrated by any health services or biomedical research.

suspended sentence In law, this is a sentence that is formally handed down for a crime committed but that is not enforced or served.

suspended solids In environmental health, these are small particles of solid pollutants that float on the surface of, or are suspended in, sewage, water, or other liquids and often resist removal by conventional means. *See total suspended solids; total suspended particulates.*

suspend the rules In formal health-care meetings, this is a parliamentary procedure rule where formal procedures are set aside to save time. A formal motion must be approved by a two-thirds vote of the board or committee.

suspension In environmental health, this is the act of suspending the use of a pesticide the EPA deems necessary to prevent an imminent hazard resulting from the continued use of the pesticide. A registrant can request a hearing before the suspension goes into effect (EPA). *See pesticide tolerance; suspension; emergency; pesticide.*

suspension, emergency In environmental health, this is the act of immediately suspending the use of a pesticide the EPA deems necessary to prevent an imminent hazard from resulting from the continued use of the pesticide. An emergency suspension takes effect immediately. *See suspension.*

suspension list A policy developed and enforced by the medical records committee and hospital administration that mandates that a physician must complete and sign all records in his or her file to have his or her name removed or kept off the suspension list. The physician who fails to complete and sign all records within a specified time period is restricted from admission of patients, scheduling surgery, and all other medical staff privileges. If the records remain incomplete for a long enough period of time, further corrective action is taken such as suspension of admitting privileges.

suspicion In law, this is being held without specific charges stated or brought against you. If not charged, by law you must be released or can be released by a writ of habeas corpus being filed with the court.

sustain 1. To maintain or uphold. 2. To suffer or undergo loss. 3. To confirm or grant. 4. To bear out.

susto (Spanish) Shock; fright. A mental and emotional disorder common to the Mexican American culture characterized by shock, fright, or sudden terror.

Sutton's law In managed care, this is to focus attention, management activities, and healthcare utilization efforts on activities that make money and enhance the long-term financial viability of the organization. The law is "Go where the money is" and is based on a folk story about the Depression-era bank robber Willy Sutton, who, when asked why he robbed banks, was supposed to have said, "That is where the money is."

suture In medical care, this is surgical sewing or use of stitches to close wounds, cuts, or injuries such as lacerations or surgical wounds in the organs or tissues of the body. Staples are also used to suture wounds; first used at the end of the World War II when penicillin was being tested experimentally to see if it would help in the healing of war wounds. For the first time in North Africa in late 1945, wounds were stitched together and then injected with penicillin. Suturing, together with the new antibiotic, caused serious battle wounds to heal rapidly. Prior to this, closing wounds meant closing in the disease-causing microorganisms.

S.W. In law, this is the South Western Reporter of the National Reporter System of case law reports.

swap maternity In managed care, this is a provision in group health insurance plans providing immediate maternity benefits to a newly covered woman but terminating coverage on pregnancies in progress on termination of a woman's coverage. *See also switch maternity; flat maternity.*

swing beds 1. The process of alternating beds between acute and long-term care. This procedure saves hospitals from going into debt and helps keep their census counts up while balancing services to meet demands, all of which increases revenue for the facility while reducing the risk of closure. This is a most useful procedure for rural hospitals, especially combination facilities. 2. In rural hospitals, these are licensed acute-care beds designated by that hospital to provide either acute- or long-term-care services. A hospital qualifying to receive Medicare and Medicaid reimbursement for care provided to swing bed patients must be located in a rural area (as defined by the U.S. Bureau of the Census), have less than 100 acute-care beds, and, where applicable, must have received a certificate of need for the provision of long-term-care services from its state health planning and development agency (Section 1883,b1 of the Social Security Act). *See sole community hospital; combination hospital.*

swing-out plan *See managed choice.*

switch maternity A provision in group health insurance plans providing maternity benefits to female employees only when their husbands are covered in the plan as their dependents; has the effect of denying maternity benefits to single women. *See also swap maternity; flat maternity.*

SWOT Strengths, Weaknesses, Opportunities, Threats. In strategic planning this is a brainstorming exercise that is used to conduct an internal and external analysis of a health-care organization. Strengths and weaknesses is the internal assessment part of the analysis. Opportunities and threats is the external analysis part of the exercise. Usually, personnel from several levels of operations and responsibility are included in the exercise, so several SWOT exercises are conducted and results recorded and analyzed. SWOT analysis results assist in understanding the operational issues and concerns of the organization and can be used to develop tactics, strategies, goals, and objectives. SWOT is one approach to internal and external analysis. *See strategic planning.*

Sydenham, Thomas A physician in England (1624–1689) who has been credited with contributing greatly to epidemiology. He wrote much on diseases that come in the form of major epidemics such as the bubonic plague, scarlet fever, and malaria. He wrote a book, *Opera Omni*, which was about the great plagues of the time.

Sydenstricker, Edgar One of the first prominent public health statisticians in the United States, Sydenstricker (1881–1936) contributed much to the areas of morbidity rates and statistics. He was appointed the first public health statistician in the U.S. Public Health Service and was a noted author in the area of public health and epidemiology.

syllabus 1. A summary or abstract of a case. 2. An outline or overview.

sym- Prefix meaning "together."

symbiosis In mental health, this is a psychological process where a dependent relationship is created between two mentally ill persons. This relationship helps to reinforce each other's pathological condition.

symbolic delivery In law, the giving of an item of value to be used as a legal symbol of ownership. For example, giving a key to an automobile to an individual is a symbolic delivery of the actual gift.

symmetrical relationship *See association; causality.*

sympathetic nervous system In medical care, this is the part of the autonomic nervous system that is reactionary rather than voluntary. In stressful situations, its response is helpful in dealing with threatening situations by preparing one's body for fight or flight.

sympathomimetic drug Any drug that can reproduce or cause the same reactions that are produced by the sympathetic nervous system. Examples are amphetamine and epinephrine.

sympathy In mental health, this is the psychological process of showing pity or some concern for another's fears by sharing their feelings, ideas, and experiences. This is opposed to empathy, is not objective, and may cause existing pathology to continue or worsen.

symptom In medical care, this is any abnormal manifestation or reaction that departs from the normal function, appearance, or sensation experienced by a patient; any sign indicative of disease. *See sign.*

symptom complex In medical care, this is when a set of symptoms run together and may indicate the existence of a disease, condition, or disorder.

symptom formation *See symptom substitution.*

symptom substitution In mental health, this is a psychological process where repressed desire shows itself and is indirectly released through psychological or behavioral symptoms. Such symptoms can include obsession, compulsion, phobia, dissociation, anxiety, depression, hallucination, and delusion. The reaction is also known as a "symptom formation."

syn- Prefix meaning "together."

syncope Being faint; having temporary loss of consciousness.

syncretic-thought In mental health, this is the psychological process of concrete and specific thought processes reached at certain stages of development (Jean Piaget).

syndicate 1. Any group of persons organized for a special undertaking. 2. A joint venture.

syndrome A group of effects, signs, and symptoms of a condition or disorder that always occur together and that constitute a typical clinical picture. *See disease.*

synergism 1. The cooperative interaction of two or more chemicals or other phenomena producing a greater total effect than the sum of their individual effects. 2. Used in health-care administration to indicate how team management approaches should work, that is, all the health facility managers working together to produce a greater total success of the facility and organization.

synergistic effect An agent or substance that affects the action of another agent or substance so that their combined effect is greater than each separately.

synopsis A summary, abstract, or overview of a document or case.

syntaxic thought In mental health, this is the psychological process of logical, goal-directed, and reality-oriented thought processes (Harry Stack Sullivan).

synthesis The combining of the elements or parts of a whole.

synthetic estimate In epidemiology and health services research, this is a statistic produced from the combining of local population data such as proportions (or means) and then using proportions (or means) from another like population as comparisons to estimate need.

synthetic organic chemicals In environmental health, these are man-made organic chemicals some of which are volatile. Some tend to stay dissolved in water rather than evaporate.

syntropy Healthy or wholesome relationships.

syphilis In public health, this is one of several STDs (sexually transmitted diseases) that is highly communicable and often in epidemic proportions in populations and that is treatable but, if left untreated, can be spread to many sexual partners. The disease can cause organic psychosis if left untreated.

system 1. Separate but related elements that are pulled together to form a common result; the coordination of various elements of a program to accomplish a goal; an organized set of components consisting of interdependent parts that make up a whole. 2. A group of components that are drawn together and work together, that can change or affect one another, and that rely on the actions or activities of each and all components to reach a goal or objective using inputs, processes, outputs, and feedback; an arrangement of interrelated and interdependent parts that have a common set of goals.

system analyses The formal assessment and evaluation of a system and the interrelationships among its various parts (including plant and hardware, policies and procedures, and personnel) to determine the real and potential problems in the system and to suggest ways to improve the system and eliminate the problems.

systematic error In epidemiology and health services research, this is an error in the statistical analysis. Biased forms of measurement error (e.g., overestimates) are not balanced by underestimates.

systematic sampling A research design sampling approach that selects every X number as a sample from a list or group of individuals. For example, a medical records administrator assisting in research may select every fifth patient record out of the master index file to examine the principal diagnosis for the research project.

Systematized Nomenclature of Medicine (SNOMED) A publication of the College of American Pathologists that is a systematized multiaxial nomenclature of medically useful terms hierarchically organized. The nomenclature is arranged in fields: topography, morphology, etiology, function, disease, and procedure, which allow for coding, computerization, sorting, and retrieving large volumes of information from medical records.

systemic Pertaining to being in or affecting the system; internal to the system or the systems of the body. For example, an infection can be in the blood of an individual and is spread throughout the entire body and thus is a systemic infection; affecting the whole body.

systemic error In epidemiology and health services research in the analysis of the findings, distorted results may occur because data are collected for a specific reason, good research protocol and uniform data collection approaches are not followed, or the data are analyzed in such a manner as to prove a point or support a cause, all resulting in distorted findings or errors in findings, results, or presentation from errors internal to the system of collection and analysis.

systems analysis In health-care administration activities or medical records administration, this is an approach to in-depth problem solving used to ascertain the most appropriate process for accomplishing an activity. The process involves planning, program development, and implementation of computer-based health-care information and data systems; the study of interdependent parts and their interrelationships in terms of the systems goals, the operating environment, resources available, tasks to be accomplished, achievement of goals and objectives, and the management of the system; the construction of models used to simulate real-life situations and then tested to observe the effects produced by changes made in the model that could not be assessed in real life situations.

systems analyst In health-care administration and information management, this is a specially trained individual who designs computerized information systems to meet the operational, information, and data needs of various departments in a health-care organization.

systems approach 1. A planning methodology, derived from engineering and computer science and adapted for use in management, health administration, medicine, health promotion, nursing, and other fields. The most basic systems approach relies on a four-phase model consisting of inputs, process, outputs, and a feedback loop to the three elements. 2. In health administration, this is one approach to managing large health-care organizations such as hospitals, where each department, program, and service interact with, depend on, and affect the work, processes, and activities of the others. If change occurs in one element of the system, it causes or affects change in other areas and possibly throughout the entire hospital. From a systems perspective, all areas of an organization have an interdependence, reliance on, interaction with, and effect and change on other programs or services in the organization. Thus, the entire hospital is viewed as a system comprised of interactive and interdependent subsystems affected by individual components inputs, processes, outputs, and feedback as well as hospitalwide outcomes.

systems management 1. The analysis, understanding, planning, coordination, and controlling of a system for maximum effectiveness and efficiency. 2. In health administration, this is the administration of a health-care organization as a system, including the management of the elements of the systems model: inputs (goals and objectives), process (planning, organizing, staffing, supervising, coordinating, controlling, and communicating), and output (productivity and results being realized with all elements adapting, improving, controlling quality, and changing as the result of feedback).

systems planning In health planning and health administration, this is also referred to as "systems approach"; the continuous planning methodology that addresses the segments of a continuum as they relate to the whole. *See system.*

systems review approach In medical records administration, this is one method of arranging the medical record by body systems. In the recording process, the physician reviews and records it in the patient's medical record, system by system.

systolic pressure In medical care, this is one component of blood pressure and its measurement, with the greatest amount of pressure exerted by the blood being forced against the arterial wall during contraction of ventricles of the heart. Systolic is just as the heart contracts and is the top number of a blood pressure reading. The bottom number, referred to as diastolic, is when the heart muscle is relaxed between beats. The average systolic reading is 120 and the average diastolic reading 80. This is considered normal blood pressure (120/80) for younger adults; 140/90 is the reading that adults should not exceed. *See Appendix VI.*

T

TA *See transactional analysis.*

T&A Tonsillectomy and adenoidectomy.

table In epidemiology, this is an organized systematic presentation of data or information for the purpose of summarizing it into a visual presentation and in a manner that is quickly reviewed; the structured organization of data with categories and frequencies, percentages, means, or other quantitative and qualitative information presented.

table rates *See age/sex rates.*

tablet A drug, medicine, or medication in solid pill form.

tacit 1. Saying nothing or making no sound. 2. Unspoken, still, or silent. 3. Implied. 4. Understood without being spoken.

tactic A method, technique, or approach to better position the organization; one element of a strategy. In strategic health planning, these are actions or activities to make a strategy work or through which a strategy is carried out.

tactile Pertaining to the sense of touch.

Taft-Hartley Act A 1947 federal law that created rights for the employer to balance union rights created by the Wagner Act. It helped control unfair union and labor practices such as forcing employees to join a union as a condition of employment.

Taft-Hartley Act injunctions In labor law, this sets forth the conditions under which the President of the United States is to seek a court order to delay a labor strike for 80 days as a cooling off period and allowing time to investigate issues of the dispute.

Taguchi technique In quality management, this is a statistical technique for optimizing design and production to increase quality. It was developed by Japanese consultant Genichi Taguchi.

tail 1. Curtailed. 2. Limited in a specific way as in an inheritance limited to only children or grandchildren. 3. To cut. 4. To set down a tally. 5. To limit, as by an entail.

talc A silicate powder used in ceramics, cosmetics, paint, and pharmaceuticals as a powder and a filler in soap, putty, and plaster. It is used on the inside of sterile rubber or latex gloves to make them go on easily.

talesman 1. A person called in to serve as a juror. 2. A person summoned as a spokesman.

tamper 1. To make changes by meddling or interfering. 2. To plot or scheme. 3. To make secret illegal arrangements. 4. To make corrupt or illegal.

tampon A cotton sponge used to plug a body cavity subject to bleeding.

tamponade A plug, usually of cotton, used to stop hemorrhage.

tangible Something real that can be held or touched.

tangible assets In health-care finance, these are land, equipment, buildings, vehicles, etc. that belong to a company and are of financial worth as opposed to goodwill; the value of a medical practice's clientele or patient list.

TAR *See treatment authorization request.*

target compound list In environmental health, this is a list of substances, chemicals, and materials under the Superfund initiative that includes 34 volatile organic chemicals, 65 semivolatile organic chemicals, 19 pesticides, 7 polychlorinated biphenyls, 23 metals, and total cyanide. In Superfund cleanups, each of these must be sampled and analyzed (EPA).

target group 1. In program development grant-writing activities, a select group of persons or a geographic area where its residents will benefit from the funding of a particular project. 2. In health services, health-care delivery, and program development, a community area chosen by the health-care organization as the recipient of a service; a service area, community, or special population that has been designated to receive services because of a demand for services or from an identified need associated with the population or location. *See service area.*

target market Any potential group or population that is the attention and focus of a health-care services marketing process.

target population In health services delivery, health-care marketing, or managed-care planning, this is a group or subgroup of people or population from specific areas or a select group having certain needs for which a program is aimed and is intended for those who can benefit from a specific program or service. *See target group.*

targets In environmental health, this is any person, objects, or animals on which any unwanted substance, agent, or dangerous energy flow may act to cause damage, injury, or death.

tariff 1. A list of items. 2. That which has a form or substance to it. 3. An explanation or information given, especially about fees to be paid. 4. To set a price or tax on an item, goods, or service; an import tax.

task analysis In health administration, this is a systematic review of a collection of actions or behaviors necessary and sufficient to complete a given task; a thorough assessment of the various and individual elements and supplemental actions constituting a task.

taskforce In health administration, health planning, and program development, this a committee-type group of individuals who have been given the responsibility to address a problem and come up with some workable solutions; a work group of individuals charged with carrying out a specific task. This task oriented work group may be ongoing but mostly is administered on an ad hoc basis with a specific time line until the specific task is completed.

task identity In health administration and the motivational aspects of management, this is when workers complete an important job, enabling them to have a sense of responsibility, importance, job satisfaction, and pride.

task significance In health administration and the motivational aspects of management, this is when a worker knows that the work he or she does is important to others in the organization and for the overall mission of the health-care organization.

TASO *See The AIDS Support Organizations.*

TASO Community Initiative In AIDS health services, this is a community based AIDS program that convenes community leaders and analyzes community problems caused by AIDS. From the community level, committees are formed to deal with community problems and oversee HIV/AIDS activities.

TAT Thematic Apperception Test. A psychological test using projective techniques in which the subject supplies interpretations of a series of pictures, revealing his or her own feelings, perceptions, and attitudes.

tautology Needless repetition of an idea using different words; redundancy.

tax 1. A compulsory payment of money to a government. 2. To assess or determine judicially the amount of levy for the support of certain government functions for public purposes; a charge or burden, usually pecuniary, laid on persons or property for public purposes; a forced contribution of wealth to meet the public needs of a government. *See also tax credit; tax deduction; regressive tax; proportional tax; progressive tax.*

taxable income 1. Money or profit gained that is legally taxable or filed under the tax laws. 2. The income against which taxes are paid.

tax, ad valorem 1. A tax according to value. 2. A portion or percentage of the value on a taxable article.

tax appropriations In some states and local governments, these are subsidies or special tax funds made available to support hospitals, nursing homes, or health-care facilities. For example, a rural town might have a 1% sales tax used to support the operation of the sole community hospital, ensuring its continued operation and preventing it from closing because of low occupancy rates.

tax avoidance Taking advantage of all legal tax breaks, deductions, exemptions, etc.

tax committee In managed care and insurance company operations, this is a subcommittee of the board of directors that is responsible for keeping abreast of changes in tax laws and structures and for assessing and evaluating the tax effect and implications of company financing policies, approaches, services, and programs.

tax credit A reduction of tax liability for federal income tax purposes. Several national health insurance proposals allow businesses and/or individuals to reduce their taxes dollar for dollar for certain defined medical expenses. The effect of using a tax credit approach rather than a tax deduction is to give persons and businesses an equal benefit for each dollar expended on health care. A tax credit favors lower over higher income people, whereas a tax deduction is worth more the higher the marginal tax rate. *See also medicredit.*

tax deduction A reduction in one's income base on which federal income tax is calculated. Health insurance expenditures are deductible by businesses as a business expense. Because the tax rate for most large businesses is 48%, this means a reduction in tax liability of nearly $1 for each $2 the business spends on health insurance. Individuals may take a medical deduction on their personal income tax of all health insurance premiums plus all medical expenses and premiums if they exceed 5% of income. Because the marginal tax rate is related to income and is higher for higher income persons and businesses, the value of a tax deduction for income spent on medical care increases as income increases. Thus, the subsidy is effectively greater for the higher income person or more profitable corporation. *See also tax credit.*

Tax Equity and Fiscal Responsibility Act of 1982 (TEFRA) Developed in the U.S. Senate and passed by Congress (P.L. 97-248) in response to the mandate of the First Concurrent Budget Resolution to increase government revenues by approximately $100 billion for the first 3 fiscal years. TEFRA's four principal objectives include the following: 1) to raise revenues to narrow anticipated budget deficits, 2) to ensure that both individual and business taxpayers pay their fair share of the total tax burden, 3) to reduce distortions in economic behavior resulting from the present tax system, and 4) to charge groups benefiting from specific government programs with the costs of those programs. Its main thrust was to develop a prospective payment system of reimbursement for hospitals receiving funds under Medicare from the Health Care Financing Administration (HCFA).

taxes on social security For elderly participants and beneficiaries of Social Security, the upper 15% of retirees pay taxes on their Social Security income, that is, those earning more than $25,000 per year. Couples with net incomes of $32,000 must include 50% of their Social Security checks in tax reports, and by law the taxes are channeled back into the Social Security fund and not used for any other purpose.

tax evasion 1. Not paying any taxes or paying fewer taxes than required by law. 2. Committing tax fraud by paying taxes in less amounts than is true or can be accounted for.

tax-exempt bond *See tax-exempt revenue bonds.*

tax-exempt revenue bonds In health-care financial management, these are revenue bonds available to hospitals or other health-care organizations in which the bond issuer (usually the government) promises to repay the bondholder (taxpayers). These are used to raise funds in anticipation of tax receipts and then are repaid from tax revenues. Most revenue bonds issues by a government are tax exempt with no federal income tax paid on earned interest.

tax expenditure budget In the federal budget, an enumeration of revenue losses resulting from tax expenditures. Section 301 of the Congressional Budget and Impoundment Control Act of 1974 requires that estimated levels of tax expenditures be presented by major functions in the congressional and presidential budgets.

tax expenditures Revenues lost to government because of any form of legal tax reduction or tax forgiveness, including tax credits and deductions. The term emphasizes that such revenues foregone for specific purposes (e.g., subsidizing private purchase of health insurance through the federal income tax deduction for health insurance) are budgetarily equivalent to actual federal expenditures. *See also tax expenditure budget.*

taxing cost Legally causing one party in a lawsuit to pay the other party's legal fees.

taxonomy In public health, epidemiology, and biomedical science, this is a systematic classification of cases, subjects, agents, diseases, or other phenomena; putting subjects or things into orderly categories according to their logical relationships as applicable to their use or discipline of study.

tax-sheltered annuity A retirement plan open to employees of certain nonprofit hospitals and school systems whereby the employee may invest in fixed or variable annuities without paying income tax on the wages or earnings until the money is received after retirement.

T binder In medical care, this a binder used in dressing wounds or surgical areas or a bandage-type cloth shaped in a T to retain dressings in the genital areas.

TB unit *See tuberculosis unit.*

TCI *See TASO Community Initiative.*

TCs Therapeutic communities.

teaching facilities Areas dedicated for use by students, faculty, or administrative personnel for clinical purposes, research activities, libraries, classrooms, offices, auditoriums, dining areas, student activities, or other related purposes necessary for and appropriate to the conduct of comprehensive programs of education. This includes interim facilities but usually does not include off-site improvements or living quarters.

teaching hospital An acute-care facility usually associated with a medical school that provides undergraduate and/or graduate medical education to interns and residents, usually with one or more medical, dental, or osteopathic (AMA, ADA, or AOA approved) internship and residency programs. Hospitals that educate nurses and other health personnel but do not train physicians are not generally thought of as teaching hospitals, nor are those that have only programs of continuing education for practicing professionals. *See also house staff; affiliated hospital.*

teaching hospital, graduate associated Teaching hospitals that have one or more training programs directed by medical school clinical departments and may also have training programs independent of the medical school.

teaching hospital, independent Teaching hospitals that conduct only their own graduate and undergraduate medical education programs.

teaching hospital, principal Teaching hospitals in which medical school clinical departments direct all aspects of graduate training programs.

teaching hospital, undergraduate associated Teaching hospitals that are tied to a school for undergraduate clinical training but conduct their own independent graduate medical education program.

teaching physician A highly experienced and trained medical doctor who has responsibilities for the training and supervision of medical students, interns, and residents. Teaching physicians are often but not necessarily salaried by the institution in which they teach. A common arrangement is that a physician in private practice must donate a certain amount of time for teaching and supervision in return for being granted staff privileges. Appropriate reimbursement of these physicians' activities has been a subject of considerable controversy. Under Medicare, hospitals are reimbursed under the hospital insurance program for the costs they incur in compensating physicians for teaching and supervisory activities and in paying the salaries of residents and interns in approved teaching programs. In addition, reasonable charges are paid under the supplementary medical insurance program for the patient care services of teaching physicians. *See also physician.*

teaching rounds Physicians in a teaching hospital taking medical students around to visit patients and discuss various cases as an educational process. Unusual cases or diseases are pointed out and discussed with the medical students in preparation for future medical practice. This educational method is also used by nurses and some allied health professions. *See ward rounds.*

team In health administration, this a group of people working together to achieve common objectives with its members willing to forego individual autonomy and personal interest to the extent necessary to achieve team and organizational goals. Two or more persons who have a specific performance objective or recognizable goal with the coordination of activity among the members of the group is required for the attainment of the group's goals and objectives. A team of five to seven persons is average, but more than eight is difficult to manage.

team leader, nurse *See nursing team leader.*

team nurse *See team nursing.*

team nursing One approach to providing nursing services to inpatients in health-care facilities. Nursing activities are organized in a manner wherein a team leader who is a registered nurse assigns nursing care activities to each nurse, LVN, or nursing assistant on the team who carries out the same activity for the duration of the shift to an assigned set of patients; an approach that is diametrically opposed to primary care nursing. *See also primary care nursing.*

teams In health administration, this is a number of persons associated together in work activity; a group of specialists or scientists functioning as a collaborative unit.

technic A rarely used word for "technician."

technical 1. Having to do with unique skills, knowledge, or terminology of a profession (e.g., X-ray technicians or medical records technicians who have special unique knowledge and skills). 2. In law, specific steps or procedures to have a case dismissed for technical reasons, usually for a failure to follow specific step-by-step procedures or rules.

technical assault In health law, this is a tort without the intent to injure such as giving an injection with a hypodermic needle to an unwilling person.

technical component Under certain circumstances, the health-care provider may make a charge for a technical procedure component alone when filing an insurance claim. Under these circumstances, the technical component charge is identified by adding a technical component modifier number to the usual procedure number as provided by the procedure coding manual.

technical information systems In health information systems and data management, this includes systems, networks, equipment and communication connections, and data collection processes necessary to detect deviations, determine rates and trends, initiate corrections, and ensure that goals are attained, all managed by researchers or project managers; providing detailed and specific information relevant to work flow, services utilization, the communication process, and quality management.

technically qualified individuals 1. In environmental health administration, this is any person who, because of education, training, or experience or a combination of these factors, is capable of understanding the health and environmental risks associated with chemical substances that are used under his or her supervision. 2. Any person who is responsible for enforcing appropriate methods of conducting scientific experimentation analysis or chemical research to minimize risks. 3. These are individuals who are responsible for the safety assessments and clearances related to the procurement, storage, use, and disposal of chemical substances as may be appropriate or required with the scope of conducting a research and development activity.

technical services In long-term care and home health care, these are the specialized, sometimes equipment-dependent, treatments and therapies, usually done by nursing personnel (under the supervision of a physician) such as IV therapy, hydration therapy, pain management, Hickman catheter nutrition therapy, total nutrition therapy, chemotherapy, and respiratory ventilation.

technical support In health administration and health planning, this is the engineering, design, specialized inspections, regulation compliance, planning, skills of specialized personnel, or other support of any capital project, maintenance, remodeling, upgrading, or repair activities.

technician 1. A person with highly specialized training in a focused area of expertise. 2. A person knowledgeable and skillful in some specific field or subject.

technicist A technician; a person skilled in techniques or having special skill or knowledge. *See technician.*

Technicon Medical Information System (TMIS) A comprehensive computerized medical information system first used at El Camino Hospital in Mountain View, California. It uses a computer to accept, store, and send medical and administrative data to physicians, nurses, technologists, clerks, etc. A broad range of medical data, physicians' orders, test results, etc., as well as administrative data such as charges, insurance coverage, etc., are all processed by the computer system.

technique 1. A specialized procedure, skill, or method. 2. A degree of expertise. 3. A rarely used word for technician.

technologist A technician; a technician with advanced skills who is knowledgeable in a specialized and focused field and who puts this knowledge to work in its practical application on the job in his or her technical area of expertise; a highly trained technician with more education and experience place in a more responsible position in a profession than a technician.

technology 1. Applied science using specialized instruments, electronics, tools, devices, and equipment with the accompanying terminology to perform specialized techniques, tasks, or skills. 2. Specialized equipment using computers, electronics, mechanical, or other means to assist in diagnosis, treatment, or procedures or to expedite work capabilities, techniques, approaches, effectiveness, or efficiency never before available without these advances.

technology assessment In health services delivery and medical care, this is the process of formally evaluating any new electronic, computer, mechanical, or other devices and materials used in medical care and patient treatment to determine if they are reliable, dependable, effective, efficient, cost-effective, safe, have any contraindications, and have user acceptability.

teenage health teaching modules program A comprehensive health education curriculum for junior and senior high school that was developed by Education Development Center, Inc., under contract with the Center for Health Promotion and Education, Centers for Disease Control and Prevention. The curriculum provides teenage students with the knowledge and skills to enable them to behave in a health-enhancing manner. The modules focus on immediate health needs and long-term consequences of behaviors established during the adolescent years.

TEFRA *See Tax Equity and Fiscal Responsibility Act of 1982.*

tele- Prefix meaning "distant" or "far."

telecommunications department The administrative unit in a health-care organization that is responsible for telephone services, paging, fire alarms, disaster warnings, and related intrafacility communication.

telecommunications manager The administrator responsible for the telecommunications department, including telephone and computer cable installation and equipment maintenance and service.

telecommuting Performing job-related work at a site away from the formal place of work, then electronically transferring (usually by computer) the work or its results to the office or another location; working whenever and from wherever work is needed, offering flexibility so the worker can work the hours most favorable when they are most productive. This saves time and expenses wasted in commuting; usually limited to managers, professional staff, specialized technicians, or positions that most effectively and efficiently lend themselves to computer use.

teleconference A business meeting or educational session between at least three or more persons in two or more different locations linked by telephone wires, satellite, microwave, or a cable system. It can be voice only or full multimedia via television cameras, television monitors, and two-way communication between sites.

telemarketing In health-care marketing, this is one direct marketing approach using the telephone system to acquire marketing information and data or to produce or increase sales.

telemedicine In medical care, this is the process of videotaping or digitally capturing, through a computer, a medical procedure, medical care activity, surgery, or related medical care process and then transmitting it as a colored television or digitized picture from one clinical setting to another or to a teleconference, educational session, or a legal proceeding via microwave, telephone line, or satellite. This process uses the most advanced electronic, computer, and multimedia technology to assist medical care as an educational medium or for diagnosis, consultation, or treatment assistance over long distances. The computer Internet and Worldwide Web has also played a major role as an electronic assistance to medical practice and education.

telephathology In medical care and biomedical research, this is the technologically driven process of transmitting images drawn from the view seen in a special microscope or electronmicroscope to a television monitor and/or video recorders, where they can be studied or used in teaching. Specially equipped and technologically advanced microscopes or electronmicroscopes are used for the taping and photographic processes.

telephone reassurance A long-term-care support service for elderly persons living alone designed to decrease social isolation by providing them with regular telephone contact on a daily basis by a trusted friend or relative.

teleprocessing The use of combination telecommunication hardware such as data processors, computers, input devices such as terminals, user communication devices such as CRTs and printers, telephone modems, and other telecommunications equipment.

teleradiology One form of telemedicine that focuses on the radiological aspects of medical care. *See telemedicine.*

TEM Transverse electromagnetic mode.

temperament An inborn predisposition to act or react in a specific way to experiences. Temperament can and does vary from person to person.

temperature 1. The level of heat of a living body as expressed in degrees. (37°C, or 98.6°F, is average for humans). 2. The balance between the heat produced and the heat lost in the body.

temporary disability An illness or injury that temporarily prevents an insured person from performing the functions of his or her regular job.

temporary disability laws In disability insurance, laws that are in effect in a select number of states (Hawaii, New Jersey, New York, California, Rhode Island, and Puerto Rico) and that offer income for disabled workers who are either on or off the job for a set or limited period of time.

temporary employment agency In health manpower and human resources management, this is an employment agency that provides companies with short-term or part-time workers such as nurses, physical therapists, respiratory therapists, certified nurse assistants, secretaries, and accountants. Also called "temporary employment pool" or "temporary help."

temporary license A licensing option offered to applicants (health-care providers or facilities) in some states that certifies that most of the minimum requirements of the law have been met but that time requirements have not. Thus, the facility is allowed to operate or the health-care provider to practice until the remainder of the requirements have been met. A nursing home administrator may manage a facility on a temporary basis until he or she has passed the licensing exam, which is offered only twice a year. *See also provisional.*

temporary restraining order (TRO) A court order causing one party or the other to take, or to refrain from taking, certain actions prior to a hearing.

temporary staff The granting of staff privileges to qualified health care providers (e.g., physicians, dentists, podiatrists, and psychologists) for a set or limited period of time.

temporary total disability Any accident or mishap resulting in trauma to the body or mind (mental state) that results in an injury or condition that cannot be totally and quickly treated, restored, or healed, resulting in impairment, restriction of abilities, and lack of capability to perform regular duties on one or more full calendar days after the injury but where full health and abilities are eventually recovered or restored.

tender 1. The act of offering money or something of value to pay for goods or services; money offered to pay a debt. 2. In contract law, to present for acceptance. 3. To officially or formally offer something of value.

tender offer 1. The offer of payment to satisfy a debt or claim; a willingness to pay. 2. To complete an offer or deal. 3. In corporate law, an offer made to the public to buy a specific number of stocks at a specific price, enabling the offeror to take over the corporation.

tenement 1. Any house, apartment, building, or place in which one could live. 2. A dwelling place. 3. Any type of permanent housing or property that is held by tenure.

tenement house A house divided into a number of living places or apartments; a word often used to refer to poorer, run-down, overcrowded, deteriorating apartments that present public health problems in central city areas.

tenor 1. A mode of continuation. 2. A general direction. 3. Of a general nature. 4. A train of thought or an idea that is basic to or runs through an issue. 5. The exact wording of a legal document. 6. An exact legal copy. 7. The tone or implication of a statement or act.

tension In mental health, these are unpleasurable emotions and anxiety characterized by a strenuous increase in mental and physical activity. *See also stress.*

teratogens In environmental health and hazardous waste, these are substances that cause malformation or serious deviation from normal development of embryos and fetuses.

teratologist A scientist who studies the result of gross malformation in a developing embryo.

teratology A branch of biological science and medicine focusing its study on malformations in utero. In particular, there is close examination of congenitally deformed fetuses and the development of an abnormal embryonic structure.

tergiversate 1. To turn one's back on an issue. 2. To use subterfuge. 3. To desert a cause. 4. To equivocate.

term 1. A fixed or definite period of time; a time period set for something to happen; a set time or date. 2. In contract law, this is a point of time to determine the beginning or ending of a period or agreement. 3. A word or words with a certain meaning. 4. In insurance, the period of time for which an insurance policy is issued and in effect.

terminal 1. In health information management and computers, this is an input-output device that includes a keyboard or other input device and a display mechanism such as CRT. 2. Having an end; to be ended and that end being permanent.

terminal care In medical care and nursing care, these are unique and specialized services and care for dying patients that include pain management and emotional and social support for a person in the final stages of a fatal disease just before death; medical and nursing care of the dying patient. More commonly called "hospice." *See hospice.*

terminal care document In medical care and health law, this is the formal and, in some states, legal document setting forth the patient's wishes concerning the use of life support technology should he or she be faced with unconsciousness and is at the brink of death where life sustaining technology and heart and lung machines might be employed to keep him or her alive. Referred to as a "living will" or the patient's "health-care power-of-attorney document."

terminal decline A decline in one's ability to think and reason, thought by some to occur shortly prior to death, perhaps a result of disruptions in the central nervous system; a marked drop in intellectual functioning as death draws near.

terminal digit filing One approach used in filing medical records using consecutively issued record numbers, divided into groups of two digits each and filed first by the last two, or terminal, digits. This method effects a near perfect distribution of the most recent records among other records in the file. For example, record 21-44-65 would be filed by the terminal digits (65), next by the middle digits (44), and finally by the first two digits (21).

terminally ill A patient with a disease or injury that will eventually cause death.

terminate 1. To end; to finish. 2. In health administration and human resource management, this is when a employee ends employment with the health-care organization with the decision to end the relationship being that of the organization; to fire an employee.

termination 1. The end. 2. The ending of an agreement or dispute. 3. Legally ending a contract without it being breached or broken by either party. 4. In human resources management, this means to end a person's employment with the health-care organization; the process of firing an employee. *See Skelly procedure.*

termination date In managed care, this is the end of the time period that an employer group contract with a health plan expires and the date when subscribers/members cease to be eligible for health services under the health plan.

termination expenses In life insurance, these are the costs incurred for processing a death benefit claim, including the cash amounts paid to the beneficiaries.

termination of employee *See terminate; termination; Skelly procedure.*

term loan In health-care finance, this a loan or a line of credit obtained from a financial institution, ranging from 1 to 10 years.

term of court The established time for a court to hold sessions or to hear cases.

territorial 1. In health administration, this is a management issue where departments or services present a noncooperative attitude and are protective of their resources, span of control, span of authority, and physical location; administratively failing to see the organization as a system and not recognizing the role of his or her department as a component of the larger system that exists to meet the overall mission of the organization. 2. Having to do with limited specific areas or jurisdictions.

territorial courts Federal courts used in each U.S. territory to serve as federal and state courts.

territorial jurisdiction The authority of a court to hear cases from within a designated or limited geographical area.

territory In managed care, health-care delivery, or home health care, this is the area that the health-care organization has exclusive responsibility for. In some health-care organizations, districts are used for large areas and are broken down to more restricted areas called "territories."

tertiary care Third level; top-level specialization. Technologically advanced and driven health-care services such as cardiac-catheterization diagnostic services, open-heart surgery; highly trained physician specialists such as cardiac surgeons, neurosurgeons, thoracic surgeons, and advanced and technologically sophisticated postoperative care intensive care units. Such services frequently require highly sophisticated technological and support facilities. The development of this level of services has largely been a function of diagnostic and therapeutic advances attained through clinical biomedical research and technological advances. *See also primary care; secondary care.*

tertiary care facility Facilities that render highly specialized services requiring highly technical resources. This type of care is usually associated with services rendered in university medical centers or specialty hospitals.

tertiary case *See tertiary care.*

tertiary prevention In public health, epidemiology, and preventive medicine, this is the third level of prevention after primary prevention and secondary prevention. The level of prevention has the purpose of retarding or blocking the progression of a disease, disability, condition, or disorder to keep it from becoming advanced and in need of excessive and unnecessary care. This consists of limiting any disability by providing rehabilitation where disease, injury, or disorder has already occurred and left damage. At this level the goal is to help diseased, disabled, or injured individuals to avoid unnecessary use of health-care services and avoid becoming dependent on health-care practitioners and health-care institutions. Prompt diagnosis and treatment, followed by proper rehabilitation and posttreatment recovery together with proper patient education, behavior change, and lifestyle changes, are all necessary so that diseases or disorders will not recur.

tertiary psychological prevention In mental health care, these are rehabilitative measures taken to reduce emotional and mental impairment or disability following a physical or emotional condition; mental and social rehabilitation.

tertiary treatment In environmental health and liquid waste management, this is advanced cleaning of wastewater that goes beyond the secondary or biological stage. It removes nutrients such as phosphorus and nitrogen and most bio-oxygen demand (BOD) and suspended solids (EPA).

testacy To create and leave a valid will. *See testate.*

testament 1. A will. 2. A legal document with instructions concerning the disposition of a person's personal property on death of the person writing it.

testamentary capacity Having the mental ability and competence necessary to make a valid will.

testate Having died and left a will.

testator One who has made a will.

test case In law, this is a lawsuit that is considered highly important because it may establish a new or important legal issue, principle, or right. Test cases are usually filed to establish the constitutionality of a new statute.

testify In health law or legal hearings or medical malpractice arbitration, this is to give verbal evidence while under oath in a hearing, in court, or to an official of the court.

testimony The evidence given by a witness while testifying under oath. *See testify.*

testing The process of assessing and evaluating individuals or groups by giving instruments, questionnaires, and test devices and taking samples from individuals for assessment and analysis, all as part of being a participant in a testing process. Testing in research is to gather data. In screening it is to separate well individuals from those who need further medical assessment. In medical care, testing means that specimens are taken and blood and serums drawn and examined in the laboratory to assist in diagnosis. Also called "laboratory procedures."

testing requirement In environmental health, this is the federal requirement that assessments be conducted on such substances or mixtures as may present an unreasonable risk of injury to health or the environment. Assessments are done to develop data with respect to health and environmental effects for which there are insufficient data and experience. Testing develops data and facts that are relevant to determining if the manufacture, distribution in commerce, processing, use, or disposal of such substance or mixture, or any combination of such activities, does or does not present an unreasonable risk of injury to health or the environment.

testing requirement rule In environmental health, this is the federal requirement that testing be conducted and include the following: 1) the identification of the chemical substance or mixture for which testing is required under the rule, 2) standards for the development of test data for such substance or mixture, and 3) with respect to chemical substances that are not new, a specification of the period (which may not be of unreasonable duration) within which the persons required to conduct the testing shall submit data developed in accordance with the standards.

test mixtures In environmental health and hazardous waste, these are substances or mixtures of chemicals administered or added to a test system in a study in which substances or mixtures are used to develop data to meet the requirements of the Toxic Substance Control Act.

test, patient liability Proposed guidelines that describe the obligations and extent of financial participation of patients in paying for physician services in a teaching setting.

test, physician role Guidelines that establish criteria for the payment of physicians on a fee-for-service basis in a teaching setting.

test reliability *See reliability.*

test-retest reliability The process of assessing, standardizing, and demonstrating the value, repeatability, and predictability of a test over time and that it is reliable each time it is used.

test systems In environmental health and hazardous waste, these are any animals, plants, microorganisms, or subparts thereof to which the test or control substance is administered or added for study. Also included are appropriate groups of components of the system not treated with the test or control substance.

test validity *See validity, test.*

tetanus An infectious disease caused by the toxic by-products of the bacteria *Clostridium tetani* and characterized by muscle spasms. Also called "lockjaw."

T-group (training group) 1. In health administration and human resources management, this is a group sensitivity training program used to increase one's awareness of and sensitivity to others with whom they work while improving skills in human relations by disclosing and discussing feelings about one another's behavior. 2. In mental health services and psychotherapy, this is a rarely used method of group therapy that emphasizes self-awareness and group dynamics; a type of encounter group that was used in the late 1960s and into the 1970s.

thanatoid Resembling dead; apparently dead; being close to or having a condition similar to death.

thanatologist A person who is an expert on the dying process or death.

thanatology 1. The study of death. 2. An account of the death process.

thanatophobia Fear of death.

thanatopsis Meditation on death.

thantos A Greek mythical figure in which death is personified; a death wish.

The AIDS Support Organizations Conceived in Uganda, this is an international AIDS treatment program that primarily provides clinics and counseling services. Because of need, it was expanded into a community-based program called the TASO Community Initiative (TCI).

theft In ethics and law, this is stealing; the dishonest act of taking something that does not belong to you. The illegal act of purposely taking something of value that does not belong to you but to the health-care organization with no intention of returning it. This can be a misdemeanor or a felony, depending on the monetary value of the property.

theory A systematic framework of constructs, concepts, principles, or paradigms to understand, predict, suggest, and explain phenomena, actions, reactions, and behavior.

theory X A management theory developed by the management theorist Douglas McGregor, who states that a theory X manager believes that workers have an inherent dislike for work and will avoid work if possible. Workers must be coerced, controlled, directed, or threatened with punishment to get them to work. The average worker prefers to be directed, wishes to avoid responsibility, has little ambition, and wants job security above all.

theory Y A management theory developed by the management theorist Douglas McGregor, who states that a theory Y manager believes that work is as natural as play or rest, individuals will exercise self-control and have commitment to objectives, the best rewards are those that satisfy needs for self-respect and personal improvement, workers will learn and seek responsibility, ingenuity and creativity is widely distributed in the population, and intellectual potentialities of workers are only partially realized.

therapeutic Having a healing or treatment effect; health enhancing. Activities, procedures, application of substances or physical agents, taking medicines, and participating in rehabilitation activities that help the patient toward recovery from an injury or illness; treatments, procedures, or activities that help restore the health of a patient.

therapeutic activity services According to JCAHO for psychiatric, alcoholism, and drug abuse facilities accreditation purposes, goal-oriented activities designed to help an individual develop expressive and/or performance skills through participation in art, crafts, dance, drama, movement, and music and prevocational, recreational, self-care, and social activities.

therapeutic agent Any substance or person that promotes healing in a maladaptive person. In group therapy, it refers mainly to people who help others.

therapeutic alternatives In medical care, these are various medicines and drugs that are different substances and have different chemical makeup but that provide the same pharmacological effect when taken by a patient in therapeutically equivalent doses (e.g., aspirin and ibuprofen).

therapeutic child care work A course of study that prepares individuals under supervision to implement activity and training programs to provide a preventive and therapeutic environment for mentally ill and emotionally disturbed children and adolescents. These workers train children in self-help skills through intensive group sessions involving structured daily activities and reinforcement of other therapeutic experiences. They also record, evaluate, and report progress of patients.

therapeutic community Any treatment setting that provides a curative or helpful environment for behavioral change through resocialization and rehabilitation; a form of group living in specialized substance abuse treatment facilities or centers used to restore former drug addicts or substance abusers to a drug-free existence based on a socially productive life centered around family and community activities.

therapeutic diet Any modified diet essential to the treatment or control of a particular disease or illness. *See special diet; modified diet.*

therapeutic environment Any social environment that is supportive of health or the restoration of physical or mental health.

therapeutic equivalents Drug products with essentially identical effects in the treatment of some disease or condition. Such products are sometimes, but not necessarily always, chemically equivalent or bioequivalent. Therapeutic equivalents are sometimes defined as chemically equivalent, and drugs with the same treatment effect that are not chemically equivalent are considered clinically equivalent.

therapeutic group In mental health services, this is a group of patients together in one location who work together for the treatment and improvement of each person's emotional disorders or maladaptive behaviors under the leadership of a psychotherapist.

therapeutic radioisotope facility In medical care, this is a special facility established for the use of radiopharmaceuticals and/or radioactive isotopes in the treatment of cancer malignancies.

therapeutic radiology services In medical care, these are services used to treat physical diseases, usually cancerous tumors, through the use of radiant energy.

therapeutic recreation *See recreational therapy.*

therapeutic recreation specialist, qualified consultant Under Medicare, a person who, if required by state law, is licensed or registered to practice and is eligible for registration as a therapeutic recreation specialist by the National Therapeutic Recreation Society under its requirements. *See also recreational therapist.*

therapeutic services Any medical care services adjunct to and supportive of medical and nursing care provided by specially trained professionals and assistants to enhance the residents' functional abilities and the quality of life.

therapist Any person whose specialized training, education, knowledge, experience, and skills are employed to assist patients or clients in the correction of a specific set of physical, emotional, social, mental, or developmental disorders as well as for improvement in the patient's health status.

therapy The treatment of physical, mental, or emotional disease; any procedure, treatment, activity, or intervention used to assist, aid, or heal a patient and restore health; to participate in a restorative, healing, or rehabilitative activity such as participating in physical therapy or psychotherapy. Sometimes used synonymously with "treatment."

-therapy Suffix meaning "treatment."

therapy services In medical care, these are therapeutic techniques used in implementing a program of habilitation or rehabilitation designed to meet the needs of an ill or disabled individual.

thermal effect In laser technology, this is when tissue and cells surrounding the treatment area are increased in heat because of exposure to a laser.

thermal trauma Injury caused from excessive heat or cold.

thermal treatment In environmental health, this is the treatment of hazardous waste in a device that uses elevated temperatures as the primary means to change the chemical, physical, or biological character or composition of a hazardous waste. Approaches used include incineration, molten salt, pyrolysis, calcination, wet air oxidation, and microwave discharge.

thermo- Prefix meaning "heat."

thermogram The picture produced by thermography.

thermography In medical care, this is a method of assessing the heat produced by different parts of the body using film that is photosensitive to infrared radiation.

thing 1. Any item, matter, issue, circumstance, object, affair, or concern. 2. A process or step-by-step procedure. 3. That which is an object of concern or discussion. 4. A tangible object, not a concept or idea. 5. An act, transaction or event, matter, or that which is done. 6. That which is mentioned but unnamed and nonspecific. 7. That which can be owned or possessed such as property. 8. That which is not a person.

third party An individual or party who is uninvolved or not associated directly with a deal, claim, dispute, or lawsuit but who may be a party to it or be affected by or subject to it; a person or party connected to or associated with the first or second party but removed from their involvement; a party one step removed from an issue, action, or direct involvement.

third-party administrator In managed care, this an independent contractor or corporate entity who administers health plan group benefits, claims, and administration for a self-insured company or employer group but does not underwrite risk.

third-party advances In health-care finance, monies paid to health-care facilities by insurance companies or other third-party payers against future health-care services waiting to be rendered, provided, and billed.

third-party beneficiary In contract law, a person who is not a party to a contract but who has a legal interest in the contract and for whose benefit it was drawn up.

third-party billing In health-care financial management, these are bills and statements prepared by a health-care practitioner, group, hospital, nursing home, or other provider and then sent to a third-party payer on behalf of the patient.

third-party claims management (TPCM) In managed care, this is the administration of self-insured employers by an insurance carrier that does administrative duties, pays employee claims, and handles checks for a set fee per employee per month.

third-party liability In managed care, this is when an organization beyond the health-care provider and health plan can be held accountable for payment of an enrollee's medical bills or can be named in a liability lawsuit.

third-party paid Patients whose health care is paid for by someone else such as an insurance company or the government. The third party pays the money for the claim to the patient or the health-care provider.

third-party payer In health-care finance, this is an insurance carrier, Medicare, and Medicaid or their government-contracted intermediary, managed-care organization, or health plan that pays for hospital or medical bills instead of the patient. Also known as a "third-party carrier." 2. Any organization, public or private, that pays or insures health or medical expenses on behalf of beneficiaries or recipients (e.g., commercial insurance companies, Medicare, and Medicaid). The individual generally pays a premium for coverage in all private and some public programs. The organization then pays bills on the patient's behalf. Such payments are called "third-party payments" and are distinguished by the separation between the individual receiving the service (the first party), the individual or institution providing it (the second party), and the organization paying for it (the third party). *See also service; indemnity benefits.*

third-party payment In health-care finance, these are any monies paid by insurance companies for the patients to health plans, managed-care plans, governmental agencies, or other organizations to cover health and medical care services provided to patients or family members.

third-party payor Same as "third-party payer."

thoracic surgery A medical specialty involving the diagnosis and operative treatment of diseases of the chest or thoracic cavity, usually involving the heart, lungs, and large blood vessels in the chest cavity; the principles and techniques of treating diseases, injuries, disorders, and deformities of the chest by surgical procedures.

thorium A naturally radioactive element; the parent of one radioactive series. Specific thorium nuclides are members of the three radionuclide series.

thought process disorder In mental health services and psychiatry, this is a symptom of schizophrenia that involves thinking complete thoughts and intellectual functioning, often manifested by incoherence in the individual's writing and verbal communication processes.

threats Conditions that, by their very nature, pose harm or injury; something or someone intending to inflict evil, injury, or damage.

three-D policy In insurance, this is used to express three areas of concern for loss. The three Ds are dishonesty, destruction, and disappearance. Insurance policies are drawn up to cover these three loss factors by providing coverage for fidelity loss, loss of money and securities, and loss from counterfeiting and depositors' forgery.

threshold 1. The level at which first effects or responses are seen or occur. 2. That point at which a person just begins to notice a sound becoming audible or the level at which a person begins to become ill because of an exposure to an agent. 3. The level or point at which a stimulus is strong enough to signal the need for an organization's response to indicator data and the beginning of the process of determining why the threshold has been approached or crossed (JCAHO).

threshold limit value (TLV) 1. In occupational health, the exposure level under which most people can work consistently for 8 hours a day, day after day, with no harmful effects. 2. In environmental health and air pollution control, this represents the air concentration of chemical substances to which it is believed that workers may be exposed daily (EPA).

threshold planning quantities 1. In environmental health and air pollution control, these are quantities designated for each chemical on the list of extremely hazardous substances that trigger notification by facilities to the state emergency planning body under Title III of the Superfund Amendments and Reauthorization Act.

tic Involuntary, repetitive behavior in a small segment of the body. Mainly psychogenic, it may be seen in certain cases of chronic encephalitis or minimal brain damage.

tidal irrigation In medical and nursing care, this is an automatic, continuous process of introducing a solution and then emptying it out (usually in the bladder) through a closed catheter system.

time In epidemiology, this is one element of the time/place/person construct used in epidemiological analysis. In all epidemiological investigations and assessments, time is considered, and the time factors as they relate to a disease outbreak or to injuries, conditions, or deaths in populations are considered and analyzed. Time factors considered in an epidemic include incubation periods, duration of the outbreak, the epidemic curve, propagation rates, infectivity, seasonal variations, cyclic variations, and long-term (secular) effects. Time factors are considered and compared with "place" and "person" factors.

time draft In health-care financial management, this is a draft bill or loan that is payable at a specified time.

time is of the essence 1. In contract law, if what is specified in the contract is not done by a specified time, a breach of the contract can occur. 2. A phrase used in contracts to ensure that certain acts are completed when time is a factor in the situation.

time-is-of-the-essence contract In contract law, this is an agreement that places emphasis on a time limitation and on expiration of the contract if not completed by a stated time.

time lagging In health services delivery and managed care, this is a method for assessing and analyzing past patterns and forecasting future utilization that uses relationships between utilization and some cause-effect relationships measured in different time periods.

time limit In managed care and insurance, this is the period of time in which a notice of an insurance claim or proof of loss must be filed.

time line In health planning and program development, this is the creation of a graphic or pictorial presentation of activities of planning or program development that need to be accomplished to implement a project or service. Every activity is listed, usually down the left side of graphs, with days, weeks, or months being laid out across the top of the graph and a bar graph drawn for each activity to show the time each activity is to begin, the length of time it is to take, and when it is scheduled to be completed. This allows a quick review of the chart to assess all activities and see if each is being completed on time and how the project is progessing.

timeliness 1. Happening at a suitable or proper time. 2. Being timely.

timeliness of care In medical care, this is a component of patient care quality consisting of the degree to which needed care is provided to the patient without undue delay (JCAHO).

time loss analysis In health and safety, this is the assessment and evaluation of the amelioration process following an accident and the positive and negative effects of intervenors on the extent of the accident.

timely 1. Well-timed; being in good time; early. 2. Completed on time. 3. Opportune timing. 4. Done at a suitable time.

time-price doctrine Allowing a higher price to be charged for items bought on credit to circumvent state usury doctrines.

time series analysis In health services delivery and in managed care, this is a predicting and forecasting technique used to identify past complex utilization patterns by trends, cycles, and seasonal variation and other causes of fluctuations that are then extrapolated into the future to attempt to predict future utilization patterns.

time-sharing An arrangement that permits two or more health-care facilities or enterprises to be users in sharing the same computer.

time studies In health-care delivery and human resource management, these are assessments and measures of work behavior, tasks, and procedures to determine length of time to complete them to increase efficiency.

time-weighted average In environmental and occupational health, this is a measure used in determining threshold limit values referred to as threshold limit values/time weighted average

(TLV/TWA), which are the time-weighted average concentrations for a normal 8-hour workday or 40-hour workweek to which nearly all workers may be repeatedly exposed, day after day, without adverse effect.

tinnitus A ringing and whistling in the ears, occasionally a side effect of some antidepressant drugs or excessive consumption of some substances such as aspirin or ibuprofen.

tissue A large group of similar cells bound together and dedicated to the performance of a particular function; the fleshy part of the human body, including the bone. In some cases, blood is considered tissue.

tissue bank In health services delivery and medical care, this is a special facility used for the retention, storage, and supply of human body tissues from donors. The highly specialized staff of this facility catalogs and distributes various types of body tissues to health-care providers for use in implantation and transplantation surgery for patients who need them.

tissue committee In medical care and hospital administration, this is formal group of health-care providers who usually function under the medical staff to review and evaluate all surgery performed in the hospital for appropriateness based on the extent of agreement among the preoperative, postoperative, and pathological diagnoses and on the relevance and acceptability of the procedures undertaken for the diagnosis. The committee derives information from the use of pathologic findings from tissue removed at surgery as a key element in the review. Findings are used to improve appropriateness, necessity, and quality and to reduce adverse events related to surgery.

tissue equivalents In environmental health, these are materials whose absorbing and scattering properties for radiation of a given type and energy simulate those of a specified biological issues.

title 1. The official document that shows the right to ownership of property. 2. Certificate of ownership.

Title III of the Older Americans Act In aging services, this is the federal law that provides for funding to states for the coordination of services to the elderly, portioned out to each state by population of those over age 60.

Title V A federal public law that created a health program for maternal and child health and crippled children's services.

Title VII In human resources management and affirmative action, this is part of the Civil Rights Act of 1964 that requires equal opportunity employment for all without regard to race, religion, sex, national origin, pregnancy, and ethnicity.

Title XVIII (18) The title of the Social Security Act that contains the principal legislative authority for the Medicare program and is therefore a common name for the program.

Title XIX (19) The title of the Social Security Act that contains the principal legislative authority for the Medicaid program and is the common name for the program.

titled patient One whose health-care services are reimbursed under Titles V, XVIII, or XIX of the Social Security Act.

titometer An instrument used to measure the depth of color in a liquid.

TLV *See threshold limit value.*

TMIS *See Technicon Medical Information System.*

toilet training In long-term care, this is also called bowel and bladder training; teaching a victim of a stroke or some other degenerative disease to hold and control his or her bowel or bladder; also applies to children who have yet to learn bladder control or who suffer from enuresis.

tolerance 1. Sympathy for beliefs or behaviors differing from one's own. 2. The capacity for endurance or adaptation. 3. In drug use or abuse, the gradually disappearing effects of a drug when it is taken in the same dose over a long period of time.

tolerance limits In environmental health, these are the criteria as to what is deemed acceptable in performance, significant error, or harmful energy.

tolerances In environmental health, these are the permissible residue levels for pesticides in raw agricultural produce and processed foods. Whenever a pesticide is registered for use on a food or a feed crop, tolerances (or exemption from the tolerance requirement) must be established. The Environmental Protection Agency establishes the tolerance levels, and the Food and Drug Administration and Department of Agriculture enforces them.

toll 1. To remove. 2. To defeat. 3. To take away. 4. To entice or allure. 5. A tax or duty paid. 6. To draw attention to. 7. A loss of a large number of items, money, or property.

tolling statute A law passed allowing the statute

of limitations to be delayed or put off or to put off its future effects.

-tome Suffix meaning "instrument to cut."

tomography An image-gathering technique using either X ray or ultrasound to produce a lineage of structures of the body at a specified depth. *See also computerized axial tomography.*

-tomy Suffix meaning "cutting," "incision," or "section."

tonometer In medical care, this is an instrument used to measure pressures in a body part (e.g., the eye) using an ophthalmotonometer.

tonsillectomy In medical care, this is the surgical removal of a tonsil or tonsils.

tontine A type of life insurance in which persons pay into an insurance fund and only those still alive by a certain time receive benefits or payments. This type of insurance approach has been outlawed in most states.

topectomy In psychiatry and neurosurgery, this is a psychosurgical procedure performed on chronic psychotic patients in cases that do not respond to psychotherapy or drug therapy.

topical Referring to the application of heat, ointment, drugs, etc. to the external surfaces of the body.

top management In health administration, this is any individual manager, group of managers, or management team responsible for overall administration, policymaking, and implementation and direction of the total health-care organization.

topo- Prefix meaning "place," "position," or "location."

topography The lay of the land; the outstanding features of the terrain, surface, and relief, including natural barriers such as rivers and mountains and man-made features and barriers. Epidemiological place implications include the concern for the spread of disease in populations that are reduced or limited by the natural barriers from the topography. *See place.*

TOPP Total Outcomes and Prediction Program. In rehabilitation, this is an outcome measures program for rehabilitation that uses as its measures the length of stay, length of therapy required, outcomes of treatment, payer expense for treatment, discharge destination, and patient satisfaction. Produced by Continental Medical Systems of Mechanicsburg, Pennsylvania.

tort 1. A main area of law and health law, this is any wrongful or negligent act done to another person or property that results in harm, injury, or damage. Torts include the areas of negligence, malpractice, battery, slander, and libel for which recovery can be sought through a civil lawsuit. When wrongful conduct on the part of one party has caused harm to a second party and those who suffer the harm seek compensation for the loss and suffering through some form of legal process or a lawsuit. 2. A civil wrong that does not involve a contract and usually is not a crime. 3. When a duty owed is breached; the twisting of the law. *See intentional tort; malpractice; slander; negligence; recovery.*

tortfeasor 1. One who does harm or damage or commits a tort. 2. A wrongdoer.

tortious Referring to a wrongful occurrence or the act of committing a tort.

to stabilize In medical care, this refers to an emergency medical condition where healthcare providers assess a patient's medical condition and render medical treatment for any disease, injury, disorder, or condition as may be needed to ensure that no deterioration of the state of the disease or injury is likely to result from a transfer to another facility.

total allowance The sum of all reimbursement categories for health-care facilities, including all allowance plus adjustment categories for the health-care facility; the sum of all separate allowance and adjustment categories.

total births, rate of In hospital administration, this is total number of deliveries (live and stillborn) plus fetal deaths in the facility. *See birth rate.*

total cases In occupational health and safety, these are all the work-related illnesses and deaths; all job-related injuries that result in loss of consciousness, restriction of work or activity, or transfer to another job or that require medical treatment beyond basic emergency care.

total current assets In health-care finance, this the sum total of all asset categories as shown on the balance sheet of the health-care organization.

total current liabilities The sum total of all liability categories as shown on the most recently produced balance sheet of the health-care organization.

total disability 1. When an illness or injury completely prevents a person from performing all duties pertaining to his or her job or occupation or from engaging in any other type of work to earn his or her livelihood. If at the end of 2 years (or other specified period) the person is prevented from working at any occupation for which they are reasonably fitted by education, training, or experience, they are considered totally disabled. 2. In managed care, this is when a disability is caused by an injury, illness, or pregnancy requiring regular medical care and attendance of a participating physician and extended rehabilitation or when disability lasts beyond 1 year and the enrollee is unable to engage in any business or occupation for which the enrollee or dependent is reasonably trained, skilled, educated, or experienced and is also unable to engage in most normal activities of daily living for their sex and age.

total expenditure In health-care finance, this is the amount of money spent for personal health services reported by clientele without the source of payment being considered.

total exposure points In epidemiology and occupational health, these are the potentials for exposure to substances or agents from more than one exposure pathway.

total hip replacement In medical care, this is a surgical operation used to treat broken hips or arthritis of the hip in elderly patients. The head of the femur and the socket (acetabulum) are replaced with metal or plastic ones.

total hospital margin In health-care financial management, this is a measure of profitability being experienced by a hospital determined by the total revenues less total costs divided by total revenues. The formula for total margin follows:

$$\frac{\text{Total revenues} - \text{Total costs}}{\text{Total revenues}}$$

total inpatient service days The sum total of all days of service provided to a person as an inpatient of a health-care facility.

total length of stay The sum total of days of stay by all persons as inpatients as determined by the number of inpatients discharged during a specified time period.

total liabilities The sum total of current and long-term liabilities of the health-care facility.

total loss constructive Any loss or damage that is of sufficient magnitude to make the cost of repairing a damaged property more than it is worth.

totally enclosed manner In occupational health and safety, this is a worker safety or hazardous waste protection process that ensures no exposure of human beings or the environment to any concentration of PCBs.

totally enclosed treatment facilities In occupational health and safety and hazardous waste management, these are hazardous waste treatment facilities that are directly connected to an industrial production process, constructed and operated in a manner that prevents the release of any hazardous waste or any constituent thereof into the environment during treatment. An example is an enclosed pipe in which acid is neutralized.

total maternity care In health-care delivery, this is the full range of usual and standard antepartum care, delivery, and postpartum care for women expecting a normal, uncomplicated delivery.

total-needs programming In insurance, this is when the agent considers all aspects of potential beneficiaries' financial needs in life. The agent considers and calculates the amount of money required to meet total financial needs and determines the amount of funds that will be available when the client dies, then figures the amount of life insurance needed to meet any differences.

total parenteral nutrition In medical care and subacute care in long-term-care facilities, this is an invasive catheter placed directly into large blood vessels to allow direct nutritional feed into elderly or seriously ill patients.

total population 1. In the United States, this includes all members of the armed forces living in foreign countries and residents of the territories of Guam, Puerto Rico, and the U.S. Virgin Islands; other Americans living and working abroad such as under contract with other governments, in the U.S. Diplomatic Service Corps, missionaries, or Peace Corps, or assigned to United Nations service. 2. In public health, health services delivery, community services, and criminal administration, illegal aliens are accounted for and considered part of the total population because they use up resources and accounts for tax expenditures. Some federal programs exclude from the total population all Americans abroad and outside the territories and boundaries of the United States.

total quality management (TQM) In health administration, this is the integration of quality and management methods, practices, concepts, and beliefs into the culture of the organization to bring about continuous quality improvement. Characteristics of a TQM system include the following: an attitude and a mindset of quality, a way of competing to give the organization a quality competitive advantage, avoiding complacency with continual improvement, and providing tools and techniques for improving quality services. The key elements of TQM are continuous quality improvement in all aspects of the organization, the idea that improvement is the responsibility of all members of the organization, the reliance on data and information gathering and analysis because knowledge and feedback are essential to improve and to make needed changes, and the idea that the customer defines quality. TQM creates an organizational culture toward quality. Top management of the health-care organization makes it clear that the organization is committed to quality in terms of commitments of personnel, time, money, and action. Programs and work tend to gravitate toward average performance, so continuous quality improvement is needed once basic quality systems are in place. TQM prevents quality problems at the onset and during the process instead of at the end, after problems occur. All employees must believe in competence and that good work is possible and can be achieved. Improvement in quality leads to lower cost by reducing waste, reworking inappropriate approaches, and reducing complexity of processes. Scientific approaches and methods improve and control quality when applied to work tasks. The needs and realistic expectations of patients, customers, consumers, and healthcare providers can and should be met through quality improvement by having quality in work, productivity, and quality services and programs. This is the application of the principles of quality control and management to integrate all process, structures, and functions of a health-care organization with the ultimate goal of customer satisfaction and continuous quality improvement. *See continuous quality improvement; quality circles; quality assurance; risk management.*

Total quality management, Deming's 14 points In health administration and quality management, the 14 points of total quality management and continuous quality improvement are as follows: 1) create constancy of purpose for the improvement of services; 2) adopt the new quality improvement philosophy; 3) cease dependence on mass inspection; 4) end the practice of awarding business on the basis of price tag alone; 5) improve constantly; 6) institute and restructure training; 7) improve supervision by helping people on the job; 8) drive out fear; 9) break down problems and barriers between departments; 10) eliminate slogans and exhortations, target the workforce, and communicate accomplishments; 11) do not rely on, and manage from, quotas; 12) remove barriers to pride of workmanship; 13) institute rigorous education and retraining; and 14) take action from the top management on down to accomplish the quality management transformation (W. Edwards Deming, 1982).

total quality management, elements of In health administration and quality management, the various components of TQM must all must be in place for it to be successful and should include the following: 1) be customer oriented; 2) be based on statistical data; 3) complete trend analysis; 4) include outcomes and process to reach customers; 5) be proactive, not reactive; 6) use cross-functional teams; 7) be organization- or hospital-wide; 8) use participative management and employee empowerment; and 9) have both good management and good leadership.

total recordable cases In occupational health and safety, these are the number of recordable injuries and illnesses per 200,000 total hours worked by all employees during a specific time period. The 200,000 hours worked are equivalent to 100 full-time workers at 40 hours per week for 50 weeks.

total recordable cases rate In occupational health and safety, these are the number of recordable injuries and illnesses per 200,000 total hours worked by all employees during a specific time period compared to the numbers of hours worked in the same period. The total recordable cases rate formula follows:

$$\frac{\text{Number of recordable injuries and illnesses} \times 200{,}000 \text{ for a specific time period}}{\text{Total hours worked in the same time period}} \times 1000$$

total suspended solids In environmental health and liquid waste management, this is a measure of the floating dirt, chemicals, and other solid materials in wastewater, effluents, or bodies of water determined by using tests for total suspended nonfilterable solids (EPA).

totten trust Placing money into an account in one's own name as a trustee for another person. The trustee can reclaim it, but if the trustee dies it becomes the property of the other person; sometimes used in nursing homes for residents with no family.

tourniquet A device that is wrapped around a limb to compress the blood vessels and completely stop the flow of blood.

to wit 1. In law, this means "namely"; to be known. The term could be replaced with "to know." 2. The use of the colon punctuation mark to introduce lists.

Towne's projection A posteroanterior X-ray film used to produce an image of the entire skull and mandible.

toxemia In medical care, this is poisoning seen in the human body by way of the bloodstream; systemic poisoning.

toxic dust In occupational health and medicine, this is any potentially harmful dust that may enter the body through the respiratory tract into the blood.

toxicity 1. A chemical agent that produces harmful effects on some biological functions. 2. The condition under which a poisonous effect occurs.

toxico- Prefix meaning "poison."

toxicologist An individual concerned with the nature and extent of the injurious response to the ingestion of chemical compounds and the determination of safe levels of exposure or ingestion in humans and other species.

toxicology 1. The study of toxic substances or poisons. 2. An educational program that describes the nature and extent of the body's response to chemical compounds and the determination of safe levels of exposure in humans and other species.

toxic psychosis In psychiatry and mental health services, this is a form of mental illness from toxic substances produced by the body itself or introduced into it (e.g., drugs).

toxin A poison; a poisonous substance that is the by-product of the metabolism of a living organism.

toxo- Prefix meaning "poison."

TPA Third-party administrator; third-party associate. *See third-party administrator.*

TPCM *See third-party claims management.*

TPL Third-party liability.

TPR Temperature, pulse, and respiration rates. *See third-party reimbursement.*

TQM *See total quality management.*

tracer disease methodology *See tracers.*

tracers In health-care delivery and quality-of-care evaluation, these are selected conditions or diseases chosen for appraisal in programs that are used to assess the quality of medical care because it is believed that the quality of care given for the tracers is representative of the general quality of care.

tracheostomy In medical care, this is a surgically created vertical slit in the windpipe in the front portion of the neck. A single or double cannula or tube airway is inserted into the opening to facilitate breathing and the adequate exchange of oxygen and carbon dioxide in the lungs. The main tube is held in place by ties around the neck.

tracheostomy care To assist in the aspiration of secretions from a patient's tracheostomy opening through use of a sterile catheter connected to a suction machine. The cleansing of the inner cannula or tube of the tracheostomy tube and the anterior part of the neck is also a part of this procedure.

traction 1. The process of placing a pulling force on injured parts of the body by means of pulleys and/or weights. 2. To support a bone by means of a strut or a pulling force on the neck or a limb as a part of the treatment process.

trade 1. To buy and sell; commerce. 2. A profession, career, technical skill, occupation, or job. 3. To barter; to swap or exchange for money. 4. The overall and collective functions, skills, and knowledge of a profession. 5. Merchandise or traffic.

trade credit In health-care finance, this is an intercompany indebtedness occurred through charging purchases to credit accounts and the seller recording them as accounts payable by the buyer. The seller then bills the health-care organization, and the bills are to be paid within the agreed-on terms such as net 30 days.

trademark A distinguishing symbol, design, mark, motto, or sign that a company can claim and reserve by law for its exclusive use in identifying its products or organization.

trade name *See brand name.*

traditional quality management Quality management systems that have been used for an extended period, addressing and focusing on quality from the assessment of and emphasis on the structure of the organization (licensure, certification, accreditation) or a process review approach (assessment of charts, generic screen, utilization review) and quality assurance based on risk management; as opposed to continuous quality improvement, total quality management, and patient-centered quality improvement. *See total quality management.*

traffic 1. To sell illegal drugs. 2. The type, amounts, and levels of patients seen on a regular basis in a clinic or screening program.

traffic accident, highway moving motor vehicle In safety and health, this is any accident that occurred on a public street or highway and that, if it occurred wholly on the highway, originated on the highway, terminated on the highway, and involved another vehicle partially on the highway.

training In health administration and human resources management, these are all applied education and learning activities that teach employees how to better perform their jobs; teaching job-related skills, methods, policies, procedures, approaches, and techniques.

training center for allied heath professions A junior college, college, or university that 1) provides programs of education leading to a bachelors or associate degree (or to the equivalent of either) or to a higher degree in medical technology, optometric technology, dental hygiene, or any of such other allied health professions curricula as are specified by regulation, for full credit toward a bachelors or equivalent degree in the allied health professions or designed to prepare the student to work as a technician in a health occupation; 2) provides training for not less than a total of twenty persons in such curricula; 3) if, in a college or university that does not include a teaching hospital or in a junior college, is affiliated with a hospital; and 4) is in a college or university accredited by a recognized body or bodies approved for such purpose by the commissioner of education or is in a junior college accredited by the regional accrediting agency for the region in which it is located or there is satisfactory assurance afforded by such accrediting agency that reasonable progress is being made toward accreditation by such a college.

training coordinator The person responsible for the education and training of personnel in a health-care facility. *See also education director; inservice education.*

training grants Monies given to health-care organizations or to colleges or universities for the education of the health-care organization staff or future staff who need to develop certain skills or to encourage students to pursue training in areas where shortages in service providers or career areas exist.

training program, approved Any graduate physician training program for interns and/or residents that is approved by the Liaison Committee on Graduate Medical Education, the Committee of Post-Doctoral Education of the American Osteopathic Association, or the Council on Dental Education of the American Dental Association.

training program, nonapproved A graduate physician training program that has not received or has not sought approval from the Liaison Committee of Post-Doctoral Education of the American Osteopathic Association or the Council on Dental Education of the American Dental Association. In nursing, this is a designation given to degree programs of nursing not approved or accredited by the National League of Nursing.

tranquilizer In psychiatry and medical care, this is a psychotropic drug that produces a calming, soothing, quieting, or pacifying effect without clouding the thought processes. Major tranquilizers are antipsychotic drugs, and the minor tranquilizers are antianxiety drugs.

trans- Prefix meaning "across."

transaction 1. A deal. 2. The making of a contract. 3. A business agreement. 4. In psychology, an interpersonal interaction between two or more persons.

transactional analysis (TA) In mental health services, this is a system of psychotherapy introduced by Eric Berne that focuses on interactions in the treatment sessions. The system includes 1) analysis of intrapsychic occurrence, 2) the determination of the dominant ego states (parent, child, or adult) of each participant, 3) identification of the games played in their interactions, and 4) uncovering the causes of the patient's emotional problems. Transactional analysis is used in individual and group psychotherapy.

transcript An official copy of a record or a court proceeding.

transdisciplinary In health-care administration and human resource management, this is when employees or professionals work together across professional boundaries or domains instead of in teams or groups of the same domain.

transfer 1. The passing or changing of a right, title, or property from one person to another or to the rightful owner. 2. Movement of a patient from one treatment service or location to another; the movement of patients between health-care facilities under the direction of the attending physician and his agents, not including any patient who goes on his or own, leaves a facility without a formal discharge, or is declared dead.

transfer agreement As used in JCAHO long-term-care facilities accreditation, a written arrangement that provides for the reciprocal transfer of patients between health-care facilities. A formal arrangement between two health-care facilities, usually between a hospital and a nursing home, two hospitals, or a hospital and a rehabilitation hospital. The agreement sets forth the conditions of the transfer such as handling the patient's medical records, sharing clinical information, and exchanging clinical records and data, discharge planning, etc.

transfer data In health services delivery, the medical record information and an abstract of a patient's care plan that are sent with a patient when transferring to another health-care facility.

transfer, discharge In health services delivery, the documents and arrangements used to provide for the discharge of a patient from one health-care facility to allow for admission to another facility.

transference 1. In Freudian psychiatric theory, this is the displacement of emotions or feelings during therapy (or otherwise) toward a psychotherapist, counselor, psychologist, or psychiatrist, stemming from one's earlier experiences with his or her father or other authority figure. 2. In education and training, this is how applicable a training program is to the actual job situation or how readily the trainee transfers the learning to his or her job. Also called "transfer of learning."

transfer in Under Medicare, this is a patient admitted to a hospital from another acute-care hospital or from the nonexempt distinct part of the same hospital to receive similar or advanced care for the same diagnosis/DRG. Thus, both hospitals or entities must share or split the reimbursement on the basis of the PPS/DRG reimbursement rate for the diagnosis.

transfer, intrahospital In hospital administration and medical care delivery, this is to move a patient in a hospital from one treatment and clinical area to another or from one nursing or patient care unit to another in the same health-care facility during the same hospital stay.

transfer out Under Medicare, this is a patient discharged from a hospital to another acute-care hospital or to the nonexempt distinct part of the same hospital to receive similar or advanced care for the same diagnosis/DRG. Thus, both hospitals or the two care units in the same hospital must share or split the reimbursement on the basis of the PPS/DRG reimbursement rate for the diagnosis. One reimbursement for a single DRG is allowed.

transfer price In health-care finance, this is revenue that is charged for a service or for goods or supplies transferred between two different services or programs in the health-care organization; services sold in-house from one administrative unit to another and the cost charged back for the services rendered. The pricing system is determined in-house and can create a complex accounting system. Prices may vary from standard and available community-based prices for the same services.

transfers In health administration and human resource management, this is when an employee is moved from one job position to another that is equal in rank, responsibility, organizational level, and pay.

transfer tax A tax placed on large transactions or the transfer of property or money. Often these transactions are made without something of value given in return. Also called a "gift tax."

transient 1. Passing away with time. 2. Transitory. 3. Not permanent.

transient situational disturbance In mental health and psychiatric care, this is a disorder that represents an acute reaction to overwhelming stress such as severe crying spells, loss of appetite, sexual dysfunction, and reaction to an unwanted situation as manifested by suicidal gestures and hostility. The disturbance generally recedes as the stress diminishes.

transillumination In medical care and diagnostic procedures, this is an information-gathering or diagnostic technique that uses a bright light shown through part of the body to allow for its examination (e.g., the sinuses of the skull).

transitional care 1. In medical and long-term care, this describes a level of care that is less acute than required by full hospitalization and more acute than found in a skilled nursing facility. Also referred to as "subacute care." 2. In mental health services or rehabilitation, this is postacute care provided in a halfway house or outpatient care arrangement until the patient transitions into mainstream living. *See subacute care; transitional care unit.*

transitional care unit A medical or nursing care unit found in a hospital for patients who need less medical or nursing attention than regular medical care units but who require more than the skilled nursing care found in a skilled nursing care facility; usually located in an acute-care hospital. Also called "subacute care."

transitional year In graduate medical education, this is the first year of clinical residency and is a transition from regular medical school. The medical residency is broad in scope, a balanced experience, and could be in two or more clinical disciplines.

transitory action 1. In health law, this is a lawsuit that may be brought to trial in one of several locales. 2. In law, this is a legal action that may be brought in any state or county as opposed to having action with a local jurisdiction.

transmission 1. In epidemiology and public health, this is the process of spreading disease. 2. In laser technology, this is the passage of radiation through a medium. *See mode of transmission; transmission of disease.*

transmission of disease In epidemiology and public health, this is the process of spreading disease from person to person or from animal to person or by fomite, vector, or any other means. *See mode of transmission.*

transpiration In environmental health, this is the process by which water vapor is lost to the atmosphere from living plants. The term can be applied to the quantity of water thus dissipated.

transplant In medical care, this is to surgically remove a living part of the body's tissue from one part of the body and reattach it in another location or to another of the body's structures or tissues; a still-healthy and living organ or tissue, donated and taken from another person, that is surgically removed and placed in or attached to another patient's body's structure or tissue (e.g., liver, cornea, heart, or kidney transplant). A transplant involving only the patient's own body and tissue is referred to as an "autograft" or "homograft," and the transplanting of a donated body part or tissue from another person is referred to as an "allograft."

transplantation services In medical care, this is the delivery of care pertaining to the surgical procedures of grafting of tissues onto a patient's body, tissues, or structures that were taken from the patient's own body or removed from another person (JCAHO).

transportation air pollution control measures In environmental health, these are the measures that are directed toward reducing emissions of air pollutants from transportation sources as mandated by Section 108(f) of the Clean Air Act.

transportation services A long-term-care support service designed to assist the mobility of the elderly. Some programs offer improved financial access by offering reduced rates and barrier-free buses or vans with ramps and lifts to assist the elderly or handicapped. Others offer subsidies for public transportation systems or operate minibus services exclusively for use by senior citizens.

transport, hazardous waste In environmental health and hazardous waste management, this is the movement of a hazardous substance by any mode, including pipeline (as defined in the Pipeline Safety Act), train, vehicle, or truck or by air. In the case of a hazardous substance that has been accepted for transportation by a common or contract carrier, routing and state mandates must be followed. Any stopping in transit that is temporary, incidental to the transportation movement, and at the ordinary operating convenience of a common or contract carrier and any such stoppage shall be considered as a continuity of movement and not as the storage of a hazardous substance.

transputer In health-care information management and computers, this is a very small computer or a computer on a silicon chip.

trash-to-energy In environmental health and solid waste management, this is to recycle solid waste through incineration; putting waste to use as energy by burning it to make steam to drive electric turbines.

T ratio A statistical method used to test significance if fewer than 30 subjects are involved. The ratio is used to determine whether the found differences could occur from chance alone.

trauma 1. Any cutting, tearing, blow, or injury to one's physical body, usually from an accident. 2. In psychiatry, a stressful and upsetting experience or event that precipitates a mental crisis. 3. Sudden stressful or psychological upset. 4. Damage.

trauma center In medical care, this is a special medical and nursing unit in a hospital that is equipped and staffed to handle emergency care services and treatment for seriously ill or injured patients. Often these units are attached to intensive care units to assist in continuity of care and ease of transfer to nonemergency status and to intensive care for recovery. *See certified trauma center.*

trauma center, certified A state-certified tertiary care facility that provides emergency and specialized intensive care to critically ill and injured patients. *See certified trauma center.*

trauma registry A hospital emergency care database that indicates the type of injury or emergency medical diagnosis presented in its emergency department and the resulting procedures and treatments used.

traumatology 1. The branch of medicine that deals with accidents and emergency surgery of wounds and disabilities as a result of traumatic injury. 2. The study of end results of accidents that can be the direct cutting, amputation, tearing, breaking, abrasion, bruising, or other tissue injury to various parts of the human body.

travel accident policy In insurance, this is a limited insurance contract or policy covering only accidents that occur while an insured person is traveling.

traverse 1. In health law and the litigation process, this is the denial of facts of a pleading by denying all facts or only certain ones. 2. To cross horizontally.

treason 1. Violating an allegiance, betraying one's country, or levying war against one's government. 2. Helping the enemy by aiding and comforting them. 3. Betrayal of trust.

treasury securities In gerontology, long-term care, and Social Security, these are the reserves in the Social Security funds lent to the federal government in exchange for special treasury notes. This allows the reserves to be used in the federal budget at below-market interest rates. The concern is that when the notes must be redeemed after the year 2018 to pay for the elder boom, they will act much like a balloon payment at the end of a mortgage because of the increased numbers of persons in old age, and the federal Social Security system taxes will have to increase to cover the shortfall.

treatability studies In environmental health and hazardous waste management, this is to assess and evaluate which hazardous waste can be subjected to a treatment process. Five factors are considered: 1) whether the waste is amenable to the treatment process; 2) what pretreatment, if any, is required; 3) the optimal process conditions needed to achieve the desired treatment; 4) the efficiency of a treatment process for a specific waste or wastes; and 5) the characteristics and volumes of residual wastes from a particular treatment process.

treatise A comprehensive written work on a subject of concern that provides a special discussion of facts, evidence, principles, and conclusions.

treatment 1. In medical care, this is the management and care of a patient for the purpose of combating disease or disorders. 2. In environmental health and hazardous waste management, this means any method, technique, or process, including neutralization, designed to change the physical, chemical, or biological character or composition of any hazardous waste so as to neutralize such waste or to render such waste nonhazardous, safer for transport, amenable for recovery or storage, or reduced in volume. Any method technique or process designed to change the physical and chemical character of waste to render it less hazardous and safer to transport, store, or dispose of or reduced in volume.

treatment authorization request In Medicaid, this is a special insurance form used in gaining authorization to render a specific service to a patient under the Medicaid program. A request sent by a physician to the Medicaid field office to obtain authorization to do surgery, hospitalize the patient, and have days of stay, procedures, treatment, or therapies approved.

treatment, extraordinary In medical care, this is an ethical decision of a health-care provider where he or she provides heroic measures in treatment or where the procedures and treatments provided have little or limited value to the patient, cannot be completed without much pain and suffering, or may be very costly with benefits being minimal.

treatment facility In health-care delivery, this is a residential or nonresidential facility or program licensed, certified, or otherwise authorized to provide treatment of substance abuse or mental illness under the care and direction of a licensed physician or other legally approved health-care providers or practitioners.

treatment plan *See patient care plan.*

treatment storage and disposal facilities (TSDs) In environmental health and hazardous materials management, these are hazardous waste storage sites. Under the Hazardous and Solid Waste Amendments (HSWA) of the Resource Conservation and Recovery Act (RCRA) of 1976, a provision was made to ensure that all facilities that handle hazardous wastes operate under the conditions specified in permits issued under HSWA/RCRA.

treatment technique requirements In environmental health and safe drinking water management, these are the requirements of the Safe Drinking Water Act and related regulations that specify which treatment techniques are to be used for each of the 83 specific contaminants that are to be treated. *See Safe Drinking Water Act.*

treatment technologies In environmental health, these are the chemical and scientific methods that alter the composition of pollutants, hazardous waste substances, or contaminants through any chemical, biological, or physical means so as to reduce toxicity, mobility, or volume of contaminated materials being treated. Treatment technologies are alternatives to landfill disposal of untreated hazardous wastes.

treatment week In managed care or medical insurance, these are four or more treatment days in a calendar week. If three treatments or less in a week are given, a "treatment day" charge is used; used mostly in radiation therapy and oncology.

treatment zones In environmental health and landfill management, these are soil areas of the unsaturated zone of a land treatment unit within which hazardous constituents are degraded, transformed, or immobilized.

treaty In a managed-care, insurance policy, or related contract, this is where risks are shared between insurance companies, often through the reinsurance method.

treble damages In health law, this is triple the amount of recovery given by the court for damages provided to the plaintiff in some lawsuit to strongly discourage certain wrongful or harmful acts. *See punitive damages.*

tree structure In medical and library literature search activities, this is an organizational structure of literature used by libraries and a computerized literature database where a hierarchical list of subjects with major categories and subcategories is used. The U.S. National Library of Medicine uses such a structure in its Medical Subject Headings publications, as do many comprehensive computerized literature sources available on CD-ROM.

trend analysis In managed care, health administration, and health planning, this is a forecasting method used by health-care administrators to project future activities and occurrences using statistical methods to analyze past data to predict future trends.

trend analysis/population projections In public health, health-care delivery, and demographics, this is a description of the population trends and the statistical measurements of the movement (growth) of the population of a state.

Trendelenburg position In medical care, this a position assumed by a patient for surgery in which the feet are lowered, the head and shoulders are slightly lowered, and the abdominal area is slightly elevated.

trend factor In health policy and health-care finance, this is the rate at which medical costs increase because of factors such as prices charged by medical care providers, changes in utilization patterns (especially frequency of visits), cost shifting, use of expensive medical technology, price gouging by insurance and pharmaceutical companies, wasting resources, or failing to recycle products.

trending 1. In managed care, health administration, and health planning, this is the process of employing trend analysis; predicting future utilization patterns of health plan members from past utilization patterns on the basis of trend factoring and calculations. 2. In environmental health, this is an analysis of parts, systems, component surveillance, performances, and operating histories to determine such things as failure causes, operational effectiveness, cost-effectiveness, and other attributes.

trespass In criminal law, this is the illegal or wrongful entry onto or into another person's property for which money damages may be sought or arrests made if local ordinances exist to cover trespass.

trespass on a case In common law, a form of action used to collect damages for injury or harm as an indirect result of a wrongful act by another party.

triad 1. Three; a group of three items, objects, or structures that are similar or alike. 2. Three symptoms or effects that occur together.

triage In medical care delivery, this is the screening of patients seeking care to determine which service is initially required and with what priority. A patient coming to a facility for care may be seen in triage screening where it is determined, possibly by a triage nurse, whether the patient has a medical or surgical problem or requires some nonphysician service such as social work consultation or which type of medical care should be rendered. In managed care and health maintenance organizations, these screening nurses, called "treatment nurses," also give vaccinations and do simple minor treatments. A screening or rapid assessment unit merely refers patients to the most appropriate treatment service or may also give treatment for minor problems. This was originally used to describe the sorting of battle casualties into groups who could wait for care, who would benefit from immediate care, and who were beyond care.

triage nurse In managed care, this is a registered nurse who has the primary responsibility of screening patients who enter a clinic to determine the type of care needed, the type of practitioner that can best treat the problem, and the urgency of the need.

trial 1. In law, these are the processes, procedures, and proceedings used for the formal examination of facts of a dispute or case by a court to decide the validity of a claim or charge. 2. In epidemiology or biomedical research, this is a research study or experiment such as a community trial or a double-blind trial.

trial balance In health-care financial management accounting practices, this is a practice run at summarizing all debits and credit balances of all accounts in the ledger; an overview of the account; ensuring the equality of debits and credits.

trial court A lower level court of law in which facts and evidence related to a dispute or crime is presented to a jury or judge for a final verdict.

trial per pais A legal trial by jury.

triangle of epidemiology See *epidemiology, triangle of*.

trichloroethylene (TCE) A stable, low boiling, colorless liquid that is toxic by inhalation. It is used as a solvent, as a metal degreasing agent, and in other industrial applications (EPA).

trichology The study of hair.

trichotillomania In psychiatry, this is a morbid compulsion to pull out one's own hair.

trickling filters In environmental health and liquid waste treatment, this is the coarse, biological treatment system in which wastewater is trickled over a bed of stones, sand, charcoal or other material covered with bacterial growth.

tricyclic drug In psychiatric and mental health services, this is an antidepressant drug that is widely used in the treatment of pathological depression.

triennial Third anniversary; anything taking place once in 3 years; happening every 3 years; lasting for or continuous for 3 years.

triennial survey In the accreditation process of the Joint Commission on Accreditation of Healthcare Facilities (JCAHO), this is the required accreditation survey conducted every 3 years.

trigger effect In psychology and marketing, this is a temporary increase in behavior often associated with television and mass media attention and focus on a concern or issue.

trigger, environmental health The report of any environmental or hazardous waste event or condition that initiates a hazard analysis or correction function.

triggers, health-care In universal coverage, these are mechanism to postpone the imposing of employer mandates to force small businesses to purchase medical insurance for their workers or pay some portion of it. The mandates will kick in if universal coverage is not being met in some future time.

triggers, patient care In long-term care, this is when a patient's health status diminishes to the point that an intervention is needed to stop the patient's diminishing health on the basis of a resident assessment protocol, which is a set of instructions established by the attending physician. Some triggers are automatic and some potential. The resident assessment protocol is a list of trigger factors that include delirium, cognitive loss/dementia, visual function, communication, activities of daily living, urinary incontinence, mental status, mood state, behavioral problems, falls, nutritional status, feeding tubes, dehydration, dental care, pressure ulcers, psychotropic drug use, and physical restraints.

trihalomethane (THM) In environmental health, this is one of a family of organic compounds named as derivatives of methane. They are generally the by-product from the chlorination of drinking water containing organic material.

trimester A 3-month period. The first 3 months (first trimester), the second 3 months (middle or second trimester), or the last 3 months (third trimester) of a pregnancy.

trim points In DRGs under Medicare, these are low and high length of stays; high or low values that describe an acceptable length of stay or cost range for each DRG. Patients who fall outside the high trim point for a particular DRG are outliers. Outliers depend on cutoff points, and the narrower the cutoff point, the larger the number of outliers or patients with unusual medical cases or anomalies. The cutoff points are based on statistical medical care criteria and policies of the organization setting the rates for reimbursement. Under the original research on DRGs, 5% of inpatients were expected to be outliers. *See also outlier.*

triple option In managed care, this is when a single carrier offers three types of medical coverage: traditional HMO, health plan, and PPO and traditional medical insurance.

triple rinse In environmental health, the flushing of containers three times, each time using a volume of the normal diluent equal to approximately 10% of the container's capacity and adding the rinse liquid to the spray mixture or disposing of it by a method prescribed for disposing of pesticides.

TRO *See temporary restraining order.*

trocar A large, hollow, sharp-pointed needle-looking instrument with openings toward the end; used to withdraw fluids and the body's flora and related bacteria from a dead body, especially from the abdominal cavity, to slow decomposition and prepare for embalming procedures.

troche Lozenge.

troika 1. A Russian term referring to a carriage drawn by three horses abreast; a team consisting of three horses. 2. In health-care administration, the three components of health-care administration, usually administration, medical staff, and nursing. The governing body, the administration, and the medical staff have also been referred to as the "hospital management troika."

trolley car policy A name for an insurance policy that is so hard to collect benefits on that it is as though it provided benefits only for injuries resulting from being hit by a trolley car; typically used in mail-order insurance.

trover 1. An action used to recover one's property or goods from someone who supposedly found them. 2. In health law, this is a writ against the wrongful holding of personal property, such as a patient's personal effects or belongings.

true bill In law, this is an indictment made by a grand jury.

true negative In epidemiology, research, or drug testing, these are the persons who a test shows do not have the disease and in fact do not have the disease; those persons who test disease free and are disease free. *See also true positive; false positive; false negative.*

true positive In epidemiology, research, or drug testing, these are the persons who a test result shows have a disease, score high on the test, and indeed have the disease. *See also true negative; false positive; false negative.*

trust 1. A fiduciary relationship. 2. An agreement where one party holds a title but controls and administers the property for the benefit of another. 3. The transfer of money or property to a second person for the benefit of another. 4. A combination of corporations in a similar industry. 5. Confidence, integrity, and honesty in a relationship.

trustee 1. One who holds, executes, or administers a trust. 2. A group, committee, or governing board appointed to manage the affairs of a hospital or other health-care facility or health service. 3. A person who has a fiduciary relationship with another person such as a physician or psychologist.

trust funds Revenue collected and used by the federal government for carrying out specific purposes and programs according to terms of a trust agreement or statute such as the Social Security and unemployment trust funds. Trust funds are administered by the government in a fiduciary capacity for those benefited and are not available for the general purposes of the government. Trust fund receipts whose use is not anticipated in the immediate future are generally invested in interest-bearing government securities. The Medicare program is financed through two trust funds: the Federal Hospital Insurance Fund, which finances Part A, and the Federal Supplementary Medical Insurance Trust Fund, which finances Part B. In health care, some unions, trade associations, and professional associations have created special trust funds to be used by members in the event a member is injured or ill and medical benefits run out. Then the member receives benefits, and medical bills are covered.

try 1. To separate or pick out. 2. To sift through or sort out facts. 3. To examine, test, or prove; to put to the test or to the proof. 4. To settle, test, or contest; to examine, argue, and decide in court of law. 5. To determine the guilt or innocence of a person within the scope of the law.

TSJI *See acupuncture.*

tuberculosis unit (TB unit) A specially staffed and equipped medical and nursing unit in a health-care facility that treats patients suffering from tuberculosis.

tumor In medical care, this is any abnormal unfocused growth of tissue and cells, usually in a lump, that is not inflammatory and has no physiological function.

tumor registry A data bank in the medical records department related to the cause, type, and characteristics of tumors, course of the disease, and treatment approaches as well as the outcome of cancer and related demographic characteristics.

turbidity 1. In environmental health, this is the cloudy condition in water caused by suspended silt or organic matter. 2. Haziness in air caused by the presence of suspended particulate matter and pollutants.

turnaround time 1. In medical insurance, this is the time it takes from receipt of claim or inquiry until an answer is provided or the bill paid. This applies to inquiries from both providers and subscribers. 2. In health administration, as a measure of productivity and efficiency, this is the lapse of time necessary to get a report back from the lab; how long it takes to get an X ray read; the time from which a pharmacist receives a prescription until it is filled and available to the patient.

turnkey system 1. In health information management, this is an arrangement in which the computer sales agency assumes all responsibilities for installing a computer, including analysis, selection, installation, maintenance, training, and documentation. When completed, the user, figuratively, has only to turn the key to have an operational system. 2. In health facility construction, this is where a new facility would be totally completed so that the new owner would only have to turn the key and open the door to have a functioning facility.

turnover 1. In health-care financial management, this is the number of times that assets such as accounts receivable are paid up during a certain time period. Accounts receivable turnover is figured by total billings on account for a period divided by the average accounts receivable balance for the period. 2. In health administration and human resource management, this is when employees leave a health-care organization because of quitting, getting terminated, or retiring; movement into and out of an organization; the loss of employees by a health-care organization who depart for a variety of reasons. Turnover is a costly experience for an organization because of hiring costs, training costs, learning curves for new persons, higher accident rates in new employees, idle equipment with no one to run it, productivity usually down, higher waste rates in new employees, overtime pay to make up for lack of workers, unmet deadlines, and new employees being more likely to leave than long-term employees.

turnover, preventable In health administration and human resource management, this is when an employee leaves a health-care organization and takes a job at a competing organization in basically the same position for similar pay and benefits and hours. Turnover that should not occur on the basis of job dissatisfaction, low morale, or no chance to get ahead rather than leaving to advance oneself, bettering oneself professionally, or leaving for personal reasons.

turnover rate In health administration and human resource management, this is an indicator of job satisfaction, morale, and motivation. Turnover rates higher than 30% have been suggested as an indicator of an organizational problem. The turnover rate is the total number of separations compared to the total number of employees. Turnover rates can be calculated on a monthly or yearly basis. The formula for turnover rate follows:

$$\frac{\text{Total number of employee separations in specific time period}}{\text{Average number of employees in the same time period}} \times 100$$

turn Q 2H In long-term care, this refers to a bed-ridden patient who is unable to roll over or move by him- or herself and must be turned over every 2 hours to avoid pressure sores.

turpitude Depravity; shameful, unjust, dishonest, or immoral activity; wickedness.

twenty-four (24)-hour nursing services In health-care facilities, these are services that require registered nurses and/or licensed practical (vocational) nurses and assistant nursing personnel on duty on a round-the-clock basis.

twenty-three (23)-hour observation unit A medical and nursing unit for patients who need limited observation, services, care, and treatment but not a full day of health-care services. By avoiding a full-day stay, the patient can be classified as an outpatient and thus reduce health-care costs. Such observations are charged on a sliding scale up to 23 hours, and patients are thus charged much less than for an inpatient stay.

twisting When an insurance agent persuades the health-care organization client to drop one insurance policy and take a different one by misrepresenting the terms of either policy to the disadvantage of the health-care organization holding the policy.

two-headed In health administration, this is when any health-care organization is managed by two administrators with equal authority or is organizationally arranged with two different heads or directors.

two-plan model In managed care and publicly funded local health-care delivery, this is a managed-care plan developed to accommodate patients who are public health, county, and Medicaid supported. These are locally developed comprehensive managed-care systems at the county level. One fork of the plan is referred to as the "local initiative," and the second the "mainstream," using one nongovernmental private managed-care program so that the members have a choice. This also avoids antitrust issues (MediCal in California).

two surgeons In managed care or health insurance, this is where under certain circumstances the skills of two surgeons (usually with different skills) may be required in the management of a specific surgical problem or be asked to give an opinion on the allowance or disallowance of a procedure (e.g., a urologist and a general surgeon in the creation of an ileal conduit).

two-thirds vote In formal health-care meetings or hearings using parliamentary procedure, the legal or accepted set level of voting needed to pass a motion or proposition.

two-tiered orientation program In health administration and human relations management, these are employee training and organization introductory meetings conducted for new employees to acquaint them with both the personnel department and the department of assignment with efforts not to duplicate information.

two-tiered wage structure In health administration and human relations management, this is an employee pay system where one type of employee is hired at and receives a different pay rate than other employees. For example, new employees may be paid lower wages than old hires who are union members to keep costs of labor down.

two–twenty-three (223) limit Section 223 of P.L. 92-603 defines the limit put on the money it would pay per discharged patient. As long as the costs or discharges of the health-care facility are under the limit, there is no financial penalty.

tying arrangement In health administration and materials management, this is when a purchase of an item can be done only if the purchase of another item is also done. The second and more desired product can be purchased only if the first item is purchased first. This may be illegal or violate antitrust laws if handled inappropriately. Also referred to as a "tie-in-sale."

type A personality This is also called the "stress personality," which describes the traits of some individuals who are prone to heart attacks because of stress when their health status should otherwise not indicate one. Some of the more common characteristics of a type A personality include time urgency; free-floating hostility; being aggressive or competitive; not being able to stand the slow rate at which events occur; trying to do several tasks at once; or failing to recognize the beauty in his or her environment; finishing the sentences of others; measuring self-worth and accomplishments in terms of things acquired or numbers of items generated such as sales for the company; and, overall, being a very driven person. The traits were identified by two cardiologists in San Francisco, Rosenman and Friedman, and first published in the book *Type A Personality and Your Heart*. Also referred to as the "heart attack personality," "type As," or "type A persons." *See type B personality; stress; stressors; dystressors; benestressors; eustress.*

type B personality This describes the traits of some individuals who are opposite of the type A personality, who have a higher quality of life, yet who are as productive and successful as the type A. These persons are more relaxed, enjoy the beautiful things in life, can relax when they are supposed to relax, can work hard when the occasion calls for it, measure life by its quality and not by numbers of things acquired, and do not put themselves under unnecessary time pressures. Also a part of Rosenman and Friedman's observations, first published in the book *Type A Personality and Your Heart*. *See type A personality*.

type of care The facilities and personnel available to apply certain approaches, levels, techniques, methods, equipment, or technology while rendering health care or carrying out the plan of care to be provided to a patient on the basis of diagnosis, disease, condition, injury, or disorder. The level of care and the approach used in treatment are components of type of care.

type of contract In managed care, this is to distinguish between employer group–contracted managed-care coverage and nongroup coverage. Under an employer group or other type of group agreement and policy, certain services are covered and benefits provided to members and their dependent, whereas in nongroup coverage the contract is directly with the individual and his or her dependents and the health plan.

type of patient *See new patient; established patient; ward patient; private patient; semiprivate patient.*

type I recommendation In the accreditation process of the Joint Commission on Accreditation of Healthcare Facilities (JCAHO), these are expectations and requirements that are expected to be recognized and followed by the healthcare organization's administration that affect adversely the accreditation decision and should be addressed in the hospital's plan for improvement. Progress in resolving this level of recommendation is monitored by the JCAHO through focused surveys, written progress reports, or both as predetermined and stated in time frames during the accreditation cycle. Failure to resolve such compliance issues within the stated time frames can result in loss of accreditation.

type II recommendation In the accreditation process of the Joint Commission on Accreditation of Healthcare Facilities (JCAHO), these suggestions are supplementary and consultative and do not affect the accreditation decision. They can, however, affect that decision at a future date if not remedied by the time of the next triennial survey.

types of accommodations In hospitals, long-term-care facilities, and other types of institutions, these are the kinds of rooms the patient occupies. *See private patient; semiprivate patient; ward patient.*

U

UB82 (Uniform Billing Code of 1982) In managed care, this is a standard form approved by the government that provides a summary of a medical care claim to a third-party payer. The form provides a comprehensive coverage of each admission of a patient to a health-care facility.

UB92 (Uniform Billing Code of 1992) In managed care, this is a standard form approved by the government (a revised form of UB82) that is based on a federal mandate that hospitals follow specific billing procedures and itemize all services included in the patient's bill.

uberrima fides (Lat.) In the utmost good faith.

ubi jus ibi remedium (Lat.) There is no wrong without a remedy.

ubiquitous background levels In environmental health, these are concentrations of chemicals that are present in the environment because of culturally and technologically derived sources such as automobiles, industry, and homes.

UCC See *Uniform Commercial Code*.

UCCC See *Uniform Consumer Credit Code*.

UCR See *usual, customary, and reasonable*.

UHDDS See *Uniform Hospital Discharge Data Set*.

ullage In environmental health and hazardous waste management, this is the amount by which packaging falls short of being full, usually expressed as percentages by volume.

ultima (Lat.) 1. The most remote. 2. The final or last answer or response; the farthest possible or ultimate response, act, or possibility.

ultima ratio (Lat.) 1. The final and last argument. 2. The last resort; final try.

ultimate fact 1. A fact, the truth of which is decided by the jury and which is essential to a case or the cause of action. 2. Basic fact based on evidence and reason.

ultimate mortality tables In insurance and vital statistics, these death tables show higher death rates than a select mortality table. By excluding the experience of an assumed select period such as 5 years, they show the mortality rates as being higher.

ultra- Prefix meaning "beyond"; excess.

ultra (Lat.) 1. Beyond the expected limit. 2. Outside of or in excess of; extreme. 3. One who proposes extreme measures or holds extreme opinions. 4. An ultraist.

ultradian rhythm A rhythm that cycles over minutes or hours.

ultrasonics The production of sound at frequencies above the audible range.

ultrasonogram The record produced by ultrasonography.

ultrasonography In medical care, this is a radiologic diagnostic technique through which deep body structures are visualized by recording the reflection or echoes of ultrasonic waves.

ultrasound High-frequency sound that causes radiant energy. In medical care, this is the use of acoustic waves above the range of 20,000 cycles per second to visualize internal body structures, tissues, or organs for medical diagnostic purposes.

ultrasound, B-color imaging A high-frequency sound-echoing system that maps and changes B-mode information into color instead of a gray scale, offering a wider range of visual images and information in the images.

ultrasound, B-mode (gray scale) In medical care, this is a high-frequency sound-echoing system used to assist in medical diagnosis through images to allow identification of the anatomy of structures with resolution of motion in two-dimensional surfaces. The final image is displayed on a TV monitor or CRT in varying shades of black and white (gray scale, as in newspaper print).

ultrasound, color-flow doppler A high-frequency sound-echoing system used to show imaging information as a color overlay to the B-mode gray scale. For example, blood is displayed in different colors depending on the direction of its flow.

ultrasound, diagnostic In medical care, this is a high-frequency sound-echoing system used to produce an image of internal body organs and structures and/or related structures such as an unborn child; a sonar device that produces acoustic sound waves beyond the range of normal human hearing when sent through the body and that results in a reflected image of body parts for diagnostic purposes.

ultrasound, duplex doppler In medical care, this is a high-frequency sound-echoing system used in medical diagnostics to produce images that combine spectral doppler with the gray scale B-mode in real time, resulting in images and doppler information at the same time.

ultrasound M-mode (motion mode) In medical care, this is a high-frequency sound-echoing system used in medical diagnostics using a linear graphic display of changes in the position of reflective structures over time. The main uses of this basic mode have been to produce images of the heart and its motion or a fetus in the uterus.

ultrasound, spectral doppler A high-frequency sound-echoing system used in medical diagnostics and presented in real time to graphically measure and display the velocity of blood flow through vessels or between chambers of the heart.

ultrasound technology A course of study connected with medical radiography training programs, which prepare individuals in the use of acoustic energy for medical diagnosis, research, and therapy.

ultraviolet A powerful type of radiation between violet rays and roentgen rays in the spectrum.

ultraviolet radiation In laser technology, this is electromagnetic radiation with wavelengths smaller than those of visible radiation (to the standard of 0.2–.04 μm).

ultraviolet rays (UV) Radiation from the sun that can be useful or potentially harmful. Rays from one part of the spectrum enhance plant life and are useful in some medical and dental procedures. Rays from other parts of the spectrum can cause skin cancer and other tissue damage in humans if exposed extensively. The ozone layer in the atmosphere provides a protective shield that limits the amount of UV rays that reach the earth's surface.

ultra vires (Lat.) 1. Beyond authority delegated to a person; beyond powers. 2. Acts performed by a corporation that are beyond the scope of its corporate power. 3. Acts that are beyond the authority of a public official or public organization such as the Environmental Protection Agency or Occupational Safety and Health Administration.

ululation In psychology and mental health care, this is the constant sobbing of a psychotic or hysterical person.

umbrella policy In liability insurance, a policy set up to supplement basic liability contracts by providing extra or excess coverage.

UMGA See Unified Medical Group Association.

unallocated benefit In managed care and medical insurance, this is a policy provision in an insurance policy providing reimbursement up to a maximum amount for the costs of all extra miscellaneous hospital services but not specifying how much will be paid for each type of service.

unanimous In formal health-care meetings and hearings using parliamentary procedure, this is when the voting process has no dissenting vote.

unanimous ballot In formal health-care board of directors meetings using parliamentary procedure, this is when an organization's bylaws or constitution allow a ballot to be cast by the secretary for a candidate who is the only one nominated for an office and there are no objections from the board.

unauthorized practice 1. Unqualified persons doing activities, practices, and skills that only specific health-care providers are trained, licensed, and permitted to do. 2. Practicing acts or providing services that may be prohibited by law unless licensed, registered, or certified.

una voce (Lat.) With one voice; unanimous.

unbundling Payment for nonphysician services furnished to inpatients in a health-care facility. Under certain conditions, payments have been made for nonphysician services that are furnished by an outside supplier or other provider and have been billed by the outside source as Part B or physician services even though furnished to a hospital inpatient. The practice of billing for physician services under Part B for these type of services has been referred to by lawmakers as "unbundling." Under some laws, this has been prohibited, and all nonphysician services provided to a patient in an inpatient setting will be paid only if they are hospital services. This is also maximizing revenue by carefully selecting health-care provider contract options or certain clinical support services.

uncertainty In safety and accident prevention, this is any nonquantifiable increase in accident probability resulting from the lack of safety program features (e.g., human factors review, hazard analysis, training); oversight and omissions in a management system. This may be termed "descriptive uncertainty." A degree of uncertainty results from a quantitative inadequacy of estimation of a stated unknown factor.

unclean-hands principle 1. A person seeking equitable relief must not have acted with bad faith, malice, or illegally, or he will not be entitled to relief. 2. Transactions must have been in good faith and with a high level of ethics.

uncompensated care 1. In health-care financial

management, these are services provided by health-care providers for which no payment is expected or no charge made; treatment, care, and therapy provided by a health-care provider on a volunteer basis. 2. The difference between reimbursement and the actual cost of providing care; the amount of money that does not get reimbursed yet expenses are incurred for it; shortfalls in compensation for care rendered.

uncompensated care costs In health-care financial management, these are the expenses and costs of providing care that have not been paid for. These are deductions from patient care revenues accounted for under bad debt, uncollectable fees, charity care, or volunteer services.

unconditioned reflex Any automatic response to a stimulus such as pulling a hand away from a hot stove. Also called a "reflex arc."

unconscionability 1. Extremely unfair sales practices. 2. Merchandising practices that a court will not permit.

unconscionable 1. Exceeding the limit of any reasonable claim or expectation. 2. Unreasonable; unscrupulous; not influenced by conscience.

unconscionable bargain 1. A bargain that is unreasonable and offends public policy. 2. To enter into a deal that exceeds the limits of a reasonable bargain.

unconscious 1. Parts of the mind in which psychic material such as repressed desires, wishes, and memories exist but are not directly accessible to one's awareness. 2. A mental state of unawareness with the absence of sensation and perception. *See also conscious; consciousness, levels of.*

unconstitutional Laws, penalties, or actions that are not permitted by the U.S. Constitution; any regulation or law passed that goes against the rights and fundamental premises set forth by the Constitution. Health regulations cannot go against, underscore, or change the rights given all citizens by the Constitution.

uncontrolled hazardous waste sites In environmental health and hazardous waste management, these are areas where an accumulation of hazardous waste creates a threat to the health and safety of individuals, the environment, or both. Some sites are found on public lands such as former municipal, county, or state landfills where illegal or poorly managed sites allowed improper waste disposal to take place. Other sites are found on private property, often belonging to the generators of the hazardous waste. Examples are surface impoundments, landfills, dumps, and tank and drum farms.

underachievement Failure to reach an adequate level of accomplishment, promotion, or work level in school because of biological or psychological underdevelopment.

underachiever A person who does not perform or function up to his or her ability or capacity; a health-care employee who does not strive for quality in his or her work; a bright child whose school grades fall below expected levels of innate capability.

undercompensated care In health-care financial management and health-care delivery, this is when a hospital, nursing home, physician, or other health-care provider receives less reimbursement than was submitted to the third-party payer or receives less reimbursement than was fair or reasonable or was less than the prevailing rate yet was ethically due to the health-care provider.

undergraduate The completion of a degree at the bachelors level from an accredited college or university; to be in the middle of a bachelors degree education program. To enter graduate school, a student must have completed his or her undergraduate education and possess a bachelors degree.

undergraduate medical education Medical education given before receipt of the doctor of medicine or equivalent degree, which is usually the 4 years of study in medical, osteopathic, dental, or podiatric school leading to a degree. This contrasts with that in general education, where undergraduate education refers to a college education leading to the bachelors degree.

underground injection In environmental health and safe water management, this is any subsurface emplacement of fluids through a dug, bored, drilled, or driven well where the depth is greater than the surface dimension; a well injection.

underground injection control In environmental health and safe water management, this is a program to prevent underground injection that endangers drinking water sources. Authorization of underground injection is controlled by the state, which issues permits followed by inspections, monitoring, record keeping, and reporting requirements.

underground sources of drinking water In environmental health and safe water management, these are aquifers, or a portion of one, that supply any public water system or that contains a sufficient quantity of groundwater to supply a public water system and currently supplies drinking water for human consumption containing fewer than 10,000 mg/l total dissolved solids and is not an exempted aquifer.

underground storage tanks In environmental health and safe water management, these are any one or combination of tanks, including underground pipes connecting them, used to contain an accumulation of regulated substances and the volume of which is 10% or more beneath the surface of the ground; tanks located totally or partially underground that are designed to hold gasoline or other petroleum products or chemical solutions.

undernutrition Inadequate intake of vitamins, minerals, calories, etc.

understudy In health administration and human resource management, this is an on-the-job training experience in management or a highly specialized area done to have the trainee become skilled enough to take over the position. *See administrative residency.*

undertaking A promise, guarantee, or assumption of responsibility.

underutilization In human resource and affirmative action management, this is when a department, unit, service, clinic, health facility, or the entire health-care organization has fewer members of a protected class as employees than are found in the organization's labor market.

underwrite 1. Bearing the financial risk for something; to assume liability to the amount specified. 2. To agree to pay or give of certain things by singing a document. 3. To insure. 4. To sign one's name to.

underwriter One who underwrites insurance; one who processes, selects, classifies, evaluates, and assumes risks according to their insurability.

underwriting In insurance, the process of selecting, classifying, evaluating, and assuming risks according to their insurability. The fundamental purpose is to make sure that the group insured has the same probability and probable amount of loss, within reasonable limits, as the universe on which premium rates were based. Because premium rates are based on an expectation of loss, the underwriting process must assess and categorize risks into classes with similar expectations of loss and risk.

underwriting department In managed care, medical insurance, or other insurance companies, this is the administrative unit that determines which kinds of policies and risks the company will insure. The staff and professional employees of this department collect and analyze mortality and morbidity rates of the beneficiaries of the organization to ensure that rates do not exceed risk. Risk factors of applicants are reviewed on the basis of an overall history of the person, age, build, physical condition, family history, habits (smoking or drinking alcohol), occupation, financial resources, and other factors that might suggest the degree of risk to determine policy type and premiums. Other activities of the department include negotiation and management of reinsurance contracts.

underwriting impairments In managed care, medical insurance, or other insurance companies, these are the risk factors, traits, characteristics, or other variables that tend to increase the applicant's risk above the norm or average beneficiary, making them a higher risk to insure and limiting the company's ability to operate profitably.

underwriting manual In managed care, medical insurance, or other insurance companies, this a review and summary of the techniques and approaches used by an insurance carrier to assess, evaluate, and rate insurable risks. This document sets forth the policies and approaches used in underwriting impairments and is a guide on the procedures of underwriting actions for specific impairments.

underwriting profit In insurance, this is the portion of the earnings of an insurance company that come from the function of underwriting. It excludes earnings from investments (other than interest earnings required by law or regulation assumed to have been earned for purposes of determining the reserves held) in the form of either income from securities or sale of securities at a profit. The remainder is found by deducting incurred losses and expenses from earned premiums.

undetermined 1. Not limited. 2. Not defined; not determined.

undo 1. To put an end to. 2. To bring to ruin. 3. To put distress on. 4. To find an answer or explanation. 5. To reverse, annul, or cancel.

undoing In mental health, this is a mental or defense mechanism in which something unacceptable and already done is symbolically acted out repetitiously in reverse in the hope of relieving anxiety.

undue 1. Not just, legal, or lawful. 2. Improper; not suitable or appropriate. 3. Excessive or unreasonable. 4. More than needed.

undue influence Controlling another to the point that he or she is no longer capable of being a free agent or is prevented from being one.

unearned premium reserve In managed care or medical insurance, this is an accounting liability on the insurance company's balance sheet for funds held by the insurance company for premiums paid in advance; revenue held by the health plan that has not been used to provide insurance coverage to members.

unemployment compensation The short-term temporary payment to individuals who have lost their jobs, continue to be unemployed, seek new employment, and are willing and able to work yet need some financial aid during the unemployment period.

unemployment compensation disability Insurance that covers off-the-job injury or sickness and is paid for by deductions from a person's paycheck. This program is administered by a state agency and is sometimes also known as "state disability insurance."

unemployment insurance A form of social insurance that operates by means of a payroll tax. The revenues are used to pay calculated benefits for defined periods to people who qualify (usually by virtue of accumulated amounts of covered employment) as being unemployed, as defined in the law. People receiving unemployment insurance are not usually eligible to receive group health insurance coverage obtained through their most recent place of employment.

unethical conduct Acts that violate a profession's standards; dishonest, questionable acts or behaviors.

unfair labor practice (ULPs) Specific acts by a union or an employer that are prohibited by law; violations of the National Labor Relations Act and its amendments.

unfinished business 1. In formal health-care meetings or hearings using parliamentary procedure, any formal activity that is put off by a motion to postpone the business for an indefinite time; incomplete business put off or not finished by the time the meeting adjourned. Unfinished business from past meetings has priority at the next official assembly of the organization. Also called "old business." 2. In mental health care, this is an emotional issue of a current or former relationship that has not been completed and still needs to be discussed to allow a more complete state of mental well-being for those involved. 3. In death and dying issues, it is important for the dying patient to clear up matters that remain incomplete prior to dying.

unfriendly takeover In health-care finance, this is a form of corporate acquisition of a publicly held for-profit health-care organization in which the management of the organization refuses the acquisition offer, yet the refusal is ignored and the acquisition is continued against the wishes of the health-care organization by the unfriendly party buying up stock in the company.

unified federal budget The budget of the U.S. government, including all expenditures and receipts. Special nonaccessible funds like Social Security are sometimes included in the calculations of the total revenue of the U.S. government. This distorts the total deficit of the U.S. government's budget because Social Security is not to be spent on running the government.

Unified Medical Group Association (UMGA) A nonprofit national professional health-care organization that unites medical groups and managed-care programs under a single organizational umbrella. Through its organizational membership structure, UMGA coordinates interactions with these entities, holds an annual conference, conducts education and training activities, and provides accreditation for large medical groups that have managed-care contracts. The name was changed to the American Medical Group Association in 1996.

uniform 1. Always the same; applying generally; regular; equally. 2. Having a consistent form, manner, or procedure.

uniform acts Laws on various subjects proposed by the Commissioners on Uniform State Laws so that most codes are adopted by most states.

Uniform Anatomical Gift Act A law passed by some states that defines conditions under which bodies approved for use as cadavers can have their tissues used as potential organ transplant material.

uniform bill-patient summary A business and medical record document combining billing information and an abstract of medical data and diagnoses.

Uniform Commercial Code (UCC) A set of laws that regulates all business transactions; a comprehensive set of laws governing business activities; statutory codes used to control business transactions that are uniformly accepted from state to state. The purposes and policies of this act are to 1) simplify, clarify, and modernize the law governing commercial transactions; 2) permit the continued expansion of commercial practices through custom, usage, and agreement of the parties; 3) make uniform the law among various jurisdictions. The act sets forth rules on sales, leases, commercial paper, bank deposits and collections, funds transfers, letters of credit, bulk transfers, warehouse receipts, bills of lading, documents of title, investment securities, secured transactions, sales of accounts, chattel papers, effective date and repealer, effective date and transition, and other important matters related to business transactions.

Uniform Consumer Credit Code (UCCC) Laws developed to protect the consumer against unscrupulous and unfair business practices.

uniform cost accounting The use of a common set of accounting definitions, procedures, terms, and methods for the accumulation and communication of quantitative data relating to the financial activities of several enterprises. The American Hospital Association, for example, encourages the use of the chart of accounts as a system that can be employed by hospitals in the United States.

Uniformed Health Services Corps (UHSC) Medical and health-care professionals who join the U.S. Public Health Service and work in public health activities in their area of expertise anywhere in the United States or its territories where there is an underserved population. The members wear military-type uniforms and have ranks similar to those of the military. Some training grants are available for medical school or certain allied health professions such as physical therapy that pay for the entire schooling. The student then must work for the Public Health Service in the UHSC for 3 years and go where assigned to work with underserved populations where there is a health manpower shortage such as on Indian reservations or central city areas of major cities.

uniform hospital abstract: minimum basic data set See Uniform Hospital Discharge Data Set.

Uniform Hospital Discharge Data Set (UHDDS) A defined set of data that gives a minimum description of a hospital episode or admission. Collection of a UHDDS is required on discharge for all hospital stays reimbursed under Medicare and Medicaid. The UHDDS was defined in a policy statement of the secretary of the old HEW and includes data on the age, sex, race, and residence of the patient; length of stay; diagnosis; responsible physicians; procedures performed; disposition of the patient; and sources of payment. The Uniform Hospital Discharge Abstract (UHDA), used to collect the UHDDS, is one example of a discharge abstract.

uniform individual policy provisions A set of provisions regarding the nature and content of individual health insurance policies developed in a recommended model law by the NAIC (National Association of Insurance Companies) and adopted (with minor variations) by almost all jurisdictions and permitted in all.

uniform reporting 1. A standardization of insurance forms and financial and hospital data reporting to allow for comparisons of data between facilities; having all health-care entities use the same standardized forms and follow set standardized reporting procedures using the same measures, protocol, and criteria. 2. In public health reporting of morbidity, mortality, and vital statistics data, all reporting organizations and reporting entities should use standardized reporting procedures established by the centralized and internationally recognized clearinghouse that sets standards (the World Health Organization).

unilateral One-sided, as in a unilateral contract.

unilateral contract 1. In contract law, this a contract in which only one side promises performance with no promise of return payment or performance by the other side. 2. A contract wherein one side performs and the other side merely promises to perform or pay; one-sided agreements that are preprepared having standardized language for all, with little option for negotiation or change in the contract, such as leases, automobile purchase agreements, or insurance policies.

unincorporated association A business or organization created without any legal process, charter, or incorporation procedures. This is often the approach used by health-care providers in solo practice or a partnership. This form of association has many similarities to a corporation: a manager, transferability of interests, and continuity of organization, with each person involved being personally legally responsible for all professional and business transactions of the association.

uninsurable risk class In managed care and medical insurance, this is a group of people who have a risk of early death that is so great or an illness so profound that an insurance company believes they cannot offer them insurance and not lose money. Under universal coverage proposals, such persons cannot be excluded from medical insurance.

union An organized group of workers united to improve benefits, economic status, and working conditions through collective bargaining with their employers. Public Law 93-360 (July 1974) extended the Labor Management Relations Act of 1947 to private health-care institutions. Passage of this law means that every health-care organization, regardless of its size, may be subject to unions organizing its employees.

union-management agreement This is a labor contract or agreement.

union members' bill of rights The specific rights of union members in dealing with their own unions as set forth in Title I of the Labor-Management Reporting and Disclosure Act of 1959.

union organizers In health administration and labor relations, these are the individuals who interact with, motivate, and assist workers in voting in a local union.

union shop A business, hospital, or other facility where all employees must eventually join a union as a condition of employment. Workers are usually given 30, 60, or 90 days to join.

union shop contract A labor agreement with an employer for continued employment being contingent on joining a union.

unit A division or area of a health-care facility that provides medical or nursing care by grouping patients according to various criteria such as age, payment method, disease, or type of care needed. Also synonymous with "program" or "services." *See also inpatient care unit; nursing care unit.*

unit assistant *See unit clerk; ward clerk.*

unit clerk An individual who serves in a support capacity in a nursing unit. He or she handles routine clerical and reception work, receives patients and visitors, schedules appointments, monitors the location of all ward staff and where hospital policy permits transcribes doctors' orders, orders supplies, and updates information on patients' charts. Also called "unit assistant," "ward clerk," "unit secretary," or "ward secretary." *See also ward clerk.*

unit dosage system In medical care, this is a method of dispensing drugs by individual packaging. Inpatients pay only for the drugs used. This is more costly, but it is a more efficient management approach.

unit dose medication system In medical care, this is a medication dispensing system in which single-dosage units of drugs are prepackaged and prelabeled in accordance with all applicable laws and regulations governing these practices and are made available separately as to patient and by dosage time. The system shall also comprise but not be limited to all equipment and appropriate records deemed necessary to make the dose available to the patient in an accurate and safe manner. A pharmacist shall be in charge of and responsible for the system (Title 22, California).

United Network for Organ Sharing (UNOS) A national organization established to be a clearinghouse for organ sharing and to serve as a organ transplantation network. Under HCFA contracts, UNOS manages and coordinates all national organ procurement activities and efforts.

United States Court of Appeals (USCA) Federal courts that hear appeals from U.S. district courts.

United States foreign medical graduate (USFMG) A graduate of a medical school outside the United States, Puerto Rico, or Canada who was a U.S. citizen at the time of graduation.

United States Government Organization Manual The official legal handbook of the U.S. government containing descriptions of the agencies of the legislative, judicial, and executive branches.

United States medical graduate (USMG) Any graduate of a U.S., Puerto Rican, or Canadian medical school regardless of citizenship.

United States Pharmacopoeia (USP) A legally recognized compendium of standards for drugs, published by the United States Pharmacopoeia Convention, Inc., and revised periodically. It also includes assays and tests for the determination of strength, quality, and purity. *See also national formulary.*

unit manager In health administration, this is an individual who supervises and coordinates administrative management functions for one or more patient care units; oversees unit clerks, initiates clerical procedures, and serves as a liaison for the unit with other hospital departments. Also referred to as "ward service manager," "ward supervisor," "charge nurse," or "supervisor nurse."

unit numbering system A medical record numbering system where only one number is permanently assigned to the patient's chart.

unit of employees In health administration, this is an administrative entity consisting of two or more employees who share a common employment environment, tasks, and conditions; a department, division, or service.

unit patient health record In medical records administration, this is a record that organizes all information on the care and treatment rendered to a patient in a health-care facility (Title 22, California).

unit record In medical records administration, this is the patient's chart (medical record), which is a comprehensive file of all hospitalizations, treatments, procedures, therapies, or patient/physician encounters kept in one file.

unit record system In medical records administration, this is one approach and method for creating and maintaining a patient's medical record as an ongoing comprehensive file of all hospitalizations or patient/physician encounters kept in a single record.

unit secretary *See ward clerk.*

unitrust A trust in which a percentage is paid each year to its beneficiaries.

units of service In health administration, these are work activities, outputs, or measures of productivity for each department or service. Units of output or work that can be measured or counted and data kept on a regular basis to assess work productivity and accomplishments and to provide feedback on effectiveness and efficiency. This develops a historical record that creates a baseline for comparison. *See line units.*

unity of command In health administration and organizational structure, this establishes a hierarchy of authority that helps workers know which employees receive commands or take orders or who has authority over whom, with each worker having only one boss and being accountable only to that boss.

universal access A national health-care insurance system in which all individuals have access to affordable coverage; a national system established to help those who need it most such as the uninsured, small-business operators and employees, the near poor, medically indigent, disabled but working, or self-employed or those who cannot afford medical insurance. The system would not tie insurance to work, and employees would be able to take the insurance with them and not have it discontinued if they lost their job.

universal coverage A national health-care insurance system in which all individuals have affordable medical coverage that is adequate to meet individual and family needs, is portable and not tied to employment, keeps health-care spending down, is sustainable, has no political constraints, improves health-care providers' ability to improve function and well-being, and has a preventive and health promotion focus; medical care insurance for all (at least 95% to 97% coverage); that point at which it can be verified that most of the nation's population is covered by medical insurance. A somewhat uncertain concept.

universal donor A person with type O blood.

universal precautions In medical care and infection control, especially in the care of AIDS and hepatitis patients, this is all human blood and certain human body fluids being treated as if known to be infectious for HIV, HBV, and other blood-borne pathogens; masking; using latex gloves and other protective clothing; exercising extreme caution in handling equipment, materials, and sharps; and avoiding slight error such as not trying to return caps to needles on syringes knowing that a slip could infect a health-care provider.

unjust enrichment In health law, this is to return money or property gained unfairly even though it was gained legally. The object is not to give so much restitution to a plaintiff as to prevent the defendant from profiting without payment; a doctrine where a defendant may sue in equity to regain that which is rightfully his or hers if it was lost because of misrepresentation, unfair practice, or incomplete disclosure.

unlawful 1. Against or contrary to law. 2. Illegal or illicit. 3. Unauthorized by law or regulation.

unlawful detainer A court order to leave property when holding onto buildings or property beyond the legal time one has a right to occupy them.

unliquidated 1. Not settled; not cleared up. 2. Undetermined; not ascertained.

unmarried In public health and vital statistics, this refers to individuals who are single and never married; divorced or widowed. *See health status; married.*

unmet need A need for which no service or resource exists or those that do exist are inadequate, inaccessible, unavailable, or inappropriate; the difference between which medical care services and resources are actually used and which are still needed.

UNOS *See United Network for Organ Sharing.*

unpalatable Distasteful, unpleasant to the taste; of poor taste.

unrelated business income tax In health-care financial management, this when nonprofit hospitals or other nonprofit health-care organizations operate for-profit side businesses and must pay income tax on business transactions not under the nonprofit tax structure of the organization.

unrestricted funds In health-care financial management, these are funds held or received by a health-care organization that have no external restrictions and can be used as seen fit by the administration of the health-care organization. *See funds, unrestricted.*

unreviewed safety questions In occupational health and safety, this is assessing the issues related to or the probability of an accident or malfunction of equipment important to safety in areas previously not assessed.

unsatisfied judgment fund In personal injury or automobile insurance, a fund set up by some states to pay for personal injury or automobile accident claims that cannot otherwise be collected.

unsaturated zones In environmental health and solid waste and hazardous waste site management, these are areas above the water table where the soil pores are not fully saturated, although some water may be present.

unsolicited In grant writing and administration, a proposal that is created and submitted by an interested applicant rather than at the request of a foundation, governmental agency, or other money-granting agency.

unstable 1. Lacking of emotional and behavioral control. 2. In health care, the unpredictable health status of an ill patient. 3. Concerning radiation, this refers to all radioactive elements because they emit particles and decay to form other elements.

unstructured interview In health administration and human resources management, this is an informal discussion with little planned structure and limited prewritten questions, thus enabling the interviewer to explore or pursue various aspects of the interviewees background and experience while observing interpersonal and communication skills and predicting the ability to meet performance on the job.

untoward Adverse.

unusually complex services *See services; levels of service.*

unusually high needs criteria In health-care delivery, these are population groups having higher levels of health and medical care problems such as poverty, unfloridated water, drug use, crime, alcoholism, unwed birth, teen pregnancies, and low prenatal care than the mainstream of society.

unusual services In managed care or medical insurance, services greater than those usually required for usual procedures listed in the procedure coding manual.

unwritten law 1. Common law; the usual acts people do that are considered right, just, expected, or usual; case law; judge-made law. *See also lex non scripta.*

upcoding In health-care financial management, this is to get the attending physician to change the diagnostic code listed in the medical record to a different DRG or reimbursement code because it more correctly represents the condition and has a higher-paying reimbursement level.

upgrades In environmental health solid waste and hazardous waste site management, this involves adding to or retrofitting some systems to make them safer or more efficient such as adding protective linings or spill overfill protection controls to improve an underground storage tank system to prevent the undesired release of a chemical and a hazardous waste spill situation.

upstream holding company In health administration and organizational structures, this is an organizational arrangement where a parent company like a hospital creates a holding company level of administration over the hospital to create or acquire other health services or facilities, which in turn controls the hospital's administration as well.

upward communication In health administration, this is any effort to share information upward with staff or management in top-level administrative positions of the health-care organization; communication that proceeds up the hierarchy to inform or influence top-level administrators.

UR *See utilization review.*

urban Relating to city dwelling. In public health and safety, this is any city that includes 5000 or more inhabitants or is classified as urban by the

U.S. Census Bureau or standard metropolitan statistical area rules. *See standard metropolitan statistical area; rural.*

urban runoff In environmental health and wastewater management, this is any storm water from city streets and adjacent domestic or commercial properties that carries pollutants of various kinds into sewer systems and receiving waters (EPA).

URC *See utilization review coordinator; utilization review committee.*

urgent Any disease, disorder, condition, or injury that demands immediate medical attention; an acute disorder in need of prompt medical action and attention; less important or less grave than an emergency but a condition or disease or injury that requires treatment in the near future to prevent death, further injury, disability, or deformity.

urgent care In health-care delivery and medical care, this is the process of providing treatment, procedures, therapy, or intervention in a timely fashion to not put life or health in jeopardy; services needed to prevent serious deterioration of the patient's health status following an injury or illness.

urgent care centers In health-care delivery, these are clinics that are strategically located in industrial areas or residential neighborhoods that serve to render lower levels of emergency care and give immediate definitive medical care for minor conditions while also serving as a feeder facility to a hospital where advanced care can be obtained by the more seriously ill or injured patients.

urgi-center *See urgent care center; freestanding emergency care center.*

urinalysis The analysis of urine by chemical or microscopic means for diagnostic purposes.

urinary incontinence In long-term care and geriatrics, this is the inability of elderly patients to control the bladder, hold urine under normal circumstances, or control urinary function. This malady is not limited to the elderly and can be found in all ages but is more prominent in older adults with certain chronic diseases.

urologist A medical doctor who has completed advanced training through a residency, is board certified in urology, and specializes in the diagnosis and treatment of conditions, disorders, and diseases of the genitourinary tract.

urology 1. The medical specialty involving the diagnosis and treatment of diseases and disorders of the kidney, the urinary system, and male reproductive organs. 2. An educational training program that prepares physicians in the structure, anatomy, physiology, care, and treatment of diseases, disorders, injuries, and conditions of the genitourinary tract.

usage 1. Well-established or continued usual practice; customary use. 2. The way a custom, act, or practice is done. 3. The known way or usual manner in which a business of a specific kind is carried out.

usage of trade The regular, usual, or customary method of dealing in a vocation or trade as to justify an expectation with respect to the transaction at hand or in question.

USC U.S. Code.

USCA U.S. Code Annotated. *See also United States Court of Appeals.*

USDA U.S. Department of Agriculture.

USDC U.S. District Court.

U.S. Department of Health and Human Services Created in 1953 as the Department of Health, Education and Welfare and reorganized in 1979 as the Department of Health and Human Services. A major department in the U.S. government, it is responsible for all preventive care, health promotion, health-care delivery, social services, aging services, and related programs for the U.S. government. Major divisions are as follows: Office of Human Development Services (HDS); Public Health Services (PHS) headed by the Surgeon General with several subdivisions—National Institutes of Mental Health, Centers for Disease Control and Prevention, Food and Drug Administration, and National Institutes of Health (National Institute of Medicine, National Cancer Institute, and National Institute on Drug Abuse), National Center for Health Statistics, National Center for Health Services Research, National Center for Infectious Disease, National Center for Chronic Disease Prevention and Health Promotion, National Institute for Occupational Safety and Health, Health Resources and Services Administration, and Bureau of Health Professions; and Substance Abuse and Mental Health Services Administration, Center for Mental Health Services. Also included are Social Security Administration (SSA), Medicare, Medicaid, Health Care Financing Administration (HCFA), Family Support Administration (FSA), Office of Civil Rights, Office of Consumer Affairs, and Environmental Protection Agency (EPA).

U.S. Department of Justice A major department in the U.S. government that serves as counsel for U.S. citizens. It represents all citizens in enforcing the law in the public's interest. It plays a key role in protection against criminals and subversion, ensuring healthy competition of business, safeguarding the consumer, and enforcing drug, immigration, and naturalization laws. The Justice Department plays a significant role in protecting citizens through law enforcement, crime prevention, and detection, prosecution, and rehabilitation of offenders. It conducts all suits in the Supreme Court in which the United States is concerned. It represents the government in legal matters generally, rendering legal advice and opinions on request, to the president and the heads of executive departments.

U.S. Department of Labor A major department in the U.S. government that has the aim to foster, promote, and develop the welfare of the wage earners of the United States, to improve working conditions, and to advance their opportunities for profitable employment. The department administers a variety of federal labor laws guaranteeing workers' rights to safe and healthful working conditions, a minimum hourly wage and overtime pay, freedom from employment discrimination, unemployment insurance, and workers' compensation. It also protects workers' pension rights and provides for job-training programs, helps workers find jobs, works to strengthen free collective bargaining, and keeps track of changes in employment, prices, and other national economic measures.

use effectiveness In medical care, this is when a medicine, procedure, or treatment falls short of its intended use and expected outcomes. Lack of effectiveness may be caused by improper use or dosage or by lack of patient compliance. The treatment is effective, but the misuse or lack of proper use renders it ineffective.

U.S. Environmental Protection Agency (EPA) The federal agency over all matters regarding environmental health, this agency protects and enhances the environment for present and future generations to the fullest extent possible under laws enacted by the U.S. Congress. The agency's mission is to control and abate pollution in the areas of air, water, solid wastes, pesticides, radiation, and toxic substances. Its mandate is to mount an integrated, coordinated attack on environmental pollution in cooperation with state and local governments.

use of outside resources For Medicare purposes, if the health-care facility does not employ a qualified professional to render a specific service to be provided by the facility, there must be arrangements for such a service through a written agreement with an outside resource: a person or agency that will render direct service to patients or act as a consultant. The responsibilities, functions, and objectives and the terms of agreement, including financial arrangements and charges, of each such outside resource are delineated in writing and signed by an authorized representative of the facility and the person or the agency providing the service. The agreement specifies that the facility retains professional and administrative responsibility for the services rendered. The financial arrangements provide that the outside resource bill the facility for covered services (either Part A or B for Medicare beneficiaries) rendered directly to the patient and that receipt of payment from the program(s) to the facility for the services discharges the liability of the beneficiary or any other person to pay for the services. The outside resource, when acting as a consultant, apprises the administrator of recommendations and plans for implementation and continuing assessment through dated, signed reports, which are retained by the administrator for follow-up action and evaluation of performance.

USFMG *See* United States foreign medical graduate.

USMG *See* United States medical graduate.

USP *See* United States pharmacopoeia.

usual and customary charge The going rate; the average rate of compensation for the same or similar care rendered in the region; in managed care and with insurance carriers that do not have contracts with physicians and cannot guarantee acceptance of payment by physician as "in full" but paid by the going rate or prevailing charges. Another approach is usual, customary, and reasonable (UCR). *See* usual, customary, and reasonable; capitation.

usual charge *See* customary charges.

usual, customary, and reasonable (UCR) In health-care financial management, this implies paid-in-full physicians' bills as long as the charge is the going rate for the specified service and is within the range of fees for that service customarily charged by other physicians in the community. The term "reasonable" has come to mean at least the average going rate or prevailing charges, a fee that meets the criteria of usual and customary, or justified in the special circumstances of the case in question. Managed care, capitation, and negotiated and contracted care are used to set rates and levels of reimbursement. Competition determines level and amounts paid by third-party payers.

usual, customary, and reasonable plans Medical insurance plans that pay a physician's full charge if it does not exceed the usual charge; if it does not exceed the amount customarily charged for the service by other physicians in the area (often defined as the 90 or 95 percentile of all charges in the community), or if it otherwise is reasonable. In this context, usual and customary charges are similar but not identical to customary and prevailing charges, respectively, under Medicare; the average going rate or prevailing charges; managed-care, capitation, negotiated, and contracted rates and set reimbursement amounts paid by third-party payers.

usufruct 1. The right to use an item just so it is not changed or used up. 2. In civil law, the right to use and make profits from property owned by another party.

usufructuary The agent or party having the usufruct of property.

usurious Pertaining to usury. *See usury.*

usury Lending money at higher rates of interest than is allowed by law.

utilities management In hospital administration, this is a component of the health-care organization's plant, technology, and safety management program designed to ensure the operational reliability, assess the special risks, and respond to failures of utility systems that support the patient care environment. In the accreditation process, standards are applied to evaluate a hospital's performance in utilities management (JCAHO for acute-care facilities).

utility In managed care and insurance, a subjective value given to monetary results. In risk situations, larger losses usually cause a greater loss of utility than small losses across a population of insured persons.

utility program Any general purpose software program included in an operating system to perform common basic functions such as copying programs or formatting disks.

utility room A room found at various locations throughout a health-care facility used for emptying and washing bedpans and commodes. Regulations in some states allow for short-term storage of dirty linens in this room prior to their transport to the soiled linen room of the laundry area.

utility systems Hospital systems for life support, infection control, environmental support, and equipment support (JCAHO for acute-care facilities).

utilization 1. In health services delivery and managed-care services, these are patterns of use or rates of use of a single service or type of service (e.g., hospital care, physician visits, prescription drugs). 2. One of the measures of a health system or health services delivery. Measurement of utilization of all medical services is usually done in terms of dollar expenditures. Use is expressed in rates per unit of population at risk for a given period (e.g., the number of admissions to a hospital per 1000 persons over age 65 per year or the number of visits to a physician per person per year for family planning services). 3. In managed care, this is the extent to which health plan members who are covered use the services offered as benefits, in which category, and how much in a specific time period, expressed as use per year or per 100 or 1000 eligible members.

utilization management In managed care, this is the administrative responsibility of monitoring, evaluating, and assessing the appropriateness and efficiency of the care and costs of physicians, hospital, and ancillary services before, during, and after the patient's care with the aim of managing resources and containing costs of health-care delivery. A professional staff member is given responsibility and authority to coordinate, gather information, tabulate data, and conduct utilization review activities to determine if the health-care providers restrain costs and remain within the established guidelines and criteria; a set of methods and approaches used on behalf of health plans, third-party payers, purchasers of medical care coverage, and members. Synonymous with "utilization review."

utilization rate In health services delivery, this is the rate at which patients use health-care services within a specific time period as compared to the total population at risk or those covered by a certain health plan. The utilization rate formula follows:

$$\frac{\text{The number of admissions per year (or month)}}{\text{Total population at risk or in health plan}} \times 1000$$

utilization review (UR) 1. Evaluation of the necessity, appropriateness, and efficiency of the use of medical services, procedures, and facilities. In a hospital this includes a review of the appropriateness of admissions, services ordered and provided, length of stay, and discharge practices on a concurrent and retrospective basis. Utilization review can be done by a utilization review committee, PRO, or public agency. 2. According to JCAHO for psychiatric, alcoholism, and drug abuse facilities accreditation purposes, the process of using predefined criteria to evaluate the necessity and appropriateness of allocated services and resources to ensure that the facility's services are necessary, cost efficient, and effectively utilized. 3. According to JCAHO for hospital accreditation, this is the examination and evaluation of the appropriateness of the utilization of resources of a hospital. Standards are applied to evaluate a hospital's performance in conducting utilization review. *See also medical review; utilization management.*

utilization review committee 1. A group of physicians, nurses, administrators, and allied health personnel from outside the hospital or nursing home who review patient records for the necessity of length-of-stay and medical and nursing procedures. This committee is a requirement for participation in Medicare. The committee studies the course of medical care and the plan of care for every patient in the facility to ensure that services received are within skilled nursing care. Any care that is more or less than skilled care would qualify a patient to be transferred to another facility to receive the level of care for which he or she is eligible. The utilization review committee not only reviews level of care and duration of stay but also conducts medical care evaluation studies to ensure the quality of care. The findings of these studies may be used to improve services in hospitals or skilled nursing facilities. The utilization review committee cannot be employed by or have an interest in the facility. A minimum of two physicians is required, and other allied health professionals or nurses may participate. A certified social worker or professional nurse can be used to help clarify matters that are not medical determinations but that affect a need for a continued stay. Facility personnel who could attend include the medical director, director of nursing, social workers, administrative director, medical records administrator, and physical therapist. 2. In JCAHO long-term-care facilities accreditation, a committee that reviews a facility's resources in striving to provide high-quality patient care in the most cost-effective manner. On the basis of this review, the committee makes recommendations, including plans for follow-up action, to the governing body of the facility. 3. According to JCAHO for hospital accreditation, this is a committee designated to carry out utilization review activities.

utilization review coordinator The administrator responsible for management of the utilization review committee and utilization review activities in the medical records department. This person is also the liaison with PROs and other agencies involved with utilization activities.

utmost good faith In insurance, a legal principle where the highest level of honesty is imposed on all parties to an insurance contract. *See also uberrima fides.*

utter 1. Unconditional; completely unqualified. 2. To put into circulation. 3. To give out or put forth. 4. To pronounce, say, or speak; to express in any way. 5. To make known; to divulge or reveal.

uxor (Lat.) Wife.

V

v. Abbreviation for "versus" or "against." In law, it is used in the title of a case (e.g., *Darling v. Charleston Community Hospital*).

VA Veterans Administration. *See Veterans Administration hospital.*

vacate 1. To annul. 2. To leave; to move out; to empty. 3. To take back. 4. To set aside.

vacate a judgment In health law, this is to set aside or completely remove a previous decision or judgment of a court, case, or hearing.

vaccination In medical care, preventive medicine, and public health, this is any immunization against infectious diseases caused by microorganisms such as a bacteria or virus.

vaccine In medical care, preventive medicine, and public health, this is a preventive care process used to reduce the susceptibility of individuals to disease-producing microorganisms by injecting biologically produced drugs designed to provide or enhance immunity into their bodies. These microorganisms, which are in a killed or attenuated (weakened) form, do not cause disease yet stimulate the formation of antibodies in the body on inoculation, enhancing immunity to a specific disease or disease families. When 85% of a population are vaccinated, epidemics can be prevented. This is called "herd immunity," a term derived from the first experience with immunizations—vaccinia virus—which is cowpox used against smallpox ("Vacca" is Latin for "cow").

VAD *See ventricular assist device.*

vagrancy 1. In mental health and psychiatry, this is wandering in thought and verbal communications. 2. A social problem constituting persons without money, home, or employment who wander through a community, going from place to place and often begging. Vagrancy is illegal in some cities. This also means shiftless, unpredictable, idle, or hanging around without money or work. Modern terminology is "street people." This is a problem for some hospital's security and the protection of patients and property because these people loiter in or around hospitals or have frequent visits to emergency rooms with no insurance or money, costing the hospital much money in charity care.

vagrant 1. A street person, bag lady, beggar, tramp, bum, vagabond, or roaming person. 2. Having no direction, plan, or course.

vague 1. Indefinite; unclear; not certain. 2. Not precise in thought or explanation.

valid 1. Good; binding; in force; legal; sound. 2. Properly completed, executed, and binding by law. 3. Well-founded in evidence.

validate To make valid.

validation point In health-care finance, managed care, and insurance, this is the point at which a service, program, or product finally makes more money than it costs to operate and adds a surplus of revenue. Also called the "break-even point."

valid criteria As used in utilization review, health-care standards are presented in objective rather than descriptive terms to provide accurate evaluation. Standards are set for diagnosis, procedures, hazardous surgery, length of stay, patient recovery, progress activities, etc.

validity 1. The extent to which results of a study are correct. 2. The extent to which a test does what it is professed or believed to do. 3. The extent to which a situation reflects the true situation. *See also reliability.*

validity, concurrent In epidemiology and health services research, in assessment of tests and research questionnaires, the researcher wants to know how well the test selected for the study correlates with other similar tests if given at the same time.

validity, construct In epidemiology and health services research, in the assessing of tests and research questionnaires, the researcher would like to know if the test represents, addresses, and taps into the concepts or relationships he or she has observed on the basis of a theory of behavior or science that the researcher wants to measure. Does the questionnaire or research instrument tap into and represent various theoretical beliefs, concepts, and ideas held by the researcher and the study?

validity, content In epidemiology and health services research, in assessment of tests and research questionnaires, the researcher must ensure that the test information and questions represent the objective the test has set out to accomplish, addressing the knowledge and skills it is supposed to assess.

validity, criterion In epidemiology and health services research, in assessment of tests and research questionnaires, the researcher wants the test to predict accurately and clearly what he or she has set out to measure. Does the test actually measure what it is meant to measure? When trying to determine patient satisfaction with clinical services, does the research instrument (questionnaire) get directly to the most important concerns and issues of patient satisfaction?

validity, external In epidemiology and health services research, in the assessment of tests and research questionnaires, the researcher wants to know if the findings of the study can be generalized to a population similar to that of the study population.

validity, predictive In epidemiology and health services research, in assessment of tests and research questionnaires, the researcher wants the test to have the ability to predict the criterion of the study.

validity, statistical In epidemiology and health services research, in assessment of tests and research questionnaires, the researcher wants to be able to measure the criterion of the test instrument against an outcome and do statistical correlations. If the correlation is high, the criterion validity is high, as is the statistical validity.

validity, test How well a test measures what it was constructed to measure. A test may be reliable even though it is not valid. A valid test is always reliable and is good at measuring what it set out to measure. *See also reliability; sensitivity; specificity.*

valuable consideration 1. The real reason, usually for money or other items of value, that a contracting party enters into an agreement. 2. In contract law, this is the worth or value of an item or material for entering into a contract; that which makes a contract valid and legal. Often referred to as "consideration," which means something of value or worth; thus, "valuable consideration" is redundant. 3. The important motive of a stipulation, reason, or cause.

valuation mortality tables In insurance, this is the use of mortality tables for computing the value of insurance policy revenue reserves. These tables have wide margins of safety, projecting higher rates of mortality than do mortality tables used for calculating premiums.

value 1. To think highly of; to esteem, prize, or hold with much respect or worth. 2. Having worth. 3. In contract law, this is consideration; something of worth that makes a contract valid. 4. A preference and belief transmitted into and shared in the health-care organization. The beliefs, expectation, and culture of the community. *See also valuable consideration; consideration.*

valued policy law A statute in some states that requires an insurance company to pay all the face value of an insurance policy covering loss caused by a peril. Thus, the insurance company must pay the full amount if a disaster occurs to the insured property.

value statements In strategic health planning, in an effort to influence corporate culture in a health-care organization and to set expectations, create direction, and influence behavior, idealistic statement(s) of what the organization believes and embraces are written, posted, distributed, and taught in the organization. Statements about what administration believes regarding employee attitudes and treatment, patient care attitudes and treatment, administrative approaches and methods, and image in the community are created. These attitudes, concepts, and beliefs embraced by the organization may be written down in a general statement and included in a strategic plan much like the mission statement and vision statement.

vapor capture system In environmental health and occupational health and safety, this is any combination of hoods and ventilation systems that capture or contain organic vapors to direct them to an abatement or recovery device.

vaporization In environmental health, this is to cause a solid or liquid to turn into gas; evaporation.

vapors In environmental health, this is the gaseous form or phase of substances that are in a solid or liquid state under normal conditions or at atmospheric temperature and pressure and may or may not contribute to air pollution when they turn to vapors.

variable 1. In epidemiology and health services research, this is the factor to be considered in a research design because it may be a focus of the research or may affect the research results if overlooked; any attribute, factor, concept, or event that differs. 2. In computers, a symbolic representation of a storage location that contains a value that changes during the computer's processing operation. 3. In health-care finance, these are elements of cost whose total varies with changes in output volume. As volume increases, the cost per service or item usually decreases, although the total revenue expended also increases.

variable annuity A retirement plan offered to employees of some health-care organizations that allows the employee to accumulate funds in savings in a life insurance company that are invested in units of common stock so that the annuity will provide retirement income with varying dollar value but constant purchasing power. This is based on the concept that the price of stocks will rise as fast as and concurrently with increases in the level of prices of consumer goods; an annuity whose value may fluctuate with the securities in which the funds are invested.

variable, antecedent In epidemiology and health services research, this is any of a number of factors that exist prior to a study yet influence various aspects of the study.

variable costs In health-care finance, this is when expenses vary directly with the level of activity. They are a function of volume, not time.

variable, independent *See independent variable.*

variable, intervening *See intervening variable.*

variance 1. In health law, this is a lack of agreement between the testimonies of the parties of a legal proceeding and evidence presented; inconsistencies between allegations and proof; not in agreement with each other. 2. In statistics, a measure arrived at by squaring the deviations in a set of measures, summing them, and then dividing them by the number of measures. Variance is helpful in analyzing how much variation in the data is caused by chance or to intervening variables or experimental treatment. 3. In environmental health law, this is governmental permission for a delay or exception in the application of a given law, ordinance, or regulation; a license, granted by the government, to pollute beyond acceptable limits in return for promises and plans on curbing pollution; releases from a standard of the type specified under the Occupational Safety and Health Act; the temporary deferral of a final compliance date for an individual source, subject to an approved regulation or a temporary change to an approved regulation as it applies to a potential source of pollution.

variation A statistical measure used to determine the different results obtained in measuring the same phenomenon. *See also variance.*

variation analysis In medical audits and utilization review activities, the assessment of compliance and variations from the review standards. The review process requires physicians to justify variations from clinical or predetermined standards such as length of stay for certain diseases; the assessment of variation about a given mean for an element of health care, procedure, or medical outcome by which an upper and a lower threshold is established beyond which a variation is considered to have an identifiable cause or is not likely to be controllable because the events or effects occur at random. *See outlier; trim points.*

variation justification In medical audits and utilization review activities, physicians must provide acceptable verification and reasons that a patient's care or length of stay is not within the standard or criterion set for the given disease or disorder.

vascular surgery A medical specialty that requires graduate medical education and advanced training and experience, including a clinical residency in conducting surgery on the heart and blood vessels.

vaso- A prefix meaning "vessel" or "duct."

V code One set of diagnostic codes in ICD-9-CM coding that represents medical care occasions other than a disease or injury classifiable under the main part of the ICD-9-CM or E codes. V codes include encounters with a health service for such purposes as being an organ donor, having a baby, or other nondisease- or noninjury-related encounter. V codes also include some past circumstances that could influence the patient's current condition.

VD *See venereal disease.*

vector In epidemiology and public health, this is a carrier, an animal (usually an arthropod), or insect that transfers an infective agent from one host to another; animals or insects that transfer pathogens from one host to another such as fleas, flies, mosquitoes, and rats. At a microscopic level, these are objects that are used to transport genes into a host cell such as plasmids, viruses, or bacteria. A gene is placed in the vector, then vector "infects" the bacterium.

vector analysis Used to determine the magnitude, nature, and direction of a moving force. For example, the electrocardiogram is used as a vector analysis to measure the movement, magnitude, nature, and force of the cycles of the heartbeat.

vector-borne infection In epidemiology and public health, this is a when a pathogen is harbored in a host such as a mosquito, flea, or tick, which is the vector. The vector passes the infection on to the host through a bite.

vegetarian Individuals who prefer to eat mostly

vegetables and avoid meat or who, in extreme cases, avoid all animal products. A full range of vegetarians exist. The most liberal will eat some meat, avoiding mostly red meat and pork products. The most strict, called "vegans," avoid all foods of animal origin.

vegetarian, lacto- Individuals who include dairy products in their diets, mainly as sources of protein. This does not make it a low-cholesterol or low-fat diet because cheese and ice cream are some of the higher fat foods. Some use low-fat and skim-milk products to reduce fat and cholesterol. Some also eat many nuts, which are also high in fat, for the protein.

vegetarian, lacto-ovo- Individuals who include dairy products and eggs in their diets, mainly as sources of protein, but avoid animal meat of all kinds.

vegetarian, ovo- Individuals who include eggs in their diets, mainly as sources of protein, but avoid all other animal products.

vegetarian, pesco- Individuals who include fish, dairy products, and eggs in their diets, mainly as sources of protein, but avoid all other animal meats.

vegetarian, semi- Individuals who include fish, dairy products, eggs, and some poultry but avoid red meats in their diets. Some people who eat meat sparingly also may consider themselves as semivegetarian.

vegetative state, permanent In medical care, this is a state or condition experienced by a patient whose physiological functions, especially the higher brain functions, are permanently suppressed, with unconsciousness or no apparent awareness.

vehicle A transporting agent or medium.

vehicle response time *See response time.*

vehicles of infection In epidemiology and public health, this is the means by which infectious agents are transported. Water, food, clothing, milk, insects, and inanimate objects (fomites) are usual vehicles of infection. Water-borne, airborne, vector-borne, fomite-borne, and person to person are the main vehicles of infection. *See also vector; fomite; transmission of disease.*

vehicles of infection transmission In epidemiology and public health, this is the spread of a contagious agent from its reservoir to a susceptible host.

vehicle spread, common In epidemiology and public health, this is the transmission of a communicable disease from a disease source that is frequently and extensively used by groups of people who are susceptible to the disease, have an exposure to it, and then get the disease. Sources that are frequently and commonly used serve as points of exposure such as swimming pools; lakes for swimming; drinking water sources; foods, milk, and shellfish from a variety of sources such as community picnics or potlucks, restaurants, stores, or street vendors; air; syringes contaminated by street drug users; and industrial noxious fumes or toxic agents.

vendee Buyer; one who purchases.

vendor 1. Seller. 2. A provider; an institution, agency, organization, or individual practitioner who provides health or medical services. Vendor payments go directly to institutions or providers from a third-party program such as Medicaid.

vendor payment Used in public assistance programs to distinguish payments made directly to vendors of service from cash income payments made directly to assistance recipients. The vendor's or health-care provider's services are reimbursed directly by the public assistance programs for services they provide to eligible recipients. Vendor payments are essentially the same as service benefits provided under health insurance and prepayment plans.

venereal disease In public health and epidemiology, this is any sexually transmitted disease. Any infectious and contagious disease that is easily transmitted from person to person (or animal to person) through sexual intercourse or other sexual acts. *See sexually transmitted diseases; AIDS.*

venire facias (Lat.) 1. Make to come. 2. A writ to the sheriff to have him or her assemble a jury.

venirefacias de novo (Lat.) 1. Make to come again. 2. A writ for a second trial resulting from some irregularity in the original trial. Also called "venire de novo."

venireman A juror.

veno- Prefix meaning "vein."

ventilation Causing fresh air to circulate to simultaneously replace foul air; the act of admitting fresh air into a space to replace stale or contaminated air, achieved by blowing air into the space (EPA).

ventilation of the lungs The act of breathing; filling the lungs with air.

ventricular assist device (VAD) In medical care, this is a technologically advanced piece of medical equipment that mechanically pumps blood for and in place of the heart during surgery or in emergency medicine circumstances such as delays or waiting periods during heart transplantation surgery. This equipment mimics the ventricles of the heart and does not replace the heart as an artificial heart would.

ventriculography In medical care, this is an X-ray or other radiological examination of the ventricles of the brain by the insertion of air or other radiopaque medium.

venue 1. Locality; region; area. 2. Jurisdiction over a geographical area. 3. In law, this is the locality in which a cause of action occurs or a crime is committed. 4. In law, this is the judicial district or area in which a case is tried and the jury selected. 5. In law, this is a writ that designates the county or geographical area in which a trial is to be held or an affidavit sworn.

verba (Lat.) Words.

verbigeration In mental health and psychiatry, this is meaningless use of words or the repetition of words or phrases. Also known as "cataphasia," which is a serious disorder common to catatonic schizophrenia.

verdict The declaration of a jury's findings, signed by the jury foreman and presented to the court.

verdict of acquittal A defense used in court to show that the evidence is not sufficient enough to proceed, so the case should be dismissed.

verdict, special The results and facts of a case with a judge or court comparing the evidence and facts to the law and how it applies.

verification The act of reviewing, inspecting, testing, checking, auditing, or otherwise determining and documenting whether items, processes, services, or documents conform to specified requirements.

verification of continuing education, training or retraining The confirmation by an auditable record of the experience, education, medical conditions, training, and testing pertinent to a candidate's specified job assignment and responsibilities.

verify 1. To establish the truth of a document. 2. To prove to be true. 3. To establish proof through facts, evidence, and testimony. 4. The truthfulness or conformity of a statement. 5. The quality of being real or actual.

vermin External animal parasites such as ticks, lice, and fleas.

vertical integration In strategic health planning, this is one of several strategic planning approaches, tactics, or strategies and is compared to horizontal integration. Vertical integration is to move certain services into the business operations of the parent organization. Instead of purchasing or contracting for outside goods or services, they are created, provided, finished, self-supplied, sold, or distributed internally in the company's own outputs; providing services or goods in-house, using them within to save money and to control costs and competition and selling excess to others; supplying some of the organization's present needs and inputs at one or several stages of services delivery.

vertical opening According to JCAHO for long-term-care facilities accreditation, a penetration in a floor slab and assembly that creates an opening between floors of a building. Examples include stairwells, elevators, chutes, and shafts.

vertical staff meetings In health administration, this is when a midmanager meets with two or more levels of subordinates to solve problems, learn of concerns, and strive to be more efficient and effective in his or her department or division.

vertigo Dizziness; the sensation that one's environment is revolving; loss of balance or equilibrium.

vesicant Anything that produces blisters.

vest 1. Fixed. 2. To place in the control of a group or organization. 3. To give full rights and power. 4. To take effect.

vested 1. Settled; absolute or complete. 2. Established; fixed. 3. Not contingent on an act or event.

vested commissions In managed care and insurance, this is when an insurance agent is guaranteed to receive commissions from past insurance contracts and policies acquired by the agent. In some cases, this includes renewal of policy commissions even if the agent is terminated from the insurance company.

vested interest In health administration and ethics, this is any personal motivation or personally favorable outcome in a business deal; personal or property gain through influence or position from a personal motivation, whether present or future; personal concern in a deal; personal gain or property, whether present or future.

vestibule training In health administration and human resource management, this is training conducted at a site removed from the workplace, with workstations (vestibules), equipment, and materials as found at the worksite when the employee arrives at his or her workplace or workstation. Many technical jobs use this approach to not disrupt operations during training.

vesting A provision in a retirement plan that gives benefits or a certain level of them to a worker who has contributed to a retirement fund after serving a specified number of years with the organization even if he or she quits or is terminated before the age of retirement.

Veterans Administration hospital A health-care facility where medical, mental health, and dental services are rendered to a veteran who has a service-related disability.

Veterans Affairs Health Services Research and Development Begun in 1958, this research started with rehabilitation and clinical research and was created to carry out more effectively the primary function of the Department of Medicine and Surgery (now the Veterans Health Administration). To contribute to the nation's knowledge about disease and disability, research activities are to carry out a program of medical research, including health services research. It currently supports a broad range of research in such areas as cost-effectiveness, clinical decision making, and innovative health-care delivery.

veterinarian An individual who is educated and skilled in preventing, diagnosing, and treating animal health problems. However, because their special knowledge and training extends into a number of closely related areas, veterinarians are involved in much more than animal medicine; a health profession with its own system of education, licensure, organization, and ethics. In taking the veterinarian's oath, the doctor solemnly swears to use his or her scientific knowledge and skills for the benefit of society through the protection of animal health, the relief of animal suffering, the conservation of livestock resources, the promotion of public health, and the advancement of medical knowledge. Some have worked as epidemiologists in public health.

veterinarian assisting A course of study that prepares persons to assist the veterinarian in providing care and treatment to animals in veterinary hospitals or clinics. The program includes instruction in preparing the animal for examination, assessing vital signs, assisting with examination and treatment, sterilizing equipment, performing routine laboratory procedures, and giving injections and other medications; also includes maintaining medical and business records and charting and scheduling activities.

veterinary medicine A course of study that prepares persons to be animal doctors and trains them in the ability to describe the nature, prevention, diagnosis, and treatment of animal diseases and the medical and surgical treatment of animals. On completion, the individual is granted the doctorate of veterinary medicine (DVM) and is licensed to provide medical treatment for and perform surgery on animals.

veterinary services Work with the care, use, production, and husbandry of animals in medical settings or in the field.

veto 1. When the president or a governor refuses to or simply does not sign a bill into law. 2. To turn down; to refuse to consent to.

vexatious 1. Troublesome; harassing; annoying. 2. Legal action instituted without legal grounds for the main purpose of causing annoyance to the defendant.

vexatious litigation In health law, this is a lawsuit filed or charge made against a person without a good reason or just cause shown.

VHA See *Voluntary Hospitals of America*.

viability Capability of living; ability to function.

viable 1. Capable of living; the power of a fetus to live outside the uterus. 2. In health administration, this is when a plan, project, or activity shows promise of implementation and successful completion.

vial A small glass bottle with a rubber stopper.

vicar 1. A term often used in a church or governmental context indicating a person who acts in the place of another. 2. One with delegated authority; a deputy.

vicarious liability In health law, this is indirect legal responsibility; legal liability of an employer for the on-the-job mistakes or negligence of his employees; legal liability suffered by the master or principal for his servants or agents. See *respondeat superior*.

vice 1. Evil or illegal conduct. 2. Immoral or depraved habits. 3. A character fault or defect such as obsessive gambling, drug use, or prostitution.

victim blaming The unfortunate occurrence in society and a form of social injustice where the victim is defined as the source of the problem.

victimization mentality A mind-set in society that allows certain outspoken or militant groups, whose values go against the norms of society, to reverse the responsibility for acceptable behavior by placing it onto the majority and blaming society and the majority for their personal problems.

vide (Lat.) See.

vide ante (Lat.) Look at the words that come before this one.

videlicet To wit; namely. *See viz.*

video conference A teleconference that uses television monitors, satellites, satellite dishes, and related equipment to link the conference with participants in one or more distant locations. An interactive component is usually used so that the distant location attendees can actively participate and get a total conference experience.

video display terminal (VDT) In health-care information management and computers, this is a special type of television monitor that can be used to view inputs and information put in by the computer operator. Some VDTs also can be input devices, with the person entering commands or data by touching a screen, keyboard, notepad, joystick, or other input medium and can view the information on the screen as it is received by the computer, making it somewhat interactive. Also called a "cathode ray tube" (CRT).

vi et armis (Lat.) With force and arms; with direct force or violence.

Vietnam Era Veteran's Readjustment Act of 1974 A federal law that prohibits certain government contractors from discriminating in employment against Vietnam-era veterans.

vinyl chloride A chemical compound, used in producing some plastics, that is believed to be carcinogenic.

virgin population In epidemiology and public health, this is a group of people or a population that has never been exposed to a specific pathogen or infectious agent, thus causing a major epidemic. The American Indians died in mass numbers when the British colonizers introduced smallpox to the American continent because they were a virgin population. If a disease has been absent from a population for a generation or more, they are susceptible to the disease and considered a virgin population.

viro- Prefix meaning "virus" or "poison."

virtue 1. Goodness; moral uprightness. 2. Chastity, especially in women. 3. By the power of; because. 4. Excellence; good quality. 5. On the grounds of.

virulence The capacity of a microorganism to produce disease; the pathogenicity of the microorganism; the disease-invoking power and strength of an infectious agent in a susceptible host.

virulent Extremely poisonous or venomous; capable of overcoming bodily defensive mechanisms; having a high disease-producing ability.

virus A class of extremely small germs (microorganisms) or infecting agents that cause many diseases. They are capable of multiplying on or in the living cells of some organisms. Viruses are usually inanimate until exposed to the right conditions and media, at which time they become active.

vis (Lat.) With force or violence.

vis à vis One who is opposed to.

viscosity The quality of being gummy or sticky; slickness caused by a lack of these factors.

viscous liquids Liquid material that has a measured viscosity in excess of 2500 centistokes at 25°C (77°F).

vis fi vis (French) One who is opposite to.

visibility impairments 1. In environmental health and air pollution control, these are any humanly perceptible changes in visual range, contrast, or coloration from that which would have existed under natural clean air conditions; reduction in visual range and atmospheric discoloration, thus posing an air pollution problem. 2. Any air pollution that interferes with the management, protection, preservation, or enjoyment of the visitor's visual experience to mandatory class I federal areas, which are national parks, preserves, and wilderness areas. Determination is made on a case-by-case basis, accounting for geographic extent, intensity, duration, frequency, and time of the visibility impairment and how these factors correlate with times of visitor use, frequency of use, and times of natural conditions that reduce visibility.

visible emissions 1. In environmental health and air pollution control, this is any smoke, vapor, or other particulate matter suspended in the air that changes the visual range, contrast, and coloration or that impairs visual range and causes atmospheric coloration, thus posing an air pollution problem. 2. In environmental health and air pollution control of particulate asbestos materials, this is any emission containing particulate asbestos material that is visually detectable without the aid of instruments. This does not include condensed, uncombined water vapor.

visible radiation In laser technology, this is electromagnetic radiation that can be detected by the human eye, usually in light wavelengths, which lie in the range of 400–700 nm.

vision, normal The normal lens of the eye is such that an object 20 feet away will be in focus without any accommodation reflex activities. If you have no difficulty reading a standard-sized letter at this distance, you are said to have normal 20/20 vision. If, however, you can see a standard-sized letter at 20 feet that a normal person can see at 40 feet, you are said to have 20/40 vision. Thus, the higher the second number, the greater your vision problem.

vision statement In strategic health planning, this is an expansion of the health-care organization's mission statement to express values, intentions, philosophy, organizational self-perception, and what the organization is to develop into.

visit 1. An encounter between a patient and a health professional that requires either the patient to travel from his or her home to the professional's usual place of practice (an office visit) or vice versa (a housecall or home visit). 2. In health insurance, a visit is an office call and is considered a personal interview between the enrolled member and the physician and shall not include telephone calls or any other situations where the enrolled member is not personally examined by the physician. This definition is used to determine benefits for office calls.

visit, home health In health-care delivery, these are all services, treatments, therapies, and nursing and other medical care activities rendered to a patient by a nurse, therapist, or other health-care provider in a single encounter at the patient's home and for which a fee is charged or reimbursed by a third-party payer or is paid in part or full by the patient.

visiting nurse association (VNA) A health agency that provides nursing services in the home, including health supervision, education, counseling, therapy, and bedside care. Physicians' orders are carried out using nurses and other appropriate health-care providers and home health aides trained for home bedside care or assistance in therapy provided in the home. *See also visiting nurse services; home health care.*

visiting nurse services (VNS) A voluntary health agency that provides nursing services in the home, including health supervision, education, and counseling; bedside care; and carrying out physicians' orders using nurses and other personnel such as home health aides who are specially trained for specific tasks of personal bedside care in the home. These agencies had their origin in the visiting nursing program provided to the sick and poor in their homes by voluntary agencies in the 1870s (e.g., the New York City Mission). The first visiting nurse associations were established in Buffalo, Boston, and Philadelphia in 1886–87. *See also home health agency; visiting nurse association.*

visiting staff Physicians, physical therapists, physician assistants, nurse practitioners, and other allied health-care providers who are in private practice yet use the hospital for the care of their patients.

visit, office In health-care delivery, these are all services, treatments, examinations, tests, and other medical care activities rendered to a patient by a health-care provider in a single encounter at the office of the health-care provider and for which a fee is charged or reimbursed by a third-party payer or is paid in part or full by the patient.

visit, outpatient In health-care delivery, these are all services, treatments, examinations, tests, surgery, and other medical care activities rendered to a patient by a health-care provider in a single encounter at an outpatient clinic or surgery center and for which a fee is charged or reimbursed by a third-party payer or is paid in part or full by the patient. *See ambulatory care; outpatient care.*

vis major (Lat.) Force majeur. An act of nature or other superior force that occurs without intervention of humans and could not have been prevented through reasonable action.

VISTA Volunteers in Service to America.

vita- Prefix meaning "life."

vital records In epidemiology and public health, these are documents, certificates, or other recording devices that create and maintain an official and formal record of marriage, birth, divorce, and death events as required by law and that are used for planning, assessment of public health initiatives, demographic purposes, assistance in epidemiological studies, and assessment of the community's health status and the need for public health services.

vital signs Various signs produced by normal body functions such as temperature, pulse, respiration, and blood pressure that reflect the physiological state of the body.

vital statistics In epidemiology and public health, these are the data, facts, and information relating to birth (natality), deaths (mortality), marriages, health, and disease (morbidity). Vital statistics for the United States are published annually by the National Center for Health Statistics of the Health Resources Administration, the Department of Health and Human Services. Each state also publishes its own vital statistics.

vitamins Organic chemical substances found in food that are essential for nutrition and normal metabolism.

vitiate 1. To make imperfect. 2. To destroy the legal effect. 3. To cause to fail; to corrupt; to weaken morally. 4. To make a document legally ineffective.

vito- Prefix meaning "life."

vivarium A facility attached to a medical research institution used to house, feed, care for, and observe all kinds of animals used in biological or medical research.

viva voce (Lat.) 1. Expressed orally; with living voice. 2. By word of mouth. 3. Oral testimony or other than written expression.

viz Short for videlicet. See *videlicet*.

VNA See *visiting nurse association*.

VNS See *visiting nurse services*.

VOA See *Volunteers of America*.

vocational assessment According to JCAHO for psychiatric, alcoholism, and drug abuse facilities accreditation purposes, this is the process of evaluating each patient's past experiences and attitudes toward work; current motivations or areas of interest; possibilities of future education, training, and/or employment.

vocational rehabilitation Long-term health and social services established to assist disabled individuals through training, education, on-the-job training, therapy, and social support to return to or acquire an occupation that is economically productive and that accommodates their limitations or disability.

vocational rehabilitation counselor A professionally trained individual, usually a psychologist or educational psychologist, social worker, or closely related professional, who provides testing, advice, and counsel on the job or employment issues to match the aptitudes, interests, and abilities of individuals with occupations suited for them.

vocational services Long-term health and social services established to assist a disabled individual with evaluation and training, aimed at assisting them to enter, reenter, or maintain employment, including training for jobs in settings that accommodate both disabled and nondisabled workers, or to work in special settings such as sheltered workshops.

void 1. Null; having no binding force. 2. Having no legal effect 3. To wipe out or destroy its validity.

voidable That which can be legally made void or declared invalid.

voidable contract A contract that may not be legally binding on either party if one party seeks to avoid it.

void contract Any legal obligation or agreement that is no longer in force because it lacks some legal element.

voir dire (French) Look-speak. To speak truthfully; the act of selecting potential jurors by lawyers and a judge to decide whether a person is unprejudiced and competent to sit on the jury of a case.

volatile Substances that evaporate rapidly.

volatile hazardous air pollutant In environmental health and air pollution control, this is substance regulated and for which a standard for equipment leaks of the substance has been proposed and promulgated (such as benzene and vinyl chloride).

volatile organic compounds In environmental health and air pollution control, these are organic substances that participate in atmospheric photochemical reactions, except for those designated by the EPA as having negligible photochemical reactivity.

volatility The relative rate of evaporation of materials to assume the vapor state.

volens (Lat.) Willing.

volenti non fit injuria (Lat.) 1. No wrong is done to the consenting person. 2. To not allow a lawsuit to be brought against another if the person originally consented to allow the act to be done that caused the harm, injury, or damage.

voluble 1. Speaking up with clarity, ease, and fluency. 2. Talkative.

voluntary health agency 1. Agencies such as nonprofit hospitals, visiting nurse associations, and other local service organizations that have both lay and professional governing boards and are supported by both voluntary contributions and fees for services provided. 2. Any nonprofit association organized on a national, state, or local level composed of lay and professional persons dedicated to the prevention, alleviation, and cure of a particular disease, disability, or group of diseases and disabilities. It is supported by voluntary contributions, primarily from the general public, and expends its resources for education, research, and service programs relevant to the disease and disabilities concerned. Examples are the American Heart Association, Red Cross, and American Lung Association (from the *Directory of National Voluntary Health Organizations of the AMA*).

voluntary health organization A nonprofit association supported by contributions dedicated to conducting research and providing education and/or services related to particular health problem or concerns such as the American Heart Association (Joint Committee on Health Education Terminology). *See voluntary health agency.*

voluntary hospital Any hospital that is owned and/or operated by any fraternal, religious, or not-for-profit community organization. *See also hospital.*

Voluntary Hospitals of America (VHA) A national nonprofit professional organization for all nonprofit hospitals in the United States that serves as an advocate, especially for religious or fraternal hospitals. The organization provides training, conferences, and educational materials for its members.

voluntary hospital system A major nonprofit corporation or other nonprofit health-care organization that is self-supported and nongovernmental.

voluntary manslaughter In criminal law, this is the act of committing a homicide in the heat of passion or when provoked.

voluntary nonsuit In law and the litigation process, this is when a plaintiff abandons the required legal procedure of his or her case and allows a judgment and costs to be brought against him or her because of failure to respond to the litigation process.

voluntary standards In health law, these are criteria or guidelines established by private-sector organizations such as research and development departments of industrial firms, research institutions, or universities that are made available for use by any person, organization, or private or governmental organization needing a standard to compare to or adopt. Also referred to as ''industrial standards'' or ''consensus standards.''

voluntary standards bodies In health law, these are nongovernmental bodies that are broadly based, multimembered, and domestic with participants from industry, industry associations, professional and technical societies, consultants, university professors, and researchers who develop, establish, or coordinate voluntary standards activities.

voluntary system of retirement A movement in America aimed at changing the Social Security deductions from one's paycheck to allow individuals to take the money deducted and put it into their own private investments for retirement instead of being forced to participate in the government-run and -controlled Social Security Administration system.

volunteer A person who works in a health-care facility or agency in an unpaid capacity; one who offers and provides services for free.

volunteer, in-service A volunteer who works in a health-care organization or agency in a regular position, does not get paid for the work, and does not replace any regular paid personnel yet holds down a responsible position.

volunteers, director of The administrator responsible for all volunteer activity in a health-care facility. This individual plans, organizes, coordinates, and directs all the volunteer activities and services for a health-care organization.

volunteer services Services donated by individuals who provide nonmedical assistance and aid in the efficient operation of the health-care facility. They assist in a variety of tasks such as delivering flowers, manning desks and reception counters, escorting families or patients, preparing bandages, or operating a gift shop or snack bar. Volunteer services in a hospital usually require a director who is paid at least half-time. *See also auxilian; auxiliary, hospital; candystripers.*

volunteer services department See volunteer services.

Volunteers of America (VOA) A nationwide organization that establishes volunteer organizations to serve a variety of areas in human services and recruits volunteers to serve in such organizations as senior citizen nutrition programs, rehabilitation centers, food distribution programs, housing, senior citizen centers, and prisons.

vote *See method of voting.*

vouch 1. To attest or give evidence. 2. To testify, affirm, or guarantee. 3. To call as a witness; to call into court to give warranty of title.

voucher 1. A document or paper that attests to facts and that can be used as evidence. 2. A receipt or evidence of payment or accuracy of the status of an account. 3. One who vouches, attests, ensures, or warrants that something is true or factual through testimony.

voucher system 1. In health-care finance and universal coverage, this is when a governmental agency or health plan gives a member a certificate that works as a credit and the holder does not have to pay for care or the premium or it is deducted from taxes. 2. Under Medicare, this is when Medicare beneficiaries have a certificate or document that allows them to enroll in a health plan of their choice or one that has been approved by Medicare.

vs. Versus. Against; as opposed to. *See also v.*

vulnerability analysis In environmental health, this is the assessment of elements in the community that are susceptible to damage should a release of hazardous materials occur, especially around an industrial plant (EPA).

vulnerability zones 1. In environmental health, this is the assessment of areas over which an airborne concentration of a chemical involved in an accidental release could reach a level of concern (EPA). 2. This is the maximum distance from the point of release of a hazardous substance in which the airborne concentration could reach a level of concern under specified weather conditions (EPA).

W

wage and salaries survey In health administration and human resource management, these are investigations conducted by a health-care organization to discover how much other health-care providers in the same labor market are paying for specific jobs.

wage assignment An agreement allowing a person to pay his or her wages directly to a creditor.

wage compression In health administration and human resource management, this is when the difference between higher paying jobs and lower paying jobs is reduced. Often this is because higher paying jobs are ignored for raises and lower paying jobs get pay raises.

wage index In health-care financial management, under Medicare, the Health Care Financing Administration (HCFA) conducts studies of hospitals. With the data supplied by the hospital and information from the research questionnaire, the HCFA adjusts payments to hospitals after considering several factors, one being the current wage structure of the regular full-time employees, including part-time workers and overtime.

wage index, rural In health-care financial management, under Medicare, the Health Care Financing Administration (HCFA) adjusts payments to hospitals on the basis of several factors, one being a rural hospital or sole community hospital in a rural setting. A special wage index is computed by the HCFA for rural hospitals.

Wagner Act The first federal act (1935) that established rights of unions by prohibiting any attempts at keeping employees out of a union, establishing the concept of unfair labor practices and creating the National Labor Relations Board.

Wagner-Murray-Dingell Bill One of the original national health insurance proposals, first introduced by Congressmen Wagner, Murray, and Dingell in the 1940s.

WAIS Wechsler Adult Intelligence Scale. An intelligence test created specifically for adults. *See Wechsler intelligence scales.*

waiting list A list of patients awaiting admission to a hospital or nursing home; the number of patients on a list to be admitted for special treatments or surgery.

waiting period 1. The time that must elapse before an indemnity is paid on health or life insurance. 2. A period of time an individual must wait either to become eligible for insurance coverage or to become eligible for a given benefit after overall coverage has commenced. This does not generally refer to the amount of time it takes to process an application for insurance but rather is a defined period before benefits become payable. Some policies will not pay maternity benefits, for example, until 9 months after the policy has been in force. Another common waiting period occurs in group insurance offered through a place of employment where coverage may not start until an employee has been with a firm for over 30 or 90 days. For disabled persons to be covered under Medicare, there is a waiting period of 2 years. A person must be entitled to Social Security disability benefits for 2 years before medical benefits start. 3. In medical insurance, this is a set amount of time following policy issue during which the insured's medical expenses are not covered by the policy. 4. In disability income insurance, this is the prescribed amount of time during which the benefits are not payable, with time starting from the onset of the disability. *See also excepted period; exclusions; indemnity.*

waive 1. To voluntarily give up a right; to relinquish a privilege. 2. To abandon or relinquish. 3. To renounce; to disclaim a right. 4. The process of setting aside a requirement; no longer requiring a person to meet a requirement.

waived 1. To have voluntarily renounced or given up a privilege. 2. To have had a requirement set aside; no longer being required to meet a standard.

waiver 1. Having given up a privilege or right. 2. Not having to meet a requirement or criteria. 3. The voluntary surrender of a claim. 4. In health law, this is to allow a policy or procedure to not be in effect or to not apply. 5. In managed care and insurance, this is an agreement attached to an insurance policy that exempts certain disabilities or injuries from coverage that are normally covered by the policy.

waiver of liability In Medicare and Medicaid, this is the legal requirement of causing an individual to pay for medical care when Medicare and Medicaid does not cover it or reimburse health-care providers for the services rendered.

waiver of premium In medical insurance or managed care, this is a provision included in some medical insurance policies that exempts the insured person from paying premiums if he or she is disabled during the period of the insurance contract.

waiving time In health law, this is to allow more time than usual to try a case or answer a legal charge.

walker A tubular frame constructed of lightweight yet sturdy materials that handicapped or elderly persons hold in front of them to steady their balance and gait. This device is more stable than a cane.

WAMI Stands for Washington, Alaska, Montana, and Idaho. These four states have entered into an agreement with regard to training of physicians, dentists, and other health-care providers. Montana, Idaho, and Alaska do not have medical or dental schools, so the University of Washington has agreed to accept a certain number of students into medical school from each of the three states.

want 1. To desire; to wish. 2. To suffer from the lack of or the need of something.

wanton 1. In need. 2. Reckless; without giving heed or caution. 3. In health law, this is any act that is negligent; malicious; undisciplined; immoral. 4. Lacking in foreseeability.

wanton negligence In health law, this is when a party acts or fails to act, is conscious and aware that his or her actions could cause injury, and has a reckless indifference to the consequences of the act or the omission of an act yet has no actual intent to cause harm. *See also negligence.*

ward 1. The guardianship of a child or other individual unable to care for him- or herself; under the care of a guardian; to be taken into custody by the courts; the court seizing custody and taking over guardianship of a person, usually a child, and caring for that person when a parent or legal guardian seems incompetent and cannot care for him- or herself. 2. A floor or large room in a health-care facility designed to accommodate more than four persons who are inpatients in a nursing or medical care unit. Some specific health-care delivery definitions state that three or more persons is considered a ward. Ward patients are usually cared for by medical residents who are supervised by staff physicians and have their medical care covered by governmental programs. 3. To fend off or turn aside. 4. A section, division, or subsection of a large geographical area or organization; a large political geographical area.

ward accommodation A hospital room with three or more beds or, in other cases, four or more beds. This is an inpatient stay arrangement with several people in one room, thus costing the health-care facility less to manage. Thus, lower income individuals or those who have their medical care covered by governmental programs are often placed in such a patient stay arrangement.

ward clerk A person who answers telephones, relays messages, receives and directs visitors, transcribes orders, types forms, and prepares requisition forms in a nursing care unit of a health-care facility under the supervision of a head nurse. *See unit clerk.*

ward manager In hospital administration, this is the administrator of a medical or nursing unit. *See also unit manager.*

ward patients Indigent or medically indigent patients who are kept in a special hospital ward that accommodates several patients; found more often in city or county hospitals or a medical school teaching hospital. In the past, these patients were kept and treated on open wards instead of in semiprivate arrangements. Ward patients are usually cared for by the medical residents who are supervised by staff physicians. *See ward.*

ward rounds When the teaching physician takes his or her medical students, interns, or residents to the bedside of patients in a teaching hospital or teaching unit to review the patients' diseases, disorders, or disabilities for the purpose of instructing and providing clinical training. Nursing education employs a similar teaching process. Also called "teaching rounds."

ward service management An educational program that prepares persons to supervise and coordinate administrative functions for one or more medical or nursing care units in a health-care facility under the direction of the director of nursing or assistant administrator of nursing care services.

warrant 1. To promise by contract or deed. 2. To ensure; to promise. 3. The legal authority by a writ to arrest a person. 4. Permission given by a judge or court to arrest a person, seize property, search a house, etc. 5. To promise that the facts of a situation are true.

warranty 1. In malpractice, actions against physicians are nominally based on negligence, but in certain circumstances the plaintiff can bring his or her action on the basis of a warranty. A warranty arises if the physician promises or seems to promise that the medical procedure to be used is safe or will be effective. One of the advantages to bringing an action on warranty grounds, rather than for negligence, is that the statute of limitations is usually longer. A warranty action may be brought and maintained if there is an express warranty offered by the physician to the patient. 2. A promise, made as part of an insurance contract on which the transaction depends. An insurance company could refuse to pay a claim if a statement is misleading, invalid, or false or if the promise is not kept. 3. In business, any representation made by a seller to a buyer on a sale of goods that items, products, equipment, or goods are fit for use and that they should last for a period of time. 4. A promise that facts are true.

warranty of fitness A promise that an item is fit for the purposes for which it is sold.

waste In health administration, this is to not conserve resources and to abuse, misuse, or use the health-care organization's supplies, materials, or possessions; in a reckless fashion, to be inefficient and ineffective in management of the health-care organization's resources.

waste load allocations In environmental health, these are maximum loads of pollutants that each discharger of waste is allowed to release into a particular waterway. Discharge limits are usually required for each specific water quality criterion being or expected to be violated (EPA).

waste management In environmental health, this is the systematic administration of activities providing for the collection, storage, transportation, transfer, processing, treatment, and disposal of waste.

waste minimization *See waste reduction and minimization.*

waste reduction and minimization In environmental health and solid waste management, this is to reduce the amount of solid waste being produced to reduce disposal problems and the continued threat to the environment that solid waste disposal poses. The place to reduce and minimize solid waste is where it is produced and accumulated. Thus, waste streams are to reduce and recycle all solid waste possible from domestic sources to industrial sources. The goal is to reduce, minimize, reuse, and recycle solid waste at its source. Under EPA mandates, all communities have to reduce the amount of waste produced by 50% by the year 2000. In addition to meeting state and federal laws, other benefits include saving money by reducing waste treatment and disposal costs and raw materials purchases and operating costs, reducing environmental liabilities, and protecting worker health and the health of the public and the environment.

wastes In environmental health, these are the unwanted materials left over from manufacturing processes; refuse, garbage, trash, or other waste products thrown away from places of human or animal habitation (EPA).

waste, special In environmental health and solid waste management, these are nonhazardous solid wastes requiring special handling beyond that normally used for municipal solid waste.

waste stream In environmental health and solid waste management, this is the continuum of waste production in modern life. One end of the continuum is the source or generator of waste, with the system having many components in the middle such as temporary domestic and industrial storage, source on-site sorting and recycling, collection, transportation, end sorting and recycling, remanufacturing, incineration, or other energy production uses with final disposal of all nonreyclable materials in landfills. This can also be defined by the identification of each and every source of waste generation, from littering to domestic sources and from small business to industrial plants through final disposal.

waste treatment plants In environmental health and liquid waste management, these are pumps, piping, conduits, and other equipment necessary to collect and transport the flow of surface water runoff resulting from precipitation or domestic, commercial, or industrial wastewater to and from retention areas or any areas where treatment is designated to occur. The collection of storm water and wastewater does not include treatment except where incidental to conveyance.

waste treatment stream In environmental health, this is the continuous movement of waste from generator to treater and disposer. *See waste stream.*

wastewater In environmental health and liquid waste management, this is spent or used water that contains dissolved or suspended matter from individual homes, communities, farms, or industries.

wastewater operations and maintenance In environmental health and liquid waste management, these are actions taken after construction to ensure that facilities constructed to treat wastewater will be properly operated, maintained, and managed to achieve efficiency levels and prescribed effluent levels in an optimum manner (EPA).

wastewater treatment processes In environmental health and liquid waste management, these are any processes that modify the characteristics of water such as BOD, COD, TSS, and pH, usually for the purpose of meeting effluent guidelines and standards, except removal requirements for vinyl chloride, which is a solvent and needs a special evaporation process.

wastewater treatment tanks In environmental health and liquid waste management, these are tanks designed to receive and treat influent wastewater through physical, chemical, or biological methods.

wastewater treatment units In environmental health and liquid waste management, these are devices designed to treat wastewater through physical, chemical, or biological methods as part of a wastewater treatment facility that is subject to regulation under the Clean Water Act; equipment and devices that receive and treat or store an influent wastewater that is a hazardous waste, that generates and accumulates a wastewater treatment sludge that is a hazardous waste, or that treats or stores a wastewater treatment sludge that is a hazardous waste and meets the definition of a tank system under various sections of the Clean Water Act (Code of Federal Regulations, Sections 260, 261, 307).

water In environmental health, this is a clear, odorless, tasteless liquid essential for most plant and animal life; descends from clouds as rain and from streams, lakes, seas, and underground aquifers used as water supplies. The chemical symbol for water is H_2O.

water-borne disease outbreak In epidemiology and public health, this is when the significant occurrences of an acute infectious illness spread through a group of people epidemiologically associated with the ingestion of water from a public source or a water system that is deficient in treatment as determined by the appropriate local and state public health and/or environmental health agencies.

water-borne disease transmission In epidemiology and public health, this when an infectious or communicable disease can be or has been spread by way of a water source such as drinking water, swimming pools, rivers, streams, ponds, lakes, water parks, fish tanks, or another water source that humans use or interface with. Water has to be the vehicle of transmission in the spread of the disease for it to be a water-borne transmission. Any cause of an epidemic would be restricted mostly to those diseases for which the microorganism/pathogen would find water conducive to good harborage and as a good environment in which to live, multiply, and spread itself.

water dumping In environmental health and safe water management, this is the unscrupulous disposal of pesticides in or on lakes, ponds, rivers, steams, sewers, or other water systems.

water pollution In environmental health, this is the contamination of water by impurities, including decaying organic matter, chemicals, dissolved gases, or suspended solids. Common sources of water pollution are suspended solids, pesticides, herbicides, fertilizers (phosphates, nitrates), PCBs (polychlorinated biphenyls), oil, gasoline, bacteria, salt, carbon-based compounds, cadmium, lead, and mercury. The Clean Drinking Water Act requires water supplies to be assessed for 83 different substances, agents, or chemicals; any undesirable foreign matter present in water that deteriorates the quality for use as drinking water, for public use, as waterways, and as sources of water supplies. According to the EPA, this is the presence in water of enough harmful or objectionable material to damage the water's quality.

water quality criteria In environmental health and safe drinking water management, these are specific levels of water quality that, if reached, are expected to render a body of water suitable for its designated use. The elements and standards that make up the criteria are based on specific levels of pollutants that would make the water harmful if used for drinking, swimming, farming, fish production, or industrial processes (EPA).

water quality standards In environmental health and safe drinking water management, national and state drinking water standards reflect the level of each substance that humans can safely consume in drinking water. State-adopted and EPA-approved ambient standards for water bodies cover the use of the water body and the water quality criteria that must be met to protect the designated use or uses.

water quality standards, primary In environmental health and safe drinking water management, these are mandatory health-related standards that measure organic and inorganic compounds, radionuclides, clarity, and microbiological elements that may be harmful to humans or affect their health if consumed for a long period of time (throughout one's lifetime).

water quality standards, secondary In environmental health and safe drinking water management, these are the aesthetic standards regarding taste, clarity, odor, and mineral content. These standards specify limits for substances that may influence consumer acceptance of the water. *See turbidity.*

water reactive materials In environmental health, these are solid substances (including sludges and pastes) that, by interaction with water, are likely to become spontaneously flammable or to give off flammable or toxic gases in dangerous quantities.

water solubility In environmental health, this is the maximum concentration of a chemical compound that can result when it is dissolved in water. If a substance is water soluble, it can very readily disperse through the environment.

Waters projection In medical care, this is a posteroanterior X ray showing parts of the face.

water supply system In environmental health, this is the collection, treatment, storage, pumping, moving, and distribution of potable water from source to consumer (EPA).

watt In laser technology, this is the unit of power or radiant flux (1 watt = 1 joule per second).

wavelength In laser technology, this is the distance between two points in a periodic wave that have the same phase.

Wechsler intelligence scales A test of individual intelligence called the Wechsler Adult Intelligence Scale (WAIS) that was initially developed to test cognitive abilities in adults. The test is organized in a series of subtests, each starting with items that are easy to do and progressing to more difficult levels. The subtests include 1) verbal subscale (general information, similarities of items, arithmetic reasoning, vocabulary, comprehension, and digit span) and 2) performance subscale (picture completion, block design, and object assembly). In addition to the adult scale, which is for persons 16 years and older, Wechsler developed two scales for children: the Wechsler Intelligence Scale for Children Revised (WAIS-R) for ages 6½ to 16½ and the Wechsler Preschool and Primary Scale of Intelligence (WPPSI) for ages 4 to 6½ years.

Wechsler IQ test *See Wechsler intelligence scales.*

weekend hospital A health-care facility used for partial hospitalization. Patients spend only weekends in the health-care facility and function in the outside world during the week.

weighted checklist In health administration and human resource management, this is used in performance appraisals where the supervisor is to use preestablished or predetermined work descriptors that are weighted according to the level or extent of performance and describe the employee's work. The supervisor is to select and weigh statements or words from the list to describe an employee's performance, productivity, or work behavior.

weighted incentive systems In health administration and human resource management, these are reward and bonus programs often used with top-level health-care executives that are based on improvements in multiple areas of a health-care organization. Part of the incentive bonus can be tied to improvements in financial savings, profit levels, cash flow, etc.

weighting factors In environmental health, occupational health and safety, and radiation monitoring, this is a measuring system that is tissue specific and represents a fraction of the total health risk resulting from uniform whole-body irradiation that could contribute to a particular tissue. These are used in the calculation of annual and committed effective dose equivalents used to equate the risk arising from the irradiation of tissue to the total risk when the whole body is uniformly irradiate. The weighting factors are gonads (0.25), breasts (0.15), red bone marrow (0.12), lungs (0.12), thyroid (0.03), bone surfaces (0.03), and remainder (0.03) (remainder means the five other organs with the next highest risk, including liver, kidney, spleen, thymus, adrenal glands, pancreas, stomach, small intestine, or upper and lower intestine but excluding skin, lens of the eye, and extremities). The weighting factor for each of these organs is 0.06 (EPA).

weight of evidence 1. In health law and the litigation process, this is the relative importance of the facts or evidence; the greater influence. 2. The consequence of the evidence given. 3. The most firm and believable evidence; the quality of evidence given. 4. In environmental health, this is an EPA classification system for characterizing the extent to which the available data indicate that an agent is a human carcinogen (EPA). *See weighting factors.*

welfare 1. The state of being well. 2. Public assistance to the poor. 3. To receive governmental aid because of poverty, sickness, unemployment, disability, or other justifiable deprivation.

well In environmental health, this is any bored, drilled, or driven shafts or dug holes whose depth is greater than the largest surface dimension.

well injection In environmental health and hazardous waste disposal, this is the subsurface emplacement of fluids in a well; the disposal of liquid wastes through a hole or shaft in the subsurface stratum of the earth (EPA); the subsurface emplacement of fluids through a bored, drilled, or driven or dug well where the depth of the dug well is greater than the largest surface dimension.

wellness The positive states or conditions of all the dimensions of humans: physical, emotional, mental, social, spiritual, and economic well-being that is necessary for one to live in harmony with the environment; having a quality of life that is conducive to a positive health status; a positive health attitude toward maintaining healthy behaviors through exercise, proper nutrition, meditation, humor and laughter, coping with stress, and positive mental health.

well pay In human resource management, this is a fringe benefit offered by some health-care organizations that pays employees for unused sick leave.

well stimulation In environmental health and water pollution, several processes are used to clean the well bore, enlarge channels, and increase pore space in the interval to be injected, thus making it possible for wastewater to move more readily into the formation, including surging, jetting, blasting, and acidizing hydraulic fracturing.

well workovers In environmental health and water pollution, this is any reentry's of an injection well, including but not limited to the cementing or casing repairs and excluding any routine maintenance.

wetlands In environmental health and water pollution, these are areas that are inundated or saturated with surface or groundwater at a frequency and duration sufficient to support a prevalence of vegetation typically adapted for life under such conditions and include sloughs, swamps, marshes, bogs, estuaries, and similar areas. Some wetlands have been turned into naturally occurring liquid wastewater treatment sites.

Western Consortium of Public Health An independent, nonprofit organization that supports the research, training, and community service activities of the schools of public health and university extensions of the University of California at Berkeley and the University of California at Los Angeles and established by these schools in 1975 with the endorsement of the University of California Regents. Their goal is to help solve critical health problems through the joint efforts of academics, practitioners, and the community.

wheelchair A specialized chair equipped with wheels for use by handicapped or invalid persons.

WHO *See World Health Organization.*

whole-body dose A radiation exposure and safety concern where the dose of radiation is received by the body in its entirety, as distinct from a dose to a limited area or part of the body.

whole law The actual laws of a state as well as other laws regarding choice-of-laws.

wholistic An integrated system of healing and well-being embracing the qualities of wholism; making and keeping one's health and well-being whole, taking into account more than disease and physiology and including the mental, emotional, spiritual, social, economic, and cultural dimensions of health. This also includes being in contact with one's own healing process and health maintenance while practicing preventive care.

wholistic health An integrated system of health care that takes into account all dimensions of the individual in addition to the entire framework of societal and cultural dimensions. Wholistic health thus meets the needs of the complete organism as it interacts with the environment. The health-care provider facilitates movement from the diseased state to a state of high-level wellness using whatever techniques or approaches that work, both traditional and nontraditional. *See also holistic; wellness.*

wholistic medicine An approach used to treat all dimensions of the whole person. Methods are not always the traditional or conventional methods. Instead, medical practice is expanded to include biofeedback, acupuncture, hypnosis, spiritual healing, etc.

WIC *See Women, Infants and Children, Supplemental Food Program for.*

wife abuse *See spousal abuse.*

wildcat strike A strike initiated without permission, support, or authorization of the union; a spontaneous work stoppage initiated by the workers in violation of the labor contract and without the support of the union leaders.

will 1. To decree or to ordain. 2. To wish, desire, or long for. 3. A legal document stating the wishes of a person concerning the disposition of his or her belongings, personal property, and estate on his or her death. 4. A command or decree.

willful 1. Intentionally done; an act deliberately and purposely done. 2. Willing and ready. 3. Following one's desires or wishes without reason or rationality; to be stubborn.

willful negligence In health law, the term is used to show a higher and more aggravated form of negligence than gross negligence; when a person has a willful determination to not perform an expected and known duty, knowing that the results will be harm or injury; a conscious and intentional omission of duty or acts of proper care so as to disregard the health, life, rights, and/or safety of another person. This definition is often rejected by the courts because it could be viewed as a criminal charge of battery rather than an act of negligence.

windfall Excessive and unexpected gain.

window In laser technology, this is a glass seal with plane-parallel sides that passes light through an optical system but keeps out contaminants.

withdrawal In mental health, this is retreating or going away, one symptom seen in a schizophrenic or depressed person. It is characterized by an unhealthy retreat from interpersonal relations, contacts, and social involvement, resulting in self-preoccupation.

withdrawal symptoms In mental health and substance abuse treatment, this is vomiting, shaking, profuse sweating, hallucinations, and other physical and emotional symptoms resulting from withdrawal from addictive or habituating drugs.

withdraw a motion In formal health-care meetings using parliamentary procedures, this is a motion allowing a previous motion to be withdrawn. The maker of the motion must agree to the withdrawal of his or her motion.

withhold In managed care, this is the portion of the monthly capitation payment to physicians withheld by a health plan until the end of the year or the contract period to create an incentive for efficient care. Physicians exceeding the levels of care determined appropriate by the HMO lose the amount held back. This is a shared-risk arrangement where the physician is at risk of losing the withheld money if the care norms are exceeded. This serves as an incentive to reduce utilization. The amount returned to the health-care provider from the withheld funds is determined by the utilization patterns of the physician, the referral patterns by the gatekeeper, and the overall participants in the panel or pool of providers.

withholding tax Withholding money by an employer from an employee's paycheck and paying it to the government as a prepaid income tax for the employee.

without day 1. An indefinite time. 2. Not final. 3. A date not given or set.

without recourse In health-care financial management, this is a conditional endorsement of a negotiable instrument. If payment is refused, the signer will not be responsible for the outcome.

witness 1. In health law, this is one who sees or is present at an event, act, situation, or occurrence; a person who provides testimony or statements under oath. 2. One who attests to the signing of a document.

witnesses Persons who have firsthand knowledge of some fact related directly or indirectly to a negligent event, crime, violation, accident, or incident.

witnessing In health law, this is to tell what one knows to be true or what one has observed or heard; testifying or providing verbal evidence.

Women, Infants and Children, Supplemental Food Program for (WIC) Recognizing the important role of nutrition during pregnancy and early childhood growth and development, Congress enacted legislation in 1972 creating the Supplemental Food Program for Women,

Infants and Children as a major nutritional intervention program for this target population. WIC serves as an adjunct to health care by providing nutritious foods to supplement a participant's diet as well as nutrition education services. As a result, it has facilitated health improvements by reducing rates of anemia, overweight, underweight, short stature, prematurity, and low birth weight infants. Pregnant, breastfeeding, and postpartum women are eligible for services if they demonstrate signs of anemia, overweight, or underweight; are younger than age 20 or over age 35; have a poor obstetrical history (miscarriages, stillbirths, previous low birth weight infants, multiple births, etc.); or have nutritionally related medical conditions such as toxemia, diabetes, and other conditions that predispose them to inadequate nutritional patterns or other nutritionally related medical conditions.

women's center In health services, this is a specialized health and medical care service in a hospital, clinic, or freestanding facility that coordinates patient counseling, education, preventive care, prenatal and perinatal care, and labor and delivery for pregnant women. The full range of obstetrical and gynecological services are provided, including birthing rooms, labor training, and patient education services.

WONCA World Organization of National Colleges, Academies and Academic Associations of General Practitioners/Family Physicians.

wood-burning stove pollution In environmental health and air pollution control, this is any air pollution caused by emissions of particulate matter, carbon monoxide, total suspended particulates, and polycyclic organic matter from wood-burning stoves or fireplaces (EPA).

word processing Computer software systems that utilize recording and retrieval of data at high speeds using a typewriter keyboard as an input device. A replacement for typewriters and typewriting, it is more flexible; has many added features such as graphics, font size, and choice of fonts; is easy to correct errors with; and writing can be changed without causing undue hardships in the process of producing a document. Final high-quality hard copies of documents are available through computer-driven printers.

Words and Phrases A set of lawbooks that provide definitions of legal words, phrases, and the actual quotes from the cases from which they were taken.

workdays lost *See incident rate; occupational health and safety; average lost workday.*

work environment In occupational health and safety, these are the surroundings in which systems operate. Includes all the conditions that may affect one or more system components such as temperature, humidity, ergonomics, noise, light, vibration, toxic materials, radioactive materials, agents that could be harmful, and indoor air pollution.

Worker Adjustment and Retraining Act In health administration and human resource management, according to this act, this is when a health-care organization with more than 100 employees must provide employees 60 days' advance written notice of the health-care facility closing or major layoffs.

workers In general, these are all persons gainfully employed, including self-employed, owners, unpaid family workers, managers, and all paid employees (excluding nonwage earners such as housewives).

workers' compensation State-run insurance programs that make cash benefits available to workers or their dependents who are injured, disabled, or die in the course of and as a result of work, regardless of who is at fault. The injured employee is entitled to benefits for some or all of the medical services necessary for his or her treatment and restoration to a useful life and a productive job. These insurance programs are mandatory under law in all states. Employees give up the right to sue employers even if injuries stem from employer negligence.

workers' compensation insurance A mandatory insurance contract that insures a person against on-the-job injury or illness. The employer pays the premium for his or her employees.

workers' compensation programs A state social unemployment health insurance program that provides cash benefits to workers or their dependents should the employee become injured, disabled, or deceased in the course of and as a result of employment. The employee is also entitled to benefits for some or all of the medical services necessary for treatment and rehabilitation and restoration to a useful life and possibly a productive job. These programs are mandatory under state laws in all states. Six objectives of workers' compensation have been identified:

1) provide adequate equitable, prompt income and medical benefits to work-related accident victims or income benefits to dependents regardless of fault; 2) provide a single remedy and reduce court delays, costs, and workloads arising out of personal injury litigation; 3) relieve public and private charities of financial drains; 4) eliminate payment of attorney and witness fees and time-consuming litigation proceedings, trials, and appeals; 5) encourage maximum employer interest in safety and rehabilitation through an appropriate experience-rating mechanism; and 6) promote the study of causes of accidents and injuries and reduction of accidents and human suffering (U.S. Chamber of Commerce). *See workers' compensation.*

work flow In health administration and human resource management, this is the assessment, evaluation, and analysis of jobs or work structure, sequence, and process to improve efficiency and effectiveness; the sequence of tasks and work activities in an organization needed to produce quality services for the health-care organization.

work-flow diagram In health administration, planning, and program implementation, this is a graphic presentation of tasks, procedures, or activities that must be accomplished to achieve work goals and objectives. The activities are expressed in the order in which they will be done to implement and manage a project, and the relationship between activities and tasks and the progress of each are illustrated. *See time lines.*

work hour The equivalent of one employee working 1 hour. Work hours is a measure of the total number of hours worked by all employees.

working capital In health administration and planning, this is the sum of an institution's investment in short-term or current assets, including cash, marketable (short-term) securities, accounts receivable, and inventories. Net working capital is defined as the excess of total current assets over total current liabilities.

working capital ratio In health-care financial-management, this is the increase in net working capital for a specific time period divided by the sum of net profit and depreciation. This indicates how much of the health-care organization's earnings flow into working capital. A positive ratio is expected, and a negative ratio would indicate either a loss from operations before depreciation or a decrease in working capital. A ratio of .30 for a fiscal year would indicate a modest profit or a goodly increase in working capital. The working capital ratio formula follows:

$$\frac{\text{Increase in working capital for the fiscal year}}{\text{Net profit + Depreciation for the same time period}}$$

working conditions In occupational health and safety, these are any negative circumstances, environments, and situations under which workers are occupationally exposed to harmful substances, work situations, treatment, or stress. The inverse is also true. These are also the positive, motivational, or job-satisfying circumstances or environments and situations that are conducive to good health, safety, low stress, and good managerial practices and policies that encourage responsibility, recognition, advancement, and satisfaction from work itself.

working poor *See near poor; medically indigent.*

working through In mental health services and psychotherapy, this is the process of obtaining insights into emotional and personal problems, personality, and behavioral changes through examination of conflicts or problems.

work injuries In occupational health and safety, these are personal injuries or occupationally related (caused) illnesses that arise out of an employee doing his or her usual job regardless of where the accident occurs. Farm and home injuries are excluded.

work-loss day A single workday on which a full-time employee or equivalent did not work at his or her job or business for a least half the normal workday because of a specific illness or injury. Workdays are based on the total number of persons presently employed by the health-care organization. *See disability.*

work plan In health administration, this is a detailed description of goals, objectives, and outcome activities of what is to be done, who is going to do it, who is responsible for various activities and outcomes, and when the work or project is to be completed.

work practices In health administration, this is the usual or set ways of doing work, following certain procedures or the way things are done in a health-care organization.

work processes All the components involved to get work done; procedures, management systems, controls, planning, scheduling, staff as-

work-product rule In health law, this a legal rule that states that one party need not show any facts discovered by the party's attorney to the other party unless the other side can show that it would be unfair or unjust for such information not to be shared.

work-sample test In health administration and human resource management, this is proof of work ability in certain technical areas where applicants are asked to provide samples of their work ability through a testing process, such as typing tests for secretaries, to prove they are qualified for the job.

work sampling 1. In health administration and human resource management, this is the process of employing various approaches to a certain job or position to measure the length of time devoted to tasks, activities, or certain phases of the job or position. 2. These are methods and approaches used for evaluating what the level, quality, and standards for each job should be.

worksheet In managed care and medical insurance, this is a computer printout or other record containing all important information and data about the proposed enrollee or potential insured and the insurance agent who submitted the request for insurance.

work simplification In health administration and human resource management, this is the assessment, evaluation, and analysis of jobs and tasks to eliminate unnecessary actions, tasks, and motions and to reduce work. Some tasks can be combined or reassigned to a more appropriate place or worker, but the goal is to remove as many tasks or motions as possible.

worksite health promotion In health promotion and health education, this is the process of screening, evaluating, and assessing a group of workers at their place of employment to determine which health-related services or programs are needed to improve the health status of the workforce. Once implemented, the health promotion services can increase the health status of the group of employees, reduce the use of medical care resources, decrease utilization of health services, and help contain costs and reduce medical insurance premiums. Health promotion activities at the worksite include testing and screening, health counseling, weight loss, fitness, back injury prevention, smoking cessation, stress management, and other health-enhancing and/or behavior change programs as determined in the testing and evaluation process. Physician referral is done as appropriate.

World Health Organization (WHO) The key international organization, an agency of the United Nations, founded in 1948 to coordinate international efforts in the field of health. The headquarters is located in Geneva, Switzerland. WHO acts as the official coordinating and directing authority on international health issues, concerns, and activities. The goal of WHO is the attainment of the highest level of health possible for all peoples of the world, to deal with disease at its origins, and to develop disease-free people living in harmony with their environment and with one another. Six regional offices are located throughout the world in New Delhi, India; Alexandria, Egypt; Washington, D.C.; Manila, Philippines; Bruzzaville (Africa); and Copenhagen, Denmark. All countries, even if they are not members of the United Nations, are open to membership in WHO.

worried well In medical care, these are patients who seem to be caught up in the sick role and who present themselves for health-care services and medical attention of physicians but who show no objective signs or symptoms of physical illness.

WPR *See written progress report.*

wraparound plan In managed care or medical insurance, this is medical care coverage used for co-payments and deductibles not covered under a health plan or medical insurance. Also called "medigap insurance" and used in conjunction with Medicare.

writ 1. A court's or judge's order; a written order issued by the authority of a court. 2. The order by a judge or court to have something done outside the actual courtroom.

write-off In health-care financial management, this is a debt that cannot be collected and thus is considered a bad debt and is deducted from gross income.

write-off method In health-care financial management, this is the health-care organization's realization that certain bills or accounts are uncollectable and a financial loss as determined by a specific time frame set for accounts receivables and are no longer collectable; identification of an uncollectable account as a loss.

write-protected In computers, this a disk or diskette that is protected by a tab or a specialized program so that no new information can be entered on it. With floppy diskettes, an adhesive tab is placed over the access notch on the edge of the diskette, or a slide tab can be adjusted.

writ of course A court order granting that which one has a right or is entitled to.

writ of entry *See entry, writ of.*

writ of prohibition 1. An order from a higher court to a lower court to stop operating out of its jurisdiction. 2. To direct a person to refrain from an act that the court has precedence over.

writ of right A legal order protecting the rights in freehold real estate.

written authorization Consent, permission, or authority given in writing, specifically empowering someone to do something.

written evidence In health law, these are all justifications and information, exclusive of oral testimony, that sets forth the positive and negative aspects of the information presented for consideration by the hearing assembly.

written law Statutes, codes, and regulations passed by a body with legislative authority. *See lex scripta.*

written premium In managed care and insurance, this is a total amount of insurance premiums obtained in a year from all policies issued by an insurance company.

written progress report In the accreditation process under JCAHO, this is a required interim report, developed and submitted to JCAHO according to JCAHO guidelines, by hospitals with a provisional accreditation status and seeking type I accreditation.

wrong 1. Not morally right. 2. Not in accordance with expected or established principles and standards; not suitable. 3. Contrary to fact and truth. 4. Incorrect acts or judgments. 5. A violation of a legal right. 6. A tort.

wrongful Injurious, unjust, and unfair; illegal; unlawful, illicit.

wrongful birth In health law, this is a legal action filed with the courts over the birth of a child who would not have been born except for professional negligence, often because of contraceptive failure, unsuccessful sterilization, failed vasectomy, unsuccessful abortion, failure to warn parents of a birth defect, or genetic risks. This is a lawsuit brought by the parents on their own behalf.

wrongful death 1. Loss of life caused by wrongful acts. 2. A lawsuit filed by the living family members of a dead person against the one who caused a death through negligence. Monetary damages are sought if the act causing the death was wanton, wrongful, negligent, or willful.

wrongful discharge *See wrongful termination.*

wrongful life In health law, this is a legal action filed with the courts over the birth of a child who would not have been born. However, because of professional negligence on the part of a health-care provider (e.g., the failure to produce a timely diagnosis), a defective child was born. Another negligent act may be the failure to warn parents of a birth defect or genetic risks so that the baby is born with a malady related to the defect or risk. A lawsuit is brought by the parents on behalf of the child.

wrongful termination In health administration and human resource management, this is when an employee is fired from his or her job without a justified reason. Employers have the right to hire and fire employees as they see fit under the "employed at will" legal principle. However, the discharge of an employee must not violate any civil rights laws or be over a circumstance where the employee was asked to put his or her health or life in jeopardy or was asked to do something illegal. To work is a privilege, not a right, and few lawsuits are successful for wrongful termination.

wry 1. Turned; bent; twisted; having a distorted meaning. 2. One-sided.

X

X 1. Roman numeral for 10. 2. A person or thing unknown or unrevealed; an unknown.

xanthine A class of chemicals containing caffeine such as coffee, cola drinks, and chocolate. Coffee and cola drinks contain caffeine, tea contains theophylline, and chocolate contains theobromine, all of which are in the xanthine group of drugs, which cause central nervous system and cardiac stimulation. As a drug group, xanthine drugs all have a cross-tolerance with one another.

xantho- Prefix meaning "yellow."

xenobiotic 1. In environmental health, these are nonnaturally occurring man-made substances found in the environment (i.e., synthetic materials, solvents, plastics) (EPA). A chemical that has a specific effect on or action in some organisms of a select species such as certain insects affected by a certain type insecticide; a herbicide affecting certain types of plants. 2. An ecologically effected relationship among species.

xenodiagnosis In medical care and pathogenic microorganism research, this is the process of investigating the existence of a disease-causing microorganism. A disease-free and germ-free vector is exposed to infected materials, and then the vector is examined to discover the existence of the pathogen and study the disease processes of the pathogen in the vector.

xenograft In medical care, this is the implanting or transplanting of tissue or an organ of one species into another (e.g., the transplantation of the heart of a baboon into a human child).

xenophobia Fear of strangers.

xero- Prefix meaning "dry."

xerography A printing process used for copying printed material or other images or pictures by the machine transferring and reproducing the exact or similar image on another sheet of paper.

Xerox A brand of photocopying that reproduces exact images on a clean sheet of paper. *See also xerography; reprography.*

X ray 1. In medical care, this is to examine or treat with X rays; a widely used imaging technique used in medical care to assist in diagnosis and treatment; electromagnetic radiation capable of penetrating soft tissue and quick to show items with high carbon content such as metals, producing pictures of the inside of the body; pictures taken with radiation. 2. Penetrating electromagnetic radiation having wavelengths shorter than those of visible light. They are usually produced by bombarding a metallic target with fast electrons in a high vacuum. In nuclear reactions, it is customary to refer to photons originating in the nucleus as gamma rays and those originating in the extranuclear part of the atom as X rays. X rays are called roentgen rays after their discoverer, W. C. Roentgen.

X-ray radiation therapy The use of roentgen rays or other radiant energy with the exception of radium, cobalt, or radioisotopes for the treatment of cancer and related diseases.

X-ray technician *See medical radiographer; radiologic technologist, registered.*

X-ray technologist *See radiologic technologist, registered; medical radiographer.*

X-ray therapy The use of radioisotopes in the treatment of cancer and other diseases. *See also X-ray radiation therapy.*

Y

yang A positive force in Chinese folk medicine that regulates health; represents the male, warmth, light, and fullness.

yea An affirmative vote or statement.

year, base In health-care financial management and Medicaid/MediCal, this is the most recent hospital accounting year ending before the effective date of the Medicaid reimbursement regulation. Reimbursement for hospital inpatient services provided to Medicaid beneficiaries is done under this time period criterion.

year, final settlement In health-care financial management and Medicaid/MediCal, this is the hospital accounting year for which final settlement is concluded. Reimbursement for hospital inpatient services provided to Medicaid beneficiaries is done under this time period criterion.

yearly renewable term reinsurance (YRT) In managed care and medical care insurance, this is a form of reinsurance where the main insurance company purchases renewable term insurance each year from a reinsurer insurance company. The amount of reinsurance coverage needed is for a year and is based on the net amount of risk on that portion of the original reinsurance policy and must be at least equal to it.

year, prior In health-care financial management and Medicaid/MediCal, this is the most recent hospital accounting year immediately preceding the year for which final settlement is concluded. Reimbursement for hospital inpatient services provided to Medicaid beneficiaries is done under this time period criterion.

years of potential life lost In epidemiology and public health, this is a measure of the untimely death of younger persons who could be productive members of society and contribute to the workforce and the economic and tax base of society and is based on the averages of the population. The age range from birth to 65 years is used to calculate the years of potential life lost. The number of deaths for each age-group is multiplied by the years of life lost, which is the difference between 65 and the midpoint of the age-group. For example, the death of a person in the age-group 15–24 counts as 45 years of life lost: 65 minus the midpoint of 20 years = 45. Potential lives lost are summed for all age-groups (CDC). It is related to the value of human life and the economic implications of the loss of individuals in a society. The improvements in death rates can cause an increase in an available workforce, which in turn benefits society by increased productivity. A count of the number of deaths occurring early in life show that such occurrences remove more years of life than one could possibly live than does a death occurring later in life. A 20-year-old who dies of an automobile accident because of drinking and driving could theoretically have lived to average life expectancy of 72 years of age. Thus, 52 years of productive life is lost. This life lost is a waste to society because it could have been prevented. When 2000 deaths like this result, 104,000 potential years of life are lost. Some sources calculate years of potential life lost on the basis of the retirement age of 65 because this concept can have a strictly economic point of view. However, the social and humane aspects need to be considered, so the example uses average life expectancy rather than age of retirement. Questions such as "What is life worth?" are often raised. The loss to society in the cost of training, manpower, and tax dollars not paid is often considered. Prevention and the decrease of the loss of unnecessary death is a major concern of public health. The value of human life is an underlying goal of public health, as are economic factors, because both issues have long-reaching societal implications.

yellow dog contract An illicit contract for employment forcing an employee to promise that he or she will not join a union.

yield 1. To give in return. 2. To submit to. 3. To give up or to surrender. 4. To give place. 5. To lose precedence. 6. To admit the truth of. 7. To admit the justice and force of. 8. To grant or to allow. 9. The amount or profits gained. 10. In epidemiology and health promotion and the use of screening tests, this is the productivity seen in the testing process; the number of cases accurately identified by the screening test.

yield management In health-care delivery and managed care, this is managing demand to meet capacity in a systematic way to decide what amount of capacity to offer and at what rate to maximize revenue for a specific time period. Several factors are taken into account: 1) assess and establish demand patterns for various case mix or population segments, 2) review overbooking policy considerations, 3) determine demand and the flexibility available for cost and pricing, and 4) evaluate availability of information management system for quick data availability and changes.

yield the floor In formal health-care meetings using parliamentary procedure, a member of the board or committee who has the floor may give it up to another member and at the time gives up his or her right to speak.

yin A negative force in Chinese folk medicine that regulates health; represents the female, coldness, darkness, and emptiness.

yttrium-90 An artificial radioactive isotope of the element yttrium. This element emits beta rays, which are used in radiation therapy.

Z

Z 1. A set of principles laid down by the Federal Reserve Board governing truth-in-lending laws. Also known as Regulation Z. 2. A mark used to fill in blank spaces left in a legal document to ensure that the blanks cannot be filled in later. 3. A management theory based on corporate culture and Japanese management styles and approaches developed by William G. Ouchi, called theory Z.

za (Greek) 1. Argumentative. 2. Intensive. 3. Used to express a high degree of quality in a scientific way.

ZEBRA See *zero balanced reimbursement account*.

Zen A Buddhist sect that seeks enlightenment through introspection and intuition rather than from scripture.

zero 1. A cipher or naught. 2. The lowest point. 3. The point halfway between positive and negative quantities. 4. A crucial or decisive moment (zero hour).

zero balanced reimbursement account In managed care and medical insurance, this is a special type of medical insurance offered as a benefit to employees by self-insured employers. This plan pays for medical care and health services as they are provided. Under this type of medical care insurance benefit, the monies paid out for medical benefits received are taxable by the Internal Revenue Service, and the employer is under mandate to withhold the proper amount of income tax for this benefit as part of the employees prepaid taxes.

zero-time shift In epidemiology, this is to identify the time or point of exposure to a disease or agent to determine survival rates or survival time span. Following the diagnosis of a disease, the epidemiologist goes back to the point of exposure or disease onset and compares that to the point in time of detection to determine length of survival.

zeumatography Sometimes used synonymously with "nuclear magnetic resonance imaging."

zip code A several-digit code number representing a postal delivery area.

zone 1. A region or area that is distinct and different in its use from other areas; any special area or district in a city or county that is restricted by law for certain and specified use (e.g., businesses, residential areas, industry, apartment complexes, or health-care facilities).

zoning When a governmental agency responsible for zoning and planning sets aside by ordinance certain sections of land for different purposes or for certain and specified use (e.g., businesses, residential areas, industry, apartment complexes, and health-care facilities); regulation of land and its use; community planning of land use. See also *zone*.

zoo- Prefix meaning "animal life."

zoonoses Plural for "zoonosis."

zoonosis In epidemiology, these are diseases and infections that are naturally transmitted between vertebrate animals and man. Also called "zoonotic disorders" or "zoonotic diseases." The transmission of diseases from animal to man; illness in humans that originated in animals or that comes from animals.

zoonotic diseases See *zoonosis*.

zoopsia Hallucination about animals or insects by intoxicated individuals or a person going through delirium tremens.

zootoxin A poisonous substance from an animal such as venom of snakes, scorpions, or spiders.

ZPG Zero population growth.

zymology The science and study of yeasts and fermentation.

APPENDICES

I   Epidemiology and Vital Statistics Rate Formulas
II   Abbreviations of Fellows of Colleges and Medical Diplomate Specialties
III   Medical Specialties and Their Abbreviations
IV   The Hospital Patient's Bill of Rights: American Hospital Association
V   Patients' Rights in Skilled Nursing Facilities
VI   Vital Signs of the Body
VII   Greek Alphabet
VIII   Numbers and Symbols Commonly Used in Charting Medical Records
IX   Abbreviations Used in Medical Records
X   Abbreviations Used in Charting in Medical Laboratories
XI   Abbreviations Used in Charting in Radiography
XII   Latin Abbreviations Commonly Used in Writing Prescriptions
XIII   Weight Equivalents: Metric and Apothecary
XIV   Volume Equivalents: Metric, Apothecary, and Household
XV   Code of Ethics for Medical Record Administration
XVI   Privacy Act of 1974

APPENDIX I

Epidemiology and Vital Statistics Rate Formulas

General Formulas:

$$\text{Crude birth rate} = \frac{\text{Number of live births to residents in an area in a calendar year}}{\text{Average population in the areas in the same year}} \times 1000$$

$$\text{RATE} = \frac{\text{Number of Cases}}{\text{Population of the Area}} \quad \text{In a period of time}$$

Mortality Formulas:

Age-specific mortality rate examples:

$$\text{Age-specific mortality rate} = \frac{\text{Number of deaths of persons ages 1–14 in a given year}}{\text{Total persons ages 1–14 in the same period (1 year)}} \times 100{,}000$$

$$\text{Age-specific mortality rate} = \frac{\text{Number of deaths of rural elderly ages 55 + in a year}}{\text{Average population of rural elderly in the same period}} \times 100{,}000$$

$$\text{Abortion rate} = \frac{\text{Number of abortions done per year}}{\text{Total number of women ages 15–44 per same year}} \times 1000$$

$$\text{Annual death rate from all causes} = \frac{\text{Total numbers of death during a specific 12-month time period}}{\text{Number of persons in the total population at middle of the time period}} \times 1000$$

$$\text{Case fatality rate} = \frac{\text{Number of deaths by a certain disease in a given time period}}{\text{Number of diagnosed cases in the same period}} \times 1000$$

Second formula for case fatality rate:

$$\text{Case fatality rate} = \frac{\text{Number of deaths by a certain disease or cause in a specified time period}}{\text{Number of cases which occurred in the same period}} \times 1000$$

$$\text{Cause-specific mortality rate} = \frac{\text{Number of deaths by a certain disease for a select subgroup in a given year}}{\text{Total subgroup population in the same period (1 year)}} \times 100{,}000$$

$$\text{Crude death rate} = \frac{\text{Total deaths per year}}{\text{Average total population of that year}} \times 100{,}000$$

$$\text{Fetal death rate} = \frac{\text{Number of fetal deaths in a time period (1 year)}}{\text{Total number of fetal deaths plus live births in the same period}} \times 1000$$

$$\text{Fetal death ratio rate} = \frac{\text{Number of fetal deaths after 28 weeks or more gestation}}{\text{Total number of live births in the same period (1 year)}} \times 1000$$

Second formula for fetal death ratio:

$$\text{Fetal death ratio rate} = \frac{\text{Number of fetal deaths in a certain period (1 year)}}{\text{Total number of live births in the same period (1 year)}} \times 1000$$

$$\text{Infant mortality rate} = \frac{\text{Number of child deaths less than 1 year old in 1 year}}{\text{Number of live births in the same year}} \times 1000$$

$$\text{Infant death rates under 1 year} = \frac{\text{Number of child deaths less than 1 year old in 1 year}}{\text{Total population}} \times 100{,}000$$

$$\text{Maternal mortality rate} = \frac{\text{Number of deaths from puerperal causes in a given year}}{\text{Total number of live births in the same period (1 year)}} \times 100{,}000$$

$$\text{Neonatal mortality rate} = \frac{\text{Number of infant deaths under 28 days old}}{\text{Number of live births in the same year}} \times 1000$$

$$\text{Perinatal mortality rate (period I)} = \frac{\text{Number of fetal deaths of 28 or more weeks gestation plus postnatal deaths (7 days)}}{\text{Total number of births in the same period}} \times 1000$$

$$\text{Perinatal mortality rate (period II)} = \frac{\text{Number of fetal deaths of 20 or more weeks gestation plus neonatal deaths}}{\text{Total number of births in the same period}} \times 1000$$

$$\text{Postneonatal mortality rate} = \frac{\text{Number of infant deaths between 28 days of age and 1 year of age}}{\text{Number of live births in the same year}} \times 1000$$

$$\text{Proportionate mortality ratio rate} = \frac{\text{Observed deaths from a specific cause}}{\text{Expected deaths from the same cause}}$$

$$\text{Proportional mortality rate} = \frac{\text{Disease death rates}}{\text{Disease death rates} + \text{Death rates for all other causes}} \times 1000$$

$$\text{Standard mortality ratio rate} = \frac{\text{Observed deaths}}{\text{Expected deaths}} \times 1000$$

Morbidity Formulas:

Attack Rates:

$$\text{Crude attack rate} = \frac{\text{Number of persons ill with the disease}}{\text{Number of persons attending the event}} \times 1000$$

$$\text{Attack rate} = \frac{\text{Number of Persons ill within the time period}}{\text{Number of persons at risk within the time period}} \times 1000$$

Appendix I

$$\text{Food-specific attack rate} = \frac{\text{Number of persons who ate a specific food and became ill}}{\text{Total number of persons who ate a specific food}} \times 1000$$

$$\text{Relative risk} = \frac{\text{Eating and sick}}{\text{Not eating and sick}}$$

$$\text{Incidence rate} = \frac{\text{Number of new cases of a disease within a population in a given time period}}{\text{Number of persons exposed to risk of developing the disease in the same time period}} \times 1000$$

$$\text{Period prevalence rate} = \frac{\text{Number of existing cases of the disease}}{\text{Average study population}} \quad \text{Within a time period}$$

$$\text{Point prevalence rate} = \frac{\text{Number of existing cases of the disease}}{\text{Total study population}} \quad \text{At a point in time}$$

$$\text{Prevalence rate} = \frac{\text{Total number of cases of the disease at a given time}}{\text{Total population at risk at a given time}} \times 1000$$

$$\text{Relative risk} = \frac{\text{Incidence rate of disease of exposed within a group}}{\text{Incidence rate of disease of nonexposed within a group}} \times 1000$$

$$\text{Risk ratio rate} = \frac{\text{Probability of a disease exposure}}{\text{Probability of a disease not yet exposed}} \times 1000$$

$$\text{Secondary attack rate} = \frac{\text{Number of exposed persons developing the disease within incubation period}}{\text{Total number of persons exposed to the primary case}} \times 1000$$

APPENDIX II

Abbreviations of Fellows of Colleges and Medical Diplomate Specialties

Fellows of Specialty Colleges

AFACAL	Associate Fellow of American College of Allergists
FAAN	Fellow of American Academy of Nursing
FACAL	Fellow of American College of Allergists
FACA	Fellow of American College of Angiology
FACAn	Fellow of American College of Anesthesiologists
FACC	Fellow of American College of Cardiology
FCCP	Fellow of American College of Chest Physicians
FACEP	Fellow of American College of Emergency Physicians
FACG	Fellow of American College of Gastroenterology
FACHCA	Fellow of American College of Health Care Administrators
FACHE	Fellow of American College of Healthcare Executives
FACMCM	Fellow of American College of Medical Care Managers
FACOG	Fellow of American College of Obstetricians and Gynecologists
FCAP	Fellow of College of American Pathologists
FACP	Fellow of American College of Physicians
FACPM	Fellow of American College of Preventive Medicine
FACR	Fellow of American College of Radiology
FACSM	Fellow of American College of Sports Medicine
FACS	Fellow of American College of Surgeons
FASHA	Fellow of American School Health Association
FCLM	Fellow of American College of Legal Medicine
FICS	Fellow of International College of Surgeons
FRSH	Fellow in the Royal Society of Health

Diplomates in Specialties

D-AI	Diplomate American Board of Allergy and Immunology
D-AN	Diplomate American Board of Anesthesiology
D-CRS	Diplomate American Board of Colon and Rectal Surgery
D-D	Diplomate American Board of Dermatology
D-FP	Diplomate American Board of Family Practice
D-M	Diplomate American Board of Internal Medicine
D-NS	Diplomate American Board of Neurological Surgery
D-NuM	Diplomate American Board of Nuclear Medicine
D-OG	Diplomate American Board of Obstetrics and Gynecology
D-OP	Diplomate American Board of Ophthalmology
D-OS	Diplomate American Board of Orthopedic Surgery
D-OT	Diplomate American Board of Otolaryngology
D-P	Diplomate American Board of Pathology
D-Pd	Diplomate American Board of Pediatrics
D-PMR	Diplomate American Board of Physical Medicine and Rehabilitation
D-PIS	Diplomate American Board of Plastic Surgery
D-PrM	Diplomate American Board of Preventive Medicine

Appendix II

D-PN	Diplomate American Board of Psychiatry and Neurology
D-R	Diplomate American Board of Radiology
D-S	Diplomate American Board of Surgery
D-TS	Diplomate American Board of Thoracic Surgery
D-U	Diplomate American Board of Urology
N-B	Diplomate certified by National Board of Medical Examiners

APPENDIX III

Medical Specialties and Their Abbreviations

A	Allergy	NA	Neuropathology
ABS	Abdominal surgery	ND	Neoplastic disease
ADL	Adolescent medicine	NEP	Nephrology
AI	Allergy and immunology	NM	Nuclear medicine
AM	Aerospace medicine	NPM	Neonatal-perinatal medicine
AN	Anesthesiology	NR	Nuclear radiation
BE	Broncho-esophagology	NS	Neurological surgery
BLB	Bloodbanking	NTR	Nutrition
CD	Cardiovascular disease	OBG	Obstetrics and gynecology
CDS	Cardiovascular surgery	OBS	Obstetrics
CHN	Child neurology	ON	Oncology
CHP	Child psychiatry	OPH	Ophthalmology
CLP	Clinical pathology	ORS	Surgery, orthopedic
CRS	Colon and rectal surgery	OT	Otology
D	Dermatology	OTO	Otorhinolaryngology
DIA	Diabetes	P	Psychiatry
DMP	Dermatopathology	PA	Pharmacology, clinical
DR	Diagnostic radiology	PD	Pediatrics
EM	Emergency medicine	PDA	Pediatrics, allergy
END	Endocrinology	PDC	Pediatrics, cardiology
FOB	Forensic pathology	PDE	Pediatric, endocrinology
FP	Family practice	PDR	Pediatric radiology
GE	Gastroenterology	PDS	Pediatric surgery
GER	Geriatrics	PH	Public health
GP	General practice	PHO	Pediatric hematology/oncology
GPM	General preventive medicine	PM	Physical medicine and rehabilitation
GS	General surgery	PNP	Pediatric nephrology
GYN	Gynecology	PS	Pediatric surgery
HEM	Hematology	PUD	Pulmonary disease
HNS	Head and neck surgery	PYA	Psychoanalysis
HS	Hand surgery	PYM	Psychosomatic medicine
HYP	Hypnosis	R	Radiology
ID	Infectious diseases	RHU	Rheumatology
IG	Immunology	RHI	Rhinology
IM	Internal medicine	RIP	Radioisotopic pathology
LAR	Laryngology	TS	Thoracic surgery
LM	Legal medicine	TRS	Traumatic surgery
MFS	Maxillofacial surgery	U	Urological surgery
N	Neurology		

APPENDIX IV

The Hospital Patient's Bill of Rights: American Hospital Association

Effective health care requires collaboration between patients and physicians and other health care professionals. Open and honest communication, respect for personal and professional values, and sensitivity to differences are integral to optimal patient care. As the setting for the provision of health services, hospitals must provide a foundation for understanding and respecting the rights and responsibilities of patients, their families, physicians, and other caregivers. Hospitals must ensure a health care ethic that respects the role of patients in decision making about treatment choices and other aspects of their care. Hospitals must be sensitive to cultural, racial, linguistic, religious, age, gender, and other differences as well as the needs of persons with disabilities.

The American Hospital Association presents *A Patient's Bill of Rights* with the expectation that it will contribute to more effective patient care and be supported by the hospital on behalf of the institution, its medical staff, employees, and patients. The American Hospital Association encourages health care institutions to tailor this bill of rights to their patient community by translating and/or simplifying the language of this bill of rights as may be necessary to ensure that patients and their families understand their rights and responsibilities.

1. The patient has the right to considerate and respectful care.

2. The patient has the right to and is encouraged to obtain from physicians and other direct caregivers relevant, current, and understandable information concerning diagnosis, treatment, and prognosis.

Except in emergencies when the patient lacks decision-making capacity and the need for treatment is urgent, the patient is entitled to the opportunity to discuss and request information related to the specific procedures and/or treatments, the risks involved, the possible length of recuperation, and the medically reasonable alternatives and their accompanying risks and benefits.

Patients have the right to know the identity of physicians, nurses, and others involved in their care, as well as when those involved are students, residents, or other trainees. The patient also has the right to know the immediate and long-term financial implications of treatment choices, insofar as they are known.

3. The patient has the right to make decisions about the plan of care prior to and during the course of treatment and to refuse a recommended treatment or plan of care to the extent permitted by law and hospital policy and to be informed of the medical consequences of this action. In case of such refusal, the patient is entitled to other appropriate care and services that the hospital provides or transfer to another hospital. The hospital should notify patients of any policy that might affect patient choice within the institution.

4. The patient has the right to have an advance directive (such as a living will, health care proxy, or durable power of attorney for health care) concerning treatment or designating a surrogate decision maker with the expectation that the hospital will honor the intent of that directive to the extent permitted by law and hospital policy.

Health care institutions must advise patients of their rights under state law and hospital policy to make informed medical choices, ask if the patient has an advance directive, and include that information in patient records. The patient has the right to timely information about hospital policy that may limit its ability to implement fully a legally valid advance directive.

5. The patient has the right to every consideration of privacy. Case discussion, consultation, examination, and treatment should be conducted so as to protect each patient's privacy.

6. The patient has the right to expect that all communications and records pertaining to his/her care will be treated as confidential by the hospital, except in cases such as suspected abuse and public health hazards when reporting is permitted or required by law. The patient has the right to expect that the hospital will emphasize the confidentiality of this information when it releases it to any other

parties entitled to review information in these records.

7. The patient has the right to review the records pertaining to his/her medical care and to have the information explained or interpreted as necessary, except when restricted by law.

8. The patient has the right to expect that, within its capacity and policies, a hospital will make reasonable response to the request of a patient for appropriate and medically indicated care and services. The hospital must provide evaluation, service, and/or referral as indicated by the urgency of the case. When medically appropriate and legally permissible, or when a patient has so requested, a patient may be transferred to another facility. The institution to which the patient is to be transferred must first have accepted the patient for transfer. The patient must also have the benefit of complete information and explanation concerning the need for, risks, benefits, and alternatives to such a transfer.

9. The patient has the right to ask and be informed of the existence of business relationships among the hospital, educational institutions, other health care providers, or payers that may influence the patient's treatment and care.

10. The patient has the right to consent to or decline to participate in proposed research studies or human experimentation affecting care and treatment or requiring direct patient involvement, and to have those studies fully explained prior to consent. A patient who declines to participate in research or experimentation is entitled to the most effective care that the hospital can otherwise provide.

11. The patient has the right to expect reasonable continuity of care when appropriate and to be informed by physicians and other caregivers of available and realistic patient care options when hospital care is no longer appropriate.

12. The patient has the right to be informed of hospital policies and practices that relate to patient care, treatment, and responsibilities. The patient has the right to be informed of available resources for resolving disputes, grievances, and conflicts, such as ethics committees, patient representatives, or other mechanisms available in the institution. The patient has the right to be informed of the hospital's charges for services and available payment methods.

The collaborative nature of health care requires that patients, or their families/surrogates, participate in their care. The effectiveness of care and patient satisfaction with the course of treatment depend, in part, on the patient fulfilling certain responsibilities. Patients are responsible for providing information about past illnesses, hospitalizations, medications, and other matters related to health status. To participate effectively in decision making, patients must be encouraged to take responsibility for requesting additional information or clarification about their health status or treatment when they do not fully understand information and instructions. Patients are also responsible for ensuring that the health care institution has a copy of their written advance directive if they have one. Patients are responsible for informing their physicians and other caregivers if they anticipate problems in following prescribed treatment.

Patients should also be aware of the hospital's obligation to be reasonably efficient and equitable in providing care to other patients and the community. The hospital's rules and regulations are designed to help the hospital meet this obligation. Patients and their families are responsible for making reasonable accommodations to the needs of the hospital, other patients, medical staff, and hospital employees. Patients are responsible for providing necessary information for insurance claims and for working with the hospital to make payment arrangements, when necessary.

A person's health depends on much more than health care services. Patients are responsible for recognizing the impact of their life-style on their personal health.

Hospitals have many functions to perform, including the enhancement of health status, health promotion, and the prevention and treatment of injury and disease; the immediate and ongoing care and rehabilitation of patients; the education of health professionals, patients, and the community; and research. All these activities must be conducted with an overriding concern for the values and dignity of patients.

Reprinted with permission of the American Hospital Association, copyright 1992.

APPENDIX V

Patients' Rights in Skilled Nursing Facilities

The governing body of the nursing home or long-term care facility establishes written policies regarding the rights and responsibilities of patients and, through the administrator, is responsible for development of and adherence to, procedures implementing such policies. These policies and procedures are made available to patients, to any guardians, next of kin, sponsoring agencies or representative payees selected pursuant to section 205(j) of the Social Security Act, and Subpart Q of CFR Part 404, and to the public. The staff of the facility is trained and involved in the implementation of these policies and procedures. These patients' rights policies and procedures ensure that, at least, each patient admitted to the facility:

1. Is fully informed, as evidenced by the patient's written acknowledgement, prior to or at the time of admission and during stay, of these rights and of all rules and regulations governing patient conduct and responsibilities;

2. If fully informed, prior to or at the time of admission and during the patient's stay, of services available in the facility, and of related charges including any charges for services not covered under Titles XVIII or XIX of the Social Security Act, or not covered by the facility's basic per diem rate.

3. Is fully informed, by a physician, of his or her medical condition unless medically contraindicated (as documented, by a physician, in his medical record), and is afforded the opportunity to participate in experimental research;

4. Is transferred or discharged only for medical reasons, or for his or her welfare or that of other patients, or for non-payment for his or her stay (except as prohibited by under Titles XVIII or XIX of the Social Security Act), and is given reasonable advance notice to ensure orderly transfer or discharge, and such actions are documented in his or her medical record.

5. Is encouraged and assisted, throughout his period of stay, to exercise his or her rights as a patient and as a citizen, and to this end may voice grievances and recommend changes in policies and services to facility staff and/or to outside representatives of his choice, free from restraint, interference, coercion, discrimination, or reprisal;

6. May manage his or her personal financial affairs, or is given at least a quarterly accounting of financial transactions made on his behalf should the facility accept his or her written delegation of this responsibility to the facility for any period of time in conformance with state law;

7. Is free from mental and physical abuse, and free from chemical and (except in emergencies) physical restraints except as authorized in writing by a physician for a specified and limited period of time, or when necessary to protect the patient from injury to himself or to others;

8. Is assured confidential treatment of his or her personal and medical records, and may approve or refuse their release to any individual outside the facility, except, in case of his or her transfer to another health care institution, or as required by law or third-party payment contract;

9. Is treated with consideration, respect, and full recognition of his or dignity and individuality, including privacy in treatment and in care for his personal needs;

10. Is not required to perform services for the facility that are not included for therapeutic purposes in his plan of care;

11. May associate and communicate privately with persons of his or her choice, and send and receive his or her personal mail unopened, unless medically contraindicated (as documented by his physician in his or her medical record);

12. May meet with, and participate in activities of social, religious and community groups at his discretion, unless medically contraindicated (as documented by his physician in his or her medical record);

13. May retain and use his or her personal clothing and possessions as space permits, unless to do so would infringe upon rights of other patients, and unless medically contraindicated (as documented by his physician in his or her medical record);

14. If married, is assured privacy for visits by his/her spouse; if both are inpatients in the facility, they are permitted to share a room, unless medically contraindicated (as documented by his physician in his or her medical record);

All rights and responsibilities specified in this law as they pertain to: a patient adjudicated incompetent in accordance with state law; patient who is found by his physician, to be medically incapable of understanding these rights; or a patient who exhibits a communication barrier—devolve to such patient's legal guardian, next of kin, sponsor or representative payee (expect when the facility itself is the payee) selected pursuant to section 205(j) of the Social Security Act, and Subpart Q of CFR Part 404.

U.S. Department of Health and Human Services for Medicare and Medicaid Participation

APPENDIX VI

Vital Signs of the Body

Temperature

Normal Body Temperature:

Children: 99°F (37.2°C)
Adults: 98.6°F (37°C)

Rectal thermometer readings tend to be half a degree higher than those recorded by mouth thermometers, with temperatures lowest on rising in the morning. One's temperature may rise as much as 1 degree toward the end of the day.

The Relationship of Temperature to Pulse:

An increase of 1 degree of temperature above 98°F is approximately equivalent to a rise of 10 beats in pulse rate.

Temperature (°F)	Pulse (beats/minute)
98	70
99	80
100	90
101	100
102	110
103	120
104	130
105	140

To convert Fahrenheit to Centigrade, subtract 32 and multiply by 5/9. To convert Centigrade to Fahrenheit, multiply by 9/5 and add 32.

Respiration

Normal Breathing Rates:

Age	Respirations/minute
Up to 1 year	25–35
12–17 years	20–25
Adult	16–18

Breathing rates tend to rise with the rate of the pulse.

Pulse Rates

Average Normal Pulse Rate:

Age	Beats/minute
Unborn	140–150
Newborn	130–140
1	110–130
2	96–105
3	86–105
7–14	76–90
14–21	76–85
21–60	70–75
60 plus	67–80

Pulse rates normally rise during emotional excitement, following physical exertion or exercise and during digestion. The pulse rate is generally more rapid for females. The pulse rate is influenced by the rate of breathing.

Blood Pressure

Average Normal Blood Pressure:

Age	Systolic pressure	Diastolic pressure
10	103	70
15	113	75
20	120	80
25	122	81
30	123	82
35	124	83
40	126	84
45	128	85
50	130	86
55	132	87
60	136	89

Systolic pressure is the pressure or force with which blood is pumped during the heart's contraction; diastolic pressure is the pressure or force with which blood is pumped during relaxation of the heart.

APPENDIX VII

Greek Alphabet

Alpha	A α	Iota	I ι	Rho	P ϱ
Beta	B β	Kappa	K ϰ	Sigma	Σ σ
Gamma	Γ γ	Lambda	Λ λ	Tau	T τ
Delta	Δ δ	Mu	M μ	Upsilon	Y υ
Epsilon	E ϵ	Nu	N ν	Phi	Φ φ
Zeta	Z ζ	Xi	Ξ ξ	Chi	X χ
Eta	H η	Omicron	O o	Psi	Ψ ψ
Theta	Θ θ	Pi	Π π	Omega	Ω ω

APPENDIX VIII

Numbers and Symbols Commonly Used in Charting Medical Records

One: i
Two: ii
Three: iii
Four: iv
Five: v
Six: vi
Seven: vii
Eight: viii
Nine: ix
Ten: x
Eleven: xi
Twelve, etc.: xii
and: et, +, &

greater than: >
less than: <
dram: ʒ
ounce: ℥
grain: gr
one-half: ss
one and one-half: iss
three ounces: ℥ iii
two drams: ʒ ii
number: #, no.
with: c̄
without: s̄

APPENDIX IX

Abbreviations Used in Medical Records

Abbreviations used in medical records should be used in a consistent manner. Personally developed abbreviations have no place in the medical record. They should appear in the medical record in places least likely to be used for legal purposes. Abbreviations do save time and space but if a word's meaning falls into question, the complete word should be written out.

Aa

aa	of each
abd	abdomen
a.c.	before meals
accom	accommodation
ACTH	adrenocorticotropic hormone
ad	to, up to
ad lib.	as desired
adm	admission
alb	albumin
alk	alkaline
A.M.	morning
amb	ambulate, ambulatory, walking
amp	ampule
amt	amount
ant.	anterior
AP	anteroposterior; arterial pressure
APC	aspirin, phenacetin, caffeine
approx	approximately, about
ASA	acetasalicylic acid (aspirin)
ASHD	arteriosclerotic heart disease
A.V. node	atrioventricular node
ax	axillary, armpit

Bb

BCG	bacillus Calmette-Guerin (tuberculosis vaccine)
b.i.d.	twice a day
bisp	bispinous or interspinous diameter (pelvic measure)
B.M.	bowel movement
BMR	basal metabolic rate
b.p.	blood pressure
BPH	benign prostatic hyperplasia
BRP	bathroom privileges

Cc

Cc	centigrade
c	with
C_1, C_2, etc.	cervical vertabra placement (i.e., first cervical vertabra)
Ca	calcium; cancer; carcinoma
CA	chronological age
cap	capsule
cath	catheter, catheterized
C.C.	chief complaint
cc.	cubic centimeter
CCU	coronary care unit; critical care unit
CD	communicable disease
CHF	congestive heart failure
CHO or carbo	carbohydrate
Cl	chloride
clysis	hypodermoclysis (fluid under the skin)
cm.	centimeter
cmp	compound
CNS	central nervous system
CO_2	carbon dioxide
c/o	complains of
COLD	chronic obstructive lung disease (referred to as COPD)
comp.	compound
cont	continued; continuous
CPR	cardiopulmonary resuscitation
C.S.	central service; cesarean section
CSF	cerebrospinal fluid
CVA	cerebrovascular accident
CVP	central venous pressure
cysto	cystoscope, cystoscopy

Dd

DC	discontinue
D.C.	diagonal conjugate (pelvic measurement)
D&C	dilatation and curettage
diab	diabetic
diag	diagnosis
diam	diameter
disc	discontinue
dist.	distil
DNP	do not publish
DNS	do not show
DOA	dead on arrival
Dr.	doctor

Appendix IX

dr.	dram	H&H	hemoglobin and hematocrit
D.Ts	delirium tremens	H&P	history and physical
D/W	distilled water	HCl	hydrochloric acid
Dx	diagnosis	HCT	hematocrit
		Hg	mercury
		Hgb	hemoglobin

Ee

ECG	electrocardiogram	hi-cal	high calorie
EDC	expected date of confinement	hi-vit	high vitamin
EEG	electroencephalogram	H_2O	water
EENT	eye, ear, nose, and throat	H_2O_2	hydrogen peroxide
EKG	electrocardiogram	HOB	head of bed
elix	elixir	hosp	hospital
EOM	extraocular movement	hr	hour
epith	epithelial	h.s.	at bedtime
ER	emergency room	ht	height
et	and		
etc.	and so forth		

Ii

exam	examination	I	iodine
exp. lap.	exploratory laparotomy	ICU	intensive care unit
expir	expiration or expiratory	I&D	incision and drainage
ext	extract or external	IICU	infant intensive care unit
		I.M.	intramuscular

Ff

F	Fahrenheit	inspir	inspiration or inspiratory
F. cath	Foley catheter	inter	between
Fe	iron	invol	involuntary, without knowledge
F.H.	family history	I&O	intake and output, input and output
FHS	fatal heart sound	IPPB	intermittent positive pressure breathing
fl.	fluid		
fld.	fluid	irrig	irrigate
fract	fracture	iss	one and one-half
ft.	feet or foot	I.T.	inhalation therapy, intertubenous (pelvic measurement)
		I.V. or IV	intravenous (within a vein)

Gg

G in W	glycerin in water		

Kk

glyc. in W	glycerin in water	K	potassium
gal	gallon	kg.	kilogram
G.B.	gallbladder	$KMnO_2$	potassium permanganate
G.C.	gonorrhea		

Ll

G.I.	gastrointestinal		
gm	gram	L	liter, left
gr.	grain	$L_1, L_2,$ etc.	placement of lumbar vertebra (i.e., first lumbar, second, etc.)
Gav. I	primigravida		
Gav. II	secundigravida	lab	laboratory
gt.	drop	lap	laparotomy
gtt.	drops	lat	lateral
G.U.	genitourinary	lb	pound
gyn	gynecology	lg	large
		liq	liquid

Hh

H or (H)	hypodermic	LLL	left lower lobe (lung)
h	hour	LLQ	left lower quadrant (left lower section of abdomen)
H et H	hemoglobin and hematocrit		

LMP	last menstrual period	occ. th.	occupational therapy
L.P.	lumbar puncture	o.d.	daily
L.R.	lactated Ringer's solution (I.V. solution)	O.D.	right eye
		oint	ointment
LUL	left upper lobe (lung)	op	operation
LUQ	left upper quadrant (left upper section of abdomen)	ophth	ophthalmology
		o.pt.	outpatient
L&W	living and well	opt	optimal
		O.R.	operating room

Mm

m.	male; meter; minimum	ortho	orthopedic
max	maximum	O.S.	left eye
mcg.	microgram	O T	occupational therapy
med	medicine, medical	oto	otology
mEq.	milliequivalent	O.U.	each eye
Mg	magnesium	oz.	ounce

Pp

mid	middle	p	after, post
mg., mgm	milligram	P	pulse; phosphorus
M.I.	myocardial infarction	P-A	posterior-anterior
min.	minimum, minute, minim (0.06 milliliter)	palp	palpable
		PAR	post anesthesia recovery
ml.	milliliter	Para I	primipara
mm.	millimeter	Para II	secundipara
Mn	manganese	paracent	paracentesis
mo.	month	path	pathology
MS	multiple sclerosis	p.c.	meals
		pedi	pediatrics

Nn

N	nitrogen	peds	pediatrics
n	normal	per	by, through
Na	sodium	percuss. & ausc.	percussion and ausculation
N.B.	newborn		
neg	negative	P.H.	past history
neuro	neurology, neurological	pH	base, alkaline/acid concentration, hydrogen concentration
no.	number		
noc. noct.	nocturnal (night)	P.I.	present illness
non repetat	do not repeat	PID	pelvic inflammatory disease
		PKU	phenylketonuria
NPN	nonprotein nitrogen	P.M.	afternoon
NPO	nothing by mouth	PMP	previous menstrual period
N.S.	neurosurgery	PNP	pediatric nurse practitioner
N/S	normal saline	P.O.	phone order
N&V	nausea and vomiting	p.o.	per os (by mouth)
		poplit	popliteal

Oo

'o'	orally	post-op	postoperative
O₂	oxygen	prep	preparation
O₂ cap	oxygen capacity	pre-op	preoperative
O₂ sat	oxygen saturation	p.r.n.	whenever necessary, as needed
OB	obstetrics	prog	prognosis
O.C.	obstetrical conjugate (pelvic measurement)	prot	protein
		psych	psychology; psychiatric
occ	occasional	pt	patient
		PT	physical therapy

Appendix IX

pulv	powder
PZI	protamine zinc insulin

Qq

q.d.	every day
q.i.d.	4 times a day
q.h.	every hour
q2H, q3H, etc.	every 2 hours, every 3 hours, etc.
q.o.d.	every other day
q.n.	every night
q.n.s.	quantity not sufficient
q.s.	sufficient quantity
qt.	quart
quant	quantity or quantitative

Rr

R	respiratory or respiration
RBC	red blood count
req	request or requisition
resp	respiratory or respiration
RHF	right heart failure
RLL	right lower lobe (lung)
RLQ	right lower quadrant (right lower section of abdomen)
RML	right middle lobe (lung)
ROM	range of motion
rt.	right
rt'd	returned
RUL	right upper lobe (lung)
RUQ	right upper quadrant (right upper section of abdomen)
Rx	therapy, treatment, drug

Ss

s	without
SAD	sugar and acetone determination
S.A. node	sinus atrial node
S.C.	subcutaneous
SCIV	subclavian intravenous
scop	scopolamine
S.H.	social history
sig	write, label
sm.	small
SMR	submucous resection
sod. bicarb.	sodium bicarbonate
sol.	solution
S.O.S.	if it is necessary
spec	specimen
sp.fl.	spinal fluid
sp.gr.	specific gravity
SS	soap suds
ss enema	soap suds enema
ss.	one half
Staph	staphylococcus
stat.	immediately, once only, at once
stillb	stillbirth
Strep	streptococcus
subcu	subcutaneous
subling	sublingual (under the tongue)
surg	surgery; surgical
sympt	symptom
syr	syru

Tt

T	temperature
T&A	tonsillectomy and adenoidectomy
tab	tablet
TAT	tetanus antitoxin
T.b.	tubercle bacillus, tuberculosis
tbsp	tablespoon
temp	temperature
t.i.d.	three times a day
tinct	tincture
T.L.	tubal ligation; team leader
TLC	total lung capacity; tender loving care
TLV	total lung volume
TPR	temperature, pulse, respirations
tr	tincture
trach	tracheostomy
tsp.	teaspoon
TUR	transurethral resection

Uu

U.	unit
U.A.	urinalysis
ung.	ointment
URI	upper respiratory infection
urol	urology; urological

Vv

vag	vaginal
VC	vital capacity
V.D.	venereal disease
V.I.	volume index
via	by the way of
vit	vitamin
vit. cap.	vital capacity
V.O.	verbal orders
vol.	volume
V.S.	vital signs

Ww

WBC	white blood count
wd	well-developed
wn	well-nourished
wt.	weight

APPENDIX X

Abbreviations Used in Charting in Medical Laboratories

Abbreviations in medical records should be used in a consistent and standardized manner. Below is the standardized way of using abbreviations in charting in medical laboratories.

acid p'tase	acid phosphatase	I	iodine
AFB	acid fast bacillus	ict. ind.	icterus index
A-G	albumin-globulin ratio	LDH	lactic dehydrogenase
alk	alkaline	L.E. cell	lupus erythematosus cell
alk p'tase	alkaline phosphatase	lymph	lymphocytes
ANA	antinuclear antibody (test for Lupus erythematosus)	MCH	mean corpuscular hemoglobin
ASO or ASTO	antistreptolysin	MCV	mean corpuscular volume
baso	basophile	mg O/O	milligrams per hundred milliliters of serum or blood
bili	bilirubin	mono	monocytes
bl. cult	blood culture	NH$_3$N	ammonia nitrogen
Bl. time	bleeding time	NPN	nonprotein nitrogen
Br.	bromine	PBI	protein bound iodine
BSP	bromosuphalein	PCO$_2$	partial pressure of carbon dioxide
BUN	blood urea nitrogen	pH	hydrogen concentration
C	carbon	PKU	phenylketonuria
Ca	calcium	PO$_4$	inorganic phosphorus
c.b.c.	complete blood count	polys	polymorphonuclear leukocytes
ceph. floc.	cephalin flocculation test	pro. time	prothrombin time
chol	cholesterol	PSP	phenolsulfonphthalein
chol. est.	cholesterol ester	RBC	red blood count
C I	color index	sed. rate	sedimentation rate
Cl	chloride	SGOT	serum glutamic: oxaloacetic transaminase
CPK	creatine phosphokinase	SGPT	serum glutamic: pyruvic transaminase
CO$_2$	carbon dioxide	SMA-12	sequential multiple analysis of 12 chemistry constituents
coag. time	coagulation time	STS	serologic test for syphilis
creat	creatinine	T3 test	triiodothyronine test
CRP	C-reactive protein	TGT	thromboplastin generation test
diff	differential count	TPI	treponema pallidum immobilization test
eos	eosinophils	U.A.	urinalysis
FBS	fasting blood sugar	VDRL	flocculation test
Fe	iron	WBC	white blood count
fib	fibrinogen	Zn	zinc
glob	globulin		
gluc	glucose		
Gm O/O	grams per hundred milliliters of serum or blood		
HCT	hematocrit		
Hgb	hemoglobin		
h.p.f.	per high powered field describes urine sediments)		

APPENDIX XI

Abbreviations Used in Charting in Radiography

Abbreviations in medical records should be used in a consistent and standardized manner. Below is the standardized way of using abbreviations in charting in radiography.

ABD	abdomen	LUQ	left upper quadrant
AC joints	acromioclavicular joints	LLQ	left lower quadrant
AP	anteroposterior	MIF	myocardial infarction
BE	barium enema	MISC	miscellaneous
BA. BE.	barium enema	MP Joints	metacarpal joints
BA swallow	barium swallow (esophagram)	MVA	motor vehicle accident
BI LAT	bilateral	NB	newborn
BPD	biparietal diameter	NMI	no middle initial
CA	cancer (carcinoma)	OP	outpatient
CHF	congestive heart failure	OR	operating room
CLAV	clavicle	O$_2$	oxygen
COPD	chronic obstructive pulmonary disease	PEDS	pediatrics
		PORT	portable
C/S	with and without contrast	PP	postpartum
CS	central supply	PREOP	preoperative
C Spine	cervical spine, cervical vertebrae	POST OP	postoperative, after a surgical operation
CXR	chest X ray		
DIP	distal interphalangeal	PROM	premature rupture of membrane
ER	emergency room	PULM	pulmonary
FU	follow-up	R/O	rule out
GB	gall bladder series	RUQ	right upper quadrant
GI	gastrointestinal	RLQ	right lower quadrant
HYSTERO	hysterosalpingogram	SI Joints	Sacral iliac joints
IV	intravenous	SOB	short of breath
IVA	Ivac intravenous monitor	SM bowel	small bowel
		SONO	sonogram
KUB	kidney, ureter, bladder (one view ABD)	T Spine	thoracic spine
		UGI	upper gastrointestinal series
LAT	lateral	UNI LAT	unilateral
L Spine	lumbar spine	US	ultrasound
LS spine	lumbar sacral spine	X-table	cross-table placement
LSP	lumbar spine		

APPENDIX XII

Latin Abbreviations Commonly Used in Writing Prescriptions

Abbreviation	Latin	English
a.c.	ante cibum	before meals
ad lib.	ad libitum	freely, as desired
agit.	agita	share, stir
aq.	aqua	water
aq.dest	aqua destillata	distilled water
b.i.d.	bis in die	twice a day
c	cum	with
cap.	capsula	capsule
comp.	compositus	compound
dil.	dilatus	dissolve, dilute
elix.	elixir	elixir
h.	hora	hour
h.s.	hora somni	at bedtime
M., m.	misce	mix
non rep.	non repatatur	do not repeat
OS	oculus sinister	in the left eye
OD	oculus dexter	in the right eye
O.U.	oculus uterque	in each eye
p.c.	post cibum	after meals
p.o.	per os	by mouth
p.r.n.	pro re nata	when needed
q.	quaque	every
q.d.	quaque die	every day
q.a.m.	quaque ante meridiem	every morning
q.h.	quaque hora	every hour
q.2h.	quaque 2 hora	every 2 hours
q.3h.	quaque 3 hora	every 3 hours
q.4h.	quaque 4 hora	every 4 hours
q.6h.	quaque 6 hora	every 6 hours
q.i.d.	quaque hora somni	every night
q.o.d.	quaque otra die	every other day
q.s.	quantum sufficiat	sufficient quantity
rept.	repetatur	may be repeated
Rx	recipe	take, drug, treatment
s	sine	without
Sig. or S.	signa	label

Appendix XII

s.o.s.	si opus sit	if it is needed
ss	semis	one-half
stat.	statim	at once
tinct.	tinctura	tincture
t.i.d.	ter in die	3 times a day
tr.	tinctura	tincture

APPENDIX XIII

Weight Equivalents: Metric and Apothecary

Metric	Apothecary
0.1 mg	1/600 grain
0.12 mg	1/500 grain
0.15 mg	1/400 grain
0.2 mg	1/300 grain
0.25 mg	1/250 grain
0.3 mg	1/200 grain
0.4 mg	1/150 grain
0.5 mg	1/120 grain
0.6 mg	1/100 grain
0.8 mg	1/80 grain
1 mg	1/60 grain
1.2 mg	1/50 grain
1.5 mg	1/40 grain
2 mg	1/30 grain
3 mg	1/20 grain
4 mg	1/15 grain
5 mg	1/12 grain
6 mg	1/10 grain
8 mg	1/8 grain
10 mg	1/6 grain
12 mg	1/5 grain
15 mg	1/4 grain
20 mg	1/3 grain
25 mg	3/8 grain
30 mg	1/2 grain
40 mg	2/3 grain
50 mg	3/4 grain
60 mg	1 grain
0.1 gm	1½ grains
0.15 gm	2½ grains
0.2 gm	3 grains
0.3 gm	5 grains
0.4 gm	6 grains
0.5 gm	7½ grains
0.6 gm	10 grains
1 gram	15 grains
1.5 gm	22 grains
2 gm	30 grains
4 gm	60 grains, or 1 dram
30 gm	1 ounce, or 8 drams
500 gm	1.34 pounds

APPENDIX XIV

Volume Equivalents: Metric, Apothecary, Household

Metric	Apothecary	Household
0.06 ml	1 minim	1 drop
0.3 ml	5 minims	
0.6 ml	10 minims	
1 ml	15 minims	15 drops
2 ml	30 minims	
3 ml	45 minims	
4 ml	60 minims (1 fluid dram)	60 drops, or 1 teaspoon
8 ml	2 fl. drams (f_3)	2 teaspoons
15 ml	4 fl. drams	4 teaspoons, or 1 tablespoon
30 ml	8 fl. drams (1 fl. oz.) (f_3)	2 tablespoons
60 ml	2 fl. ounces	
90 ml	3 fl. ounces	
200 ml	7 fl. ounces	1 teacup
250 ml	8 fl. ounces	1 glass (average size)
500 ml	16 fl. ounces	1 pint
750 ml	1½ pints	
1000 ml (1 liter)	about 2 pints	1.05 quarts
4000 ml	4.20 quarters	1⅕ gallons

APPENDIX XV

Code of Ethics for American Health Information Management Association

The health information management professional abides by a set of ethical principles developed to safeguard the public and to contribute within the scope of the profession to quality and efficiency in health care. This Code of Ethics, adopted by the members of the American Health Information Management Association, defines the standards of behavior which promote ethical conduct.

1. The Health Information Management Profession demonstrates behavior that reflects integrity, supports objectivity, and fosters trust in professional activities.

2. The Health Information Management Profession respects the dignity of each human being.

3. The Health Information Management Profession strives to improve personal competence and quality of services.

4. The Health Information Management Professional respresents truthfully and accurately professional credentials, education, and experience.

5. The Health Information Management Professional refuses to participate in illegal or unethical acts and also refuses to conceal the illegal, incompetent, or unethical acts of others.

6. The Health Information Management Professional protects the confidentiality of primary and secondary health records as mandated by law, professional standards, and the employer's policies.

7. The Health Information Management Professional promotes to others the tenets of confidentiality.

8. The Health Information Management Professional adheres to pertinent laws and regulations while advocating changes which serve the best interest of the public.

9. The Health Information Management Professional encourages appropriate use of health record information and advocates policies and systems that advance the management of health records and health information.

10. The Health Information Management Professional recognizes and supports the Association's mission.

Used with permission of the American Health Information Management Association

APPENDIX XVI

Privacy Act of 1974

The Freedom of Information Act of 1967 gave the right to the public to be informed about most all that the government does and makes information available to anyone who wants it, for whatever reason. Congress recognized that some information should be withheld from public scrutiny with nine exemptions made. One exemptions sets forth that certain records such as personnel and medical records are to be considered privileged. The Privacy Act of 1974 as applicable to federal hospitals and clinics has six elements:

1. An individual may request access to any records or files pertaining to him or her.

2. The request must be in writing and signed by requestor, stating what portion of records, date of visit, and/or particular tests, reports, etc., are desired for viewing.

3. The patient's record is pulled and referred to the patient's physician (or designee) for determination as to whether or not direct access to the information would be detrimental to the patient.

4. If there is approval, the requested portion of the record is given to the patient for perusal. Copies are made for a set fee per page.

5. Should the patient's physician feel it is not in the best interests of the patient to view the record, the patient may designate a third party to review the record and that person may determine whether the patient should view the record.

6. If a patient wishes a correction in the record it may made by addendum only, not by crossing out and initialing. The correction may be done only upon concurrence of the person making the entry. If that person refuses, then the patient may appeal.

(Individual federal facilities maintain detailed policies and procedures which are periodically reviewed and updated governing the process and access.)